Book 3

The Bedford Anthology of *World Literature*

The Early Modern World, 1450–1650

EDITED BY

Paul Davis
Gary Harrison
David M. Johnson
Patricia Clark Smith
John F. Crawford

THE UNIVERSITY OF NEW MEXICO

BEDFORD / ST. MARTIN'S **Boston ♦ N York**

For Bedford/St. Martin's

Executive Editor: Alanya Harter
Associate Developmental Editor: Joshua Levy
Production Editor: Stasia Zomkowski
Senior Production Supervisor: Nancy Myers
Marketing Manager: Jenna Bookin Barry
Art Editor: Genevieve Hamilton
Editorial Assistant: Jeffrey Voccola
Production Assistants: Kerri Cardone, Kendra LeFleur
Copyeditor: Janet Renard
Map Coordinator: Tina Samaha
Text and Cover Design: Anna George
Cover Art: Printing Press, engraving after a miniature from the beginning of the sixteenth century. Bibliothèque Nationale, Paris / Bridgeman Art Library.
Composition: Stratford Publishing Services, Inc.
Printing and Binding: R. R. Donnelley & Sons Company

President: Joan E. Feinberg
Editorial Director: Denise B. Wydra
Editor in Chief: Karen S. Henry
Director of Marketing: Karen Melton
Director of Editing, Design, and Production: Marcia Cohen
Managing Editor: Elizabeth M. Schaaf

Library of Congress Control Number: 2002112262

Manufactured in the United States of America.

9 8
f

For information, write: Bedford / St. Martin's, 75 Arlington Street, Boston, MA 02116 (617-399-4000)

ISBN-10: 0-312-40262-7
ISBN-13: 978-0-312-40262-4

Acknowledgments

Appar, "An Earring of Bright New Gold Glows in One Ear," "See the God!," "The Unholy Town Where No Temple Stands," and "Why Was I Born?" from *The Tevaram,* translated by Indira Viswanathan Peterson, from *Poems to Siva: The Hymns of the Tamil Saints.* Copyright © 1989 by Princeton University Press. Reprinted with the permission of the publishers.

Acknowledgments and copyrights are continued at the back of the book on pages 998–1000, which constitute an extension of the copyright page. It is a violation of the law to reproduce these selections by any means whatsoever without the written permission of the copyright holder.

PREFACE

The Bedford Anthology of World Literature has a story behind it. In 1985, a group of us received a grant from the National Endowment for the Humanities. Our task: to develop and team teach a new kind of literature course—one that drew from the rich literary traditions of Asia, India, the Middle East, and the Americas as well as from the masterpieces of the Western world. We learned so much from that experience—from our students and from each other—that we applied those lessons to an anthology published in 1995, *Western Literature in a World Context.*

In that first edition of our anthology, our goal was to add works that truly represented *world* literature to the list of Western classics and to place great literary works in their historical and cultural contexts. We've kept that focus in the newly titled *Bedford Anthology*—but we've also drastically reshaped, redesigned, and reimagined it to make it the book you hold today. We talked to hundreds of instructors and students in an effort to identify and confirm what they considered challenging about the world literature course. The design and content of these pages represent our attempt to meet these challenges.

The study and teaching of world literature have changed significantly in the past twenty to thirty years. Formerly, most world literature courses consisted of masterpieces of Western literature, while the literary traditions of Asia, Africa, and Latin America were virtually ignored. The movement to broaden the canon to more accurately represent our world—and to better represent oral and marginalized traditions in the West—has greatly increased the number of texts taught in world literature courses today. Although the specifics remain controversial, nearly all teachers of literature are committed to the ongoing revaluation and expansion of the canon.

The last few decades have also seen instructors reconsidering the traditional methods of teaching world literature. In the past, most world literature courses were designed along formalistic or generic principles. But the expanded canon has complicated both of these approaches. There are no developed criteria for defining masterworks in such formerly ignored genres as letters and diaries or for unfamiliar forms from non-Western cultures, and we are frequently reminded that traditional approaches sometimes impose inappropriate Eurocentric perspectives on such works. As content and methodology for the course have been evolving, recent critical theory has reawakened interest in literature's historical and cultural contexts. All of these factors have both complicated and enriched the study of world literature. With this multivolume literature anthology, we don't claim to be presenting the definitive new canon of world literature or the last word on how to teach it. We have, however, tried to open new perspectives and possibilities for both students and teachers.

One anthology — six individual books. *The Bedford Anthology of World Literature* is now split into six separate books that correspond to the six time periods most commonly taught. These books are available in two packages: Books 1–3 and Books 4–6. Our motivation for changing the packaging is twofold and grows out of the extensive market research we did before shaping the development plan for the book. In our research, instructors from around the country confirmed that students just don't want to cart around a 2,500-page book — who would? Many also said that they focus on ancient literatures in the first semester of the course and on the twentieth

The Bedford Anthology of World Literature *has been dynamically reimagined, redesigned, and restructured. We've added a second color, four hundred images, three hundred pronunciation guides, forty maps, six comparative time lines — and much more.*

The Eighteenth Century
1650 - 1800
Portuguese Caravels Leaving to Explore the World, 1775 The eighteenth century was a time of unprecedented global communication — political, social, economic, and literary. These painted blue tiles are found on the walls of the town of Paco de Arcos, near Lisbon, Portugal. (The Art Archive / Dagli Orti.)

century in the second semester. In addition, many instructors teach an introduction to world literature that is tailored specifically to the needs of their students and their institution and thus want a text that can be adapted to *many* courses.

We believe that the extensive changes we've made to *The Bedford Anthology of World Literature*—breaking the anthology into six books rather than only two, creating a new two-color design, increasing the trim size, and adding maps, illustrations, numerous pedagogical features, an expanded instructor's manual, and a new companion Web site—will make the formidable task of teaching and taking a world literature course both manageable and pleasurable.

An expanded canon for the twenty-first century. In each of the six books of *The Bedford Anthology,* you'll find a superb collection of complete longer works, plays, prose, and poems—the best literature available in English or English translation. Five of the books are organized geographically and then by author in order of birth date. The exception to this rule is Book 6, which, reflecting our increasingly global identities, is organized by author without larger geographical groupings.

Aphra Behn's Oroonoko *is one of the texts we include in its entirety—highlighting important issues of race, gender, and slavery in the eighteenth century.*

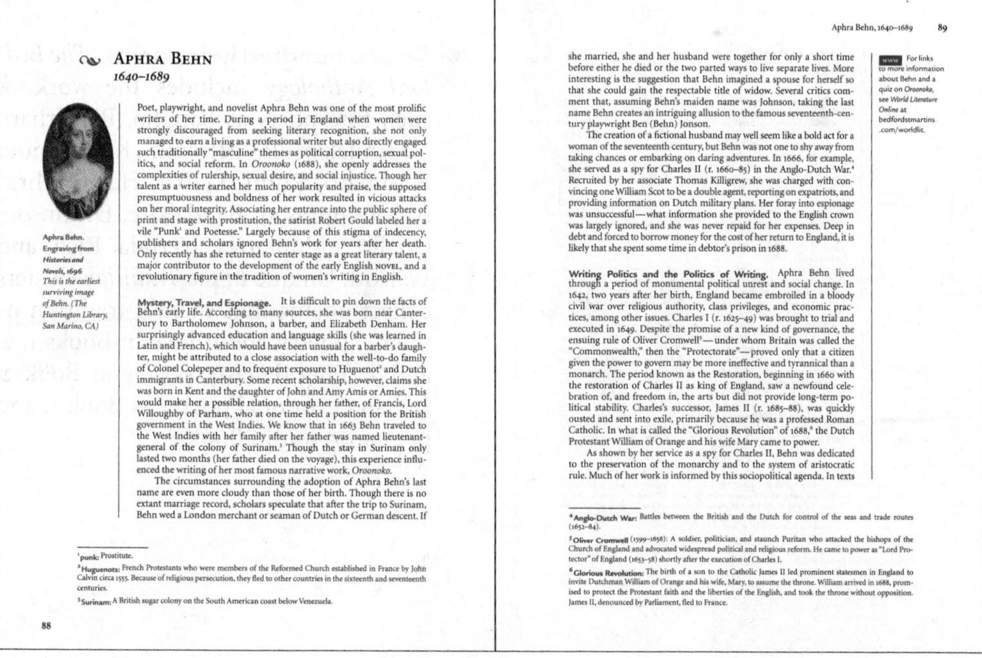

APHRA BEHN
1640–1689

Aphra Behn. Engraving from *Histories and Novels,* 1696
This is the earliest surviving image of Behn. (The Huntington Library, San Marino, CA)

Poet, playwright, and novelist Aphra Behn was one of the most prolific writers of her time. During a period in England when women were strongly discouraged from seeking literary recognition, she not only managed to earn a living as a professional writer but also directly engaged such traditionally "masculine" themes as political corruption, sexual politics, and social reform. In *Oroonoko* (1688), she openly addresses the complexities of rulership, sexual desire, and social injustice. Though her talent as a writer earned her much popularity and praise, the supposed presumptuousness and boldness of her work resulted in vicious attacks on her moral integrity. Associating her entrance into the public sphere of print and stage with prostitution, the satirist Robert Gould labeled her a vile "Punk[1] and Poetesse." Largely because of this stigma of indecency, publishers and scholars ignored Behn's work for years after her death. Only recently has she returned to center stage as a great literary talent, a major contributor to the development of the early English NOVEL, and a revolutionary figure in the tradition of women's writing in English.

Mystery, Travel, and Espionage. It is difficult to pin down the facts of Behn's early life. According to many sources, she was born near Canterbury to Bartholomew Johnson, a barber, and Elizabeth Denham. Her surprisingly advanced education and language skills (she was learned in Latin and French), which would have been unusual for a barber's daughter, might be attributed to a close association with the well-to-do family of Colonel Colepeper and to frequent exposure to Huguenot[2] and Dutch immigrants in Canterbury. Some recent scholarship, however, claims she was born in Kent and the daughter of John and Amy Amis or Amies. This would make her a possible relation, through her father, of Francis, Lord Willoughby of Parham, who at one time held a position for the British government in the West Indies. We know that in 1663 Behn traveled to the West Indies with her family after her father was named lieutenant-general of the colony of Surinam.[3] Though the stay in Surinam only lasted two months (her father died on the voyage), this experience influenced the writing of her most famous narrative work, *Oroonoko.*

The circumstances surrounding the adoption of Aphra Behn's last name are even more cloudy than those of her birth. Though there is no extant marriage record, scholars speculate that after the trip to Surinam, Behn wed a London merchant or seaman of Dutch or German descent. If

[1] **punk:** Prostitute.

[2] **Huguenots:** French Protestants who were members of the Reformed Church established in France by John Calvin circa 1555. Because of religious persecution, they fled to other countries in the sixteenth and seventeenth centuries.

[3] **Surinam:** A British sugar colony on the South American coast below Venezuela.

88

Aphra Behn, 1640–1689 89

she married, she and her husband were together for only a short time before either he died or the two parted ways to live separate lives. More interesting is the suggestion that Behn imagined a spouse for herself so that she could gain the respectable title of widow. Several critics comment that, assuming Behn's maiden name was Johnson, taking the last name Behn creates an intriguing allusion to the famous seventeenth-century playwright Ben (Behn) Jonson.

The creation of a fictional husband may well seem like a bold act for a woman of the seventeenth century, but Behn was not one to shy away from taking chances or embarking on daring adventures. In 1666, for example, she served as a spy for Charles II (r. 1660–85) in the Anglo-Dutch War.[4] Recruited by her associate Thomas Killigrew, she was charged with convincing one William Scot to be a double agent, reporting on expatriots, and providing information on Dutch military plans. Her foray into espionage was unsuccessful—what information she provided to the English crown was largely ignored, and she was never repaid for her expenses. Deep in debt and forced to borrow money for the cost of her return to England, it is likely that she spent some time in debtor's prison in 1688.

WWW For links to more information about Behn and a quiz on *Oroonoko,* see *World Literature Online* at bedfordstmartins.com/worldlit.

Writing Politics and the Politics of Writing. Aphra Behn lived through a period of monumental political unrest and social change. In 1642, two years after her birth, England became embroiled in a bloody civil war over religious authority, class privileges, and economic practices, among other issues. Charles I (r. 1625–49) was brought to trial and executed in 1649. Despite the promise of a new kind of governance, the ensuing rule of Oliver Cromwell[5]—under whom Britain was called the "Commonwealth," then the "Protectorate"—proved only that a citizen given the power to govern may be more ineffective and tyrannical than a monarch. The period known as the Restoration, beginning in 1660 with the restoration of Charles II as king of England, saw a newfound celebration of, and freedom in, the arts but did not provide long-term political stability. Charles's successor, James II (r. 1685–88), was quickly ousted and sent into exile, primarily because he was a professed Roman Catholic. In what is called the "Glorious Revolution" of 1688,[6] the Dutch Protestant William of Orange and his wife Mary came to power.

As shown by her service as a spy for Charles II, Behn was dedicated to the preservation of the monarchy and to the system of aristocratic rule. Much of her work is informed by this sociopolitical agenda. In texts

[4] **Anglo-Dutch War:** Battles between the British and the Dutch for control of the seas and trade routes (1652–84).

[5] **Oliver Cromwell** (1599–1658): A soldier, politician, and staunch Puritan who attacked the bishops of the Church of England and advocated widespread political and religious reform. He came to power as "Lord Protector" of England (1653–58) shortly after the execution of Charles I.

[6] **Glorious Revolution:** The birth of a son to the Catholic James II led prominent statesmen in England to invite Dutchman William of Orange and his wife, Mary, to assume the throne. William arrived in 1688, promised to protect the Protestant faith and the liberties of the English, and took the throne without opposition. James II, denounced by Parliament, fled to France.

We've tried to assemble a broad selection of the world's literatures. We've updated our selection of European texts; we have also included American writers who have had significant contact with world culture and who have influenced or defined who we are as Americans. And of course we have added many works from non-Western traditions, both frequently anthologized pieces and works unique to this anthology, including texts from Mesopotamia, Egypt, Israel, India, Persia, China, Japan, Arab countries of the Middle East, Africa, native America, Latin America, and the Caribbean.

Over thirty-five complete, longer works. These include Homer's *Odyssey* and *The Epic of Gilgamesh* in Book 1, Dante's *Inferno* and Kalidasa's *Shakuntala* in Book 2, Marlowe's *Doctor Faustus* and Shakespeare's *The Tempest* in Book 3, Bashō's *Narrow Road through the Backcountry* in Book 4, Dostoevsky's *Notes from Underground* in Book 5, and Achebe's *Things Fall Apart* in Book 6.

When a work is too long to be produced in its entirety, we've presented carefully edited selections from it; examples include the Rig Veda, *Ramayana, Mahabharata,* Qur'an, *The Song of Roland,* Ibn Hazm's *The Dove's Necklace, The Book of Margery Kempe,* Attar's *Conference of the Birds,* Cervantes's *Don Quixote,* Swift's *Gulliver's Travels,* Equiano's *Interesting Narrative,* Benjamin Franklin's *Autobiography,* Chikamatsu's *The Love Suicides at Amijima,* and Cao Xueqin's *The Story of the Stone.* In most cases the excerpts are not fragments but substantial selections wherein the structure and themes of the whole work are evident. The anthology also contains a generous selection of prose writing—short stories, letters, and essays.

RAMPRASAD SEN
1718–1775

The intensely religious village life of India produced not only storytellers—whose primary purpose was transmitting the stories of gods, goddesses, heroes, and heroines—but also poets who expressed ordinary people's spiritual longing for God. Emotional worship or surrender to God in Hinduism is called ***bhakti***, a term that has its origins in the Upanishads. Bhakti became a religious movement in India during the religious reforms of the eighth, ninth, and tenth centuries. A particular version of bhakti was devoted to feminine divinity; in India there had been a long history of worshiping the greatgoddess **Shakti**[1]—also known as **Kali** and Durga—but a resurgence of her worship, led by the poet **Ramprasad** Sen, took place in Bengal[2] during the eighteenth century. Like medieval Christian poets devoted to the Virgin Mother, Bengal poets of this time favored the feminine dimension of God, which seemed to invite a personal relationship, an opportunity for conversation, and expressions of sadness and longing.

BAHK-tee

SHAHK-tee; KAH-lee

RAHM-pruh-sahd

Ramprasad's poems, primarily songs to Kali, were extremely popular at the end of the eighteenth century when Bengal was in a time of darkness and despair. The region had been under Muslim rule for about five hundred years when the British defeated the Mughal army in the Battle of Plassey in 1757.[3] Robber barons controlled large parts of Bengal, and Kali was their patron deity. Regional kings promoted Kali worship by supporting court poets who composed and sang songs to the goddess. The songs became part of an extremely precarious village life. Bengal is a region of extremes, feast or famine, due to unpredictable rains. Some years bring little rain or droughts, while others have heavy rain and flooding. Occasionally there are years when just the right amount of rain falls at the appropriate times; these times are thought to be blessed by Kali.

Ramprasad's simple lyricism and familiar images touched a broad range of listeners; his songs appealed to scholars and peasants alike. His poetic skills influenced succeeding generations of Indian poets. Rabindranath Tagore,[4] the most famous Bengali writer of the late nineteenth cen-

WWW For links to more information about Ramprasad and a quiz on his poetry, see *World Literature Online* at bedfordstmartins.com/worldlit.

[1] **Shakti:** Shakti is the collective name for the consort of Shiva who has several names. **Shakti** is the feminine dynamic energy by which God creates, preserves, and dissolves the world. **Kali** is usually portrayed as terrifying: blue-black, three-eyed, and four-armed, with a necklace of human heads and a girdle of severed hands. **Durga,** "the unfathomable one," is one of the oldest versions of the Great Mother: fair complexioned and riding a lion, she releases humans from rebirth with her touch.

[2] **Bengal:** A region in the northeast Indian peninsula, now divided between India and Bangladesh.

[3] **Battle of Plassey:** Plassey is a village in West Bengal state where the British defeated the Bengal army in 1757, leading to Britain's control of northeast India.

[4] **Rabindranath Tagore** (1861–1941): A native of Bengal anxious to preserve the cultural richness of traditional village life while at the same time bridging the philosophical and literary gap between East and West. (See Book 5.)

612

Several hundred lyric poems. *The Bedford Anthology* includes the work of such fine poets as Sappho, Bhartrhari, Nezahualcoyotl, Petrarch, Kakinomoto Hitomaro, Rumi, Li Bai, Heine, Mirabai, Ramprasad, Baudelaire, Dickinson, Ghalib, Akhmatova, Neruda, Rich, and Walcott. Unique *In the Tradition* clusters collect poems that share a tradition or theme: poetry about love in Books 1, 2, and 3, Tang dynasty poetry in Book 2, Indian devotional poetry in Book 3, and poetry on war in Book 6.

Literature in context. In addition to individual authors presented in chronological order, *The Bedford Anthology* features two types of cross-cultural literary groupings. In the more than thirty ***In the World*** clusters, five to six in each book, writings around a single theme—such as the history of religions, science, love, human rights, women's rights, colonialism, the meeting of East and West, imperialism, and existentialism—and from different countries and cultural traditions are presented side by side, helping students understand that people of every culture have had their public gods, heroes, and revolutions, their private loves, lives, and losses. Titles include "Changing Gods: From Religion to Philosophy," in Book 1; "Muslim and Christian at War," in Book 2; "Humanism, Learning, and Education," in Book 3; "Love, Marriage, and the Education of Women," in Book 4; "Emancipation," in Book 5; and "Imagining Africa," in Book 6. The second type of grouping, ***In the Tradition,*** presents poetry on love in Books 1, 2, and 3 and literature on war and American multiculturalism in Book 6. These clusters gather together such widely disparate writers as Hammurabi, Heraclitus, Marcus Aurelius, Ibn Battuta, Marco Polo, Sei Shonagon, Galileo, Bartolomé de las Casas, Mary Wollstonecraft, Mary Astell, Shen Fu, Karl Marx, Elizabeth Cady Stanton, Swami Vivekananda, Aimé Césaire, and Bharati Mukherjee.

In the World *clusters bring together texts from different literary traditions and help students make thematic connections and comparisons.*

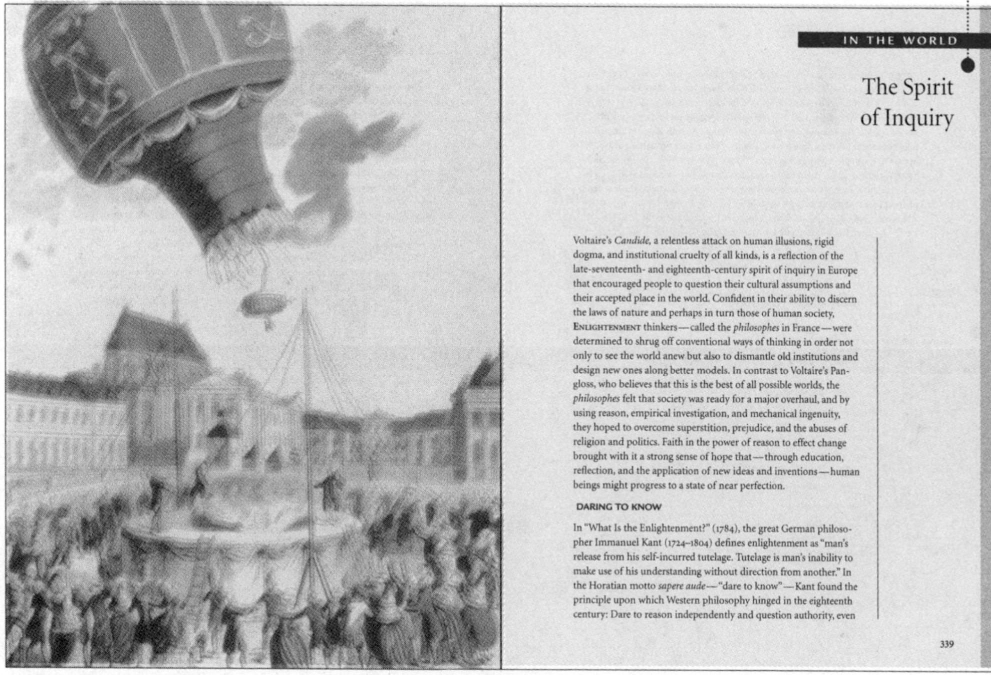

IN THE WORLD

The Spirit of Inquiry

Voltaire's *Candide*, a relentless attack on human illusions, rigid dogma, and institutional cruelty of all kinds, is a reflection of the late-seventeenth- and eighteenth-century spirit of inquiry in Europe that encouraged people to question their cultural assumptions and their accepted place in the world. Confident in their ability to discern the laws of nature and perhaps in turn those of human society, Enlightenment thinkers—called the *philosophes* in France—were determined to shrug off conventional ways of thinking in order not only to see the world anew but also to dismantle old institutions and design new ones along better models. In contrast to Voltaire's Pangloss, who believes that this is the best of all possible worlds, the *philosophes* felt that society was ready for a major overhaul, and by using reason, empirical investigation, and mechanical ingenuity, they hoped to overcome superstition, prejudice, and the abuses of religion and politics. Faith in the power of reason to effect change brought with it a strong sense of hope that—through education, reflection, and the application of new ideas and inventions—human beings might progress to a state of near perfection.

DARING TO KNOW

In "What Is the Enlightenment?" (1784), the great German philosopher Immanuel Kant (1724–1804) defines enlightenment as "man's release from his self-incurred tutelage. Tutelage is man's inability to make use of his understanding without direction from another." In the Horatian motto *sapere aude*—"dare to know"—Kant found the principle upon which Western philosophy hinged in the eighteenth century: Dare to reason independently and question authority, even

339

Helping students and teachers navigate the wide world of literature. The hundreds of instructors we talked to before embarking on *The Bedford Anthology* shared with us their concerns about teaching an introduction to world literature course, no matter what their individual agendas were. One concern was the sheer difficulty for students of reading literature that not only spans the period from the beginning of recorded literatures to the present but also hails from vastly different cultures and historical moments. Another was the fact that no one instructor is an expert in *all* of world literature. We've put together *The Bedford Anthology of World Literature* with these factors in mind and hope that the help we offer both around and with the selected texts goes a long way toward bringing clarity to the abundance and variety of world writings.

Helping students understand the where and when of the literature in the anthology. Each book of *The Bedford Anthology* opens with an extended overview of its time period as well as with a **comparative time line** that lists what happened, where, and when in three overarching categories: history and politics; literature; and science, culture, and technology. An interactive version of each time line serves as the portal to the online support offered on our Book Companion Site. In addition,

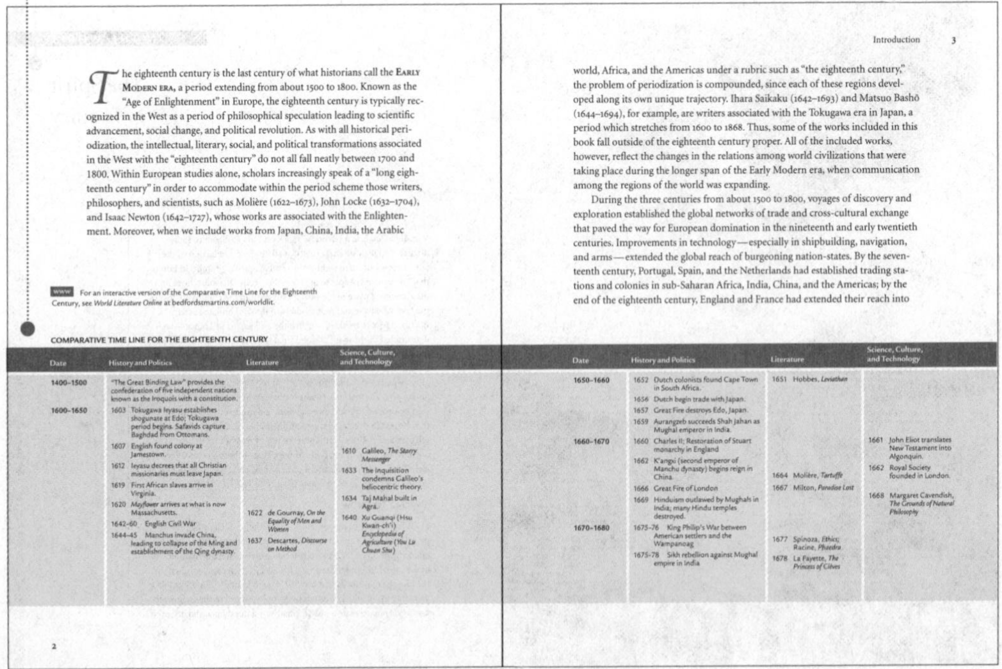

The eighteenth century is the last century of what historians call the **Early Modern era**, a period extending from about 1500 to 1800. Known as the "Age of Enlightenment" in Europe, the eighteenth century is typically recognized in the West as a period of philosophical speculation leading to scientific advancement, social change, and political revolution. As with all historical periodization, the intellectual, literary, social, and political transformations associated in the West with the "eighteenth century" do not all fall neatly between 1700 and 1800. Within European studies alone, scholars increasingly speak of a "long eighteenth century" in order to accommodate within the period scheme those writers, philosophers, and scientists, such as Molière (1622–1673), John Locke (1632–1704), and Isaac Newton (1642–1727), whose works are associated with the Enlightenment. Moreover, when we include works from Japan, China, India, the Arabic

WWW For an interactive version of the Comparative Time Line for the Eighteenth Century, see *World Literature Online* at bedfordstmartins.com/worldlit.

COMPARATIVE TIME LINE FOR THE EIGHTEENTH CENTURY

Date	History and Politics	Literature	Science, Culture, and Technology
1400–1500	"The Great Binding Law" provides the confederation of five independent nations known as the Iroquois with a constitution.		
1600–1650	1603 Tokugawa Ieyasu establishes shogunate at Edo; Tokugawa period begins. Safavids capture Baghdad from Ottomans. 1607 English found colony at Jamestown. 1612 Ieyasu decrees that all Christian missionaries must leave Japan. 1619 First African slaves arrive in Virginia. 1620 *Mayflower* arrives at what is now Massachusetts. 1642–60 English Civil War 1644–45 Manchus invade China, leading to collapse of the Ming and establishment of the Qing dynasty.	1622 de Gournay, *On the Equality of Men and Women* 1637 Descartes, *Discourse on Method*	1610 Galileo, *The Starry Messenger* 1633 The Inquisition condemns Galileo's heliocentric theory. 1634 Taj Mahal built in Agra. 1640 Xu Guangqi (Hsu Kwan-ch'i) *Encyclopedia of Agriculture* (*You Lu Chuan Shu*)

2

world, Africa, and the Americas under a rubric such as "the eighteenth century," the problem of periodization is compounded, since each of these regions developed along its own unique trajectory. Ihara Saikaku (1642–1693) and Matsuo Bashō (1644–1694), for example, are writers associated with the Tokugawa era in Japan, a period which stretches from 1600 to 1868. Thus, some of the works included in this book fall outside of the eighteenth century proper. All of the included works, however, reflect the changes in the relations among world civilizations that were taking place during the longer span of the Early Modern era, when communication among the regions of the world was expanding.

During the three centuries from about 1500 to 1800, voyages of discovery and exploration established the global networks of trade and cross-cultural exchange that paved the way for European domination in the nineteenth and early twentieth centuries. Improvements in technology—especially in shipbuilding, navigation, and arms—extended the global reach of burgeoning nation-states. By the seventeenth century, Portugal, Spain, and the Netherlands had established trading stations and colonies in sub-Saharan Africa, India, China, and the Americas; by the end of the eighteenth century, England and France had extended their reach into

Date	History and Politics	Literature	Science, Culture, and Technology
1650–1660	1652 Dutch colonists found Cape Town in South Africa. 1656 Dutch begin trade with Japan. 1657 Great Fire destroys Edo, Japan. 1659 Aurangzeb succeeds Shah Jahan as Mughal emperor in India.	1651 Hobbes, *Leviathan*	
1660–1670	1660 Charles II; Restoration of Stuart monarchy in England 1662 K'angxi (second emperor of Manchu dynasty) begins reign in China. 1666 Great Fire of London 1669 Hinduism outlawed by Mughals in India; many Hindu temples destroyed.	1664 Molière, *Tartuffe* 1667 Milton, *Paradise Lost*	1661 John Eliot translates New Testament into Algonquin. 1662 Royal Society founded in London. 1668 Margaret Cavendish, *The Grounds of Natural Philosophy*
1670–1680	1675–76 King Philip's War between American settlers and the Wampanoag 1675–78 Sikh rebellion against Mughal empire in India	1677 Spinoza, *Ethics*; Racine, *Phaedra* 1678 La Fayette, *The Princess of Clèves*	

"Time and Place" boxes in the introductions to the different geographical groupings of writers further orient students in the era and culture connected with the literature they're reading by spotlighting something interesting and specific about a certain place and time.

Maps included throughout the anthology show students where in the world various literatures came from. Besides the maps that open each geographical section and show countries in relation to the larger world at a given time in history, we've supplied maps that illustrate the shifting of national boundaries; industrial growth; the effects of conquest, conquerors, and colonialism; and the travels of Odysseus, Ibn Battuta, and Bashō.

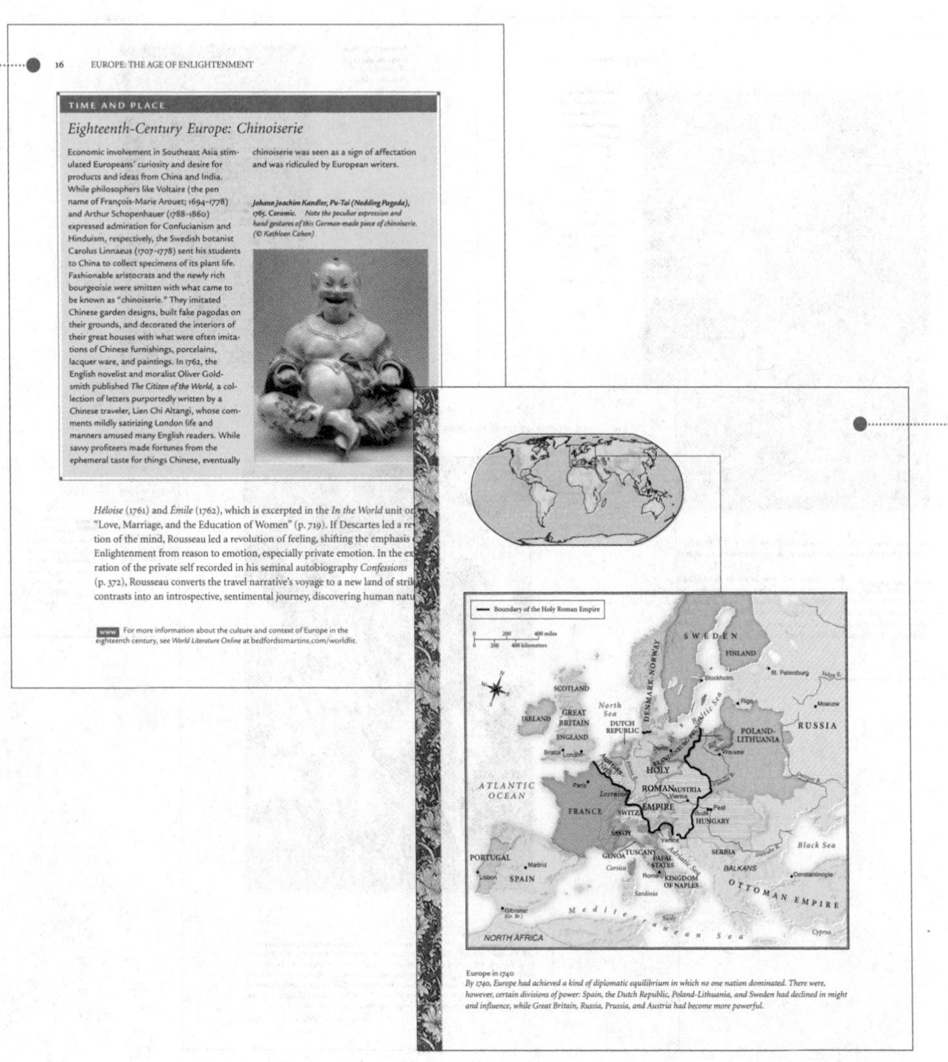

16 EUROPE: THE AGE OF ENLIGHTENMENT

TIME AND PLACE

Eighteenth-Century Europe: Chinoiserie

Economic involvement in Southeast Asia stimulated Europeans' curiosity and desire for products and ideas from China and India. While philosophers like Voltaire (the pen name of François-Marie Arouet; 1694–1778) and Arthur Schopenhauer (1788–1860) expressed admiration for Confucianism and Hinduism, respectively, the Swedish botanist Carolus Linnaeus (1707–1778) sent his students to China to collect specimens of its plant life. Fashionable aristocrats and the newly rich bourgeoisie were smitten with what came to be known as "chinoiserie." They imitated Chinese garden designs, built fake pagodas on their grounds, and decorated the interiors of their great houses with what were often imitations of Chinese furnishings, porcelains, lacquer ware, and paintings. In 1762, the English novelist and moralist Oliver Goldsmith published *The Citizen of the World*, a collection of letters purportedly written by a Chinese traveler, Lien Chi Altangi, whose comments mildly satirizing London life and manners amused many English readers. While savvy profiteers made fortunes from the ephemeral taste for things Chinese, eventually chinoiserie was seen as a sign of affectation and was ridiculed by European writers.

Johann Joachim Kandler, Pu-Tai (Nodding Pagoda), 1765. Ceramic. *Note the peculiar expression and hand gestures of this German-made piece of chinoiserie. (© Kathleen Cohen)*

Héloise (1761) and *Émile* (1762), which is excerpted in the *In the World* unit o[n] "Love, Marriage, and the Education of Women" (p. 719). If Descartes led a re[volu]tion of the mind, Rousseau led a revolution of feeling, shifting the emphasis [of the] Enlightenment from reason to emotion, especially private emotion. In the ex[plo]ration of the private self recorded in his seminal autobiography *Confessions* (p. 372), Rousseau converts the travel narrative's voyage to a new land of stri[king] contrasts into an introspective, sentimental journey, discovering human natu[re]

www For more information about the culture and context of Europe in the eighteenth century, see *World Literature Online* at bedfordstmartins.com/worldlit.

Europe in 1740

By 1740, Europe had achieved a kind of diplomatic equilibrium in which no one nation dominated. There were, however, certain divisions of power: Spain, the Dutch Republic, Poland-Lithuania, and Sweden had declined in might and influence, while Great Britain, Russia, Prussia, and Austria had become more powerful.

The anthology's many illustrations — art, photographs, frontispieces, cartoons, and cultural artifacts — are meant to bring immediacy to literature that might otherwise feel spatially and temporally remote. A few examples are a photo of the Acropolis today juxtaposed with an artist's rendering of what it looked like newly built, a sketch of the first seven circles of Dante's hell, a scene from Hogarth's *Marriage à la Mode,* the ad Harriet Jacobs's owner ran for her capture and return, an editorial cartoon mocking Darwin's evolutionary theories, and a woodcut depicting Japanese boats setting out to greet Commodore Perry's warship in their harbor.

Ramprasad Sen, 1718–1775 613

The Holy Family: Shiva, Parvati, and Their Children on Mount Kailasa, c. 1800
An androgynous, naked Shiva is attended by Parvati, his spouse, who offers him liquid refreshment. The bull represents Shiva; the lion, Parvati; and the elephant-headed creature is Ganesha, a popular Hindu god. (Courtesy of the British Museum)

tury, composed Kali songs even though he was not a worshipe
himself; he merged the goddess's image with nationalistic devoti

Poet and Legend. Ramprasad Sen was born in Kumarhatt
twenty-five miles from Calcutta. His father, Ramram Sen, wa
Vaidyas caste — that of physicians. Ramprasad had a minimal e
and was versed in Sanskrit, Persian, and Hindi as well as Beng
young man he got a job in Calcutta as a clerk with an estate
Valulachandra Ghosal. Rather than paying attention to the a

Pu Song-Ling, 1640–1715 773

Pu Song-Ling, Page from *Liao-zhai zhi-yi*
(University of Wisconsin-Madison Library)

service exam at
n, he remained
tales, and writ-
l then as a pri-

Pu Song-Ling
to the tales cir-
began writing
pear until 1679,
mpendium first
ld not afford to
revise the tales;
nd lyrics to be
venty years old,
of his literary
he final version

WWW For more information about Pu Song-Ling, "The Wise Neighbor," and "The Mural," see *World Literature Online* at bedfordstmartins.com/worldlit.

236 EUROPE: THE AGE OF ENLIGHTENMENT

Aubrey Beardsley, *The Rape of the Lock*, 1896
A nineteenth-century depiction of the title act. (Courtesy of the trustees of the Boston Public Library)

■ CONNECTIONS
Virgil, *Aeneid* (Book 1). As a mock epic, *The Rape of the Lock* demands comparison with the epics it mocks. Virgil's use of such conventions of the epic as the plea to a muse for aid, the summary of the poem's grand subject matter at the beginning, the involvement of the gods in the action, heroic epithets, or names, for the characters, and elaborate similes is imitated in Pope's epic. Consider how the differences in the subject matter of the two poems — the founding of Rome (*Aeneid*) and the theft of a lock of hair — changes the impact of these literary devices.

Practical and accessible editorial apparatus helps students understand what they read. Each author in the anthology is introduced by an informative and accessible literary and biographical discussion. The selections themselves are complemented with generous footnotes, marginal notes, cross-references, and critical quotations. Phonetic pronunciation guides are supplied in the margins of introductory material and before the selections for unfamiliar character and place names. Providing help with literary and historical vocabulary, bold-faced key terms throughout the text refer students to the comprehensive glossary at the end of each book.

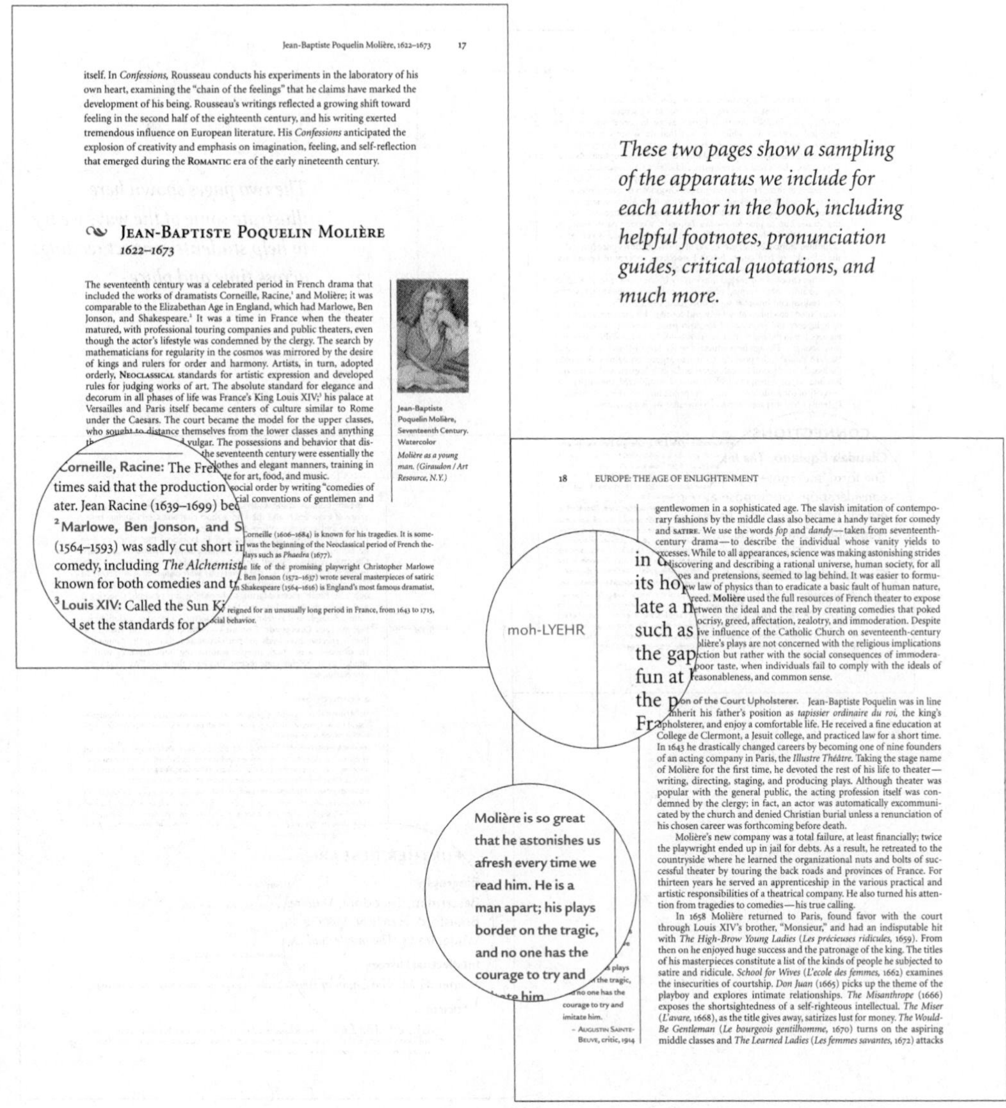

Jean-Baptiste Poquelin Molière, 1622–1673 17

itself. In *Confessions,* Rousseau conducts his experiments in the laboratory of his own heart, examining the "chain of the feelings" that he claims have marked the development of his being. Rousseau's writings reflected a growing shift toward feeling in the second half of the eighteenth century, and his writing exerted tremendous influence on European literature. His *Confessions* anticipated the explosion of creativity and emphasis on imagination, feeling, and self-reflection that emerged during the ROMANTIC era of the early nineteenth century.

JEAN-BAPTISTE POQUELIN MOLIÈRE
1622–1673

The seventeenth century was a celebrated period in French drama that included the works of dramatists Corneille, Racine,[1] and Molière; it was comparable to the Elizabethan Age in England, which had Marlowe, Ben Jonson, and Shakespeare.[2] It was a time in France when the theater matured, with professional touring companies and public theaters, even though the actor's lifestyle was condemned by the clergy. The search by mathematicians for regularity in the cosmos was mirrored by the desire of kings and rulers for order and harmony. Artists, in turn, adopted orderly, NEOCLASSICAL standards for artistic expression and developed rules for judging works of art. The absolute standard for elegance and decorum in all phases of life was France's King Louis XIV;[3] his palace at Versailles and Paris itself became centers of culture similar to Rome under the Caesars. The court became the model for the upper classes, who sought to distance themselves from the lower classes and anything ... vulgar. The possessions and behavior that dis... the seventeenth century were essentially the ...lothes and elegant manners, training in ...te for art, food, and music. ...social order by writing "comedies of ...cial conventions of gentlemen and

Jean-Baptiste Poquelin Molière, Seventeenth Century. Watercolor
Molière as a young man. (Giraudon / Art Resource, N.Y.)

...Corneille (1606–1684) is known for his tragedies. It is some- ...was the beginning of the Neoclassical period of French the- ...lays such as *Phaedra* (1677).
...e life of the promising playwright Christopher Marlowe ... Ben Jonson (1572–1637) wrote several masterpieces of satiric ...n Shakespeare (1564–1616) is England's most famous dramatist,
... reigned for an unusually long period in France, from 1643 to 1715, ...cial behavior.

18 EUROPE: THE AGE OF ENLIGHTENMENT

gentlewomen in a sophisticated age. The slavish imitation of contemporary fashions by the middle class also became a handy target for comedy and SATIRE. We use the words *fop* and *dandy*—taken from seventeenth-century drama—to describe the individual whose vanity yields to excesses. While to all appearances, science was making astonishing strides ...discovering and describing a rational universe, human society, for all ...pes and pretensions, seemed to lag behind. It was easier to formu...w law of physics than to eradicate a basic fault of human nature, ...reed. **Molière** used the full resources of French theater to expose ...tween the ideal and the real by creating comedies that poked ...ocrisy, greed, affectation, zealotry, and immoderation. Despite ...ive influence of the Catholic Church on seventeenth-century ...lière's plays are not concerned with the religious implications ...ction but rather with the social consequences of immodera...poor taste, when individuals fail to comply with the ideals of ...easonableness, and common sense.

...on of the Court Upholsterer. Jean-Baptiste Poquelin was in line ...inherit his father's position as *tapissier ordinaire du roi,* the king's upholsterer, and enjoy a comfortable life. He received a fine education at College de Clermont, a Jesuit college, and practiced law for a short time. In 1643 he drastically changed careers by becoming one of nine founders of an acting company in Paris, the *Illustre Théâtre.* Taking the stage name of Molière for the first time, he devoted the rest of his life to theater—writing, directing, staging, and producing plays. Although theater was popular with the general public, the acting profession itself was condemned by the clergy; in fact, an actor was automatically excommunicated by the church and denied Christian burial unless a renunciation of his chosen career was forthcoming before death.

Molière's new company was a total failure, at least financially; twice the playwright ended up in jail for debts. As a result, he retreated to the countryside where he learned the organizational nuts and bolts of successful theater by touring the back roads and provinces of France. For thirteen years he served an apprenticeship in the various practical and artistic responsibilities of a theatrical company. He also turned his attention from tragedies to comedies—his true calling.

In 1658 Molière returned to Paris, found favor with the court through Louis XIV's brother, "Monsieur," and had an indisputable hit with *The High-Brow Young Ladies* (*Les précieuses ridicules,* 1659). From then on he enjoyed huge success and the patronage of the king. The titles of his masterpieces constitute a list of the kinds of people he subjected to satire and ridicule. *School for Wives* (*L'ecole des femmes,* 1662) examines the insecurities of courtship. *Don Juan* (1665) picks up the theme of the playboy and explores intimate relationships. *The Misanthrope* (1666) exposes the shortsightedness of a self-righteous intellectual. *The Miser* (*L'avare,* 1668), as the title gives away, satirizes lust for money. *The Would-Be Gentleman* (*Le bourgeois gentilhomme,* 1670) turns on the aspiring middle classes and *The Learned Ladies* (*Les femmes savantes,* 1672) attacks

...plays ...the tragic, ...no one has the courage to try and imitate him.
– AUGUSTIN SAINTE-BEUVE, critic, 1914

These two pages show a sampling of the apparatus we include for each author in the book, including helpful footnotes, pronunciation guides, critical quotations, and much more.

These terms cover the generic conventions of fiction, poetry, and drama; historical forms such as epic, epigram, and myth; and relevant historical periods such as the European Enlightenment or the Edo period in Japan.

Making connections among works from different times and places. At the end of each author introduction are two catalysts for further thought and discussion. **Questions** in the Connections apparatus tie together Western and world texts, both those within a single book and selections from other centuries, making the six books more of a unit and aiding in their interplay. **Further Research bibliographies**

Aphra Behn, 1640–1689 93

human relations. The narrator is a member of the dominant class of white colonists, but as a woman she is not in a particularly privileged position. She initially describes herself as an impartial observer and recorder of events. But while it is clear that she is not impartial, it is unclear exactly where her sympathies lie or to what extent she is a responsible participant in the unfolding events. Her description of Prince Oroonoko, who is first a slave-owner and then a slave, resembles depictions of heroes in European romances. Educated by a French tutor and conversant in three European languages, Oroonoko is courageous, witty and genteel. His features are Roman rather than African, he is highly skilled in the arts of war, and he is the possessor of an extreme sensibility that causes him to pine for the fair Imoinda. Working partly from the concept of the "noble savage," which celebrates an idealized version of "primitive" human beings as symbols of innate goodness uncorrupted by the influence of civilization, Behn's Eurocentric concept of beauty and nobility complicates the status and function of her hero.

After Oroonoko is tricked into slavery by the captain of an English ship, his story, while keeping many of its romantic elements, takes on a dark realism and broaches some disturbing aspects of human interaction. Oroonoko's inherent nobility and courage, for example, bring him compliments and promises of freedom from his white associates and masters, but in the end neither his friends nor his own nobility saves him from savagery. Though he is educated in the language and reasoning of Western thought, the powerful Christian arguments he uses to protest the bloody practices of the colonizers make little impact. And in the violent and unjust system to which Oroonoko is subjected, the purity and integrity of romantic love—which the prince honors in his dedication to Imoinda when they meet again as fellow slaves—is undermined.

CONNECTIONS

Olaudah Equiano, *The Int* ***ing Narrative of the Life of Olaudah Equiano,* p. 405.** The form and content of a work are always influenced to some degree by considerations of purpose a ence. It might be argued that *Oroonoko* Westernizes its hero in order to m fficult lesson more palatable to a European readership. Consider the way ose and approach of Behn's work compare with those in *The Interesting N e Life of Olaudah Equiano.*

oyinka, *The Lion and the Jewel,* (Book 6). In England, the status and role of women as en up in literature. Behn's interest in gender her description of the powers of Imoinda, the brave prince Oroonoko so completely atment of the female sex with the position and

Chinua Achebe, *Things Fall* *Fall Apart* and Soyinka's *The Lion and the Jewel.*

aptivity and Restoration of Mrs. Mary Rowlandson, late seventeenth- and eig zed the concept of the "noble savage." In *Oroonoko,* oko experience and record their exposure to unfamiliar of the social who In addition, Behn's text is famous for its portrayal of the use of Christian doctrine to argue for compassionate understanding among cultures. Look at Rowlandson's style of description, characterization of the "savage," and use of Christian doctrine in contrast with Behn's.

The two pages shown here illustrate some of the ways we try to help students connect readings across time and place.

274 EUROPE: THE AGE OF ENLIGHTENMENT

officials, military commanders, and religious professionals. This wide range of experiences and the work's short chapters keep *Candide* entertaining and engaging. When the protagonist and his valet, Cacambo, finally arrive in the famed utopia of El Dorado,[10] they discover it to be boring; naturally they find a commonsense religion, about which Cacambo remarks, "What! you have no monks to teach, argue, govern, intrigue, and burn at the stake everyone who disagrees with them?" In Candide's search for situations that would confound Pangloss's philosophy, he finally meets Martin, a thoroughgoing pessimist. Steering a philosophical course between the two extremes, Candide arrives in Constantinople and is rejoined by his former comrades, including his beloved Lady **Cunégonde**. Candide's adjustments to all the changes in their respective lives leads to conclusions about living the simple life. He proposes a practical, modest realism; the importance of work is alluded to in the enigmatic dictum that ends the work: "We must cultivate our garden."

koo-nay-GOHND

■ CONNECTIONS

Tu Fu (Book 2). In his work, eighth-century Chinese poet Tu Fu critiques the incompetent bureaucrats of the Tang dynasty. Which parts of society does Voltaire single out for criticism in *Candide*?

Jonathan Swift, *Gulliver's Travels,* p. 147. Both Swift and Voltaire use their narrators as agents through which they can view and satirize reality. A narrator may mirror or discover a society's weaknesses and defects. How does Voltaire's use of the innocent Candide differ from Swift's use of Gulliver, the ordinary seaman?

Alexander Pope, *The Rape of the Lock,* p. 238. One tool of satire is hyperbole: the exaggeration of a character trait or social defect. The hyperbole in Pope's *The Rape of the Lock* highlights the shallowness of social vanity and upper-class manners. What does the hyperbole Voltaire employs in his portrayal of clergymen say about ution of religion?

FURTHER RESEARCH

Biography

Besterman, Theodore. *Voltaire.* 1976.
Brailsford, Henry N. *Voltaire.* 1935.
Wade, Ira O. *The Intellectual Development of Voltaire.* 1969.

Intellectual History

Keener, F. M. *The Chain of Being.* 1983.
tenment and the Comic Mode. 1990.
: The Poet as Realist. 1959.
nd Candide: *A Study in the Fusion of History, Art, and Philosophy.*

ticism

M., ed. *The En*

onquistadors believed that *El Dorado* ("the golden man") was a kingdom of unlimited gold—so much gold that the king covered himself with it daily—located somewhere in the Americas. The name became synonymous with a hidden or lost paradise.

provide sources for students who want to read more critical, biographical, or historical information about an author or a work.

Print and online ancillaries further support the anthology's material. Two instructor's manuals, *Resources for Teaching* THE BEDFORD ANTHOLOGY OF WORLD LITERATURE, accompany Books 1–3 and Books 4–6 (one for each package), providing additional information about the anthology's texts and the authors, suggestions for discussion and writing prompts in the classroom and beyond, and additional connections among texts in the six books.

We are especially enthusiastic about our integrated Book Companion Site, *World Literature Online*, which provides a wealth of content and information that only the interactive medium of the Web can offer. **Web links** throughout the anthology direct

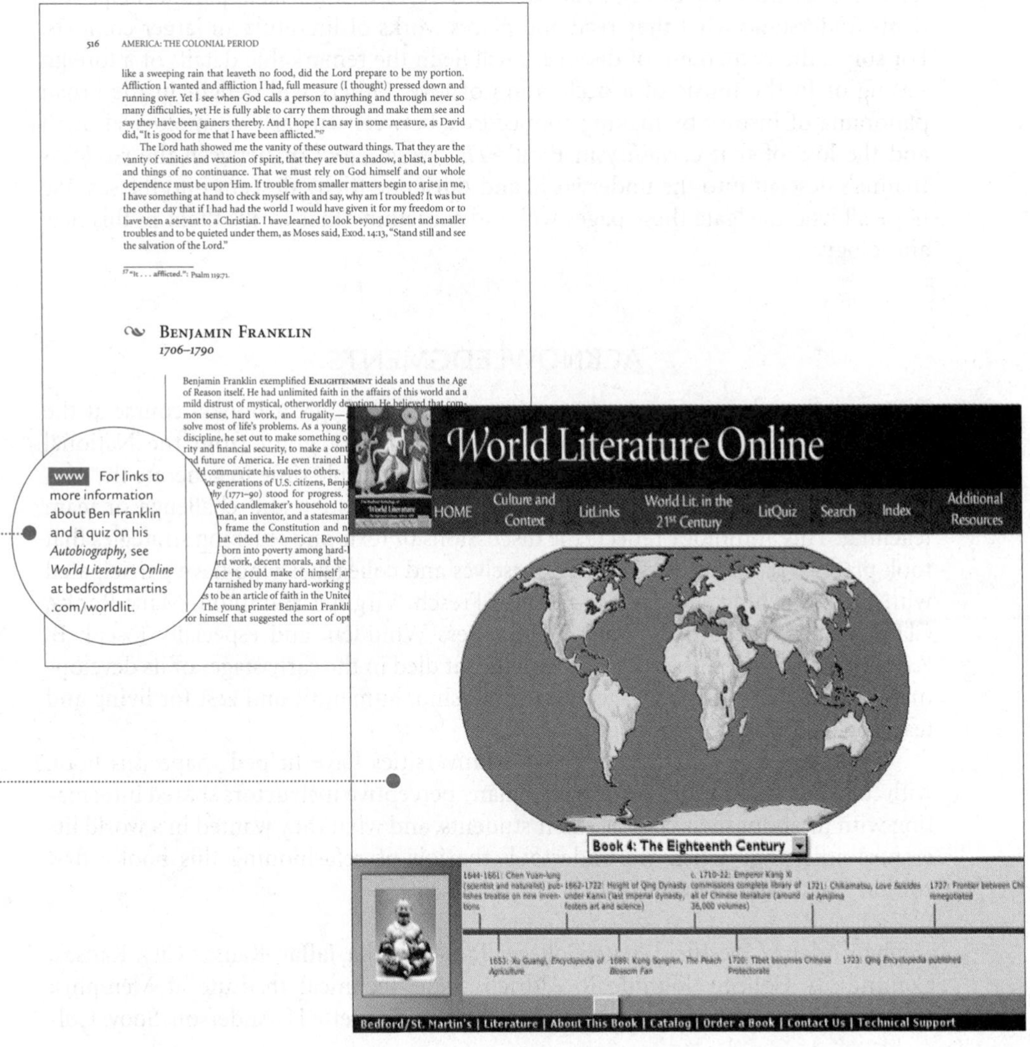

students to additional content on the Web site, where interactive illustrated time lines and maps serve as portals to more information about countries, texts, and authors. Culture and Context overviews offer additional historical background and annotated research links that students can follow to learn more on their own. Illustrated World Literature in the Twenty-First Century discussions trace the enduring presence in contemporary culture of the most frequently taught texts in world literature courses. Maps from the book are available online. Quizzes in LitQuiz offer an easy way for instructors to assess students' reading and comprehension. And LitLinks—annotated research links—provide a way for students to learn more about individual authors.

This wide variety of supplementary materials, as well as the broad spectrum of literary texts, offers teachers choices for navigating the familiar and the unfamiliar territories of world literature. Practical and accessible editorial apparatus helps students understand what they read and places works of literature in larger contexts. For some, the excitement of discovery will lie in the remarkable details of a foreign setting or in the music of a declaration of love. Others will delight in the broad panorama of history by making connections between an early cosmological myth and the loss of that certainty in Eliot's *The Waste Land* or between the Goddess Inanna's descent into the underworld and Adrienne Rich's descent into the sea. We hope all who navigate these pages will find something that thrills them in this new anthology.

ACKNOWLEDGMENTS

This anthology began in a team-taught, multicultural "great books" course at the University of New Mexico, initially developed with a grant from the National Endowment for the Humanities. The grant gave us ample time to generate the curriculum for the course, and it also supported the luxury and challenge of team teaching. This anthology reflects the discussions of texts and teaching strategies that took place over many years among ourselves and colleagues who have participated with us in teaching the course—Cheryl Fresch, Virginia Hampton, Mary Rooks, Claire Waters, Richard K. Waters, Mary Bess Whidden, and especially Joseph B. Zavadil, who began this anthology with us but died in the early stages of its development. Joe's spirit—his courage, wit, scholarship, humanity, and zest for living and teaching—endures in this book.

Reviewers from many colleges and universities have helped shape this book with their advice and suggestions. And many perceptive instructors shared information with us about their courses, their students, and what they wanted in a world literature anthology when we undertook the job of refashioning this book's first edition. We thank them all:

Stephen Adams, Westfield State College; Tamara Agha-Jaffar, Kansas City, Kansas, Community College; Johnnie R. Aldrich, State Technical Institute at Memphis; Allison Alison, Southeastern Community College; Jannette H. Anderson, Snow College; Kit Andrews, Western Oregon University; Joan Angelis, Woodbury University; Shirley Ariker, Empire State College; Sister Elena F. Arminio, College of Saint Elizabeth; Rose Lee Bancroft, Alice Lloyd College; John Bartle, Hamilton College; Amy M. Bawcom, University of Mary Hardin-Baylor; M. Susan Beck, University of Wisconsin-River Falls; Frank Beesley, Dalton State College; Peter Benson, Farleigh Dickinson University; Michael Bielmeier, Silver Lake College; Dale B. Billingsley, University of Louisville; Mark Bingham, Union University; Stephen Black, Dyersburg State Community College; Neil Blackadder, Knox College; Tyler Blake, MidAmerica Nazarene University; Gene Blanton, Jacksonville State University; James Boswell Jr., Harrisburg Area Community College; Lisa S. Bovelli, Itasca Community College; Lois Bragg, Gallaudet University; Kristin Ruth Brate, Arizona Western College; Marie Brenner, Bethel College; Linda Brown, Coastal Georgia Community College; Keith Callis, Crichton College; Charles P. Campbell, New Mexico Tech.; Zuoya Cao, Lincoln University; William Carpenter, College of ME Atlantic; May Charles, Wheeling Jesuit College; R. J. Clougherty, Tennessee Technical College; Helen Connell, Barry University; Lynn Conroy, Seton Hill College; Sue Coody, Weatherford College; Thomas A. Copeland, Youngstown State University; Peter Cortland, Quinnipiac College; R. Costomiris, Georgia Southern University; H. J. Coughlin, Eastern Connecticut State University; Marc D. Cyr, Georgia Southern University; Sarah Dangelantonio, Franklin Pierce College; James Davis, Troy State University; Barbara Dicey, Wallace College; Wilfred O. Dietrich, Blinn College; Michael Dinielli, Chaffey College; Matt Djos, Mesa State College; Marjorie Dobbin, Brewton-Parker College; Brian L. Dose, Martin Luther College; Dawn Duncan, Concordia College; Bernie Earley, Tompkins-Cortland Community College; Sarah M. Eichelman, Walters State Community College; Robert H. Ellison, East Texas Baptist University; Joshua D. Esty, Harvard University; Robert J. Ewald, University of Findlay; Shirley Felt, Southern California College; Lois Ferrer, CSU Dominguez Hills; Patricia Fite, University of the Incarnate Word; Sr. Agnes Fleck, St. Scholastica College; Robert Fliessner, Central State University; M. L. Flynn, South Dakota State University; Keith Foster, Arkansas State University; John C. Freeman, El Paso Community College; Doris Gardenshire, Trinity Valley Community College; Susan Gardner, University of North Carolina-Charlotte; Jerry D. Gibbens, Williams Baptist College; Susan Gilbert, Meredith College; Diana Glyer, Azusa Pacific University; Irene Gnarra, Kean University; R. C. Goetter, Glouster Community College; Nancy Goldfarb, Western Kentucky University; Martha Goodman, Central Virginia Community College; Lyman Grant, Austin Community College; Hazel Greenberg, San Jacinto College South; Janet Grose, Union University; Sharon Growney-Seals, Ouachita Technical College; Rachel Hadas, Rutgers University; Laura Hammons, East Central Community College; Carmen Hardin, University of Louisville; Darren Harris-Fain, Shawnee State University; Patricia B. Heaman, Wilkes University; Charles Heglan, University of South Florida; Dennis E. Hensley, Taylor University; Kathleen M. Herndon, Weber State University; Betty Higdon, Reedley College; David Hoegberg, Indiana University; Diane Long Hoeveler, Marquette University; Tyler Hoffman, Rutgers University; Lynn Hoggard, Midwestern State University; Greg Horn, Southwest VA Community College; Roger Horn, Charles County Community

College; Malinda Jay-Bartels, Gulf Coast Community College; Mell Johnson, Wallace State Community College; Kathryn Joyce, Santa Barbara City College; Steven Joyce, Ohio State University-Mansfield; Ronald A. T. Judy, University of Pittsburgh; Alan Kaufman, Bergen Community College; Tim Kelley, Northwest-Shoals Community College; Shoshanna Knapp, Virginia Technical College; Jim Knox, Roane State Community College; Mary Kraus, Bob Jones University; F. Kuzman, Bethel College; Kate Kysa, Anoka-Ramsey Community College; Linda L. Labin, Husson College; Barbara Laman, Dickinson State University; R. Scott Lamascus, GA-Southwestern State University; Sandi S. Landis, St. Johns River Community College; Ben Larson, York College; Craig Larson, Trinidad State Junior College; Linda M. Lawrence, Georgia Military College; Simon Lewis, C. of Charleston; Gary L. Litt, Moorhead State University; H. W. Lutrin, Borough of Manhattan Community College; Dennis Lynch, Elgin Community College; Donald H. Mager, Johnson C. Smith University; Barbara Manrique, California State University; W. E. Mason, Mid-Continent College; Judith Matsunobu, Atlantic Community College; Noel Mawer, Edward Waters College; Patrick McDarby, St. John's University; Judy B. McInnis, University of Delaware; Becky McLaughlin, University of Southern Alabama; Edward E. Mehok, Notre Dame College of Ohio; Patricia Menhart, Broward Community College; Arthur McA. Miller, New College of Florida; Mark James Morreale, Marist College; Toni Morris, University of Indianapolis; Philip Mosley, Penn State–Worthington; George Mower, Community College of Alleghany County; L. Carl Nadeau, University of St. Francis; Walter Nelson, Red Rocks Community College; Steven Neuwirth, Western Connecticut State University; Carol H. Oliver, St. Louis College of Pharmacy; Richard Orr, York Technical College; Geoffrey Orth, Longwood College; Ramenga M. Osotsi, James Madison University; Bonnie Pavlis, Riverside Community College; Craig Payne, Indian Hills College; Leialoha Perkins, University of Hawaii; Ralph Perrico, Mercyhurst College; Charles W. Pollard, Calvin College; Michael Popkin, Touro College; Victoria Poulakis, Northern Virginia Community College; Alan Powers, Bristol Community College; Andrew B. Preslar, Lamar University; Evan Radcliffe, Villanova University; Belle Randall, Cornish College of the Arts; Elaine Razzano, Lyndon State College; Lucia N. Robinson, Okaloosa-Walton Community College; John Rooks, Morris College; William T. Ross, University of South Florida; Andrew Rubenfeld, Stevens Institute of Technology; Elizabeth S. Ruleman, Tennessee Wesleyan College; Olena H. Saciuk, Inter-American University; Mary Lynn Saul, Worcester State College; MaryJane Schenck, University of Tampa; Kevin Schilbrack, Wesleyan College; Deborah Schlacks, University of Wisconsin; Michael Schroeder, Savannah State University; Helen Scott, Wilkes University; Asha Sen, University of Wisconsin; Mary Sheldon, Washburn University; Lisa Shoemaker, State Technical Community College; Jack Shreve, Allegany College of Maryland; Meg Simonton, Albertson College; Susan Sink, Joliet Junior College; Henry Sloss, Anne Arundel Community College; T. Sluberski, Concordia University; Betty Smith, The Criswell College; Jane Bouman Smith, Winthrop University; John Somerville, Hillsdale College; Claudia Stanger, Fullerton College; Patrick Sullivan, Manchester Community-Technical College; Joan S. Swartz, Baptist

Bible College of PA; Leah Swartz, Maryville University; Sister Renita Tadych, Silver Lake College; Janet Tarbuck, Kennebee Valley Technical College; Gina Teel, Southeast Arkansas College; Daniel Thurber, Concordia University; John Paul Vincent, Asbury College; Paul Vita, Morningside College; Tim Walsh, Otera Junior College; Julia Watson, Ohio State University; Patricia J. Webb, Maysville Community College; Lynne Weller, John Wood Community College; Roger West, Trident Technical College; Katherine Wikoff, Milwaukee School of Engineering; Evelyn M. Wilson, Tarrant County College; Carmen Wong, John Lyle Community College; Paul D. Wood, Paducah Community College; Fay Wright, North Idaho College; and finally, Pamela G. Xanthopoulos, Jackson State Community College.

We also want to thank a special group of reviewers who looked in depth at the manuscript for each book, offering us targeted advice about its strengths and weaknesses:

Cora Agatucci, Central Oregon Community College; Michael Austin, Shepherd College; Maryam Barrie, Washtenaw Community College; John Bartle, Hamilton College; Jeffry Berry, Adrian College; Lois Bragg, Gallaudet University; Ron Carter, Rappahannock Community College; Robin Clouser, Ursinus College; Eugene R. Cunnar, New Mexico State University; Karen Dahr, Ellsworth Community College; Kristine Daines, Arizona State University; Sarah Dangelantonio, Franklin Pierce College; Jim Doan, Nova SE University; Melora Giardetti, Simpson College; Audley Hall, North West Arkansas Community College; Dean Hall, Kansas State University; Wail Hassan, Illinois State University; Joris Heise, Sinclair Community College; Diane Long Hoeveler, Marquette University; Glenn Hopp, Howard Payne University; Mickey Jackson, Golden West College; Feroza Jussawalla, University of New Mexico; Linda Karch, Norwich University; David Karnos, Montana State University; William Laskowski, Jamestown College; Pat Lonchar, University of the Incarnate Word; Donald Mager, The Mott University; Judy B. McInnis, University of Delaware; Becky McLaughlin, University of South Alabama; Tony J. Morris, University of Indianapolis; Deborah Schlacks, University of Wisconsin; James Snowden, Cedarville University; David T. Stout, Luzerne County Community College; Arline Thorn, West Virginia State College; Ann Volin, University of Kansas; Mary Wack, Washington State University; Jayne A. Widmayer, Boise State University; and William Woods, Wichita State University.

No anthology of this size comes into being without critical and supportive friends and advisors. Our thanks go to the Department of English at the University of New Mexico (UNM); its chair, Scott Sanders, who encouraged and supported our work; and Margaret Shinn and the office staff, who provided administrative and technical assistance. Among our colleagues at UNM, we particularly want to thank Gail Baker, Helen Damico, Reed Dasenbrock, Patrick Gallacher, Feroza Jussawalla, Michelle LeBeau, Richard Melzer, Mary Power, Diana Robin, and Hugh Witemeyer. Several graduate students also helped with this project: Jana Giles contributed the final section on American multicultural literature; Mary Rooks wrote the sections on Aphra Behn and Wole Soyinka and served heroically as our assistant, record keeper, all-purpose editor, and consultant.

We have benefited from the knowledge and suggestions of those who have corrected our misunderstandings, illuminated topics and cultures with which we were unfamiliar, critiqued our work, and suggested ways to enrich the anthology: Paula Gunn Allen, Reynold Bean, Richard Bodner, Machiko Bomberger, Robert Dankoff, Kate Davis, Robert Hanning, Arthur Johnson, Dennis Jones, James Mischke, Harlan Nelson, Barrett Price, Clayton Rich, Julia Stein, Manjeet Tangri, William Witherup, Diane Wolkstein, and William Woods.

Resources for Teaching THE BEDFORD ANTHOLOGY OF WORLD LITERATURE was expertly developed, edited, and assembled by Mary Rooks, assisted by Julia Berrisford. Along with Mary, Shari Evans, Gabriel Gryffyn, Rick Mott, Susan Reese, Kenneth Kitchell, Randall Colaizzi, Bainard Cowan, William Flesch, Fidel Fajardo-Acosta, Yigal Levin, and John Phillips each wrote a section of the manual. The manual itself was a large and challenging endeavor; we are grateful to its authors for their enthusiasm and hard work.

A six-volume anthology is an undertaking that calls for a courageous, imaginative, and supportive publisher. Chuck Christensen, Joan Feinberg, Karen Henry, and Steve Scipione at Bedford/St. Martin's possess these qualities; we especially appreciate their confidence in our ability to carry out this task. Our editor, Alanya Harter, and her associate, Joshua Levy, have guided the project throughout, keeping us on track with a vision of the whole when we were discouraged and keeping the day-to-day work moving forward. In particular, they helped us to reconceptualize the anthology's format and content. Without their suggestions, unacknowledged contributions, and guidance, this anthology would not be what it is today. They were assisted by many others who undertook particular tasks: The brilliant design was conceived by Anna George; Genevieve Hamilton helped to manage the art program, and together with Julia Berrisford she managed the final stages of development. Martha Friedman served as photo researcher, and Tina Samaha was design consultant and map coordinator. Jeff Voccola acted as editorial assistant, taking on many tasks, including the onerous ones of pasting up and numbering the manuscript. Ben Fortson expertly and efficiently supplied the pronunciation guides. Harriet Wald tirelessly and imaginatively oversaw the content and production of the Web site, an enormous task; she was helped along the way by Coleen O'Hanley, Chad Crume, and Dave Batty. Jenna Bookin Barry enthusiastically developed and coordinated the marketing plan, especially challenging when six books publish over a span of six months.

We were blessed with a superb production team who took the book from manuscript to final pages. For Books 4 and 6, we owe special thanks to Senior Production Editor Karen Baart, whose dedication and eye for detail made the project better in every way. Stasia Zomkowski efficiently served as production editor for Books 3 and 5, Ara Salibian for Book 1, and Paula Carroll for Book 2; they were ably assisted by Courtney Jossart, Kerri Cardone, and Tina Lai. Melissa Cook's and Janet Renard's careful and thoughtful copyediting helped to give consistency and clarity to the different voices that contributed to the manuscript. Managing Editor Elizabeth Schaaf oversaw the whole process and Senior Production Supervisor Nancy Myers realized our final vision of design and content in beautifully bound and printed books.

Most of all, we thank our families, especially Mary Davis, Marlys Harrison, and Mona Johnson, for their advice, stamina, and patience during the past three years while this book has occupied so much of our time and theirs.

Paul Davis
Gary Harrison
David M. Johnson
Patricia Clark Smith
John F. Crawford

A NOTE ON TRANSLATION

Some translators of literary works into English tended to sacrifice form for literal meaning, while others subordinated literal meaning to the artistry of the original work. With the increasing number of translations of world literature available by a range of translators, it has become possible to select versions that are clear and accessible as well as literally and aesthetically faithful to the original. Thus our choice of Horace Gregory's poems by Catullus, Mary Barnard's poems by Sappho, Theodore Morrison's *Canterbury Tales,* Edward Seidensticker's *Tale of Genji,* and Willa and Edwin Muir's *The Metamorphosis,* among others.

There are those who question whether poetry can ever be adequately translated from one language and culture into another; our concern, however, is not with what might be lost in a translation but with what is gained. The best translations do not merely duplicate a work but re-create it in a new idiom. Coleman Barks's poems of Rumi, Stephen Mitchell's poems of Rilke, Miguel León-Portilla's translations of Nahuatl poetry, and David Hinton's poems of the Tang dynasty are in a way outstanding English poems in their own right. And William Kelly Simpson's love poems of ancient Egypt, Robert and Jean Hollander's *Inferno,* Richard Wilbur's *Tartuffe,* W. S. Merwin's poems of Ghalib, Judith Hemschemeyer's poems of Anna Akhmatova, and Robert Bly's poems of Pablo Neruda are examples of translations done by major poets whose renderings are now an important part of their own body of work.

Barbara Stoler Miller's translation of the Bhagavad Gita and Donald Keene's translation of Chikamatsu's *Love Suicides at Amijima* communicate the complexity of a literary work. Richard Bodner's contemporary translation of Bashō's *Narrow Road through the Backcountry,* especially commissioned, does justice to both the prose and the resonant haiku in that work. David Luke's excellent translation of *Death in Venice* pays tribute to Thomas Mann's original German and is at the same time very readable.

More is said about the translations in this book in the notes for individual works.

About the Editors

Paul Davis (Ph.D., University of Wisconsin), professor emeritus of English at the University of New Mexico, has been the recipient of several teaching awards and academic honors, including that of Master Teacher. He has taught courses since 1962 in composition, rhetoric, and nineteenth-century literature and has written and edited many scholarly books, including *The Penguin Dickens Companion* (1999), *Dickens A to Z* (1998), and *The Life and Times of Ebeneezer Scrooge* (1990). He has also written numerous scholarly and popular articles on solar energy and Victorian book illustration.

Gary Harrison (Ph.D., Stanford University), professor and director of undergraduate studies at the University of New Mexico, has won numerous fellowships and awards for scholarship and teaching. He has taught courses in world literature, British Romanticism, and literary theory at the University of New Mexico since 1987. Harrison's publications include a critical study on William Wordsworth, *Wordsworth's Vagrant Muse: Poetry, Poverty and Power* (1994); and many articles on the literature and culture of the early nineteenth century.

David M. Johnson (Ph.D., University of Connecticut), professor emeritus of English at the University of New Mexico, has taught courses in world literature, mythology, the Bible as literature, philosophy and literature, and creative writing since 1965. He has written, edited, and contributed to numerous scholarly books and collections of poetry, including *Fire in the Fields* (1996) and *Lord of the Dawn: The Legend of Quetzalcoatl* (1987). He has also published scholarly articles, poetry, and translations of Nahuatl myths.

Patricia Clark Smith (Ph.D., Yale University), professor emerita of English at the University of New Mexico, has taught courses in world literature, creative writing, American literature, and Native American literature since 1971. Her many publications include a collection of poetry, *Changing Your Story* (1991); the biography *As Long as the Rivers Flow* (1996); and *On the Trail of Elder Brother* (2000).

John F. Crawford (Ph.D., Columbia University), associate professor of English at the University of New Mexico–Valencia, has taught medieval, world, and other literature courses since 1965 at a number of institutions, including California Institute of Technology, Herbert Lehmann College of CUNY, and, most recently, the University of New Mexico. The publisher of West End Press, Crawford has also edited *This Is About Vision: Interviews with Southwestern Writers* (1990) and written articles on multicultural women poets of the Southwest.

Pronunciation Key

This key applies to the pronunciation guides that appear in the margins and before most selections in *The Bedford Anthology of World Literature*. The syllable receiving the main stress is CAPITALIZED.

a	mat, alabaster, laugh	MAT, AL-uh-bas-tur, LAF
ah	mama, Americana, Congo	MAH-mah, uh-meh-rih-KAH-nuh, KAHNG-goh
ar	cartoon, Harvard	kar-TOON, HAR-vurd
aw	saw, raucous	SAW, RAW-kus
ay (or a)	may, Abraham, shake	MAY, AY-bruh-ham, SHAKE
b	bet	BET
ch	church, matchstick	CHURCH, MACH-stik
d	desk	DESK
e	Edward, melted	ED-wurd, MEL-tid
ee	meet, ream, petite	MEET, REEM, puh-TEET
eh	cherub, derriere	CHEH-rub, DEH-ree-ehr
f	final	FIGH-nul
g	got, giddy	GAHT, GIH-dee
h	happenstance	HAP-un-stans
i	mit, Ipswich, impression	MIT, IP-swich, im-PRESH-un
igh (or i)	eyesore, right, Anglophile	IGH-sore, RITE, ANG-gloh-file
ih	Philippines	FIH-luh-peenz
j	judgment	JUJ-mint
k	kitten	KIT-tun
l	light, allocate	LITE, AL-oh-kate
m	ramrod	RAM-rahd
n	ran	RAN
ng	rang, thinker	RANG, THING-ker
oh (or o)	open, owned, lonesome	OH-pun, OHND, LONE-sum
ong	wrong, bonkers	RONG, BONG-kurz
oo	moot, mute, super	MOOT, MYOOT, SOO-pur
ow	loud, dowager, how	LOWD, DOW-uh-jur, HOW
oy	boy, boil, oiler	BOY, BOYL, OY-lur
p	pet	PET
r	right, wretched	RITE, RECH-id
s	see, citizen	SEE, SIH-tuh-zun
sh	shingle	SHING-gul
t	test	TEST
th	thin	THIN
th	this, whether	*TH*IS, WEH-*th*ur
u	until, sumptuous, lovely	un-TIL, SUMP-choo-us, LUV-lee
uh	about, vacation, suddenly	uh-BOWT, vuh-KAY-shun, SUH-dun-lee
ur	fur, bird, term, beggar	FUR, BURD, TURM, BEG-ur
v	vacuum	VAK-yoo-um
w	western	WES-turn
y	yesterday	YES-tur-day
z	zero, loser	ZEE-roh, LOO-zur
zh	treasure	TREH-zhur

Where a name is given two pronunciations, usually the first is the most familiar pronunciation in English and the second is a more exact rendering of the native pronunciation.

In the pronunciations of French names, nasalized vowels are indicated by adding "ng" after the vowel.

Japanese words have no strong stress accent, so the syllables marked as stressed are so given only for the convenience of English speakers.

CONTENTS

Sandro Boticelli, La Primavera, 1485 *Sometimes called "Allegory of Spring,"* La Primavera *was painted for the great Renaissance prince and patron of the arts, Lorenzo de'Medici. While scholars have not fully agreed upon the painting's meaning, most agree that its depiction of mythological figures reflects the revival of classical learning and the Italian humanist tradition. The central figure of Venus, the goddess of Love, flanked by the three Graces and Flora, the goddess of Fecundity, has been understood to symbolize life, beauty, and knowledge united by love. (Alinari / Art Resource, NY)*

The Early Modern World

1450 - 1650

The **Early Modern** Period encompasses the two hundred years from about 1450 to around 1650. The trends of modernization that give the period its name include the expansion of global networks of trade and European colonialism; the formation of strong, centralized monarchies and empires; the shift from feudal societies based on agriculture to urban societies based on commerce and industry; and the increasing secularization of political, social, and cultural life.

Of course, such changes did not occur all at once, at equal rates of acceleration, or to the same degree even within Europe, much less across the globe. The German states of the Holy Roman Empire and the Italian city-states, for example, did not undergo centralization until the nineteenth century, though early modern Italy did see the rise of an urban middle class and the growth of fortunes from

www For an interactive version of the Comparative Time Line for the Early Modern World, see *World Literature Online* at bedfordstmartins.com/worldlit.

COMPARATIVE TIME LINE FOR THE EARLY MODERN WORLD

Date	History and Politics	Literature	Science, Culture, and Technology
500–1000		6th–7th centuries Campantar Appar in India	
	7th century Islam takes hold in northern Africa	7th–8th centuries Cuntara in India	
	9th century Islam takes hold in Horn of Africa		
		980 Ibn Sina (Avicenna) (980–1037)	
1000–1300		1018 Nizam al-Mulk (1018–1092)	
	c. 1100 Founding of Timbuktu	12th century Basavanna Mahdeviyakka Jayadeva	
	c. 1100 Mexica begin migration toward the Valley of Mexico		
		1130 Zhu Xi (1130–1200)	
	c. 1200 Rise of Mali empire		
	1281 Rule of Osman of Ottoman Empire		
1300–1350	14th to mid-15th century Height of culture and power in Zimbabwe	14th century Sunjata	14th century Djingareyber and Sankore Mosques built at Timbuktu
		14th century Vidyapati	
	1312 Mansa Musa (r. 1312–37) takes power in Mali	1304 Francesco Petrarch (1304–1374)	
	1322 Visconti family takes hold of power in Milan		
	1324 Mansa Musa's famous pilgrimage to Meca creates legendary view of Timbuktu and the Mali empire		
	1325 Mexica arrive in the Valley of Mexico; establish Tenochtitlán		
		1332 Ibn Khaldun (1332–1406)	

trade and banking. Similarly, the origins of the Italian **Renaissance** date back to the mid-1300s, but Renaissance ideas and practices did not reach northern Europe until well into the 1400s.

The Early Modern Period may well be considered a transitional phase between cultural isolation and global interdependence. By the end of the 1600s, in no small part due to the European voyages of discovery that took place during these two hundred years, cultural, economic, and political exchanges—many of which were fraught with conflict—would begin to erode the autonomy of individual cultures in most regions of the world and lead to a bona fide era of world history.

EXPANSION OF GLOBAL NETWORKS OF TRADE AND EUROPEAN COLONIALISM

The European voyages of discovery and conquest between 1450 and 1650 forever altered the patterns of economic exchange, the distribution of wealth, and the

Date	History and Politics	Literature	Science, Culture, and Technology
1350–1400	1360 Rule of Murat (r. 1360–89) conquered all of Byzantine Empire except Constantinople 1368 Zhu Yuanzhang (1328–1398) becomes Hongwu (r. 1368–98) emperor of Ming dynasty (1368–1644) 1372 Acamapichtli (r. 1372–91), first of the Aztec rulers, ascends the throne c. 1375 Rise of Songhai 1389 Battle of Kosovo: Ottomans defeat the Serbian army, leading to Ottoman control of southeastern Europe 1398 Tamerlane sacks Delhi		1380 Jan van Eyck (1380–1441)
1400–1450	15th century Heyday of Aztec and Inca empires 1403 Zhu Di becomes Yongle (r. 1403–24) emperor of Ming dynasty 1405–33 Voyages of Zheng He (c. 1371–1433)	15th century Govindadasa	1400–30 Period of "Civic Humanism" in Europe 1401 Masaccio (1401–28), painter of frescoes in the Brancacci Chapel in the Santa Maria del Carmine church of Florence 1403 Movable type first used for printing in Korea 1407 Construction begins on the "Forbidden City" in Beijing

alignments of political authority throughout the world. Led by Spain and Portugal, European countries opened up direct lines of trade with Africa, India, and China, and occupied—often by force—vast areas of Africa, India, and Indonesia, as well as the Americas, which the Europeans began in the 1500s to call the New World. This European expansion into global trade meant that Muslims and Hindus in port towns along the Indian Ocean lost much of the control they had held over the exchange of goods. For their part, the Portuguese—the first Europeans to sail around the southern tip of Africa and into the Indian Ocean—seized Calicut, in India, and Malacca, on the Malay Peninsula. Meanwhile, Spanish voyagers, spearheaded by Christopher Columbus (1451–1506), had landed in America, where the abundance of gold, silver, and land spurred the acquisitive desires of the English, Dutch, and French, among others. In the sixteenth century, the Europeans' desire for riches led to colonial expansion (and, concurrently, the spread of Christianity)

Date	History and Politics	Literature	Science, Culture, and Technology
1400–1450 (cont.)	1415 Jan Hus (1372–1415) burned at the stake for heresy; Portuguese capture Ceunta on the northern tip of Morocco 1417 Council of Constance brings end to the Great Schism, that had divided the Catholic Church into two papacies—at Avignon and Rome—since 1378 1421 Yongle moves capital from Nanjing to Beijing 1427 Under Itzcoatl (1427–40) Aztecs begin military expansion, forcing neighboring cities into their tributary network 1434 Cosimo de' Medici (1389–1464) takes control of Florence (until 1464) 1441 Portuguese arrive at the Senegal River; first European cargo of African Slaves	1414 Jami (1414–92) Seven Thrones 1421 Vespasiano da Bisticci (1421–1498) 1433 Marsilio Ficino (1433–1499) 1440 Kabir (1440–1518)	1434 Lateen sail adapted for ocean travel; enables Portuguese to begin exploration along coast of West Africa
1450–1500	1450 Sforzas dominate Milan (until 1494) 1451–81 Rule of Mehmet II over Ottoman empire 1453 Ottomans overtake Constantinople, bringing end to Byzantine Empire 1453 End of Hundred Years' War in Europe; Ottoman Turks seize Constantinople	1451 Christopher Columbus (1451–1506)	c. 1445–50 Johannes Gutenberg (c. 1307–1468) of Mainz, Germany, develops process for printing using movable type

in nearly every region in the world. The areas most powerfully affected were coastal Africa, the Americas, India, and the Spice Islands (East Indies), but even China, Japan, and what are now the Philippines and Hawaii would feel the repercussions of this sea change in global relations.

TOWNS, CITIES, COMMERCE, AND TRADE

While the majority of the world's people, including Europeans, worked in agriculture and lived in rural areas during the fifteenth and sixteenth centuries, the profits from trade and commerce, as well as from colonial expansion, promoted the growth of great cities and city-states in many parts of the world. In Europe, prosperous merchant and commercial classes emerged first in Italy, Portugal, and Spain, and then in the Netherlands and England. Port and trading towns in China, the Spice Islands, Africa, the Ottoman empire, and eventually even Japan also ben-

Date	History and Politics	Literature	Science, Culture, and Technology
1450–1500 (cont.)		1455–56 Gutenberg's bible, first book produced using movable metal type	1455 Kamal al-Din, Persian painter of miniatures (c. 1455–1536)
		1463 Giovanni Pico della Mirandola (1463–1494)	
	1468 Songhai empire conquers Timbuktu	1466 Desidarius Erasmus (1466–1536)	
		1469 Nanak (1469–1538)	
		1469 Niccolò Machiavelli (1469–1527)	
	1471–1521 The Renaissance papacy with popes Sixtus IV (1471–84), Alexander VI (1492–1503), Julius II (1503–13), and Leo X (1513–21)	1474 Bartolomé de Las Casas (1474–1549)	1471 Albrecht Dürer (1471–1528)
			1473 Nicholas Copernicus (1473–1543)
	1480 Ivan III of Russia (1440–1505) ends Mongol control of Russia	1478 Baldesar Castiglione (1478–1529)	1475 Michelangelo (1475–1564)
	1482 Portuguese establish trading post at Elmina in the Gulf of Guinea	1480 Fuzuli (1480–1556)	1483 Raphael (1483–1520)
		1483 Martin Luther (1483–1546)	
		François Rabelais (1483–1553)	
	1487–88 Bartholomeu Dias rounds Cape of Good Hope (c. 1450–1500)	1485 Hernán Cortés (1485–1547)	
		1490 Nzinga Mbemba (1490–1543), ruler in Africa	
	1492 Columbus arrives in America; met by the Taino	1492 Marguerite de Navarre (1492–1549)	

efited from international trade. Over time, this trade fostered the growth of a fairly prosperous urban middle class of traders and bankers, as well as manufacturers of exported goods and suppliers of resources.

Venice, Lisbon, Antwerp, Seville, and Amsterdam in Europe grew in fortune and influence, as did Calicut and Goa in India, Mombasa and Sofala in Africa, Canton and Macao in China, and Rio de Janeiro and Buenos Aires in South America. In Africa, important trading centers in the kingdoms of Mali, Songhai, and Hausa also had a thriving commercial class, and cities such as Timbuktu, on the trade routes between West Africa and the Mediterranean, enjoyed great prosperity. Much like its European counterparts, Timbuktu also became an important center for education, scholarship, and the arts.

Population increases in the towns and cities began to influence social patterns. In Europe and many other parts of the world, the clergy and the nobility were traditionally the most respected, powerful, and wealthy members of society. Beneath

Date	History and Politics	Literature	Science, Culture, and Technology
1450–1500 (cont.)	1494 Treaty of Tordesillas divides New World into two parts, giving Brazil to Portugal and the rest of the Americas to Spain		
	1494 France invades Italy		
	1497 John Cabot (c. 1450–99) lands on Newfoundland		
	1497–99 Voyage of Vasco da Gama (c. 1460–1524) opens European sea route to Indian Ocean		
	1498 Portuguese led by Vasco da Gama reach Calicut along India's Malabar Coast	1498 Mirabai (1498–1547)	
1500–1550		16th century Ancient Mexicans	
	1500 Height of culture and society in Benin	16th century Chandidasa	
	1501 Ismail (r. 1501–24) founds the Safavid Empire (1501–1736) in Persia (now Iran); officially adopts Shi'ism, setting Safavids apart from the Ottomans who were Sunnis	1501 Garcilaso de la Vega (c. 1501–1536) Maurice Scève (1501–1564)	
	1502 Moctezuma II (r. 1502–20) emperor of Aztecs		
	1502 Portuguese attack Calicut on the Malabar coast of India		
		1503 Sir Thomas Wyatt (1503–1542)	1503 Leonardo da Vinci (1452–1519), *Mona Lisa*
	1505 Portuguese capture Mombasa on east coast of Africa		
		1506 Wu Chengen (c. 1500–1582)	

these two powerful ranks lay what was known in France as the third estate, the supposedly undifferentiated mass of merchants, shopkeepers, artisans, craftsmen, farmers, peasants, and others who by dint of birth were allotted a life of unrelenting labor. Of course, there were vast differences in occupation and fortune within this group of people, and in the early modern period many bankers, merchants, and manufacturers found their incomes equaling or surpassing those of the nobles. In Europe, wealthy families, such as the Medicis in Florence and the Fuggers in Augsburg, became the effective leaders of their cities, exercising a social and political influence akin to that of hereditary royalty. The blurring of boundaries between the gentry and the newly well-to-do families led to a proliferation of treatises like Baldesar Castiglione's *The Courtier* (1528), which spelled out the ideal virtues and characteristics of the gentleman.

Outside of Europe, the commercial classes generally did not see their social standing increase as their fortunes grew. Nevertheless, in India, China, and Japan,

Date	History and Politics	Literature	Science, Culture, and Technology
1500–1550 (cont.)			1508 Pope Julius II commissions Michelangelo to decorate the ceiling of the Sistine Chapel in Rome; completed in 1512
	1510 Spanish take Tripoli in northern Africa		
	1510 Portuguese take over Goa, establishing their trading base there		
	1511 Portuguese seize Malacca, the major Indonesian trading center	1511 Erasmus, *In Praise of Folly*	
	1513 Portuguese arrive in Canton	1513 Machiavelli, *The Prince*	1513–21 Pope Leo X in Rome becomes leading patron of the arts
	1514 Ottomans defeat the Safavids		
	1517 Capture of Egypt by Ottomans ends Mamluk dynasty	1517 Luther, Ninety-Five Theses	
	1517 Luther's Ninety-Five Theses launch the Protestant Reformation		
	1518 First shipment of slaves leaves for Americas		
	1518 Charles I of Spain (1500–58) elected Holy Roman Emperor as Charles V (r. 1519–58)		
	1519–21 Hernán Cortés (1485–1587) arrives on Yucatan Peninsula and conquers Aztec empire		
	1520–66 Rule of Suleyman I the Magnificent over Ottoman empire	1520 Luther, *On the Freedom of a Christian Man*	
	1521 Catholic Church excommunicates Martin Luther		
	1522 Magellan's sailors complete the first European voyage circumnavigating the world		

wealthy merchants enjoyed a great deal of respect and influence. After the sack of Constantinople in 1453, the sultan Mehmet II (r. 1451–81) invited merchants and artisans—Christians, Muslims, and Jews—to occupy the emptied houses of the city, thereby promoting wealth and trade in his new capital. And though the lives of peasants and workers during this time probably remained consistent with those of their forebears in the Middle Period, even these groups were caught up (unfortunately, often as victims) in the wars over territory, trade, and commerce that swept through Europe and other parts of the world.

WAR, EMPIRE, AND MONARCHY

Competition in the fifteenth and sixteenth centuries for control of trade routes, markets, territories, and resources led to conflict—often violent—not only among European powers but also between European and non-European nations. Powerful kings competed, and conflicts between them ranged from the plundering of mer-

Date	History and Politics	Literature	Science, Culture, and Technology
1500–1550 (cont.)	1524 Reign begins of Shah Tahmasp I (r. 1524–76), Safavid emperor and patron of the arts	1524 Pierre de Ronsard (1524–1585) Louise Labé (1524–1566)	
	1526 Mughals under Babur (1483–1530) seize Delhi and establish the Mughal empire		
	1527–13 Civil war among the Inca	1527 Li Zhi (1527–1602)	
	1527 Sack of Rome by army of Charles V, Holy Roman Emperor and King of Spain (as Charles I)	1528 Castiglione, *The Book of the Courtier*	
	1529 Hapsburg armies defeat Turks at Vienna		
	1531–36 Pizarro (c. 1475–1541) arrives in Peru and conquers the Inca	1533 Michel Eyquem de Montaigne (1533–1592) Gaspara Stampa (c. 1523–1554)	1530s Rise of Mannerism
	1534 Act of Supremacy declares that the English King (Henry VIII r. 1509–47) is supreme head of the church, effectively breaking Anglican Church from Roman Catholic Church; followed by dissolution of Catholic monasteries in England		
	1534 Ignatius of Loyola (1491–1556) founds the Jesuit Order (Society of Jesus), which is sanctioned by the pope in 1540		
	1536 John Calvin, *Institutes of the Christian Religion*		
	1539 Hernando de Soto (c. 1500–42) arrives in Florida		

chant ships to devastating wars at home and abroad. Among the latter were France's ongoing war with the Holy Roman Empire, civil wars in England and in France, the Thirty Years' War, and Spain's wars of conquest in the Americas. At the same time, the Holy Roman Empire was fighting the Ottoman Turks, who were trying to expand into eastern Europe, and the Turks in turn were also fighting with their Persian neighbors, the Safavid empire.

India and Japan, too, were beset by wars during this time. In India, rival Hindu kingdoms in the south battled among themselves over land, while in the north and northwest Hindus fought against the invading Muslims of Turkish and Mongol descent known as the Mughals, who in about 1526 established an empire that would bring relative peace to the region. In Japan, the Onin War (1467–77) brought down the Ashikaga shogunate, or military government, and left a power vacuum until the Tokugawa shogunate was established in 1603. In between, the country was torn with ongoing conflicts between rival warlords, or daimyo, assisted by their

Date	History and Politics	Literature	Science, Culture, and Technology
1500–1550 (cont.)	1540 Mongol leader Sher Shah seizes Delhi, overthrowing Mughal dynasty until it is restored in 1555 by emperor Humayun 1542 Portuguese merchants reach Japan 1545 Council of Trent; Catholic (Counter) Reformation 1549 Jesuit priest Francis Xavier (1506–1552) arrives in Japan	1540 Abd al-Qadir Bada' uni (1540–c. 1615) 1547 Miguel de Cervantes Saavedra (1547–1616)	1541 El Greco (Dominico Theotocopuli; 1541–1614), chief artist of the Mannerism movement 1543 Copernicus, *On the Revolution of the Celestial Spheres;* Andreas Vesalius, *On the Fabric of the Human Body* 1546 Shaykh-I Bahai (1546–1631) great scholar of the Safavid empire in Persia
1550–1600	1550 Ivan IV the Terrible (1533–84) creates the Zemsky Sobor, a Russian parliament 1555 Peace of Augsburg; legitimates Lutheranism and gives rulers of individual German states within the Holy Roman Empire the right to determine their religion 1556 Akbar (r. 1556–1605) becomes emperor of Mughal empire (1526–1707) 1557 Portuguese establish trading center at Macao 1558 Queen Elizabeth I of England ascends the throne; rules until 1603 1559 Pope Paul IV introduces the Index of Forbidden (Prohibited) Books	1551 Abu'l Fazl (1551–1602) 1552 Matteo Ricci (1552–1610)	1555–56 Mercury amalgamation process for mining silver introduced in Mexico, by German mining engineers increases production of silver

military retainers, known as *SAMURAI.* Only China, at the height of the Ming empire (1368–1644), enjoyed a time of peace during the fifteenth century, but famine and disease in the sixteenth century led to civil uprisings that weakened the Ming, who were overrun by the Manchus from the northeast in 1644.

As a result of the wars in Europe during the fifteenth and sixteenth centuries, monarchies became centralized and the royalty gained great power. To raise money for their costly wars, European kings levied heavy taxes on their subjects. Resentment of such taxes led the kings, in turn, to improve the efficiency of their courts and bureaucracies. The monarchies of Spain, France, England, and the Holy Roman Empire became especially strong during this period of conflict. Although Portugal, Spain, and the Holy Roman Empire entered the mid-1400s as the powers with the most promise, the balance shifted over time, leaving France and England to emerge at the beginning of the 1700s as the two strongest kingdoms—the first an absolute monarchy, the second a constitutional monarchy.

Date	History and Politics	Literature	Science, Culture, and Technology
1550–1600 (cont.)	1561 Jesuit priests arrive in the court of Mwene Metapa, East African dynasty controlling gold trade along Zambezi River		
	1562–98 Civil war in France between the Huguenots and Catholics	1562 Lope de Vega (1562–1635)	
	1562 Teresa of Avila founds Carmelite convent	1564 Christopher Marlowe (1564–1593) William Shakespeare (1564–1616)	1564 Galileo Galilei (1564–1642) 1565 Humayun's Mausoleum built at Agra; Akbar begins to build his palace, the Red Fort at Agra
	1568 Oda Nobunaga controls Kyoto	1567 Francis Bacon (1567–1626)	1570s Rise of Baroque art
	1571 Battle of Lepanto; Philip II of Spain defeats Turkish fleet in Mediterranean	1570 Wu Chengen's *Monkey* first published	1571–86 Construction of Fatehpur Sikri
	1576 Mughals take control of Bengal	1572 John Donne (1572–1626)	1571 Johannes Kepler (1571–1630)
	1580 Jesuits arrive in the court of Akbar 1581 Morocco begins southern expansion 1582 Nobunaga assassinated: rise of Hideyoshi		1577 Peter Paul Rubens (1577–1640), key artist of the Baroque movement
	1583 Arrival of Jesuit priest Matteo Ricci (1552–1610) in China	1583 Hayashi Razan (Doshun) (1583–1657)	
	1588 English navy, assisted by a fortuitous storm, defeats the Spanish Armada		
	1590 Moroccan forces capture Timbuktu, bringing end to the Songhai empire		

INCREASING SECULARIZATION OF POLITICAL, SOCIAL, AND CULTURAL LIFE

Despite the constant turmoil, the Early Modern Period ushered in great cultural innovation and production, especially in Europe, which went through a period of renewal and proliferation in the arts and humanities known as the Renaissance. This rebirth in Europe followed closely on the heels of a similar renaissance in the Arabic world. As early as the tenth century, a spirit of learning had flourished during the Abbasid empire, centered in Baghdad, and in some of the great Islamic and Byzantine centers of learning, such as Cordova (in Andalusia) and Constantinople. From these cities came many of the Greek, Latin, Arabic, and Hebrew manuscripts that scholars took to the flourishing commercial and urban centers of Italy.

The renewed interest in Greco-Roman literature, art, and philosophy, particularly the works of Plato, quickly spread northward and eastward to neighboring countries. The early writers of the Italian Renaissance, including Francesco

Date	History and Politics	Literature	Science, Culture, and Technology
1560–1600 (cont.)	1597 First persecution of Christians in Japan 1598 Death of Toyotomi Hideyoshi leads to rising power of Tokugawa Ieyasu, founder of Tokugawa empire in 1603 Edict of Nantes, issued by King Henry IV of France (r. 1589–1610), makes Catholicism official religion of France while tolerating Huguenots	1592 Wu Chengen's *Monkey* published in final form	1598 Gian Lorenzo Bernini (1598–1680), key Baroque sculptor and architect
1600–1650	1600 English East India Company founded 1600 Tokugawa Ieyasu victor at Sekigahara 1602 Dutch East India Company founded 1603 Tokugawa Period begins (1603–1867) 1605 Death of Akbar, who is replaced by his son Jahangir (r. 1605–27) 1608 English arrive at Surat 1612 Tokugawa Ieyasu evicts missionaries from Japan 1616 British establish embassy at the imperial court in Agra 1618–48 Thirty Years' War	1611 Evliya Çelebi (1611–84) 1612 Anne Bradstreet (1612–1672) 1618 Yamazaki Ansai (1618–1682) 1621 Andrew Marvell (1621–1678)	1604 Tung-lin Academy founded for Confucian Studies 1610 Galileo, *The Starry Messenger*

Petrarch (1304–1374), Leonardo Bruni (c. 1370–1444), and Marsilio Ficino (1433–1499), inaugurated a sense of individualism, known as **HUMANISM**, that was genuinely new in the history of the European mind. Painters and sculptors, similarly inspired by classical models, took a new interest in the human form and in mythological and secular themes. By the end of the fifteenth century, many educated Europeans had begun to believe that they were both intellectually and spiritually freer than their medieval counterparts had been. They welcomed the chance to exercise their curiosity and test their strength in the worlds—old and new—that lay before them.

A test of the humanist philosophy arose in 1517 when the Augustinian friar Martin Luther (1483–1546) nailed his Ninety-Five Theses on the door of the church in Wittenberg, setting off what came to be known as the **PROTESTANT REFORMATION**. Luther opposed the Catholic Church's corrupt practice of selling indulgences (by which priests promised to forgive sins in exchange for money) and argued that

Date	History and Politics	Literature	Science, Culture, and Technology
1600–1650 (cont.)	1622 Shah Abbas drives Portuguese from Ormuz (Hormuz), fortified port on Persian Gulf, restoring control of trade with India for Persia	1622 Yamaga Soko (1622–1685)	
	1626 French begin establishing colonies on west coast of Africa at the mouth of the Senegal River and on Madagascar		
	1627 Death of Jahangir; replaced by Shah Jahan (r. 1627–58)		
	1639 English establish trading factory and fort at Madras		
	1640 Exclusion policies in effect in Japan		
	1642–48 Civil Wars in England		
	1644 Rebellion of Li Zicheng and occupation of China by Manchus bring end to Ming dynasty; beginning of Qing dynasty (1644–1924)		
	1648 Shah Jahan moves capital from Agra to Delhi		
	1648 Peace of Westphalia ends the Thirty Years' War; breakup of the Holy Roman Empire gives autonomy to independent German states and leads way to rise of Prussia and Austria as major powers; The series of civil uprisings known as the Fronde begins in France	1648 Kong Shangren (1648–1718)	1648 Construction completed on Shah Jahan's palace, the Red Fort, at Delhi

instead of following rituals, performing good works, and trusting in the authority of the pope, Christian souls could be saved by faith alone. Luther was soon followed by other reformers, such as Huldrych Zwingli (1484–1531) and John Calvin (1509–1564), and a schism spread eventually divided Europe into two regions: the mostly Protestant north and the mostly Catholic south. Luther's challenge helped to set off within the Catholic Church an era of introspection and self-conscious reaffirmation of Catholic doctrine known as the Counter-Reformation. From the 1520s onward, the divide between Catholicism and Protestantism figured into the political conflicts between and within European nations.

Renaissance Europe's revolutions in science, religion, learning, art, and literature were mirrored in other parts of the world. The expansion of trade discussed earlier promoted the exchange of not just goods and commodities but also technologies, such as papermaking and printing; scientific knowledge, especially about navigation and astronomy; and philosophical and religious ideas, including the

Date	History and Politics	Literature	Science, Culture, and Technology
1600–1650 (cont.)	1649 Execution of King Charles I (r. 1625–49) of England; Commonwealth of England		
1650–1700	1658 Dutch settlers found Capetown in southern Africa 1658 Aurangzeb (r. 1658–1707), overthrows his father Shah Jahan to seize power over Mughal empire 1660 Restoration of Charles II (r. 1660–85) returns Stuart dynasty to England 1661 Louis XIV, King of France (r. 1661–1715) 1661 Bombay ceded to England	1651 Sor Juana Inés de la Cruz (1651–1695)	1651 Thomas Hobbes (1588–1697), *Leviathan* 1653 Construction completed on the Taj Mahal at Agra
		1667 Milton, *Paradise Lost* 1672 Zhang Ting-yu (1672–1755)	
	1680 Ashanti kingdom rises in West Africa 1683 Ottomans defeated at Vienna, Austria 1688 Glorious Revolution in England 1688–1704 Cultural renaissance during Genroku era in Japan		1687 Sir Isaac Newton (1642–1727), *Principia*

doctrines of **Buddhism**, **Islam**, and Christianity. In China and Japan, scholar-officials and philosophers vigorously debated the tenets of **Confucianism**, often attempting to blend Confucianist ideas with those of other native religions, such as **Taoism** in China and **Shintoism** in Japan, or of Buddhism, which came to both countries from India. In India, the arrival of the Mughals led to conflicts between Muslim and Hindu, and within Hinduism itself, rival groups following charismatic mystics and poets who practiced a form of devotion known as ***bhakti*** grew up at first in the south and then in the northern parts of India. In the Americas, where Spanish Catholicism met native religions among the Mexican Indians, a rich hybrid culture developed. Christianity also spread in Africa, meeting indigenous religions as well as Islam, which had been long established especially in the northern and eastern territories. Thus, many orthodoxies and traditions throughout the world were being questioned and challenged in the fifteenth and sixteenth centuries.

LITERATURE AND THE ARTS

Literature and the arts of the Early Modern Period were characterized by innovation. An early trend in literature was the move toward using vernacular, or regional, languages, especially in Europe, China, and India. Combined with the improvement of the printing press brought about by German inventor Johannes Gutenberg (c. 1397–1468) around 1450, the use of common languages enabled literature to reach a wider audience—and to do so far more rapidly and efficiently—than in the Middle Period. With the wider availability of printed materials and the need (as cities grew) for more extensive bureaucratic institutions, literacy rates rose, especially in areas where new schools, colleges and universities had been established. Lyric poetry—including hymns, devotional poems, and love songs—was popular in many regions. Following the popularity of Francesco Petrarch, lyric poets in Italy, Spain, France, England, and New Spain (Mexico) produced a dizzying array of imitations and genuinely innovative love poems celebrating the torments and joys of both physical and spiritual love. In India, the many bhakti saints such as Chandidasa (1500s), Kabir (1440–1518), and Mirabai (1498–1547) produced countless songs of mystic devotion to the gods Krishna and Shiva, as well as to the ineffable essence of the divine.

Drama was an important genre of the fifteenth and sixteenth centuries, and Spain and England in particular enjoyed what is now considered a golden age of theater. In both countries actors organized into professional performing companies, new playhouses were built, and some of the most celebrated playwrights of all time, such as Pedro Calderón de la Barca (1600–1681), and William Shakespeare (1564–1616) had their heyday. By the late sixteenth century, dramas such as *The*

Peach Blossom Fan of Kong Shangren (1648–1718) brought new life into the drama in China, and in the early part of the Tokugawa era, Japanese drama reached a new height with the plays of Chikamatsu Monzaemon (1653–1724), whose work we include in Book 4. The novel was another important genre emerging in this period, reaching new levels of perfection in Miguel de Cervantes Saavedra's *Don Quixote* in Spain and Wu Chengen's *Monkey* in China (1570).

Among the other varieties of literature that proliferated in this era were travel narratives spurred by the voyages of exploration and discovery, as well as a new form, the essay, first practiced in Europe by Michel Eyquem de Montaigne (1533–1592). This nonfiction prose genre, a loose combination of personal reflection, philosophical speculation, and classical and historical thought, had some parallels in other parts of the world, as in China, where in the late sixteenth century the ***xiaopin***, a form of autobiographical essay, became an important medium. The essays of the Chinese neo-Confucian philosopher Li Zhi (1527–1602) anticipate this genre. In the Ottoman empire, where literary production centered primarily on biographies, histories, and Qur'anic (Koranic) studies, as well as in Europe, philosophical treatises and political works also arose. Ibn Khaldun's *Il Muqaddimah* (1377) and Niccolò Machiavelli's *The Prince* (1532), for example, two of the most important works of political and social theory of this era, both demonstrate a strikingly pragmatic and level-headed approach to the study of relations of power and authority. Overall, the fifteenth and sixteenth centuries left behind a great legacy of important works in a wide variety of genres, and some of the greatest writers of world literature, including Shakespeare, Cervantes, Calderón, Wu Chengen, and Mirabai were active during these years.

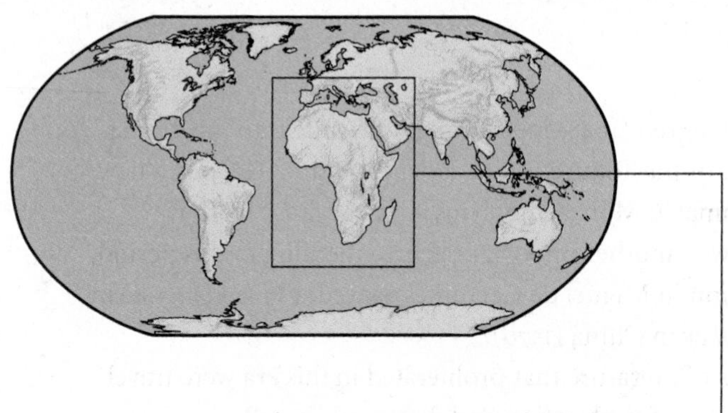

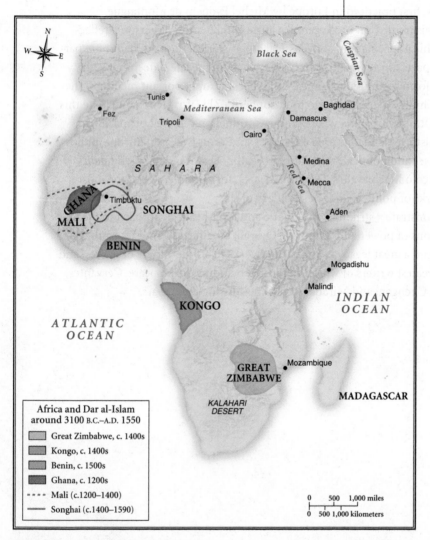

African Peoples and Kingdoms, 1500–1800

Before the advent of European colonization, Africa was composed of many kingdoms, rather than states. The richest developed in the West African savanna, an area of semi-arid grassland that was especially well suited to agriculture. Three principal kingdoms arose there over the course of about a thousand years: Ghana (c. 600–1100), Mali (c. 1200–1320), and Songhai (c. 1350–1591).

AFRICA
Epic and Empire in Mali

For centuries our knowledge of early African civilization depended on the written records of Muslim soldiers, merchants, and visitors: tribesmen from the northern Sahara Desert, visiting the region of the Sudan in the tenth and eleventh centuries; Almoravid warriors invading Ghana in the latter half of the eleventh century; merchants and emissaries traveling throughout West Africa, especially in the thirteenth and fourteenth centuries; and traders along the east coast of Africa from Arabia and the Persian Gulf. But recent archeological and linguistic studies show that deep in the African interior the richness of the soil, the dispersal of food crops, and the spread of agricultural knowledge had, before the Muslim arrivals, already produced a flourishing trading economy native to the region. The entire African continent was crisscrossed with trade routes; and wherever trade developed, kingdoms arose. So the movement of Muslims from the northern deserts connected with the developing African agricultural economy to the south, helping to create a remarkably homogeneous African culture between the twelfth and sixteenth centuries. During this period, the richest kingdoms were situated in the West African savanna, a semi-arid grassland abundant in both farmland and iron ore. The three principal West African kingdoms were Ghana (c. 600–1100), Mali (c. 1200–1320), and Songhai (c. 1350–1591).

GHANA, MALI, AND SONGHAI: THREE KINGDOMS OF WEST AFRICA

The first major encounter between Muslims and West Africans occurred in Ghana, and it was, arguably, also the bloodiest. Between 1050 and 1080 the Almoravids, a group of North African nomads united under a militant version of Islam, warred against Ghana, which collapsed in 1076. The major reason for the military posture of the Muslims was the area's rich gold trade, which continued unabated after Ghana's military defeat. In a few years the Almoravid invaders had spent their forces, but Muslim influence prevailed in Africa for centuries on the strength of trade. With the combination of their shipping activities along the eastern coast of Africa from Arabia and the Persian Gulf and the march of their armies through Ethiopia from Egypt, the Muslims had successfully opened up most of Africa by the beginning of the twelfth century.

Muslim influence remained partially dependent on internal struggles in West Africa after the fall of Ghana. Only the scantiest oral traditions remain concerning the late eleventh and twelfth centuries in this part of Africa; for more information we must await the rise of Mande society in the early thirteenth century. In a climactic battle, Sunjata, king of the Mande people, defeated Sumaguru, king of the Susu, in 1235, founding the new Mali empire. The epic legends hail Sunjata as a cultural hero, but it is also important to understand his policies of reopening the area to Muslim commerce and culture and restoring the great trade routes across the Sahara through the Sudan. Sunjata's successors are known to history because Muslims once again were available to record their discoveries. Mali culture entered a golden age in the fourteenth century, during which the ruler Mansa Musa (r. 1312–37) entertained such important visitors as the author and scholar Ibn Battuta and made his own pilgrimage to Mecca in 1324.

Later in the century, however, the Mali empire underwent a long period of decline. Muslim influence, greatly extended by Mansa Musa, eventually proved destabilizing to the government, and gradually the Mande rulers lost control of the sub-Saharan trade. By the end of the fifteenth century, Portuguese influence from the coastal regions had also begun to undermine Mande culture. But the biggest impact came from the rise of the Songhai, an ancient people based along the Niger River. Among the Songhai the Sunni dynasty rose to power in the fifteenth century. In 1468 the Sunni ruler Ali Ber conquered the trading center of Timbuktu. He centralized control of the conquered regions and firmly directed the economic and political development of the Niger River territory. Never a good Muslim, Ali Ber fought for independence from outside authority. After his death in 1492, his successor, Askia Mohammed I, reconciled with the Muslim authority and extended Songhai territory to the southern Sahara early in the sixteenth century.

The cultural center of Songhai life was Timbuktu. This city included three great mosques as well as a great university. The decentralized university curriculum included Islamic studies, theology, law, the sciences, the scholastic method, and, above all, the humanities. The city itself, which had served as a major trading center for several centuries, witnessed its rise and fall as a major center of learning, paralleling the experience of the great university cities of Baghdad and Cordova hundreds of years before.

ASPECTS OF WEST AFRICAN CULTURE

The empires of Ghana, Mali, and Songhai were on the whole rather uniform. Their leadership consisted of a king, supposedly of divine origins; a ruling body of wise men; and a group of women who supervised many of the traditional elements of the culture. An important cultural feature was the ***GRIOT***, the singer who kept traditions alive and often performed before the king's council in a constant process of revisiting the ancient legends. At one end of the spectrum, the griot could be an esteemed adviser to the king, indispensable to his rule; at the other, a mercenary schemer, willing to abandon patrons for the promise of money.

The traditional aspects of West African culture can easily be seen in the emphasis on stories about naming, practical lore, and proper social behavior. One way listeners measured the truth of the epics that were told and retold was to judge how well they described practical life. The songs of the griot were expected not only to reinforce cultural beliefs in, for example, the nature of witchcraft, protection against one's foes, and the importance of family lineage but also to present the rationale behind social conventions of all sorts. While listeners may already have known the general dimensions of the story of a hero like Sunjata, the success or failure of the griot's performance rested in the details of the presentation. Beyond this, the epic formulas of West African stories share with other world epics the kind of reflection that ennobles thought and invokes the experience of a warrior culture. The modern-day griot Bamba Suso addresses his character, the king Sunjata, as follows:

> You are right, many great matters have passed,
> Let us enjoy our time upon the earth.
> A time for action, a time for speaking, a time for dying;
> knowing the world is not easy.
> If you call a great man, no great man answers your call;
> You must lay your hand upon the earth;
> Many a great man is under the ground, a youthful king.

THE SHOCK OF CULTURES

The Mali epic *Sunjata* is placed in the Early Modern Period largely because it points to the clash with the new society of Europe arriving on African shores during the sixteenth century. West African societies had survived the Muslim incursion of the Middle Period with comparatively little cultural damage: The native society had absorbed Islamic culture while retaining many of its original beliefs. But the advent of slavery on a major economic scale, beginning with the arrival of the Portuguese in 1440 but increasing greatly in the next century, would

TIME AND PLACE

Fourteenth Century Africa: Timbuktu

The West African city of Timbuktu, now in Mali, was founded about 1100 C.E. by nomadic peoples who settled down at this site on the southern edge of the Sahara Desert, about ninety miles from the Niger River. Named after its legendary founder, a Tuareg woman named Buktu (*Timbuktu* means "the well of Buktu"), the city soon became an important caravan center, where traders from the Sahara exchanged salt (one of the most valuable of all commodities in Africa) for gold, kola nuts, ivory, and eventually slaves from the south. By the late fourteenth century, Timbuktu had become a part of the great Mali empire, after which time it evolved into a key center for trade, Islamic culture, and the arts. One of the early Mande kings, Mansa Musa (r. 1312–37), created a sense of mystique for his city, known as the Pearl of Africa, when he made his *hajj*, the pilgrimage to Mecca that is the religious duty of Muslims, with a retinue of nearly twelve thousand servants and eighty camels bearing nearly two tons of gold to be distributed as alms. Upon his return from Mecca, Musa brought back many Islamic scholars, intellectuals, and books, and founded several libraries and Islamic schools, known as *madrasas.*

René-Auguste Caillié,* Timbuktu, *1799–1833. *This engraving depicting Timbuktu was made by the French explorer René-Auguste Caillié in the early nineteenth century. (The Art Archive/Musée des Arts Africains et Océaniens/Dagli Orti)*

Musa oversaw the construction of several impressive monuments of African-Islamic architecture, including the Djingareyber and Sankore Mosques and the Madagu, his residential palace. In 1468, Timbuktu became part of the Songhai empire, and under the leadership of Askia Mohammed I (r. 1493–1528), Timbuktu prospered economically and culturally, rivaling cities like Cairo and Mecca, and creating an atmosphere conducive to scholarship and the arts comparable to that of Florence in Italy. By the mid-1500s, Timbuktu, with its three universities and over 180 madrasas, was enjoying its golden age. According to Leo Africanus, who visited the city during Askia's reign, traders earned more profits from hand-printed books made in Barbary than from other goods. Timbuktu's fortunes would run out in 1591, when it was captured by invaders from Morocco. In an era of the emergence of great cities around the world, Timbuktu must be included as a key center for commerce, scholarship, and the arts, and the legend of a golden Timbuktu survived long after its golden age of the sixteenth century.

WWW For more information about the culture and context of Africa in the Early Modern Period, see *World Literature Online* at bedfordstmartins.com/worldlit.

prove too shocking to allow the traditional culture to survive intact. The instruction and the traditional wisdom represented by the songs of the griot would eventually suffer not only from the competition of European culture in general but also from the dilution of these songs into mere entertainment. Old values would soon give way to new, and African society would lose much more than it had gained. It was a pattern that was to be repeated elsewhere.

Sunjata
Fourteenth Century

Of all the African epics known today, the West African story of **Sunjata**, the Mande king, commands the most attention. According to oldest legends, Sunjata united the territories surrounding his kingdom into the greatest state in Africa, the Mali empire, in the middle of the thirteenth century.[1] His story has been celebrated since at least the fourteenth century. The modern versions of the epic come from the region stemming from the headwaters of the **Niger** River that includes western Mali and eastern Guinea. While a number of separate versions are still available through the recitations of bards called ***griots*** (or ***jali*** or ***jeli*** in the **Mande** languages), they suggest the existence of a "composite version" of the story that tells of the rivalry of two great leaders, both magical kings, for the territory of ancient Mali and beyond. Sunjata, the culture hero, possesses the significant virtues of strength, courage, humility, filial piety, and a sense of justice. In the end he prevails over his enemy, the Susu (Sudanese) king **Sumanguru**. While the modern versions of the story vary in emphasis, to the Mali people the "truth" of the tale undoubtedly lay both in its celebration of the Mali triumph and in its fidelity to its community's folkways and practices. European recognition of this epic came slowly, but due to the work of anthropologists, linguists, folklorists, and literary scholars, it finally found its way into printed literature in the twentieth century.

soon-JAH-tah

NIGH-jur

gree-OHS, GREE-ohs, GREE-ahts; JAH-lee; JEH-lee; MAHN-day

soo-mahng-GOO-roo

Historical and Legendary Origins. In the history of West Africa, the Mali empire of the thirteenth and fourteenth centuries was the region's second great civilization. It followed that of Ghana, a kingdom made wealthy through its gold trade with the Arab states to the north. After the decline of the Ghanian empire in the eleventh century, the earliest Mali

www For links to more information and a quiz on *Sunjata*, see *World Literature Online* at bedfordstmartins .com/worldlit.

[1] **Sunjata, Mali, Mande:** Variants of all three terms are common, for linguistic, political, and cultural reasons. We will use Sunjata for the famous king; Mali for the empire of the thirteenth and fourteenth centuries; and Mande for its people, their language, and their culture.

The Manden looks back to its period of unification and glory under the emperor Sunjata. In his time (generally dated to the early thirteenth century), the separate kingdoms (or territories) of Do, Kri, and Tabon, and Sibi became one; he ended the oppression of Sumanguru Kante and the Sosso around 1325 and made the Malinka the rulers of their world. To speak of the Manden is, of necessity, to evoke the time and space of Sunjata's rule; thus, the Manden is also an idea spread across West Africa.

– Stephen Belcher, *Epic Traditions of Africa*, 1999

Mande Staff Finial, Seventeenth–Nineteenth Centuries
Believed to have originated with the Mande peoples of the Mali empire in West Africa, iron staffs surmounted by cast brass sculptures have been in use as recently as the mid-twentieth century. (Copper alloy, H x W x D: 7⅜ x 2½ x 3½ in. Museum purchase 3/12/83. Photograph by Franko Koury, National Museum of African Art, Smithsonian Institution.)

rulers gradually united a number of fragmented kingdoms in order to confront their chief rival, the Susu kingdom, early in the thirteenth century. Legends state that the final struggle for the region took place between the Susu king Sumanguru and the initially reluctant Mali leader Sunjata. After the Mali victory in approximately 1235, the empire was consolidated, reaching its height under **Mansa Musa** in the first quarter of the fourteenth century. Mansa Musa was well known to the Muslim world, having invited Islamic dignitaries to see his kingdom; he himself journeyed to Mecca on a holy pilgrimage in 1324.[2]

MAHN-sah MOO-sah

An approach to the story of Sunjata the king must rely on oral tradition. The legends state that he grew up in the small kingdom of Niane in what is now eastern Guinea. Born to Sukulung Konte, a deformed woman reputed to have magical powers and one of the wives of King Makhang, Sunjata grew up bent and crippled like his mother. He literally rose to power by pulling himself to his full stature after uprooting a

[2] **well known to the Muslim world:** Later in the fourteenth century, Islamic authors of the first rank visited Mali. Ibn Battuta (1304–1368 or 1369) visited the Mali court in 1352, and Ibn Khaldun (1332–1406) followed late in the fourteenth century. Ibn Battuta commented on the performances of the griots, and both writers alluded to the legend of Sunjata.

baobab tree, an impossible feat of strength even for a man, much less a crippled boy. Although not first in the line of succession to be king, Sunjata showed many royal virtues while still a youth. Denied even his rightful inheritance (the ownership of his favorite musician) by his half-brother following his father's death, Sunjata fled Niane with his mother. Later, the kingdom was seized by the Susu king Sumanguru. After the death of his mother, whom he attended to the end, Sunjata returned to fight Sumanguru on behalf of his people. Sunjata's sister **Nyakhaleng Juma Suukho**, visited Sumanguru's camp and seduced the chief into betraying the secret of his magical powers. Allying with Sumanguru's half-brother, Sunjata fought many battles against the Susu until he finally defeated Sumanguru by use of a magical arrow. After his defeat, Sumanguru was transformed into a whirlwind, a palm tree, an ant hill, and a **coucal** (a bird). He finally eluded his pursuers and vacated the kingdom.

BAY-oh-bahb

NY-AH-kah JOO-mah

KOO-kul

The Role of the Storytellers. In European culture, written history is privileged over oral tales. The opposite is true for many tribal peoples, and this fact is exemplified in the story of Sunjata. This extremely popular tale spread across West Africa with the dispersal of the Mali people in the fifteenth century; versions of it can now be found in Guinea, the Upper Volta, Mali, Senegal, and the Gambia. Indeed, tribal leaders of these societies affirm their common identity by tracing their descent from Sunjata himself. The modern-day griots, or tribal singers, are defined not as a separate class but according to their families; one may come from a family of historians, another from a family of hunters, and so on. Like Sunjata's favorite musician, they accompany their stories on one of several instruments: a twenty-one-stringed harp, a xylophone, or a small plucked lute, among others. Traditionally, the lowest griot on the social scale has been the *mbo jalo,* or public entertainer, with his repertoire of popular songs and stories about Sunjata and other heroes. Increasingly, however, even the most privileged griots have been employed for entertainment at social functions rather than performances before the tribal nobility. Thus, their art has become diluted, less necessary for the maintenance of tribal culture.

In 1968 the Mali historian **Djibril Tamsir Niane** compiled a version of the Sunjata epic made up of stories recited by the Guinean griot Mammatu Kouyate. This encyclopedic version reconstructs the epic to its fullest known length. At first the Niane text was taken to be the authoritative version of the epic. However, it is written in a prose style that uses relatively few of the rhetorical devices, much less the poetic structure, of performance versions. More recently, scholars have returned to study some of the versions of other griots as both unique works of art and parts of a greater tradition. With the Niane prose version available for reference, these scholars now are able to see how much of the entire story is accounted for in an individual performance.

ji-BRIL tahm-SEER nee-AH-nay

The Version of Bamba Suso. The version presented in this book is a slightly edited text of the account of Bamba Suso (d. 1974), a Gambian griot with a broad knowledge of the oral traditions of his people. It

When I was discussing with Mr. Sidibe [a griot] the reason that people listen to the Sunjata epic, he replied [that] . . . though Sunjata is undoubtedly braver and stronger than we are, he is nevertheless a human being like ourselves. The qualities which he has are the qualities which we ourselves have, in however diminished a form. Sunjata shows us of what a man is capable.

– Gordon Innes, *Sunjata: Three Mandinka Versions,* 1974

recounts the legendary story from the birth of Sunjata through the defeat of Sumanguru. While it features oral conventions such as repetition, digressions, and other connections with the past, this version of *Sunjata* moves along rapidly, providing not a full epic in the sense of Homer's *Iliad* or *Odyssey,* but what might be considered an abridged version in the same form as the original. Also, Suso's mastery of his craft reveals the griot behind the story, a quality missing today in textual versions of classical Near Eastern, Greek, Roman, and Old English epics. It might thus be more accurate to refer to this work as an epic lay, or narrative ballad, rather than a full-blown epic. Also, its complete performance time is about an hour—hardly epic length in the traditional sense.

The version of Bamba Suso differs from the encyclopedic version of the Sunjata story in several respects. Sunjata does not rise up from the ground by pulling over a baobab tree, but simply by leaning on his mother's shoulder. He does not take his favorite griot with him when he departs from his father's kingdom, but all the king's former griots. Later, the narrative conforms to the encyclopedic version more closely. Sumanguru reveals his mortal weakness to Nyakhaleng Juma Suukho, Sunjata's clever sister, and she conveys the knowledge to Sunjata, who destroys Sumanguru's power with a magic arrow. Sumanguru himself appears to escape, though the bard also refers in passing to the hero's death. The episodic treatment of the story as a whole by Bamba Suso covers the major details of the legendary history but stresses the folklore of the Mande people. Thus, it is both a historical and a popular version.

■ CONNECTIONS

***The Epic of Gilgamesh,* Book 1.** Gilgamesh is the culture hero of the Babylonian people. They celebrate his birth, his maturation, and his many deeds, while they need him to defend them militarily and to maintain their kingdom. In the same way, Sunjata must return to the Mande people and save them. Yet there are significant differences between the two culture heroes. How would you compare Sunjata's relationship to his society with that of the epic figure Gilgamesh to his?

Ibn Battuta, *The Travels of Ibn Battuta,* Book 2. Imagine you are the famous Muslim traveler Ibn Battuta, hearing a popular version of the story of Sunjata for the first time. What would you make of the story of Sunjata and the creation of the Mali empire? What questions would you ask your host about the story?

Machiavelli, *The Prince* (p. 124). Machiavelli's book is a guide for the instruction of a Renaissance prince. A study of how to rule, it advocates the use of coercion and persuasion. Machiavelli stresses the use of logic in the fashioning of statecraft. Sunjata often acts by instinct rather than reason, and his life consists of a number of feats of daring connected to magic. Could Machiavelli and the griot telling Sunjata's exploits find common ground in their notion of the proper function of the ruler?

■ FURTHER RESEARCH

Translation and Commentary

Innes, Gordon, trans. *Sunjata: Gambian Versions of the Mande Epic.* 1999. 1–31, 95–108.
———. *Sunjata: Three Mandinka Versions.* 1974. 34–135.

Other Versions in Translation

Niane, D. T., trans. *Sundiata: An Epic of Old Mali.* 1980.

Johnson, John W., trans. *The Epic of Son-Jara: A West African Tradition.* 1992.

History

Boahen, Adu. *Topics in West African History.* 1990.

Trimingham, J. S. *A History of Islam in West Africa.* 1970.

History of the Oral Epic

Bowra, C. M. *Heroic Poetry.* 1952.

Lord, Albert B. *The Singer of Tales,* 2nd ed. (Stephen Mitchell and Gregory Nagy, eds.). 2000.

Literary History and Criticism

Austen, Ralph, ed. *In Search of Sunjata: The Mande Oral Epic as History, Literature, and Performance.* 1999.

Belcher, Stephen. *Epic Traditions in Africa.* 1999.

Biebuyck, Daniel P. "The African Oral Epic." In Felix J. Oinas, *Heroic Epic and Saga.* 1978. 336–367.

Kunene, Daniel. *Heroic Poetry of the Basotho.* 1971.

Okpewho, Isidore. *The Epic in Africa.* 1979.

■ PRONUNCIATION

baobab: BAY-oh-bahb
coucal: KOO-kul
Djibril Tamsir Niane: ji-BRIL tahm-SEER nee-AH-nay
griot: gree-OH; GREE-oh; GREE-aht
jali, jeli: JAH-lee; JEH-lee
Mammatu Kouyate
Mande: MAHN-day
Mansa Musa: MAHN-sah MOO-sah
Niger: NIGH-jur
Nyakhaleng Juma Suukho: NY-AH-kah JOO-mah
Sumanguru: soo-mahng-GOO-roo
Sunjata: soon-JAH-tah

Sunjata

Translated by Gordon Innes

It is I, Bamba Suso, who am talking,
Along with Amadu Jebate;
It is Amadu Jebate who is playing the *kora*,[1]
And it is I, Bamba Suso, who am doing the talking.
Our home is at Sotuma;[2]
That is where we both were born;
This tune that I am now playing,
I learned it from my father,
And he learned it from my grandfather.
Our grandfather's name—Koriyang Musa.
That Koriyang Musa

Sunjata. Our text was collected and translated by Gordon Innes of the School of Oriental and African Studies at London University in 1974. His informant, Bamba Suso, died shortly after Innes finished transcribing Suso's performance of the epic. The nature of the performance is somewhat unusual; it was conducted before senior pupils of a public school in Brikama. Bamba Suso was accompanied by Amadu Jebate, playing on a twenty-one-string harp-lute. Because of the school setting, Mr. Jebate broke into the performance on several occasions to ask Bamba Suso questions intended to clarify a point raised by the griot.

The text itself is normally divided among three "performance modes": speech, recitation, and song. Speech is the narrative flow of the griot, who includes some highly traditional poetic devices, however informal and lacking in self-consciousness he appears. These devices will be noted where they affect the meaning of the story. Recitation includes formal names such as praise-names and their elaboration. (Sunjata, for example, is named by a formula, "Cats on the shoulder, Simbong and Jata are at Naarena.") Recitation also includes common sayings, such as "The world does not belong to one person." Songs are distinguished from the other two modes by rhythm, and they contain a repeated melody. In this text, recitation and songs are set in italics and are distinguished from one another in a note where necessary.

It should be remembered that since *Sunjata* is an ancient story still relevant to West African audiences today, the griot may occasionally offer an updating or commentary within the text. Storytelling is not solely intended to produce textual fidelity but also to adapt a traditional message to the needs and interests of the audience. The stability of the story lies in its cultural purpose. In particular, Sunjata himself must remain a culture hero; his growth and development in the story from a headstrong young man to a wise leader must be communicated in a modern enough idiom for the audience to understand. One gets somewhat the same impression from summertime Shakespeare in the Park performances in the United States. Hardly scholarly productions, these versions of Shakespeare plays belong to the audience, and allowances are made for that purpose.

All notes are adapted from the translator's.

---

[1] **the *kora*:** A twenty-one-stringed harp-lute, the most common instrument employed by the Mande griots.

[2] **Sotuma:** A village in the Upper River division of the Gambia.

Went to Sanimentereng[3] and spent a week there;
He met the *jinns*, and brought back a *kora*.
The very first *kora*
Was like a *simbingo*.[4]
The *kora* came from the *jinns*.
Amadu Jebate's father's name was Griot Fili Jebate.
He came from Gaali in the East,
But the name of the area was Gaadugu.
My father, Griot Musa,
And Griot Fili were the sons of two sisters.
When my own father died it was Griot Fili who took my mother;
It was he whom I knew as my father.
All right,
I am going to tell you the story of Sunjata,
And you must pay attention.
Sunjata's father's name was Fata Kung Makhang.[5]
He went to Sankarang Madiba Konte.
The soothsayers had said, "If you go to Sankarang Madiba Konte
And find a wife there,
She will give birth to a child
Who will become king of the black people."
He went there.
They had told him the name of this woman;
They called her Sukulung.[6]
Nine Sukulungs were brought forward,
And a soothsayer consulted the omens,
And then declared, "No, I do not see the woman among these ones."
They said to Sankarang Madiba Konte,
"Now, is there not another Sukulung?"
He answered, "There is, but she is ugly.
She is my daughter."
He told him, "Go and bring her here; I wish to see her."
When they had brought her,
A soothsayer consulted the omens and then told him, "This is the one."
When Fata Kung Makhang had married her in Manding,
Then he and she went away.

---

[3] **Sanimentereng:** A small, uninhabited island off the coast of the Gambia, believed to be the home of many *jinns*, or evil spirits.

[4] ***simbingo:*** A smaller harp-lute, with only six strings, used by hunter griots.

[5] **Fata Kung Makhang:** Sunjata's legitimate father, the previous king. Note that he is given another name in line 75, and again in 293 ff., later in the poem.

[6] **Sukulung [Konte]:** Sunjata's mother, a deformed magician.

She became pregnant, and for seven years
Sunjata's mother was pregnant with him.
She did not get a fright even once,
Except for one occasion.[7]
Her husband called her,
During the rainy season, and he happened to speak at the same time that thunder sounded,
So that she did not hear him speak, and he repeated the call.
Then she went in trepidation to her husband.
That was the only fright that she ever got;
For seven years she never got a fright,
Except for that one occasion.
She gave birth to Sunjata.
The king had declared,
Fata Kung Makhang had declared, "If any of my wives gives birth to a son,
I shall give my kingship to him."
Sukulung Konte eventually gave birth—
Sunjata's mother.
They sent a slave, with the instructions, "Go and tell Sunjata's father."
At that time he had built a compound out on the farm land.
When the slave came he found them eating,
And they said to him, "All right, sit down and have something to eat."
The slave sat down.
It was not long before a co-wife of Sukulung's also gave birth.
When her co-wife gave birth, they sent a griot.
When the griot arrived he said, "Greetings!"
They said to him, "Come and have something to eat before you say anything."
He said, "No!"
The griot said, "Naareng Daniyang Konnate,
Your wife has given birth—a boy."
The slave was sitting; he said, "They sent me first.
It was Sukulung Konte who gave birth first."
Fata Kung Makhang declared,
"The one I heard of first,[8]
He it is who is my son, the firstborn."
That made Sunjata angry.
For seven years he crawled on all fours,
And refused to get up.
Those seven years had passed,

[7] **She did not get a fright even once, / Except for one occasion:** It was believed that the child of a mother who has been frightened will be less brave.

[8] **"The one I heard of first":** This story of the two messengers is a common motif among African folk tales, often associated with the coming of death as a result of the failure of the first messenger to speak in time.

And the time had come for the boys who were to be circumcised to go into the circumcision shed.
People said, "But Sunjata is crawling on all fours and has not got up;
The time to go into the circumcision shed has arrived, and all his brothers are going in."
At that time they used to smelt ore and make iron from it,
The smiths put bellows to the ore,
And when they had smelted the ore they made it into iron,
And they forged the iron and made it into rods—
Two rods.
They put one into one of his hands,
And they put the other into his other hand,
And said that he must get up.
When he had grasped the rods, they both broke.
They said, "How will Sunjata get up?"
He himself said to them, "Call my mother;
When a child has fallen down, it is his mother who picks him up."
When his mother came,
He laid his hand upon his mother's shoulder,
And he arose and stood up.[9]
It is from that incident that the griots say,
"*The Lion has arisen,*" they say, "*The Lion of Manding has arisen,*
The mighty one has arisen."
There were trousers in Manding;
Whoever was to be king of Manding,
If they put those trousers on you,
And you were able to get up with them on,
Then you would become king of Manding.
But if they put those trousers on you,
And you did not get up with them on,
Then you would not be king of Manding.
They brought those trousers,
But whichever of his brothers they put them on,
He was unable to get up with them on.
When they brought them to Sunjata,
They were trying to put them on Sunjata,
But the trousers did not fit Sunjata—they were too small—
Until a bit was added.[10]
After that had happened they went into the circumcision shed.

---

[9] **And he arose and stood up:** This version of Sunjata's emergence from his crippled state differs from the standard version of his toppling of a baobab tree.

[10] **Until a bit was added:** This appears to be a recognition story based on the exact fitting of clothes. It may also suggest virility.

After they had come out of there,
It was not long before his father died.
Sunjata announced, "As for myself,
However extensive my father's property may be,
I want no part of it except the griots."
They asked him, "Do you want the griots?"
They said, "Leave it;
A person who has nothing will not have griots for long."
The griots said, "Since he has let all his inheritance go,
And says that it is only us that he wants,
We will not abandon him.
If he does not die, we shall not desert him."
The griots were at his side.[11]
It happened that three things were distinctive in Sunjata's family;
They had three hairs on their body, and if you spoke their names,
Whoever was a legitimate child would die that year.
The griots said, "Ah, he has absolutely nothing,
So let us employ some guile and if he dies, then we can take it easy,
And go to men of substance."
They went and begged from him.
When they went and begged from him,
He did not have anything.
He went and got honey in the bush,
And brought it back for the griots.
Whatever he gave them, they did not scorn it.
They went off; that is why the griots call him
"Bee, little bee, Makhara Makhang Konnate, Haimaru and Yammaru."[12]
Next morning they came and begged from him.
He had nothing,
So he went and caught a cat and gave it to them;
That is why the griots call him
"Cats on the shoulder Simbong."[13]
The griots came and begged from him again.
And he had nothing,
So he went and found some firewood in the bush and came back and gave it
to them.
From that incident the griots say,

---

[11] **The griots were at his side:** The attachment of the griots to Sunjata is qualified by their plans to test his ability to provide for him.

[12] ***"Bee, little bee, . . .":*** This chant praises Sunjata's discovery of the honey. His full given name is Makhara Makhang Konnate. See line 170, below it, and elsewhere.

[13] ***"Cats on the shoulder Simbong":*** Another praise song, for the cat he has captured. *Simbong* means "master hunter" in eastern Mande languages.

"Firewood Makhara Makhang Konnate, Haimaru and Yammaru,
The lion has his fill of followers, the big-footed hunter."[14]
The griots came and begged from him again.
He went and took a strip of cloth.
What he took was to the value of one shilling and sixpence.
It belonged to his brothers,
But no one dared to apprehend him
Because no one dared to stand up to him.
He gave it to the griots,
Who said, "Jata has committed a theft";
It was that which gave him the name Sunjata;[15]
His name was Makhang Konnate.
His name became Sunjata
When he took the one-and-sixpenny strip of cloth
And gave it to the griots.
They knew that he had taken it,
But no one dared to ask him about it.
The griots said, "Jata has committed theft";
It was that which gave him the name Sunjata;
His name was Makhang Konnate.
Naareng Makhang Konnate—
That was his name.

Then that is how things were;
His brothers got together,
And then they went to a sorcerer
And told him, "Attack him with *korte* till he dies."[16]
They gave a bull to the sorcerers.
They took this bull onto a hillside;
The sorcerers congregated,
Their leader was sitting;
One was saying, "If I attack him in the morning, by evening he will be dead."
Another was saying, "If I attack him,
When he sees the roofs of the town, he will die."
From that the Easterners say even today "Home-person-taking."
He himself was a hunter at that time.
He left the hunting area, having killed two elephants,
Whose tails he had in his hand.

---

[14] ***"The lion has his fill of followers . . .":*** An alternative translation is "The lion is full of dignity."

[15] **It was that which gave him the name Sunjata:** The etymology Bamba Suso proposes is *sung*, "thief," and *jata*, "lion."

[16] **"Attack him with *korte* till he dies":** *Korte* is a powdery poison, often contained in a horn by the same name. The animosity between Sunjata and his brothers is a theme common to other versions of the story.

He encountered the sorcerers on the hillside,
And he greeted them, but they did not answer him.
To the leader of the sorcerers he said,
"You ought to return my greeting.
When one freeman greets another freeman,
He should return the greeting.
I have killed two elephants,
One of which is lying on the hillside."
He took its tail out of his bag and threw it to them,
He said, "I give it to you,
For you to add to your own meat.[17]
But what you were sent to do,
Just do it!"
As he was about to go,
The leader of the sorcerers called him.
When he came, he said to him,
"You must leave Manding.
If someone says he will kill you,
A man's life is not in another man's hands,
But if he says he will ruin you,
Even if he does not ruin you, he could greatly hinder the fulfilment of your destiny,
It could be greatly delayed."
Sunjata said, "I cannot go,
My mother is at home."
That was Sukulung Kutuma.
Hence the griots say "*Sukulung Kutuma's child Sukulung Yaamaru,*
Cats on the shoulder Simbong and Jata are at Naarena."
Sunjata said, "I cannot go;
My sister is at home."
That was Nyakhaleng Juma Suukho.[18]
He said, "My horn is at home,
My wine gourd is at home,
My bow is at home."
The sorcerer said to him, "I will summon all of them to the *korte* horn,
And they will answer the call."
He called all of them to the *korte* horn and they answered the call.[19]
He told Sunjata, "Go!"

[17] **"For you to add to your own meat":** By throwing the sorcerers the tail of the elephant, Sunjata is signifying that he will give them one of the two dead elephants.

[18] **That was Nyakhaleng Juma Suukho:** As in other versions of the story, Sunjata's devotion to his mother and sister and his refusal to leave Mali because of them is one mark of his virtue.

[19] **He called all of them to the *korte* horn and they answered the call:** The *korte* horn, besides being the repository of poison, also contains magical powers of assistance when called upon. In this way Sunjata's family is summoned together and they leave the kingdom for safety.

Sunjata's leaving Manding
And going to foreign lands came about in this manner.

On his way he came to a fork in the road,
He put down the *korte* horn and consulted it.
It told him, "This road goes to Sankarang Madiba Konte,
This other road leads to Tamaga Jonding Keya"—
He was the ancestor of the Darbos.
Sunjata said, "I shall go to Tamaga Jonding Keya's place,
Because if I go to my uncle's residence,
My cousins and I are bound to end up quarrelling."
He set off.
He reached Tamaga Jonding Keya's place,
And he found that they had put beeswax in a pot,
And the pot was boiling.
They took a ring and threw it into the hot wax,
And they were making their boasts on it.
This is what they were saying,
"If I am to become king of Manding,
When I plunge my hand into this boiling wax,
Let it not burn me.
But if I am not to be king of Manding,
When I plunge my hand into it,
Let my hand be destroyed."
He found them making this declaration.
That was a public challenge.
Sunjata came and when he reached them,
He plunged his hand into that hot wax,
And took out the ring,
Threw it into cold water,
And gave it to Tamaga Jonding Keya.
Tamaga Jonding Keya was angry.
He said to Sunjata, "There is a silk-cotton tree here;
If you are a freeman,
If you are legitimate—
We must go and shoot that silk-cotton tree.
Whoever misses that silk-cotton tree,
Whose arrow does not touch it,
Is not a freeman,
Is not legitimate."
Sunjata was outraged,
At the very thought that anyone should say to him in Manding,
"You are not legitimate."
He went and drew his bow and shot the silk-cotton tree.
Tamaga Jonding Keya also drew his bow

And shot the silk-cotton tree.
Sunjata went and pulled out his arrow,
And said, "If my mother was pregnant with me for seven years,
And she never had a fright,
Then when I shoot this silk-cotton tree, let it fall down."
He shot the silk-cotton tree—
The tree remained standing.
He drew his knife,
He went and grabbed his mother's arm,
And said to her, "Tell me about myself;
Tell me about the circumstances of my birth in Manding,
Otherwise I will kill you."
Master of the lion! Master of the maga! *Master of the rhinoceros!*
Ah, cats on the shoulder,
Simbong and Jata are at Naarena.
Maabirama Konnate is no more.
Before Daniyang Konnate returned to the next world—
Naareng Daniyang Konnate has perished—
His griots were saying, "Daniyang Konnate,
Are you afraid of death?"
He said, "Death is not the thing I fear;
My griots must cross four great rivers,
They must cross four great swamps,
They will come to a worthless man and an even more worthless,
And he will say, 'Go away,
I swear I have nothing,
You are a griot,
You must get it from someone else.
Go away.' "
He said, "The dog was standing—may God lay him low,
When he is laid low, may God make him never rise again."
Cats on the shoulder,
Simbong and Jata are at Naarena.
The world does not belong to any man.[20]
Sunjata said to his mother,
"If I am a bastard,
Make it clear to me,
And I will kill you and kill myself.
If I am not a bastard in Manding,
Make it clear to me,
Because I shot the silk-cotton tree and it did not fall down,

[20] ***The world does not belong to any man:*** This chorus relates the death of Sunjata's father, while noting his concern for his griots.

And I had made my boast."
She said to him. "You went too far in your boast;
For seven years I was pregnant with you,
And I never had a fright,
But during the rainy season it was thundering,
And when your father called me I did not hear him,
And he called a second time.
That day I went in trepidation to your father.
Go and take that out of your boast and then see what happens."
When he had removed that declaration from his boast,
He shot the silk-cotton tree,
And the tree leant over and was about to fall.
Tamaga Jonding Keya was standing nearby,
He shouted at the silk-cotton tree,
And the tree was about to rise up straight again,
Then Sunjata bellowed at the tree,
And it split down the middle and fell to the ground.
Even to this day when a silk-cotton tree is drying up,
It begins at the top,
It never dries up at the foot,
It begins at the top.
Tamaga Jonding Keya was angry,
And he boxed Sunjata's ear.
When he boxed Sunjata's ear,
Sunjata grabbed his arm and was about to cut his throat,
But Sunjata's sister came running up and stood beside him,
And said to him, "When you were leaving Manding,
The soothsayers told you that you would have three causes for anger,
But that if you assuaged your anger by retaliating you would never be king of Manding.
This is one of those occasions for anger—leave it."
That is why the wrists of the members of the Darbo family are not thick.
Tamaga Jonding Keya said to Sunjata, "You are not going to remain here in my town,
Because anyone who is a greater man than I am
Will not remain here."
Sunjata passed through that area
And went to Faring Burema Tunkara at Neema.
He stayed there; he was engaged in hunting,
He was engaged in hunting.

Of his brothers who were installed as king,
Any whom Susu Sumanguru did not kill by witchcraft,
He would kill in war.

If they made anyone king on Monday,
By the following Monday he would be dead,
Till all his brothers were finished,
And there remained only children.
Sunjata had a younger brother,
And they called him and told him, "Go after your older brother;
His brothers are all finished,
The kingship has come to him."
He set off.
He kept on till he reached Neema.
When he reached Neema,
He was approaching it in the heat of the day.
He was quite exhausted when his sister caught sight of him.
One loves one's brother,
Especially after a long absence.
She ran to him
And had just taken hold of her brother,
When they both fell down.
He pushed her,
And his sister fell down.
Sunjata arrived,
Having just come from the bush,
And he saw his sister sitting with an unhappy look on her face,
And he asked her, "What is the matter?"
She said, "My brother pushed me and I fell down."
Sunjata looked at his younger brother and he said to him, "Fofana,
You will never be king of Manding."
That was how the surname Fofana originated.
It happened that his mother was ill.
When Fofana had explained the reason for his journey, he said to Sunjata,
"Our brothers are all finished.
Susu Sumanguru has finished our brothers;
I was told to go for you,
So that you would come back;
The kingship of Manding has come to you."
Sunjata stood by his mother's head
And said to her, "If I am to be king of Manding,
Before dawn breaks tomorrow, may you be dead.
If I am not to be king of Manding,
May you remain ill,
Because I will not leave you here in illness."
Before dawn broke, Sukulung Konte died.
Sunjata said that he would bury Sukulung Konte.
Faring Burema Tunkara told him,

"You will not bury her until you have bought the burial plot."[21]
Sunjata asked him, "How am I to buy it?"
He said, "You must fit earrings together,
And lay one upon her forehead,
And lay one upon her big toe,
And then measure the length on the ground;
However long the chain is, that is what you must dig,
And you will bury your mother there."
When he had done that, he put the gold earrings together,
And he laid one upon his mother's forehead,
And he laid another upon her big toe,
And he measured it on the ground.[22]
The gravediggers were about to go,
But he said to them, "Wait!"
He took the gold and laid it on a new winnowing tray,
And he laid a broken pot on it,
He laid a bush fowl's egg on it,
He laid some old thatching grass on it,
And then he gave it to Faring Burema Tunkara.
When it had been given to Faring Burema Tunkara,
One of the latter's men was there who was called Makhang Know All,
And he declared, "I know what this means."
Makhang Say All was there;
Makhang Say All declared, "But I will say it."
Faring Burema Tunkara ordered him, "Say it!"
He said, "What Sunjata has said here
Is that a day will come
When he will smash this town of yours just like this broken pot;
A day will come
When old thatch will not be seen in this town of yours
Because he will burn it all;
A day will come
When bush fowls will lay their eggs on the site of your deserted town.
He says here is your gold."
When he had done that, Sunjata buried his mother;
Then he and Nyakhaleng Juma Suukho,
And his younger brother,

[21] **"You will not bury her until you have bought the burial plot":** In other versions, this harsh demand by the king of Neema comes because he was counting on Sunjata to defend his kingdom.

[22] **And he measured it on the ground:** Sunjata joins gold earrings together in a chain stretching from his mother's head to her feet, marking the length of the burial plot. The chain will be the payment for the plot Sunjata has to make.

And Bala Faaseega Kuyate
Rose up and went.

When he and Bala Faaseega Kuyate were on their way,
They had gone far into the bush,
And they had been travelling for a long time when Bala said, "I am terribly hungry."
Sunjata said, "Wait here."
He went into a clump of thick bush,
He examined the calf of his leg where there was plenty of flesh and he cut some off.
When he had cut it into thin strips, he cooked it,
Then he pounded the leaves of a medicinal shrub and then tied up his leg,
He applied *kuna fito* to the wound and tied it up.
He came back,
And he said to Bala, "Here is some meat."[23]
He chewed the meat,
Had a drink,
And then said, "Let's go."
They went on for a long time;
When the wound turned septic, Sunjata was limping.
When Sunjata was limping,
Bala Faaseega Kuyate said to him,
"Naareng, why are you limping?"
Sunjata replied, "Just let's go on."
Bala said, "I will not move from here until you tell me what the matter is.
Since the day I first met you,
I have never seen you
In the grip of such pain
That people were aware of it from your appearance;
But now you are limping."
Sunjata said to him, "You said you were hungry."
He thrust his leg out of his gown,
And he told him, "This is what I cut off and gave to you."
There is a special relationship
Between the members of the Keita family and the members of the Kuyate family.
Even today, if a member of the Kuyate family deceives a member of the Keita family,
Things will go badly for him.
If a member of the Keita family deceives a member of the Kuyate family,
Things will go badly for him.

They carried on till they came to Dakhajala.
They stayed at Dakhajala.
Sunjata said to Bala Faaseega Kuyate,

[23] **And he said to Bala, "Here is some meat":** This folk motif is used here to establish the closeness between Sunjata and his griot Bala Faaseega Kuyate.

"Haven't you called the horses for me?"
Bala asked, "What sort of a thing is a horse?"
Sunjata said to him, "A griot is an impatient fellow;
Just call the horses."
Horses oh, ah horses, mighty Sira Makhang,
A person who could argue with him.
Horses oh, mighty Sira Makhang,
Being dragged does not humiliate a great beast.
A long, long way through the bush, an outstanding stallion and a saddle,
Go quickly and come back quickly,
Giver of news from far away.
A horse is something that goes far away,
A horseman is someone who goes far away,
A horse is something that goes far away,
A horse's rein is something that goes far away,
A horse is something that goes far away,
A horseman is someone who goes far away.
A man who buys a horse never regrets it.
Ah, mighty war king,
A man who likes making deserted villages.
Many great matters have passed from the world.
Ah, you have an army.
You seize, you slay.
Maabirama Konnate, fighting goes well with you.
When he called the horses,
A white stallion appeared,
And Sunjata said, "This is a fine looking horse,
But if it falls ill, it will not recover."
The griot called the horses,
And a brownish horse with white lower legs appeared,
And Sunjata said, "I did not say this one."
The griot called the horses,
A brownish horse with a white circle on its forehead appeared,
And Sunjata leapt on it first.
That is why the griots say,
"Oh horses, brownish horse."
Sunjata told his griot, "You must summon my leading men."
Those who were known as leading men
Are what we Mandinka call army commanders,
And what the Easterners call men of death.
When he had summoned the leading men,
Kurang Karang[24] Kama Fofana came—

[24] **Kurang Karang:** Words indicating the clanking sound of the rider's armor.

A far-seeing man and a man who speaks with authority,
Kama crossed to the other side of the river with iron shoes,
Kama crossed the river with iron shoes.
He and one thousand,
Four hundred
And forty-four bowmen.
Sunjata declared, "The time for battle has not yet arrived, Tira Makhang has not come."[25] [. . .]

[Other commanders are called, and take their places.]

Sunjata said to him, "The time for fighting has not yet come, Tira Makhang has not come."
Sankarang Madiba Konte demanded, "Is Tira Makhang better than all the rest of us?"
Sunjata replied, "He is not better than all the rest of you,
But he fights a morning battle,
He fights an evening battle,
And we join with him in the big battle."
Sankarang Madiba Konte was Sunjata's grandfather;
He was angry, and he took out an arrow and fired it.
The arrow hit Muru,
It hit Murumuru,
It hit Gembe,
It hit Gembe's bold son,
It hit Seega, the Fula, in his navel.
That is why the griots say to members of the Konte family,
"Arrow on the navel Faa Ganda."
They say that if you see an arrow on a forehead,
It is Faa Ganda's arrow,
Because anyone who is shot in the forehead—
If anything has cut his head open—
Will not live.
Any serious illness which attacks you in the abdomen also never leaves you alive.
That is why they say, *"Arrow in the navel Faa Ganda,*
Arrow in the forehead Faa Ganda."
They call him "Firer of the red arrow."
He it was who shot the arrow[26]
And slew Susu Sumanguru's father upon the hill.

[25] **"Tira Makhang has not come":** Tira Makhang was Sunjata's greatest commander. Here his lateness in arriving provides the opportunity for more description of the assembling of the troops.

[26] **He it was who shot the arrow:** This statement foreshadows later events in the story. Sankarang Madiba Konte, Sunjata's grandfather, will shoot Susu Sumanguru's father, a *jinn* or sorcerer, with a magical arrow, thereby curtailing Sumanguru's power.

All seven heads,
It was his arrow which smashed them all.
Sukulung Kutuma's child Sukulung Yammaru,
You are right, many great matters have passed,
Let us enjoy our time upon the earth.
A time for action, a time for speaking, a time for dying; knowing the world is not easy.
If you call a great man, no great man answers your call;
You must lay your hand upon the earth;
Many a great man is under the ground, a youthful king.
Had the ground a mouth, it would say, "Many great men are under me."
Maabirama Konnate, cats on the shoulder, Simbong and Jata are at Naarena,
Your griots suffered when you were not there.
Ah, you have an army,
You seize and you slay,
Sheikh 'Umar, man of war, war goes well for you.
(*Amadu asks:* At that time was he preparing to wage war against Susu Sumanguru?
Bamba: He declared that he would not become king of Manding
Until he and Susu Sumanguru had first joined battle.)
[. . .]
When Tira Makhang was coming,
He said, "Wrap me in a shroud,
Because when I see Susu Sumanguru, either I put him in a shroud or he puts me in a shroud.
That is my declaration."
He called his wives,
And he put them in mourning,
And he declared, "When I see Susu Sumanguru,
If he does not do this to my wives, then this is what I will do to his wives."
He then lay down upon a bier,
And they carried it on their heads and came and laid it at Sunjata's feet,
And Tira Makhang said to him, "There is no need to make a speech;
As you see me,
When I see Susu Sumanguru,
Either he will kill me and they will wrap me in a shroud and lay me upon a bier
Or else I will kill him and they will wrap him in a shroud and lay him upon a bier."
(*Amadu:* At that time they were preparing for battle, but they had not yet set out.
Bamba: War had not yet broken out.
At that time they were preparing for battle.)

When the leading men had responded,
The army rose up
And battle was joined at Taumbaara.
That day the fighting went well for the smith, Susu Sumanguru.
They met next at Umbaara,

And the fighting went well for Susu Sumanguru.
Then they met at Kankinyang.
Susu Sumanguru took a bow
And shot at Sunjata.
When the arrows fell upon his gown,
He did this with his gown [i.e., shook it].
The griots said to him, "Are you afraid?"
That is why the griots call him
"Kubang Kubang Makhara Makhang Konnate Haimaru and Yammaru."
Sumanguru once shot at him with an arrow,
He dodged the arrow, and the griots said to him,
"Are you afraid of death, Naareng?"
It is from that incident that they call him *"Dendending*[27] *Makhara Makhang Konnate,*
Haimaru and Yammaru,
The lion has its fill of followers, resilient hunter."
There was one occasion
When Sunjata walked very quickly,
And people thought that he was running away.
The griots said to him, "Naareng, are you running away?"
The griots said to him, "Kubang Kubang Makhara Makhang Konnate,
Haimara and Yammaru,
The lion has its fill of followers, resilient hunter;
If a lion had not broken his bones, a fool's wife would not be in need of strength."
Fighting went on till the sun had set,
When it was evening, Sunjata's sister came to him — Nyakhaleng Juma Suukho —
And said, "To be sure, hot water kills a man,
But cold water too kills a man.
Leave the smith and me together."[28]
She was the best looking woman in both Susu and Manding.
When she had got herself ready,
She left the land of Manding and went to the land of Susu.
When the woman had gone some distance she reached Susu,
She reached Susu Sumanguru.
The gates of his fortified town —
The griots call smiths
"Big kuku *Tree,*
Big Silk-cotton Tree,[29]
Push-in-front Expert,
And Lift the Hammer."

[27] ***Dendending:*** Perhaps another word imitating a sound; meaning "otherwise unknown."

[28] **"Leave the smith and me together"**: Susu Sumanguru was famed as a blacksmith.

[29] ***"Big kuku Tree"*** . . . : Praise song for smiths. Smiths often set up shop in the shade of *kuku* and silk-cotton trees.

Those were the names of the gateways of the fort,
They were gateways with porches.
Whenever the woman reached a gateway,
When she knocked, the guards would ask her,
"Where are you going?";
Inevitably they were all smitten with love for her,
But she would tell them, "I am not your guest;
I am the guest of Susu Sumanguru."
She would go and knock at another door,
Till she had passed through all the doorways.
They took her to Susu Sumanguru.
When Susu Sumanguru saw her,
He greatly desired the woman.
He welcomed her to the house,
And gave her every kind of hospitality.
Night fell,
And he and the woman were in his house.
Now, a princess of Manding
And a smith would not sleep together.
They were chatting,
Till the smith's mind turned in a certain direction,
And then she said to him, "I am a guest;
I have come to you—
Don't be impatient."
She said to him, "There is something that greatly puzzles me;
Any army which comes to this town of yours is destroyed."
Susu Sumanguru said to her,
"Ah, my father was a *jinn.*"
When he said that, his mother heard it,
Because Susu Sumanguru's
Mother was a human being,
But his father was a *jinn.*
Two women had conceived him;
As you may know, the griots praise smiths in terms of this,
Saying, "Between Susuo and Dabi, take suck from two mothers."
Two women had conceived him;
When he was inside one of them,
She was fit and people saw her going about
For a week or ten days, and the other one was ill;
When he returned to the other one,
The one he came out of became ill.
He would return inside her
For a week or ten days and people saw her around too.
That is why they called him *"Between Susuo and Dabi, take suck from two mothers."*
But when these events were taking place,

Dabi was still alive.
When Sumanguru said to Sunjata's sister, "My father is a *jinn*,"
The old lady appeared,
And said to him, "Don't give away all your secrets to a one-night woman."
When Susu Sumanguru's mother said that, the woman got up and said to him,
"I'm going, because your mother is driving me away."
He said, "Wait!"
He went and gave his mother some palm wine,
And she drank it, became drunk and fell asleep.
He said to Sunjata's sister, "Let us continue with our chat.
She is an old lady."
They were chatting,
And she said to him, "Did you say that your father is a *jinn*?"
He said, "My father is a *jinn*, and he lives on this hill.
This *jinn* has seven heads.
So long as he is alive, war will never damage this country."
She said to him, "Your father,
How can he be killed?"
He said, "You must go and find a white chicken,
Then they must remove the spur of the white chicken,
They must pick the leaves of self-seeded guinea-corn,
They must put *korte* powder in it.
If they put that on the tip of an arrow,
And shoot it at this hill,
They will kill my father.
That is the only thing that will kill him."
She asked him, "Supposing they kill him?"
He replied, "If war came, this country would be destroyed."
She asked, "Supposing this land were destroyed, what would happen to you?"
He said, "I would become a whirlwind."
She said, "Supposing people went into the whirlwind with swords?"
He said, "I would become a rhun palm."
She said to him, "What if people were about to fell the palm?"
He said, "I would become an ant-hill."
She asked, "Supposing people were about to scatter the ant-hill?"
He said, "I would become a Senegalese cou . . ."
His heart palpitated,
And he fell silent.
The woman said to him, "Wait,
I am going to the wash-place,
Because a woman and a man do not go to bed together dirty."
(*Amadu:* That "Senegalese cou . . ."—what was it he cut short there?
Bamba: He had cut short the name "Senegalese coucal."
Even today, if you fire at a Senegalese coucal in the bush,
Quite often the gun will shatter in your hands.)

Nyakhaleng Juma was in the wash-place,
And Susu Sumanguru was in bed inside the house.
After some time, he would say to her,
"Aren't you coming back today?"
At that time in Manding
They had a *korte* ring,
And when they laid it down,
And the person for whom it had been laid down
Spoke, it would answer him.
It did not answer everybody,
But it would answer the person for whom it had been laid down.
She took off that *korte* ring
And threw it into the pot of ablution water.
When Sumanguru said, "Aren't you coming?"
It would say to him, "Wait;
Such is this fort of yours
That a guest who comes to you
Is completely in your hands.
You are king;
Why are you so impatient?"
When she had thrown the ring in there,
She climbed over the wall of the fort and off she went.
When she had gone, Sumanguru lay for a long time,
He had a short nap,
Then he awoke with a start
And went and looked inside the wash-place.
He said, "I think there is more to this than just a visit to the wash-place."
He did not find anyone there.
At length he came upon the *korte* ring,
But he did not see anyone.
He wept,
She reached Sunjata,
And she told him all that Sumanguru had said.
They went and found a white cock,
They found self-seeded guinea-corn,
They found *korte* powder.
That is why the members of the Kante family do not eat white chicken.
When they had prepared this arrow,
They gave it to Sankarang Madiba Konte.
It was Sankarang Madiba Konte who fired the arrow.
That is why the griots say "*The head and neck of an arrow both with red* mananda,
Arrow on the forehead Faa Ganda."
It was he who slew the *jinn* on the hill.
When he had slain the *jinn* on the hill in Susu,
The griots called him the red arrow firer of Manding.

Next morning the army rose up and flung itself against the fortified town;
It was not yet two o'clock when they smashed it.
Nyakhaleng Juma Suukho was with the army,
Since the soldiers were searching for Sumanguru.
When the head of a snake is cut off,
What remains is just a piece of rope.
They were searching for the king;
They were engaged on that, when she saw a great whirlwind arise,
And she shouted to them, "That's him, don't let him get away!"
They rushed upon that whirlwind,
Armed men were entering it, when they saw a rhun palm standing.
She said to them, "This is him!"
They rushed, and were about to fell the palm tree,
When he changed into an ant-hill.
She shouted to them, "This is him!"
They took axes and were just about to smash the ant-hill to pieces,
When they saw a Senegalese coucal fly up
And go into an area of thick bush.
Manda Kante,
Saamagha Kante,
Tunkang Kante,
Baayang Kante,
Sege and Sirimang,
It is forging and the left hand,
Between Susuo and Dabi,
Frustrater of plots.
It went into thick bush.
This was how Susu Sumanguru's career ended.
That is where my own knowledge ends.
Then Sunjata took control of Susu and Manding.
The mode of life of people at that time
And our mode of life at the present day are not the same.
Surnames did not exist.
All the surnames with which we are familiar
Were given by Sunjata,
Because he was an extraordinary person.
If you had done anything noteworthy,
Then, when you appeared before him,
He would greet you with a name related to that.
At that time these Danso surnames—
There is an animal in the East,
Which is there even today, and which they call *dango.*
That *dango* denied people passage along the road;
People did not pass that way.
It was a rhinoceros; what we Westerners call a rhinoceros,

And which the Easterners call *dango.*
The ancestor of the Damfas killed that creature;
When he came to Sunjata, the latter called him Damfagha.
That was the origin of the surname Damfa.
The ancestor of the Dansos—a snake was lying across the road,
No one passed by that way.
The road from east to west was cut,
And it was that snake which had cut it.
The ancestor of the Dansos killed that snake;
When he came, Sunjata said to him, "*Kenyeramatigi, road-clearing lion.*"
He added, "It was you who opened up the road."
He said to him, "*Road-clearing lion.*"
Even today the Mandinka say, "So-and-so has cleared the road in front of us."
That was he,
That was the ancestor of the Dansos.
When Sunjata had taken over the kingship,
He told Tamaga Jonding Keya, "Daabo,
You must give up your interest in the kingship of Manding now."
As you know, they call the members of the Suso family *Red Bureng Gold.*
Sora Musa had been king of Manding,
And when Sunjata became king,
The old king and the new king did not trust one another.
Sora Musa gave Sunjata a great quantity of gold.
At Tabaski, Sunjata said to him, "*Eye red as Bureng gold.*"
That was Sora Musa.
When they had killed Susu Sumanguru,[30]
Sunjata became master of both countries.
He did not have any enemies,
He did not have any rivals.
Susu and Manding both belonged to Sunjata,
And his reign endured for a long time.

[30] **When they had killed Susu Sumanguru:** Apparently Bamba Suso sang this line in error. When asked later whether Susu Sumanguru was killed, Bamba said no.

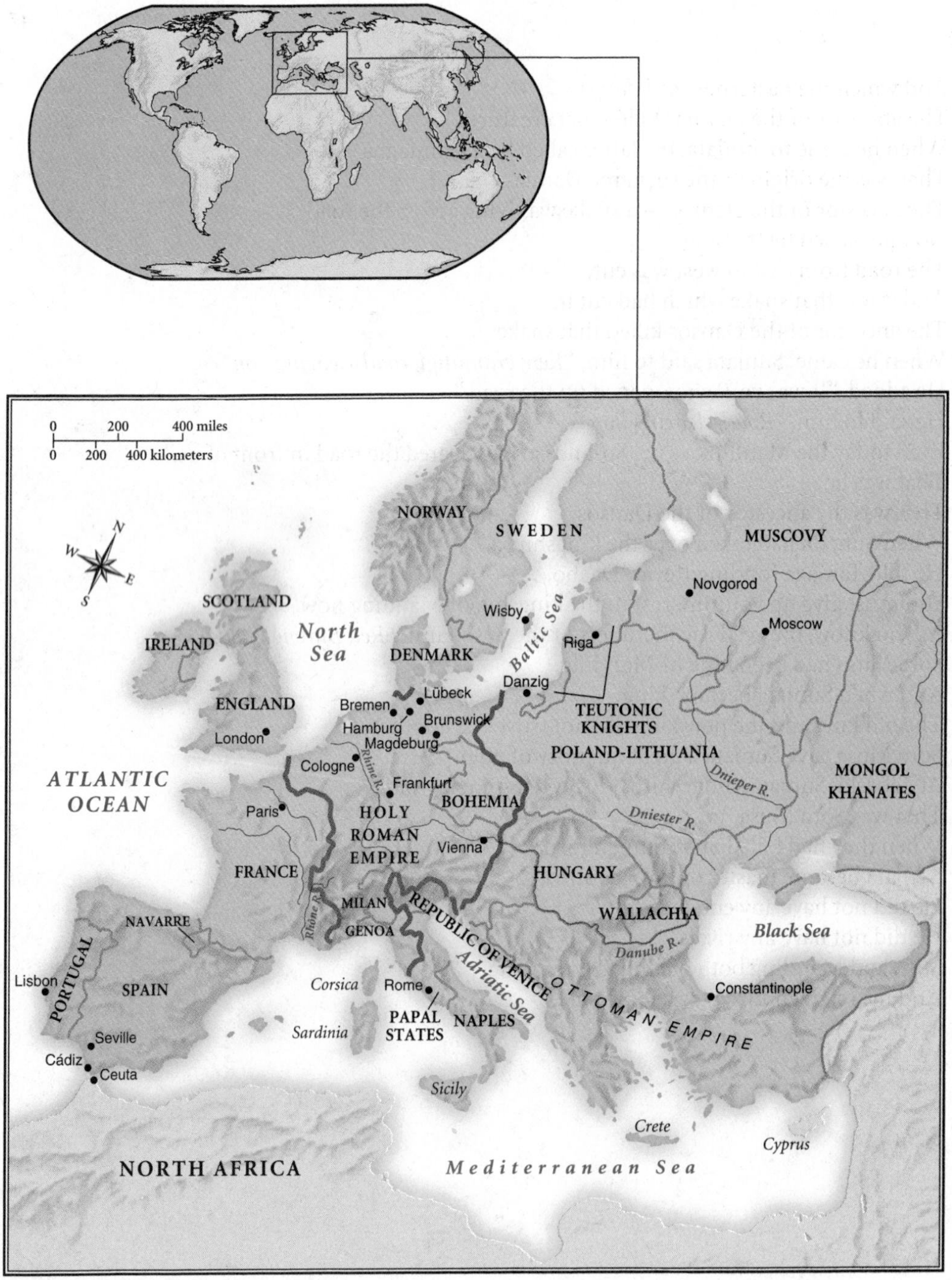

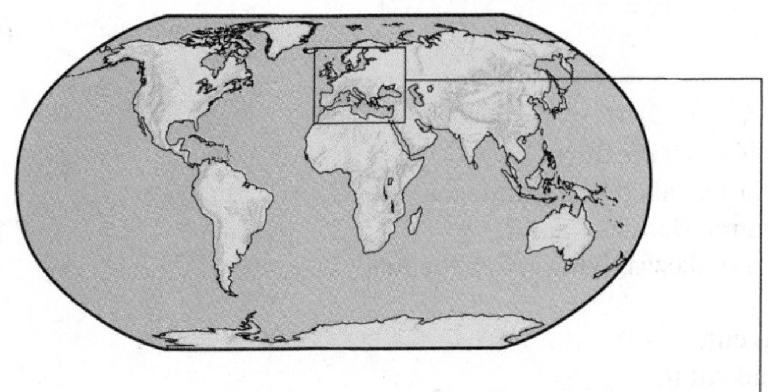

Renaissance Europe, c. 1500

By 1500, the boundaries of early modern Europe were largely established and would remain relatively stable until the 1700s.

EUROPE
Renaissance and Reformation

The year 1453 is important to European history for two reasons: It marked the end of the Hundred Years' War (1337–1453) between England and France, and it saw the fall of Constantinople, the last stronghold of the Byzantine empire, to the Ottoman Turks. After that date, Europe saw many significant transformations of its political, social, religious, and cultural life: the "discovery" and subsequent colonization of the Americas; the opening of direct trade with India, the Spice Islands, China, and Japan; the centralization of monarchies; various religious and political wars; and the **Renaissance** and the Protestant **Reformation**. As the spread of Protestantism weakened the authority of the Catholic Church, particularly influential people outside the clergy began to shape events, following a logic of individualism and secularism that began in fifteenth-century Italy, the birthplace of the European Renaissance.

VOYAGES OF DISCOVERY AND CONFRONTATION

Before the fifteenth century, Arabs and Mongols controlled most of the trade between Europe and the Far East. Spices, silk, jewels, dyes, and perfumes from China, India, and what is now Indonesia reached the Mediterranean trading centers of Italy, France, and Spain via Constantinople, the westernmost destination of the overland caravan routes, and via Alexandria and Beirut, the culminating points of the Muslim-controlled Indian Ocean trade. In 1453, the Ottomans, members of the Turkish dynasty founded in the late thirteenth century, seized Constantinople; soon after, they also took control of Ormuz, a major port city on the Persian Gulf. Some European leaders, such as the Portuguese prince Henry the Navigator (1394–1460), hoped to end what they saw as a Muslim monopoly over goods from the Far East. Though his immediate goal was to eliminate the Muslim middlemen and find direct access to gold that was being imported from Guinea,

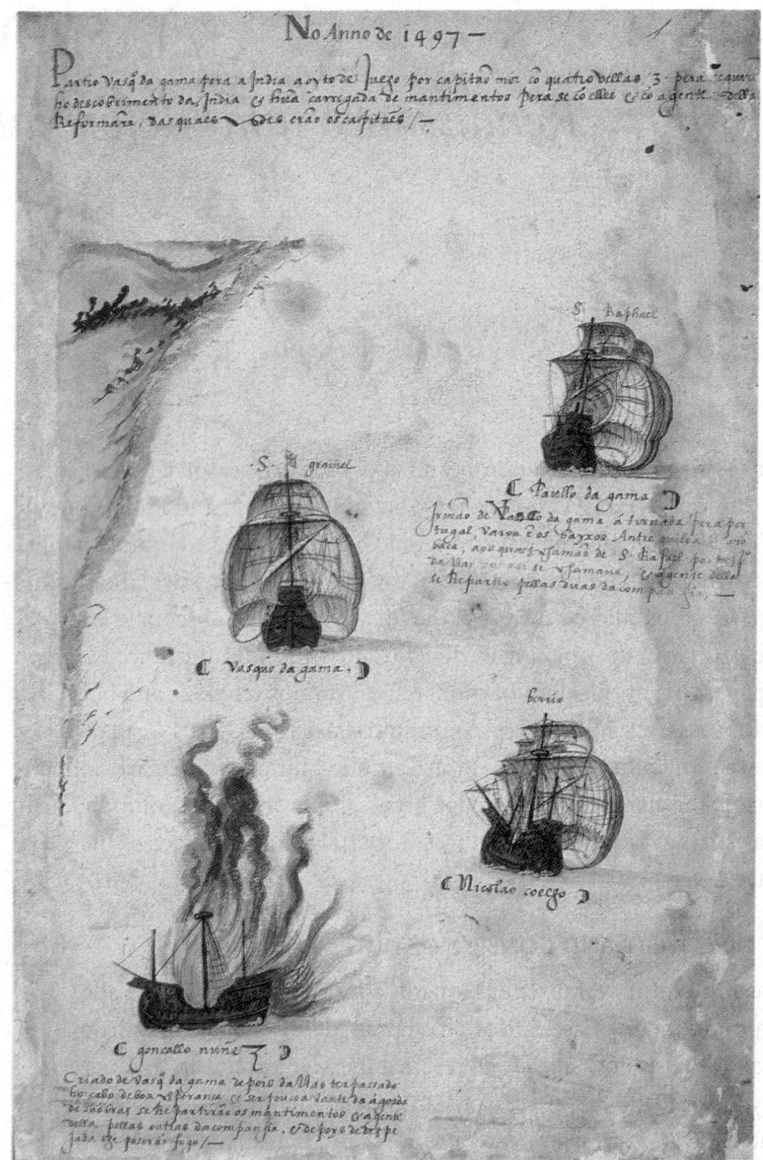

***Departure of Vasco da Gama,* Sixteenth Century**

This illustration depicts the first voyage of Vasco da Gama, the Portuguese navigator who set sail from Lisbon in 1497 with four ships and became famous for opening up a sea route between Europe and the East via the Cape of Good Hope. (Academia das Ciencias da Lisboa, Lisbon, Portugal/Bridgeman Art Library)

Prince Henry launched a series of voyages along the western coast of Africa, where the Portuguese established fortified trading posts and tried to gain control over the gold trade. The Portuguese eventually rounded the Cape of Good Hope and placed heavily armed vessels in the Indian Ocean, where they defeated a combined Muslim and Indian naval force and supplanted the Muslim and Hindu merchants and traders who had exchanged goods there for centuries. The Dutch and the English soon followed and by the mid sixteenth century had begun to challenge the Portuguese. By the end of the sixteenth century, both the English and the Dutch had formed East India companies, financing trade expeditions to India and the Spice Islands.

In 1492, the Genoese sailor Christopher Columbus (c. 1451–1506), sailing under the Spanish flag, crossed the Atlantic Ocean in search of a passage to the Indies. Columbus reached the island of Guanahani, named San Salvador by the Spanish, in what are now the Bahamas; he traveled from there to other islands in the region before returning to Spain to spread the news and gather resources for a second voyage. There were likely more comings and goings between continents than have been recorded, but Columbus's voyage of 1492 was the one that not only provided Europeans sure knowledge of the existence of the lands and the peoples of what came to be called the New World but also marked the beginning of a permanent change in the way of life for all the indigenous people there. The arrival of the Europeans in the Western Hemisphere often meant confrontation and clash of cultures, as well as death, devastation, and disease. On his second voyage Columbus found that the Taino people he had met before had been nearly wiped out. More broadly, by the middle of the 1500s, over half of thirty-five million Native Americans who had contact with Europeans had died as a result of violence perpetrated by their colonizers and from such illnesses as smallpox, cholera, influenza, measles, and whooping cough.

For Europeans, however, Columbus's first voyage meant opportunity. The early Spanish conquistadors—including Hernán Cortés (1485–1547), the conqueror of the Aztec empire, and Francisco Pizarro (c. 1475–1541), who conquered the Inca empire—were bent on acquiring new lands and amassing vast quantities of gold and silver for themselves and for the Crown, as well as on saving pagan souls. Spanish settlement and conquest of the Americas spread north and south along the Atlantic coast, and the Spanish and Portuguese, who conquered what is now Brazil, were soon joined by the English, French, and Dutch, who were not to be outdone by their neighbors. These countries commissioned voyages to find a northwest passage to the Indies, and to explore the coastal waters along the Atlantic seaboard. Their efforts led to the discovery and eventual settlement (in the seventeenth century) of lands from what is now Virginia and Georgia up to the Hudson Bay.

After Vasco de Balboa (1475–1519) sighted the ocean we know as the Pacific from a hill in Panama, Ferdinand Magellan (c. 1480–1521) sailed from Spain in 1519 and rounded the southern tip of South America into the Pacific Ocean. Two years later Magellan and his crew became the first Europeans to reach the Philippines. Though Magellan himself was killed there, the survivors of his expedition sailed on to the Indian Ocean, rounded the Cape of Good Hope, and returned to Cadiz, Spain, in 1522. Others were soon to circumnavigate the globe, including the English admiral Sir Francis Drake (1540 or 1543–1596) in the 1580s. By the end of the sixteenth century, Europe had extended its reach across the world—from Africa to the Americas, India, China, and the Spice Islands. The colonization that followed, as well as competition for resources, territories, and trade, would lead Europe—and much of the world—into a succession of costly and devastating wars over the next two centuries.

ITALY

During the fifteenth and sixteenth centuries, Italy was divided into several independent city-states. Some of these states were more or less self-consciously modeled on the city-states of ancient Greece, though they were actually controlled by powerful religious or secular leaders. Rome, for example, was the center of the Papal States or States of the Church; a small oligarchy of powerful merchants ran Venice; and Florence and Milan answered to the Medici and Sforza families, respectively. After the Treaty of Lodi in 1454 established a balance of power, many of the city-states and republics of Italy amassed great wealth from trade, banking, and commerce. Strategically located in the middle of the European trade with Constantinople and the Islamic port towns in the eastern Mediterranean, the cities of Florence, Genoa, Pisa, and Rome, among others, saw the rise of powerful families who controlled the banking and trade networks. The Medicis in Florence were bankers, secular and religious leaders, and patrons of the arts.

The relative stability under the Treaty of Lodi was short-lived, and political rivalries—especially among Florence, Venice, and Milan—as well as competing claims to Italian territories by France and Spain and the territorial ambitions of the Papacy in Rome, dragged Italy into a state of constant turmoil. Milan invited France to help protect its interests against Florence and Naples, and the French king Charles VIII (r. 1483–98) answered the call by invading the peninsula with more than thirty thousand troops. After forcing the Medicis to flee Florence, Charles pushed south to capture Naples in 1494. Fearing it might lose Sicily to France, Spain joined with the Papal States, the Holy Roman Empire, and Venice against France, thereby plunging Italy into continuing warfare and a succession of changing alliances among the republics from 1499 until 1529.

Benozzo di Lese di Sandro Gozzoli, *Lorenzo de' Medici*, 1460
Scion of the great Florentine banking family, Lorenzo de' Medici, known as "the Magnificent," was a great patron of the arts during the Italian Renaissance. Artists under his protection included Botticelli, Leonardo da Vinci, and Michelangelo. (Palazzo Medici-Riccardi, Florence, Italy/Bridgeman Art Library)

Eventually, Charles V, the Hapsburg emperor (r. 1519–58), restored the Medici family to power in Florence and imposed a kind of captive peace to the Italian peninsula. With the "new monarchies" in the Italian city-states, the papacy's rule over Europe declined and the princes of small territories were threatened. In this atmosphere emerged a ***REALPOLITIK***—that is, ideal philosophical principles gave way to a system of doing politics based on the realities of power and conflict. One of Italy's great Renaissance thinkers and writers, Niccolò Machiavelli (1469–1527) articulated the practical rules of the new, calculating political game in his masterful political treatise *The Prince* (p. 124).

Despite their tumultuous politics, the Italian city-states and republics fostered the renewal in the arts, in letters, and in classical scholarship that became the Renaissance. The Medicis of Florence, the Sforza of Milan, and the papacy in Rome, as well as wealthy leaders of other smaller cities, lavished their considerable wealth on artists, scholars, and writers to promote a revival of classical learning with a philosophical focus on individualism—known as **HUMANISM**—to bring about a period of innovation and proliferation in painting, sculpture, architecture, and literature. As the birthplace of the Renaissance forerunners Dante (1265–1321) and Boccaccio (1313–1375), as well as Francis Petrarch (1304–1374) and Machiavelli, Florence was the flash point for the intellectual fire that gradually spread northward, eastward, and westward throughout Europe and across the Atlantic. The city was also home to the artists Giotto (c. 1266–1337), Donatello (c. 1386–1466), Botticelli (c. 1445–1510), and Leonardo da Vinci (1452–1519).

SPAIN AND THE AMERICAS

Between 1474 and 1504 Spain became a relatively unified Catholic nation under the joint rule of Ferdinand V (r. 1474–1516) of Aragon and Isabella I (r. 1474–1504) of Castile. Their marriage in 1469 brought about political stability in the country. At home Isabella and Ferdinand worked to unify the Iberian peninsula, weakening the autonomy of the Spanish nobles and implementing a set of policies known as the Spanish inquisition to police and punish the *Marranos* and *Moriscos*—Jews and Muslims who posed as Christian converts but who secretly practiced their own faith. Abroad, these two monarchs sponsored explorers such as Christopher Columbus and thereby expanded Spain's empire to the Americas. Moreover, in the fateful year of 1492, Isabella and Ferdinand oversaw the fall of Granada, the last stronghold of Turkish power in Spain.

After Ferdinand's death in 1516, the crown passed to his grandson, Charles I (r. 1516–56), who three years later would join the Hapsburg dynasty and become the Holy Roman Emperor Charles V. Under Charles, who extended the Spanish empire in the Americas, Spain entered a golden age when its economy, otherwise struggling under the cost of Charles's wars, was enriched by the wealth from its colonial holdings in the Americas. The patronage of Charles and his immediate successors helped the arts and intellectual life flourish in Spain and in the colony known as New Spain. By the end of the sixteenth century, Spain had established a vast empire encompassing Florida, the southwestern part of what is now the United States, Mexico, Central America, the Caribbean Islands, and all of South America, except Brazil, which the Portuguese claimed.

In 1556, the Spanish and Italian possessions of Charles V, including the Spanish Americas, passed to his son, Philip II (r. 1556–98). An ardent Catholic with a crusader mentality, Philip hoped at whatever cost to spread Catholicism throughout his dominions, to put down Protestantism wherever it rose up, and to defeat the Ottoman Turks, whom he perceived as infidels. Under his reign, the **Inquisition** was reinvigorated in Spain and in Spanish America, and he led an alliance known as the Holy League against the Ottomans, defeating the Turkish fleet at Lepanto in 1571. When trying to stamp out Protestantism in Spanish-held parts of the Netherlands in 1581, however, Philip encountered tough resistance from Dutch Calvinists supported by England and in 1588 the English navy defeated the Spanish Armada, a fleet of 130 ships, wielding a severe blow to Spain.

After the defeat of the Armada, Spanish power entered a long period of decline. Despite the flow of silver, gold, and goods from the Americas, Spain faced financial problems, including inflation and the high cost of prosecuting its part in the **Thirty Years' War** (1618–48), a series of conflicts that grew out of religious tensions and encompassed most of western Europe. Afterward, Spain continued to fight against France for another twenty years, until the Treaty of Aix-la-Chapelle in 1668 dealt the Spanish further losses of power and prestige. By the end of the War of the Spanish Succession (1701–14), Spain was a shadow of its former self, while France and England had emerged as the two most powerful European states.

FRANCE, THE HOLY ROMAN EMPIRE, AND THE OTTOMANS

After winning back disputed territories from England at the end of the Hundred Years' War, the French kings Louis XI (r. 1461–83) and his son Charles VIII (r. 1483–98) began consolidating their power and increasing their dominions. Part of that quest involved ongoing wars with the Hapsburg dynasty, who ruled the Holy Roman Empire. Through a series of strategic marriages, the Hapsburgs had extended their control to Spain and its holdings overseas; Austria and other central European duchies; parts of Burgundy in the north of France; Luxembourg; and the Low Countries (the Netherlands). In 1494, Charles VIII sent his forces into Italy, ostensibly to assist the duke of Milan but more pointedly to protect his claims to Naples against the Hapsburg leader, Charles V (r. 1519–58), who had been given the title of Holy Roman Emperor. This invasion set off a war between France and the Holy Roman Empire, because Charles V, in his capacity as King Charles I of Spain, also laid claim to Naples, as well as to Sardinia and Sicily.

To assist them in their struggle against Charles V, the French enlisted aid from the Ottoman Turks, who had their own agenda to pursue against the Hapsburgs. In 1453, the Ottomans under the leadership of Mehmet II (r. 1451–81) had taken over Constantinople; here they shored up their holdings along the Black Sea and in the Balkans south of the Danube. Over the next century, the Ottoman emperors, including Suleiman the Magnificent (r. 1520–66), attacked the Safavid empire in Persia, as well as Syria, Egypt, and western Arabia. Acquisitions in those areas put the Ottomans in control of the overland trading centers along the Mediterranean and the Persian Gulf, including the port of Ormuz. The Ottomans also warred against the easternmost European states, including Serbia, Hungary, and Austria, the seat of the Hapsburg dynasty. Thus, the Ottomans welcomed the struggle between France and the Holy Roman Empire. They attacked Vienna, the Hapsburg capital, in 1529 and seven years later the Ottomans joined the French in a joint attack against Hapsburg forces gathered in Italy. Though these efforts to defeat the Hapsburgs failed, the Ottomans did not give up their advances against Europe until the late seventeenth century, when they again tried to seize Vienna and failed.

In 1559, the French throne passed to the ten-year-old Charles IX (r. 1560–74), placing effective leadership in the hands of the new king's mother, the powerful and clever Catherine de Medici (1519–1589); in the preceding year the Holy Roman Emperor Charles V had abdicated his throne, and his brother Ferdinand I (r. 1559–64) had been elected in his place. Both events led to a long period of further troubles at home and abroad. In France, fighting between Catholics and French Calvinists, known as **HUGUENOTS**, erupted into bloody violence, culminating in the St. Bartholomew's Day Massacre of August 24, 1572. This bloodbath was followed a decade later by the War of the Three Henrys, which ended with the ascension of Henry Navarre of the Bourbon dynasty as King Henry IV of France in 1589.

In the Holy Roman Empire, a dispute over Ferdinand I's title to Bohemia embroiled the Hapsburgs in the Thirty Years' War, which eventually drew Protestant Sweden and Catholic France into an unprecedented alliance against the Hapsburgs. The war nearly devastated parts of Germany and Bohemia, affecting primarily the peasants and the poor. Outmaneuvered by the brilliant military leadership of the Swedish king, Gustavus Adolphus (r. 1611–32), as well as the political and diplomatic strategies of the French, the Hapsburg armies retreated in 1648. The Peace of Westphalia, which settled the conflict, put an end to the Hapsburgs' dream of a Catholic Europe united under their auspices and elevated France as one of the most powerful kingdoms in Europe.

ENGLAND

After the Hundred Years' War cooled the territorial ambitions of the English, the Tudor king Henry VII (r. 1485–1509) focused his energies on building up royal authority at home and promoting trade abroad. Like other northern European countries in the age of discovery, England was eager to compete with its Spanish and Portuguese neighbors. Just five years after Columbus's landing in the Americas, Henry commissioned the Venetian sailor John Cabot (c. 1450–c. 1499) to find a northwest passage to the Indies. Cabot undertook two voyages in 1497–98 that took him to the coast of North America, establishing a precedent for England's later claim to the Atlantic seaboard. Though the English found no gold or silver to rival that of Spain's new territories, their discoveries along the Atlantic, like those of the French explorer Jacques Cartier up the St. Lawrence River, would eventually prove to be extremely valuable.

Henry VII's successor, Henry VIII (r. 1509–47), for reasons of state more than of religion, took the most extraordinary measure of cutting England's ties to the Roman Catholic Church and declaring himself the supreme head of his own Church of England. To stymie Catholic power at home, the king dissolved the Catholic monasteries in England and appropriated their lands and revenues. Though England did become involved in the wars of France, Spain, and the Holy Roman Empire, its early separation from the Roman Catholic Church, as well as its relative geographic isolation, enabled it to remain somewhat aloof from the wars of religion sweeping the Continent in the sixteenth and seventeenth centuries. Nonetheless, the schism between Catholic and Protestant, as well as the divisions with Protestantism itself, would eventually bear down hard on England's internal affairs.

The power and prosperity of the Tudor monarchs culminated in the reign of Elizabeth I (r. 1558–1603), who presided over the victory against the Spanish Armada in 1588, signaling the rise of England as a formidable naval power. Elizabeth embraced Protestantism and underscored the Anglican Church's independence from Rome, but she also broadened Anglican doctrine to keep different religious sects from fighting. During Elizabeth's reign, the English Renaissance reached its apex, and the Elizabethan era witnessed a flowering of the arts, culminating in the works of William Shakespeare (1564–1616), England's greatest

Henry Bone, *Queen Elizabeth I, 1755–1834*
This is a miniature copy in enamel of the famous Ditchley portrait of Queen Elizabeth painted in 1572 by Marcus Gheerhaerts. The Tudor monarch under whose reign the English Renaissance reached its peak is shown standing on a map of England. (National Trust / Art Resource, NY)

playwright, who, in such plays as *Othello, Hamlet, Henry IV, King Lear,* and *The Tempest* (p. 495), thematized England's position as a great power, the troublesome issues of dynastic succession, and the duties of kings, queens, and their subjects.

With the accession of James I (r. 1603–25), who, as James VI, was also the king of Scotland, the royal house of Tudor passed over to the house of Stuart, inaugurating a period of troubles between the English monarchy and its Parliamentary subjects. By the time Charles I (r. 1625–49) became king, the animosity between the Crown and the nobles and gentry was nearly at an impasse. The civil war that broke out in England in 1642 lasted until January 1649, when opposition forces took the extraordinary measure of putting the king on trial and beheading him. The opposing forces in the civil war divided along religious lines: The king and his supporters came largely from Catholic and High Church Anglicans, while those who supported Parliament were largely Protestants and Low Church Anglicans. The Parliamentary forces, known as the Roundheads, were led by Oliver Cromwell (1599–1658), who became the leader of what was known as the English Commonwealth or Protectorate, which lasted from 1649 to 1660. Under Cromwell, Puritanism permeated all of English society and culture. Catholics were not allowed to worship in public, Anglicans could not use the Book of Common Prayer, newspapers were censored, and most of the theaters were closed. Nonetheless, debates about religion and government were vigorous, involving a dynamic exchange of ideas about the relationship between the state and religion, the authority of the Church, religious tolerance, and civil liberty. The great poet and man of letters John Milton (1608–1674), who served as Cromwell's Latin secretary, contributed extensively to these debates, and his *Areopagitica* (p. 680), arguing for a principled liberty and freedom of the press, is one of the most important treatises to emerge from them. In 1660, two years after the death of Cromwell, Parliament recalled the Stuart heir, Charles II (r. 1660–85), to become king of England. Though the English revolution was not yet over, theaters reopened and Charles vowed to practice religious toleration and to heed Parliament—vows he did not always keep. Following Charles's reign, the Glorious Revolution of 1688–89, a relatively bloodless change from the Stuart to the Hanover dynasty, set the stage for England to emerge along with France as the leading European nation in the eighteenth century.

RELIGIOUS CRISIS IN EUROPE: THE REFORMATION

Throughout the fifteenth century, the Catholic popes in Rome enjoyed great prosperity from their business interests and also served as generous patrons of the arts. As the Papacy became increasingly involved in political intrigues and secular enterprises, some popes, such as the Milanese Roderigo Borgia, Pope Alexander VI (r. 1492–1503), gained a reputation for lavish and hedonistic ways. Nepotism, bribery, and the sale of offices were common at the highest levels of the Church, and corruption among priests and monks was widespread. The moral decay led to skepticism, confusion, and eventually reaction from laity and clergy alike. The greatest challenge of all came in 1517 when the Augustinian monk and professor of theology Martin Luther (1483–1546) tacked his Ninety-Five Theses against indulgences onto the door of the church at Wittenberg.

As the writers and artists of the Renaissance were reaching into the past and studying Greco-Roman classics, religious reformers such as Luther, Huldrych Zwingli (1484–1531), and John Calvin (1509–1564) were looking back to the days of the apostles to recover a simpler, more accurate, and more immediate Christian faith than that offered by the vast, complex, and often corrupt machinery of the Roman Catholic Church. Unlike previous reform movements, the major Protestant sects that emerged after 1517—Lutheranism, Zwinglianism, Calvinism, and Anabaptism—challenged the very doctrines upon which the Catholic hierarchy rested. Luther and others maintained that Christian truth was revealed directly in the Scriptures themselves and did not require the intervention of popes, priests, or church doctrine. All Christians, under the direct inspiration of the Holy Spirit, could turn immediately to the Bible for spiritual guidance.

Though none of the major Protestant reformers were political revolutionaries, the idea that salvation came solely from faith and God's grace undermined the power and authority of Catholic priests and the Papacy. Luther himself was conservative in political matters, but his ideas opened the door for other people to interpret the Bible more radically than he did—and some of these people saw a connection between spiritual and physical freedom. This connection was felt strongly in England, France, and the German states of the Holy Roman Empire. Here, empowered by the advances in printing that made possible a proliferation of tracts and pamphlets—as well as editions of the Bible translated into vernacular languages, such as German, French, and Italian—Protestantism took hold quickly. Thus, the Reformation, however unintentionally, set the stage for a hundred years or more of bloody wars, rebellions, and civil disturbances throughout Europe. Political and social struggles—both within and between kingdoms and cities—increasingly played on the antipathy between Catholics and Protestants, and even between various factions of Protestants.

COUNTER-REFORMATION

As Protestantism spread throughout northern and central Europe, the Roman Catholic Church underwent a period of self-scrutiny and reform known as the **Counter-Reformation**. Under Pope Paul III (r. 1534–49) and his immediate successors, the papacy shored up its moral strength and generated a new energy and sense of mission within its ranks. From 1545 to 1563, a general council of Catholic bishops met in the city of Trent, near the border of Italy and Austria, to investigate corruption in the Church and determine strategies for meeting the Protestant challenge. The Council of Trent rejected Protestant positions on such matters as transubstantiation, confession, absolution, and tradition. As far as the council was concerned only ordained priests could properly interpret Scripture, perform the Eucharist, and hear confession.

To help spread the reformed Catholic faith, the Church in 1540 sanctioned a new missionary order—the Society of Jesus. Originating a few years earlier under the leadership of Ignatius of Loyola (1491–1556), the **Jesuits**, as the new order was called, became the chief missionary and military wing of the Catholic Church. Highly educated and well trained, the Jesuits led the assault against paganism in the New World and Protestantism in the old, seeking to reclaim souls lost to Protestantism in Poland, England, and Austria. Thus, in the mid sixteenth century the lines were drawn that would, as noted earlier, pit Catholics against Protestants in more than a century of violence.

THE EUROPEAN RENAISSANCE: HUMANISM AND THE ARTS

While the Middle Ages should not be regarded as a period of dormancy, the dynamic transformation that came to be called the European Renaissance is often described as a reawakening. The fifteenth and sixteenth centuries were characterized by a desire to recover the classical past, an impulse to relish and explore the world, a passion for discovery and invention, and an interest in personal knowledge and power in the hands of charismatic individuals. The love of classical learning and scholarship in Europe began in fourteenth-century Italy with Francesco Petrarch (1304–1374), a Christian writer who took great pride in his scholarly research into Roman classics, as well as in his own Latin writings, and with Leonardo Bruni (c. 1370–1444), whose studies of the Roman philosopher Cicero gave rise to what is known as civic humanism—basically, putting one's scholarship, learning, and taste into the service of the state. Later writers such as Marsilio Ficino (1433–1499) and Giovanni Pico della Mirandola (1463–1494) studied the Greeks, especially Plato, whose work had fallen into neglect during the Middle Ages. The works of these and other humanist writers led people to reorient their thoughts and actions from the heavenly realm to the human world.

To the humanists, the potential for creative thought and action seemed to be unlimited. The hero most interesting to the Renaissance intellectual was not, as in the Middle Period, the Christian soul making its way toward the heavenly city; instead it was the charismatic, curious, and learned man (less often the woman) who studied, theorized about, and eventually controlled all manner of materials, enterprises, and earthly realms. The belief in the godlike potential of human beings, perhaps most succinctly articulated in Pico's *On the Dignity of Man* (p. 468), led to a sense of exhilaration but also to one of trepidation. Later European writers, particularly religious ones, came to question the scientific and intellectual potential of their Italian forebears.

Christopher Marlowe's *Dr. Faustus* (1604; p. 389) attacks the arcane scholasticism of the Middle Ages but also points to the consequences of human overreaching and raises the question of whether limits should be imposed on human knowledge and power. Gifted with a prodigious intellect and possessed of unlimited knowledge, the learned Dr. Faustus stepped out of his proper place in the order of things and set loose forces he ultimately could not control. John Milton's Adam and Eve in his great epic *Paradise Lost* (1667; p. 575) are similar figures, in that they succumb to the temptation to acquire the knowledge of good and evil and thereby disobey God. Thus, even as Renaissance learning inspired confidence in human ingenuity, it also posed questions about the place and purpose of humanity in the cosmic order.

The humanist writers' emphasis on the dignity and value of human beings had parallels in the visual arts, as evidenced by a trend toward realism. In *Lives of the Most Eminent Painters, Sculptors, and Architects,* the artist and biographer Giorgio Vasari (1511–1574)—the first to use the term *Renaissance*—speaks of how the artists of his own time were recovering classical aesthetics and creating new ways to depict nature accurately. A group of Florentine painters and sculptors, including Giotto (c. 1266–1337), Donatello (c. 1386–1466), and Masaccio (1401–1428), experimented with perspective—the realistic depiction of spatial relations between figure and ground—and thereby exerted a profound influence on later artists. Moving beyond their predecessors, the Renaissance artists learned to work with perspective on two-dimensional surfaces to create the illusion of three-dimensional space, and they experimented boldly with *chiaroscuro,* the play of light and shade on solid surfaces, a realistic technique that lent flashes of drama and emotion to a painted scene. Perhaps most significantly, however, artists were once again paying attention, as classical artists and sculptors had, to the human body. The intricate anatomical drawings of Leonardo da Vinci and of the Flemish anatomist Andreas Vesalius (1514–1564) are the most obvious examples of the new emphasis on direct observation; the sculptor Donatello's *David* offers another. This nearly life-sized figure of the biblical hero, the first nude statue by a Renaissance artist, bears a realistic pose but, at the same time, an ideal beauty that seems to glorify its human subject.

The humanist trends of the Renaissance led to renewed interest not only in the arts and literature but also in the scientific and mathematical texts from Greece,

Rome, and Arabia. Perhaps nowhere were the limits of human knowledge tested more powerfully than in the areas of astronomy and cosmology. By directly observing the planets and stars, and carefully measuring their movements, the astronomers Nicolas Copernicus (1473–1543), Galileo Galilei (1564–1642), and Johannes Kepler (1571–1630) developed theories that challenged the Catholic Church and the **Scholastic** thinkers. Copernicus's *On the Revolutions of Heavenly Bodies* (1543; p. 685) set forth the theory that the planets orbit the sun (heliocentrism), which conflicted with the Church's cosmology, rooted in the earth-centered theories (geocentrism) of Ptolemy and Aristotle.

Although when Galileo advocated Copernicus's theory, the Catholic Church tried him by Inquisition and placed him under house arrest, the Catholic hold on European thought was being challenged during this period on many other fronts, especially by the Protestant Reformation, discussed earlier. Eventually, like the Protestant reformers, the scientists prevailed over the Church. Their success may in part be measured by the founding of the Royal Society, an English organization established to promote scientific studies, in 1660.

FROM RENAISSANCE TO BAROQUE

In one way or another, European art and literature of the mid-fifteenth through the early seventeenth centuries reflect—or reflect on—the humanist values that characterize the age of the Renaissance. *Humanism* is an elastic term, but Renaissance humanists generally embraced the idea that human beings, endowed with a great deal of autonomy and self-determination, are the central and most fascinating subjects of all creation. They also believed in the perfectibility of individuals and societies. Many writers, as noted earlier, challenged or questioned some of those assumptions, and during and after the Reformation the idea of human perfectibility and self-determination came under severe scrutiny. Nonetheless, even in many Protestant works, such as Milton's *Paradise Lost,* the emphasis falls on men's and women's ability to determine their own fate, even when that fate may have been foreseen by God.

Despite their similarities of theme, however, the art and literature of the late sixteenth and early seventeenth centuries differ in mood and form from that of the fourteenth and fifteenth centuries. In comparison to the balance and symmetry of Renaissance art, much of the art and literature of the late sixteenth and seventeenth centuries is characterized by a wider range of emotion. Known as the **Baroque**, this general trend in art, architecture, and literature began in Italy in the late sixteenth century and spread through other parts of Europe and to New Spain in the Americas. Some have suggested that the Baroque embodies the spirit of the Counter-Reformation, others that it expresses the tensions and stresses of the wars of religion sweeping through Europe. In art, the symmetries and balance of Michelangelo's *David* (1501–04) or Raphael's *Madonna del Granduca* (c. 1505) gave way to the more contorted forms of Bernini's *David* (1623) and Rubens's *The Raising of the Cross* (1609–10); in poetry, the sweet melodies of Petrarch's lyric love poems gave way to the acerbic wit and wrenching conceits (that is, elaborate metaphors) of John Donne.

EUROPEAN LITERATURE

Epic and Novel. Humanist values are reflected in the treatment of the **EPIC**, the earliest of literary forms, which traditionally expresses the ethos of its age, and the novel. These genres are represented in the Early Modern Period by John Milton's *Paradise Lost* (p. 575) and Miguel de Cervantes Saavedra's *Don Quixote* (p. 262). Self-consciously alluding to his classical predecessors, Milton paints intimate psychological portraits of his protagonists, Adam and Eve (revealing their individual personalities), and of their self-tormented but superhuman foe, Satan. For his part Cervantes captures in writing, as his contemporary Diego Velazquez did in painting, a sense of the proud but diminishing estate of the Spanish empire after the defeat of the Spanish Armada in 1588. But the work is not just a reflection on contemporary politics; *Don Quixote* is also a satire on the medieval romance literature that was popular at the time. The novel explores the conflict between the idealism attributed to the historical past and the pragmatism necessary to survive the Machiavellian realities of the present.

Drama. Renaissance Europe saw the flourishing of drama, in both its tragic and comic modes, for the first time since fifth-century Greece. These **TRAGEDIES**, **COMEDIES**, and **HISTORIES**, written by such dramatists as Lope de Vega (1562–1635), William Shakespeare (1564–1616), Christopher Marlowe (1564–1593), and Pedro Calderón de la Barca (1600–1681) were influenced by the many Greek and Roman plays that had been recovered and translated during the Renaissance, as well as the medieval Christian and folk plays, with their cosmic scope, rousing characters, and homely personal touches given to the lives of saints and biblical figures. Spain and England, in particular, enjoyed golden ages of the stage, especially during the sixteenth and seventeenth centuries. In both countries professional acting companies formed, and stage productions grew far more sophisticated and spectacular than in the past. The conflicted personality of Dr. Faustus could now gradually reveal itself not on a bare stage, but within scenery that would credibly pass as a humanist's study; Prospero's magic would call up not only a tempest but also a variety of special effects. The first **OPERAS**—stage spectacles that combined dance, lyric, music, and drama—began to appear in Italy during this period.

TIME AND PLACE

Renaissance Europe: Johannes Gutenberg and the Printing Press

The Renaissance would not have spread as widely and as quickly as it did without the advent of new methods of printing, developed in about 1450 by Johannes Gutenberg (c. 1397–1468) of Mainz. Woodblock printing—the art of carving a text on a wooden block, inking it, and transferring the ink to a new surface—had been invented in China in the seventh century during the Tang dynasty (618–907 C.E.), and by the eleventh century the Chinese had developed a movable type made from clay. Block printing, along with papermaking, had spread from China through Central Asia into Europe by the twelfth century. What was unique to Gutenberg was his method of casting movable metal type, which enabled the printer to rearrange and reuse the letters that made up a given piece of writing. Gutenberg then adapted a wine press so that the type could be arranged on an inked metal plate, then pressed down onto blank sheets of paper.

The Gutenberg press made it possible for printers to quickly produce inexpensive texts in a wide variety of forms. Everything from Bibles to love poems, books of travelers' tales to scientific treatises, political and religious pamphlets to playing cards could now be given mass distribution. Within fifty years of Gutenberg's first book, the Bible, produced in 1455, more than nine million books had been printed on European printing presses alone.

The flood of books was so "troublesome" that in 1559 Pope Paul IV published the *Index Librorum Prohibitorum*, a list of forbidden books, among which were many of the pamphlets and books of the Protestant reformers. Gutenberg's printing press effected a revolution in the production and dissemination of information equivalent to or greater than the development of the personal computer and the Internet in our own time.

Gutenberg Printing Press, 1468. *A replica of the printing press designed by Johannes Gutenberg, the German inventor of the method of printing from movable type, is on display at the Gutenberg Museum in Mainz. (The Art Archive / Musée Gutenberg Mayence / Dagli Orti)*

WWW For more information about the culture and context of Europe in the Early Modern Period, see *World Literature Online* at bedfordstmartins.com/worldlit.

Lyric and the Essay. Two genres during the Early Modern Period particularly embodied the humanist interest in the individual: Italian writer Francesco Petrarch (1304–1374) revitalized the LYRIC in the fourteenth century, and French writer Michel de Montaigne (1533–1592) invented the ESSAY, a brand-new genre that grew out of the political conflicts sweeping through France in the sixteenth century. Drawing from the courtly love tradition of the medieval troubadours and the poems of Dante's *Vita Nuova,* and writing in SONNETS and other lyric forms, Petrarch intimately chronicled his shifting feelings toward life, art, and, above all, love. His lyrics dramatize the most minute details of his relationship with his beloved Laura, the smallest alteration in his emotional temperature, and the intensity of his unrequited desire. Petrarch set the standard in Europe for the lyric's typical mixture of sensuality and idealism. Like Petrarch, other poets of this period, such as Louise Labé (c. 1524–1566), John Donne (1572–1631), and Anne Bradstreet (1612–1672) often blended the bodily and the spiritual, and—like the devotional poets of the *bhakti* tradition in India—wrote of sexual love in terms of divine adoration or vice versa.

No less than the lyric, the essay also captures the restlessness and intellectual curiosity of the Early Modern Period. Montaigne, like other Renaissance intellectuals, read widely. He eventually prepared lists of quotations from his reading and made personal annotations on them; gradually, the annotations came to outweigh the quotations and evolved into the essay, which in French—*essai*—means "attempt." In his essays, Montaigne confides particulars about his personal life, tells anecdotes, and cites the observations of his friends, all while circling loosely around a central (often serious) subject such as colonialism or human freedom. His humanist assumption is clearly that his opinions matter, especially inasmuch as they draw on historical events and classical works to comment on the present day.

Francesco Petrarch
1304–1374

Although only forty years separate Francesco **Petrarch** from his countryman Dante, Petrarch is often described as the first Renaissance man, partly because of the breadth of his interests. Even more than Dante, he was multitalented: a poet in both his native Italian and in Latin, a classical scholar who recovered and edited manuscripts of Cicero and Livy[1] and wrote the biographies of a number of Roman heroes, an unofficial diplomat who gave advice to the Doge of Venice and the Holy Roman Emperor, a traveler who knew the Rhineland, the Netherlands, and most of France and Italy, a landscape gardener, a fisherman, a lutanist, and a climber of mountains. But more than the multiplicity of his interests, the shape those interests took marks him as a Renaissance figure. Observing at close hand the corruption of the papal court in Avignon, Petrarch grew concerned with how a person might learn to lead a moral life through guidance and pursuits that lay beyond as well as within the Church, specifically through the study of the pre-Christian writers of Greece and Rome and through one's own practice of arts and letters. Petrarch does not simply make his HUMANISTIC studies the handmaidens of Christian doctrine. His work grants this world its own value and does not scorn the pleasures and the beauty it offers. He pays a highly self-conscious attention to the drama of his own personal life as a lover, scholar, and aspiring man of letters.

PEE-trark

A Lifelong Exile. Petrarch was born on July 20, 1304, "on a Monday, at dawn," as he tells us in his autobiography. His birthplace was Arezzo, a small town in Tuscany. Like Dante's, Petrarch's parents, Pietro Petrarca and Elleta Canigiani, had been exiled from Florence in 1301 for being on the wrong side of one of the many factional disputes that troubled the city, although whether Dante's and Petrarch's families were exiled over the same incident is not known. Although Petrarch was never even to visit Florence for any length of time, that urban center of Renaissance culture always claimed to be his home. In truth, the fact that Petrarch knew no single stable home from very early childhood on may have helped to make him the universally-minded, pan-European figure he became.

While Petrarch was still a child, his lawyer father moved the family first to Incisa and then to Pisa in Italy before settling in southern France in the Provençal city of Avignon in 1312, when Petrarch was eight. In 1309, Pope Clement V, pressured by the increasingly powerful French monarchy to center the Catholic Church in France rather than in Rome, had moved the Papacy to Avignon. The small city was overcrowded because

WWW For links to more information about Petrarch, a quiz on the *Canzoniere,* and information about the twenty-first-century relevance of Petrarch, see *World Literature Online* at bedfordstmartins.com/worldlit.

[1] **Cicero and Livy:** Marcus Tullius Cicero (106–43 B.C.E.), Roman orator, republican politician, and Stoic philosopher, admired during the Renaissance for his philosophical and political views and for the purity of his prose style. Titus Livius (59 B.C.E.–17 C.E.), Roman historian; 35 of the 142 books of his history of Rome survive.

Andrea del Castagno, *Petrarch,* Fifteenth Century
The humanist scholar-poet Francesco Petrarch is shown here with a book under his arm. (Scala/Art Resource, NY)

of the presence of the papal court, and Petrarch was taken to live with his mother and younger brother **Gherardo** in the little village of Carpentras, fifteen miles to the northeast. There followed four idyllic years when he studied grammar, logic, and rhetoric under a Tuscan schoolmaster, read the Cicero and Virgil he learned early to love, and roamed the beautiful Provençal countryside with Gherardo, to whom he would always remain close.

geh-RAR-doh

Studying the Law. The childhood that Petrarch remembered as a dreamy time of security and peace, of "freedom in the town and . . . silence in the countryside," came to an end when he turned twelve and his father sent him southeast to Montpellier to begin his studies for the law, the profession his father chose for him. But even in his early teens it was clear that the law was not to be Petrarch's real vocation, and he neglected his studies to read the Latin classics in secret. His father, visiting him at school, discovered his hidden hoard of books and burned them, but the boy's grief made him relent in time to save Virgil and Cicero from the flames. Petrarch also suffered his first profound experience of human loss at Montpellier in 1319 when his mother died; his earliest surviving poem is an elegy to her written in Virgilian hexameters.

At the age of sixteen, in 1320, he was sent to the University of Bologna, then the leading European center for legal studies, where he remained for the next six years. In his autobiographical *Letter to Posterity* (c. 1373), Petrarch tells us that although he revered the law for its power and its roots in Roman antiquity, he thought its practitioners corrupt, and says, "I hated the idea of learning an art which I would not practice dishonestly, and could hardly hope to practice otherwise."

Entering the Church. At his father's death in 1326, the twenty-two-year-old was suddenly free to do as he pleased, and for the next four years he moved in Avignon's faster social circles. He and Gherardo, living the life of young fops, were preoccupied with the latest styles in fancy gowns and shoes and fashionable entertainment; they even hesitated to go outside in windy weather for fear of mussing their modishly curled hair. By 1330, most of their estate had been squandered, and Petrarch took minor orders in the Church, accepting a post as private chaplain to Cardinal Giovanni Colonna, who respected Petrarch's classical learning and allowed him time for study. Petrarch would remain attached to Colonna's household until 1348. This change to a steadier life may well have been precipitated not only by personal finances but also by Petrarch's first glimpse of the woman he calls Laura. He first saw her in the Church of Saint Claire in Avignon on April 6, 1327, and he was anxious to be worthy of her, however unattainable she might be.

Who Laura was, whether she was married, how well she and Petrarch knew one another, what kept them from becoming lovers, even whether she was an actual person rather than an idealized composite woman—these are all questions for which scholars have no definitive answers. We know Laura only from the ***Canzoniere*** (*The Songbook,* c. 1330–1374), the collection of 366 Italian lyrics that celebrate her in life and in death.

kahn-tsoh-NYEY-ray

He helped to define and form the modern sensibility, in its appreciation of the beauty in nature, in its sense of the mystery and marvel in everyday reality, in its idealization of romantic love, in its refinement of self-scrutiny.

– MORRIS BISHOP, critic, 1963

Petrarch sometimes dismissed these vernacular poems as "bagatelles," or trifles, but he kept writing and reworking them from the 1330s until his own death in 1374, and it is for these poems rather than for his more ambitious Latin works that Petrarch is best remembered.

From 1330 on, Petrarch continued to hold minor clerical offices that left him time for writing, editing, and scholarship; throughout his life he several times declined higher posts that would interfere with his studies. Despite his love for Laura, Petrarch fathered at least two children by an unknown woman; in time, he had them declared legitimate. In 1337, after his first trip to Rome, he established a residence at Vaucluse, a small town near Avignon where he would reside off and on for the next twenty years, attempting to live a life of disciplined simplicity. About this time Petrarch began what he thought would be his major work, an epic poem on the Roman general Scipio Africanus;[2] he believed that if he were to be the fit heir of Virgil and Dante, he would have to produce an epic poem, for epics were what the greatest poets wrote. Petrarch's *Africa* is seldom read today, but in 1341 that work-in-progress earned him simultaneous bids from both Paris and Rome to crown him as poet laureate. In accord with his devotion to classical ideals he chose Rome, and in the month of April, always a significant season for him, Petrarch was crowned on the Capitoline Hill in a ceremony that seemed to affirm the growing interest of many citizens in newly revering the classical heritage of arts and letters.

In 1343, Petrarch's brother Gherardo became a Carthusian monk; Petrarch was both admiring and somewhat chagrined, for he had never felt similarly able to renounce the world. Five years later, in 1348, while he was traveling in Parma, Petrarch received news of Laura's death on April 6, the anniversary of their meeting. Both of these events affected him deeply, and probably influenced his *Secretum (The Secret)* begun in 1342, a work in the form of a dialogue between Petrarch and Saint Augustine. In it, he explores the problems of reconciling his Christianity with his keen appetite for worldly fame and his love for Laura and for literature written by pagan authors.

Petrarch returned to Rome in 1350 for the Papal Jubilee, and on his way he stopped in Florence to meet Boccaccio. In the following year, the Pope begged Petrarch to return to Avignon to work for the Curia, while at the same time Boccaccio entreated him to accept a professorship at the University in Florence, promising to restore the family property that had been seized. Petrarch chose to go to Avignon, but he soon regretted that decision, given the "seething, obscene, terrible" corruption he observed in the "New Babylon" of the French Papacy, corruption he lambasted in a series of writings titled *Letters without a Name.* Between 1353 and 1361 he lived largely in Milan under the patronage of Giovanni Visconti,[3] performing minor diplomatic missions, writing and studying, and produc-

[2] **Scipio Africanus:** Roman general (234?–183 B.C.E.) who defeated Hannibal, the Carthaginian general, in the Second Punic War (218–202 B.C.E.).

[3] **Visconti family:** The Ghibelline family that ruled Milan and was the arch-enemy of Florence.

ing a number of pleas for peace among the fractious Italian cities and states. In 1361 he moved to Padua to escape a new outbreak of the plague in which his son and a number of close friends died, and for the remainder of his life he used Padua and Venice as his bases for travel and study. His patron in Padua, Francesco de Carrera, of the ruling family in the city, gave him a plot of land south of Padua in the Eugenaean Hills, and there Petrarch built a villa, where he retired in 1370. He continued to work on the *Canzoniere* and other pieces up until his death, which came on the night before his seventieth birthday, July 19, 1374.

The Ascent of Mount Ventoux. Presented here are samples of Petrarch's prose and poetry. His letter to his friend Dionisio Da Borga San Sepolchro, describing his ascent of Mount **Ventoux** ("Windy Mountain") in about 1336 in company with his brother Gherardo, suggests his Renaissance sensibilities. First, in this letter Petrarch gives us a world that is quite solid and material. To be sure, Petrarch fashions an allegory out of the ascent, contrasting, for example, the climbing styles of himself and his more determined brother: Gherardo climbs as vertically as possible, choosing the steeper but shorter path, while Petrarch makes his circuitous way to the top, ultimately wearying himself more. Petrarch makes the inevitable comparison between climbing the mountain and attaining "the blessed life" through spiritual discipline. But this mountain is a genuine peak in the French Alps, as opposed to Dante's wholly symbolic Mount Purgatory. Mount Ventoux is made of real rock; real shepherds dwell in its foothills; and Petrarch does not let us forget that he is describing with relish an actual physical feat.

vawng-TOO

Second, Petrarch makes this climb he has dreamed of since childhood not because he thinks any spiritual, military, or scientific purpose will be served, but because of "the wish to see what so great a height had to offer"—in other words, because it is there. Petrarch's is the first recorded Western expression of the desire to climb a mountain for the sheer sake of doing so, and an early example of the Renaissance European's zest for discovery and adventure. Private impulse and personal desire are for Petrarch valid reasons for undertaking a project others might deem silly, reckless, or unnecessary.

Third, even this vigorous outdoor excursion is saturated with and partly determined by appeals to both classical and Christian authority; Petrarch is presenting himself here equally as an alpinist and as a Christian humanist. He makes plans to climb the peak after reading a passage in Livy describing Philip of Macedon ascending Mount Haemus in the Balkans and surveying two seas at once from that summit. In the course of the letter, Petrarch casually alludes to many other classical authors, texts, and historical figures, confident his readers will not have to strain to catch his allusions. Finally, once atop Mount Ventoux, Petrarch pulls his copy of St. Augustine's *Confessions* out of his pocket and reproaches himself for taking such delight and pride in a physical feat; St. Augustine is the voice of conscience that impels him to vow to give up such worldly vanity. But it is very like the moment in *The Tempest* when Prospero, who has shown us so many rich wonders, vows to drown his book and meditate upon his death. Petrarch has evoked already the thrill of ascending those windy heights; the appeal of the physical world has already been thoroughly set forth, and cannot wholly be called back.

Canzoniere. The tug of war in the human heart between contending authorities that is characteristic of the Renaissance also marks Petrarch's most famous work, the *Canzoniere,* the Italian lyrics in honor of Laura that occupied him from his twenties until his death. These poems borrow their form and their themes from the earlier medieval poetry of courtly love. Petrarch was not the first to discover the sonnet form,[4] nor the first to write in Italian rather than in Latin, and certainly he was not the first to make an unattainable beloved the central image of a body of poems, but he was the first to show others how supple the sonnet form could be, and how richly suited to poetry the Italian language might be in the hands of a master. In a manner that almost seems to anticipate the romantic writers of centuries to come, Petrarch brings his own personality to the fore, insisting upon writing in his own name, preserving and revising his manuscripts, and keeping a poetic record of the minutely detailed shifts in his emotions and physical sensations and the contrasts between the outer world and his own inner state.

Petrarch's sonnets often seem stale to modern readers because so many writers of love poems who have come after Petrarch have borrowed his themes and techniques. *Petrarchan* has become a pejorative word among critics because Petrarch did what he did so well that writers are still copying him; we are too accustomed in poems and popular song lyrics to catalogues of the wonders of a beloved woman's lips and eyes and voice and hair, to hyperbole and paradox and pledges of undying love. Moreover, it is difficult for any English translation to suggest Petrarch's intricate music; English has far fewer rhyming words than Italian, and if a translator tries to replicate in English Petrarch's rhyme schemes, the result often sounds jangling and unnatural, more like a snappy Gilbert and Sullivan[5] patter song than a sensuous or anguished love lyric. Our translations abandon the elaborate rhyme scheme in hopes of suggesting in English the pace and texture of Petrarch's Italian.

The real delight of the *Canzoniere* sonnets for modern readers, and their most intensely Renaissance quality, lies in the way they form a kind of private psychic and spiritual journal over Petrarch's lifetime. Taken together, they record his wavering among his sense of his own sinfulness, his longing for peace and salvation, his craving for adventure and honor, his pride in the work that signals him the heir of Dante and Virgil, his

[4] **sonnet form:** The Italian or Petrarchan sonnet is a fourteen-line poem of eleven syllables per line in Italian (ten in English). Its two parts are the octave (the first eight lines), rhymed *abba abba,* and the sestet (the last six lines), which use either two or three more rhymes.

[5] **Gilbert and Sullivan:** English playwright William Schwenck Gilbert (1836–1911) collaborated with composer Arthur Sullivan (1842–1900) to produce a series of popular satiric and comic operas, including *H.M.S. Pinafore* (1878) and *The Mikado* (1885).

impassioned response to the call of all that is lovely and mortal, and, above all, his acceptance of his own vacillation. Throughout the *Canzoniere,* Petrarch refuses to come down on any side of all the varied conflicts his life presents to him; he does not pass any final judgment, but he does create for us with power and tenderness the contradictions of the physical and moral world he knew.

■ CONNECTIONS

Dante, *The Inferno,* Book 2. Mount Ventoux is described as a real place, even though Petrarch does make symbolic use of the differences between himself and his brother as climbers. The "little hill" Dante encounters at the beginning of *The Inferno* and his Mount Purgatory are creations of the medieval imagination. What elements make Petrarch's account "real"? How is Dante's imaginative? In what ways are these differences those of the Middle Ages and the Renaissance?

Augustine, *Confessions,* Book 2; Li Bai, *Poems,* Book 2; Basho, *Narrow Road through the Deep Interior,* Book 4. At the top of Mount Ventoux Petrarch meditates on Augustine's moment of conversion, two events we would now describe as "peak experiences," life-changing moments. Such experiences often happen in solitude and in a strange or unfamiliar place. Consider Li Bai's experiences in the mountains. Could they be described as peak experiences? What moments on Basho's journey to the "deep interior" might be considered peak experiences?

***In the Tradition,* "Courtly Love," Book 2; *In the Tradition,* "European Love Lyrics," p. 85.** The conventions of the love sonnet and the idealized lady in the *Canzoniere* also define many of the love poems in the *In the Tradition* sections "Courtly Love" and "European Love Lyrics." Describe the characteristics of the lady. Could the poets who address their poems to these ladies be said to have a common attitude toward women and about love?

■ FURTHER RESEARCH

Bergin, Thomas. *Petrarch.* 1970.
Bishop, Morris. *Petrarch and His World.* 1963.
Foster, Kenelm. *Petrarch: Poet and Humanist.* 1984.
Mann, Nicholas. *Petrarch.* 1984.
O'Rourke, Marjorie. *Petrarch's Genius: Pentimento and Prophesy.* 1991.
Waller, Marguerite R. *Petrarch's Poetics and Literary History.* 1980.

■ PRONUNCIATION

Canzoniere: kahn-tsoh-NYEH-ray, -nee-EH-ray
Gherardo: geh-RAR-doh
Petrarch: PEE-trark
Ventoux: vawng-TOO

The Ascent of Mount Ventoux

Translated by Mark Musa

Today I climbed the highest mountain in this region, which is not improperly called Ventosum (Windy). The only motive for my ascent was the wish to see what so great a height had to offer. I had had the project in mind for many years, for, as you know, I have lived in these parts from childhood on, having been cast there by the fate which determines human affairs. And so the mountain, which is visible from a great distance, was always before my eyes, and for a long time I planned on doing what I have finally done today. The impulse to make the climb actually took hold of me while I was reading Livy's *History of Rome*[1] yesterday, and I happened upon the place where Philip of Macedon,[2] the one who waged the war against the Romans, climbed Mount Haemus in Thessaly. From its summit, it was reported that he was able to see two seas, the Adriatic and the Euxine. Whether this is true or false I do not know, for the mountain is too far away, and there is disagreement among the commentators. Pomponius Mela,[3] the cosmographer—not to mention the many others who have talked about this occurrence—accepts the truth of this statement without hesitation while Livy, on the other hand, thinks it false. I, certainly, would not have left the question long in doubt if that mountain had been as easy to explore as this one. But let us drop the matter and return to my mountain here: I thought it proper for a young man in private life to attempt what no one would criticize in an aged king.

When I thought about looking for a companion for the ascent I realized, strangely enough, that hardly any of my friends were suitable—so rarely does one find, even among those most dear to one, the perfect combination of character and purpose. One was too phlegmatic, another too anxious; one too slow, another too hasty; one too sad, another too happy; one too simple, another more sagacious than I would like. I was frightened by the fact that one never spoke while another talked too much; the heavy deliberation of some repelled me as much as the lean incapacity of others. I rejected some for their cold lack of interest and others for their excessive enthusiasm. Such defects as these, however grave, are tolerable enough at home (for charity suffers all things, and friendship rejects no burden), but it is another matter

---

The Ascent of Mount Ventoux. When Petrarch wrote this letter on April 26, 1336, to the Augustinian monk Father Dionigi da Borgo San Sepolero, his former confessor and a professor of theology at the University of Paris, the author was thirty-two years old. His expedition to climb the mountain was the culmination of a long-harbored curiosity and was prompted specifically by reading Livy's *History of Rome,* two motivations characteristic of the European Renaissance.

---

[1] **Livy's *History of Rome:*** Titus Livius (59 B.C.E.–17 C.E.) spent his life writing a history of Rome from the city's founding in 753 B.C.E. to 9 B.C.E.

[2] **Philip of Macedon:** Philip V (238–179 B.C.E.), king of Macedon.

[3] **Pomponius Mela:** Roman geographer of the first century C.E. His description of the known world of his time, *De situ orbis,* was published in Latin in 1471.

on a journey, where such weaknesses become more serious. So, with only my own pleasure in mind, with great care I looked about weighing the various characteristics of my friends against one another without committing any breach of friendship and silently condemning any trait which might prove to be disagreeable on my journey. And would you believe it? I finally turned to my own family for help and proposed the ascent to my younger brother, the only one I have, and whom you know well. He was delighted beyond measure and gratified by the thought of acting at the same time as a friend as well as a brother.

On the appointed day we left the house and by evening reached Malaucène which lies at the foot of the mountain on the north side. We rested there a day and finally this morning made the ascent with no one except two servants. And it is a most difficult task indeed, for the mountain is a very steep and almost inaccessible mass of rocky terrain. But, as a poet once put it well: "Remorseless labour conquers all."[4] The day was long and the air invigorating, our spirits were high and our agile bodies strong, and everything else necessary for such an undertaking helped us on our way. The only difficulty we had to face was the nature of the place itself. We found an old shepherd among the mountain's ridges who tried at great length to discourage us from the ascent, saying that some fifty years before he had, in the same ardour of youth, climbed to the summit and had got nothing from it except fatigue and repentance and torn clothes and scratches from the rocks and briars. Never, according to what he or his friends knew, had anyone ever tried the ascent before or after him. But his counsels merely increased our eagerness to go on, as a young man's mind is usually suspicious of warnings. So the old man, finding his efforts were useless, went along with us a little way and pointed out a steep path among the rocks, continuing to cry out admonitions even after we had left him behind. Having left him with those garments and anything else we thought might prove burdensome to us, we made ready for the ascent and started to climb at a good pace. But, as often happens, fatigue soon followed upon our strenuous effort, and before long we had to rest on some rock. Then we started on again, but more slowly, I especially taking the rocky path at a more modest pace. My brother chose the steepest course straight up the ridge, while I weakly took an easier one which turned along the slopes. And when he called me back showing me the shorter way, I replied that I hoped to find an easier way up on the other side, and that I did not mind taking a longer course if it were not so steep. But this was merely an excuse for my laziness; and when the others had already reached a considerable height I was still wandering in the hollows, and having failed to find an easier means of ascent, I had only lengthened the journey and increased the difficulty of the ascent. Finally I became disgusted with the tedious way I had chosen, and decided to climb straight up. By the time I reached my brother, who had managed to have a good rest while waiting for me, I was tired and irritated. We walked along together for a while, but hardly had we left that rise when I forgot all about the circuitous route I had just taken and again tended to take a lower one. Thus, once again I found myself taking the easy way, the roundabout path

[4] **"Remorseless labour . . .":** Virgil, *Georgics*, I, 145.

of winding hollows, only to find myself soon back in my old difficulty. I was simply putting off the trouble of climbing; but no man's wit can alter the nature of things, and there is no way to reach the heights by going downward. In short, I tell you that I made this same mistake three or more times within a few hours, much to my brother's amusement and my anger.

After being misled in this way a number of times, I finally sat down in a hollow and my thoughts quickly turned from material things to the spiritual, and I said to myself more or less what follows: "What you have experienced so often today in the ascent of this mountain, certainly happens to you as it does to many others in their journey toward the blessèd life. But this is not so easily perceived by men, for the movements of the body are out in the open while those of the soul are invisible and hidden. The life we call blessèd is to be sought on a high level, and straight is the way that leads to it. Many, also, are the hills that stand in the way that leads to it, and we must ascend from virtue to virtue up glorious steps. At the summit is both the end of our struggles and the goal of our journey's climb. Everyone wishes to reach this goal, but, as Ovid says: 'To wish is not enough; you must yearn with ardent eagerness to gain your end.' And you certainly both wish and ardently yearn, unless you are deceiving yourself in this matter, as you so often do. What, then, is holding you back? Nothing, surely, except that you take a path which seems at first sight easier leading through low and worldly pleasures. Nevertheless in the end, after long wanderings, you will either have to climb up the steeper path under the burden of labours long deferred to its blessèd culmination, or lie down in the valley of your sins; and—I shudder to think of it!—if the shadow of death finds you there, you will spend an eternal night in constant torment." These thoughts stimulated my body and mind to a remarkable degree and made me face up to the difficulties which still remained. Oh, that my soul might follow that other road for which I long day and night, even as today I conquered material obstacles by bodily force! And why should it not be far easier: after all, the agile, immortal soul can reach its goal in the twinkling of an eye without intermediate space, while progress today had to be slow because my feeble body was burdened by its heavy members.

One mountain peak, the highest of all, the country people call Filiolus ("Sonny"); why, I do not know, unless by antiphrasis, as is sometimes the case, for the peak in question seems to be the father of all the surrounding ones. At its top is a little level place, and it was there that we could, at last, rest our weary bodies.

My good father, since you have listened to the troubles mounting in the heart of a man who ascends, listen now to the rest of the story, and devote one hour, I pray you, to reviewing the events of my day. At first, because I was not accustomed to the quality of the air and the effect of the wide expanse of view spread out before me, I stood there like a dazed person. I could see the clouds under our feet, and the tales I had read of Athos and Olympus[5] seemed less incredible as I myself was witnessing the very same things from a less famous mountain. I turned my eyes toward Italy, the

[5] **Athos and Olympus:** Mountains in Greece; Mount Athos is the site of many monasteries of the Eastern Church; Mount Olympus was the home of the gods in ancient Greece.

place to which my heart was most inclined. The great and snow-capped Alps seemed to rise close by, though they were far away—those same Alps through which that fierce enemy of the Roman name[6] once made his way, splitting the rocks, if we can believe the story, by means of vinegar. I sighed, I must admit, for Italian skies which I beheld more with my thought than with my eyes, and an inexpressible longing came over me to see once more my friend and my country, though at the same time I reproached myself for this double weakness which came from a soul not yet up to manly resistance—and yet there were excuses for both my desires, and several excellent authorities could be cited to support me.

Then a new idea came to me, and I started thinking in terms of time rather than space. I thought: "Today marks ten years since you completed your youthful studies and left Bologna. Oh, eternal God! Oh, immutable wisdom! Think of all the changes in your character these intervening years have seen! I suppress a great deal, for I have not yet reached a safe harbour where I can calmly recall past storms. The time, perhaps, will come when I can review all the experiences of the past in their order saying with the words of your St Augustine: 'I wish to recall my foul past and the carnal corruption of my soul, not that I love them, but that I may the more love you, O my God.'[7] Much that is dubious and evil still clings to me, but what I once loved, I love no longer. Come now, what am I saying? I still love it, but more moderately. No, not so, but with more shame, with more heaviness of heart. Now, at last, I have told the truth. The fact is I love, but I love what I long not to love, what I would like to hate. Though I hate to do so, though constrained, though sad and sorrowing, I love none the less, and I feel in my miserable self the meaning of the well-known words: 'I will hate if I can; if not, I will love against my will!' Not three years have passed since that perverse and wicked desire which had me in tight hold and held undisputed sway in my heart began to discover a rebellious opponent who was no longer willing to yield in obedience. These two adversaries have joined in close combat for supremacy, and for a long time now a gruelling war, the outcome of which is still doubtful, has been waging in the field of my mind."

Thus my thoughts turned back over the last ten years, and then with concentrated thought on the future, I asked myself: "If you should, by chance, prolong this uncertain life of yours for another ten years, advancing toward virtue in proportion to the distance from which you departed from your original infatuation during the past two years since the new longing first encountered the old, could you not face death on reaching forty years of age, if not with complete assurance at least with hopefulness, calmly dismissing from your thoughts the residuum of life that fades into old age?"

Such thoughts as these, father, occurred to me. I rejoiced in my progress, mourned for my weaknesses, and took pity on universal inconstancy of human conduct. I had

[6]**fierce enemy of the Roman name:** Hannibal (247–182 B.C.E.), the Carthaginian general who attacked Rome during the Punic Wars by crossing the Alps with elephants, heated rocks and melted them with vinegar to get through the mountains in winter. See Livy, *History of Rome,* Book 21.

[7]**"I wish . . .":** St. Augustine, *Confessions,* II, 1.

by this time forgotten where I was and why we had come; then, dismissing my anxieties to a more appropriate occasion, I decided to look about me and see what we had come to see. The sun was sinking and the shadows of the mountain were already lengthening below, warning us that the time for us to go was near at hand. As if suddenly roused from sleep, I turned to gaze at the west. I could not see the tops of the Pyrenees, which form the barrier between France and Spain, not because of any intervening obstacle that I know of but simply because of the inadequacy of mortal vision. But off to the right I could see most clearly the mountains of the region around Lyons and to the left the bay of Marseilles and the sea that beats against the shores of Aigues-Mortes, though all these places were at a distance requiring a journey of several days to reach them. The Rhône was flowing under our very eyes.

While my thoughts were divided thus, now turning my attention to thoughts of some worldly object before me, now uplifting my soul, as I had done my body, to higher planes, it occurred to me to look at Augustine's *Confessions,* a gift of your love that I always keep with me in memory of the author and the giver. I opened the little volume, small in size but infinitely sweet, with the intention of reading whatever came to hand, for what else could I happen upon if not edifying and devout words. Now I happened by chance to open it to the tenth book. My brother stood attentively waiting to hear what St Augustine would say from my lips. As God is my witness and my brother too, the first words my eyes fell upon were: "And men go about admiring the high mountains and the mighty waves of the sea and the wide sweep of rivers and the sound of the ocean and the movement of the stars, but they themselves they abandon."[8] I was ashamed, and asking my brother, who was anxious to hear more, not to bother me, I closed the book, angry with myself for continuing to admire the things of this world when I should have learned a long time ago from the pagan philosophers themselves that nothing is admirable but the soul beside whose greatness nothing can be as great. Then, having seen enough of the mountain I turned an inward eye upon myself, and from that moment on not a syllable passed my lips until we reached the bottom. The words I had read had given me enough food for thought and I could not believe that I happened to turn to them by mere chance. I believed that what I had read there was written for me and no one else, and I remembered that St Augustine had once thought the same thing in his own case, as he himself tells us when opening the book of the Apostle, the first words he saw were: "Not in rioting and drunkenness, not in chambering and wantonness, not in strife and envy, but put ye on the Lord Jesus Christ, and make not provision for the flesh in its concupiscences." The same thing happened earlier to St Anthony, as he listened to the Gospel where it is written, "If thou wilt be perfect, go and sell what thou hast, and give to the poor, and thou shalt have treasure in heaven; and come follow me." He believed this scripture to have been spoken specifically for him, and by means of it he guided himself to the Kingdom of Heaven, as the biographer Athanasius tells

---

[8] **"And men go . . .":** St. Augustine, *Confessions,* VIII, 12; Augustine compares his revelation to that of St. Anthony (251–350) in the same passage. St. Athanasius (297–373) is Anthony's original biographer.

us. And as Anthony on hearing these words asked for nothing more, and as Augustine after reading the Apostle's admonition sought no farther, so did I conclude my reading after the few words which I have recorded. I thought in silence of the vanity in us mortals who neglect what is noblest in ourselves in a vain show only because we look around ourselves for what can be found only within us. I wondered at the natural nobility of that human soul which unless degenerate has deserted its original state and turned to dishonour what God has given it for its honour. How many times I turned back that day to look at the mountain top which seemed scarcely more than a cubit high compared with the height of human contemplation, unless it is immersed in the foulness of earth? As I descended I asked myself: "If we are willing to endure so much sweat and labour in order to raise our bodies a little closer to heaven, how can a soul struggling toward God, up the steeps of human pride and mortal destiny, fear any cross or prison or sting of fortune?" How few, I thought, are they who are not diverted from this path for fear of hardship or the love of ease! And how happy those few, if any such there be! It is they, I feel, the poet had in mind when he wrote:

> Blessèd the man who is skilled to understand
> The hidden cause of things; who beneath his feet
> All fear casts, and death's relentless doom,
> And the howlings of greedy Acheron.[9]

How earnestly should we strive to trample beneath our feet not mountain-tops but the appetites which spring from earthly impulses!

In the middle of the night, unaware of the difficulties of the way back and amid the preoccupations which I have so frankly revealed, we came by the friendly light of a full moon to the little inn which we had left that morning before day-break. Then, while the servants were busy preparing our supper, I spent my time in a secluded part of the house, hurriedly and extemporaneously writing all this down, fearing that if I were to put off the task, my mood would change on leaving the place, and I would lose interest in writing to you.

You see, dearest father, that I wish to conceal nothing of myself from you. I describe to you not only the course of my life but even my individual thoughts. And I ask for your prayers that these vague and wandering thoughts of mine may some day become coherent and, having been so vainly cast in all directions, that they may direct themselves at last to the one, true, certain, and never-ending good.

[9] **"Blessèd the man . . .":** Virgil, *Georgics,* II, 490–93.

Canzoniere

Translated by Patricia Clark Smith

1: Oh you, who in these scattered rhymes may find

Oh you, who in these scattered rhymes may find
echoes of sighs that I once fed my heart
when I was young, when I was still in part
this man you see, that boy now left behind;

if you yourself have had one turn to writhe
in love's extremes of harsh delight, soft pain,
balanced between false hope, sweet love-in-vain,
I pray you'll read and pity and forgive.

There's talk of me on every street in town,
and I know why; although I feel that shame,
shame's not the deepest reason why I weep,

nor even penitence, but that stark dawn
of understanding how it's all a dream,
all that we love, all that we ache to keep.

Canzoniere. In the *Canzoniere* Petrarch perfected the form of the Italian sonnet, which is also often called the Petrarchan sonnet. Tradition had established the sonnet as a love poem addressed to an ideal lady who both inspires and often frustrates the poet's adoration. Formally the sonnet is divided into two parts, the octave (the first eight lines) and the sestet (the last six). It employs only four or five rhymes, the octave rhyming *abba abba,* and the sestet *cde, cde, cdc, cdc,* or *cde dce.* The limited number of rhymes is possible because there are so many more rhyming words in Italian than in English. Like most English translators, Patricia Clark Smith has increased the number of rhymes in rendering the poems into English.

Working within the conventions of the sonnet, Petrarch is able to create poems that reveal the inner life of the poet and make real his idealized Laura.

In sonnet 164 of the *Canzoniere,* the night world may lie in halcyon calm, but Petrarch's inner landscape is quite different:

> But I, I wake and brood, rage, weep, my eyes
> Always behold my love, my foe, my pain.
> I *am* a war. Here wrath and sorrow reign,
> Yet solely in her image I find peace.

3: It was the very day the sun's own light

It was the very day the sun's own light
grew dim to mark the passion of Our Lord
when I myself succumbed without a word,
struck down, my lady, simply by your sight.[1]

That one day least auspicious for romance
I walked unwary through the people's sorrow,
through grieving streets, all open to the blow
Love dealt amid that universal penance.

Love found its way to my heart through my eyes;
now my tears pool and gather, overflow
outward through those same gates where I was breached.

But you, my love, were never so surprised,
and I ask whether it is fair, or no,
Love laid me low, and left you so untouched?

Petrarch invents paradoxical similes and metaphors to describe the lady who simultaneously hurts and ennobles him:

> It was her healing hand gave me my wound,
> And where the pure and living spring wells forth
> I drink at once sweet water, bitter gall . . .

In 148, she is both the source of the love that turns him into a battered victim stumbling dazed through life, and the green laurel tree that sweetly shelters him, takes on his sorrow, and inspires his poems. There is a piquant element of sin and shame in his love for Laura, yet it is in part through his celebration of her in his poems that Petrarch envisions himself as gaining salvation. Through his words, the world "may better learn her grace / and love her" (333). If he has written of her truly, Petrarch's prayer will be granted, and her spirit will be the watcher at his own deathbed, accompanying him into Paradise.

Although Dante's Beatrice and Petrarch's Laura are related in the sense that they are both the female ideals of male poets, women whose real personalities and histories are nearly unknown to us, Laura is more clearly a living, earthly woman than Beatrice, both in life and in death. Even though, like Beatrice, she represents beauty, purity, and inspiration, Laura's physical presence is always evident, and its power to elate and torment Petrarch persists even after her death. In 292, more than half the sonnet evokes her living appearance so vividly she scarcely seems gone; in other poems she comes, sits by the poet's bed, and carries on conversations with him.

---

[1] **It was the . . . your sight:** The day Petrarch first saw Laura was April 6, 1327, then supposed to be the exact anniversary of the crucifixion, as opposed to the movable feast of Good Friday. He also tells us Laura died of plague on that same date in 1348.

90: Sometimes she'd comb her yellow braids out loose

Sometimes she'd comb her yellow braids out loose
for winds to tease and tangle in bright air,
and all that light caught in her eyes, her hair.
Most things have faded now. But once I used

to see her gauging me with thoughtful eyes:
with pity true or false, it's all the same.
My soul dry kindling, waiting for her flame,
and could I help it I was set ablaze?

I tell you, she was like a goddess walking,
a pulsing sun to keep a man from cold,
radiant, gold, that spirit danced abroad;

when she spoke, I divined the angels talking.
You say she's just a woman growing old?
Her bow's gone slack, her arrow's in my side.

148: Not Tiber, Tesin, Po, nor Arno, Rhône

Not Tiber, Tesin, Po, nor Arno, Rhône,
Tigris, Euphrates, Nile, Erme, Indus, Seine,
Alphaeus, Elbe; not breaking sea, nor Rhine,
Ebro, Loire, Garonne, Don, Danube—none

can quench me! What's more, no pine,
spruce, ivy, juniper can shelter
me from sun! And yet there is one river
who shares my grief; one sapling bears my pain.[2]

They succor me through every heavy blow
of Love, who still compels me to bear arms
as I go reeling headlong far abroad.

[2] **one sapling . . . my pain:** The stream that consoles Petrarch as none of the great storied rivers of the world can is the Sorgue, which flows through the town of Vaucluse in southern France, near Avignon, where Petrarch often made his home. The sapling is almost certainly a real laurel tree he planted, for he loved gardening and landscape design. But the laurel tree also puns on the name of Laura, who sustains him even as his love for her wounds him. The tree also symbolizes Petrarch's growing body of poems, for in European tradition the laurel is the tree sacred to poets. Its leaves are like pages, and a laurel wreath is the prize for the poet who has written well.

Grow green, dear laurel, by this riverflow;
let me who planted you inscribe true poems
here where sweet water ripples in your shade.

164: All silent now lie earth and wind and sky

All silent now lie earth and wind and sky,
And sleep enfolds all animals and birds.
Night turns the wheel of stars. No wave disturbs
The wide unrippled sameness of the sea.

But I, I wake and brood, rage, weep, my eyes
always behold my love, my foe, my pain.
I *am* a war! Here wrath and sorrow reign,
Yet solely in her image I find peace.

It was her healing hand gave me my wound,
And where the pure and living spring wells forth
I drink at once sweet water, bitter gall;

Storm-driven and extreme, remote from land,
A thousand times I suffer birth and death,
Swept far from any salvage of my soul.

292: Those eyes I raved about in ardent rhyme

Those eyes I raved about in ardent rhyme,
the arms, the hands, the feet, the loving face
that split my soul in two, and made me pass
my life apart from all the common throng,

the tumbled mane of uncut gold that shone,
that angel smile whose flash made me surmise
the very earth had turned to Paradise,
have come to dust: no life, no sense. Undone.

And I live on, in sorrow and self-scorn
here where the light I steered by gleams no more
for my dismasted ship, wracked by the storm.

Let there be no more love songs! The dear spring
of my accustomed art has been drained dry,
my lyre itself dissolved in so much weeping.

310: West Wind comes leading into warmth and light

West Wind comes leading into warmth and light
his whole sweet family of flowers and grass,
and Sparrow's chirp, and Nightingale's *alas*,
and Springtime born again in red and white.

The meadows smile, the sky burns blue above,
and Jove beams with delight upon his daughter.
Love animates the air, the earth, the water;
all creatures yield their beings up to Love!

All that returns for me are weary sighs
drawn from the most profound depths of my heart
by her who kept its keys to Paradise;

so birdsong, and the softly blooming leas,
and lovely women, generous and wise,
seem only deserts, forests, savage beasts.

333: Go forth, my elegies, to that hard stone

Go forth, my elegies, to that hard stone
beneath whose weight my dearest treasure lies.
Call her, and she may answer from the skies,
but here lies only rotting flesh and bone.

Tell her how I grow weary of my life,
of navigating through this dark expanse;
only these scattered pages save my sense,
these stepping-stones to lead me out of grief.

I'll go on telling how she lived and died,
and how she's living now, beyond all death,
so that the world may better learn her grace

and love her. Let her linger by my side
at my death, which grows nearer as I breathe,
to beckon me toward her transcendent peace.

European Love Lyrics

As in the Aztec, Chinese, Japanese, Ottoman, and Mughal cultures—which placed a high value on learning, rhetoric, and writing among the courtly elite—the court circles of Europe considered the writing of poetry to be a manifestation of noble character and good breeding, and it was an art to be carefully cultivated. According to Castiglione in *The Courtier*, ladies and gentlemen at court were supposed to be able to compose poetry for both the enjoyment and the favor it might bring them. The earliest model of the Renaissance courtly poet was Francesco Petrarch (1304–1374), whose celebrated sonnets to Laura invested the European lyric with a personal intensity and depth of feeling rarely achieved even by his Italian predecessor Dante or by the **TROUBADOURS** in France. Petrarch's crafted poems reflect both the balance and harmony and the unresolved tension between physical desire and ideal, **PLATONIC LOVE** that would later be associated with the resurgence of classical values in the **HUMANIST** tradition. Widely translated and imitated in all the vernacular languages of Europe, Petrarch's work had such an extensive and profound influence that later writers of lyrics found it difficult to avoid being seen as mere imitators. And there were plenty of imitators; in France and Italy alone upward of three hundred thousand sonnets following Petrarch were composed in the sixteenth century. Soon the term *Petrarchism* entered the vocabulary to denote the stock metaphors and turns of phrase that lesser poets borrowed shamelessly from Petrarch's *Canzoniere*.

p. 171

Of the forms perfected by Petrarch, perhaps the **SONNET** is the most popular and well known. The **PETRARCHAN SONNET** is a

Niccolo dell'Abate, ***Eros and Psyche***, 1560

The poetry of love gained particular fluency in the sixteenth and seventeenth centuries. Using the Petrarchan sonnet as a starting point, European poets took it in innovative directions, producing a memorable body of romantic poetry. (Niccolo dell'Abate Founders Society Purchase, Robert H. Tannahill Foundation Fund. Photograph © 1978 The Detroit Institute of Arts)

fourteen-line poem divided into an OCTAVE of eight lines and a SESTET of six lines. The two-part structure of the Petrarchan form allows for a double perspective on a subject, or for an extended development of two different aspects of a theme. As in some of the sonnets in this section, the octave is often broken into two quatrains (stanzas of four lines), and the sestet into two TERCETS (stanzas of three lines), which allows the poet greater flexibility. In the English, or Shakespearean, sonnet, the fourteen lines break out into four parts: three quatrains, followed by a couplet (a two-line unit). This form of the sonnet allows the poet to develop three different perspectives on a theme, followed by a statement or question that either affirms or challenges what has come before. While the rhyme scheme of a sonnet may vary, it tends to be fairly formal, with the Petrarchan sonnet rhyming *abbaabba, cdecde* (or *cdcdcd*) and the Shakespearean sonnet rhyming *abab cdcd efef gg.* Sir Thomas Wyatt's sonnets were rhymed *abba abba cdcd ee,* indicating that the form is more flexible than it may first appear.

In addition to fixed formal structures, Petrarchan poetry introduced certain conventional motifs, or thematic elements, into European love lyrics, although some of these had appeared in courtly love lyrics of the Middle Ages. In order to emphasize certain paradoxes—the presence of love but absence of the lover, the bittersweet quality of longing which suggests presence but springs from absence—Petrarch often uses OXYMORONS (combinations of seemingly contradictory words). Moreover, in what is known as the PETRARCHAN CONCEIT—a metaphor, sometimes an extended metaphor of surprising value—the poet would spend considerable time describing the imagined thoughts of his or her lover, usually conceived as thoughts of rejection or cold indifference. Indeed, a convention of Petrarchan love lyrics is to describe a situation in which the beloved has no feelings whatsoever for the enthusiastic lover, whom she or he may or may not even know.

Another feature of some of the love lyrics inherited from the courtly love tradition of the Middle Ages was the BLAZON, a catalog of similes or metaphors comparing the fair parts of the lover's body to images drawn from nature, the biblical Song of Songs, or earlier love poems. Truly innovative poets eventually grew weary of the clichéd tropes derived from Petrarch's once-vital innovations, and William Shakespeare challenged the tradition most obviously in his

To a degree not generally recognized, women shared in the great literary flowering of the two successive ages that we know as the Renaissance and Baroque. The field in which they contributed the most distinguished work was lyric poetry, and that fact in itself may explain to some extent the failure of even the greatest of these women—Louise Labé, Gaspara Stampa, and Sor Juana Inés de la Cruz—to achieve a broadly international reputation.

– FRANK J. WARNKE, critic, 1987

The sonnet represents the single most important Italian contribution to the development of the European lyric, and the overwhelming majority of the poems in [Petrarch's] *Canzoniere* are in this form.

– Steven Minta, critic, 1980

Sonnet 130, which begins by categorically stating "My mistress' eyes are nothing like the sun."

Of course, some of Petrarch's followers produced mechanical efforts filled with literal borrowings, whereas others managed brilliant organic efforts, imitating not so much the Italian master's poems as the spirit behind them. Such imitations are filled with the personality of the poet, his or her feelings and sensibility, and thereby achieve greatness in their own right. Among the poets who achieve this status in the Renaissance lyric are Garcilaso de la Vega (c. 1501–1536), from Spain; Pierre de Ronsard (1524–1585), Maurice Scève (c. 1501–1564), and Louise Labé (c. 1524–1566), from France; Gaspara Stampa (c. 1523–1554), from Italy; and Sir Thomas Wyatt (1503–1542), from England. Each of these poets takes up the theme of balance between physical desire and spiritual longing, sensual and Platonic love. As in Arabic love poetry, the beloved is often a composite figure, symbolizing a beautiful, usually elusive woman or man, as well as an equally or even more elusive spiritual destiny.

In the fifteenth and sixteenth centuries, the Renaissance love lyric evolved both stylistically and thematically. Beyond the sonnet, many European poets adopted and adapted TERZA RIMA, OTTOVA RIMA (three- and eight-line rhyming forms, respectively), and other forms originating in Italy. They also explored the pastoral, mythological, and erotic themes that were becoming increasingly well known as the result of humanist scholarship, translation, and dissemination of books and manuscripts.

Peter Paul Rubens, *The Garden of Love*, 1633
Love was a preoccupation not only among the poets of the Early Modern Period but also of painters. (The Art Archive / Museo del Prado Madrid / Dagli Orti (A))

BAROQUE AND METAPHYSICAL POETRY

Like Renaissance art and architecture, the poetry of the late sixteenth and seventeenth centuries departed from that of the earlier Renaissance and became designated as **Baroque**. The Baroque poem employs extravagance of theme, language, and form; mingles appearance and reality; and often addresses controversies, especially in religion and science. At its far limit lies personal subjectivity, the idea that the feelings, logical inventions, and poetic inspiration of the artist are the best sources of knowledge. Like their Renaissance antecedents, Baroque poems can take either a secular or religious turn—or sometimes both, as in the work of the English poet John Donne (1572–1631). In place of melodious continuities and harmonies, the late-sixteenth-century lyric is characterized by often wrenching or tortuous lines of logic, flashes of wit, and even bits of satire. Besides Donne, the poets whose work, or at least some of it, may be considered Baroque include Lope de Vega (1562–1635), from Spain, and Sor Juana Inés de la Cruz (1651–1695), from New Spain.

The Petrarchan lover, as Shakespeare well knew, frequently found a beautiful and *cruel* mistress.

– Cleanth Brooks, literary critic, 1951

The extravagance of Baroque poetry lies partly in the use of striking metaphor and partly in its attention to extreme states of mind and feeling arising from such matters as physical love, mystical communion, and death. Sometimes these states are joined together, as in John Donne's image of rape as a metaphor of the religious vision in his sonnet "Batter my heart, three person'd God." This forcing of language, called a *conceit,* was generally praised at the time, though it was later often held as excessive by writers more oriented to the Latin classical tradition. **Metaphysical poetry**, one strain of Baroque, is characterized by dramatic images of logical and emotional incongruity that arise from the poet's wit. Here the stress is on the inventiveness of the artist. The Metaphysical poets used the language of the new sciences and of colonialism; religious poems may juxtapose sacred and profane images. These intellectual poems are often either arguments for the beloved's favor or evocations of mystical communion with God. John Donne was a master of the conceit in both his religious and his secular poetry, and like Shakespeare he invented puns and unexpected images to enrich his poems.

Although the main current in poetry of the late sixteenth and seventeenth centuries was Baroque, many poems did in fact preserve the classical balance and formal symmetries associated with the earlier Renaissance and with Petrarch. The poems of Shakespeare, for example, do not fall precisely within either category, Renaissance or Baroque. Similarly, in "A Letter to Her Husband, Absent Upon Public Employment," the English-born American poet Anne Bradstreet (1612–1672) manages both a certain formality and a sense of familiarity that makes her one of the first recognizably American poets. Other poems slightly at variance from the Baroque tradition include satires against the traditional mores of society. Andrew Marvell (1621–1678) wrote "To His Coy Mistress" in a satirical vein. Overall, the greatest examples of the European Renaissance lyric present a range of moods, styles, and themes; almost all of them, however, are characterized by an intensity of feeling and an individual, personal expression that captures the humanist spirit of the age.

■ CONNECTIONS

***In the Tradition: Indian Devotional Poetry,* p. 929.** The Renaissance and Baroque love lyrics often conflate spiritual and physical love, the longing for spiritual ecstasy with that for sexual consummation. Similarly, many of the devotional poems of India's bhakti movement blur the boundaries between physical and spiritual desire. In the European tradition, both Christian and Platonic ideas of love contributed to this fusion, whereas in India, of course, it was the tradition of Hindu religion and Sufi mysticism. How do these two traditions combine sensuality with spirituality? What common motifs, conceits, or metaphors do they use to create such synthesis?

***In the World: Courtly Love Lyrics,* Book 2.** Renaissance and Baroque love lyrics draw on, even as they transform, many of the motifs, themes, stylistic devices, and conventions—such as the blazon—from earlier courtly love traditions. Comparing the poems in these two sections, explain what is new in the lyric poetry of the fifteenth and sixteenth centuries. What social conditions do these changes in the poetry reflect?

Sappho, poems, Book 1. Gaspara Stampa was called "the Italian Sappho" in her own time, and that epithet might well have applied equally to Louise Labé, and, for certain poems, to Sor Juana Inés de la Cruz. Sappho, of course, was a lyric poet who was celebrated in her own time as the poet of love and desire. What qualities does Sappho's poetry—or what elements of her life, what we know of it—share with that of the three women represented in this section? You might contrast their work with that of Catullus, whose poetry is also included in Book 1, to consider how the poetry of love is gendered in both the ancient world and the Renaissance.

■ FURTHER RESEARCH

Criticism and History

Krailsheimer, A. J., ed. *The Continental Renaissance.* 1971.

Minta, Stephen. *Petrarch and Petrarchism: The English and French Traditions.* 1980.

Collections of European Poetry

Barnstone, Aliki, and Willis Barnstone, eds. *A Book of Women Poets from Antiquity to Now.* 1992.

Gardner, Helen. *The Metaphysical Poets.* 1966.
Priest, Howard Martin. *Renaissance and Baroque Lyrics.* 1962.
Segel, Harold B. *The Baroque Poem.* 1974.
Warnke, Frank J., ed. *European Metaphysical Poetry.* 1961.
———. *Three Women Poets: Louise Labé, Gaspara Stampa, and Sor Juana Inés de la Cruz.* 1987.
Wilson, Katharina M. *Women Writers of the Renaissance and Reformation.* 1987.

Garcilaso de la Vega
c. 1501–1536

Italian forms of lyric poetry entered Spain through the work of Juan Boscán (c. 1490–1542) and his younger friend Garcilaso de la Vega, who was the better poet and the founder of the Renaissance lyric tradition in Spain. Garcilaso was born in 1501 in Toledo into a noble family. His father was a diplomat and courtier to King Ferdinand and Queen Isabella, and just before he turned eighteen Garcilaso entered into the service of Charles V, to whom he was a bodyguard. A distinguished soldier, Garcilaso took part in many of Charles V's campaigns in Germany and Italy, and he participated in the battle against the Ottoman Turks at Vienna in 1529. Serving as a soldier, agent, and diplomat all his life, he was killed in battle in 1536. After Vega's death, Boscán took charge of his friend's poems, and he was working on an edition of them when he himself died in 1542.

In 1543, a joint edition of the two friends' poetry appeared, leading to a new sensibility in Spanish lyric poetry. As in the case of San Juan de la Cruz, the overall number of Garcilaso's poems is small—thirty-eight sonnets, three eclogues, two elegies, a verse epistle, and five songs. Nonetheless, his adaptation of Italian verse forms and metrical arrangements created a sensation, and his works were emulated by later Spanish poets. In 1574, his poetry was published in a volume of its own and went through several editions during the sixteenth century. The two sonnets, or *sonetos,* included here give an example of the range of Garcilaso's feelings. "While There Is Still the Color of a Rose" invokes the motif of *carpe diem*—seize the day—that came down from the Latin elegy. The poem praises the lover's beauty as it cautions that those beauties will fall victim to the ravages of time. "Your Face Is Written in My Soul" expresses the lover's total absorption in the beloved, describing an intensity of devotion that anticipates the Baroque expressions of the next century.

While There Is Still the Color of a Rose

Translated from the Spanish by Edwin Morgan

While there is still the color of a rose
And of a lily in your countenance,
And you with such an ardent candid glance
Can fire the heart, and check the flames it shows;

And while that golden hair of yours that flows
Into a knot can leap into a dance
As the wind blows with livelier dalliance
Upon the fairest proud white neck it knows:

Gather together from your happy spring
Fruits that are sweet, before time ravages
With angry snow the beauty of your head.

The rose will wither as the cold wind rages,
And age come gently to change everything,
Lest our desire should change old age instead.

Your Face Is Written in My Soul

Translated from the Spanish by Edwin Morgan

Your face is written in my soul, and when
I want to write about you, you alone
Become the writer, I but read the line;
I watch you where you still watch me, within.

This state I am and always will be in.
For though my soul imprints a half-design
Of what I see in you, the good unknown
Is taken on a trusting regimen.

What was I born for if not to adore you?
My ills have shaped you to the bent they give.
I love you by a daily act of soul.

All that I have I must confess I owe you.
For you I came to life, for you I live,
For you I'd die, and do die, after all.

Sir Thomas Wyatt
1503–1542

One of the leading English Renaissance poets, Sir Thomas Wyatt the Elder, was born at Allington Castle in Kent, and eventually studied at St. John's College at Cambridge. After graduation he served as a diplomat in the court of Henry VIII of England, where he cultivated the life of a model Renaissance courtier and gentleman. In addition to composing his own poetry, he translated and imitated the great Italian poets, especially Petrarch, and he was the first to introduce the sonnet form into English verse. His reworking of Petrarch's Song 157, "Whoso List to Hunt," equals or excels the original. Wyatt refashions some elements of Petrarch's poem to conform to the rather dangerous life of the English court. In this version, the "hind," or deer, most likely refers to Anne Boleyn, a young lady of the court under the watchful eye of Henry VIII and therefore off-limits to any lowly courtiers ("*Noli me tangere,* for Caesar's I am"). Another Wyatt poem, "They Flee from Me," is an English dance-song that shows at its best the author's somewhat cynical attitude combined with his graceful method of composition.

Whoso List to Hunt[1]

Whoso list° to hunt, I know where is an hind, — wishes
But as for me, alas, I may no more;
The vain travail hath wearied me so sore,
I am of them that furthest come behind.
Yet may I by no means my wearied mind
Draw from the deer, but as she fleeth afore
Fainting I follow; I leave off therefore,
Since in a net I seek to hold the wind.
Who list her hunt, I put him out of doubt,
As well as I, may spend his time in vain.
And graven with diamonds in letters plain,
There is written her fair neck round about,
"*Noli me tangere,*[2] for Caesar's I am,
And wild for to hold, though I seem tame."

[1] **"Whoso List to Hunt"**: Adapted from Petrarch, Rime 90.

[2] **"*Noli me tangere,* . . . tame"**: "Touch me not." Caesar's hinds were said to be fitted with collars so inscribed, to keep them safe from poachers. Wyatt is thought to be referring to the young Anne Boleyn, whom Henry VIII had marked for his future bride.

They Flee from Me

They flee from me, that sometime did me seek,
With naked foot stalking in my chamber.
I have seen them, gentle, tame, and meek,
That now are wild, and do not remember
That sometime they put themselves in danger
To take bread at my hand; and now they range,
Busily seeking with a continual change.

Thanked be Fortune it hath been otherwise,
Twenty times better; but once in special,
In thin array, after a pleasant guise,
When her loose gown from her shoulders did fall,
And she caught me in her arms long and small,° slender
And therewith all sweetly did me kiss
And softly said, "Dear heart, how like you this?"

It was no dream, I lay broad waking.
But all is turned, through my gentleness,
Into a strange fashion of forsaking;
And I have leave to go, of her goodness,
And she also to use newfangleness.° fickleness, infidelity
But since that I so kindely am served,
I fain would know what she hath deserved.

MAURICE SCÈVE
c. 1510–1564

Maurice Scève was part of a poetic circle based in Lyons, France, that sought to infuse French poetry with a new, personal spirit. A follower of Petrarch, he adopted the French form called the *dizain*—a ten-line, ten-syllable poem with an intricate rhyme scheme. His major work, a sequence of 450 dizains titled *Delie,* was probably inspired by his infatuation with a real-life disciple, Pernette du Guillet. The compression of thought and syntax in Scève's poetry looks forward to the metaphysical English poetry of John Donne. The poem "The Day We Passed Together for a While" is characteristic of the *Delie* sequence in expressing the unrequited longing of the poet for his departed lover.

The Day We Passed Together for a While

Translated from the French by Patricia Clark Smith

The day we passed together for a while
Seemed a bright fire on a winter's night,
And showed me how your absence is the dark,
A shadow more oppressive to my soul
Than life is to my frame, that weary weight
Of life, which even now seeks to depart.
For ever since that time you went away
I've been a rabbit burrowed in the wood;
I cock my ear, strain at each distant cry,
All lost within some deep Egyptian shade.

Gaspara Stampa
c. 1523–1554

Among the hundreds of women poets writing in the wake of Petrarch, the Italian Gaspara Stampa—once called "the Italian Sappho"—is among the most important. Born in Padua in about 1523, she was raised in Venice by her father, a jeweler, who moved to Venice after the death of her mother. A talented musician and songwriter, she would entertain guests at her father's house, which became a kind of gathering place for poets after her brother Baldassare, himself a poet, entered the university at Venice. Though critics dispute the question, Stampa appears to have become a *cortigiana onestia,* a courtesan of the highest rank, something like a geisha in Japan. At some point around the late 1540s, Stampa met and fell in love with Count Collaltino di Collalto, to whom she dedicates many of her most important love lyrics.

Following in the tradition of Petrarch, Stampa primarily wrote sonnets, often closely modeled on Petrarch's own, and *canzonieri,* or songs, which some critics believe represent her finest work. Writing on the pleasures and joys, torment and folly of love, Stampa often alludes to classical mythology and modifies the Petrarchan conceit to establish a strong sense of her own identity and power.

Only three of her poems were published during her lifetime, but shortly after Stampa died her sister Cassandra arranged to have a volume of her works published. As with many women writers of the Renaissance, her work fell into neglect until it was rediscovered in the late eighteenth century, when Antonio Rambaldo wrote a laudatory and largely fictional biography that turned Gaspara Stampa into a legend. Other important women writers of the Italian lyric tradition include Vittoria Colonna (1490–1547), Tullia D'Aragona (1510–1556), and Isabella di Morra (1520–1546).

Both sonnets we include here demonstrate the passion Gaspara Stampa brings to the love lyric. In "Love, Having Elevated Her to Him, Inspires Her Verses," Stampa proclaims that it is the intensity of her love, not the attributes of the beloved, that brings her to song. As translator and commentator Frank J. Warnke points out, in centering the source of her inspiration in herself rather than in the lover, she overturns the conventions derived from Petrarch by creating a motif whereby "the love . . . elevates the lover above the beloved." This motif appears again in "She Does Not Fear Amorous Pain, but Rather Its End," which begins with an apostrophe, or address, to Love, which brings her a special power that she hopes is not merely an illusion.

Love, Having Elevated Her to Him, Inspires Her Verses

Translated from the Italian by Frank J. Warnke

If, being a woman so abject and vile,
I nonetheless can bear so high a flame,
Why should I not give to the world the same,
At least in part, in proper wealth and style?

If Love, with a new, unprecedented spark,
Could raise me to a place I could not reach,
Why cannot pain and pen combine to teach
Such arts as, never known, shall find their mark?

And if this does not lie in Nature's art,
Then let it be by miracle, whose power
Can conquer, transcend, and every limit break.
How this may be I cannot say for sure,
But well I know the fortune I partake,
And through it a new style engraves my heart.

She Does Not Fear Amorous Pain, but Rather Its End

Translated from the Italian by Frank J. Warnke

Love, by your mighty arrows thus I swear,
And by the sacred, potent torch you carry:
Though the latter burn me, make my heart its quarry,
And the former wound me, still I do not care;

Delve in the past or in the future gaze,
You'll never find a woman who love's anguish
Could feel as I have, or like me could languish
In the arrows' sharpness, the torch's furious blaze;

For of these pains a special virtue is born,
Which dulls and conquers every sense of sorrow,
So that it doesn't hurt, does scarcely gnaw.
And that, which does both soul and body harrow,
Is the fear that leads me to my death forlorn:
That my fire may prove to be a fire of straw.

Pierre de Ronsard

1524–1585

By many accounts, the greatest poet of the French Renaissance was Pierre de Ronsard, the founder of the *Pléiade* school, a group of French humanist poets who were determined to produce a truly original French literature that would compete against other literatures. Ronsard was born into a noble family residing at the Château de la Poissonniere near Couture, a village in the province of Vendôme. His father, Loys de Ronsard, was in the service of King Francis I and was himself a man of letters. Sent to school in Paris, Ronsard became a page to the king's eldest son, and later to the duke of Orleans. From 1537 to 1539 he was in Scotland, after the marriage of James V to Madeleine of France, during which time he traveled to England. He advanced in his courtly appointments, traveling more, until in 1541 deafness caused him to give up his courtly ambitions and turn to study and poetry. Enrolling at the College Coqueret in Paris,

Toussaint Dubreuil, ***Hyante and Climène at Their Toilette,*** **Sixteenth Century**
This painting shows a scene from Ronsard's Franciade, *conceived as a national epic modeled on Virgil's* Aeneid. *(The Art Archive / Musée du Louvre Paris / Dagli Orti)*

he met Jean Dorat, a humanist, whose influence inspired the *Pléiade* to revolutionize French poetry through a close study of Greek and Roman models, as well as Petrarch's work. Ronsard soon made it his life's project to become a master of all the classical genres of poetry, from the epic to the epigram. In 1550, Ronsard published a collection of odes, followed two years later by *The Loves,* a collection of sonnets. These and other publications brought him instant fame (as well as bitter criticism from rivals), and he eventually became the court poet for Charles IX. He also published panegyric and heroic poems celebrating France and the French monarchs, and began work on an epic called the *Franciade.* One of his last collections to be published before his death, *Sonnets for Helen,* contains many of his greatest love lyrics. Poor health in his later years led finally to his death in 1585. As indicated here in "To Cassandre" and "To Hélène," Ronsard invokes the motif of ***carpe diem*** in poems that otherwise are marked by a sense of delicacy and beauty. "To Hélène" wittily projects an image of the beloved as an old woman reflecting, regretfully, on the lost opportunity to consummate her love for the poet.

To Cassandre

Translated from the French by David Sanders

I'm sending you this fresh bouquet of flowers
Which, if my fingers hadn't picked them tonight,
Would all be withered up and shriveled tight,
And have dropped their petals in a few short hours.

There is in this a lesson meant for you:
The delicate flower your beauty has become
Will also wither up and drop in time
And someday, like these flowers, perish too.

Time goes on, my dearest, time goes on.
Alas! not time, it's we who have to go,
And we who'll lie beneath the family stone.

And the love of which we've both been talking so
Will mean just nothing when our lives are through;
So love me, while your beauty is still new.

To Hélène

Translated from the French by David Sanders

When you are old and sitting by the fire,
Spinning your threads of yarn by candlelight,
Singing my songs, you'll say to yourself one night,
"Ronsard praised me when I was his desire."

You'll have no maid who hears you tell this story
Though already half-asleep from working hard,
Who won't wake up at the sound of the name Ronsard,
Blessing your name with songs of lasting glory.

By then I'll be a ghost, long since dead,
Buried in the shade of the myrtle overhead,
And you'll be an old crone crouching at the fire

Regretting my lost love and your cold scorning.
Live now, if you believe me, don't wait till morning;
Come out and cut the roses from your brier.

Louise Labé
c. 1524–1566

Louise Labé was the daughter of a wealthy rope-maker from Lyons. After her mother died, her father saw to it that she received a liberal education. Eventually she became a celebrated intellectual, a prodigious beauty, an extraordinary horsewoman and archer, and a champion of free love. She is said to have dressed as a man in order to fight in military campaigns against Spain. Eventually she married a wealthy man in her father's profession, earning herself the nickname *la belle cordiere*—the beautiful rope-maker. By and large her poems, published in 1555 but written somewhat earlier, celebrate all aspects of love and desire. After the publication of her work—consisting of just a dedicatory epistle, twenty-three sonnets, a prose "Debate Between Folly and Love," and three elegies—she moved away from Lyons. She died, possibly of the plague, in 1566. Though her ouevre is small, the passion of her work and the unique perspective she brings to otherwise traditional themes drew attention in her own time and in ours. Though she writes in the form of the Petrarchan sonnet, she presents emotion directly and with very little artifice, as in "Oh, That I Could Be Crushed to That Dear Breast," which unabashedly celebrates the immediacy and ecstasy of sensual love. "Kiss Me Again, Again, Kiss Me Again!" similarly presents an unblinking celebration of love, even as the poem acknowledges that passion, after it subsides, may bring certain suffering.

Detail from *Woman between the Two Ages of Man*, Sixteenth Century
This painting by an unknown French artist shows a woman accepting the amorous advances of a man. (The Art Archive / Musée Granet Aix-en-Provence / Dagli Orti)

Kiss Me Again, Again, Kiss Me Again!

Translated from the French by Frank J. Warnke

Kiss me again, again, kiss me again!
Give me one of the luscious ones you have,
Give me one of the loving ones I crave:
Four hotter than burning coals I shall return.

What, are you moaning? Let me soothe the pain,
Giving you now ten kisses more, but sweetly;
Thus, our happy kisses joining meetly,
Let us enjoy each other to our gain.

A double life for each of us ensues.
Each in the self and in the lover lives.
Allow me, Love, to feign a pleasing folly:
Living as one, I'm always ill at ease,
And sweet content within me never thrives
Unless outside myself I sometimes sally.

Oh, That I Could Be Crushed to That Dear Breast

Translated from the French by Frank J. Warnke

Oh, that I could be crushed to that dear breast
Of him for whom in every way I die!
If only I could spend with him the rest
Of my short days, but spiteful tongues deny!

If, holding me, he were to say, "Dear Love,
Let's make each other happy," telling me
That the storms that dread Euripus'[1] current move
Could not disjoin us, long as life might be;

If, holding him encircled by my arms
As the tree is by the ivy all embraced,
I were caught up, by envious Death prevented,
I should, while soft I felt his kisses' charms,
And while upon his lips my spirit raced,
Die willingly, more than alive, contented.

---

[1] **Euripus:** A strait dividing the island Euboea from Greece.

Lope de Vega

1562–1635

Lope Félix de Vega Carpio is best known, along with Pedro Calderón de la Barca (1600–1681), as one of the greatest playwrights of Spain's golden age; it was his drama that inaugurated the great age of theater in Spain, drawing packed audiences to the newly built playhouses in the sixteenth century. One of the most prolific of all Spanish writers, Lope wrote more than fifteen hundred plays, many narrative poems, pastoral romances, and short religious plays known as *autos,* as well as hundreds of shorter poems in the form of ballads, sonnets, odes, and elegies. Born in Madrid in 1562, Lope went on to study at the University of Alcalá, after which he served in the Spanish army, participating in the ill-fated battle of 1588 in which England defeated the Spanish Armada.

Lope became legendary in his time for his numerous and passionate love affairs, yet he was also ardently involved in the Catholic Church. At the age of fifty-two, his reputation somewhat tarnished by scandalous affairs, he entered a religious order and became a judge of the Inquisition. He continued to write *comedias* after taking orders, and though the Church officially frowned on his plays, Pope Urban III honored him by appointing him to the Order of St. John of Jerusalem and awarding him an honorary degree in theology. Something of an authority on love (he was twice married, had countless affairs, and had sixteen children, of which only six were legitimate), Lope expressed his feelings toward his lovers in his lyrics. Known for their variety and intensity of emotion, as well as their hybrid constructions from classical and popular traditions, Lope's love lyrics represent the fluctuations of mood and feeling and the dramatic dynamism of the Baroque.

The three poems of different genres presented here characterize Lope de Vega's range of style and feeling, as well as his blending of spiritual and sensual love. The sonnet "Woman Is of Man the Best" sees its subject through the eyes of a man whose view vacillates between the idealized notions of woman as preserver and destroyer, mother and lover. Invoking the imagery of the Song of Songs, "Stranger to Love, Whoever Loves Not Thee," another sonnet in the Petrarchan form, contrasts, even as it confuses, worldly and spiritual love. Finally, "A Sonnet All of a Sudden" mixes love with a self-conscious play on the act of writing, showing the poet steering between his feelings and the formal requirements of the sonnet form.

Woman Is of Man the Best

Translated from the Spanish by Perry Higman

Woman is of man the best,
and insane it is to say the worst;
his life she is and his great gift,
his poison is she and his death.

Heaven to the eyes chaste and serene,
Which often to hell I compare,
for her courage, I tell the world she is rare,
for false to man her rigor I condemn.

She gives us her blood, she rears us all:
Heaven has not made a more ungrateful thing;
she is an angel, and sometimes she's the devil.

She loves, abhors, treats well, treats ill,
and it's woman, after all, like a bleeding,
that sometimes cures, and sometimes kills.

Stranger to Love, Whoever Loves Not Thee

Translated from the Spanish by Iain Fletcher

Stranger to love, whoever loves not Thee,
Thou Holy Beauty, Friend and my fair Spouse,
Whose head drops gold, whose radiant hair shades me
As the young leaves, down of the palm's boughs.

Like lily-flowering fountains, thy lips distil
Rich torrents to the dawn; thy neck, a white-sided plinth,
Thy hand the lathe, and in its palm that seal
My soul dissembling sensed as hyacinth.

Ah, God, how much deluded I, in leaving
So just a Beauty, and mortal loves befriending,
Losing that Beauty ever wide in flower:

But if for time lost I linger grieving,
I'll make such haste that by one loving hour
I will root out the years I lived pretending.

A Sonnet All of a Sudden

Translated by Doreen Bell

Violante has commanded me to write
A sonnet. Oh! what trouble I am in!
Though here go three lines, eager to begin,
A sonnet's lines must number fourteen, quite!

I never thought that I should find a rhyme,
And look! the second quatrain is begun:
But nothing in the quatrains would I shun
If I reach the first tercet in good time.

I enter the first tercet in effect,
And I came in on the right foot, it seems,
Because the end of this verse is in sight.

Already in the second, I suspect
That I am finishing just thirteen lines:
Count them! If there are fourteen, it is right.

William Shakespeare
1564–1616

England's greatest playwright, William Shakespeare was born in Stratford-on-Avon, where he received a decent grammar-school education. When he was eighteen years old, he married Anne Hathaway and soon thereafter moved to London. By 1592 he was already regarded with jealousy by his fellow playwrights; one of his rival critics, Robert Greene, referred to Shakespeare as "an upstart crow, beautified with our feathers." By 1598, he had written a dozen plays, mostly histories and comedies, with his great tragedies to come in the next decade. Although, like Lope de Vega, Shakespeare is best known for his plays, he was also a master of the longer narrative poem and the lyric, and he was celebrated in his own time as a great poet. Shakespeare privately circulated a collection of his sonnets for many years, finally publishing them in 1609. Some of the poems are highly mysterious in their references, and they have given rise to much speculation about the person or persons to whom they are addressed and about Shakespeare's sexuality. Although one might read them as philosophical poems, many of the sonnets are simply personal poetry written to note particular occasions.

Sonnet 18, "Shall I compare thee to a summer's day," is one of the great love poems of the English Renaissance. The first line of the poem invokes the convention of the blazon only to disappoint the reader's expectations—the following lines abandon the anticipated cataloging of the lover's body for an elaboration on the theme of love's transcendence, enabled by the verse itself. Sonnet 116, which also praises the power of love to confer a kind of permanence, points forward to the logical complexities of a poet like John Donne. Another poem with a kind of tortuous logic, Sonnet 129, "Th' expense of spirit in a waste of shame," focuses on the torments of passion, with fierce expectation beforehand and bitter woe afterward. The word *expense* suggests multiple meanings, including sexual expenditure but also revenge or physical violence. Sonnet 130, "My mistress' eyes are nothing like the sun," is a spoof of the Petrarchan sonnet, with its habit of praising the parts of a lady in a poetic catalog; Shakespeare calls for more honest expression.

Sonnet 18

Shall I compare thee to a summer's day?
Thou art more lovely and more temperate:
Rough winds do shake the darling buds of May,
And summer's lease hath all too short a date:
Sometime too hot the eye of heaven shines,
And often is his gold complexion dimm'd;
And every fair from fair° sometime declines, beauty
By chance or nature's changing course untrimm'd;° unadorned
But thy eternal summer shall not fade,
Nor lose possession of that fair thou owest;° own, have
Nor shall Death brag thou wander'st in his shade,
When in eternal lines to time thou grow'st:
　　So long as men can breathe, or eyes can see,
　　So long lives this, and this gives life to thee.

Sonnet 116

Let me not to the marriage of true minds
Admit impediments. Love is not love
Which alters when it alteration finds,
Or bends with the remover to remove:
O, no! it is an ever-fixed mark,

That looks on tempests and is never shaken;
It is the star to every wandering bark,° ship
Whose worth's unknown, although his height be taken.° measured
Love's not Time's fool, though rosy lips and cheeks
Within his bending sickle's compass come;
Love alters not with his brief hours and weeks,
But bears it out even to the edge of doom.
If this be error and upon me proved,
I never writ, nor no man ever loved.

Sonnet 129

Th' expense of spirit in a waste of shame
Is lust in action;[1] and till action, lust
Is perjured, murderous, bloody, full of blame,
Savage, extreme, rude, cruel, not to trust;
Enjoyed no sooner but despiséd straight:
Past reason hunted; and no sooner had,
Past reason hated, as a swallowed bait,
On purpose laid to make the taker mad:
Mad in pursuit, and in possession so;
Had, having, and in quest to have, extreme;
A bliss in proof,[2] and proved, a very woe;
Before, a joy proposed; behind, a dream.
All this the world well knows; yet none knows well
To shun the heaven that leads men to this hell.

Sonnet 130

My mistress' eyes are nothing like the sun;
Coral is far more red than her lips' red;
If snow be white, why then her breasts are dun;
If hairs be wires, black wires grow on her head.
I have seen roses damasked, red and white,
But no such roses see I in her cheeks;
And in some perfumes is there more delight

[1] **Th' expense . . . action:** The first one and one-half lines might be paraphrased, "Lust, when acted upon, wastes the spirit (life, soul, vital force) in a waste (a desert, as well as a squandering) of shame."

[2] **bliss in proof:** Blissful at the moment it is experienced.

Than in the breath that from my mistress reeks.
I love to hear her speak, yet well I know
That music hath a far more pleasing sound;
I grant I never saw a goddess go;
My mistress, when she walks, treads on the ground.
And yet, by heaven, I think my love as rare
As any she belied with false compare.

John Donne
1572–1631

John Donne acknowledged he had lived two lives: first as Jack Donne, a seducer of women and universal cynic, and then as an Anglican priest, dean of St. Paul's Cathedral in London. Actually, rather like his Spanish contemporary Lope de Vega, Donne embodied a little of both the rogue and the God-haunted man. Born a Catholic during the worst years of anti-Catholic prejudice in England, Donne attended Oxford and Cambridge as well as the law school at Lincoln's Inn, but never finished a degree. During this time he spent his father's small inheritance, traveling abroad when he could. After he won a court appointment in 1598, Donne compromised his chances of success by secretly marrying the niece of his benefactor. Briefly imprisoned as a result, he relied afterward on whatever patronage he could find. Finally, giving in to the combined pleading and threats of King James in 1615, Donne entered the Anglican ministry and became the Dean of St. Paul's in 1621. Obsessed by death, he preached his own funeral sermon in 1631 and posed for his last portrait wrapped in a shroud.

Donne's poetry borrows from the Petrarchan and Shakespearean traditions, but goes further in developing a highly concentrated structure and poetic logic, as well as a sometimes tortuous set of highly wrought and surprisingly unlikely metaphors, known as conceits. The conceits of his early love poems were designed to shock and arouse the reader. Later he employed the same language mix—formal and colloquial, sacred and profane—in his religious poetry. At the same time, Donne compressed English syntax to the breaking point. His love poems, such as "A Valediction Forbidding Mourning," were often argumentative poems, presenting the lover with an impeccable case to comply with the desires of the speaker. "Valediction," in particular, contains one of Donne's most famous conceits, the comparison of the separating lovers to the feet of a draftsman's compass. Though the feet of the compass may be pulled far apart, they are always joined at the head—and this joining represents the spiritual level of love. In the more carnal poem "To His Mistress Going to Bed," Donne describes his lady undressing and presenting herself to him.

Gian Lorenzo Bernini, *The Ecstasy of Saint Theresa*, 1644–51
Baroque and Metaphysical poetry took as its subject a mystical communion with God, an intense religious experience like that expressed in Bernini's classic of Baroque sculpture, the transformation of Saint Theresa. (The Art Archive / Dagli Orti)

He addresses her as "O my America! my new-found-land," suggesting how close fantasies of sexual conquest were to the waking thoughts of the first European explorers of the New World. "Holy Sonnet 14" transforms the most violent of imagery into a profession of devotion.

The Good Morrow

I wonder, by my troth, what thou and I
Did till we loved? were we not weaned till then,
But sucked on country pleasures, childishly?
Or snorted we in the Seven Sleepers' den?[1]
'Twas so; but this, all pleasures fancies be.

---

[1] **the Seven Sleepers' den:** Early Christian folklore tells of seven young Christian men of Ephesus who hid in a cave from the persecutions of the emperor Decius; after a miraculous sleep of 187 years, they awoke to find Europe had become Christianized.

Peter Paul Rubens, *The Rape of Ganymede by Eagle of Zeus,* Late Sixteenth/Early Seventeenth Century
Baroque poets like John Donne and artists such as the Flemish painter Rubens (1577–1640) explored extreme states of mind and sometimes employed violent metaphors to evoke the intensity of mystical feeling. (The Art Archive/Museo del Prado Madrid/The Art Archive)

If ever any beauty I did see
Which I desired, and got, 'twas but a dream of thee.

And now good morrow to our waking souls,
Which watch not one another out of fear;
For love all love of other sights controls,
And makes one little room an everywhere.

Let sea-discoverers to new worlds have gone;
Let maps to other, worlds on worlds have shown;
Let us possess one world; each hath one, and is one.

My face in thine eye, thine in mine appears,
And true, plain hearts do in the faces rest;
Where can we find two better hemispheres
Without sharp north, without declining west?
Whatever dies, was not mixed equally;[2]
If our two loves be one, or thou and I
Love so alike that none do slacken, none can die.

[2] **not mixed equally:** Alchemy taught that matter in which the elements were not perfectly mixed was subject to change, decay, and death.

A Valediction Forbidding Mourning

As virtuous men passe mildly'away,
    And whisper to their soules, to goe,
Whilst some of their sad friends doe say,
    The breath goes now, and some say, no.

So let us melt, and make no noise,
    No teare-floods, nor sigh-tempests move,
T'were prophanation of our joyes
    To tell the layetie our love.

Moving of th'earth brings harmes and feares,
    Men reckon what it did and meant,
But trepidation of the spheares,[1]
    Though greater farre, is innocent.

Dull sublunary[2] lovers love
    (Whose soule[3] is sense) cannot admit

[1] **trepidation of the spheares:** The movement of the spheres; Donne refers to the Ptolemaic structure of the cosmos, which described nine spheres circling the earth, at the center of the universe.

[2] **sublunary:** Literally, "below or beneath the moon"; Donne's poem compares earthly and therefore transient love to spiritual or intellectual love that transcends the temporal and physical limits of the body.

[3] **soule:** Essential element or nature.

Absence, because it doth remove
Those things which elemented it.[4]

But we by'a love, so much refin'd,
That our selves know not what it is,
Inter-assured of the mind,
Care lesse, eyes, lips, and hands to misse.

Our two soules therefore, which are one,
Though I must goe, endure not yet
A breach, but an expansion,
Like gold to ayery thinnesse beate.

If they be two, they are two so
As stiffe twin compasses[5] are two,
Thy soule the fixt foot, makes no show
To move, but doth, if the'other doe.

And though it in the center sit,
Yet when the other far doth rome,
It leanes, and hearkens after it,
And growes erect, as that comes home.

Such wilt thou be to mee, who must
Like th'other foot, obliquely runne.
Thy firmnes makes my circle just,
And makes me end, where I begunne.

[4] **Those things which elemented it:** Those things of which it is composed.

[5] **twin compasses:** An artist's or draftsman's compass.

To His Mistress Going to Bed

Come, Madam, come, all rest my powers defy,
Until I labor, I in labor lie.[1]
The foe oft-times having the foe in sight,
Is tired with standing, though he never fight.

[1] **Until . . . lie:** Until I can get to work at making love, I'm in pain.

Off with that girdle, like heaven's zone[2] glittering,
But a far fairer world encompassing.
Unpin that spangled breastplate which you wear,
That th' eyes of busy fools may be stopped there.
Unlace yourself, for that harmonious chime,
Tells me from you that now it is bed time.
Off with that happy busk,° which I envy, bodice or corset
That still can be, and still can stand so nigh.
Your gown going off, such beauteous state reveals,
As when from flowery meads th'hills shadow steals.
Off with that wiry coronet and show
The hairy diadem which on you doth grow:
Now off with those shoes, and then safely tread
In this love's hallowed temple, this soft bed.
In such white robes, heaven's angels used to be
Received by men; Thou, Angel, bringst with thee
A heaven like Mahomet's Paradise;[3] and though
Ill spirits walk in white, we easily know,
By this these angels from an evil sprite,
Those set our hairs, but these our flesh upright.
　　Licence my roving hands, and let them go,
Before, behind, between, above, below.
O my America! my new-found-land,
My kingdom, safeliest when with one man manned,
My mine of precious stones, my empery,
How blest am I in this discovering thee!
To enter in these bonds, is to be free;
Then where my hand is set, my seal[4] shall be.
　　Full nakedness! All joys are due to thee,
As souls unbodied, bodies unclothed must be,
To taste whole joys. Gems which you women use
Are like Atalanta's balls,[5] cast in men's views,
That when a fool's eye lighteth on a gem,
His earthly soul may covet theirs, not them.
Like pictures, or like books' gay coverings made
For lay-men, are all women thus arrayed;
Themselves are mystic books, which only we
(Whom their imputed grace will dignify)

[2] **heaven's zone:** The zodiac.

[3] **Mahomet's Paradise:** The Islamic paradise contains beautiful female spirits who reward the faithful.

[4] **seal:** The physical impression of him, and the sign of his ownership.

[5] **Atalanta's balls:** The swift-footed Atalanta was reluctant to marry Hippomenes, but she agreed to do so if he could outrun her. Hippomenes scattered golden apples in her path and distracted her from their race.

Must see revealed. Then since that I may know;[6]
As liberally as to a midwife, show
Thyself: cast all, yea, this white linen hence,
There is no penance due to innocence.
To teach thee, I am naked first; why then
What needst thou have more covering than a man?

[6] **know:** *Know* here means both to learn and to know sexually.

Holy Sonnet 14

Batter my heart, three-personed God; for You
As yet but knock, breathe, shine, and seek to mend;
That I may rise, and stand, o'erthrow me, and bend
Your force, to break, blow, burn and make me new.
I, like an usurped town, to another due,
Labor to admit You, but O, to no end,
Reason Your viceroy in me, me should defend,
But is captived and proves weak or untrue,
Yet dearly I love You, and would be loved fain,
But am betrothed unto Your enemy,
Divorce me, untie, or break that knot again,
Take me to You, imprison me, for I,
Except You enthrall me, never shall be free,
Nor ever chaste, except You ravish me.

Anne Bradstreet
1612–1672

Anne Bradstreet was born in England in 1612 and educated by private tutors, using the extensive library of the Earl of Lincoln. She married in 1628 and left England in 1630 with a group of Nonconformist Puritans planning to found the Massachusetts Bay Colony. She recorded her many adventures in America in diaries, letters, and poetry. Moving from Boston to Ipswich and later North Andover, Massachusetts, she raised eight children and wrote poetry. Her first volume was published in London in 1650, but her most substantial poetry was not published until 1678, six years after her death. In these poems she insisted on keeping her personal voice, negotiating between her Puritan background and her obvious attachment to the physical world around her. Her love poetry to her husband, while discreet, is also candid, and her lyrics fall within the tradition of English Renaissance love lyrics stemming back to Sir Thomas Wyatt and Sir Philip Sydney. "A Letter to Her Husband, Absent upon Public Employment" bears comparison with John Donne's "A Valediction Forbidding Mourning," inasmuch as it challenges to some degree, even as it affirms, the notion in Donne's poem that woman is the "fixed foot" that stabilizes the otherwise roving male.

A Letter to Her Husband, Absent upon Public Employment

My head, my heart, mine eyes, my life, nay, more,
My joy, my magazine° of earthly store, storehouse
If two be one, as surely thou and I,
How stayest thou there, whilst I at Ipswich[1] lie?
So many steps, head from the heart to sever,
If but a neck, soon should we be together.
I, like the Earth this season, mourn in black,
My Sun is gone so far in's zodiac,
Whom whilst I' joyed, nor storms, nor frost I felt,
His warmth such frigid colds did cause to melt.
My chilled limbs now numbed lie forlorn;
Return, return, sweet Sol, from Capricorn;[2]
In this dead time, alas, what can I more
Than view those fruits which through thy heat I bore?
Which sweet contentment yield me for a space,
True living pictures of their father's face.
O strange effect! now thou art southward gone,
I weary grow the tedious day so long;
But when thou northward to me shalt return,
I wish my Sun may never set, but burn
Within the Cancer[3] of my glowing breast,
The welcome house of him my dearest guest.
Where ever, ever stay, and go not thence,
Till nature's sad decree shall call thee hence;
Flesh of thy flesh, bone of thy bone,
I here, thou there, yet both but one.

[1] **Ipswich:** A town north of Boston in Massachusetts.

[2] **Return, sweet Sol, from Capricorn:** The sun is in the constellation Capricorn during the winter.

[3] **Within the Cancer:** The constellation of the sun, "Sol," in the summer.

ANDREW MARVELL
1621–1678

Andrew Marvell was born at Winstead, Yorkshire, in 1621, and attended Cambridge University, graduating in 1638. After spending several years traveling, he was by 1650 the tutor to Mary Fairfax, daughter of Sir Thomas Fairfax, the Lord General of Parliamentary forces who resided at the magnificent Nunn Appleton House, where Marvell wrote many of his poems. In 1657, Marvell became the assistant to John Milton, then Latin secretary for Oliver Cromwell, and two years later he was sent up to Parliament. Marvell lived most of his life in the shadow of the English Civil War, keeping in good standing with the parties in power, so that he eventually served as intercessor on Milton's behalf after the Puritan defeat. While serving as M.P. for Hull, Marvell continued to write poems until his death in 1678. His poetry, virtually unknown outside of narrow circles during his lifetime, was published three years after his death.

One of Marvell's most famous poems, "To His Coy Mistress," is a love poem cast in the form of an argument. It invokes the familiar theme of *carpe diem*—seize the day—which permeates much Renaissance love poetry: since tomorrow we grow old and die, we must seize the sweet fullness of life in the present. In the vein of John Donne, however, Marvell elaborates the theme, and invokes the spirit of discovery—"the Indian Ganges"—to add an exotic element to the poem and underscore the gulf between the lovers who would be separated. The violence of the final image—"tear[ing] our pleasures with rough strife"—heightens the urgency of their situation, and is one of Marvell's most complex conceits.

To His Coy Mistress

Had we but world enough, and time,
This coyness, lady, were no crime.
We would sit down, and think which way
To walk, and pass our long love's day.
Thou by the Indian Ganges'[1] side
Shouldst rubies find; I by the tide
Of Humber[2] would complain. I would
Love you ten years before the flood,
And you should, if you please, refuse

[1] **Ganges':** The most important holy river of India.

[2] **Humber:** A river in England that flows through Marvell's hometown of Hull.

Till the conversion of the Jews.[3]
My vegetable° love should grow slow-moving
Vaster than empires and more slow;
An hundred years should go to praise
Thine eyes, and on thy forehead gaze;
Two hundred to adore each breast,
But thirty thousand to the rest;
An age at least to every part,
And the last age should show your heart.
For, lady, you deserve this state,
Nor would I love at lower rate.
    But at my back I always hear
Time's wingèd chariot hurrying near;
And yonder all before us lie
Deserts of vast eternity.
Thy beauty shall no more be found;
Nor, in thy marble vault, shall sound
My echoing song; then worms shall try
That long-preserved virginity,
And your quaint honor turn to dust,
And into ashes all my lust:
The grave's a fine and private place,
But none, I think, do there embrace.
    Now therefore, while the youthful hue
Sits on thy skin like morning glow,
And while thy willing soul transpires
At every pore with instant fires,
Now let us sport us while we may,
And now, like amorous birds of prey,
Rather at once our time devour
Than languish in his slow-chapped° power. slow-jawed
Let us roll all our strength and all
Our sweetness up into one ball,
And tear our pleasures with rough strife
Thorough the iron gates of life:
Thus, though we cannot make our sun
Stand still, yet we will make him run.

---

[3] **conversion of the Jews:** The Jews, it was popularly believed, would be converted just before the Last Judgment.

Sor Juana Inés de la Cruz
1648–1695

The greatest poet of New Spain during the Colonial era, Sor Juana Inés de la Cruz was born in San Miguel Mepantla, a small village southeast of Mexico City. She was the illegitimate child of Isabel Ramirez de Santillana, from Mexico, and Pedro Manuel de Asbaje, from the Basque region of Spain. She lived with her mother on a small hacienda; her father, who did not live with them, did not play a role in her life. Sor Juana began attending school at the age of three, and as a young girl she demonstrated a tremendous gift and ardent desire for learning. As a teenager she studied Latin on her own, because her mother would not allow her to disguise herself as a boy in order to attend the University of Mexico.

At an early age, she began serving in the court of Marqués de Mancera (1664–1673), the Viceroy of New Spain in Mexico City. Astonished at the young girl's learning and intelligence, the court turned their brilliant maid-in-waiting into something of a spectacle, and she began writing occasional poetry for social and political events. All this time she continued her studies, extending her reach to subjects normally outside the realm of women's education, such as mathematics, logic, and theology. Persuaded by officials in the Order of the Discalced Carmelites, the order for which San Juan de la Cruz in Spain had been an advocate, Sor Juana joined their convent in 1667. After two years, she left for the convent of

Miguel Cabrera, 1695–1768, *Sor Juana Inés de la Cruz*

The great writer of New Spain is shown here in her habit at a writing desk with a rosary in one hand and a book in the other. (The Art Archive / National History Museum Mexico City / Dagli Orti)

the Order of Saint Jerome, which she found more hospitable and suitable for her interests and needs. Although she maintained ties with the court, she remained in the convent for the rest of her life, absorbed in her studies, writing, and teaching. She died of the plague in 1695.

As an intellectual, Sor Juana surpassed the wisest men of Mexico, and she devoted herself to learning throughout her life despite the censure and jealousy of authorities. Besides poetry, she wrote learned treatises, plays, and a long allegorical poem, *The First Dream* (c. 1685). The three sonnets printed here represent some of her finest love poetry. "Love, at First, Is Fashioned of Agitation" is reminiscent of Shakespeare's sonnets; it invokes an atmosphere of baroque tension and anatomizes love rather than describing the beauties of a lover. "In Which She Restrains a Fantasy, Satisfying It with Decent Love" blurs the boundaries between real and ideal love and inverts the Petrarchan conceit in such a way that the speaker of the poem, not the imagined lover, is the central agent of the poem. The lover here is imprisoned in a fantasy, vexing the reality of the dynamic situation and underscoring the elusive nature of love. In "The Rhetoric of Tears" Sor Juana creates a stunning conceit in the image of her tears becoming the molten substance of her heart—a palpable testimony to the intensity of her love.

Love, at First, Is Fashioned of Agitation

Translated from the Spanish by S. G. Morley

Love, at first, is fashioned of agitation,
Ardors, anxiety, and wakeful hours;
By danger, risk, and fear it spreads its power,
And feeds on weeping and on supplication.

It learns from coolness and indifference,
Preserves its life beneath faithless veneers,
Until, with jealousy or with offense,
It extinguishes its fire in its tears.

Love's beginning, middle, and its end are these:
Then why, Alcino, does it so displease
That Celia, who once loved you, now should leave you?

Is that a cause for sorrow and remorse?
Alcino mine, no, love did not deceive you:
It merely ran its customary course.

In Which She Restrains a Fantasy, Satisfying It with Decent Love

Translated from the Spanish by Frank J. Warnke

Stay, elusive shadow that I cherish,
Image of the enchantment which I love,
Illusion fair for which I gladly perish,
Sweet fiction for whose sake in pain I live.

If my breast responds to your attractive graces
As to the magnet the obedient steel,
Why woo me with your flattering embraces,
To flee me later, mocking my appeal?

But you cannot in satisfaction boast
That your tyranny has triumphed over me:
Even if you escape the noose I fashioned
To bind the form of your evasive ghost,
It matters not to flee my arms impassioned,
If you're imprisoned in my fantasy.

The Rhetoric of Tears

Translated from the Spanish by Frank J. Warnke

Tonight, my dearest, when I spoke to thee,
I noted in thy bearing and thy face
That words of mine could not thy doubts erase,
Or prove I wanted thee my heart to see;

Then love, which my avowals came to prop,
Conquered, and the impossible occurred:
I fell to weeping tears which sorrow poured,
Which my melting heart distilled in copious drop.

No more reproaches, ah my love, forbear;
Let doubt not hold thee in tormenting bonds,
Nor let vile jealousy thy peace impair
With foolish shades, with vain and useless wounds,
Since thou hast seen and touched a liquid rare—
My molten heart caught up between thy hands.

ꝏ NICCOLÒ MACHIAVELLI
1469–1527

Giorgione, *Cesare Borgia*, 1500 *Machiavelli considered the Italian aristocrat Cesare Borgia (1476–1507) an example of a new kind of "prince." (Hulton Archive)*

Niccolò Machiavelli has been called the "Galileo of politics," a title well suited for the thinker who transformed political writing and is sometimes thought to be the founder of modern political science. Abandoning the examples of Aristotle and Plato,[1] whose political works construct a model of an ideal society, Machiavelli turned directly to the turbulent and corrupt affairs of state in his native fifteenth-century Florence to construct a model of society as it actually was. Drawing on his experience as a public official, military analyst, diplomat, and political exile, Machiavelli was in a perfect position to observe the political and historical events sweeping through Florence and the other Italian city-states. The picture that he drew of the strategies a prince must exercise in order to maintain power during such times has earned him the reputation of cynic, pessimist, and genius from his own time down to ours. What is certain is that Machiavelli's work continues to be read and to generate debate over questions of power, authority, and the administration of the modern state.

Modest Origins. Niccolò Machiavelli was born into a family struggling to gain a secure footing among the Florentine aristocracy to whom the family linked its ancestry. Although his father, Bernardo di Niccolò di Buoninsegna, received a small inheritance and practiced law in Florence, the family did not enjoy a secure or large fortune, so Machiavelli received only a modest education in Latin, grammar, and mathematics from a series of tutors. Machiavelli gives us a mere glimpse of his early life, about which little has been recorded, when he writes, "I was born poor, and I learned to know want before enjoyment."

WWW For links to more information about Machiavelli, a quiz on *The Prince*, and information about the twenty-first-century relevance of Machiavelli, see *World Literature Online* at bedfordstmartins.com/worldlit.

Hard Lessons in Politics. From his modest origins, Machiavelli rose to be elected Secretary to the Second Chancery, beginning a fourteen-year career as civil servant, military adviser, and diplomat for the Florentine republic, which had been reestablished by the French monarch Charles VIII (r. 1483–98), after ousting the Medici family[2] from Florence in 1494. In this position, which he held from 1498 to 1512, Machiavelli served as a kind of secretary and emissary, concerned with matters of domestic and foreign policy. During his visits to the various Italian city-states and the

[1] **Aristotle and Plato:** Aristotle (384–322 B.C.E.) and Plato (427?–347 B.C.E.), Greek philosophers and authors of two founding works of political philosophy, *The Politics* and *The Republic*, respectively. Aristotle was Plato's student.

[2] **Medici family:** An Italian family whose enormous wealth from trade and banking enabled them to gain control of political power in Florence, beginning in 1434 with Cosimo de' Medici (1389–1464). The Medicis were well known as patrons of the arts: Cosimo de' Medici founded the Platonic Academy in Florence; Lorenzo (the Magnificent) de' Medici (1449–1492) was the patron of Leonardo da Vinci (1452–1519).

courts of other European rulers, such as Louis XII,[3] king of France, and Maximilian,[4] emperor of the Holy Roman Empire, Machiavelli witnessed firsthand the political intrigue that he describes in *The Art of War* (1521), *The Discourses* (1531), *The History of Florence* (1532), and, most famously, *The Prince* (1513; published 1532). When the Medicis returned to power in 1512, they removed Machiavelli from office and forced him to abandon hopes of any political preferment. Because his name had appeared on a list of possible conspirators, Machiavelli was unjustly imprisoned and tortured for crimes against the state and then banished from Florence. Experiencing with painful immediacy the manipulations of power he so brilliantly analyzes, Machiavelli retired to his home at Sant'Andrea, seven miles from Florence, and began writing *The Prince* and *Discourses on the First Decade of Titus Livius,* partly in hopes of regaining the grace of the Medicis. Explaining to his friend Francesco Vettori why he dedicated *The Prince* to Giuliano de' Medici, Machiavelli gives us a sense of his hopes for that work: "If they read this work of mine, they would see that the fifteen years I have spent in the study of politics, I have not wasted or gambled away; and anyone ought to be glad to use a man who has gained a great deal of experience at other people's expense."

This book has often been thrown aside in disgust, as replete with the maxims of the most revolting tyranny; but nothing worse can be urged against it than that the writer, having the profound consciousness of the necessity for the formation of a State, has here exhibited the principles on which alone states could be founded in the circumstances of the times.

– George W. F. Hegel, philosopher, *The Philosophy of History,* 1837

Writer and Historian. Over the next few years Machiavelli turned to more literary pursuits, writing a satirical poem, *The Ass;* a comedy, *Mandragola*; and a few short tales, including *Belfagor* and *Life of Castruccio Castracani.* In 1520 he completed *On the Art of War,* a study of military tactics characterized by his application of reading in the classics to his observation of contemporary affairs—a typical strategy in his writings overall. After being commissioned to write the history of Florence, Machiavelli attained a partial reconciliation with the Medici family, who in 1526 placed him in charge of a commission overseeing the fortification of Florence, newly threatened by hostilities between France and the Holy Roman Empire. After the sack of Rome in May 1527, Republican factions in Florence drove the Medicis into exile. Although Machiavelli had long sympathized with the Republicans, he had been too closely bound to the Medicis to maintain a place in the new government. Shortly after he was passed by for his old position at the Second Chancery, Machiavelli became ill; he died on June 21, 1527, after telling a story to those gathered at his bedside about a man who preferred going to hell, where he could discuss politics with Plato, Plutarch, Tacitus, and other men of noble minds, than to paradise with a beggarly crowd of blessed saints.

The Prince. Combined with a fascination for, if not obsession with, the history of ancient Rome, Machiavelli's realistic observations on warfare, diplomacy, and the workings of power in *The Prince* and other writings

[3] **Louis XII:** (r. 1498–1515), successor to Charles VIII as king of France; he continued Charles's invasion of Italian states, including Milan and Genoa.

[4] **Maximilian:** Maximilian I (r. 1493–1519), a member of the powerful Hapsburg family who became Holy Roman Emperor and king of Germany.

Machiavelli represents in Italy the realization that there can be no real Renaissance without the foundation of a national state.

– ANTONIO GRAMSCI, political theorist, *Prison Notebooks*, 1929–35

set him apart from earlier political thinkers. Aristotle in *The Politics* and Plato in *The Republic* had sought to create a philosophical vision of the ideal republic, to construct politics as they should be. In contrast, Machiavelli seeks in *The Prince* to create a practical vision of the actual republic as he saw it, to construct politics as they really are. Machiavelli explains his departure from earlier writers on the rules of conduct for a prince when he writes: "It being my intention to write a thing which shall be useful to him who apprehends it, it appears to me more appropriate to follow up the real truth of a matter than the imagination of it; for many have pictured republics and principalities which in fact have never been known or seen, because how one lives is so far distant from how one ought to live, that he who neglects what is done for what ought to be done, sooner effects his ruin than his preservation." For philosophical speculation, Machiavelli substitutes practical observation, and for this shift in focus his work has sometimes been considered—with some qualification—to be the forerunner of political science.

Expediency and Power. *The Prince* sets out to enumerate the necessary strategies of a prince who wants to gain power in a state and then to keep it. Indeed, Machiavelli's matter-of-factness and his evasion of questions about the morality of the actions he describes have earned him the severe criticism of thinkers from his own day down to the present time. Espousing efficiency as an end in itself, Machiavelli describes how a ruler can successfully secure and maintain power while arousing the least amount of resistance from the ruled. Although a prince should hope for the chance to practice kindness and generosity to his subjects, to govern with honesty and compassion, when pressed the prince must do whatever is necessary to remain in control by keeping a good name even when circumstances force him to resort to vices such as deception, parsimony, and terror. As Machiavelli puts it, "anyone who determines to act in all circumstances the part of a good man must come to ruin among so many who are not good. Hence, if a prince wishes to maintain himself, he must learn how to be not good, and to use that ability or not as is required." This emphasis on expedience in Machiavelli's treatise suggests, as has often been remarked, that the end—staying in power—justifies whatever means the prince must use, however devious or unscrupulous they may be.

Given the political turbulence of Machiavelli's Italy, one can see why he might be interested above all in presenting a guide to achieve stability in government; yet Machiavelli's basic outlook on human nature—one later followed by Thomas Hobbes[5] and to a lesser degree by Adam Smith[6]—has caused critics to label him a cynic. Insisting that human

[5] **Thomas Hobbes:** (1588–1679), an English philosopher and author of *Leviathan* (1651), which presents the state of human nature as an arena of brutal competition.

[6] **Adam Smith:** (1723–1790), a Scottish philosopher and economist whose book *The Wealth of Nations* (1776) promotes the doctrine of laissez-faire competition.

beings act in the last instance out of self-interest and therefore cannot be trusted, *The Prince* advises would-be rulers to use deceit, cunning, and force, if necessary, to achieve their ultimate objective—to remain in power. Above all, the ruler must keep up the appearance of being in control and acting for the benefit of the governed, when in fact he may be primarily concerned to preserve his own power.

Whether *The Prince* is amoral or immoral and whether Machiavelli is a realist or a pessimist, the significance of his work as a testament of the Renaissance preoccupation with secular power and conquest cannot be denied. Indeed, his name has been memorialized as a household word, *Machiavellian,* signifying an act of sheer expedience without regard for scruples. In those ages (or in those institutions) where power protects its interests through the presentation of spectacle, like that conjured up by Prospero in Shakespeare's ***The Tempest***, for example, accusations of Machiavellianism are sure to be heard once the smoke clears and the mirrors are exposed.

Dante is Italy's greatest poet, Niccolò her greatest writer of prose.

– Sebastian de Grazia, critic, *Machiavelli in Hell,* 1989

p. 495

■ CONNECTIONS

William Shakespeare, *The Tempest,* p. 495; Christopher Columbus, *Diario,* p. 773. *The Prince* discusses some of the problems the prince faces when acquiring new territories, and it emphasizes the need to create a spectacle of either fairness and virtue or, when necessary, terror and martial power. Prospero and Columbus both rely to some degree on creating spectacles of power to control or subdue the inhabitants (or invaders) of their newly acquired colonies, and both exhibit some of the characteristics of Machiavelli's prince. Consider Prospero and Columbus as Machiavellian rulers. In what ways do they both indicate that Machiavelli's advice to the prince is correct, and in what ways do they indicate that the advice may need to be qualified?

"In the World: Declarations of Rights and Independence," Jean-Jacques Rousseau, *The Social Contract,* Book 4. While Machiavelli's *The Prince* is most often read as a handbook for self-interested rulers, some readers, such as Rousseau, have read the book as a satire. Hence, in *The Social Contract,* Rousseau claims that "*The Prince* is the book of republicans," since it opens the eyes of the people to the wicked abuses and hypocrisy of monarchs. Putting aside Machiavelli's intentions, to what degree is Rousseau right? How does *The Prince* alert its readers to leaders' potential for abusing their power? Compare the republican principles in the selections from *Declarations of Rights and Independence* to those guiding Machiavelli's prince.

Bhagavad Gita, Book 1. Machiavelli's *The Prince* advises the ruler that he (or possibly she) must do everything possible to remain in power; to do so is to fulfill the role, the duty, of the prince. In the Bhagavad Gita, Krishna advises the warrior prince Arjuna that he must do his duty to his office of warrior, no matter the extenuating circumstances and no matter whether he may have to kill members of his own kin. What advice might Arjuna give to Machiavelli, or vice versa?

■ FURTHER RESEARCH

Biography

Hale, J. R. *Machiavelli and Renaissance Italy.* 1972.
Ridolfi, Roberto. *The Life of Niccolo Machiavelli.* 1954; trans. 1963.

Criticism
Bondanella, Peter E. *Machiavelli and the Art of Renaissance History.* 1973.
De Grazia, Sebastian. *Machiavelli in Hell.* 1989.
Kahn, Victoria. *Machiavellian Rhetoric: From the Counter-Reformation to Milton.* 1994.
Rebhorn, Wayne A. *Foxes and Lions: Machiavelli's Confidence Man.* 1988.
Ruffo Fiore, Silvia. *Niccolò Machiavelli.* 1982.

The Prince

Translated by Allan H. Gilbert

Chapter 2

On Hereditary Principates

I shall omit any discussion of republics, because I have elsewhere dealt with them at length.[1] I shall concern myself only with princely governments, and shall proceed to spin my web about the classes mentioned, and discuss how these princely governments can be managed and maintained.

I say, then, that hereditary states, being accustomed to the family of their prince, are maintained with fewer difficulties than new ones, because it is enough for the hereditary ruler merely not to go beyond the customs of his ancestors, and otherwise to deal with accidents by moving slowly and cautiously. This is so true that if such a prince is of ordinary diligence, he will always maintain himself in his position, unless some extraordinary and excessive force deprives him of it; and even if he is deprived of it, he will get it back whenever the conqueror falls into misfortune.

We have in Italy, for example, the Duke of Ferrara, who sustained the assaults of the Venetians in 1484 and of Pope Julius[2] in 1510 for no other reason than that he had long been established in that dominion. For a hereditary prince has fewer causes for doing injury and less necessity for it than a new one; hence it is normal that he will

---

The Prince. Portraying human beings as essentially base, greedy, self-interested, deceitful, and concerned primarily with the maintenance of power at any cost, *The Prince* is one of the most well-known and controversial political treatises in the West, if not the world. While Machiavelli first mentions this work—called *Of Principates*—in a letter of 1513, it was first printed as *The Prince* in 1532, five years after his death. The work's twenty-six chapters may be divided into roughly four parts. The first eleven chapters discuss the characteristics of, and the most appropriate means to rule, various kinds of principalities, from hereditary states to newly acquired ones. The second part, Chapters 12 through 14, provides an overview and analysis of the various kinds of militias and

---

[1] **elsewhere . . . at length:** While some scholars believe this sentence refers to *Discourses on the First Decade of Titus Livius,* written sometime between 1513 and 1521, others believe that Machiavelli had finished *The Prince* before starting to write the *Discourses.*

[2] **Duke of Ferrara . . . Pope Julius:** Under Duke of Ferrara, Machiavelli refers to both Ercole d'Este (1431–1505), defeated by the Venetians in 1484, and Alfonso d'Este (1476–1534), who fell to Pope Julius II in 1510; Giuliano della Rovere (1443–1513), Pope Julius II, reigned from 1503 to 1513.

be more loved, and if extraordinary vices do not make him hated, it is reasonable that he will naturally have the good wishes of his people. Moreover, if his government is old and has long been settled, new measures and their causes have been forgotten; for one change always leaves points of attachment for the building of another.

Chapter 3

On Mixed Principates

A new princely government, however, encounters difficulties. And first, if it is not wholly new but a member of a larger unit (so that the whole may be called a mixed principate), changes originate chiefly in a natural difficulty found in all new principalities; namely that men are glad to change their rulers, in the belief that they will better themselves, and this belief makes them take arms against the prince; but they deceive themselves in it, because afterwards they learn from experience that they are worse off. This depends on another natural and normal necessity, which makes it always necessary for a new ruler to harm those over whom he places himself, because he must employ soldiers and inflict various injuries incident to his new acquisition. Hence as a new prince you make enemies of all those you have damaged in occupying your position as ruler, and are not able to keep as friends those who have placed you there, because you cannot satisfy them in the manner they have been looking forward to, and you cannot use strong medicine against them because you are under obligation to them; it is always true, even when one's armies are very powerful, that one who is to enter a province needs the favor of the inhabitants. For these reasons Louis XII, the king of France, quickly occupied Milan and quickly lost it. The forces of Lodovico[3] himself were enough to take it away from him the first time, because the people who had opened the gates of the city, finding themselves deceived in their

---

armies, since states must be based on a strong and loyal army. Machiavelli then moves on to the most controversial part of his treatise, Chapters 15 through 19, wherein he surveys the reasons for which a prince may be praised or blamed. In this third part of the book, from which most of the selection here has been taken, Machiavelli shows that rulers must use any means at their disposal to gain and to maintain power. Although he notes that rulers should always appear to be virtuous and good in the eyes of their people, he argues that history shows that they must compromise the standards of virtue and goodness whenever necessary. In the remaining chapters, Machiavelli offers more practical advice for princes—on the use of fortresses, on choosing advisers, on the role of "Fortune" in their affairs. In Chapter 26 he focuses particularly on what should be done to protect Italy from foreign invaders. Included here is part of the famous chapter on Fortune, where Machiavelli accounts for the power of luck in the governance of the state but suggests that the prince can arm himself against this power (personified as a woman).

The translation is by Allan H. Gilbert, whose English version gives some sense of the power of Machiavelli's plain style.

---

[3] **Lodovico:** Ludovico Sforza, Duke of Milan from 1494 to 1499, lost Milan to Louis XII in September 1499; he recaptured it in the next year, only to lose it again to Pope Julius II and the Holy League in 1502.

opinions and in the benefits they had looked forward to, were not able to endure the annoyances caused by the new prince.

It is indeed quite true that when a country that has rebelled is acquired for the second time, it is less easily lost, because the ruler, taking his opportunity from the rebellion, is less hesitant in making himself solid by punishing those who failed him, getting at the truth about those he suspects, and strengthening his weakest points. So then, the disturbance Duke Lodovico made on the borders was enough to cause the French king to lose Milan the first time, but if the King was to lose the city a second time he had to have all the world against him and his armies had to be destroyed or driven from Italy. This all resulted from the causes mentioned above. Nevertheless, the city was taken from him both the first time and the second.

The general causes of the first loss have been discussed; it now remains to give those of the second, and to see what means of prevention he had, and what one in his condition can do, to enable him to maintain himself in his acquisition better than the king of France did. I say, then, that those states which, when they are gained, are joined to the old dominion of him who gains them, either are of the same region and the same language, or they are not. When they are, it is very easy to hold them, especially when they are not accustomed to independence. In order to have secure possession, it is enough to extirpate the line of the prince who was ruling them, because, when their methods of government are kept up and there is no dissimilarity in customs, men live quietly enough with respect to other things. It can be seen that this has been done in Burgundy, Brittany, Gascony, and Normandy, which have long been under the king of France; and though there is some unlikeness of language, yet the customs are similar, and the peoples can easily tolerate each other. He who acquires such new provinces and wishes to hold them, ought to be attentive to two matters: one is that the race of the old prince be wiped out; the other is that there be no change in laws or taxes, so that in a very short time the new province and the old become one body.

But when states are acquired in a region different in language, customs, and laws, there are many difficulties. He who will retain them needs to have great good fortune and great shrewdness. One of the most important and effective devices is that the person who acquires them should go into them to live. This will make his possession more secure and more durable. The Turk has used this method in Greece; if, in addition to all the other methods practised by him to hold that country, he had not gone there to live, he could not possibly have held it. The reason is that, since he lives there, he can see troubles when they arise and can remedy them quickly; but if he is not there, he learns of them when they are already big and there is no remedy for them. In addition, the province cannot be plundered by his officials, and the subjects are pleased by having easy access to their prince; hence they have good cause to love him if they intend to be good, and to fear him if they intend to be otherwise. Any foreigner who wishes to assail that state is therefore more hesitant about it. Hence a prince who lives in a new province can lose it only with the greatest difficulty.

Another excellent remedy is to send colonies into one or two places, to serve as fetters for that state. It is necessary either to do this or to keep there sufficient men-at-arms and infantry. Not much is spent on colonies; they can be sent out and kept up without any expense, or very little; this method damages only those—and they are a very small part of the new state—whose fields and houses are taken away in order to give them to the new inhabitants; those whom the prince damages, since they are scattered and poor, can do no harm, and all the others are undisturbed and uninjured. For this reason the latter are likely to be quiet, and on the other hand they are afraid of doing something wrong, and fear that the same thing may happen to them as to those who have been plundered. I conclude that such colonies are not expensive, are very faithful, and do little damage; those who are harmed are unable to do injury, since they are poor and dispersed, as has been said. From this it may be concluded that men should be either caressed or exterminated, because they can avenge light injuries, but not severe ones. The damage done to a man should be such that there is no fear of revenge. But if a prince keeps men-at-arms in his new province, instead of sending colonies, he will spend much more, since he will consume all the revenues of his state in guarding it; hence his acquisition will cause him loss; and he does much more damage, because he injures the whole state by shifting the encampments of his army. Everybody feels something of this annoyance, and the enemies he makes by it are able to injure him because, if they are beaten, they remain at home. In every way then, this method of protection is useless, but the colonial method is useful.

He who goes into a region unlike his own, such as has been spoken of, ought also to make himself head and defender of the neighboring minor rulers of the region, endeavor to weaken the powerful ones, and take precautions against any accident that might cause the entrance of a foreigner as powerful as himself. Those in the province who are discontented, either through too great ambition or through fear, will always try to bring in such a foreigner, as was seen long ago when the Etolians[4] brought the Romans into Greece; in fact the natives of every country the Romans occupied brought them into it. And the course of things is such that as soon as a powerful foreigner enters a land, all the less powerful rulers adhere to him, moved by their envy against the one who has been in power over them. This is so true that the foreigner has to take no trouble to win the lesser rulers, because at once and all together they willingly unite in one body with the supporters he has gained there. He has only to see to it that they do not grasp too much power and too much authority; then, with his forces and their favor, he can put down those who are powerful, and remain in every way master of that land. And he who does not attend carefully to this matter will quickly lose what he has acquired; and while he holds his territory he will have countless difficulties and troubles within it.

The Romans fully observed these requirements in the lands they took; they sent colonies, they sheltered the less powerful men without increasing the latter's power, they weakened the more powerful, and did not allow powerful foreigners to obtain prestige. I think the province of Greece alone will be a sufficient example: the

[4] **Etolians:** Inhabitants of Aetolia, a region in ancient Greece; in the second century B.C.E. it allied with Rome to defeat Philip V of Macedonia (207–192 B.C.E.), who was making incursions into Greek provinces.

Achaeans and the Aetolians were received, the kingdom of Macedonia was weakened; Antiochus was driven out of Greece; the merits of the Achaeans and the Aetolians did not cause Rome to permit their influence to grow; the persuasions of Philip did not ever induce her to be his friend without lessening his importance; the power of Antiochus could not force her to consent to his having any authority in that province.[5] In fact, the Romans did in these matters what all wise princes ought to do, for they are obliged to take thought not merely about immediate rebellions but about future ones, and to use every effort to forestall them, because if they are foreseen they can easily be remedied, but if they are awaited until they are near at hand, medicine cannot be given in time, because the malady has become incurable. The same thing happens in hectic fever: the physicians say that at the beginning the disease is easy to cure and hard to diagnose, but if it is not diagnosed and treated at the beginning, and a long time elapses, it grows easy to diagnose and hard to cure. So it is in matters of state, for if the ills of a policy are recognized early (something that can be done only by a prudent man), they are soon cured; but when, not being diagnosed early, they are allowed to increase in such fashion that everybody recognizes them, no remedy can then be found.

So the Romans, seeing difficulties in advance, always remedied them, and did not let them go on in order to escape a war, because they knew that war could not be avoided but would be deferred to the advantage of others. Hence they determined to make war with Philip and Antiochus in Greece in order not to have to make it with them in Italy, yet at that time they were able to escape both wars; but they did not wish to do so. Nor were they ever satisfied with the saying that is always in the mouths of the wise men of our days, about enjoying the benefit the day brings with it, but preferred what they could derive from their own vigor and prudence, because Time sweeps everything before him, and can bring along good as well as evil, and evil as well as good.

. . .

Chapter 15

On the Things for Which Men, and Especially Princes, Are Praised or Censured

It now remains to see what should be the methods and conduct of a prince in dealing with his subjects and his friends. And because I know that many have written on this topic, I fear that when I too write I shall be thought presumptuous, because, in discussing it, I break away completely from the principles laid down by my predecessors. But since it is my purpose to write something useful to an attentive reader, I think it more effective to go back to the practical truth of the subject than to depend

[5] **The Achaeans . . . that province:** Like the Aetolians, the Achaeans, who lived in a region of Greece just south of Aetolia, fought to drive Philip V from their territories; Rome intervened, defeating Philip. When Rome refused to punish Philip, the Aetolians turned against Rome and allied with Antiochus III, "The Great," ruler of Syria from 223 to 187 B.C.E.; Rome defeated this alliance at Thermopylae in 191 B.C.E., thus preventing Syria from gaining a foothold in Greece.

on my fancies about it. And many have imagined republics and principalities that never have been seen or known to exist in reality. For there is such a difference between the way men live and the way they ought to live, that anybody who abandons what is for what ought to be will learn something that will ruin rather than preserve him, because anyone who determines to act in all circumstances the part of a good man must come to ruin among so many who are not good. Hence, if a prince wishes to maintain himself, he must learn how to be not good, and to use that ability or not as is required.

Leaving out of account, then, things about an imaginary prince, and considering things that are true, I say that all men, when they are spoken of, and especially princes, because they are set higher, are marked with some of the qualities that bring them either blame or praise. To wit, one man is thought liberal, another stingy (using a Tuscan word, because *avaricious* in our language is still applied to one who desires to get things through violence, but *stingy* we apply to him who refrains too much from using his own property); one is thought open-handed, another grasping; one cruel, the other compassionate; one is a breaker of faith, the other reliable; one is effeminate and cowardly, the other vigorous and spirited; one is philanthropic, the other egotistic; one is lascivious, the other chaste; one is straight-forward, the other crafty; one hard, the other easy to deal with; one is firm, the other unsettled; one is religious, the other unbelieving; and so on.

And I know that everybody will admit that it would be very praiseworthy for a prince to possess all of the above-mentioned qualities that are considered good. But since he is not able to have them or to observe them completely, because human conditions do not allow him to, it is necessary that he be prudent enough to understand how to avoid getting a bad name because he is given to those vices that will deprive him of his position. He should also, if he can, guard himself from those vices that will not take his place away from him, but if he cannot do it, he can with less anxiety let them go. Moreover, he should not be troubled if he gets a bad name because of vices without which it will be difficult for him to preserve his position. I say this because, if everything is considered, it will be seen that some things seem to be virtuous, but if they are put into practice will be ruinous to him; other things seem to be vices, yet if put into practice will bring the prince security and well-being.

Chapter 16

On Liberality and Parsimony

Beginning, then, with the first of the above-mentioned qualities, I assert that it is good to be thought liberal.[6] Yet liberality, practiced in such a way that you get a reputation for it, is damaging to you, for the following reasons: If you use it wisely and as it ought to be used, it will not become known, and you will not escape being censured for the opposite vice. Hence, if you wish to have men call you liberal, it is necessary not to omit any sort of lavishness. A prince who does this will always be

[6] **good to be . . . liberal:** Generous.

obliged to use up all his property in lavish actions; he will then, if he wishes to keep the name of liberal, be forced to lay heavy taxes on his people and exact money from them, and do everything he can to raise money. This will begin to make his subjects hate him, and as he grows poor he will be little esteemed by anybody. So it comes about that because of this liberality of his, with which he has damaged a large number and been of advantage to but a few, he is affected by every petty annoyance and is in peril from every slight danger. If he recognizes this and wishes to draw back, he quickly gets a bad name for stinginess.

Since, then, a prince cannot without harming himself practice this virtue of liberality to such an extent that it will be recognized, he will, if he is prudent, not care about being called stingy. As time goes on he will be thought more and more liberal, for the people will see that because of his economy his income is enough for him, that he can defend himself from those who make war against him, and that he can enter upon undertakings without burdening his people. Such a prince is in the end liberal to all those from whom he takes nothing, and they are numerous; he is stingy to those to whom he does not give, and they are few. In our times we have seen big things done only by those who have been looked on as stingy; the others have utterly failed. Pope Julius II,[7] though he made use of a reputation for liberality to attain the papacy, did not then try to maintain it, because he wished to be able to make war. The present King of France[8] has carried on great wars without laying unusually heavy taxes on his people, merely because his long economy has made provision for heavy expenditures. The present King of Spain,[9] if he had continued liberal, would not have carried on or completed so many undertakings.

Therefore a prince ought to care little about getting called stingy, if as a result he does not have to rob his subjects, is able to defend himself, does not become poor and contemptible, and is not obliged to become grasping. For this vice of stinginess is one of those that enables him to rule. Somebody may say: Caesar,[10] by means of his liberality, became emperor, and many others have come to high positions because they have been liberal and have been thought so. I answer: Either you are already a prince, or you are on the way to become one. In the first case liberality is dangerous; in the second it is very necessary to be thought liberal. Caesar was one of those who wished to attain dominion over Rome. But if, when he had attained it, he had lived for a long time and had not moderated his expenses, he would have destroyed his authority. Somebody may answer: Many who have been thought very liberal have been princes and done great things with their armies. I answer: The prince spends either his own property and that of his subjects or that of others. In the first case he ought to be frugal; in the second he ought to abstain from no sort of liberality. When

---

[7] **Pope Julius II:** See note 2.

[8] **King of France:** Louis XII (1462–1515), king of France from 1498 to 1515.

[9] **King of Spain:** King Ferdinand "the Catholic" (1452–1516) jointly ruled Spain with Isabella I from 1474 to 1504, and was also king of Aragon, Sicily, and Naples.

[10] **Caesar:** Julius Caesar (100–44 B.C.E.), powerful member of the First Triumvirate of Rome, was appointed dictator of Rome in 44 B.C.E., the year of his famous assassination on the Ides of March by Marcus Brutus.

he marches with his army and lives on plunder, loot, and ransom, a prince controls the property of others. To him liberality is essential, for without it his soldiers would not follow him. You can be a free giver of what does not belong to you or your subjects, as were Cyrus,[11] Caesar, and Alexander, because to spend the money of others does not decrease your reputation but adds to it. It is only the spending of your own money that hurts you.

There is nothing that eats itself up as fast as does liberality, for when you practice it you lose the power to practice it, and become poor and contemptible, or else to escape poverty you become rapacious and therefore are hated. And of all the things against which a prince must guard himself, the first is being an object of contempt and hatred. Liberality leads you to both of these. Hence there is more wisdom in keeping a name for stinginess, which produces a bad reputation without hatred, than in striving for the name of liberal, only to be forced to get the name of rapacious, which brings forth both bad reputation and hatred.

Chapter 17

On Cruelty and Pity, and Whether It Is Better to Be Loved or to Be Feared, and Vice Versa

Coming then to the other qualities already mentioned, I say that every prince should wish to be thought compassionate and not cruel; still, he should be careful not to make a bad use of the pity he feels. Cesare Borgia[12] was considered cruel, yet this cruelty of his pacified the Romagna, united it, and changed its condition to that of peace and loyalty. If the matter is well considered, it will be seen that Cesare was much more compassionate than the people of Florence, for in order to escape the name of cruel they allowed Pistoia[13] to be destroyed. Hence a prince ought not to be troubled by the stigma of cruelty, acquired in keeping his subjects united and faithful. By giving a very few examples of cruelty he can be more truly compassionate than those who through too much compassion allow disturbances to continue, from which arise murders or acts of plunder. Lawless acts are injurious to a large group, but the executions ordered by the prince injure a single person. The new prince, above all other princes, cannot possibly avoid the name of cruel, because new states are full of perils. Dido in Vergil puts it thus: "Hard circumstances and the newness of my realm force me to do such things, and to keep watch and ward over all my lands."[14]

All the same, he should be slow in believing and acting, and should make no one afraid of him, his procedure should be so tempered with prudence and humanity

[11] **Cyrus:** Cyrus the Great (d. 529 B.C.E.), king of Persia from 559 B.C.E. and ruler of the Persian empire from 550 to 529 B.C.E.

[12] **Cesare Borgia:** The son of Pope Alexander VI, Borgia (1476–1507) resigned his cardinalship to lead a treacherous campaign to seize power over the cities of Romagna.

[13] **Pistoia:** A city under Florentine rule that was plagued with bloody factional rioting while Florentine authorities looked on without taking definitive action against the rival parties.

[14] **"Hard . . . my lands":** *Aeneid* I, 563–64.

that too much confidence does not make him incautious, and too much suspicion does not make him unbearable.

All this gives rise to a question for debate: Is it better to be loved than to be feared, or the reverse? I answer that a prince should wish for both. But because it is difficult to reconcile them, I hold that it is much more secure to be feared than to be loved, if one of them must be given up. The reason for my answer is that one must say of men generally that they are ungrateful, mutable, pretenders and dissemblers, prone to avoid danger, thirsty for gain. So long as you benefit them they are all yours; as I said above, they offer you their blood, their property, their lives, their children, when the need for such things is remote. But when need comes upon you, they turn around. So if a prince has relied wholly on their words, and is lacking in other preparations, he falls. For friendships that are gained with money, and not with greatness and nobility of spirit, are deserved but not possessed, and in the nick of time one cannot avail himself of them. Men hesitate less to injure a man who makes himself loved than to injure one who makes himself feared, for their love is held by a chain of obligation, which, because of men's wickedness, is broken on every occasion for the sake of selfish profit; but their fear is secured by a dread of punishment which never fails you.

Nevertheless the prince should make himself feared in such a way that, if he does not win love, he escapes hatred. This is possible, for to be feared and not to be hated can easily coexist. In fact it is always possible, if the ruler abstains from the property of his citizens and subjects, and from their women. And if, as sometimes happens, he finds that he must inflict the penalty of death, he should do it when he has proper justification and evident reason. But above all he must refrain from taking property, for men forget the death of a father more quickly than the loss of their patrimony. Further, causes for taking property are never lacking, and he who begins to live on plunder is always finding cause to seize what belongs to others. But on the contrary, reasons for taking life are rarer and fail sooner.

But when a prince is with his army and has a great number of soldiers under his command, then above all he must pay no heed to being called cruel, because if he does not have that name he cannot keep his army united or ready for duty. It should be numbered among the wonderful feats of Hannibal[15] that he led to war in foreign lands a large army, made up of countless types of men, yet never suffered from dissension, either among the soldiers or against the general, in either bad or good fortune. His success resulted from nothing else than his inhuman cruelty, which, when added to his numerous other strong qualities, made him respected and terrible in the sight of his soldiers. Yet without his cruelty his other qualities would not have been adequate. So it seems that those writers have not thought very deeply who on one side admire his accomplishment and on the other condemn the chief cause for it.

The truth that his other qualities alone would not have been adequate may be

[15] **Hannibal:** Carthaginian general (247–182 B.C.E.), one of Rome's greatest threats, who led his troops over the Alps from Spain into Italy.

learned from Scipio,[16] a man of the most unusual powers not only in his own times but in all ages we know of. When he was in Spain his armies mutinied. This resulted from nothing other than his compassion, which had allowed his soldiers more license than befits military discipline. This fault was censured before the Senate by Fabius Maximus,[17] and Scipio was called by him the corruptor of the Roman soldiery. The Locrians[18] were destroyed by a lieutenant of Scipio's, yet he did not avenge them or punish the disobedience of that lieutenant. This all came from his easy nature, which was so well understood that one who wished to excuse him in the Senate said there were many men who knew better how not to err than how to punish errors. This easy nature would in time have overthrown the fame and glory of Scipio if, in spite of his weakness, he had kept on in independent command. But since he was under the orders of the Senate, this bad quality was not merely concealed but was a glory to him.

Returning, then, to the debate on being loved and feared, I conclude that since men love as they please and fear as the prince pleases, a wise prince will evidently rely on what is in his own power and not on what is in the power of another. As I have said, he need only take pains to avoid hatred.

Chapter 18

In What Way Faith Should Be Kept by Princes

Everybody knows how laudable it is in a prince to keep his faith and to be an honest man and not a trickster. Nevertheless, the experience of our times shows that the princes who have done great things are the ones who have taken little account of their promises and who have known how to addle the brains of men with craft. In the end they have conquered those who have put their reliance on good faith.

You must realize, then, that there are two ways to fight. In one kind the laws are used, in the other, force. The first is suitable to man, the second to animals. But because the first often falls short, one has to turn to the second. Hence a prince must know perfectly how to act like a beast and like a man. This truth was covertly taught to princes by ancient authors, who write that Achilles and many other ancient princes were turned over for their up-bringing to Chiron the centaur,[19] that he might keep them under his tuition. To have as teacher one who is half beast and half man means nothing else than that a prince needs to know how to use the qualities of both creatures. The one without the other will not last long.

Since, then, it is necessary for a prince to understand how to make good use of

[16] **Scipio:** Publius Cornelius Scipio, Africanus Major (236–182 B.C.E.), Roman general who defeated Hannibal and Carthage; the mutiny took place in 206 B.C.E.

[17] **Fabius Maximus:** Quintus Fabius Maximus Verrucosus (d. 203 B.C.E.), Roman general called "the Delayer" for his cat-and-mouse tactics against Hannibal.

[18] **Locrians:** Citizens of Locri, in Sicily.

[19] **Chiron the centaur:** Mythical half man, half horse; said to be the tutor of legendary heroes Achilles, Theseus, Jason, and Hercules.

the conduct of the animals, he should select among them the fox and the lion, because the lion cannot protect himself from traps, and the fox cannot protect himself from the wolves. So the prince needs to be a fox that he may know how to deal with traps, and a lion that he may frighten the wolves. Those who act like the lion alone do not understand their business. A prudent ruler, therefore, cannot and should not observe faith when such observance is to his disadvantage and the causes that made him give his promise have vanished. If men were all good, this advice would not be good, but since men are wicked and do not keep their promises to you, you likewise do not have to keep yours to them. Lawful reasons to excuse his failure to keep them will never be lacking to a prince. It would be possible to give innumerable modern examples of this and to show many treaties and promises that have been made null and void by the faithlessness of princes. And the prince who has best known how to act as a fox has come out best. But one who has this capacity must understand how to keep it covered, and be a skilful pretender and dissembler. Men are so simple and so subject to present needs that he who deceives in this way will always find those who will let themselves be deceived.

I do not wish to keep still about one of the recent instances. Alexander VI[20] did nothing else than deceive men, and had no other intention; yet he always found a subject to work on. There never was a man more effective in swearing that things were true, and the greater the oaths with which he made a promise, the less he observed it. Nonetheless his deceptions always succeeded to his wish, because he thoroughly understood this aspect of the world.

It is not necessary, then, for a prince really to have all the virtues mentioned above, but it is very necessary to seem to have them. I will even venture to say that they damage a prince who possesses them and always observes them, but if he seems to have them they are useful. I mean that he should seem compassionate, trustworthy, humane, honest, and religious, and actually be so; but yet he should have his mind so trained that, when it is necessary not to practice these virtues, he can change to the opposite, and do it skilfully. It is to be understood that a prince, especially a new prince, cannot observe all the things because of which men are considered good, because he is often obliged, if he wishes to maintain his government, to act contrary to faith, contrary to charity, contrary to humanity, contrary to religion. It is therefore necessary that he have a mind capable of turning in whatever direction the winds of Fortune and the variations of affairs require, and, as I said above, that he should not depart from what is morally right, if he can observe it, but should know how to adopt what is bad, when he is obliged to.

A prince, then, should be very careful that there does not issue from his mouth anything that is not full of the above-mentioned five qualities. To those who see and hear him he should seem all compassion, all faith, all honesty, all humanity, all religion. There is nothing more necessary to make a show of possessing than this last quality. For men in general judge more by their eyes than by their hands; everybody is fitted to see, few to understand. Everybody sees what you appear to be; few make

---

[20] **Alexander VI:** Cardinal Rodrigo Borgia, pope from 1492 to 1503 and father of Cesare Borgia.

out what you really are. And these few do not dare to oppose the opinion of the many, who have the majesty of the state to confirm their view. In the actions of all men, and especially those of princes, where there is no court to which to appeal, people think of the outcome. A prince needs only to conquer and to maintain his position. The means he has used will always be judged honorable and will be praised by everybody, because the crowd is always caught by appearance and by the outcome of events, and the crowd is all there is in the world; there is no place for the few when the many have room enough. A certain prince of the present day,[21] whom it is not good to name, preaches nothing else than peace and faith, and is wholly opposed to both of them, and both of them, if he had observed them, would many times have taken from him either his reputation or his throne.

Chapter 19

On Avoiding Contempt and Hatred

But because I have spoken of the more important of the qualities above, I wish to cover the others briefly with this generality. To wit, the prince should give his attention, as is in part explained above, to avoiding the things that make him hateful and contemptible. As long as he escapes them, he will have done his duty, and will find no danger in other injuries to his reputation. Hatred, as I have said, comes upon him chiefly from being rapacious and seizing the property and women of his subjects. He ought to abstain from both of these, for the majority of men live in contentment when they are not deprived of property or honor. Hence the prince has to struggle only with the ambition of the few, which can be restrained in many ways and with ease. Contempt is his portion if he is held to be variable, volatile, effeminate, cowardly, or irresolute. From these a prince should guard himself as from a rock in the sea. He should strive in all his actions to give evident signs of greatness, spirit, gravity, and fortitude. Also in the private affairs of his subjects he should make it understood that his opinion is irrevocable. In short he should keep up such a reputation that nobody thinks of trying to deceive him or outwit him.

The prince who makes people hold that opinion has prestige enough. And if a prince has a high reputation, men hesitate to conspire against him and hesitate to attack him, simply because he is supposed to be of high ability and respected by his subjects. For a prince must needs have two kinds of fear: one within his state, because of his subjects; the other without, because of foreign rulers. From these dangers he defends himself with good weapons and good friends. And if his weapons are good, he will always have good friends. Conditions within the state, too, will always remain settled when those without are settled, if they have not already been unsettled by some conspiracy. And when things without are in movement, if he has ruled and lived as I have said, and does not fail himself, he will surely repel every attack, as I said Nabis the Spartan[22] did.

[21] **A certain prince . . . day:** Ferdinand II of Spain.

[22] **Nabis the Spartan:** A tyrant of Sparta (r. 207–192 B.C.E.), noted for his cruelty.

But with respect to his subjects, when there is no movement without, he has to fear that they will make a secret conspiracy. From this the prince protects himself adequately if he avoids being hated and despised and keeps the people satisfied with him. The latter necessarily follows the former, as was explained above at length. Indeed one of the most potent remedies the prince can have against conspiracies is not to be hated by the majority of his subjects. The reason for this is that a man who conspires always thinks he will please the people by killing the prince; but when he thinks he will offend them by it, he does not pluck up courage to adopt such a plan, because the difficulties that fall to the portion of conspirators are numerous. Experience shows that there have been many conspiracies and that few have come out well. They fail because the conspirator cannot be alone, and he can get companions only from those who, he thinks, are discontented. But as soon as you have revealed your purpose to a malcontent, you have given him an opportunity to become contented, because he evidently can hope to gain every advantage from his knowledge. Such is his position that, seeing on the one hand certain gain, and on the other gain that is uncertain and full of danger, he must needs be a rare friend, or, at any rate, an obstinate enemy of the prince, if he keeps faith with you. To put the thing briefly, I say that on the part of those who conspire there is nothing but fear, jealousy, and the expectation of punishment, which terrifies them. But on the part of the prince are the majesty of his high office, the laws, the power of his friends and his party that protects him. Evidently when the popular good-will is joined to all these things, it is impossible that anybody can be so foolhardy as to conspire against him. Ordinarily the conspirator must be afraid before the execution of his evil deed, but in this case he also has reason to fear after his transgression, because he will have the people against him and therefore cannot hope for any escape.

On this subject numerous examples might be given. But I have decided to be content with one alone, which happened in the memory of our fathers. Messer Annibale Bentivogli, grandfather of the present Messer Annibale, prince of Bologna,[23] was murdered by the Canneschi, who conspired against him. He left no heir save Messer Giovanni, who was in the cradle. Yet immediately after that murder, the people rose up and killed all the Canneschi. This act was the result of the popular good-will that the house of the Bentivogli had in those days, as is shown by what followed. After the death of Annibale, no member of the family who could rule the state was left in Bologna. The Bolognese, however, got a hint that there was in Florence a scion of the Bentivogli[24] who had been supposed until then to be the son of a smith. They came to Florence after him and gave him control of their city, which he governed from that time until Messer Giovanni reached an age capable of ruling it.

I conclude, therefore, that a prince need not pay much attention to conspiracies when the people are well-disposed to him. But when they are unfriendly and hate him, he must fear everything and everybody. Further, well-organized governments

---

[23] **Messer . . . Bologna:** The Bentivoglis were a powerful ruling family in Bologna. Annibale Sr. died in 1445 at the hands of the Canneschi, a rival family. Giovanni Bentivogli (1447–1508) ruled Bologna from 1462 to 1506, when he was driven out by Julius II.

[24] **Bentivogli:** Santi Bentivoglio of Florence, who ruled Bologna from 1446 to 1462, when Giovanni came of age.

and wise princes have striven with all diligence not to make the upper classes feel desperate, and to satisfy the populace and keep them contented. In fact this is one of the most important matters a prince has to deal with.

Among the kingdoms well organized and well governed in our times is France. In this country there are numerous good institutions on which depend the liberty and security of the king. The first of these is the parliament and its authority. He who organized this kingdom[25] set up the parliament because he knew the ambition of the nobles and their arrogance, and judged it necessary that the nobility should have a bit in its mouth to restrain it. On the other hand, he knew the hatred, founded on fear, of the generality of men for the nobles, and intended to secure the position of the latter. Yet he did not wish this to be the special concern of the king, because he wished to relieve the king from the hatred he would arouse among the great if he favored the people, and among the people if he favored the nobles. Therefore he set up a third party as judge, to be the one who, without bringing hatred on the king, should restrain the nobles and favor the people. This institution could not be better or more prudent, nor could there be a stronger cause for the security of the king and the realm. From this can be deduced another important idea: To wit, princes should have things that will bring them hatred done by their agents, but should do in person those that will give pleasure. Once more I conclude that a prince should esteem the nobles, but should not make himself hated by the populace.

. . .

Chapter 25

The Power of Fortune in Human Affairs, and to What Extent She Should Be Relied On

It is not unknown to me that many have been and still are of the opinion that the affairs of this world are so under the direction of Fortune and of God that man's prudence cannot control them; in fact, that man has no resource against them. For this reason many think there is no use in sweating much over such matters, but that one might as well let Chance take control. This opinion has been the more accepted in our times, because of the great changes in the state of the world that have been and now are seen every day, beyond all human surmise. And I myself, when thinking on these things, have now and then in some measure inclined to their view. Nevertheless, because the freedom of the will should not be wholly annulled, I think it may be true that Fortune is arbiter of half of our actions, but that she still leaves the control of the other half, or about that, to us.

I liken her to one of those raging streams that, when they go mad, flood the plains, ruin the trees and the buildings, and take away the fields from one bank and put them down on the other. Everybody flees before them; everybody yields to their onrush without being able to resist anywhere. And though this is their nature, it does

[25] **He . . . kingdom:** Possibly Louis IX (1214–1270), who promoted the use of Roman law in France and set up the Parlement de Paris.

not cease to be true that, in calm weather, men can make some provision against them with walls and dykes, so that, when the streams swell, their waters will go off through a canal, or their currents will not be so wild and do so much damage. The same is true of Fortune. She shows her power where there is no wise preparation for resisting her, and turns her fury where she knows that no walls and dykes have been made to hold her in. And if you consider Italy—the place where these variations occur and the cause that has set them in motion—you will see that she is a country without dykes and without any wall of defence. If, like Germany, Spain, and France, she had had a sufficient bulwark of military vigor, this flood would not have made the great changes it has, or would not have come at all.

And this, I think, is all I need to say on opposing oneself to Fortune, in general. But limiting myself more to particulars, I say that a prince may be seen prospering today and falling in ruin tomorrow, though it does not appear that he has changed in his nature or any of his qualities. I believe this comes, in the first place, from the causes that have been discussed at length in preceding chapters. That is, if a prince bases himself entirely on Fortune, he will fall when she varies. I also believe that a ruler will be successful who adapts his mode of procedure to the quality of the times, and likewise that he will be unsuccessful if the times are out of accord with his procedure. Because it may be seen that in things leading to the end each has before him, namely glory and riches, men proceed differently. One acts with caution, another rashly; one with violence, another with skill; one with patience, another with its opposite; yet with these different methods each one attains his end. Still further, two cautious men will be seen, of whom one comes to his goal, the other does not. Likewise you will see two who succeed with two different methods, one of them being cautious and the other rash. These results are caused by nothing else than the nature of the times, which is or is not in harmony with the procedure of men. It also accounts for what I have mentioned, namely, that two persons, working differently, chance to arrive at the same result; and that of two who work in the same way, one attains his end, but the other does not.

On the nature of the times also depends the variability of the best method. If a man conducts himself with caution and patience, times and affairs may come around in such a way that his procedure is good, and he goes on successfully. But if times and circumstances change, he is ruined, because he does not change his method of action. There is no man so prudent as to understand how to fit himself to this condition, either because he is unable to deviate from the course to which nature inclines him, or because, having always prospered by walking in one path, he cannot persuade himself to leave it. So the cautious man, when the time comes to go at a reckless pace, does not know how to do it. Hence he comes to ruin. Yet if he could change his nature with the times and with circumstances, his fortune would not be altered.

Pope Julius II proceeded rashly in all his actions, and found the times and circumstances so harmonious with his mode of procedure that he was always so lucky as to succeed. Consider the first enterprise he engaged in, that of Bologna, while Messer Giovanni Bentivogli was still alive. The Venetians were not pleased with it; the King of Spain felt the same way; the Pope was debating such an enterprise with the King of France. Nevertheless, in his courage and rashness Julius personally undertook that expedition. This movement made the King of Spain and the Venetians stand irresolute and motionless, the latter for fear, and the King because of his wish to recover the entire kingdom of Naples. On the other side, the King of France was dragged behind Julius, because the King, seeing that the Pope had moved and wishing to make him a friend in order to put down the Venetians, judged he could not refuse him soldiers without doing him open injury. Julius, then, with his rash movement, attained what no other pontiff, with the utmost human prudence, would have attained. If he had waited to leave Rome until the agreements were fixed and everything arranged, as any other pontiff would have done, he would never have succeeded, for the King of France would have had a thousand excuses, and the others would have raised a thousand fears. I wish to omit his other acts, which are all of the same sort, and all succeeded perfectly. The brevity of his life did not allow him to know anything different. Yet if times had come in which it was necessary to act with caution, they would have ruined him, for he would never have deviated from the methods to which nature inclined him.

I conclude, then, that since Fortune is variable and men are set in their ways, they are successful when they are in harmony with Fortune and unsuccessful when they disagree with her. Yet I am of the opinion that it is better to be rash than overcautious, because Fortune is a woman and, if you wish to keep her down, you must beat her and pound her. It is evident that she allows herself to be overcome by men who treat her in that way rather than by those who proceed coldly. For that reason, like a woman, she is always the friend of young men, because they are less cautious, and more courageous, and command her with more boldness.

Fashioning the Prince

Like Machiavelli, many writers from Europe, India, Turkey, and Japan, among other places, explored enduring questions about power, justice, and leadership. In the fourteenth and early fifteenth centuries, not only the city-states of Italy but all of Europe, like much of the rest of the world, was experiencing a great deal of political instability and turmoil. In Persia and India a successive series of recent invasions had led to sweeping changes in the character and form of leadership. As political conditions were changing and old loyalties broke down in the face of new ones, the fashioning of the prince became a preoccupation for many writers. From Nizam al-
p. 146 Mulk's ***The Book of Government*** through Baldesar Castiglione's
p. 171 ***The Courtier***, literary works offered both practical and ideal models of policy and etiquette for rulers and the ruling classes.

Literature offering moral and strategic advice takes on a variety of literary forms, from mixed prose and verse to historical plays and tragedies to philosophical treatises, like Machiavelli's *The Prince*. In addition, some memoirs and biographies offer us detailed portraits of exemplary leaders, such as Vespasiano da Bisticci's description of
p. 165 **Cosimo de' Medici**. However these texts may differ in form, policy, historical context, and culture, they all have in common at least two aims: to reconcile ideals with realities in the theater of politics, and

***Falconer*, 1600–05** ▶
Originally thought to be the Mughal emperor Akbar, the richly dressed young man in this portrait is almost certainly a member of the Mughal imperial family. (Los Angeles County Museum of Art, from the Nasli and Alice Heeramanek Collection, Museum Associates Purchase. Photograph © 2003 Museum Associates/LACMA)

to give readers a sense of a ruler's responsibilities to his or her subjects (and vice versa).

SELJUK AND OTTOMAN RULERSHIP

This section stretches the chronological framework of the Early Modern Period in order to bring like works together. Nizam al-Mulk p. 146 (1018–1092) wrote ***The Book of Government*** in the eleventh century. A vizier, or adviser, to the Seljuk Turk rulers Alp Arslan and his son Sultan Malikshah, Nizam al-Mulk, a Persian, hoped to show the sultan the way to increase his power. Like Machiavelli, he was mainly interested in implementing reforms in policy that would place the king in favor with his people. Closer in time, spirit, and content to p. 154 Machiavelli's *The Prince* is the ***Il Muqaddimah,*** by Ibn Khaldun (1332–1406). Written in the fourteenth century, this treatise—often described as the first work of sociology or historiography—offers a farsighted analysis of the organization of society and one of the earliest critical reflections on historical method. Ibn Khaldun, as if anticipating Machiavelli's work, discusses the principles on which royal authority is grounded and analyzes the means by which the ruler should manipulate public sentiment—what he calls group feeling—in order to establish and maintain power.

COSIMO DE' MEDICI AND *THE COURTIER*

Following the two Arabic works described above is a selection from the *Memoirs* of Vespasiano da Bisticci (1421–1498): a portrait of Cosimo de' Medici, the Florentine who ruled from 1434 to 1464 and whose patronage promoted the flourishing of the arts and letters in fifteenth-century Italy. A philosopher, statesman, and soldier, Cosimo de' Medici, as drawn by Bisticci, displays the features of an ideal Renaissance prince. He also shows some of the characteristics of Machiavelli's prince: He relies on secret diplomacy and violent force when necessary, but promotes a sense of goodwill and patron- p. 171 izes religion and the arts when possible. In ***The Courtier*** Baldesar Castiglione (1478–1529) moves down a notch in social rank to observe what he believes are the ideal virtues of the court gentleman. Castiglione's ideals not only contrast with Machiavelli's realities but also seem quite out of alignment with the court intrigues displayed p. 495 in other works, such as Shakespeare's ***The Tempest.***

THE MUGHAL EMPEROR AKBAR

Sixteenth-century India at the time of the Mughal emperor Akbar (1542–1605) was a period of cultural efflorescence, comparable to the Italian Renaissance. A master of martial strategy and statecraft, Akbar gathered under him shrewd advisers, such as Abu'l Fazl (1551–1602), a witty and learned courtier whose synthesis of Islamic teachings and **Platonic** ideas invite comparison with Castiglione's synthesis of Christianity and Platonism. The ***Institutes of Akbar***, written by Abu'l Fazl, provides a theory of rulership that unites the philosopher-statesman-soldier with the seeker of divine wisdom. Abu'l Fazl's emphasis on love, tolerance, trust, and prayer make an interesting contrast with the more aggressive features of Machiavelli's prince.

p. 176

HAYASHI RAZAN AND NEO-CONFUCIAN RULERSHIP IN JAPAN

The selection by Hayashi Razan (1583–1657), **"On Mastery of the Arts of Peace and War,"** is also a work of practical advice to a ruler. Hayashi's goal was to reconcile the pressures of politics and war with the ethical principles of **neo-Confucian** teachings. Hayashi emphasized the scrupulous study of first principles, history, and human affairs from an objective point of view (as in Machiavelli), while insisting that the ruler's strategies should follow in accord with the moral strictures of the Chinese philosopher Zhu Xi (Chu Hsi; 1130–1200). Like some of the other writers included here, Hayashi fashioned a new model for the prince—a scholar-soldier-bureaucrat, with a knowledge of history, literature, economy, and leadership as well as a mastery of the sword.

p. 179

■ CONNECTIONS

Homer, *Iliad*, Book 1; Ramayana, Book 1; Bhagavad Gita, Book 1; Virgil, *The Aeneid*, Book 1. Some of the texts in this "In the World" unit present models of the ideal leader or ruler. The larger-than-life heroes engaged in wars to protect their honor or homelands or embarked on nation-founding quests. Greco-Roman and Indian epic poetry similarly present exemplary, if sometimes flawed, models of leaders and rulers. How do the epic heroes—Achilles, Odysseus, Rama, Arjuna, Aeneas—compare to the Renaissance hero? What qualities of the epic heroes are preserved in the Renaissance? How do the models of leaders and heroes change over time and across cultures?

William Shakespeare, *The Tempest*, p. 495; Christopher Columbus, *Diario*, p. 773. Many of the texts in this unit enumerate the desired characteristics of the ideal leader, and some give strategic advice regarding the formation of states, warfare, and conquest. Both *The Tempest* and the *Diario,* directly and indirectly, raise questions about leadership and the appropriate limits of power. In what ways are Prospero and Columbus Renaissance heroes?

John Milton, *Paradise Lost,* p. 575. Many readers, especially in the early nineteenth century, saw Satan as the true hero of Milton's *Paradise Lost.* His proud defiance, his martial prowess, his command of rhetoric, and even his mental anguish made him seem a more dynamic and noble character than Adam, God, or the Son. In light of the advice to princes and rulers in this section, consider Satan as a Renaissance hero: What qualities of leadership does he demonstrate? How does he meet or fulfill the ideal standards of the scholar-soldier-prince delineated in these texts?

■ PRONUNCIATION

Aeneas: uh-NEE-us
Aeneid: uh-NEE-id
Alp Arslan: AHLP ars-LAHN
Arjuna: AR-joo-nuh
Cosimo de Medici: KOH-see-moh day-MED-ih-chee
Hayashi: high-YAH-shee
Malikshah: muh-LIK-shuh
Mughal: MOO-guhl
Muqaddimah: moo-KAH-dih-muh
Nizam al-Mulk: nee-ZAHM ahl-MOOK
Seljuk: SEL-juk, -jook
Zhu Xi: joo-SHEE

Nizam al-Mulk
1018–1092

nee-ZAHM ahl-MOOK

AB-uh-sid; SOO-nii

GAZ-nuh-vidz

koo-rah-SAHN

muh-LIK-shuh

Nizam al-Mulk, which means "Regulator of the Kingdom," is the title given to Abu Ali Hasan ibn Ali. He was a Persian in the employ of the Seljuk Turks, converts to Islam from Central Asia who by the middle of the eleventh century occupied some of the former territory of the central **Abassid** empire, including Persia, Armenia, and Turkey. A devout **Sunni Moslem**, he was one of the most formidable statesmen of the Muslim world in the eleventh century. Having served as an official for the **Ghaznavids**, who had ruled in Turkey before the Seljuks took power, he became the chief administrator of **Khurasan** and eventually a powerful vizier in the courts of the second and third sultans of the Seljuk Turks, Alp Arslan (r. 1063–72) and Alp Arslan's son, **Malikshah** (r. 1072–92). Taking the lead in setting policy for both sultans, Nizam al-Mulk introduced many administrative reforms and founded the Nizamiyya Madrasa, an institute for Islamic education, in Baghdad. His institute promoted edu-

***Seljuk Sultan,* Thirteenth Century**
From a Turkish manuscript titled "The Best Maxims and Most Precious Dictums of al-Mubashir," this illustration shows the sultan on a throne flanked by two servants. (The Art Archive / Topkapi Museum Istanbul / Dagli Orti)

cation in Orthodox Sunni theology as well as in the sciences and philosophy, and its success led to the proliferation of similar schools providing free secondary and higher education in the Arab world. Nizam al-Mulk eventually lost favor, became the butt of several satires, and was ousted from power with the fall of Malikshah in 1092. At the age of seventy-three, Nizam al-Mulk was assassinated by an agent of one of his enemies.

Like Machiavelli, Nizam al-Mulk drew on his vast education and experience to write a treatise on government. Unlike *The Prince,* however, *The Book of Government* aims to establish an ideal model for a centralized monarchy as well as to serve as a book of practical advice for a king. Beginning with an exposition of the divine sanction of the king and his mission to govern with wisdom, charity, and justice, *The Book of Government* moves to enumerate the measures a ruler must take in order to maintain his power and rule according to the precepts of Islamic law and scripture. The book recommends that the ruler seek out well-informed advisers, that he ensure his agents act fairly, and that he remain responsive to the needs of his subjects. It further advises the king on how best to choose companions, how to treat ambassadors, how to win the loyalty of his troops, and to be wary of their wives. Above all, *The Book of Government* urges the king to maintain a constant vigilance.

FROM

The Book of Government or Rules for Kings

Translated by Hubert Darke

Chapter One

On the turn of Fortune's wheel and in praise of The Master of the World — may Allah confirm his sovereignty

1. In every age and time God (be He exalted) chooses one member of the human race and, having adorned and endowed him with kingly virtues, entrusts him with the interests of the world and the well-being of His servants; He charges that person to close the doors of corruption, confusion, and discord, and He imparts to him such dignity and majesty in the eyes and hearts of men, that under his just rule they may live their lives in constant security and ever wish for his reign to continue.

2. Whenever — Allah be our refuge! — there occurs any disobedience or disregard of divine laws on the part of His servants, or any failure in devotion and attention to the commands of The Truth (be He exalted), and He wishes to chasten them and make them taste the retribution for their deeds — may God not deal us such a fate, and keep us far from such a calamity! — verily the wrath of The Truth overtakes those people and He forsakes them for the vileness of their disobedience; anarchy rears its head in their midst, opposing swords are drawn, blood is shed, and whoever has the stronger hand does whatever he wishes, until those sinners are all destroyed in tumults and bloodshed, and the world becomes free and clear of them; and through the wickedness of such sinners may innocent persons too perish in the tumults; just as, by analogy, when a reed-bed catches fire every dry particle is consumed and much wet stuff is burnt also, because it is near to that which is dry.

3. Then by divine decree one human being acquires some prosperity and power, and according to his deserts The Truth bestows good fortune upon him and gives him wit and wisdom, wherewith he may employ his subordinates every one according to his merits and confer upon each a dignity and a station proportionate to his powers. He selects ministers and their functionaries from among the people, and giving a rank and post to each, he relies upon them for the efficient conduct of affairs spiritual and temporal. If his subjects tread the path of obedience and busy themselves with their tasks he will keep them untroubled by hardships, so that they may pass their time at ease in the shadow of his justice. If one of his officers or ministers commits any impropriety or oppression, he will only keep him at his post provided that he responds to correction, advice, or punishment, and wakes up from the sleep of negligence; if he fails to mend his ways, he will retain him no longer, but change him for someone who is deserving; and when his subjects are ungrateful for benefits and do not appreciate security and ease, but ponder treachery in their hearts, shewing unruliness and overstepping their bounds, he will admonish them for their misdeeds, and punish them in proportion to their crimes. Having done that

he will cover their sins with the skirt of pardon and oblivion. Further he will bring to pass that which concerns the advance of civilization, such as constructing underground channels, digging main canals, building bridges across great waters, rehabilitating villages and farms, raising fortifications, building new towns, and erecting lofty buildings and magnificent dwellings; he will have inns built on the highways and schools for those who seek knowledge; for which things he will be renowned for ever; he will gather the fruit of his good works in the next world and blessings will be showered upon him. [. . .]

Chapter Two

On recognizing the extent of God's grace towards kings

1. It is for kings to observe His pleasure (His name be glorified) and the pleasure of The Truth is in the charity which is done to His creatures and in the justice which is spread among them. A kingdom which is blessed by its people will endure and increase from day to day, while its king will enjoy power and prosperity; in this world he will acquire good fame, in the next world salvation, and his reckoning will be the easier. Great men have said, "A kingdom may last while there is irreligion, but it will not endure when there is oppression." [. . .]

Chapter Eight

On enquiry and investigation into matters of religion, religious law, and suchlike

1. It is incumbent upon the king to enquire into religious matters, to be acquainted with the divine precepts and prohibitions and put them into practice, and to obey the commands of God (be He exalted); it is his duty to respect doctors of religion and pay their salaries out of the treasury, and he should honour pious and abstemious men. Furthermore it is fitting that once or twice a week he should invite religious elders to his presence and hear from them the commands of The Truth; he should listen to interpretations of the Qur'an and traditions of The Prophet (may Allah pray for him and give him peace); and he should hear stories about just kings and tales of the prophets (upon them be peace). During that time he should free his mind from worldly cares and give his ears and attention [wholly] to them. Let him bid them take sides and hold a debate, and let him ask questions about what he does not understand; when he has learnt the answers let him commit them to memory. After this has gone on for some time it will become a habit, and it will not be long before he has learnt and memorized most of the precepts of divine law, the meanings of the Quran and the traditions of The Prophet (upon him be peace). Then the way of prudence and rectitude in both spiritual and temporal affairs will be open to him; no heretic or innovator will be able to turn him from that path. His judgment will be strengthened and he will increase in justice and equity; vanity and heresy will vanish from his kingdom and great works will spring from his hands. The roots of wickedness, corruption, and discord will be cut out in the time of his empire. The hand of the righteous shall become strong and the wicked shall be no more. In this

world he shall have fame, and in the next world he shall find salvation, high degree, and inestimable reward. In his age men will more than ever delight in gaining knowledge. [. . .]

Chapter Ten

Concerning intelligence agents and reporters and [their importance in] administering the affairs of the country

1. It is the king's duty to enquire into the condition of his peasantry and army, both far and near, and to know more or less how things are. If he does not do this he is at fault and people will charge him with negligence, laziness, and tyranny, saying, "Either the king knows about the oppression and extortion going on in the country, or he does not know. If he knows and does nothing to prevent it and remedy it, that is because he is an oppressor like the rest and acquiesces in their oppression; and if he does not know then he is negligent and ignorant." Neither of these imputations is desirable. Inevitably therefore he must have postmasters; and in every age in the time of ignorance and of Islam, kings have had postmasters, through whom they have learnt everything that goes on, good and bad. For instance if anybody wrongly took so much as a chicken or a bag of straw from another—and that five hundred farsangs [about 1500 miles] away—the king would know about it and have the offender punished, so that others knew that the king was vigilant. In every place they appointed informers and so far checked the activities of oppressors that men enjoyed security and justice for the pursuit of trade and cultivation. But this is a delicate business involving some unpleasantness; it must be entrusted to the hands and tongues and pens of men who are completely above suspicion and without self-interest, for the weal or woe of the country depends on them. They must be directly responsible to the king and not to anyone else; and they must receive their monthly salaries regularly from the treasury so that they may do their work without any worries. In this way the king will know of every event that takes place and will be able to give his orders as appropriate, meting out unexpected reward, punishment, or commendation to the persons concerned. When a king is like this, men are always eager to be obedient, fearing the king's displeasure, and nobody can possibly have the audacity to disobey the king or plot any mischief. Thus the employment of intelligence agents and reporters contributes to the justice, vigilance, and prudence of the king, and to the prosperity of the country. [. . .]

Chapter Thirteen

On sending spies and using them for the good of the country and the people

1. Spies must constantly go out to the limits of the kingdom in the guise of merchants, travellers, sufis, pedlars (of medicines), and mendicants, and bring back reports of everything they hear, so that no matters of any kind remain concealed,

and if anything [untoward] happens it can in due course be remedied. In the past it has often happened that governors, assignees, officers and army-commanders have planned rebellion and resistance, and plotted mischief against the king; but spies forestalled them and informed the king, who was thus enabled to set out immediately with all speed and, coming upon them unawares, to strike them down and frustrate their plans; and if any foreign king or army was preparing to attack the country, the spies informed the king, and he took action and repelled them. Likewise they brought news, whether good or bad, about the condition of the peasants, and the king gave the matter his attention, as did ʿAdud ad Daula on one occasion. [. . .]

Chapter Seventeen

Concerning boon-companions and intimates of the king and the conduct of their affairs

1. A king cannot do without suitable boon-companions with whom he can enjoy complete freedom and intimacy. The constant society of nobles [such as] margraves and generals tends to diminish the king's majesty and dignity because they become too arrogant. As a general rule people who are employed in any official capacity should not be admitted as boon-companions nor should those who are accepted for companionship be appointed to any public office, because by virtue of the liberty they enjoy in the king's company they will indulge in high-handed practices and oppress the people. Officers should always be in a state of fear of the king, while boon-companions need to be familiar. If an officer is familiar he tends to oppress the peasantry; but if a boon-companion is not familiar the king will not find any pleasure or relaxation in his company. Boon-companions should have a fixed time for their appearance; after the king has given audience and the nobles have retired, then comes the time for their turn.

2. There are several advantages in having boon-companions: firstly they are company for the king; secondly since they are with him day and night, they are in the position of bodyguards, and if any danger (we take refuge with Allah!) should appear, they will not hesitate to shield the king from it with their own bodies; and thirdly the king can say thousands of different things, frivolous and serious, to his boon-companions which would not be suitable for the ears of his wazir or other nobles, for they are his officials and functionaries; and fourthly all sorts of sundry tidings can be heard from boon-companions, for through their freedom they can report on matters, good and bad, whether drunk or sober; and in this there is advantage and benefit.

3. A boon-companion should be well-bred, accomplished and of cheerful face. He should have pure faith, be able to keep secrets and wear good clothes. He must possess an ample fund of stories and strange tales both amusing and serious, and be able to tell them well. He must always be a good talker and a pleasant partner; he should know how to play backgammon and chess, and if he can play a musical instrument and use a weapon, so much the better. He must always agree with the king, and

whatever the king says or does, he must exclaim, "Bravo!" and "Well done!" He should not be didactic with "Do this" and "Don't do that" for it will displease the king and lead to dislike. Where pleasure and entertainment are concerned, as in feasting, drinking, hunting, polo and wrestling—in all matters like these it is right that the king should consult with his boon-companions, for they are there for this purpose. On the other hand in everything to do with the country and its cultivation, the military and the peasantry, warfare, raids, punishments, gifts, stores and travels, it is better that he should take counsel with the ministers and nobles of the state and with experienced elders, for they are more skilled in these subjects. In this way matters will take their proper course. [. . .]

Chapter Eighteen

On having consultation with learned and experienced men

1. Holding consultations on affairs is a sign of sound judgment, high intelligence, and foresight. Every person has some knowledge and in every branch of knowledge one knows more and another less. One may have knowledge and never have put it into practice or tested it; another has that same knowledge, and has used it and tried it. For example one may have read in medical books the cure of this pain or that sickness and know by heart the names of all the specific medicines, but no more; while another knows these same medicines and has used them in treatment and tried them many times. Never will the first be on a level with the second. Likewise a man who has travelled widely and seen the world and experienced heat and cold and been in the midst of affairs is not to be compared with one who is untravelled and inexperienced. Thus it has been said that one ought to take counsel with the wise, the old and the experienced. Further, some people have sharper wits and quicker perception of affairs; others have duller intellects. The wise have said, "The counsel of one man is like the strength of one man, and the counsel of ten persons is as the strength of ten." Everybody in the world agrees that there has never been any mortal wiser than The Prophet (upon him be peace); and with all the wisdom that he had—for he could see behind him as well as in front; and the skies and the earth, the tablet and the pen, the throne and seat [of God], paradise and hell and all things in between were revealed to him, and Gabriel (upon him be peace) often used to visit him, bringing inspiration and giving news of things past and things to come—in spite of all this perfection, in spite of all his miracles, God (be He exalted) said to him [in the Qur'an 3. 153], "Consult them in affairs." ("O Muhammad, when you do any work or when you are confronted with an important matter, confer with your companions.") Since God commanded him to seek advice and even he needed counsel, it is obvious that nobody can need it less than he. [. . .]

Chapter Twenty-One
Concerning ambassadors and their treatment

1. When ambassadors come from foreign countries nobody is aware of their movements until they actually arrive at the city gates; nobody gives any information [that they are coming] and nobody makes any preparation for them; and they will surely attribute this to our negligence and indifference. So officers at the frontiers must be told that whenever anyone approaches their stations they should at once despatch a rider and find out who it is who is coming, how many men there are with him, mounted and unmounted, how much baggage and equipment he has, and what is his business. A trustworthy person must be appointed to accompany them and conduct them to the nearest big city; there he will hand them over to another agent who will likewise go with them to the next city (and district), and so on until they reach the court. Whenever they arrive at a place where there is cultivation, it must be a standing order that officers, tax-collectors, and assignees should give them hospitality and entertain them well so that they depart satisfied. When they return, the same procedure is to be followed. Whatever treatment is given to an ambassador, whether good or bad, it is as if it were done to the very king who sent him; and kings have always shewn the greatest respect to one another and treated envoys well, for by this their own dignity has been enhanced. And if at any time there has been disagreement or enmity between kings, and if ambassadors have still come and gone as occasion requires, and discharged their missions according to their instructions, never have they been molested or treated with less than usual courtesy. Such a thing would be disgraceful, as God (to Him be power and glory) says [in the Qur'an 24. 53], "The messenger has only to convey the message plainly."

2. It should also be realized that when kings send ambassadors to one another their purpose is not merely the message or the letter which they communicate openly, but secretly they have a hundred other points and objects in view. In fact they want to know about the state of roads, mountain-passes, rivers and grazing grounds, to see whether an army can pass or not; where fodder is available and where not; who are the officers in every place; what is the size of that king's army and how well it is armed and equipped; what is the standard of his table and his company; what is the organization and etiquette of his court and audience-hall; does he play polo and hunt; what are his qualities and manners, his designs and intentions, his appearance and bearing; is he cruel or just, old or young; is his country flourishing or decaying; are his troops contented or not; are the peasants rich or poor; is he avaricious or generous; is he alert or negligent in affairs; is his wazir competent or the reverse, of good faith and high principles or of impure faith and bad principles; are his generals experienced and battle-tried or not; are his boon-companions polite and worthy; what are his likes and dislikes, in his cups is he jovial and good-natured or not; is he strict in religious matters and does he shew magnanimity and mercy or is he careless; does he incline more to jesting or to gravity; and does he prefer boys or women. So that, if at any time they want to win over that king, or oppose his designs or criticize his faults, being informed of all his affairs they can think out their plan of

campaign, and being aware of all the circumstances, they can take effective action, as happened to your humble servant in the time of The Martyr Sultan Alp Arslan[1] (may Allah sanctify his soul). [. . .]

Chapter Forty-Two

On the subject of those who wear the veil, and keeping underlings in their place

1. The king's underlings must not be allowed to assume power, for this causes the utmost harm and destroys the king's splendour and majesty. This particularly applies to women, for they are wearers of the veil and have not complete intelligence. Their purpose is the continuation of the lineage of the race, so the more noble their blood the better, and the more chaste their bearing the more admirable and acceptable they are. But when the king's wives begin to assume the part of rulers, they base their orders on what interested parties tell them, because they are not able to see things with their own eyes in the way that men constantly look at the affairs of the outside world. They give orders following what they are told by those who work amongst them such as chamberlains and servants. Naturally their commands are the opposite of what is right, and mischief ensues; the king's dignity suffers and the people are afflicted with trouble; ruin comes to the state and the religion; men's wealth is dissipated and the ruling class are put to vexation. In all ages nothing but disgrace, infamy, discord, and corruption have resulted when kings have been dominated by their wives. Let us discuss a little of this subject in the hope that much will be made clear.

2. The first man who suffered loss and underwent pain and trouble for obeying a woman was Adam (upon him be peace) who did the bidding of Eve and ate the wheat, with the result that he was expelled from paradise, and wept for two hundred years until God had mercy on him and accepted his repentance.

[1] **Sultan Alp Arslan** (1029–1072): The second sultan of the Seljuk Turks, who had captured Baghdad in 1055; Arslan ruled from 1063 to 1072, during which time he extended the boundaries of the Seljuk empire into Armenia, Georgia, and Syria.

IBN KHALDUN
1332–1406

Born into an aristocratic family in Tunis in 1332, **Abd-al-Rhman ibn Khaldun** received an extraordinary education in the **QUR'AN** (**KORAN**), the **HADITH**, law, and Arabic poetry and language at the hands of tutors and scholars. In his early twenties he left Tunis for Fez, where he began his long political career. A talented and gifted scholar, thinker, and observer of human affairs, Ibn Khaldun had a turbulent career, working under several different rulers in Spain and in Northern Africa, until about 1375, when he was forced to take refuge in a village in Oran, Algeria. There he began his *Universal History,* which many readers celebrate as the first great work of historical writing in world literature. In 1377 he completed the work's famous introduction, known as *The Muqaddimah.* In 1383, Ibn Khaldun set out to make his ***HAJJ,*** the Muslim's required pilgrimage to Mecca, but was detained in Cairo by the Egyptian ruler **al-Malik az-Zahir Barquq**, who was drawn to the writer's considerable abilities as an administrator and legal adviser. Ibn Khaldun spent the rest of his life

ib-un kahl-DOON

ha-DEETH

ahl-mah-LEEK
ah zah-HEER
bar-KOOK

***Sultan,* Fourteenth Century**
This miniature from an illuminated manuscript shows a sultan dispensing justice. (Giraudon / Art Resource, NY)

in Cairo, where he became professor of law at Qamhiyah College and was appointed to various offices, including a prestigious judgeship.

The Muqaddimah, sometimes translated as "Introduction" or "Prolegomena," is one of the first books to reflect critically on the sociological, geographical, cultural, and even psychological factors that play into the making of history. For this reason Ibn Khaldun is sometimes called the "father of sociology." The selections included here draw from Chapter 3 of his great treatise, where Ibn Khaldun discusses the origins of dynasties and royal authority, the various ways in which such authority may be eroded, and the relations between the ruler and his ministers and subjects. Like Machiavelli in *The Prince,* Ibn Khaldun is concerned to show the mechanisms by which a ruler maintains and loses his authority, and he supports his analysis with historical examples. For Ibn Khaldun the consequences of a breakdown of authority are not just the loss of power but the breakdown of civilization itself.

The text is from *The Muqaddimah: An Introduction to History,* translated by Franz Rosenthal and abridged and edited by N. J. Dawood, Princeton University Press, 1967. Unless otherwise indicated, the notes are those of the editors.

Il Muqaddimah

Translated by Franz Rosenthal

FROM

Chapter 3

On dynasties, royal authority, and the caliphate

1 ROYAL AUTHORITY AND LARGE-SCALE DYNASTIC POWER ARE ATTAINED ONLY THROUGH A GROUP AND GROUP FEELING

This is because aggressive and defensive strength is obtained only through group feeling which means affection and willingness to fight and die for each other.

Now, royal authority is a noble and enjoyable position. It comprises all the good things of the world, the pleasures of the body, and the joys of the soul. Therefore, there is, as a rule, great competition for it. It rarely is handed over (voluntarily), but it may be taken away. Thus, discord ensues. It leads to war and fighting, and to attempts to gain superiority. Nothing of all this comes about except through group feeling, as we have also mentioned.

This situation is not at all understood by the great mass. They forget it, because they have forgotten the time when the dynasty first became established. They have grown up in settled areas for a long time. They have lived there for successive generations. Thus, they know nothing about what took place with God's help at the beginning of the dynasty. They merely notice that the colouring of the men of the dynasty is determined, that people have submitted to them, and that group feeling is no longer needed to establish their power. They do not know how it was at the beginning and what difficulties had to be overcome by the founder. The inhabitants of Spain especially have forgotten group feeling and its influence, because so long a time has passed, and because as a rule they have no need of the power of group feeling, since their country has been annihilated and is depleted of tribal groups.

2 WHEN A DYNASTY IS FIRMLY ESTABLISHED, IT CAN DISPENSE WITH GROUP FEELING

The reason for this is that people find it difficult to submit to general dynastic (power) at the beginning, unless they are forced into submission by strong superiority. The new government is something strange. People are not familiar with, or used to, its rule. But once leadership is firmly vested in the members of the family qualified to exercise royal authority in the dynasty, and once (royal authority) has been passed on by inheritance over many generations and through successive dynasties, the beginnings are forgotten, and the members of that family are clearly marked as leaders. It has become a firmly established article of faith that one must be subservient and submissive to them. People will fight with them in their behalf, as they would fight for the articles of faith. By this time, (the rulers) will not need much group (feeling to maintain) their power. It is as if obedience to the government were a divinely revealed book that cannot be changed or opposed.

(The rulers) maintain their hold over the government and their own dynasty with the help, then, either of clients and followers who grew up in the shadow and power of group feeling, or of tribal groups of a different descent who have become their clients.

Something of the sort happened to the ʿAbbâsids.[1] The group feeling of the Arabs had been destroyed by the time of the reign of al-Muʿtaṣim and his son, al-Wâthiq. They tried to maintain their hold over the government thereafter with the help of Persian, Turkish, Daylam, Saljûq,[2] and other clients. Then, the (non-Arabs) and their clients gained power over the provinces (of the realm). The influence of the dynasty grew smaller, and no longer extended beyond the environs of Baghdad. Eventually, the Daylam closed in upon and took possession of (that area). The caliphs were ruled by them. Then (the Daylam), in turn, lost control. The Saljûqs seized power after the Daylam, and the (caliphs) were ruled by them. Then (the Saljûqs), in turn, lost control. Finally, the Tatars closed in. They killed the caliph and wiped out every vestige of the dynasty. [. . .]

[1] **ʿAbbâsids:** The Abbâsid caliphate, under which Islamic culture flourished especially in the early years, was founded in 750 and lasted until 1258, when the Mongols (Tatars) sacked Baghdad. Muhammad al-Mu'tasim (r. 833–42) assumed the caliphate at Baghdad after the death of his father, al-Ma'mum, the founder of the House of Wisdom and patron of the arts. He was succeeded by his son al-Wathiq (r. 842–47).

[2] **Saljûq:** Ibn Khaldun provides a capsulated history of the rise and decline of the great Abbasid empire here. At its height, with the help of client governments such as the Seljuk Turks and mercenaries from Daylam, a region along the southern shore of the Caspian Sea, the Abbâsid caliphate exercised authority over a wide area extending outward from the political and religious center at Baghdad. Eventually, in 1258, the caliphate fell to the Mongols (Tatars), who sacked Baghdad and brought the empire to a close.

3 MEMBERS OF A ROYAL FAMILY MAY BE ABLE TO FOUND A DYNASTY THAT CAN DISPENSE WITH GROUP FEELING

This is because the group feeling in which (a member of a royal family) shares may have much power over nations and races, and the inhabitants of remote regions who support his power may be obedient (to that family) and submissive. So, when such a person secedes, leaving the seat of his rule and the home of his might, and joins those inhabitants of remote regions, they adopt him. They support his rule and help him. They take care of establishing his dynasty on a firm basis. They hope that he will be confirmed in his family (rights) and take the power away from his kinsmen. They do not desire to share in any way in his rule, as they subject themselves to his group feeling and submit to the colouring of material superiority firmly belonging to him and his people. They believe, as in an article of faith, in being obedient to (him and his people). Were they to desire to share his rule with him or to rule without him, "the earth would be shaken."[3] . . .

20 THOSE WHO GAIN POWER OVER THE RULER DO NOT SHARE WITH HIM IN THE SPECIAL TITLE THAT GOES WITH ROYAL AUTHORITY

This is because the first men to achieve royal and governmental authority at the beginning of the dynasty do so with the help of the group feeling of their people and with the help of their own group feeling which causes their people to follow them until they and their people have definitely adopted the colouring of royal authority and superiority. The colouring, then, continues to exist. Through it the identity and persistence of the dynasty are assured.

The person who gains superiority (over the ruler) may have a share in the group feeling that belongs to the tribe which has gained royal authority or to its clients and followers. However, his group feeling still is comprised by, and subordinate to, the group feeling of the family of the ruler. He cannot (take on) the colouring of royal authority. Thus, in gaining control, he does not plan to appropriate royal authority for himself openly, but only to appropriate its fruits, that is, the exercise of administrative, executive, and all other power. He gives the people of the dynasty the impression that he merely acts for the ruler and executes the latter's decisions from behind the curtain. He carefully refrains from using the attributes, emblems, or titles of royal authority. He avoids throwing any suspicion upon himself in this respect, even though he exercises full control. For, in his exercise of full control, he takes cover behind the curtain the ruler and his ancestors had set up to protect themselves from their own tribe when the dynasty came into being. He disguises his exercise of control under the form of acting as the ruler's representative.

Should he undertake to adopt (any of the royal prerogatives), the people who represent the group feeling and tribe of the ruler would resent it and contrive to appropriate (such prerogatives) for themselves, to his exclusion. He has no definite

[3] **"the earth would be shaken":** Qur'an 99.1 (1). [Translator's note.]

colouring to (make him appear suited for the royal prerogatives) or cause others to submit to him and obey him. (Any attempt by him to appropriate the royal prerogatives) would, thus, instantly precipitate his doom. . . .

21 THE TRUE CHARACTER AND DIFFERENT KINDS OF ROYAL AUTHORITY

Royal authority is an institution that is natural to mankind. We have explained before that human beings cannot live and exist except through social organization and co-operation for the purpose of obtaining their food and other necessities of life. When they have organized, necessity requires that they deal with each other and satisfy their needs. Each one will stretch out his hand for whatever he needs and (try simply to) take it, since injustice and aggressiveness are in the animal nature. The others, in turn, will try to prevent him from taking it, motivated by wrathfulness and spite and the strong human reaction when one's own property is menaced. This causes dissension, which leads to hostilities, and hostilities lead to trouble and bloodshed and loss of life, which lead to the destruction of the species. Now, (the human species) is one of the things the Creator has especially (enjoined us) to preserve.

People, thus, cannot persist in a state of anarchy and without a ruler who keeps them apart. Therefore, they need a person to restrain them. He is their ruler. As is required by human nature, he must be a forceful ruler, one who exercises authority. In this connection, group feeling is absolutely necessary, for as we have stated before, aggressive and defensive enterprises can succeed only with the help of group feeling. As one can see, royal authority of this kind is a noble institution, toward which all claims are directed, and one that needs to be defended. Nothing of the sort can materialize except with the help of group feelings, as has been mentioned before.

Group feelings differ. Each group feeling exercises its own authority and superiority over the people and family adhering to it. Not every group feeling has royal authority. Royal authority, in reality, belongs only to those who dominate subjects, collect taxes, send out (military) expeditions, protect the frontier regions, and have no one over them who is stronger than they. This is generally accepted as the real meaning of royal authority.

There are people whose group feeling falls short of accomplishing (one or another of these things which constitute) part of (real royal authority), such as protecting the frontier regions, or collecting taxes, or sending out (military) expeditions. Such royal authority is defective and not royal authority in the real meaning of the term.

Then, there are people whose group feeling is not strong enough to gain control over all the other group feelings or to stop everyone, so that there exists an authority superior to theirs. Their royal authority is also defective, and not royal authority in the real meaning of the term. It is exercised, for instance, by provincial amirs and regional chieftains who are all under one dynasty. This situation is often found in far-flung dynasties. I mean that there are rulers of provincial and remote regions who rule their own people but also obey the central power of the dynasty.

22 EXAGGERATED HARSHNESS IS HARMFUL TO ROYAL AUTHORITY AND IN MOST CASES CAUSES ITS DESTRUCTION

The interest subjects have in their ruler is not interest in his person and body, for example, in his good figure, handsome face, large frame, wide knowledge, good handwriting, or acute mind. Their interest in him lies in his relation to them. Royal and governmental authority is something relative, a relationship between ruler and subjects. Government becomes a reality when (a ruler) rules over subjects and handles their affairs. A ruler is he who has subjects, and subjects are persons who have a ruler. The quality accruing to the ruler from the fact of his correlative relation with his subjects is called "rulership." That is, he rules them, and if such rulership and its concomitants are of good quality, the purpose of government is most perfectly achieved. If such rulership is good and beneficial, it will serve the interests of the subjects. If it is bad and unfair, it will be harmful to them and cause their destruction.

Good rulership is equivalent to mildness. If the ruler uses force and is ready to mete out punishment and eager to expose the faults of people and to count their sins, (his subjects) become fearful and depressed and seek to protect themselves against him through lies, ruses, and deceit. This becomes a character trait of theirs. Their mind and character become corrupted. They often abandon (the ruler) on the battlefield and (fail to support his) defensive enterprises. The decay of (sincere) intentions causes the decay of (military) protection. The subjects often conspire to kill the ruler. Thus, the dynasty decays, and the fence (that protects it) lies in ruin. If the ruler continues to keep a forceful grip on his subjects, group feeling will be destroyed. If the ruler is mild and overlooks the bad sides of his subjects, they will trust him and take refuge with him. They love him heartily and are willing to die for him in battle against his enemies. Everything is then in order in the state.

The concomitants of good rulership are kindness to, and protection of, one's subjects. The true meaning of royal authority is realized when the ruler defends his subjects. To be kind and beneficent toward them is part of being mild to them and showing an interest in the way they live. These things are important for the ruler in gaining the love of his subjects.

An alert and very shrewd person rarely has the habit of mildness. Mildness is usually found in careless and unconcerned persons. The least (of the many drawbacks) of alertness (in a ruler) is that he imposes tasks upon his subjects that are beyond their ability, because he is aware of things they do not perceive and, through his genius, foresees the outcome of things at the start. (The ruler's excessive demands) may lead to his subjects' ruin. Muḥammad[4] said: "Follow the pace of the weakest among you."

Muḥammad therefore made it a condition that the ruler should not be too shrewd. For this quality is accompanied by tyrannical and bad rulership and by a tendency to make the people do things that it is not in their nature to do.

---

[4] **Muḥammad:** (c. 570–632), the great prophet and founder of Islam to whom Allah dictated the sacred scriptures of the Qur'an.

The conclusion is that it is a drawback in a political leader to be (too) clever and shrewd. Cleverness and shrewdness imply that a person thinks too much, just as stupidity implies that he is too rigid. In the case of all human qualities, the extremes are reprehensible, and the middle road is praiseworthy. This is, for instance, the case with generosity in relation to waste and stinginess, or with bravery in relation to foolhardiness and cowardice. And so it is with all the other human qualities. For this reason, the very clever person is said to have the qualities of a devil. He is called a "satan," or "a would-be satan," and the like. [. . .]

38 COMMERCIAL ACTIVITY ON THE PART OF THE RULER IS HARMFUL TO HIS SUBJECTS AND RUINOUS TO THE TAX REVENUE

A dynasty may find itself in financial straits, as we have mentioned before, on account of the number of (its luxurious) habits and on account of its expenditure and the insufficiency of the tax revenue to pay for its needs. It may require more money and higher revenues. Then, it sometimes imposes customs duties on the commercial activities of its subjects. Sometimes, it increases the kinds of customs duties, if (customs duties as such) had been introduced before. Sometimes, it applies torture to its officials and tax collectors and sucks their bones dry. (This happens) when officials and tax collectors are observed to have appropriated a good deal of tax money, which their accounts do not show.

Sometimes, the ruler himself may engage in commerce and agriculture, from desire to increase his revenues. He sees that merchants and farmers make (large) profits and have plenty of property and that their gains correspond to the capital they invest. Therefore, he starts to acquire livestock and fields in order to cultivate them for profit, purchase goods, and expose himself to fluctuations of the market. He thinks that this will improve his revenues and increase his profits.

However this is a great error. It causes harm to the subjects in many ways. First, farmers and merchants will find it difficult to buy livestock and merchandise and to procure cheaply the things that belong to (farming and commerce). The subjects have all the same or approximately the same amount of wealth. Competition between them already exhausts, or comes close to exhausting, their financial resources. Now, when the ruler, who has so much more money than they, competes with them, scarcely a single one of them will any longer be able to obtain the things he wants, and everybody will become worried and unhappy.

Furthermore, the ruler can appropriate much of (the agricultural produce and the available merchandise), if it occurs to him. (He can do this) by force or by buying things up at the cheapest possible price. Further, there may be no one who would dare to bid against him. Thus, he will be able to force the seller to lower his price. Further, when agricultural products such as corn, silk, honey, and sugar, etc., or goods of any kind, become available, the ruler cannot wait for a favourable market and a boom, because he has to take care of government needs. Therefore, he forces the merchants or farmers who deal in these particular products to buy from him. He will be satisfied only with the highest prices and more. (The merchants and farmers, on the other hand), will exhaust their liquid capital in such transactions. The merchandise they thus acquire will remain useless on their hands. They themselves will no longer be able to trade, which is what enables them to earn something and make their living. Often, they need money. Then, they have to sell the goods (that they were forced to buy from the ruler), at the lowest prices, during a slump in the market. Often, the merchant or farmer has to do the same thing over again. He thus exhausts his capital and has to go out of business.

This becomes an oft-repeated process. The trouble and financial difficulties and the loss of profit that it causes the subjects take away from them all incentives to effort, thus ruining the fiscal (structure). Most of the revenue from taxes comes from farmers and merchants, especially once customs duties have been introduced and the tax revenue has been augmented by means of them. Thus, when the farmer gives up agriculture and the merchant goes out of business, the revenue from taxes vanishes altogether or becomes dangerously low.

Were the ruler to compare the revenue from taxes with the small profits (he reaps from trading himself), he would find the latter negligible in comparison with the former. Even if (his trading) were profitable, it would still deprive him of a good deal of his revenue from taxes, so far as commerce is concerned. It is unlikely that customs duties would be levied on (the ruler's commercial activities). If, however, the same deals were made by others, the customs duties would be included in the tax total.

Furthermore (the trading of the ruler) may cause the destruction of civilization and hence the disintegration of the dynasty. When the subjects can no longer make their capital larger through agriculture and commerce, it will decrease and disappear as the result of expenditure. This will ruin their situation.

The Persians made no one king except members of the royal house. Further, they chose him from among those who possessed virtue, religion, education, liberality, bravery, and nobility. Then, they stipulated in addition that he should be just. Also, he was not to take a farm, as this would harm his neighbours. He was not to engage in trade, as this would of necessity raise the prices of all goods. And he was not to use slaves as servants, since they would not give good and beneficial advice.

It should be known that the finances of a ruler can be increased, and his financial resources improved, only through the revenue from taxes. This can be improved only through the equitable treatment of people with property and regard for them, so that their hopes rise, and they have the incentive to start making their capital bear fruit and grow. This, in turn, increases the ruler's revenues in taxes.

Amirs and other men in power in a country who engage in commerce and agriculture, reach a point where they undertake to buy agricultural products and goods from their owners who come to them, at prices fixed by themselves as they see fit. Then, they resell these things to the subjects under their control, at the proper times, at prices fixed by themselves. This is even more dangerous, harmful, and ruinous for the subjects than the aforementioned (procedure). The ruler is often influenced to choose such a (course) by those sorts of people—I mean, merchants and farmers—who bring him into contact with the profession in which they have been reared. They work with him, but for their own profit, to garner quickly as much money as they may wish, especially through profits reaped from doing business without having to pay taxes and customs duties. Exemption from taxes and customs duties is more likely than anything else to cause one's capital to grow, and it brings quick profits. These people do not understand how much damage is caused the ruler by each decrease in the revenue from taxes. The ruler, therefore, must guard against such persons, and not pay any attention to suggestions that are harmful to his revenues and his rule. [. . .]

41 INJUSTICE BRINGS ABOUT THE RUIN OF CIVILIZATION

Attacks on people's property remove the incentive to acquire and gain property. People, then, become of the opinion that the purpose and ultimate destiny of (acquiring property) is to have it taken away from them. The extent and degree to which property rights are infringed upon determines the extent and degree to which the efforts of the subjects to acquire property slacken. When attacks on (property) are extensive and general, affecting all means of making a livelihood, business inactivity, too, becomes general. If the attacks upon property are but light, the stoppage of gainful activity is correspondingly slight. Civilization and its well-being as well as business prosperity depend on productivity and people's efforts in all directions in their own interest and profit. When people no longer do business in order to make a living, and when they cease all gainful activity, the business of civilization slumps, and everything decays. People scatter everywhere in search of sustenance, to places outside the jurisdiction of their present government. The population of the particular region becomes sparse. The settlements there become empty. The cities lie in ruins. The disintegration causes the disintegration of the status of dynasty and ruler, because (their peculiar status) constitutes the form of civilization and the form necessarily decays when its matter (in this case, civilization) decays.

One may compare here the story that al-Mas'ûdî[5] tells in connection with the history of the Persians. In the days of King Bahrâm b. Bahrâm, the Môbedhân, the chief religious dignitary among the Persians, expressed to the King his disapproval of the latter's injustice and indifference to the consequences that his injustice must bring upon the dynasty. He did this through a parable, which he placed in the mouth of an owl. The King, hearing an owl's cry, asked the Môbedhân whether he understood what it was saying. He replied: "A male owl wanted to marry a female owl. The female owl, as a condition prior to consent, asked the male owl for the gift of twenty villages ruined in the days of Bahrâm, that she might hoot in them. (The male owl) accepted her condition and said to her: 'If the King continues to rule, I shall give you a thousand ruined villages. This is of all wishes the easiest to fulfil.' "

The King was stirred out of his negligence by that story. He had a private (talk) with the Môbedhân and asked him what he had in mind. He replied: "O King, the might of royal authority materializes only through the religious law, obedience toward God, and compliance with His commands and prohibitions. The religious law persists only through royal authority. Mighty royal authority is achieved only

[5] **al Mas'ûdî:** Hassan ibn Ali al-Mas'udi (c. 890–957) Muslim historian, geographer, and traveler, whose historical reflection and critical analysis anticipates the work of Ibn Khaldun. King Bahram (Varhran) was a third-century ruler of the Sassanian empire that stretched over what is now Iran and Iraq.

through men. Men persist only with the help of property. The only way to property is through cultivation. The only way to cultivation is through justice. Justice is a balance set up among mankind. The Lord set it up and appointed an overseer of it, and that is the ruler. You, O King, went after the farms and took them away from their owners and cultivators. They are the people who pay the land tax and from whom one gets money. You gave their farms as fiefs to your entourage and servants and to sluggards. They did not cultivate them and did not heed the consequences. (They did not look for the things) that would be good for the farms. They were leniently treated with regard to the land tax (and were not asked to pay it), because they were close to the king. The remaining landowners who did pay the land tax and cultivated their farms had to carry an unjust burden. Therefore, they left their farms and abandoned their settlements. They took refuge in farms that were far away or difficult (of access), and lived on them. Thus, cultivation slackened, and the farms were ruined. There was little money, and soldiers and subjects perished. Neighbouring rulers coveted the Persian realm, because they were aware of the fact that the basic materials that alone maintain the foundation of a realm had been cut off."

When the King heard that, he proceeded to look into (the affairs of) his realm. The farms were taken away from the intimates of the ruler and restored to their owners. They were again treated, as they had formerly been treated. They began again to cultivate (their farms). Those who had been weak gained in strength. The land was cultivated, and the country became prosperous. There was much money for the collectors of the land tax. The army was strengthened. The enemies' sources of (strength) were cut off. The frontier garrisons were manned. The ruler proceeded to take personal charge of his affairs. His days were prosperous, and his realm was well organized.

The lesson this teaches is that injustice ruins civilization, which has as its consequence the complete destruction of the dynasty. In this connection, one should disregard the fact that dynasties (centred) in great cities often infringe upon justice and still are not ruined. It should be known that this is the result of a relationship that exists between such infringements and the situation of the urban population. When a city is large and densely populated and unlimited in the variety of its conditions, the loss it suffers from hostile acts and injustice is small, because such losses take place gradually. Because of the great variety of conditions and the manifold productivity of a particular city, any loss may remain concealed. Its consequences will become visible only after some time. Thus, the dynasty which committed the infringements (of justice) may be replaced before the city is ruined. Another dynasty may make its appearance and restore the city with the help of its wealth. Thus, the (previous) loss which had remained concealed is made up and is scarcely noticed. This, however, happens only rarely. The proven fact is that civilization inevitably suffers losses through injustice and hostile acts, as we have mentioned, and it is the dynasty that suffers consequently.

Injustice should not be understood to imply only the confiscation of money or other property from the owners, without compensation and without cause. It is commonly understood in that way, but it is something more general than that.

Whoever takes someone's property, or uses him for forced labour, or presses an unjustified claim against him, or imposes upon him a duty not required by the religious law, does an injustice to that particular person. People who collect unjustified taxes commit an injustice. Those who infringe upon property commit an injustice. Those who take away property commit an injustice. Those who deny people their rights commit an injustice. Those who, in general, take property by force, commit an injustice. It is the dynasty that suffers from all these acts, inasmuch as civilization, which is the substance of the dynasty, is ruined when people have lost all incentive.

This is what Muḥammad actually had in mind when he forbade injustice. He meant the resulting destruction and ruin of civilization, which ultimately permits the eradication of the human species. This is what the religious law quite generally and wisely aims at in emphasizing five things as necessary: the preservation of (1) religion, (2) the soul (life), (3) the intellect, (4) progeny, and (5) property.

Since, as we have seen, injustice calls for the eradication of the species by leading to the ruin of civilization, it contains in itself a good reason for being prohibited. Consequently, it is important that it be forbidden.

If injustice were to be committed by every individual, the list of deterring punishments that would then have been given for it (in the religious law) would be as large as that given for the other (crimes) which lead to the destruction of the human species and which everybody is capable of committing, such as adultery, murder, and drunkenness. However, injustice can be committed only by persons who cannot be touched, only by persons who have power and authority. Therefore, injustice has been very much censured, and repeated threats against it have been expressed in the hope that perhaps the persons who are able to commit injustice will find a restraining influence in themselves.

One of the greatest injustices and one contributing most to the destruction of civilization is the unjustified imposition of tasks and the use of the subjects for forced labour. This is so because labour belongs to the things that constitute capital. Gain and sustenance represent the value realized from labour among civilized people. By their efforts and all their labours they (acquire) capital and (make a) profit. They have no other way to make a profit except (through labour). Subjects employed in cultural enterprises gain their livelihood and profit from such activities. Now, if they are obliged to work outside their own field and are used for forced labour unrelated to their (ordinary ways of) making a living, they no longer have any profit and are thus deprived of the price of their labour, which is their capital (asset). They suffer, and a good deal of their livelihood is gone, or even all of it. If this occurs repeatedly, all incentive to cultural enterprise is destroyed, and they cease utterly to make an effort. This leads to the destruction and ruin of civilization.

An injustice even greater and more destructive of civilization and the dynasty is the appropriation of people's property by buying their possessions as cheaply as possible and then reselling the merchandise to them at the highest possible prices by means of forced sales and purchases. Often, people have to accept (high) prices with the privilege of later payment. They console themselves for the loss they suffer with the hope that the market will fluctuate in favour of the merchandise that had been sold to them at such a high price, and that their loss will be cancelled later on. But then, they are required to make payment at once, and they are forced to sell the merchandise at the lowest possible price. The loss involved in the two transactions affects their capital.

This (situation) affects all kinds of merchants, those resident in town and those who import merchandise from elsewhere, the pedlars and shopkeepers who deal in food and fruit, and the craftsmen who deal in the instruments and implements that are in general use. The loss affects all professions and classes quite generally. This goes on from hour to hour. It causes capital funds to dwindle. The only possibility that remains is for the merchants to go out of business, because their capital is gone, as it can no longer be restored by the profits. Merchants who come from elsewhere for the purchase and sale of merchandise are slow to come, because of that situation. Business declines, and the subjects lose their livelihood, which, generally, comes from trading. Therefore, if no (trading) is being done in the markets, they have no livelihood, and the tax revenue of the ruler decreases or deteriorates, since, in the middle (period) of a dynasty and later on, most of the tax revenue comes from customs duties on commerce. This leads to the dissolution of the dynasty and the decay of urban civilization. The disintegration comes about gradually and imperceptibly.

This happens whenever the ways and means of seizing property described above are used. On the other hand, if it is taken outright and if the hostile acts are extended to affect the property, the wives, the lives, the skins, and the honour of people, it will lead to sudden disintegration and decay and the quick destruction of the dynasty. It will result in disturbances leading to complete destruction.

On account of these evil consequences, all such (unfair activities) are prohibited by the religious law. The religious law legalizes the use of cunning in trading, but forbids depriving people of their property illegally. The purpose is to prevent such evil (consequences), which would lead to the destruction of civilization through disturbances or the lack of opportunity to make a living.

It should be known that all these (practices) are caused by the need for more money on the part of dynasty and ruler, because they have become accustomed to luxurious living. Their expenditure increases, and much spending is done. Their ordinary income does not meet (the expenditures). Therefore, the ruler invents new sorts and kinds of taxes, in order to increase the revenues and to be able to balance the budget. But luxury continues to grow, and spending increases on account of it. The need for (appropriating) people's property becomes stronger and stronger. In this way, the authority of the dynasty shrinks until its influence is wiped out and its identity lost and it is defeated by an attacker. [. . .]

Vespasiano da Bisticci
1421–1498

A seller of rare and fine books, a librarian, an important collector of books and manuscripts, and a writer, Vespasiano da Bisticci in many ways typifies the humanist-artist-entrepreneur. As such, he compares to figures such as **Benvenuto Cellini** (1500–1571) who rose to the top of their game by means not solely of intelligence, education, and literary or artistic talent but also of entrepreneurial genius. The books in Bisticci's collection were so well known that important men, including Cosimo de' Medici and the Duke of Urbino, would meet at his bookshop. Bisticci helped supply and organize many of the private libraries that were springing up in Italy along with the desire for humanistic learning. In his workshop — one of the growing numbers of scriptoria in fourteenth-century Europe — he maintained an operation where teams of copyists could write up to forty manuscript copies at a time. His copyists once produced nearly two hundred volumes for Cosimo de' Medici in less than two years.

ben-vay-NOO-toh

cheh-LEE-nee

When the developments in the printing press made his workshop obsolete, Bisticci gave up his business to devote his time fully to writing his memoirs and the life histories of many of the luminaries of his time. Though Bisticci was by no means disinterested in his approach to his subjects, his pieces capture the spirit of the age and present a kind of portrait in words of fifteenth-century Florence as a whole. Among the most important of the many lives Bisticci documented is that of Cosimo de' Medici (1389–1464), who inherited the banking and trading fortune of his father, Giovanni de' Medici (1360–1429).

The Medici family was one of the most powerful and influential dynasties in Italy, and Cosimo's son, Lorenzo the Magnificent (1449–1492), was one of the great patrons of learning and the arts in the Italian Renaissance. Cosimo, who has been called the "merchant prince," exemplifies some of the qualities of the Renaissance hero, and while he was a shrewd businessman who expanded the family fortune, he was also a Latinist, a collector of books, and a patron to men of letters.

Memoirs

Translated by William George and Emily Waters

[Cosimo de' Medici]

Cosimo di Giovanni de' Medici was of most honourable descent, a very prominent citizen, and one of great weight in the republic. He was well versed in Latin letters, both sacred and secular, of capable judgment in all matters and able to argue thereupon. His teacher was Roberto dei Rossi, a good Greek and Latin scholar and of excellent carriage. At this time many other youths of good station were his fellow-pupils: Domenico di Lionardo Buoninsegni, Bartolo Tebaldi, Luca di Messer Maso degli Albizzi, Messer Alessandro degli Alessandri, and many others who came together regularly for instruction. Roberto lived in his own house, unmarried, and when he went out he was usually accompanied by the above-named, who were held in much esteem both for their good conduct and learning: moreover, Roberto would often entertain his pupils at table. He made a most excellent will which divided his large library of books written by his own hand—and he was one of the finest of scribes—amongst his pupils.

Returning to Cosimo, he had a knowledge of Latin which would scarcely have been looked for in one occupying the station of a leading citizen engrossed with affairs. He was grave in temperament, prone to associate with men of high station who disliked frivolity, and averse from all buffoons and actors and those who spent time unprofitably. He had a great liking for men of letters and sought their society, chiefly conversing with the Fra Ambrogio degli Agnoli, Messer Lionardo d' Arezzo, Nicolao Nicoli, Messer Carlo d' Arezzo, and Messer Poggio. His natural bent was to discuss matters of importance; and, although at this time the city was full of men of distinction, his worth was recognised on account of his praiseworthy qualities, and he began to find employment in affairs of every kind. By his twenty-fifth year he had gained great reputation in the city, and, as it was recognised that he was aiming at a high position, feeling ran strong against him, and the report of those who knew roused a fear that he would win success. The Council of Constance,[1] gathered from all parts of the world, was then sitting; and Cosimo, who was well acquainted with foreign affairs as well as those of the city, went thither with two objects: one to allay the ill-feeling against him, and the other to see the Council which had in hand the reform of the Church, now greatly vexed by divisions. After staying some time at Constance, and witnessing the procedure of the Council, he visited almost all parts of Germany and France, spending some two years in travel. He hoped thus to let cool the ill-feeling against him which had greatly increased. He understood his own disposition which made him discontented with low estate, and made him seek to rise out of the crowd of men of small account. Many people remarked this tendency, and warned him that it might lead him into danger of death or exile. By way of lessening this resentment he began to absent himself from the palace, and to consort with men of low estate without either money or position, all by way of temporising; but his foes took this in bad part, affirming that what he did was a mere pretence to abate the suspicions of others. [. . .]

Cosimo having come back to Florence, to the great satisfaction of the citizens and of his own party, his friends procured the banishment of divers of those who had opposed his recall, and of those who were neutral; at the same time bringing forward new people. He rewarded those who had brought him back, lending to one

[1] **Council of Constance:** A meeting of bishops from all over Europe called in 1414 by the Pisan pope John XXIII (r. 1400–15) to try to end the schism that had divided the Catholic Church since 1378, as well as to deal with corruption in the Church and the heresies of reformers John Wycliff and John Hus. The council issued an edict condemning Wycliff, but it did not resolve the problem of corruption or division within the Church.

a good sum of money, and making a gift to another to help marry his daughter or buy lands, while great numbers were banished as rebels. He and his party took every step to strengthen their own position, following the example of those of the government of 1433. In Florence there were many citizens who were men of weight in the state; and, as they were friendly to Cosimo and had helped to recall him, they retained their influence. Cosimo found that he must be careful to keep their support by temporising and making believe that he was fain they should enjoy power equal to his own. Meantime he kept concealed the source of his influence in the city as well as he could. I have no wish to set down here everything that I could tell, for what I write is only by way of memorandum. I leave the rest to anyone who may write his life. But I say that anyone who may be fain to bring new forms into the state, that those who wrought the changes in 1433, brought ruin to themselves and to the state also. Many leading citizens, men of weight, never wished for these changes, declaring they had no wish to dig their own graves. [. . .]

Now Cosimo, having applied himself to the temporal affairs of the state, the conduct of which was bound to leave him with certain matters on his conscience—as is the case with all those who are fain to govern states and take the leading place—awoke to a sense of his condition, and was anxious that God might pardon him, and secure to him the possession of his earthly goods. Wherefore he felt he must needs turn to pious ways, otherwise his riches would be lost to him. He had prickings of conscience that certain portions of his wealth—where it came from I cannot say—had not been righteously gained, and to remove this weight from his shoulders he held conference with Pope Eugenius,[2] who was then in Florence, as to the load which lay on his conscience. Pope Eugenius had settled the Observantist Order in S. Marco; but, as their lodging there was inadequate, he remarked to Cosimo that, if he was bent on unburdening his soul, he might build a monastery. After he had spent ten thousand without providing all that was wanted, he afterwards completed the monastery, spending more than forty thousand florins over the work. Beyond building the house he fitted it with everything necessary for residence. He gave all the musical books for the church and the greater part of those are now in the library, and furthermore provided the sacristy with everything needful for Divine worship. And because the Dominican brothers may not hold goods of their own, he paid all the charges of their life in common in order that they might enjoy their fine convent during their lives. For the daily outlay he settled with his bank what weekly sum should be paid to them, thus providing all they wanted. To save personal application to himself, much occupied with affairs, he gave orders to the bank that whatever sum of money might be marked on the bill should be paid and charged to his account. [. . .]

I once heard Cosimo say that the great mistake of his life was that he did not begin to spend his wealth ten years earlier; because, knowing well the disposition of his fellow-citizens, he was sure that, in the lapse of fifty years, no memory would remain of his personality or of his house save the few fabrics he might have built. He went on, "I know that after my death my children will be in worse case than those of

---

[2] **Pope Eugenius:** Pope Eugene IV (r. 1431–47).

any other Florentine who has died for many years past; moreover, I know I shall not wear the crown of laurel more than any other citizen." He spake thus because he knew the difficulty of ruling a state as he had ruled Florence, through the opposition of influential citizens who had rated themselves his equals in former times. He acted privately with the greatest discretion in order to safeguard himself, and whenever he sought to attain an object he contrived to let it appear that the matter had been set in motion by someone other than himself and thus he escaped envy and unpopularity. His manner was admirable; he never spoke ill of anyone, and it angered him greatly to hear slander spoken by others. He was kind and patient to all who sought speech with him: he was more a man of deeds than of words: he always performed what he promised, and when this had been done he sent to let the petitioner know that his wishes had been granted. His replies were brief and sometimes obscure, so that they might be made to bear a double sense.

He had a very long memory which retained everything. One evening at home, when he wished for the love of God to give some more books to S. Marco—which books had lain for a long time in a press—he recalled all the books by name, and noted especially one of them, the *Digesto vecchio,*[3] and said: "Make a note mentally that there is thereon the singular name of a certain German who formerly possessed it," remembering thus both the name of the book and of the German. When he came upon it he said, "I once owned it forty years ago and I have never seen it since." So great was his knowledge of all things, that he could find some matter of discussion with men of all sorts; he would talk literature with a man of letters and theology with a theologian, being well versed therein through his natural liking, and for the reading of the Holy Scripture. With philosophy it was just the same, also with astrology, of which he had complete knowledge from having practised it with Maestro Pagolo and other astrologers. Indeed, he put faith in it, and always made use of it in his affairs. He took kindly notice of all musicians, and delighted greatly in their art. He had dealings with painters and sculptors and had in his house works of divers masters. He was especially inclined towards sculpture and showed great favour to all worthy craftsmen, being a good friend to Donatello[4] and all sculptors and painters; and because in his time the sculptors found scanty employment, Cosimo, in order that Donatello's chisel might not be idle, commissioned him to make the pulpits of bronze in S. Lorenzo and the doors of the sacristy. He ordered the bank to pay every week enough money to Donatello for his work and for that of his four assistants. And because Donatello was wont to go clad in a fashion not to Cosimo's taste, Cosimo gave him a red mantle and a cowl, with a cloak to go under the mantle, all new, and one festal day in the morning he sent them in order that Donatello might wear them. After a day or two of wear he put them aside, saying that he would not wear them again as they were too fine for him. Cosimo was thus liberal to all men of worth through his great liking for them. He had good knowledge of architecture, as

[3] ***Digesto vecchio:*** Many bound works that might be known as "old digests" circulated during this time, so it is uncertain what this book might be.

[4] **Donatello:** (c. 1386–1466), one of the great Italian sculptors of the Renaissance. A Florentine, Donatello is known in particular for his *David, St. Mark,* and *Magdalen.*

may be seen from the buildings he left, none of which were built without consulting him; moreover, all those who were about to build would go to him for advice.

Of agriculture he had the most intimate knowledge, and he would discourse thereupon as if he had never followed any other calling. At S. Marco the garden, which was a most beautiful one, was laid out after his instructions. Hitherto it had been a vacant field belonging to some friars who had held it before the reformation of the order by Pope Eugenius. In all his possessions there were few farming operations which were not directed by him. He did much fruit planting and grafting; and, wonderful as it may seem, he knew about every graft that was made on his estates; moreover, when the peasants came into Florence, he would ask them about the fruit trees and where they were planted. He loved to do grafting and lopping with his own hand. One day I had some talk with him when, being then a young man, he had gone from Florence — where there was sickness — to Careggi. It was then February, when they prune the vines, and I found him engaged in two most excellent tasks. One was to prune the vines every morning for two hours as soon as he rose (in this he imitated Pope Boniface IX, who would prune certain vines in the vineyard of the papal palace at Rome every year in due season. Moreover, at Naples they have preserved till this day his pruning-knife with two silver rings, in memory of Pope Boniface). Cosimo's other employment, when he had done with pruning, was to read the *Moralia* of S. Gregory, an excellent work in thirty-five books, which task occupied him for six months. Both at his villa and in Florence he spent his time well; taking pleasure in no game, save chess, of which he would occasionally play a game or two after supper by way of pastime. He knew Magnolino, who was the best chess player of his age. [. . .]

Having spoken of the praiseworthy way of life followed by Cosimo, specially in his management of things spiritual and temporal as well as of those appertaining to the honour of God, I will add that his fame was known throughout the world so that all men of worship passing that way desired to visit him. There was at Ferrara a bishop of Fünfkirchen, a Hungarian, a man of great learning and high station, who, having finished his studies, was recalled to his country, but was unwilling to depart till he should first have visited Florence and seen the three illustrious men who then dwelt there, Cosimo de' Medici, Messer Giovanni Argiropolo, and Messer Poggio. When he arrived in Florence he told me he desired to see all three before leaving, and as Cosimo was then at Careggi I accompanied him thither. I told Cosimo of his wish, and introduced him, and the two conversed a long time. After the bishop had left, Cosimo told me he was the most remarkable ultramontane he had ever met. The bishop was greatly struck with Cosimo's marvellous presence and ready wit, saying that in all his life he had never conversed with a more extraordinary man. The presence of Cosimo took nothing away from his fame, which greatly increased, and numberless men of worship sought him through his worldwide reputation. [. . .]

Cosimo used to say that in most gardens there grew a weed which should never be watered but left to dry up. Most men, however, watered it instead of letting it die of drought. This weed was that worst of all weeds, Envy, and that there were few except the truly wise who did not make shipwreck through it. In his latter days Cosimo fell into irresolute mood, and would often sit for hours without speaking, sunk in thought. In reply to his wife who remarked on his taciturnity he said, "When you propose to go into the country, you trouble yourself for fifteen days in settling what you will do when you get there. Now that the time has come for me to quit this world and pass into another, does it not occur to you that I ought to think about it?" For about a year before he died his humour was to have Aristotle's Ethics[5] read to him by Messer Bartolomeo da Colle, the chancellor of the palace, and he brought Donato Acciaiuoli to arrange in order the writings on the Ethics which he had collected under Messer Giovanni, and when these came to Cosimo, Messer Bartolomeo read them to him, after emendation by Donato, and this emended text of the Ethics is the one now in use. Many other things might be told of Cosimo by one who purposed to write his Life, but I am not set on this task. I have only set down matters concerning him which I myself have seen or heard from trustworthy witnesses. I leave all the rest to anyone who may undertake the work of writing the Life of so worthy a citizen, the ornament of his age. What I have written is the actual truth according to what I have heard and seen, neither adding nor omitting anything. Whoever may put together this Life may be vastly more lengthy than I have been, and let things be more clearly portrayed.

[5] **Ethics:** A treatise by the Greek philosopher Aristotle (384–322 B.C.E.).

Baldesar Castiglione

1478–1529

BAHL-deh-sar kah-stee-LYOH-nee, lee-OH-nee

loh-doh-VEE-koh SFORE-tsah

kohn-ZAH-gah, kohn-*THAH*;

MAN-too-uh, MAHN-too-uh

Baldesar Castiglione was born near Mantua in 1478 into an aristocratic family. He received a classical education, studying Latin and Greek, and as a young man served in the courts of **Lodovico Sforza** at Milan and **Francesco Conzaga** at Mantua. After serving as a soldier fighting against Spain, he moved to Rome, where the Duke of Urbino recruited his services for a diplomatic mission to Henry VII of England, who knighted the young emissary. Upon his return from England in 1507, Castiglione remained in the service of Urbino until the duke's death in 1513. Among his acquaintances at this time was Raphael (1483–1520), the great Italian artist, who painted Castiglione's portrait. Known for his good manners, efficiency, learning, and intelligence, Castiglione went on to other courts, eventually entering into the service of the Pope Clement VII, to whom he was an ambassador and adviser. He died while visiting Toledo, Spain, on February 2, 1529, a year after the publication of *The Book of the Courtier* (1528).

The Courtier offers an exemplary portrait of the manners, demeanor, and qualities of an idealized aristocratic gentleman. A model of good birth, grace, talent, taste, learning, and both physical and moral strength, the courtier is above all characterized by *SPREZZATURA*, a term that has no equivalent in English but suggests a quality of perfect composure and nonchalance, the ability to act with studied artifice while giving the appearance of effortless spontaneity. The book takes the form of a conversation among seven men and women—all named after Castiglione's friends and acquaintances—led by **Count Ludovico da Canossa** (1476–1532), whose ideas appear to be those of Castiglione himself. Though Castiglione finished the book in 1518, it was not published until ten years later; upon publication, it became a tremendous success and was translated into several European languages.

lood-VEE-koh dah-koh-NAW-sah

The Book of the Courtier

Translated by Charles S. Singleton

[The Qualities of the Courtier]

"I[1] would have our Courtier born of a noble and genteel family; because it is far less becoming for one of low birth to fail to do virtuous things than for one of noble birth, who, should he stray from the path of his forebears, stains the family name, and not only fails to achieve anything but loses what has been achieved already. For noble birth is like a bright lamp that makes manifest and visible deeds both good and bad, kindling and spurring on to virtue as much for fear of dishonor as for hope of praise. And since this luster of nobility does not shine forth in the deeds of the lowly born, they lack that spur, as well as that fear of dishonor, nor do they think themselves obliged to go beyond what was done by their forebears; whereas to the wellborn it seems a reproach not to attain at least to the mark set them by their ancestors. Hence, it almost always happens that, in the profession of arms as well as in other worthy pursuits, those who are most distinguished are men of noble birth, because nature has implanted in everything that hidden seed which gives a certain force and quality of its own essence to all that springs from it, making it like itself: as we can see not only in breeds of horses and other animals, but in trees as well, the shoots of which nearly always resemble the trunk; and if they sometimes degenerate, the fault lies with the husbandman. And so it happens with men, who, if they are tended in the right way, are almost always like those from whom they spring, and often are better; but if they lack someone to tend them properly, they grow wild and never attain their full growth.

"It is true that, whether favored by the stars or by nature, some men are born endowed with such graces that they seem not to have been born, but to have been fashioned by the hands of some god, and adorned with every excellence of mind and body; even as there are many others so inept and uncouth that we cannot but think that nature brought them into the world out of spite and mockery. And just as the

[1] **"I"**: Count Ludovico da Canossa (1476–1532), one of the interlocutors in the conversations through which Castiglione sketches the ideal model of the courtier. Ludovico was one of Castiglione's friends.

latter, for the most part, yield little fruit even with constant diligence and good care, so the former with little labor attain to the summit of the highest excellence. And take, as an example, Don Ippolito d'Este,[2] Cardinal of Ferrara, who enjoyed such a happy birth that his person, his appearance, his words, and all his actions are so imbued and ruled by this grace that, although he is young, he evinces among the most aged prelates so grave an authority that he seems more fit to teach than to be taught. Similarly, in conversing with men and women of every station, in play, in laughter, in jest, he shows a special sweetness and such gracious manners that no one who speaks with him or even sees him can do otherwise than feel an enduring affection for him.

"But, to return to our subject, I say that there is a mean to be found between such supreme grace on the one hand and such stupid ineptitude on the other, and that those who are not so perfectly endowed by nature can, with care and effort, polish and in great part correct their natural defects. Therefore, besides his noble birth, I would wish the Courtier favored in this other respect, and endowed by nature not only with talent and with beauty of countenance and person, but with that certain grace which we call an 'air,' which shall make him at first sight pleasing and lovable to all who see him; and let this be an adornment informing and attending all his actions, giving the promise outwardly that such a one is worthy of the company and the favor of every great lord." [. . .]

"But to come to some particulars: I hold that the principal and true profession of the Courtier must be that of arms; which I wish him to exercise with vigor; and let him be known among the others as bold, energetic, and faithful to whomever he serves. And the repute of these good qualities will be earned by exercising them in every time and place, inasmuch as one may not ever fail therein without great blame. And, just as among women the name of purity, once stained, is never restored, so the reputation of a gentleman whose profession is arms, if ever in the least way he sullies himself through cowardice or other disgrace, always remains defiled before the world and covered with ignominy. Therefore, the more our Courtier excels in this art, the more will he merit praise; although I do not deem it necessary that he have the perfect knowledge of things and other qualities that befit a commander, for since this would launch us on too great a sea, we shall be satisfied, as we have said, if he have complete loyalty and an undaunted spirit, and be always seen to have them. For oftentimes men are known for their courage in small things rather than in great. And often in important perils and where there are many witnesses, some men are found who, although their hearts sink within them, still, spurred on by fear of shame or by the company of those present, press forward with eyes shut, as it were, and do their duty, God knows how; and in things of little importance and when they think they can avoid the risk of danger, they are glad to play safe. But those men who, even when they think they will not be observed or seen or recognized by anyone, show courage and are not careless of anything, however slight, for which they could be blamed, such have the quality of spirit we are seeking in our Courtier.

[2] **Don Ippolito d'Este:** (1509–1572), the son of Lucrezia Borgia and Alfonso I, Duke of Ferrara; grandson of Pope Alexander VI; eventually became a cardinal.

"However, we do not wish him to make a show of being so fierce that he is forever swaggering in his speech, declaring that he has wedded his cuirass, and glowering with such dour looks as we have often seen Berto do; for to such as these one may rightly say what in polite society a worthy lady jestingly said to a certain man (whom I do not now wish to name) whom she sought to honor by inviting him to dance, and who not only declined this but would not listen to music or take any part in the other entertainments offered him, but kept saying that such trifles were not his business. And when finally the lady said to him: 'What then is your business?' he answered with a scowl: 'Fighting.' Whereupon the lady replied at once: 'I should think it a good thing, now that you are not away at war or engaged in fighting, for you to have yourself greased all over and stowed away in a closet along with all your battle harness, so that you won't grow any rustier than you already are'; and so, amid much laughter from those present, she ridiculed him in his stupid presumption. Therefore, let the man we are seeking be exceedingly fierce, harsh, and always among the first, wherever the enemy is; and in every other place, humane, modest, reserved, avoiding ostentation above all things as well as that impudent praise of himself by which a man always arouses hatred and disgust in all who hear him." [. . .]

"If I well remember, Count, it seems to me you have repeated several times this evening that the Courtier must accompany his actions, his gestures, his habits, in short, his every movement, with grace. And it strikes me that you require this in everything as that seasoning without which all the other properties and good qualities would be of little worth. And truly I believe that everyone would easily let himself be persuaded of this, because, by the very meaning of the word, it can be said that he who has grace finds grace. But since you have said that this is often a gift of nature and the heavens, and that, even if it is not quite perfect, it can be much increased by care and industry, those men who are born as fortunate and as rich in such treasure as some we know have little need, it seems to me, of any teacher in this, because such benign favor from heaven lifts them, almost in spite of themselves, higher than they themselves had desired, and makes them not only pleasing but admirable to everyone. Therefore I do not discuss this, it not being in our power to acquire it of ourselves. But as for those who are less endowed by nature and are capable of acquiring grace only if they put forth labor, industry, and care, I would wish to know by what art, by what discipline, by what method, they can gain this grace, both in bodily exercises, in which you deem it to be so necessary, and in every other thing they do or say. Therefore, since by praising this quality so highly you have, as I believe, aroused in all of us an ardent desire, according to the task given you by signora Emilia, you are still bound to satisfy it."

"I am not bound," said the Count, "to teach you how to acquire grace or anything else, but only to show you what a perfect Courtier ought to be. Nor would I undertake to teach you such a perfection; especially when I have just now said that the Courtier must know how to wrestle, vault, and so many other things which, since I never learned them myself, you all know well enough how I should be able to teach them. Let it suffice that just as a good soldier knows how to tell the smith what shape, style, and quality his armor must have, and yet is not able to teach him to make it, nor how to hammer or temper it; just so I, perhaps, shall be able to tell you what a perfect Courtier should be, but not to teach you what you must do to become one. Still, in order to answer your question in so far as I can (although it is almost proverbial that grace is not learned), I say that if anyone is to acquire grace in bodily exercises (granting first of all that he is not by nature incapable), he must begin early and learn the principles from the best of teachers. [. . .]

"[. . .] whoever would be a good pupil must not only do things well, but must always make every effort to resemble and, if that be possible, to transform himself into his master. And when he feels that he has made some progress, it is very profitable to observe different men of that profession; and, conducting himself with that good judgment which must always be his guide, go about choosing now this thing from one and that from another. And even as in green meadows the bee flits about among the grasses robbing the flowers, so our Courtier must steal this grace from those who seem to him to have it, taking from each the part that seems most worthy of praise; not doing as a friend of ours whom you all know, who thought he greatly resembled King Ferdinand the Younger[3] of Aragon, but had not tried to imitate him in anything save in the way he had of raising his head and twisting one side of his mouth, which manner the King had contracted through some malady. And there are many such, who think they are doing a great thing if only they can resemble some great man in something; and often they seize upon that which is his only bad point.

"But, having thought many times already about how this grace is acquired (leaving aside those who have it from the stars), I have found quite a universal rule which in this matter seems to me valid above all others, and in all human affairs whether in word or deed: and that is to avoid affectation in every way possible as though it were some very rough and dangerous reef; and (to pronounce a new word perhaps) to practice in all things a certain *sprezzatura*, so as to conceal all art and make whatever is done or said appear to be without effort and almost without any thought about it. And I believe much grace comes of this: because everyone knows the difficulty of things that are rare and well done; wherefore facility in such things causes the greatest wonder; whereas, on the other hand, to labor and, as we say, drag forth by the hair of the head, shows an extreme want of grace, and causes everything, no matter how great it may be, to be held in little account.

"Therefore we may call that art true art which does not seem to be art; nor must one be more careful of anything than of concealing it, because if it is discovered, this robs a man of all credit and causes him to be held in slight esteem. [. . .]"

[3] **King Ferdinand the Younger:** (1503–1564) King Ferdinand I, Holy Roman Emperor from 1558 to 1564.

ABU'L FAZL
1551–1602

One of the most gifted advisers of the Mughal emperor Akbar (r. 1556–1605), **Abu'l Fazl 'Allami** was born in Agra, India, in 1551. The son of **Shaikh Mubarak**, an important scholar and mystic, Abu'l Fazl proved to be a gifted student whose learning and considerable talents enabled him to advance quickly into the innermost circle of Akbar's court. Entering the court in 1574, Abu'l Fazl soon became Akbar's most important political and religious adviser, as well as a friend and companion. His genius lies behind many of the celebrated reforms undertaken during Akbar's reign, especially the practice of *sulahkul,* or universal religious tolerance. Akbar eliminated both the *jizya,* the hated tax on non-Muslims, as well as the tax on Hindu pilgrims. In addition, Akbar included non-Muslims in his government and allowed the Hindus to exercise greater control in local government and in legal matters.

AH-bool FAH-zul

SHIKE moo-BAH-rahk

Abu'l Fazl encouraged Akbar to consolidate his power and to take greater control than previous Muslim rulers had in deciding religious questions. Such questions had customarily been deferred to the Sharia—Islamic law—and were decided by Muslim religious men. Drawing on Shia traditions as well as on Plato's idea of the "philosopher-king," Abu'l Fazl argued that Akbar was the imam, the chosen man who, according to Shia belief, had inherited the divine light of God passed down from the creation of Adam and served as the spiritual guide of his age. Akbar evolved the idea of his divinity into the form of a new religion, the ***Din-i Ilahi*** ("Divine Faith"), which emphasized the unity of all religions under God and focused on his own spiritual enlightenment. The major exponent of this new faith was Abu'l Fazl, who celebrated Akbar's divinity in the ***Akbar-nama,*** his chronicle of Akbar's reign. Abu'l Fazl's influence over Akbar was resented by many orthodox Sunni Muslims who believed Akbar's policies were too liberal. Among the detractors was prince Salim (Jahangir), Akbar's oldest son. In 1601 Prince Salim declared himself emperor, and the next year he ordered the assassination of Abu'l Fazl.

DEEN-ee ee-LAH-hee, ee-lah-HEE

AHK-bar NAH-muh

In addition to the *Akbar-nama,* as well as the *Institutes of Akbar,* an encyclopedic compendium of important facts and figures about Akbar's reign, Abu'l Fazl also left behind many letters. All of his works, written in Persian, are recognized for the high quality of their prose. In the selection that follows, from the preface to the *Institutes of Akbar,* Abu'l Fazl describes the features of the ideal ruler, exemplified in his view by Akbar. For Abu'l Fazl, the marks of a true king—a king who in spirit and in deeds embodies the divine spirit of the perfect man—are justice and virtue, made visible in the king's love for his subjects and humility before God.

FROM

Institutes of Akbar

Translated by Peter Hardy

No dignity is higher in the eyes of God than royalty, and those who are wise drink from its auspicious fountain. A sufficient proof of this, for those who require one, is the fact that royalty is a remedy for the spirit of rebellion, and the reason why subjects obey. Even the meaning of the word *Pādshāh*[1] shows this; for *pād* signifies stability and possession. If royalty did not exist, the storm of strife would never subside, nor selfish ambition disappear. Mankind, being under the burden of lawlessness and lust, would sink into the pit of destruction; this world, this great market place, would lose its prosperity, and the whole world become a barren waste. But by the light of imperial justice, some follow with cheerfulness the road of obedience, while others abstain from violence through fear of punishment; and out of necessity make choice of the path of rectitude. *Shāh* is also a name given to one who surpasses his fellows, as you may see from words like *shāh-suwār, shāh-rāh;*[2] it is also a term applied to a bridegroom—the world, as the bride, betrothes herself to the king, and becomes his worshiper.

Silly and shortsighted men cannot distinguish a true king from a selfish ruler. Nor is this remarkable, as both have in common a large treasury, a numerous army, clever servants, obedient subjects, an abundance of wise men, a multitude of skillful workmen, and a superfluity of means of enjoyment. But men of deeper insight remark a difference. In the case of the former, these things just now enumerated are lasting, but in that of the latter, of short duration. The former does not attach himself to these things, as his object is to remove oppression and provide for everything which is good. Security, health, chastity, justice, polite manners, faithfulness, truth, and increase of sincerity, and so forth, are the result. The latter is kept in bonds by the external forms of royal power, by vanity, the slavishness of men, and the desire of enjoyment; hence everywhere there is insecurity, unsettledness, strife, oppression, faithlessness, robbery.

Royalty is a light emanating from God, and a ray from the sun, the illuminator of the universe, the argument of the book of perfection, the receptacle of all virtues. Modern language calls this light the divine light, and the tongue of antiquity called it the sublime halo. It is communicated by God to kings without the intermediate assistance of anyone, and men, in the presence of it, bend the forehead of praise toward the ground of submission.

Again, many excellent qualities flow from the possession of this light:

1. A paternal love toward the subjects. Thousands find rest in the love of the king, and sectarian differences do not raise the dust of strife. In his wisdom, the king will understand the spirit of the age, and shape his plans accordingly.

---

[1] ***Pādshāh:*** Emperor.

[2] ***shāh-rāh:*** Royal road; *shah-suwar* means royal horseman.

2. A large heart. The sight of anything disagreeable does not unsettle him, nor is want of discrimination for him a source of disappointment. His courage steps in. His divine firmness gives him the power of requittal, nor does the high position of an offender interfere with it. The wishes of great and small are attended to, and their claims meet with no delay at his hands.

3. A daily increasing trust in God. When he performs an action, he considers God as the real doer of it [and himself as the medium] so that a conflict of motives can produce no disturbance.

4. Prayer and devotion. The success of his plans will not lead him to neglect, nor will adversity cause him to forget God and madly trust in man. He puts the reins of desire into the hands of reason; in the wide field of his desires he does not permit himself to be trodden down by restlessness; nor will he waste his precious time in seeking after that which is improper. He makes wrath, the tyrant, pay homage to wisdom, so that blind rage may not get the upper hand, and inconsiderateness overstep the proper limits. He sits on the eminence of propriety, so that those who have gone astray have a way left to return, without exposing their bad deeds to the public gaze. When he sits in judgment, the petitioner seems to be the judge, and he himself, on account of his mildness, the suitor for justice. He does not permit petitioners to be delayed on the path of hope; he endeavors to promote the happiness of the creatures in obedience to the will of the Creator, and never seeks to please the people in contradiction to reason. He is forever searching after those who speak the truth and is not displeased with words that seem bitter, but are in reality sweet. He considers the nature of the words and the rank of the speaker. He is not content with committing violence, but he must see that no injustice is done within his realm.

Hayashi Razan (Doshun)

1583–1657

Hayashi Razan, also known as Doshun, was born in Kaga, Japan, in 1583. As a young man he moved to Kyoto, where he studied the Japanese and Chinese classics, and became a follower of **Fujiwara Seika** (1561–1619), the founder of neo-Confucianism in Japan. Originating with Chinese philosopher **Zhu Xi** (Chu Hsi; 1130–1200), neo-Confucianism was a rationalistic philosophy emphasizing the importance of history and tradition, duty and loyalty to the family and state, and the empirical study of nature and human society. **Hayashi Razan** adapted these essentially Chinese principles to Japanese society and culture, and set out to promote neo-Confucianism in the early Tokugawa period (1603–1867).

foo-jee-WAH-rah
SAY-kah
joo-SHEE

high-YAH-shee
rah-ZAHN

Around 1605, Hayashi was invited to **Edo**, where he became the Confucian adviser to the first Tokugawa shogun, **Tokugawa Ieyasu**; after

AY-doh, EH-doh
toh-koo-GAH-wah

Toyotomi Hideyoshi (1536–98) *This popular print of Hideyoshi shows the well-known samurai lord and chief imperial minister of Japan in action in full warrior dress. (The Art Archive)*

ee-ay-YAH-soo

oo-AY-noh

Ieyasu's death, Hayashi lived on to serve as an adviser under three successive shoguns, enabling him to play a powerful role in the adoption of neo-Confucian ideas and practices in Japan. In 1630, he established a school in **Ueno**, Edo, where many of the government officials were trained. Among other things, as the selection here shows, Hayashi encouraged the warrior class, the samurai, to balance their study of martial arts with the pursuit of learning and to adopt a code of conduct that would maintain their dignity and status in peacetime. Hayashi Razan died in 1657, but his sons continued the tradition of education he had started, and members of the Hayashi family were the effective leaders of the State University until 1906.

The text presented here is from *Sources of Japanese Tradition*, compiled, edited, and translated by William Theodore de Bary and Donald Keene. The notes are adapted from those of the editor and translators.

On Mastery of the Arts of Peace and War

Translated by William Theodore de Bary and Donald Keene

Someone asked for an explanation of the samurai's mastering both the arts of peace and the arts of war. The reply was: "Armies achieve victory by the arts of war. That by which they achieve victory is strategy. Strategy is derived from the arts of peace. This is why the precepts of T'ai Kung included a chapter on civil arts as well as a chapter on military arts.[1] These two together make up the art of the general. When one is unable to combine one with the other, as in the cases of Chuang Hou and Kuan Ying, who lacked the arts of peace, and Sui Ho and Lu Chia, who lacked the arts of war, there will be cause for regret. Warfare involves knowledge of one's opportunity. Stratagems involve secrecy. Opportunities are not easy to see, but one can learn them through stratagems so long as the stratagems are not divulged. Therefore, those who are adept at the handling of troops regard the arts of peace and the arts of war as their left and right hands.

"Let us consider [the teaching of] the Sage[2] that 'to lead an untaught people into war is to throw them away.' Teaching the people is a civil art, but warfare is a military art. Without both of them, the people would be thrown away. Therefore it is said that the man of civil affairs must also have military preparedness. There may be no lack of daring in hunting a tiger unarmed or in crossing a river without a boat, but this is not the same thing as prowess in the arts of war. There may be no lack of magnanimity in refraining from making old people prisoners of war, but this is not the same thing as mastery of the arts of peace. To have the arts of peace, but not the arts of war, is to lack courage. To have the arts of war, but not the arts of peace, is to lack wisdom. Keeping both in mind, generals employ or disperse their troops and advance or retreat according to the proper time. This is the Way of the general. A general is no other than a true man. A man who is dedicated and has a mission to perform is called a samurai (or *shi*). A man who is of inner worth and upright conduct, who has moral principles and mastery of the arts is also called a samurai. A man who pursues learning, too, is called a samurai. A man who serves [at court] without neglecting the mountains and forests is also called a samurai. The term samurai (or *shi*) is indeed broad. Thus of ranks [in the Chou dynasty][3] it was said that they ascended from officer [*shi*] to high official; from high official to chief minister; and from chief minister to prince. Nevertheless, when a man became a chief minister and entered the service of the king to administer the government, he was also called a 'minister-officer' *(kyō-shi)*.[4] At court he was a statesman; in the field he was a general. The Book of Odes says: 'Mighty in peace and war is Chi-fu / A pattern to all the peoples.'[5] How can a man discharge the duties of his rank and position without combining the peaceful and military arts?"

[1] **"military arts":** Refers to the *Liu Tao,* an ancient Chinese treatise on war attributed to T'ai Kung, also known as Lu Wang (twelfth century B.C.E.). [2] **Sage:** Confucius (Kong Fuzi; 551–479 B.C.E.), Chinese philosopher to whom is attributed the *Analects,* a collection of aphorisms and dialogues recorded by his disciples. The quote is from *Analects* 13.30. [3] **[Chou dynasty]:** Zhou dynasty, c. 1027–256 B.C.E. [4] **[*kyō-shi*]:** The term *shi* designates the lowest rank in the feudal aristocracy, but it is also in the titles of the highest officials. [5] **'all the peoples':** From the ancient Chinese collection of poetry known as *The Book of Songs.*

Marguerite de Navarre
1492–1549

François Clouet, *Marguerite de Navarre*, 1544
The educated and aristocratic Marguerite de Navarre is shown here in a late portrait. Her Heptameron *was modeled on Boccaccio's* Decameron, *taking up themes of Platonic and spiritual love. (Musée Conde, Chantilly, France / Bridgeman Art Library)*

www For links to more information about Marguerite de Navarre and a quiz on *The Heptameron*, see *World Literature Online* at bedfordstmartins.com/worldlit.

A member of the French royal family, Marguerite de Navarre was at the center of the political and cultural life of her time. With her brother, Francis I, who ruled France from 1515 to 1547, she participated in bringing the learning and culture of Italy to France and facilitating the French **Renaissance**. She acted as much more than a cultural messenger. Her interest in religious issues contributed to reform movements in the Catholic Church that would become the **Reformation**. In her literary works she recasts established literary forms from a distinctively feminine point of view. Modeled on Boccaccio's *Decameron* (1353), her best-known literary work, *The Heptameron* (1558), explores conflicting ideals of love and male and female codes of sexuality, courtship, and marriage, and contrasts the conventions of the Middle Ages with the emerging individualism of the Renaissance.

Sister to the King. The daughter of Charles of Orléans, Count of Angoulême, and Louise of Savoy, Marguerite, as the sister of an heir to the throne, received an extraordinary education for a woman of her time. She was especially proficient in languages and studied Latin, Italian, Spanish, German, Greek, and Hebrew. There were unsuccessful negotiations to marry her to Prince Henry of England (Henry VIII) and to Charles of Austria, who would later become the Holy Roman Emperor Charles V (1500–1558), but the king of France at the time of her marriage, Louis XII (1462–1515), insisted that she marry Charles, Duke of Alençon. The two were never particularly compatible and her brother Francis remained a more important figure in her life than her first husband. When Francis I (1494–1547) was crowned King of France in 1515, Marguerite became one of the most important persons in his court, advising him, carrying out diplomatic missions and treaty negotiations, and meeting the many important visitors who came to the court, including such artists as Leonardo da Vinci and Benvenuto Cellini.[1] Francis and Marguerite were the two central figures in bringing the Italian Renaissance to France, presiding over a court inspired by the art and literature of Italy.

When Francis went to Italy in 1524 to pursue the French war with the Holy Roman Emperor, Charles V of Spain, Marguerite and her mother, the two remaining members of the ruling family "trinity," as it was called, governed France in his absence. After Francis's defeat and capture at the Battle of Pavia in 1525, Marguerite went to Madrid to negotiate the treaty

[1] **Leonardo da Vinci, Benvenuto Cellini:** Leonardo de Vinci (1452–1519), Florentine artist, inventor, scientist, engineer, musician, and architect; best known, perhaps, for the painting *Mona Lisa.* Benvenuto Cellini (1500–1571), Italian sculptor, metalsmith, and author; best known for his *Autobiography* and for his sculpture *Perseus with the Head of Medusa.*

that ended the hostilities and secured her brother's release. In the same year her first husband, Charles, Duke of Alençon, died.

A Courtly Salon in Navarre. Her second marriage in 1527 to **Henri d'Albret**, King of Navarre (1503–1555), was also an arranged union, but one that took account of her wishes. Henri, ten years her junior, was a military hero who had made a daring escape from imprisonment in Italy after the Battle of Pavia. Although she married him for love as well as position, he was not her intellectual equal. Nevertheless, Marguerite was able to establish a courtly salon in Navarre, his kingdom on the Atlantic coast at the western end of the Pyrenees; here intellectuals and religious reformers met and exchanged ideas. As she became increasingly engaged in intellectual and literary pursuits, Marguerite became a supporter and protector of artists and thinkers, particularly of such religious reformers as Clement Marot, Gerard Roussel, and Lefèvre d'Etaples.[2] She corresponded with Erasmus and Calvin;[3] **Rabelais**[4] dedicated the third volume of *Gargantua and Pantagruel* to her. Although she was particularly interested in the writings of Martin Luther,[5] she did not leave the Church; she remained convinced that reform could take place within it.

aw-REE dahl-BRAY

RAB-uh-lay

Her first published work, *The Mirror of the Sinful Soul* (1531), a devotional poem, was attacked for Protestant "heresy" by the theologians at the Sorbonne, and her brother had to intervene on her behalf. Although she never left the Catholic faith, her acquaintance with Protestant reformers and with intellectuals within the Church made her suspect in the eyes of conservative theologians, especially at a time when the differences between Catholics and Protestants were the basis for continuing civil strife.

During the last decade of her life, strains in her relationships with Francis and especially with Henri II (1519–1559), his successor, led to her attending the French court for only brief periods. She spent most of her time in Navarre and in retreat in a convent at Tusson. The mystical and devotional character of much of her later work, in many of the plays and poems collected in *Pearls of the Pearl of Princesses* (1547), for example, reveals her growing concern for spiritual issues. Her long poem, *Prisons* (c. 1548), describes a mystical journey from the various prisons of this

[2] **Clement Marot, Gerard Roussel, Lefèvre d'Etaples:** Clement Marot (1496?–1544), French court poet imprisoned for many years for heresy. Gerard Roussel (d. 1555), a churchman who was one of Lefèvre d'Etaples's followers and Marguerite's private chaplain. Both men were protected from prosecution for heresy for a time by Marguerite. Lefèvre d'Etaples (c. 1455–1536), French philosopher, biblical commentator, and theologian who inspired French protestantism even though he stayed within the Church.

[3] **Erasmus, Calvin:** Desiderius Erasmus (1466–1536), Dutch scholar and humanist; he attacked the abuses of the Roman Catholic Church but remained within it. John Calvin (1509–1564), French protestant theologian who broke from the Catholic Church in 1533 and developed his theological ideas in *Institutes of the Christian Religion* (1536).

[4] **Rabelais:** François Rabelais (c. 1490–1553), French writer, humanist, and physician, best known for his satiric romances recounting the legends of the giants Gargantua and Pantagruel.

[5] **Luther:** Martin Luther (1483–1546), German leader of the Protestant Reformation. See p. 666.

world to ascend to unity with God. She died in Navarre in 1549, two years after Francis, with her husband at her side. Their only surviving child, Jeanne, born in 1527, would become the mother of Henry IV of France (1553–1610).

The Heptameron. Boccaccio's *Decameron* was the model for *The Heptameron.* Marguerite had commissioned a French translation of Boccaccio's work from Antoine Le Maçon, one of Francis I's councilors, and a member of her literary coterie. It appeared in 1545, just a few years before her death, and is mentioned in the Prologue to *The Heptameron.* The frame story[6] for Marguerite's work is similar to Boccaccio's. A group of travelers is brought together by traumatic experiences and natural disasters. Assaulted by bandits, chased by bears, and nearly drowned in torrential rivers, five men and five women find themselves gathered for safety in a remote monastery. There they must wait for ten days while a rude bridge is constructed to enable them to escape the floods. They decide to while away the time pleasurably by reenacting *The Decameron:* Each of them will tell a story each day and by the end of their stay they will have made another collection of one hundred tales. But unlike Boccaccio's stories, all their tales are to be true. Modern scholarship has confirmed that nearly a third of the tales are based in historical fact.

Even though Marguerite had not completed her original plan for a hundred stories and had not organized the manuscript by the time of her death, most contemporary scholars think that she wrote most of the seventy-two tales included in modern editions of the work. Her maid reported that Marguerite found time to write the stories in between her many courtly duties or while she was traveling, scribbling them on scraps of paper or dictating them to companions. The tales were first published nine years after her death. Since *The Heptameron*'s first edition, the stories have been placed in different orders and varying numbers of tales have been included by different editors. The sexual subject matter and the many tales dealing with the sexual indulgences of monks have seemed to some readers inconsistent with the pietistic and devotional tone of much of Marguerite's other work and have led to speculation that Marguerite did not compose many of the tales. However, one has only to look at *The Decameron; The Canterbury Tales,* by English poet Geoffrey Chaucer (c. 1340–1400); or the poetry of English poet John Donne to see how Marguerite's melding of carnal and spiritual themes was characteristic of her time.

Like Boccaccio's, the stories here address love and sexual relationships; Marguerite's storytellers, modeled on real people, engage in an ongoing discussion of the relations between men and women. These conversations frame the tales and frequently boil over into a battle between the sexes. The tale included here, for example, is told by **Parlamente**, the female narrator usually identified as Marguerite's representation of her-

par-lah-MAWNT

[6] **frame story:** A story that encloses another story or stories, most fully developed in such works as *The Canterbury Tales* and *The Arabian Nights.* In *The Heptameron* the frame tells about the ten storytellers and how they came together to tell their stories.

self, in response to a male challenge to tell a story of a faithful woman. Parlamente does much more than meet the challenge. She turns the conventional "male" love story on its head and redefines faithfulness from a female point of view.

Amador and Florida. The story of **Amador** and Florida also reveals the changes taking place in Marguerite's time. It begins as a chivalric romance, like *Amadis of Gaul* or *Launcelot,* the fantastic stories that so distorted Don Quixote's[7] sense of reality. Amador is described as the perfect knight, handsome, self-possessed, daring, and articulate. But he is left speechless when he first meets Florida, even though she is only twelve years old, and she becomes the object of his knightly intentions. He is too far beneath her socially to hope to marry her, but he plans to serve her, to win her love, and to make her his lady. His goals are altogether consistent with the medieval code of courtly love, and his success will be measured by how far he is faithful to his lady and the chivalric ideal she represents.

ah-mah-DOR

To fulfill his quest, Amador undertakes a secret strategy. He marries Florida's best friend, **Avanturada**, so that he will have access to Florida, and he attaches himself to the man she loves and will probably marry, the son of the Fortunate Infante. Amador's secret stratagems are not apparent to Florida; she accepts him as a pure and courtly servitor. But his machinations warn the reader that he is not all he appears to be and that this courtly romance may have a dark underside. By the time of the crisis in the story, when Avanturada's death threatens to separate Amador from Florida and he attempts to rape her, the sexuality suppressed by the romantic story comes to the surface. The rest of the story is a proto-novel exploring Florida's psychology as she attempts to reconcile her love for Amador with his threatening sexuality. The second half of the story looks forward to novels such as *The Princess of Clèves,*[8] where psychological issues predominate.

ah-vahn-too-RAH-*th*ah

The conflict in the story is between two ideas of love and two ideas of honor. Florida—and Marguerite de Navarre—affirm Platonic love, love purified of its sexuality, that transforms the earthly into the spiritual. Marguerite described "perfect lovers [are] those who seek some perfection in the object of their love, be it beauty, kindness, or good grace, tending to virtue, and who have such high and honest hearts that they will not even for fear of death do base things that honour and conscience blame." Although Amador's courtship seems to promise such transforming love,

The Heptameron, **standing as it were mid-way between the neo-classical and individualistic tendencies of the Renaissance, makes its valid, original, and entertaining contribution to culture. Like all classics, it tries to civilize the human animal.**

–JULES GELERNT, critic, 1966

[7] **chivalric romance, like *Amadis of Gaul,* or *Launcelot,* . . . Don Quixote:** Medieval romances are adventure stories about knights, kings, and ladies that articulate a chivalric worldview and usually have a love theme. They first appeared, written in French, in the twelfth century. In France most romances were based on materials from the legends of Charlemagne, although the thirteenth-century French romance *Launcelot* drew on Arthurian materials that would also inspire many English romances. *Amadis of Gaul* (1508), a Spanish romance based on French sources, was one of the books that infected Don Quixote's imagination with chivalric ideas in Cervantes's novel *Don Quixote* (1605, 1615).

[8] ***The Princess of Clèves:*** A novel published in 1679 by Madame de LaFayette (1634–1693), often considered the first French novel and the first psychological novel in Western literature. It recounts the conflict between love and duty of a woman caught in an arranged marriage.

Perfect lovers [are] those who seek some perfection in the object of their love, be it beauty, kindness, or good grace, tending to virtue, and who have such high and honest hearts that they will not even for fear of death do base things that honour and conscience blame.

– Marguerite de Navarre

his underlying motives prove to be sensual. He cannot control the love that drives him to attempt to take Florida by force and that prompts him to threaten to kill himself if she does not give herself bodily to him. In this struggle with Amador, Florida is alone. Avanturada is dead and even her mother seems sympathetic to Amador's cause. The established chivalric code has turned against her and she has nothing to rely on but her own conscience. Florida is like the Protestant reformer who, betrayed by the corrupt practices of the Church, had only an inner voice to trust.

By the end of the story, a female perspective has replaced the male perspective with which the story began. Instead of Amador and his quest as its heroic subject matter, Florida and her conscience have become the focus. The discussion in the frame-narrative following the story concentrates on this shift. When Parlamente asks Hircan to confirm her reading that the story shows "a lady . . . tried to the utmost . . . [who] resisted virtuously," he responds by praising Amador for doing "his duty" by attempting to "master" Florida. Clearly the tale has not resolved the conflict between these opposing views of male and female honor, but it has brought the powerful struggle between men and women and between tradition and the individual conscience into clear definition.

■ CONNECTIONS

Geoffrey Chaucer, *The Canterbury Tales,* Book 2. Like other collections of tales—Boccaccio's *Decameron,* Chaucer's *Canterbury Tales,* or *The Arabian Nights,* for example—*The Heptameron* places its stories within a frame. How does the frame of *The Heptameron* in relation to the story of Florida and Amador compare to the frames for Chaucer's "Wife of Bath's Tale"? How do Chaucer's views on love and sexuality seem to differ from Marguerite's?

Giovanni Boccaccio, *The Decameron,* Book 2. Compare Boccaccio's story of Ghismonda and Tancred with Marguerite's story of Florida and Amador: How do the attitudes of the two heroines differ? Would you explain this difference as philosophical or as a conflict between a man's story and a woman's story? Would you consider the stories, both of which involve suffering and death, to be tragedies? If so, who would be the "tragic hero" in each story?

Chikamatsu Monzaemon, *The Love Suicides at Amijima,* Book 4. Like the story of Florida and Amador, Chikamatsu's drama of the love of Kamiya Jihei and Koharu involves a conflict between passion and duty, a conflict that has inspired many literary tragedies. What social and ethical codes come into play in each work? How does the Japanese code differ from the chivalric code in Marguerite de Navarre's tale? How are the reasons for and the expectations connected with the suicides in both stories different?

■ FURTHER RESEARCH

Biography and Criticism

Cholakian, Patricia Francis. *Rape and Writing in the Heptameron of Marguerite de Navarre.* 1991.

Gelernt, Jules. *World of Many Loves: The Heptameron of Marguerite de Navarre.* 1966.

Lyons, John D., and Mary B. McKinley, eds. *Critical Tales: New Studies of the Heptameron and Early Modern Culture.* 1993.

Putnam, Samuel. *Marguerite of Navarre.* 1935.

Tetel, Marcel. *Marguerite de Navarre's "Heptameron": Themes, Language, and Structure.* 1973.

■ **PRONUNCIATION**

Alençon: ah-lawng-SAWNG
Amador: ah-mah-DOR
Avanturada: ah-vahn-too-RAH-*th*ah
Dagoucin: dah-goo-SANG
Geburon: zheh-boo-RAWNG
Henri d'Albret: aw-REE dahl-BRAY
Nájera: NAH-heh-rah
Oisille: wah-ZEEL
Parlamente: par-lah-MAWNT
Perpignan: pehr-peen-YAWNG
Rabelais: RAB-uh-lay
Saffredent: sah-fruh-DAWNG
Salces: SAHLS

The Heptameron

Translated by P. A. Chilton

FROM

Story Nine

[On the Virtue of Women]

"Now, Gentlemen," concluded Dagoucin, "you who refused to believe what I said before, do you not find this case enough to force you to admit that perfect love can, through being too carefully concealed and too little known, lead lovers to their death? There isn't one among you who doesn't know the families concerned, so you can have no doubts as to the facts, though no one who has not had personal experience may actually believe them."

The Heptameron. The tale of Florida and Amador, the last tale on the first day of *The Heptameron,* is told by Parlamente, an idealistic young woman who defends Platonic love. In the frame narrative that precedes the tale, the participants are discussing the previous story. That tale is of a poor lover who, awed by the purity of the lady he desires and aware of his own unworthiness, is unable to reveal his love. Finally, when he is on his deathbed, he confesses his love to his sweetheart and requests one final embrace. He dies holding her in his arms. The first speaker among the group of storytellers, Dagoucin, who has just finished telling this tale, is a self-effacing man who puts women on a pedestal. The other two young men, Hircan and Saffredent, are cynical misogynists. Geburon, an older man, cautions the women against their masculine aggressiveness, while the masculine view is countered by Oisille, an older woman, who celebrates spirituality, and the younger women, Longarine and Parlamente, who defend an idealized Platonic love.

Parlamente's story begins as a **chivalric romance** describing the attempts of the perfect knight, Amador, to win Florida as his lady. However, the chivalric code of manners proves inadequate to accommodate a woman who prefers to rely solely on her own resources. By the end of the story Florida has become the protagonist, replacing the chivalric knight with the woman of conscience as its center of interest.

A Note on the Translation: P. A. Chilton's 1984 translation seeks to render the variety of voices in *The Heptameron.* Some storytellers use an elevated, biblical diction while others have a plain style, accessible to modern readers.

There was not a lady present who did not have tears in her eyes. But Hircan said: "I've never heard of such a fool in all my life! Does it make sense, I ask you, that we men should die for the sake of women, when women are made solely for our benefit? And does it make sense to hesitate to demand from them what God Himself has commanded that they should let us have? I'm not speaking for myself, of course, or for other married men. As far as women and so forth are concerned, I'm quite satisfied already—more than satisfied! But I mean those who aren't—they're very stupid to be afraid of women, when it's women who should be afraid of them! And as for the girl, don't you see how much she regretted having been so silly? She was happy enough to kiss the corpse, repugnant to nature though it is. So she wouldn't have refused physical contact if the man had had a little more nerve while he was alive, and been a little bit less pathetic on his deathbed!"

"Nevertheless," said Oisille, "the gentleman clearly showed that the love he bore her was noble and good, and for that he deserves high praise before all men. For chastity in a lover's heart is a thing more divine than human."

"Madame, I support Hircan's point of view," said Saffredent, "and if you want confirmation of what Hircan says, bear in mind that Fortune favours the bold. There was never a man, you know, who didn't in the end get what he wanted from any lady who really loved him, so long as he went about wooing her ardently and astutely. But because of ignorance and some sort of stupid timidity there are men who miss many a good opportunity in love. Then they attribute their failures to their lady's virtue, even though they never get anywhere near testing it. To put it another way, you've only got to attack your fortress in the right way, and you can't fail to take it in the end!"

"I'm shocked that you two can talk like that!" exclaimed Parlamente. "From what you've just said, the ladies you've been in love with can scarcely have been very faithful to you—or else you've only gone for immoral women anyway, and think that all the others are like them!"

"Mademoiselle, I do not have the good fortune to be able to boast of my conquests," Saffredent replied, "but I attribute my misfortune less to ladies' virtue than to my own failure to undertake my ventures with the right degree of care and astuteness. I don't want to quote the learned doctors to you. My sole authority is the old woman in the *Roman de la Rose*, who said:

Remember, sir, it's Nature's plan,
It's every man for every maid,
And every maid for every man!

So I shall always believe that once a woman has love in her heart the outcome cannot fail to be happy for the man concerned, provided he does not persist in his own stupidity."

"And just suppose," said Parlamente, "that I were able to name a lady who had been truly in love, who had been desired, pursued and wooed, and yet had remained an honest woman, victorious over the feelings of her heart, victorious over her body, victorious over her love and victorious over her would-be lover? Would you admit that such a thing were possible?"

"Certainly I should," replied Saffredent.

"Then if Saffredent can accept a case like that," she concluded, "the rest of you would be hard to convince indeed, if you didn't accept it also."

"Madame," said Dagoucin, "I have proved to you by means of an example that a man may continue in the way of virtuous love even unto death. If you know of a lady to whom similar honour is due, then I should like to ask you to finish our day of stories by telling us about her. We shall not mind if the story is a long one. We have time enough to listen to a good tale."

"Since I am allotted what time is left," she began, "I shall not delay my story by giving you a wordy preamble. It's such a true, such a lovely story, that I'm anxious for you to hear it without more ado. I was not an eye-witness to the facts, but they were recounted to me by a very close friend of mine, a man who was devoted to the hero of the story and wished to sing his praises. He made me swear, however, that if I should ever tell the story to anyone else, I would alter the names of the people involved. So everything that I shall tell you is true to life, except the names of the people and the places."

Story Ten

[Florida and Amadour]

In Aragon, in the province of Aranda, there once lived a lady. She was the widow of the Count of Aranda, who had died while she was still very young, and left her with a son and a daughter, who was called Florida. As was right and proper for the children of a noble lord, they were brought up by her according to the strictest codes of virtue and honour. So carefully did she school them that her house was known far and wide as the most honourable in the whole of Spain. She would often go to Toledo, which was then the seat of the King of Spain, and when she visited Saragossa, which was not far from the family home, she would spend her time at the Queen's court, where she was as highly esteemed as any lady could be.

One day, when the King was in residence at his castle in Saragossa, the Castillo de la Aljaferia, the Countess, on her way to pay her respects as was her wont, was passing through a little village that belonged to the Viceroy of Catalonia.[1] Normally the Viceroy never moved from the border at Perpignan, where he was in command during the war between France and Spain, but peace had just been declared, and he returned with his officers in order to do homage to his King.[2] He knew that the Countess would be passing through his lands, and went to meet her, not only to do her the honour that was her due as the King's kinswoman, but also because of the goodwill that he had long borne her. Now in the Viceroy's entourage there were not a few noblemen of outstanding valour, courageous men, who, after long service in the wars had earned such heroic reputations that there was no one in the land who was not anxious to meet them and be seen in their company. Amongst these men there was one by the name of Amador.

[1] **Viceroy of Catalonia:** Duke of Segorbe and Count of Ribagorce, Henry of Aragon was Viceroy of Catalonia at this time. He was called the Infante of Fortune because his father died before he was born in 1445.

[2] **his King:** Ferdinand II of Aragon (1452–1516). The tale takes place at the end of the fifteenth and the beginning of the sixteenth century when Spain, during the reign of Ferdinand and Isabella, was engaged in an ongoing border war with France for control of the Pyrenees. Ferdinand II of Aragon was also Ferdinand V of Spain.

Although he was only eighteen or nineteen years of age, he had such confidence, and such sound judgement, that you could not have failed to regard him as one of those rare men fit to govern any state. Not only was he a man of sound judgement, he was also endowed with an appearance so handsome, so open and natural, that he was a delight for all to behold. This was not all, for his handsome looks were equally matched by the fairness of his speech. Poise, good looks, eloquence—it was impossible to say with which gift he was more richly blessed. But what gained him even higher esteem was his fearlessness, which, despite his youth, was famed throughout all lands. For he had already in many different places given evidence of his great abilities. Not only throughout the kingdoms of Spain, but also in France and Italy people looked upon him with admiration. Not once during the recent wars had he shrunk from battle, and when his country had been at peace, he had gone to seek action in foreign parts, and there too had been loved and admired by friend and foe alike.

This young nobleman had devotedly followed his commander back home, to meet the Countess of Aranda. He could not fail to notice her daughter, Florida, who was then but twelve years of age. Never, he thought to himself, as he contemplated her grace and beauty, had he beheld so fair and noble a creature. If only she might look with favour upon him, that alone would give him more happiness than anything any other woman in the world could ever give him. For a long while he gazed at her. His mind was made up. He would love her. The promptings of reason were in vain. He would love her, even though she was of far higher birth than he. He would love her, even though she was not yet of an age to hear and understand the words of love. But his misgivings were as nothing against the firm hope that grew within him, as he promised himself that time and patient waiting would in the end bring his toils to a happy conclusion. Noble Love, through the power that is its own, and for no other cause, had entered Amador's breast and now held out to him the promise of a happy end, and the means of attaining it.

The greatest obstacle was the distance that separated his own homeland from that of Florida, and the lack of opportunity to see her. To [overcome] this problem he decided, contrary to his previous intentions, to marry some lady from Barcelona or Perpignan. His reputation stood so high there that there was little or nothing anyone would refuse him. Moreover, he had spent so long on the frontier during the wars, that although he came from the region of Toledo, he was more like a Catalan than a Castilian. His family was rich and distinguished, but he was the youngest son, and possessed little in the way of inheritance. But Love and Fortune, seeing him ill-provided for by his parents, and resolving to make him their paragon, bestowed upon him through the gift of virtue and valour that which the laws of the land denied him. He was experienced in matters of war, and much sought after by noble lords and princes. He did not have to go out of his way to ask for rewards. More often than not he had to refuse them.

The Countess meanwhile continued on her way, and arrived at Saragossa, where she was well received by the King and the whole court. The Viceroy of Catalonia visited her frequently, and Amador took the opportunity of accompanying him. In this way he might at least have the chance of looking at Florida, for there was no way in which he might be able to speak to her. In order to introduce himself into the society of the Countess, he approached the daughter of an old knight, who came from his home town. Her name was Avanturada, and she [had been brought up alongside] Florida, so that she knew the innermost secrets of her heart. Since she was a good, respectable girl, and expected to receive three thousand ducats a year by way of dowry, Amador made up his mind to address himself to her as a suitor, and seek her hand in marriage. She was only too willing to listen. But her father was a rich man, and she felt that he would never consent to her marriage with a man as poor as Amador unless she enlisted the aid of the Countess. So she first approached Florida.

"My lady, you have seen the Castilian gentleman, who often talks to me," she said. "I believe that it is his intention to ask my hand in marriage. But you know what my father is like. You know that he will never consent, unless the Countess and yourself persuade him."

Florida, who loved the young lady dearly, assured her that she would do everything she could for her, just as if her own interests were at stake. Then Avanturada presented Amador to Florida. As he kissed her hand, he almost fainted in rapture. He, the most eloquent man in Spain, was speechless as he stood before her. This somewhat surprised Florida, for, although she was only twelve years of age, she knew well enough that there was not a man in Spain who could express his mind more eloquently than Amador. He stood there in silence, so she said to him:

"Señor Amador, your reputation has spread through all the kingdoms of Spain, and it would be surprising indeed if you were not known to us also. All of us who have heard about you are anxious to find some way in which we can be of service. So if there is anything I can do, I hope you will not be afraid to ask."

Amador stood gazing at his lady's beauty. He was transported with joy, and was only just able to utter a few words of grateful thanks. Florida was astonished to see that he was still incapable of making any kind of reply, but she attributed it to some momentary whim, completely failing to see that the true cause of his behaviour lay in the violence of his love. She ignored his silence, and said no more.

Amador, for his part, had perceived what great virtue was beginning to appear in Florida, young as she was, and later he said to the lady he was planning to marry: "Avanturada, do not be surprised that I couldn't speak a word in front of Lady Florida. She is so young, yet she speaks so well and so wisely, and behind her tender years there clearly lie hidden such virtues, that I was overcome with admiration and didn't know what to say to her. Tell me, Avanturada, since you are her friend and must know her closest secrets, how is it possible that she hasn't stolen the heart of every single man at court? Any man who has met her, and hasn't fallen in love with her, must be a dumb beast or made of stone!"

Avanturada, who by now was much in love with Amador, could keep nothing from him. She told him that the Lady Florida was indeed greatly loved by everyone, but that very few people actually spoke with her, that being the custom in that part of the land. There were only two men who seemed to show any inclination—Don Alfonso, son of Henry of Aragon, otherwise known as the Infante of Fortune, and the young Duke of Cardona.

"Tell me," said Amador, "which of the two do you think she likes the best?"

"She is so good and wise," replied Avanturada, "that she would never confess to anything that was not in accordance with the wishes of her mother. But, as far as we can judge, she prefers the son of the Infante of Fortune to the Duke of Cardona, although it is the Duke of Cardona her mother prefers, because with him she would stay closer to home. But you are a man of perception and sound judgement, so perhaps you would help us decide what the truth of the matter is. It's like this. The son of the Infante of Fortune was brought up at this court, and he is one of the most handsome and most accomplished young princes in Christendom. What I and the other girls think is that he is the one she should marry—they'd make the loveliest couple in the whole of Spain. And I ought to tell you as well that although they're both very young—she's only twelve and he's fifteen—they've been in love for three years already. If you want to get in her good books you ought to make a friend of him and enter into his service."

Amador was relieved to hear that his lady was capable of love at all. One day, he hoped, he might win the right to become her true and devoted servant, even though he might never become her husband. Of her virtue he was not afraid. His sole anxiety had been that she might reject love completely. From this conversation onwards, Amador made friends with the son of the Infante of Fortune. He had little difficulty in gaining his goodwill, for he was versed in all the sports and diversions that the young prince enjoyed, being an excellent horseman, skilled in the use of arms and indeed good at everything that a young man ought to be able to do.

War broke out again in Languedoc, and Amador was obliged to return with the governor. His sorrow was great, the more so as he had no means of ensuring that he would return to a post where he would still be able to see his Florida. So before his departure, he spoke to a brother of his, who was major-domo in the household of the Queen. He told him what an excellent match he had found in the Lady Avanturada while in the Countess's household, and asked him to do everything in his power during his absence to bring the marriage about, by drawing on the influence of the Queen, the King and all his other friends. The brother, who was very fond of Amador, not only because of their common blood, but because he admired his prowess, promised to do as he was bidden. He was as good as his word. The Countess of Aranda, the young Count, who was growing to appreciate virtue and valour, and above all the beautiful Florida, joined in singing the praises of Amador. The result was that Avanturada's miserly old father put aside his grasping habits for once and was brought to recognize Amador's excellent qualities. The marriage was duly agreed upon by the parents of the couple, and, during the truce that had been declared by the two warring kings, Amador was summoned home by his brother.

It was at that time that the King of Spain withdrew to Madrid, where he was safe from the unhealthy air that was affecting a number of places throughout the country. Acting on the advice of his Council, but also at the request of the Countess, he had arranged a marriage between her son, the little Count, and a rich heiress, the Duchess of Medinaceli, in order to bring the two families together in an advantageous union and to please the Countess herself, whose interests were very dear to his heart. In accordance with his wishes the marriage was celebrated in the King's palace at Madrid. Amador was present, and was able to pursue his own matrimonial plans so successfully that he too was married—to Avanturada, in whom he inspired a good deal more love than he returned. His marriage was no more than a cover, no more than a convenient excuse to enable him to visit her on whom his mind constantly dwelled.

After his marriage he made himself so familiar in the Countess's household that no one took any more notice of him than if he had been a woman. He was only twenty-two at this time, but had such good sense that the Countess used to keep him informed of all her business affairs. She even instructed her son and her daughter to listen carefully to his conversation, and heed any advice he might give. Having reached these heights in the Countess's esteem, he behaved in such a sensible, such a restrained manner, that even the lady whom he loved so dearly failed to perceive his feelings. In fact, being so fond of Amador's wife, she hid nothing from Amador himself, not even her most intimate thoughts, [and went so far as] to tell him about her love for the son of the Infante of Fortune. Amador's sole concern was to win her completely, and he talked to her constantly about the Infante's son. Provided he was able to converse with her, he did not care what was the topic of their conversation. However, he had been there hardly a month after his marriage when he was obliged to go back to the wars. Not once, during the two years that followed, did he return to see his wife, who waited for him, living as she always had done in the household of the Countess. Throughout this time Amador would write to his wife, but his letters consisted principally of messages for Florida. She for her part would reply, and even insert something amusing in her own hand in Avanturada's letters—which alone was enough to make Amador very conscientious in writing to his wife. But throughout all this Florida was aware of nothing, except perhaps that she was as fond of Amador as if he had been her own brother.

Several times Amador came and went, but for five whole years he never saw Florida for two months together. Yet in spite of these long absences, and the long distances that separated them, his love grew. At last he was able to travel to see his wife. He found the Countess far from the court, for the King had gone into Andalusia, taking with him the young Count of Aranda, who had already started to bear arms. The Countess had moved to a country house she owned on the borders of Aragon and Navarre. She was delighted to see Amador, who had been away now for three years, and commanded that he was to be treated like a son. There was nobody who did not make him welcome. During his stay, the Countess told him all her domestic business, and asked his advice on almost every aspect of it. The family's regard for him was unbounded. Wherever he went, there was always an open door. He was looked upon as a man of such integrity that he was trusted in everything. Had he been a saint or an angel, he could hardly have been trusted more. Florida, fond as she was of Avanturada, went straight to Amador whenever she saw him. Having not the slightest suspicion as to his true intentions, she was quite unreserved in her behaviour towards him. There was not a trace of passion in her heart, unless it was a feeling of contentment at being by his side. Nothing else occurred to her. But there are people who can guess from the expression in a man's eyes whether that man is in love or not, and Amador was constantly anxious lest he be thus found out. When Florida came to speak to him alone, in complete innocence, the fire that burned in his breast would flare up so violently that, do what he might, the colour would mount to his cheeks and the flames of passion would gleam in his eyes.

In order that no one should guess from his intimacy with Florida that he was in love with her, he began to make approaches to an extremely attractive lady called Paulina, whose charms were highly celebrated in her day, and from whose snares few men managed to escape. She had heard how Amador had been successful with the ladies in Barcelona and Perpignan, and how he had won the hearts of the most beautiful and most noble ladies in the land; in particular she had heard how a certain Countess of Palamos, who was regarded as the most beautiful woman in Spain, had lost her heart to him. So she told him how deeply she pitied him for having married such an ugly wife, after all his past good fortunes in love. Amador realized from what she said that she was ready to provide him with any consolation he might require, and replied with as encouraging words as he was able, thinking that it would be possible to cover up the truth of his real feelings by making her believe a lie. But she was shrewd, experienced in the ways of love, and not a woman to make do with mere words. She sensed that his heart was not entirely taken up with love for her, and suspected that he wanted to use her as a cover. She watched him so closely that not a single glance escaped her. Amador's eyes were well-practised in the art of dissembling, however, and Paulina could get no further than her vague suspicions. But it was only with extreme difficulty that he was able to hide his feelings, especially when Florida, who had not the slightest idea of the game he was playing, talked to him with her customary intimacy in front of Paulina herself. It was only by making the most painful effort that on such occasions he was able to control the expression in his eyes, and prevent them reflecting the feelings in his heart. So to forestall any unfortunate consequences in the future, he said to her one day as he leaned against the window where they had been chatting: "Tell me, [my Lady], is it better to speak or to die?"

"I would always advise my friends to speak," she replied quickly, "because there are very few words that can't be remedied, but once you've lost your life, there's no way of getting it back."

"So will you promise that you will not only not be angry at what I am going to say, but also, if you are shocked, that you will not say anything until I have finished?"

"Say whatever you please," she said, "because if *you* shock me, then there's no one in the world who could reassure me."

So he began.

"My Lady, there are two reasons why I have not yet told you of the feelings I have for you. One reason is that I hoped to give you proof of my love through long and devoted service. The other is that I feared that you would consider it [overweening presumption] that I, an ordinary nobleman, should dare to aspire to the love of a lady of birth so high. Even if I were, like you, my Lady, of princely estate, a heart so true and loyal as your own would not suffer such talk of love from anyone but the son of the Infante of Fortune, who has taken possession of your heart. Yet, my Lady, just as in the hardships of war one may be compelled to destroy one's own land, to lay waste one's rising crops, in order to prevent the enemy taking advantage of them, even so do I now seek to anticipate the fruit that I had hoped to reap only in the fullness of time, in order to prevent our enemies from taking advantage of it to your loss. I must tell you, my Lady, that from the time I first saw you, when you were still so young, I have wholly consecrated myself to your service. I have never ceased to seek the means to obtain your good grace, and it was for this reason alone that I married the very lady who is your own dearest friend. Knowing, too, that you loved the son of the Infante, I did my utmost to serve him, to become his friend. In short, I have striven to do everything that I thought would give you pleasure. You have seen how the Countess, your mother, has looked favourably upon me, as has the Count your brother, and all those of whom you are fond, with the result that I am treated in this house, not as a man serving his superiors, but as a son. All the efforts that I made five years ago were for no other end than to live my whole life by you. But you must believe me, my Lady, when I tell you that I am not one of those men who would exploit this advantage. I desire no favour, nor pleasure, from you, except what is in accordance with the dictates of virtue. I know that I cannot marry you. And even if I could, I should not seek to do so, for your love is given to another, and it is he whom I long to see your husband. Nor is my love a base love. I am not one of those men who hope that if they serve their lady long enough they will be rewarded with her dishonour. Such intentions could not be further from my heart, for I would rather see you dead, than have to admit that my own gratification had sullied your virtue, had, in a word, made you less worthy to be loved. I ask but one thing in recompense of my devotion and my service. I ask only that you might be my true and faithful Lady, so true, so faithful, that you will never cast me from your good grace, that you will allow me to continue in my present estate, and that you will place your trust in me above all others. And if your honour, or any cause close to your heart, should demand that a noble gentleman lay down his life, then mine will I gladly lay down for your sake. On this you may depend. Know, too, that whatsoever deeds of mine may be counted noble, good or brave, these deeds will be performed for love of you alone. Yes, and if for ladies less exalted my deeds have met acclaim, then be you assured that for a lady such as you I shall perform such deeds of greatness, that acts which once I deemed impossible I shall now perform with ease. But if you will not accept me as wholly yours, my Lady, then I shall make up my mind to abandon my career at arms. I shall renounce the valour and the virtue that were mine, for they will have availed me nought. Wherefore, my Lady, I do humbly beseech that my just demand might be granted, since your honour and your conscience cannot refuse it."

The young Lady Florida changed colour at this speech, the like of which she had never heard before. Then she lowered her gaze, like a mature woman, her modesty shocked. Then, with all the virtue and good sense that was hers, she said:

"If, as seems to be the case, Amador, you're only asking me for something that you already have, then why do you insist on making such a long, high-flown speech about it? I am rather afraid that there is some evil intent hidden away underneath all these fine words, and that you're trying to beguile me because I'm young and innocent. It makes me very uncertain as to how I should reply to you. If I were to reject the noble love that you offer me, I would only be contradicting the way I've behaved towards you up till now, because in you I've placed more trust than in any other man in the world. Neither my honour nor my conscience stand in the way of your request. Nor does the love I bear the son of the Infante of Fortune, for my love for him is founded on marriage, to which you lay no claim. In fact I can think of no reason why I should not grant your wishes, except perhaps for one anxiety that troubles my mind. You have no reason to address me in the way you do. If you already have what you desire, what can it be that now makes you tell me about it in such an emotional manner?"

Amador was ready with his reply.

"My Lady, you speak most prudently," he said, "and do me great honour to place in me such trust as you declare. If I were not happy to receive this blessing from you, I should be unworthy indeed to receive any other. But let me explain, my Lady, that the mall who desires to build an edifice that will endure throughout eternity should take the utmost care to lay a safe and sure foundation. So it is that I, who desire most earnestly to serve you through all eternity, should take the greatest care that I have the means to ensure not only that I shall remain always by you, but that I shall be able to prevent all others from knowing of the great love I bear you. For, though my love is pure and noble enough to be announced to the whole world, yet there are people who will never understand a lover's soul, and whose pronouncements will always belie the truth. The rumours that result are none the less unpleasant for being untrue. The reason why I have made so bold as to say all this to you, is that Paulina has become very suspicious. She senses in her heart that I am unable to give her my love, and she is constantly on the watch for me to give myself away. And when you come to talk to me alone in your affectionate way, I am so nervous lest she discern something in my expression to confirm her suspicions that I find myself in just the awkward situation that I am most anxious to avoid. So I made up my mind to beg you not to take me unawares when Paulina is present, or anyone else whom you know to have an equally malicious disposition. For I would die rather than let any living creature know of my feelings. Were it not that your honour is so dear to me, I should never have entertained the idea of speaking to you in the way I have spoken. For I feel myself so content in the love that you have for me, that there is nothing further that I desire, unless it be that you should continue in the same for ever."

At these words Florida was filled with delight beyond bounds. Deep within her heart she began to feel stirrings that she had never felt before. And as she could see that the arguments he brought forth were honourable and good, she was able to grant his request, saying that virtue and honour answered for her. Amador was transported with joy, as anyone who has ever truly loved will understand.

However, Florida took his advice too seriously. She became nervous, not only in the presence of Paulina, but in other circumstances too, until she began not to seek Amador's company at all in the way she had in the past. Moreover, she took it badly that he spent so much time with Paulina, who seemed so attractive that she felt it impossible for Amador not to be in love with her. To relieve her distress she would talk at great length with Avanturada, who was herself beginning to be jealous of her husband and Paulina, and often bemoaned her lot to her friend. Florida, suffering from the same affliction, would offer what consolation she was able. It was not long before Amador noticed Florida's strange behaviour, and concluded that she was keeping away from him, not just as a result of his advice, but because she was displeased with him. One day, as they were returning from vespers at a monastery, he said to her: "My Lady, why do you treat me the way you do?"

"Because that is the way I thought you wanted it," she replied.

Then, suspecting the truth of the matter, and wishing to know whether he was right, Amador said: "My Lady, because of the time I have spent with her, Paulina no longer suspects you."

"Then you couldn't have done better, either for yourself or for me," she answered, "for in giving yourself a little pleasure, you are acting in the interests of my honour."

Amador understood from these words that she thought he derived pleasure from talking with Paulina. So hurt was he that he could not restrain his anger:

"Ah! My Lady, so you're starting already to torment your servant, by hurling abuse at him for [acting in your interests!] There's nothing more irksome and distressing than being obliged to spend one's time with a woman one isn't even in love with! Since you take exception to tasks I undertake solely in your service, I'll never speak to her again. And let the consequences take care of themselves! To cover up my anger, just as in the past I've hidden my joy, I shall go away to a place not far from here, and wait until your mood has passed. But I hope that when I get there I shall receive orders from my commanding officer to return to the wars, where I shall stay long enough to prove to you that nothing keeps me here but you, my Lady."

So saying, he went, without even waiting for her reply. Florida was left utterly dejected and downcast. Love, having been thwarted, was aroused now, and began to demonstrate its power. She acknowledged that she had wronged Amador, and wrote to him over and over again, beseeching him to come back to her—as indeed he did several days later, once his anger had subsided. I could not begin to tell you in detail what they said to one another to resolve their jealousies. To cut a long story short, he won the day. She promised that she would never again suspect him of being in love with Paulina. More than that, she swore she was and would remain convinced that it was for Amador almost unbearable to have to speak with Paulina or any other woman, nay that it was a martyrdom suffered for no other reason than to render service to his lady.

No sooner had Love overcome these first suspicions and jealousies, no sooner had the two lovers begun to take more pleasure than ever from talking together, than word came that the King of Spain was sending the entire army to Salces.[3] Amador, who was accustomed to be the first to join the royal standards, was as eager as ever to follow the path of honour and glory. Yet this time it was with particular regret, a regret deeper than that which he had experienced before, for not only was he relinquishing the one pleasure of his life, but he now feared that Florida might change during his absence. She had already reached the age of fifteen or sixteen, and was wooed by lords and princes from far and wide. He feared that she might be married while he was away, and that he might never see her again. He had one safeguard, however—that the Countess should make his wife the special companion to Florida. Accordingly, he employed his influence to obtain promises both from the Countess and from Florida herself that wherever she should go after her marriage Avanturada should go with her. And so, in spite of the fact that the talk at that time was of a marriage in Portugal, Amador was certain in his mind that she would never abandon him. With this assurance, yet none the less filled with sorrow beyond words, he departed for the wars, leaving his wife with the Countess.

---

[3] **Salces:** A fortress town in the Corbière Mountains between Spain and France, Salces was a site of frequent battles in the wars between the two countries. The battle in question here took place in 1503.

After her faithful servant had left, Florida found herself quite alone. She set herself to perform all manner of good and virtuous deeds, hoping thereby to acquire the reputation of being the most perfect lady in the land, and worthy to have a man such as Amador devoted to her service. As for Amador himself, when he arrived at Barcelona, he was, as he had been in the past, greeted with delight by all the ladies. But they found him a changed man. They would never have thought that marriage had such a hold over a man, for he now seemed to have nothing but distaste for all the things that before he had pursued. Even the Countess of Palamos, of whom he had once been so enamoured, could no longer find a way of luring him even as far as the door of her residence. Anxious to be away to the scene of battle [where glory was to be won], Amador spent as little time as possible in Barcelona. No sooner had he arrived at Salces, than war did indeed break out between the two kings. It was a great and merciless war. I have no intention of relating the course of events in detail, or even of recounting the many heroic deeds accomplished by Amador, for to tell you all this I should need a whole day. Suffice it to say that Amador won renown above all his comrades in arms. The Duke of Nájera arrived at Perpignan in charge of two thousand men, and invited Amador to be his second-in-command. He answered the call of duty, and led his men with such success that in every skirmish the air rang with shouts of "Nájera! Nájera!"

Now it came to the ears of the King of Tunis that the kings of Spain and France were waging war on the border between Perpignan and Narbonne. He had long been at war himself with the King of Spain, and he now saw that he could not wish for a better opportunity to harass him more. So he sent a large fleet of galleys and other vessels to pillage and lay waste every inch of unguarded territory that he could find along the Spanish coasts. When the inhabitants of Barcelona saw the vast number of sailing ships looming on the horizon, they immediately sent word to their Viceroy at Salces, who reacted by sending the Duke of Nájera to Palamos[4] without delay. The Moors arrived to find the coasts well garrisoned and acted as if they were sailing on. But towards midnight they returned, and put large numbers of men ashore. The Duke was taken completely by surprise, and was in fact taken prisoner. Amador, vigilant as ever, had heard the noise, marshalled as many of his men as he could and defended himself so effectively that it was a long time before the stronger forces of the enemy were able to make any inroads. In the end, however, realizing that the Duke of Nájera had been captured, and that the Turks were determined to set fire to the whole of Palamos, and destroy the building which he had defended against them, he thought it better to surrender than to be the cause of the annihilation of his valiant comrades. It was also in his mind that if he were held to ransom, there would be some hope of seeing Florida again. Without more ado, he gave himself up to the Turkish chief-in-command, a man called Dorlin, who took Amador before the King of Tunis himself. He was received respectfully and treated well. He was guarded well, too, for the Turkish King was aware that the man he had in his hands was the veritable Achilles of Spain.

[4] **Palamos:** A village on the Mediterranean coast north of Barcelona.

For two years Amador remained the prisoner of the King of Tunis. When the news reached Spain, the family of the Duke of Nájera was stricken with grief, but people who held the honour of their country dear judged the capture of Amador an even greater loss. It was broken to the Countess of Aranda and her household at a time when the poor Avanturada lay seriously ill. The Countess (who had guessed how Amador felt about her daughter, and had kept quiet, raising no objections, because she appreciated the young man's qualities) called Florida to one side to tell her the distressing news. But Florida knew how to hide her true feelings, and merely said that it was a great loss for all the family, and that she felt especially sorry for Amador's poor wife lying sick in bed. But seeing her mother weeping bitterly, she shed a few tears with her, lest her secret be discovered by being too well disguised. From this time on the Countess often spoke to Florida about Amador, but never once was she able to draw from her any reaction that would confirm her thoughts. I shall leave aside for now the pilgrimages, the prayers, the devotions, the fasts, which Florida began regularly to offer for Amador's salvation. As for Amador himself, as soon as he reached Tunis, he lost no time in sending messengers to his friends. To Florida he naturally sent the most trustworthy man he could find, to let her know that he was well and living in the hope of seeing her again. This was all she had to sustain her in her distress, but you may be sure that since she was allowed to write to him, she assiduously performed this task, and Amador did not go without the consolation of her letters.

The Countess of Aranda was summoned to Saragossa, where the King had taken up residence. There she found the young Duke of Cardona, who had been actively seeking the support of the King and Queen in his suit for the hand of Florida. Pressed by the King to agree to the marriage, the Countess, as a loyal subject, could not refuse his request. She was sure that her daughter, still so young in years, could have no other will than that of her mother, and, once the agreement was concluded, she took her on one side to explain how she had chosen for her the match which was most fitting. Florida knew that the matter was already settled and that further deliberation was useless. "May the Lord be praised in everything," was all she could bring herself to say, for her mother looked so stern, and she judged it preferable to obey rather than indulge in self-pity. To crown all her sorrows, she then heard that the son of the Infante of Fortune had fallen sick and was close to death. But never once in the presence of her mother, or of anyone else, did she show any sign of how she felt. So hard indeed did she repress her feelings that her tears, having been held back in her heart by force, caused violent bleeding from the nose which threatened her life. And all the cure she got was marriage to a man she would gladly have exchanged for death. After the marriage was over she went to the Duchy of Cardona. With her went Avanturada, to whom she was able to unburden herself, bemoaning the harsh treatment she had received from her mother and the sorrow she nursed in her heart at the loss of the son of the Infante. But never once did she mention the fact that she missed Amador, except by way of consoling Avanturada herself. In short, the young Lady Florida resolved to have God and honour constantly before her eyes, and she so carefully hid her troubles, that no one had the slightest suspicion that her husband gave her no pleasure.

For a long time Florida lived this life, a life that seemed to her little better than death. She wrote of her woe to her servant Amador, who, knowing how great and noble was his lady's heart, and how deep was her love for the son of the Infante, could only think her end was nigh. This new anguish heightened his affliction, and he grieved bitterly, for Florida's plight seemed already worse than death. Yet he knew what torment his beloved must be suffering, and his own paled into insignificance. Gladly would he have stayed a slave to the end of his days, if only that might have ensured Florida the husband of her desires. One day he learned from a friend he had made at the court of Tunis that the King, who would have liked to keep Amador in his service, provided he could make a good Turk of him, was planning to threaten him with impalement if he did not renounce his faith. To forestall this move, therefore, he prevailed upon the man who had captured him and had become his master to let him go on parole, without informing the King. The ransom was set so high that the Turk reckoned no one as poor as Amador could ever possibly find the money to pay it.

So, having been allowed to depart, he went to the court of the King of Spain, from where, as soon as he was able, he set off again to seek his ransom amongst his friends. He went straight to Barcelona, where the young Duke of Cardona, his mother and Florida were staying on account of some family business. As soon as Amador's wife, Avanturada, heard the news, she told Florida, who, as if for Avanturada's sake, expressed her joy. But she was afraid lest the joy she felt at seeing him again should show in her face, and lest people who did not know her well should put a bad interpretation on it. So instead of going to meet him, she stood at a window to watch his arrival from afar. Immediately he came into sight she went down by way of a staircase, which was dark enough to prevent anybody seeing whether her cheeks changed colour. She embraced Amador, took him to her room, and then to meet her husband's mother, who had not yet made his acquaintance. Needless to say, he had not been there two days before he had endeared himself to the whole household, exactly as he had in the house of the Countess of Aranda. I shall leave you to imagine the words that passed between him and Florida, and how Florida sorrowfully told of all that she had been through during his absence. She wept bitterly at having had to marry against her inclinations, and at having lost the man whom she loved so dearly, without hope of ever seeing him again. Then she made up her mind to take consolation in her love for Amador and the sense of security it afforded her, though she never once dared declare to him her intent. Amador guessed, however, and never lost an opportunity to make known to her how great was his love for her.

Florida was almost won. She was almost at the point where she was ready not merely to accept Amador as a devoted servant, but to admit him as a sure and perfect lover. But it was then that a most unhappy accident occurred. Amador had received word from the King to go to him immediately on urgent business. Avanturada was very upset at the news, and fainted. Unfortunately she happened to be standing at the top of a flight of stairs. She fell, and injured herself so badly that she never recovered. Florida was deeply affected by Avanturada's death. There could be no consolation for her now. It was as if she felt herself bereft of all relatives and friends. She went into deep mourning for her loss. To Amador the blow was even more overwhelming, for not only had he lost one of the most virtuous wives who ever lived, but he had also lost all hope now of continuing to be near Florida. He sank into a state of such dejection, that he thought he himself had not long to live. The old Duchess of Cardona visited him at frequent intervals, and quoted the sayings of the philosophers, in the hope of inducing him to bear the death of his wife with fortitude. But to no avail. The spectre of death tormented him from one side. From the other, his martyrdom was made more painful by the force of his love. His wife was dead and buried. His sovereign lord had called him. What further reason could he have for staying where he was? In his heart was such despair that he thought he would lose his reason. Florida sought to give consolation, but desolation was all she brought him. One whole afternoon she spent in an attempt to console him with gentle words, doing all she would to lessen the pain of his grief, and assuring him that she would find a way of seeing him far more often than he supposed. Since he was due to depart the following morning, and since he was so weak that he was unable to move from his bed, he begged her to come and visit him again that same evening, when everyone else had gone. This she promised to do, not realizing that such extremity of love as Amador's knew no rational bounds. He had served her long and well, without any reward other than what I have described in my story. Now he despaired of ever being able to return to see her again, and, racked by a love that had been hidden away within him, he made up his mind to make one last desperate gamble—to risk losing all, or to gain everything and treat himself to one short hour of the bliss that he considered he had earned. He had his bed hung with heavy curtains, so that it was impossible for anyone in the room to see in, and when his visitors came he moaned even more than before, so that people thought that he must surely die before another day passed.

In the evening, when all the visitors had gone, Florida came, with the full approval of her husband, who had encouraged her to tend the sick man. She hoped to give him consolation by declaring her feelings and her desire to love him within the limits permitted by honour. She sat down on a chair at the head of his bed, and began, as she thought, to comfort him, by joining her tears to his. Seeing her so overcome with sorrow and regret, Amador judged that it was now, while she was in this state of torment, that his intentions would most easily be accomplished. He rose from his bed. Florida, thinking he was too weak for such exertions, tried to stop him. But he fell on his knees in front of her, saying, "Must I lose you for ever from my sight?" Whereupon he collapsed into her arms, as if all his strength had suddenly drained from him. The poor Florida put her arms around him and supported him for a while, doing her utmost to console him. He said not a word, and pretending still that he was at the brink of death, began to pursue the path that leads to the forbidden goal of a lady's honour. When Florida realized that his intentions were not pure, she found it beyond belief. Had not his conversation in the past always been pure and good? She asked him what he was trying to do. Amador still said nothing. He did not want to receive a reply that could not but be virtuous and chaste. He struggled with all the strength in his body to have his way. Florida, terrified, thought he must be out of his mind. Rather that, than have to admit he had desired to stain her honour. She called out to a gentleman who she knew would be in the room. Amador, now utterly despairing, threw himself back on the bed with such violence that the other man thought he had breathed his last. Florida, who had now got up from her chair, said: "Quick, go and fetch some fresh vinegar!"

While the gentleman was doing as he had been bidden, she turned to Amador.

"What kind of madness is this, Amador? Are you beginning to lose your mind? What did you think you were trying to do?"

"What cruelty!" exclaimed Amador, now bereft of all reason through the violence of love. "Is this the only reward I deserve after serving you so long?"

"And what," she replied, "has become of the honour you preached about so often?"

"Ah! my Lady," he said, "no one in the world could possibly hold your honour as dear as I do! Before you were married I was able to overcome the desires of my heart so successfully that you knew nothing at all of my feelings. But now you are a married woman. You have a cover and your honour is safe. So what wrong can I possibly be doing you in asking for what is truly mine? It is I who have really won you, through the power of my love. The man who first won your heart so irresolutely pursued your body that he well deserved to lose both. As for the man who now possesses your body—he's not worthy of the smallest corner in your heart. So you do not really belong to him, even in body. But consider, my Lady, what trials and tribulations I have gone through in the last five or six years for your sake. Surely you cannot fail to realize that it is to me alone that you belong, body and heart, for is it not for you that I have refused to give thought to my own body and my own heart? And if you are thinking that you can justify yourself on grounds of conscience, bear in mind that no sin may be imputed when the heart and the body are constrained by the power of love. When men kill themselves in a violent fit of madness, in no way do they commit a sin. For passion leaves no room for reason. And if it is the case that the passion of love is the most difficult to bear of all, if it is—as indeed it is—the passion that most completely blinds the senses, then what sin can you impute to a man who merely lets himself be swept along by an insuperable force? Now I must depart. All hope of seeing you again is gone. Had I but the guarantee that my great love deserves, I would have all the strength I need to endure in patience what will surely be a long and painful absence. If, however, you do not deign to grant me my request, then ere long you shall hear that your severity has brought me to a cruel and unhappy end!"

Florida was as distressed as she was taken aback to hear a speech like this from a man of whom she would never have expected anything of the kind, and her tears flowed.

"Alas! Amador," she began, "what has happened to all the virtuous things you used to say to me when I was young? Is this the honour, is this the conscience, for which you so often told me to die, rather than lose my soul? Have you forgotten all the lessons you taught me from examples of virtuous ladies who resisted senseless and wicked passion? Have you forgotten how you have always spoken with scorn of women who succumb to it? It is hard, Amador, to believe that you have left your former self so far behind that all regard for God, for your conscience, and for my honour is completely dead. But if it really is as you seem to say, then I thank God that in His goodness He has forewarned me of the disaster that was about to befall me. By the words you have uttered God has revealed to me what your heart is really like. How could I have remained ignorant for so long? I lost the son of the Infante of Fortune, not just because I was obliged to marry somebody else, but because I knew that he really loved another woman. Now I am married to a man whom I cannot love and cherish however hard I try. That is why I had made up my mind to give you all the love that is in me, to love you with my whole heart. And the foundation of this love was to have been virtue, that virtue which holds honour and conscience dearer than life itself, that virtue which I first found in you, and which, through you, I think I have now attained. Thus it was that I came to you, Amador, firmly resolved to build upon this rock of honour. But in this short space of time you have clearly demonstrated to me that I would have been building not upon the solid rock of purity, but upon the shifting sands, nay, upon a treacherous bog of vice. I had begun to build a dwelling in which I could live for evermore, but with a single blow you have razed it to the ground. So now you must abandon hope. You must be resolved never again, wherever it may be, to seek to speak to me or look into my eyes. Nor may you hope that one day I could change my mind, even should I so desire. My heart brims with sorrow for what might have been. But had it come to pass that I had sworn myself to you in the bond of perfect love, my poor heart would have been wounded unto death by what has transpired. To think that I have been so deceived! If it does not bring me to an early grave, I shall surely suffer for the rest of my days. This is my final word to you. Adieu. For ever more adieu!"

I shall not try to describe Amador's feelings as he listened to these words. It would be impossible to set such anguish down in writing. It is difficult even for anyone to imagine such anguish, unless they have experienced the same kind of suffering themselves. What a cruel end! Realizing that she was going to leave him on this note, and that he would lose her for ever if he did not clear his name, he seized her by the arm.

"My Lady," he said, putting on the most convincing expression he could manage, "for as long as I can remember I have longed to love a good and honourable woman. But I have found few who are truly virtuous, and that is why I wanted to test you out—to see if you were as worthy to be admired for your virtue, as you are to be loved for your other attributes. And now I know for certain that you are. For this I praise God, and give Him thanks that He has brought my heart to love such consummate perfection! So I beseech you, forgive this whim, pardon my rash behaviour. For as you can see, all has turned out for the best. Your honour is vindicated, and I am happy indeed that this should be so!"

But Florida was beginning to understand the evil ways of men. If she had before found it hard to believe that Amador's intentions were bad, she now found it even harder to believe him when he said that in reality they were good.

"Would to God that you were speaking the truth!" she said. "But I am a married woman, and I am not so ignorant that I do not clearly realize that it was violent passion that drove you to do what you did. If God had not stood by me, and my hold on the reins had slackened, I am not at all convinced that you would have been the one to tighten the bridle. Those who truly seek virtue do not take the route that you took. But enough has been said. I was too ready to believe you were a good man. It is time that I recognized the truth, for it is by truth that now I am delivered from your clutches."

With these words, Florida left the room. The whole night long she wept. This sudden change caused her such pain that her heart was hard pressed to withstand the assaults of bitter regret which love hurled against it. For, while in accordance with reason she was determined to love him no more, the heart, over which none of us has control, would never yield. Thus, unable to love him less than before, she resolved to propitiate love, since love it was that was the cause. She resolved, in short, to go on loving Amador with all her heart, but, in order to obey the dictates of honour, never to let it be known, either to him or to anyone.

The next morning Amador departed in a state of mind which I leave to your imagination. But no one in the world had a more valiant heart than he, and, instead of sinking into despair, he began to seek new ways of seeing Florida again, and winning her. So, being due to present himself to the King of Spain, who at that time was in residence at Toledo, he went by way of the County of Aranda. He arrived late one night at the castle of the Countess, and found her ailing, and pining for her daughter. When she saw Amador she put her arms around him and kissed him, as if he were her own son, for she loved him dearly, and had guessed that he was in love with Florida. She pressed him for news, and he told her as much as he could without telling the whole truth. Then he told her what her daughter had always concealed, and confessed their love, begging the Countess to help him have news of Florida, and to bring her soon to live with her.

The next morning he left, and continued on his journey. When his business with the King had been dispatched, he went off to join the army on active service. He was downcast and so changed in every respect that the ladies and officers whose company he had always kept no longer recognized him. He continually dressed himself in clothes of coarse black cloth, much more austere than was called for by the death of his wife. But the death of his wife served merely as a cover for a much deeper grief. Three or four years went by, and Amador never once returned to court. The Countess meanwhile had word that such a change had come over her daughter that she was piteous to behold. She summoned Florida to her, in the hope that she might want to come back and live with her permanently. But Florida would not hear of it. When she heard that Amador had told her mother about their love, and that her mother, good and wise as she was, had confided in Amador and told him she approved, her consternation was great indeed. On the one hand, she could see that her mother had considerable admiration for Amador, and that if she had the truth told to her, it might bring him harm. That was the last thing she wanted, and in any case, she felt quite well able to punish him for his outrageous behaviour without help from her family. On the other hand, she could see that if she concealed the bad things she knew about him, she would be obliged by her mother and all her friends to talk with him and receive him favourably. That, she feared, could only strengthen him in his base intentions. However, he was in distant parts, so she made little fuss, and wrote him letters whenever the Countess asked her to do so. But when she did write, she made sure that he would realize that they were written out of obedience, and not from any inclination of her own. There had once been a time when her letters had brought him transports of joy. Now he felt nothing but sorrow as he read them.

Three years went by, during which time Amador performed so many glorious deeds that no writer could ever hope to set them all down, even if he had all the paper in Spain. It was now that he devised his grand scheme—not a scheme to win back Florida's heart, for he deemed her lost for ever, but a scheme to score a victory over her as his mortal enemy, for that was how she now appeared. Throwing all reason to the winds, and setting aside all fear of death, he took the greatest risk of his life. His mind was made up. He was not to be deterred from his aim. Since his credit stood high with the governor, he was able to get himself appointed to a mission to the King for the purpose of discussing some secret campaign directed against the town of Leucate.[5] He also managed to get himself issued with orders to inform the Countess of Aranda of the plan, and to take her advice before meeting the King. Knowing that Florida was there, he went post-haste into Aranda, and on his arrival sent a friend in secrecy to tell the Countess that he wished to see her, and that they must meet only at dead of night, without anyone else knowing about it. Overjoyed to hear that Amador was in the neighbourhood, the Countess told Florida, and sent her to undress in her husband's room, so that she should be ready to be called once everyone had retired. Florida made no objection. But she had not yet recovered from her earlier terrifying experience, and, instead of doing as she was bidden, went straight to an oratory to commend herself to our Lord, and to pray to Him that He might preserve her heart from all base affections. Remembering that Amador had often praised her beauty, which in spite of long sickness had in no way diminished, she could not bear the thought that this beauty of hers should kindle so base a fire in the heart of a man who was so worthy and so good. Rather than that she would disfigure herself, impair her beauty. She seized a stone that lay on the chapel floor, and struck herself in the face with great force, severely injuring her mouth, nose and eyes. Then, so that no one would suspect her when she was summoned, she deliberately threw herself against a [large piece of stone] as she left the chapel. She lay with her face to the ground, screaming, and was found in this appalling state by the Countess, who immediately had her wounds dressed and her face swathed in bandages.

Once she had been made comfortable, the Countess took her into her chamber and told her that she wanted her to go and talk to Amador in her private room till she had dismissed her attendants. Thinking that Amador would not be unaccompanied, Florida obeyed, but, once the door closed behind her, she was horrified to find herself completely alone with him. Amador, for his part, was not at all displeased, for now, he thought, he would by fair means or foul surely get what he had so long desired. A few words were sufficient to tell him that her attitude was the same as when he had last seen her, and that she would die rather than change her mind. In a state of utter desperation he said:

"Almighty God, Florida, I'm not going to have the just deserts of all my efforts frustrated by your scruples! Seeing that all my love, all my patient waiting, all my begging and praying are useless, I shall use every ounce of strength in my body to get the one thing that will make life worth living! Without it I shall die!"

His whole expression, his face, his eyes, had changed as he spoke. The fair

[5] **Leucate:** A fortified town near Salces.

complexion was flushed with fiery red. The kind, gentle face was contorted with a terrifying violence, as if there was some raging inferno belching fire in his heart and behind his eyes. One powerful fist roughly seized hold of her two weak and delicate hands. Her feet were held in a vice-like grip. There was nothing she could do to save herself. She could neither fight back, nor could she fight free. She had no other recourse than to see if there might not yet be some trace of his former love, for the sake of which he might relent and have mercy.

"Amador," she gasped, "even if you think I'm your enemy now, I beg you, in the name of that pure love which I used to think you felt for me in your heart, please listen to me, before you torture me!"

Seeing that he was prepared to hear her out, she continued: "Alas, Amador! What is it that drives you to seek that which can give you no satisfaction, and to cause me the greatest sorrow anyone could ever cause me? You came to know my feelings so well in the days when I was young, when my beauty was at its most fresh, and when your passion might have had some excuse, that I marvel now that at the age I am, ugly as I am, ravaged by deepest sorrow as I am, you should seek that which you know you cannot find. I am certain that you can have no doubt but that my feelings remain as they have always been, and that [only by use of force therefore can you obtain that which you ask]. If you will look at the way my face is now adorned, you will lose all memory of the delights that once you found there, you will lose all your desire to approach it nearer! If there is the slightest trace in you of the love you used to bear me, you must surely have pity on me and overcome this violent madness. In the name of all the [pity and noble virtue] that I have known in you in the past, I plead with you, and beg you for mercy. Just let me live in peace! Let me live the life of honour and virtue to which, as you yourself once urged me, I have committed myself. And if your former love for me really has turned to hatred, and if, more out of a desire for revenge than some form of love, your intention is to make me the most wretched woman on earth, then I tell you plainly that you will not have your way. I shall be forced, against all my previous intentions, to make known your vicious designs to the very lady, who hitherto has held you in the highest esteem. You will realize that if I take this action, you will be in danger of your life . . ."

"If I am to die anyway," Amador broke in, "then the agony will be over all the sooner! Nor am I going to be deterred because you've disfigured your face! I'm quite sure you did it yourself, of your own volition. No! If all I could get were your bare bones, still I should want to hold them close!"

Florida could see that neither tears, nor entreaties, nor reasoning were to any avail. She could see that he was going to act out his evil desires, unmoved and merciless. Exhausted and unable to struggle any more, there was only one thing left she could do to save herself, the one thing that she had shrunk from as from death itself. With a heart-rending cry, she shouted out to her mother with all the strength that was in her. There was something in Florida's voice that made the Countess go cold with horror. Suspecting what had happened, she flew to the room with all possible haste. Amador, not quite so ready to die as he had just declared, had had enough time to gather himself together. When the Countess entered, there he was standing by the door, with Florida at a distance.

"Amador, what's the matter?" she demanded, "Tell me the truth!"

Amador was never at loss when it came to finding his way out of a difficult situation. Looking shocked and pale, he gave his answer.

"Alas! Madame, what has come over Florida? I've never been so astonished as I am at this moment. I used to think, as you know, that I had some share in her goodwill. But now I see that I have none at all. I do not think that she was any less modest, any less virtuous in the days when she was living in your household than she is now, but she used not to have such scruples about seeing men and talking to them. I only have to look at her now, and she can't bear it! I thought it was a dream or a trance, when I saw her acting like that, and I asked her if I could kiss her hand, which after all is quite normal in this part of the world, but she completely refused! I am prepared to admit that I was in the wrong over one thing, Madame, and for this I do ask your forgiveness: I'm afraid I did hold her hand as you might say by force, and kissed it. But that was the only thing I asked of her. But she seems to be so determined that I should die, that she called out to you, as you must have heard. I can't understand why she did it, unless she was afraid that I had other intentions. Anyway, whatever the reason, Madame, I take the blame for it. She really ought to show affection for all your loyal servants. But such is fate! I happen to be the one who's in love, and yet I'm the only one who loses favour! Of course, I'll always feel the same way about you, Madame, and about your daughter, as I have in the past, and I hope and pray that I shan't lose your good opinion, even if, through no fault of my own, I have lost hers."

The Countess, who half believed, half doubted these words, turned to Florida. "Why did you call out for me like that?" she asked.

Florida replied that she had been afraid, and, in spite of her mother's insistent and repeated questions, she refused ever to give more details. It was enough for her that she had been delivered from the hands of her enemy, and as far as she was concerned Amador had been quite sufficiently punished by being thwarted in his attempt. The Countess had a long talk with Amador, and then let him speak again to Florida, though she stayed in the room while he did so, in order to observe from a distance how he would comport himself. He had little to say, though he did thank Florida for not telling her mother the whole truth, and he did ask her that since he was banished from her heart for ever, she would at least not admit a successor.

"If I had had any other way of protecting myself," came her reply, "I would not have shouted out, and no one would have heard anything about what happened. Provided that you don't drive me to it, that is the worst you will have from me. And you need have no fear that I shall give my love to some other man. For since I have not found that which I desired in the heart which I regarded as the most virtuous in the world, I shall never believe it is to be found in any man. Thanks to what has happened I shall be free for ever more from the passions that can arise from love."

So saying, she bade Amador farewell. The Countess had been watching closely, but she could come to no conclusion, except that her daughter plainly no longer felt any affection for Amador. She was convinced that Florida was just being perverse, and had taken it into her head to dislike anyone that her mother was fond of. From that time on, the Countess became so hostile towards her daughter, that for seven whole years she did not speak to her except in anger—and all this for the sake of Amador.

Up till this time Florida had had a horror of being with her husband, but during this period her attitude changed, and, in order to [escape] the harshness of her mother, she refused to move from his side. But this did not help her in her plight, so she conceived a plan which involved deceiving Amador. Dropping for a day or two her hostile air, she advised Amador to make amorous overtures to a certain woman, who, she said, had spoken of their love. The woman in question was a lady by the name of Loretta, who was attached to the household of the Queen. Amador believed Florida, and in the hope of eventually regaining her favour, he made advances to Loretta, who was only too pleased to have such an eminently desirable servant. Indeed she made it so obvious by her simperings, that the whole court soon got to hear of it. The Countess herself was at court at this time, and when she heard the rumours, she began to be less severe than she had been with her daughter. One day, however, it came to Florida's ears that Loretta's husband, who was a high-ranking officer in the army, and one of the King of Spain's highest governors, had become so jealous, that he had sworn to stop at nothing to kill Amador. Now Florida was incapable of wishing harm on Amador, however harsh a mask she might wear, and she informed him immediately of the danger he was in. Amador, anxious to return to her, replied that he would never again speak a word to Loretta, provided that Florida would agree to see him for three hours each day. To that she could not give her consent.

"Then why," said Amador to her, "if you do not wish to give me life, do you wish to save me from death? There can only be one reason—that you want to keep me alive in order to torture me, and hope thereby to cause me greater pain than a thousand deaths could ever do. Death may shun me, yet I shall seek it out, and I shall find it, for only in death shall I have repose!"

Even as they spoke, news arrived that the King of Granada had declared war on the King of Spain, and had attacked so fiercely that the King had had to send his son, the Prince, to the front, together with two old and experienced lords, the Constable of Castile and the Duke of Alba. The Duke of Cardona, too, and the Count of Aranda, were anxious to join the campaign, and petitioned the King for a commission. His majesty granted their requests, appointing each to the command appropriate to his birth. Amador was appointed to lead them. His exploits during that campaign were so extraordinary that they had more the appearance of acts of desperation than acts of bravery. Indeed, to bring my story to its conclusion, this bravery, going beyond all bounds, was demonstrated at the last in death.

The Moors had indicated that they were about to join battle. Then, seeing the size of the Christian forces, they had staged a sham retreat. The Spaniards had been about to follow in hot pursuit. But the old Constable and the Duke of Alba, realizing that it was a trap, had managed to restrain the Prince from crossing the river. The Count of Aranda and the Duke of Cardona, however, had defied orders. The Moors, seeing their pursuers were reduced in number, had wheeled round. Cardona had been killed, cut down by thrusts from Moorish scimitars. Aranda had been left gravely wounded, and as good as dead. In the midst of the carnage Amador arrived, riding furiously, and forcing his way like a madman through the thick of the battle. He had the two bodies transported back to the Prince's encampment. The Prince was as overcome as if they had been his own brothers. When the wounds were examined, however, it was found that the Count of Aranda was still alive, so he was carried back in a litter to the family home, where he lay ill for a very long time. The Duke's corpse was sent back to Cardona. Amador, having rescued the two bodies, was so heedless of his own safety that he found himself surrounded by vast numbers of Moors. He made up his mind what he should do. His enemies would not enjoy the glory either of capturing him alive or of slaying him. Even as he had failed to take his lady, so now his enemies would be frustrated in taking him. His faith to her he had broken. His faith to God he would not break. He knew, too, that if he was taken before the King of Granada, he would have to abjure Christianity, or die a horrible death. Commending body and soul to God, he kissed the cross of his sword, and plunged it with such force into his body that he killed himself in one fell blow.

Thus died poor Amador, his loss bemoaned as his virtue and prowess deserved. The news of his death spread throughout Spain, and eventually reached Florida, who was at Barcelona, where her husband had expressed his wish to be buried. She conducted the obsequies with due honour. Then, saying not a word either to her own mother or to the mother of her dead husband, she entered the Convent of Jesus. Thus she took Him as lover and as spouse who had delivered her from the violent love of Amador and from the misery of her life with her earthly husband. All her affections henceforth were bent on the perfect love of God. As a nun she lived for many long years, until at last she commended her soul to God with the joy of the bride who goes to meet her bridegroom.

"I'm afraid, Ladies, that this story has been rather long, and that some of you might have found it somewhat tedious—but it would have been even longer if I'd done justice to the person who originally told it to me. I hope you will take Florida's example to heart, but at the same time I would beg you to be less harsh, and not to have so much faith in men that you end up being disappointed when you learn the truth, drive them to a horrible death and give yourselves a miserable life."

Parlamente had had a patient and attentive audience. She now turned to Hircan, and said: "Don't you think that this woman was tried to the limits of her endurance, and that she put up a virtuous resistance in the face of it all?"

"No," replied Hircan, "for screaming is the least resistance a woman can offer. If she'd been somewhere where nobody could have heard her, I don't know what she'd have done. And as for Amador, if he'd been more of a lover and less of a coward, he wouldn't have been quite so easily put off. The example of Florida is not going to make me change my opinion on this matter. I still maintain that no man who loved perfectly, or who was loved by a lady, could fail in his designs, provided he went about things in a proper manner. All the same, I must applaud Amador for at least partly fulfilling his duty."

"What duty?" demanded Oisille. "Do you call it duty when a man who devotes himself to a lady's service tries to take her by force, when what he owes to her is obedience and reverence?"

"Madame," replied Saffredent, "when our ladies are holding court and sit in state like judges, then we men bend our knees before them, we timidly invite them to dance, we serve them so devotedly that we anticipate their every wish. Indeed, we have the appearance of being so terrified of offending them, so anxious to serve their every whim, that anybody else observing us would think we must be either out of our minds, or struck dumb, so idiotic is our animal-like devotion. Then all the credit goes to the ladies, because they put on such haughty expressions and adopt such refined ways of speaking, that people who see nothing but their external appearance go in awe of them, and feel obliged to admire and love them. However, in private it is quite another matter. Then Love is the only judge of the way we behave, and we soon find out that they are just women, and we are just men. The title 'lady' is soon exchanged for 'mistress,' and her 'devoted servant' soon becomes her 'lover.' Hence the well-known proverb: 'loyal service makes the servant master.' "

"They have honour, just as men, who can give it to them or take it away, have honour; and they see the things we patiently endure; but it is therefore only right that our long-suffering should be rewarded when honour cannot be injured."

"But you are not talking about true honour," intervened Longarine, "true honour which alone gives true contentment in this world. Suppose that everybody said I was a decent woman, while I knew that the opposite was true—then their praise would only increase my dishonour and make me feel inwardly ashamed. Equally, if everybody criticized me, while I knew that I was completely innocent, I would only derive contentment from their criticism. For no one is truly contented, unless he is contented within himself."

"Well, whatever you all might say," said Geburon, "in my opinion Amador was the most noble and valiant knight that ever lived. I think I recognize him beneath his fictitious name, but since Parlamente has preferred not to disclose the identities of her characters, I shall not disclose them either. Suffice it to say that if it's the man I think it is, then he's a man who never experienced fear in his life, a man whose heart was never devoid of love or the desire for courageous action."

Then Oisille turned to them all and said: "I think it has been a delightful day, and if the remaining days are equally enjoyable, then we shall have seen how swiftly the time can be made to pass in refined conversation. See how low the sun is already. And listen to the Abbey bell calling us to vespers! It started ringing a while ago, but I didn't draw your attention to it because your desire to hear the end of the story was more devout than your desire to hear vespers!"

Upon these words they all got up and made their way to the Abbey, where they found the monks had been waiting for them for a good hour. After hearing vespers, they had their supper, and spent the evening discussing the stories they had heard that day and racking their brains for new stories to make the next day as enjoyable as the first. Then, after playing not a few games in the meadow, they retired to bed, thus bringing the first day to a happy and contented close.

End of the First Day

Michel Eyquem de Montaigne

1533–1592

Reading **Montaigne**, one is immediately struck by the apparent modernity of his views, especially his skepticism about absolute truth, his questioning of the shifting grounds of identity, his acceptance of the limits of human understanding, and his tolerant recognition of cultural differences. Yet, as his biographers and critics have noted, the author of the *Essays* (1580–88), a collection of desultory and unpretentious reflections on his own life, is rooted firmly in the material and intellectual experience of the European **Renaissance**. Montaigne's renunciation of human claims to knowledge, power, and authority seems to fly in the face of the great celebrations of those qualities in Leonardo da Vinci, Niccolò Machiavelli, and Giovanni Pico della Mirandola,[1] but his *Essays* combine the nobleman's graceful poise, the humanist's love of the classics, and the explorer's ardent curiosity. Above all, he shares with his age its desire for self-understanding, characterized most notably in an epithet Montaigne had engraved on a medallion: *"Que scais je?"*—"What do I know?" His *Essays,* composed over the last twenty years of his life and in the midst of relentless political turmoil, not only represent Montaigne's attempts to answer that question but also introduce a new literary genre in the West. In his *essais,* or "attempts," Montaigne suggests that all he can say with certainty is that "there is no end to our investigations."

mone-TEN

Early Love of Latin. Montaigne's father, Pierre Eyquem de Montaigne, descended from a trading family who had acquired enough wealth and property to claim status as nobles, which ensured that his son would be able to experience diversity. When Michel de Montaigne was born on February 28, 1533, his father brought him up for two years among peasants in order to bond him with people of the lowest class before hiring a German tutor and two attendants to care for his son and to speak to him only in Latin. Montaigne tells us that he was six years old before he understood his native French, and he praises his father for enabling him to acquire a flawless Latin "without the whip and tears" of a grammar school. From age six to twelve Montaigne attended the College de Guyenne in Bordeaux, where he says he learned to love the works of the Latin writers Ovid, Virgil, and Horace, which he read as a kind of confection to sweeten the standard school fare of Cicero (106–43 B.C.E.). Once he left school, Montaigne probably spent a good deal of time in Paris before beginning his career as a lawyer in the high court of Bordeaux; there he formed a strong friendship with his colleague and erudite classicist Étienne de La Boétie (1530–1563), a bond that lasted until his friend's

WWW For links to more information about Montaigne, a quiz on "Of Cannibals," and information about the twenty-first century relevance of Montaigne, see *World Literature Online* at bedfordstmartins .com/worldlit.

[1] **Leonardo da Vinci, Niccolò Machiavelli and Giovanni Pico della Mirandola:** Leonardo da Vinci (1452–1519), Italian painter, scientist, and inventor, whose works include the *Adoration of the Magi* and *Mona Lisa;* Niccolò Machiavelli, see p. 120; Giovanni Pico della Mirandola, see p. 471.

Jean-Baptiste Mauzaisse, *Michel de Montaigne*
This portrait of the French humanist and author Montaigne was painted in the nineteenth century. (The Art Archive / Musée du Château de Versailles / Dagli Orti)

untimely death. As a magistrate, Montaigne was necessarily involved in the growing conflict between the Catholics and Protestants in France, which eventually amounted to religious civil war, culminating in the War of the Three Henries.[2] Although he was a Catholic loyalist, Montaigne disagreed with the cruel punishments the government dealt to the Protestant **Huguenots**,[3] and his outrage at these sufferings is echoed in his appeals for tolerance and moderation in the *Essays*.

HYOO-guh-nahts

Marriage and Retirement. Two years after La Boétie's death, the grieving Montaigne married Françoise de La Chassaigne. Shortly thereafter, his father asked him to translate a Latin work, *The Book of Creatures, or Natural Theology*, by the fifteenth-century Spanish writer Raymond

[2] **War of the Three Henries:** (1584–89) A war over succession to the French throne involving the Catholics Henry III of Valois (r. 1574–89), Henry of Guise (founder of the Catholic League), and the Protestant Henry of Navarre. When in 1584 Navarre became presumptive heir to the throne, Guise and Henry III, backed by the pope, sought to keep Navarre from becoming king. In a tangle of political intrigue, first Guise and then Henry III were assassinated, and Navarre became the first of the Bourbon monarchs, ruling from 1589 to 1610, when he too was assassinated.

[3] **Huguenots:** French Calvinists, who were members of the Reformed Church, founded about 1555 in France by the Protestant reformer John Calvin. The Huguenots were condemned as heretics and subject to persecution in predominantly Catholic France in the fifteenth and sixteenth centuries.

Sebond. After his father died in 1568, Montaigne inherited the family estate, the Château de Montaigne, about thirty miles from Bordeaux. Two years later, perhaps disappointed with a lack of political preferment, Montaigne retired to his beloved book-lined study in the tower at the château in order to devote his time to reading and writing. It was here that he began his *Essays,* after having completed an edition of La Boétie's works, in 1572.

Despite his hope to retire, Montaigne continued to be involved in public and state affairs. He received the Order of Saint Michael in 1571 and was appointed gentleman-in-ordinary of the king's chamber in 1573. He served in the army at the siege of La Fère in Normandy in 1580, and from September 1580 to November 1581 he toured Germany, Switzerland, Austria, and Italy, partly to see Venice and Rome, but partly to seek relief in the baths at Lucca from a painful kidney stone that would torment him for the rest of his life. Called back to Bordeaux to serve as mayor from 1581 to 1585, a time of plague and religious fighting in the city, Montaigne resigned, only to become embroiled in attempts to strengthen the alliance against the Catholic League, whose soldiers had pillaged his land when they attacked Castillon in 1587. Over the next few years Montaigne continued to be involved in the struggles for power among the three Henries. Amid these public responsibilities, Montaigne wrote and revised his essays, the first edition of which was published in 1580. Montaigne revised and added to his *Essays* until the end of his life, publishing three editions before his death in 1592, after which appeared the complete four-book version we read today.

Montaigne resists simple definitions. He is the first essayist, a skeptic, an acute student of himself and of man, a champion of a man-based morality, a vivid and charming stylist, and many other things besides. No one description tells nearly enough, and indeed it is hard to see which one to place at the center.

– Donald Frame, critic, 1943

The Essays. Montaigne's essays were unique to the literary world of the Renaissance; indeed, Montaigne is often known as the "father of the essay" for his invention of this casual, exploratory form. In the essay, Montaigne discovered a form with which to set down his thoughts and observations with a subjectivity and gentle irony that allows for further exploration. Montaigne describes his method best in "Of Democritus and Heraclitus" (1580), noting that "I take the first subject that chance offers. They are all equally good for me. And I never plan to develop them completely. For I do not see the whole of anything; nor do those who promise to show it to us." There is something here of the nobleman's **SPREZZATURA,** a poised casualness and practiced spontaneity; yet he is sincere, more so than Rousseau in *The Confessions,* when he describes in "Of Coaches" (1588) the limits of our knowledge in a phrase that equally characterizes his essay style: "We do not go in a straight line; we rather ramble and turn this way and that. We retrace our steps." Moreover, the *Essays* give us not just a sense of the ostensible subject but, most important, the personality and character of the writer. As he explains his intentions, "I want to be seen here in my simple, natural, and ordinary fashion, without straining or artifice; for it is myself that I portray." To this end, Montaigne thinks out loud in a language that is accessible and plain, and he entertains ideas with a personal and playful openness. Thus, many of the essays show Montaigne fusing an event or idea with personal reflection

I have no more made my book than my book has made me.
– MONTAIGNE

without making claims to some absolute truth, yet each essay demonstrates the breadth of Montaigne's reading and experience, marking him as a true man of the Renaissance.

Montaigne's *Essays* takes a somewhat skeptical view toward the authority of texts and the authority of reason and the senses. His skepticism emerges most prominently in the famous and ironically titled essay "Apology for Raymond Sebond" (1580). In that essay, the longest in his collection, Montaigne criticizes Sebond's faith in natural reason and holds instead that we cannot know anything for certain. In *The Book of Creatures,* which had been placed on the Catholic Church's Index of 1558–59, Sebond had argued that God's existence could be derived from a study of nature. In contrast, in his so-called apology Montaigne argues that we can rely on neither our senses nor our reason to give us reliable knowledge of God or the world. Acknowledging the shake-up in the foundations of beliefs resulting from Europeans' encounter with the New World and from new scientific discoveries, Montaigne encourages readers to give up their presumptuous claims to knowledge, as well as their sense of dominion over other creatures and peoples of the world, and to acknowledge their inherent ignorance. As he puts it, perhaps more simply, in "Of the Education of Children" (1580), "Wonderful brilliance may be gained for human judgment by getting to know men. We are all huddled and concentrated within ourselves, and our vision is reduced to the length of our nose." Prescient in his belief in the fallibility and imperfection of human reason, Montaigne anticipates the satirists of the eighteenth century in his critique of the vanity of human wishes, institutions, and values, all of which, in his view, vary according to differences in time and place. As he says in "Of Presumption" (1580), "We are nothing but ceremony; ceremony carries us away, and we leave the substance of things." And even when we do pay attention to them, he might add from "On the Uncertainty of Our Judgement" (1580), unreliable fortune "involves our reason . . . in her uncertainties and confusion" to the degree that our judgment, as Timaeus says in Plato, " 'has in it a large element of chance.' "

"Of Cannibals." "Of Cannibals" (1580) reveals a cautious, but nonetheless genuine, respect for cultural values and practices of non-European people. Montaigne engages the question of cultural difference evident between the various human communities, especially here along the gradient between the primitive and the civilized. What Montaigne notices is that human perception of other cultures is relative to the perspective of the beholder, and he wonders characteristically whether it is not the so-called civilized peoples who are the true barbarians. Despite his love of classical learning, Montaigne entertains the possibility that native peoples might be able to teach Europeans something about human relationships, politics, and philosophy. Breaking with the view, sometimes linked to Machiavelli, that Greco-Roman history and philosophy should serve up the only models for European states, Montaigne sees possible models for statecraft in the new world. As he says in "Of Cannibals," "I am sorry that Lycurgus and Plato[4] did not know [the natives]; for it seems to me that what we actually see in these nations surpasses not only all the pictures in which poets have idealized the golden age and all their inventions in imagining a happy state of man, but also the conceptions and the very desire of philosophy. They could not imagine a naturalness so pure and simple as we see by experience; nor could they believe that our society could be maintained with so little artifice and human solder." This tolerance, respect for others, and acceptance of the limits of knowledge typify Montaigne's version of Renaissance humanism.

■ CONNECTIONS

William Shakespeare, *The Tempest*, p. 495; Christopher Columbus, *Diario*, p. 773; Denis Diderot, Supplement to Bougainville's Travels, Book 4. With its tolerant, if not entirely sympathetic, view of cannibals based on reports about the natives of Brazil, Montaigne's "Of Cannibals" takes part in a growing discussion of the "noble savage," a view of native peoples of the New World that acknowledges their difference from Europeans but often risks oversimplification or idealization. How do Shakespeare's presentation of Caliban—in part based on Montaigne's essay, which Shakespeare knew in John Florio's translation—and Diderot's view of the natives of Tahiti support or refute the idea of the noble savage? Columbus's description of the Taino reflects his actual encounter with peoples from the Americas. How do Montaigne's attitudes toward cannibals compare to Shakespeare's treatment of Caliban and/or Diderot's treatment of the Tahitians?

Jonathan Swift, *Gulliver's Travels*, Book 4; Voltaire, *Candide*, Book 4; "In the World: Spirit of Inquiry," Book 4. Because of his skepticism and tolerance, Montaigne is often said to anticipate the thought of the Enlightenment. Swift, Voltaire, and the Enlightenment thinkers included in the "Spirit of Inquiry" section accept some limits to human knowledge, but generally tend to have faith in reason. Descartes, in particular, argued against Montaigne's skepticism, suggesting that we could arrive at some certain truths. How do Montaigne's ideas about the limits of human knowledge compare to those of some of these later thinkers?

Wu Chengen, *Monkey*, p. 837. Wu Chengen's novel is a fictionalized account of the travels of the Buddhist pilgrim Xuanzang to India. How does the novel appear to represent Tripitaka's encounters with people and places who are different from the Chinese? How do these strategies of handling difference compare to Montaigne's?

■ FURTHER RESEARCH

Biography

Frame, Donald. *Montaigne: A Biography.* 1965.
Friedrich, Hugo. *Montaigne.* 1991.

Criticism

Bencivenga, Ermanno. *The Discipline of Subjectivity: An Essay on Montaigne.* 1990.
Burke, Peter. *Montaigne.* 1981.

[4] **Lycurgus and Plato:** Lycurgus (ninth century B.C.E.), the lawgiver, perhaps mythic, of Sparta; Plato (427?–347 B.C.E.), Greek philosopher and author of *The Republic.* Montaigne associates both Lycurgus and Plato with creating ideal models of society.

Frame, Donald. *Montaigne's Essais: A Study.* 1969.
Saynce, R. A. *The Essays of Montaigne: A Critical Exploration.* 1972.
Shklar, Judith. *Ordinary Vices.* 1984.
Starobinski, Jean. *Montaigne in Motion.* 1982; trans. Arthur Goldhammer, 1985.
Tetel, Marcel. *Montaigne.* 1990.

■ **PRONUNCIATION**

Huguenots: HYOO-guh-nahts
Montaigne: mone-TEN

Essays

Translated by Donald M. Frame

Of Cannibals

When King Pyrrhus[1] passed over into Italy, after he had reconnoitered the formation of the army that the Romans were sending to meet him, he said: "I do not know what barbarians these are" (for so the Greeks called all foreign nations), "but the formation of this army that I see is not at all barbarous." The Greeks said as much of the army that Flaminius brought into their country, and so did Philip, seeing from a knoll the order and distribution of the Roman camp, in his kingdom, under Publius Sulpicius Galba.[2] Thus we should beware of clinging to vulgar opinions, and judge things by reason's way, not by popular say.

Essays. Montaigne began writing his *Essays* after 1570 and published the first collection in two volumes in 1580, followed by a third volume in 1588. Known for their unaffected and graceful style, loose structure, and familiar or personal character, the essays follow a sometimes playful pattern of free associations, moving blithely from one topic to another, combining aphoristic reflections with short anecdotes, thus mirroring the mind's search for knowledge and meaning. "Of Cannibals" is perhaps Montaigne's most well-known essay, in part because it broaches the idea of cultural relativism, inviting its readers to question whether barbarism is only an epithet we apply to anyone whose customs we do not understand. Montaigne—whose essay influenced Shakespeare's *The Tempest*—contrasts the purported barbarism of the cannibals in Brazil with the warlike manners of his fellow Europeans, only to suggest that Europeans are the true barbarians. Perhaps more fundamentally, the essay challenges readers to question received knowledge—opinion—in general, cautioning that "we should beware of clinging to vulgar opinions, and judge things by reason's way, not by popular say."

The selection here is from Donald Frame's highly acclaimed translation of Montaigne's *Essays;* Frame's work captures the verbal play and the unaffected charm of Montaigne's style. Notes are the editors'.

---

[1] **King Pyrrhus:** King of Epirus (c. 318–272 B.C.E.), who invaded Rome in 280 B.C.E. at a high cost of lives among his soldiers.

[2] **Flaminius . . . Galba:** Roman generals who fought against Philip V, king of Macedon (221–179 B.C.E.).

I had with me for a long time a man who had lived for ten or twelve years in that other world which has been discovered in our century, in the place where Villegaignon landed, and which he called Antarctic France.[3] This discovery of a boundless country seems worthy of consideration. I don't know if I can guarantee that some other such discovery will not be made in the future, so many personages greater than ourselves having been mistaken about this one. I am afraid we have eyes bigger than our stomachs, and more curiosity than capacity. We embrace everything, but we clasp only wind.

Plato[4] brings in Solon, telling how he had learned from the priests of the city of Saïs in Egypt that in days of old, before the Flood, there was a great island named Atlantis, right at the mouth of the Strait of Gibraltar, which contained more land than Africa and Asia put together, and that the kings of that country, who not only possessed that island but had stretched out so far on the mainland that they held the breadth of Africa as far as Egypt, and the length of Europe as far as Tuscany, undertook to step over into Asia and subjugate all the nations that border on the Mediterranean, as far as the Black Sea; and for this purpose crossed the Spains, Gaul, Italy, as far as Greece, where the Athenians checked them; but that some time after, both the Athenians and themselves and their island were swallowed up by the Flood.

It is quite likely that the extreme devastation of waters made amazing changes in the habitations of the earth, as people maintain that the sea cut off Sicily from Italy—

> 'Tis said an earthquake once asunder tore
> These lands with dreadful havoc, which before
> Formed but one land, one coast
>
> –VIRGIL[5]

—Cyprus from Syria, the island of Euboea from the mainland of Boeotia; and elsewhere joined lands that were divided, filling the channels between them with sand and mud:

> A sterile marsh, long fit for rowing, now
> Feeds neighbor towns, and feels the heavy plow.
>
> –HORACE[6]

But there is no great likelihood that that island was the new world which we have just discovered; for it almost touched Spain, and it would be an incredible result of a flood to have forced it away as far as it is, more than twelve hundred leagues; besides, the travels of the moderns have already almost revealed that it is not an island, but a

---

[3] **Antarctic France:** Nicolas Durand de Villegaignon (1510–1571?), a French explorer, landed in Brazil (Antarctic France) in 1555.

[4] **Plato** (427?–347 B.C.E.): Greek philosopher and author of dialogues on various topics, including the *Timaeus*, in which he mentions the myth of Atlantis.

[5] **Virgil:** Publius Vergilius Maro (70–19 B.C.E.), the greatest of the Roman epic poets and author of *The Aeneid*, from which the quote is taken (3:414–15).

[6] **Horace:** Horatius Flaccus (65–8 B.C.E.), Roman lyric poet and author of *Art of Poetry*, from which these lines are taken (65–66).

mainland connected with the East Indies on one side, and elsewhere with the lands under the two poles; or, if it is separated from them, it is by so narrow a strait and interval that it does not deserve to be called an island on that account.

It seems that there are movements, some natural, others feverish, in these great bodies, just as in our own. When I consider the inroads that my river, the Dordogne, is making in my lifetime into the right bank in its descent, and that in twenty years it has gained so much ground and stolen away the foundations of several buildings, I clearly see that this is an extraordinary disturbance; for if it had always gone at this rate, or was to do so in the future, the face of the world would be turned topsy-turvy. But rivers are subject to changes: now they overflow in one direction, now in another, now they keep to their course. I am not speaking of the sudden inundations whose causes are manifest. In Médoc,[7] along the seashore, my brother, the sieur d'Arsac, can see an estate of his buried under the sands that the sea spews forth; the tops of some buildings are still visible; his farms and domains have changed into very thin pasturage. The inhabitants say that for some time the sea has been pushing toward them so hard that they have lost four leagues of land. These sands are its harbingers; and we see great dunes of moving sand that march half a league ahead of it and keep conquering land.

The other testimony of antiquity with which some would connect this discovery is in Aristotle,[8] at least if that little book *Of Unheard-of Wonders* is by him. He there relates that certain Carthaginians, after setting out upon the Atlantic Ocean from the Strait of Gibraltar and sailing a long time, at last discovered a great fertile island, all clothed in woods and watered by great deep rivers, far remote from any mainland; and that they, and others since, attracted by the goodness and fertility of the soil, went there with their wives and children, and began to settle there. The lords of Carthage, seeing that their country was gradually becoming depopulated, expressly forbade anyone to go there any more, on pain of death, and drove out these new inhabitants, fearing, it is said, that in course of time they might come to multiply so greatly as to supplant their former masters and ruin their state. This story of Aristotle does not fit our new lands any better than the other.

This man I had was a simple, crude fellow—a character fit to bear true witness; for clever people observe more things and more curiously, but they interpret them; and to lend weight and conviction to their interpretation, they cannot help altering history a little. They never show you things as they are, but bend and disguise them according to the way they have seen them; and to give credence to their judgment and attract you to it, they are prone to add something to their matter, to stretch it out and amplify it. We need a man either very honest, or so simple that he has not the stuff to build up false inventions and give them plausibility; and wedded to no theory. Such was my man; and besides this, he at various times brought sailors and merchants, whom he had known on that trip, to see me. So I content myself with his information, without inquiring what the cosmographers say about it.

[7] **Médoc:** A region in southwestern France.

[8] **Aristotle** (384–322 B.C.E.): Greek philosopher and author of treatises on physics, logic, ethics, rhetoric, and poetics; he did not write the book mentioned here.

We ought to have topographers who would give us an exact account of the places where they have been. But because they have over us the advantage of having seen Palestine, they want to enjoy the privilege of telling us news about all the rest of the world. I would like everyone to write what he knows, and as much as he knows, not only in this, but in all other subjects; for a man may have some special knowledge and experience of the nature of a river or a fountain, who in other matters knows only what everybody knows. However, to circulate this little scrap of knowledge, he will undertake to write the whole of physics. From this vice spring many great abuses.

Now, to return to my subject, I think there is nothing barbarous and savage in that nation, from what I have been told, except that each man calls barbarism whatever is not his own practice; for indeed it seems we have no other test of truth and reason than the example and pattern of the opinions and customs of the country we live in. *There* is always the perfect religion, the perfect government, the perfect and accomplished manners in all things. Those people are wild, just as we call wild the fruits that Nature has produced by herself and in her normal course; whereas really it is those that we have changed artificially and led astray from the common order, that we should rather call wild. The former retain alive and vigorous their genuine, their most useful and natural, virtues and properties, which we have debased in the latter in adapting them to gratify our corrupted taste. And yet for all that, the savor and delicacy of some uncultivated fruits of those countries is quite as excellent, even to our taste, as that of our own. It is not reasonable that art should win the place of honor over our great and powerful mother Nature. We have so overloaded the beauty and richness of her works by our inventions that we have quite smothered her. Yet wherever her purity shines forth, she wonderfully puts to shame our vain and frivolous attempts:

> Ivy comes readier without our care;
> In lonely caves the arbutus grows more fair;
> No art with artless bird song can compare.
>
> —PROPERTIUS[9]

All our efforts cannot even succeed in reproducing the nest of the tiniest little bird, its contexture, its beauty and convenience; or even the web of the puny spider. All things, says Plato,[10] are produced by nature, by fortune, or by art; the greatest and most beautiful by one or the other of the first two, the least and most imperfect by the last.

These nations, then, seem to me barbarous in this sense, that they have been fashioned very little by the human mind, and are still very close to their original naturalness. The laws of nature still rule them, very little corrupted by ours; and they are in such a state of purity that I am sometimes vexed that they were unknown earlier, in the days when there were men able to judge them better than we. I am sorry

[9] **Propertius:** Sextus Propertius (c. 50–c. 16 B.C.E.), Roman poet noted for his moving elegiac poems; the quote is from *Elegies* 1:2.10–12.

[10] **Plato:** In the *Laws*.

that Lycurgus[11] and Plato did not know of them; for it seems to me that what we actually see in these nations surpasses not only all the pictures in which poets have idealized the golden age and all their inventions in imagining a happy state of man, but also the conceptions and the very desire of philosophy. They could not imagine a naturalness so pure and simple as we see by experience; nor could they believe that our society could be maintained with so little artifice and human solder. This is a nation, I should say to Plato, in which there is no sort of traffic, no knowledge of letters, no science of numbers, no name for a magistrate or for political superiority, no custom of servitude, no riches or poverty, no contracts, no successions, no partitions, no occupations but leisure ones, no care for any but common kinship, no clothes, no agriculture, no metal, no use of wine or wheat. The very words that signify lying, treachery, dissimulation, avarice, envy, belittling, pardon—unheard of.[12] How far from this perfection would he find the republic that he imagined: *Men fresh sprung from the gods* [Seneca].[13]

> These manners nature first ordained.
>
> –VIRGIL[14]

For the rest, they live in a country with a very pleasant and temperate climate, so that according to my witnesses it is rare to see a sick man there; and they have assured me that they never saw one palsied, bleary-eyed, toothless, or bent with age. They are settled along the sea and shut in on the land side by great high mountains, with a stretch about a hundred leagues wide in between. They have a great abundance of fish and flesh which bear no resemblance to ours, and they eat them with no other artifice than cooking. The first man who rode a horse there, though he had had dealings with them on several other trips, so horrified them in this posture that they shot him dead with arrows before they could recognize him.

Their buildings are very long, with a capacity of two or three hundred souls; they are covered with the bark of great trees, the strips reaching to the ground at one end and supporting and leaning on one another at the top, in the manner of some of our barns, whose covering hangs down to the ground and acts as a side. They have wood so hard that they cut with it and make of it their swords and grills to cook their food. Their beds are of a cotton weave, hung from the roof like those in our ships, each man having his own; for the wives sleep apart from their husbands.

They get up with the sun, and eat immediately upon rising, to last them through the day; for they take no other meal than that one. Like some other Eastern peoples, of whom Suidas[15] tells us, who drank apart from meals, they do not drink then; but they drink several times a day, and to capacity. Their drink is made of some root, and

---

[11] **Lycurgus:** A Spartan lawgiver (perhaps mythic) of the ninth century B.C.E. who wrote about ideal societies.

[12] **This is a nation . . . unheard of:** Shakespeare borrowed from this entire passage in Florio's translation of *The Tempest,* Act II, scene 1, lines 137–58 (see pages 520–21).

[13] **[Seneca]:** Lucius Annaeus Seneca (c. 3 B.C.E.–c. 65 C.E.), Roman statesman and dramatist; the quote is from his *Epistles* 90.

[14] **Virgil:** From his *Georgics,* a poem about agricultural life (Book 2:20).

[15] **Suidas:** A Greek lexicographer from the tenth century C.E.

is of the color of our claret wines. They drink it only lukewarm. This beverage keeps only two or three days; it has a slightly sharp taste, is not at all heady, is good for the stomach, and has a laxative effect upon those who are not used to it; it is a very pleasant drink for anyone who is accustomed to it. In place of bread they use a certain white substance like preserved coriander. I have tried it; it tastes sweet and a little flat.

The whole day is spent in dancing. The younger men go to hunt animals with bows. Some of the women busy themselves meanwhile with warming their drink, which is their chief duty. Some one of the old men, in the morning before they begin to eat, preaches to the whole barnful in common, walking from one end to the other, and repeating one single sentence several times until he has completed the circuit (for the buildings are fully a hundred paces long). He recommends to them only two things: valor against the enemy and love for their wives. And they never fail to point out this obligation, as their refrain, that it is their wives who keep their drink warm and seasoned.

There may be seen in several places, including my own house, specimens of their beds, of their ropes, of their wooden swords and the bracelets with which they cover their wrists in combats, and of the big canes, open at one end, by whose sound they keep time in their dances. They are close shaven all over, and shave themselves much more cleanly than we, with nothing but a wooden or stone razor. They believe that souls are immortal, and that those who have deserved well of the gods are lodged in that part of heaven where the sun rises, and the damned in the west.

They have some sort of priests and prophets, but they rarely appear before the people, having their home in the mountains. On their arrival there is a great feast and solemn assembly of several villages—each barn, as I have described it, makes up a village, and they are about one French league from each other. The prophet speaks to them in public, exhorting them to virtue and their duty; but their whole ethical science contains only these two articles: resoluteness in war and affection for their wives. He prophesies to them things to come and the results they are to expect from their undertakings, and urges them to war or holds them back from it; but this is on the condition that when he fails to prophesy correctly, and if things turn out otherwise than he has predicted, he is cut into a thousand pieces if they catch him, and condemned as a false prophet. For this reason, the prophet who has once been mistaken is never seen again.

Divination is a gift of God; that is why its abuse should be punished as imposture. Among the Scythians,[16] when the soothsayers failed to hit the mark, they were laid, chained hand and foot, on carts full of heather and drawn by oxen, on which they were burned. Those who handle matters subject to the control of human capacity are excusable if they do the best they can. But these others, who come and trick us with assurances of an extraordinary faculty that is beyond our ken, should they not be punished for not making good their promise, and for the temerity of their imposture?

---

[16] **Scythians:** Nomadic people noted for barbarity who occupied southeastern Europe until about 300 B.C.E.

They have their wars with the nations beyond the mountains, further inland, to which they go quite naked, with no other arms than bows or wooden swords ending in a sharp point, in the manner of the tongues of our boar spears. It is astonishing what firmness they show in their combats, which never end but in slaughter and bloodshed; for as to routs and terror, they know nothing of either.

Each man brings back as his trophy the head of the enemy he has killed, and sets it up at the entrance of his dwelling. After they have treated their prisoners well for a long time with all the hospitality they can think of, each man who has a prisoner calls a great assembly of his acquaintances. He ties a rope to one of the prisoner's arms, by the end of which he holds him, a few steps away, for fear of being hurt, and gives his dearest friend the other arm to hold in the same way; and these two, in the presence of the whole assembly, kill him with their swords. This done, they roast him and eat him in common and send some pieces to their absent friends. This is not, as people think, for nourishment, as of old the Scythians used to do; it is to betoken an extreme revenge. And the proof of this came when they saw the Portuguese, who had joined forces with their adversaries, inflict a different kind of death on them when they took them prisoner, which was to bury them up to the waist, shoot the rest of their body full of arrows, and afterward hang them. They thought that these people from the other world, being men who had sown the knowledge of many vices among their neighbors and were much greater masters than themselves in every sort of wickedness, did not adopt this sort of vengeance without some reason, and that it must be more painful than their own; so they began to give up their old method and follow this one.

I am not sorry that we notice the barbarous horror of such acts, but I am heartily sorry that, judging their faults rightly, we should be so blind to our own. I think there is more barbarity in eating a man alive than in eating him dead; and in tearing by tortures and the rack a body still full of feeling, in roasting a man bit by bit, in having him bitten and mangled by dogs and swine (as we have not only read but seen within fresh memory, not among ancient enemies, but among neighbors and fellow citizens, and what is worse, on the pretext of piety and religion), than in roasting and eating him after he is dead.

Indeed, Chrysippus and Zeno,[17] heads of the Stoic sect, thought there was nothing wrong in using our carcasses for any purpose in case of need, and getting nourishment from them; just as our ancestors, when besieged by Caesar in the city of Alésia, resolved to relieve their famine by eating old men, women, and other people useless for fighting.

The Gascons once, 'tis said, their life renewed
By eating of such food.

– JUVENAL[18]

---

[17] **Chrysippus and Zeno:** Chrysippus (280–206 B.C.E.) and Zeno of Cittium (c. 333–264 B.C.E.), Greek philosophers and founders of Stoicism, a philosophy emphasizing the importance of virtuous action in accordance with nature.

[18] **Juvenal:** Decimus Junius Juvenalis (fl. second century C.E.), Roman poet known for his harsh satires; the quote is from *Satires* 15:93–94.

And physicians do not fear to use human flesh in all sorts of ways for our health, applying it either inwardly or outwardly. But there never was any opinion so disordered as to excuse treachery, disloyalty, tyranny, and cruelty, which are our ordinary vices.

So we may well call these people barbarians, in respect to the rules of reason, but not in respect to ourselves, who surpass them in every kind of barbarity.

Their warfare is wholly noble and generous, and as excusable and beautiful as this human disease can be; its only basis among them is their rivalry in valor. They are not fighting for the conquest of new lands, for they still enjoy that natural abundance that provides them without toil and trouble with all necessary things in such profusion that they have no wish to enlarge their boundaries. They are still in that happy state of desiring only as much as their natural needs demand; anything beyond that is superfluous to them.

They generally call those of the same age, brothers; those who are younger, children; and the old men are fathers to all the others. These leave to their heirs in common the full possession of their property, without division or any other title at all than just the one that Nature gives to her creatures in bringing them into the world.

If their neighbors cross the mountains to attack them and win a victory, the gain of the victor is glory, and the advantage of having proved the master in valor and virtue; for apart from this they have no use for the goods of the vanquished, and they return to their own country, where they lack neither anything necessary nor that great thing, the knowledge of how to enjoy their condition happily and be content with it. These men of ours do the same in their turn. They demand of their prisoners no other ransom than that they confess and acknowledge their defeat. But there is not one in a whole century who does not choose to die rather than to relax a single bit, by word or look, from the grandeur of an invincible courage; not one who would not rather be killed and eaten than so much as ask not to be. They treat them very freely, so that life may be all the dearer to them, and usually entertain them with threats of their coming death, of the torments they will have to suffer, the preparations that are being made for that purpose, the cutting up of their limbs, and the feast that will be made at their expense. All this is done for the sole purpose of extorting from their lips some weak or base word, or making them want to flee, so as to gain the advantage of having terrified them and broken down their firmness. For indeed, if you take it the right way, it is in this point alone that true victory lies:

> It is no victory
> Unless the vanquished foe admits your mastery.
>
> – CLAUDIAN[19]

The Hungarians, very bellicose fighters, did not in olden times pursue their advantage beyond putting the enemy at their mercy. For having wrung a confession

[19] **Claudian:** Claudius Claudianus (c. 370–c. 404 C.E.), Roman lyric and epic poet; author of the epic *Rape of Proserpine* and the panegyric poem *Of the Sixth Consulate of Honorius,* from which the quote is taken (ll. 248–49).

from him to this effect, they let him go unharmed and unransomed, except, at most, for exacting his promise never again to take up arms against them.

We win enough advantages over our enemies that are borrowed advantages, not really our own. It is the quality of a porter, not of valor, to have sturdier arms and legs; agility is a dead and corporeal quality; it is a stroke of luck to make our enemy stumble, or dazzle his eyes by the sunlight; it is a trick of art and technique, which may be found in a worthless coward, to be an able fencer. The worth and value of a man is in his heart and his will; there lies his real honor. Valor is the strength, not of legs and arms, but of heart and soul; it consists not in the worth of our horse or our weapons, but in our own. He who falls obstinate in his courage, *if he has fallen, he fights on his knees* [Seneca]. He who relaxes none of his assurance, no matter how great the danger of imminent death; who, giving up his soul, still looks firmly and scornfully at his enemy—he is beaten not by us, but by fortune; he is killed, not conquered.

The most valiant are sometimes the most unfortunate. Thus there are triumphant defeats that rival victories. Nor did those four sister victories, the fairest that the sun ever set eyes on—Salamis, Plataea, Mycale, and Sicily—ever dare match all their combined glory against the glory of the annihilation of King Leonidas and his men at the pass of Thermopylae.[20]

Who ever hastened with more glorious and ambitious desire to win a battle than Captain Ischolas to lose one? Who ever secured his safety more ingeniously and painstakingly than he did his destruction? He was charged to defend a certain pass in the Peloponnesus against the Arcadians. Finding himself wholly incapable of doing this, in view of the nature of the place and the inequality of the forces, he made up his mind that all who confronted the enemy would necessarily have to remain on the field. On the other hand, deeming it unworthy both of his own virtue and magnanimity and of the Lacedaemonian name to fail in his charge, he took a middle course between these two extremes, in this way. The youngest and fittest of his band he preserved for the defense and service of their country, and sent them home; and with those whose loss was less important, he determined to hold this pass, and by their death to make the enemy buy their entry as dearly as he could. And so it turned out. For he was presently surrounded on all sides by the Arcadians, and after slaughtering a large number of them, he and his men were all put to the sword. Is there a trophy dedicated to victors that would not be more due to these vanquished? The role of true victory is in fighting, not in coming off safely; and the honor of valor consists in combating, not in beating.

To return to our story. These prisoners are so far from giving in, in spite of all that is done to them, that on the contrary, during the two or three months that they are kept, they wear a gay expression; they urge their captors to hurry and put them to the test; they defy them, insult them, reproach them with their cowardice and the number of battles they have lost to the prisoners' own people.

---

[20] **Salamis . . . Thermopylae:** Sites of famous Greek victories against the Persians and Carthaginians in the fifth century B.C.E.; Leonidas was the Spartan king who led the famous standoff against the Persians at Thermopylae in 480 B.C.E.

I have a song composed by a prisoner which contains this challenge, that they should all come boldly and gather to dine off him, for they will be eating at the same time their own fathers and grandfathers, who have served to feed and nourish his body. "These muscles," he says, "this flesh and these veins are your own, poor fools that you are. You do not recognize that the substance of your ancestors' limbs is still contained in them. Savor them well; you will find in them the taste of your own flesh." An idea that certainly does not smack of barbarity. Those that paint these people dying, and who show the execution, portray the prisoner spitting in the face of his slayers and scowling at them. Indeed, to the last gasp they never stop braving and defying their enemies by word and look. Truly here are real savages by our standards; for either they must be thoroughly so, or we must be; there is an amazing distance between their character and ours.

The men there have several wives, and the higher their reputation for valor the more wives they have. It is a remarkably beautiful thing about their marriages that the same jealousy our wives have to keep us from the affection and kindness of other women, theirs have to win this for them. Being more concerned for their husbands' honor than for anything else, they strive and scheme to have as many companions as they can, since that is a sign of their husbands' valor.

Our wives will cry "Miracle!" but it is no miracle. It is a properly matrimonial virtue, but one of the highest order. In the Bible, Leah, Rachel, Sarah,[21] and Jacob's wives gave their beautiful handmaids to their husbands; and Livia seconded the appetites of Augustus, to her own disadvantage; and Stratonice, the wife of King Deiotarus,[22] not only lent her husband for his use a very beautiful young chambermaid in her service, but carefully brought up her children, and backed them up to succeed to their father's estates.

And lest it be thought that all this is done through a simple and servile bondage to usage and through the pressure of the authority of their ancient customs, without reasoning or judgment, and because their minds are so stupid that they cannot take any other course, I must cite some examples of their capacity. Besides the warlike song I have just quoted, I have another, a love song, which begins in this vein: "Adder, stay; stay, adder, that from the pattern of your coloring my sister may draw the fashion and the workmanship of a rich girdle that I may give to my love; so may your beauty and your pattern be forever preferred to all other serpents." This first couplet is the refrain of the song. Now I am familiar enough with poetry to be a judge of this: not only is there nothing barbarous in this fancy, but it is altogether Anacreontic.[23] Their language, moreover, is a soft language, with an agreeable sound, somewhat like Greek in its endings.

---

[21] **Leah, Rachel, Sarah:** See Genesis 30 for the stories of Jacob's wives Leah and Rachel; see Genesis 16 for the story of Abraham's wife Sarah and her handmaid Hagar.

[22] **King Deiotarus:** The story of Livia is told in *Life of Augustus* by the Roman writer Suetonius (c. 69–c. 149), author of *Lives of the Caesars;* the story of Stratonice and Deiotarus, the Tetrarch of Galatia, is told in *On the Bravery of Women,* by the Roman writer Plutarch (46?–c. 120), author of *Moralia* and *Parallel Lives.*

[23] **Anacreontic:** Anacreon (c. 563–c. 478 B.C.E.), Greek poet celebrated for his love poetry.

Three of these men, ignorant of the price they will pay some day, in loss of repose and happiness, for gaining knowledge of the corruptions of this side of the ocean; ignorant also of the fact that of this intercourse will come their ruin (which I suppose is already well advanced: poor wretches, to let themselves be tricked by the desire for new things, and to have left the serenity of their own sky to come and see ours!) — three of these men were at Rouen, at the time the late King Charles IX was there. The king talked to them for a long time; they were shown our ways, our splendor, the aspect of a fine city. After that, someone asked their opinion, and wanted to know what they had found most amazing. They mentioned three things, of which I have forgotten the third, and I am very sorry for it; but I still remember two of them. They said that in the first place they thought it very strange that so many grown men, bearded, strong, and armed, who were around the king (it is likely that they were talking about the Swiss of his guard) should submit to obey a child, and that one of them was not chosen to command instead. Second (they have a way in their language of speaking of men as halves of one another), they had noticed that there were among us men full and gorged with all sorts of good things, and that their other halves were beggars at their doors, emaciated with hunger and poverty; and they thought it strange that these needy halves could endure such an injustice, and did not take the others by the throat, or set fire to their houses.

I had a very long talk with one of them; but I had an interpreter who followed my meaning so badly, and who was so hindered by his stupidity in taking in my ideas, that I could get hardly any satisfaction from the man. When I asked him what profit he gained from his superior position among his people (for he was a captain, and our sailors called him king), he told me that it was to march foremost in war. How many men followed him? He pointed to a piece of ground, to signify as many as such a space could hold; it might have been four or five thousand men. Did all his authority expire with the war? He said that this much remained, that when he visited the villages dependent on him, they made paths for him through the underbrush by which he might pass quite comfortably.

All this is not too bad — but what's the use? They don't wear breeches.

Discovery and Confrontation

Montaigne's "Of Cannibals" announces one of the most important themes of literature in the Early Modern Period: the encounter between Europe and other countries of the world. In a time of unprecedented travel, discovery, and exploration, Montaigne offers an extraordinarily humane and open-minded perspective on contact between peoples of different cultures. While few shared his cultural relativism, many shared his curiosity and interest in the opening of diplomatic, economic, and cultural ties to the expanding world. Between 1450 and 1700, the opening of overseas trade routes and improvements in shipbuilding and navigation began to make the world a smaller place, and the shift toward a global network of commercial and cultural exchange led to violent struggles over territory, resources, religious belief, and power. Most of these struggles continued well into the eighteenth and nineteenth centuries; some have continued into the twenty-first.

The desire to open up and control markets around the globe, accompanied by a sense of religious mission, national zeal, and personal pride, inspired much of the European exploration and discovery in the fifteenth and sixteenth centuries. By 1500, European explorers such as Bartolomeu Dias, Christopher Columbus, John Cabot, Vasco da Gama, and Amerigo Vespucci expanded European contact to the east coast of Africa, the West Indies, Newfoundland, India, and South America, respectively. In the early years of European discovery, Portugal gained ascendancy. Encouraged by Prince Henry the Navigator (1394–1460), who financed maritime expeditions along the West African coast and promoted improvements in cartography and navigation, the Portuguese opened a direct sea

***The Arrival of Vasco da Gama in Calicut,* Sixteenth Century**
This rich tapestry shows the formal arrival of Vasco da Gama in Calicut, India. The Portuguese were a great seafaring people and dominated the early voyages of discovery. (Banco Nacional Ultramarino, Portugal / Bridgeman Art Library)

route around the Cape of Good Hope in Southern Africa into the Indian Ocean. Here they found a flourishing sea trade controlled by Muslims extending along the east coast of Africa to the west coast of India. Fifteen years after Vasco da Gama (c. 1460–1524) first sailed along the West African coast to India, the Portuguese had seized the Muslim trading centers of Goa, Hormuz, and Malacca on the west coast of India; defeated the Muslim fleet; and taken control of trade in the Indian Ocean.

Meanwhile the Spanish had been active in establishing colonial footholds in Mexico, Peru, and the Philippines. In 1492, six years before da Gama reached the Indian Ocean, Christopher Columbus (1451–1506) sailed across the Atlantic Ocean and stumbled onto the Americas, which he mistook for Asia. As we discuss further in the unit on the Ancient Mexicans, Columbus was soon followed by

Hernán Cortés (1485–1547) and Francisco Pizarro (c. 1475–1541), who established colonial territories in Mexico and Peru. John Cabot (c. 1450–c. 1499), searching for a route to China, also crossed the Atlantic at the same time of da Gama's initial voyage, 1497–98, and found instead the teeming fishing banks off Newfoundland. Cabot's discovery set the grounds for England to make claims in North America, where it began to settle colonies by 1600. The French, not to be left behind, laid claims in North America in the 1530s when Jacques Cartier (1491–1557) sailed up the St. Lawrence River. At the same time, the French began to challenge the Portuguese claims to territories in West Africa. Moreover, in the early 1600s, the founding of the English East India Company (1600) and the Netherlands East India Company (1602) changed the character of European exploration and discovery by downplaying national and religious goals and emphasizing commercial ones. In the sixteenth century the Portuguese had upset the monopoly on Eastern goods held by the Arabs, Venetians, and Genoans, but in the seventeenth century the powerful Dutch and English trading companies eventually displaced the Portuguese and seized control of the rich trade in spices, silks, and other luxuries with India and China.

The phrase "age of discovery and confrontation"—coined by the historian J. M. Roberts—refers primarily to the expansion of European powers onto the global scene. But Europe was not alone in claiming new territories and extending its reach. Well before the fifteenth century, the Chinese, for example, had enjoyed two centuries of dominance as a sea power in southeast Asia. During the early years of the Ming dynasty (1368–1644), China experienced the height of its maritime power with the seven voyages of the Chinese admiral **Zheng He** (Cheng Ho; c. 1371–c. 1433), which extended China's influence and the source of tribute flowing into China from Vietnam to the east coast of Africa. Chinese ships were up to 517 feet long and 212 feet wide, and the spectacle of these huge ships and their crews astounded observers all along the route from Java to Aden to Mogadishu. Zheng He's voyages took him from China all the way to the east coast of Africa, by way of the Indian Ocean. By the time the voyages ended in 1433, China was receiving tribute from more than twenty kingdoms or nations, and Zheng He, as noted in the ***History of the Ming*** by **Zhang Ting-yu** (Chang T'ing-yü), became one of the celebrated figures of the early Ming dynasty. Zheng He's description

jung-HUH

p. 253

jahng-ting-YOO

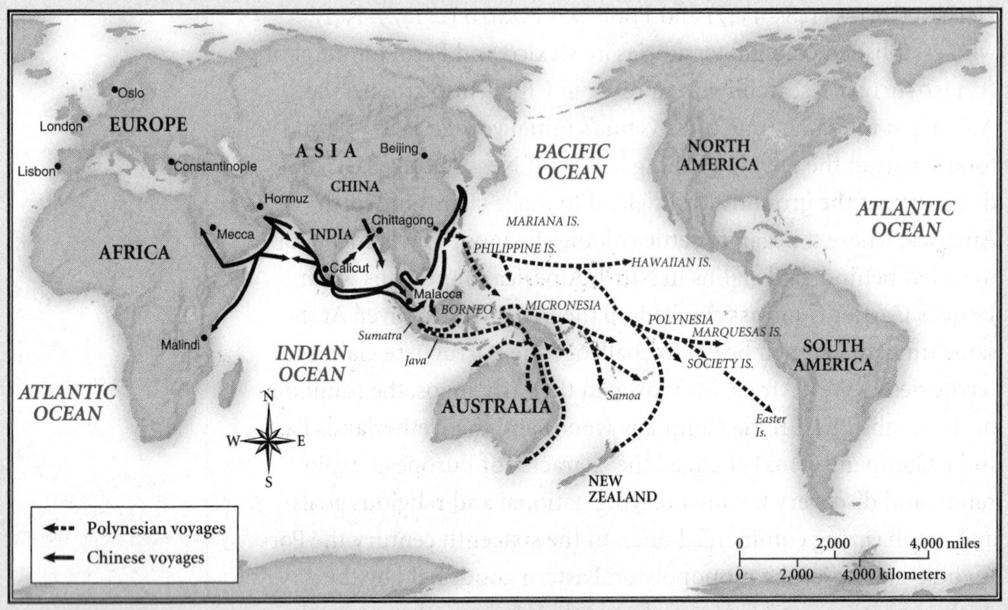

Early Voyages of World Exploration
Over the course of the fifteenth and early sixteenth centuries, shipping in the Atlantic Ocean was dominated by Europeans, led by the pioneering voyages of the Portuguese, who also first sailed around the Cape of Good Hope to the Indian Ocean and Cape Horn to the Pacific.

of the greed of foreign merchants reveals a unique perspective on the trade with the Orient. In addition, in the fifteenth and sixteenth centuries there were some Europeans, including Jesuit missionaries such as Matteo Ricci (1552–1610), living in China. Ricci's ***Diary,*** like the accounts of Marco Polo (1254–1324), became an important resource for details of Western impressions of Chinese culture and society.

p. 239

As Europe and China expanded, so too did the Ottoman empire, which had been established in the late thirteenth century. After the defeat of Constantinople in 1453, the Ottomans vigorously expanded their control over Syria, Anatolia, Egypt, the northern states of Africa, much of the Balkan region, Greece, and even parts of Hungary and Austria, where the forces of Suleiman the Magnificent (1520–1566) were defeated in 1529. Islamic travelers on diplomatic missions, as well as soldiers, merchants, and pilgrims making the

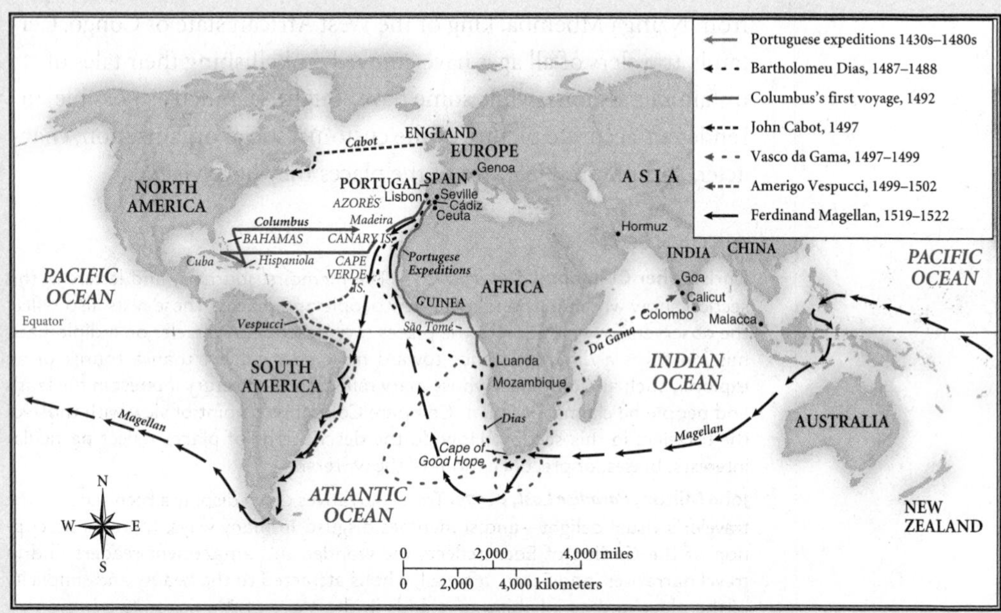

HAJJ to Mecca, sometimes covered the broad expanses of the empire, and a few, like **Evliya Çelebi**, left behind records of their travels. As in European travel narratives, Evliya's ***Book of Travels*** works a fine line between documentary and invention, presenting fantastic tales as well as minute descriptions of the customs and character of the places he visits.

ev-lee-YAH
cheh-leh-BEE
p. 248

Many travelers—both European and non-European—from the late fifteenth through the seventeenth centuries were dramatically surprised during their travels by their encounters with other people and other cultures. Their writings record wonder, amusement, and sometimes terror in the face of the unfamiliar. While most travelers made some effort to naturalize the differences they observed, they also filled their accounts with localized and particular stories of "brave new worlds." Evliya Çelebi, a lively narrator, exaggerated the marvelous and placed himself as a hero in various dangerous episodes.

In addition to the accounts of Ricci and Evliya, and the history of Zhang Ting-yu, this section includes an anonymous journal from Vasco da Gama's first voyage and the appeal to the king of Portugal from Nzinga Mbemba, king of the West African state of Congo. Certainly travelers of all ages have enjoyed embellishing their tales of unfamiliar regions, while some have sought, as much as possible, to render an accurate picture of the customs, social organization, character, and physical features of the places they have visited.

■ CONNECTIONS

Christopher Columbus, *Diario*, p. 773. The memoirs, journals, and letters in this section show writers responding to new people and places. These texts also reflect the observers' own relation to the places they describe. A traveler on a diplomatic mission takes a different stance toward his or her subject than a tourist or an explorer, such as Columbus, whose diary reflects a proprietary interest in the lands and people he claims for Spain. Compare Columbus's point of view with those of the travelers in this section: How do the descriptions of places reflect particular interests, biases, or preconceptions of the writers?

John Milton, *Paradise Lost*, p. 575. Travel narratives often display a keen sense of the traveler's visual delight—and sometimes disgust. In many ways, Milton's description of the Garden of Eden reflects the wonder and amazement readers find in travel narratives, and Satan, after all, who is attracted to the beauty and simplicity of the place and its inhabitants, stands in the place of the visitor to a brave new world. How does Milton's description of Satan's first landing in the Garden of Eden compare to these accounts of travel to new countries and regions?

William Shakespeare, *The Tempest*, p. 495. Nzinga Mbemba's "Letter to the King of Portugal" criticizes the Portuguese whose arrival in the Congo has led to critical problems and disrupted the lives of the indigenous people. Similarly, Caliban accuses Prospero, who attempts to "civilize" him, of upsetting the order of things on his island and alienating him from its natural beauty. Compare Nzinga Mbemba's appeal to the king of Portugal to Caliban's attempts to free himself from Prospero's control. How does Caliban serve as a symbol for the victims of colonization?

■ PRONUNCIATION

Evliya Çelebi: ev-lee-YAH cheh-leh-BEE
Zhang Ting-yu: jahng-ting-YOO
Zheng He: jung-HUH

Anonymous

FIFTEENTH CENTURY

Roughly ten years after Bartolomeu Dias sailed around the Cape of Good Hope in 1488, Vasco da Gama (c. 1460–1524) set out under the command of four ships with the goal of reaching Calicut (or, as it is spelled in the journal printed here, Calecut), one of the major trading ports on the southwestern coast of India. Though da Gama's voyage was ostensibly for purposes of discovery and the improvement of charts (as well as to keep an eye open for signs of the legendary king Prester John), the opening of this route into the Indian Ocean led the way for the Portuguese monopoly of trade in the Indian Ocean. Da Gama's pilots did keep scrupulous records of their journey and made accurate maps for further travel and exploration. Following Dias's route around the southern tip of Africa, da Gama sailed into the midst of an extensive Muslim trade extending along the East African coast to the Persian Gulf and India, whose port cities linked up with the overland trade to China. Ironically, it was one of the great Muslim navigators, Ibn Majid, the "Lion of the Sea," who guided da Gama from Malindi, on the East African coast, to India.

The journal of this first voyage of Vasco da Gama was kept by an anonymous author, most likely an officer or a seaman who served aboard the *S. Raphael*, one of the ships in the fleet. The journal was first printed in 1838, edited by Diogo Kopke and Dr. Antonio da Costa Paiva, at the Academia Polytechnica of Oporto, with a second Portuguese edition published in Lisbon in 1861, edited by A. Herculano and Baron do Castello de Paiva.

The text of the journal presented here was translated by E. G. Ravenstein, a member of the Geographical Society of Lisbon, and first printed by the Hakluyt Society. The notes, kept to a minimum in order to emphasize readability rather than geography, are based on the translator's.

A Journal of the First Voyage of Vasco da Gama, 1497–99

Translated by E. G. Ravenstein

[*Calecut.*][1]

[*Arrival.*] That night [May 20] we anchored two leagues from the city of Calecut, and we did so because our pilot mistook *Capua*, a town at that place, for Calecut. Still further there is another town called *Pandarani.*[2] We anchored about a league and a half from the shore. After we were at anchor, four boats *(almadias)* approached

[1] ***Calecut:*** Calicut, an important port and trading city on the Malabar coast of southeastern India.

[2] ***Pandarani:*** A city fourteen miles northwest of Calicut.

us from the land, who asked of what nation we were. We told them, and they then pointed out Calecut to us.

On the following day [May 21] these same boats came again alongside, when the captain-major sent one of the convicts to Calecut, and those with whom he went took him to two Moors from Tunis, who could speak Castilian and Genoese. The first greeting that he received was in these words: "May the Devil take thee! What brought you hither?" They asked what he sought so far away from home, and he told them that we came in search of Christians and of spices. They said: "Why does not the King of Castile, the King of France, or the Signoria of Venice send hither?" He said that the King of Portugal would not consent to their doing so, and they said he did the right thing. After this conversation they took him to their lodgings and gave him wheaten bread and honey. When he had eaten he returned to the ships, accompanied by one of the Moors, who was no sooner on board, than he said these words: "A lucky venture, a lucky venture! Plenty of rubies, plenty of emeralds! You owe great thanks to God, for having brought you to a country holding such riches!" We were greatly astonished to hear his talk, for we never expected to hear our language spoken so far away from Portugal.

[*A Description of Calecut.*] The city of Calecut is inhabited by Christians. They are of a tawny complexion. Some of them have big beards and long hair, whilst others clip their hair short or shave the head, merely allowing a tuft to remain on the crown as a sign that they are Christians. They also wear moustaches. They pierce the ears and wear much gold in them. They go naked down to the waist, covering their lower extremities with very fine cotton stuffs. But it is only the most respectable who do this, for the others manage as best they are able.

The women of this country, as a rule, are ugly and of small stature. They wear many jewels of gold round the neck, numerous bracelets on their arms, and rings set with precious stones on their toes. All these people are well-disposed and apparently of mild temper. At first sight they seem covetous and ignorant. [. . .]

[*Gama Goes to Calecut.*] On the following morning, which was Monday, May 28th, the captain-major set out to speak to the king, and took with him thirteen men, of whom I was one. We put on our best attire, placed bombards in our boats, and took with us trumpets and many flags. On landing, the captain-major was received by the *alcaide,*[3] with whom were many men, armed and unarmed. The reception was friendly, as if the people were pleased to see us, though at first appearances looked threatening, for they carried naked swords in their hands. A palanquin[4] was provided for the captain-major, such as is used by men of distinction in that country, as also by some of the merchants, who pay something to the king for this privilege. The captain-major entered the palanquin, which was carried by six men by turns.

---

[3] ***alcaide:*** From the Arabic *al-Qa'id,* meaning leader. Here the term refers to the *Wa'li,* called in this text the *bale,* the civil governor of the city and chief of the police.

[4] **palanquin:** A litter, equipped with canopy and seat, suspended on poles and carried by two or more men.

Attended by all these people we took the road of Qualecut, and came first to another town, called Capua. The captain-major was there deposited at the house of a man of rank, whilst we others were provided with food, consisting of rice, with much butter, and excellent boiled fish. The captain-major did not wish to eat, and when we had done so, we embarked on a river close by, which flows between the sea and the mainland, close to the coast. The two boats in which we embarked were lashed together, so that we were not separated. There were numerous other boats, all crowded with people. As to those who were on the banks I say nothing; their number was infinite, and they had all come to see us. We went up that river for about a league, and saw many large ships drawn up high and dry on its banks, for there is no port here.

When we disembarked, the captain-major once more entered his palanquin. The road was crowded with a countless multitude anxious to see us. Even the women came out of their houses with children in their arms and followed us.

[*A Christian Church.*] When we arrived [at Calecut] they took us to a large church, and this is what we saw:—

The body of the church is as large as a monastery, all built of hewn stone and covered with tiles. At the main entrance rises a pillar of bronze as high as a mast, on the top of which was perched a bird, apparently a cock. In addition to this, there was another pillar as high as a man, and very stout. In the centre of the body of the church rose a chapel,[5] all built of hewn stone, with a bronze door sufficiently wide for a man to pass, and stone steps leading up to it. Within this sanctuary stood a small image which they said represented Our Lady.[6] Along the walls, by the main entrance, hung seven small bells. In this church the captain-major said his prayers, and we with him.

We did not go within the chapel, for it is the custom that only certain servants of the church, called *quafees,*[7] should enter. These *quafees* wore some threads passing over the left shoulder and under the right arm, in the same manner as our deacons wear the stole. They threw holy water over us, and gave us some white earth, which the Christians of this country are in the habit of putting on their foreheads, breasts, around the neck, and on the forearms. They threw holy water upon the captain-major and gave him some of the earth, which he gave in charge of someone, giving them to understand that he would put it on later.

Many other saints were painted on the walls of the church, wearing crowns. They were painted variously, with teeth protruding an inch from the mouth, and four or five arms.

Below this church there was a large masonry tank, similar to many others which we had seen along the road. [. . .]

[5] **chapel:** A translation of *corucheo,* which means, literally, "spire" or "minaret." [Translator's note.]

[6] **Our Lady:** The sailors here appear to have mistaken an image of a Hindu mother figure or goddess for the Virgin Mary.

[7] ***quafees:*** Brahmin priests; the priests ring the bells at the entrance when they enter the temple. [Translator's note.]

[*The King's Palace.*] The further we advanced in the direction of the king's palace, the more did they increase in number. And when we arrived there, men of much distinction and great lords came out to meet the captain, and joined those who were already in attendance upon him. It was then an hour before sunset. When we reached the palace we passed through a gate into a courtyard of great size, and before we arrived at where the king was, we passed four doors, through which we had to force our way, giving many blows to the people. When, at last, we reached the door where the king was, there came forth from it a little old man, who holds a position resembling that of a bishop, and whose advice the king acts upon in all affairs of the church. This man embraced the captain when he entered the door. Several men were wounded at this door, and we only got in by the use of much force.

[*A Royal Audience, May 28.*] The king was in a small court, reclining upon a couch covered with a cloth of green velvet, above which was a good mattress, and upon this again a sheet of cotton stuff, very white and fine, more so than any linen. The cushions were after the same fashion. In his left hand the king held a very large golden cup [spittoon], having a capacity of half an almude [8 pints]. At its mouth this cup was two palmas [16 inches] wide, and apparently it was massive. Into this cup the king threw the husks of a certain herb which is chewed by the people of this country because of its soothing effects, and which they call *atambor.*[8] On the right side of the king stood a basin of gold, so large that a man might just encircle it with his arms: this contained the herbs. There were likewise many silver jugs. The canopy above the couch was all gilt.

The captain, on entering, saluted in the manner of the country: by putting the hands together, then raising them towards Heaven, as is done by Christians when addressing God, and immediately afterwards opening them and shutting the fists quickly. The king beckoned to the captain with his right hand to come nearer, but the captain did not approach him, for it is the custom of the country for no man to approach the king except only the servant who hands him the herbs, and when anyone addresses the king he holds his hand before the mouth, and remains at a distance. When the king beckoned to the captain he looked at us others, and ordered us to be seated on a stone bench near him, where he could see us. He ordered that water for our hands should be given us, as also some fruit, one kind of which resembled a melon, except that its outside was rough and the inside sweet, whilst another kind of fruit resembled a fig, and tasted very nice. There were men who prepared these fruits for us; and the king looked at us eating, and smiled; and talked to the servant who stood near him supplying him with the herbs referred to.

Then, throwing his eyes on the captain, who sat facing him, he invited him to address himself to the courtiers present, saying they were men of much distinction, that he could tell them whatever he desired to say, and they would repeat it to him (the king). The captain-major replied that he was the ambassador of the King of Portugal, and the bearer of a message which he could only deliver to him personally.

[8] ***atambor:*** Betel nut.

The king said this was good, and immediately asked him to be conducted to a chamber. When the captain-major had entered, the king, too, rose and joined him, whilst we remained where we were. All this happened about sunset. An old man who was in the court took away the couch as soon as the king rose, but allowed the plate to remain. The king, when he joined the captain, threw himself upon another couch, covered with various stuffs embroidered in gold, and asked the captain what he wanted.

And the captain told him he was the ambassador of a King of Portugal, who was Lord of many countries and the possessor of great wealth of every description, exceeding that of any king of these parts; that for a period of sixty years his ancestors had annually sent out vessels to make discoveries in the direction of India, as they knew that there were Christian kings there like themselves. This, he said, was the reason which induced them to order this country to be discovered, not because they sought for gold or silver, for of this they had such abundance that they needed not what was to be found in this country. He further stated that the captains sent out travelled for a year or two, until their provisions were exhausted, and then returned to Portugal, without having succeeded in making the desired discovery. There reigned a king now whose name was Dom Manuel, who had ordered him to build three vessels, of which he had been appointed captain-major, and who had ordered him not to return to Portugal until he should have discovered this King of the Christians, on pain of having his head cut off. That two letters had been intrusted to him to be presented in case he succeeded in discovering him, and that he would do so on the ensuing day; and, finally, he had been instructed to say by word of mouth that he [the King of Portugal] desired to be his friend and brother.

In reply to this the king said that he was welcome; that, on his part, he held him as a friend and brother, and would send ambassadors with him to Portugal. This latter had been asked as a favour, the captain pretending that he would not dare to present himself before his king and master unless he was able to present, at the same time, some men of this country. [. . .]

[*Presents for the King.*] On Tuesday [May 29] the captain got ready the following things to be sent to the king, viz., twelve pieces of *lambel,*[9] four scarlet hoods, six hats, four strings of coral, a case containing six wash-hand basins, a case of sugar, two casks of oil, and two of honey. And as it is the custom not to send anything to the king without the knowledge of the Moor, his factor, and of the *bale,* the captain informed them of his intention. They came, and when they saw the present they laughed at it, saying that it was not a thing to offer to a king, that the poorest merchant from Mecca, or any other part of India, gave more, and that if he wanted to make a present it should be in gold, as the king would not accept such things. When the captain heard this he grew sad, and said that he had brought no gold, that, moreover, he was no merchant, but an ambassador; that he gave of that which he had, which was his own [private gift] and not the king's; that if the King of Portugal ordered him

[9] ***lambel:*** Striped cloth.

to return he would intrust him with far richer presents; and that if King Camolim would not accept these things he would send them back to the ships. Upon this they declared that they would not forward his presents, nor consent to his forwarding them himself. When they had gone there came certain Moorish merchants, and they all depreciated the present which the captain desired to be sent to the king.

When the captain saw that they were determined not to forward his present, he said, that as they would not allow him to send his present to the palace he would go to speak to the king, and would then return to the ships. They approved of this, and told him that if he would wait a short time they would return and accompany him to the palace. And the captain waited all day, but they never came back. The captain was very wroth at being among so phlegmatic and unreliable a people, and intended, at first, to go to the palace without them. On further consideration, however, he thought it best to wait until the following day. As to us others, we diverted ourselves, singing and dancing to the sound of trumpets, and enjoyed ourselves much.

Nzinga Mbemba
[1490?–1543?]

Nzinga Mbemba, also known as Affonso of Congo, was the king of that West African state from 1506 to 1543. Mbemba was the son of King Nzinga a Kuwu, who after the Portuguese first arrived in the Congo in 1483 sent some members of his court to Lisbon to find out more about Portugal and its ways. In his letters, Mbemba explains how the Portuguese traders—and slave traders in particular—are upsetting the balance within his state and disobeying his laws. Having been baptized in 1491, Mbemba appeals to Christian principles as he suggests the Portuguese are not following the will of God, and he urges the Portuguese king to encourage useful trade and stop the exchange of slaves that was taking place in the coastal settlements. Twenty-four of these letters from Nzinga Mbemba survive, giving an account of the increasingly devastating effects of Portuguese imperialism in West Africa.

The letter of Nzinga Mbemba to the king of Portugal presented here was extracted and translated by Basil Davidson from original text in Viconde de Paiva-Manso's *History of the Congo: Documents,* published in Lisbon in 1877. The letter, dated October 18, 1526, was written out by João Teixeira.

Letter to the King of Portugal

Translated by Basil Davidson

[The Consequences of the Slave Trade]

Sir, Your Highness [of Portugal] should know how our Kingdom is being lost in so many ways that it is convenient to provide for the necessary remedy, since this is caused by the excessive freedom given by your factors and officials to the men and merchants who are allowed to come to this Kingdom to set up shops with goods and many things which have been prohibited by us, and which they spread throughout our Kingdoms and Domains in such an abundance that many of our vassals, whom we had in obedience, do not comply because they have the things in greater abundance than we ourselves; and it was with these things that we had them content and subjected under our vassalage and jurisdiction, so it is doing a great harm not only to the service of God, but the security and peace of our Kingdoms and State as well.

And we cannot reckon how great the damage is, since the mentioned merchants are taking every day our natives, sons of the land and the sons of our noblemen and vassals and our relatives, because the thieves and men of bad conscience grab them wishing to have the things and wares of this Kingdom which they are ambitious of; they grab them and get them to be sold; and so great, Sir, is the corruption and licentiousness that our country is being completely depopulated, and Your Highness should not agree with this nor accept it as in your service. And to avoid it we need from those [your] Kingdoms no more than some priests and a few people to teach in schools, and no other goods except wine and flour for the holy sacrament. That is why we beg of Your Highness to help and assist us in this matter, commanding your factors that they should not send here either merchants or wares, because it is *our will that in these Kingdoms there should not be any trade of slaves nor outlet for them.* Concerning what is referred above, again we beg of Your Highness to agree with it, since otherwise we cannot remedy such an obvious damage. Pray Our Lord in His mercy to have Your Highness under His guard and let you do for ever the things of His service. I kiss your hands many times.

At our town of Congo, written on the sixth day of July.
João Teixeira did it in 1526.
The King. Dom Affonso.

The Origins of Slaving

Moreover, Sir, in our Kingdoms there is another great inconvenience which is of little service to God, and this is that many of our people, keenly desirous as they are of the wares and things of your Kingdoms, which are brought here by your people, and in order to satisfy their voracious appetite, seize many of our people, freed and exempt men; and very often it happens that they kidnap even noblemen and the sons of noblemen, and our relatives, and take them to be sold to the white men who are in our Kingdoms; and for this purpose they have concealed them; and others are brought during the night so that they might not be recognized.

And as soon as they are taken by the white men they are immediately ironed and branded with fire, and when they are carried to be embarked, if they are caught by our guards' men the whites allege that they have bought them but they cannot say from whom, so that it is our duty to do justice and to restore to the freemen their freedom, but it cannot be done if your subjects feel offended, as they claim to be.

And to avoid such a great evil we passed a law so that any white man living in our Kingdoms and wanting to purchase goods in any way should first inform three of our noblemen and officials of our court whom we rely upon in this matter, and these are Dom Pedro Manipanza and Dom Manuel Manissaba, our chief usher, and Gonçalo Pires our chief freighter, who should investigate if the mentioned goods are captives or free men, and if cleared by them there will be no further doubt nor embargo for them to be taken and embarked. But if the white men do not comply with it they will lose the aforementioned goods. And if we do them this favor and concession it is for the part Your Highness has in it, since we know that it is in your service too that these goods are taken from our Kingdom, otherwise we should not consent to this. [. . .]

A Call for Aid

Sir, Your Highness has been kind enough to write to us saying that we should ask in our letters for anything we need, and that we shall be provided with everything, and as the peace and the health of our Kingdom depend on us, and as there are among us old folks and people who have lived for many days, it happens that we have continuously many and different diseases which put us very often in such a weakness that we reach almost the last extreme; and the same happens to our children, relatives and natives owing to the lack in this country of physicians and surgeons who might know how to cure properly such diseases. And as we have got neither dispensaries nor drugs which might help us in this forlornness, many of those who had been already confirmed and instructed in the holy faith of Our Lord Jesus Christ perish and die; and the rest of the people in their majority cure themselves with herbs and breads and other ancient methods, so that they put all their faith in the mentioned herbs and ceremonies if they live, and believe that they are saved if they die; and this is not much in the service of God.

And to avoid such a great error and inconvenience, since it is from God in the first place and then from your Kingdoms and from Your Highness that all the good and drugs and medicines have come to save us, we beg of you to be agreeable and kind enough to send us two physicians and two apothecaries and one surgeon, so that they may come with their drug-stores and all the necessary things to stay in our kingdoms, because we are in extreme need of them all and each of them. We shall do them all good and shall benefit them by all means, since they are sent by Your Highness, whom we thank for your work in their coming. We beg of Your Highness as a great favor to do this for us, because besides being good in itself it is in the service of God as we have said above.

Matteo Ricci

1552–1610

After strictly limiting contacts with the world after the last voyages of Zheng He in the mid fifteenth century, the Chinese in 1557 allowed the Portuguese to set up a trading post in the port town of Macao and lifted the ban on foreign trade in 1567. At about the same time, the Jesuit mission to China was established by highly educated priests such as Alessandro Valignano (1539–1606), who arrived in 1577, and Matteo Ricci, who established a residence at Beijing in 1582. Ricci spent more than twenty years in China, where he recorded his observations of Chinese culture and society in a diary intended for the Father General of the Society of Jesus. A man of extensive scientific, mathematical, and philosophical learning, Ricci was accepted among the educated elite in Beijing, where he remained until his death in 1610. Aside from the chronicle of Marco Polo's travels that first appeared in the fourteenth century and was not translated into English until 1579, Europeans had no detailed descriptions of China. Thus, when Ricci's diaries were translated into Latin in 1615, they immediately went through several editions and translations into vernacular languages, and inspired a renewed European interest in China.

A note on the text: The selections from Ricci's journals presented here were translated from the Latin by Louis J. Gallagher, S.J.; the notes are the editors'.

The Diary of Matthew Ricci

Translated by Louis J. Gallagher, S.J.

[The Art of Printing and the Making of Fans]

The art of printing was practiced in China at a date somewhat earlier than that assigned to the beginning of printing in Europe, which was about 1405. It is quite certain that the Chinese knew the art of printing at least five centuries ago, and some of them assert that printing was known to their people before the beginning of the Christian era, about 50 B.C. Their method of printing differs widely from that employed in Europe, and our method would be quite impracticable for them because of the exceedingly large number of Chinese characters and symbols. At present they cut their characters in a reverse position and in a simplified form, on a comparatively small tablet made for the most part from the wood of the pear tree or the apple tree, although at times the wood of the jujube tree is also used for this purpose.

Their method of making printed books is quite ingenious. The text is written in ink, with a brush made of very fine hair, on a sheet of paper which is inverted and pasted on a wooden tablet. When the paper has become thoroughly dry, its surface is

P. Matthæus Riccius Macerat. è Soc. Jesu
prim.° Chrīanæ Fidei in Regno Sinarum
propagator
Li Paulus Magnus Sinarum Colaus
Legis Christiana propagator.

Athanasius Kircher, *Matteo Ricci*, 1667

This engraving shows Matteo Ricci with Li Paul, Mandarin Colao, prominent convert and champion of the faith. (Private Collection / The Stapleton Collection / Bridgeman Art Library)

scraped off quickly and with great skill, until nothing but a fine tissue bearing the characters remains on the wooden tablet. Then, with a steel graver, the workman cuts away the surface following the outlines of the characters until these alone stand out in low relief. From such a block a skilled printer can make copies with incredible speed, turning out as many as fifteen hundred copies in a single day. Chinese printers are so skilled in engraving these blocks, that no more time is consumed in making one of them than would be required by one of our printers in setting up a form of type and making the necessary corrections. This scheme of engraving wooden blocks is well adapted for the large and complex nature of the Chinese characters, but I do not think it would lend itself very aptly to our European type which could hardly be engraved upon wood because of its small dimensions.

Their method of printing has one decided advantage, namely, that once these tablets are made, they can be preserved and used for making changes in the text as often as one wishes. Additions and subtractions can also be made as the tablets can be readily patched. Again, with this method, the printer and the author are not obliged to produce here and now an excessively large edition of a book, but are able to print a book in smaller or larger lots sufficient to meet the demand at the time. We have derived great benefit from this method of Chinese printing, as we employ the domestic help in our homes to strike off copies of the books on religious and scientific subjects which we translate into Chinese from the languages in which they were written originally. In truth, the whole method is so simple that one is tempted to try it for himself after once having watched the process. The simplicity of Chinese printing is what accounts for the exceedingly large numbers of books in circulation here and the ridiculously low prices at which they are sold. Such facts as these would scarcely be believed by one who had not witnessed them.

They have another odd method of reproducing reliefs which have been cut into marble or wood. An epitaph, for example, or a picture set out in low relief on marble or on wood, is covered with a piece of moist paper which in turn is overlayed with several pieces of cloth. Then the entire surface is beaten with a small mallet until all the lineaments of the relief are impressed upon the paper. When the paper dries, ink or some other coloring substance is applied with a light touch, after which only the impression of the relief stands out on the original whiteness of the paper. This method cannot be employed when the relief is shallow or made in delicate lines.

The Chinese use pictures extensively, even in the crafts, but in the production of these and especially in the making of statuary and cast images they have not at all acquired the skill of Europeans. They decorate their magnificent arches with the figures of men and beasts, and enrich their temples with the images of gods and with brass bells. Indeed, if my deductions have been rightly made, it seems to me that the Chinese, who in other respects are so ingenious, and by nature in no way inferior to any other people on earth, are very primitive in the use of these latter arts, because they have never come into intimate contact with the nations beyond their borders. Such intercourse would undoubtedly have been most helpful to them in making progress in this respect. They know nothing of the art of painting in oil or of the use of perspective in their pictures, with the result that their productions are likely to resemble the dead rather than the living. It seems also that they have not been very successful in the production of statuary, in which they follow rules of symmetry determined by the eye only. This, of course, frequently results in illusions and causes glaring defects in their works of larger proportions. Yet this does not prevent them from fashioning huge, ugly monsters in marble and brass and clay. Their bells are made of brass and sounded with wooden mallets. They cannot tolerate bells sounded with iron tongues on hammers, and consequently their bells do not compare with ours in quality of tone. [. . .]

One particular trade here is far more universal than elsewhere, namely, that of making fans. Ordinarily these fans are used to temper the breezes during the season of greater heat, and they are carried by every class and by both sexes. It would be considered a lack of taste to appear in public without a fan, even though the weather should prompt one to ward off breezes rather than to stir them up. Perhaps the reason for this particular custom is that fans are used more for ornamental display than for any necessity. There is a great variety of fashion in Chinese fans and in the material from which they are made. Ordinarily they consist of ribs of reed, wood, ivory, or ebony, covered with paper or perhaps with cotton and at times even with a sweet-scented straw. Some are round, some oval, and some square. Those used by the upper classes are generally made of bright paper decorated with a design, beautifully traced in gold, and they are carried either spread out or folded up. Sometimes, too, these fans are inscribed with certain maxims or even with whole poems. The gift most frequently exchanged as a sign of friendship and esteem is a fan. We have at our house a box full of these gift fans which have been given to us by our friends as a mark of esteem and which we in turn give to others as a proof of friendship. It is easy to imagine the number of artisans everywhere employed in the manufacture of these fans. It has always seemed to me that the use of the fan among the Chinese is like our own use of gloves. Although, the chief purpose of each seems to be quite opposite, one being used to ward off heat and the other to protect against cold; yet, both alike seem to be employed much more frequently either as a matter of display or as a small gift token of friendship.

In the practice of the arts and the crafts we have mentioned, the Chinese are certainly different from all other people, but for the most part their practice of the other arts and sciences is quite the same as our own, despite the great distance that separates them from our civilization. In fact, the similarity of customs is rather remarkable when we consider their methods of eating and sitting and sleeping, in which they alone of all nations outside of Europe are quite in accord with the West. Their use of tables, chairs, and beds is wholly unknown to any of the peoples of the states that border on China, all of whom place straw mats on the ground or floor and use them in place of chair, bed, or table. This difference of custom is quite remarkable, and I am somewhat at a loss to explain it, but I shall proceed no further with this matter lest it weary the patience of the reader. One may gather from what has been said that there are numerous points of advantageous contact between ourselves and the Chinese people. [. . .]

[Chinese Medicine and Education]

The practice of the art of medicine in China differs very much from what we are accustomed to. Their method of taking the pulse is the same as ours and they are quite successful in bringing about cures. In general, they make use of very simple remedies, such as herbs, roots, and other such things. In fact, the whole art of Chinese medicine is practically contained in the rules we ourselves follow for the use of herbs. There are no public schools for the teaching of medicine. Each aspirant is taught by someone skilled in the art. In both kingdoms (Pekin and Nankin)[1] examinations may be taken for degrees in medicine. This, however, is a mere formality as there is no advantage attached to it. A man with a degree in medicine enjoys no more authority or esteem than one without it, because no one is prohibited from attempting to cure the sick, whether he be skilled in medicine or not.

It is evident to everyone here that no one will labor to attain proficiency in mathematics or in medicine who has any hope of becoming prominent in the field of philosophy. The result is that scarcely anyone devotes himself to these studies, unless he is deterred from the pursuit of what are considered to be the higher studies, either by reason of family affairs or by mediocrity of talent. The study of mathematics and that of medicine are held in low esteem, because they are not fostered by honors as is the study of philosophy, to which students are attracted by the hope of the glory and the rewards attached to it. This may be readily seen in the interest taken in the study of moral philosophy. The man who is promoted to the higher degrees in this field, prides himself on the fact that he has in truth attained to the pinnacle of Chinese happiness.

I think it will be as interesting as it is new to the reader to treat somewhat more fully of this phase of their studies. Confucius,[2] called the Prince of Chinese Philosophers, compiled four volumes of the works of more ancient philosophers and wrote five books of his own. These five he entitled "The Doctrines," and they contain the ethical principles of right living, precepts governing the conduct of political life, customs, and examples of the ancients, their rites and sacrifices, and even samples of their poetry and other subjects of this nature. Besides these five books there is another one composed of the precepts of the great philosopher and of his disciples and compiled without particular arrangement. These are chiefly directions for proper moral proceedings, in the light of human reason, with a view to virtuous conduct on the part of the individual, of the family and of the kingdom in general. This volume, being a summary in excerpts from the four books mentioned, is called the Tetrabiblion.[3] The nine books of Confucius, making up the most ancient of Chinese libraries, of which all others are a development, are written mostly in hieroglyphic characters, and present a collection of moral precepts for the future good and development of the kingdom.

There is a law in the land, handed down from ancient kings and confirmed by the custom of centuries, stating that he who wishes to be learned, and to be known as such, must draw his fundamental doctrine from these same books. In addition to this it is not sufficient for him to follow the general sense of the text, but what is far more difficult, he must be able to write aptly and exactly of every particular doctrine contained in these books. To this end he must commit the entire Tetrabiblion to memory, so as to be a recognized authority thereon. Contrary to what has been

[1] **(Pekin and Nankin):** Beijing (Peking) and Nanking.

[2] **Confucius** (Kongfuzi, 551–479 B.C.E.): Chinese philosopher, whose *Analects,* a collection of maxims and parables, provided the basis for China's most important tradition, Confucianism.

[3] **Tetrabiblion:** Greek for "The Four Books."

stated by some of our writers, there are no schools or public academies in which these books are taught or explained by masters. Each student selects his own master by whom he is instructed in his own home and at his personal expense.

The number of such private teachers, of course, is great, partly because it would be hard for one master to teach many at a time, owing to the difficulty of handling the Chinese characters, and partly because it is an old custom here for each home to have a private school for its own children. At times it happens that tutors, other than the one regularly employed, may be called in, as it would seem, to prevent the custom of bidding for the position from interfering with the interest of their profession.

In the field of philosophy there are three degrees, conferred upon those who pass the written examinations assigned for each degree. The first degree is awarded in the larger cities and in a public academy, by some prominent scholar, appointed by the emperor for that purpose. In virtue of his office this dignitary is known as Tihio, and the first degree, corresponding to our baccalaureate, is called Lieucai. The Tihio visits the various cities of his province in which the degree is to be conferred and for which a triple examination is required. Upon the arrival of this chancellor, as we would call him, the candidates assemble for the examinations. The preliminary examination is conducted by the local teachers who have attained to the baccalaureate and are preparing for a higher degree, and they are paid from the royal treasury for these particular examinations. Anyone may be admitted to the preliminary examinations, and sometimes four or five thousand from a single district will take them. Those who pass the first test are recommended by the teachers to the four city prefects, who are themselves learned men, otherwise they would not be in office. The prefects then select the candidates who are to be presented to the chancellor. Not more than two hundred may be thus presented, and these are chosen for the excellence of their written composition.

The third examination is conducted by the chancellor, himself, and is far more rigid than those preceding it. Of the two hundred admitted to this examination, the twenty or thirty obtaining the highest grades are granted the degree, depending upon the size of the district from which the candidates are drawn. They are then known as academic bachelors, a distinguished class representing the advanced citizenry of their particular town, and their company is cultivated by all who hope to attain to the same dignity. Their particular insignia is an ankle-long gown, a cap, and leggings, which no class other than their own is permitted to wear. They are given seats of honor at the conventions of the magistrates, and with them they may employ the more intimate rites of address which the common people are never permitted to use. In their home cities they enjoy a great many civil privileges and are looked upon as inferior to none, save the chancellor and the four city prefects, nor is it easy for other magistrates to pass judgment upon the cases they present or on charges made against them.

The duty of the chancellor is not confined to the class of new bachelors. He is also responsible for the conduct of those who attained to the degree in former years, weighing in a strict balance what progress they have made and what laxity they have suffered. To this end he institutes five different grades or classes, which are adjudged according to the caliber of their writings. Those who are listed in the first category are awarded with a public office, but not one of superior grade. The second class is also awarded but with lesser honors. The third class is held as indifferent, with neither reward nor punishment. Class number four is considered as negligent and must pay a penalty for their shortcomings. Finally, if a bachelor is unfortunate enough to fall into the fifth or last class, he is stripped of his bachelor's insignia and reduced to the ranks of an ordinary citizen. This is done to prevent those who become bachelors from losing interest and forgetting in a life of ease what they have labored so hard to acquire.

The second degree of the Chinese literati is called Kiugin and may be compared to our licentiate. This degree is conferred with considerable solemnity in each metropolitan province but only every third year and at the eighth moon. This degree is not open to all who may aspire to it. Only those of the highest ranking are selected for it and their number depends upon the dignity or celebrity of the province. In the districts of Nankin and Pekin one hundred and fifty bachelors are called for the licentiate. From Cequin (Chekiang), Quiamsi (Kiangsi), and Fuquiam (Fu-kien), ninety-five are called and fewer in other provinces, according to the standing of the province and of the number of degrees already granted in the province. As has been stated, only the bachelors are called for this second degree, and not all of these. The selection is made by the chancellor of bachelors, who summons thirty or at most forty from each city or study center of the province, and this choice is made by written tests. Yet, despite this strict selection, in some of the larger provinces the number of those aspiring to the licentiate is frequently in excess of four thousand. [. . .]

[The Literati]

In this chapter, we shall treat only of the triple cult of the Chinese as distinguished from all other pagan sects. The traces of Saracen, Judaic, and of Christian worship evident in China we shall leave for later consideration. Chinese books enumerate only three cults or systems of religious observance for the whole world and this people knows of no others. These are, the Literati, the Sciequia, and the Laucu. All Chinese and all people of the surrounding nations who make use of Chinese writing—the Japanese, the Koreans, the Leuquici or Formosans, and the Cochin Chinese—belong to one or other of these three sects.

The sect of the Literati is proper to China and is the most ancient in the kingdom. They rule the country, have an extensive literature, and are far more celebrated than the others. Individually, the Chinese do not choose this sect; they rather imbibe the doctrine of it in the study of letters. No one who attains honors in the study of letters or who even undertakes the study would belong to any other sect. Confucius is their Prince of Philosophers, and according to them, it was he who discovered the art of philosophy. They do not believe in idol worship. In fact they have no idols. They do, however, believe in one deity who preserves and governs all things on earth. Other spirits they admit, but these are of less restricted domination and receive only minor honors. The real Literati teach nothing relative to the time, the manner, or the author of the creation of the world. We use the word real, or true, because there are some of them, less celebrated, who interpret dreams, but not much faith is placed in them as they deal mostly with trifles and improbable things. Their law contains a doctrine of reward for good done and of punishment for evil, but they seem to limit it to the present life and to apply it to the evil-doer and to his descendants, according to their merits. The ancients scarcely seem to doubt about the immortality of the soul because, for a long time after a death, they make frequent reference to the departed as dwelling in heaven. They say nothing, however, about punishment for the wicked in hell. The more recent Literati teach that the soul ceases to exist when the body does, or a short time after it. They, therefore, make no mention of heaven or of hell. To some of them this seems to be rather a severe doctrine and so this school teaches that only the souls of the just survive. They say that the soul of a man is strengthened by virtue and solidified to endure, and since this is not true of the wicked, their souls vanish, like thin smoke, immediately after leaving the body.

The doctrine most commonly held among the Literati at present seems to me to have been taken from the sect of idols, as promulgated about five centuries ago. This doctrine asserts that the entire universe is composed of a common substance; that the creator of the universe is one in a continuous body, a corpus continuum as it were, together with heaven and earth, men and beasts, trees and plants, and the four elements, and that each individual thing is a member of this body. From this unity of substance they reason to the love that should unite the individual constituents and also that man can become like unto God because he is created one with God. This philosophy we endeavor to refute, not only from reason but also from the testimony of their own ancient philosophers to whom they are indebted for all the philosophy they have. [. . .]

Evliya Çelebi
1611–c. 1684

One of the world's great travelers, Evliya Çelebi was born in Istanbul in 1611, the son of the wealthy Mehmet Zilli, the court goldsmith, and his wife, who was related to Melek Ahmed Pasha, a man who would eventually become the grand vizier. As he was growing up, Evliya learned his father's trade, but he also received a comprehensive education in the Islamic sciences and the Qur'an (Koran), becoming an accomplished singer of Qur'anic verses. When Evliya was twenty years old, the prophet Muhammad appeared to him in a dream and gave his blessing to Evliya's wanderlust. This blessing was soon to become relevant, for after completing his education at the palace school of Sultan Murat IV, Evliya entered into the service of various *pashas,* high-ranking officials, whose missions took him to the remotest boundaries of the Ottoman empire and beyond to Austria and Iran. Over his lifetime, Evliya traveled from Istanbul to the Caucasus Mountains, to Crimea and Crete, throughout

Anatolia and to Syria, and to the Balkans. In 1655, he went to Vienna in the company of Kara Mehmed Pasha, who was making an embassy there; and in 1671 he took the pilgrimage to Mecca. After making the ***HAJJ***, Evliya settled in Egypt, where he lived for the rest of his life.

In Egypt Evliya began writing his *Book of Travels*, working from copious notes that he had kept during his years of traveling, as well as drawing from other writings and from his memory. The manuscript he left behind was not published until 1843, when an Arabic version of selected passages appeared in print. This edition was followed by the first eight volumes published from 1896 to 1928 and the final two volumes in 1935 to 1938. The book's popularity in the Arabic world quickly rose, and Evliya is now considered one of the greatest of the Ottoman writers, valued for his detailed descriptions as well as for his exaggerated and fantastic accounts of people and events. Evliya's tendency to embellish his accounts is in good evidence in the passage presented here, in which he describes the thousand skills of the seventy-year-old Abdal Khan and the palace gardens at Bitlis, a city in the southeastern corner of what is now Turkey.

A note on the text: Evliya was in Bitlis on three separate occasions in 1655 and 1656, and he describes these visits in Books 4 and 5. The translator and editor of the selections that follow, Robert Dankoff, has compiled these materials into a single volume for the series of partial editions of Evliya Çelebi's travels published by E. J. Brill and under the general editorship of Klaus Kreiser (1990). The notes to the text are based on the translator's (indicated in parentheses), with additions of the editors'.

***Ottoman Court*, Seventeenth Century**
This Turkish manuscript shows Venetian ambassador Jacopo Soranzo being received at the Ottoman court in Constantinople for peace negotiations. (The Art Archive/Museo Correr Venice/Dagli Orti)

The Book of Travels

Translated by Robert Dankoff

[The Court of Abdal Khan, Governor of Bitlis]

Abdal Khan's[1] *thousand skills.* Aside from being versed in alchemy and magic and several hundred occult philosophical sciences, he is—according to the Hadith,[2] "Science is two, the science of bodies, and the science of religions"—a master physician, next to whom the ancient physicians such as Galen and Hippocrates and Socrates and Philekos[3] are not even schoolboys; for they were reckoned physicians according to the men of their time, but this Khan is a master pulse-taker and bloodletter according to the nature of the sick and the weakly of the present age.

He even treated an eighty-year-old sick and weakly opium addict, who had turned into a wishbone, giving him decoctions and hot baths and cures beggaring description, so that this meager fellow found new life and became fresh and ruddy as a Tebkani apple within three days. He has, like Jesus, given life to some thousands of individuals such as this.

He is also an incomparable surgeon, and has set and wrapped many a man who has tumbled from his horse or fallen from his roof, so that the fellow was on his feet in seven days. He even has a kind of mummy-powder which, if ingested by an emaciated man, his slender waist fills out to Iskender's sash.

He is such a fine horseman that, when he mounts his swift steed, playing jereed or polo, or engaging in battle, he is like Rüstem of Zabulistan or Shaghad of Iran. [...]

We spent the ten-day halt in his palace with our lord the Pasha. Each day from dawn to dusk there was a constant stream of musicians and buffoons and acrobats, displaying their wares and receiving gifts from the Khan and the Pasha. Because of the Khan's reputation as patron of the arts and sciences, skilled men would come to him from every country, and if they were well-rounded and cultivated individuals, the Khan would give them gardened palaces and slavegirls and timars and dye works in order that he might keep them tied down in the valley of Bitlis and so acquire some of their skills. Thus the Khan became a second Cemshid, spending all his free time learning new skills. And thus the city of Bitlis was filled with skilled masters.

As for the master players on the shawm and the trumpet and the kettle drum and the cymbals in the Khan's band, their like is not to be found in the imperial workshop itself, let alone in that of a vizier. For he himself performs concerts *(pīşrev)* and is knowledgeable in the various musical sciences. And he has masters in his band

[1] ***Abdal Khan:*** The governor of the city of Bitlis (in what is now southeastern Turkey).

[2] **Hadith:** The traditional record or collection of sayings and deeds of Muhammad, second only in importance to the Qu'ran in Islamic tradition. The translator notes that "Evliya always cites this dubious Hadith when he mentions medicine."

[3] **Philekos:** Galen, Hippocrates, Socrates, Philekos.

who perform *küll-i külliyāt, zencīr* in the twenty-four rhythmic cycles, *shükūfe-zār,* and *peshrevs* in the *ṣabā* mode and the *ẓarb-i fetiḥ* rhythmic cycle.[4] Each one is like Cemshid who invented the shawm. When they perform in the evening, or in the predawn when no one is stirring, they delight the listener.

The Khan's pleasure garden. On the harem side of this garden palace there is a garden as long and broad as the range of a bowshot. If the seas were ink and the trees were pens, and all the scribes gathered, they could not record a drop in the ocean or a mote in the sunlight of due description and praise of this garden. Suffice it to say that all the fruit-bearing trees are planted in rows, each one swaying with the zephyr breeze like beauties with girded loins. Aside from the fig, the sycamore, the banana, and the cypress, all varieties are present. In some nooks and crannies there are even lemon and orange saplings which are protected with felt coverings during the winter. There are also charming and lavish pleasure-domes, like so many castles of Khavarnak, each one difference in style from the others, and each the work of a master of a different land.

The pools and jets and fountains here are not to be found in Turkey. Each pool is surrounded by a mosaic floor of varicolored marble, like Indian-style mother-of-pearl and marquetry inlay. Streams of water as thick as a man's neck flow into the pools from the mouths of various demons, lions, and dragons; then pour down into the reticulated garden beds. There is also water springing up from jets. In certain cases, forty or fifty streams jet out of a single hole and mingle together like a beauty's tresses. The marvelous thing is that they all issue from one mouth. Some of the pleasure-domes have suspended glass and crystal bowls, which give a melancholy sound when the water jets strike them, while the larger ones channel the water so that it cascades like rain. Some of the jets have a wheel suspended above, which turns when the jet stream strikes. Others have a hollow ball the size of a watermelon, which turns and bobs in the air. In short, the master craftsmen of every land have created such wonders that the tongue cannot express.

There are beds with thousands of flowers of various sorts, including rose, hyacinth, sweet basil, violet, judas-tree, jonquil, *nebatī* (?), camel's neck, camphor-tree, peony, Roman musk, carnation, syringa, lily, iris, narcissus, cyclamen, jasmine, tulip, and hollyhock. Each bed is laid out differently, and they intoxicate with the scent of jonquils and other blossoms. As for the varieties of fruit trees, there are saplings from as far away as Isfahan, Tebriz, and Nakhshevan. Even though this garden was constructed only recently, when Sultan Murad IV saw it during the Revan campaign, he was astounded.

The Khan's artificial lake. Behind the aforementioned garden on the northern side there was a flowing spring called Ayn-i Taklaban. The Khan dammed up the lower part of the stream and made a sea-like lagoon. The dam is like the Wall of Iskender or the Wall of Magog, and myriad fishes swim in the lake. The Khan had

---

[4] ***küll-i . . . cycle:*** These terms refer to different types of musical styles distinguished by different compound rhythms.

caiques constructed and decked out, and he himself used to row alone, or else he would take his household out for excursions, thereby dissipating his longing for the sea.

One day, by God's wisdom, the women were not sitting properly in the caique and it capsized, leaving several slavegirls drowned. After that he gave up the sport, only occasionally going fishing. The lake is very deep. Once, when the flood waters were severe, one side of the dam broke and the rushing waters destroyed quite a few houses in the Taklaban quarter. When the Kurds cursed the Khan, wishing that he too would be ruined, he reconstructed all of their houses.

The garden bath. A delightful bath goes off the treasury room of the above-mentioned Khan's palace, and gives onto a dressing-room. It has gardens on three sides, and the dressing-room has windows overlooking the gardens, all with bronze and iron grating like Fakhri cut-outs, also shutters of Arab-style carved (wood), which the khans of Persia sent from Tebriz as gifts. The shutter carvings are filled in with raw black ambergris, and as the zephyr breeze strikes them from without, the men within enjoy the fragrance.

All four walls of this dressing-room are covered with varicolored porcelain tiles. And going all around the lofty dome and over the upper sills of the windows, in calligraphy written enchantingly on the tiles by the hand of Mehemmed Riza of Tebriz, is Fuzuli's[5] "Bath Kaside." [. . .]

In the very center of this dressing-room are fountains full of water shooting toward the dome from three hundred places. Its floor is paved with Egyptian-style varicolored marble. The jet in the center of the pool strikes the glass bowl at the peak of the dome and then rains down. All the servants here are lovely Circassian, Abkhazian and Georgian ghulams,[6] each outfitted with a jewelled belt worth a thousand piasters, adorned with daggers and knives, and walking about on clogs with inlaid mother-of-pearl, like so many peacocks of paradise. They give the bathers silk waist-wrappers and clogs like their own, and serve them respectfully.

When one enters the bath from the dressing-room, one finds oneself in a large domed room called the tepidarium *(ṣovuḳluḳ),* but the water of the pools and fountains in the middle of this room is all hot, and the walls are all covered with varicolored tiles. The floor here too is paved with marble mosaic "China-rose" while the sturdy enamel dome is brightened by porcelain tiles and ornamented with numerous chandeliers.

The next room is the caldarium *(ḥammām-i germā).* It is as though one entered a pool of light, for there is no sign of a wall rising on all sides to the lofty dome. Rather, this great round dome is perched on tall columns, and between the columns are windows of clear and polished rock crystal and Murano cut glass. When the sun strikes the windows, the inside of the bath become "light upon light."[7] In the garden of Irem outside these windows a thousand nightingales wail and cry, as the bathers within listen and watch them feed their chicks, and observe the flowering trees

---

[5] **Fuzuli** (1495–1556): A Turkish poet of the Ottoman empire; the poem mentioned is a famous ghazal of his.

[6] **ghulams:** Slaves.

[7] **"light upon light":** An allusion to the Qur'an 24:35. [Translator's note.]

and the singing birds' nests and the tall and brightly colored flowers arrayed on the ground.

In the middle of this bath is a large pool with jets spouting up on all sides, the jet in the center reaching as high as the bowl in the dome and then pouring down into the hot water. Ruby-colored petals of rose and carnation are floating in the pool and stick to the bathers' skin, imparting their perfume. Each cubicle has a two-jar sarcophagus bath. This room also is paved with marble that dazzles the eye, since it is inlaid with precious stones, like the eye of a bird: jade, turquoise, onyx, amber, fish-eye, agate, *yemenī,* and garnets. And attached to the columns that are between the windows are wash basins of onyx, porphyry, *yereḳān* stone, *feraḥ* stone, and Chinese porcelain, carved to such perfection that the marble cutters of today could not even strike a chisel at it. The craftsmen made the water flow out of the marble columns into the basins in a marvelous manner. All the spouts are gold and silver, the bowls as well, and the jet pipes are pure silver. The atmosphere is so delightful, one seems to be enjoying eternal life. As the fountain streams strike the various chandeliers and wheels and suspended crystal bowls, they turn in the air, which is also a rare sight. On the lower level (lit., skirts) of this dome are fine calligraphic inscriptions with verses relating to the bath. Lovely slaveboys, with silken indigo waistbands wrapped round their naked bodies, service the bathers with *fütūnī* bathgloves and scented soaps. When they loosen their tresses, the distraught lover goes out of his mind. Some of them light censers and incense-burners with aloes and ambergris, so the bath is filled with fragrance.

In sum, the tongue falls short in describing this bath, or the grand palace, or the garden of Irem. For in the expenditure of filigree-work in these buildings, and in grace and elegance and cleanliness, it is a peerless bath of unique design whose like I have not seen in forty-one years of travel.

The master builder in each of his works brought forth such marvels of art that no former architect under the sun achieved such a construction. Only God knows what it cost to make such a wondrous mansion. Even Sultan Murad, during the Revan campaign, when he entered this bath and found the cold water flowing with rose-water, and the hot with steam; and in one cubicle five lovely male attendants with black tresses, and in another five fairy-graced and angel-faced virgin maiden attendants;—even he exclaimed with delight: "If only this bath were in *my* palace!" It is truly a wonderful and charming bath.

Zhang Ting-yu (Chang T'ing-yü)
1672–1755

jahng-ting-YOO

Zhang Ting-yu (Chang T'ing-yü) was one of the most important historians of the late Ming dynasty. He was the leader of the team of scholars that produced the *History of the Ming,* a compilation of 336 scrolls, describing sometimes in minute detail the customs and culture of the Ming dynasty. Among the subjects covered by this work are the seven maritime expeditions of the admiral **Zheng He** (Cheng Ho; c. 1371–c. 1433) undertaken between 1405 and 1433. Although the history does not give us the account of a direct observer, the discussion of Zheng He's travels provides us with a good sense of the importance of these officially commissioned voyages of exploration and discovery.

jung-HUH

During the reign of the third emperor of the Ming dynasty, Zhu Di (Chu Ti; 1360–1424), who reigned under the title Yongle (Yung-lo) from 1403 to 1424, the Chinese were involved in expanding their tributary network and in broadening their knowledge about remote regions. Like their Ming predecessors, **Yongle** and his successor **Xuande** (Hsüan-te; r. 1425–35) sent emissaries to several areas outside of China, including Japan, Java, central Asia, Tibet, and India, in part to bring back religious texts and in part simply to learn more about the culture, resources, and social practices of such places. The expeditions were thus religious, economic, and political. Beginning in 1403, Yongle commissioned Zheng He to undertake the first of what would be seven voyages. The vast fleet, consisting of two hundred or more Chinese junks—the largest ocean-going vessels of their time—and carrying nearly twenty-eight thousand men, was designed to display China's considerable maritime prowess. The spectacle of this flotilla and its vast retinues astounded those who saw it and did much to raise the prestige of China throughout the Indian Ocean region. The voyages also promoted trade, extended China's tributary network, and led to the emigration of many Chinese to places in Southeast Asia.

yohng-LUH; schwen-DUH

Zheng He's first voyage, from 1405 to 1407, took him along the southeast coast of Vietnam, then on to Calicut on the southwestern coast of India, by way of Java, Sumatra, and Ceylon. In the six subsequent voyages, Zheng He sailed to the Persian Gulf and beyond, reaching Ormuz and the coast of Somalia. He declared that the kingdoms he reached were under the dominion of the Ming emperors, and he carried sufficient numbers of troops to enforce his claims. By the end of the seventh voyage, Zheng He had established diplomatic or economic relations, primarily in the form of tribute flowing into China, from more than twenty kingdoms reaching from Vietnam, Java, and Sumatra to Aden and Jiddah (on the Red Sea), and on to Mogadishu and Mombasa on the eastern coast of Africa. Although the records of Zheng He's achievements do not survive, the account in the *History of the Ming* gives some sense of their importance at the time and creates a strong image of the power of China's navies, which had been a force since the twelfth century.

***The Emperor Yongle,* 1360–1424**
The Ming dynasty ruler Zhu Di (Chu Ti), who reigned under the name Yongle (Yung-lo), is shown here on a sedan chair, being fanned by servants. (Private Collection / Bridgeman Art Library)

History of the Ming

Translated by Dun J. Li

[The Voyages of Zheng He]

Cheng Ho [Zheng He], a native of Yunnan,[1] was popularly known as San-pao the Grand Eunuch *(San-pao t'ai-chien)*. At one time he served as a staff member in the feudatory of King Ch'eng;[2] later he was promoted to the position of grand eunuch in recognition of his contribution to King Ch'eng's successful revolt against Emperor

[1] **Yunnan:** Yünnan; southwestern province of China.

[2] **King Ch'eng:** Chengzu, the family name of Zhu Di (Chu Ti), the prince who overthrew the second Ming emperor in 1401; he then took the dynastic name Yongle and ruled as the third and most effective emperor of the Ming dynasty from 1402 to 1424.

Ming Hui-ti.[3] After his accession to the throne, Emperor Yung-lo,[4] the former King Ch'eng, suspected that his defeated predecessor Hui-ti might have escaped from Nanking and be residing somewhere in the South Seas and wanted very much to know his whereabouts. Besides, he wished to glorify Chinese arms in the remote regions and show off the wealth and power of the Central Kingdom. It was this combination of motives that prompted him to launch Cheng Ho's voyages.

In the sixth month of the third year[5] of Yung-lo Cheng Ho and his deputy Wang Ching-hung, as ordered by the emperor, proceeded with their journey to the Western Ocean.[6] Well furnished with treasure and accompanied by more than 27,800 officers and men, they sailed in sixty-two giant ships, each of which measured forty-four *chang* [ca. 517 feet] in length and eighteen *chang* [ca. 212 feet] in width. The ships left the Liuchia River[7] for the sea and then sailed southward to Fukien wherefrom they proceeded with sails full-blown to Champa. From Champa the Chinese envoys visited one country after another. They read the imperial decree that demanded the submission of the kingdoms they visited and rewarded generously those rulers who agreed to submit. As for those who chose not to obey, force was used to assure their compliance.

In the ninth month of the fifth year[8] of Yung-lo Cheng Ho returned to the capital and presented to the emperor tribute-bearing envoys from the kingdoms he had visited. The emperor was greatly pleased and granted titles and financial rewards to all of those who had been presented to him. Cheng Ho also brought back many prisoners of war, including the captured king of Palembang.[9]

Palembang was formally known as Sanfuch'i whose ruler, a Chinese named Ch'en Tsu-yi, had been active as a pirate in the South Seas before he was captured by Cheng Ho. When Cheng Ho demanded his surrender, he said he would, but in secret he was planning to launch an attack upon Cheng Ho's ships. Once the perfidy was recognized, Cheng Ho attacked and won a decisive victory. Ch'en Tsu-yi was captured alive and later brought to Peking. He was executed shortly afterward.

In the ninth month of the sixth year[10] of Yung-lo Cheng Ho sailed again for Ceylon. Upon his arrival, the king of Ceylon, a man named Alagakkonara, invited him to visit his city with fine promises. Once inside the city, Cheng Ho was presented with a demand for gold and silk; moreover, Alagakkonara had already ordered an attack on the Chinese ships. Taking advantage of the fact that practically all the Ceylonese troops had been out of the city for this attack, Cheng Ho personally

[3] **Ming Hui-ti:** (r. 1399–1402), the second Ming emperor; his policies were to reduce the power of local lords, including the prince Zhu Di (Chu Ti); see note 2.

[4] **Yung-lo:** Yongle (r. 1402–1424), the third Ming emperor; see note 2.

[5] **third year:** 1405.

[6] **Western Ocean:** The seas of Southeast Asia.

[7] **Liuchia River:** A river in the vicinity of Shanghai.

[8] **fifth year:** 1407.

[9] **Palembang:** Kingdom on the eastern coast of Sumatra.

[10] **sixth year:** 1408.

led two thousand soldiers to attack the city itself. The surprise worked, and Alagakkonara and his family, together with many high-ranking officials, were captured alive. The Ceylonese troops hurried back to rescue their king, only to be routed by the Chinese. In the sixth month of the ninth year[11] of Yung-lo the captured Ceylonese, including their king, were presented to the Chinese emperor for a determination of their fate. The emperor decided to forgive them and ordered them to be returned to Ceylon. By then all of Indochina had been pacified and brought under Chinese jurisdiction. Frightened by Chinese might, more and more kingdoms sent envoys to China to pay their tribute.

In the eleventh month of the tenth year[12] of Yung-lo the emperor again ordered Cheng Ho to proceed to Sumatra. Cheng Ho arrived at a time when Sekander, son of a former ruler of that kingdom, was plotting the overthrow of the reigning prince so as to establish himself as the king. Resenting Cheng Ho for having failed to give him any gold or silk, he ordered his men to attack Chinese troops. Cheng Ho responded vigorously, defeated his army, and pursued him until he, together with his family, was captured at Lambri. The Chinese envoy returned to Peking in the seventh month of the thirteenth year,[13] to be welcomed by a pleased emperor who rewarded all the officers and men for their efforts.

In the winter of the fourteenth year[14] of Yung-lo Malacca, Calicut, and seventeen other nations sent envoys to China to pay their tribute. The emperor ordered Cheng Ho to accompany them on their return trip after they had successfully completed their own mission in China. Having granted gifts, in the name of the emperor, to each of the kings who had sent tribute missions to China, Cheng Ho returned to Peking in the seventh month of the seventeenth year.[15]

In the spring of the nineteenth year[16] of Yung-lo Cheng Ho again visited the kingdoms that had sent tribute missions to China. He returned in the eighth month of the following year.

In the first month of the twenty-second year[17] of Yung-lo Shih Chi-sun, king of Palembang, requested the honor of being appointed a pacification commissioner. The emperor granted the request and ordered Cheng Ho to bring to him the appropriate seal to make the appointment official. The emperor died before Cheng Ho's return to China.

In the sixth month of the fifth year of Hsüan-teh the reigning emperor, Hsüan-teh,[18] was greatly annoyed that many of China's tributary states had so far failed to pay tribute to him. He, consequently, dispatched Cheng Ho and Wang Ching-hung

[11] **ninth year:** 1411.

[12] **tenth year:** 1412.

[13] **thirteenth year:** 1415.

[14] **fourteenth year:** 1416.

[15] **seventeenth year:** 1419.

[16] **nineteenth year:** 1421.

[17] **twenty-second year:** 1424.

[18] **Hsüan-teh:** Xuande (r. 1425–1435), the fourth Ming emperor; the year is 1430.

to these states for an inquiry. The Chinese envoys visited Hormus and sixteen other states before returning home.

Cheng Ho served three emperors with distinction and conducted seven voyages altogether. Among the more than thirty kingdoms he had visited were the following: Champa, Java, Camboja, Palembang, Siam, Calicut, Malacca, Borneo, Sumatra, Aru, Cochin, Quilon, Chola, Cail, Jurfattan, Koyampadi, Ceylon, Lambri, Pahang, Kelantan, Hormus, Brawa, Maldives, Sunda, Mogedoxu, Malinde, Sana, Zufar, Juba, Bengal, Mecca, Lide, and Battak. The amount of treasure he brought to China from these kingdoms was of course enormous, but the expense to China herself was even more staggering. Beginning in the Hsüan-teh period [1426–35] these kingdoms, occasionally, still sent tribute missions to China, but they could not be compared with the tribute missions of the Yung-lo period [1403–24] that were not only more sumptuous but also more frequent. By then Cheng Ho had become too old to undertake any strenuous task. Long after his death, however, his achievement was still so highly regarded that Chinese generals and admirals, whenever serving abroad, kept mentioning it as a way to impress foreigners. Even laymen spoke of the Seven Voyages of the Grand Eunuch as a most outstanding event of the Ming dynasty.

MIGUEL DE CERVANTES SAAVEDRA
1547–1616

One of the great works of world literature, characterized by the French literary critic Charles Sainte-Beuve as the "bible of humanity," ***Don Quixote*** (1605, 1615) has been translated into more languages than any other book except the Bible. The lean and angular protagonist Don Quixote and his rotund companion Sancho Panza have entered the visual iconography of our culture, and we use the adjective *QUIXOTIC* and the phrase *tilting at windmills* to describe impractical idealism of the sort exemplified by the knight of La Mancha. *Don Quixote* is usually considered the first Western novel. Its story of a wanderer encountering a series of adventures, its use of a hero and a contrasting foil, its challenge to romantic conventions and ideas, and its thematic conflict between illusion and reality have become commonplaces of later novels.

kee-HOH-tay

Don Quixote begins as a story that will reveal the absurdity of romantic idealism, but by the end it apparently reverses itself. For as foolish and mistaken as Don Quixote is, he nevertheless wins the love and allegiance of those he meets—and of the reader. The novel may begin with a Machiavellian intent, to make us more aware of the realities of the world, but by the end we are celebrating idealism and imagination, no matter how impractical they are. Thus *Don Quixote* tests the realism and individualism of its time by celebrating an impossible chivalric dream, an idealistic mythology of a golden age inherited from the past and kept alive in an age of iron by an absurd and improbable knight. This unlikely hero does not prove himself like Hernán Cortés by seeking new lands to

WWW For links to more information about Cervantes, a quiz on *Don Quixote,* and information about the twenty-first-century relevance of Cervantes, see *World Literature Online* at bedfordstmartins.com/worldlit.

***Don Quixote* poster**
The story of Don Quixote has captured readers' imaginations, through the centuries. Here, in an advertisement for a nineteenth-century play based on Cervantes's novel, the title character is shown with his faithful horse against the symbolic windmill. (The Art Archive / Victoria and Albert Museum London / Sally Chappell)

Cervantes smiled Spain's chivalry away.

– LORD BYRON, *Don Juan*, 1824

rule, nor does he revel like Dr. Faustus in playing tricks on those in power. True to his inner vision, Don Quixote represents the triumph of the ideal that challenges the worldliness and realism informing many of the texts of the period.

A Life of Adventure. The life of Miguel de Cervantes Saavedra reads like an improbable romance played out on the stage of Spain at the height of its GOLDEN AGE.[1] The fourth of seven children of a poor doctor, Cervantes spent his childhood fleeing with his family from his father's creditors. After a brief formal education in Córdoba and at a Jesuit school in Seville, he was convicted of dueling and fled to Italy to avoid his sentence. In Rome he served the Cardinal Nuncio Acquaviva for a time before enlisting in the Spanish army, then engaged in battling the Turks for control of the Mediterranean. At the Battle of Lepanto in 1571, Cervantes got up from his sick bed to fight heroically. He was decorated for his bravery, but battle wounds left him permanently disabled in his left hand. Nevertheless he went on to participate in campaigns at Tunis, Sardinia, Naples, Sicily, and Genoa before returning to Spain. On the return trip in 1575, his ship was captured by pirates and he and his brother Rodrigo were both sold into slavery in Algiers. During five years in slavery, Cervantes made five unsuccessful escape attempts; his daring so impressed the Dey of Algiers, Hassan Pacha, that his life was spared after each attempt. Finally, in 1580, he was ransomed and returned to Spain.

Penniless, disabled, and desperate, Cervantes turned to the stage to make money, but he was not a successful playwright, even after writing twenty or thirty plays. After he married Catalina Salaza y Vozmediano in 1584, to support his growing family he accepted a civil service job as a commissary collecting food for the Spanish navy. The post of provisioner for the Armada afforded opportunities for creative accounting, and Cervantes spent several stints in jail as a result of disputes with the Treasury Department, which claimed he had illegally appropriated wheat or money for himself.

During his time in jail, as legend has it, Cervantes wrote the first part of *Don Quixote,* which was published in 1605. With this novel he achieved the recognition he had failed to find writing for the theater. In the next decade *Don Quixote* went through ten editions, and it inspired an imitator (writing under the pen name Alonzo Fernandez de Avellaneda) to publish a sequel. This pseudo-Quixote was partly responsible for prompting Cervantes to write his own continuation of the story. *Don Quixote,* Part II, appeared in 1615, not long before he died, the same day as William Shakespeare, April 23, 1616. Besides *Don Quixote,* Cervantes's most notable

[1] **Spain . . . golden age:** The latter part of the sixteenth century and most of the seventeenth century is known as the golden age of Spanish literature, during the period when Spain was also a dominant European power. Besides Cervantes, the great authors of the period were poets Garcilaso de la Vega (c. 1501–1536), Juan Boscán Almogaver (c. 1490–1542), and Luis de Góngora y Argote (1561–1627); novelists Mateo Alemán (1547–c. 1614) and Francisco Gómez de Quevedo y Villegas (1580–1645); dramatists Tirso de Molina (c. 1580–1648), Lope de Vega (1562–1635), and Pedro Calderón de la Barca (1600–1681).

works are *Persiles and Sigismunda,* a romance published after his death in 1617, and *Exemplary Novels* (1613), a collection of twelve short romantic adventure tales that illustrate various kinds of behavior to avoid.

> It can be said that all prose fiction is a variation on the theme of *Don Quixote*. . . . The poverty of the Don suggests that the novel is born with the appearance of money, as a social element — money, the great solvent of the solid fabric of the old society, the great generator of illusion. Or, which is to say the same thing, the novel is born in response to snobbery.
>
> – Lionel Trilling, "Manners, Morals and the Novel," 1948

An Age of Transition. At the end of the sixteenth century, when *Don Quixote* was written, the traditional feudal system in Spain was disappearing and being replaced by a modern capitalist system. The small landowners, the *hidalgos,* the class to which Don Quixote belonged, were being forced into poverty and many were driven off the land and into the cities, where they gave up their precarious status as "gentlemen" to enter the mercantile BOURGEOISIE. Caught in this historic change, Don Quixote, at the beginning of the novel, sells some of his land so that he can remain a while longer in the country. He uses some of this money to buy books, CHIVALRIC ROMANCES, which allow him to escape the distressing economic realities of his situation. These popular stories—works like *Amadis of Gaul* (1508), *Launcelot* (early thirteenth century), and others based on them—featured romantic knights and ladies, perilous adventures, mysterious spells, heroic deeds, and miraculous escapes and were the pulp fiction of the day.

Don Quixote. Cervantes uses the conceit of Quixote's addiction to romances as a way to contrast medieval idealism with RENAISSANCE REALISM. The Don has read so many chivalric romances that he has decided to undertake his own knightly quest. In rusty armor and a makeshift helmet, he sets out to aid damsels in distress and to fight for the glory of his imaginary lady Dulcinea. He has been so imbued with the tales of adventure he has read that everything he sees is transformed in the romantic filter of his mind: Windmills become giants, a herd of sheep becomes an attacking army, country inns are castles. Don Quixote does not look like a hero. Tall and gaunt and leaning on his lance, he is physically unprepossessing. He is a comic imitation of a medieval knight, who, in spite of his armor, is not a Renaissance man of power. He is not a prince, nor is he a trickster or magician. When tricks are played in *Don Quixote,* they are usually played on the Don. He is the butt, not the perpetrator. The Duke and Duchess invite him to their castle, for example, so that they can contrive a series of practical jokes to play on him.

Unlike his Renaissance compatriots—whether politicians, scientists, or explorers—Quixote does not seek to master external reality. He is uncomfortable in his time and he does not relish the struggle for power and supremacy. His speech to Sancho in Book I, Chapter 11, describes the lost golden age that embodied the chivalric ideals he pursues. In that time, he tells Sancho, "Fraud, deceit, or malice had not yet mingled with truth and sincerity. Justice held her ground, undisturbed and unassailed by the efforts of favor and interest, that now so much impair, pervert, and beset her. Arbitrary law had not yet established itself in the mind of the judge, for then there was no cause to judge and no one to be judged." His mission as knight-errant is to attack the wickedness of his age of iron and remain true to his vision of a past golden age. The symbol of Quixote's idealism is Dulcinea, the lady for whom he undertakes his

Quixote's exploits are his last hurrah. He has one last chance to make the world as interesting as he dreams it to be.
– TERRY GILLIAM, director, 2003

knightly quest. Although she turns out to be a figment of his imagination or just a peasant girl, Dulcinea is nonetheless real as an ideal for him to believe in. Unlike the Renaissance sonneteers[2] who blamed their lovers for the pains of love, Quixote never blames Dulcinea for the frustrations of his quest. When he loses his vision and realizes that Dulcinea is an illusion, the knight has nothing to live for and he dies.

His squire, the peasant Sancho Panza, recognizes the common reality in Quixote's adventures, but he is unable to make his master see what he sees. So this unlikely duo—the gaunt and doleful idealist and his rotund and realistic squire—become an anomalous pair of chivalric adventurers in a world of con men, government agents, shrewd innkeepers, and cunning shopkeepers; their adventures degenerate into a series of misunderstandings, miscommunications, slapstick encounters, and practical jokes. On more than one occasion Don Quixote makes things worse by his chivalric interference. Yet through it all he retains his belief in himself, his mistress, and his mission.

Sancho Panza goes on the road for more down-to-earth reasons. As a realist—a person of common sense who knows that windmills are windmills—he has a large stock of folk sayings and proverbs that explain any situation, and he is savvy enough to survive a host of dangerous encounters. He accompanies Quixote to better himself. His dream is the Renaissance dream of power: he wants, like Prospero, to rule an island. Near the end of Part II, his dream comes true, if only as part of an elaborate practical joke. There are wonderful parodic echoes of Machiavelli's advice to the prince in Quixote's advice to Sancho as he goes off to govern Baratario. Sancho is a surprisingly successful governor, especially shrewd when faced with impossible judicial decisions. But just as surprisingly, he gives up his kingdom and returns to serve again as Don Quixote's squire. He learns the limitations of power and leaves his "island" to rejoin Quixote and his ideals.

In the end, Sancho's realism is transformed by the Don's idealism, and *Don Quixote* seems to have reversed its original intent. Instead of being a critique of chivalric idealism, it has become a celebration of Quixote's idealistic madness. Even the practical Sancho is won over to the impossible ideals of his master: he believes in the imaginary Dulcinea and is ready to start out on another journey. Don Quixote, no longer mad, is at last aware that Dulcinea was an illusion, a disillusionment that costs him his life. He and Sancho have changed places, and the final pages of the novel make us aware of the loss when such divine madness is gone from the world.

[2] **Renaissance sonneteers:** Two types of the Renaissance sonnet are commonly identified, the Italian and the English, or the Petrarchan, after the Italian poet Francesco Petrarch (1300–1374), who originated the form, and the Shakespearean, after its preeminent English practitioner. The major difference between the two forms is in the number of rhymes, usually five in the Italian and seven in the English. Both Italian and English sonneteers collected their poems into groups known as sonnet sequences.

■ CONNECTIONS

William Shakespeare, *The Tempest*, p. 495; Christopher Marlowe, *Doctor Faustus*, p. 389; Wu Chengen, *Monkey*, p. 837. In many works of literature the hero has a double who either complements or contrasts with him or her. In westerns, cowboy heroes have their "sidekicks," and in mystery stories Sherlock Holmes almost inevitably has his Dr. Watson. Although Sancho's realism, practicality, and earthiness contrast with Quixote's idealism, impracticality, and spaciness, the two can also be seen as two dimensions in every human being, so that their reversal in the course of the novel describes a change that experience can effect for anyone. Consider the following as doubles: Prospero and Caliban, Faust and Mephistopheles, Tripitaka and Monkey. What does each character represent? Can the two characters in each pair be seen as "halves" of a single personality? Does the conflict between realism and idealism explain their differences?

Niccolò Machiavelli, *The Prince*, p. 124; "The Ancient Mexicans," p. 708. Europeans during the Renaissance were obsessed with power, conquest, and discovery. Sancho Panza's desire to rule an island and his chance to do so – at least virtually – is one of Cervantes's ways of commenting on this impulse of his time. Sancho is not so rebellious in his desire for power as Caliban, nor so ruthless and single-minded as Hernán Cortés. And even though he gets his wish, he, like Prospero, gives up his rulership to return to serving the Don. Consider these various aspirants and rulers in the light of Machiavelli's advice in *The Prince:* Can Don Quixote's counsels to Sancho be considered Machiavellian? How would Machiavelli view Prospero and Cortés?

■ FURTHER RESEARCH

Biography

Byron, William. *Cervantes: A Biography.* 1978.

Commentary

Canavaggio, Jean. *Cervantes.* 1990.
Close, A. J. *Don Quixote.* 1990.
Gilman, Stephen. *The Novel According to Cervantes.* 1989.
Mancing, Howard. *The Chivalric World of Don Quijote: Style, Structure, and Narrative Technique.* 1982.
Nelson, Lowry, ed. *Cervantes: A Collection of Critical Essays.* 1969.
Riley, E. C. *Don Quixote.* 1986.

■ PRONUNCIATION

Carrasco: kah-RAHS-koh
Cascajo: kahs-KAH-hoh
Durandarte: doo-rahn-DAR-tay
Orbaneja: ore-bah-NAY-hah
Quixote: kee-HOH-tay
Rocinante: roh-thee-NAHN-tay, roh-zee-NAN-tee
Siguenza: see-GWEN-sah
Tirteafuera: teer-tay-ah-FWEH-rah

Don Quixote

Translated by John Ormsby

Part I

Chapter 1

WHICH TREATS OF THE CHARACTER AND PURSUITS OF THE FAMOUS GENTLEMAN DON QUIXOTE OF LA MANCHA

In a village of La Mancha, the name of which I have no desire to call to mind, there lived not long since one of those gentlemen that keep a lance in the lance-rack, an old buckler, a lean hack, and a greyhound for coursing. An olla of rather more beef than mutton, a salad on most nights, scraps on Saturdays, lentils on Fridays, and a pigeon or so extra on Sundays, made away with three-quarters of his income. The rest of it went in a doublet of fine cloth and velvet breeches and shoes to match for holidays, while on week-days he made a brave figure in his best homespun. He had in his house a housekeeper past forty, a niece under twenty, and a lad for the field and market-place, who used to saddle the hack as well as handle the bill-hook. The age of this gentleman of ours was bordering on fifty, he was of a hardy habit, spare, gaunt-featured, a very early riser and a great sportsman. They will have it his surname was Quixada or Quesada (for here there is some difference of opinion among the authors who write on the subject), although from reasonable conjectures it seems plain that he was called Quixana. This, however, is of but little importance to our tale; it will be enough not to stray a hair's breadth from the truth in the telling of it.

You must know, then, that the above-named gentleman whenever he was at leisure (which was mostly all the year round) gave himself up to reading books of chivalry with such ardor and avidity that he almost entirely neglected the pursuit of his field-sports, and even the management of his property; and to such a pitch did his eagerness and infatuation go that he sold many an acre of tillage-land to buy books of chivalry to read, and brought home as many of them as he could get. But of all there were none he liked so well as those of the famous

---

Don Quixote. *Don Quixote* is a big book; its 124 chapters add up to nearly a thousand pages. Even a substantial selection from so large a novel can only serve as a teasing introduction to the wonderful riches of the story. The selections presented here from John Ormsby's translation comprise only about ten percent of the novel. They trace the relationship between Quixote and Sancho and follow the motif of Sancho's desire to become governor of an island. In doing so, they make the novel seem simpler and more thematically focused than it actually is. In the original, the particular strand of the novel that is presented here is woven into a complex fabric of stories tracing the progress of Don Quixote's madness, his search for the ideal, his adventures throughout Spain, and the stories of many other characters he encounters on the road. Interspersed amid these stories are ongoing discussions of literature, imagination, ideals, history, and many other topics. The selection in this book can follow only a few of the threads in Cervantes's rich literary tapestry.

Feliciano de Silva's[1] composition, for their lucidity of style and complicated conceits were as pearls in his sight, particularly when in his reading he came upon courtships and cartels, where he often found passages like *"the reason of the unreason with which my reason is afflicted so weakens my reason that with reason I murmur at your beauty"*; or again, *"the high heavens, that of your divinity divinely fortify you with the stars, render you deserving of the desert your greatness deserves."* Over conceits of this sort the poor gentleman lost his wits, and used to lie awake striving to understand them and worm the meaning out of them; what Aristotle himself could not have made out or extracted had he come to life again for that special purpose. He was not at all easy about the wounds which Don Belianis[2] gave and took, because it seemed to him that, great as were the surgeons who had cured him, he must have had his face and body covered all over with seams and scars. He commended, however, the author's way of ending his book with the promise of that interminable adventure, and many a time was he tempted to take up his pen and finish it properly as is there proposed, which no doubt he would have done, and made a successful piece of work of it too, had not greater and more absorbing thoughts prevented him.

Many an argument did he have with the curate of his village (a learned man, and a graduate of Siguenza[3]) as to which had been the better knight, Palmerin of England or Amadis of Gaul.[4] Master Nicholas, the village barber, however, used to say that neither of them came up to the Knight of Phœbus, and that if there was any that could compare with *him* it was Don Galaor, the brother of Amadis of Gaul, because he had a spirit that was equal to every occasion, and was no finikin knight, nor lachrymose like his brother, while in the matter of valor he was not a whit behind him. In short, he became so absorbed in his books that he spent his nights from sunset to sunrise, and his days from dawn to dark, poring over them; and what with little sleep and much reading his brains got so dry that he lost his wits. His fancy grew full of what he used to read about in his books, enchantments, quarrels, battles, challenges, wounds, wooings, loves, agonies, and all sorts of impossible nonsense; and it so possessed his mind that the whole fabric of invention and fancy he read of was true, that to him no history in the world had more reality in it. He used to say the Cid Ruy Diaz was a very good knight, but that he was not to be compared with the Knight of the Burning Sword who with one back-stroke cut in half two fierce and monstrous giants. He thought more of Bernardo del Carpio because at Roncesvalles he slew Roland in spite of enchantments, availing himself of the artifice of Hercules when he strangled Antæus the son of Terra in his arms. He approved highly of the giant Morgante, because, although of the giant breed which is always arrogant and ill-conditioned, he alone was affable and well-bred. But above all he

[1] **Feliciano de Silva:** A writer of romances, best known for the chronicle of *Don Florisel de Niquea* (1532) and *Amadis of Gaul* (1535). The quotation is from *Don Florisel.*

[2] **Don Belianis:** A character in a romance by Jerónimo Fernández.

[3] **Siguenza:** A minor university often mocked by the Spanish humorists.

[4] **Palmerin . . . Amadis:** The heroes of two famous romances, as are the Knight of Phœbus, Don Galaor, Cid Ruy Diaz, the Knight of the Burning Sword, Bernardo del Carpio, Morgante, and Reinaldos of Montalbán.

admired Reinaldos of Montalban, especially when he saw him sallying forth from his castle and robbing every one he met, and when beyond the seas he stole that image of Mahomet which, as his history says, was entirely of gold. And to have a bout of kicking at that traitor of a Ganelon[5] he would have given his housekeeper, and his niece into the bargain.

In short, his wits being quite gone, he hit upon the strangest notion that every madman in this world hit upon, and that was that he fancied it was right and requisite, as well for the support of his own honor as for the service of his country, that he should make a knight-errant of himself, roaming the world over in full armor and on horseback in quest of adventures, and putting in practice himself all that he had read of as being the usual practices of knights-errant; righting every kind of wrong, and exposing himself to peril and danger from which, in the issue, he was to reap eternal renown and fame. Already the poor man saw himself crowned by the might of his arm Emperor of Trebizond at least; and so, led away by the intense enjoyment he found in these pleasant fancies, he set himself forthwith to put his scheme into execution.

The first thing he did was to clean up some armor that had belonged to his great-grandfather, and had been for ages lying forgotten in a corner eaten with rust and covered with mildew. He scoured and polished it as best he could, but he perceived one great defect in it, that it had no closed helmet, nothing but a simple morion.[6] This deficiency, however, his ingenuity supplied, for he contrived a kind of half-helmet of pasteboard which, fitted on to the morion, looked like a whole one. It is true that, in order to see if it was strong and fit to stand a cut, he drew his sword and gave it a couple of slashes, the first of which undid in an instant what had taken him a week to do. The ease with which he had knocked it to pieces disconcerted him somewhat, and to guard against that danger he set to work again, fixing bars of iron on the inside until he was satisfied with its strength; and then, not caring to try any more experiments with it, he passed it and adopted it as a helmet of the most perfect construction.

He next proceeded to inspect his hack, which, with more quartos than a real[7] and more blemishes than the steed of Gonela, that *tantum pellis et ossa fuit,*[8] surpassed in his eyes the Bucephalus of Alexander or the Babieca of the Cid.[9] Four days were spent in thinking what name to give him, because (as he said to himself) it was not right that a horse belonging to a knight so famous, and one with such merits of his own, should be without some distinctive name, and he strove to adapt it so as to indicate what he had been before belonging to a knight-errant, and what he then

---

[5] **Ganelon:** The knight who betrayed Roland.

[6] **morion:** A helmet, like those worn by the Spanish conquistadores, that covered only the top of the head. The gentleman wants one that also covers his face, like those worn by medieval knights.

[7] **real:** A coin worth about five cents. There were eight quartos in a real.

[8] ***tantum . . . fuit:*** "Was all skin and bones." Pedro Gonela, the clown of the Duke of Ferrara in the fifteenth century, had a horse that was the butt of many jokes.

[9] **Babieca of the Cid:** The horse of Ruy Diaz, hero of *The Cid,* a twelfth-century Spanish epic.

was; for it was only reasonable that, his master taking a new character, he should take a new name, and that it should be a distinguished and full-sounding one, befitting the new order and calling he was about to follow. And so, after having composed, struck out, rejected, added to, unmade, and remade a multitude of names out of his memory and fancy, he decided upon calling him Rocinante, a name, to his thinking, lofty, sonorous, and significant of his condition as a hack before he became what he now was, the first and foremost of all the hacks in the world.

Having got a name for his horse so much to his taste, he was anxious to get one for himself, and he was eight days more pondering over this point, till at last he made up his mind to call himself Don Quixote, whence, as has been already said, the authors of this veracious history have inferred that his name must have been beyond a doubt Quixada, and not Quesada as others would have it. Recollecting, however, that the valiant Amadis was not content to call himself curtly Amadis and nothing more, but added the name of his kingdom and country to make it famous, and called himself Amadis of Gaul, he, like a good knight, resolved to add on the name of his, and to style himself Don Quixote of La Mancha, whereby, he considered, he described accurately his origin and country, and did honor to it in taking his surname from it.

So then, his armor being furbished, his morion turned into a helmet, his hack christened, and he himself confirmed, he came to the conclusion that nothing more was needed now but a look out for a lady to be in love with; for a knight-errant without love was like a tree without leaves or fruit, or a body without a soul. As he said to himself, "If, for my sins, or by my good fortune, I come across some giant hereabouts, a common occurrence with knights-errant, and overthrow him in one onslaught, or cleave him asunder to the waist, or, in short, vanquish and subdue him, will it not be well to have some one I may send him to as a present, that he may come in and fall on his knees before my sweet lady, and in a humble, submissive voice say, 'I am the giant Caraculiambro, lord of the island of Malindrania, vanquished in single combat by the never sufficiently extolled knight Don Quixote of La Mancha, who has commanded me to present myself before your Grace, that your Highness dispose of me at your pleasure?'" Oh, how our good gentleman enjoyed the delivery of this speech, especially when he had thought of some one to call his Lady! There was, so the story goes, in a village near his own a very good-looking farm girl with whom he had been at one time in love, though, so far as is known, she never knew it nor gave a thought to the matter. Her name was Aldonza Lorenzo, and upon her he thought fit to confer the title of Lady of his Thoughts; and after some search for a name which should not be out of harmony with her own, and should suggest and indicate that of a princess and great lady, he decided upon calling her Dulcinea del Toboso—she being of El Toboso—a name, to his mind, musical, uncommon, and significant, like all those he had already bestowed upon himself and the things belonging to him.

Chapter 2

WHICH TREATS OF THE FIRST SALLY THE INGENIOUS DON QUIXOTE MADE FROM HOME

These preliminaries settled, he did not care to put off any longer the execution of his design, urged on to it by the thought of all the world was losing by his delay, seeing what wrongs he intended to right, grievances to redress, injustices to repair, abuses to remove, and duties to discharge. So, without giving notice of his intention to any one, and without anybody seeing him, one morning before the dawning of the day (which was one of the hottest of the month of July) he donned his suit of armor, mounted Rocinante with his patched-up helmet on, braced his buckler, took his lance, and by the back door of the yard sallied forth upon the plain in the highest contentment and satisfaction at seeing with what ease he had made a beginning with his grand purpose. But scarcely did he find himself upon the open plain, when a terrible thought struck him, one all but enough to make him abandon the enterprise at the very outset. It occurred to him that he had not been dubbed a knight, and that according to the law of chivalry he neither could nor ought to bear arms against any knight; and that even if he had been, still he ought, as a novice knight, to wear white armor, without a device upon the shield until by his prowess he had earned one. These reflections made him waver in his purpose, but his craze being stronger than any reasoning he made up his mind to have himself dubbed a knight by the first one he came across, following the example of others in the same case, as he had read in the books that brought him to this pass. As for white armor, he resolved, on the first opportunity, to scour his until it was whiter than an ermine; and so comforting himself he pursued his way, taking that which his horse chose, for in this he believed lay the essence of adventures.

Thus setting out, our new-fledged adventurer paced along, talking to himself and saying, "Who knows but that in time to come, when the veracious history of my famous deeds is made known, the sage who writes it, when he has to set forth my first sally in the early morning, will do it after this fashion? 'Scarce had the rubicund Apollo spread o'er the face of the broad spacious earth the golden threads of his bright hair, scarce had the little birds of painted plumage attuned their notes to hail with dulcet and mellifluous harmony the coming of the rosy Dawn, that, deserting the soft couch of her jealous spouse, was appearing to mortals at the gates and balconies of the Manchegan horizon, when the renowned knight Don Quixote of La Mancha, quitting the lazy down, mounted his celebrated steed Rocinante and began to traverse the ancient and famous Campo de Montiel' ";[10] which in fact he was actually traversing. "Happy the age, happy the time," he continued, "in which shall be made known my deeds of fame, worthy to be moulded in brass, carved in marble, limned in pictures, for a memorial forever. And thou, O sage magician, whoever thou art, to whom it shall fall to be the chronicler of this wondrous history, forget not, I entreat thee, my good Rocinante, the constant companion of my ways and wanderings." Presently he broke out again, as if he were love-stricken in earnest, "O

---

[10] **Campo de Montiel:** Site of a famous battle in 1369.

Princess Dulcinea, lady of this captive heart, a grievous wrong hast thou done me to drive me forth with scorn, and with inexorable obduracy banish me from the presence of thy beauty. O lady, deign to hold in remembrance this heart, thy vassal, that thus in anguish pines for love of thee."

So he went on stringing together these and other absurdities, all in the style of those his books had taught him, imitating their language as well as he could; and all the while he rode so slowly and the sun mounted so rapidly and with such fervor that it was enough to melt his brains if he had any. Nearly all day he travelled without anything remarkable happening to him, at which he was in despair, for he was anxious to encounter some one at once upon whom to try the might of his strong arm.

Writers there are who say the first adventure he met with was that of Puerto Lápice; others say it was that of the windmills; but what I have ascertained on this point, and what I have found written in the annals of La Mancha, is that he was on the road all day, and towards nightfall his hack and he found themselves dead tired and hungry, when, looking all around to see if he could discover any castle or shepherd's shanty where he might refresh himself and relieve his sore wants, he perceived not far out of his road an inn, which was welcome as a star guiding him to the portals if not the palaces, of his redemption; and quickening his pace he reached it just as night was setting in. At the door were standing two young women, girls of the district as they call them, on their way to Seville with some carriers who had chanced to halt that night at the inn; and as, happen what might to our adventurer, everything he saw or imagined seemed to him to be and to happen after the fashion of what he had read of, the moment he saw the inn he pictured it to himself as a castle with its four turrets and pinnacles of shining silver, not forgetting the drawbridge and moat and all the belongings usually ascribed to castles of the sort. To this inn, which to him seemed a castle, he advanced, and at a short distance from it he checked Rocinante, hoping that some dwarf would show himself upon the battlements, and by sound of trumpet give notice that a knight was approaching the castle. But seeing that they were slow about it, and that Rocinante was in a hurry to reach the stable, he made for the inn door, and perceived the two gay damsels who were standing there, and who seemed to him to be two fair maidens or lovely ladies taking their ease at the castle gate.

At this moment it so happened that a swineherd who was going through the stubbles collecting a drove of pigs (for, without any apology, that is what they are called) gave a blast of his horn to bring them together, and forthwith it seemed to Don Quixote to be what he was expecting, the signal of some dwarf announcing his arrival; and so with prodigious satisfaction he rode up to the inn and to the ladies, who, seeing a man of this sort approaching in full armor and with lance and buckler, were turning in dismay into the inn, when Don Quixote, guessing their fear by their flight, raising his pasteboard visor, disclosed his dry, dusty visage, and with courteous bearing and gentle voice addressed them, "Your ladyships need not fly or fear any rudeness, for that it belongs not to the order of knighthood which I profess to offer to any one, much less to high-born maidens as your appearance proclaims you to be." The girls were looking at him and straining their eyes to make out the features which the clumsy visor obscured, but when they heard themselves called maidens, a thing so much out of their line, they could not restrain their laughter, which made Don Quixote wax indignant, and say, "Modesty becomes the fair, and moreover laughter that has little cause is great silliness; this, however, I say not to pain or anger you, for my desire is none other than to serve you."

The incomprehensible language and the unpromising looks of our cavalier only increased the ladies' laughter, and that increased his irritation, and matters might have gone farther if at that moment the landlord had not come out, who, being a very fat man, was a very peaceful one. He, seeing this grotesque figure clad in armor that did not match any more than his saddle, bridle, lance, buckler, or corselet, was not at all indisposed to joint the damsels in their manifestations of amusement; but, in truth, standing in awe of such a complicated armament, he thought it best to speak him fairly, so he said, "Señor Caballero, if your worship wants lodging, bating the bed (for there is not one in the inn) there is plenty of everything else here." Don Quixote, observing the respectful bearing of the Alcaide of the fortress (for so innkeeper and inn seemed in his eyes), made answer, "Sir Castellan, for me anything will suffice, for

My armor is my only wear,
My only rest the fray."

The host fancied he called him Castellan[11] because he took him for a "worthy of Castile," though he was in fact an Andalusian, and one from the Strand of San Lucar, as crafty a thief as Casus[12] and as full of tricks as a student or a page. "In that case," said he,

"Your bed is on the flinty rock,
Your sleep to watch alway;

and if so, you may dismount and safely reckon upon any quantity of sleeplessness under this roof for a twelvemonth, not to say for a single night." So saying, he advanced to hold the stirrup for Don Quixote, who got down with great difficulty and exertion (for he had not broken his fast all day), and then charged the host to take great care of his horse as he was the best bit of flesh that ever ate bread in this world. The landlord eyed him over, but did not find him as good as Don Quixote said, nor even half as good, and putting him up in the stable, he returned to see what might be wanted by his guest, whom the damsels, who had by this time made their peace with him, were now relieving of his armor. They had taken off his breastplate and backpiece, but they neither knew nor saw how to open his gorget or remove his make-shift helmet, for he had fastened it with green ribbons, which, as there was no untying the knots, required to be cut. This, however, he would not by any means consent to, so he remained all the evening with his helmet on, the drollest and oddest figure that can be imagined; and while they were removing his armor, taking the

[11] **Alcaide . . . Castellan:** *Alcaide* and *castellano* both mean governor of a castle or fortress, but the latter also means "a Castilian."

[12] **Casus:** The son of Vulcan who robbed the Italians of their cattle; hence, a thief.

baggages who were about it for ladies of high degree belonging to the castle, he said to them with great sprightliness:

> "Oh, never, surely, was there knight
> So served by hand of dame,
> As served was he, Don Quixote hight,
> When from his town he came;
> With maidens waiting on himself,
> Princesses on his hack—

—or Rocinante, for that, ladies mine, is my horse's name, and Don Quixote of La Mancha is my own; for though I had no intention of declaring myself until my achievements in your service and honor had made me known, the necessity of adapting that old ballad of Lancelot to the present occasion has given you the knowledge of my name altogether prematurely. A time, however, will come for your ladyships to command and me to obey, and then the might of my arm will show my desire to serve you."

The girls, who were not used to hearing rhetoric of this sort, had nothing to say in reply: they only asked him if he wanted anything to eat. "I would gladly eat a bit of something," said Don Quixote, "for I feel it would come very seasonably." The day happened to be a Friday, and in the whole inn there was nothing but some pieces of the fish they call in Castile *abadejo,* in Andalusia *bacallao,* and in some places *curadillo,* and in others *troutlet;* so they asked him if he thought he could eat troutlet, for there was no other fish to give him. "If there be troutlets enough," said Don Quixote, "they will be the same thing as a trout; for it is all one to me whether I am given eight reals in small change or a piece of eight; moreover, it may be that these troutlets are like veal, which is better than beef, or kid, which is better than goat. But whatever it be let it come quickly, for the burden and pressure of arms cannot be borne without support to the inside." They laid a table for him at the door of the inn for the sake of the air, and the host brought him a portion of ill-soaked and worse cooked stockfish, and a piece of bread as black and mouldy as his own armor; but a laughable sight it was to see him eating, for having his helmet on and the beaver up, he could not with his own hands put anything into his mouth unless some one else placed it there, and this service one of the ladies rendered him. But to give him anything to drink was impossible, or would have been so had not the landlord bored a reed, and putting one end in his mouth poured the wine into him through the other; all which he bore with patience rather than sever the ribbons of his helmet.

While this was going on there came up to the inn a pig-gelder, who, as he approached, sounded his reed pipe four or five times, and thereby completely convinced Don Quixote that he was in some famous castle, and that they were regaling him with music, and that the stockfish was trout, the bread the whitest, the wenches ladies, and the landlord the castellan of the castle; and consequently he held that his enterprise and sally had been to some purpose. But still it distressed him to think he had not been dubbed a knight, for it was plain to him he could not lawfully engage in any adventure without receiving the order of knighthood.

. . .

FROM

Chapter 7

OF THE SECOND SALLY OF OUR WORTHY KNIGHT DON QUIXOTE OF LA MANCHA

. . . Meanwhile Don Quixote worked upon a farm laborer, a neighbor of his, an honest man (if indeed that title can be given to him who is poor), but with very little wit in his pate. In a word, he so talked him over, and with such persuasions and promises, that the poor clown made up his mind to sally forth with him and serve him as esquire. Don Quixote, among other things, told him he ought to be ready to go with him gladly, because any moment an adventure might occur that might win an island in the twinkling of an eye and leave him governor of it. On these and the like promises Sancho Panza (for so the laborer was called) left wife and children, and engaged himself as esquire to his neighbor. Don Quixote next set about getting some money; and selling one thing and pawning another, and making a bad bargain in every case, he got together a fair sum. He provided himself with a buckler, which he begged as a loan from a friend, and, restoring his battered helmet as best he could, he warned his squire Sancho of the day and hour he meant to set out, that he might provide himself with what he thought most needful. Above all, he charged him to take *alforjas*[13] with him. The other said he would, and that he meant to take also a very good ass he had, as he was not much given to going on foot. About the ass, Don Quixote hesitated a little, trying whether he could call to mind any knight-errant taking with him an esquire mounted on ass-back, but no instance occurred to his memory. For all that, however, he determined to take him, intending to furnish him with a more honorable mount when a chance of it presented itself, by appropriating the horse of the first discourteous knight he encountered. Himself he provided with shirts and such other things as he could, according to the advice the host had given him; all which being settled and done, without taking leave, Sancho Panza of his wife and children, or Don Quixote of his housekeeper and niece, they sallied forth unseen by anybody from the village one night, and made such good way in the course of it that by daylight they held themselves safe from discovery, even should search be made for them.

Sancho rode on his ass like a patriarch with his *alforjas* and *bota,*[14] and longing to see himself soon governor of the island his master had promised him. Don Quixote decided upon taking the same route and road he had taken on his first journey, that over the Campo de Montiel, which he travelled with less discomfort than on the last occasion, for, as it was early morning and the rays of the sun fell on them obliquely, the heat did not distress them.

And now said Sancho Panza to his master, "Your worship will take care, Señor Knight-errant, not to forget about the island you have promised me, for be it ever so big I'll be equal to governing it."

To which Don Quixote replied, "Thou must know, friend Sancho Panza, that it

[13] ***alforjas:*** Saddlebags that were often carried slung across the shoulder.

[14] ***bota:*** A leather wine-bag.

was a practice very much in vogue with the knights-errant of old to make their squires governors of the islands or kingdoms they won, and I am determined that there shall be no failure on my part in so liberal a custom; on the contrary, I mean to improve upon it, for they sometimes, and perhaps most frequently, waited until their squires were old, and then when they had had enough of service and hard days and worse nights, they gave them some title or other, of count, or at the most marquis, of some valley or province more or less; but if thou livest and I live, it may well be that before six days are over, I may have won some kingdom that has others dependent upon it, which will be just the thing to enable thee to be crowned king of one of them. Nor needst thou count this wonderful, for things and chances fall to the lot of such knights in ways so unexampled and unexpected that I might easily give thee even more than I promise thee."

"In that case," said Sancho Panza, "if I should become a king by one of those miracles your worship speaks of, even Juana Gutierrez, my old woman, would come to be queen and my children infantas."

"Well, who doubts it?" said Don Quixote.

"I doubt it," replied Sancho Panza, "because for my part I am persuaded that though God should shower down kingdoms upon earth, not one of them would fit the head of Mari Gutierrez.[15] Let me tell you, señor, she is not worth two maravedís for a queen; countess will fit her better, and that only with God's help."

"Leave it to God, Sancho," returned Don Quixote, "for he will give her what suits her best; but do not undervalue thyself so much as to come to be content with anything less than being governor of a province."

"I will not, señor," answered Sancho, "especially as I have a man of such quality for a master in your worship, who will be able to give me all that will be suitable for me and that I can bear."

FROM
Chapter 8

OF THE GOOD FORTUNE WHICH THE VALIANT DON QUIXOTE HAD IN THE TERRIBLE AND UNDREAMT-OF ADVENTURE OF THE WINDMILLS, WITH OTHER OCCURRENCES WORTHY TO BE FITLY RECORDED

At this point they came in sight of thirty or forty windmills that there are on that plain, and as soon as Don Quixote saw them he said to his squire, "Fortune is arranging matters for us better than we could have shaped our desires ourselves, for look there, friend Sancho Panza, where thirty or more monstrous giants present themselves, all of whom I mean to engage in battle and slay, and with whose spoils we shall begin to make our fortunes; for this is righteous warfare, and it is God's good service to sweep so evil a breed from off the face of the earth."

"What giants?" said Sancho Panza.

[15] **"Mari Gutierrez":** Gutierrez is the maiden name of Juana (or Mari) Panza. In Part II, Cervantes (apparently forgetting how he named her in Part I) gives her the maiden name of Teresa Cascajo.

"Those thou seest there," answered his master, "with the long arms, and some have them nearly two leagues long."

"Look, your worship," said Sancho "what we see there are not giants but windmills, and what seem to be their arms are the sails that turned by the wind make the millstone go."

"It is easy to see," replied Don Quixote, "that thou are not used to this business of adventures; those are giants; and if thou art afraid, away with thee out of this and betake thyself to prayer while I engage them in fierce and unequal combat."

So saying, he gave the spur to his steed Rocinante, heedless of the cries his squire Sancho sent after him, warning him that most certainly they were windmills and not giants he was going to attack. He, however, was so positive they were giants that he neither heard the cries of Sancho, nor perceived, near as he was, what they were, but made at them shouting, "Fly not, cowards and vile beings, for it is a single knight that attacks you."

A slight breeze at this moment sprang up, and the great sails began to move, seeing which Don Quixote exclaimed, "Though ye flourish more arms than the giant Briareus,[16] ye have to reckon with me."

So saying, and commending himself with all his heart to his lady Dulcinea, imploring her to support him in such a peril, with lance in rest and covered by his buckler, he charged at Rocinante's fullest gallop and fell upon the first mill that stood in front of him; but as he drove his lance-point into the sail the wind whirled it round with such force that it shivered the lance to pieces, sweeping with it horse and rider, who went rolling over on the plain, in a sorry condition. Sancho hastened to his assistance as fast as his ass could go, and when he came up found him unable to move, with such a shock had Rocinante fallen on him.

"God bless me!" said Sancho, "did I not tell your worship to mind what you were about, for they were only windmills? And no one could have made any mistake about it but one who had something of the same kind in his head."

"Hush, friend Sancho," replied Don Quixote, "the fortunes of war more than any other are liable to frequent fluctuations; and moreover I think, and it is the truth, that that same sage Friston who carried off my study and books, has turned these giants into mills in order to rob me of the glory of vanquishing them, such is the enmity he bears me; but in the end his wicked arts will avail but little against my good sword."

"God order it as he may," said Sancho Panza, and helping him to rise got him up again on Rocinante, whose shoulder was half out; and then, discussing the late adventure, they followed the road to Puerto Lápice, for there, said Don Quixote, they could not fail to find adventures in abundance and variety, as it was a great thoroughfare. For all that, he was much grieved at the loss of his lance, and saying so to his squire, he added, "I remember having read how a Spanish knight, Diego Perez de Vargas by name, having broken his sword in battle, tore from an oak a ponderous bough or branch, and with it did such things that day, and pounded so many Moors,

[16] **"Briareus":** In Greek mythology, a giant with a hundred arms.

that he got the surname of Machuca, and he and his descendants from that day forth were called Vargas y Machuca.[17] I mention this because from the first oak I see I mean to rend such another branch, large and stout like that, with which I am determined and resolved to do such deeds that thou mayest deem thyself very fortunate in being found worthy to come and see them, and be an eye-witness of things that will with difficulty be believed."

"Be that as God will," said Sancho, "I believe it all as your worship says it; but straighten yourself a little, for you seem all on one side, maybe from the shaking of the fall."

"That is the truth," said Don Quixote, "and if I make no complaint of the pain it is because knights-errant are not permitted to complain of any wound, even though their bowels be coming out through it."

"If so," said Sancho, "I have nothing to say; but God knows I would rather your worship complained when anything ailed you. For my part, I confess I must complain however small the ache may be; unless indeed this rule about not complaining extends to the squires of knights-errant also."

Don Quixote could not help laughing at his squire's simplicity, and he assured him he might complain whenever and however he chose, just as he liked, for, so far, he had never read of anything to the contrary in the order of knighthood.

Sancho bade him remember it was dinnertime, to which his master answered that he wanted nothing himself just then, but that he might eat when he had a mind. With this permission Sancho settled himself as comfortably as he could on his beast, and taking out of the *alforjas* what he had stowed away in them, he jogged along behind his master munching deliberately, and from time to time taking a pull at the *bota* with a relish that the thirstiest tapster in Malaga might have envied; and while he went on in this way, gulping down draught after draught, he never gave a thought to any of the promises his master had made him, nor did he rate it as hardship but rather as recreation going in quest of adventures, however dangerous they might be. Finally they passed the night among some trees, from one of which Don Quixote plucked a dry branch to serve him after a fashion as a lance, and fixed on it the head he had removed from the broken one. All that night Don Quixote lay awake thinking of his lady Dulcinea, in order to conform to what he had read in his books, how many a night in the forests and deserts knights used to lie sleepless supported by the memory of their mistresses. Not so did Sancho Panza spend it, for having his stomach full of something stronger than chiccory water he made but one sleep of it, and, if his master had not called him, neither the rays of the sun beating on his face nor all the cheery notes of the birds welcoming the approach of day would have had power to waken him. On getting up he tried the *bota* and found it somewhat less full than the night before, which grieved his heart because they did not seem to be on the way to remedy the deficiency readily. Don Quixote did not care to break his fast, for, as has been already said, he confined himself to savory recollections for nourishment.

[17] **"Machuca":** "The Crusher," the hero of a popular ballad.

They returned to the road they had set out with, leading to Puerto Lápice, and at three in the afternoon they came in sight of it. "Here, brother Sancho Panza," said Don Quixote when he saw it, "we may plunge our hands up to the elbows in what they call adventures; but observe, even shouldst thou see me in the greatest danger in the world, thou must not put a hand to thy sword in my defence, unless, indeed, thou perceivest that those who assail me are rabble or base folk; for in that case thou mayest very properly aid me; but if they be knights it is on no account permitted or allowed thee by the laws of knighthood to help me until thou has been dubbed a knight."

"Most certainly, señor," replied Sancho, "your worship shall be fully obeyed in this matter; all the more as of myself I am peaceful and no friend to mixing in strife and quarrels: it is true that as regards the defence of my own person I shall not give much heed to those laws, for laws human and divine allow each one to defend himself against any assailant whatever."

"That I grant," said Don Quixote, "but in this matter of aiding me against knights thou must put a restraint upon thy natural impetuosity."

"I will do so, I promise you," answered Sancho, "and I will keep this precept as carefully as Sunday."

While they were thus talking there appeared on the road two friars of the order of St. Benedict, mounted on two dromedaries, for not less tall were the two mules they rode on. They wore travelling spectacles and carried sunshades; and behind them came a coach attended by four or five persons on horseback and two muleteers on foot. In the coach there was, as afterwards appeared, a Biscay lady on her way to Seville, where her husband was about to take passage for the Indies with an appointment of high honor. The friars, though going the same road, were not in her company; but the moment Don Quixote perceived them he said to his squire, "Either I am mistaken, or this is going to be the most famous adventure that has ever been seen, for those black bodies we see there must be, and doubtless are, magicians who are carrying off some stolen princess in that coach, and with all my might I must undo this wrong."

"This will be worse than the windmills," said Sancho. "Look, señor; those are friars of St. Benedict, and the coach plainly belongs to some travellers: mind, I tell you to mind well what you are about and don't let the devil mislead you."

"I have told thee already, Sancho," replied Don Quixote, "that on the subject of adventures thou knowest little. What I say is the truth, as thou shalt see presently."

So saying, he advanced and posted himself in the middle of the road along which the friars were coming, and as soon as he thought they had come near enough to hear what he said, he cried aloud, "Devilish and unnatural beings, release instantly the high-born princesses whom you are carrying off by force in this coach, else prepare to meet a speedy death as the just punishment of your evil deeds."

The friars drew rein and stood wondering at the appearance of Don Quixote as well as at his words, to which they replied, "Señor Caballero, we are not devilish or unnatural, but two brothers of St. Benedict following our road, nor do we know whether or not there are any captive princesses coming in this coach."

"No soft words with me, for I know you, lying rabble," said Don Quixote, and without waiting for a reply he spurred Rocinante and with levelled lance charged the first friar with such fury and determination that, if the friar had not flung himself off the mule, he would have brought him to the ground against his will, and sore wounded, if not killed outright. The second brother, seeing how his comrade was treated, drove his heels into his castle of a mule and made off across the country faster than the wind.

Sancho Panza, when he saw the friar on the ground, dismounting briskly from his ass, rushed towards him and began to strip off his gown. At that instant the friars' muleteers came up and asked what he was stripping him for. Sancho answered them that this fell to him lawfully as spoil of the battle which his lord Don Quixote had won. The muleteers, who had no idea of a joke and did not understand all this about battles and spoils, seeing that Don Quixote was some distance off talking to the travellers in the coach, fell upon Sancho, knocked him down, and leaving hardly a hair in his beard, belabored him with kicks and left him stretched breathless and senseless on the ground; and without any more delay helped the friar to mount, who, trembling, terrified, and pale, as soon as he found himself in the saddle, spurred after his companion, who was standing at a distance looking on, watching the result of the onslaught; then, not caring to wait for the end of the affair just begun, they pursued their journey making more crosses than if they had the devil after them.

Don Quixote was, as has been said, speaking to the lady in the coach: "Your beauty, lady mine," said he, "may now dispose of your person as may be most in accordance with your pleasure, for the pride of your ravishers lies prostrate on the ground through this strong arm of mine; and lest you should be pining to know the name of your deliverer, know that I am called Don Quixote of La Mancha, knight-errant and adventurer, and captive to the peerless and beautiful lady Dulcinea del Toboso; and in return for the service you have received of me I ask no more than that you should return to El Toboso, and on my behalf present yourself before that lady and tell her what I have done to set you free."

One of the squires in attendance upon the coach, a Biscayan, was listening to all Don Quixote was saying, and, perceiving that he would not allow the coach to go on, but was saying it must return at once to El Toboso, he made at him, and seizing his lance addressed him in bad Castilian and worse Biscayan after this fashion, "Begone, caballero, and ill go with thee; by the God that made me, unless thou quittest coach, slayest thee as art here a Biscayan."

Don Quixote understood him quite well, and answered him very quietly, "If thou wert a knight, as thou art none, I should have already chastised thy folly and rashness, miserable creature." To which the Biscayan returned, "I no gentleman!—I swear to God thou liest as I am Christian: if thou droppest lance and drawest sword, soon shalt thou see thou art carrying water to the cat: Biscayan on land, hidalgo at sea, hidalgo at the devil, and look, if thou sayest otherwise thou liest."

"'You will see presently,' said Agrajes,"[18] replied Don Quixote; and throwing his

---

[18] **"'You . . . ,' said Agrajes":** Quixote is quoting Agrajes from *Amadis of Gaul;* the challenge has become the conventional opener for a fight.

lance on the ground he drew his sword, braced his buckler on his arm, and attacked the Biscayan, bent upon taking his life.

The Biscayan, when he saw him coming on, though he wished to dismount from his mule, in which, being one of those sorry ones let out for hire, he had no confidence, had no choice but to draw his sword; it was lucky for him, however, that he was near the coach, from which he was able to snatch a cushion that served him for a shield; and then they went at one another as if they had been two mortal enemies. The others strove to make peace between them, but could not, for the Biscayan declared in his disjointed phrase that if they did not let him finish his battle he would kill his mistress and every one that strove to prevent him. The lady in the coach, amazed and terrified at what she saw, ordered the coachman to draw aside a little, and set herself to watch this severe struggle, in the course of which the Biscayan smote Don Quixote a mighty stroke on the shoulder over the top of his buckler, which, given to one without armor, would have cleft him to the waist. Don Quixote, feeling the weight of this prodigious blow, cried aloud, saying: "O lady of my soul, Dulcinea, flower of beauty, come to the aid of this your knight who, in fulfilling his obligations to your beauty, finds himself in this extreme peril." To say this, to lift his sword, to shelter himself well behind his buckler, and to assail the Biscayan was the work of an instant, determined as he was to venture all upon a single blow. The Biscayan, seeing him come on in this way, was convinced of his courage by his spirited bearing, and resolved to follow his example, so he waited for him keeping well under cover of his cushion, being unable to execute any sort of manœuvre with his mule, which, dead tired and never meant for this kind of game, could not stir a step. [. . .]

FROM

Chapter 10

OF THE PLEASANT DISCOURSE THAT PASSED BETWEEN DON QUIXOTE AND HIS SQUIRE SANCHO PANZA

Now by this time Sancho had risen, rather the worse for the handling of the friars' muleteers, and stood watching the battle of his master, Don Quixote, and praying to God in his heart that it might be his will to grant him the victory, and that he might thereby win some island to make him governor of, as he had promised. Seeing, therefore, that the struggle was now over, and that his master was returning to mount Rocinante, he approached to hold the stirrup for him, and, before he could mount, he went on his knees before him, and taking his hand, kissed it saying, "May it please your worship, Señor Don Quixote, to give me the government of that island which has been won in this hard fight, for be it ever so big I feel myself in sufficient force to be able to govern it as much and as well as any one in the world who has ever governed islands."

To which Don Quixote replied, "Thou must take notice, brother Sancho, that this adventure and those like it are not adventures of islands, but of cross-roads, in which nothing is got except a broken head or an ear the less: have patience, for adventures will present themselves from which I may make you not only a governor, but something more."

Sancho gave him many thanks, and again kissing his hand and the skirt of his hauberk, helped him to mount Rocinante, and mounting his ass himself, proceeded to follow his master, who at a brisk pace, without taking leave, or saying anything further to the ladies belonging to the coach, turned into a wood that was hard by. Sancho followed him at his ass's best trot, but Rocinante stepped out so that, seeing himself left behind, he was forced to call to his master to wait for him. Don Quixote did so, reining in Rocinante until his weary squire came up, who on reaching him said, "It seems to me, señor, it would be prudent in us to go and take refuge in some church, for, seeing how mauled he with whom you fought has been left, it will be no wonder if they give information of the affair to the Holy Brotherhood[19] and arrest us, and, faith, if they do, before we come out of gaol we shall have to sweat for it."

"Peace," said Don Quixote; "where hast thou ever seen or heard that a knight-errant has been arraigned before a court of justice, however many homicides he may have committed?"

"I know nothing about omecils,"[20] answered Sancho, "nor in my life have had anything to do with one; I only know that the Holy Brotherhood looks after those who fight in the fields, and in that other matter I do not meddle."

"Then thou needest have no uneasiness, my friend," said Don Quixote, "for I will deliver thee out of the hands of the Chaldeans, much more out of those of the Brotherhood. But tell me, as thou livest, hast thou seen a more valiant knight than I in all the known world; hast thou read in history of any who has or had higher mettle in attack, more spirit in maintaining it, more dexterity in wounding or skill in over-throwing?"

"The truth is," answered Sancho, "that I have never read any history, for I can neither read nor write, but what I will venture to bet is that a more daring master than your worship I have never served in all the days of my life, and God grant that this daring be not paid for where I have said; what I beg of your worship is to dress your wound, for a great deal of blood flows from that ear, and I have here some lint and a little white ointment in the *alforjas.*"

"All that might be well dispensed with," said Don Quixote, "if I had remembered to make a vial of the balsam of Fierabras,[21] for time and medicine are saved by one single drop."

"What vial and what balsam is that?" said Sancho Panza.

"It is a balsam," answered Don Quixote, "the receipt[22] of which I have in my memory, with which one need have no fear of death, or dread dying of any wound;

[19] **"Holy Brotherhood":** A tribunal for highway robbers, established by Ferdinand and Isabella at the end of the fifteenth century.

[20] **"omecils":** Grudges.

[21] **Fierabras:** In Roman legend, a giant who stole the liquid with which Jesus was embalmed, which could miraculously heal wounds.

[22] **"receipt":** Recipe.

and so when I make it and give it to thee thou hast nothing to do when in some battle thou seest they have cut me in half through the middle of the body—as is wont to happen frequently—but neatly and with great nicety, ere the blood congeal, to place that portion of the body which shall have fallen to the ground upon the other half which remains in the saddle, taking care to fit it on evenly and exactly. Then thou shalt give me to drink but two drops of the balsam I have mentioned, and thou shalt see me become sounder than an apple."

"If that be so," said Panza, "I renounce henceforth the government of the promised island, and desire nothing more in payment of my many and faithful services than that your worship give me the receipt of this supreme liquor, for I am persuaded it will be worth more than two reals an ounce anywhere, and I want no more to pass the rest of my life in ease and honor; but it remains to be told if it costs much to make it."

"With less than three reals six quarts of it may be made," said Don Quixote.

"Sinner that I am!" said Sancho, "then why does your worship put off making it and teaching it to me."

"Peace, friend," answered Don Quixote; "greater secrets I mean to teach thee and greater favors to bestow upon thee; and for the present let us see to the dressing, for my ear pains me more than I could wish."

Sancho took out some lint and ointment from the *alforjas;* but when Don Quixote came to see his helmet shattered, he was like to lose his senses, and, clapping his hand upon his sword and raising his eyes to heaven, he said, "I swear by the Creator of all things and the four Gospels in their fullest extent, to do as the great Marquis of Mantua did when he swore to avenge the death of his nephew Baldwin (and that was not to eat bread from a table-cloth, nor embrace his wife, and other points which, though I cannot now call them to mind, I here grant as expressed), until I take complete vengeance upon him who has committed such an offence against me."

Hearing this, Sancho said to him, "Your worship should bear in mind, Señor Don Quixote, that if the knight has done what was commanded him in going to present himself before my lady Dulcinea del Toboso, he will have done all that he was bound to do, and does not deserve further punishment unless he commits some new offence."

"Thou hast said well and hit the point," answered Don Quixote; "and so I recall the oath in so far as relates to taking fresh vengeance on him, but I make and confirm it anew to lead the life I have said until such time as I take by force from some knight another helmet such as this and as good; and think not, Sancho, that I am raising smoke with straw in doing so, for I have one to imitate in the matter, since the very same thing to a hair happened in the case of Mambrino's helmet,[23] which cost Sacripante so dear."

"Señor," replied Sancho, "let your worship send all such oaths to the devil, for they are very pernicious to salvation and prejudicial to the conscience; just tell me now, if for several days to come we fall in with no man armed with a helmet, what

[23] **"Mambrino's helmet":** Mambrino, a Moorish king in the epic poem *Roland in Love,* by Matteo Maria Boiardo, has his enchanted helmet stolen by Rinaldo.

are we to do? Is the oath to be observed in spite of all the inconvenience and discomfort it will be to sleep in your clothes, and not to sleep in a house, and a thousand other mortifications contained in the oath of that old fool, the Marquis of Mantua, which your worship is now wanting to revive? Let your worship observe that there are no men in armor travelling on any of these roads, nothing but carriers and carters, who not only do not wear helmets, but perhaps never heard tell of them all their lives."

"Thou art wrong there," said Don Quixote, "for we shall not have been two hours among these cross-roads before we see more men in armor than came to Albraca to win the fair Angelica."[24]

"Enough," said Sancho; "so be it then, and God grant us success, and that the time for winning that island which is costing me so dear may soon come, and then let me die."

"I have already told thee, Sancho," said Don Quixote, "not to give thyself any uneasiness on that score; for if an island should fail, there is the kingdom of Denmark, or of Sobradisa, which will fit thee as a ring fits the finger, and all the more that being on *terra firma* thou wilt all the better enjoy thyself. But let us leave that to its own time; see if thou hast anything for us to eat in those *alforjas,* because we must presently go in quest of some castle where we may lodge tonight and make the balsam I told thee of, for I swear to thee by God, this ear is giving me great pain."

"I have here an onion and a little cheese and a few scraps of bread," said Sancho, "but they are not victuals fit for a valiant knight like your worship."

"How little thou knowest about it," answered Don Quixote; "I would have thee know, Sancho, that it is the glory of knights-errant to go without eating for a month, and even when they do eat, that it should be of what comes first to hand; and this would have been clear to thee hadst thou read as many histories as I have, for, though they are very many, among them all I have found no mention made of knights-errant eating, unless by accident or at some sumptuous banquets prepared for them, and the rest of the time they passed in dalliance. And though it is plain they could not do without eating and performing all the other natural functions, because, in fact, they were men like ourselves, it is plain too that, wandering as they did the most part of their lives through woods and wilds and without a cook, their most usual fare would be rustic viands such as those thou dost now offer me; so that, friend Sancho, let not that distress thee which pleases me, and do not seek to make a new world or pervert knight-errantry."

"Pardon me, your worship," said Sancho, "for, as I can not read or write, as I said just now, I neither know nor comprehend the rules of the profession of chivalry: henceforward I will stock the *alforjas* with every kind of dry fruit for your worship, as you are a knight; and for myself, as I am not one, I will furnish them with poultry and other things more substantial."

"I do not say, Sancho," replied Don Quixote, "that it is imperative on knights-errant not to eat anything else but the fruits thou speakest of; only that their more

[24] **"Angelica":** Also in *Roland in Love.*

usual diet must be those, and certain herbs they found in the fields which they knew and I know too."

"A good thing it is," answered Sancho, "to know those herbs, for to my thinking it will be needful some day to put that knowledge into practice."

And here taking out what he said he had brought, the pair made their repast peaceably and sociably. But anxious to find quarters for the night, they with all despatch made an end of their poor dry fare, mounted at once, and made haste to reach some habitation before night set in. [. . .]

Chapter 20

OF THE UNEXAMPLED AND UNHEARD-OF ADVENTURE WHICH WAS ACHIEVED BY THE VALIANT DON QUIXOTE OF LA MANCHA WITH LESS PERIL THAN ANY EVER ACHIEVED BY ANY FAMOUS KNIGHT IN THE WORLD

"It can not be, señor, but that this grass is a proof that there must be hard by some spring or brook to give it moisture, so it would be well to move a little farther on, that we may find some place where we may quench this terrible thirst that plagues us, which beyond a doubt is more distressing than hunger."

The advice seemed good to Don Quixote, and, he leading Rocinante by the bridle and Sancho the ass by the halter, after he had packed away upon him the remains of the supper, they advanced up the meadow feeling their way, for the darkness of the night made it impossible to see anything; but they had not gone two hundred paces when a loud noise of water, as if falling from great high rocks, struck their ears. The sound cheered them greatly; but halting to make out by listening from what quarter it came they heard unseasonably another noise which spoiled the satisfaction the sound of the water gave them, especially for Sancho, who was by nature timid and faint-hearted; they heard, I say, strokes falling with a measured beat, and a certain rattling of iron and chains that, together with the furious din of the water, would have struck terror into any heart but Don Quixote's. The night was, as has been said, dark, and they had happened to reach a spot in among some tall trees, whose leaves stirred by a gentle breeze made a low ominous sound; so that, what with the solitude, the place, the darkness, the noise of the water, and the rustling of the leaves, everything inspired awe and dread; more especially as they perceived that the strokes did not cease, nor the wind lull, nor morning approach; to all which might be added their ignorance as to where they were.

But Don Quixote, supported by his intrepid heart, leaped on Rocinante, and bracing his buckler on his arm, brought his pike to the slope, and said, "Friend Sancho, know that I by Heaven's will have been born in this our iron age to revive in it the age of gold, or the golden as it is called; I am he for whom perils, mighty achievements, and valiant deeds are reserved; I am, I say again, he who is to revive the Knights of the Round Table, the Twelve of France and the Nine Worthies; and he who is to consign to oblivion the Platirs, the Tablantes, the Olivantes and Tirantes, the Phœbuses and Belianises, with the whole herd of famous knights-errant of days gone by, performing in these in which I live such exploits, marvels, and feats of arms as shall obscure their brightest deeds. Thou dost mark well, faithful and trusty squire, the gloom of this night, its strange silence, the dull confused murmur of these trees, the awful sound of that water in quest of which we came, that seems as though it were precipitating and dashing itself down from the lofty mountains of the moon, and that incessant hammering that wounds and pains our ears; which things all together and each of itself are enough to instil fear, dread, and dismay into the breast of Mars himself, much more into one not used to hazards and adventures of the kind. Well, then, all this that I put before thee is but an incentive and stimulant to my spirit, making my heart burst in my bosom through eagerness to engage in this adventure, arduous as it promises to be; therefore tighten Rocinante's girths a little, and God be with thee; wait for me here three days and no more, and if in that time I come not back, thou canst return to our village, and thence, to do me a favor and a service, thou wilt go to El Toboso, where thou shalt say to my incomparable lady Dulcinea that her captive knight hath died in attempting things that might make him worthy of being called hers."

When Sancho heard his master's words he began to weep in the most pathetic way, saying, "Señor, I know not why your worship wants to attempt this so dreadful adventure; it is night now, no one sees us here, we can easily turn about and take ourselves out of danger, even if we don't drink for three days to come; and as there is no one to see us, all the less will there be any one to set us down as cowards; besides, I have many a time heard the curate of our village, whom your worship knows well, preach that he who seeks danger perishes in it; so it is not right to tempt God by trying so tremendous a feat from which there can be no escape save by a miracle, and Heaven has performed enough of them for your worship in delivering you from being blanketed as I was,[25] and bringing you out victorious and safe and sound from among all those enemies that were with the dead man; and if all this does not move or soften that hard heart, let this thought and reflection move it, that you will have hardly quitted this spot when from pure fear I shall yield my soul up to any one that will take it. I left home and wife and children to come and serve your worship, trusting to do better and not worse; but, as covetousness bursts the bag, it has rent my hopes asunder, for just as I had them highest about getting that wretched unlucky island your worship has so often promised me, I see that instead and in lieu of it you mean to desert me now in a place so far from human reach; for God's sake, master mine, deal not so unjustly by me, and if your worship will not entirely give up attempting this feat, at least put it off till morning, for by what the lore I learned when I was a shepherd tells me it can not want three hours of dawn now, because the mouth of the Horn is overhead and makes midnight in the line of the left arm."[26]

"How canst thou see, Sancho," said Don Quixote, "where it makes that line, or where the mouth or head is that thou talkest of, when the night is so dark that there is not a star to be seen in the whole heaven?"

"That's true," said Sancho, "but fear has sharp eyes, and sees things underground,

---

[25] **blanketed as I was:** Sancho had been tossed in a blanket at an inn on one of their adventures.

[26] **"the Horn . . . arm":** The Little Dipper resembles a curved hunting horn. One could tell the hour by facing the horn and extending one's arms horizontally. The time was told by the position of the horn relative to the arms.

much more above in the heavens; besides, there is good reason to show that it now wants but little of day."

"Let it want what it may," replied Don Quixote, "it shall not be said of me now or at any time that tears or entreaties turned me aside from doing what was in accordance with knightly usage; and so I beg of thee, Sancho, to hold thy peace, for God, who has put it into my heart to undertake now this so unexampled and terrible adventure, will take care to watch over my safety and console thy sorrow; what thou hast to do is to tighten Rocinante's girths well, and wait here, for I shall come back shortly, alive or dead."

Sancho perceiving it his master's final resolve, and how little his tears, counsels, and entreaties prevailed with him, determined to have recourse to his own ingenuity and compel him if he could to wait till daylight; and so, while tightening the girths of the horse, he quietly and without being felt, tied both Rocinante's fore-legs, so that when Don Quixote strove to go he was unable as the horse could only move by jumps. Seeing the success of his trick, Sancho Panza said, "See there, señor! Heaven, moved by my tears and prayers, has so ordered it that Rocinante can not stir; and if you will be obstinate, and spur and strike him, you will only provoke fortune, and kick, as they say, against the pricks."

Don Quixote at this grew desperate, but the more he drove his heels into the horse, the less he stirred him; and not having any suspicion of the tying, he was fain to resign himself and wait till daybreak or until Rocinante could move, firmly persuaded that all this came of something other than Sancho's ingenuity. So he said to him, "As it is so, Sancho, and as Rocinante can not move, I am content to wait till dawn smiles upon us, even though I weep while it delays its coming."

"There is no need to weep," answered Sancho, "for I will amuse your worship by telling stories from this till daylight, unless, indeed, you like to dismount and lie down to sleep a little on the green grass after the fashion of knights-errant, so as to be fresher when day comes and the moment arrives for attempting this extraordinary adventure you are looking forward to."

"What art thou talking about dismounting or sleeping for?" said Don Quixote. "Am I, thinkest thou, one of those knights that take their rest in the presence of danger? Sleep thou who art born to sleep, or do as thou wilt, for I will act as I think most consistent with my character."

"Be not angry, master mine," replied Sancho, "I did not mean to say that"; and coming close to him he laid one hand on the pommel of the saddle and the other on the cantle, so that he held his master's left thigh in his embrace, not daring to separate a finger's length from him; so much afraid was he of the strokes which still resounded with a regular beat. Don Quixote bade him tell some story to amuse him as he had proposed, to which Sancho replied that he would if his dread of what he heard would let him; "Still," said he, "I will strive to tell a story which, if I can manage to relate it, and it escapes me not, is the best of stories, and let your worship give me your attention, for here I begin. What was, was; and may the good that is to come be for all, and the evil for him who goes to look for it—your worship must know that the beginning the old folk used to put to their tales was not just as each one pleased;

it was a maxim of Cato Zonzorino the Roman[27] that says 'the evil for him that goes to look for it,' and it comes as pat to the purpose now as ring to finger, to show that your worship should keep quiet and not go looking for evil in any quarter, and that we should go back by some other road, since nobody forces us to follow this in which so many terrors affright us."

"Go on with thy story, Sancho," said Don Quixote, "and leave the choice of our road to my care."

"I say then," continued Sancho, "that in a village of Estremadura there was a goat-shepherd—that is to say, one who tended goats—which shepherd or goat-herd, as my story goes, was called Lope Ruiz, and this Lope Ruiz was in love with a shepherdess called Torralva, which shepherdess called Torralva was the daughter of a rich grazier, and this rich grazier"—

"If that is the way thou tellest thy tale, Sancho," said Don Quixote, "repeating twice all thou hast to say, thou wilt not have done these two days; go straight on with it, and tell it like a reasonable man, or else say nothing."

"Tales are always told in my country in the very way I am telling this," answered Sancho, "and I can not tell it in any other, nor is it right of your worship to ask me to make new customs."

"Tell it as thou wilt," replied Don Quixote; "and as fate will have it that I can not help listening to thee, go on."

"And so, lord of my soul," continued Sancho, "as I have said, this shepherd was in love with Torralva the shepherdess, who was a wild buxom lass with something of the look of a man about her, for she had little mustaches; I fancy I see her now."

"Then you knew her?" said Don Quixote.

"I did not know her," said Sancho, "but he who told me the story said it was so true and certain that when I told it to another I might safely declare and swear I had seen it all myself. And so in course of time, the devil, who never sleeps and puts everything in confusion, contrived that the love the shepherd bore the shepherdess turned into hatred and ill-will, and the reason, according to evil tongues, was some little jealousy she had caused him that crossed the line and trespassed on forbidden ground; and so much did the shepherd hate her from that time forward that, in order to escape from her, he determined to quit the country and go where he should never set eyes on her again. Torralva, when she found herself spurned by Lope, was immediately smitten with love for him, though she had never loved him before."

"That is the natural way of women," said Don Quixote, "to scorn the one that loves them, and love the one that hates them: go on, Sancho."

"It came to pass," said Sancho, "that the shepherd carried out his intention, and driving his goats before him took his way across the plains of Estremadura to pass over into the Kingdom of Portugal. Torralva, who knew of it, went after him, and on foot and barefooted followed him at a distance, with a pilgrim's staff in her hand and

[27] **"Cato Zonzorino the Roman":** Cato Censorino, or Cato the Censor. "Cato Zonzorino" would derive from *zonzo*, Spanish for "stupid."

a scrip round her neck, in which she carried, it is said, a bit of looking-glass, and a piece of a comb and some little pot or other of paint for her face; but let her carry what she did, I am not going to trouble myself to prove it; all I say is, that the shepherd, they say, came with his flock to cross over the river Guadiana, which was at that time swollen and almost overflowing its banks, and at the spot he came to there was neither ferry nor boat nor any one to carry him or his flock to the other side, at which he was much vexed, for he perceived that Torralva was approaching and would give him great annoyance with her tears and entreaties; however, he went looking about so closely that he discovered a fisherman who had alongside of him a boat so small that it could only hold one person and one goat; but for all that he spoke to him and agreed with him to carry himself and his three hundred goats across. The fisherman got into the boat and carried one goat over; he came back and carried another over; he came back again, and again brought over another—let your worship keep count of the goats the fisherman is taking across, for if one escapes the memory there will be an end of the story, and it will be impossible to tell another word of it. To proceed, I must tell you the landing place on the other side was miry and slippery, and the fisherman lost a great deal of time in going and coming; still he returned for another goat, and another, and another."

"Take it for granted he brought them all across," said Don Quixote, "and don't keep going and coming in this way, or thou wilt not make an end of bringing them over this twelve-month."

"How many have gone across so far?" said Sancho.

"How the devil do I know?" replied Don Quixote.

"There it is," said Sancho, "what I told you, that you must keep a good count; well then, by God, there is an end of the story, for there is no going any farther."

"How can that be?" said Don Quixote; "is it so essential to the story to know to a nicety the goats that have crossed over, that if there be a mistake of one in the reckoning, thou canst not go on with it?"

"No, señor, not a bit," replied Sancho; "for when I asked your worship to tell me how many goats had crossed, and you answered you did not know, at that very instant all I had to say passed away out of my memory, and faith, there was much virtue in it, and entertainment."

"So, then," said Don Quixote, "the story has come to an end?"

"As much as my mother has," said Sancho.

"In truth," said Don Quixote, "thou hast told one of the rarest stories, tales, or histories, that any one in the world could have imagined, and such a way of telling it and ending it was never seen nor will be in a lifetime; though I expected nothing else from thy excellent understanding. But I do not wonder, for perhaps those ceaseless strokes may have confused thy wits."

"All that may be," replied Sancho, "but I know that as to my story, all that can be said is that it ends there where the mistake in the count of the passage of the goats begins."

"Let it end where it will, well and good," said Don Quixote, "and let us see if Rocinante can go"; and again he spurred him, and again Rocinante made jumps and remained where he was, so well tied was he.

Just then, whether it was the cold of the morning that was now approaching, or that he had eaten something laxative at supper, or that it was only natural (as is most likely), Sancho felt a desire to do what no one could do for him; but so great was the fear that had penetrated his heart, he dared not separate himself from his master by so much as the black of his nail; to escape doing what he wanted was, however, also impossible; so what he did for peace' sake was to remove his right hand, which held the back of the saddle, and with it to untie gently and silently the running string which alone held up his breeches, so that on loosening it they at once fell down round his feet like fetters; he then raised his shirt as well as he could and bared his hind quarters, no slim ones. But this accomplished, which he fancied was all he had to do to get out of this terrible strait and embarrassment, another still greater difficulty presented itself, for it seemed to him impossible to relieve himself without making some noise, and he ground his teeth and squeezed his shoulders together, holding his breath as much as he could; but in spite of his precautions he was unlucky enough after all to make a little noise, very different from that which was causing him so much fear.

Don Quixote, hearing it, said, "What noise is that, Sancho?"

"I don't know, señor," said he; "it must be something new, for adventures and misadventures never begin with a trifle." Once more he tried his luck, and succeeded so well, that without any further noise or disturbance he found himself relieved of the burden that had given him so much discomfort. But as Don Quixote's sense of smell was as acute as his hearing, and as Sancho was so closely linked with him that the fumes rose almost in a straight line, it could not be but that some should reach his nose, and as soon as they did he came to its relief by compressing it between his fingers, saying in a rather snuffling tone, "Sancho, it strikes me thou art in great fear."

"I am," answered Sancho; "but how does your worship perceive it now more than ever?"

"Because just now thou smellest stronger than ever, and not of ambergris," answered Don Quixote.

"Very likely," said Sancho, "but that's not my fault, but your worship's, for leading me about at unseasonable hours and at such unwonted paces."

"Then go back three or four, my friend," said Don Quixote, all the time with his fingers to his nose; "and for the future pay more attention to thy person and to what thou owest to mine; for it is my great familiarity with thee that has bred this contempt."

"I'll bet," replied Sancho, "that your worship thinks I have done something I ought not with my person."

"It makes it worse to stir it, friend Sancho," returned Don Quixote.

With this and other talk of the same sort master and man passed the night, till Sancho, perceiving that daybreak was coming on apace, very cautiously untied Rocinante and tied up his breeches. As soon as Rocinante found himself free, though by nature he was not at all mettlesome, he seemed to feel lively and began pawing—for as to capering, begging his pardon, he knew not what it meant. Don Quixote, then, observing that Rocinante could move, took it as a good sign and a signal that he should attempt the dread adventure. By this time day had fully broken and everything showed distinctly, and Don Quixote saw that he was among some tall trees, chestnuts, which cast a very deep shade; he perceived likewise that the sound of the strokes did not cease, but could not discover what caused it, and so without any further delay he let Rocinante feel the spur, and once more taking leave of Sancho, he told him to wait for him there three days at most, as he had said before, and if he should not have returned by that time, he might feel sure it had been God's will that he should end his days in that perilous adventure. He again repeated the message and commission with which he was to go on his behalf to his lady Dulcinea, and said he was not to be uneasy as to the payment of his services, for before leaving home he had made his will, in which he would find himself fully recompensed in the matter of wages in due proportion to the time he had served; but if God delivered him safe, sound, and unhurt out of that danger, he might look upon the promised island as much more than certain. Sancho began weeping afresh on again hearing the affecting words of his good master, and resolved to stay with him until the final issue and end of the business. From these tears and this honorable resolve of Sancho Panza's the author of this history infers that he must have been of good birth and at least an old Christian;[28] and the feeling he displayed touched his master somewhat, but not so much as to make him show any weakness; on the contrary, hiding what he felt as well as he could, he began to move towards that quarter whence the sound of the water and of the strokes seemed to come.

Sancho followed him on foot, leading by the halter, as his custom was, his ass, his constant comrade in prosperity or adversity; and advancing some distance through the shady chestnut trees they came up on a little meadow at the foot of some high rocks, down which a mighty rush of water flung itself. At the foot of the rocks were some rudely constructed houses looking more like ruins than houses, from among which came, they perceived, the din and clatter of blows, which still continued without intermission. Rocinante took fright at the noise of the water and of the blows, but quieting him Don Quixote advanced step by step towards the houses, commending himself with all his heart to his lady, imploring her support in that dread pass and enterprise, and on the way commended himself to God, too, not to forget him. Sancho, who never quitted his side, stretched his neck as far as he could and peered between the legs of Rocinante to see if he could now discover what it was that caused him such fear and apprehension. They went it might be a hundred paces farther, when on turning a corner the true cause, beyond the possibility of any mistake, of that dread-sounding and to them awe-inspiring noise that had kept them all the night in such fear and perplexity, appeared plain and obvious; and it was (if, reader, thou art not disgusted and disappointed) six fulling hammers which by their alternate strokes made all the din.[29]

When Don Quixote perceived what it was, he was struck dumb and rigid from head to foot. Sancho glanced at him and saw him with his head bent down upon his breast in manifest mortification; and Don Quixote glanced at Sancho and saw him

[28] **old Christian:** One who had no trace of Moorish or Jewish blood in his veins.

[29] **noise . . . din:** The sound came from a wool-finishing mill, where heavy hammers pounded cloth for hours on end.

with his cheeks puffed out and his mouth full of laughter, and evidently ready to explode with it, and in spite of his vexation he could not help laughing at the sight of him; and when Sancho saw his master begin he let go so heartily that he had to hold his sides with both hands to keep himself from bursting with laughter. Four times he stopped, and as many times did his laughter break out afresh with the same violence as at first, whereat Don Quixote grew furious, above all when he heard him say mockingly, "Thou must know, friend Sancho, that of Heaven's will I was born in this our iron age to revive in it the golden or age of gold; I am he for whom are reserved perils, mighty achievements, valiant deeds"; and here he went on repeating all or most of the words that Don Quixote uttered the first time they heard the awful strokes.

Don Quixote, then, seeing that Sancho was turning him into ridicule, was so mortified and vexed that he lifted up his pike and smote him two such blows that if, instead of catching them on his shoulders, he had caught them on his head, there would have been no wages to pay, unless indeed to his heirs. Sancho seeing that he was getting an awkward return in earnest for his jest, and fearing his master might carry it still further, said to him very humbly, "Calm yourself, sir, for by God I am only joking."

"Well, then, if you are joking I am not," replied Don Quixote. "Look here, my lively gentleman, if these, instead of being fulling hammers, had been some perilous adventure, have I not, think you, shown the courage required for the attempt and achievement? Am I, perchance, being, as I am, a gentleman, bound to know and distinguish sounds and tell whether they come from fulling mills or not; and that, when perhaps, as is the case, I have never in my life seen any as you have, low boor as you are, that have been born and bred among them? But turn me these six hammers into six giants, and bring them to beard me, one by one or all together, and if I do not knock them head over heels, then make what mockery you like of me."

"No more of that, señor," returned Sancho; "I own I went a little far with the joke. But tell me, your worship, now that peace is made between us (and may God bring you out of all the adventures that may befall you as safe and sound as He has brought you out of this one), was it not a thing to laugh at, and is it not a good story, the great fear we were in?—at least that I was in; for as to your worship I see now that you neither know nor understand what either fear or dismay is."

"I do not deny," said Don Quixote, "that what happened to us may be worth laughing at, but it is not worth making a story about, for it is not every one that is shrewd enough to hit the right point of a thing."

"At any rate," said Sancho, "your worship knew how to hit the right point with your pike, aiming at my head and hitting me on the shoulders, thanks be to God and my own smartness in dodging it. But let that pass; all will come out in the scouring; for I have heard say 'he loves thee well that makes thee weep'; and moreover that it is the way with great lords after any hard words they give a servant to give him a pair of breeches; though I do not know what they give after blows, unless it be that knights-errant after blows give islands, or kingdoms on the mainland."

"It may be on the dice," said Don Quixote, "that all thou sayest will come true; overlook the past, for thou art shrewd enough to know that our first movements are not in our own control; and one thing for the future bear in mind, that thou curb and restrain thy loquacity in my company; for in all the books of chivalry that I have read, and they are innumerable, I never met with a squire who talked so much to his lord as thou dost to thine; and in fact I feel it to be a great fault of thine and of mine: of thine, that thou hast so little respect for me; of mine, that I do not make myself more respected. There was Gandalin, the squire of Amadis of Gaul, that was Count of the Insula Firme, and we read of him that he always addressed his lord with his cap in his hand, his head bowed down and his body bent double, *more turquesco.*[30] And then, what shall we say of Gasabal, the squire of Galaor, who was so silent that in order to indicate to us the greatness of his marvellous taciturnity his name is only once mentioned in the whole of that history, as long as it is truthful? From all I have said thou wilt gather, Sancho, that there must be a difference between master and man, between lord and lackey, between knight and squire: so that from this day forward in our intercourse we must observe more respect and take less liberties, for in whatever way I may be provoked with you it will be bad for the pitcher. The favors and benefits that I have promised you will come in due time, and if they do not your wages at least will not be lost, as I have already told you."

"All that your worship says is very well," said Sancho, "but I should like to know (in case the time of favors should not come, and it might be necessary to fall back upon wages) how much did the squire of a knight-errant get in those days, and did they agree by the month, or by the day like bricklayers?"

"I do not believe," replied Don Quixote, "that such squires were ever on wages, but were dependent on favor; and if I have now mentioned thine in the sealed will I have left at home, it was with a view to what may happen; for as yet I know not how chivalry will turn out in these wretched times of ours, and I do not wish my soul to suffer for trifles in the other world; for I would have thee know, Sancho, that in this there is no condition more hazardous than that of adventures."

"That is true," said Sancho, "since the mere noise of the hammers of a fulling mill can disturb and disquiet the heart of such a valiant errant adventurer as your worship; but you may be sure I will not open my lips henceforward to make light of anything of your worship's, but only to honor you as my master and natural lord."

"By so doing," replied Don Quixote, "shalt thou live long on the face of the earth; for next to parents, masters are to be respected as though they were parents."

...

FROM
Chapter 25
WHICH TREATS OF THE STRANGE THINGS THAT HAPPENED TO THE STOUT KNIGHT OF LA MANCHA IN THE SIERRA MORENA, AND OF HIS IMITATION OF THE PENANCE OF BELTENEBROS

... They reached the foot of a high mountain which stood like an isolated peak among the others that surrounded it. Past its base there flowed a gentle brook, all around it

[30] ***"more turquesco":*** "In Turkish fashion."

spread a meadow so green and luxuriant that it was a delight to the eyes to look upon it, and forest trees in abundance, and shrubs and flowers, added to the charms of the spot. Upon this place the Knight of the Rueful Countenance fixed his choice for the performance of his penance, and as he beheld it exclaimed in a loud voice as though he were out of his senses, "This is the place, oh, ye heavens, that I select and choose for bewailing the misfortune in which ye yourselves have plunged me: this is the spot where the overflowings of mine eyes shall swell the waters of yon little brook, and my deep and endless sighs shall stir unceasingly the leaves of these mountain trees, in testimony and token of the pain my persecuted heart is suffering. Oh, ye rural deities, whoever ye be that haunt this lone spot, give ear to the complaint of a wretched lover whom long absence and brooding jealousy have driven to bewail his fate among these wilds and complain of the hard heart of that fair and ungrateful one, the end and limit of all human beauty! Oh, ye wood nymphs and dryads, that dwell in the thickets of the forest, so may the nimble wanton satyrs by whom ye are vainly wooed never disturb your sweet repose, help me to lament my hard fate or at least weary not at listening to it! Oh, Dulcinea del Toboso, day of my night, glory of my pain, guide of my path, star of my fortune, so may Heaven grant thee in full all thou seekest of it, bethink thee of the place and condition to which absence from thee has brought me, and make that return in kindness that is due to my fidelity! Oh, lonely trees, that from this day forward shall bear me company in my solitude, give me some sign by the gentle movement of your boughs that my presence is not distasteful to you! Oh, thou, my squire, pleasant companion in my prosperous and adverse fortunes, fix well in thy memory what thou shalt see me do here, so that thou mayest relate and report it to the sole cause of all," and so saying he dismounted from Rocinante, and in an instant relieved him of saddle and bridle, and giving him a slap on the croup, said, "He gives thee freedom who is bereft of it himself, oh steed as excellent in deed as thou art unfortunate in thy lot; begone where thou wilt, for thou bearest written on thy forehead that neither Astolfo's hippogriff, nor the famed Frontino that cost Bradamante so dear, could equal thee in speed."[31]

Seeing this Sancho said, "Good luck to him who has saved us the trouble of stripping the pack-saddle off Dapple! By my faith he would not have gone without a slap on the croup and something said in his praise; though if he were here I would not let any one strip him, for there would be no occasion, as he had nothing of the lover or victim of despair about him, inasmuch as his master, which I was while it was God's pleasure, was nothing of the sort; and indeed, Sir Knight of the Rueful Countenance, if my departure and your worship's madness are to come off in earnest, it will be as well to saddle Rocinante again in order that he may supply the want of Dapple, because it will save me time in going and returning; for if I go on foot I don't know when I shall get there or when I shall get back, as I am, in truth, a bad walker."

"I declare, Sancho," returned Don Quixote, "it shall be as thou wilt, for thy plan

[31] **"Astolfo's . . . speed":** In Aristo's *Orlando Furioso,* Astolfo's hippogriff was a winged horse; Frontino was the horse of Ruggiero, Bradamante's lover.

does not seem to me a bad one, and three days hence thou wilt depart, for I wish thee to observe in the mean time what I do and say for her sake, that thou mayest be able to tell it." . . .

Don Quixote took out the note-book, and, retiring to one side, very deliberately began to write the letter, and when he had finished it he called to Sancho, saying he wished to read it to him, so that he might commit it to memory, in case of losing it on the road; for with evil fortune like his anything might be apprehended. To which Sancho replied, "Write it two or three times there in the book and give it to me, and I will carry it very carefully, because to expect me to keep it in my memory is all nonsense, for I have such a bad one that I often forget my own name; but for all that repeat it to me, as I shall like to hear it, for surely it will run as if it was in print."

"Listen," said Don Quixote, "this is what it says:"

DON QUIXOTE'S LETTER TO DULCINEA DEL TOBOSO

> SOVEREIGN AND EXALTED LADY, The pierced by the point of absence, the wounded to the heart's core, sends thee, sweetest Dulcinea del Toboso, the health that he himself enjoys not. If thy beauty despises me, if thy worth is not for me, if thy scorn is my affliction, though I be sufficiently long-suffering, hardly shall I endure this anxiety, which, besides being oppressive, is protracted. My good Squire Sancho will relate to thee in full, fair ingrate, dear enemy, the condition to which I am reduced on thy account; if it be thy pleasure to give me relief, I am thine; if not, do as may be pleasing to thee; for by ending my life I shall satisfy thy cruelty and my desire.
>
> Thine till death,
>
> THE KNIGHT OF THE RUEFUL COUNTENANCE

"By the life of my father," said Sancho, when he heard the letter, "it is the loftiest thing I ever heard. Body of me! how your worship says everything as you like in it! And how well you fit in 'The Knight of the Rueful Countenance' into the signature. I declare your worship is indeed the very devil, and there is nothing you don't know."

"Everything is needed for the calling I follow," said Don Quixote.

"Now then," said Sancho, "let your worship put the order for the three ass-colts on the other side, and sign it very plainly, that they may recognize it at first sight."

"With all my heart," said Don Quixote, and as soon as he had written it he read it to this effect:

> MISTRESS NIECE, By this first of ass-colts please pay to Sancho Panza, my squire, three of the five I left at home in your charge: said three ass-colts to be paid and delivered for the same number received here in hand, which upon this and upon his receipt shall be duly paid. Done in the heart of the Sierra Morena, the twenty-seventh of August of this present year.

"That will do," said Sancho; "now let your worship sign it."

"There is no need to sign it," said Don Quixote, "but merely to put my flourish, which is the same as a signature, and enough for three asses, or even three hundred."

"I can trust your worship," returned Sancho; "let me go and saddle Rocinante, and be ready to give me your blessing, for I mean to go at once without seeing the fooleries your worship is going to do; I'll say I saw you do so many that she will not want any more." [. . .]

"Do you know what I am afraid of?" said Sancho upon this; "that I shall not be able to find my way back to this spot where I am leaving you, it is such an out-of-the-way place."

"Observe the landmarks well," said Don Quixote, "for I will try not to go far from this neighborhood, and I will even take care to mount the highest of these rocks to see if I can discover thee returning; however, not to miss me and lose thyself, the best plan will be to cut some branches of the broom that is so abundant about here, and as thou goest to lay them at intervals until thou hast come out upon the plain; these will serve thee, after the fashion of the clew in the labyrinth of Theseus, as marks and signs for finding me on thy return."

"So I will," said Sancho Panza, and having cut some, he asked his master's blessing, and not without many tears on both sides took his leave of him, and mounting Rocinante, of whom Don Quixote charged him earnestly to have as much care as of his own person, he set out for the plain, strewing at intervals the branches of broom as his master had recommended him; and so he went his way, though Don Quixote still entreated him to see him do were it only a couple of mad acts. He had not gone a hundred paces, however, when he returned and said, "I must say, señor, your worship said quite right, that in order to be able to swear without a weight on my conscience that I had seen you do mad things, it would be well for me to see if it were only one; though in your worship's remaining here I have seen a very great one."

"Did I not tell thee so?" said Don Quixote. "Wait, Sancho, and I will do them in the saying of a *credo*," and pulling off his breeches in all haste he stripped himself to his skin and his shirt, and then, without more ado, he cut a couple of *gambados* in the air, and a couple of somersaults, heels over head, making such a display that, not to see it a second time, Sancho wheeled Rocinante round, and felt easy, and satisfied in his mind that he could swear he had left his master mad; and so we will leave him to follow his road until his return, which was a quick one.

. . .

FROM

Chapter 31

OF THE DELECTABLE DISCUSSION BETWEEN DON QUIXOTE AND SANCHO PANZA, HIS SQUIRE, TOGETHER WITH OTHER INCIDENTS

"All that is not unsatisfactory to me," said Don Quixote. "Go on; thou didst reach her; and what was that queen of beauty doing? Surely thou didst find her stringing pearls, or embroidering some device in gold thread for this her enslaved knight."

"I did not," said Sancho, "but I found her winnowing two bushels of wheat in the yard of her house."

"Then depend upon it," said Don Quixote, "the grains of that wheat were pearls when touched by her hands; and didst thou look, friend? was it white wheat or brown?"

"It was neither, but red," said Sancho.

"Then I promise thee," said Don Quixote, "that, winnowed by her hands, beyond a doubt the bread it made was of the whitest; but go on; when thou gavest her my letter, did she kiss it? Did she place it on her head? Did she perform any ceremony befitting such a letter, or what did she do?"

"When I went to give it to her," replied Sancho, "she was hard at it swaying from side to side with a lot of wheat she had in the sieve, and she said to me, 'Lay the letter, friend, on the top of that sack, for I can not read it until I have done sifting all this.'"

"Discreet lady!" said Don Quixote; "that was in order to read it at her leisure and enjoy it; proceed, Sancho; while she was engaged in her occupation what converse did she hold with thee? What did she ask about me, and what answer didst thou give? Make haste; tell me all, and let not an atom be left behind in the ink-bottle."

"She asked me nothing," said Sancho; "but I told her how your worship was left doing penance in her service, naked from the waist up, in among these mountains like a savage, sleeping on the ground, not eating bread off a tablecloth nor combing your beard, weeping and cursing your fortune."

"In saying I cursed my fortune thou saidst wrong," said Don Quixote; "for rather do I bless it and shall bless it all the days of my life for having made me worthy of aspiring to love so lofty a lady as Dulcinea del Toboso."

"And so lofty she is," said Sancho, "that she overtops me by more than a hand's-breadth."

"What! Sancho," said Don Quixote, "didst thou measure with her?"

"I measured in this way," said Sancho; "going to help her to put a sack of wheat on the back of an ass, we came so close together that I could see she stood more than a good palm over me."

"Well!" said Don Quixote, "and doth she not of a truth accompany and adorn this greatness with a thousand million charms of mind! But one thing thou wilt not deny, Sancho; when thou camest close to her didst thou not perceive a Sabæan[32] odor, an aromatic fragrance, a, I know not what, delicious, that I can not find a name for; I mean a redolence, an exhalation, as if thou wert in the shop of some dainty glover?"

"All I can say is," said Sancho, "that I did perceive a little odor, something goaty; it must have been that she was all in a sweat with hard work."

"It could not be that," said Don Quixote, "but thou must have been suffering from cold in the head, or must have smelt thyself; for I know well what would be the scent of that rose among thorns, that lily of the field, that dissolved amber."

"Maybe so," replied Sancho; "there often comes from myself that same odor which then seemed to me to come from her grace the lady Dulcinea; but that's no wonder, for one devil is like another."

"Well then," continued Don Quixote, "now she has done sifting the corn and sent it to the mill; what did she do when she read the letter?"

"As for the letter," said Sancho, "she did not read it, for she said she could neither read nor write; instead of that she tore it up into small pieces, saying that she did not want to let any one read it lest her secrets should become known in the village, and that what I had told her by word of mouth about the love your worship bore her, and

[32] **Sabæan:** From Saba or Sheba, an area known for perfume.

the extraordinary penance you were doing for her sake, was enough; and, to make an end of it, she told me to tell your worship that she kissed your hands, and that she had a greater desire to see you than to write to you; and that therefore she entreated and commanded you, on sight of this present, to come out of these thickets, and to have done with carrying on absurdities, and to set out at once for El Toboso, unless something else of greater importance should happen, for she had a great desire to see your worship. She laughed greatly when I told her how your worship was called the Knight of the Rueful Countenance; I asked her if that Biscayan the other day had been there; and she told me he had, and that he was a very honest fellow; I asked her too about the galley slaves, but she said she had not seen any yet."

"So far all goes well," said Don Quixote; "but tell me what jewel was it that she gave thee on taking thy leave, in return for thy tidings of me? For it is a usual and ancient custom with knights and ladies errant to give the squires, damsels, or dwarfs who bring tidings of their ladies to the knights, or of their knights to the ladies, some rich jewel as a guerdon for good news, and acknowledgment of the message."

"That is likely," said Sancho, "and a good custom it was, to my mind; but that must have been in days gone by, for now it would seem to be the custom only to give a piece of bread and cheese; because that was what my lady Dulcinea gave me over the top of the yard-wall when I took leave of her; and more by token it was sheep's-milk cheese."

"She is generous in the extreme," said Don Quixote, "and if she did not give thee a jewel of gold, no doubt it must have been because she had not one to hand there to give thee, but sleeves are good after Easter; I shall see her and all shall be made right. But knowest thou what amazes me, Sancho? It seems to me thou must have gone and come through the air, for thou has taken but little more than three days to go to El Toboso and return, though it is more than thirty leagues from here to there. From which I am inclined to think that the sage magician who is my friend, and watches over my interests (for of necessity there is and must be one, or else I should not be a right knight-errant), that this same, I say, must have helped thee to travel without thy knowledge; for some of these sages will catch up a knight-errant sleeping in his bed, and without his knowing how or in what way it happened, he wakes up the next day more than a thousand leagues away from the place where he went to sleep. And if it were not for this, knights-errant would not be able to give aid to one another in peril, as they do at every turn. For a knight, maybe, is fighting in the mountains of Armenia with some dragon, or fierce serpent, or another knight, and gets the worst of the battle, and is at the point of death; but when he least looks for it, there appears over against him on a cloud, or chariot of fire, another knight, a friend of his, who just before had been in England, and who takes his part, and delivers him from death; and at night he finds himself in his own quarters supping very much to his satisfaction; and yet from one place to the other will have been two or three thousand leagues. And all this is done by the craft and skill of the sage enchanters who take care of those valiant knights; so that, friend Sancho, I find no difficulty in believing that thou mayest have gone from this place to El Toboso and returned in such a short time, since, as I have said, some friendly sage must have carried thee through the air without thee perceiving it." [. . .]

FROM

Chapter 50

OF THE SHREWD CONTROVERSY WHICH DON QUIXOTE AND THE CANON HELD, TOGETHER WITH OTHER INCIDENTS

"A good joke, that!" returned Don Quixote. "Books that have been printed with the king's license, and with the approbation of those to whom they have been submitted, and read with universal delight, and extolled by great and small, rich and poor, learned and ignorant, gentle and simple, in a word by people of every sort, of whatever rank or condition they may be—that these should be lies! And above all when they carry such an appearance of truth with them; for they tell us the father, mother, country, kindred, age, place, and the achievements, step by step, and day by day, performed by such and such a knight or knights! Hush, sir; utter not such blasphemy; trust me I am advising you now to act as a sensible man should; only read them, and you will see the pleasure you will derive from them. For, come, tell me, can there be anything more delightful than to see, as it were, here now displayed before us a vast lake of bubbling pitch with a host of snakes and serpents and lizards, and ferocious and terrible creatures of all sorts swimming about in it, while from the middle of the lake there comes a plaintive voice saying: 'Knight, whosoever thou art who beholdest this dread lake, if thou wouldst win the prize that lies hidden beneath these dusky waves, prove the valor of thy stout heart and cast thyself into the midst of its dark burning waters, else thou shalt not be worthy to see the mighty wonders contained in the seven castles of the seven Fays that lie beneath this black expanse'; and then the knight, almost ere the awful voice has ceased, without stopping to consider, without pausing to reflect upon the danger to which he is exposing himself, without even relieving himself of the weight of his massive armor, commending himself to God and to his lady, plunges into the mist of the boiling lake, and when he little looks for it, or knows what his fate is to be, he finds himself among flowery meadows, with which the Elysian fields are not to be compared. The sky seems more transparent there, and the sun shines with a strange brilliancy, and a delightful grove of green leafy trees presents itself to the eyes and charms the sight with its verdure, while the ear is soothed by the sweet untutored melody of the countless birds of gay plumage that flit to and fro among the interlacing branches. Here he sees a brook whose limpid waters, like liquid crystal, ripple over fine sands and white pebbles that look like sifted gold and purest pearls. There he perceives a cunningly wrought fountain of many-colored jasper and polished marble; here another of rustic fashion where the little mussel-shells and the spiral white and yellow mansions of the snail disposed in studious disorder, mingled with fragments of glittering crystal and mock emeralds, make up a work of varied aspect, where art, imitating nature, seems to have outdone it. Suddenly there is presented to his sight a strong castle or gorgeous palace with walls of massy gold, turrets of diamond and gates of jacinth; in short, so marvellous is its structure that though the materials of which it is built are nothing less than diamonds, carbuncles, rubies, pearls, gold, and emeralds, the workmanship is still more rare. And after having seen all this, what can be more charming than to see how a bevy of damsels comes forth from the gate of the castle in gay and gorgeous attire, such that, were I to set myself now to depict it as the histories describe it to us, I should never have done; and then how she who seems to be the first among them all takes the bold knight who plunged into the boiling lake by the hand, and without addressing a word to him leads him into the rich palace or castle, and strips him as naked as when his mother bore him, and bathes him in lukewarm water, and anoints him all over with sweet-smelling unguents, and clothes him in a shirt of the softest sendal, all scented and perfumed, while another damsel comes and throws over his shoulders a mantle which is said to be worth at the very least a city, and even more? How charming it is, then, when they tell us how, after all this, they lead him to another chamber where he finds the tables set out in such style that he is filled with amazement and wonder; to see how they pour out water for his hands distilled from amber and sweet-scented flowers; how they seat him on an ivory chair; to see how the damsels wait on him all in profound silence; how they bring him such a variety of dainties so temptingly prepared that the appetite is at a loss which to select; to hear the music that resounds while he is at table, by whom or whence produced he knows not. And then when the repast is over and the tables removed, for the knight to recline in the chair, picking his teeth perhaps as usual, and a damsel, much lovelier than any of the others, to enter unexpectedly by the chamber door, and seat herself by his side, and begin to tell him what the castle is, and how she is held enchanted there, and other things that amaze the knight and astonish the readers who are perusing his history. But I will not expatiate any further upon this, as it may be gathered from it that whatever part of whatever history of a knight-errant one reads, it will fill the reader, whoever he be, with delight and wonder; and take my advice, sir, and, as I said before, read these books and you will see how they will banish any melancholy you may feel and raise your spirits should they be depressed. For myself I can say that since I have been a knight-errant I have become valiant, polite, generous, well-bred, magnanimous, courteous, dauntless, gentle, patient, and have learned to bear hardships, imprisonments, and enchantments; and though it be such a short time since I have seen myself shut up in a cage like a madman, I hope by the might of my arm, if Heaven aid me and fortune thwart me not, to see myself king of some kingdom where I may be able to show the gratitude and generosity that dwell in my heart; for by my faith, señor, the poor man is incapacitated from showing the virtue of generosity to any one, though he may possess it in the highest degree; and gratitude that consists of disposition only is a dead thing, just as faith without works is dead. For this reason I should be glad were fortune soon to offer me some opportunity of making myself an emperor, so as to show my heart in doing good to my friends, particularly to this poor Sancho Panza, my squire, who is the best fellow in the world; and I would gladly give him a county I have promised him this ever so long, only that I am afraid he has not the capacity to govern his realm."

Sancho partly heard these last words of his master, and said to him, "Strive hard you, Señor Don Quixote, to give me that county so often promised by you and so long looked for by me, for I promise you there will be no want of capacity in me to govern it; and even if there is, I have heard say there are men in the world who farm seigniories, paying so much a year, and they themselves taking charge of the government, while the lord, with his legs stretched out, enjoys the revenue they pay him, without troubling himself about anything else. That's what I'll do, and not stand haggling over trifles, but wash my hands at once of the whole business, and enjoy my rents like a duke, and let things go their own way."

"That, brother Sancho," said the canon, "only holds good as far as the enjoyment of the revenue goes; but the lord of the seigniory must attend to the administration of justice, and here capacity and sound judgment come in, and above all a firm determination to find out the truth; for if this be wanting in the beginning, the middle and the end will always go wrong; and God as commonly aids the honest intentions of the simple as he frustrates the evil designs of the crafty."

"I don't understand those philosophies," returned Sancho Panza; "all I know is I would I had the county as soon as I shall know how to govern it; for I have as much soul as another, and as much body as any one, and I shall be as much king of my realm as any other of his; and being so I should do as I liked, and doing as I liked I should please myself, and pleasing myself I should be content, and when one is content he has nothing more to desire, and when one has nothing more to desire there is an end of it; so let the county come, and God be with you, and let us see one another, as one blind man said to the other."

"That is not bad philosophy thou art talking, Sancho," said the canon; "but for all that there is a good deal to be said on this matter of counties."

To which Don Quixote returned, "I know not what more there is to be said; I only guide myself by the example set me by the great Amadis of Gaul, when he made his squire count of the Insula Firme; and so, without any scruples of conscience, I can make a count of Sancho Panza, for he is one of the best squires that ever knight-errant had."

The canon was astonished at the methodical nonsense (if nonsense be capable of method) that Don Quixote uttered, at the way in which he had described the adventure of the knight of the lake, at the impression that the deliberate lies of the books he read had made upon him, and lastly he marvelled at the simplicity of Sancho, who desired so eagerly to obtain the county his master had promised him. [. . .]

Part II

Chapter 3

OF THE LAUGHABLE CONVERSATION THAT PASSED BETWEEN DON QUIXOTE, SANCHO PANZA, AND THE BACHELOR SAMSON CARRASCO

Don Quixote remained very deep in thought, waiting for the bachelor Carrasco,[33] from whom he was to hear how he himself had been put into a book as Sancho said; and he could not persuade himself that any such history could be in existence, for the blood of the enemies he had slain was not yet dry on the blade of his sword, and now they wanted to make out that his mighty achievements were going about in print. For all that, he fancied some sage, either a friend or an enemy, might, by the

[33] **Carrasco:** A young man from La Mancha who has just earned his bachelor's degree at the University of Salamanca and returned home. He informs the Don that his story has been published in a book.

aid of magic, have given them to the press; if a friend, in order to magnify and exalt them above the most famous ever achieved by any knight-errant; if an enemy, to bring them to naught and degrade them below the meanest ever recorded of any low squire, though, as he said to himself, the achievements of squires never were recorded. If, however, it were the fact that such a history were in existence, it must necessarily, being the story of a knight-errant, be grandiloquent, lofty, imposing, grand and true. With this he comforted himself somewhat, though it made him uncomfortable to think that the author was a Moor, judging by the title of "Cid";[34] and that no truth was to be looked for from Moors, as they are all impostors, cheats, and schemers. He was afraid he might have dealt with his love affairs in some indecorous fashion, that might tend to the discredit and prejudice of the purity of his lady Dulcinea del Toboso; he would have had him set forth the fidelity and respect he had always observed towards her, spurning queens, empresses, and damsels of all sorts, and keeping in check the impetuosity of his natural impulses. Absorbed and wrapped up in these and divers other cogitations, he was found by Sancho and Carrasco, whom Don Quixote received with great courtesy.

The bachelor, though he was called Samson, was of no great bodily size, but he was a very great wag; he was of a sallow complexion, but very sharp-witted, somewhere about four-and-twenty years of age, with a round face, flat nose, and a large mouth, all indications of a mischievous disposition and a love of fun and jokes; and of this he gave a sample as soon as he saw Don Quixote, by falling on his knees before him and saying, "Let me kiss your mightiness's hand, Señor Don Quixote of La Mancha, for, by the habit of St. Peter that I wear, though I have no more than the first four orders, your worship is one of the most famous knights-errant that have ever been, or will be, all the world over. A blessing on Cid Hamet Benengeli, who has written the history of your great deeds, and a double blessing on that connoisseur who took the trouble of having it translated out of the Arabic into our Castilian vulgar tongue for the universal entertainment of the people!"

Don Quixote made him rise, and said, "So, then, it is true that there is a history of me, and that it was a Moor and a sage who wrote it?"

"So true is it, señor," said Samson, "that my belief is there are more than twelve thousand volumes of the said history in print this very day. Only ask Portugal, Barcelona, and Valencia, where they have been printed, and moreover there is a report that it is being printed at Antwerp, and I am persuaded there will not be a country or language in which there will not be a translation of it."

"One of the things," here observed Don Quixote, "that ought to give most pleasure to a virtuous and eminent man is to find himself in his lifetime in print and in type, familiar in people's mouths with a good name; I say with a good name, for if it be the opposite, then there is no death to be compared to it."

"If it goes by good name and fame," said the bachelor, "your worship alone bears away the palm from all the knights-errant; for the Moor in his own language,

[34] **Moor . . . "Cid":** Carrasco has told Sancho that the author of Don Quixote's adventures is called Cid Hamet Benengele.

and the Christian in his, have taken care to set before us your gallantry, your high courage in encountering dangers, your fortitude in adversity, your patience under misfortunes as well as wounds, the purity and continence of the platonic loves of your worship and my lady Doña Dulcinea del Toboso"—

"I never heard my lady Dulcinea called Doña," observed Sancho here; "nothing more than the lady Dulcinea del Toboso; so here already the history is wrong."

"That is not an objection of any importance," replied Carrasco.

"Certainly not," said Don Quixote; "but tell me, señor bachelor, what deeds of mine are they that are made most of in this history?"

"On that point," replied the bachelor, "opinions differ, as tastes do; some swear by the adventure of the windmills that your worship took to be Briareuses and giants; others by that of the fulling mills; one cries up the description of the two armies that afterwards took the appearance of two droves of sheep; another that of the dead body on its way to be buried at Segovia; a third says the liberation of the galley slaves is the best of all, and a fourth that nothing comes up to the affair with the Benedictine giants, and the battle with the valiant Biscayan."[35]

"Tell me, señor bachelor," said Sancho at this point, "does the adventure with the Yanguesans come in, when our good Rocinante went hankering after dainties?"

"The sage has left nothing in the ink-bottle," replied Samson; "he tells all and sets down everything, even to the capers the worthy Sancho cut in the blanket."

"I cut no capers in the blanket," returned Sancho; "in the air I did, and more of them than I liked."

"There is no human history in the world, I suppose," said Don Quixote, "that has not its ups and downs, but more than others such as deal with chivalry, for they can never be entirely made up of prosperous adventures."

"For all that," replied the bachelor, "there are those who have read the history who say they would have been glad if the author had left out some of the countless cudgellings that were inflicted on Señor Don Quixote in various encounters."

"That's where the truth of the history comes in," said Sancho.

"At the same time they might fairly have passed them over in silence," observed Don Quixote; "for there is no need of recording events which do not change or affect the truth of a history, if they tend to bring the hero of it into contempt. Æneas was not in truth and earnest so pious as Virgil represents him, nor Ulysses so wise as Homer describes him."

"That is true," said Samson; "but it is one thing to write as a poet, another to write as a historian; the poet may describe or sing things, not as they were, but as they ought to have been; but the historian has to write them down, not as they ought to have been, but as they were, without adding anything to the truth or taking anything from it."

"Well then," said Sancho, "if this señor Moor goes in for telling the truth, no doubt among my master's drubbings mine are to be found; for they never took the measure of his worship's shoulders without doing the same for my whole body; but I

[35] **"the adventure . . . Biscayan":** These are all episodes from Part I.

have no right to wonder at that, for, as my master himself says, the members must share the pain of the head."

"You are a sly dog, Sancho," said Don Quixote; "i' faith, you have no want of memory when you choose to remember."

"If I were to try to forget the thwacks they gave me," said Sancho, "my weals would not let me, for they are still fresh on my ribs."

"Hush, Sancho," said Don Quixote, "and don't interrupt the bachelor, whom I entreat to go on and tell me all that is said about me in this same history."

"And about me," said Sancho, "for they say, too, that I am one of the principal presonages in it."

"Personages, not presonages, friend Sancho," said Samson.

"What! Another word-catcher!" said Sancho; "if that's to be the way we shall not make an end in a lifetime."

"May God shorten mine, Sancho," returned the bachelor, "if you are not the second person in the history, and there are even some who would rather hear you talk than the cleverest in the whole book; though there are some, too, who say you showed yourself over-credulous in believing there was any possibility in the government of that island offered you by Señor Don Quixote here."

"There is still sunshine on the wall," said Don Quixote; "and when Sancho is somewhat more advanced in life, with the experience that years bring, he will be fitter and better qualified for being a governor than he is at present."

"By God, master," said Sancho, "the island that I can not govern with the years I have, I'll not be able to govern with the years of Methuselam; the difficulty is that the said island keeps its distance somewhere, I know not where; and not that there is any want of head in me to govern it."

"Leave it to God, Sancho," said Don Quixote, "for all will be well, and perhaps better than you think; no leaf on the tree stirs but by God's will."

"That is true," said Samson; "and if it be God's will, there will not be any want of a thousand islands, much less one, for Sancho to govern."

"I have seen governors in these parts," said Sancho, "that are not to be compared to my shoesole; and for all that they are called 'your lordship' and served on silver."

"Those are not governors of islands," observed Samson, "but of other governments of an easier kind: those that govern islands must at least know grammar."

"I could manage the gram well enough," said Sancho; "but for the mar I have neither leaning nor liking, for I don't know what it is; but leaving this matter of the government in God's hands, to send me wherever it may be most to his service, I may tell you, señor bachelor Samson Carrasco, it has pleased me beyond measure that the author of this history should have spoken of me in such a way that what is said of me gives no offence; for, on the faith of a true squire, if he had said anything about me that was at all unbecoming an old Christian, such as I am, the deaf would have heard of it."

"That would be working miracles," said Samson.

"Miracles or no miracles," said Sancho, "let every one mind how he speaks or writes about people, and not set down at random the first thing that comes into his head."

"One of the faults they find with this history," said the bachelor, "is that its author inserted in it a novel called *The Ill-advised Curiosity;* not that it is bad or ill-told, but that it is out of place and has nothing to do with the history of his worship Señor Don Quixote."

"I will bet the son of a dog has mixed the cabbages and the baskets," said Sancho.

"Then, I say," said Don Quixote, "the author of my history was no sage, but some ignorant chatterer, who, in a haphazard and heedless way, set about writing it, let it turn out as it might, just as Orbaneja, the painter of Úbeda, used to do, who, when they asked him what he was painting, answered 'What it may turn out.' Sometimes he would paint a cock in such a fashion, and so unlike, that he had to write alongside of it in Gothic letters, 'This is a cock'; and so it will be with my history, which will require a commentary to make it intelligible."

"No fear of that," returned Samson, "for it is so plain that there is nothing in it to puzzle over; the children turn its leaves, the young people read it, the grown men understand it, the old folk praise; in a word, it is so thumbed, and read, and got by heart by people of all sorts, that the instant they see any lean hack, they say, 'There goes Rocinante.' And those that are most given to reading it are the pages, for there is not a lord's ante-chamber where there is not a *Don Quixote* to be found; one takes it up if another lays it down; this one pounces upon it, and that begs for it. In short, the said history is the most delightful and least injurious entertainment that has been hitherto seen, for there is not to be found in the whole of it even the semblance of an immodest word, or a thought that is other than Catholic."

"To write in any other way," said Don Quixote, "would not be to write truth, but falsehood, and historians who have recourse to falsehood, ought to be burned, like those who coin false money; and I know not what could have led the author to have recourse to novels and irrelevant stories, when he had so much to write about in mine; no doubt he must have gone by the proverb 'with straw or with hay, etc.,'[36] for by merely setting forth my thoughts, my sighs, my tears, my lofty purposes, my enterprises, he might have made a volume as large, or larger than all the works of El Tostado[37] would make up. In fact, the conclusion I arrive at, señor bachelor, is, that to write histories, or books of any kind, there is need of great judgment and a ripe understanding. To give expression to humor, and write in a strain of graceful pleasantry, is the gift of great geniuses. The cleverest character in comedy is the clown, for he who would make people take him for a fool, must not be one. History is in a measure a sacred thing, for it should be true, and where the truth is, there God is, so far as truth is concerned; but notwithstanding this, there are some who write and fling books broadcast on the world as if they were fritters."

"There is no book so bad but it has something good in it," said the bachelor.

"No doubt of that," replied Don Quixote; "but it often happens that those who have acquired and attained a well-desired reputation by their writings, lose it entirely, or damage it in some degree, when they give them to the press."

---

[36] **" 'with . . . hay' ":** ". . . fill my belly all the way."

[37] **"El Tostado":** An author of many devotional works.

"The reason of that," said Samson, "is, that as printed works are examined leisurely, their faults are easily seen; and the greater the fame of the writer, the more closely are they scrutinized. Men famous for their genius, great poets, illustrious historians, are always, or most commonly, envied by those who take a particular delight and pleasure in criticising the writings of others, without having produced any of their own."

"That is no wonder," said Don Quixote; "for there are many divines who are no good for the pulpit, but excellent in detecting the defects or excesses of those who preach."

"All that is true, Señor Don Quixote," said Carrasco; "but I wish such fault-finders were more lenient and less exacting, and did not pay so much attention to the spots on the bright sun of the work they grumble at; for if *aliquando bonus dormitat Homerus,*[38] they should remember how long he remained awake to shed the light of his work with as little shade as possible; and perhaps it may be that what they find fault with may be moles, that sometimes heighten the beauty of the face that bears them; and so I say very great is the risk to which he who prints a book exposes himself, for of all impossibilities the greatest is to write one that will satisfy and please all readers."

"That which treats of me must have pleased few," said Don Quixote.

"Quite the contrary," said the bachelor; "for, as *stultorum infinitus est numerus,*[39] innumerable are those who have relished the said history; but some have brought a charge against the author's memory, inasmuch as he forgot to say who the thief was who stole Sancho's Dapple; for it is not stated there, but only to be inferred from what is set down, that he was stolen, and a little farther on we see Sancho mounted on the same ass, without any re-appearance of it. They say, too, that he forgot to state what Sancho did with those hundred crowns that he found in the valise in the Sierra Morena, as he never alludes to them again, and there are many who would be glad to know what he did with them, or what he spent them on, for it is one of the serious omissions of the work."

"Señor Samson, I am not in a humor now for going into accounts or explanations," said Sancho; "for there's a sinking of the stomach come over me, and unless I doctor it with a couple of sups of the old stuff it will put me on the thorn of Santa Lucia.[40] I have it at home, and my old woman is waiting for me; after dinner I'll come back, and will answer you and all the world every question you may choose to ask, as well about the loss of the ass as about the spending of the hundred crowns"; and without another word or waiting for a reply he made off home.

Don Quixote begged and entreated the bachelor to stay and do penance with him. The bachelor accepted the invitation and remained, a couple of young pigeons were added to the ordinary fare, at dinner they talked chivalry, Carrasco fell in with his host's humor, the banquet came to an end, they took their afternoon sleep, Sancho returned, and the previous conversation was resumed.

---

[38] ***"aliquando . . . Homerus":*** "Worthy Homer sometimes nods" (Horace, *Art of Poetry*).

[39] ***"stultorum . . . numerus":*** "Infinite is the number of fools" (*Ecclesiastes,* I:15).

[40] **"put . . . Lucia":** Make me weak with hunger.

FROM

Chapter 4

IN WHICH SANCHO PANZA GIVES A SATISFACTORY REPLY TO THE DOUBTS AND QUESTIONS OF THE BACHELOR SAMSON CARRASCO, TOGETHER WITH OTHER MATTERS WORTH KNOWING AND MENTIONING

. . . "Does the author promise a second part at all?" said Don Quixote.

"He does promise one," replied Samson; "but he says he has not found it, nor does he know who has got it; and we can not say whether it will appear or not; and so, on that head, as some say that no second part has ever been good, and others that enough has been already written about Don Quixote, it is thought there will be no second part; though some, who are jovial rather than saturnine, say, 'Let us have more Quixotades, let Don Quixote charge and Sancho chatter, and no matter what it may turn out, we shall be satisfied with that.' "

"And what does the author mean to do?" said Don Quixote.

"What?" replied Samson; "why, as soon as he has found the history which he is now searching for with extraordinary diligence, he will at once give it to the press, moved more by the profit that may accrue to him from doing so than by any thought of praise."

Whereat Sancho observed, "The author looks for money and profit, does he? It will be a wonder if he succeeds, for it will be only hurry, hurry, with him, like the tailor on Easter Eve; and works done in a hurry are never finished as perfectly as they ought to be. Let Master Moor, or whatever he is, pay attention to what he is doing, and I and my master will give him as much grouting ready to his hand, in the way of adventures and accidents of all sorts, as would make up not only one second part, but a hundred. The good man fancies, no doubt, that we are fast asleep in the straw here, but let him hold up our feet to be shod and he will see which foot it is we go lame on. All I say is, that if my master would take my advice, we would be now afield, redressing outrages and righting wrongs, as is the use and custom of good knights-errant."

Sancho had hardly uttered these words when the neighing of Rocinante fell upon their ears, which neighing Don Quixote accepted as a happy omen, and he resolved to make another sally in three or four days from that time. Announcing his intention to the bachelor, he asked his advice as to the quarter in which he ought to commence his expedition, and the bachelor replied that in his opinion he ought to go to the kingdom of Aragon, and the city of Saragossa, where there were to be certain solemn joustings at the festival of St. George, at which he might win renown above all the knights of Aragon, which would be winning it above all the knights of the world. He commended his very praiseworthy and gallant resolution, but admonished him to proceed with greater caution in encountering dangers, because his life did not belong to him, but to all those who had need of him to protect and aid them in their misfortunes.

"There's where it is, what I abominate, Señor Samson," said Sancho here; "my master will attack a hundred armed men as a greedy boy would a half dozen melons. Body of the world, señor bachelor! there is a time to attack and a time to retreat, and it is not to be always 'Santiago, and close Spain!' Moreover, I have heard it said (and I think by my master himself, if I remember rightly) that the mean of valor lies between the extremes of cowardice and rashness; and if that be so, I don't want him to fly without having good reason, or to attack when the odds make it better not. But, above all things, I warn my master that if he is to take me with him it must be on the condition that he is to do all the fighting, and that I am not to be called upon to do anything except what concerns keeping him clean and comfortable; in this I will dance attendance on him readily; but to expect me to draw sword, even against rascally churls of the hatchet and hood, is idle. I don't set up to be a fighting man, Señor Samson, but only the best and most loyal squire that ever served knight-errant; and if my master Don Quixote, in consideration of my many faithful services, is pleased to give me some island of the many his worship says one may stumble on in these parts, I will take it as a great favor; and if he does not give it to me, I was born like every one else, and a man must not live in dependence on any one except God; and what is more, my bread will taste as well, and perhaps even better, without a government than if I were a governor; and how do I know but that in these governments the devil may have prepared some trip for me, to make me lose my footing and fall and knock my grinders out? Sancho I was born and Sancho I mean to die. But for all that, if Heaven were to make me a fair offer of an island or something else of the kind, without much trouble and without much risk, I am not such a fool as to refuse it; for they say, too, 'when they offer thee a heifer, run with a halter'; and 'when good luck comes to thee, take it in.'"

"Brother Sancho," said Carrasco, "you have spoken like a professor; but, for all that, put your trust in God and in Señor Don Quixote, for he will give you a kingdom, not to say an island."

"It is all the same, be it more or be it less," replied Sancho; "though I can tell Señor Carrasco that my master would not throw the kingdom he might give me into a sack all in holes; for I have felt my own pulse and I find myself sound enough to rule kingdoms and govern islands; and I have before now told my master as much."

"Take care, Sancho," said Samson; "honors change manners, and perhaps when you find yourself a governor you won't know the mother that bore you."

"That may hold good of those that are born in the ditches," said Sancho, "not of those who have the fat of an old Christian four fingers deep on their souls, as I have. Nay, only look at my disposition, is that likely to show ingratitude to any one?"

"God grant it," said Don Quixote; "we shall see when the government comes; and I seem to see it already."

He then begged the bachelor, if he were a poet, to do him the favor of composing some verses for him conveying the farewell he meant to take of his lady Dulcinea del Toboso, and to see that a letter of her name was placed at the beginning of each line, so that, at the end of the verses, "Dulcinea del Toboso" might be read by putting together the first letters. The bachelor replied that although he was not one of the famous poets of Spain, who were, they said, only three and a half, he would not fail to compose the required verses; though he saw a great difficulty in the task, as the letters which made up the name were seventeen; so, if he made four ballad stanzas of four lines each, there would be a letter over, and if he made them of five, what they called *decimas* or *redondillas,* there were three letters short; nevertheless he would try to drop a letter as well as he could, so that the name "Dulcinea del Toboso" might be got into four ballad stanzas.

"It must be, by some means or other," said Don Quixote, "for unless the name stands there plain and manifest, no woman would believe the verses were made for her."

They agreed upon this, and that the departure should take place in three days from that time. Don Quixote charged the bachelor to keep it a secret, especially from the curate and Master Nicholas, and from his niece and the housekeeper, lest they should prevent the execution of his praiseworthy and valiant purpose. Carrasco promised all, and then took his leave, charging Don Quixote to inform him of his good or evil fortunes whenever he had an opportunity; and thus they bade each other farewell, and Sancho went away to make the necessary preparations for their expedition.

Chapter 5

OF THE SHREWD AND DROLL CONVERSATION THAT PASSED BETWEEN SANCHO PANZA AND HIS WIFE TERESA PANZA, AND OTHER MATTERS WORTHY OF BEING DULY RECORDED

The translator of this history, when he comes to write this fifth chapter, says that he considers it apocryphal, because in it Sancho Panza speaks in a style unlike that which might have been expected from his limited intelligence, and says things so subtle that he does not think it possible he could have conceived them; however, desirous of doing what his task imposed upon him, he was unwilling to leave it untranslated, and therefore he went on to say:

Sancho came home in such glee and spirits that his wife noticed his happiness a bowshot off, so much so that it made her ask him, "What have you got, Sancho friend, that you are so glad?"

To which he replied, "Wife, if it were God's will, I should be very glad not to be so well pleased as I show myself."

"I don't understand you, husband," said she, "and I don't know what you mean by saying you would be glad, if it were God's will, not to be well pleased; for, fool as I am, I don't know how one can find pleasure in not having it."

"Hark ye, Teresa," replied Sancho, "I am glad because I have made up my mind to go back to the service of my master Don Quixote, who means to go out a third time to seek for adventures; and I am going with him again, for my necessities will have it so, and also the hope that cheers me with the thought that I may find another hundred crowns like those we have spent; though it makes me sad to have to leave thee and the children; and if God would be pleased to let me have my daily bread, dry-shod and at home, without taking me out into the byways and cross-roads—and he could do it at small cost by merely willing it—it is clear my happiness would be more solid and lasting, for the happiness I have is mingled with sorrow at leaving thee; so that I was right in saying I would be glad, if it were God's will, not to be well pleased."

"Look here, Sancho," said Teresa; "ever since you joined on to a knight-errant you talk in such a roundabout way that there is no understanding you."

"It is enough that God understands me, wife," replied Sancho; "for he is the understander of all things; that will do; but mind, sister, you must look to Dapple carefully for the next three days, so that he may be fit to take arms; double his feed and see to the pack-saddle and other harness, for it is not to a wedding we are bound, but to go round the world, and play at give and take with giants and dragons and monsters, and hear hissings and roarings and bellowings and howlings; and even all this would be lavender, if we had not to reckon with Yanguesans and enchanted Moors."

"I know well enough, husband," said Teresa, "that squires-errant don't eat their bread for nothing, and so I will be always praying to our Lord to deliver you speedily from all that hard fortune."

"I can tell you, wife," said Sancho, "if I did not expect to see myself governor of an island before long, I would drop down dead on the spot."

"Nay, then, husband," said Teresa, "let the hen live, though it be with her pip; live, and let the devil take all the governments in the world; you came out of your mother's womb without a government, you have lived until now without a government, and when it is God's will you will go, or be carried, to your grave without a government. How many there are in the world who live without a government, and continue to live all the same, and are reckoned in the number of the people. The best sauce in the world is hunger, and as the poor are never without that, they always eat with a relish. But mind, Sancho, if by good luck you should find yourself with some government, don't forget me and your children. Remember that Sanchico is now full fifteen, and it is right he should go to school, if his uncle the abbot has a mind to have him trained for the Church. Consider, too, that your daughter Mari-Sancha will not die of grief if we marry her; for I have my suspicions that she is as eager to get a husband as you to get a government; and, after all, a daughter looks better ill-married than well kept."

"By my faith," replied Sancho, "if God brings me to get any sort of a government, I intend, wife, to make such a high match for Mari-Sancha that there will be no approaching her without calling her 'my lady.'"

"Nay, Sancho," returned Teresa, "marry her to her equal, that is the safest plan; for if you put her out of wooden clogs into high-heeled shoes, out of her gray flannel petticoat into hoops and silk gowns, out the plain 'Marica' and 'thou,' into 'Doña So-and-so' and 'my lady,' the girl won't know where she is, and at every turn she will fall into a thousand blunders that will show the thread of her coarse homespun stuff."

"Tut, you fool," said Sancho; "it will be only to practise it for two or three years; and then dignity and decorum will fit her as easily as a glove; and if not, what matter? Let her be 'my lady,' and never mind what happens."

"Keep to your own station, Sancho," replied Teresa; "don't try to raise yourself higher, and bear in mind the proverb that says, 'wipe the nose of your neighbor's son, and take him into your house.' A fine thing it would be, indeed, to marry our Maria to some great count or grand gentleman, who, when the humor took him, would abuse her and call her clown-bred and clodhopper's daughter and spinning wench. I have not been bringing up my daughter for that all this time, I can tell you, husband. Do you bring home money, Sancho, and leave marrying her to my care; there is Lope Tocho, Juan Tocho's son, a stout, sturdy young fellow that we know, and I can see he does not look sour at the girl; and with him, one of our own sort, she will be well married, and we shall have her always under our eyes, and be all one family, parents and children, grandchildren and sons-in-law, and the peace and blessing of God will dwell among us; so don't you go marrying her in those courts and grand palaces where they won't know what to make of her, or she what to make of herself."

"Why, you idiot and wife for Barabbas," said Sancho, "what do you mean by trying, without why or wherefore, to keep me from marrying my daughter to one who will give me grandchildren that will be called 'your lordship?' Look ye, Teresa, I have always heard my elders say that he who does not know how to take advantage of luck when it comes to him, has no right to complain if it gives him the go-by; and now that it is knocking at our door, it will not do to shut it out; let us go with the favoring breeze that blows upon us." (It is this sort of talk, and what Sancho says lower down, that made the translator of the history say he considered this chapter apocryphal.) "Don't you see, you animal," continued Sancho, "that it will be well for me to drop into some profitable government that will lift us out of the mire, and marry Mari-Sancha to whom I like; and you yourself will find yourself called 'Doña Teresa Panza,' and sitting in church on a fine carpet and cushions and draperies, in spite and in defiance of all the born ladies of the town? No, stay as you are, growing neither greater nor less, like a tapestry figure—Let us say no more about it, for Sanchia shall be a countess, say what you will."

"Are you sure of all you say, husband?" replied Teresa. "Well, for all that, I am afraid this rank of countess for my daughter will be her ruin. You do as you like, make a duchess or a princess of her, but I can tell you it will not be with my will and consent. I was always a lover of equality, brother, and I can't bear to see people give themselves airs without any right. They called me Teresa at my baptism, a plain, simple name, without any additions or tags or fringes of Dons or Doñas; Cascajo was my father's name, and as I am your wife, I am called Teresa Panza, though by right I ought to be called Teresa Cascajo; but 'kings go where laws like,' and I am content with this name without having the 'Don' put on top of it to make it so heavy that I can not carry it; and I don't want to make people talk about me when they see me go dressed like a countess or governor's wife; for they will say at once, 'See what airs the slut gives herself! Only yesterday she was always spinning flax, and used to go to Mass with the tail of her petticoat over her head instead of a mantle, and there she goes today in a hooped gown with her brooches and airs, as if we didn't know her!' If God keeps me in my seven senses, or five, or whatever number I have, I am not going to bring myself to such a pass; go you, brother, and be a government or an island man, and swagger as much as you like; for by the soul of my mother, neither my daughter nor I are going to stir a step from our village; a respectable woman should have a broken leg and keep at home; and to be busy at something is a virtuous damsel's holiday; be off to your adventures along with your Don Quixote, and leave us to our misadventures, for God will mend them for us according as we deserve it. I don't know, I'm sure, who fixed the 'Don' to him, what neither his father nor grandfather ever had."

"I declare thou hast a devil of some sort in thy body!" said Sancho. "God help thee, woman, what a lot of things thou hast strung together, one after the other, without head or tail! What have Cascajo, and the brooches and the proverbs and the airs, to do with what I say? Look here, fool and dolt (for so I may call you, when you don't understand my words, and run away from good fortune), if I had said that my daughter was to throw herself down from a tower, or go roaming the world, as the Infanta Doña Urraca[41] wanted to do, you would be right in not giving way to my will; but if in an instant, in less than the twinkling of an eye, I put the 'Don' and 'my lady' on her back, and take her out of the stubble, and place her under the canopy, on a daïs, and on a couch, with more velvet cushions than all the Almohades of Morocco[42] ever had in their family, why won't you consent and fall in with my wishes?"

"Do you know why, husband?" replied Teresa; "because of the proverb that says 'who covers thee, discovers thee.' At the poor man people only throw a hasty glance; on the rich man they fixed their eyes; and if the said rich man was once on a time poor, it is then there is the sneering and the tattle and spite of backbiters; and in the streets here they swarm as thick as bees."

"Look here, Teresa," said Sancho, "and listen to what I am now going to say to you; maybe you never heard it in all your life; and I do not give my own notions, for what I am about to say are the opinions of his reverence the preacher, who preached in this town last Lent, and who said, if I remember rightly, that all things present that our eyes behold, bring themselves before us, and remain and fix themselves on our memory much better and more forcibly than things past." (These observations which Sancho makes here are the other ones on account of which the translator says he regards this chapter as apocryphal, inasmuch as they are beyond Sancho's capacity.) "Whence it arises," he continued, "that when we see any person well-dressed and making a figure with rich garments and retinue of servants, it seems to lead and impel us perforce to respect him, though memory may at the same moment recall to us some lowly condition in which we have seen him, but which, whether it may have been poverty or low birth, being now a thing of the past, has no existence; while the only thing that has any existence is what we see before us; and if this person whom fortune has raised from his original lowly state (these were the very words the padre used) to his present height of prosperity, be well bred, generous, courteous to all, without seeking to vie with those whose nobility is of ancient date, depend upon it, Teresa, no one will remember what he was, and every one will respect what he is, except indeed the envious, from whom no fair fortune is safe."

"I do not understand you, husband," replied Teresa; "do as you like, and don't break my head with any more speechifying and rhetoric; and if you have revolved to do what you say"—

---

[41] **"Doña Urraca:"** When Doña Urraca was left out of her father's will, she threatened to take up a disreputable life on the streets. He then changed his will and left her the city of Zamora.

[42] **"Almohades of Morocco":** Sancho confuses the Spanish word for cushion *(almohada)* with an Islamic sect from North Africa, the Almohades.

"Resolved, you should say, woman," said Sancho, "not revolved."

"Don't set yourself to wrangle with me, husband," said Teresa; "I speak as God pleases, and don't deal in out-of-the-way phrases; and I say if you are bent upon having a government, take your son Sancho with you, and teach him from this time on how to hold a government; for sons ought to inherit and learn the trades of their fathers."

"As soon as I have the government," said Sancho, "I will send for him by post, and I will send thee money, of which I shall have no lack, for there is never any want of people to lend it to governors when they have not got it; and do thou dress him so as to hide what he is and make him look what he is to be."

"You send the money," said Teresa, "and I'll dress him up for you as fine as you please."

"Then we are agreed that our daughter is to be a countess," said Sancho.

"The day that I see her a countess," replied Teresa, "it will be the same to me as if I was burying her; but once more I say do as you please, for we women are born to this burden of being obedient to our husbands, though they be blockheads"; and with this she began to weep in downright earnest, as if she already saw Sanchica dead and buried.

Sancho consoled her by saying that though he must make her a countess, he would put it off as long as possible. Here their conversation came to an end, and Sancho went back to see Don Quixote, and make arrangements for their departure. . . .

FROM
Chapter 22

WHEREIN IS RELATED THE GRAND ADVENTURE OF THE CAVE OF MONTESINOS IN THE HEART OF LA MANCHA, WHICH THE VALIANT DON QUIXOTE BROUGHT TO A HAPPY TERMINATION

. . . Don Quixote begged the fencing licentiate to find him a guide to show him the way to the cave of Montesinos, as he had a great desire to enter it and see with his own eyes if the wonderful tales that were told of it all over the country were true. The licentiate said he would get him a cousin of his own, a famous scholar, and one very much given to reading books of chivalry, who would have great pleasure in conducting him to the mouth of the very cave, and would show him the lakes of Ruidera, which were likewise famous all over La Mancha, and even all over Spain; and he assured him he would find him entertaining, for he was a youth who could write books good enough to be printed and dedicated to princes. The cousin arrived at last, leading an ass in foal, with a pack-saddle covered with a party-colored carpet or sackcloth; Sancho saddled Rocinante, got Dapple ready, and stocked his *alforjas,* along with which went those of the cousin, likewise well filled; and so, commending themselves to God and bidding farewell to all, they set out, taking the road for the famous cave of Montesinos.

On the way Don Quixote asked the cousin of what sort and character his pursuits, avocations, and studies were, to which he replied that he was by profession a humanist, and that his pursuits and studies were making books for the press, all of great utility and no less entertainment to the nation. One was called *The Book of Liveries,* in which he described seven hundred and three liveries, with their colors, mottoes, and ciphers, from which gentlemen of the court might pick and choose any they fancied for festivals and revels, without having to go a begging for them from any one, or puzzling their brains, as the saying is, to have them appropriate to their objects and purposes; "for," said he, "I give the jealous, the rejected, the forgotten, the absent, what will suit them, and fit them without fail. I have another book, too, which I shall call *Metamorphoses, or the Spanish Ovid,*[43] one of rare and original invention; for, imitating Ovid in burlesque style, I show in it who the Giralda of Seville and the Angel of the Magdalena were, what the sewer of Vecinguerra at Cordova was, what the bulls of Guisando, the Sierra Morena, the Leganitos and Lavapiés fountains at Madrid, not forgetting those of el Piojo, of the Caño Dorado, and of the Priora; and all with their allegories, metaphors, and changes, so that they are amusing, interesting, and instructive, all at once. Another book I have which I call *The Supplement to Polydore Vergil,*[44] which treats of the invention of things, and is a work of great erudition and research, for I establish and elucidate elegantly some things of great importance which Polydore omitted to mention. He forgot to tell us who was the first man in the world that had a cold in his head, and who was the first to try salivation for the French disease, but I give it accurately set forth, and quote more than five-and-twenty authors in proof of it, so your worship may perceive I have labored to good purpose and that the book will be of service to the whole world."

Sancho, who had been very attentive to the cousin's words, said to him, "Tell me, señor,—and God give you luck in printing your books,—can you tell me (for of course you know, as you know everything) who was the first man that scratched his head? For to my thinking it must have been our father Adam."

"So it must," replied the cousin; "for there is no doubt but Adam had a head and hair; and being the first man in the world he would have scratched himself sometimes."

"So I think," said Sancho; "but now tell me, who was the first tumbler in the world?"

"Really, brother," answered the cousin, "I could not at this moment say positively without having investigated it; I will look it up when I go back to where I have my books, and will satisfy you the next time we meet, for this will not be the last time."

"Look here, señor," said Sancho, "don't give yourself any trouble about it, for I have just this minute hit upon what I asked you. The first tumbler in the world, you must know, was Lucifer, when they cast or pitched him out of heaven; for he came tumbling into the bottomless pit."

"You are right, friend," said the cousin; and said Don Quixote, "Sancho, that question and answer are not thine own; thou hast heard them from some one else."

---

[43] ***"Metamorphoses . . . Ovid":*** Ovid's *Metamorphoses* told Greek and Roman legends, many of which explained the origins of place names.

[44] ***"The Supplement . . . Vergil":*** Polydore Vergil (1470–1555) compiled a list of discoveries from classical sources.

"Hold your peace, señor," said Sancho; "faith, if I take to asking questions and answering, I'll go on from this till tomorrow morning. Nay! to ask foolish things and answer nonsense I needn't go looking for help from my neighbors."

"Thou hast said more than thou art aware of, Sancho," said Don Quixote; "for there are some who weary themselves out in learning and proving things that, after they are known and proved, are not worth a farthing to the understanding or memory."

In this and other pleasant conversation the day went by, and that night they put up at a small hamlet whence it was not more than two leagues to the cave of Montesinos, so the cousin told Don Quixote, adding that if he was bent upon entering it, it would be requisite for him to provide himself with ropes, so that he might be tied and lowered into its depths. Don Quixote said that even if it reached to the bottomless pit he meant to see where it went to; so they bought about a hundred fathoms of rope, and the next day at two in the afternoon they arrived at the cave, the mouth of which is spacious and wide, but full of thorn and wild-fig bushes and brambles and briers, so thick and matted that they completely close it up and cover it over.

On coming within sight of it the cousin, Sancho, and Don Quixote dismounted, and the first two immediately tied the latter very firmly with the ropes, and as they were girding and swathing him Sancho said to him, "Mind what you are about, master mine; don't go burying yourself alive, or putting yourself where you'll be like a bottle put to cool in a well; it's no affair or business of your worship's to become the explorer of this, which must be worse than a Moorish dungeon."

"Tie me and hold thy peace," said Don Quixote, "for an emprise like this, friend Sancho, was reserved for me"; and said the guide, "I beg of you, Señor Don Quixote, to observe carefully and examine with a hundred eyes everything that is within there; perhaps there may be some things for me to put into my book of transformations."

"The drum is in hands that will know how to beat it well enough," said Sancho Panza.

When he had said this and finished the tying (which was not over the armor, but only over the doublet) Don Quixote observed, "It was careless of us not to have provided ourselves with a small cattle-bell to be tied on the rope close to me, the sound of which would show that I was still descending and alive; but as this is out of the question now, in God's hand be it to guide me"; and forthwith he fell on his knees and in a low voice offered up a prayer to Heaven, imploring God to aid him and grant him success in this to all appearance perilous and untried adventure, and then exclaimed aloud, "O mistress of my actions and movements, illustrious and peerless Dulcinea del Toboso, if so be the prayers and supplications of this thy fortunate lover can reach thy ears, by thy incomparable beauty I entreat thee to listen to them, for they but ask thee not to refuse me thy favor and protection now that I stand in such need of them. I am about to precipitate, to sink, to plunge myself into the abyss that is here before me, only to let the world know that while thou dost favor me there is no impossibility I will not attempt and accomplish." With these words he approached the cavern, and perceived that it was impossible to let himself down or effect an entrance except by sheer force or cleaving a passage; so drawing his sword he began to demolish and cut away the brambles at the mouth of the cave, at the noise of which a vast multitude of crows and choughs flew out of it so thick and so fast that they knocked Don Quixote down; and if he had been as much of a believer in augury as he was a Catholic Christian he would have taken it as a bad omen and declined to bury himself in such a place. He got up, however, and as there came no more crows, or nightbirds like the bats that flew out at the same time with the crows, the cousin and Sancho giving him rope, he lowered himself into the depths of the dread cavern; and as he entered it Sancho sent his blessing after him, making a thousand crosses over him and saying, "God, and the Peña de Francia, and the Trinity of Gaeta[45] guide thee, O flower and cream of knights-errant. There thou goest, thou dare-devil of the earth, heart of steel, arm of brass; once more, God guide thee and send thee back safe, and sound, and unhurt to the light of this world thou art leaving to bury thyself in the darkness thou art seeking there"; and the cousin offered up almost the same prayers and supplications.

Don Quixote kept calling to them to give him rope and more rope, and they gave it out little by little, and by the time the calls, which came out of the cave as out of a pipe, ceased to be heard they had let down the hundred fathoms of rope. They were inclined to pull Don Quixote up again, as they could give him no more rope; however, they waited about half an hour, at the end of which time they began to gather in the rope again with great ease and without feeling any weight, which made them fancy Don Quixote was remaining below; and persuaded that it was so, Sancho wept bitterly, and hauled away in great haste in order to settle the question. When, however, they had come to, as it seemed, rather more than eighty fathoms they felt a weight, at which they were greatly delighted; and at last, at ten fathoms more, they saw Don Quixote distinctly, and Sancho called out to him, saying, "Welcome back, señor, for we had begun to think you were going to stop there to found a family." But Don Quixote answered not a word, and drawing him out entirely they perceived he had his eyes shut and every appearance of being fast asleep.

They stretched him on the ground and untied him, but still he did not awake; however, they rolled him back and forwards and shook and pulled him about, so that after some time he came to himself, stretching himself just as if he were waking up from a deep and sound sleep, and looking about him as if scared he said, "God forgive you, friends; ye have taken me away from the sweetest and most delightful existence and spectacle that ever human being enjoyed or beheld. Now indeed do I know that all the pleasures of this life pass away like a shadow and a dream, or fade like the flower of the field. O ill-fated Montesinos! O sore-wounded Durandarte! O unhappy Belerma! O tearful Guadiana, and ye O hapless daughters of Ruidera who show in your waves the tears that flowed from your beauteous eyes!"

The cousin and Sancho Panza listened with deep attention to the words of Don Quixote, who uttered them as though with immense pain he drew them up from his

[45] **"Peña de Francia . . . Trinity of Gaeta":** La Peña de Francia is a mountain near Ciudad Rodrigo, where an image of the Virgin is said to have appeared in the fifteenth century. The Trinity of Gaeta is a chapel dedicated to the Trinity.

very bowels. They begged of him to explain himself, and tell them what he had seen in that hell down there.

"Hell do you call it?" said Don Quixote; "call it by no such name, for it does not deserve it, as ye shall soon see."

He then begged them to give him something to eat, as he was very hungry. They spread the cousin's sackcloth on the grass, and put the stores of the *alforjas* into requisition, and all three sitting down lovingly and sociably, they made a luncheon and a supper of it all in one; and when the sackcloth was removed, Don Quixote of La Mancha said, "Let no one rise; and attend to me, my sons, both of you."

Chapter 23

OF THE WONDERFUL THINGS THE INCOMPARABLE DON QUIXOTE SAID HE SAW IN THE PROFOUND CAVE OF MONTESINOS, THE IMPOSSIBILITY AND MAGNITUDE OF WHICH CAUSE THIS ADVENTURE TO BE DEEMED APOCRYPHAL

It was about four in the afternoon when the sun, veiled in clouds, with subdued light and tempered beams, enabled Don Quixote to relate, without heat or inconvenience, what he had seen in the cave of Montesinos to his two illustrious hearers, and he began as follows:

"A matter of some twelve or fourteen times a man's height down in this pit, on the left-hand side, there is a recess or space, roomy enough to contain a large cart with its mules. A little light reaches it through some chinks or crevices, communicating with it and open to the surface of the earth. This recess or space I perceived when I was already growing weary and disgusted at finding myself hanging suspended by the rope, travelling downwards into that dark region without any certainty or knowledge of where I was going to, so I resolved to enter it and rest myself for a while. I called out, telling you not to let out more rope until I bade you, but you can not have heard me. I then gathered in the rope you were sending me, and making a coil or pile of it I seated myself upon it, ruminating and considering what I was to do to lower myself to the bottom, having no one to hold me up; and I was thus deep in thought and perplexity, suddenly and without provocation a profound sleep fell upon me, and when I least expected it, I know not how, I awoke and found myself in the midst of the most beautiful, delicious, delightful meadow that nature could produce or the most lively human imagination conceive. I opened my eyes, I rubbed them, and found I was not asleep, but thoroughly awake. Nevertheless, I felt my head and breast to satisfy myself whether it was I myself who was there or some empty delusive phantom; but touch, feeling, the collected thoughts that passed through my mind, all convinced me that I was the same then and there that I am this moment. Next there presented itself to my sight a stately royal palace or castle, with walls that seemed built of clear transparent crystal; and through two great doors that opened wide therein, I saw coming forth and advancing towards me a venerable old man, clad in a long gown of mulberry-colored serge that trailed upon the ground. On his shoulders and breast he had a green satin collegiate hood, and covering his head a black Milanese bonnet, and his snow-white beard fell below his girdle. He carried no arms whatever, nothing but a rosary of beads bigger than fair-sized filberts, each tenth bead being like a moderate ostrich egg; his bearing, his gait, his dignity and imposing presence held me spellbound and wondering. He approached me, and the first thing he did was to embrace me closely, and then he said to me, 'For a long time now, O valiant knight Don Quixote of La Mancha, we who are here enchanted in these solitudes have been hoping to see thee, that thou mayest make known to the world what is shut up and concealed in this deep cave, called the cave of Montesinos, which thou hast entered, an achievement reserved for thy invincible heart and stupendous courage alone to attempt. Come with me, illustrious sir, and I will show thee the marvels hidden within this transparent castle, whereof I am the *alcaide* and perpetual warden; for I am Montesinos himself, from whom the cave takes its name.'[46]

"The instant he told me he was Montesinos, I asked him if the story they told in the world above here was true, that he had taken out the heart of his great friend Durandarte from his breast with a little dagger, and carried it to the lady Belerma, as his friend when at the point of death had commanded him. He said in reply that they spoke the truth in every respect except as to the dagger, for it was not a dagger, nor little, but a burnished poniard sharper than an awl."

"That poniard must have been made by Ramon de Hoces the Sevillian," said Sancho.

"I do not know," said Don Quixote; "it could not have been by that poniard maker, however, because Ramon de Hoces was a man of yesterday, and the affair of Roncesvalles, where this mishap occurred, was long ago; but the question is of no great importance, nor does it affect or make any alteration in the truth or substance of the story."

"That is true," said the cousin; "continue, Señor Don Quixote, for I am listening to you with the greatest pleasure in the world."

"And with no less do I tell the tale," said Don Quixote: "and so, to proceed—the venerable Montesinos led me into the palace of crystal, where, in a lower chamber, strangely cool and entirely of alabaster, was an elaborately wrought marble tomb, upon which I beheld, stretched at full length, a knight, not of bronze, or marble, or jasper, as are seen on other tombs, but of actual flesh and bone. His right hand (which seemed to me somewhat hairy and sinewy, a sign of great strength in its owner) lay on the side of his heart; but before I could put any question to Montesinos, he, seeing me gazing at the tomb in amazement, said to me, 'This is my friend Durandarte, flower and mirror of the true lovers and valiant knights of his time. He is held enchanted here, as I myself and many others are, by that French enchanter Merlin, who, they say, was the devil's son; but my belief is, not that he was the devil's son, but that he knew, as the saying is, a point more than the devil. How or why he enchanted us, no one knows, but time will tell, and I suspect that time is not far off. What I marvel at is, that I know it to be as sure as that it is now day, that Durandarte ended his life in my arms, and that, after his death, I took out his heart with my own hands; and indeed it must have weighed more than two pounds, for,

[46] **Montesinos . . . name:** Montesinos, hero of half a dozen ballads, was a Peer and a grandson of Charlemagne.

according to naturalists, he who has a large heart is more largely endowed with valor than he who has a small one. Then, as this is the case, and as the knight did really die, how comes it that he now moans and sighs from time to time, as if he were still alive?'

"As he said this, the wretched Durandarte cried out in a loud voice:

O cousin Montesinos!
'Twas my last request of thee,
When my soul hath left the body,
And that lying dead I be,
With thy poniard or thy dagger
Cut the heart from out my breast,
And bear it to Belerma.
This was my last request.

On hearing which, the venerable Montesinos fell on his knees before the unhappy knight, and with tearful eyes exclaimed, 'Long since, O Señor Durandarte, my beloved cousin, long since have I done what you bade me on that sad day when I lost you; I took out your heart as well as I could, not leaving an atom of it in your breast, I wiped it with a lace handkerchief, and I took the road to France with it, having first laid you in the bosom of the earth with tears enough to wash and cleanse my hands of the blood that covered them after wandering among your bowels; and more by token, O cousin of my soul, at the first village I came to after leaving Roncesvalles, I sprinkled a little salt upon your heart to keep it sweet, and bring it, if not fresh, at least pickled, into the presence of the lady Belerma, whom, together with you, myself, Guadiana your squire, the duenna Ruidera and her seven daughters and two nieces, and many more of your friends and acquaintances, the sage Merlin has been keeping enchanted here these many years; and although more than five hundred have gone by, not one of us has died; Ruidera and her daughters and nieces alone are missing, and these, because of the tears they shed, Merlin, out of the compassion he seems to have felt for them, changed into so many lakes, which to this day in the world of the living, and in the province of La Mancha, are called the lakes of Ruidera. The seven daughters belong to the kings of Spain, and the two nieces to the knights of a very holy order called the Order of St. John. Guadiana your squire, likewise bewailing your fate, was changed into a river of his own name, but when he came to the surface and beheld the sun of another heaven, so great was his grief at finding he was leaving you, that he plunged into the bowels of the earth; however, as he can not help following his natural course, he from time to time comes forth and shows himself to the sun and the world. The lakes aforesaid send him their waters, and with these, and others that come to him, he makes a grand and imposing entrance into Portugal; but for all that, go where he may, he shows his melancholy and sadness, and takes no pride in breeding dainty choice fish, only coarse and tasteless sorts, very different from those of the golden Tagus. All this that I tell you now, O cousin mine, I have told you many times before, and as you make no answer, I fear that either you believe me not, or do not hear me, whereat I feel God knows what grief. I have now news to give you, which, if it serves not to alleviate your sufferings, will not in any wise increase them. Know that you have here before you (open your eyes and you will see) that great knight of whom the sage Merlin has prophesied such great things; that Don Quixote of La Mancha I mean, who has again, and to better purpose than in past times, revived in these days knight-errantry, long since forgotten, and by whose intervention and aid it may be we shall be disenchanted; for great deeds are reserved for great men.'

"'And if that may not be,' said the wretched Durandarte in a low and feeble voice, 'if that may not be, then, O my cousin, I say "patience and shuffle"'; and turning over on his side, he relapsed into his former silence without uttering another word.

"And now there was heard a great outcry and lamentation, accompanied by deep sighs and bitter sobs. I looked round and through the crystal wall I saw passing through another chamber a procession of two lines of fair damsels all clad in mourning, and with white turbans of Turkish fashion on their heads. Behind, in the rear of these, there came a lady, for so from her dignity she seemed to be, also clad in black, with a white veil so long and ample that it swept the ground. Her turban was twice as large as the largest of any of the others; her eyebrows met, her nose was rather flat, her mouth was large but with ruddy lips, and her teeth, of which at times she allowed a glimpse, were seen to be sparse and ill-set, though as white as peeled almonds. She carried in her hands a fine cloth, and in it, as well as I could make out, a heart that had been mummied, so parched and dried was it. Montesinos told me that all those forming the procession were the attendants of Durandarte and Belerma, who were enchanted there with their master and mistress, and that the last, she who carried the heart in the cloth, was the lady Belerma, who, with her damsels, four days in the week went in procession singing, or rather weeping, dirges over the body and miserable heart of his cousin; and that if she appeared to me somewhat ill-favored, or not so beautiful as fame reported her, it was because of the bad nights and worse days that she passed in that enchantment, as I could see by the great dark circles round her eyes, and her sickly complexion; 'her sallowness, and the rings round her eyes,' said he, 'are not caused by the periodical ailment usual with women, for it is many months and even years since she has had any, but by the grief her own heart suffers because of that which she holds in her hand perpetually, and which recalls and brings back to her memory the sad fate of her lost lover; were it not for this, hardly would the great Dulcinea del Toboso, so celebrated in all these parts, and even in all the world, come up to her for beauty, grace, and gayety.'

"'Hold hard!' said I at this, 'tell your story as you ought, Señor Don Montesinos, for you know very well that all comparisons are odious, and there is no occasion to compare one person with another; the peerless Dulcinea del Toboso is what she is, and the lady Doña Belerma is what *she* is and has been, and that's enough.' To which he made answer, 'Forgive me, Señor Don Quixote; I own I was wrong and spoke unadvisedly in saying that the lady Dulcinea could scarcely come up to the lady Belerma; for it were enough for me to have learned, by what means I know not, that you are her knight, to make me bite my tongue out before I compared her to anything save heaven itself.' After this apology which the great Montesinos made me, my heart recovered itself from the shock I had received in hearing my lady compared with Belerma."

"Still I wonder," said Sancho, "that your worship did not get upon the old fellow and bruise every bone of him with kicks, and pluck his beard until you didn't leave a hair in it."

"Nay, Sancho, my friend," said Don Quixote, "it would not have been right in me to do that, for we are all bound to pay respect to the aged, even though they be not knights, but especially those who are, and who are enchanted; I only know I gave him as good as he brought in the many other questions and answers we exchanged."

"I can not understand, Señor Don Quixote," remarked the cousin here, "how it is that your worship, in such a short space of time as you have been below there, could have seen so many things, and said and answered so much."

"How long is it since I went down?" asked Don Quixote.

"Little better than an hour," replied Sancho.

"That can not be," returned Don Quixote, "because night overtook me while I was there, and day came, and it was night again and day again three times; so that, by my reckoning, I have been three days in those remote regions beyond our ken."

"My master must be right," replied Sancho; "for as everything that has happened to him is by enchantment, maybe what seems to us an hour would seem three days and nights there."

"That's it," said Don Quixote.

"And did your worship eat anything all that time, señor?" asked the cousin.

"I never touched a morsel," answered Don Quixote, "nor did I even feel hunger, or think of it."

"And do the enchanted eat?" said the cousin.

"They neither eat," said Don Quixote; "nor are they subject to the greater excrements, though it is thought that their nails, beards, and hair grow."

"And do the enchanted sleep, now, señor?" asked Sancho.

"Certainly not," replied Don Quixote; "at least, during those three days I was with them not one of them closed an eye, nor did I either."

"The proverb, 'Tell me what company thou keepest and I'll tell thee what thou art,' is to the point here," said Sancho; "your worship keeps company with enchanted people that are always fasting and watching; what wonder is it, then, that you neither eat nor sleep while you are with them? But forgive me, señor, if I say that of all this you have told us now, may God take me—I was just going to say the devil—if I believe a single particle."

"What!" said the cousin, "has Señor Don Quixote, then, been lying? Why, even if he wished it he has not had time to imagine and put together such a host of lies."

"I don't believe my master lies," said Sancho.

"If not, what dost thou believe?" asked Don Quixote.

"I believe," replied Sancho, "that this Merlin, or those enchanters who enchanted the whole crew your worship says you saw and discoursed with down there, stuffed your imagination or your mind with all this rigmarole you have been treating us to, and all that is still to come."

"All that might be, Sancho," replied Don Quixote; "but it is not so, for everything that I have told you I saw with my own eyes, and touched with my own hands. But what will you say when I tell you now how, among the countless other marvellous things Montesinos showed me (of which at leisure and at the proper time I will give thee an account in the course of our journey, for they would not be all in place here), he showed me three country girls who went skipping and capering like goats over the pleasant fields there, and the instant I beheld them I knew one to be the peerless Dulcinea del Toboso, and the other two those same country girls that were with her and that we spoke to on the road from El Toboso! I asked Montesinos if he knew them, and he told me he did not, but he thought they must be some enchanted ladies of distinction, for it was only a few days before that they had made their appearance in those meadows; but I was not to be surprised at that, because there were a great many other ladies there of times past and present, enchanted in various strange shapes, and among them he had recognized Queen Guinevere and her dame Quintañona, she who poured out the wine for Lancelot when he came from Britain."

When Sancho Panza heard his master say this he was ready to take leave of his senses, or die with laughter; for, as he knew the real truth about the pretended enchantment of Dulcinea, in which he himself had been the enchanter and concocter of all the evidence, he made up his mind at last that, beyond all doubt, his master was out of his wits and stark mad, so he said to him, "It was an evil hour, a worse season, and a sorrowful day, when your worship, dear master mine, went down to the other world, and an unlucky moment when you met with Señor Montesinos, who has sent you back to us like this. You were well enough here above in your full senses, such as God had given you, delivering maxims and giving advice at every turn, and not as you are now, talking the greatest nonsense that can be imagined."

"As I know thee, Sancho," said Don Quixote, "I heed not thy words."

"Nor I your worship's," said Sancho, "whether you beat me or kill me for those I have spoken, and will speak if you don't correct and mend your own. But tell me, while we are still at peace, how or by what did you recognize the lady our mistress; and if you spoke to her, what did you say, and what did she answer?"

"I recognized her," said Don Quixote, "by her wearing the same garments she wore when thou didst point her out to me. I spoke to her, but she did not utter a word in reply; on the contrary, she turned her back on me and took to flight, at such a pace that a crossbow bolt could not have overtaken her. I wished to follow her, and would have done so had not Montesinos recommended me not to take the trouble as it would be useless, particularly as the time was drawing near when it would be necessary for me to quit the cavern. He told me, moreover, that in course of time he would let me know how he and Belerma, and Durandarte, and all who were there, were to be disenchanted. But of all I saw and observed down there, what gave me most pain was, that while Montesinos was speaking to me, one of the two companions of the hapless Dulcinea approached me on one side, without my having seen her coming and with tears in her eyes said to me, in a low, agitated voice, 'My lady Dulcinea del Toboso kisses your worship's hands and entreats you to do her the favor of letting her know how you are; and, being in great need, she also entreats your worship as earnestly as she can to be so good as to lend her half a dozen reals, or as much as you may have about you, on this new dimity petticoat that I have here; and she promises to repay them very speedily.' I was amazed and taken aback by such a message, and turning to Señor Montesinos I asked him, 'Is it possible, Señor

Montesinos, that persons of distinction under enchantment can be in need?' To which he replied, 'Believe me, Señor Don Quixote, that which is called need is to be met with everywhere, and penetrates all quarters and reaches every one, and does not spare even the enchanted; and as the lady Dulcinea del Toboso sends to beg those six reals, and the pledge is to all appearance a good one, there is nothing for it but to give them to her, for no doubt she must be in some great strait.' 'I will take no pledge of her,' I replied, 'nor yet can I give her what she asks, for all I have is four reals'; which I gave (they were those which thou, Sancho, gavest me the other day to bestow in alms upon the poor I met along the road), and I said, 'Tell your mistress, my dear, that I am grieved to the heart because of her distresses, and wish I was a Fucar[47] to remedy them, and that I would have her know that I can not be, and ought not be, in health while deprived of the happiness of seeing her and enjoying her discreet conversation, and that I implore her as earnestly as I can, to allow herself to be seen and addressed by this her captive servant and forlorn knight. Tell her, too, that when she least expects it she will hear it announced that I have made an oath and vow after the fashion of that which the Marquis of Mantua made to avenge his nephew Baldwin, when he found him at the point of death in the heart of the mountains, which was, not to eat bread off a table-cloth, and the other trifling matters which he added, until he had avenged him; and I will make the same to take no rest, and to roam the seven regions of the earth more thoroughly than the Infante Don Pedro of Portugal ever roamed them, until I have disenchanted her.' 'All that, and more, you owe my lady,' was the damsel's answer to me, and taking the four reals, instead of making me a courtesy she cut a caper, springing two full yards into the air."

"O blessed God!" exclaimed Sancho aloud at this, "is it possible that such things can be in the world, and that enchanters and enchantments can have such power in it as to have changed my master's right senses into a craze so full of absurdity! O señor, señor, for God's sake, consider yourself, have a care for your honor, and give no credit to this silly stuff that has left you scant and short of wits."

"Thou talkest in this way because thou lovest me, Sancho," said Don Quixote; "and not being experienced in the things of the world, everything that has some difficulty about it, seems to thee impossible; but time will pass, as I said before, and I will tell thee some of the things I saw down there which will make thee believe what I have related now, the truth of which admits of neither reply nor question."

. . .

FROM

Chapter 28

OF MATTERS THAT BENENGELI SAYS HE WHO READS THEM WILL KNOW, IF HE READS THEM WITH ATTENTION

. . . "When I worked for Tomé Carrasco, the father of the bachelor Samson Carrasco that your worship knows," replied Sancho, "I used to earn two ducats a month

[47] **"Fucar":** Fucar (or Fugger) was a German banking family of the sixteenth century.

besides my food; I can't tell what I can earn with your worship, though I know a knight-errant's squire has harder times of it than he who works for a farmer; for after all, we who work for farmers, however much we toil all day, at the worst, at night, we have our olla supper and sleep in a bed, which I have not slept in since I have been in your worship's service, if it wasn't the short time we were in Don Diego de Miranda's house, and the feast I had with the skimmings I took off Camacho's pots, and what I ate, drank, and slept in Basilio's house; all the rest of the time I have been sleeping on the hard ground under the open sky, exposed to what they call the inclemencies of heaven, keeping life in me with scraps of cheese and crusts of bread, and drinking water either from the brooks or from the springs we come to on these by-paths we travel."

"I own, Sancho," said Don Quixote, "that all thou sayest is true; how much, thinkest thou, ought I to give thee over and above what Tomé Carrasco gave thee?"

"I think," said Sancho, "that if your worship was to add on two reals a month I'd consider myself well paid; that is, as far as the wages of my labor go; but to make up to me for your worship's pledge and promise to give me the government of an island, it would be fair to add six reals more, making thirty in all."

"Very good," said Don Quixote; "it is twenty-five days since we left our village, so reckon up, Sancho, according to the wages you have made out for yourself, and see how much I owe you in proportion, and pay yourself, as I said before, out of your own hand."

"O body o' me!" said Sancho, "but your worship is very much out in that reckoning; for when it comes to the promise of the island we must count from the day your worship promised it to me to this present hour we are at now."

"Well, how long is it, Sancho, since I promised it to you?" said Don Quixote.

"If I remember rightly," said Sancho, "it must be over twenty years, three days more or less."

Don Quixote gave himself a great slap on the forehead and began to laugh heartily, and said he, "Why, I have not been wandering, either in the Sierra Morena or in the whole course of our sallies, but barely two months, and thou sayest, Sancho, that it is twenty years since I promised thee the island. I believe now thou wouldst have all the money thou hast of mine go in thy wages. If so, and if that be thy pleasure, I give it to thee now, once and for all, and much good may it do thee, for so long as I see myself rid of such a good-for-nothing squire, I'll be glad to be left a pauper without a rap. But tell me, thou perverter of the squirely rules of knight-errantry, where hast thou ever seen or read that any knight-errant's squire made terms with his lord, 'you must give me so much a month for serving you'? Plunge, O scoundrel, rogue, monster—for such I take thee to be—plunge, I say, into the *mare magnum*[48] of their histories; and if thou shalt find that any squire ever said or thought what thou has said now, I will let thee nail it on my forehead, and give me, over and above, four sound slaps in the face. Turn the rein, or the halter, of thy Dapple, and begone home; for one single step farther thou shalt not make in my company. O bread

[48] ***"mare magnum":*** The great sea.

thanklessly received! O promises ill-bestowed! O man more beast than human being! Now, when I was about to raise thee to such a position, that, in spite of thy wife, they would call thee 'my lord,' thou art leaving me? Thou art going now when I had a firm and fixed intention of making thee lord of the best island in the world? Well, as thou thyself hast said before now, honey is not for the mouth of the ass. Ass thou art, ass thou wilt be, and ass thou wilt end when the course of thy life is run; for I know it will come to its close before thou dost perceive or discern that thou art a beast."

Sancho regarded Don Quixote earnestly while he was giving him his rating, and was so touched by remorse that the tears came to his eyes, and in a piteous and broken voice he said to him, "Master mine, I confess that, to be a complete ass, all I want is a tail; if your worship will only fix one on to me, I'll look on it as rightly placed, and I'll serve you as an ass all the remaining days of my life. Forgive me and have pity on my folly, and remember I know but little, and, if I talk much, it's more from infirmity than malice; but he who sins and mends commends himself to God."

"I should have been surprised, Sancho," said Don Quixote, "if thou hadst not introduced some bit of proverb into thy speech. Well, well, I forgive thee, provided thou dost mend and not show thyself in future so fond of thine own interest, but try to be of good cheer and take heart, and encourage thyself to look forward to the fulfilment of my promises, which, by being delayed, does not become impossible."

Sancho said he would do so, and keep up his heart as best he could. They then entered the grove, and Don Quixote settled himself at the foot of an elm, and Sancho at that of a beech, for trees of this kind and others like them always have feet but no hands. Sancho passed the night in pain, for with the evening dews the blow of the staff made itself felt all the more. Don Quixote passed it in his never-failing meditations; but, for all that, they had some winks of sleep, and with the appearance of daylight they pursued their journey in quest of the banks of the famous Ebro, where that befell them which will be told in the following chapter.

. . .

FROM

Chapter 30

OF DON QUIXOTE'S ADVENTURE WITH A FAIR HUNTRESS

. . . It so happened that the next day towards sunset, on coming out of a wood, Don Quixote cast his eyes over a green meadow, and at the far end of it observed some people, and as he drew nearer saw that it was a hawking party. Coming closer, he distinguished among them a lady of graceful mien, on a pure white palfrey or hackney caparisoned with green trappings and a silver-mounted side-saddle. The lady was also in green, and so richly and splendidly dressed that splendor itself seemed personified in her. On her left hand she bore a hawk, a proof to Don Quixote's mind that she must be some great lady and the mistress of the whole hunting party, which was the fact; so he said to Sancho, "Run, Sancho, my son, and say to that lady on the palfrey with the hawk that I, the Knight of the Lions, kiss the hands of her exalted beauty, and if her excellence will grant me leave I will go and kiss them in person and place myself at her service for aught that may be in my power and her highness may command; and mind, Sancho, how thou speakest, and take care not to thrust in any of thy proverbs into thy message."

"You've got a likely one here to thrust any in!" said Sancho; "leave me alone for that! Why, this is not the first time in my life I have carried messages to high and exalted ladies."

"Except that thou didst carry to the lady Dulcinea," said Don Quixote, "I know not that thou hast carried any other, at least in my service."

"That is true," replied Sancho; "but pledges don't distress a good paymaster, and in a house where there's plenty supper is soon cooked; I mean there's no need of telling or warning me about anything; for I'm ready for everything and know a little of everything."

"That I believe, Sancho," said Don Quixote; "go and good luck to thee, and God speed thee."

Sancho went off at top speed, forcing Dapple out of his regular pace, and came to where the fair huntress was standing, and dismounting knelt before her and said, "Fair lady, that knight that you see there, the Knight of the Lions by name, is my master, and I am a squire of his, and at home they call me Sancho Panza. This same Knight of the Lions, who was called not long since the Knight of the Rueful Countenance, sends by me to say may it please your highness to give him leave that, with your permission, approbation, and consent, he may come and carry out his wishes, which are, as he says and I believe, to serve your exalted loftiness and beauty; and if you give it, your ladyship will do a thing which will redound to your honor, and he will receive a most distinguished favor and happiness."

"You have indeed, worthy squire," said the lady, "delivered your message with all the formalities such messages require; rise up, for it is not right that the squire of a knight so great as he of the Rueful Countenance, of whom we have already heard a great deal here, should remain on his knees; rise, my friend, and bid your master welcome to the services of myself and the duke my husband, in a country house we have here."

Sancho got up, charmed as much by the beauty of the good lady as by her high-bred air and her courtesy, but, above all, by what she had said about having heard of his master, the Knight of the Rueful Countenance; for if she did not call him Knight of the Lions it was no doubt because he had so lately taken the name. "Tell me, brother squire," asked the duchess (whose title, however, is not known), "this master of yours, is he not one of whom there is a history extant in print, called *The Ingenious Gentleman, Don Quixote of La Mancha,* who has for the lady of his heart a certain Dulcinea del Toboso?"

"He is the same, señora," replied Sancho; "and that squire of his who figures, or ought to figure, in the said history under the name of Sancho Panza, is myself, unless they have changed me in the cradle, I mean in the press."

"I am rejoiced at this," said the duchess; "go, brother Panza, and tell your master that he is welcome to my estate, and that nothing could happen to me that could give me greater pleasure."

Sancho returned to his master mightily pleased with this gratifying answer, and told him all the great lady had said to him, lauding to the skies, in his rustic phrase, her rare beauty, her graceful gayety, and her courtesy. Don Quixote drew himself up briskly in his saddle, fixed himself in his stirrups, settled his visor, gave Rocinante the spur, and with an easy bearing advanced to kiss the hands of the duchess, who, having sent to summon the duke her husband, told him while Don Quixote was approaching all about the message; and as both of them had read the First Part of this history, and from it were aware of Don Quixote's crazy turn, they awaited him with the greatest delight and anxiety to make his acquaintance, meaning to fall in with his humor and agree with everything he said, and, so long as he stayed with them, to treat him as a knight-errant, with all the ceremonies usual in the books of chivalry they had read, for they themselves were very fond of them.

Don Quixote now came up with his visor raised, and as he seemed about to dismount Sancho made haste to go and hold his stirrup for him; but getting down off Dapple he was so unlucky as to hitch his foot in one of the ropes of the pack-saddle in such a way that he was unable to free it, and was left hanging by it with his face and breast on the ground. Don Quixote, who was not used to dismount without having the stirrup held, fancying that Sancho had by this time come to hold it for him, threw himself off with a lurch and brought Rocinante's saddle after him, which was no doubt badly girthed, and saddle and he both came to the ground; nor without discomfiture to him and abundant curses muttered between his teeth against the unlucky Sancho, who had his foot still in the shackles. The duke ordered his huntsmen to go to the help of knight and squire, and they raised Don Quixote sorely shaken by his fall; and he, limping, advanced as best he could to kneel before the noble pair. This, however, the duke would by no means permit; on the contrary, dismounting from his horse, he went and embraced Don Quixote, saying, "I am grieved, Sir Knight of the Rueful Countenance, that your first experience on my ground should have been such an unfortunate one as we have seen; but the carelessness of squires is often the cause of worse accidents."

"That which has happened me in meeting you, mighty prince," replied Don Quixote, "can not be unfortunate, even if my fall had not stopped short of the depths of the bottomless pit, for the glory of having seen you would have lifted me up and delivered me from it. My squire, God's curse upon him, is better at unloosing his tongue in talking impertinence than in tightening the girths of a saddle to keep it steady; but however I may be, fallen or raised up, on foot or on horseback, I shall always be at your service and that of my lady the duchess, your worthy consort, worthy queen of beauty and paramount princess of courtesy."

"Gently, Señor Don Quixote of La Mancha," said the duke; "where my lady Doña Dulcinea del Toboso is, it is not right that other beauties should be praised."

Sancho, by this time released from his entanglement, was standing by, and before his master could answer he said, "There is no denying, and it must be maintained, that my lady Dulcinea del Toboso is very beautiful; but the hare jumps up where one least expects it; and I have heard say that what we call nature is like a potter that makes vessels of clay, and he who makes one fair vessel can as well make two, or three, or a hundred; I say so because, by my faith, my lady the duchess is in no way behind my mistress the lady Dulcinea del Toboso."

Don Quixote turned to the duchess and said, "Your highness may conceive that never had knight-errant in this world a more talkative or a droller squire than I have, and he will prove the truth of what I say, if your highness is pleased to accept of my services for a few days."

To which the duchess made answer, "That worthy Sancho is droll I consider a very good thing, because it is a sign that he is shrewd; for drollery and sprightliness, Señor Don Quixote, as you very well know, do not take up their abode with dull wits; and as good Sancho is droll and sprightly I here set him down as shrewd."

"And talkative," added Don Quixote.

"So much the better," said the duke, "for many droll things can not be said in few words; but not to lose time in talking, come, great Knight of the Rueful Countenance"—

"Of the Lions, your highness must say," said Sancho, "for there is no Rueful Countenance nor any such character now."

"He of the Lions be it," continued the duke; "I say, let Sir Knight of the Lions come to a castle of mine close by, where he shall be given that reception which is due to so exalted a personage, and which the duchess and I are wont to give to all knights-errant who come there."

By this time Sancho had fixed and girthed Rocinante's saddle, and Don Quixote having got on his back and the duke mounted a fine horse, they placed the duchess in the middle and set out for the castle. The duchess desired Sancho to come to her side, for she found infinite enjoyment in listening to his shrewd remarks. Sancho required no pressing, but pushed himself in between them and made a fourth in the conversation, to the great amusement of the duchess and the duke, who thought it rare good fortune to receive such a knight-errant and such a homely squire in their castle.

. . .

FROM

Chapter 32

OF THE REPLY DON QUIXOTE GAVE HIS CENSURER, WITH OTHER INCIDENTS, GRAVE AND DROLL

. . . The duchess begged Don Quixote, as he seemed to have a retentive memory, to describe and portray to her the beauty and features of the lady Dulcinea del Toboso, for, judging by what fame trumpeted abroad of her beauty, she felt sure she must be the fairest creature in the world, nay in all La Mancha.

Don Quixote sighed on hearing the duchess's request, and said, "If I could pluck out my heart, and lay it on a plate on this table here before your highness's eyes, it would spare my tongue the pain of telling what can hardly be thought of, for in it your excellence would see her portrayed in full. But why should I attempt to depict and describe in detail, and feature by feature, the beauty of the peerless Dulcinea, the g one worthy of other shoulders than mine, an enterprise wherein the arrhasius, Timantes, and Apelles, and the graver of Lysippus[49] ought to ed, to paint it in pictures and carve it in marble and bronze, and Cicero-Demosthenian eloquence to sound its praises?"

nat does Demosthenian mean, Señor Don Quixote?" said the duchess; "it is a never heard in all my life."

Demosthenian eloquence," said Don Quixote "means the eloquence of Demosthenes, as Ciceronian means that of Cicero, who were the two most eloquent orators in the world."

"True," said the duke; "you must have lost your wits to ask such a question. Nevertheless, Señor Don Quixote would greatly gratify us if he would depict her to us; for never fear, even in an outline or sketch she will be something to make the fairest envious."

"I would do so certainly," said Don Quixote, "had she not been blurred to my mind's eye by the misfortune that fell upon her a short time since, one of such a nature that I am more ready to weep over it than to describe it. For your highnesses must know that, going a few days back to kiss her hands and receive her benediction, approbation, and permission for this third sally, I found her altogether a different being from the one I sought; I found her enchanted and changed from a princess into a peasant, from fair to foul, from an angel into a devil, from fragrant to pestiferous, from refined to clownish, from a dignified lady into a jumping tomboy, from a light to darkness, and, in a word, from Dulcinea del Toboso into a coarse Sayago wench."

"God bless me!" said the duke aloud at this, "who can have done the world such an injury? Who can have robbed it of the beauty that gladdened it, of the grace and gayety that charmed it, of the modesty that shed a lustre upon it?"

"Who?" replied Don Quixote; "who could it be but some malignant enchanter of the many that persecute me out of envy—that accursed race born into the world to obscure and bring to naught the achievements of the good, and glorify and exalt the deeds of the wicked? Enchanters have persecuted me, enchanters persecute me still, and enchanters will continue to persecute me until they have sunk me and my lofty chivalry in the deep abyss of oblivion; and they injure and wound me where they know I feel it most. For to deprive a knight-errant of his lady is to deprive him of the eyes he sees with, of the sun that gives him light, of the food whereby he lives. Many a time before have I said it, and I say it now once more, a knight-errant without a lady is like a tree without leaves, a building without a foundation, or a shadow without the body that causes it."

"There is no denying it," said the duchess; "but still, if we are to believe the history of Don Quixote that has come out here lately with general applause, it is to be inferred from it, if I mistake not, that you never saw the lady Dulcinea, and that the said lady is nothing in the world but an imaginary lady, one that you yourself begot and gave birth to in your brain, and adorned with whatever charms and perfections you chose."

[49] **"Parrhasius . . . Lysippus":** Artists of ancient Greece.

"There is a good deal to be said on that point," said Don Quixote; "God knows whether there be any Dulcinea or not in the world, or whether she is imaginary or not imaginary; these are things the proof of which must not be pushed to extreme lengths. I have not begotten nor given birth to my lady, though I behold her as she needs must be, a lady who contains in herself all the qualities to make her famous throughout the world, beautiful without blemish, dignified without haughtiness, tender and yet modest, gracious from courtesy and courteous from good breeding, and lastly of exalted lineage, because beauty shines forth and excels with a higher degree of perfection upon good blood than in the fair of lowly birth."

"That is true," said the duke; "but Señor Don Quixote will give me leave to say what I am constrained to say by the story of his exploits that I have read, from which it is to be inferred that, granting there is a Dulcinea in El Toboso, or out of it, and that she is in the highest degree beautiful as you have described her to us, as regards the loftiness of her lineage she is not on a par with the Orianas, Alastrajareas, Madasimas, or others of that sort, with whom, as you well know, the histories abound."

"To that I may reply," said Don Quixote, "that Dulcinea is the daughter of her own works, and that virtues rectify blood, and that lowly virtue is more to be regarded and esteemed than exalted vice. Dulcinea, besides, has that within her that may raise her to be a crowned and sceptred queen; for the merit of a fair and virtuous woman is capable of performing greater miracles; and virtually, though not formally, she has in herself higher fortunes."

"I protest, Señor Don Quixote," said the duchess, "that in all you say, you go most cautiously and lead in hand, as the saying is; henceforth I will believe myself, and I will take care that every one in my house believes, even my lord the duke if needs be, that there is a Dulcinea in El Toboso, and that she is living to-day, and that she is beautiful and nobly born and deserves to have such a knight as Señor Don Quixote in her service, and that is the highest praise that it is in my power to give her or that I can think of. But I can not help entertaining a doubt, and having a certain grudge against Sancho Panza; the doubt is this, that the aforesaid history declares that the said Sancho Panza, when he carried a letter on your worship's behalf to the said lady Dulcinea, found her sifting a sack of wheat: and more by token it says it was red wheat: a thing which makes me doubt the loftiness of her lineage."

To this Don Quixote made answer, "Señora, your highness must know that everything or almost everything that happens to me transcends the ordinary limits of what happens to other knights-errant; whether it be that it is directed by the inscrutable will of destiny, or by the malice of some jealous enchanter. Now it is an established fact that all or most famous knights-errant have some special gift, one that of being proof against enchantment, another that of being made of such invulnerable flesh that he can not be wounded, as was the famous Roland, one of the twelve peers of France, of whom it is related that he could not be wounded except in the sole of his left foot, and that it must be with the point of a stout pin and not with any other sort of weapon whatever; and so, when Bernardo del Carpio slew him at Roncesvalles, finding that he could not wound him with steel, he lifted him up from the ground in his arms and strangled him, calling to mind seasonably the death which Hercules inflicted on Antæus, the fierce giant that they say was the son of Terra. I would infer from what I have mentioned that perhaps I may have some gift of this kind, not that of being invulnerable, because experience has many times proved to me that I am of tender flesh and not at all impenetrable; nor that of being proof against enchantment, for I have already seen myself thrust into a cage, in which all the world would not have been able to confine me except by force of enchantments. But as I delivered myself from that one, I am inclined to believe that there is no other that can hurt me; and so, these enchanters, seeing that they can not exert their vile craft against my person, revenge themselves on what I love most, and seek to rob me of life by maltreating that of Dulcinea in whom I live; and therefore I am convinced that when my squire carried my message to her, they changed her into a common peasant girl, engaged in such a mean occupation as sifting wheat; I have already said, however, that that wheat was not red wheat, nor wheat at all, but grains of orient pearl. And as a proof of all this, I must tell your highnesses that, coming to El Toboso a short time back, I was altogether unable to discover the palace of Dulcinea; and that the next day, though Sancho, my squire, saw her in her own proper shape, which is the fairest in the world, to me she appeared to be a coarse, ill-favored, farm-wench, and by no means a well-spoken one, she who is propriety itself. And so, as I am not and, so far as one can judge, can not be enchanted, she it is that is enchanted, that is smitten, that is altered, changed, and transformed; in her have my enemies revenged themselves upon me, and for her shall I live in ceaseless tears, until I see her in her pristine state. I have mentioned this lest anybody should mind what Sancho said about Dulcinea's winnowing or sifting; for, as they changed her to me, it is no wonder if they changed her to him. Dulcinea is illustrious and well-born, and of one of the gentle families of El Toboso, which are many, ancient, and good. Therein, most assuredly, not small is the share of the peerless Dulcinea, through whom her town will be famous and celebrated in ages to come, as Troy was through Helen, and Spain through La Cava,[50] though with a better title and tradition. For another thing; I would have your graces understand that Sancho Panza is one of the drollest squires that ever served knight-errant; sometimes there is a simplicity about him so acute that it is an amusement to try and make out whether he is simple or sharp; he has mischievous tricks that stamp him rogue, and blundering ways that prove him a booby; he doubts everything and believes everything; when I fancy he is on the point of coming down headlong from sheer stupidity, he comes out with something shrewd that sends him up to the skies. After all, I would not exchange him for another squire, though I were given a city to boot, and therefore I am in doubt whether it will be well to send him to the government your highness has bestowed upon him; though I perceive in him a certain aptitude for the work of governing, so that, with a little trimming of his understanding, he would manage any government as easily as the king does his taxes; and moreover, we know already by ample experience that it does not require much cleverness or much learning to be a

[50] **"La Cava":** Daughter of Count Julian, La Cava was seduced by Rodrigo, the last king of the Visigoths.

governor, for there are a hundred round about us that scarcely know how to read, and govern like gerfalcons. The main point is that they should have good intentions and be desirous of doing right in all things, for they will never be at a loss for persons to advise and direct them in what they have to do, like those knight-governors who, being no lawyers, pronounce sentences with the aid of an assessor. My advice to him will be to take no bribe and surrender no right, and I have some other little matters in reserve, that shall be produced in due season for Sancho's benefit and the advantage of the island he is to govern." [. . .]

Chapter 33

OF THE DELECTABLE DISCOURSE WHICH THE DUCHESS AND HER DAMSELS HELD WITH SANCHO PANZA, WELL WORTH READING AND NOTING

The history records that Sancho did not sleep that afternoon, but in order to keep his word came, before he had well done dinner, to visit the duchess, who, finding enjoyment in listening to him, made him sit down beside her on a low seat, though Sancho, out of pure good breeding, wanted not to sit down; the duchess, however, told him he was to sit down as governor and talk as squire, as in both respects he was worthy of even the chair of the Cid Ruy Diaz the Campeador. Sancho shrugged his shoulders, obeyed, and sat down, and all the duchess's damsels and duennas gathered round him, waiting in profound silence to hear what he would say. It was the duchess, however, who spoke first, saying, "Now that we are alone, and that there is nobody here to overhear us, I should be glad if the señor governor would relieve me of certain doubts I have, rising out of the history of the great Don Quixote that is now in print. One is: inasmuch as worthy Sancho never saw Dulcinea, I mean the lady Dulcinea del Toboso, nor took Don Quixote's letter to her, for it was left in the memorandum book in the Sierra Morena, how did he dare to invent the answer and all that about finding her sifting wheat, the whole story being a deception and falsehood, and so much to the prejudice of the peerless Dulcinea's good name, a thing that is not at all becoming the character and fidelity of a good squire?"

At these words, Sancho, without uttering one in reply, got up from his chair, and with noiseless steps, with his body bent and his finger on his lips, went all round the room lifting up the hangings; and this was done, he came back to his seat and said, "Now, señora, that I have seen that there is no one except the bystanders listening to us on the sly, I will answer what you have asked me, and all you may ask me, without fear or dread. And the first thing I have got to say is, that for my own part I hold my master Don Quixote to be stark mad, though sometimes he says things that, to my mind, and indeed everybody's that listens to him, are so wise, and run in such a straight furrow, that Satan himself could not have said them better; but for all that, really, and beyond all question, it's my firm belief he is cracked. Well, then, as this is clear to my mind, I can venture to make him believe things that have neither head nor tail, like that affair of the answer to the letter, and that other of six or eight days ago, which is not yet in history, that is to say, the affair of the enchantment of my lady

Dulcinea; for I made him believe she is enchanted, though there's no more truth in it than over the hills of Úbeda."[51]

The duchess begged him to tell her about the enchantment or deception, so Sancho told the whole story exactly as it had happened, and his hearers were not a little amused by it; and then resuming, the duchess said, "In consequence of what worthy Sancho has told me, a doubt starts up in my mind, and there comes a kind of whisper to my ear that says, 'If Don Quixote be mad, crazy, and cracked, and Sancho Panza his squire knows it, and, notwithstanding, serves and follows him, and goes trusting to his empty promises, there can be no doubt he must be still madder and sillier than his master; and that being so, it will be cast in your teeth, señora duchess, if you give the said Sancho an island to govern; for how will he who does not know how to govern himself know how to govern others?' "

"By God, señora," said Sancho, "but that doubt comes timely; but your grace may say it out, and speak plainly, or as you like; for I know what you say is true, and if I were wise I should have left my master long ago; but this was my fate, this was my bad luck; I can't help it. I must follow him; we're from the same village, I have eaten his bread, I'm fond of him, I'm grateful, he gave me his ass-colts, and above all I'm faithful; so it's quite impossible for anything to separate us, except the pickaxe and shovel. And if your highness does not like to give me the government you promised, God made me without it, and maybe your not giving it to me will be all the better for my conscience, for fool as I am I know the proverb 'to her hurt the ant got wings,' and it may be that Sancho the squire will get to heaven sooner than Sancho the governer. 'They make as good bread here as in France,' and 'by night all cats are gray,' and 'a hard case enough his, who hasn't broken his fast at two in the afternoon,' and 'there's no stomach a hand's breadth bigger than another,' and the same can be filled 'with straw or hay,' as the saying is, and 'the little birds of the field have God for their purveyor and caterer,' and 'four yards of Cuenca frieze keep one warmer than four of Segovia broadcloth,' and 'when we quit this world and are put underground the prince travels by as narrow a path as the journeyman,' and 'the Pope's body does not take up more feet of earth than the sacristan's,' for all that the one is higher than the other; for when we go to our graves we all pack ourselves up and make ourselves small, or rather they pack us up and make us small in spite of us, and then—good night to us. And I say once more, if your ladyship does not like to give me the island because I'm a fool, like a wise man I will take care to give myself no trouble about it; I have heard say that 'behind the cross there's the devil,' and that 'all that glitters is not gold,' and that from among the oxen, and the ploughs, and the yokes, Wamba the husbandman was taken to be made King of Spain, and from among brocades, and pleasures, and riches, Roderick was taken to be devoured by adders, if the verses of the old ballads don't lie."[52]

"To be sure they don't lie!" exclaimed Doña Rodriguez, the duenna, who was one of the listeners. "Why, there's a ballad that says they put King Rodrigo alive into a

---

[51] **"hills of Úbeda":** There are no hills near Úbeda; hence, the story is a fiction.

[52] **"Roderick . . . lie":** A reference to old ballads telling the story of King Rodrigo, last king of the Visigoths.

tomb full of toads, and adders, and lizards, and that two days afterwards the King, in a plaintive, feeble voice, cried out from within the tomb—

They gnaw me now, they gnaw me now,
There where I most did sin.

And according to that the gentleman has good reason to say he would rather be a laboring man than a king, if vermin are to eat him."

The duchess could not help laughing at the simplicity of her duenna, or wondering at the language and proverbs of Sancho, to whom she said, "Worthy Sancho knows very well that when once a knight has made a promise he strives to keep it, though it should cost him his life. My lord and husband the duke, though not one of the errant sort, is none the less a knight for that reason, and will keep his word about the promised island, in spite of the envy and malice of the world. Let Sancho be of good cheer; for when he least expects it he will find himself seated on the throne of his island and seat of dignity, and will take possession of his government that he may discard it for another of three-bordered brocade. The charge I give him is to be careful how he governs his vassals, bearing in mind that they are all loyal and well-born."

"As to governing them well," said Sancho, "there's no need of charging me to do that, for I'm kind-hearted by nature, and full of compassion for the poor; 'there's no stealing the loaf from him who kneads and bakes'; and by my faith it won't do to throw false dice with me; I am an old dog, and I know all about '*tus, tus*'; I can be wide awake if need be, and I don't let clouds come before my eyes, for I know where the shoe pinches me; I say so, because with me the good will have support and protection, and the bad neither footing nor access. And it seems to me that, in governments, to make a beginning is everything; and maybe, after having been governor a fortnight, I'll take kindly to the work and know more about it than the field labor I have been brought up to."

"You are right, Sancho," said the duchess, "for no one is born ready taught, and the bishops are made out of men and not out of stones. But to return to the subject we were discussing just now, the enchantment of the lady Dulcinea, I look upon it as certain, and something more than evident, that Sancho's idea of practising a deception upon his master, making him believe that the peasant girl was Dulcinea and that if he did not recognize her it must be because she was enchanted, was all a device of one of the enchanters that persecute Don Quixote. For in truth and earnest, I know from good authority that the coarse country wench who jumped up on the ass was and is Dulcinea del Toboso, and that worthy Sancho, though he fancies himself the deceiver, is the one that is deceived; and that there is no more reason to doubt the truth of this, than of anything else we never saw. Señor Sancho Panza must know that we too have enchanters here that are well disposed to us, and tell us what goes on in the world, plainly and distinctly, without subterfuge or deception; and believe me, Sancho, that agile country lass was and is Dulcinea del Toboso, who is as much enchanted as the mother that bore her; and when we least expect it, we shall see her in her own proper form, and then Sancho will be disabused of the error he is under at present."

"All that's very possible," said Sancho Panza; "and now I'm willing to believe what my master says about what he saw in the cave of Montesinos, where he says he saw the lady Dulcinea del Toboso in the very same dress and apparel that I said I had seen her in when I enchanted her all to please myself. It must be all exactly the other way, as your ladyship says; because it is impossible to suppose that out of my poor wit such a cunning trick could be concocted in a moment, nor do I think my master is so mad that by my weak and feeble persuasion he could be made to believe a thing so out of all reason. But, señora, your excellence must not therefore think me ill-disposed, for a dolt like me is not bound to see into the thoughts and plots of those vile enchanters. I invented all that to escape my master's scolding, and not with any intention of hurting him; and if it has turned out differently, there is a God in heaven who judges our hearts."

"That is true," said the duchess; "but tell me, Sancho, what is this you say about the cave of Montesinos, for I should like to know."

Sancho upon this related to her, word for word, what has been said already touching that adventure, and having heard it the duchess said, "From this occurrence it may be inferred that, as the great Don Quixote says he saw there the same country wench Sancho saw on the way from El Toboso, it is, no doubt, Dulcinea, and that there are some very active and exceedingly busy enchanters about."

"So I say," said Sancho, "and if my lady Dulcinea is enchanted, so much the worse for her, and I'm not going to pick a quarrel with my master's enemies, who seem to be many and spiteful. The truth is that the one I saw was a country wench, and I set her down to be a country wench; and if that was Dulcinea it must not be laid at my door, nor should I be called to answer for it or take the consequences. But they must go nagging at me every step—'Sancho said it, Sancho did it, Sancho here, Sancho there,' as if Sancho was nobody at all, and not that same Sancho Panza that's now going all over the world in books, so Samson Carrasco told me, and he's at any rate one that's a bachelor of Salamanca; and people of that sort can't lie, except when the whim seizes them or they have some very good reason for it. So there's no occasion for anybody to quarrel with me; and then I have a good character, and, as I have heard my master say, 'a good name is better than great riches'; let them only stick me into this government and they'll see wonders, for one who has been a good squire will be a good governor."

"All worthy Sancho's observations," said the duchess, "are Catonian sentences, or at any rate out of the very heart of Michael Verino himself, who *florentibus occidit annis.*[53] In fact, to speak in his own style, 'under a bad cloak there's often a good drinker.'"

"Indeed, señora," said Sancho, "I never yet drank out of wickedness; from thirst I have very likely, for I have nothing of the hypocrite in me; I drink when I'm inclined, or, if I'm not inclined, when they offer it to me, so as not to look either strait-laced or ill-bred; for when a friend drinks one's health what heart can be so hard as not to return it? But if I put on my shoes I don't dirty them; besides, squires to knights-errant mostly drink water, for they are always wandering among woods, forests and meadows, mountains and crags, without a drop of wine to be had if they gave their eyes for it."

"So I believe," said the duchess; "and now let Sancho go and take his sleep, and

[53] ***"florentibus . . . annis":*** "Died in the flower of his youth." Michael Verino was the author of a poem written in the style of Cato.

we will talk by-and-by at greater length, and settle how he may soon go and stick himself into the government, as he says."

Sancho once more kissed the duchess's hand, and entreated her to be so kind as to let good care be taken of his Dapple, for he was the light of his eyes.

"What is Dapple?" said the duchess.

"My ass," said Sancho, "which, not to mention him by that name, I'm accustomed to call Dapple; I begged this lady duenna here to take care of him when I came into the castle, and she got as angry as if I had said she was ugly or old, though it ought to be more natural and proper for duennas to feed asses than to ornament chambers. God bless me! what a spite a gentleman of my village had against these ladies!"

"He must have been some clown," said Doña Rodriguez the duenna; "for if he had been a gentleman and well-born he would have exalted them higher than the horns of the moon."

"That will do," said the duchess; "no more of this; hush, Doña Rodriguez, and let Señor Panza rest easy and leave the treatment of Dapple in my charge, for as he is a treasure of Sancho's, I'll put him on the apple of my eye."

"It will be enough for him to be in the stable," said Sancho, "for neither he nor I are worthy to rest a moment in the apple of your highness's eye, and I'd as soon stab myself as consent to it; for though my master says that in civilities it is better to lose by a card too many than a card too few, when it comes to civilities to asses we must mind what we are about and keep within due bounds."

"Take him to your government, Sancho," said the duchess, "and there you will be able to make as much of him as you like, and even release him from work and pension him off."

"Don't think, señora duchess, that you have said anything absurd," said Sancho; "I have seen more than two asses go to governments, and for me to take mine with me would be nothing new."

Sancho's words made the duchess laugh again and gave her fresh amusement, and dismissing him to sleep she went away to tell the duke the conversation she had had with him, and between them they plotted and arranged to play a joke upon Don Quixote that was to be a rare one and entirely in knight-errantry style, and in that same style they practised several upon him, so much in keeping and so clever that they form the best adventures this great history contains.

. . .

FROM

Chapter 42

OF THE COUNSELS WHICH DON QUIXOTE GAVE SANCHO PANZA BEFORE HE SET OUT TO GOVERN THE ISLAND, TOGETHER WITH OTHER WELL-CONSIDERED MATTERS

The duke and duchess . . . having laid their plans and given instructions to their servants and vassals how to behave to Sancho in his government of the promised island, the next day, . . . the duke told Sancho to prepare and get ready to go and be governor, for his islanders were already looking out for him as for the showers of May.

Sancho made him an obeisance, and said, "Ever since I came down from heaven, and from the top of it beheld the earth, and saw how little it is, the great desire I had to be a governor has been partly cooled in me; for what is there grand in being ruler on a grain of mustard seed, or what dignity or authority in governing half a dozen men about as big as hazel nuts; for, so far as I could see, there were no more on the whole earth? If your lordship would be so good as to give me ever so small a bit of heaven, were it no more than half a league, I'd rather have it than the best island in the world."

"Take notice, friend Sancho," said the duke, "I can not give a bit of heaven, no not so much as the breadth of my nail, to any one; rewards and favors of that sort are reserved for God alone. What I can give I give you, and that is a real, genuine island, compact, well-proportioned, and uncommonly fertile and fruitful, where, if you know how to use your opportunities, you may, with the help of the world's riches, gain those of heaven."

"Well then," said Sancho, "let the island come; and I'll try and be such a governor, that in spite of scoundrels I'll go to heaven; and it's not from any craving to quit my own humble condition or better myself, but from the desire I have to try what it tastes like to be a governor."

"If you once make trial of it, Sancho," said the duke, "you'll eat your fingers off after the government, so sweet a thing is it to command and be obeyed. Depend upon it when your master comes to be emperor (as he will beyond a doubt from the course his affairs are taking), it will be no easy matter to wrest the dignity from him, and he will be sore and sorry at heart to have been so long without becoming one."

"Señor," said Sancho, "it is my belief it's a good thing to be in command, if it's only over a drove of cattle."

"May I be buried with you, Sancho," said the duke, "but you know everything; I hope you will make as good a governor as your sagacity promises, and that is all I have to say; and now remember to-morrow is the day you must set out for the government of the island, and this evening they will provide you with the proper attire for you to wear, and all things requisite for your departure."

"Let them dress me as they like," said Sancho; "however I'm dressed I'll be Sancho Panza."

"That's true," said the duke; "but one's dress must be suited to the office or rank one holds; for it would not do for a jurist to dress like a soldier, or a soldier like a priest. You, Sancho, shall go partly as a lawyer, partly as a captain, for, in the island I am giving you, arms are needed as much as letters, and letters as much as arms."

"Of letters I know but little," said Sancho, "for I don't even know the A B C; but it is enough for me to have the Christus[54] in my memory to be a good governor. As for arms, I'll handle those they give me till I drop, and then, God be my help!"

"With so good a memory," said the duke, "Sancho can not go wrong in anything."

Here Don Quixote joined them; and learning what passed, and how soon Sancho was to go to his government, he with the duke's permission took him by the

[54] **"Christus":** A cross prefixed to the alphabet in schoolbooks.

hand, and retired to his room with him for the purpose of giving him advice as to how he was to demean himself in his office. As soon as they had entered the chamber he closed the door after him, and almost by force made Sancho sit down beside him, and in a quiet tone thus addressed him: "I give infinite thanks to Heaven, friend Sancho, that before I have met with any good luck, fortune has come forward to meet thee. I who counted upon my good fortune to discharge the recompense of thy services, find myself still waiting for advancement, while thou, before the time, and contrary to all reasonable expectation, seest thyself blessed in the fulfilment of thy desires. Some will bribe, beg, solicit, rise early, entreat, persist, without attaining the object of their suit; while another comes, and without knowing why or wherefore, finds himself invested with the place or office so many have sued for; and here it is that the common saying, 'There is good luck as well as bad luck in suits,' applies. Thou, who, to my thinking, art beyond all doubt a dullard, without early rising or night watching or taking any trouble, with the mere breath of knight errantry that has breathed upon thee, seest thyself without more ado governor of an island, as though it were a mere matter of course. This I say, Sancho, that thou attribute not the favor thou hast received to thine own merits, but give thanks to Heaven that disposes matters beneficently, and secondly thanks to the great power the profession of knight-errantry contains in itself. With a heart, then, inclined to believe what I have said to thee, attend, my son, to thy Cato here who would counsel thee and be thy pole-star and guide to direct and pilot thee to a safe haven out of this stormy sea wherein thou art about to ingulf thyself; for offices and great trusts are nothing else but a mighty gulf of troubles.

"First of all, my son, thou must fear God, for in the fear of him is wisdom, and being wise thou canst not err in aught.

"Secondly, thou must keep in view what thou art, striving to know thyself, the most difficult thing to know that the mind can imagine. If thou knowest thyself, it will follow thou wilt not puff thyself up like the frog that strove to make himself as large as the ox; if thou dost, the recollection of having kept pigs in thine own country will serve as the ugly feet for the wheel of thy folly."

"That's the truth," said Sancho; "but that was when I was a boy; afterwards when I was something more of a man it was geese I kept, not pigs. But to my thinking that has nothing to do with it; for not all who are governors come of kingly stock."

"True," said Don Quixote, "and for that reason those who are not of noble origin should take care that the dignity of the office they hold be accompanied by a gentle suavity, which wisely managed will save them from the sneers of malice that no station escapes.

"Glory in thy humble birth, Sancho, and be not ashamed of saying thou art peasant-born; for when it is seen thou art not ashamed no one will set himself to put thee to the blush; and pride thyself rather upon being one of lowly virtue than a lofty sinner. Countless are they who, born of mean parentage, have risen to the highest dignities, pontifical and imperial, and of the truth of this I could give thee instances enough to weary thee.

"Remember, Sancho, if thou make virtue thy aim, and take a pride in doing virtuous actions, thou wilt have no cause to envy those who are born princes and lords, for blood is an inheritance, but virtue an acquisition, and virtue has in itself a worth that blood does not possess.

"This being so, if perchance any one of thy kinsfolk should come to see thee when thou art in thine island, thou art not to repel or slight him, but on the contrary to welcome him, entertain him, and make much of him; for in so doing thou wilt be approved of Heaven (which is not pleased that any should despise what it hath made), and wilt comply with the laws of well-ordered nature.

"If thou carriest thy wife with thee (and it is not well for those that administer governments to be long without their wives), teach and instruct her, and strive to smooth down her natural roughness; for all that may be gained by a wise governor may be lost and wasted by a boorish stupid wife.

"If perchance thou art left a widower—a thing which may happen—and in virtue of thy office seekest a consort of higher degree, choose not one to serve thee for a hook, or for a fishing-rod, or for the hood of thy 'won't have it';[55] for verily, I tell thee, for all the judge's wife receives, the husband will be held accountable at the general calling to account; where he will have to repay in death fourfold, items that in life he regarded as naught.

"Never go by arbitrary law, which is so much favored by ignorant men who plume themselves on cleverness.

"Let the tears of the poor man find with thee more compassion, but not more justice, than the pleadings of the rich.

"Strive to lay bare the truth, as well amid the promises and presents of the rich man, as amid the sobs and entreaties of the poor.

"When equity may and should be brought into play, press not the utmost rigor of the law against the guilty; for the reputation of the stern judge stands not higher than that of the compassionate.

"If perchance thou permittest the staff of justice to swerve, let it be not by the weight of a gift, but by that of mercy.

"If it should happen to thee to give judgment in the cause of one who is thine enemy, turn thy thoughts away from thy injury and fix them on the justice of the case.

"Let not thine own passion blind thee in another man's cause; for the errors thou wilt thus commit will be most frequently irremediable; or if not, only to be remedied at the expense of thy good name and fortune.

"If any handsome woman come to seek justice of thee, turn away thine eyes from her tears and thine ears from her lamentations, and consider deliberately the merits of her demand, if thou wouldst not have thy reason swept away by her weeping, and thy rectitude by her sighs.

"Abuse not by word him whom thou hast to punish in deed, for the pain of punishment is enough for the unfortunate without the addition of thine objurgations.

"Bear in mind that the culprit who comes under thy jurisdiction is but a miserable man subject to all the propensities of our depraved nature, and so far as may be

[55] **hood . . . "won't have it":** An allusion to a popular joke about begging friars, who were said to make a pretense of refusing gifts, while hinting that gifts might be thrown into the hoods of their robes.

in thy power show thyself lenient and forbearing; for though the attributes of God are all equal, to our eyes that of mercy is brighter and loftier than that of justice.

"If thou followest these precepts and rules, Sancho, thy days will be long, thy fame eternal, thy reward abundant, thy felicity unutterable; thou wilt marry thy children as thou wouldst; they and thy grandchildren will bear titles; thou wilt live in peace and concord with all men; and, when life draws to a close, death will come to thee in calm and ripe old age, and the light and loving hands of thy great-grandchildren will close thine eyes.

"What I have thus far addressed to thee are instructions for the adornment of thy mind; listen now to those which tend to that of the body."

Chapter 43

OF THE SECOND SET OF COUNSELS DON QUIXOTE GAVE SANCHO PANZA

Who, hearing the foregoing discourse of Don Quixote, would not have set him down for a person of great good sense and greater rectitude of purpose? But, as has been frequently observed in the course of this great history, he only talked nonsense when he touched on chivalry, and in discussing all other subjects showed that he had a clear and unbiassed understanding; so that at every turn his acts gave the lie to his intellect, and his intellect to his acts; but in the case of these second counsels that he gave Sancho he showed himself to have a lively turn of humor, and displayed conspicuously his wisdom, and also his folly.

Sancho listened to him with the deepest attention, and endeavored to fix his counsels in his memory, like one who meant to follow them and by their means bring the full promise of his government to a happy issue. Don Quixote, then, went on to say:

"With regard to the mode in which thou shouldst govern thy person and thy house, Sancho, the first charge I have to give thee is to be clean, and to cut thy nails, not letting them grow as some do, whose ignorance makes them fancy that long nails are an ornament to their hands, as if those excrescences they neglect to cut were nails, and not the talons of a lizard-catching kestrel—a filthy and unnatural abuse.

"Go not ungirt and loose, Sancho; for disordered attire is a sign of an unstable mind, unless indeed the slovenliness and slackness is to be set down to craft, as was the common opinion in the case of Julius Cæsar.

"Ascertain cautiously what thy office may be worth; and if it will allow thee to give liveries to thy servants, give them respectable and serviceable, rather than showy and gay ones, and divide them between thy servants and the poor; that is to say, if thou canst clothe six pages, clothe three and three poor men, and thus thou wilt have pages for heaven and pages for earth; the vainglorious never think of this new mode of giving liveries.

"Eat not garlic nor onions, lest they find out thy boorish origin by the smell; walk slowly and speak deliberately, but not in such a way as to make it seem thou art listening to thyself; for all affectation is bad.

"Dine sparingly and sup more sparingly still; for the health of the whole body is forged in the workshop of the stomach.

"Be temperate in drinking, bearing in mind that wine in excess keeps neither secrets nor promises.

"Take care, Sancho, not to chew on both sides, and not to eruct in anybody's presence."

"Eruct!" said Sancho; "I don't know what that means."

"To eruct, Sancho," said Don Quixote, "means to belch, and that is one of the filthiest words in the Spanish language, though a very expressive one; and therefore nice folk have had recourse to the Latin, and instead of belch say eruct, and instead of belches say eructations; and if some do not understand these terms it matters little, for custom will bring them into use in the course of time, so that they will be readily understood; that is the way a language is enriched; custom and the public are all-powerful there."

"In truth, señor," said Sancho, "one of the counsels and cautions I mean to bear in mind shall be this, not to belch, for I'm constantly doing it."

"Eruct, Sancho, not belch," said Don Quixote.

"Eruct, I shall say henceforth, and I swear not to forget it," said Sancho.

"Likewise, Sancho," said Don Quixote, "thou must not mingle such a quantity of proverbs in thy discourse as thou dost; for though proverbs are short maxims, thou dost drag them in so often by the head and shoulders that they savor more of nonsense than of maxims."

"God alone can cure that," said Sancho; "for I have more proverbs in me than a book, and when I speak they come so thick together into my mouth that they fall to fighting among themselves to get out; that's why my tongue lets fly the first that come, though they may not be pat to the purpose. But I'll take care henceforward to use such as befit the dignity of my office; for 'in a house where there's plenty, supper is soon cooked,' and 'he who binds does not wrangle,' and 'the bell-ringer's in a safe berth,' and 'giving and keeping require brains.'"

"That's it, Sancho!" said Don Quixote; "pack, tack, string proverbs together; nobody is hindering thee! 'My mother beats me, and I go on with my tricks.' I am bidding thee avoid proverbs, and here in a second thou hast shot out a whole litany of them, which have as much to do with what we are talking about as 'over the hills of Úbeda.' Mind, Sancho, I do not say that a proverb aptly brought in is objectionable; but to pile up and string together proverbs at random makes conversation dull and vulgar.

"When thou ridest on horseback, do not go lolling with thy body on the back of the saddle, nor carry thy legs stiff or sticking out from the horse's belly, nor yet sit so loosely that one would suppose thou wert on Dapple; for the seat on a horse makes gentlemen of some and grooms of others.

"Be moderate in thy sleep; for he who does not rise early does not get the benefit of the day; and remember, Sancho, diligence is the mother of good fortune, and indolence, its opposite, never yet attained the object of an honest ambition.

"The last counsel I will give thee now, though it does not tend to bodily improvement, I would have thee carry carefully in thy memory, for I believe it will be no less useful to thee than those I have given thee already, and it is this—never engage in a dispute about families, at least in the way of comparing them one with another; for necessarily one of those compared will be better than the other, and thou wilt be hated by the one thou hast disparaged, and get nothing in any shape from the one thou hast exalted.

"Thy attire shall be hose of full length, a long jerkin, and a cloak a trifle longer; loose breeches by no means, for they are becoming neither for gentlemen nor for governors.

"For the present, Sancho, this is all that has occurred to me to advise thee; as time goes by and occasions arise my instructions shall follow, if thou take care to let me know how thou art circumstanced."

"Señor," said Sancho, "I see well enough that all these things your worship has said to me are good, holy, and profitable; but what use will they be to me if I don't remember one of them? To be sure that about not letting my nails grow, and marrying again if I have the chance, will not slip out of my head; but all that other hash, muddle, and jumble—I don't and can't recollect any more of it than of last year's clouds; so it must be given me in writing; for though I can't either read or write, I'll give it to my confessor to drive it into me and remind me of it whenever it is necessary."

"Ah, sinner that I am!" said Don Quixote, "how bad it looks in governors not to know how to read or write; for let me tell thee, Sancho, when a man knows not how to read, or is left-handed, it argues one of two things; either that he was the son of exceedingly mean and lowly parents, or that he himself was so incorrigible and ill-conditioned that neither good company nor good teaching could make any impression on him. It is a great defect that thou laborest under, and therefore I would have thee learn at any rate to sign thy name."

"I can sign my name well enough," said Sancho, "for when I was steward of the brotherhood in my village I learned to make certain letters, like the marks on bales of goods, which they told me made out my name. Besides I can pretend my right hand is disabled and make some one else sign for me, for 'there's a remedy for everything except death'; and as I shall be in command and hold the staff, I can do as I like; moreover, 'he who has the alcalde for his father—,'[56] and I'll be governor, and that's higher than alcalde. Only come and see! Let them make light of me and abuse me; 'they'll come for wool and go back shorn'; 'whom God loves, his house is sweet to him'; 'the silly sayings of the rich pass for saws in the world'; and as I'll be rich, being a governor, and at the same time generous, as I mean to be, no fault will be seen in me. 'Only make yourself honey and the flies will suck you'; 'as much as thou hast so much art thou worth,' as my grandmother used to say; and 'thou canst have no revenge of a man of substance.'"

"Oh, God's curse upon thee, Sancho!" here exclaimed Don Quixote; "sixty thousand devils fly away with thee and thy proverbs! For the last hour thou hast been stringing them together and inflicting the pangs of torture on me with every one of them. Those proverbs will bring thee to the gallows one day, I promise thee; thy subjects will take the government from thee, or there will be revolts among them, all

[56] **"'he . . . father'":** The full proverb is "He who has the alcalde for his father goes into court with an easy mind."

because of them. Tell me, where dost thou pick them up, thou booby? How dost thou apply them, thou blockhead? For with me, to utter one and make it apply properly, I have to sweat and labor as if I were digging."

"By God, master mine," said Sancho, "your worship is making a fuss about very little. Why the devil should you be vexed if I make use of what is my own? And I have got nothing else, nor any other stock in trade except proverbs and more proverbs; and here are four just this instant come into my head, pat to the purpose and like pears in a basket; but I won't repeat them, for 'Sage silence is called Sancho.'"

"That, Sancho, thou art not," said Don Quixote; "for not only art thou not sage silence, but thou art pestilent prate and perversity; still I would like to know what four proverbs have just now come into thy memory, for I have been turning over mine own—and it is a good one—and not one occurs to me."

"What can be better," said Sancho, "than 'never put thy thumbs between two back teeth'; and 'to *"get out of my house"* and *"what do you want with my wife?"* there is no answer'; and 'whether the pitcher hits the stone, or the stone the pitcher, it's a bad business for the pitcher'; all which fit to a hair? For no one should quarrel with his governor, or him in authority over him, because he will come off the worst, as he does who puts his finger between two back teeth, and if they are not back teeth it makes no difference, so long as they are teeth; and to whatever the governor may say there's no answer, any more than to 'get out of my house' and 'what do you want with my wife?' and then, as for that about the stone and the pitcher, a blind man could see that. So that he who sees the mote in another's eye had need to see the beam in his own, that it be not said of himself, 'the dead woman was frightened at the one with her throat cut'; and your worship knows well that the fool knows more in his own house than the wise man in another's."

"Nay, Sancho," said Don Quixote, "the fool knows nothing, either in his own house or in anybody else's, for no wise structure of any sort can stand on a foundation of folly; but let us say no more about it, Sancho, for if thou governest badly, thine will be the fault and mine the shame; but I comfort myself with having done my duty in advising thee as earnestly and as wisely as I could; and thus I am released from my obligations and my promise. God guide thee, Sancho, and govern thee in thy government, and deliver me from the misgiving I have that thou wilt turn the whole island upside down, a thing I might prevent by explaining to the duke what thou art and telling him that all that fat little person of thine is nothing else but a sack full of proverbs and sauciness."

"Señor," said Sancho, "if your worship thinks I'm not fit for this government, I give it up on the spot; for the mere black of the nail of my soul is dearer to me than my whole body; and I can live just as well, simple Sancho, on bread and onions, as governor, on partridges and capons; and what's more, while we're asleep we're all equal, great and small, rich and poor. But if your worship looks into it, you will see it was your worship alone that put me on to this business of governing; for I know no more about the government of islands than a buzzard; and if there's any reason to think that because of my being a governor the devil will get hold of me, I'd rather go Sancho to heaven than governor to hell."

"By God, Sancho," said Don Quixote, "for those last words thou hast uttered alone, I consider thou deservest to be governor of a thousand islands. Thou hast good natural instincts, without which no knowledge is worth anything; commend thyself to God, and try not to swerve in the pursuit of thy main object; I mean, always make it thy aim and fixed purpose to do right in all matters that come before thee, for Heaven always helps good intentions; and now let us go to dinner, for I think my lord and lady are waiting for us."

. . .

FROM

Chapter 45

OF HOW THE GREAT SANCHO PANZA TOOK POSSESSION OF HIS ISLAND, AND OF HOW HE MADE A BEGINNING IN GOVERNING

O perpetual discoverer of the antipodes, torch of the world, eye of heaven, sweet stimulator of the water-coolers! Thymbræus here, Phœbus there, now archer, now physician, father of poetry, inventor of music; thou that always risest and, notwithstanding appearances, never settest! To thee, O Sun, by whose aid man begetteth man, to thee I appeal to help me and lighten the darkness of my wit that I may be able to proceed with scrupulous exactitude in giving an account of the great Sancho Panza's government; for without thee I feel myself weak, feeble, and uncertain.

To come to the point, then—Sancho with all his attendants arrived at a village of some thousand inhabitants, and one of the largest the duke possessed. They informed him that it was called the island of Barataria, either because the name of the village was Baratario, or because of the joke by way of which the government had been conferred upon him.[57] On reaching the gates of the town, which was a walled one, the municipality came forth to meet him, the bells rang out a peal, and the inhabitants showed every sign of general satisfaction; and with great pomp they conducted him to the principal church to give thanks to God, and then with burlesque ceremonies they presented him with the keys of the town, and acknowledged him as perpetual governor of the island of Barataria. The costume, the beard, and the fat squat figure of the new governor astonished all those who were not in the secret, and even all who were, and they were not a few. Finally, leading him out of the church they carried him to the judgment seat and seated him on it, and the duke's majordomo said to him, "It is an ancient custom in this island, señor governor, that he who comes to take possession of this famous island is bound to answer a question which shall be put to him, and which must be a somewhat knotty and difficult one; and by his answer the people take the measure of their new governor's wit, and hail with joy or deplore his arrival accordingly."

While the majordomo was making this speech Sancho was gazing at several large letters inscribed on the wall opposite his seat, and as he could not read he asked

[57] **Barataria . . . him:** *Barato,* in old Spanish, is a trick or practical joke.

what that was painted on the wall. The answer was, "Señor, there is written and recorded the day on which your lordship took possession of this island, and the inscription says, *This day, the so-and-so of such-and-such a month and year, Señor Don Sancho Panza took possession of this island; many years may he enjoy it.*"

"And whom do they call Don Sancho Panza?" asked Sancho.

"Your lordship," replied the majordomo; "for no other Panza but the one who is now seated in that chair has ever entered this island."

"Well then, let me tell you, brother," said Sancho, "I haven't got the 'Don,' nor has any one of my family ever had it; my name is plain Sancho Panza, and Sancho was my father's name, and Sancho was my grandfather's, and they were all Panzas, without any Dons or Doñas tacked on; I suspect that in this island there are more Dons than stones; but never mind; God knows what I mean, and maybe if my government lasts four days I'll weed out these Dons that no doubt are as great a nuisance as the midges, they're so plenty. Let the majordomo go on with his question, and I'll give the best answer I can, whether the people deplore or not."

At this instant there came into court two old men, one carrying a cane by way of a walking-stick, and the one who had no stick said, "Señor, some time ago I lent this good man ten gold-crowns in gold to gratify him and do him a service, on the condition that he was to return them to me whenever I should ask for them. A long time passed before I asked for them, for I would not put him to any greater straits to return them than he was in when I lent them to him; but thinking he was growing careless about payment I asked for them once and several times; and not only will he not give them back, but he denies that he owes them, and says I never lent him any such crowns; or if I did, that he repaid them; and I have no witnesses either of the loan, or of the payment, for he never paid me; I want your worship to put him to his oath, and if he swears he returned them to me I forgive him the debt here and before God."

"What say you to this, good old man, you with the stick?" said Sancho.

To which the old man replied, "I admit, señor, that he lent them to me; but let your worship lower your staff, and as he leaves it to my oath, I'll swear that I gave them back, and paid him really and truly."

The governor lowered the staff, and as he did so the old man who had the stick handed it to the other old man to hold for him while he swore, as if he found it in his way; and then laid his hand on the cross of the staff, saying that it was true the ten crowns that were demanded of him had been lent him; but that he had with his own hand given them back into the hand of the other, and that he, not recollecting it, was every minute asking for them.

Seeing this the great governor asked the creditor what answer he had to make to what his opponent said. He said that no doubt his debtor had told the truth, for he believed him to be an honest man and a good Christian, and he himself must have forgotten when and how he had given him back the crowns; and that from that time forth he would make no further demand upon him.

The debtor took his stick again, and bowing his head left the court. Observing this, and how, without another word, he made off, and observing too the resignation of the plaintiff, Sancho buried his head in his bosom and remained for a short space in deep thought, with the forefinger of his right hand on his brow and nose; then he raised his head and bade them call back the old man with the stick, for he had already taken his departure. They brought him back, and as soon as Sancho saw him he said, "Honest man, give me that stick, for I want it."

"Willingly," said the old man; "here it is, señor," and he put it into his hand.

Sancho took it and handing it to the other old man, said to him, "Go, and God be with you; for now you are paid."

"I, señor!" returned the old man; "why, is this cane worth ten gold-crowns?"

"Yes," said the governor, "or if not I am the greatest dolt in the world; now you will see whether I have got the head-piece to govern a whole kingdom"; and he ordered the cane to be broken in two, there, in the presence of all. It was done, and in the middle of it they found ten gold-crowns. All were filled with amazement, and looked upon their governor as another Solomon. They asked him how he had come to the conclusion that the ten crowns were in the cane; he replied that, observing how the old man who swore gave the stick to his opponent while he was taking the oath, and swore that he had really and truly given him the crowns, and how as soon as he had done swearing he asked for the stick again, it came into his head that the sum demanded must be inside it; and from this he said it might be seen that God sometimes guides those who govern in their judgments, even though they may be fools; besides he had heard the curate himself mention just such another case, and he had so good a memory, that if it was not that he forgot everything he wished to remember, there would not be such a memory in all the island. To conclude, the old men went off, one crestfallen, and the other in high contentment, all who were present were astonished, and he who was recording the words, deeds, and movements of Sancho could not make up his mind whether he was to look upon him and set him down as a fool or as a man of sense.

As soon as this case was disposed of, there came into court a woman holding on with a tight grip to a man dressed like a well-to-do cattle dealer, and she came forward making a great outcry and exclaiming, "Justice, señor governor, justice! and if I don't get it on earth I'll go look for it in heaven. Señor governor of my soul, this wicked man caught me in the middle of the fields here and used my body as if it was an ill-washed rag, and, woe is me! got from me what I had kept these three-and-twenty years and more, defending it against Moors and Christians, natives and strangers; and I always as hard as an oak, and keeping myself as pure as a salamander in the fire, or wool among the brambles, for this good fellow to come now with clean hands to handle me!"

"It remains to be proved whether this gallant has clean hands or not," said Sancho; and turning to the man he asked him what he had to say in answer to the woman's charge.

He all in confusion made answer, "Sirs, I am a poor pig dealer, and this morning I left the village to sell (saving your presence) four pigs, and between dues and cribbings they got out of me little less than the worth of them. As I was returning to my village I fell in on the road with this good dame, and the devil who makes a coil and a mess out of everything, yoked us together. I paid her fairly, but she not contented laid hold of me and never let go until she brought me here; she says I forced her, but she lies by the oath I swear or am ready to swear; and this is the whole truth and every particle of it."

The governor on this asked him if he had any money in silver about him; he said he had about twenty ducats in a leather purse in his bosom. The governor bade him take it out and hand it to the complainant; he obeyed trembling; the woman took it, and making a thousand salaams to all and praying to God for the long life and health of the señor governor who had such regard for distressed orphans and virgins, she hurried out of court with the purse grasped in both her hands, first looking, however, to see if the money it contained was silver.

As soon as she was gone Sancho said to the cattle dealer, whose tears were already starting and whose eyes and heart were following his purse, "Good fellow, go after that woman and take the purse from her, by force even, and come back with it here"; and he did not say it to one who was a fool or deaf, for the man was off at once like a flash of lightning, and ran to do as he was bid.

All the bystanders waited anxiously to see the end of the case, and presently both man and woman came back at even closer grips than before, she with her petticoat up and the purse in the lap of it, and he struggling hard to take it from her, but all to no purpose, so stout was the woman's defence, she all the while crying out, "Justice from God and the world! see here, señor governor, the shamelessness and boldness of this villain, who in the middle of the town, in the middle of the street, wanted to take from me the purse your worship bade him give me."

"And did he take it?" asked the governor.

"Take it!" said the woman; "I'd let my life be taken from me sooner than the purse. A pretty child I'd be! It's another sort of cat they must throw in my face, and not that poor scurvy knave. Pincers and hammers, mallets and chisels would not get it out of my grip; no, nor lions' claws; the soul from out of my body first!"

"She is right," said the man; "I own myself beaten and powerless; I confess I haven't the strength to take it from her"; and he let go his hold of her.

Upon this the governor said to the woman, "Let me see that purse, my worthy and sturdy friend." She handed it to him at once, and the governor returned it to the man, and said to the unforced mistress of force, "Sister, if you had shown as much, or only half as much, spirit and vigor in defending your body as you have shown in defending that purse, the strength of Hercules could not have forced you. Be off, and God speed you, and bad luck to you, and don't show your face in all this island, or within six leagues of it on any side, under pain of two hundred lashes; be off at once, I say, you shameless, cheating shrew."

The woman was cowed and went off disconsolately, hanging her head; and the governor said to the man, "Honest man, go home with your money, and God speed you; and for the future, if you don't want to lose it, see that you don't take it into your head to yoke with anybody." The man thanked him as clumsily as he could and went his way, and the bystanders were again filled with admiration at their new governor's judgments and sentences.

Next, two men, one apparently a farm-laborer, and the other a tailor, for he had a pair of shears in his hand, presented themselves before him, and the tailor said, "Señor governor, this laborer and I come before your worship by reason of this honest man coming to my shop yesterday (for saving everybody's presence I'm a passed tailor, God be thanked), and putting a piece of cloth into my hands and asking me, 'Señor, will there be enough in this cloth to make me a cap?' Measuring the cloth I said there would. He probably suspected—as I supposed, and I supposed right—that I wanted to steal some of the cloth, led to think so by his own roguery and the bad opinion people have of tailors; and he told me to see if there would be enough for two. I guessed what he would be at, and I said 'yes.' He, still following up his original unworthy notion, went on adding cap after cap, and I 'yes' after 'yes,' until we got as far as five. He has just this moment come for them; and I gave them to him, but he won't pay me for the making; on the contrary, he calls upon me to pay *him,* or else return his cloth."

"Is all this true, brother?" said Sancho.

"Yes, señor," replied the man; "but will your worship make him show the five caps he has made me?"

"With all my heart," said the tailor; and drawing his hand from under his cloak he showed five caps stuck upon the five fingers of it, and said, "there are the five caps this good man asks for; and by God and upon my conscience I haven't a scrap of cloth left, and I'll let the work be examined by the inspectors of the trade."

All present laughed at the number of caps and the novelty of the suit; Sancho set himself to think for a moment, and then said, "It seems to me that in this case it is not necessary to deliver long-winded arguments, but only to give off-hand the judgment of an honest man; and so my decision is that the tailor lose the making and the laborer the cloth, and that the caps go to the prisoners in the jail, and let there be no more about it."

If the previous decision about the cattle dealer's purse excited the admiration of the bystanders, this provoked their laughter; however, the governor's orders were after all executed. All this, having been taken down by his chronicler, was at once despatched to the duke, who was looking out for it with great eagerness. [. . .]

FROM

Chapter 47

WHEREIN IS CONTINUED THE ACCOUNT OF HOW SANCHO PANZA CONDUCTED HIMSELF IN HIS GOVERNMENT

The history says that from the justice court they carried Sancho to a sumptuous palace, where in a spacious chamber there was a table laid out with royal magnificence. The clarions sounded as Sancho entered the room, and four pages came forward to present him with water for his hands, which Sancho received with great dignity. The music ceased, and Sancho seated himself at the head of the table, for there was only that seat placed, and no more than the one cover laid. A personage, who it appeared afterwards was a physician, placed himself standing by his side with a whalebone wand in his hand. They then lifted up a fine white cloth covering fruit and a great variety of dishes of different sorts; one who looked like a student said grace, and a page put a laced bib on Sancho, while another who played the part of head carver placed a dish of fruit before him. But hardly had he tasted a morsel when the man with the wand touched the plate with it, and they took it away from before him with the utmost celerity. The carver, however, brought him another dish, and Sancho proceeded to try it; but before he could get at it, not to say taste it, already the wand had touched it and a page had carried it off with the same promptitude as the fruit. Sancho seeing this was puzzled, and looking from one to another asked if this dinner was to be eaten after the fashion of a jugglery trick.

To this he with the wand replied, "It is not to be eaten, señor governor, except as is usual and customary in other islands where there are governors. I, señor, am a physician, and I am paid a salary in this island to serve its governors as such, and I have a much greater regard for their health than for my own, studying day and night making myself acquainted with the governor's constitution, in order to be able to cure him when he falls sick. The chief thing I have to do is to attend at his dinners and suppers and allow him to eat what appears to me to be fit for him and keep from him what I think will do him harm and be injurious to his stomach; and therefore I ordered that plate of fruit to be removed as being too moist, and that other dish I ordered to be removed as being too hot and containing many spices that stimulate thirst; for he who drinks much kills and consumes the radical moisture wherein life consists."

"Well then," said Sancho, "that dish of roast partridges there that seems so savory will not do me any harm."

To this the physician replied, "Of those my lord the governor shall not eat so long as I live."

"Why so?" said Sancho.

"Because," replied the doctor, "our master Hippocrates, the polestar and beacon of medicine, says in one of his aphorisms *omnis saturatio mala, perdicis autem pessima,* which means 'all repletion is bad, but that of partridge is the worst of all.'"

"In that case," said Sancho, "let señor doctor see among the dishes that are on the table what will do me most good and least harm, and let me eat it, without tapping it with his stick; for by the life of the governor, and so may God suffer me to enjoy it, but I'm dying of hunger; and in spite of the doctor and all he may say, to deny me food is the way to take my life instead of prolonging it."

"Your worship is right, señor governor," said the physician; "and therefore your worship, I consider, should not eat of those stewed rabbits there, because it is a furry kind of food; if that veal were not roasted and served with pickles, you might try it; but it is out of the question."

"That big dish that is smoking farther off," said Sancho, "seems to me to be an *olla podrida,*[58] and out of the diversity of things in such *ollas,* I can't fail to light upon something tasty and good for me."

"*Absit,*" said the doctor; "far from us be any such base thought! There is nothing in the world less nourishing than an *olla podrida;* to canons, or rectors of colleges, or peasants' weddings with your *ollas podridas,* but let us have none of them on the

[58] ***"olla podrida":*** A stew.

tables of governors, where everything that is present should be delicate and refined; and the reason is, that always, everywhere and by everybody, simple medicines are more esteemed than compound ones, for we cannot go wrong in those that are simple, while in the compound we may, by merely altering the quantity of the things composing them. But what I am of opinion the governor should eat now in order to preserve and fortify his health is a hundred or so of wafer cakes and a few thin slices of conserve of quinces, which will settle his stomach and help his digestion."

Sancho on hearing this threw himself back in his chair and surveyed the doctor steadily, and in a solemn tone asked him what his name was and where he had studied.

He replied, "My name, Señor Governor, is Doctor Pedro Recio de Aguero, I am a native of a place called Tirteafuera which lies between Caracuel and Almodóvar del Campo, on the right-hand side, and I have the degree of doctor from the university of Osuna."

To which Sancho, glowing all over with rage, returned, "Then let Doctor Pedro Recio de Mal-aguero, native of Tirteafuera,[59] a place that's on the right-hand side as we go from Caracuel to Almodóvar del Campo, graduate of Osuna, get out of my presence at once; or I swear by the sun I'll take a cudgel, and by dint of blows, beginning with him, I'll not leave a doctor in the whole island; at least of those I know to be ignorant; for as to learned, wise, sensible physicians, them I will reverence and honor as divine persons. Once more I say let Pedro Recio get out of this or I'll take this chair I am sitting on and break it over his head. And if they call me to account for it, I'll clear myself by saying I served God in killing a bad doctor—a general executioner. And now give me something to eat, or else take your government; for a trade that does not feed its master is not worth two beans."

The doctor was dismayed when he saw the governor in such a passion, and he would have made a *Tirteafuera* out of the room but that the same instant a posthorn sounded in the street; and the carver putting his head out of the window turned round and said, "It's a courier from my lord the duke, no doubt with some despatch of importance."

The courier came in all sweating and flurried, and taking a paper from his bosom, placed it in the governor's hands. Sancho handed it to the majordomo and bade him read the superscription, which ran thus:

TO DON SANCHO PANZA, GOVERNOR OF THE ISLAND OF
BARATARIA, INTO HIS OWN HANDS OR THOSE OF HIS SECRETARY.

Sancho when he heard this said, "Which of you is my secretary?" "I am, señor," said one of those present, "for I can read and write, and am a Biscayan." "With that addition," said Sancho, "you might be secretary to the emperor himself; open this paper and see what it says." The new-born secretary obeyed, and having read the contents said the matter was one to be discussed in private. Sancho ordered the chamber to be

[59] **"Recio . . . Tirteafuera":** *Recio* means "obstinate"; *mal-aguero* means "evil omen"; *Tirteafuera* means, literally, "take thyself off."

cleared, the majordomo and the carver only remaining; so the doctor and the others withdrew, and then the secretary read the letter, which was as follows:

> It has come to my knowledge, Señor Don Sancho Panza, that certain enemies of mine and of the island are about to make a furious attack upon it some night, I know not when. It behooves you to be on the alert and keep watch, that they surprise you not. I also know by trustworthy spies that four persons have entered the town in disguise in order to take your life, because they stand in dread of your great capacity; keep your eyes open and take heed who approaches you to address you, and eat nothing that is presented to you. I will take care to send you aid if you find yourself in difficulty, but in all things you will act as may be expected of your judgment. From this place, the Sixteenth of August, at four in the morning.
>
> Your friend,
> THE DUKE.

Sancho was astonished, and those who stood by made believe to be so too, and turning to the majordomo he said to him, "What we have got to do first, and it must be done at once, is to put Doctor Recio in the lock-up; for if anyone wants to kill me it is he, and by a slow death and the worst of all, which is hunger."

"Likewise," said the carver, "it is my opinion your worship should not eat anything that is on this table, for the whole was a present from some nuns; and as they say, 'behind the cross there's the devil.'"

"I don't deny it," said Sancho; "so for the present give me a piece of bread and four pound or so of grapes; no poison can come in them; for the fact is I can't go on without eating; and if we are to be prepared for these battles that are threatening us we must be well provisioned; for it is the tripes that carry the heart and not the heart the tripes. And you, secretary, answer my lord the duke and tell him that all his commands shall be obeyed to the letter, as he directs; and say from me to my lady the duchess that I kiss her hands, and that I beg her not to forget to send my letter and bundle to my wife Teresa Panza by a messenger; and I will take it as a great favor and will not fail to serve her in all that may lie within my power; and as you are about it you may enclose a kiss of the hand to my master Don Quixote that he may see I am grateful bread; and as a good secretary and a good Biscayan you may add whatever you like, and whatever will come in best; and now take away this cloth and give me something to eat, and I'll be ready to meet all the spies and assassins and enchanters that may come against me or my island."

At this instant a page entered saying, "Here is a farmer on business, who wants to speak to your lordship on a matter of great importance, he says."

"It's very odd," said Sancho, "the ways of these men on business; is it possible they can be such fools as not to see that an hour like this is no hour for coming on business? We who govern and we who are judges—are we not men of flesh and blood, are we not to be allowed the time required for taking rest, unless they'd have us made of marble? By God and on my conscience, if the government remains in my hands (which I have a notion it won't), I'll bring more than one man on business to order. However, tell this good man to come in; but take care first of all that he is not some spy or one of my assassins."

"No, my lord," said the page, "for he looks like a simple fellow, and either I know very little or he is as good as good bread."

"There is nothing to be afraid of," said the majordomo, "for we are all here."

"Would it be possible, carver," said Sancho, "now that Doctor Pedro Recio is not here, to let me eat something solid and substantial, if it were even a piece of bread and an onion?"

"To-night at supper," said the carver, "the shortcomings of the dinner shall be made good, and your lordship shall be fully satisfied and contented."

"God grant it," said Sancho.

The farmer now came in, a well-favored man that one might see a thousand leagues off was an honest fellow and a good soul. The first thing he said was, "Which is the señor governor here?"

"Which should it be," said the secretary, "but he who is seated in the chair?"

"Then I humble myself before him," said the farmer; and going on his knees he asked for his hand, to kiss it. Sancho refused it, and bade him stand up and say what he wanted. The farmer obeyed, and then said, "I am a farmer, señor, a native of Miguelturra, a village two leagues from Ciudad Real."

"Another Tirteafuera!" said Sancho; "say on, brother; I know Miguelturra very well I can tell you, for it's not very far from my own town."

"The case is this, señor," continued the farmer, "that by God's mercy I am married with the leave and license of the holy Roman Catholic Church; I have two sons, students, and the younger is studying to become bachelor, and the elder to be licentiate; I am a widower, for my wife died, or more properly speaking, a bad doctor killed her on my hands, giving her a purge when she was with child; and if it had pleased God that the child had been born, and was a boy, I would have put him to study for doctor, that he might not envy his brothers the bachelor and the licentiate."

"So that if your wife had not died, or had not been killed, you would not now be a widower," said Sancho.

"No, señor, certainly not," said the farmer.

"We've got that much settled," said Sancho; "get on, brother, for it's more bedtime than business-time."

"Well then," said the farmer, "this son of mine who is going to be a bachelor fell in love in the said town with a damsel called Clara Perlerina, daughter of Andres Perlerino, a very rich farmer, and this name of Perlerines does not come to them by ancestry or descent, but because all the family are paralytics, and for a better name they call them Perlerines though to tell the truth the damsel is as fair as an Oriental pearl, and like a flower of the field, if you look at her on the right side; on the left not so much, for on that side she wants an eye that she lost by smallpox; and though her face is thickly and deeply pitted, those who love her say they are not pits that are there, but the graves where the hearts of her lovers are buried. She is so cleanly that not to soil her face she carries her nose turned up, as they say, so that one would fancy it was running away from her mouth; and with all this she looks extremely well, for she has a wide mouth; and but for wanting ten or a dozen teeth and grinders she might compare and compete with the comeliest. Of her lips I say nothing, for they are so fine and thin that, if lips might be reeled, one might make a skein of them; but being of a different color from ordinary lips they are wonderful for they are mottled, blue, green, and purple—let my lord the governor pardon me for painting so minutely the charms of her who some time or other will be my daughter; for I love her, and I don't find her amiss."

"Paint what you will," said Sancho; "I enjoy your painting, and if I had dined there could be no dessert more to my taste than your portrait."

"That I have still to furnish," said the farmer; "but a time may come when we may be able if we are not now; and I can tell you, señor, if I could paint her gracefulness and her tall figure, it would astonish you; but that is impossible because she is bent double with her knees up to her mouth; but for all that it is easy to see that if she could stand up she'd knock her head against the ceiling; and she would have given her hand to my bachelor ere this, only that she can't stretch it out, for it's contracted; but still one can see its elegance and fine make by its long furrowed nails."

"That will do, brother," said Sancho; "consider you have painted her from head to foot; what is it you want now? Come to the point without all this beating about the bush, and all these scraps and additions."

"I want your worship, señor," said the farmer, "to do me the favor of giving me a letter of recommendation to the girl's father, begging him to be so good as to let this marriage take place, as we are not ill-matched either in the gifts of fortune or of nature; for to tell the truth, señor governor, my son is possessed of a devil, and there is not a day but the evil spirits torment him three or four times; and from having once fallen into the fire, he has his face puckered up like a piece of parchment, and his eyes watery and always running; but he has the disposition of an angel, and if it was not for belaboring and pummelling himself he'd be a saint."

"Is there anything else you want, good man?" said Sancho.

"There's another thing I'd like," said the farmer, "but I'm afraid to mention it; however, out it must; for after all I can't let it be rotting in my breast, come what may. I mean, señor, that I'd like your worship to give me three hundred or six hundred ducats as a help to my bachelor's portion, to help him in setting up house, I mean; for they must, in short, live by themselves, without being subject to the interferences of their fathers-in-law."

"Just see if there's anything else you'd like?" said Sancho, "and don't hold back from mentioning it out of bashfulness or modesty."

"No, indeed there is not," said the farmer.

The moment he said this the governor started to his feet, and seizing the chair he had been sitting on exclaimed, "By all that's good you ill-bred, boorish Don Bumpkin, if you don't get out of this at once and hide yourself from my sight, I'll lay your head open with this chair. You whoreson rascal, you devil's own painter, and is it at this hour you come to ask me for six hundred ducats! How should I have them, you stinking brute? And why should I give them to you if I had them, you knave and blockhead? What have I to do with Miguelturra or the whole family of the Perlerines? Get out I say, or by the life of my lord the duke I'll do as I said. You're not from Miguelturra, but some knave sent here from hell to tempt me. Why, you villain, I have not yet had the government half a day, and you want me to have six hundred ducats already!"

The carver made signs to the farmer to leave the room, which he did with his head down, and to all appearance in terror lest the governor should carry his threats into effect, for the rogue knew very well how to play his part. [. . .]

FROM
Chapter 49

OF WHAT HAPPENED TO SANCHO IN MAKING THE ROUND OF HIS ISLAND

. . . Night came, and with the permission of Doctor Pedro Recio, the governor had supper. They then got ready to go the rounds, and he started with the majordomo, the secretary, the head-carver, the chronicler charged with recording his deeds, and *alguacils*[60] and notaries enough to form a fair-sized squadron. In the midst marched Sancho with his staff, as fine a sight as one could wish to see, and but a few streets of the town had been traversed when they heard a noise as of a clashing of swords. They hastened to the spot, and found that the combatants were but two, who seeing the authorities approaching stood still, and one of them exclaimed, "Help, in the name of God and the king! Are men to be allowed to rob in the middle of this town, and rush out and attack people in the very streets?"

"Be calm, my good man," said Sancho, "and tell me what the cause of this quarrel is; for I am the governor."

Said the other combatant, "Señor governor, I will tell you in a very few words. Your worship must know that this gentleman has just now won more than a thousand reals in that gambling house opposite, and God knows how. I was there, and gave more than one doubtful point in his favor, very much against what my conscience told me. He made off with his winnings, and when I made sure he was going to give me a crown or so at least by way of a present, as it is usual and customary to give men of quality of my sort who stand by to see fair or foul play, and back up swindles, and prevent quarrels, he pocketed his money and left the house. Indignant at this I followed him, and speaking him fairly and civilly asked him to give me if it were only eight reals, for he knows I am an honest man and that I have neither profession nor property, for my parents never brought me up to any or left me any; but the rogue, who is a greater thief than Cacus and a greater sharper than Andradilla, would not give me more than four reals; so your worship may see how little shame and conscience he has. But by my faith if you had not come up I'd have made him disgorge his winnings, and he'd have learned what the range of the steelyard was."

"What say you to this?" asked Sancho. The other replied that all his antagonist said was true, and that he did not choose to give him more than four reals because he very often gave him money; and that those who expected presents ought to be civil and take what is given them with a cheerful countenance, and not make any claim against winners unless they know them for certain to be sharpers and their winnings to be unfairly won; and that there could be no better proof that he himself was an

[60] ***alguacils:*** Bailiffs.

honest man than his having refused to give anything; for sharpers always pay tribute to lookers-on who know them.

"This is true," said the majordomo; "let your worship consider what is to be done with these men."

"What is to be done," said Sancho, "is this; you, the winner, be you good, bad, or indifferent, give this assailant of yours a hundred reals at once, and you must disburse thirty more for the poor prisoners; and you who have neither profession nor property, and hang about the island in idleness, take these hundred reals now, and some time of the day tomorrow quit the island under sentence of banishment for ten years, and under pain of completing it in another life if you violate the sentence, for I'll hang you on a gibbet, or at least the hangman will by my orders; not a word from either of you, or I'll make him feel my hand."

The one paid down the money and the other took it, and the latter quitted the island, while the other went home; and then the governor said, "Either I am not good for much, or I'll get rid of these gambling houses, for it strikes me they are very mischievous."

"This one at least," said one of the notaries, "your worship will not be able to get rid of, for a great man owns it, and what he loses every year is beyond all comparison more than what he makes by the cards. On the minor gambling houses your worship may exercise your power, and it is they that do most harm and shelter the most barefaced practices; for in the houses of lords and gentlemen of quality the notorious sharpers dare not attempt to play their tricks; and as the vice of gambling has become common, it is better that men should play in houses of repute than in some tradesman's, where they catch an unlucky fellow in the small hours of the morning and skin him alive."

"I know already, notary, that there is a good deal to be said on that point," said Sancho.

And now a tipstaff came up with a young man in his grasp, and said, "Señor governor, this youth was coming towards us, and as soon as he saw the officers of justice he turned about and ran like a deer, a sure proof that he must be some evil-doer; I ran after him, and had it not been that he stumbled and fell, I should never have caught him."

"What did you run for, fellow?" said Sancho.

To which the young man replied, "Señor, it was to avoid answering all the questions officers of justice put."

"What are you by trade?"

"A weaver."

"And what do you weave?"

"Lance heads, with your worship's good leave."

"You're facetious with me! You plume yourself on being a wag? Very good; and where were you going just now?"

"To take the air, señor."

"And where does one take the air in this island?"

"Where it blows."

"Good! your answers are very much to the point; you are a smart youth; but take notice that I am the air, and that I blow upon you astern, and send you to jail. Ho there! lay hold of him and take him off; I'll make him sleep there tonight without air."

"By God," said the young man, "your worship will make me sleep in jail just as soon as make me king."

"Why shan't I make thee sleep in jail?" said Sancho. "Have I not the power to arrest thee and release thee whenever I like?"

"All the power your worship has," said the young man, "won't be able to make me sleep in jail."

"How? not able!" said Sancho; "take him away at once where he'll see his mistake with his own eyes, even if the jailer is willing to exert his interested generosity on his behalf; for I'll lay a penalty of two thousand ducats on him if he allows him to stir a step from the prison."

"That's ridiculous," said the young man; "the fact is, all the men on earth will not make me sleep in prison."

"Tell me, you devil," said Sancho, "have you got any angel that will deliver you, and take off the irons I am going to order them to put upon you?"

"Now, señor governor," said the young man in a sprightly manner, "let us be reasonable and come to the point. Granted your worship may order me to be taken to prison, and have irons and chains put on me, and to be shut up in a cell, and may lay heavy penalties on the jailer if he lets me out, and that he obeys your orders; still, if I don't choose to sleep, and choose to remain awake all night without closing an eye, will your worship with all your power be able to make me sleep if I don't choose?"

"No, truly," said the secretary, "and the fellow has made his point."

"So then," said Sancho, "it would be entirely of your own choice you would keep from sleeping; not in opposition to my will?"

"No, señor," said the youth, "certainly not."

"Well then, go, and God be with you," said Sancho; "be off home to sleep, and God give you sound sleep, for I don't want to rob you of it; but for the future, let me advise you don't joke with the authorities, because you may come across some one who will bring down the joke on your own skull."

The young man went his way, and the governor continued his round, and shortly afterwards two tipstaffs came up with a man in custody, and said, "Señor governor, this person, who seems to be a man, is not so, but a woman, and not an ill-favored one, in man's clothes." They raised two or three lanterns to her face, and by their light they distinguished the features of a woman to all appearance of the age of sixteen or a little more, with her hair gathered into a gold and green silk net, and fair as a thousand pearls. They scanned her from head to foot, and observed that she had on red silk stockings with garters of white taffety bordered with gold and pearl; her breeches were of green and gold stuff, and under an open jacket or jerkin of the same she wore a doublet of the finest white and gold cloth; her shoes were white and such as men wear; she carried no sword at her belt, but only a richly ornamented dagger, and on her fingers she had several handsome rings. In short, the girl seemed fair to look at in the eyes of all, and none of those who beheld her knew her, the people of the town said they could not imagine who she was, and those who were in the secret of the jokes that were to be practised upon Sancho were the ones who were most surprised, for this incident or discovery had not been arranged by them; and they watched anxiously to see how the affair would end.

Sancho was fascinated by the girl's beauty, and he asked her who she was, where she was going, and what had induced her to dress herself in that garb. She with her eyes fixed on the ground answered in modest confusion, "I cannot tell you, señor, before so many people what it is of such consequence to me to have kept secret; one thing I wish to be known, that I am no thief or evil-doer, but only an unhappy maiden whom the power of jealousy has led to break through the respect that is due to modesty."

Hearing this the majordomo said to Sancho, "Make the people stand back, señor governor, that this lady may say what she wishes with less embarrassment."

Sancho gave the order, and all except the majordomo, the head-carver, and the secretary fell back. Finding herself then in the presence of no more, the damsel went on to say, "I am the daughter, sirs, of Pedro Perez Mazorca, the wool-farmer of this town, who is in the habit of coming very often to my father's house."

"That won't do, señora," said the majordomo; "for I know Pedro Perez very well, and I know he has no child at all, either son or daughter; and besides, though you say he is your father you add then that he comes very often to your father's house."

"I have already noticed that," said Sancho.

"I am confused just now, sirs," said the damsel, "and I don't know what I am saying; but the truth is that I am the daughter of Diego de la Llana, whom you must all know."

"Ay, that will do," said the majordomo; "for I know Diego de la Llana, and know that he is a gentleman of position and a rich man, and that he has a son and a daughter, and that since he was left a widower nobody in all this town can speak to having seen his daughter's face; for he keeps her so closely shut up that he does not give even the sun a chance of seeing her; and for all that report says she is extremely beautiful."

"It is true," said the damsel, "and I am that daughter; whether report lies or not as to my beauty, you, sirs, will have decided by this time, as you have seen me"; and with this she began to weep bitterly.

On seeing this the secretary leant over to the head-carver's ear, and said to him in a low voice, "Something serious has no doubt happened to this poor maiden, that she goes wandering from home in such a dress and at such an hour, and one of her rank too." "There can be no doubt about it," returned the carver, "and moreover her tears confirm your suspicion." Sancho gave her the best comfort he could, and entreated her to tell them without any fear what had happened to her, as they would all earnestly and by every means in their power endeavor to relieve her.

"The fact is, sirs," said she, "that my father has kept me shut up these ten years, for so long is it since the earth received my mother. Mass is said at home in a sumptuous chapel, and all this time I have seen but the sun in the heaven by day, and the moon and the stars by night; nor do I know what streets are like, or plazas, or churches, or even men, except my father and a brother I have, and Pedro Perez the wool-farmer; whom, because he came frequently to our house, I took it into my head to call my father, to avoid naming my own. This seclusion and the restrictions laid upon my going out, were it only to church, have been keeping me unhappy for many a day and month past; I longed to see the world, or at least the town where I was born, and it did not seem to me that this wish was inconsistent with the respect maidens of good quality should have for themselves. When I heard them talking of bull-fights taking place, and of javelin games, and of acting plays, I asked my brother, who is a year younger than myself, to tell me what sort of things these were, and many more that I had never seen; he explained them to me as well as he could, but the only effect was to kindle in me a still stronger desire to see them. At last, to cut short the story of my ruin, I begged and entreated my brother—O that I had never made such an entreaty"—And once more she gave way to a burst of weeping.

"Proceed, señora," said the majordomo, "and finish your story of what has happened to you, for your words and tears are keeping us all in suspense."

"I have but little more to say, though many a tear to shed," said the damsel; "for ill-placed desires can only be paid for in some such way."

The maiden's beauty had made a deep impression on the head-carver's heart, and he again raised his lantern for another look at her, and thought they were not tears she was shedding, but seed-pearl or dew of the meadow, nay, he exalted them still higher, and made Oriental pearls of them, and fervently hoped her misfortune might not be so great a one as her tears and sobs seemed to indicate. The governor was losing patience at the length of time the girl was taking to tell her story, and told her not to keep them waiting any longer; for it was late, and there still remained a good deal of the town to be gone over.

She, with broken sobs and half-suppressed sighs, went on to say, "My misfortune, my misadventure, is simply this, that I entreated my brother to dress me up as a man in a suit of his clothes, and take me some night, when our father was asleep, to see the whole town; he, overcome by my entreaties, consented, and dressing me in this suit and himself in clothes of mine that fitted him as if made for him (for he has not a hair on his chin, and might pass for a very beautiful young girl), to-night, about an hour ago, more or less, we left the house, and guided by our youthful and foolish impulse we made the circuit of the whole town, and then, as we were about to return home, we saw a great troop of people coming, and my brother said to me, 'Sister, this must be the round, stir your feet and put wings to them, and follow me as fast as you can, lest they recognize us, for that would be a bad business for us'; and so saying he turned about and began, I cannot say to run but to fly; in less than six paces I fell from fright, and then the officer of justice came up and carried me before your worships, where I find myself put to shame before all these people as whimsical and vicious."

"So then, señora," said Sancho, "no other mishap has befallen you, nor was it jealousy that made you leave home, as you said at the beginning of your story?"

"Nothing has happened to me," said she, "nor was it jealousy that brought me out, but merely a longing to see the world, which did not go beyond seeing the streets of this town."

The appearance of the tipstaffs with her brother in custody, whom one of them had overtaken as he ran away from his sister, now fully confirmed the truth of what the damsel said. He had nothing on but a rich petticoat and a short blue damask cloak with fine gold lace, and his head was uncovered and adorned only with its own hair, which looked like rings of gold, so bright and curly was it. The governor, the majordomo, and the carver went aside with him, and, unheard by his sister, asked him how he came to be in that dress, and he with no less shame and embarrassment told exactly the same story as his sister, to the great delight of the enamoured carver; the governor, however, said to them, "In truth, young lady and gentleman, this has been a very childish affair, and to explain your folly and rashness there was no necessity for all this delay and all these tears and sighs; for if you had said we are so-and-so, and we escaped from our father's house in this way in order to ramble about, out of mere curiosity and with no other object, there would have been an end of the matter, and none of these little sobs and tears and all the rest of it."

"That is true," said the damsel, "but you see the confusion I was in was so great it did not let me behave as I ought."

"No harm has been done," said Sancho; "come, we will leave you at your father's house; perhaps they will not have missed you; and another time don't be so childish or eager to see the world; for a respectable damsel and a broken leg should keep at home; and the woman and the hen by gadding about are soon lost; and she who is eager to see is also eager to be seen; I say no more."

The youth thanked the governor for his kind offer to take them home, and they directed their steps towards the house, which was not far off. On reaching it the youth threw a pebble up at a grating, and immediately a woman-servant who was waiting for them came down and opened the door to them, and they went in, leaving the party marvelling as much at their grace and beauty as at the fancy they had for seeing the world by night and without quitting the village; which, however, they set down to their youth.

The head-carver was left with a heart pierced through and through, and he made up his mind on the spot to demand the damsel in marriage of her father on the morrow, making sure she would not be refused him as he was a servant of the duke's; and even to Sancho ideas and schemes of marrying the youth to his daughter Sanchica suggested themselves, and he resolved to open the negotiation at the proper season, persuading himself that no husband could be refused to a governor's daughter. And so the night's round came to an end, and a couple of days later the government, whereby all his plans were over-thrown and swept away, as will be seen farther on.

Chapter 50

WHEREIN IS SET FORTH WHO THE ENCHANTERS AND EXECUTIONERS WERE WHO FLOGGED THE DUENNA AND PINCHED DON QUIXOTE, AND ALSO WHAT BEFELL THE PAGE WHO CARRIED THE LETTER TO TERESA PANZA, SANCHO PANZA'S WIFE

Cid Hamet, the painstaking investigator of the minute points of this veracious history, says that when Doña Rodriguez left her own room to go to Don Quixote's, another duenna who slept with her observed her, and as all duennas are fond of pry-ing, listening, and sniffing, she followed her so silently that the good Rodriguez never perceived it; and as soon as the duenna saw her enter Don Quixote's room, not to fail in a duenna's invariable practice of tattling, she hurried off that instant to report to the duchess how Doña Rodriguez was closeted with Don Quixote. The duchess told the duke, and asked him to let her and Altisidora go and see what the said duenna wanted with Don Quixote. The duke gave them leave, and the pair cautiously and quietly crept to the door of the room and posted themselves so close to it that they could hear all that was said inside. But when the duchess heard how Rodriguez had made public the Aranjuez of her issues she could not restrain herself, nor Altisidora either; and so, filled with rage and thirsting for vengeance, they burst into the room and tormented Don Quixote and flogged the duenna in the manner already described; for indignities offered to their charms and self-esteem mightily provoke the anger of women and make them eager for revenge. The duchess told the duke what had happened, and he was much amused by it; and she, in pursuance of her design of making merry and diverting herself with Don Quixote, despatched the page who had played the part of Dulcinea in the negotiations for her disenchantment (which Sancho Panza in the cares of government had forgotten all about) to Teresa Panza his wife with her husband's letter and another from herself, and also a great string of fine coral beads as a present.

Now the history says this page was very sharp and quick-witted; and eager to serve his lord and lady he set off very willingly for Sancho's village. Before he entered it he observed a number of women washing in a brook, and asked them if they could tell him whether there lived there a woman of the name of Teresa Panza, wife of one Sancho Panza, squire to a knight called Don Quixote of La Mancha. At the question a young girl who was washing stood up and said, "Teresa Panza is my mother, and that Sancho is my father, and that knight is our master."

"Well then, miss," said the page, "come and show me where your mother is, for I bring her a letter and a present from your father."

"That I will with all my heart, señor," said the girl, who seemed to be about fourteen, more or less; and leaving the clothes she was washing to one of her companions, and without putting anything on her head or feet, for she was bare-legged and had her hair hanging about her, away she skipped in front of the page's horse, saying, "Come, your worship, our house is at the entrance of the town, and my mother is there, sorrowful enough at not having had any news of my father this ever so long."

"Well," said the page, "I am bringing her such good news that she will have reason to thank God for it."

And then, skipping, running, and capering, the girl reached the town, but before going into the house she called out at the door, "Come out, mother Teresa, come out, come out; here's a gentleman with letters and other things from my good father." At these words her mother Teresa Panza came out spinning a bundle of flax, in a gray petticoat (so short was it one would have fancied "they to her shame had cut it short"[61]), a gray bodice of the same stuff, and a smock. She was not very old, though

[61] **("they . . . short"):** Docking the skirts was a punishment for misconduct.

plainly past forty, strong, healthy, vigorous, and sun-dried; and seeing her daughter and the page on horseback, she exclaimed, "What's this, child? What gentleman is this?"

"A servant of my lady, Doña Teresa Panza," replied the page; and suiting the action to the word he flung himself off his horse, and with great humility advanced to kneel before the lady Teresa, saying, "Let me kiss your hand, Señora Doña Teresa, as the lawful and only wife of Señor Don Sancho Panza, rightful governor of the island of Barataria."

"Ah, señor, get up, don't do that," said Teresa; "for I'm not a bit of a court lady, but only a poor countrywoman, the daughter of a clod-crusher, and the wife of a squire-errant and not of any governor at all."

"You are," said the page, "the most worthy wife of a most arch-worthy governor; and as a proof of what I say accept this letter and this present"; and at the same time he took out of his pocket a string of coral beads with gold clasps, and placed it on her neck, and said, "This letter is from his lordship the governor, and the other as well as these coral beads from my lady the duchess, who sends me to your worship."

Teresa stood lost in astonishment, and her daughter just as much, and the girl said, "May I die but our master Don Quixote's at the bottom of this; he must have given father the government or country he so often promised him."

"That is the truth," said the page; "for it is through Señor Don Quixote that Señor Sancho is now governor of the island of Barataria, as will be seen by this letter."

"Will your worship read it to me, noble sir?" said Teresa; "for though I can spin I can't read, not a scrap."

"Nor I either," said Sanchica; "but wait a bit, and I'll go and fetch some one who can read it, either the curate himself or the bachelor Samson Carrasco, and they'll come gladly to hear any news of my father."

"There is no need to fetch anybody," said the page; "for though I can't spin I can read, and I'll read it"; and so he read it through, but as it has already been given it is not inserted here; and then he took out the other one from the duchess, which ran as follows:

> Friend Teresa, Your husband Sancho's good qualities, of heart as well as of head, induced and compelled me to request my husband the duke to give him the government of one of his many islands. I am told he governs like a gerfalcon, of which I am very glad, and my lord the duke, of course, also; and I am very thankful to Heaven that I have not made a mistake in choosing him for that same government; for I would have Señora Teresa know that a good governor is hard to find in this world, and may God make me as good as Sancho's way of governing. Herewith I send you, my dear, a string of coral beads with gold clasps; I wish they were Oriental pearls; but "he who gives thee a bone does not wish to see thee dead"; a time will come when we shall become acquainted and meet one another, but God knows the future. Commend me to your daughter Sanchica, and tell her from me to hold herself in readiness, for I mean to make a high match for her when she least expects it. They tell me there are big acorns in your village; send me a couple of dozen or so, and I shall value them greatly as coming from your hand; and write to me at length to assure me of

your health and well-being; and if there be anything you stand in need of, it is but to open your mouth, and that shall be the measure; and so God keep you.

From this place.
Your loving friend,
THE DUCHESS

"Ah, what a good, plain, lowly lady!" said Teresa when she heard the letter; "that I may be buried with ladies of that sort, and not the gentlewomen we have in this town, that fancy because they are gentlewomen the wind must not touch them, and go to church with as much airs as if they were queens, no less, and seem to think they are disgraced if they look at a farmer's wife! And see here how this good lady, for all she's a duchess, calls me 'friend,' and treats me as if I was her equal—and equal may I see her with the tallest church-tower in La Mancha! And as for the acorns, señor, I'll send her ladyship a peck and such big ones that one might come to see them as a show and a wonder. And now, Sanchica, see that the gentleman is comfortable; put up his horse, and get some eggs out of the stable, and cut plenty of bacon, and let's give him his dinner like a prince; for the good news he has brought, and his own bonny face deserve it all; and meanwhile I'll run out and give the neighbors the news of our good luck, and father curate, and Master Nicholas the barber, who are and always have been such friends of thy father's."

"That I will, mother," said Sanchica; "but mind, you must give me half of that string; for I don't think my lady the duchess could have been so stupid as to send it all to you."

"It is all for thee, my child," said Teresa; "but let me wear it round my neck for a few days; for verily it seems to make my heart glad."

"You will be glad, too," said the page, "when you see the bundle there is in this portmanteau, for it is a suit of the finest cloth, that the governor only wore one day out hunting and now sends, all for Señora Sanchica."

"May he live a thousand years," said Sanchica, "and the bearer as many, nay two thousand, if needful."

With this Teresa hurried out of the house with the letters, and with the string of beads round her neck, and went along thrumming the letters as if they were a tambourine, and by chance coming across the curate and Samson Carrasco she began capering and saying, "None of us poor now, faith! We've got a little government! Ay, let the finest fine lady tackle me, and I'll give her a setting down!"

"What's all this, Teresa Panza," said they; "what madness is this, and what papers are those?"

"The madness is only this," said she, "that these are the letters of duchesses and governors, and these I have on my neck are fine coral beads, with ave marias and paternosters of beaten gold, and I am a governess."

"God help us," said the curate, "we don't understand you, Teresa, or know what you are talking about."

"There, you may see it yourselves," said Teresa, and she handed them the letters.

The curate read them out for Samson Carrasco to hear, and Samson and he regarded one another with looks of astonishment at what they had read, and the bachelor asked who had brought the letters. Teresa in reply bade them come with her to her house and they would see the messenger, a most elegant youth, who had brought another present which was worth as much more. The curate took the coral beads from her neck and examined them again and again, and having satisfied himself as to their fineness he fell to wondering afresh, and said, "By the gown I wear I don't know what to say or think of these letters and presents; on the one hand I can see and feel the fineness of these coral beads, and on the other I read how a duchess sends to beg for a couple of dozen acorns."

"Square that if you can," said Carrasco; "well, let's go and see the messenger, and from him we'll learn something about this mystery that has turned up."

They did so, and Teresa returned with them. They found the page sifting a little barley for his horse, and Sanchica cutting a rasher of bacon to be paved with eggs for his dinner. His looks and his handsome apparel pleased them both greatly; and after they had saluted him courteously, and he them, Samson begged him to give them his news, as well of Don Quixote as of Sancho Panza, for, he said, though they had read the letters from Sancho and her ladyship the duchess, they were still puzzled and could not make out what was meant by Sancho's government, and above all of an island, when all or most of those in the Mediterranean belonged to his majesty.

To this the page replied, "As to Señor Sancho Panza's being a governor there is no doubt whatever; but whether it is an island or not that he governs, with that I have nothing to do; suffice it that it is a town of more than a thousand inhabitants; with regard to the acorns I may tell you my lady the duchess is so unpretending and unassuming that, not to speak of sending to beg for acorns from a peasant woman, she has been known to send to ask for the loan of a comb from one of her neighbors; for I would have your worships know that the ladies of Aragon, though they are just as illustrious, are not so punctilious and haughty as the Castilian ladies; they treat people with greater familiarity."

In the middle of this conversation Sanchica came in with her skirt full of eggs, and said she to the page, "Tell me, señor, does my father wear trunk-hose since he has been governor?"

"I have not noticed," said the page; "but no doubt he wears them."

"Ah! my God!" said Sanchica, "what a sight it must be to see my father in tights! Isn't it odd that ever since I was born I have had a longing to see my father in trunk-hose?"

"As things go you will see that if you live," said the page; "by God, he is in the way to take the road with a sunshade if the government only lasts him two months more."

The curate and the bachelor could see plainly enough that the page spoke in a waggish vein; but the fineness of the coral beads, and the hunting suit that Sancho sent (for Teresa had already shown it to them) did away with the impression; and they could not help laughing at Sanchica's wish, and still more when Teresa said, "Señor curate, look about if there's anybody here going to Madrid or Toledo, to buy me a hooped petticoat, a proper fashionable one of the best quality; for indeed and indeed I must do honor to my husband's government as well as I can; nay, if I am put to it, I'll go to court and set up a coach like all the world; for she who has a governor for her husband may very well have one and keep one."

"And why not, mother!" said Sanchica; "would to God it were to-day instead of to-morrow, even though they were to say when they saw me seated in the coach with my mother, 'See that rubbish, that garlic-stuffed fellow's daughter, how she goes stretched at her ease in a coach as if she was a she-pope!' But let them tramp through the mud, and let me go in my coach with my feet off the ground. Bad luck to back-biters all over the world; 'let me go warm and the people may laugh.' Do I say right, mother?"

"To be sure you do, my child," said Teresa; "and all this good luck, and even more, my good Sancho foretold me; and thou wilt see, my daughter, he won't stop till he has made me a countess; for to make a beginning is everything in luck; and as I have heard thy good father say many a time (for besides being thy father he's the father of proverbs too), 'When they offer thee a heifer, run with a halter; when they offer thee a government, take it; when they would give thee a country, seize it; when they say "Here, here!" to thee with something good, swallow it.' Oh no! go to sleep, and don't answer the strokes of good fortune and the lucky chances that are knocking at the door of your house!"

"And what do I care," added Sanchica, "whether anybody says when he sees me holding my head up, 'The dog saw himself in hempen breeches,' and the rest of it?"

Hearing this the curate said, "I do believe that all this family of the Panzas are born with a sackful of proverbs in their insides, every one of them; I never saw one of them that does not pour them out at all times and on all occasions."

"That is true," said the page, "for Señor Governor Sancho utters them at every turn; and though a great many of them are not to the purpose, still they amuse one, and my lady the duchess and the duke praise them highly."

"Then you still maintain that all this about Sancho's government is true, señor," said the bachelor, "and that there actually is a duchess who sends him presents and writes to him? Because we, although we have handled the presents and read the letters, don't believe it, and suspect it to be something in the line of our fellow-townsman Don Quixote, who fancies that everything is done by enchantment; and for this reason I am almost ready to say that I'd like to touch and feel your worship to see whether you are a mere ambassador of the imagination or a man of flesh and blood."

"All I know, sirs," replied the page, "is that I am a real ambassador, and that Señor Sancho Panza is governor as a matter of fact, and that my lord and lady the duke and duchess can give, and have given him this same government, and that I have heard the said Sancho Panza bears himself very stoutly therein; whether there be any enchantment in all this or not, it is for your worships to settle between you; for that's all I know by the oath I swear, and that is by the life of my parents whom I have still alive, and love dearly."

"It may be so," said the bachelor, "but *dubitat Augustinus.*"[62]

"Doubt who will," said the page; "what I have told you is the truth, and that will always rise above falsehood as oil above water; if not *operibus credite, et non verbis.*[63]

---

[62] ***"dubitat Augustinus":*** "But Augustine doubts it." Carrasco means that he is not convinced.

[63] ***"operibus . . . verbis":*** "Believe in my actions, not my words."

Let one of you come with me, and he will see with his eyes what he does not believe with his ears."

"It's for me to make that trip," said Sanchica; "take me with you, señor, behind you on your horse; for I'll go with all my heart to see my father."

"Governors' daughters," said the page, "must not travel along the roads alone, but accompanied by coaches and litters and a great number of attendants."

"By God," said Sanchica, "I can go just as well mounted on a she-ass as in a coach; what a dainty lass you must take me for!"

"Hush, girl," said Teresa; "you don't know what you're talking about; the gentleman is quite right, for 'as the time so the behavior'; when it was Sancho it was 'Sancha'; when it is governor it's 'señora'; I don't know if I'm right."

"Señora Teresa says more than she is aware of," said the page; "and now give me something to eat and let me go at once, for I mean to return this evening."

"Come and do penance with me," said the curate at this; "for Señora Teresa has more will than means to serve so worthy a guest."

The page refused, but had to consent at last for his own sake; and the curate took him home with him very gladly, in order to have an opportunity of questioning him at leisure about Don Quixote and his doings. The bachelor offered to write the letters in reply for Teresa; but she did not care to let him mix himself up in her affairs, for she thought him somewhat given to joking; and so she gave a cake and a couple of eggs to a young acolyte who was a penman, and he wrote for her two letters, one for her husband and the other for the duchess, dictated out of her own head, and these are not the worst inserted in this great history, as will be seen farther on.

Chapter 51

OF THE PROGRESS OF SANCHO'S GOVERNMENT, AND OTHER SUCH ENTERTAINING MATTERS

Day came after the night of the governor's round; a night which the head-carver passed without sleeping, so full were his thoughts of the face and air and beauty of the disguised damsel, while the majordomo spent what was left of it in writing an account to his lord and lady of all Sancho said and did, being as much amazed at his sayings as at his doings, for there was a mixture of shrewdness and simplicity in all his words and deeds. The señor governor got up, and by Doctor Pedro Recio's directions they made him break his fast on a little conserve and four sups of cold water, which Sancho would have readily exchanged for a piece of bread and a bunch of grapes; but seeing there was no help for it, he submitted with no little sorrow of heart and discomfort of stomach; Pedro Recio having persuaded him that light and delicate diet enlivened the wits, and that was what was most essential for persons placed in command and in responsible situations, where they have to employ not only the bodily powers but those of the mind also.

By means of this sophistry Sancho was made to endure hunger, and hunger so keen that in his heart he cursed the government, and even him who had given it to him; however, with his hunger and his conserve he undertook to deliver judgments that day, and the first thing that came before him was a question that was submitted to him by a stranger, in the presence of the majordomo and the other attendants, and it was in these words: "Señor, a large river separated two districts of one and the same lordship—will your worship please to pay attention, for the case is an important and a rather knotty one? Well then, on this river there was a bridge, and at one end of it a gallows, and a sort of tribunal, where four judges commonly sat to administer the law which the lord of the river, the bridge and the lordship had enacted, and which was to this effect, 'If any one crosses by this bridge from one side to the other he shall declare on oath where he is going and with what object; and if he swears truly, he shall be allowed to pass, but if falsely, he shall, without any remission, be put to death for it by hanging on the gallows erected there.' Though the law and its severe penalty were known, many persons crossed, but in their declarations it was easy to see at once they were telling the truth, and the judges let them pass free. It happened, however, that one man, when they came to take his declaration, swore and said that by the oath he took he was going to die upon that gallows that stood there, and nothing else. The judges held a consultation over the oath, and they said, 'If we let this man pass free he has sworn falsely, and by the law he ought to die; but if we hang him, as he swore he was going to die on that gallows, and therefore swore the truth, by the same law he ought to go free.' It is asked of your worship, señor governor, what are the judges to do with this man? For they are still in doubt and perplexity; and having heard of your worship's acute and exalted intellect, they have sent me to entreat your worship on their behalf to give your opinion on this very intricate and puzzling case."

To this Sancho made answer, "Indeed those gentlemen the judges that send you to me might have spared themselves the trouble, for I have more of the obtuse than the acute in me; however, repeat the case over again, so that I may understand it, and then perhaps I may be able to hit the point."

The querist repeated again and again what he had said before, and then Sancho said, "It seems to me I can set the matter right in a moment, and in this way; the man swears that he is going to die upon the gallows; but if he dies upon it, he has sworn the truth, and by the law enacted deserves to go free and pass over the bridge; but if they don't hang him, then he has sworn falsely, and by the same law deserves to be hanged."

"It is as the señor governor says," said the messenger; "and as regards a complete comprehension of the case, there is nothing left to desire or hesitate about."

"Well then I say," said Sancho, "that of this man they should let pass the part that has sworn truly, and hang the part that has lied; and in this way the conditions of the passage will be fully complied with."

"But then, señor governor," replied the querist, "the man will have to be divided into two parts; and if he is divided of course he will die; and so none of the requirements of the law will be carried out, and it is absolutely necessary to comply with it."

"Look here, my good sir," said Sancho; "either I'm a numskull or else there is the same reason for this passenger dying as for his living and passing over the bridge; for if the truth saves him the falsehood equally condemns him; and that being the case it is my opinion you should say to the gentlemen who sent you to me that as the arguments for condemning him and for absolving him are exactly balanced, they should let him pass freely, as it is always more praiseworthy to do good than to do evil; this I would give signed with my name if I knew how to sign; and what I have said in this case is not out of my own head, but one of the many precepts my master Don Quixote gave me the night before I left to become governor of this island, that came into my mind, and it was this, that when there was any doubt about the justice of a case I should lean to mercy; and it is God's will that I should recollect it now, for it fits this case as if it was made for it."

"That is true," said the majordomo; "and I maintain that Lycurgus himself, who gave laws to the Lacædemonians, could not have pronounced a better decision than the great Panza has given; let the morning's audience close with this, and I will see that the señor governor has dinner entirely to his liking."

"That's all I ask for — fair play," said Sancho; "give me my dinner, and then let it rain cases and questions on me, and I'll despatch them in a twinkling."

The majordomo kept his word, for he felt it against his conscience to kill so wise a governor by hunger; particularly as he intended to have done with him that same night, playing off the last joke he was commissioned to practise upon him.

It came to pass, then, that after he had dined that day, in opposition to the rules and aphorisms of Doctor Tirteafuera, as they were taking away the cloth there came a courier with a letter from Don Quixote for the governor. Sancho ordered the secretary to read it to himself, and if there was nothing in it that demanded secrecy to read it aloud. The secretary did so, and after he had skimmed the contents he said, "It may well be read aloud, for what Señor Don Quixote writes to your worship deserves to be printed or written in letters of gold, and it is as follows."

DON QUIXOTE OF LA MANCHA'S LETTER TO SANCHO PANZA, GOVERNOR OF THE ISLAND OF BARATARIA.

When I was expecting to hear of thy stupidities and blunders, friend Sancho, I have received intelligence of thy displays of good sense, for which I give special thanks to Heaven that can raise the poor from the dunghill and of fools to make wise men. They tell me thou dost govern as if thou wert a man, and art a man as if thou wert a beast, so great is the humility wherewith thou dost comport thyself. But I would have thee bear in mind, Sancho, that very often it is fitting and necessary for the authority of office to resist the humility of the heart; for the seemly array of one who is invested with grave duties should be such as they require and not measured by what his own humble tastes may lead him to prefer. Dress well; a stick dressed up does not look like a stick; I do not say thou shouldst wear trinkets or fine raiment, or that being a judge thou shouldst dress like a soldier, but that thou shouldst array thyself in the apparel thy office requires, and that at the same time it be neat and handsome. To win the good-will of the people thou governest there are two things, among others, that thou must do; one is to be civil to all (this, however, I told thee before) and the other to take care that food be abundant, for there is nothing that vexes the heart of the poor more than hunger and high prices. Make not many proclamations; but those thou makest take care that they be good ones, and above all that they be observed and carried out; for proclamations that are not observed are the same as if they did not exist; nay, they encourage the idea that the prince who had the wisdom and authority to make them had not the power to enforce them; and laws that threaten and are not enforced come to be like the log, the king of the frogs, that frightened them at first, but that in time they despised and mounted upon. Be a father to virtue and a step-father to vice. Be not always strict, nor yet always lenient, but observe a mean between these two extremes, for in that is the aim of wisdom. Visit the jails, the slaughter-houses, and the market-places; for the presence of the governor is of great importance in such places; it comforts the prisoners who are in hopes of a speedy release, it is the bugbear of the butchers who have then to give just weight, and it is the terror of the market-women for the same reason. Let it not be seen that thou art (even if perchance thou art, which I do not believe) covetous, a follower of women, or a glutton; for when the people and those that have dealings with thee become aware of thy special weakness they will bring their batteries to bear upon thee in that quarter, till they have brought thee down to the depths of perdition. Consider and reconsider, con and con over again the advice and the instructions I gave thee before thy departure hence to thy government, and thou wilt see that in them, if thou dost follow them, thou hast a help at hand that will lighten for thee the troubles and difficulties that beset governors at every step. Write to thy lord and lady and show thyself grateful to them, for ingratitude is the daughter of pride, and one of the greatest sins we know of; and he who is grateful to those who have been good to him shows that he will be so to God also who has bestowed and still bestows so many blessings upon him.

My lady the duchess sent off a messenger with thy suit and another present to thy wife Teresa Panza; we expect the answer every moment. I have been a little indisposed through a certain cat-scratching I came in for, not very much to the benefit of my nose; but it was nothing; for if there are enchanters who maltreat me, there are also some who defend me. Let me know if the majordomo who is with thee had any share in the Trifaldi performance, as thou didst suspect; and keep me informed of everything that happens to thee, as the distance is so short; all the more as I am thinking of giving over very shortly this idle life I am now leading, for I was not born for it. A thing has occurred to me which I am inclined to think will put me out of favor with the duke and duchess; but though I am sorry for it I do not care, for after all I must obey my calling rather than their pleasure, in accordance with the common saying *amicus Plato, sed magis amica veritas.*[64] I quote this Latin to thee because I conclude that since thou hast been a governor thou wilt have learned it. Adieu; God keep thee from being an object of pity to any one.

Thy friend,

Don Quixote of La Mancha

Sancho listened to the letter with great attention, and it was praised and considered wise by all who heard it; he then rose up from table, and calling his secretary shut himself in with him in his own room, and without putting it off any longer set about answering his master Don Quixote at once; and he bade the secretary write down what he told him without adding or suppressing anything, which he did, and the answer was to the following effect.

SANCHO PANZA'S LETTER TO DON QUIXOTE OF LA MANCHA.

The pressure of business is so great upon me that I have no time to scratch my head or even to cut my nails; and I wear them so long—God send a remedy for it. I say

[64] ***"amicus . . . veritas":*** "Plato is a friend, but Truth is a better friend."

this, master of my soul, that you may not be surprised if I have not until now sent you word of how I fare, well or ill, in this government, in which I am suffering more hunger than when we two were wandering through the woods and wastes.

My lord the duke wrote to me the other day to warn me that certain spies had got into this island to kill me; but up to the present I have not found out any except a certain doctor who receives a salary in this town for killing all the governors that come here; he is called Doctor Pedro Recio, and is from Tirteafuera; so you see what a name he has to make me dread dying under his hands. This doctor says of himself that he does not cure diseases when there are any, but prevents them coming, and the medicines he uses are diet and more diet, until he brings one down to bare bones; as if leanness was not worse than fever.

In short he is killing me with hunger, and I am dying myself of vexation; for when I thought I was coming to this government to get my meat hot and my drink cool, and take my ease between holland sheets on feather beds, I find I have come to do penance as if I was a hermit; and as I don't do it willingly I suspect that in the end the devil will carry me off.

So far I have not handled any dues or taken any bribes, and I don't know what to think of it; for here they tell me that the governors that come to this island, before entering it have plenty of money either given to them or lent to them by the people of the town, and that this is the usual custom not only here but with all who enter upon governments.

Last night going the rounds I came upon a fair damsel in man's clothes, and a brother of hers dressed as a woman; my head-carver has fallen in love with the girl, and has in his own mind chosen her for a wife, so he says, and I have chosen the youth for a son-in-law; to-day we are going to explain our intentions to the father of the pair, who is one Diego de la Llana, a gentleman and an old Christian as much as you please.

I have visited the market-places, as your worship advises me, and yesterday I found a stall-keeper selling new hazelnuts and proved her to have mixed a bushel of old empty rotten nuts with a bushel of new; I confiscated the whole for the children of the charity school, who will know how to distinguish them well enough, and I sentenced her not to come into the market-place for a fortnight; they told me I did bravely. I can tell your worship it is commonly said in this town that there are no people worse than the marketwomen, for they are all barefaced, unconscionable, and impudent, and I can well believe it from what I have seen of them in other towns.

I am very glad my lady the duchess has written to my wife Teresa Panza and sent her the present your worship speaks of; and I will strive to show myself grateful when the time comes; kiss her hands for me, and tell her I say she has not thrown it into a sack with a hole in it, as she will see in the end. I should not like your worship to have any difference with my lord and lady; for if you fall out with them it is plain it must do me harm; and as you give me advice to be grateful it will not do for your worship not to be so yourself to those who have shown you such kindness, and by whom you have been treated so hospitably in their castle.

That about the cat-scratching I don't understand; but I suppose it must be one of the ill-turns the wicked enchanters are always doing your worship; when we meet I shall know all about it. I wish I could send your worship something; but I don't know what to send, unless it be some very curious clyster pipes, to work with bladders, that they make in this island; but if the office remains with me I'll find out something to send, one way or another. If my wife Teresa Panza writes to me, pay the postage and send me the letter, for I have a very great desire to hear how my house and wife and children are going on. And so, may God deliver your worship from evil-minded enchanters, and bring me well and peacefully out of this government, which I doubt, for I expect to take leave of it and my life together, from the way Doctor Pedro Recio treats me.

Your worship's servant,
SANCHO PANZA THE GOVERNOR

The secretary sealed the letter, and immediately dismissed the courier; and those who were carrying on the joke against Sancho putting their heads together arranged how he was to be dismissed from the government. Sancho spent the afternoon in drawing up certain ordinances relating to the good government of what he fancied the island; and he ordained that there were to be no provision hucksters in the State, and that men might import wine into it from any place they please, provided they declared the quarter it came from, so that a price might be put upon it according to its quality, reputation, and the estimation it was held in; and he that watered his wine, or changed the name, was to forfeit his life for it. He reduced the prices of all manner of shoes, boots, and stockings, but of shoes in particular, as they seemed to him to run extravagantly high. He established a fixed rate for servants' wages, which were becoming recklessly exorbitant. He laid extremely heavy penalties upon those who sang lewd or loose songs either by day or night. He decreed that no blind man should sing of any miracle in verse, unless he could produce authentic evidence that it was true, for it was his opinion that most of those the blind men sing are trumped up, to the detriment of the true ones. He established and created an *alguacil* of the poor, not to harass them, but to examine them and see whether they really were so; for many a sturdy thief or drunkard goes about under cover of a make-believe crippled limb or a sham sore. In a word, he made so many good rules that to this day they are preserved there, and are called *The constitutions of the great governor Sancho Panza.*

FROM
Chapter 52
WHEREIN IS RELATED THE ADVENTURES OF THE SECOND DISTRESSED OR AFFLICTED DUENNA, OTHERWISE CALLED DOÑA RODRIGUEZ

Cid Hamet relates that Don Quixote being now cured of his scratches felt that the life he was leading in the castle was entirely inconsistent with the order of chivalry he professed, so he determined to ask the duke and duchess to permit him to take his departure for Saragossa, as the time of the festival was now drawing near, and he hoped to win there the suit of armor which is the prize at festivals of the sort. But one day at table with the duke and duchess, just as he was about to carry his resolution into effect and ask for their permission, [. . .] the page who had carried the letters and presents to Teresa Panza, the wife of the governor Sancho, entered the hall; and the duke and duchess were very well pleased to see him, being anxious to know the result of his journey; but when they asked him the page said in reply that he could not give it before so many people or in a few words, and begged their excellences to be pleased to let it wait for a private opportunity, and in the meantime amuse themselves with these letters; and taking out the letters he placed them in the duchess's hand. One bore by way of address, *Letter for my lady the Duchess So-and-so, of I don't know where;* and the other, *To my husband Sancho Panza, governor of the island of Barataria, whom God prosper longer than me.* The duchess's bread would not bake, as the saying is, until she had read her letter; and having looked over it herself and seen that it might be read aloud for the duke and all present to hear, she read out as follows.

TERESA PANZA'S LETTER TO THE DUCHESS.

> The letter your highness wrote me, my lady, gave me great pleasure, for indeed I found it very welcome. The string of coral beads is very fine, and my husband's hunting suit does not fall short of it. All this village is very much pleased that your ladyship has made a governor of my good man Sancho; though nobody will believe it, particularly the curate, and Master Nicholas the barber, and the bachelor Samson Carrasco; but I don't care for that, for so long as it is true, as it is, they may all say what they like; though, to tell the truth, if the coral beads and the suit had not come I would not have believed it either; for in this village everybody thinks my husband a numskull, and except for governing a flock of goats, they cannot fancy what sort of government he can be fit for. God grant it, and direct him according as he sees his children stand in need of it. I am resolved with your worship's leave, lady of my soul, to make the most of this fair day, and go to Court to stretch myself at ease in a coach, and make all those I have envying me already burst their eyes out; so I beg your excellence to order my husband to send me a small trifle of money, and to let it be something to speak of, because one's expenses are heavy at the Court; for a loaf costs a real, and meat thirty maravedís a pound, which is beyond everything; and if he does not want me to go let him tell me in time, for my feet are on the fidgets to be off; and my friends and neighbors tell me that if my daughter and I make a figure and a brave show at Court, my husband will come to be known far more by me than I by him, for of course plenty of people will ask, "Who are those ladies in that coach?" and some servant of mine will answer, "The wife and daughter of Sancho Panza, governor of the island of Barataria"; and in this way Sancho will become known, and I'll be thought well of, and 'to Rome for everything.' I am as vexed as vexed can be that they have gathered no acorns this year in our village; for all that I send your highness about half a peck that I went to the wood to gather and pick out one by one myself, and I could find no bigger ones; I wish they were as big as ostrich eggs.
>
> Let not your high mightiness forget to write to me; and I will take care to answer, and let you know how I am, and whatever news there may be in this place, where I remain, praying our Lord to have your highness in his keeping and not to forget me.
>
> Sancha, my daughter, and my son, kiss your worship's hands.
>
> She who would rather see your ladyship than write to you,
>
> Your servant,
> TERESA PANZA

All were greatly amused by Teresa Panza's letter, but particularly the duke and duchess; and the duchess asked Don Quixote's opinion whether they might open the letter that had come for the governor, which she suspected must be very good. Don Quixote said that to gratify them he would open it, and did so, and found that it ran as follows.

TERESA PANZA'S LETTER TO HER HUSBAND SANCHO PANZA.

I got thy letter, Sancho of my soul, and I promise thee and swear as a Catholic Christian that I was within two fingers' breadth of going mad, I was so happy. I can tell thee, brother, when I came to hear that thou wert a governor I thought I should have dropped dead with pure joy; and thou knowest they say sudden joy kills as well as great sorrow; and as for Sanchica thy daughter, she leaked from sheer happiness. I had before me the suit thou didst send me, and the coral beads my lady the duchess sent me round my neck, and the letters in my hands, and there was the bearer of them standing by, and in spite of all this I verily believed and thought that what I saw and handled was all a dream; for who could have thought that a goatherd would come to be a governor of islands? Thou knowest, my friend, what my mother used to say, that one must live long to see much; I say it because I expect to see more if I live longer; for I don't expect to stop until I see thee a farmer of taxes or a collector of revenue, which are offices where, though the devil carries off those who make a bad use of them, still they make and handle money. My lady the duchess will tell thee the desire I have to go to the Court; consider the matter and let me know thy pleasure; I will try to do honor to thee by going in a coach.

Neither the curate, nor the barber, nor the bachelor, not even the sacristan, can believe that thou art a governor, and they say the whole thing is a delusion or an enchantment affair, like everything belonging to thy master Don Quixote; and Samson says he must go in search of thee and drive the government out of thy head and the madness out of Don Quixote's skull; I only laugh, and look at my string of beads, and plan out the dress I am going to make for our daughter out of thy suit. I sent some acorns to my lady the duchess; I wish they had been gold. Send me some strings of pearls if they are in fashion in that island. Here is the news of the village; La Berrueca has married her daughter to a good-for-nothing painter, who came here to paint anything that might turn up. The council gave him an order to paint his Majesty's arms over the door of the town hall; he asked two ducats, which they paid him in advance; he worked for eight days, and at the end of them had nothing painted, and then said he had no turn for painting such trifling things; he returned the money, and for all that has married on the pretence of being a good workman; to be sure he has now laid aside his paintbrush and taken a spade in hand, and goes to the field like a gentleman. Pedro Lobo's son has received the first orders and tonsure, with the intention of becoming a priest. Minguilla, Mingo Silvato's granddaughter, found it out, and has gone to law with him on the score of having given her promise of marriage. Evil tongues say she is with child by him, but he denies it stoutly. There are no olives this year, and there is not a drop of vinegar to be had in the whole village. A company of soldiers passed through here; when they left they took away with them three of the girls of the village; I will not tell thee who they are; perhaps they will come back, and they will be sure to find those who will take them for wives with all their blemishes, good or bad. Sanchica is making bonelace; she earns eight maravedís a day clear, which she puts into a money-box as a help towards house furnishing; but now that she is a governor's daughter thou wilt give her a portion without her working for it. The fountain in the plaza has run dry. A flash of lightning struck the gibbet, and I wish they all lit there. I look for an answer to this, and to know thy mind about my going to the Court; and so, God keep thee longer than me, or as long, for I would not leave thee in this world without me.

Thy wife,
TERESA PANZA

The letters were applauded, laughed over, relished, and admired; and then, as if to put the seal to the business, the courier arrived, bringing the one Sancho sent to Don Quixote, and this, too, was read out, and it raised some doubts as to the governor's simplicity. The duchess withdrew to hear from the page about his adventures in Sancho's village, which he narrated at full length without leaving a single circumstance unmentioned. He gave her the acorns, and also a cheese which Teresa had given him as being particularly good and superior to those of Tronchon. The duchess received it with greatest delight, in which we will leave her, to describe the end of the government of the great Sancho Panza, flower and mirror of all governors of islands.

Chapter 53

OF THE TROUBLOUS END AND TERMINATION SANCHO PANZA'S GOVERNMENT CAME TO

To fancy that in this life anything belonging to it will remain forever in the same state, is an idle fancy; on the contrary, in it everything seems to go in a circle, I mean round and round. The spring succeeds the summer, the summer the fall, the fall the autumn, the autumn the winter, and the winter the spring, and so time rolls with never-ceasing wheel. Man's life alone, swifter than time, speeds onward to its end without any hope of renewal, save it be in that other life which is endless and boundless. Thus saith Cid Hamet the Mahometan philosopher, for there are many that by the light of nature alone, without the light of faith, have a comprehension of the fleeting nature and instability of this present life and the endless duration of that eternal life we hope for; but our author is here speaking of the rapidity with which Sancho's government came to an end, melted away, disappeared, vanished as it were in smoke and shadow. For as he lay in bed on the night of the seventh day of his government, sated, not with bread and wine, but with delivering judgments and giving opinions and making laws and proclamations, just as sleep, in spite of hunger, was beginning to close his eyelids, he heard such a noise of bell-ringing and shouting that one would have fancied the whole island was going to the bottom. He sat up in bed and remained listening intently to try if he could make out what could be the cause of so great an uproar; not only, however, was he unable to discover what it was, but as countless drums and trumpets now helped to swell the din of the bells and shouts, he was more puzzled than ever, and filled with fear and terror; and getting up he put on a pair of slippers because of the dampness of the floor, and without throwing a dressing-gown or anything of the kind over him he rushed out of the door of his room, just in time to see approaching along a corridor a band of more than twenty persons with lighted torches and naked swords in their hands, all shouting out, "To arms, to arms, Señor Governor, to arms! The enemy is in the island in countless numbers, and we are lost unless your skill and valor come to our support."

Keeping up this noise, tumult, and uproar, they came to where Sancho stood dazed and bewildered by what he saw and heard, and as they approached one of them called out to him, "Arm at once, your lordship, if you would not have yourself destroyed and the whole island lost."

"What have I to do with arming?" said Sancho. "What do I know about arms or supports? Better leave all that to my master Don Quixote, who will settle it and make all safe in a trice; for I, sinner that I am, God help me, don't understand these scuffles."

"Ah, Señor Governor," said another, "what slackness of mettle this is! Arm yourself; here are arms for you, offensive and defensive; come out to the plaza and be our leader and captain; it falls upon you by right to be so, for you are our governor."

"Arm me then, in God's name," said Sancho, and they at once produced two large shields they had come provided with; and placed them upon him over his shirt, without letting him put on anything else, one shield in front and the other behind, and passing his arms through openings they had made, they bound him tight with ropes, so that there he was walled and boarded up as straight as a spindle and unable to bend his knees or stir a single step. In his hand they placed a lance, on which he leant to keep himself from falling, and as soon as they had him thus fixed, they bade him march forward and lead them on and give them all courage; for with him for their guide and lamp and morning star, they were sure to bring their business to a successful issue.

"How am I to march, unlucky being that I am?" said Sancho, "when I can't stir my kneecaps, for these boards I have bound so tight to my body won't let me. What you must do is to carry me in your arms, and lay me across or set me upright in some postern, and I'll hold it either with this lance or with my body."

"On, Señor Governor!" cried another, "it is fear more than the boards that keeps you from moving; make haste, stir yourself, for there is no time to lose; the enemy is increasing in numbers, the shouts grow louder, and the danger is pressing."

Urged by these exhortations and reproaches the poor governor made an attempt to advance, but fell to the ground with such a crash that he fancied he had broken himself all to pieces. There he lay like a tortoise enclosed in its shell, or a side of bacon between two kneading-troughs, or a boat bottom up on the beach; nor did the gang of jokers feel any compassion for him when they saw him down; so far from that, extinguishing their torches they began to shout afresh and to renew the calls to arms with such energy, trampling on poor Sancho, and slashing at him over the shield with their swords in such a way that, if he had not gathered himself together and made himself small and drawn in his head between the shields, it would have fared badly with the poor governor, as, squeezed into that narrow compass, he lay, sweating and sweating again, and commending himself with all his heart to God to deliver him from his present peril. Some stumbled over him, others fell upon him, and one there was who took up a position on top of him for some time, and from thence as if from a watch-tower issued orders to the troops, shouting out, "Here, our side! Here the enemy is thickest! Hold the breach there! Shut that gate! Barricade those ladders! Here with your stink-pots of pitch and resin, and kettles of boiling oil! Block the streets with feather beds!" In short, in his ardor he mentioned every little thing, and every implement and engine of war by means of which an assault upon a city is warded off, while the bruised and battered Sancho, who heard and suffered all, was saying to himself, "O if it would only please the Lord to let the island be lost at once, and I could see myself either dead or out of this torture!" Heaven heard his prayer, and when he least expected it he heard voices exclaiming, "Victory, victory! The enemy retreats beaten! Come, Señor Governor, get up, and come and enjoy the victory, and divide the spoils that have been won from the foe by the might of that invincible arm."

"Lift me up," said the wretched Sancho in a woe-begone voice. They helped him to rise, and as soon as he was on his feet he said, "The enemy I have beaten you may nail to my forehead; I don't want to divide the spoils of the foe, I only beg and entreat some friend, if I have one, to give me a sup of wine, for I'm parched with thirst, and wipe me dry, for I'm turning to water."

They rubbed him down, fetched him wine and unbound the shields, and he seated himself upon his bed, and with fear, agitation, and fatigue he fainted away. Those who had been concerned in the joke were now sorry they had pushed it so far; however, the anxiety his fainting away had caused them was relieved by his returning to himself. He asked what o'clock it was; they told him it was just daybreak. He said no more, and in silence began to dress himself, while all watched him, waiting to see what the haste with which he was putting on his clothes meant.

He got himself dressed at last, and then, slowly, for he was sorely bruised and could not go fast, he proceeded to the stable, followed by all who were present, and going up to Dapple embraced him and gave him a loving kiss on the forehead, and said to him, not without tears in his eyes, "Come along, comrade and friend and partner of my toils and sorrows; when I was with you and had no cares to trouble me except mending your harness and feeding your little carcass, happy were my hours, my days, and my years; but since I left you, and mounted the towers of ambition and pride, a thousand miseries, a thousand troubles, and four thousand anxieties have entered into my soul"; and all the while he was speaking in this strain he was fixing the pack-saddle on the ass, without a word from any one. Then having Dapple saddled, he, with great pain and difficulty, got up on him, and addressing himself to the majordomo, the secretary, the head-carver, and Pedro Recio the doctor and several others who stood by, he said, "Make way, gentlemen, and let me go back to my old freedom; let me go look for my past life, and raise myself up from this present death. I was not born to be a governor or protect islands or cities from the enemies that choose to attack them. Ploughing and digging, vine-dressing and pruning, are more in my way than defending provinces or kingdoms. Saint Peter is very well at Rome; I mean each of us is best following the trade he was born to. A reaping-hook fits my hand better than a governor's sceptre; I'd rather have my fill of *gazpacho* than be subject to the misery of a meddling doctor who kills me with hunger, and I'd rather lie in summer under the shade of an oak, and in winter wrap myself in a double sheepskin jacket in freedom, than go to bed between holland sheets and dress in sables under the restraint of a government. God be with your worships, and tell my lord the duke that 'naked I was born, naked I find myself, I neither lose nor gain'; I mean that without a farthing I came into this government, and without a farthing I go out of it, very different from the way governors commonly leave other islands. Stand aside and let me go; I have to plaster myself, for I believe every one of my ribs is crushed, thanks to the enemies that have been trampling over me to-night."

"That is unnecessary, Señor Governor," said Doctor Recio, "for I will give your worship a draught against falls and bruises that will soon make you as sound and strong as ever; and as for your diet I promise your worship to behave better, and let you eat plentifully of whatever you like."

"You spoke late," said Sancho. "I'd as soon turn Turk as stay any longer. Those jokes won't pass a second time. By God I'd as soon remain in this government, or take another, even if it was offered me between two plates, as fly to heaven without wings. I am of the breed of the Panzas, and they are every one of them obstinate, and if they once say 'odds,' odds it must be, no matter if it is evens, in spite of all the world. Here in this stable I leave the ant's wings that lifted me up into the air for the swifts and other birds to eat me, and let's take to level ground and our feet once more; and if they're not shod in pinked shoes of cordovan, they won't want for rough sandals of hemp; 'every ewe to her like,' 'and let no one stretch his leg beyond the length of the sheet'; and now let me pass, for it's growing late with me."

To this the majordomo said, "Señor Governor, we would let your worship go with all our hearts, though it sorely grieves us to lose you, for your wit and Christian conduct naturally make us regret you; but it is well known that every governor, before he leaves the place where he has been governing, is bound first of all to render an account. Let your worship do so for the ten days you have held the government, and then you may go and the peace of God go with you."

"No one can demand it of me," said Sancho, "but he whom my lord the duke shall appoint; I am going to meet him, and to him I will render an exact one; besides, when I go forth naked as I do, there is no other proof needed to show that I have governed like an angel."

"By God the great Sancho is right," said Doctor Recio, "and it is my opinion we should let him go, for the duke will be beyond measure glad to see him."

They all agreed to this, and allowed him to go, first offering to bear him company and furnish him with all he wanted for his own comfort or for the journey. Sancho said he did not want anything more than a little barley for Dapple, and half a cheese and half a loaf for himself; for the distance being so short there was no occasion for any better or bulkier provant. They all embraced him, and he with tears embraced all of them, and left them filled with admiration not only at his remarks but at his firm and sensible resolution.

...

FROM

Chapter 55

OF WHAT BEFELL SANCHO ON THE ROAD, AND OTHER THINGS THAT CANNOT BE SURPASSED

The length of time he delayed . . . prevented Sancho from reaching the duke's castle that day, though he was within half a league of it when night, somewhat dark and cloudy, overtook him. This, however, as it was summer time, did not give him much uneasiness, and he turned aside out of the road intending to wait for morning; but his ill luck and hard fate so willed it that as he was searching about for a place to make himself as comfortable as possible, he and Dapple fell into a deep dark hole that lay among some very old buildings. As he fell he commended himself with all his heart to God, fancying he was not going to stop until he reached the depths of the bottomless pit; but it did not turn out so, for at little more than thrice a man's height Dapple touched bottom, and he found himself sitting on him without having received any hurt or damage whatever. He felt himself all over and held his breath to try whether he was quite sound or had a hole made in him anywhere, and finding himself all right and whole and in perfect health he was profuse in his thanks to God our Lord for the mercy that had been shown him, for he thought surely he had been broken into a thousand pieces. He also felt along the sides of the pit with his hands to see if it were possible to get out of it without help, but he found they were quite smooth and afforded no hold anywhere, at which he was greatly distressed, especially when he heard how pathetically and dolefully Dapple was bemoaning himself, and no wonder he complained, nor was it from ill-temper, for in truth he was not in a very good case.

"Alas," said Sancho, "what unexpected accidents happen at every step to those who live in this miserable world! Who would have said that one who saw himself yesterday sitting on a throne, governor of an island, giving orders to his servants and his vassals, would see himself to-day buried in a pit without a soul to help him, or servant or vassal to come to his relief! Here must we perish with hunger, my ass and myself, if indeed we don't die first, he of his bruises and injuries, and I of grief and sorrow. At any rate I shall not be as lucky as my master Don Quixote of La Mancha, when he went down into the cave of that enchanted Montesinos, where he found people to make more of him than if he had been in his own house; for it seems he came in for a table laid out and a bed ready made. There he saw fair and pleasant visions, but here I shall see, I imagine, toads and adders. Unlucky wretch that I am, what an end my follies and fancies have come to! They'll take up my bones out of this, when it is Heaven's will that I'm found, picked clean, white and polished, and my good Dapple's with them, and by that, perhaps, it will be found out who we are, at least by such as have heard that Sancho Panza never separated from his ass, nor his ass from Sancho Panza. Unlucky wretches, I say again, that our hard fate should not let us die in our own country and among our own people, where if there was no help for our misfortune, at any rate there would be some one to grieve for it and to close our eyes as we passed away! O comrade and friend, how ill have I repaid thy faithful services! Forgive me, and entreat Fortune, as well as thou canst, to deliver us out of this miserable strait we are both in; and I promise to put a crown of laurel on thy head, and make thee look like a poet laureate, and give thee double feeds."

In this strain did Sancho bewail himself, and his ass listened to him, but answered him never a word, such was the distress and anguish the poor beast found himself in. At length, after a night spent in bitter moanings and lamentations, day came, and by its light Sancho perceived that it was wholly impossible to escape out of that pit without help, and he fell to bemoaning his fate and uttering loud shouts to find out if there was any one within hearing; but all his shouting was only crying in the wilderness, for there was not a soul anywhere in the neighborhood to hear him, and then at last he gave himself up for dead. Dapple was lying on his back, and Sancho helped him to his feet, which he was scarcely able to keep; and then taking a piece of bread out of his *alforjas* which had shared their fortunes in the fall, he gave it to the ass, to whom it was not unwelcome, saying to him as if he understood him, "With bread all sorrows are less."

And now he perceived on one side of the pit a hole large enough to admit a person if he stooped and squeezed himself into a small compass. Sancho made for it, and entered it by creeping, and found it wide and spacious on the inside, which he was able to see as a ray of sunlight that penetrated what might be called the roof showed it all plainly. He observed, too, that it opened and widened out into another spacious cavity; seeing which he made his way back to where the ass was, and with a stone began to pick away the clay from the hole until in a short time he had made room for the beast to pass easily, and this accomplished, taking him by the halter, he proceeded to traverse the cavern to see if there was any outlet at the other end. He advanced, sometimes in the dark, sometimes with light, but never without fear; "God Almighty help me!" said he to himself; "this that is a misadventure to me would make a good adventure for my master Don Quixote. He would have been sure to take these depths and dungeons for flowery gardens or the palaces of Galiana,[65] and would have counted upon issuing out of this darkness and imprisonment into some blooming meadow; but I, unlucky that I am, hopeless and spiritless, expect at every step another pit deeper than the first to open under my feet and swallow me up for good; 'welcome evil, if thou comest alone.'"

In this way and with these reflections he seemed to himself to have travelled rather more than half a league, when at last he perceived a dim light that looked like daylight and found its way in on one side, showing that this road, which appeared to him the road to the other world, led to some opening.

Here Cid Hamet leaves him, and returns to Don Quixote, who, . . . as he was putting Rocinante through his paces or pressing him to the charge, he brought his feet so close to a pit that but for reining him in tightly it would have been impossible for him to avoid falling into it. He pulled him up, however, without a fall, and coming a little closer examined the hole without dismounting; but as he was looking at it he heard loud cries proceeding from it, and by listening attentively was able to make out that he who uttered them was saying, "Ho, above there! is there any Christian

[65] **"Galiana"**: A legendary Moorish princess.

that hears me, or any charitable gentleman that will take pity on a sinner buried alive, or an unfortunate disgoverned governor?"

It struck Don Quixote that it was the voice of Sancho Panza he heard, whereat he was taken aback and amazed, and raising his own voice as much as he could, he cried out, "Who is below there? Who is that complaining?"

"Who should be here, or who should complain," was the answer, "but the forlorn Sancho Panza, for his sins and for his ill-luck governor of the island of Barataria, squire that was to the famous knight Don Quixote of La Mancha?"

When Don Quixote heard this his amazement was redoubled and his perturbation grew greater than ever, for it suggested itself to his mind that Sancho must be dead, and that his soul was in torment down there; and carried away by this idea he exclaimed, "I conjure thee by everything that as a Catholic Christian I can conjure thee by, tell me who thou art; and if thou art a soul in torment, tell me what thou wouldst have me do for thee; for as my profession is to give aid and succor to those that need it in this world, it will also extend to aiding and succoring the distressed of the other, who cannot help themselves."

"In that case," answered the voice, "your worship who speaks to me must be my master Don Quixote of La Mancha; nay, from the tone of the voice it is plain it can be nobody else."

"Don Quixote I am," replied Don Quixote, "he whose profession it is to aid and succor the living and the dead in their necessities; wherefore tell me who thou art, for thou art keeping me in suspense; because, if thou art my squire Sancho Panza, and art dead, since the devils have not carried thee off, and thou art by God's mercy in purgatory, our holy mother the Roman Catholic Church has intercessory means sufficient to release thee from the pains thou art in; and I for my part will plead with her to that end, so far as my substance will go; without further delay, therefore, declare thyself, and tell me who thou art."

"By all that's good," was the answer, "and by the birth of whomsoever your worship chooses, I swear, Señor Don Quixote of La Mancha, that I am your squire Sancho Panza, and that I have never died all my life; but that, having given up my government for reasons that would require more time to explain, I fell last night into this pit where I am now, and Dapple is witness and won't let me lie, for more by token he is here with me."

Nor was this all; one would have fancied the ass understood what Sancho said, because that moment he began to bray so loudly that the whole cave rang again.

"Famous testimony!" exclaimed Don Quixote; "I know that bray as well as if I was its mother, and thy voice, too, my Sancho. Wait while I go to the duke's castle, which is close by, and I will bring some one to take thee out of this pit into which thy sins no doubt have brought thee."

"Go, your worship," said Sancho, "and come back quick for God's sake; for I cannot bear being buried alive here any longer, and I'm dying of fear."

Don Quixote left him, and hastened to the castle to tell the duke and duchess what had happened to Sancho, and they were not a little astonished at it, although they could easily understand his having fallen, from the confirmatory circumstance of the cave which had been in existence there from time immemorial; but they could not imagine how he had quitted the government without their receiving any intimation of his coming. To be brief, they fetched ropes and tackle, as the saying is, and by dint of many hands and much labor they drew up Dapple and Sancho Panza out of the darkness into the light of day. A student who saw him remarked, "That's the way all bad governors should come out of their governments, as this sinner comes out of the depths of the pit, dead with hunger, pale, and I suppose without a farthing."

Sancho overheard him and said, "It is eight or ten days, brother growler, since I entered upon the government of the island they gave me, and all that time I never had a bellyfull of victuals, no not for an hour; doctors persecuted me and enemies crushed my bones; nor had I any opportunity of taking bribes or levying taxes; and if that be the case, as it is, I don't deserve, I think, to come out in this fashion, but 'man proposes and God disposes'; and God knows what is best, and what suits each one best; and 'as the occasion, so the behaviour'; and 'let nobody say "I won't drink of this water" '; and 'where one thinks there are flitches, there are no pegs'; God knows my meaning and that's enough; I say no more, though I could."

"Be not angry or annoyed at what thou hearest, Sancho," said Don Quixote, "or there will never be an end of it; keep a safe conscience and let them say what they like; for trying to stop slanderers' tongues is like trying to put gates to the open plain. If a governor comes out of his government rich, they say he has been a thief; and if he comes out poor, that he has been a noodle and a blockhead."

"They'll be pretty sure this time," said Sancho, "to set me down for a fool rather than a thief."

Thus talking, and surrounded by boys and a crowd of people, they reached the castle, where in one of the corridors the duke and duchess stood waiting for them; but Sancho would not go up to see the duke until he had first put up Dapple in the stable, for he said he had passed a very bad night in his last quarters; then he went upstairs to see his lord and lady, and kneeling before them he said, "Because it was your highnesses' pleasure, not because of any desert of my own, I went to govern your island of Barataria, which I entered naked, 'and naked I find myself; I neither lose nor gain.' Whether I have governed well or ill, I have had witnesses who will say what they think fit. I have answered questions, I have decided causes, and always dying of hunger, for Dr. Pedro Recio of Tirteafuera, the islandish and governorish doctor, would have it so. Enemies attacked us by night and put us in a great quandary, but the people of the island say they came off safe and victorious by the might of my arm; and may God give them as much health as there's truth in what they say. In short, during that time I have weighed the cares and responsibilities governing brings with it, and by my reckoning I find my shoulders can't bear them, nor are they a load for my loins or arrows for my quiver; and so, before the government threw me over, I preferred to throw the government over; and yesterday morning I left the island as I found it, with the same streets, houses, and roofs it had when I entered it. I asked no loan of anybody, nor did I try to fill my pocket; and though I meant to make some useful laws, I made hardly any, as I was afraid they would not be kept; for in that case it comes to the same thing to make them or not to make them. I quitted the island, as I said, without any escort except my ass; I fell into a pit, I pushed on through it, until this morning by the light of the sun I saw an outlet, but not so easy a one but that, had not Heaven sent me my master Don Quixote, I'd have stayed there till the end of the world. So now, my lord and lady duke and duchess, here is your governor Sancho Panza, who in the bare ten days he has held the government has come by the knowledge that he would not give anything to be governor, not to say of an island, but of the whole world; and that point being settled, kissing your worships' feet, and imitating the game of the boys when they say 'leap thou, and give me one,' I take a leap out of the government and pass into the service of my master Don Quixote; for after all, though in it I eat my bread in fear and trembling, at any rate I take my fill; and for my part, so long as I'm full, it's all alike to me whether it's with carrots or with partridges."

Here Sancho brought his long speech to an end, Don Quixote having been the whole time in dread of his uttering a host of absurdities; and when he found him leave off with so few, he thanked Heaven in his heart. The duke embraced Sancho and told him he was heartily sorry he had given up the government so soon, but that he would see that he was provided with some other post on his estate less onerous and more profitable. The duchess also embraced him, and gave orders that he should be taken good care of, as it was plain to see he had been badly treated and worse bruised.

. . .

Chapter 73

OF THE OMENS DON QUIXOTE HAD AS HE ENTERED HIS OWN VILLAGE, AND OTHER INCIDENTS THAT EMBELLISH AND GIVE A COLOR TO THIS GREAT HISTORY

At the entrance of the village, so says Cid Hamet, Don Quixote saw two boys quarrelling on the village threshing-floor, one of whom said to the other, "Take it easy, Periquillo; thou shalt never see it again as long as thou livest."

Don Quixote heard this, and said he to Sancho, "Dost thou not mark, friend, what that boy said, 'Thou shalt never see it again as long as thou livest'?"

"Well," said Sancho, "what does it matter if the boy said so?"

"What!" said Don Quixote, "dost thou not see that, applied to the object of my desires, the words mean that I am never to see Dulcinea more?"

Sancho was about to answer, when his attention was diverted by seeing a hare come flying across the plain pursued by several greyhounds and sportsmen. In its terror it ran to take shelter and hide itself under Dapple. Sancho caught it alive and presented it to Don Quixote, who was saying, "*Malum signum, malum signum!*[66] a hare flies, greyhounds chase it. Dulcinea appears not."

"Your worship's a strange man," said Sancho; "let's take it for granted that this hare is Dulcinea, and these greyhounds chasing it the malignant enchanters who turned her into a country wench; she flies, and I catch her and put her into your worship's hands, and you hold her in your arms and cherish her; what bad sign is that, or what ill omen is there to be found here?"

---

[66] ***"Malum . . . signum!":*** "A bad sign, a bad sign!"

The two boys who had been quarrelling came over to look at the hare, and Sancho asked one of them what their quarrel was about. He was answered by the one who had said, "Thou shalt never see it again as long as thou livest," that he had taken a cage full of crickets from the other boy, and did not mean to give it back to him as long as he lived. Sancho took out four cuartos from his pocket and gave them to the boy for the cage, which he placed in Don Quixote's hands, saying, "There, señor! there are the omens broken and destroyed, and they have no more to do with our affairs, to my thinking, fool as I am, than with last year's clouds; and if I remember rightly I have heard the curate of our village say that it does not become Christians or sensible people to give any heed to these silly things; and even you yourself said the same to me some time ago, telling me that all Christians who minded omens were fools; but there's no need of making words about it; let us push on and go into our village."

The sportsmen came up and asked for their hare, which Don Quixote gave them. They then went on, and upon the green at the entrance of the town they came upon the curate and the bachelor Samson Carrasco busy with their breviaries. It should be mentioned that Sancho had thrown, by way of a sumpter-cloth, over Dapple and over the bundle of armor, the buckram robe painted with flames which they had put upon him at the duke's castle the night Altisidora came back to life. He had also fixed the mitre on Dapple's head, the oddest transformation and decoration that ever ass in the world underwent. They were at once recognized by both the curate and the bachelor, who came towards them with open arms. Don Quixote dismounted and received them with a close embrace; and the boys, who are lynxes that nothing escapes, spied out the ass's mitre and came running to see it, calling out to one another, "Come here, boys, and see Sancho Panza's ass rigged out finer than Mingo, and Don Quixote's beast leaner than ever."

So at length, with the boys capering round them, and accompanied by the curate and the bachelor, they made their entrance into the town, and proceeded to Don Quixote's house, at the door of which they found his housekeeper and niece, whom the news of his arrival had already reached. It had been brought to Teresa Panza, Sancho's wife, as well, and she with her hair all loose and half naked, dragging Sanchica her daughter by the hand, ran out to meet her husband; but seeing him coming in by no means as good case as she thought a governor ought to be, she said to him, "How is it you come this way, husband? It seems to me you come tramping and footsore, and looking more like a disorderly vagabond than a governor."

"Hold your tongue, Teresa," said Sancho; "often where there are pegs there are no flitches; let's go into the house and there you'll hear strange things. I bring money, and that's the main thing, got by my own industry without wronging anybody."

"You bring the money, my good husband," said Teresa, "and no matter whether it was got this way or that; for, however you may have got it, you'll not have brought any new practice into the world."

Sanchica embraced her father and asked him if he brought her anything, for she had been looking out for him as for the showers of May; and she taking hold of him by the girdle on one side, and his wife by the hand, while the daughter led Dapple, they made for their house, leaving Don Quixote in his, in the hands of his niece and housekeeper, and in the company of the curate and the bachelor.

Don Quixote at once, without any regard to time or season, withdrew in private with the bachelor and the curate, and in a few words told them of his defeat, and of the engagement he was under not to quit his village for a year,[67] which he meant to keep to the letter without departing a hair's breadth from it, as became a knight-errant bound by scrupulous good faith and the laws of knight-errantry; and of how he thought of turning shepherd for that year, and taking his diversion in the solitude of the fields, where he could with perfect freedom give range to his thoughts of love while he followed the virtuous pastoral calling; and he besought them, if they had not a great deal to do and were not prevented by more important business, to consent to be his companions, for he would buy sheep enough to qualify them for shepherds; and the most important point of the whole affair, he could tell them, was settled, for he had given them names that would fit them to a T. The curate asked what they were. Don Quixote replied that he himself was to be called the shepherd Quixotiz and the bachelor the shepherd Carrascon, and the curate the shepherd Curiambro, and Sancho Panza the shepherd Pancino.

Both were astounded at Don Quixote's new craze; however, lest he should once more make off out of the village from them in pursuit of chivalry, they, trusting that in the course of the year he might be cured, fell in with his new project, applauded his crazy idea as a bright one, and offered to share the life with him. "And what's more," said Samson Carrasco, "I am, as all the world knows, a very famous poet, and I'll be always making verses, pastoral, or courtly, or as it may come into my head, to pass away our time in those secluded regions where we shall be roaming. But what is most needful, sirs, is that each of us should choose the name of the shepherdess he means to glorify in his verses, and that we should not leave a tree, be it ever so hard, without writing up and carving her name on it, as is the habit and custom of love-smitten shepherds."

"That's the very thing," said Don Quixote; "though I am relieved from looking for the name of an imaginary shepherdess, for there's the peerless Dulcinea del Toboso, the glory of these brook-sides, the ornament of these meadows, the mainstay of beauty, the cream of all the graces, and, in a word, the being to whom all praise is appropriate, be it ever so hyperbolical."

"Very true," said the curate; "but we the others must look about for accommodating shepherdesses that will answer our purpose one way or another."

"And," added Samson Carrasco, "if they fail us, we can call them by the names of the ones in print that the world is filled with, Filidas, Amarilises, Dianas, Fleridas, Galateas, Belisardas; for as they sell them in the market-places we may fairly buy them and make them our own. If my lady, or I should say my shepherdess, happens to be called Ana, I'll sing her praises under the name of Anarda, and if Francisca, I'll call her Francenia, and if Lucia, Lucinda, for it all comes to the same thing; and Sancho Panza, if he joins this fraternity, may glorify his wife Teresa Panza as Teresaina."

---

[67] **his defeat . . . a year:** Before being defeated in a single combat with the White Knight (Samson Carrasco in disguise), Quixote has agreed that if he loses the fight he will return to La Mancha and stay there for a year.

Don Quixote laughed at the adaptation of the name, and the curate bestowed vast praise upon the worthy and honorable resolution he had made, and again offered to bear him company all that he could spare from his imperative duties. And so they took their leave of him, recommending and beseeching him to take care of his health and treat himself to a generous diet.

It so happened his niece and the housekeeper overheard all the three of them said; and as soon as they were gone they both of them came in to Don Quixote, and said the niece, "What's this, uncle? Now that we were thinking you had come back to stay at home and lead a quiet respectable life there, are you going to get into fresh entanglements, and turn 'young shepherd, thou that comest here, young shepherd going there'? Nay! indeed 'the straw is too hard now to make pipes of.'"

"And," added the housekeeper, "will your worship be able to bear, out in the fields, the heats of summer, and the chills of winter, and the howling of the wolves? Not you; for that's a life and a business for hardy men, bred and seasoned to such work almost from the time they were in swaddling-clothes. Why, to make choice of evils, it's better to be a knight-errant than a shepherd! Look here, señor; take my advice—and I'm not giving it to you full of bread and wine, but fasting, and with fifty years upon my head—stay at home, look after your affairs, go often to confession, be good to the poor, and upon my soul be it if any evil comes to you."

"Hold your peace, my daughters," said Don Quixote; "I know very well what my duty is; help me to bed, for I don't feel very well; and rest assured that, knight-errant now or wandering shepherd to be, I shall never fail to have a care for your interests, as you will see in the end." And the good wenches (for that they undoubtedly were), the housekeeper and niece, helped him to bed, where they gave him something to eat and made him as comfortable as possible.

Chapter 74

OF HOW DON QUIXOTE FELL SICK, AND OF THE WILL HE MADE, AND HOW HE DIED

As nothing that is man's can last forever, but all tends ever downwards from its beginning to its end, and above all man's life, and as Don Quixote's enjoyed no special dispensation from Heaven to stay its course, its end and close came when he least looked for it. For—whether it was of the dejection the thought of his defeat produced, or of Heaven's will that so ordered it—a fever settled upon him and kept him in his bed for six days, during which he was often visited by his friends the curate, the bachelor, and the barber, while his good squire Sancho Panza never quitted his bedside. They, persuaded that it was grief at finding himself vanquished, and the object of his heart, the liberation and disenchantment of Dulcinea, unattained, that kept him in this state, strove by all the means in their power to cheer him up; the bachelor bidding him take heart and get up to begin his pastoral life, for which he himself, he said, had already composed an eclogue that would take the shine out of all Sannazaro had ever written, and had bought with his own money two famous dogs to guard the flock, one called Barcino and the other Butron, which a herdsman of Quintanar had sold him.

But for all this Don Quixote could not shake off his sadness. His friends called in the doctor, who felt his pulse and was not very well satisfied with it, and said that in any case it would be well for him to attend to the health of his soul, as that of his body was in a bad way. Don Quixote heard this calmly; but not so his housekeeper, his niece, and his squire, who fell weeping bitterly, as if they had him lying dead before them. The doctor's opinion was that melancholy and depression were bringing him to his end. Don Quixote begged them to leave him to himself, as he had a wish to sleep a little. They obeyed, and he slept at one stretch, as the saying is, more than six hours, so that the housekeeper and niece thought he was going to sleep forever. But at the end of that time he woke up, and in a loud voice exclaimed, "Blessed be Almighty God, who has shown me such goodness. In truth his mercies are boundless, and the sins of men can neither limit them nor keep them back!"

The niece listened with attention to her uncle's words, and they struck her as more coherent than what usually fell from him, at least during his illness, so she asked, "What are you saying, señor? Has anything strange occurred? What mercies or what sins of men are you talking of?"

"The mercies, niece," said Don Quixote, "are those that God has this moment shown me, and with him, as I said, my sins are no impediment to them. My reason is now free and clear, rid of the dark shadows of ignorance that my unhappy constant study of those detestable books of chivalry cast over it. Now I see through their absurdities and deceptions, and it only grieves me that this destruction of my illusions has come so late that it leaves me no time to make some amends by reading other books that might be a light to my soul. Niece, I feel myself at the point of death, and I would fain meet it in such a way as to show that my life has not been so ill that I should leave behind me the name of a madman; for though I have been one, I would not that the fact should be made plainer at my death. Call in to me, my dear, my good friends the Curate, the Bachelor Samson Carrasco, and Master Nicholas the barber, for I wish to confess and make my will." But his niece was saved the trouble by the entrance of the three. The instant Don Quixote saw them he exclaimed, "Good news for you, good sirs, that I am no longer Don Quixote of La Mancha, but Alonso Quixano, whose way of life won for him the name of Good. Now am I the enemy of Amadis of Gaul and of the whole countless troop of his descendants, odious to me now are all the profane stories of knight-errantry; now I perceive my folly, and the peril into which reading them brought me; now, by God's mercy schooled into my right senses, I loathe them."

When the three heard him speak in this way, they had no doubt whatever that some new craze had taken possession of him; and said Samson, "What? Señor Don Quixote! Now that we have intelligence of the lady Dulcinea being disenchanted, are you taking this line; now, just as we are on the point of becoming shepherds, to pass our lives singing, like princes, are you thinking of turning hermit? Hush for Heaven's sake, be rational, and let's have no more nonsense."

"All that nonsense," said Don Quixote, "that until now has been a reality to my hurt, my death will, with Heaven's help, turn to my good. I feel, sirs, that I am rapidly drawing near death; a truce to jesting; let me have a confessor to confess me, and a notary to make my will; for in extremities like this, man must not trifle with his soul; and while the curate is confessing me let some one, I beg, go for the notary."

They looked at one another, wondering at Don Quixote's words; but, though uncertain, they were inclined to believe him, and one of the signs by which they came to the conclusion he was dying was this so sudden and complete return to his senses after having been mad; for to the words already quoted he added much more, so well expressed, so devout, and so rational, as to banish all doubt and convince them that he was sound of mind. The curate turned them all out, and left alone with him confessed him. The bachelor went for the notary and returned shortly afterwards with him and with Sancho, who, having already learned from the bachelor the condition his master was in, and finding the housekeeper and niece weeping, began to blubber and shed tears.

The confession over, the curate came out saying, "Alonso Quixano the Good is indeed dying, and is indeed in his right mind; we may now go in to him while he makes his will."

This news gave a tremendous impulse to the brimming eyes of the housekeeper, the niece, and Sancho Panza his good squire, making the tears burst from their eyes and a host of sighs from their hearts; for of a truth, as has been said more than once, whether as plain Alonso Quixano the Good, or as Don Quixote of La Mancha, Don Quixote was always of a gentle disposition and kindly in all his ways, and hence he was beloved, not only by those of his own house, but by all who knew him.

The notary came in with the rest, and as soon as the preamble of the will had been set out and Don Quixote had commended his soul to God with all the devout formalities that are usual, coming to the bequests, he said, "Item, it is my will that, touching certain moneys in the hands of Sancho Panza (whom in my madness I made my squire), inasmuch as between him and me there have been certain accounts and debits and credits, no claim be made against him, nor any account demanded of him in respect of them; but that if anything remain over and above, after he has paid himself what I owe him, the balance, which will be but little, shall be his, and much good may it do him; and if, as when I was mad I had a share in giving him the government of an island, so, now that I am in my senses, I could give him that of a kingdom, it should be his, for the simplicity of his character and the fidelity of his conduct deserve it." And then, turning to Sancho, he said, "Forgive me, my friend, that I led thee to seem as mad as myself, making thee fall into the same error I myself fell into, that there were and still are knights-errant in the world."

"Ah!" said Sancho weeping, "don't die, master, but take my advice and live many years; for the foolishest thing a man can do in this life is to let himself die without rhyme or reason, without anybody killing him, or any hands but melancholy's making an end of him. Come, don't be lazy, but get up from your bed and let us take to the fields in shepherd's trim as we agreed. Perhaps behind some bush we shall find the lady Dulcinea disenchanted, as fine as fine can be. If it be that you are dying of vexation at having been vanquished, lay the blame on me, and say you were overthrown because I had girthed Rocinante badly; besides you must have seen in your books of chivalry that it is a common thing for knights to upset one another, and for him who is conquered to-day to be conqueror to-morrow."

"Very true," said Samson, "and good Sancho Panza's view of these cases is quite right."

"Sirs, not so fast," said Don Quixote, "'in last year's nests there are no birds this year.' I was mad, now I am in my senses; I was Don Quixote of La Mancha, I am now, as I said, Alonso Quixano the Good; and may my repentance and sincerity restore me to the esteem you used to have for me; and now let Master Notary proceed.

"Item, I leave all my property absolutely to Antonia Quixana my niece, here present, after all has been deducted from the most available portion of it that may be required to satisfy the bequests I have made. And the first disbursement I desire to be made is the payment of the wages I owe for the time my housekeeper has served me, with twenty ducats, over and above for a gown. The curate and the bachelor Samson Carrasco, now present, I appoint my executors.

"Item, it is my wish that if Antonia Quixana, my niece, desires to marry, she shall marry a man of whom it shall be first of all ascertained by information taken that he does not know what books of chivalry are; and if it should be proved that he does, and if, in spite of this, my niece insists upon marrying him, and does marry him, then that she shall forfeit the whole of what I have left her, which my executors shall devote to works of charity as they please.

"Item, I entreat the aforesaid gentlemen my executors, that if any happy chance should lead them to discover the author who is said to have written a history now going about under the title of *Second Part of the Achievements of Don Quixote of La Mancha,* they beg of him on my behalf as earnestly as they can to forgive me for having been, without intending it, the cause of his writing so many and such monstrous absurdities as he has written in it; for I am leaving the world with a feeling of compunction at having provoked him to write them."

With this he closed his will, and a faintness coming over him he stretched himself out at full length on the bed. All were in a flutter and made haste to relieve him, and during the three days he lived after that on which he made his will he fainted away very often. The house was all in confusion; but still the niece ate and the housekeeper drank and Sancho Panza enjoyed himself; for inheriting property wipes out or softens down in the heir the feeling of grief the dead man might be expected to leave behind him.

At last Don Quixote's end came, after he had received all the sacraments, and had in full and forcible terms expressed his detestation of books of chivalry. The notary was there at the time, and he said that in no book of chivalry had he ever read of any knight-errant dying in his bed so calmly and so like a Christian as Don Quixote, who amid the tears and lamentations of all present yielded up his spirit, that is to say died. On perceiving it the curate begged the notary to bear witness that Alonso Quixano the Good, commonly called Don Quixote of La Mancha, had passed away from his present life, and died naturally; and said he desired this testimony in order to remove the possibility of any other author save Cid Hamet Benengeli bringing him to life again falsely and making interminable stories out of his achievements.

Such was the end of the Ingenious Gentleman of La Mancha, whose village Cid Hamet would not indicate precisely, in order to leave all the towns and villages of

La Mancha to contend among themselves for the right to adopt him and claim him as a son, as the seven cities of Greece contended for Homer. The lamentations of Sancho and the niece and housekeeper are omitted here, as well as the new epitaphs upon his tomb; Samson Carrasco, however, put the following:

A doughty gentleman lies here;
A stranger all his life to fear;
Nor in his death could Death prevail,
In that lost hour, to make him quail.

He for the world but little cared;
And at his feats the world was scared;
A crazy man his life he passed,
But in his senses died at last.

And said most sage Cid Hamet to his pen, "Rest here, hung up by this brass wire, upon this shelf, O my pen, whether of skilful make or clumsy cut I know not; here shalt thou remain long ages hence, unless presumptuous or malignant story-tellers take thee down to profane thee. But ere they touch thee warn them, and, as best thou canst, say to them:

Hold off! ye weaklings; hold your hands!
    Adventure it let none,
For this emprise, my lord the king,
    Was meant for me alone.

For me alone was Don Quixote born, and I for him; it was his to act; mine to write; we two together make but one, notwithstanding and in spite of that pretended Tordesillesque writer who has ventured or would venture with his great, coarse, ill-trimmed ostrich quill to write the achievements of my valiant knight;—no burden for his shoulders, nor subject for his frozen wit: whom, if perchance thou shouldst come to know him, thou shalt warn to leave at rest where they lie the weary mouldering bones of Don Quixote, and not to attempt to carry him off, in opposition to all the privileges of death, to Old Castile, making him rise from the grave where in reality and truth he lies stretched at full length, powerless to make any third expedition or new sally; for the two that he has already made, so much to the enjoyment and approval of everybody to whom they have become known, in this as well as in foreign countries, are quite sufficient for the purpose of turning into ridicule the whole of those made by the whole set of the knights-errant; and so doing shalt thou discharge thy Christian calling, giving good counsel to one that bears ill-will to thee. And I shall remain satisfied, and proud to have been the first who has ever enjoined the fruit of his writings as fully as he could desire; for my desire has been no other than to deliver over to the detestation of mankind the false and foolish tales of the books of chivalry, which, thanks to that of my true Don Quixote, are even now tottering, and doubtless doomed to fall forever. Farewell."

Christopher Marlowe

1564–1593

During his brief career Christopher Marlowe raised important questions about traditional beliefs and social change, and explored new ideas about personality and power. During the European **Renaissance**, individuals could pursue writing as a profession, and Marlowe joined other professionals in England, including Edmund Spenser (1552–1599), Ben Jonson (1572–1637), William Shakespeare (1564–1616), and John Milton (1608–1674). Marlowe's poetic dramas explore essential themes of the Renaissance; he is especially adept at showing how the quest for political or intellectual power is inevitably compromised by human limitations.

The consciousness of Europeans in the fifteenth and sixteenth centuries was changing, and an inevitable conflict arose between the sacred worldview of the past and the secular horizons of the present. The medieval Catholic Church fostered a concern with one's inward state, its relation to a transcendent deity, and the eternal salvation of one's soul. The material world was meaningful only as a reflection of the spiritual world. As long as one's eye was ultimately focused on the rewards of the next world, the dichotomy between heaven above and the temptations of earthly life was perhaps bearable, but just as soon as human beings learned to love and care for earthly existence, its beauty and transience, the worldview of the Church would inevitably be questioned by the laity. In the Renaissance, thinkers celebrated external, physical existence for its own sake. Explorers were as occupied with finding the routes to countries and peoples halfway around the globe as they were with articulating the pathway to heaven.

The dialogues contrasting good and evil, old and new, church and state, spirit and flesh, the collective and the individual—carried on both in the universities and in the culture at large—became the polarized conversations of Marlowe's play *Doctor Faustus.* Faustus epitomizes the struggle involved with leaving the medieval world of sin and salvation and entering the **humanistic** frontiers of the Renaissance. Faustus has a foot in both worlds. At least in the first half of the play, he challenges the goal of redemption as the exclusive criterion for measuring the progress of human life.

Life as a Writer. The facts about Marlowe's life are few and ambiguous, but enough is known to indicate his personal rebellion against social mores and his contribution to British theater. He was born into a prosperous middle-class family in Canterbury on February 6, 1564. He was given a scholarship to Cambridge and received a BA in 1584, but the university authorities intended to withhold his MA because they suspected that Marlowe was going to convert to Roman Catholicism at a seminary in France. However, the Queen's Privy Council, a powerful group, intervened with a letter that commended him for service "in matters touching the benefit of the country" and insisted that Marlowe receive his degree "this next Commencement," in 1587. While at Cambridge Marlowe apparently had been employed abroad in secret service for the government.

Although his student scholarship pointed toward a vocation as a clergyman, Marlowe moved to London, where he made his living as a professional writer—a new cultural phenomenon—and aggravated conventional morality with his liberal opinions and free spirit. His entire career was squeezed into the period between 1587 and 1593. His earliest play was probably *Dido, Queen of Carthage,* but his four major dramas began with the two-part *Tamburlaine the Great* (c. 1587), where with his "mighty line" he established blank verse—unrhymed lines of ten syllables each—as the preferred poetic form for Elizabethan tragedy. Marlowe captures the spirit of the Renaissance with his hero's conquering might and dreams of power, although Tamburlaine's obsession becomes tiring by the end of the second part. In his second major play, *The Jew of Malta* (c. 1588), Marlowe creates a villain who is greedy and treacherous, a Machiavellian figure wholly devoted to self-advancement. *The Troublesome Raigne and Lamentable Death of Edward the Second* (c. 1592) contributed to the genre of the history play with a portrayal of a character whose weaknesses are, nevertheless, sympathetic. *Doctor Faustus* (1592–93) is Marlowe's most famous and most important play. Unlike the rather static character of Tamburlaine, Faustus captures the dramatic conflict of a man who steps beyond the accepted boundaries of his day; this play became a model for the great poetic tragedies of the Elizabethan Age.

WWW For links to more information about Marlowe and a quiz on *Doctor Faustus,* see *World Literature Online* at bedfordstmartins.com/worldlit.

In addition to a translation of Ovid's *Amores* that was so erotic it was burned by the Archbishop of Canterbury in 1599, Marlowe wrote a long poem, *Hero and Leander* (1598); although incomplete, it is notable for the passionate descriptions of the lovers and their meetings.

In 1593, there were political rumblings in the London literary scene caused by subversive comments about religion. When the playwright Thomas Kyd was arrested, he attributed a paper denying the divinity of Christ to possessions left behind by Christopher Marlowe when they had roomed together two years earlier. A spy, Richard Baines, made a list of heretical ideas associated with one "Christopher Marly." "Marly" was said to have claimed that Jesus had illicit affairs with two women of Samaria and with St. John the Evangelist, and that religion came into being to "keep men in awe." On May 18, the Privy Council issued orders for Marlowe's arrest. On May 30, Marlowe had an argument over the payment of a bill with one Ingram Frizer at a Deptford tavern, a few miles from London. Marlowe apparently grabbed Frizer's dagger, but as Frizer defended himself the dagger pierced Marlowe's eye, killing him.

Doctor Faustus. *Doctor Faustus,* first published in 1604 and then again in 1616, is a dramatization of a book, the *Historia von D. Iohan Fausten,* published in German in 1587 and translated into English as *The History of the damnable life and deserved death of Dr. John Faustus* in 1592, the earliest version available to Marlowe.

The legendary German prototype of Faustus was born in the late fifteenth century. He learned numerous languages such as Persian, Hebrew, Arabic, and Greek in order to study the "infernal arts" of "necromancy,

The Tragicall Hiftory
of the Life and Death
of Doctor Fauftus.
Written by Ch. Marklin.

***Doctor Faustus,* Seventeenth Century**
The frontispiece of the first edition of The Tragicall History of the Life and Death of Doctor Faustus, *by Christopher Marlowe, bears a woodcut showing the doctor standing within a "magic circle." (Private Collection / Bridgeman Art Library)*

charms, soothsaying, witchcraft, enchantment." This Faustus, who reportedly sold his soul to the devil for twenty-four years of earthly power, wandered through Germany gaining a reputation as a magician and astrologer. After practicing his secret arts for a number of years in Wittenberg, he died from a chemical explosion in 1540 or 1541, and according to legend went to hell. His reputation quickly spread, and his biography—known as the *German Faust Book*—was published anonymously. The English translation—the *English Faust Book*—contains most of the plot material for Marlowe's play. Scholars have noted an unknown collaborator and the possibility of additions to the play after Marlowe's death. Nevertheless, the depth of psychological insight with the character of Faustus and the struggles of Marlowe himself with the strictures of his culture continue to provoke relevant issues for a modern, technological age.

Marlowe's play is fully rooted in the complexities of his time. The prologue prepares us for the conflict in Faustus's personality; born of "base stock," reflecting a new middle class, he is educated, especially in theology. But he is discontented and wants to exceed his reach by leaving the earth like Icarus and mounting into the sky, risking life and limb in the face of the sun. We first see Faustus in his study—a symbol of learning and the intellectual aspirations of the Renaissance—where he debates with himself about the state of his own education and decides to risk even his soul in order to break out of the limits of the traditional, humanistic education associated with Greek philosophy, physics, Roman law, and the Vulgate Bible. Faustus wants to gain new understanding through the power and exotic trappings of magic and necromancy—a course consistent with Marlowe's own youthful intellect and imagination. In addition, the "metaphysics of magicians" suggests theatrical spectacle for Elizabethan audiences.

Marlowe next introduces the mechanism of a medieval morality play by including a dialogue between Good Angel and Bad Angel, a device illustrative of Faustus's own inner struggle between piety and profligacy and an indication of the larger dialogue between religion and the rising spirit of secularism. The use of the two Scholars and the two Angels is reminiscent of the chorus in Greek tragedy; they reflect on the course of Faustus's life and discuss options open for him, debating the ongoing question of whether he can be saved. Faustus is not unlike the Greek figure of Prometheus, who discovers that there is a price for challenging authority and cherishing the fire of intellect.

The play gathers intensity as Faustus stabs his arm for the blood necessary for signing a compact with the devil; some part of him, however, resists this ultimate act. He admits, "My blood congeals, and I can write no more." Mephistophilis, Lucifer's assistant, brings fire—plainly symbolic—to dissolve the blood, and the pact is sealed. What can Faustus possibly request that will compensate for his damnation? He asks for a curious mixture of knowledge, power, and pranks. The answer to his question about the location of hell is surprisingly modern in its implications:

Hell hath no limits nor is circumscribed
In one self place, but where we are is hell,
And where hell is there must we ever be.

When Faustus wants to blame Mephistophilis for being deprived of heaven, his attention, in true Renaissance fashion, is redirected to the earth and the wonder of human beings:

But think'st thou heaven is such a glorious thing?
I tell thee, Faustus, it is not half so fair
As thou or any man that breathe on earth.

Some of the wonder associated with an age of travel and discovery, of explorers and new worlds, is reflected in Faustus's speeches about his travels from Paris to Germany, to "Venice, Padua and the rest," and finally to Rome. There are interludes of comedy and slapstick, tricks that seem inappropriate perhaps for the magnitude of Faustus's soulful compact; he seems to waste his time with trivialities. Rather than complete any grand projects, Faustus abuses his powers with selfish whims. After all, the Helen who evokes Faustus's immortal lines is a ghost and not the real thing.

Was this the face that launch'd a thousand ships,
And burnt the topless towers of Ilium?—
Sweet Helen, make me immortal with a kiss.—

Has Faustus sold his immortal soul for frippery?

The end of the play, with Faustus's struggle with death and damnation, again reaches toward the grandeur of authentic tragedy and is intensified by Marlowe's own poetic powers. The emptiness of Faustus's tricks lends poignancy to the ultimate rejection of his educational training.

> O would I had never seen Wittenberg, never read book! And what wonders I have done all Germany can witness, yea all the world, for which Faustus had lost both Germany and the world, yea heaven itself—heaven the seat of God, the throne of the blessed, the kingdom of joy, and must remain in hell forever.

Medieval morality plays tend to end with the sinner repenting and the promise of salvation, but Faustus is a tragic hero who appears to remain true to his agreement and courageously faces a vision of hell and eternal punishment, as if he were a necessary sacrifice to the old order. The modern witness to Faustus's agonizing spiritual deliberations does not have to literally believe in a fiery pit to appreciate Faustus's sense of despair and estrangement. Is it courage or foolhardiness that allows him to face his own demise?

Regardless of any faults in Marlowe's portrayal of Faustus, there is something very modern and compelling about this Renaissance figure. The Faustus figures of each succeeding age would carry less baggage from the past and extend in ever-widening circles the frontiers of imagination and possibility as well as the potential for destruction. Later writers such as Goethe with his *Faust* (1832) and Thomas Mann with his *Doctor Faustus* (1947) re-created his questioning, iconoclastic personality for their own periods in history. In the twenty-first century, the growing distance between technological marvels and the human capacity to use or integrate them seems to reflect a modern Faustian bargain with the unknown. The devilish figures might wear different masks in today's version, but there is a definite unease—even misgiving—about the complexities of modern knowledge, especially with weapons, chemicals, genetic engineering, and medicine, and their capacity to do harm and even destroy the planet.

■ CONNECTIONS

Socrates in Plato's *Apology,* Book 1. From the classical world comes the warning that the overreacher—the person of excessive zeal, power, or knowledge—can expect to pay a price for his or her immoderation. Socrates was charged with impiety and corrupting the youth of his day, but some commentators suggest that he was condemned to death because of his intellectual arrogance. How does Marlowe suggest that, in addition to the religious reasons for his death, Faustus was overly zealous in his pursuit of knowledge and power, and thus offensive to his peers?

"In the World: Humanism, Learning, and Education," p. 452. One of the qualities of the European Renaissance is the apparent focus on the physical (versus spiritual) world as the primary arena within which the individual makes choices and creates relationships. The focus on this world is seen in writers like Machiavelli, Pico della Mirandola, and Bacon. Marlowe's play is a reminder, however, that some people believed in a larger context for life; R. M. Dawkins states that the play tells "the story of a Renaissance man who had to pay the medieval price for being one." What are the differences between the worldviews of the Renaissance and the Middle Ages?

John Milton, *Paradise Lost,* p. 575. The angels' revolt in heaven, the fall of Lucifer, and the punishments of hell play important parts in both *Doctor Faustus* and *Paradise Lost.* What are the sources of these stories? What are some possible metaphorical interpretations of them (beyond the literal ones)? What roles might such interpretations play in Marlowe's and Milton's works?

■ FURTHER RESEARCH

Biography and Background

Boas, Frederick S. *Christopher Marlowe: A Biographical and Critical Study.* 1940.
Harrison, G. B. *Elizabethan Plays & Players.* 1956.
Hopkins, Lisa. *Christopher Marlowe: A Literary Life.* 2000.
Rowse, A. L. *Christopher Marlowe: A Biography.* 1964.
Sanders, Wilbur. *The Dramatist and the Received Idea.* 1968.

Criticism

Eliot, T. S. *The Sacred Wood.* 1920.
Farnham, Willard, ed. *Twentieth Century Interpretations of Doctor Faustus.* 1969.
Levin, Harry. *The Overreacher: A Study of Christopher Marlowe.* 1952.
Tydeman, William, and Vivien Thomas. *Christopher Marlowe: A Guide through the Critical Maze.* 1989.

Doctor Faustus

DRAMATIS PERSONAE:

THE CHORUS
DOCTOR FAUSTUS
WAGNER, *his servant*
VALDES, CORNELIUS — *friends to* FAUSTUS
THREE SCHOLARS
AN OLD MAN

THE POPE
RAYMOND, *King of Hungary*
BRUNO
TWO CARDINALS
ARCHBISHOP OF RHEIMS
CARDINAL OF LORRAINE
CHARLES, *Emperor of Germany*
MARTINO, FREDERICK, BENVOLIO — *Gentlemen of his Court*
A KNIGHT
DUKE OF SAXONY
DUKE OF ANHOLT
DUCHESS OF ANHOLT
BISHOPS, MONKS, FRIARS, SOLDIERS, *and* ATTENDANTS

CLOWN
ROBIN, *an ostler*
DICK
RALPH
A VINTNER
A HORSE-COURSER
A CARTER
HOSTESS

GOOD ANGEL
BAD ANGEL
EVIL ANGEL
MEPHISTOPHILIS
LUCIFER
BELZEBUB
DEVILS
THE SEVEN DEADLY SINS
ALEXANDER THE GREAT, PARAMOUR OF ALEXANDER, DARIUS, HELEN, TWO CUPIDS — *Spirits*

Doctor Faustus. Marlowe's play was published in 1604, but the date of its first production is uncertain. Some scholars say it was produced in 1589, but that would suggest that the play was written before Marlowe had access to the English translation of the book about Johann Faustus. A safer date for the first production is 1592. The version of the play included here is not the original; in 1602, William Birde and Samuel Rowley were hired to make additions, such as the scenes of low comedy. The text has been edited for a modern audience by Frederick S. Boas.

Act I

Prologue

[*Enter* CHORUS.]

CHORUS:

Not marching in the fields of Thrasimen,
Where Mars did mate the warlike Carthagens;[1]
Nor sporting in the dalliance of love,
In courts of kings, where state° is over-turn'd; political power
Nor in the pomp of proud audacious deeds,
Intends our Muse to vaunt his heavenly verse:
Only this, Gentles—we must now perform
The form of Faustus' fortunes, good or bad:
And now to patient judgments we appeal,
And speak for Faustus in his infancy.
Now is he born, of parents base of stock,
In Germany, within a town call'd Rhode:[2]
At riper years, to Wittenberg[3] he went,
Whereas his kinsmen chiefly brought him up.
So much he profits in divinity,
The fruitful plot of scholarism grac'd,
That shortly he was grac'd with Doctor's name,
Excelling all and sweetly can dispute
In th' heavenly matters of theology;
Till swoln with cunning, of a self-conceit,
His waxen wings did mount above his reach,[4]
And, melting, heavens conspir'd his overthrow;
For, falling to a devilish exercise,
And glutted now with learning's golden gifts,
He surfeits upon cursed necromancy;
Nothing so sweet as magic is to him,
Which he prefers before his chiefest bliss:° eternal salvation
And this the man that in his study sits.

[*Exit.*]

---

[1] **Carthagens:** Hannibal, the Carthaginian, won one of his greatest victories over the Romans in the battle of Lake Trasimene in 217 B.C.E.

[2] **Rhode:** The town of Roda in the Duchy of Saxe-Altenburg.

[3] **Wittenberg:** The famous university attended by Martin Luther.

[4] **His waxen . . . reach:** The Greek myth about how Daedalus invented wax wings for himself and his son, Icarus, who then flew too close to the sun.

Scene 1

FAUSTUS *in his Study.*

FAUSTUS:

Settle thy studies, Faustus, and begin
To sound the depth of that thou wilt profess:
Having commenc'd,° be a divine in show, graduated
Yet level° at the end of every art, aim
And live and die in Aristotle's works.
Sweet Analytics,[5] 'tis thou hast ravish'd me!
Bene disserere est finis logices.[6]
Is, to dispute well, logic's chiefest end?
Affords this art no greater miracle?
Then read no more; thou hast attain'd that end.
A greater subject fitteth Faustus' wit:
Bid ὂν χαὶ μὴ ὂν[7] farewell; and Galen come;
Seeing, *Ubi desinit philosophus ibi incipit medicus,*[8]
Be a physician, Faustus; heap up gold,
And be eternis'd for some wondrous cure!
Summum bonum medicinæ sanitas,[9]
The end of physic is our body's health.
Why, Faustus, hast thou not attain'd that end?
Is not thy common talk sound aphorisms?° medical opinions
Are not thy bills hung up as monuments,
Whereby whole cities have escap'd the plague,
And thousand desp'rate maladies been cur'd?
Yet art thou still but Faustus, and a man.
Couldst thou make men to live eternally,
Or, being dead, raise them to life again,
Then this profession were to be esteem'd.
Physic, farewell! Where is Justinian?[10] [*Reads.*]
"Si una eademque res legatur duobus
Alter rem, alter valorem rei,"[11] *etc.*
A petty case of paltry legacies! [*Reads.*]

---

[5] **Analytics:** Aristotle's treatise on logic.

[6] ***Bene . . . logices:*** Latin for "To argue well is the end of logic."

[7] **ὂν . . . ὂν:** A Greek phrase, "Being and not being," representing philosophy.

[8] ***Ubi . . . medicus:*** Where the philosopher leaves off the physician begins.

[9] ***Summum . . . sanitas:*** Good health is the object of medicine.

[10] **Justinian:** (482–565 C.E.), Byzantine emperor and codifier of Roman law in the *Institutes.*

[11] ***"Si . . . rei":*** "If something is bequeathed to two persons, one shall have the thing itself, the other something of equal value."

"Exhæreditare filium non potest pater nisi"[12]—
Such is the subject of the Institute,
And universal body of the law.
This study fits a mercenary drudge,
Who aims at nothing but external trash;
Too servile and illiberal for me.
When all is done, divinity is best:
Jeromë's Bible,[13] Faustus; view it well. [*Reads.*]
"Stipendium peccati mors est." Ha! *"Stipendium," etc.*
The reward of sin is death: that's hard. [*Reads.*]
"Si peccasse negamus, fallimur
Et nulla est in nobis veritas."[14]
If we say that we have no sin,
We deceive ourselves, and there is no truth in us.
Why, then, belike we must sin,
And so consequently die:
Ay, we must die an everlasting death.
What doctrine call you this, *Che sera, sera:*
What will be, shall be? Divinity, adieu!
These metaphysics of magicians,
And necromantic books are heavenly;
Lines, circles, letters, and characters;
Ay, these are those that Faustus most desires.
O, what a world of profit and delight,
Of power, of honour, and omnipotence,
Is promised to the studious artizan![15]
All things that move between the quiet poles
Shall be at my command: emperors and kings
Are but obey'd in their several provinces,
Nor can they raise the wind, or rend the clouds;
But his dominion that exceeds in this,
Stretcheth as far as doth the mind of man;
A sound magician is a demigod:
Here, tire my brain to get a deity!

[*Enter* WAGNER.]

Wagner, commend me to my dearest friends,
The German Valdes and Cornelius;
Request them earnestly to visit me.

---

[12] ***"Exhæreditare . . . nisi":*** "A father cannot disinherit his son unless."

[13] **Jeromë's Bible:** St. Jerome's translation of the Bible: the Latin or Vulgate translation (fourth century C.E.).

[14] ***"Si . . . veritas":*** I John 1:8, translated in the next two lines.

[15] **artizan:** A master of the higher arts.

WAGNER:
I will, sir.

[*Exit.*]

FAUSTUS:
Their conference will be a greater help to me
Than all my labours, plot I ne'er so fast.

[*Enter the* GOOD ANGEL *and* BAD ANGEL.]

GOOD ANGEL:
O, Faustus, lay that damned book aside,
And gaze not on it, lest it tempt thy soul,
And heap God's heavy wrath upon thy head!
Read, read the Scriptures: — that is blasphemy.

BAD ANGEL:
Go forward, Faustus, in that famous art
Wherein all Nature's treasure is contain'd:
Be thou on earth as Jove is in the sky,
Lord and commander of these elements.

[*Exeunt* ANGELS.]

FAUSTUS:
How am I glutted with conceit of[16] this!
Shall I make spirits fetch me what I please,
Resolve me of all ambiguities,
Perform what desperate enterprise I will?
I'll have them fly to India for gold,
Ransack the ocean for orient pearl,
And search all corners of the new-found world
For pleasant fruits and princely delicates;
I'll have them read me strange philosophy,
And tell the secrets of all foreign kings;
I'll have them wall all Germany with brass,
And make swift Rhine circle fair Wittenberg.
I'll have them fill the public schools° with silk, university classrooms
Wherewith the students shall be bravely clad;
I'll levy soldiers with the coin they bring,
And chase the Prince of Parma[17] from our land,
And reign sole king of all the Provinces;
Yea, stranger engines for the brunt of war,
Than was the fiery keel[18] at Antwerp's bridge,
I'll make my servile spirits to invent. [*He calls within.*]

[16] **glutted . . . conceit of:** Filled with the idea of attaining.

[17] **Prince of Parma:** The Spanish governor of the Low Countries from 1579 to 1592.

[18] **fiery keel:** A burning ship sent into Antwerp's bridge.

[*Enter* VALDES *and* CORNELIUS.]

Come, German Valdes, and Cornelius,
And make me blest with your sage conference!
Valdes, sweet Valdes, and Cornelius,
Know that your words have won me at the last
To practise magic and concealed arts:
Yet not your words only, but mine own fantasy,
That will receive no object,[19] for my head
But ruminates on necromantic skill.
Philosophy is odious and obscure;
Both law and physic are for petty wits;
Divinity is basest of the three,
Unpleasant, harsh, contemptible, and vile:
'Tis magic, magic, that hath ravish'd me.
Then, gentle friends, aid me in this attempt
And I, that have with subtle syllogisms
Gravell'd° the pastors of the German church, confounded
And made the flowering pride of Wittenberg
Swarm to my problems, as the infernal spirits
On sweet Musaeus when he came to hell,
Will be as cunning as Agrippa[20] was,
Whose shadows made all Europe honour him.

VALDES:

Faustus, these books, thy wit, and our experience
Shall make all nations to canonize us.
As Indian Moors° obey their Spanish lords, American Indians
So shall the spirits of every element
Be always serviceable to us three;
Like lions shall they guard us when we please;
Like Almain rutters° with their horsemen's staves, German horsemen
Or Lapland giants, trotting by our sides;
Sometimes like women, or unwedded maids,
Shadowing more beauty in their airy brows
Than has the white breasts of the queen of love;
From Venice shall they drag huge argosies,
And from America the golden fleece
That yearly stuffs old Philip's[21] treasury;
If learned Faustus will be resolute.

[19] **That . . . object:** That will entertain no academic objection.

[20] **Agrippa:** Cornelius Agrippa (1486–1535), a German necromancer, thought to be able to summon up the spirits of the dead.

[21] **Philip's:** Philip II (1527–1598), king of Spain.

FAUSTUS:
Valdes, as resolute am I in this
As thou to live: therefore object it not.
CORNELIUS:
The miracles that magic will perform
Will make thee vow to study nothing else.
He that is grounded in astrology,
Enrich'd with tongues, well seen in minerals,
Hath all the principles magic doth require:
Then doubt not, Faustus, but to be renown'd,
And more frequented for this mystery,
Than heretofore the Delphian oracle.[22]
The spirits tell me they can dry the sea,
And fetch the treasure of all foreign wrecks,
Yea, all the wealth that our forefathers hid
Within the massy entrails of the earth:
Then tell me, Faustus, what shall we three want?
FAUSTUS:
Nothing, Cornelius. O, this cheers my soul!
Come, show me some demonstrations magical,
That I may conjure in some bushy grove,
And have these joys in full possession.
VALDES:
Then haste thee to some solitary grove,
And bear wise Bacon's and Albertus'[23] works,
The Hebrew Psalter, and New Testament;[24]
And whatsoever else is requisite
We will inform thee ere our conference cease.
CORNELIUS:
Valdes, first let him know the words of art;
And then, all other ceremonies learn'd,
Faustus may try his cunning by himself.
VALDES:
First I'll instruct thee in the rudiments,
And then wilt thou be perfecter than I.
FAUSTUS:
Then come and dine with me, and, after meat,
We'll canvass every quiddity° thereof; essential element

[22] **Delphian oracle:** In ancient Greece, Apollo's oracle at Delphi was frequently consulted.

[23] **Bacon, Albertus:** Roger Bacon (c. 1220–1292), a monk and scientist thought to be a magician; Albertus Magnus, a thirteenth-century magician.

[24] **New Testament:** Both the Psalms and the Gospel of John (New Testament) were used for summoning spirits.

For, ere I sleep, I'll try what I can do:
This night I'll conjure, though I die therefore.

[*Exeunt omnes.*]

Scene 2

Before FAUSTUS' *house.*

[*Enter* TWO SCHOLARS.]

FIRST SCHOLAR: I wonder what's become of Faustus, that was wont to make our schools ring with *sic probo.*[25]

[*Enter* WAGNER.]

SECOND SCHOLAR: That shall we presently know; here comes his boy.
FIRST SCHOLAR: How now, sirrah! where's thy master?
WAGNER: God in heaven knows.
SECOND SCHOLAR: Why, dost not thou know, then?
WAGNER: Yes, I know; but that follows not.
FIRST SCHOLAR: Go to, sirrah! leave your jesting, and tell us where he is.
WAGNER: That follows not by force of argument, which you, being Licentiates,[26] should stand upon; therefore acknowledge your error, and be attentive.
SECOND SCHOLAR: Then you will not tell us?
WAGNER: You are deceiv'd, for I will tell you: yet, if you were not dunces, you would never ask me such a question; for is he not *corpus naturale*? and is not that *mobile*?[27] Then wherefore should you ask me such a question? But that I am by nature phlegmatic, slow to wrath, and prone to lechery (to love, I would say), it were not for you to come within forty foot of the place of execution,[28] although I do not doubt but to see you both hanged the next sessions. Thus having triumph'd over you, I will set my countenance like a precisian,[29] and begin to speak thus: — Truly, my dear brethren, my master is within at dinner, with Valdes and Cornelius, as this wine, if it could speak, would inform your worships: and so, the Lord bless you, preserve you, and keep you, my dear brethren.

[*Exit.*]

FIRST SCHOLAR:
O Faustus. Then I fear that which I have long suspected,
That thou are fallen into that damned art
For which they two are infamous through the world.

SECOND SCHOLAR:
Were he a stranger, not allied to me,
The danger of his soul would make me mourn.
But, come, let us go and inform the Rector,° — head of the university
It may be his grave counsel may reclaim him.

---

[25] ***sic probo:*** Thus I prove. [26] **Licentiates:** Graduate students. [27] ***corpus naturale, mobile:*** Natural, movable matter: a scholastic definition of the physical world. [28] **place of execution:** Dining room. [29] **precisian:** Puritan.

FIRST SCHOLAR:
I fear me nothing will reclaim him now!
SECOND SCHOLAR:
Yet let us see what we can do.
[*Exeunt.*]

Scene 3

A grove.

[*Enter* FAUSTUS *to conjure.*]
FAUSTUS:
Now that the gloomy shadow of the night,
Longing to view Orion's[30] drizzling look,
Leaps from th' antarctic world unto the sky,
And dims the welkin with her pitchy breath,
Faustus, begin thine incantations,
And try if devils will obey thy hest,
Seeing thou hast pray'd and sacrific'd to them.
Within this circle is Jehovah's name,
Forward and backward anagrammatiz'd;
Th' abbreviated names of holy saints,
Figures of every adjunct to the heavens,
And characters of signs and erring stars,
By which the spirits are enforc'd to rise:
Then fear not, Faustus, to be resolute,
And try the utmost magic can perform. [*Thunder.*]
"Sint mihi Dii Acherontis propitii! Valeat numen triplex Jehovœ! Ignis, aeris, aquœ, terrae spiritus, salvete! Orientis princeps, Belzebub, inferni ardentis monarcha, et Demogorgon, propitiamus vos, ut appareat et surgat Mephistophilis. [*Enter* DRAGON *above.*] *Quid tu moraris? per Jehovam, Gehennam, et consecratam aquam quam nunc spargo, signumque crucis quod nunc facio, et per vota nostra, ipse nunc surgat nobis dicatus Mephistophilis!"*[31]

[*Enter* MEPHISTOPHILIS.][32]
I charge thee to return, and change thy shape;
Thou art too ugly to attend on me:
Go, and return an old Franciscan friar;
That holy shape becomes a devil best.

[30] **Orion:** A winter constellation.

[31] ***"Sint . . . Mephistophilis":*** "Unto me be the gods of Acheron propitious. May the triple name of Jehovah prevail. Spirits of fire, air, water, and earth, hail! Belzebub, Prince of the East, Sovereign of burning Hell and Demogorgon, we propitiate you, that Mephistophilis may appear and rise. Why do you delay? By Jehovah, Gehenna, and the holy water which now I sprinkle, and the sign of the cross which now I make, and by our prayer, may Mephistophilis, by us summoned, now arise."

[32] **Mephistophilis:** One of the many devils of medieval legend.

[*Exit* MEPHISTOPHILIS.]

I see there's virtue in my heavenly words:
Who would not be proficient in this art?
How pliant is this Mephistophilis,
Full of obedience and humility!
Such is the force of magic and my spells:
Now, Faustus, thou art conjuror laureat,
That canst command great Mephistophilis.
Quin redis, Mephistophilis, fratris imagine![33]

[*Re-enter* MEPHISTOPHILIS *like a Franciscan friar.*]

MEPHISTOPHILIS:
Now, Faustus, what would'st thou have me do?

FAUSTUS:
I charge thee wait upon me whilst I live,
To do whatever Faustus shall command,
Be it to make the moon drop from her sphere,
Or the ocean to overwhelm the world.

MEPHISTOPHILIS:
I am a servant to great Lucifer,[34]
And may not follow thee without his leave;
No more than he commands must we perform.

FAUSTUS:
Did not he charge thee to appear to me?

MEPHISTOPHILIS:
No, I came now hither of mine own accord.

FAUSTUS:
Did not my conjuring raise thee? speak.

MEPHISTOPHILIS:
That was the cause, but yet *per accidens;*[35]
For, when we hear one rack the name of God,
Abjure the Scriptures and his Saviour Christ,
We fly, in hope to get his glorious soul;
Nor will we come, unless he use such means
Whereby he is in danger to be damn'd.
Therefore the shortest cut for conjuring
Is stoutly to abjure the Trinity,
And pray devoutly to the prince of hell.

FAUSTUS:
So Faustus hath
Already done; and holds this principle,

---

[33] ***Quin . . . imagine:*** Mephistophilis, return in the likeness of a friar.

[34] **Lucifer:** That is, "Light-bringer"; see lines 63 ff. for his story.

[35] ***per accidens:*** By the accidental cause (not the ultimate cause).

There is no chief but only Belzebub;
To whom Faustus doth dedicate himself.
This word "damnation" terrifies not me,
For I confound hell in Elysium:[36]
My ghost be with the old philosophers![37]
But, leaving these vain trifles of men's souls,
Tell me what is that Lucifer thy lord?

MEPHISTOPHILIS:
Arch-regent and commander of all spirits.

FAUSTUS:
Was not that Lucifer an angel once?

MEPHISTOPHILIS:
Yes, Faustus, and most dearly lov'd of God.

FAUSTUS:
How comes it then that he is prince of devils?

MEPHISTOPHILIS:
O, by aspiring pride and insolence;
For which God threw him from the face of heaven.

FAUSTUS:
And what are you that live with Lucifer?

MEPHISTOPHILIS:
Unhappy spirits that fell with Lucifer,
Conspir'd against our God with Lucifer,
And are for ever damn'd with Lucifer.

FAUSTUS:
Where are you damn'd?

MEPHISTOPHILIS:
In hell.

FAUSTUS:
How comes it then that thou art out of hell?

MEPHISTOPHILIS:
Why this is hell, nor am I out of it:
Think'st thou that I, that saw the face of God,
And tasted the eternal joys of Heaven,
Am not tormented with ten thousand hells,
In being depriv'd of everlasting bliss?
O, Faustus, leave these frivolous demands,
Which strikes a terror to my fainting soul!

FAUSTUS:
What, is great Mephistophilis so passionate
For being deprived of the joys of heaven?

---

[36] **Elysium:** In Greek mythology, the place for virtuous souls.

[37] **old philosophers:** Pre-Christian philosophers.

Learn thou of Faustus manly fortitude,
And scorn those joys thou never shalt possess.
Go bear these tidings to great Lucifer:
Seeing Faustus hath incurr'd eternal death
By desperate thoughts against Jove's deity,
Say, he surrenders up to him his soul,
So he will spare him four-and-twenty years,
Letting him live in all voluptuousness;
Having thee ever to attend on me,
To give me whatsoever I shall ask,
To tell me whatsoever I demand,
To slay mine enemies, and to aid my friends,
And always be obedient to my will.
Go, and return to mighty Lucifer,
And meet me in my study at midnight,
And then resolve me of thy master's mind.

MEPHISTOPHILIS:
I will, Faustus.

[*Exit.*]

FAUSTUS:
Had I as many souls as there be stars,
I'd give them all for Mephistophilis.
By him I'll be great Emperor of the world,
And make a bridge through the moving air,
To pass the ocean with a band of men;
I'll join the hills that bind the Afric shore,
And make that country continent to° Spain, bordering
And both contributory to my crown:
The Emperor shall not live but by my leave,
Nor any potentate of Germany.
Now that I have obtain'd what I desir'd,
I'll live in speculation of this art,
Till Mephistophilis return again.

[*Exit.*]

Scene 4

[*Enter* WAGNER *and the* CLOWN.[38]]

WAGNER: Come hither, sirrah boy.

CLOWN: Boy! O disgrace to my person. Zounds, boy in your face! You have seen many boys with beards, I am sure.

[38] CLOWN: A rustic or buffoon.

WAGNER: Sirrah, hast thou no comings in?[39]

CLOWN: Yes, and goings out too, you may see, sir.

WAGNER: Alas, poor slave! see how poverty jests in his nakedness! I know the villain's out of service, and so hungry, that I know he would give his soul to the devil for a shoulder of mutton, though it were blood-raw.

CLOWN: Not so, neither. I had need to have it well-roasted, and good sauce to it, if I pay so dear, I can tell you.

WAGNER: Sirrah, wilt thou be my man and wait on me, and I will make thee go like *Qui mihi discipulus*?[40]

CLOWN: What, in verse?

WAGNER: No slave; in beaten silk and stavesacre.[41]

CLOWN: Stavesacre! that's good to kill vermin. Then, belike, if I serve you, I shall be lousy.

WAGNER: Why, so thou shalt be, whether thou do'st it or no. For, sirrah, if thou do'st not presently bind thyself to me for seven years, I'll turn all the lice about thee into familiars,[42] and make them tear thee in pieces.

CLOWN: Nay, sir, you may save yourself a labour, for they are as familiar with me as if they had paid for their meat and drink, I can tell you.

WAGNER: Well, sirrah, leave your jesting and take these guilders.

CLOWN: Yes, marry, sir, and I thank you too.

WAGNER: So, now thou art to be at an hour's warning, whensoever and wheresoever the devil shall fetch thee.

CLOWN: Here, take your guilders again, I'll none of 'em.

WAGNER: Not I, thou art pressed,[43] for I will presently raise up two devils to carry thee away—Banio, Belcher!

CLOWN: Belcher! and Belcher come here, I'll belch him. I am not afraid of a devil.

[*Enter two* DEVILS.]

WAGNER: How now, sir, will you serve me now?

CLOWN: Ay, good Wagner, take away the devil then.

WAGNER: Spirits, away! Now, sirrah, follow me.

[*Exeunt* DEVILS.]

CLOWN: I will, sir, but hark you, master, will you teach me this conjuring occupation?

WAGNER: Ay, sirrah, I'll teach thee to turn thyself to a dog, or a cat, or a mouse, or a rat, or any thing.

CLOWN: A dog, or a cat, or a mouse, or a rat, O brave Wagner!

WAGNER: Villain, call me Master Wagner, and see that you walk attentively and let your right eye be always diametrally fixed upon my left heel, that thou may'st *quasi vestigias nostras insistere.*[44]

CLOWN: Well, sir, I warrant you.

[*Exeunt.*]

---

[39] **comings in:** Income. [40] ***Qui . . . discipulus:*** "One who is my pupil." [41] **stavesacre:** A powder used to kill vermin. [42] **familiars:** Devils. [43] **pressed:** Enlisted, hired. [44] ***quasi . . . insistere:*** As if to tread my tracks.

Act II

Scene 1

[*Enter* FAUSTUS *in his study.*]

FAUSTUS:
Now, Faustus, must
Thou needs be damn'd, and canst thou not be sav'd.
What boots° it, then, to think on God or heaven? avails
Away with such vain fancies, and despair;
Despair in God, and trust in Belzebub:
Now go not backward; Faustus, be resolute:
Why waver'st thou? O, something soundeth in mine ear,
"Abjure this magic, turn to God again!"
Ay, and Faustus will turn to God again.
To God? he loves thee not;
The God thou serv'st is thine own appetite,
Wherein is fix'd the love of Belzebub:
To him I'll build an altar and a church,
And offer lukewarm blood of newborn babes.

[*Enter the two* ANGELS.]

BAD ANGEL:
Go forward, Faustus, in that famous art.

GOOD ANGEL:
Sweet Faustus, leave that execrable art.

FAUSTUS:
Contrition, prayer, repentance—what of these?

GOOD ANGEL:
O, they are means to bring thee unto heaven!

BAD ANGEL:
Rather illusions, fruits of lunacy,
That make them foolish that do use them most.

GOOD ANGEL:
Sweet Faustus, think of heaven and heavenly things.

BAD ANGEL:
No, Faustus; think of honour and of wealth.

[*Exeunt* ANGELS.]

FAUSTUS:
Wealth! Why, the signiory of Emden[45] shall be mine.
When Mephistophilis shall stand by me,
What power can hurt me? Faustus, thou art safe:
Cast no more doubts—Mephistophilis, come!
And bring glad tidings from great Lucifer;—

[45] **Emden:** A wealthy German city.

Is't not midnight?—come, Mephistophilis,
Veni,[46] *veni, Mephistophile!*

[*Enter* MEPHISTOPHILIS.]

Now tell me what saith Lucifer, thy lord?

MEPHISTOPHILIS:
That I shall wait on Faustus while he lives,
So he will buy my service with his soul.

FAUSTUS:
Already Faustus hath hazarded that for thee.

MEPHISTOPHILIS:
But now thou must bequeath it solemnly,
And write a deed of gift with thine own blood;
For that security craves Lucifer.
If thou deny it, I must back to hell.

FAUSTUS:
Stay, Mephistophilis, tell me what good
Will my soul do thy lord?

MEPHISTOPHILIS:
Enlarge his kingdom.

FAUSTUS:
Is that the reason why he tempts us thus?

MEPHISTOPHILIS:
Solamen miseris socios habuisse doloris.[47]

FAUSTUS:
Why, have you any pain that torture others?

MEPHISTOPHILIS:
As great as have the human souls of men.
But tell me, Faustus, shall I have thy soul?
And I will be thy slave, and wait on thee,
And give thee more than thou hast wit to ask.

FAUSTUS:
Ay, Mephistophilis, I'll give it him.

MEPHISTOPHILIS:
Then, Faustus, stab thy arm courageously,
And bind thy soul, that at some certain day
Great Lucifer may claim it as his own;
And then be thou as great as Lucifer.

FAUSTUS [*stabbing his arm*]:
Lo, Mephistophilis, for love of thee,
I cut mine arm, and with my proper blood
Assure my soul to be great Lucifer's,
Chief lord and regent of perpetual night!

---

[46] ***Veni:*** Come. [47] ***Solamen . . . doloris:*** Misery loves company.

View here this blood that trickles from mine arm,
And let it be propitious for my wish.

MEPHISTOPHILIS:
But, Faustus,
Write it in manner of a deed of gift.

FAUSTUS:
Ay, so I do. [*Writes.*] But, Mephistophilis,
My blood congeals, and I can write no more.

MEPHISTOPHILIS:
I'll fetch thee fire to dissolve it straight.

[*Exit.*]

FAUSTUS:
Why might the staying of my blood portend?
Is it unwilling I should write this bill?
Why streams it not, that I may write afresh?
Faustus gives to thee his soul: oh, there it stay'd!
Why shouldst thou not? is not thy soul thine own?
Then write again, *Faustus gives to thee his soul.*

[*Re-enter* MEPHISTOPHILIS *with a chafer of fire.*]

MEPHISTOPHILIS:
See, Faustus, here is fire, set it on.

FAUSTUS:
So, now the blood begins to clear again;
Now will I make an end immediately. [*Writes.*]

MEPHISTOPHILIS:
What will not I do to obtain his soul? [*Aside.*]

FAUSTUS:
Consummatum est![48] this bill is ended,
And Faustus hath bequeath'd his soul to Lucifer.
But what is this inscription on mine arm?
Homo, fuge![49] Whither should I fly?
If unto God, he'll throw me down to hell.
My senses are deceiv'd; here's nothing writ:—
O yes, I see it plain; even here is writ,
Homo, fuge! Yet shall not Faustus fly.

MEPHISTOPHILIS: I'll fetch him somewhat to delight his mind.

[*Aside, and then exit.*]

[*Enter* DEVILS, *giving crowns and rich apparel to* FAUSTUS. *They dance, and then depart.*]
[*Enter* MEPHISTOPHILIS.]

FAUSTUS:
What means this show? Speak, Mephistophilis.

[48] ***Consummatum est!:*** It is finished! [49] ***Homo, fuge!:*** Man, fly!

MEPHISTOPHILIS:

Nothing, Faustus, but to delight thy mind,
And let thee see what magic can perform.

FAUSTUS:

But may I raise such spirits when I please?

MEPHISTOPHILIS:

Ay, Faustus, and do greater things than these.

FAUSTUS:

Then there's enough for a thousand souls.
Here, Mephistophilis, receive this scroll,
A deed of gift of body and of soul:
But yet conditionally that thou perform
All articles prescrib'd between us both.

MEPHISTOPHILIS:

Faustus, I swear by hell and Lucifer
To effect all promises between us made!

FAUSTUS:

Then hear me read it, Mephistophilis.

On these conditions following.
First, that Faustus may be a spirit in form and substance.
Secondly, that Mephistophilis shall be his servant, and at his command.
Thirdly, that Mephistophilis shall do for him, and bring him whatsoever.
Fourthly, that he shall be in his chamber or house invisible.
Lastly, that he shall appear to the said John Faustus at all times, in what form or shape soever he please.
I, John Faustus, of Wittenberg, Doctor, by these presents, do give both body and soul to Lucifer Prince of the East, and his minister Mephistophilis; and furthermore grant unto them that, four and twenty years being expired, and these articles above written being inviolate, full power to fetch or carry the said John Faustus, body and soul, flesh, blood, or goods, into their habitation wheresoever.

By me, John Faustus.

MEPHISTOPHILIS:

Speak, Faustus, do you deliver this as your deed?

FAUSTUS:

Ay, take it, and the devil give thee good of it!

MEPHISTOPHILIS:

So, now, Faustus, ask me what thou wilt.

FAUSTUS:

First I will question with thee about hell.
Tell me, where is the place that men call hell?

MEPHISTOPHILIS:

Under the heavens.

FAUSTUS:

Ay, so are all things else, but whereabouts?

MEPHISTOPHILIS:

Within the bowels of these elements,
Where we are tortur'd and remain for ever:
Hell hath no limits, nor is circumscrib'd,
In one self place; but where we are is hell,
And where hell is, there must we ever be:
And, to be short, when all the world dissolves,
And every creature shall be purified,
All places shall be hell that is not heaven.

FAUSTUS:

I think hell's a fable.

MEPHISTOPHILIS:

Ay, think so, till experience change thy mind.

FAUSTUS:

Why, dost thou think that Faustus shall be damn'd?

MEPHISTOPHILIS:

Ay, of necessity, for here's the scroll
In which thou hast given thy soul to Lucifer.

FAUSTUS:

Ay, and body too: but what of that?
Think'st thou that Faustus is so fond° to imagine — foolish
That, after this life, there is any pain?
No, these are trifles and mere old wives' tales.

MEPHISTOPHILIS:

But I am an instance to prove the contrary;
For I tell thee I am damn'd, and now in hell.

FAUSTUS:

Nay, and this be hell, I'll willingly be damn'd:
What! sleeping, eating, walking, and disputing!
But, leaving off this, let me have a wife,
The fairest maid in Germany, for I
Am wanton and lascivious
And cannot live without a wife.

MEPHISTOPHILIS:

I prithee, Faustus, talk not of a wife.

FAUSTUS:

Nay, sweet Mephistophilis, fetch me one, for I will have one.

MEPHISTOPHILIS:

Well, Faustus, thou shalt have a wife.

[*He fetches in a* WOMAN-DEVIL.]

FAUSTUS:

What sight is this?

MEPHISTOPHILIS:
Now, Faustus, wilt thou have a wife?
FAUSTUS:
Here's a hot whore indeed! No, I'll no wife.
MEPHISTOPHILIS:
Marriage is but a ceremonial toy:
And if thou lovest me, think no more of it.
I'll cull thee out the fairest courtesans,
And bring them ev'ry morning to thy bed:
She whom thine eye shall like, thy heart shall have,
Were she as chaste as was Penelope,
As wise as Saba,[50] or as beautiful
As was bright Lucifer before his fall.
Here, take this book, and peruse it well:
The iterating of these lines brings gold;
The framing of this circle on the ground
Brings thunder, whirlwinds, storm and lightning;
Pronounce this thrice devoutly to thyself,
And men in harness° shall appear to thee, armor
Ready to execute what thou command'st.
FAUSTUS:
Thanks, Mephistophilis, for this sweet book.
This will I keep as chary° as my life. carefully
[*Exeunt.*]

Scene 2

[*Enter* FAUSTUS *in his study and* MEPHISTOPHILIS.]
FAUSTUS:
When I behold the heavens, then I repent,
And curse thee, wicked Mephistophilis,
Because thou hast depriv'd me of those joys.
MEPHISTOPHILIS:
'Twas thine own seeking, Faustus, thank thyself.
But think'st thou heaven is such a glorious thing?
I tell thee, Faustus, it is not half so fair
As thou, or any man that breathes on earth.
FAUSTUS:
How prov'st thou that?
MEPHISTOPHILIS:
'Twas made for man; then he's more excellent.
FAUSTUS:
If heaven was made for man, 'twas made for me:

[50] **Saba:** The Queen of Sheba.

I will renounce this magic and repent.

[*Enter the two* ANGELS.]

GOOD ANGEL:

Faustus, repent; yet God will pity thee.

BAD ANGEL:

Thou art a spirit;° God cannot pity thee. evil spirit

FAUSTUS:

Who buzzeth in mine ears, I am a spirit?
Be I a devil, yet God may pity me;
Yea, God will pity me, if I repent.

BAD ANGEL:

Ay, but Faustus never shall repent.

[*Exeunt* ANGELS.]

FAUSTUS:

My heart is harden'd, I cannot repent:
Scarce can I name salvation, faith, or heaven,
But fearful echoes thunders in mine ears,
"Faustus, thou art damn'd!" Then swords, and knives,
Poison, guns, halters, and envenom'd steel
Are laid before me to despatch myself;
And long ere this I should have done the deed,
Had not sweet pleasure conquer'd deep despair.
Have not I made blind Homer sing to me
Of Alexander's[51] love and Oenon's death?
And hath not he,[52] that built the walls of Thebes,
With ravishing sound of his melodious harp,
Made music with my Mephistophilis?
Why should I die, then, or basely despair?
I am resolv'd; Faustus shall not repent.—
Come, Mephistophilis, let us dispute again,
And reason of divine astrology.
Speak, are there many spheres above the moon?
Are all celestial bodies but one globe,
As is the substance of this centric earth?[53]

MEPHISTOPHILIS:

As are the elements, such are the heavens,
Even from the moon unto the imperial orb,
Mutually folded in each others' spheres,
And jointly move upon one axletree,

---

[51] **Alexander:** Another name for Paris, Helen of Troy's and Oenon's lover.

[52] **he:** The musician Amphion.

[53] **centric earth:** Faustus appears to be asking whether all the apparently different heavenly bodies are part of a single interconnected system.

Whose termine is termed the world's wide pole;
Nor are the names of Saturn, Mars, or Jupiter
Feign'd but are erring stars.[54]

FAUSTUS:
But have they all
One motion, both *situ et tempore*?[55]

MEPHISTOPHILIS: All move from east to west in four and twenty hours upon the poles of the world, but differ in their motions upon the poles of the zodiac.

FAUSTUS:
These slender questions Wagner can decide:
Hath Mephistophilis no greater skill?
Who knows not the double motion of the planets?
That the first is finish'd in a natural day;
The second thus: Saturn in thirty years;
Jupiter in twelve; Mars in four; the Sun, Venus, and Mercury in a year; the Moon in twenty-eight days. These are freshmen's questions. But, tell me, hath every sphere a dominion or intelligentia?[56]

MEPHISTOPHILIS: Ay.

FAUSTUS: How many heavens or spheres are there?

MEPHISTOPHILIS: Nine; the seven planets, the firmament, and the imperial heaven.

FAUSTUS: But is there not *coelum igneum, et cristallinum*?[57]

MEPHISTOPHILIS: No, Faustus, they be but fables.

FAUSTUS: Resolve me then in this one question: why are not conjunctions, oppositions, aspects, eclipses, all at one time, but in some years we have more, in some less?

MEPHISTOPHILIS: *Per inaequalem motum respectus totius.*[58]

FAUSTUS: Well, I am answer'd. Now tell me who made the world.

MEPHISTOPHILIS: I will not.

FAUSTUS: Sweet Mephistophilis, tell me.

MEPHISTOPHILIS: Move me not, Faustus.

FAUSTUS: Villain, have not I bound thee to tell me any thing?

MEPHISTOPHILIS:
Ay, that is not against our kingdom.
This is: thou art damn'd; think thou of hell.

FAUSTUS:
Think, Faustus, upon God that made the world.

MEPHISTOPHILIS:
Remember this.

[*Exit.*]

---

[54] **erring stars:** Wandering stars, planets.

[55] ***situ et tempore:*** In both the direction and the duration of their revolutions.

[56] **intelligentia:** A ruling spirit or angel.

[57] ***coelum . . . cristallinum:*** The heaven of fire and the crystalline sphere.

[58] ***Per . . . totius:*** Because of their uneven speeds within the system.

FAUSTUS:
Ay, go, accursed spirit, to ugly hell!
'Tis thou hast damn'd distressed Faustus' soul.
Is't not too late?

[*Enter the two* ANGELS.]

BAD ANGEL:
Too late.

GOOD ANGEL:
Never too late, if Faustus will repent.

BAD ANGEL:
If thou repent, devils will tear thee in pieces.

GOOD ANGEL:
Repent, and they shall never raze° thy skin. touch

[*Exeunt* ANGELS.]

FAUSTUS:
O, Christ, my Saviour, my Saviour,
Help to save distressed Faustus' soul!

[*Enter* LUCIFER, BELZEBUB, *and* MEPHISTOPHILIS.]

LUCIFER:
Christ cannot save thy soul, for he is just:
There's none but I have interest in the same.

FAUSTUS:
O, what art thou that look'st so terribly?

LUCIFER:
I am Lucifer,
And this is my companion prince in hell.

FAUSTUS:
O, Faustus, they are come to fetch thy soul!

BELZEBUB:
We are come to tell thee thou dost injure us.

LUCIFER:
Thou call'st on Christ, contrary to thy promise.

BELZEBUB:
Thou shouldst not think on God.

LUCIFER:
Think on the devil.

BELZEBUB:
And his dam too.

FAUSTUS:
Nor will I henceforth: pardon me in this,
And Faustus vows never to look to heaven,
Never to name God, or to pray to him,
To burn his Scriptures, slay his ministers,
And make my spirits pull his churches down.

LUCIFER:
So shalt thou show thyself an obedient servant,
And we will highly gratify thee for it.

BELZEBUB: Faustus, we are come from hell in person to show thee some pastime: sit down, and thou shalt behold the Seven Deadly Sins appear to thee in their own proper shapes and likeness.

FAUSTUS:
That sight will be as pleasing unto me,
As Paradise was to Adam, the first day
Of his creation.

LUCIFER:
Talk not of Paradise or creation; but mark the show.
Go, Mephistophilis, fetch them in.

[*Enter the* SEVEN DEADLY SINS.]

BELZEBUB: Now, Faustus, question them of their names and dispositions.

FAUSTUS: That shall I soon. What are thou, the first?

PRIDE: I am Pride. I disdain to have any parents. I am like Ovid's flea;[59] I can creep into every corner of a wench; sometimes, like a periwig, I sit upon her brow; next, like a necklace I hang about her neck; then, like a fan of feathers, I kiss her lips, and then turning myself to a wrought smock do what I list. But, fie, what a smell is here! I'll not speak another word, unless the ground be perfum'd, and cover'd with cloth of arras.[60]

FAUSTUS: Thou art a proud knave, indeed! What are thou, the second?

COVETOUSNESS: I am Covetousness, begotten of an old churl in a leather bag: and might I now obtain my wish, this house, you and all, should turn to gold, that I might lock you safe into my chest. O my sweet gold!

FAUSTUS: And what are thou, the third?

ENVY: I am Envy, begotten of a chimney-sweeper and an oyster-wife. I cannot read, and therefore wish all books burn'd. I am lean with seeing others eat. O, that there would come a famine over all the world, that all might die, and I live alone! then thou should'st see how fat I'd be. But must thou sit, and I stand? come down, with a vengeance!

FAUSTUS: Out, envious wretch!—But what art thou, the fourth?

WRATH: I am Wrath. I had neither father nor mother: I leapt out of a lion's mouth when I was scarce an hour old; and ever since have run up and down the world with these case of rapiers, wounding myself when I could get none to fight withal. I was born in hell; and look to it, for some of you shall be my father.

FAUSTUS: And what are thou, the fifth?

GLUTTONY: I am Gluttony. My parents are all dead, and the devil a penny they have left me, but a small pension, and that buys me thirty meals a day and ten bevers[61]—a small trifle to suffice nature. I come of a royal pedigree! my father

[59] **Ovid's flea:** *The Flea,* a lewd medieval poem, was mistakenly attributed to Ovid. [60] **arras:** Tapestry cloth woven in Flanders. [61] **bevers:** Snacks.

was a Gammon of Bacon,[62] and my mother was a Hogshead of Claret wine; my godfathers were these, Peter Pickled-herring and Martin Martlemas-beef.[63] But my godmother, O she was an ancient gentlewoman; her name was Margery March-beer. Now, Faustus, thou hast heard all my progeny; wilt thou bid me to supper?

FAUSTUS: Not I.

GLUTTONY: Then the devil choke thee.

FAUSTUS: Choke thyself, glutton!—What art thou, the sixth?

SLOTH: Heigh ho! I am Sloth. I was begotten on a sunny bank, where I have lain ever since; and you have done me great injury to bring me from thence: let me be carried thither again by Gluttony and Lechery. Heigh ho! I'll not speak a word more for a king's ransom.

FAUSTUS: And what are you, Mistress Minx, the seventh and last?

LECHERY: Who, I, sir? I am one that loves an inch of raw mutton[64] better than an ell of fried stockfish, and the first letter of my name begins with Lechery.

LUCIFER: Away, to hell, away, on Piper!

[*Exeunt the* SEVEN SINS.]

FAUSTUS: O, how this sight doth delight my soul!

LUCIFER: But, Faustus, in hell is all manner of delight.

FAUSTUS: O, might I see hell, and return again safe, how happy were I then!

LUCIFER:

Faustus, thou shalt. At midnight I will send for thee.
Meanwhile peruse this book and view it thoroughly,
And thou shalt turn thyself into what shape thou wilt.

FAUSTUS:

Thanks, mighty Lucifer!
This will I keep as chary as my life.

LUCIFER:

Now, Faustus, farewell.

FAUSTUS:

Farewell, great Lucifer. Come, Mephistophilis.

[*Exeunt omnes several ways.*]

Scene 3

An inn yard.

[*Enter* ROBIN *with a book.*]

ROBIN: What, Dick, look to the horses there, till I come again. I have gotten one of Doctor Faustus' conjuring books, and now we'll have such knavery, as't passes.[65]

[*Enter* DICK.]

DICK: What, Robin, you must come away and walk the horses.

---

[62] **Gammon of Bacon:** Lower side of bacon. [63] **Martlemas-beef:** Martinmas (November 11) was the traditional time for salting beef. [64] **inch . . . mutton:** Penis. [65] **as't passes:** As is possible.

ROBIN: I walk the horses? I scorn't, 'faith, I have other matters in hand, let the horses walk themselves and they will. [*Reads.*] *A per se;*[66] *a, t.h.e. the: o per se; o deny orgon, gorgon.*[67] Keep further from me, O thou illiterate and unlearned hostler.

DICK: 'Snails, what hast thou got there? a book? why, thou canst not tell ne'er a word on't.

ROBIN: That thou shalt see presently. Keep out of the circle, I say, lest I send you into the ostry[68] with a vengeance.

DICK: That's like, 'faith: you had best leave your foolery, for an my master come, he'll conjure you, 'faith.

ROBIN: My master conjure me? I'll tell thee what, an my master come here, I'll clap as fair a pair of horns[69] on's head as e'er thou sawest in thy life.

DICK: Thou need'st not do that, for my mistress hath done it.

ROBIN: Ay, there be of us here that have waded as deep into matters as other men, if they were disposed to talk.

DICK: A plague take you, I thought you did not sneak up and down after her for nothing. But I prithee, tell me, in good sadness,[70] Robin, is that a conjuring book?

ROBIN: Do but speak what thou'lt have me to do, and I'll do't: If thou'lt dance naked, put off thy clothes, and I'll conjure thee about presently: or if thou'lt go but to the tavern with me, I'll give thee white wine, red wine, claret wine, sack, muscadine, malmesey, and whippin-crust,[71] hold belly, hold, and we'll not pay one penny for it.

DICK: O brave, prithee let's to it presently, for I am as dry as a dog.

ROBIN: Come then, let's away.

[*Exeunt.*]

Act III

Prologue

[*Enter the* CHORUS.]

CHORUS:

Learned Faustus,
To find the secrets of astronomy
Graven in the book of Jove's high firmament,
Did mount him up to scale Olympus' top,
Where sitting in a chariot burning bright,
Drawn by the strength of yoked dragons' necks,
He views the clouds, the planets, and the stars,
The tropic zones, and quarters of the sky,
From the bright circle of the hornèd moon,
E'en to the height of *Primum Mobile:*[72]

---

[66] ***A per se:*** A by itself—a beginner's method of reading the alphabet. [67] ***o . . . gorgon:*** A parody of Faustus when he invoked the Demogorgon. [68] **ostry:** Stable. [69] **pair of horns:** A cuckold's horns. [70] **sadness:** Seriousness. [71] **whippin-crust:** Hippocras, a type of wine. [72] ***Primum Mobile:*** The empyrean—in medieval cosmology, the highest heaven.

And whirling round with this circumference,
Within the concave compass of the pole;
From east to west his dragons swiftly glide,
And in eight days did bring him home again.
Not long he stayed within his quiet house,
To rest his bones after his weary toil,
But new exploits do hale him out again,
And mounted then upon a dragon's back,
That with his wings did part the subtle air,
He now is gone to prove cosmography,
That measures coasts, and kingdoms of the earth:
And, as I guess, will first arrive at Rome,
To see the Pope and manner of his court,
And take some part of holy Peter's feast,
The which this day is highly solemniz'd.

[*Exit.*]

Scene 1

The Pope's privy chamber.

[*Enter* FAUSTUS *and* MEPHISTOPHILIS.]

FAUSTUS:

Having now, my good Mephistophilis,
Pass'd with delight the stately town of Trier,[73]
Environ'd round with airy mountain tops,
With walls of flint, and deep entrenched lakes,° moats
Not to be won by any conquering prince;
From Paris next, coasting the realm of France,
We saw the river Maine fall into Rhine,
Whose banks are set with groves of fruitful vines;
Then up to Naples, rich Campania,
Whose buildings fair and gorgeous to the eye,
The streets straight forth, and paved with finest brick,
Quarters the town in four equivalents;
There saw we learned Maro's golden tomb,[74]
The way he cut, an English mile in length,
Through a rock of stone, in one night's space;
From thence to Venice, Padua, and the East,
In one of which a sumptuous temple[75] stands,

[73] **Trier:** Town now called Treves, in Prussia.

[74] **Maro's golden tomb:** Near Virgil's tomb (d. 19 B.C.E.) in Naples was a tunnel thought to be the work of Virgil's magic powers.

[75] **temple:** St. Mark's in Venice.

That threats the stars with her aspiring top,
Whose frame is paved with sundry coloured stones,
And roof'd aloft with curious work in gold.
Thus hitherto hath Faustus spent his time:
But tell me now, what resting place is this?
Hast thou, as erst I did command,
Conducted me within the walls of Rome?

MEPHISTOPHILIS:
I have, my Faustus, and for proof thereof
This is the goodly Palace of the Pope;
And cause we are no common guests
I choose his privy chamber for our use.

FAUSTUS:
I hope his Holiness will bid us welcome.

MEPHISTOPHILIS:
All's one, for we'll be bold with his venison.
But now, my Faustus, that thou may'st perceive
What Rome contains for to delight thine eyes,
Know that this city stands upon seven hills
That underprop the groundwork of the same:
Just through the midst runs flowing Tiber's stream,
With winding banks that cut it in two parts;
Over the which four stately bridges lean,
That make safe passage to each part of Rome:
Upon the bridge called Ponte Angelo
Erected is a castle passing strong,
Where thou shalt see such store of ordinance,
As that the double cannons, forg'd of brass,
Do match the number of the days contain'd
Within the compass of one complete year:
Beside the gates, and high pyramides,° obelisks
That Julius Caesar brought from Africa.

FAUSTUS:
Now, by the kingdoms of infernal rule,
Of Styx, of Acheron, and the fiery lake
Of ever-burning Phlegethon,[76] I swear
That I do long to see the monuments
And situation of bright splendent Rome:
Come, therefore, let's away.

MEPHISTOPHILIS:
Nay, stay, my Faustus; I know you'd see the Pope
And take some part of holy Peter's feast,

[76] **Styx . . . Phlegethon:** Underworld rivers in classical mythology.

The which, in state and high solemnity,
This day is held through Rome and Italy,
In honour of the Pope's triumphant victory.

FAUSTUS:

Sweet Mephistophilis, thou pleasest me,
Whilst I am here on earth, let me be cloy'd
With all things that delight the heart of man.
My four-and-twenty years of liberty
I'll spend in pleasure and in dalliance,
That Faustus' name, whilst this bright frame doth stand,
May be admired through the furthest land.

MEPHISTOPHILIS:

'Tis well said, Faustus, come then, stand by me
And thou shalt see them come immediately.

FAUSTUS:

Nay, stay, my gentle Mephistophilis,
And grant me my request, and then I go.
Thou know'st within the compass of eight days
We view'd the face of heaven, of earth and hell.
So high our dragons soar'd into the air,
That looking down, the earth appear'd to me
No bigger than my hand in quantity.
There did we view the kingdoms of the world,
And what might please mine eye, I there beheld.
Then in this show let me an actor be,
That this proud Pope[77] may Faustus' cunning see.

MEPHISTOPHILIS:

Let it be so, my Faustus, but, first stay,
And view their triumphs, as they pass this way.
And then devise what best contents thy mind
By cunning in thine art to cross the Pope,
Or dash the pride of this solemnity;
To make his monks and abbots stand like apes,
And point like antics at his triple crown:
To beat the beads about the friars' pates,
Or clap huge horns upon the Cardinals' heads;
Or any villainy thou canst devise,
And I'll perform it, Faustus: Hark! they come:
This day shall make thee be admir'd in Rome.

---

[77] **Pope:** Possibly Adrian VI or Clement VII, sixteenth-century popes and contemporaries of the historical Faustus; they ruled during a time of papal excess.

[*Enter the* CARDINALS *and* BISHOPS, *some bearing crosiers, some the pillars,*[78] MONKS *and* FRIARS *singing their procession. Then the* POPE, *and* RAYMOND, *King of Hungary, with* BRUNO[79] *led in chains.*]

POPE:

Cast down our footstool.

RAYMOND:

Saxon Bruno, stoop,
Whilst on thy back his Holiness ascends
Saint Peter's chair and state pontifical.

BRUNO:

Proud Lucifer, that state belongs to me:
But thus I fall to Peter, not to thee.

POPE:

To me and Peter shalt thou grovelling lie,
And crouch before the Papal dignity;
Sound trumpets, then, for thus Saint Peter's heir,
From Bruno's back, ascends Saint Peter's chair.

[*A flourish while he ascends.*]

Thus, as the gods creep on with feet of wool,
Long ere with iron hands they punish men,
So shall our sleeping vengeance now arise,
And smite with death thy hated enterprise.
Lord Cardinals of France and Padua,
Go forthwith to our holy Consistory,
And read amongst the Statutes Decretal,
What, by the holy Council held at Trent,[80]
The sacred synod hath decreed for him
That doth assume the Papal government
Without election, and a true consent:
Away, and bring us word with speed.

FIRST CARDINAL:

We go, my lord.

[*Exeunt* CARDINALS.]

POPE:

Lord Raymond.

FAUSTUS:

Go, haste thee, gentle Mephistophilis,
Follow the Cardinals to the Consistory;

[78] **crosiers, pillars:** Objects symbolizing their official ranks.

[79] **BRUNO:** Fictitious figure; the emperor's nominee for the papacy.

[80] **Council . . . Trent:** Councils held between 1545 and 1563.

And as they turn their superstitious books,
Strike them with sloth, and drowsy idleness;
And make them sleep so sound, that in their shapes
Thyself and I may parley with this Pope,
This proud confronter of the Emperor:[81]
And in despite of all his Holiness
Restore this Bruno to his liberty,
And bear him to the States of Germany.

MEPHISTOPHILIS:
Faustus, I go.

FAUSTUS:
Despatch it soon,
The Pope shall curse that Faustus came to Rome.

[*Exeunt* FAUSTUS *and* MEPHISTOPHILIS.]

BRUNO:
Pope Adrian, let me have right of law,
I was elected by the Emperor.

POPE:
We will depose the Emperor for that deed,
And curse the people that submit to him;
Both he and thou shalt stand excommunicate,
And interdict from Church's privilege
And all society of holy men:
He grows too proud in his authority,
Lifting his lofty head above the clouds,
And like a steeple overpeers the Church:
But we'll pull down his haughty insolence.
And as Pope Alexander,[82] our progenitor,
Trod on the neck of German Frederick,[83]
Adding this golden sentence to our praise:—
"That Peter's heirs should tread on Emperors,
And walk upon the dreadful adder's back,
Treading the lion and the dragon down,
And fearless spurn the killing basilisk":[84]
So will we quell that haughty schismatic;
And by authority apostolical
Depose him from his regal government.

---

[81] **Emporer:** Holy Roman Emperor.

[82] **Pope Alexander:** Alexander III (1159–1181).

[83] **Frederick:** Alexander III forced submission from the emperor Frederick Barbarossa (1123–1190).

[84] **basilisk:** A legendary monster that was said to kill by its looks.

BRUNO:

Pope Julius swore to princely Sigismond,[85]
For him, and the succeeding Popes of Rome,
To hold the Emperors their lawful lords.

POPE:

Pope Julius did abuse the Church's rites,
And therefore none of his decrees can stand.
Is not all power on earth bestowed on us?
And therefore, though we would, we cannot err.
Behold this silver belt, whereto is fix'd
Seven golden keys fast sealed with seven seals
In token of our sevenfold power from Heaven,
To bind or loose, lock fast, condemn, or judge,
Resign, or seal, or whatso pleaseth us.
Then he and thou, and all the world shall stoop,
Or be assured of our dreadful curse,
To light as heavy as the pains of hell.

[*Enter* FAUSTUS *and* MEPHISTOPHILIS *like the* CARDINALS.]

MEPHISTOPHILIS:

Now tell me, Faustus, are we not fitted well?

FAUSTUS:

Yes, Mephistophilis, and two such Cardinals
Ne'er serv'd a holy Pope as we shall do.
But whilst they sleep within the Consistory,
Let us salute his reverend Fatherhood.

RAYMOND:

Behold, my Lord, the Cardinals are return'd.

POPE:

Welcome, grave Fathers, answer presently,
What have our holy Council there decreed,
Concerning Bruno and the Emperor,
In quittance of their late conspiracy
Against our state and Papal dignity?

FAUSTUS:

Most sacred Patron of the Church of Rome
By full consent of all the synod
Of priests and prelates, it is thus decreed:
That Bruno and the German Emperor
Be held as Lollards[86] and bold schismatics

---

[85] **Pope Julius, Sigismond:** There were popes named Julius in the fourth and sixteenth centuries; Sigismond (1368–1437) was a German emperor.

[86] **Lollards:** Followers of the English religious reformer John Wycliffe (c. 1330–1384).

And proud disturbers of the Church's peace.
And if that Bruno, by his own assent,
Without enforcement of the German peers,
Did seek to wear the triple diadem,
And by your death to climb Saint Peter's chair,
The Statutes Decretal have thus decreed,
He shall be straight condemn'd of heresy,
And on a pile of fagots burnt to death.

POPE:

It is enough: Here, take him to your charge,
and bear him straight to Ponte Angelo,
And in the strongest tower enclose him fast;
Tomorrow, sitting in our Consistory
With all our college of grave Cardinals,
We will determine of his life or death.
Here, take his triple crown along with you,
And leave it in the Church's treasury.
Make haste again, my good Lord Cardinals,
And take our blessing apostolical.

MEPHISTOPHILIS:

So, so; was never devil thus blessed before.

FAUSTUS:

Away, sweet Mephistophilis, be gone,
The Cardinals will be plagu'd for this anon.

[*Exeunt* FAUSTUS *and* MEPHISTOPHILIS, *with* BRUNO.]

POPE:

Go presently and bring a banquet forth,
That we may solemnize Saint Peter's feast,
And with Lord Raymond, King of Hungary,
Drink to our late and happy victory.

[*Exeunt.*]

Scene 2

A sennet[87] *while the banquet is brought in; and then enter* FAUSTUS *and* MEPHISTOPHILIS *in their own shapes.*

MEPHISTOPHILIS:

Now, Faustus, come, prepare thyself for mirth:
The sleepy Cardinals are hard at hand
To censure Bruno, that is posted hence,
and on a proud-pac'd steed, as swift as thought,
Flies o'er the Alps to fruitful Germany,
There to salute the woeful Emperor.

---

[87] ***sennet:*** A signal by a trumpet.

FAUSTUS:
The Pope will curse them for their sloth today,
That slept both Bruno and his crown away:
But now, that Faustus may delight his mind,
And by their folly make some merriment,
Sweet Mephistophilis, so charm me here,
That I may walk invisible to all,
And do whate'er I please, unseen of any.
MEPHISTOPHILIS:
Faustus, thou shalt, then kneel down presently:

Whilst on thy head I lay my hand,
And charm thee with this magic wand.
First wear this girdle, then appear
Invisible to all are here:
The Planets seven, the gloomy air,
Hell and the Furies' forked hair,
Pluto's blue fire, and Hecate's tree,
With magic spells so compass thee,
That no eye may thy body see.

So, Faustus, now for all their holiness,
Do what thou wilt, thou shalt not be discern'd.
FAUSTUS:
Thanks, Mephistophilis; now, friars, take heed,
Lest Faustus make your shaven crowns to bleed.
MEPHISTOPHILIS:
Faustus, no more: see where the Cardinals come.

[*Enter* POPE *and all the* LORDS. *Enter the* CARDINALS *with a book.*]
POPE:
Welcome, Lord Cardinals: come, sit down.
Lord Raymond, take your seat. Friars, attend,
And see that all things be in readiness,
As best beseems this solemn festival.
FIRST CARDINAL:
First, may it please your sacred Holiness
To view the sentence of the reverend synod,
Concerning Bruno and the Emperor?
POPE:
What needs this question? Did I not tell you,
Tomorrow we would sit i' th' Consistory,
And there determine of his punishment?
You brought us word even now, it was decreed
That Bruno and the cursed Emperor
Were by the holy Council both condemn'd

For loathed Lollards and base schismatics:
Then wherefore would you have me view that book?

FIRST CARDINAL:
Your Grace mistakes, you gave us no such charge.

RAYMOND:
Deny it not, we all are witnesses
That Bruno here was late deliver'd you,
With his rich triple crown to be reserv'd
And put into the Church's treasury.

BOTH CARDINALS:
By holy Paul, we saw them not.

POPE:
By Peter, you shall die,
Unless you bring them forth immediately:
Hale them to prison, lade their limbs with gyves:° — prisoners' shackles
False prelates, for this hateful treachery,
Curs'd be your souls to hellish misery.

[*Exeunt* ATTENDANTS *with the two* CARDINALS.]

FAUSTUS:
So, they are safe: now, Faustus, to the feast,
The Pope had never such a frolic guest.

POPE:
Lord Archbishop of Reames, sit down with us.

ARCHBISHOP:
I thank your Holiness.

FAUSTUS:
Fall to, the devil choke you an you spare.

POPE:
How now? Who's that which spake?—Friars, look about.

FRIAR:
Here's nobody, if it like your Holiness.

POPE:
Lord Raymond, pray fall to. I am beholding
To the Bishop of Milan for this so rare a present.

FAUSTUS:
I thank you, sir. [*Snatches the dish.*]

POPE:
How now? who's that which snatch'd the meat from me?
Villains, why speak you not?—
My good Lord Archbishop, here's a most dainty dish,
Was sent me from a Cardinal in France.

FAUSTUS:
I'll have that too. [*Snatches the dish.*]

POPE:
What Lollards do attend our Holiness,

That we receive such great indignity?
Fetch me some wine.

FAUSTUS:
Ay, pray do, for Faustus is adry.

POPE:
Lord Raymond, I drink unto your grace.

FAUSTUS:
I pledge your grace. [*Snatches the cup.*]

POPE:
My wine gone too?—ye lubbers, look about
And find the man that doth this villainy,
Or by our sanctitude, you all shall die.
I pray, my lords, have patience at this
Troublesome banquet.

ARCHBISHOP:
Please it your Holiness, I think it be
Some ghost crept out of Purgatory, and now
Is come unto your Holiness for his pardon.

POPE:
It may be so:
God then command our priests to sing a dirge,
To lay the fury of this same troublesome ghost.

[*Exit an* ATTENDANT.]

Once again, my Lord, fall to. [*The* POPE *crosseth himself.*]

FAUSTUS:
How now?
Must every bit be spicéd with a cross?
Nay then, take that. [*Strikes the* POPE.]

POPE:
O I am slain, help me, my lords;
O come and help to bear my body hence:—
Damn'd be his soul for ever for this deed!

[*Exeunt the* POPE *and his train.*]

MEPHISTOPHILIS: Now, Faustus, what will you do now, for I can tell you you'll be curs'd with bell, book, and candle.[88]

FAUSTUS:
Bell, book, and candle,—candle, book, and bell,—
Forward and backward, to curse Faustus to hell!

[*Enter the* FRIARS *with bell, book, and candle for the Dirge.*]

FIRST FRIAR: Come, brethren, let's about our business with good devotion. [*Sing this.*]

[88] **candle:** An excommunication concludes with the tolling of a bell, the closing of the book, and the extinguishing of the candle.

Cursed be he that stole his Holiness' meat from the table!
Maledicat Dominus![89]
Cursed be he that struck his Holiness a blow on the face!
Maledicat Dominus!
Cursed be he that took Friar Sandelo a blow on the pate!
Maledicat Dominus!
Cursed be he that disturbeth our holy dirge!
Maledicat Dominus!
Cursed be he that took away his Holiness' wine!
Maledicat Dominus!
Et omnes Sancti![90] *Amen!*

[MEPHISTOPHILIS *and* FAUSTUS *beat the* FRIARS, *fling fireworks among them, and exeunt.*]

Scene 3

A street, near an inn.

[*Enter* ROBIN *and* DICK, *with a cup.*]

DICK: Sirrah Robin, we were best look that your devil can answer the stealing of this same cup, for the vintner's boy follows us at the hard heels.[91]

ROBIN: 'Tis no matter! let him come; and he follow us I'll so conjure him as he was never conjured in his life. I warrant him. Let me see the cup.

[*Enter* VINTNER.]

DICK: Here 't is. Yonder he comes. Now, Robin, now or never show thy cunning.

VINTNER: O are you here? I am glad I have found you, you are a couple of fine companions; pray, where's the cup you stole from the tavern?

ROBIN: How, how? we steal a cup? Take heed what you say; we look not like cup-stealers, I can tell you.

VINTNER: Never deny 't, for I know you have it, and I'll search you.

ROBIN: Search me? Ay, and spare not. Hold the cup, Dick [*aside to* DICK].
Come, come, search me, search me! [VINTNER *searches him.*]

VINTNER [*to* DICK]: Come on, sirrah, let me search you now!

DICK: Ay, ay, do! Hold the cup, Robin [*aside to* ROBIN]. I fear not your searching; we scorn to steal your cups, I can tell you. [VINTNER *searches him.*]

VINTNER: Never outface me for the matter, for, sure, the cup is between you two.

ROBIN: Nay, there you lie, 'tis beyond us both.

VINTNER: A plague take you! I thought 't was your knavery to take it away; come, give it me again.

ROBIN: Ay much; when? can you tell? Dick, make me a circle, and stand close at my back, and stir not for thy life. Vintner, you shall have your cup anon. Say nothing, Dick. [*Reads.*] *O per se, o Demogorgon, Belcher and Mephistophilis!*

[89] ***Maledicat Dominus!*:** May the Lord curse him! [90] ***Et omnes Sancti!*:** And all the saints! [91] **hard heels:** Closely.

[*Enter* MEPHISTOPHILIS.]

MEPHISTOPHILIS:

You princely legions of infernal rule,
How am I vexed by these villains' charms!
From Constantinople have they brought me now
Only for pleasure of these damned slaves.

[*Exit* VINTNER.]

ROBIN: By Lady, sir, you have had a shrewd journey of it. Will it please you to take a shoulder of mutton to supper, and a tester[92] in your purse, and go back again?

DICK: Aye, aye. I pray you heartily, sir, for we call'd you but in jest, I promise you.

MEPHISTOPHILIS:

To purge the rashness of this cursed deed,
First be thou turned to this ugly shape,
For apish deeds transformed to an ape.

ROBIN: O brave! an Ape! I pray, sir, let me have the carrying of him about to show some tricks.

MEPHISTOPHILIS: And so thou shalt: be thou transformed to a dog, And carry him upon thy back. Away, be gone!

ROBIN: A dog! that's excellent; let the maids look well to their porridge-pots, for I'll into the kitchen presently. Come, Dick, come.

[*Exeunt the* TWO CLOWNS.]

MEPHISTOPHILIS:

Now with the flames of ever-burning fire,
I'll wing myself, and forthwith fly amain
Unto my Faustus, to the Great Turk's Court.

[*Exit.*]

ACT IV

Prologue

[*Enter* CHORUS.]

CHORUS:

When Faustus had with pleasure ta'en the view
Of rarest things, and royal courts of kings,
He stay'd his course, and so returned home;
Where such as bear his absence but with grief,
I mean his friends and near'st companions,
Did gratulate his safety with kind words,
And in their conference of what befell,
Touching his journey through the world and air,
They put forth questions of astrology,
Which Faustus answer'd with such learned skill

[92] **tester:** Sixpence.

As they admir'd and wonder'd at his wit.
Now is his fame spread forth in every land:
Amongst the rest the Emperor is one,
Carolus the Fifth,[93] at whose palace now
Faustus is feasted 'mongst his noblemen.
What there he did, in trial of his art,
I leave untold; your eyes shall see perform'd.

[*Exit.*]

Scene 1

A room in the Emperor's Court at Innsbruck.

[*Enter* MARTINO *and* FREDERICK *at several doors.*]

MARTINO:

What ho, officers, gentlemen,
Hie to the presence to attend the Emperor,
Good Frederick, see the rooms be voided straight,
His majesty is coming to the hall;
Go back, and see the state° in readiness. throne

FREDERICK:

But where is Bruno, our elected Pope,
That on a fury's back came post from Rome?
Will not his Grace consort the Emperor?

MARTINO:

O yes, and with him comes the German conjuror,
The learned Faustus, fame of Wittenberg,
The wonder of the world for magic art;
And he intends to show great Carolus
The race of all his stout progenitors;
And bring in presence of his Majesty
The royal shapes and warlike semblances
Of Alexander and his beauteous paramour.[94]

FREDERICK:

Where is Benvolio?

MARTINO:

Fast asleep, I warrant you,
He took his rouse with stoups of Rhenish wine
So kindly yesternight to Bruno's health,
That all this day the sluggard keeps his bed.

---

[93] **Carolus the Fifth:** Charles V was emperor from 1519 to 1556, then retired to a monastery.

[94] **Alexander . . . paramour:** Alexander the Great and Thais.

FREDERICK:
See, see, his window's ope, we'll call to him.

MARTINO:
What ho, Benvolio!

[*Enter* BENVOLIO *above, at a window, in his nightcap; buttoning.*]

BENVOLIO:
What a devil ail you two?

MARTINO:
Speak softly, sir, lest the devil hear you:
For Faustus at the court is late arriv'd,
And at his heels a thousand furies wait,
To accomplish whatsoever the Doctor please.

BENVOLIO:
What of this?

MARTINO:
Come, leave thy chamber first, and thou shalt see
This conjuror perform such rare exploits,
Before the Pope[95] and royal Emperor,
As never yet was seen in Germany.

BENVOLIO:
Has not the Pope enough of conjuring yet?
He was upon the devil's back late enough;
And if he be so far in love with him,
I would he would post with him to Rome again.

FREDERICK:
Speak, wilt thou come and see this sport?

BENVOLIO:
Not I.

MARTINO:
Wilt thou stand in thy window, and see it then?

BENVOLIO:
Ay, an I fall not asleep i' th' meantime.

MARTINO:
The Emperor is at hand, who comes to see
What wonders by black spells may compass'd be.

BENVOLIO: Well, go you attend the Emperor: I am content for this once to thrust my head out at a window; for they say if a man be drunk overnight the devil cannot hurt him in the morning; if that be true, I have a charm in my head shall control him as well as the conjuror, I warrant you.

[*Exeunt* FREDERICK *and* MARTINO.]

[95] **Pope:** Bruno.

Scene 2

The Presence Chamber in the Court.

[*A sennet. Enter* CHARLES, *the* GERMAN EMPEROR, BRUNO, DUKE OF SAXONY, FAUSTUS, MEPHISTOPHILIS, FREDERICK, MARTINO, *and* ATTENDANTS.]

EMPEROR:

Wonder of men, renown'd magician,
Thrice-learned Faustus, welcome to our Court.
This deed of thine, in setting Bruno free
From his and our professed enemy,
Shall add more excellence unto thine art,
Than if by powerful necromantic spells,
Thou couldst command the world's obedience:
For ever be belov'd of Carolus,
And if this Bruno thou hast late redeem'd,
In peace possess the triple diadem,
And sit in Peter's chair, despite of chance,
Thou shalt be famous through all Italy,
And honour'd of the German Emperor.

FAUSTUS:

These gracious words, most royal Carolus,
Shall make poor Faustus, to his utmost power,
Both love and serve the German Emperor,
And lay his life at holy Bruno's feet.
For proof whereof, if so your Grace be pleas'd,
The Doctor stands prepar'd by power of art
To cast his magic charms, that shall pierce through
The ebon gates of ever-burning hell,
And hale the stubborn Furies from their caves,
To compass whatsoe'er your Grace commands.

BENVOLIO [*above*]: 'Blood, he speaks terribly: but for all that I do not greatly believe him: he looks as like a conjuror as the Pope to a costermonger.

EMPEROR:

Then, Faustus, as thou late did'st promise us,
We would behold that famous conqueror,
Great Alexander and his paramour
In their true shapes and state majestical,
That we may wonder at their excellence.

FAUSTUS:

Your Majesty shall see them presently.
Mephistophilis, away.
And with a solemn noise of trumpets' sound
Present before this royal Emperor,
Great Alexander and his beauteous paramour.

MEPHISTOPHILIS: Faustus, I will.

BENVOLIO: Well, Master Doctor, an your devils come not away quickly, you shall have me asleep presently: zounds, I could eat myself for anger, to think I have been such an ass all this while to stand gaping after the devil's governor, and can see nothing.

FAUSTUS:
I'll make you feel something anon, if my art fail me not.—
My lord, I must forewarn your Majesty,
That when my spirits present the royal shapes
Of Alexander and his paramour,
Your Grace demand no questions of the king,
But in dumb silence let them come and go.

EMPEROR:
Be it as Faustus please, we are content.

BENVOLIO: Ay, ay, and I am content too; and thou bring Alexander and his paramour before the Emperor, I'll be Acteon[96] and turn myself to a stag.

FAUSTUS: And I'll play Diana, and send you the horns presently.

[*Sennet. Enter at one door the* EMPEROR ALEXANDER, *at the other* DARIUS; *they meet.* DARIUS *is thrown down.* ALEXANDER *kills him; takes off his crown and offering to go out, his paramour meets him, he embraceth her, and sets Darius' crown upon her head; and coming back, both salute the* EMPEROR, *who, leaving his state, offers to embrace them, which,* FAUSTUS *seeing, suddenly stays him. Then trumpets cease, and music sounds.*]

My gracious lord, you do forget yourself,
These are but shadows, not substantial.

EMPEROR:
O pardon me, my thoughts are so ravished
With sight of this renowned Emperor,
That in mine arms I would have compass'd him.
But, Faustus, since I may not speak to them,
To satisfy my longing thoughts at full,
Let me this tell thee: I have heard it said,
That this fair lady whilst she liv'd on earth,
Had on her neck, a little wart, or mole;
How may I prove that saying to be true?

FAUSTUS:
Your Majesty may boldly go and see.

EMPEROR:
Faustus, I see it plain,
And in this sight thou better pleasest me,
Than if I gain'd another monarchy.

FAUSTUS: Away, be gone!

[*Exit show.*]

[96] **Acteon:** In Greek mythology, the hunter Acteon spied on Diana while she was bathing and was consequently turned into a stag.

See, see, my gracious lord, what strange beast is yon, that thrusts his head out at window?

EMPEROR:

O wondrous sight: see, Duke of Saxony,
Two spreading horns most strangely fastened
Upon the head of young Benvolio.

SAX:

What, is he asleep, or dead?

FAUSTUS:

He sleeps, my lord, but dreams not of his horns.

EMPEROR:

This sport is excellent; we'll call and wake him.
What ho, Benvolio.

BENVOLIO: A plague upon you, let me sleep a while.

EMPEROR: I blame thee not to sleep much, having such a head of thine own.

SAX: Look up, Benvolio, 'tis the Emperor calls.

BENVOLIO: The Emperor? where—O zounds, my head!

EMPEROR: Nay, and thy horns hold, 'tis no matter for thy head, for that's arm'd sufficiently.

FAUSTUS: Why, how now, Sir Knight, what, hang'd by the horns? this is most horrible: fie, fie, pull in your head for shame, let not all the world wonder at you.

BENVOLIO: Zounds, Doctor, is this your villainy?

FAUSTUS:

O say not so, sir: the Doctor has no skill,
No art, no cunning, to present these lords,
Or bring before this royal Emperor
The mighty monarch, warlike Alexander.
If Faustus do it, you are straight resolv'd
In bold Acteon's shape to turn a stag.
And therefore, my lord, so please your Majesty,
I'll raise a kennel of hounds, shall hunt him so,
As all his footmanship shall scarce prevail
To keep his carcase from their bloody fangs.
Ho, Belimote, Argiron, Asterote.

BENVOLIO:

Hold, hold! Zounds, he'll raise up a kennel of devils,
I think, anon: good, my lord, entreat for me: 'sblood,
I am never able to endure these torments.

EMPEROR:

Then, good Master Doctor,
Let me entreat you to remove his horns,
He has done penance now sufficiently.

FAUSTUS: My gracious lord, not so much for injury done to me, as to delight your Majesty with some mirth, hath Faustus justly requited this injurious[97] knight,

[97] **injurious:** Insulting.

which being all I desire, I am content to remove his horns. Mephistophilis, transform him [MEPHISTOPHILIS *removes the horns*], and hereafter, sir, look you speak well of scholars.

BENVOLIO: Speak well of ye? 'sblood, and scholars be such cuckold-makers to clap horns of honest men's head o' this order, I'll e'er trust smooth faces and small ruffs[98] more. But an I be not reveng'd for this, would I might be turn'd to a gaping oyster, and drink nothing but salt water.

[*Aside, and then exit above.*]

EMPEROR:

Come, Faustus, while the Emperor lives,
In recompense of this thy high desert,
Thou shalt command the state of Germany,
And live belov'd of mighty Carolus.

[*Exeunt omnes.*]

Scene 3

Near a grove, outside Innsbruck.

[*Enter* BENVOLIO, MARTINO, FREDERICK, *and* SOLDIERS.]

MARTINO:

Nay, sweet Benvolio, let us sway thy thoughts
From this attempt against the conjuror.

BENVOLIO:

Away, you love me not, to urge me thus.
Shall I let slip so great an injury,
When every servile groom jests at my wrongs,
And in their rustic gambols proudly say,
"Benvolio's head was graced with horns today"?
O may these eyelids never close again,
Till with my sword I have that conjuror slain.
If you will aid me in this enterprise,
Then draw your weapons, and be resolute:
If not, depart: here will Benvolio die,
But Faustus' death shall quit° my infamy. avenge

FREDERICK:

Nay, we will stay with thee, betide what may,
And kill that Doctor if he come this way.

BENVOLIO:

Then, gentle Frederick, hie thee to the grove,
And place our servants and our followers
Close in an ambush there behind the trees.
By this (I know) the conjuror is near;
I saw him kneel and kiss the Emperor's hand,
And take his leave laden with rich rewards.

[98] **ruffs:** Beardless scholars in academic garb did not typically wear large ruffs or collars.

Then, soldiers, boldly fight; if Faustus die,
Take you the wealth, leave us the victory.

FREDERICK:
Come, soldiers, follow me unto the grove;
Who kills him shall have gold and endless love.
[*Exit* FREDERICK *with the* SOLDIERS.]

BENVOLIO:
My head is lighter than it was by th' horns,
But yet my heart's more ponderous than my head,
And pants until I see that conjuror dead.

MARTINO:
Where shall we place ourselves, Benvolio?

BENVOLIO:
Here will we stay to bide the first assault.
O were that damned hellhound but in place,
Thou soon shouldst see me quit my foul disgrace.

[*Enter* FREDERICK.]

FREDERICK:
Close, close, the conjuror is at hand,
And all alone comes walking in his gown;
Be ready then, and strike the peasant down.

BENVOLIO:
Mine be that honour then: now, sword, strike home,
For horns he gave I'll have his head anon.

[*Enter* FAUSTUS *with the false head.*]

MARTINO:
See, see, he comes.

BENVOLIO:
No words: this blow ends all,
Hell take his soul, his body thus must fall. [*Stabs* FAUSTUS.]

FAUSTUS [*falling*]:
Oh!

FREDERICK:
Groan you, Master Doctor?

BENVOLIO:
Break may his heart with groans: dear Frederick, see,
Thus will I end his griefs immediately.

MARTINO:
Strike with a willing hand. [BENVOLIO *strikes off* FAUSTUS' *false head.*]
His head is off.

BENVOLIO:
The devil's dead, the Furies now may laugh.

FREDERICK:
Was this that stern aspect, that awful frown,

Made the grim monarch of infernal spirits
Tremble and quake at his commanding charms?

MARTINO:
Was this that damned head, whose art conspir'd
Benvolio's shame before the Emperor?

BENVOLIO:
Ay, that's the head, and here the body lies,
Justly rewarded for his villainies.

FREDERICK:
Come, let's devise how we may add more shame
To the black scandal of his hated name.

BENVOLIO:
First, on his head, in quittance of my wrongs,
I'll nail huge forked horns, and let them hang
Within the window where he yok'd me first,
That all the world may see my just revenge.

MARTINO: What use shall we put his beard to?

BENVOLIO: We'll sell it to a chimney-sweeper; it will wear out ten birchen brooms. I warrant you.

FREDERICK: What shall his eyes do?

BENVOLIO: We'll put out his eyes, and they shall serve for buttons to his lips, to keep his tongue from catching cold.

MARTINO: An excellent policy: and now, sirs, having divided him, what shall the body do? [*Faustus rises.*]

BENVOLIO: Zounds, the devil's alive again.

FREDERICK:
Give him his head, for God's sake.

FAUSTUS:
Nay, keep it: Faustus will have heads and hands,
Ay, all your hearts to recompense this deed.
Knew you not, traitors, I was limited° — given a fixed period of time
For four-and-twenty years to breathe on earth?
And had you cut my body with your swords,
Or hew'd this flesh and bones as small as sand,
Yet in a minute had my spirit return'd,
And I had breath'd a man made free from harm.
But wherefore do I dally my revenge?
Asteroth, Belimoth, Mephistophilis,

[*Enter* MEPHISTOPHILIS *and other* DEVILS.]

Go, horse these traitors on your fiery backs,
And mount aloft with them as high as heaven,
Thence pitch them headlong to the lowest hell:
Yet, stay, the world shall see their misery,
And hell shall after plague their treachery.

Go, Belimoth, and take this caitiff hence,
And hurl him in some lake of mud and dirt:
Take thou this other, drag him through the woods,
Amongst the pricking thorns, and sharpest briers,
Whilst with my gentle Mephistophilis,
This traitor flies unto some steepy rock,
That, rolling down, may break the villain's bones,
As he intended to dismember me.
Fly hence, despatch my charge immediately.

FREDERICK:
Pity us, gentle Faustus, save our lives!

FAUSTUS:
Away!

FREDERICK:
He must needs go that the devil drives.

[*Exeunt* SPIRITS *with the* KNIGHTS.]

[*Enter the ambushed* SOLDIERS.]

FIRST SOLDIER:
Come, sirs, prepare yourselves in readiness,
Make haste to help these noble gentlemen,
I heard them parley with the conjuror.

SECOND SOLDIER:
See where he comes, despatch, and kill the slave.

FAUSTUS:
What's here? an ambush to betray my life:
Then, Faustus, try thy skill: base peasants, stand:
For lo! these trees remove at my command,
And stand as bulwarks 'twixt yourselves and me,
To shield me from your hated treachery:
Yet to encounter this your weak attempt,
Behold an army comes incontinent.° — immediately

[FAUSTUS *strikes the door, and enter a devil playing on a drum, after him another bearing an ensign; and divers with weapons,* MEPHISTOPHILIS *with fireworks; they set upon the* SOLDIERS, *and drive them out. Exit* FAUSTUS.]

Scene 4

[*Enter at several doors* BENVOLIO, FREDERICK, *and* MARTINO, *their heads and faces bloody, and besmear'd with mud and dirt, all having horns on their heads.*]

MARTINO:
What ho, Benvolio!

BENVOLIO:
Here, what, Frederick, ho!

FREDERICK:

O help me, gentle friend; where is Martino?

MARTINO:

Dear Frederick, here,
Half smother'd in a lake of mud and dirt,
Through which the furies dragg'd me by the heels.

FREDERICK:

Martino, see Benvolio's horns again.

MARTINO:

O misery, how now, Benvolio?

BENVOLIO:

Defend me, heaven, shall I be haunted still?

MARTINO:

Nay, fear not, man; we have no power to kill.

BENVOLIO:

My friends transformed thus! O hellish spite,
Your heads are all set with horns.

FREDERICK:

You hit it right:
It is your own you mean, feel on your head.

BENVOLIO:

'Zounds, horns again!

MARTINO:

Nay, chafe not, man, we all are sped.° done for

BENVOLIO:

What devil attends this damn'd magician,
That, spite of spite, our wrongs are doubled?

FREDERICK:

What may we do, that we may hide our shames?

BENVOLIO:

If we should follow him to work revenge,
He'd join long asses' ears to these huge horns,
And make us laughingstocks to all the world.

MARTINO:

What shall we then do, dear Benvolio?

BENVOLIO:

I have a castle joining near these woods,
And thither we'll repair and live obscure,
Till time shall alter these our brutish shapes:
Sith black disgrace hath thus eclips'd our fame,
We'll rather die with grief than live with shame.

[*Exeunt omnes.*]

Scene 5

At the entrance to the house of FAUSTUS.

[*Enter* FAUSTUS *and the* HORSE-COURSER.[99]]

HORSE-COURSER: I beseech, your worship, accept of these forty dollars.

FAUSTUS: Friend, thou canst not buy so good a horse, for so small a price. I have no great need to sell him, but if thou likest him for ten dollars more take him, because I see thou hast a good mind to him.

HORSE-COURSER: I beseech you, sir, accept of this; I am a very poor man and have lost very much of late by horseflesh, and this bargain will set me up again.

FAUSTUS: Well, I will not stand with thee, give me the money. [HORSE-COURSER *gives* FAUSTUS *the money.*] Now, sirrah, I must tell you that you may ride him o'er hedge and ditch, and spare him not; but, do you hear? in any case ride him not into the water.

HORSE-COURSER: How, sir, not into the water? Why, will he not drink of all waters?

FAUSTUS: Yes, he will drink of all waters, but ride him not into the water; o'er hedge and ditch, or where thou wilt, but not into the water. Go, bid the ostler deliver him unto you, and remember what I say.

HORSE-COURSER: I warrant you, sir. O joyful day, now am I a made man for ever. [*Exit.*]

FAUSTUS:

What art thou, Faustus, but a man condemn'd to die?
Thy fatal time draws to a final end,
Despair doth drive distrust into my thoughts.
Confound these passions with a quiet sleep.
Tush! Christ did call the thief upon the Cross;
Then rest thee, Faustus, quiet in conceit.[100] [*He sits to sleep.*]

[*Re-enter the* HORSE-COURSER *wet.*]

HORSE-COURSER: O what a cozening Doctor was this? I was riding my horse into the water, thinking some hidden mystery had been in the horse, I had nothing under me but a little straw, and had much ado to escape drowning. Well, I'll go rouse him, and make him give me my forty dollars again. Ho, sirrah Doctor, you cozening scab! Master Doctor, awake and rise, and give me my money again, for your horse is turned to a bottle[101] of hay, master Doctor. [*He pulls off his leg.*] Alas! I am undone, what shall I do? I have pull'd off his leg.

FAUSTUS: O, help, help, the villain hath murder'd me.

HORSE-COURSER: Murder, or not murder, now he has but one leg, I'll outrun him, and cast this leg into some ditch or other. [*Aside, and then runs out.*]

FAUSTUS: Stop him, stop him, stop him!—ha, ha, ha, Faustus hath his leg again, and the horse-courser a bundle of hay for his forty dollars.

[99] **HORSE-COURSER:** Horse trader. [100] **in conceit:** In his thoughts. [101] **bottle:** Bundle.

[*Enter* WAGNER.]

How now, Wagner, what news with thee?

WAGNER: If it please you, the Duke of Anholt doth earnestly entreat your company, and hath sent some of his men to attend you with provision fit for your journey.

FAUSTUS: The Duke of Anholt's an honourable gentleman, and one to whom I must be no niggard of my cunning. Come away!

[*Exeunt.*]

Scene 6

An Inn.

[*Enter* ROBIN, DICK, *the* HORSE-COURSER, *and a* CARTER.]

CARTER: Come, my masters, I'll bring you to the best beer in Europe. What ho, hostess! — where be these whores?

[*Enter* HOSTESS.]

HOSTESS: How now, what lack you? What, my old guests, welcome.

ROBIN: Sirra Dick, dost thou know why I stand so mute?

DICK: No, Robin, why is't?

ROBIN: I am eighteenpence on the score,[102] but say nothing, see if she have forgotten me.

HOSTESS: Who's this, that stands so solemnly by himself? what, my old guest?

ROBIN: O hostess, how do you? I hope my score stands still.

HOSTESS: Ay, there's no doubt of that, for methinks you make no haste to wipe it out.

DICK: Why, hostess, I say, fetch us some beer.

HOSTESS: You shall presently: look up in th' hall there, ho!

[*Exit.*]

DICK: Come, sirs, what shall we do now till mine hostess comes?

CARTER: Marry, sir, I'll tell you the bravest tale how a conjuror served me; you know Doctor Fauster?

HORSE-COURSER: Ay, a plague take him, here's some on's have cause to know him; did he conjure thee too?

CARTER: I'll tell you how he serv'd me: As I was going to Wittenberg t'other day, with a load of hay, he met me, and asked me what he should give me for as much hay as he could eat; now, sir, I thinking that a little would serve his turn, bade him take as much as he would for three farthings; so he presently gave me my money, and fell to eating; and, as I am a cursen man,[103] he never left eating, till he had eat up all my load of hay.

ALL: O monstrous, eat a whole load of hay!

ROBIN: Yes, yes, that may be; for I have heard of one that has eat a load of logs.[104]

HORSE-COURSER: Now sirs, you shall hear how villainously he serv'd me: I went to him yesterday to buy a horse of him, and he would by no means sell him under forty dollars; so, sir, because I knew him to be such a horse as would run over

---

[102] **score:** Account. [103] **cursen man:** A christen man — that is, a Christian. [104] **eat . . . logs:** Been drunk.

hedge and ditch and never tire, I gave him his money. So when I had my horse, Doctor Fauster bade me ride him night and day, and spare him no time; but, quoth he, in any case, ride him not into the water. Now, sir, I thinking the horse had had some rare quality that he would not have me know of, what did I but rid him into a great river, and when I came just in the midst, my horse vanish'd away, and I sat straddling upon a bottle of hay.

ALL: O brave Doctor!

HORSE-COURSER: But you shall hear how bravely I serv'd him for it; I went me home to his house, and there I found him asleep; I kept a hallooing and whooping in his ears, but all could not wake him: I seeing that, took him by the leg, and never rested pulling, till I had pull'd me his leg quite off, and now 'tis at home in mine hostry.

DICK: And has the Doctor but one leg then? that's excellent, for one of his devils turn'd me into the likeness of an ape's face.

CARTER: Some more drink, hostess.

ROBIN: Hark you, we'll into another room and drink a while, and then we'll go seek out the Doctor.

[*Exeunt omnes.*]

Scene 7

The Court of the DUKE OF ANHOLT.

[*Enter the* DUKE OF ANHOLT, *his* DUCHESS, FAUSTUS, *and* MEPHISTOPHILIS.]

DUKE: Thanks, master Doctor, for these pleasant sights. Nor know I how sufficiently to recompense your great deserts in erecting that enchanted castle in the air, the sight whereof so delighted me,
As nothing in the world could please me more.

FAUSTUS: I do think myself, my good Lord, highly recompensed in that it pleaseth your Grace to think but well of that which Faustus hath performed. But gracious lady, it may be that you have taken no pleasure in those sights; therefore, I pray you tell me, what is the thing you most desire to have; be it in the world, it shall be yours. I have heard that great-bellied women do long for things are rare and dainty.

DUCHESS: True, master Doctor, and since I find you so kind, I will make known unto you what my heart desires to have; and were it now summer, as it is January, a dead time of the winter, I would request no better meat than a dish of ripe grapes.

FAUSTUS: This is but a small matter. Go, Mephistophilis, away!

[*Exit* MEPHISTOPHILIS.]

Madam, I will do more than this for your content.

[*Enter* MEPHISTOPHILIS *again with the grapes.*]

Here now taste ye these, they should be good,
For they come from a far country, I can tell you.

DUKE:

This makes me wonder more than all the rest
That at this time of the year, when every tree

Is barren of his fruit, from whence you had
These ripe grapes.

FAUSTUS: Please it your Grace the year is divided into two circles over the whole world, so that when it is winter with us, in the contrary circle it is likewise summer with them, as in India, Saba[105] and such countries that lie far east, where they have fruit twice a year. From whence, by means of a swift spirit that I have, I had these grapes brought, as you see.

DUCHESS: And trust me, they are the sweetest grapes that e'er I tasted.

[*The* CLOWNS *bounce*[106] *at the gate within.*]

DUKE:
What rude disturbers have we at the gate?
Go, pacify their fury, set it ope,
And then demand of them what they would have.

[*They knock again, and call out to talk with* FAUSTUS.]

A SERVANT:
Why, how now, masters, what a coil[107] is there?
What is the reason you disturb the Duke?

DICK: We have no reason for it, therefore a fig[108] for him.

SERVANT: Why, saucy varlets, dare you be so bold?

HORSE-COURSER: I hope, sir, we have wit enough to be more bold than welcome.

SERVANT: It appears so, pray be bold elsewhere, and trouble not the Duke.

DUKE: What would they have?

SERVANT: They all cry out to speak with Doctor Faustus.

CARTER: Ay, and we will speak with him.

DUKE: Will you, sir? Commit[109] the rascals.

DICK: Commit with us! he were as good commit with his father as commit with us.

FAUSTUS:
I do beseech your Grace let them come in,
They are good subject for a merriment.

DUKE:
Do as thou wilt, Faustus, I give thee leave.

FAUSTUS:
I thank your Grace.

[*Enter* ROBIN, DICK, CARTER, *and* HORSE-COURSER.]

Why, how now, my good friends?
Faith you are too outrageous, but come near,
'I have procur'd your pardons: welcome all.

ROBIN: Nay, sir, we will be welcome for our money, and we will pay for what we take. What ho, give's half a dozen of beer here, and be hang'd.

FAUSTUS: Nay, hark you, can you tell me where you are?

---

[105] **Saba:** The Queen of Sheba's land. [106] ***bounce:*** Bang. [107] **coil:** Disturbance. [108] **fig:** Obscene gesture.
[109] **Commit:** Take to prison, but with a pun suggesting "have intercourse with."

CARTER: Ay, marry can I; we are under heaven.

SERVANT: Ay, but, sir sauce-box, know you in what place?

HORSE-COURSER: Ay, ay, the house is good enough to drink in: Zounds, fill us some beer, or we'll break all the barrels in the house, and dash out all your brains with your bottles.

FAUSTUS:

Be not so furious: come, you shall have beer.
My lord, beseech you give me leave a while,
I'll gage my credit 'twill content your Grace.

DUKE:

With all my heart, kind Doctor, please thyself;
Our servants and our Court's at thy command.

FAUSTUS:

I humbly thank your Grace: then fetch some beer.

HORSE-COURSER: Ay, marry, there spake a Doctor indeed, and, 'faith, I'll drink a health to thy wooden leg for that word.

FAUSTUS: My wooden leg! what dost thou mean by that?

CARTER: Ha, ha, ha, dost hear him, Dick? He has forgot his leg.

HORSE-COURSER: Ay, ay, he does not stand much upon that.

FAUSTUS: No, 'faith not much upon a wooden leg.

CARTER: Good Lord, that flesh and blood should be so frail with your Worship. Do not you remember a horse-courser you sold a horse to?

FAUSTUS: Yes, I remember I sold one a horse.

CARTER: And do you remember you bid he should not ride him onto the water?

FAUSTUS: Yes, I do very well remember that.

CARTER: And do you remember nothing of your leg?

FAUSTUS: No, in good sooth.

CARTER: Then, I pray, remember your curtsy.

FAUSTUS: I thank you, sir.

CARTER: 'Tis not so much worth; I pray you tell me one thing.

FAUSTUS: What's that?

CARTER: Be both your legs bedfellows every night together?

FAUSTUS: Wouldst thou make a Colossus of me, that thou askest me such questions?

CARTER: No, truly, sir: I would make nothing of you, but I would fain know that.

[*Enter* HOSTESS *with drink.*]

FAUSTUS: Then I assure thee certainly they are.

CARTER: I thank you, I am fully satisfied.

FAUSTUS: But wherefore dost thou ask?

CARTER: For nothing, sir: but methinks you should have a wooden bedfellow of one of 'em.

HORSE-COURSER: Why, do you hear, sir, did not I pull off one of your legs when you were asleep?

FAUSTUS: But I have it again, now I am awake: look you here, sir.

ALL: O horrible, had the Doctor three legs?

CARTER: Do you remember, sir, how you cozened me and ate up my load of—

[FAUSTUS *charms him dumb.*]

DICK: Do you remember how you made me wear an ape's—

HORSE-COURSER: You whoreson conjuring scab, do you remember how you cozened me with a ho—

ROBIN: Ha' you forgotten me? you think to carry it away with your *hey-pass* and *re-pass*,[110] do you remember the dog's fa—

[*Exeunt* CLOWNS.]

HOSTESS: Who pays for the ale? hear you, Master Doctor, now you have sent away my guests, I pray who shall pay me for my a—

[*Exit* HOSTESS.]

LADY:

My Lord,
We are much beholding to this learned man.

DUKE:

So are we, Madam, which we will recompense
With all the love and kindness that we may.
His artful sport drives all sad thoughts away.

[*Exeunt.*]

ACT V

Scene 1

Thunder and lightning.

[*Enter* DEVILS *with cover'd dishes.* MEPHISTOPHILIS *leads them into Faustus' study. Then enter* WAGNER.]

WAGNER:

I think my master means to die shortly,
He has made his will, and given me his wealth,
His house, his goods, and store of golden plate,
Besides two thousand ducats ready coin'd.
I wonder what he means; if death were nigh
He would not frolic thus. He's now at supper
With the scholars, where there's such belly-cheer
As Wagner in his life ne'er saw the like.
And see where they come, belike the feast is done.

[*Exit.*]

[*Enter* FAUSTUS, MEPHISTOPHILIS, *and two or three* SCHOLARS.]

FIRST SCHOLAR: Master Doctor Faustus, since our conference about fair ladies, which was the beautifullest in all the world, we have determined with ourselves that Helen of Greece was the admirablest lady that ever liv'd: therefore, Master Doctor, if you will do us so much favour, as to let us see that peerless dame of Greece, we should think ourselves much beholding unto you.

[110] ***hey-pass, re-pass:*** Expressions used by a conjurer.

FAUSTUS:

Gentlemen,
For that I know your friendship is unfeign'd,
It is not Faustus' custom to deny
The just request of those that wish him well,
You shall behold that peerless dame of Greece,
No otherwise for pomp or majesty
Than when Sir Paris cross'd the seas with her,
And brought the spoil to rich Dardania.[111]
Be silent, then, for danger is in words.

[*Music sounds,* MEPHISTOPHILIS *brings in* HELEN, *she passeth over the stage.*]

SECOND SCHOLAR:

Was this fair Helen, whose admired worth
Made Greece with ten years' wars afflict poor Troy?
Too simple is my wit to tell her praise,
Whom all the world admires for majesty.

THIRD SCHOLAR:

No marvel though the angry Greeks pursued
With ten years' war the rape of such a queen,
Whose heavenly beauty passeth all compare.

FIRST SCHOLAR:

Now we have seen the pride of Nature's work,
And only paragon of excellence,
We'll take our leaves; and for this glorious deed
Happy and blest be Faustus evermore!

FAUSTUS:

Gentlemen, farewell: the same wish I to you.

[*Exeunt* SCHOLARS.]

[*Enter an* OLD MAN.]

OLD MAN:

O gentle Faustus, leave this damned art,
This magic, that will charm thy soul to hell,
And quite bereave° thee of salvation. deprive
Though thou hast now offended like a man,
Do not persever in it like a devil;
Yet, yet, thou hast an amiable soul,
If sin by custom grow not into nature:
Then, Faustus, will repentance come too late,
Then thou art banish'd from the sight of heaven;
No mortal can express the pains of hell.
It may be this my exhortation

[111] **Dardania:** Troy.

Seems harsh and all unpleasant; let it not,
For, gentle son, I speak it not in wrath,
Or envy of thee, but in tender love,
And pity of thy future misery.
And so have hope, that this my kind rebuke,
Checking thy body, may amend thy soul.

FAUSTUS:

Break heart, drop blood, and mingle it with tears,
Tears falling from repentant heaviness
Of thy most vile and loathsome filthiness,
The stench whereof corrupts the inward soul
With such flagitious crimes of heinous sins
As no commiseration may expel,
But mercy, Faustus, of thy Saviour sweet,
Whose blood alone must wash away thy guilt—
Where art thou, Faustus? wretch, what has thou done?
Damn'd art thou, Faustus, damn'd; despair and die!

[MEPHISTOPHILIS *gives him a dagger.*]

Hell claims his right, and with a roaring voice
Says, "Faustus, come; thine hour is almost come";
And Faustus now will come to do thee right.

OLD MAN:

Oh, stay, good Faustus, stay thy desperate steps!
I see an angel hover o'er thy head,
And, with a vial full of precious grace,
Offers to pour the same into thy soul:
Then call for mercy, and avoid despair.

FAUSTUS:

O friend, I feel
Thy words to comfort my distressed soul!
Leave me a while to ponder on my sins.

OLD MAN:

Faustus, I leave thee; but with grief of heart,
Fearing the enemy of thy hapless soul.

[*Exit.*]

FAUSTUS:

Accursed Faustus, where is mercy now?
I do repent; and yet I do despair:
Hell strives with grace for conquest in my breast:
What shall I do to shun the snares of death?

MEPHISTOPHILIS:

Thou traitor, Faustus, I arrest thy soul
For disobedience to my sovereign lord:
Revolt, or I'll in piecemeal tear thy flesh.

FAUSTUS:

I do repent I e'er offended him.
Sweet Mephistophilis, entreat thy lord
To pardon my unjust presumption,
And with my blood again I will confirm
The former vow I made to Lucifer.

MEPHISTOPHILIS:

Do it, then, Faustus with unfeigned heart,
Lest greater dangers do attend thy drift.

[FAUSTUS *stabs his arm, and writes on a paper with his blood.*]

FAUSTUS:

Torment, sweet friend, that base and aged man
That durst dissuade me from thy Lucifer,
With greatest torments that our hell affords.

MEPHISTOPHILIS:

His faith is great; I cannot touch his soul;
But what I may afflict his body with
I will attempt, which is but little worth.

FAUSTUS:

One thing, good servant, let me crave of thee,
To glut the longing of my heart's desire,—
That I may have unto my paramour
That heavenly Helen which I saw of late,
Whose sweet embraces may extinguish clean
Those thoughts that do dissuade me from my vow,
And keep my oath I made to Lucifer.

MEPHISTOPHILIS:

This, or what else, my Faustus shall desire,
Shall be perform'd in twinkling of an eye.

[*Enter* HELEN *again, passing over the stage between two* CUPIDS.]

FAUSTUS:

Was this the face that launch'd a thousand ships,
And burnt the topless towers of Ilium?—
Sweet Helen, make me immortal with a kiss.—[*She kisses him.*]
Her lips suck forth my soul: see where it flies!—
Come, Helen, come, give me my soul again.
Here will I dwell, for heaven is in these lips
And all is dross that is not Helena. [*Enter* OLD MAN.]
I will be Paris, and for love of thee,
Instead of Troy, shall Wittenberg be sack'd;
And I will combat with weak Menelaus,
And wear thy colours on my plumed crest:
Yea, I will wound Achilles in the heel,
And then return to Helen for a kiss.

O, thou art fairer than the evening's air
Clad in the beauty of a thousand stars;
Brighter art thou than flaming Jupiter
When he appear'd to hapless Semele;
More lovely than the monarch of the sky
In wanton Arethusa's[112] azured arms;
And none but thou shalt be my paramour!

[*Exeunt* FAUSTUS, HELEN, *and* CUPIDS.]

OLD MAN:

Accursed Faustus, miserable man,
That from thy soul exclud'st the grace of Heaven,
And fliest the throne of his tribunal-seat!

[*Enter the* DEVILS.]

Satan begins to sift° me with his pride: test
As in this furnace God shall try my faith,
My faith, vile hell, shall triumph over thee.
Ambitious fiends, see how the heavens smiles
At your repulse, and laughs your state to scorn!
Hence, hell! for hence I fly unto my God.

[*Exeunt.*]

Scene 2

FAUSTUS' *Study. Thunder.*

[*Enter above* LUCIFER, BELZEBUB, *and* MEPHISTOPHILIS.]

LUCIFER:

Thus from infernal Dis do we ascend
To view the subjects of our monarchy,
Those souls which sin seals the black sons of hell,
'Mong which as chief, Faustus, we come to thee,
Bringing with us lasting damnation
To wait upon thy soul; the time is come
Which makes it forfeit.

MEPHISTOPHILIS:

And this gloomy night,
Here in this room will wretched Faustus be.

BELZEBUB:

And here we'll stay,
To mark him how he doth demean himself.

MEPHISTOPHILIS:

How should he, but in desperate lunacy?
Fond worldling, now his heart-blood dries with grief,

[112] **Arethusa:** A nymph of a fountain.

His conscience kills it and his labouring brain
Begets a world of idle fantasies,
To overreach the Devil; but all in vain,
His store of pleasures must be sauc'd with pain.
He and his servant, Wagner, are at hand.
Both come from drawing Faustus' latest will.
See where they come!

[*Enter* FAUSTUS *and* WAGNER.]

FAUSTUS:

Say, Wagner, thou hast perus'd my will,
How dost thou like it?

WAGNER:

Sir, so wondrous well,
As in all humble duty, I do yield
My life and lasting service for your love.

[*Enter the* SCHOLARS.]

FAUSTUS: Gramercies, Wagner. Welcome, gentlemen.

[*Exit* WAGNER.]

FIRST SCHOLAR: Now, worthy Faustus, methinks your looks are changed.

FAUSTUS: O, gentlemen!

SECOND SCHOLAR: What ails Faustus?

FAUSTUS: Ah, my sweet chamber-fellow,[113] had I liv'd with thee, then had I lived still! but now must die eternally. Look, sirs, comes he not? comes he not?

FIRST SCHOLAR: O my dear Faustus, what imports this fear?

SECOND SCHOLAR: Is all our pleasure turn'd to melancholy?

THIRD SCHOLAR: He is not well with being over-solitary.

SECOND SCHOLAR:

If it be so, we'll have physicians
And Faustus shall be cur'd.

THIRD SCHOLAR: 'Tis but a surfeit,[114] sir; fear nothing.

FAUSTUS: A surfeit of deadly sin, that hath damn'd both body and soul.

SECOND SCHOLAR: Yet, Faustus, look up to heaven; remember God's mercies are infinite.

FAUSTUS: But Faustus' offence can ne'er be pardoned: the serpent that tempted Eve may be saved, but not Faustus. O, gentlemen, hear me with patience, and tremble not at my speeches! Though my heart pant and quiver to remember that I have been a student here these thirty years, O, would I had never seen Wittenberg, never read book! and what wonders I have done, all Germany can witness, yea, all the world; for which Faustus hath lost both Germany and the world; yea, heaven itself, heaven, the seat of God, the throne of the blessed, the kingdom of joy; and must remain in hell for ever—hell, oh, hell for ever! Sweet friends, what shall become of Faustus, being in hell for ever?

---

[113] **chamber-fellow:** Roommate. [114] **surfeit:** Indigestion.

SECOND SCHOLAR: Yet, Faustus, call on God.

FAUSTUS: On God, whom Faustus hath abjur'd! on God, whom Faustus hath blasphem'd! Oh, my God, I would weep! but the devil draws in my tears. Gush forth blood, instead of tears! yea, life and soul—Oh, he stays my tongue! I would lift up my hands; but see, they hold 'em, they hold 'em!

ALL: Who, Faustus?

FAUSTUS: Why, Lucifer and Mephistophilis. O, gentlemen, I gave them my soul for my cunning!

ALL: Oh, God forbid!

FAUSTUS: God forbade it, indeed; but Faustus hath done it: for the vain pleasure of four and twenty years hath Faustus lost eternal joy and felicity. I writ them a bill with mine own blood: the date is expired; this is the time, and he will fetch me.

FIRST SCHOLAR: Why did not Faustus tell us of this before, that divines might have pray'd for thee?

FAUSTUS: Oft have I thought to have done so; but the devil threaten'd to tear me in pieces, if I nam'd God; to fetch me, body and soul, if I once gave ear to divinity: and now 'tis too late. Gentlemen, away, lest you perish with me.

SECOND SCHOLAR: O, what may we do to save Faustus?

FAUSTUS: Talk not of me, but save yourselves, and depart.

THIRD SCHOLAR: God will strengthen me; I will stay with Faustus.

FIRST SCHOLAR: Tempt not God, sweet friend; but let us into the next room, and pray for him.

FAUSTUS: Ay, pray for me, pray for me; and what noise soever you hear, come not unto me, for nothing can rescue me.

SECOND SCHOLAR: Pray thou, and we will pray that God may have mercy upon thee.

FAUSTUS: Gentlemen, farewell: if I live till morning, I'll visit you; if not, Faustus is gone to hell.

ALL: Faustus, farewell.

[*Exeunt* SCHOLARS.]

MEPHISTOPHILIS [*above*]:

Ay, Faustus, now thou hast no hope of heaven;
Therefore despair, think only upon hell,
For that must be thy mansion, there to dwell.

FAUSTUS:

O thou bewitching fiend, 'twas thy temptation
Hath robb'd me of eternal happiness.

MEPHISTOPHILIS:

I do confess it, Faustus, and rejoice;
'Twas I, that when thou wert i' the way to heaven,
Damm'd up thy passage; when thou took'st the book,
To view the Scriptures, then I turn'd the leaves,
And led thine eye.—
What, weep'st thou? 'tis too late, despair, farewell!
Fool that will laugh on earth, must weep in hell.

[*Exeunt* LUCIFER, BELZEBUB, MEPHISTOPHILIS.]

[*Enter the* GOOD ANGEL *and the* BAD ANGEL *at several doors.*]

GOOD ANGEL:

Oh, Faustus, if thou hadst given ear to me,
Innumerable joys had followed thee.
But thou didst love the world.

BAD ANGEL:

Gave ear to me,
And now must taste hell's pains perpetually.

GOOD ANGEL:

O what will all thy riches, pleasures, pomps,
Avail thee now?

BAD ANGEL:

Nothing but vex thee more,
To want in hell, that had on earth such store.

[*Music while the throne descends.*[115]]

GOOD ANGEL:

O thou hast lost celestial happiness,
Pleasures unspeakable, bliss without end.
Hadst thou affected° sweet divinity, — devoted yourself to
Hell, or the devil, had had no power on thee.
Hadst thou kept on that way, Faustus, behold,
In what resplendent glory thou hadst sit
In yonder throne, like those bright shining saints,
And triumph'd over hell: that hast thou lost:
And now, poor soul, must thy good angel leave thee,

[*The throne ascends.*]

The jaws of hell are open to receive thee.

[*Exit.*]

[*Hell is discovered.*[116]]

BAD ANGEL:

Now, Faustus, let thine eyes with horror stare
Into that vast perpetual torture-house.
There are the Furies tossing damned souls
On burning forks; their bodies boil in lead:
There are live quarters° broiling on the coals, — bodies
That ne'er can die: this ever-burning chair
Is for o'er-tortured souls to rest them in;
These that are fed with sops of flaming fire,
Were gluttons and lov'd only delicates,
And laugh'd to see the poor starve at their gates:

[115] ***throne descends:*** The throne of authority descends from the "heavens" by ropes.

[116] ***Hell is discovered:*** A curtain is drawn to reveal a scene in hell.

But yet all these are nothing; thou shalt see
Ten thousand tortures that more horrid be.

FAUSTUS:

O, I have seen enough to torture me.

BAD ANGEL:

Nay, thou must feel them, taste the smart of all:
He that loves pleasure, must for pleasure fall:
And so I leave thee, Faustus, till anon;
Then wilt thou tumble in confusion.

[*Exit.*]

[*Hell disappears.*]
[*The clock strikes eleven.*]

FAUSTUS:

Ah, Faustus,
Now hast thou but one bare hour to live,
And then thou must be damn'd perpetually!
Stand still, you ever moving spheres of heaven,
That time may cease, and midnight never come;
Fair Nature's eye, rise, rise again, and make
Perpetual day; or let this hour be but
A year, a month, a week, a natural day,
That Faustus may repent and save his soul!
O lente, lente currite, noctis equi![117]
The stars move still, time runs, the clock will strike,
The devil will come, and Faustus must be damn'd.
O, I'll leap up to my God!—Who pulls me down?—
See, see, where Christ's blood streams in the firmament!
One drop would save my soul, half a drop: ah, my Christ!—
Ah, rend not my heart for naming of my Christ!
Yet will I call on him: O, spare me, Lucifer!—
Where is it now? 'tis gone: and see, where God
Stretcheth out his arm, and bends his ireful brows!
Mountains and hills, come, come, and fall on me,
And hide me from the heavy wrath of God!
No, no!
Then will I headlong run into the earth:
Earth, gape! O, no, it will not harbour me!
You stars that reign'd at my nativity,
Whose influence hath allotted death and hell,
Now draw up Faustus, like a foggy mist,
Into the entrails of yon lab'ring cloud
That, when you vomit forth into the air,

[117] ***O . . . equi!:*** O slowly slowly run, horses of the night! The line is from Ovid's *Amores.*

My limbs may issue from your smoky mouths,
So that my soul may but ascend into heaven!

[*The clock strikes.*]

Ah, half the hour is past! 'twill all be passed anon.
O God,
If thou wilt not have mercy on my soul,
Yet for Christ's sake, whose blood hath ransom'd me,
Impose some end to my incessant pain;
Let Faustus live in hell a thousand years,
A hundred thousand, and at last be sav'd!
O, no end is limited to damned souls!
Why wert thou not a creature wanting soul?
Or why is this immortal that thou hast?
Ah, Pythagoras' *metempsychosis,*[118] were that true,
This soul should fly from me, and I be changed
Unto some brutish beast! all beasts are happy,
For, when they die,
Their souls are soon dissolved in elements;
But mine must live still to be plagu'd in hell.
Curs'd be the parents that engender'd me!
No, Faustus, curse thyself, curse Lucifer
That hath depriv'd thee of the joys of heaven.

[*The clock striketh twelve.*]

O, it strikes, it strikes! Now, body, turn to air,
Or Lucifer will bear thee quick° to hell! alive
O soul, be changed into little water drops,
And fall into the ocean, ne'er be found!

[*Thunder and enter the* DEVILS.]

My God, my God, look not so fierce on me!
Adders and serpents, let me breathe a while!
Ugly hell, gape not! come not, Lucifer!
I'll burn my books!—Ah, Mephistophilis!

[*Exeunt with him.*]

Scene 3

A room next to FAUSTUS' *study.*

[*Enter the* SCHOLARS.]

FIRST SCHOLAR:

Come, gentlemen, let us go visit Faustus,
For such a dreadful night was never seen,

[118] ***metempsychosis:*** Pythagorus's doctrine of the transmigration of souls (sixth century B.C.E.) appealed to Marlowe's audience.

Since first the world's creation did begin.
Such fearful shrieks and cries were never heard:
Pray heaven the Doctor have escap'd the danger.

SECOND SCHOLAR:
O help us heaven! see, here are Faustus' limbs,
All torn asunder by the hand of death.

THIRD SCHOLAR:
The devils whom Faustus serv'd have torn him thus:
For 'twixt the hours of twelve and one, methought
I heard him shriek and call aloud for help:
At which self° time the house seem'd all on fire, same
With dreadful horror of these damned fiends.

SECOND SCHOLAR:
Well, gentlemen, though Faustus' end be such
As every Christian heart laments to think on,
Yet for he was a scholar, once admired
For wondrous knowledge in our German schools,
We'll give his mangled limbs due burial;
And all the students, clothed in mourning black,
Shall wait upon his heavy° funeral. sorrowful

[*Exeunt.*]

Epilogue

[*Enter* CHORUS.]

CHORUS:
Cut is the branch that might have grown full straight,
And burned is Apollo's laurel bough,[119]
That sometime grew within this learned man.
Faustus is gone: regard his hellish fall,
Whose fiendful fortune may exhort the wise,
Only to wonder at unlawful things,
Whose deepness doth entice such forward wits
To practise more than heavenly power permits.

[*Exit.*]

Terminat hora diem; terminat Author opus.[120]

---

[119] **Apollo's laurel bough:** A symbol of victory and accomplishment linked to Apollo, the god of oracles and divination.

[120] ***Terminat . . . opus:*** The hour ends the day, the author finishes his work.

Humanism, Learning, and Education

Marlowe's *Doctor Faustus* dramatizes the divide between the Medieval worldview, with its eye upon God and salvation in the afterlife, and the new orientation of the European Renaissance, with its emphasis upon humanism and the worldly opportunities of the present. Although Doctor Faustus ultimately is damned for trading his soul for knowledge and power, which he lacks the wisdom to use responsibly, his ambition and insatiable desire to master all the fields of learning affiliate him with the **Renaissance man**—a person who has mastered the liberal arts and sciences and whose thirst for knowledge is unquenchable. Beginning with the golden age of Islamic arts and sciences in the early Abbasid empire, and then in China, India, and Europe, a powerful and vital love of learning and spirit of humanism, albeit in various forms, rose up in many places throughout the world. In China, this phenomenon was associated with the rise of new interpretations of **Confucianism** in the late Song dynasty (960–1279); in Europe, it was known as humanism, a revival of the Latin and Greek classics of philosophy, poetry, rhetoric, and history, that swept northward from Italy in the fourteenth and fifteenth centuries; and in India, it was connected to the enlightened rule of Akbar (r. 1556–1605), who sanctioned greater religious tolerance and promoted philosophical and religious debate in his court.

IBN SINA AND THE GOLDEN AGE OF THE ABBASID EMPIRE

The European Renaissance was partly indebted to the Islamic world's preservation of Greek and Latin works in great libraries as well as to the presence of Arabic treatises on mathematics, medicine, and astronomy dating from the eighth century. Even before the advent of the Ottoman empire in 1280 under Osman I (r. 1281–1326), the Islamic world was a major center for the development of the arts and sciences. The early part of the Abbasid dynasty (750–1258) is identified with the golden age of Islamic arts and sciences. Under the Abbasids, a succession of caliphs who claimed descent from Abbas, the uncle of Muhammad, a center for higher education known as the House of Wisdom (Bayt al Hikma) was founded at Baghdad in the ninth century and soon housed one of the great libraries of the world. The House of Wisdom produced translations of works from Greece, Persia, India, and elsewhere. From other such centers—in Cairo, Constantinople (part of the Byzantine empire at this time), and Toledo, in Islamic Spain—came the Greek and Latin works that stimulated the revival of classical learning in Europe in the fourteenth and fifteenth centuries. Moreover, the works of Arabic astronomers and mathematicians, such as Muhammad ibn Musa al-Khwarizmi (780–850), would later influence European astronomers such as Copernicus and Galileo. Islamic students of chemistry and pharmacy advanced the world's understanding of those sciences and led to the founding of the first institute for the study of pharmacy and the licensing of medical practitioners. A further contribution to the intellectual atmosphere of the European Renaissance came from the refinement of papermaking, which Islamic craftsmen had learned from the Chinese after the Talas River Battle of 751.

Let us struggle toward the heavenly . . . and let us fly beyond the chambers of the world to the chamber nearest the most lofty divinity.

– Pico della Mirandola

Among the greatest of the learned men of the Abbasid golden age was Abu Ali al-Husein Ibn Sina (980–1037), known in the West as Avicenna. A master of many sciences, including astronomy, chemistry, medicine, and botany, as well as a student of philosophy, literature, and the arts, Ibn Sina wrote medical treatises that became well known in Europe where they were used up until the eighteenth century. In his philosophical works, Ibn Sina sought to synthesize Islamic religion with Greek philosophy. Other important philosophers of his era, which is sometimes called the Golden Age of Islamic Science, include the great scientist, astronomer, and philosopher Abu Raihan al-Biruni (973–1048), the medical doctor Abul Qasim Al-Zahrawi (936–1013), and the philosopher and scholar Abu Hamid al-Ghazali (1058–1128). Although Ibn Sina's work predates the Early Modern Period, he is included in this section because his

Grammatica.
Dialectica
The seaven liberall sciences:
Grammatica, teacheth men to speake aptlye, and to make congruetye of speach, in all langueges, and to ioyne perfect sentences to geather:
Dialectica. teacheth men to reason and dispute, and by arguments to prove, the truthe, from falsehode, whose rules being observed, they doo shewe an order to all other arts:
Rhetorica
Arithmetria
i·2·3·
4·5·6
7·8·9·
10:20
100·
1000
10000
Rhetorice teacheth men to delate, and
Arithmaticke teacheth men to num-

love of learning and respect for the classics of Greece and the Arabic world anticipate, influence, and demonstrate an affinity with the humanistic orientation of the writers included here from other countries, including China, where in the twelfth century a small revolution was taking place in Confucian thinking.

NEO-CONFUCIANISM IN CHINA

The humanistic tendencies of China and Japan in the Early Modern Period did not derive from the Greek and Latin classics, but from the Chinese classics, particularly the writings of the great philosopher Confucius (Kongfuzi; 551–479 B.C.E.). Emphasizing duty to the family and state, self-discipline, and reverence for tradition, Confucian thought oriented its followers toward a study of the ancient masters and toward a focus on ethics in a way that roughly parallels the civic humanism of Leonardo Bruni, who in his own time and place had redirected the study of classical literature and history toward the active life of politics and civil society. As an exemplary figure, Confucius himself, often called "the first teacher," articulates a love of learning strikingly similar to that of some of the European and Arabic scholars and writers excerpted here: "At fifteen I wanted to learn. At thirty I had a foundation. At forty, a certitude. At fifty, knew the orders of heaven. At sixty, was ready to listen to them. At seventy, could follow my own heart's desire without overstepping the law" (*Analects* II.iv). Despite these resemblances, it is important to keep in mind that while the European humanists distinguished clearly between the secularism of the Greco-Roman classics and the spirituality of the Judeo-Christian scriptures, the writings of Confucius, despite their emphasis upon this world, had both philosophical and religious significance. They outlined ritual practices and ceremonies for spiritual as well as for moral and ethical development.

While Confucianism had grown into an official doctrine in China during the Qin and Han dynasties (221 B.C.E. to 220 C.E.), from the end of the Han through the Tang dynasty (618–907 C.E.) it lost some of its status in the face of a revival of Taoism and the rise

◀ **Page from *The Commonplace Book*, 1608**

The humanist tradition emphasizes the Greco-Roman ideals of art, literature, and society and celebrates human potential in the here and now. (Courtesy of the Folger Shakespeare Library)

I am still learning.
– MICHELANGELO, his *favorite saying* (1475–1564)

of Buddhism in China. The popularity of Buddhism in particular led Confucian scholars in the late Song dynasty (960–1279) to launch a studied and aggressive defense of Confucian ideas. One of the greatest of these defenders was the scholar Zhu Xi (Chu Hsi; 1130–1200), the founder of what is called neo-Confucianism. Like St. Thomas Aquinas, who reconciled Aristotle with Christian theology, or Marsilio Ficino, who did the same with Platonism, Zhu Xi reconciled Confucianism with Buddhism. He threw himself into the study of the classics of his tradition, wrote commentaries on them, and restructured the canon. Zhu Xi's revision of the canon of Confucian texts profoundly influenced the education of Chinese and Japanese scholars, officials, and intellectuals for many generations. It was Zhu Xi who selected what are called the Four Books — The Analects, The Mencius, The Great Learning, and The Doctrine of the Mean — which would become not only the foundation of the civil service examinations in China but also the focus of study for Japanese neo-Confucians, such as Nakae Toju (1608–1648) and Yamazaki Ansai (1618–1682), who helped to introduce Zhu Xi's ideas into Japan. Zhu Xi emphasized the cultivation of the individual mind by means of the critical, not deferential, study of the masters; devotion to social order; and an application of the principles derived from study and thought to social and political life. Zhu Xi's ardent study and revisionary interpretations of the classics point to a love of learning comparable to that of his Arabic and European counterparts.

HUMANISM IN EUROPE

In contrast to Dr. Faustus, whose learning was rooted in the philosophy of the Greek philosopher Aristotle, in biblical scholarship, and in alchemy, the Humanists of the Renaissance were men and women devoted to the Greco-Roman ideals of literature, art, and society. They turned from Aristotle to Plato and from the contemplation of theological mysteries to the celebration of human potential in the here and now. As its name suggests, humanism shifted the focus of philosophy, art, and literature from God to "man." In the words of Giovanni Pico della Mirandola (1463–1494), man is "a great marvel and the animal really worthy of wonder." Among the first Europeans to capture the new spirit of humanism and to ardently pursue the Latin classics was the Florentine poet and scholar Francesco Petrarch (1304–1474). Along with his protegé and companion Giovanni Boccaccio (1313–1375), Petrarch led the movement to revive classical Latin, which he used for his prose as well as for many of his poems.

While Latin language and literature fueled the imaginations of early humanists, the advent of the study of classical Greek stimulated a new wave of inquiry in the late fourteenth century. It was not until the Greek scholar and diplomat Manuel Chrysoloras (c. 1350–1415) arrived from Constantinople, then the major center in the world for Greek studies and a major repository for Greek manuscripts, that the study of Greek began to flourish in Europe. One of Chrysoloras's students, Leonardo Bruni (1370–1444), the founder of "civic humanism," was one of the leading figures in the translation of Greek, especially the works of Plato. While Petrarch advocated a quiet life of scholarly retirement and study, Bruni sought to bring the study of the classics to bear on the active life of the scholar-soldier-statesman. Though his place among the humanists has been debated, Niccolò Machiavelli (1469–1527), whose love for the classics is well demonstrated in the letter to Francesco Vettori excerpted below, squarely follows from Bruni's efforts to draw exemplary lessons from the Greco-Roman past and apply them to contemporary civil and political situations.

Under the Medici leader Lorenzo the Magnificent (1449–1492), Florence became one of the key centers outside of Byzantium for the translation of both Greek and Latin texts. The Council of Greek and Latin Churches, which Lorenzo sponsored in 1439, brought businessmen as well as scholars from Constantinople, and he commissioned one of the greatest of the humanist scholars, Marsilio Ficino (1433–1499), to translate the complete works of Plato into Latin. In his own writing, Ficino attempted to reconcile the apparently divergent traditions of Christianity and Platonism, just as Ibn Sina four centuries earlier had attempted to reconcile Platonist ideas with the revelations of Islam. One of Ficino's students, Giovanni Pico della Mirandola took Ficino's synthetic project even further by attempting to reconcile Greek, Christian, Hebrew, and Islamic ideas. Pico's *On the Dignity of Man,* a kind of summation of his ideals and a celebration of the almost infinite potential of human beings, is one of the crowning achievements of European humanist thought. Pico's humanism expresses the faith that by devoting one's life to study and

[. . . i]t is important to gain knowledge. Grasp of the intelligibles determines the fate of the rational soul in the hereafter, and therefore is crucial to human activity.
– Ibn Sina (980–1037)

A student who wishes to comprehend the basic truth of things yet fails to study [the classics] might as well place himself in front of a wall — he will not get anywhere.
–Zhu Xi (1130–1200), *Memorial on the Principles of Study*

thought, human beings can attain an almost godlike understanding of the world and the mysteries of religion and the universe.

Renaissance humanism led the way to the empirical thought and rational skepticism that characterizes the age of Enlightenment associated with eighteenth-century Europe. At the end of the Renaissance, the ideas of Francis Bacon serve as a kind of transition between the two eras. Unlike many of his Renaissance contemporaries who associated science with magic, Bacon described science as the careful and controlled observation of nature. Marlowe's Doctor Faustus learns his "science" by studying old books, but the scholars in Salomon's House in Bacon's *New Atlantis* (1621) develop their knowledge through controlled observation and experiment. Similar to the Chinese philosopher Li Zhi's (1527–1602) attempt to loosen the hold of deductive reasoning in Confucian thought, Bacon argued in *The Advancement of Learning* (1605) and the *Novum Organum* (1620) that we must clear our thinking from the habits of mind that interfere with our habits of learning. Along with his Renaissance contemporaries, Bacon believed that knowledge is power, and, as his description of the activities in New Atlantis shows, he was interested in both empirical investigation and the practical applications of science.

ENLIGHTENED RULERSHIP IN INDIA: AKBAR

By the sixteenth century India was divided between the Hindu south and Muslim north. In 1526 Babur, a descendant of the Mongol leaders Tamerlane and Genghis Khan, invaded Muslim India from the north to establish what is known as the Mughal empire. Babur's grandson, the legendary and enlightened Akbar (1542–1605), expanded the empire southward to a line just north of Bombay on the west coast across to the Bay of Bengal. Although he could not read, as explained in the excerpt from his biography written by Abd al-Qadir Bada'uni (1540–c. 1615), Akbar patronized the arts and surrounded himself with sages and learned clerics from all religions, engaging them in a critical dialogue about spirituality and theology. He also entertained a variety of artists, intellectuals, and writers from many traditions, including Persian and Hindu. Drawing upon the knowledge he gained from interviewing Hindus, Christians, Sufis, Zoroastrians, and others, later in life Akbar created a new religion that, in his view, crystallized the essential spirituality common to all faiths. Some argue that because he did not try to force his subjects into accepting his beliefs as a state religion, it was doomed to dwindle away, as it did, after his death. While not a humanist in the European sense, Akbar, as Bada'uni's portrait shows, embodied a spirit of statesmanship, martial prowess, and love of ideas that may be compared to that of his European and Asian contemporaries.

■ CONNECTIONS

William Shakespeare, *The Tempest,* p. 495. Prospero in Shakespeare's *The Tempest* displays a kind of "civic humanism": he uses his classical and arcane learning to manipulate the appearance of things on the island and exercise power over others. At the end of the play, Prospero drowns his book—a symbol of giving up his mastery and accepting, perhaps, a more humble position in society. In what ways is Prospero like the humanist scholars, poets, and rulers depicted in this section?

John Milton, *Paradise Lost,* p. 575. John Milton was one of the great humanists of England. His prose treatise *Areopagitica* offers an important defense of the free dissemination of knowledge, and his epic *Paradise Lost* deals with the themes of freedom and knowledge. How does *Paradise Lost* represent Milton's love of learning and his engagement with the classics of Greece, Rome, and Israel? In what ways do Adam and Eve display the human desire for insight and knowledge? What are the consequences (according to Milton) of such desire?

Ibn Khaldun, *The Muqaddimah,* p. 154. One of the Arabic writers who carried on the scholarly tradition into the fifteenth century was Ibn Khaldun, author of what some describe as the first treatise on historiography and sociology, *The Muqaddimah.* Compare Khaldun's treatise to the humanist precepts, both European and Arabic, that appear in this section. How does his work represent the spirit of inquiry, love of learning, and engagement with both the classical past and the present that form the core of humanist inquiry?

Ibn Sina (Avicenna)

980–1037

One of the most influential of all Islamic philosophers, Abu Ali al-Husein Ibn Sina, known in the West as Avicenna, was born in the village of Afshana, near Bukhara. At the time Bukhara was in the region of Transoxania (now in Uzbekistan), which was ruled nominally by the Abbasid caliphs in Baghdad but governed in practice by the Samanid ruler Nuh ibn Mansur (Nuh II; r. 976–97). Here the intellectually gifted Ibn Sina undertook his education. At age ten, he had already mastered the Qur'an (Koran) and the traditional sciences; he then took up the study of law and medicine. At age eighteen, he was more skilled in medicine than other doctors and was thus invited into Nuh II's court, where he took advantage of the considerable resources of the library, which contained, among other works, rare Greek manuscripts on science. After the death of his father, Ibn Sina left Bukhara and after several years of moving from place to place joined the court of the Shamsud al-Daula (r. 1016–22) at Hamadan in Persia in 1016. Here he served as an adviser and as vizier and wrote his most influential book on medicine, *The Canon.* When political intrigue led to his imprisonment and once again forced him to flee, he moved to Isfahan, where he spent the remainder of his life.

Ibn Sina's greatest works are *The Canon* and the *Book of Healing,* a compendium of scientific and philosophical observations with commentary. He wrote several other treatises on science and philosophy, as well as poetry. Somewhat like St. Thomas Aquinas or Erasmus, both of whom attempted to reconcile Christian theology with Greek philosophy, Ibn Sina attempted to reconcile Greek philosophy, particularly Aristotelian and neo-Platonic ideas, with the revelations of the Qur'an and the doctrines of the Hadith, the collected sayings of Muhammad. Like later European humanists, Ibn Sina believed in the power of the human intellect to reach to almost godlike heights of reason and understanding through a combination of disciplined study and ascetic practices. Ibn Sina's emphasis on free thinking contradicted orthodox Islamic views about revelation and led other philosophers, such as Abu Hamid al-Ghazali (1058–1111), to oppose him. Though he lived four centuries before the European humanists, Ibn Sina is clearly one of their founding spirits.

The selection here is from the "Autobiography of Avicenna," translated by Arthur J. Arberry for the Wisdom of the East Series from John Murray Publishers in London.

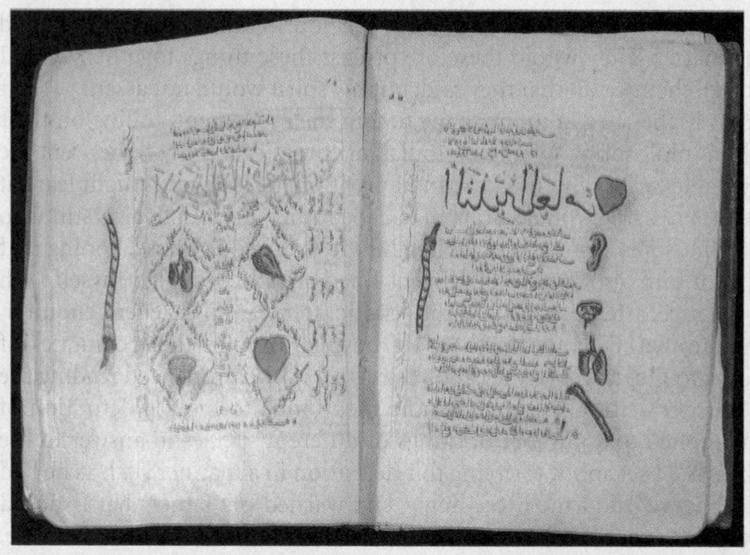

***The Canon*, Fourteenth Century**
This photo shows two pages from a Syrian copy of The Canon, *a treatise on medicine by the tenth-century Persian physician and writer Ibn Sina (Avicenna). (The Art Archive / National Museum Damascus Syria / Dagli Orti)*

FROM

Autobiography of Avicenna

Translated by Arthur J. Arberry

My father was a man of Balkh, and he moved from there to Bukhara[1] during the days of Nūḥ ibn Manṣūr;[2] in his reign he was employed in the administration, being governor of a village-centre in the outlying district of Bukhara called Kharmaithan. Nearby is a village named Afshana, and there my father married my mother and took up his residence; I was also born there, and after me my brother. Later we moved to Bukhara, where I was put under teachers of the Koran[3] and of letters. By the time I was ten I had mastered the Koran and a great deal of literature, so that I was marvelled at for my aptitude.

Now my father was one of those who had responded to the Egyptian propagandist (who was all Ismaili);[4] he, and my brother too, had listened to what they had to

[1] **Bukhara:** A city in Transoxania (now in Uzbekistan), a region in Central Asia and the northeasternmost area nominally under the control of the Abbasid caliphs in Baghdad.

[2] **Nūḥ ibn Manṣūr:** (r. 976–97), the Samanid ruler of the Central Asian region of Khurasan (what is now northern Iran and part of Afghanistan).

[3] **Koran:** (Qur'an), the sacred book of Islam, containing the scriptures revealed to Muhammad (c. 570–632) by Allah.

[4] **Ismaili:** A branch of the Shia movement, which in general opposed the established caliphate. The Ismailis believed the imamate should have fallen to Ismail (d. 760), the oldest son of Ja'far al-Sadiq, whom the Ismailis believe to be the sixth imam. They conducted extensive missionary activities throughout the Abbasid empire, including the remote regions of Khurasan and Transoxania. One such Ismaili missionary in Khurasan was Nasir-i Khusraw (1004–1077), a poet and traveler.

say about the Spirit and the Intellect, after the fashion in which they preach and understand the matter. They would therefore discuss these things together, while I listened and comprehended all that they said; but my spirit would not assent to their argument. Presently they began to invite me to join the movement, rolling on their tongues talk about philosophy, geometry, Indian arithmetic; and my father sent me to a certain vegetable-seller who used the Indian arithmetic, so that I might learn it from him. Then there came to Bukhara a man called Abū ʿAbd Allāh al-Nātilī who claimed to be a philosopher; my father invited him to stay in our house, hoping that I would learn from him also. Before his advent I had already occupied myself with Muslim jurisprudence, attending Ismāʿīl the Ascetic; so I was an excellent enquirer, having become familiar with the methods of postulation and the techniques of rebuttal according to the usages of the canon lawyers. I now commenced reading the *Isagoge* (of Porphyry)[5] with al-Nātilī: when he mentioned to me the definition of *genus* as a term applied to a number of things of different species in answer to the question "What is it?" I set about verifying this definition in a manner such as he had never heard. He marvelled at me exceedingly, and warned my father that I should not engage in any other occupation but learning; whatever problem he stated to me, I showed a better mental conception of it than he. So I continued until I had read all the straightforward parts of Logic with him; as for the subtler points, he had no acquaintance with them.

From then onward I took to reading texts by myself; I studied the commentaries, until I had completely mastered the science of Logic. Similarly with Euclid[6] I read the first five or six figures with him, and thereafter undertook on my own account to solve the entire remainder of the book. Next I moved on to the *Almagest* (of Ptolemy);[7] when I had finished the prolegomena and reached the geometrical figures, al-Nātilī told me to go on reading and to solve the problems by myself; I should merely revise what I read with him, so that he might indicate to me what was right and what was wrong. The truth is that he did not really teach this book; I began to solve the work, and many were the complicated figures of which he had no knowledge until I presented them to him, and made him understand them. Then al-Nātilī took leave of me, setting out for Gurganj.

I now occupied myself with mastering the various texts and commentaries on natural science and metaphysics, until all the gates of knowledge were open to me. Next I desired to study medicine, and proceeded to read all the books that have been written on this subject. Medicine is not a difficult science, and naturally I excelled

---

[5] ***Isagoge* (of Porphyry):** Porphyry (c. 234–305 C.E.) was a philosopher from Tyre (now in Lebanon) who studied in his native Syria and in Athens, then went to Rome, where he studied with the neo-Platonic philosopher Plotinus, and later to Sicily, where he became one of the most important neo-Platonic philosophers of the early Middle Ages. *Isagoge,* which means "Introduction," is a study of Aristotle's philosophy.

[6] **Euclid:** (fl. fourth century B.C.E.), Greek mathematician and author of *Elements,* a foundational work in geometry.

[7] ***Almagest* (of Ptolemy):** (fl. second century C.E.), Greek-Egyptian astronomer, geographer, and mathematician; his *Almagest* provided a systematic survey of the scientific knowledge of Alexandria. Ptolemy's geocentric (earth-centered) cosmology dominated Western thought until Copernicus (1473–1543) provided evidence that the sun was the center of our planetary system.

in it in a very short time, so that qualified physicians began to read medicine with me. I also undertook to treat the sick, and methods of treatment derived from practical experience revealed themselves to me such as baffle description. At the same time I continued between whiles to study and dispute on law, being now sixteen years of age.

The next eighteen months I devoted entirely to reading; I studied Logic once again, and all the parts of philosophy. During all this time I did not sleep one night through, nor devoted my attention to any other matter by day. I prepared a set of files; with each proof I examined, I set down the syllogistic premisses and put them in order in the files, then I examined what deductions might be drawn from them. I observed methodically the conditions of the premisses, and proceeded until the truth of each particular problem was confirmed for me. Whenever I found myself perplexed by a problem, or could not find the middle term in any syllogism, I would repair to the mosque and pray, adoring the All-Creator, until my puzzle was resolved and my difficulty made easy. At night I would return home, set the lamp before me, and busy myself with reading and writing; whenever sleep overcame me or I was conscious of some weakness, I turned aside to drink a glass of wine until my strength returned to me; then I went back to my reading. If ever the least slumber overtook me, I would dream of the precise problem which I was considering as I fell asleep; in that way many problems revealed themselves to me while sleeping. So I continued until I had made myself master of all the sciences; I now comprehended them to the limits of human possibility. All that I learned during that time is exactly as I know it now; I have added nothing more to my knowledge to this day.

I was now a master of Logic, natural sciences and mathematics. I therefore returned to metaphysics; I read the *Metaphysica* (of Aristotle),[8] but did not understand its contents and was baffled by the author's intention; I read it over forty times, until I had the text by heart. Even then I did not understand it or what the author meant, and I despaired within myself, saying, "This is a book which there is no way of understanding." But one day at noon I chanced to be in the booksellers' quarter, and a broker was there with a volume in his hand which he was calling for sale. He offered it to me, but I returned it to him impatiently, believing that there was no use in this particular science. However he said to me, "Buy this book from me: it is cheap, and I will sell it to you for four dirhams. The owner is in need of the money." So I bought it, and found that it was a book by Abū Naṣr al-Fārābī *On the Objects of the Metaphysica.*[9] I returned home and hastened to read it; and at once the objects of that book became clear to me, for I had it all by heart. I rejoiced at this, and upon the next day distributed much in alms to the poor in gratitude to Almighty God.

Now the Sultan of Bukhara at that time was Nūḥ ibn Manṣūr, and it happened that he fell sick of a malady which baffled all the physicians. My name was famous

[8] ***Metaphysica* (of Aristotle):** The Greek philosopher Aristotle (384–322 B.C.E.) wrote *The Metaphysics* in about 350 B.C.E.; it is an inquiry into the nature of being, cause, universals, identity, and change.

[9] **Abū Naṣr al-Fārābī *On the Objects of the Metaphysica*:** Abū Naṣr al-Fārābī (Al Pharabius; 870–950) was a Turkish philosopher known as the "second teacher"; his work sought to reconcile Plato and Aristotle's philosophy with the theology of Sufism.

among them because of the breadth of my reading; they therefore mentioned me in his presence, and begged him to summon me. I attended the sick-room, and collaborated with them in treating the royal patient. So I came to be enrolled in his service. One day I asked his leave to enter their library, to examine the contents and read the books on medicine; he granted my request, and I entered a mansion with many chambers, each chamber having chests of books piled one upon another. In one apartment were books on language and poetry, in another law, and so on; each apartment was set aside for books on a single science. I glanced through the catalogue of the works of the ancient Greeks, and asked for those which I required; and I saw books whose very names are as yet unknown to many—works which I had never seen before and have not seen since. I read these books, taking notes of their contents; I came to realize the place each man occupied in his particular science.

So by the time I reached my eighteenth year I had exhausted all these sciences. My memory for learning was at that period of my life better than it is now, but today I am more mature; apart from this my knowledge is exactly the same, nothing further having been added to my store since then.

There lived near me in those days a man called Abu 'l-Ḥasan the Prosodist; he requested me to compose a comprehensive work on this science, and I wrote for him the *Majmū'* ("Compendium") which I named after him, including in it all the branches of knowledge except mathematics. At that time I was twenty-one. Another man lived in my neighbourhood called Abū Bakr al-Barqī, a Khwarizmian by birth; he was a lawyer at heart, his interests being focused on jurisprudence, exegesis and asceticism, to which subjects he was extremely inclined. He asked me to comment on his books, and I wrote for him *al-Ḥāṣil wa'l-maḥṣūl* ("The Import and the Substance") in about twenty volumes, as well as a work on ethics called *al-Birr wa'l-ithm* ("Good Works and Sin"); these two books are only to be found in his library, and are unknown to anyone else, so that they have never been copied.

Then my father died, and my circumstances changed. I accepted a post in the Sultan's employment, and was obliged to move from Bukhara to Gurganj, where Abu 'l-Ḥusain al-Sahlī was a minister, being a man devoted to these sciences. I was introduced to the Amir, 'Alī ibn al-Ma'mūn, being at that time dressed in the garb of lawyers, with scarf and chin-wrap; they fixed a handsome salary for me, amply sufficient for the like of me. Then I was constrained to move to Nasa, and from there to Baward, and thence successively to Tus, Shaqqan, Samanqan, Jajarm the frontier-post of Khurasan, and Jurjan. My entire purpose was to come to the Amir Qābūs;[10] but it happened meanwhile that Qābūs was taken and imprisoned in a fortress, where he died.

After this I went to Dihistan, where I fell very ill. I returned to Jurjan, and there made friends with Abū 'Ubaid al-Jūzjānī.[11]

---

[10] **Amir Qābūs:** Qabus ibn Woshmgir (Amir Shams al-Ma'ali; d. 1012), the Ziyarid ruler of Jurjan (Gorgan), on the southern shore of the Caspian Sea.

[11] **Abū 'Ubaid al-Jūzjānī:** (fl. early eleventh century), Ibn Sina's student and companion.

Zhu Xi (Chu Hsi)

1130–1200

Zhu Xi (Chu Hsi) was one of China's most important philosophers after Confucius and Mencius. His reworking of Confucian doctrine led to the foundation of neo-Confucianism. His compilation of and commentaries on the Four Books—*The Analects, The Mencius, The Great Learning,* and *The Doctrine of the Mean*—became basic texts for the study of Confucianism in China from the early fourteenth through the early nineteenth centuries. (The Yüan dynasty made his commentaries the source for imperial examinations, which were abolished only in 1905.) Zhu Xi wrote in the vernacular, aiming to reach a large audience. *Master Zhu's Family Rituals* modified the ceremonies of everyday life—important rituals such as funeral rites and birth rituals. He also published an anthology, *Reflections on Things at Hand,* that served as an introduction to moral philosophy. In his philosophical works, Zhu Xi explored the connection between the principles of the universe and the material world, calling new attention to the external world. He believed that philosophers should study the physical objects of the world in order to determine their underlying laws; such study, he thought, would lead to the conclusion that the principles governing the human intellect and the phenomenal world would be one and the same.

Memorial on the Principles of Study

Translated by Clara Yu

Of all the methods of learning, the first is to explore the basic principle of things.[1] To get at the basic principle of things, one must study. The best way to study is to proceed slowly and in sequence, so as to learn everything well. In order to learn everything well, one must be serious-minded and able to concentrate. These are the unchanging principles of study.

There is a principle for everything under the sun: there is a principle behind the relationship between an Emperor and his subjects, between a father and his son, between brothers, between friends, and between man and wife. Even in such trivial matters as entering and leaving a house, rising in the morning and going to bed at night, dealing with people and conducting daily affairs, there are set principles. Once we have explored the basic principles of things, we will understand all phenomena as well as the reasons behind them. There no longer will be doubts in our minds. We

[1] **basic principle of things:** Neo-Confucianism emphasizes the notion that the understanding of things must be based upon an understanding of an underlying principle, known as *li.*

will naturally follow good and reject evil. Such are the reasons why learning should begin with the exploration of the true principles of things.

There are many theories about the principles of things in our world, some simple, others subtle, some clear, others obscure. Yet only the ancient sages were able to formulate a constant, eternal theory of the world, and their words and deeds have become the model for the ages. If we follow the teachings of these ancient sages, we can become superior men; if not, we will become ignorant fellows. We are inspired by the superior men who govern the realm within the four seas; we are frightened by the ignorant ones who lose their lives. All these deeds and results are recorded in the classics, historical writings, and memorials to the throne. A student who wishes to comprehend the basic truth of things yet fails to study these materials might as well place himself in front of a wall—he will not get anywhere. This is why I say that study is the only key to the comprehension of the principles of the world.

People who dislike studying are often indolent, careless, and without perseverance. On the other hand, those who like studying often tend to be too ambitious with regard to volume and range. The latter, barely having begun a subject, are already eager to probe into its ultimate meaning; before they have thoroughly understood one work, they already are anxious to start another. For this reason, they are busy studying all the time yet always feel hurried and unsettled, as if they were chasing or being chased by something. They can never achieve the serenity of leisure and confidence, nor can they feel contented. Furthermore, they are never able to retain a prolonged interest in learning. Consequently, they are essentially no different from those who are indolent, careless, or without perseverance. This is what Confucius[2] meant when he said, "Speeding will not get you to your destination," and what Mencius meant when he said, "One who advances too fast will retreat just as quickly."

If we take care to avoid these pitfalls, correct our study habits, and concentrate on one subject at a time, eventually all the works we have studied will begin to make sense in a larger context, in the same way that all the blood vessels are connected in a complicated system. Gradually, we will become naturally involved in our studies, and our minds will become one with the principle of things. Then to follow good and avoid evil will become the most natural course. Such a gradual process of acquiring essential knowledge is the ideal method for learning.

The comprehension of essential knowledge depends on the mind. The mind is the most abstract, most mysterious, most delicate, and most unpredictable of all things. It is always the master of a person, for everything depends on it, and it cannot be absent for even a second. Once a person's mind wanders beyond his body, he will no longer have control over himself. Even in movements and perception he will not be the master of himself, let alone in the comprehension of the teachings of ancient sages or in the investigation of the true nature of the myriad things. Therefore Confucius said, "If a gentleman is not serious-minded, he will not inspire awe and his learnings will not be solid." And Mencius said, "There is no principle in learning

[2] **Confucius:** (Kongfuzi; 551–479 B.C.E.), the great Chinese philosopher whose religious, philosophical, and moral principles have provided a foundation for Chinese thought and life from his time through today.

other than the freeing of the mind." If a person can really concentrate his mind on learning and observation and not be distracted by various desires and temptations, there will be no obstacles to his comprehension of the nature of things, nor any impropriety in his contacts with people. This is why concentration is the basis of learning. I, your humble subject, have tried these principles in the course of my own studies and found them most effective. I believe that even if the ancient sages should return to life, they would have no better methods for educating people. I believe these principles are fit even for the education of Kings and Emperors.

Giovanni Pico della Mirandola
1463–1494

Giovanni Pico, a child prodigy, was the youngest son of the ruler of Mirandola, a principality in northern Italy. At the age of sixteen he began studying at the University of Ferrara, then moved on to those at Padua and Paris. Here he absorbed the Greek and Latin classics, the Hebrew Kabala and Talmud, Arabic philosophy, and Christian theology. Synthesizing these various traditions, the young man planned treatises that would exhibit not only their compatibility but also the basic unity of truth. Like the Arabic philosopher Ibn Sina and Doctor Faustus in Marlowe's play, Pico took the world's learning as his domain—but there was a price to pay for challenging the establishment. When he was just twenty-three, he published 900 theses as a kind of compendium of philosophical assertions to be debated in Rome by the best intellects of Europe. The Roman Catholic Church, however, under Pope Innocent VIII (r. 1484–92), declared thirteen of the theses to be heretical and prevented the debate from taking place. Pico retired from public view and wrote an *Apology* (1488) to defend his religious ideas. While in retirement at Fiesole, he wrote *Heptaplus* (1489), commentaries on the Psalms, *On Being and the One* (1491), and *Disputations against Astrology* (1494). In the end Pico submitted to the authority of the Church, and Pope Alexander VI (r. 1492–1503) removed the ban on his writings shortly before his death.

Pico described himself as an *explorator,* and the depth of his learning led him to value the wisdom of all ages and cultures. He believed that beneath the symbolic surfaces of differing philosophical and religious traditions was a unitary thread binding them together. At the center of this intellectual complex was Pico's belief in the virtually unlimited intellectual potential of human beings. The work in which he argues for that potential is his oration *On the Dignity of Man* (1486), which is excerpted here.

FROM

On the Dignity of Man

Translated by Charles Glenn Wallis

Most venerable fathers, I have read in the records of the Arabians that Abdul the Saracen,[1] on being asked what thing on, so to speak, the world's stage, he viewed as most greatly worthy of wonder, answered that he viewed nothing more wonderful than man. And Mercury's, "a great wonder, Asclepius,[2] is man!" agrees with that opinion. On thinking over the reason for these sayings, I was not satisfied by the many assertions made by many men concerning the outstandingness of human nature: that man is the messenger between creatures, familiar with the upper and king of the lower; by the sharpsightedness of the senses, by the hunting-power of reason, and by the light of intelligence, the interpreter of nature; the part in between the standstill of eternity and the flow of time; and, as the Persians say, the bond tying the world together, nay, the nuptial bond; and, according to David,[3] "a little lower than the angels." These reasons are great but not the chief ones, that is, they are not reasons for a lawful claim to the highest wonder as to a prerogative. Why should we not wonder more at the angels themselves and at the very blessed heavenly choirs?

Finally, it seemed to me that I understood why man is the animal that is most happy, and is therefore worthy of all wonder; and lastly, what the state is that is allotted to man in the succession of things,[4] and that is capable of arousing envy not only in the brutes but also in the stars and even in minds beyond the world. It is wonderful and beyond belief. For this is the reason why man is rightly said and thought to be a great marvel and the animal really worthy of wonder. Now hear what it is, fathers; and with kindly ears and for the sake of your humanity, give me your close attention:

Now the highest Father, God the master-builder, had, by the laws of His secret wisdom, fabricated this house, this world which we see, a very superb temple of divinity. He had adorned the super-celestial region with minds. He had animated the celestial globes with eternal souls; He had filled with a diverse throng of animals the cast-off and residual parts of the lower world. But, with the work finished, the Artisan desired that there be someone to reckon up the reason of such a big work, to love its beauty, and to wonder at its greatness. Accordingly, now that all things had been completed, as Moses and Timaeus[5] testify, He lastly considered creating man.

---

[1] **Abdul the Saracen:** Probably Abd Allah, Muhammad's cousin (c. seventh century C.E.).

[2] **Asclepius:** The legendary Greek healer and physician. He is a speaker in Mercury's (Hermes Trismegistus) dialogue. Hermes Trismegistus is a legendary sage associated with arcane teachings of neo-Platonism and the Kabala.

[3] **David:** King David, Psalm 8:5.

[4] **the succession of things:** That is, the great chain of being, or hierarchical pattern from God down to the smallest organism.

[5] **Timaeus:** A speaker in one of Plato's dialogues.

But there was nothing in the archetypes from which He could mold a new sprout, nor anything in His storehouses which He could bestow as a heritage upon a new son, nor was there an empty judiciary seat where this contemplator of the universe could sit. Everything was filled up; all things had been laid out in the highest, the lowest, and the middle orders. But it did not belong to the paternal power to have failed in the final parturition, as though exhausted by childbearing; it did not belong to wisdom, in a case of necessity, to have been tossed back and forth through want of a plan; it did not belong to the loving-kindness which was going to praise divine liberality in others to be forced to condemn itself. Finally, the best of workmen decided that that to which nothing of its very own could be given should be, in composite fashion, whatsoever had belonged individually to each and every thing. Therefore He took up man, a work of indeterminate form; and, placing him at the midpoint of the world, He spoke to him as follows:

"We have given to thee, Adam, no fixed seat, no form of thy very own, no gift peculiarly thine, that thou mayest feel as thine own, have as thine own, possess as thine own the seat, the form, the gifts which thou thyself shalt desire. A limited nature in other creatures is confined within the laws written down by Us. In conformity with thy free judgment, in whose hands I have placed thee, thou art confined by no bounds; and thou wilt fix limits of nature for thyself. I have placed thee at the center of the world, that from there thou mayest more conveniently look around and see whatsoever is in the world. Neither heavenly nor earthly, neither mortal nor immortal have We made thee. Thou, like a judge appointed for being honorable, art the molder and maker of thyself; thou mayest sculpt thyself into whatever shape thou dost prefer. Thou canst grow downward into the lower natures which are brutes. Thou canst again grow upward from thy soul's reason into the higher natures which are divine."

O great liberality of God the Father! O great and wonderful happiness of man! It is given him to have that which he chooses and to be that which he wills. As soon as brutes are born, they bring with them, "from their dam's bag," as Lucilius[6] says, what they are going to possess. Highest spirits have been, either from the beginning or soon after, that which they are going to be throughout everlasting eternity. At man's birth the Father placed in him every sort of seed and sprouts of every kind of life. The seeds that each man cultivates will grow and bear their fruit in him. If he cultivates vegetable seeds, he will become a plant. If the seeds of sensation, he will grow into brute. If rational, he will come out a heavenly animal. If intellectual, he will be an angel, and a son of God. And if he is not contented with the lot of any creature but takes himself up into the center of his own unity, then, made one spirit with God and settled in the solitary darkness of the Father, who is above all things, he will stand ahead of all things. Who does not wonder at this chameleon which we are? Or who at all feels more wonder at anything else whatsoever? It was not unfittingly that Asclepius the Athenian said that man was symbolized by Proteus[7] in the secret rites,

[6] **Lucilius:** A Roman satirical poet (second century B.C.E.).

[7] **Proteus:** Greek god of the sea who eluded his opponents by shape-shifting.

by reason of our nature sloughing its skin and transforming itself; hence metamorphoses were popular among the Jews and the Pythagoreans.[8] For the more secret Hebrew theology at one time reshapes holy Enoch[9] into an angel of divinity, whom they call *malach hashechina,* and at other times reshapes other men into other divinities. According to the Pythagoreans, wicked men are deformed into brutes and, if you believe Empedocles,[10] into plants too. And copying them, Maumeth[11] often had it on his lips that he who draws back from divine law becomes a brute. And his saying so was reasonable: for it is not the rind which makes the plant, but a dull and non-sentient nature; not the hide which makes a beast of burden, but a brutal and sensual soul; not the spherical body which makes the heavens, but right reason; and not a separateness from the body but a spiritual intelligence which makes an angel. For example, if you see a man given over to his belly and crawling upon the ground, it is a bush not a man that you see. If you see anyone blinded by the illusions of his empty and Calypso-like[12] imagination, seized by the desire of scratching, and delivered over to the senses, it is a brute not a man that you see. If you come upon a philosopher winnowing out all things by right reason, he is a heavenly not an earthly animal. If you come upon a pure contemplator, ignorant of the body, banished to the innermost places of the mind, he is not an earthly, not a heavenly animal; he more superbly is a divinity clothed with human flesh.

Who is there that does not wonder at man? And it is not unreasonable that in the Mosaic and Christian holy writ man is sometimes denoted by the name "all flesh" and at other times by that of "every creature"; and man fashions, fabricates, transforms himself into the shape of all flesh, into the character of every creature. Accordingly, where Evantes the Persian tells of the Chaldaean theology, he writes that man is not any inborn image of himself, but many images coming in from the outside: hence that saying of the Chaldaeans:[13] *enosh hu shinuy vekamah tevaoth baal chayim,* that is, man is an animal of diverse, multiform, and destructible nature.

But why all this? In order for us to understand that, after having been born in this state so that we may be what we will to be, then, since we are held in honor, we ought to take particular care that no one may say against us that we do not know that

[8] **Pythagoreans:** The followers of the Greek philosopher and mathematician Pythagoras (c. 582–c. 507 B.C.E.). They believed in the transmigration of souls and in the need to follow rituals to prepare for the next life.

[9] **Enoch:** Genesis 5:18–24 describes Enoch, the father of Methusaleh; Hebrews 11:5 suggests that he was taken by God without experiencing death.

[10] **Empedocles:** (c. 492–435 B.C.E.), Greek natural philosopher who believed that the basic elements of all substance were earth, air, fire, and water and that change is generated by the cyclic and opposing forces of love and strife.

[11] **Maumeth:** Muhammad (c. 570–632), the great Prophet of Islam to whom Allah dictated the sacred scriptures of the Qur'an.

[12] **Calypso-like:** Pico is perhaps confusing Calypso with Circe from *The Odyssey.*

[13] **Chaldaeans:** An ancient Semitic people who invaded Babylon in the tenth century B.C.E.; Pico uses the term here to mean the priest-astronomers or astrologers associated with ancient Babylonian literature and lore.

we are made similar to brutes and mindless beasts of burden. But rather, as Asaph the prophet says: "Ye are all gods, and sons of the most high," unless by abusing the very indulgent liberality of the Father, we make the free choice, which he gave to us, harmful to ourselves instead of helpful toward salvation. Let a certain holy ambition invade the mind, so that we may not be content with mean things but may aspire to the highest things and strive with all our forces to attain them: for if we will to, we can. Let us spurn earthly things; let us struggle toward the heavenly. Let us put in last place whatever is of the world; and let us fly beyond the chambers of the world to the chamber nearest the most lofty divinity. There, as the sacred mysteries reveal, the seraphim, cherubim, and thrones[14] occupy the first places. Ignorant of how to yield to them and unable to endure the second places, let us compete with the angels in dignity and glory. When we have willed it, we shall be not at all below them.

[14] **seraphim . . . thrones:** In the medieval Christian hierarchy, seraphim, cherubim, and thrones constitute the highest order of angels.

NICCOLÒ MACHIAVELLI
1469–1527

Although the great political theorist Niccolò Machiavelli received a relatively modest education, he was well grounded in the study of Latin, grammar, and mathematics. During his life as a civil servant, military adviser, diplomat, and writer, Machiavelli pursued his reading in the Latin classics, and his works such as *The Art of War* (1521), *Discourses* (1531), and *The Prince* (1513; published 1532) display Machiavelli's prodigious knowledge of the ancient world—especially the history of Rome. As mentioned in the introduction to Machiavelli's ***The Prince,*** upon his p. 124 deathbed he told those gathered around that instead of joining the beggarly crowds of monks and saints in heaven, he would prefer to go to hell, where he could meet other great thinkers and the pagan philosophers such as Plato, Plutarch, and Tacitus. In his famous letter of 10 December 1513 to his friend and benefactor Francesco Vettori (1499–1585), Machiavelli describes the joy and serious character of his reading, an act that he portrays as joining the company of great minds.

The translation of Machiavelli's letter printed here is by Allan H. Gilbert; the notes are those of the editors.

Letter to Francesco Vettori, 10 December 1513

Translated by Allan H. Gilbert

Magnificent Ambassador:

... I am living on my farm, and since I had my last bad luck, I have not spent twenty days, putting them all together, in Florence. I have until now been snaring thrushes with my own hands. I got up before day, prepared birdlime, went out with a bundle of cages on my back, so that I looked like Geta when he was returning from the harbor with Amphitryo's books.[1] I caught at least two thrushes and at most six. And so I did all September. Later this pastime, pitiful and strange as it is, gave out, to my displeasure. And of what sort my life is, I shall tell you.

I get up in the morning with the sun and go into a grove I am having cut down, where I remain two hours to look over the work of the past day and kill some time with the cutters, who have always some bad-luck story ready, about either themselves or their neighbors. And as to this grove I could tell you a thousand fine things that have happened to me, in dealing with Frosino da Panzano and others who wanted some of this firewood. And Frosino especially sent for a number of cords without saying a thing to me, and on payment he wanted to keep back from me ten lire, which he says he should have had from me four years ago, when he beat me at *cricca* at Antonio Guicciardini's. I raised the devil, and was going to prosecute as a thief the waggoner who came for the wood, but Giovanni Machiavelli came between us and got us to agree. Battista Guicciardini, Filippo Ginori, Tommaso del Bene, and some other citizens, when that north wind was blowing, each ordered a cord from me. I made promises to all and sent one to Tommaso, which at Florence changed to half a cord, because it was piled up again by himself, his wife, his servant, his children, so that he looked like Gabburra when on Thursday with all his servants he cudgels an ox. Hence, having seen for whom there was profit, I told the others I had no more wood, and all of them were angry about it, and especially Battista, who counts this along with his misfortunes at Prato.

Leaving the grove, I go to a spring, and thence to my aviary. I have a book in my pocket, either Dante or Petrarch,[2] or one of the lesser poets, such as Tibullus, Ovid,[3] and the like. I read of their tender passions and their loves, remember mine, enjoy myself a while in that sort of dreaming. Then I move along the road to the inn; I speak with those who pass, ask news of their villages, learn various things, and note the various tastes and different fancies of men. In the course of these things comes the hour for dinner, where with my family I eat such food as this poor farm of mine

---

[1] **Amphitryo's books:** In a popular story found in Plautus, upon his return to Thebes from Athens, Amphitryo sends his servant Geta, burdened down with Amphitryo's books, to tell his wife, Almene, of his arrival.

[2] **Dante or Petrarch:** Two of the greatest Italian poets and writers. Dante (1265–1321) is the author of the *Divine Comedy* (see Book 2); Petrarch (1304–1374), of the *Canzoniere* and other works (see p. 67).

[3] **Tibullus, Ovid:** Both important Roman elegiac poets. Albius Tibullus (c. 55–c. 19 B.C.E.) wrote two books of elegiac lyric poems. Ovid (43 B.C.E. to 17 C.E.) is the author of *Metamorphoses* and many elegiac lyric poems.

and my tiny property allow. Having eaten, I go back to the inn; there is the host, usually a butcher, a miller, two furnace tenders. With these I sink into vulgarity for the whole day, playing at *cricca* and at trich-trach,[4] and then these games bring on a thousand disputes and countless insults with offensive words, and usually we are fighting over a penny, and nevertheless we are heard shouting as far as San Casciano.[5] So, mixed up with these lice, I keep my brain from growing mouldy, and satisfy the malice of this fate of mine, being glad to have her drive me along this road, to see if she will be ashamed of it.

On the coming of evening, I return to my house and enter my study; and at the door I take off the day's clothing, covered with mud and dust, and put on garments regal and courtly; and reclothed appropriately, I enter the ancient courts of ancient men, where, received by them with affection, I feed on that food which only is mine and which I was born for, where I am not ashamed to speak with them and to ask them the reason for their actions; and they in their kindness answer me; and for four hours of time I do not feel boredom, I forget every trouble, I do not dread poverty, I am not frightened by death; entirely I give myself over to them.

And because Dante says it does not produce knowledge when we hear but do not remember, I have noted everything in their conversation which has profited me, and have composed a little work *On Princedoms,* where I go as deeply as I can into considerations on this subject, debating what a princedom is, of what kinds they are, how they are gained, how they are kept, why they are lost. If ever you can find any of my fantasies pleasing, this one should not displease you; and by a prince, and especially by a new prince, it ought to be welcomed. Hence I am dedicating it to His Magnificence Giuliano. Filippo Casavecchia has seen it; he can give you some account in part of the thing in itself and of the discussions I have had with him, though I am still enlarging and revising it.

You wish, Magnificent Ambassador, that I leave this life and come to enjoy yours with you. I shall do it in any case, but what tempts me now are certain affairs that within six weeks I shall finish. What makes me doubtful is that the Soderini we know so well are in the city, whom I should be obliged, on coming there, to visit and talk with. I should fear that on my return I could not hope to dismount at my house but should dismount at the Bargello, because though this government has mighty foundations and great security, yet it is new and therefore suspicious, and there is no lack of wiseacres who, to make a figure, like Pagolo Bertini, would place others at the dinner table and leave the reckoning to me. I beg you to rid me of this fear, and then I shall come within the time mentioned to visit you in any case.

I have talked with Filippo about this little work of mine that I have spoken of, whether it is good to give it or not to give it; and if it is good to give it, whether it would be good to take it myself, or whether I should send it there. Not giving it would make me fear that at the least Giuliano will not read it and that this rascal

[4] ***cricca,* trich-trach:** Cricca was a popular card game; trich-trach, a popular dice game in which the throw of the dice determined the movement of pawns on a chessboard.

[5] **San Casciano:** A village near the country estate where Machiavelli lived after being dismissed from public office by the Medicis in 1512.

Ardinghelli will get himself honor from this latest work of mine. The giving of it is forced on me by the necessity that drives me, because I am using up my money, and I cannot remain as I am a long time without becoming despised through poverty. In addition, there is my wish that our present Medici lords will make use of me, even if they begin by making me roll a stone; because then if I could not gain their favor, I should complain of myself; and through this thing, if it were read, they would see that for the fifteen years while I have been studying the art of the state, I have not slept or been playing; and well may anybody be glad to get the services of one who at the expense of others has become full of experience. Of my honesty there should be no doubt, because having always preserved my honesty, I shall hardly now learn to break it; he who has been honest and good for forty-three years, as I have, cannot change his nature; and as a witness to my honesty and goodness I have my poverty.

I should like, then, to have you also write me what you think best on this matter, and I give you my regards. Be happy.

Niccolò Machiavelli, in Florence.

Abd al-Qadir Bada'uni

1540–c. 1615

An important scholar and historian of the Mughal period, Abd al-Qadir Bada'uni was born in Toda, India. Bada'uni was raised and educated in Baswar, Sambhal, and Agra, where he moved with his father Muluk Shah in 1558–59. After his father's death in 1562, Bada'uni moved to Bada'un, from which he took his name, and began working for the regional governor Husayn Khan. He served as the governor's *sadr,* an official overseeing religious affairs, and traveled frequently to study with various sages and teachers from whom he learned more about Islam. In 1574 Bada'uni joined the court of the Mughal emperor Akbar (1542–1605) as an *ulama,* or scholar. Despite being passed over for preferment, Bada'uni served as a historian, translator, and biographer for Akbar. Nonetheless, in part because of his disappointment and in part because of his Sunni religious beliefs, he was suspicious and critical of Akbar's reforms. These criticisms may have led him to keep secret one of his most important works, *Selected Histories,* an account of the Muslims in India. The excerpt here from that work indicates that, despite its negative tone, Bada'uni's text provides a lively account of the dialogues Akbar had with representatives of the various religious groups present in India at the time.

Akbar is considered one of the greatest of India's rulers. According to p. 176 Abul Faz'l's ***Institutes of Akbar,*** a laudatory chronicle that often exaggerates, as a child Akbar had a gift for mathematics and sciences; moreover, he could recite Hindi and Persian poetry, and he tried his own hand at writing verses. Renowned for prodigious intelligence and acute memory,

Mughal Court Scene, 1565
The powerful Mughal emperor Akbar is shown here being entertained by court dancers. (The Art Archive / Bodleian Library Oxford / The Bodleian)

Akbar gained a reputation as an enlightened ruler, and though he was more than capable of exercising brutal force to increase his dominion, he was noted for his religious tolerance, his efficient and humane policies, and his patronage of the arts. Under Akbar, a Muslim, the hated taxes on Hindus were abolished and the empire achieved the stability needed for the development of the arts. Unlike previous Muslim rulers, Akbar married a Hindu woman and counted Hindus among his most important advisers and ministers at court. Among Akbar's cultural accomplishments was the building of Fatehpur Sikri, a fabulous palace and capital city west of Agra. Built to show his gratitude to the Sufi mystic Shaykh Salim Chisti, who had foretold the birth of Akbar's son, this elaborate city made of red sandstone was finished in 1586. Akbar imagined Fatehpur Sikri as the "perfect city," symbolizing balance, order, and God's light. Unfortunately, an inadequate supply of water led to the abandonment of the city, though it stands today and is the site of a beautiful mosque and the tomb of Shaykh Salim Chisti.

A great military strategist and politician, Akbar was nonetheless a well-informed and highly intelligent man who pursued his studies not by poring over dusty tomes but by engaging the best and the brightest people of his generation in conversation. Akbar's inclusive approach to spiritual matters led him to invite Sufis, Hindus, Jains, Zoroastrians, Christians, and Muslims (divided between the Sunni and Shia branches) to his court to discuss matters of religion and philosophy. Synthesizing what he learned from these ministers and sages, Akbar founded his own religion, the *Din-i-Ilahi,* or Divine Faith, which involved, among other ideas, a doctrine of the infallibility of the emperor, even in point of religious matters—a doctrine contrary to Islamic law. According to the Divine Faith, there was one god, a Sun God, to whom worshippers had direct access, without need of priests or ulama, as in Hindu or Muslim religions, respectively. Though Akbar's attempt to form an inclusive religion ultimately failed, his spirit of curiosity and emphasis on learning came through in Bada'uni's account.

The text presented here is from the *Muntakhab ut-Tawarikh* of Bada'uni in *Sources of Indian Tradition,* 2nd edition, edited and revised by Christopher Brunner and David Lelyveld, published in 1988. Notes are those of the editors.

FROM

Selected Histories

Translated by Peter Hardy; revised by Christopher Brunner and David Lelyveld

[Akbar in the Company of Learned Men]

And later that day the emperor came to Fatehpur.[1] There he used to spend much time in the Hall of Worship in the company of learned men and shaikhs and especially on Friday nights, when he would sit up there the whole night continually occupied in discussing questions of religion, whether fundamental or collateral. The learned men used to draw the sword of the tongue on the battlefield of mutual con-

[1] **Fatehpur:** Fatehpur Sikri, the capital city, complete with palace and mosque, that Akbar built in memory to the Sufi mystic Shaykh Salim Chisti, who had foretold the birth of Akbar's son; this elaborate and beautiful city made of red sandstone was finished in 1586.

tradiction and opposition, and the antagonism of the sects reached such a pitch that they would call one another fools and heretics. The controversies used to pass beyond the differences of Sunni, and Shī'a,[2] Hanafī and Shāfi'ī,[3] of lawyer and divine, and they would attack the very bases of belief. And Makhdūm-ul-Mulk wrote a treatise to the effect that Shaikh 'Abd-al-Nabī had unjustly killed Khizr Khān Sarwānī, who had been suspected of blaspheming the Prophet [peace be upon him!], and Mīr Habsh, who had been suspected of being a Shī'a, and saying that it was not right to repeat the prayers after him, because he was undutiful toward his father, and was himself afflicted with hemorrhoids. Shaikh 'Abd-al-Nabī replied to him that he was a fool and a heretic. Then the mullās[4] became divided into two parties, and one party took one side and one the other, and became very Jews and Egyptians for hatred of each other. And persons of novel and whimsical opinions, in accordance with their pernicious ideas and vain doubts, coming out of ambush, decked the false in the garb of the true, and wrong in the dress of right, and cast the emperor, who was possessed of an excellent disposition, and was an earnest searcher after truth, but very ignorant and a mere tyro, and used to the company of infidels and base persons, into perplexity, till doubt was heaped upon doubt, and he lost all definite aim, and the straight wall of the clear law and of firm religion was broken down, so that after five or six years not a trace of Islam was left in him: and everything was turned topsy-turvy. [. . .]

And samanas[5] and brāhmans (who as far as the matter of private interviews is concerned gained the advantage over everyone in attaining the honor of interviews with His Majesty, and in associating with him, and were in every way superior in reputation to all learned and trained men for their treatises on morals, and on physical and religious sciences, and in religious ecstasies, and stages of spiritual progress and human perfections) brought forward proofs, based on reason and traditional testimony, for the truth of their own, and the fallacy of our religion, and inculcated their doctrine with such firmness and assurance, that they affirmed mere imaginations as though they were self-evident facts, the truth of which the doubts of the sceptic could no more shake "Than the mountains crumble, and the heavens be cleft!" And the Resurrection, and Judgment, and other details and traditions, of

[2] **Sunni, and Shī'a:** The two great divisions of Islam, whose ceremonies and interpretations of the Qur'an and Hadith differ in several aspects. The schism originated in questions of the legitimacy of the caliphate, the temporal leaders of Islam, after the death of Muhammad in 632 left open the question of his proper successor. The Shia, whose name means "party of Ali," believed that Muhammad's cousin and son-in-law Muhammad Ali was the only legitimate ruler. Ali's son Hussein led a revolt against the Umayyads in 680 in the name of reclaiming the caliphate for the *shi'at Ali,* leading to the division between the Shia and Sunni Muslims that exists today.

[3] **Hanafī and Shāfi'ī:** Two schools of Islamic legal thought, taking their names after Abu Hanifa (c. 699–767) and al-Shāfi'i (767–820). Al-Shāfi'i believed in a literal interpretation of the Qur'an, the dictates of which he valued equally with the *sunna,* or practice of Muhammad as recorded in the Hadith. The Hanafi school, which allowed for more interpretive freedom on the part of individual scholars, was more predominant in Asia and India.

[4] **mullās:** Muslim theologians.

[5] **samanas:** Hindu and Buddhist ascetics.

which the Prophet was the repository, he laid all aside. And he made his courtiers continually listen to those revilings and attacks against our pure and easy, bright and holy faith. [. . .]

Some time before this a brāhman, named Puruk'hotam, who had written a commentary on the Book, *Increase of Wisdom* (*Khirad-afzā*),[6] had had private interviews with him, and he had asked him to invent particular Sanskrit names for all things in existence. And at one time a brāhman, named Debi, who was one of the interpreters of the *Mahābhārata,*[7] was pulled up the wall of the castle sitting on a bedstead till he arrived near a balcony, which the emperor had made his bed-chamber. Whilst thus suspended he instructed His Majesty in the secrets and legends of Hinduism, in the manner of worshiping idols, the fire, the sun and stars, and of revering the chief gods of these unbelievers, such as Brahma, Mahadev, Bishn, Kishn, Ram, and Mahama[8] (whose existence as sons of the human race is a supposition, but whose nonexistence is a certainty, though in their idle belief they look on some of them as gods, and some as angels). His Majesty, on hearing further how much the people of the country prized their institutions, began to look upon them with affection. [. . .]

Sometimes again it was Shaikh Tāj ud-dīn whom he sent for. This shaikh was son of Shaikh Zakarīya of Ajodhan. . . . He had been a pupil of Rashīd Shaikh Zamān of Panipat, author of a commentary on the *Paths (Lawā'ih),*[9] and of other excellent works, was most excellent in Sufism, and in the knowledge of theology second only to Shaikh Ibn ʿArabī and had written a comprehensive commentary on the *Joy of the Souls (Nuzhat ul-Arwāh).*[10] Like the preceding he was drawn up the wall of the castle in a blanket, and His Majesty listened the whole night to his Sufic obscenities and follies. The shaikh, since he did not in any great degree feel himself bound by the injunctions of the law, introduced arguments concerning the unity of existence, such as idle Sufis discuss, and which eventually led to license and open heresy. [. . .]

Learned monks also from Europe, who are called *Padre,*[11] and have an infallible head, called *Papa,* who is able to change religious ordinances as he may deem advisable for the moment, and to whose authority kings must submit, brought the Gospel, and advanced proofs for the Trinity. His Majesty firmly believed in the truth of the Christian religion, and wishing to spread the doctrines of Jesus, ordered

---

[6] ***Increase of Wisdom* (*Khirad-afzā*):** Bada'uni refers to this book, which so far remains lost, as a translation of Hindu stories into Persian made by Shamsuddin Altamish with the help of some Hindu pundits.

[7] ***Mahābhārata:*** The great Sanskrit epic, dating between 400 B.C.E. and 400 C.E., recounting the wars between the descendants of the legendary King Bharata, the Pandavas and the Kauravas.

[8] **Brahma . . . Mahama:** Bada'uni here lists the chief gods of the Hindus, a panoply of which he is skeptical. Mahadev is Shiva, Bishn is Vishnu, and Kishn is Krishna.

[9] ***Paths* (*Lawā'ih*):** A treatise on Sufism by the Persian mystic poet Jami (1414–1492).

[10] ***Nuzhat ul-Arwāh:*** A biographical dictionary of Islamic and Greek philosophers, scientists, and medical doctors composed by Shams al-din Muhammad ibn Mahmud al-Shahrazuri in the thirteenth century.

[11] ***Padre:*** (father); Bada'uni refers to the Portuguese Catholic missionaries from Goa from whom Akbar learned about Christianity. The *Papa,* of course, denotes the Roman Catholic pope.

Prince Murād to take a few lessons in Christianity under good auspices, and charged Abū 'l Fazl[12] to translate the Gospel. [. . .]

Fire worshipers also came from Nousarī in Gujarat, proclaimed the religion of Zardusht[13] as the true one, and declared reverence to fire to be superior to every other kind of worship. They also attracted the emperor's regard, and taught him the peculiar terms, the ordinances, the rites and ceremonies of the Kaianians.[14] At last he ordered that the sacred fire should be made over to the charge of Abū'l Fazl, and that after the manner of the kings of Persia, in whose temples blazed perpetual fires, he should take care it was never extinguished night or day, for that it is one of the signs of God, and one light from His lights. [. . .]

His Majesty also called some of the yogis, and gave them at night private interviews, inquiring into abstract truths; their articles of faith; their occupation; the influence of pensiveness; their several practices and usages; the power of being absent from the body; or into alchemy, physiognomy, and the power of omnipresence of the soul.

---

[12] **Abū'l Fazl:** (1551–1602), one of Akbar's most important and gifted advisers and author of the *Institutes of Akbar* and the *Book of Akbar*, which illuminate the policies of Akbar and chronicle the history of his reign (see p. 175).

[13] **Zardusht:** Zarathustra, or Zoroaster, is the legendary prophet and teacher from Bactria (ancient Persia) who founded a religion centered on the belief that the world is the site of a great battle between the supernatural forces of good and evil.

[14] **Kaianians:** A pre-Muslim dynasty centered in Seistan (Sejestan) in Persia.

Francis Bacon
1561–1626

Lawyer, politician, and philosopher of science, Francis Bacon was the son of the Lord Keeper of the Great Seal under Elizabeth I. As a young man he studied at Trinity College at Cambridge and then moved on to Gray's Inn, where he studied law. He spent his working years as a member of Parliament, which he entered at age twenty-three, and as a legal adviser. Bacon made his literary debut in 1597 with the publication of the *Essays*, which he supplemented and revised for later editions in 1612 and 1625. Combining speculative reflection and aphoristic expression, Bacon's essays cover a wide range of topics — from truth, death, and unity, to marriage, gardens, and reading. Objective and reserved, Bacon's essays offer a striking contrast to those of Montaigne. In 1618 he was named Lord Chancellor of England under King James I (r. 1603–25). His tenure was brief, however, for after only three years he was convicted of taking bribes and lost his position and reputation. The last five years of his life were the only time during his maturity that he spent outside the corridors of power. Perhaps appropriately—or ironically—he died as the result of a scientific experiment. Trying to determine the effect of cold on the decay of meat, Bacon went into the country in winter and stuffed the carcass of a fowl with snow. While doing so, he took a sudden chill that led to a fatal case of bronchitis; he died in March 1626.

Bacon was not a scientist by profession, yet he set out to free the science of his time from the deductive methods—reasoning from principles or laws to facts, in contrast to reasoning from observations of facts to laws—that medieval Scholasticism had derived from Aristotle. To break the hold of deductive science and inaugurate a new method for discovering truth, Bacon argued, people must become aware of the four "idols" of the mind—Idols of the Tribe, the Cave, the Marketplace, and the Theater—that interfere with direct observation of natural phenomena. If people can free themselves from preconceptions that they acquire through habit and conventional ideas, they may begin to see the world for what it is and develop appropriate experiments to increase their knowledge of it. Though he was better at identifying the weaknesses of his predecessors than in defining precisely the new method, Bacon pointed natural philosophers, as scientists were called, toward the importance of empirical observation, and he is remembered today as one of the founders of the scientific method. Among his scientific writings are *The Advancement of Learning* (1605), *Novum Organum* (1620), and *New Atlantis* (1626).

New Atlantis, excerpted here, is one of a number of Renaissance works describing ideal communities that began with Sir Thomas More's *Utopia* (1516), the work that introduced the word ***UTOPIA*** (no-place) into the language. *New Atlantis* shows both the Renaissance and **ENLIGHTENMENT** sides of Bacon's character. It describes the imaginary country of Bensalem, whose ideal society is based on a blend of Christian humanism, respect for tradition, and scientific observation and experimentation. On the one hand, the religion and social order of Bensalem is grounded in the study of ancient texts; on the other hand, the society is enriched by the discoveries and experiments of Salomon's House, a scientific research center that is its most important institution. Devoted to the orderly and controlled pursuit of empirical knowledge, the researchers at Salomon's House have made this "new Atlantis" into an advanced society, a scientific utopia. Although the work does not discuss the apparent contradictions of the two sides of this utopia—how, for example, the inevitable conflicts between revealed religion and experimental science would be resolved—it certainly points toward the Enlightenment spirit of inquiry. The text itself remains unfinished, its incompleteness suggesting the open-endedness of the scientific point of view.

FROM

New Atlantis

[Salomon's House]

[. . .] And as we were thus in conference, there came one that seemed to be a messenger, in a rich huke,[1] that spake with the Jew; whereupon he turned to me, and said, "You will pardon me, for I am commanded away in haste." The next morning he came to me again, joyful as it seemed, and said, "There is word come to the Governor of the city, that one of the fathers of Salomon's House[2] will be here this day sevennight; we have seen none of them this dozen years. His coming is in state; but the cause of his coming is secret. I will provide you and your fellows of a good standing to see his entry." I thanked him, and told him I was most glad of the news.

The day being come he made his entry. He was a man of middle stature and age, comely of person, and had an aspect as if he pitied men. He was clothed in a robe of fine black cloth, with wide sleeves, and a cape: his under garment was of excellent white linen down to the foot, girt with a girdle of the same; and a sindon or tippet of the same about his neck. He had gloves that were curious,[3] and set with stone; and shoes of peach-coloured velvet. His neck was bare to the shoulders. His hat was like a helmet, or Spanish montero;[4] and his locks curled below it decently: they were of colour brown. His beard was cut round and of the same colour with his hair, somewhat lighter. He was carried in a rich chariot, without wheels, litterwise, with two horses at either end, richly trapped in blue velvet embroidered; and two footmen on each side in the like attire. The chariot was all of cedar, gilt, and adorned with crystal; save that the fore-end had panels of sapphire, set in borders of gold, and the hinder-end the like of emeralds of the Peru colour. There was also a sun of gold, radiant upon the top, in the midst; and on the top before, a small cherub of gold, with wings displayed. The chariot was covered with cloth of gold tissued upon blue. He had before him fifty attendants, young men all, in white satin loose coats to the midleg; and stockings of white silk, and shoes of blue velvet; and hats of blue velvet, with fine plumes of divers colours, set round like hat-bands. Next before the chariot went two men, bare-headed, in linen garments down to the foot, girt, and shoes of blue velvet, who carried the one a crosier, the other a pastoral staff like a sheep-hook: neither of them of metal, but the crosier of balm-wood, the pastoral staff of cedar. Horsemen he had none, neither before nor behind his chariot: as it seemeth, to avoid all tumult and trouble. Behind his chariot went all the officers and principals of the companies

---

[1] **huke:** A cape with a hood.

[2] **Salomon's House:** Earlier in the text, this institution, what we might today call a center for advanced research, has been described as the "noblest foundation" and the "lantern of the kingdom." It is also called the "College of the Six Day's Works," and its purpose is to discover the "true nature of all things" and to transmit what is useful knowledge to the people of Bensalem.

[3] **curious:** Carefully made.

[4] **montero:** A hat with ear flaps.

of the city. He sat alone, upon cushions, of a kind of excellent plush, blue; and under his foot curious carpets of silk of divers colours, like the Persian, but far finer. He held up his bare hand, as he went, as blessing the people, but in silence. The street was wonderfully well kept; so that there was never any army had their men stand in better battle-array than the people stood. The windows likewise were not crowded, but every one stood in them, as if they had been placed.

When the show was passed, the Jew said to me, "I shall not be able to attend you as I would, in regard of some charge the city hath laid upon me for the entertaining of this great person." Three days after the Jew came to me again, and said, "Ye are happy men; for the father of Salomon's House taketh knowledge of your being here, and commanded me to tell you, that he will admit all your company to his presence, and have private conference with one of you, that ye shall choose; and for this hath appointed the next day after to-morrow. And because he meaneth to give you his blessing, he hath appointed it in the forenoon."

We came at our day and hour, and I was chosen by my fellows for the private access. We found him in a fair chamber, richly hanged, and carpeted under foot, without any degrees to the state.[5] He was set upon a low throne richly adorned, and a rich cloth of state over his head, of blue satin embroidered. He was alone, save that he had two pages of honour, on either hand one, finely attired in white. His under garments were the like that we saw him wear in the chariot; but instead of his gown, he had on him a mantle with a cape, of the same fine black, fastened about him. When we came in, as we were taught, we bowed low at our first entrance; and when we were come near his chair, he stood up, holding forth his hand ungloved, and in posture of blessing; and we every one of us stooped down, and kissed the hem of his tippet. That done, the rest departed, and I remained. Then he warned the pages forth of the room, and caused me to sit down beside him, and spake to me thus in the Spanish tongue:

"God bless thee, my son; I will give thee the greatest jewel I have. For I will impart unto thee, for the love of God and men, a relation of the true state of Salomon's House. Son, to make you know the true state of Salomon's House, I will keep this order. First, I will set forth unto you the end of our foundation. Secondly, the preparations and instruments we have for our works. Thirdly, the several employments and functions whereto our fellows are assigned. And fourthly, the ordinances and rites which we observe.

"The end of our foundation is the knowledge of causes, and secret motions of things; and the enlarging of the bounds of human empire, to the effecting of all things possible.

"The preparations and instruments are these. We have large and deep caves of several depths: the deepest are sunk six hundred fathoms; and some of them are digged and made under great hills and mountains; so that if you reckon together the depth of the hill, and the depth of the cave, they are, some of them, above three miles deep. For we find that the depth of a hill, and the depth of a cave from the flat, is the same thing; both remote alike from the sun and heaven's beams, and from the open

---

[5] **without . . . state:** Without any steps leading up to the throne.

air. These caves we call the lower region, and we use them for all coagulations, indurations, refrigerations, and conservations of bodies. We use them likewise for the imitation of natural mines, and the producing also of new artificial metals, by compositions and materials which we use, and lay there for many years. We use them also sometimes (which may seem strange) for curing of some diseases, and for prolongation of life, in some hermits that choose to live there, well accommodated of all things necessary, and indeed live very long; by whom also we learn many things.

"We have burials in several earths, where we put divers cements, as the Chinese do their porcelain. But we have them in greater variety, and some of them more fine. We also have great variety of composts and soils, for the making of the earth fruitful.

"We have high towers, the highest about half a mile in height, and some of them likewise set upon high mountains, so that the vantage of the hill, with the tower, is in the highest of them three miles at least. And these places we call the upper region, accounting the air between the high places and the low as a middle region. We use these towers, according to their several heights and situations, for insulation, refrigeration, conservation, and for the view of divers meteors[6]—as winds, rain, snow, hail; and some of the fiery meteors also. And upon them, in some places, are dwellings of hermits, whom we visit sometimes, and instruct what to observe.

"We have great lakes, both salt and fresh, whereof we have use for the fish and fowl. We use them also for burials of some natural bodies, for we find a difference in things buried in earth, or in air below the earth, and things buried in water. We have also pools, of which some do strain fresh water out of salt, and others by art do turn fresh water into salt. We have also some rocks in the midst of the sea, and some bays upon the shore for some works, wherein is required the air and vapour of the sea. We have likewise violent streams and cataracts, which serve us for many motions; and likewise engines for multiplying and enforcing[7] of winds to set also on divers motions.

"We have also a number of artificial wells and fountains, made in imitation of the natural sources and baths, as tincted upon vitriol, sulphur, steel, brass, lead, nitre, and other minerals; and again, we have little wells for infusions of many things, where the waters take the virtue quicker and better than in vessels or basins. And amongst them we have a water, which we call Water of Paradise, being by that we do to it made very sovereign for health and prolongation of life.

"We have also great and spacious houses, where we imitate and demonstrate meteors—as snow, hail, rain, some artificial rains of bodies, and not of water, thunders, lightnings; also generations of bodies in air—as frogs, flies, and divers others.

"We have also certain chambers, which we call chambers of health, where we qualify the air as we think good and proper for the cure of divers diseases, and preservation of health.

"We have also fair and large baths, of several mixtures, for the cure of diseases, and the restoring of man's body from arefaction;[8] and others for the confirming of it in strength of sinews, vital parts, and the very juice and substance of the body.

---

[6] **meteors:** In the Renaissance, a meteor was anything that fell from the sky. [7] **enforcing:** Reinforcing. [8] **arefaction:** Drying up.

"We have also large and various orchards and gardens, wherein we do not so much respect beauty as variety of ground and soil, proper for divers trees and herbs, and some very spacious, where trees and berries are set, whereof we make divers kinds of drinks, besides the vineyards. In these we practise likewise all conclusions of grafting and inoculating, as well of wild-trees as fruit-trees, which produceth many effects. And we make by art, in the same orchards and gardens, trees and flowers, to come earlier or later than their seasons, and to come up and bear more speedily than by their natural course they do. We make them also by art greater much than their nature; and their fruit greater and sweeter, and of differing taste, smell, colour, and figure, from their nature. And many of them we so order as they become of medicinal use.

"We have also means to make divers plants rise by mixtures of earths without seeds, and likewise to make divers new plants, differing from the vulgar, and to make one tree or plant turn into another.

"We have also parks, and enclosures of all sorts, of beasts and birds; which we use not only for view or rareness, but likewise for dissections and trials, that thereby we may take light what may be wrought upon the body of man. Wherein we find many strange effects: as continuing life in them, though divers parts, which you account vital, be perished and taken forth; resuscitating of some that seem dead in appearance, and the like. We try also all poisons, and other medicines upon them, as well of chirurgery[9] as physic. By art likewise we make them greater or taller than their kind is, and contrariwise dwarf them and stay their growth; we make them more fruitful and bearing than their kind is, and contrariwise barren and not generative. Also we make them differ in colour, shape, activity, many ways. We find means to make commixtures and copulations of divers kinds, which have produced many new kinds, and them not barren, as the general opinion is. We make a number of kinds, of serpents, worms, flies, fishes, of putrefaction, whereof some are advanced (in effect) to be perfect creatures, like beasts or birds, and have sexes, and do propagate. Neither do we this by chance, but we know beforehand of what matter and commixture, what kind of those creatures will arise.

"We have also particular pools where we make trials upon fishes, as we have said before of beasts and birds.

"We have also places for breed and generation of those kinds of worms and flies which are of special use; such as are with you your silkworms and bees.

"I will not hold you long with recounting of our brew-houses, bake-houses, and kitchens, where are made divers drinks, breads and meats, rare and of special effects. Wines we have of grapes, and drinks of other juice, of fruits, of grains, and of roots, and of mixtures with honey, sugar, manna, and fruits dried and decocted;[10] also of the tears or woundings of trees, and of the pulp of canes. And these drinks are of several ages, some to the age or last[11] of forty years. We have drinks also brewed with several herbs, and roots and spices; yea, with several fleshes and white-meats; whereof some of the drinks are such as they are in effect meat and drink both, so that divers, especially in age, do desire to live with them with little or no meat or bread.

[9] **chirurgery:** Surgery. [10] **decocted:** Dissolved in water. [11] **last:** Duration.

And above all we strive to have drinks of extreme thin parts, to insinuate into the body, and yet without all biting, sharpness, or fretting; insomuch as some of them, put upon the back of your hand, will with a little stay pass through to the palm, and taste yet mild to the mouth. We have also waters, which we ripen in that fashion, as they become nourishing, so that they are indeed excellent drinks, and many will use no other. Bread we have of several grains, roots, and kernels; yea, and some of flesh, and fish, dried; with divers kinds of leavenings and seasonings; so that some do extremely move appetites, some do nourish so, as divers do live of them, without any other meat, who live very long. So for meats, we have some of them so beaten, and made tender, and mortified,[12] yet without all corrupting, as a weak heat of the stomach will turn them into good chilus,[13] as well as a strong heat would meat otherwise prepared. We have some meats also, and breads, and drinks, which taken by men, enable them to fast long after; and some other, that used make the very flesh of men's bodies sensibly more hard and tough, and their strength far greater than otherwise it would be.

"We have dispensatories or shops of medicines; wherein you may easily think, if we have such variety of plants, and living creatures, more than you have in Europe (for we know what you have), the simples,[14] drugs and ingredients of medicines, must likewise be in so much the greater variety. We have them likewise of divers ages, and long fermentations. And for their preparations, we have not only all manner of exquisite distillations and separations, and especially by gentle heats, and percolations through divers strainers, yea, and substances; but also exact forms of composition, whereby they incorporate almost as they were natural simples.

"We have also divers mechanical arts, which you have not; and stuffs made by them, as papers, linen, silks, tissues, dainty works of feathers of wonderful lustre, excellent dyes, and many others: and shops likewise, as well for such as are not brought into vulgar use amongst us, as for those that are. For you must know, that of the things before recited, many of them are grown into use throughout the kingdom, but yet, if they did flow from our invention, we have of them also for patterns and principles.

"We have also furnaces of great diversities, and that keep great diversity of heats: fierce and quick, strong and constant, soft and mild; blown, quiet, dry, moist, and the like. But above all we have heats, in imitation of the sun's and heavenly bodies' heats, that pass divers inequalities, and (as it were) orbs, progresses, and returns, whereby we produce admirable effects. Besides, we have heats of dungs, and of bellies and maws of living creatures and of their bloods and bodies, and of hays and herbs laid up moist, of lime unquenched, and such like. Instruments also which generate heat only by motion. And farther, places for strong insulations; and again, places under the earth, which by nature or art yield heat. These divers heats we use as the nature of the operation which we intend requireth.

"We have also perspective houses, where we make demonstrations of all lights and radiations, and of all colours; and out of things uncoloured and transparent, we can represent unto you all several colours, not in rainbows (as it is in gems and

[12] **mortified:** Softened. [13] **chilus:** Food softened by heat into a digestible form. [14] **simples:** Herbs.

prisms), but of themselves single. We represent also all multiplications of light, which we carry to great distance, and make so sharp, as to discern small points and lines. Also all colourations of light; all delusions and deceits of the sight, in figures, magnitudes, motions, colours; all demonstrations of shadows. We find also divers means yet unknown to you, of producing of light, originally from divers bodies. We procure means of seeing objects afar off, as in the heaven and remote places; and represent things near as afar off, and things afar off as near; making feigned distances. We have also helps for the sight, far above spectacles and glasses in use. We have also glasses and means to see small and minute bodies, perfectly and distinctly; as the shapes and colours of small flies and worms, grains, and flaws in gems which cannot otherwise be seen, observations in urine and blood not otherwise to be seen. We make artificial rainbows, halos, and circles about light. We represent also all manner of reflections, refractions, and multiplications of visual beams of objects.

"We have also precious stones of all kinds, many of them of great beauty and to you unknown; crystals likewise, and glasses of divers kinds; and amongst them some of metals vitrificated, and other materials, besides those of which you make glass. Also a number of fossils and imperfect minerals, which you have not. Likewise loadstones of prodigious virtue: and other rare stones, both natural and artificial.

"We have also sound-houses, where we practise and demonstrate all sounds and their generation. We have harmonies which you have not, of quarter-sounds and lesser slides of sounds. Divers instruments of music likewise to you unknown, some sweeter than any you have; together with bells and rings that are dainty and sweet. We represent small sounds as great and deep; likewise great sounds, extenuate and sharp; we make divers tremblings and warblings of sounds, which in their original are entire. We represent and imitate all articulate sounds and letters, and the voices and notes of beasts and birds. We have certain helps, which set to the ear do further the hearing greatly. We have also divers strange and artificial echoes, reflecting the voice many times, and as it were tossing it; and some that give back the voice louder than it came, some shriller and some deeper; yea, some rendering the voice, differing in the letters or articulate sound from that they receive. We have also means to convey sounds in trunks and pipes, in strange lines and distances.

"We have also perfume-houses, wherewith we join also practices of taste. We multiply smells, which may seem strange: we imitate smells, making all smells to breathe out of other mixtures than those that give them. We make divers imitations of taste likewise, so that they will deceive any man's taste. And in this house we contain also a confiture-house, where we make all sweetmeats, dry and moist, and divers pleasant wines, milks, broths, and salads, far in greater variety than you have.

"We have also engine-houses, where are prepared engines and instruments for all sorts of motions. There we imitate and practise to make swifter motions than any you have, either out of your muskets or any engine that you have; and to make them and multiply them more easily and with small force, by wheels and other means, and to make them stronger and more violent than yours are, exceeding your greatest cannons and basilisks.[15] We represent also ordnance and instruments of war and

[15] **basilisks:** Large cannons.

engines of all kinds; and likewise new mixtures and compositions of gunpowder, wild-fires burning in water and unquenchable, also fire-works of all variety, both for pleasure and use. We imitate also flights of birds; we have some degrees of flying in the air. We have ships and boats for going under water and brooking of seas, also swimming-girdles and supporters. We have divers curious clocks, and other like motions of return, and some perpetual motions. We imitate also motions of living creatures by images of men, beasts, birds, fishes, and serpents; we have also a great number of other various motions, strange for equality, fineness, and subtilty.

"We have also a mathematical-house, where are represented all instruments, as well of geometry as astronomy, exquisitely made.

"We have also houses of deceits of the senses, where we represent all manner of feats of juggling, false apparitions, impostures, and illusions, and their fallacies. And surely you will easily believe that we, that have so many things truly natural which induce admiration, could in a world of particulars deceive the senses if we would disguise those things, and labour to make them seem more miraculous. But we do hate all impostures and lies, insomuch as we have severely forbidden it to all our fellows, under pain of ignominy and fines, that they do not show any natural work or thing adorned or swelling, but only pure as it is, and without all affectation of strangeness.

"These are, my son, the riches of Salomon's House.

"For the several employments and offices of our fellows, we have twelve that sail into foreign countries under the names of other nations (for our own we conceal) who bring us the books and abstracts, and patterns of experiments of all other parts. These we call Merchants of Light.

"We have three that collect the experiments which are in all books. These we call Depredators.

"We have three that collect the experiments of all mechanical arts, and also of liberal sciences, and also of practises which are not brought into arts. These we call Mystery-men.

"We have three that try new experiments, such as themselves think good. These we call Pioneers or Miners.

"We have three that draw the experiments of the former four into titles and tables, to give the better light for the drawing of observations and axioms out of them. These we call Compilers.

"We have three that bend themselves, looking into the experiments of their fellows, and cast about how to draw out of them things of use and practice for man's life and knowledge, as well for works as for plain demonstration of causes, means of natural divinations, and the easy and clear discovery of the virtues and parts of bodies. These we call Dowry-men or Benefactors.

"Then after divers meetings and consults of our whole number, to consider of the former labours and collections, we have three that take care out of them to direct new experiments, of a higher light, more penetrating into Nature than the former. These we call Lamps.

"We have three others that do execute the experiments so directed, and report them. These we call Inoculators.

"Lastly, we have three that raise the former discoveries by experiments into greater observations, axioms, and aphorisms. These we call Interpreters of Nature.

"We have also, as you must think, novices and apprentices, that the succession of the former employed men do not fail; besides a great number of servants and attendants, men and women. And this we do also: we have consultations, which of the inventions and experiences which we have discovered shall be published, and which not: and take all an oath of secrecy for the concealing of those which we think fit to keep secret: though some of those we do reveal sometimes to the State, and some not.

"For our ordinances and rites, we have two very long and fair galleries: in one of these we place patterns and samples of all manner of the more rare and excellent inventions: in the other we place the statues of all principal inventors. There we have the statue of your Columbus, that discovered the West Indies: also the inventor of ships: your Monk that was the inventor of ordnance and of gunpowder: the inventor of music: the inventor of letters: the inventor of printing: the inventor of observations of astronomy: the inventor of works in metal: the inventor of glass: the inventor of silk of the worm: the inventor of wine: the inventor of corn and bread: the inventor of sugars: and all these by more certain tradition than you have. Then we have divers inventors of our own, of excellent works, which since you have not seen, it were too long to make descriptions of them; and besides, in the right understanding of those descriptions you might easily err. For upon every invention of value we erect a statue to the inventor, and give him a liberal and honourable reward. These statues are some of brass, some of marble and touchstone, some of cedar and other special woods gilt and adorned; some of iron, some of silver, some of gold.

"We have certain hymns and services, which we say daily, of laud and thanks to God for His marvellous works. And forms of prayer, imploring His aid and blessing for the illumination of our labours, and the turning of them into good and holy uses.

"Lastly, we have circuits or visits, of divers principal cities of the kingdom; where, as it cometh to pass, we do publish such new profitable inventions as we think good. And we do also declare natural divinations of diseases, plagues, swarms of hurtful creatures, scarcity, tempests, earthquakes, great inundations, comets, temperature of the year, and divers other things; and we give counsel thereupon, what the people shall do for the prevention and remedy of them."

And when he had said this he stood up; and I, as I had been taught, knelt down; and he laid his right hand upon my head, and said, "God bless thee, my son, and God bless this relation which I have made. I give thee leave to publish it, for the good of other nations; for we here are in God's bosom, a land unknown." And so he left me; having assigned a value of about two thousand ducats for a bounty to me and my fellows. For they give great largesses, where they come, upon all occasions.

The rest was not perfected

WILLIAM SHAKESPEARE
1564–1616

In the 1623 Folio, the first collected edition of William Shakespeare's works, fellow poet and critic Ben Jonson (1572–1637) paid tribute to his great contemporary:

> Triumph, my *Britaine,* thou hast one to showe,
> To whom all scenes of *Europe* homage owe.
> He was not of an age, but for all time!

Jonson's lines do not exaggerate, for from the sixteenth century to the present Shakespeare's tragedies, comedies, histories, and romances throughout the world have been performed on stage, adapted for film, and studied for their dramatic techniques, the complexity of their characters, their history, and their philosophy. From the noble magnanimity of King Lear and the mean vindictiveness of Iago, through the hopeless innocence of Juliet and the sprightly savvy of Beatrice, to the deep vexation of Hamlet, Shakespeare's plays evoke a full range of human passions and experiences. The plays allow viewers to see the **RENAISSANCE** mind in all its complexity, as characters vie for love and power in an atmosphere shot through with a tragic sense that forces beyond human reckoning may at any moment thwart the best of human efforts. Against the forces of "Devouring Time," as Shakespeare calls it in Sonnet 19, each person must seize those moments of fulfillment, hope, love, and self-esteem before they vanish; yet in his work, Shakespeare the poet held one stop against mutability, and his concluding couplet has proved to be self-prophetic: "Yet do thy worst, old Time: despite thy wrong, / My love shall in my verse ever live young."

WWW For links to more information about Shakespeare and a quiz on *The Tempest,* see *World Literature Online* at bedfordstmartins.com/worldlit.

Shakespeare was no deep reader. True; but in the Greece of Pindar and Sophocles, in the England of Shakespeare, the poet lived in a current of ideas in the highest degree animating and nourishing to the creative power; society was, in the fullest measure, permeated by fresh thought, intelligent and alive.

– MATTHEW ARNOLD, "The Function of Criticism at the Present Time," 1864

Stratford-on-Avon. About William Shakespeare's early life little is known, but much has been invented. He was born in Stratford-on-Avon, a market town in Warwickshire, just northwest of London, in April 1564. William's father, John Shakespeare, was a glove maker and leather worker who through his trade and a fortunate marriage to Mary Arden, heiress of a small estate, rose to become a member of the city council and Bailiff at Stratford. As the son in a respectable family, young William most likely received the standard education in Latin grammar, reading, and writing at the Stratford grammar school. Biographers have speculated that Shakespeare must have enjoyed the bustling life of Stratford, with its renowned local fairs, visiting theater companies, and ample countryside in which a young imaginative boy could exercise his fancy. All we know for certain is that on November 27, 1582, the Bishop of Worcester issued a marriage license to William Shakespeare and Anne Hathaway; the parish records show the birth of a daughter in 1583 and a set of twins, a son and daughter, in 1585. Sometime between 1582 and 1592, Shakespeare began to take an active part in the theater in London, for which Robert Greene in a letter called the young actor and writer "an upstart Crow," a player so bold as to think he could write plays.

Robert Deighton, *Prospero*, 1777
This watercolor depicts the eighteenth-century actor Robert Bensley as Prospero in The Tempest. *(The Art Archive / Garrick Club / Garrick Club)*

A Man of the Theater. When London theaters reopened in 1594 after being closed for two years by an outbreak of the plague, Shakespeare was performing with one of the most prominent acting companies, the Lord Chamberlain's Men, along with the great actors Richard Burbage and William Kemp. During the lull in dramatic activity, Shakespeare had written his two important nondramatic poems, *Venus and Adonis* (1593) and *The Rape of Lucrece* (1594), both dedicated to the Earl of Southampton and showing his debt to, and command of, the classical education he had received as a youth. Proceeds from his theatrical endeavors, Southampton's patronage, and various business transactions were proving remarkably profitable for the young actor and writer, and in 1597 Shakespeare purchased New Place, one of the finest houses in Stratford. Two years later Shakespeare joined Richard Burbage and others to found the Globe Theatre, one of the most important playhouses in London, which was built to the specifications of the actor–proprietors, members of the Chamberlain's Men. After Queen Elizabeth's death in 1603, this troupe, now called the King's Men and fast becoming the preeminent company at Court and in the city, received the sponsorship of James I, who made them Grooms of the Chamber.

Shakespeare approximates the remote, and familiarizes the wonderful; the event which he represents will not happen, but if it were possible, its effects would probably be such as he has assigned.
– SAMUEL JOHNSON, *Preface to Shakespeare*, 1765

The King's Men. By this time, Shakespeare was already celebrated as a writer. In 1598, Francis Mere compared Shakespeare favorably to Plautus and Seneca, noting in his *Palladis Tamia: Wit's Treasury* that whereas these writers are known for comedy and tragedy, respectively, "Shakespeare among the English is the most excellent in both kinds for the stage." Among the plays written up to this time are many of the histories, including Parts One through Three of *Henry the Sixth, Richard III, King John,* and Parts One and Two of *Henry IV; The Comedy of Errors, A Midsummer Night's Dream,* and *The Taming of the Shrew* among other comedies; and *Titus Andronicus* and *Romeo and Juliet* among the tragedies. Between 1598 and 1609, a period of incredible artistic productivity for the poet–dramatist, Shakespeare completed more than fifteen major plays, including *Hamlet, Othello,* and *King Lear,* among the tragedies; *As You Like It* and *All's Well That Ends Well,* among the comedies; and *Pericles Prince of Tyre,* a romance. The King's Men now had established a veritable stronghold over London theater, having acquired in 1608 Blackfriar's Theatre. Unlike the Globe, Blackfriar's was an enclosed playhouse, which enabled the players to hold winter performances. Around 1610, Shakespeare retired from London to his home at Stratford, where he wrote his final plays—*Cymbeline, The Winter's Tale, The Tempest,* and *Henry VIII*—and where he died April 23, 1616.

But it exceeds all imagination to conceive what would have been the moral condition of the world if neither Dante, Petrarch, Boccaccio, Chaucer, Shakespeare, Calderón, Lord Bacon, nor Milton, had ever existed.

– Percy Bysshe Shelley, *A Defence of Poetry,* 1821

The Plays. The vast range of Shakespeare's dramatic production, the diversity of characters, and the variations of dramatic form among the plays do not admit to much generalization. As Ben Jonson's tribute points out, Shakespeare was at home writing both tragedies and comedies, but he was equally adept at writing history plays and what some call romances; most important, however, many of his greatest dramas blur the boundaries among these genres. Like many other **Elizabethan** dramatists, Shakespeare often disregarded the classical "unities," derived from Aristotle's *Poetics,*[1] refusing to limit the action to a single day and to a single place. English theater during this period did not look to Sophocles, Aristophanes, Terence, or Plautus for its models.

What distinguishes Shakespeare's plays are their intricacy of plot, brilliant display of language, and presentation of complex characters that, despite their historical particularity, have fascinated and served the interests of readers throughout the world for four hundred years. Prince Hal from *Henry IV,* Hamlet, and Rosalind from *As You Like It* come to us as visitations from a political and social reality constructed entirely differently from ours; yet with their differences as well as their similarities they exert a lively, almost palpable presence even to contemporary readers and spectators. Through his art, Shakespeare transformed stock dramatic types, such as the *miles gloriosus*—the boastful soldier—into likable characters, such as Falstaff in *Henry IV.*

The Great Chain of Being. It is important to keep in mind that the Elizabethan England in which Shakespeare wrote his plays operated on a

[1] **Aristotle's *Poetics*:** The *Poetics* is one of the earliest works of literary criticism in the West, compiled from the notes of students who attended the lectures of the Greek philosopher Aristotle (384–322 B.C.E.). The *Poetics* offers definitions of epic poetry and of tragedy that influenced later generations of critics and writers.

Historical arguments claiming that Shakespeare could not have intended Prospero to be seen as unattractive or Caliban as sympathetic are denying to the Renaissance's greatest playwright precisely that complexity of sensibility which is what we have come to value most in Shakespearian drama.

– Stephen Orgel, critic, 1987

model of hierarchical stratification—the **Great Chain of Being**—that was thought to stretch from the lowliest form of inert matter up to God, the purest form of active spirit. Ulysses's often-quoted speech on degree from *Troilus and Cressida* describes the systematic correspondence between heaven and earth, cautioning that any transgression of the vested degrees sends a fault along the entire system: "Take but degree away, untune that string, / And hark what discord follows" (I.iii.109–10). At the center of the universal ladder stood humanity, fraught with the physical limitations of the animal kingdom, yet endowed with the spiritual and intellectual essence of the higher forms of life. In *The Tempest,* Caliban and Ariel symbolize the two sides of this imperfect match in human nature, and Prospero's manipulation of them suggests the balance that humanity can achieve between its physical and spiritual elements. In some plays, such as *Hamlet,* Shakespeare thematizes the consequences of a world untuned and the vexation that such duality can impose upon human beings. Thus, Hamlet complains to Ophelia, "what should such fellows as I do, crawling between earth and heaven?" (III.ii.127–28).

The Globe Theatre. The Globe Theatre itself, for which Shakespeare's plays were written, was a slice of the Elizabethan's stratified society. Built in the shape of a polyhedron around an open courtyard, the theater had galleries on its sides, with the stage extending from one side out into the center of the courtyard. Wealthier spectators occupied the three floors of galleries, and those with less money, the groundlings, stood in the courtyard, or pit, and looked across to the stage that stood five feet above the ground. The stage itself embodied the structure of the religious cosmos. The area under the stage was called Hell (from which ghosts and devils emerged by means of a trap door); the area above the stage, a covered ceiling space from which gods and angels descended, was called the Heavens. At the back of the stage was another enclosed area that could be used in the productions, and behind that the "tiring house," where actors waited for their cues. Just above the back of the stage was a gallery for musicians, when called for in the play, or on which to stage balcony scenes. In the cosmic scheme of its design, the stage obviously represented the world, a point that Shakespeare toys with repeatedly in his drama, perhaps most familiarly in *As You Like It,* where Jacques declares "All the world's a stage, / And all the men and women merely players . . ." (II.vii.139–40). In *The Tempest,* Shakespeare again depends on the audience's awareness that the Globe Theatre could symbolize the world in miniature, when Prospero points to the transience of life and the products of human labor:

> . . . the great globe itself,
> Yea, all which it inherit, shall dissolve,
> And, like this insubstantial pageant faded,
> Leave not a rack behind. (IV.i.153–56)

Thus, the Globe was a microcosm of the ordered universe, reproducing in its design and in its organization of spectators the cosmic and social divisions along a structured gradient of high and low. The mixing of high and low at the Globe and other theaters had important consequences for Elizabethan playwrights, who took care to address all levels of the mixed audience in their plays. As evidenced in *The Tempest,* dramatists offered a blend of subtle and crude humor, refined and coarse language, serious and comic plots and subplot, to engage the variety of spectators.

> **. . . the direction of *The Tempest* is toward forgiveness. And if that forgiveness is itself the manifestation of supreme power, the emblem of that power remains marriage rather than punishment.**
> **– Stephen Greenblatt, critic, 1988**

The Tempest. *The Tempest* was first performed at Court in 1611 and published in what is known as the First Folio of 1623.[2] Listed among the Comedies in the First Folio, *The Tempest* eludes categorization and has been called a romance, a romantic comedy, a tragicomedy, and a romantic tragicomedy; modern editors generally list *The Tempest* as a romance, along with *Pericles Prince of Tyre, Cymbeline,* and *The Winter's Tale.* Its transgressive spirit and deliberate mixing of forms—tragedy, comedy, masque, satire—suggest that *The Tempest* self-consciously addresses the playwright's art and celebrates the artist's power to transcend the social and aesthetic codes and conventions of the time, even as it questions the moral consequences of breaking such boundaries. The play more generally questions the relationship between nature and art, especially as that relationship is negotiated by the playwright, here compared to a magician. Indeed, Prospero becomes a composite figure of the forms of power, assembling in his various guises the prince, the playwright, the magician, and the father, thus blurring the distinctions and highlighting the resemblances among those roles. The comic subplot involving Stephano and Trinculo parodies, as it mirrors, the important questions about the responsibilities of princes, the governance of state, the building of empires, and the treatment (and nature) of the prince's subjects. Although Prospero shapes the events that take place on his island and even exerts dominion over nature, as when he conjures up the storm that sets the plot in motion, unlike Faustus he recognizes and accepts the limitations of his legitimate power. Thus, like Marlowe's *Doctor Faustus,*[3] *The Tempest* raises questions about knowledge and power—for the artist as well as the prince.

Although many of Shakespeare's plays are based on earlier plays or popular stories, *The Tempest* may have its origins in the story of the wreck of a ship, the *Sea Adventurer,* off the coast of Bermuda in 1609. En route to Virginia from Plymouth, the *Sea Adventurer*'s passengers included the new governor of Virginia, Sir Thomas Gates. After being stranded for

[2] **First Folio of 1623:** The First Folio, printed between February 1622 and November 1623, was the first printed collection of Shakespeare's plays. Divided into comedies, histories, and tragedies, the Folio serves as the foundation for all subsequent editions of the plays, except *Pericles,* which was not included. The First Folio was published by Edward Blount and the printers William and Isaac Jaggard, with editorial assistance from the actors and co-owners of Shakespeare's company, the King's Men, particularly Jon Heminge and Henry Condell, who wrote a dedication and preface. The Folio was based on previously printed (quarto) versions of some of the plays and from manuscript fragments, transcripts, and players' prompt-books for the eighteen plays that had not been printed before.

[3] **Marlowe's *Doctor Faustus*:** The English playwright Christopher Marlowe (1564–1593) wrote several important Elizabethan tragedies, including *Tamburlaine* (published 1590) and his most famous play, *Doctor Faustus* (published 1604). (See p. 389.)

The Tempest . . . declares no all-embracing triumph for colonialism. Rather it serves as a limit text in which the characteristic operations of colonialist discourse may be discerned—as an instrument of exploitation, a register of beleaguerment and a site of radical ambivalence.

– Paul Brown, critic, 1985

nine months, the entire group of 150 crew and passengers managed to sail back to Jamestown on two smaller boats that they had built. Accounts of these adventures began to appear in 1610, leading to speculation that Shakespeare either had read the accounts or may have been acquainted with one of the authors. What is important, however, is that Shakespeare constructs out of such an adventure a play that engages key questions about the nature of power, politics, art, and humanity.

■ CONNECTIONS

Niccolò Machiavelli, *The Prince*, p. 124. Like many Renaissance texts, *The Tempest* raises questions about the limits of human power, legitimate authority, and the duties and responsibilities of leaders. By manipulating natural forces, Prospero creates a counterfeit world, a spectacle or theater by means of which his shipwrecked friends and foes reveal their true natures. In creating his spectacle and manipulating events on the island, Prospero seems to follow some of the principles established in Machiavelli's *The Prince.* Consider Prospero as a Machiavellian prince. Do his ends justify his means? How do his principles qualify or differ from those Machiavelli describes?

Christopher Columbus, *Diario*, p. 773; "In the World: Colonialism," Book 6. For many contemporary writers from former colonies, *The Tempest* has become a central focus of critical debate and creative appropriation. Seeing Prospero as a colonial power occupying a colonial territory and subordinating its resources and inhabitants to his own ends, these writers show how the play mirrors—not necessarily for critical purposes—the colonial relation between centralized European powers and their colonial peripheries. How does the colonial relation as it appears in the play compare to that we see in Columbus's *Diario*? Consider too Césaire's rewriting of the play from Caliban's point of view, or Chinweizu's appropriation of the Caliban and Ariel as figures in his "Decolonizing of the African Mind."

Sophocles, *Antigone*, Book 1; Aristotle, *Poetics*, Book 1; Molière, *Tartuffe*, Book 4; Chikamatsu, *Love Suicides at Amijima*, Book 4. In the First Folio, *The Tempest* was classified as a comedy; like many comedies, the play culminates in marriage and a favorable resolution for the main characters of the play. Modern editors, however, tend to classify the drama as a romance, because it lacks the lighthearted tone of comedy, takes place in an exotic setting, and suggests something of the mythic and supernatural. The play, then, raises questions about the classification of genre in drama, both within Western literary tradition and in the context of world literature. Compare *The Tempest* to Sophocles's classic tragedy (theorized in Aristotle's *Poetics*), to Molière's comedy, and/or to Chikamatsu's tragedy: What tragic and comic elements do we find in *The Tempest*? Why is it not a comedy or a tragedy? Do these categories as defined in Western poetics apply to the Japanese stage?

■ FURTHER RESEARCH

Biography

Burgess, Anthony. *Shakespeare.* 1970.

Schoenbaum, S. *William Shakespeare: A Compact Documentary Life.* 1977.

Background

Bradbrook, Muriel. *The Rise of the Common Player.* 1964.

Gurr, Andrew. *The Shakespearean Stage: 1574–1642.* 3rd ed. 1992.

Robinson, Randal. *Unlocking Shakespeare's Language: Help for the Teacher and Student.* 1989.

Taylor, Gary. *Reinventing Shakespeare: A Cultural History from the Restoration to the Present.* 1989.

Criticism

Felperin, Howard. *Shakespearean Romance.* 1972.

Fiedler, Leslie. *The Stranger in Shakespeare.* 1972.

Graff, Gerald, and James Phelan. *William Shakespeare: The Tempest: A Case Study in Critical Controversy.* 2000.

Greenblatt, Stephen J. *Shakespearean Negotiations.* 1988.

———. *Learning to Curse: Essays in Early Modern Culture.* 1990.

Hillman, Richard. *Shakespearean Subversions: The Trickster and the Play-Text.* 1992.

Hulme, Peter, and William H. Sherman, eds. *The Tempest and Its Travels.* 2000.

Kermode, Frank. *The Tempest.* 1954.

Kernan, Alvin B. *The Playwright as Magician: Shakespeare's Image of the Poet in the English Public Theater.* 1979.

Vaughan, Alden T., and Virginia Mason Vaughan. *Shakespeare's Caliban: A Cultural History.* 1991.

The Tempest

THE SCENE: *An uninhabited island.*

NAMES OF THE ACTORS

ALONSO, *King of Naples*
SEBASTIAN, *his brother*
PROSPERO, *the right Duke of Milan*
ANTONIO, *his brother, the usurping Duke of Milan*
FERDINAND, *son to the King of Naples*
GONZALO, *an honest old councilor*
ADRIAN *and* FRANCISCO, *lords*
CALIBAN, *a savage and deformed slave*
TRINCULO, *a jester*
STEPHANO, *a drunken butler*
MASTER OF A SHIP
BOATSWAIN
MARINERS
MIRANDA, *daughter to Prospero*
ARIEL, *an airy spirit*
IRIS, CERES, JUNO, NYMPHS, REAPERS — *[presented by] spirits*
[OTHER SPIRITS ATTENDING ON PROSPERO]

The Tempest. *The Tempest* was first performed in 1611 and first published in the 1623 Folio printed by William and Isaac Jaggard. As with all of Shakespeare's plays, no manuscript version of the play has survived. Shakespeare's next-to-last play, *The Tempest* has been called his valedictory play, summing up his art, celebrating the power of the playwright, and, like Prospero, announcing his retirement. The play addresses questions about the limits of human power, the human place in the cosmos, and, like many of Shakespeare's plays, about the nature of theater—of spectacle and imagination—as an agency in shaping thought and behavior. Moreover, taking place on an island symbolizing the "brave" New World, the play places these questions about the nature of power, politics, art, and humanity into the context of European colonization. Drawing on John Florio's translation of Montaigne's "Of Cannibals," the play speculates on the nature of human beings in the New World, their place in the Great Chain of Being, and their relationship to Europe. Like a Renaissance magician, operating within the parameters nature's laws impose on him, Prospero manipulates the ethereal spirit Ariel as well as the supposedly baser Caliban. Caliban symbolizes, on the one hand, nature and natural processes (he is attuned to the beauty and music of his native island) and, on the other hand, native peoples of the New World. Standing in the place of nature and native, Caliban becomes subject to Prospero's attempts first to tame or civilize him, and then

ACT I

Scene 1

On a ship at sea.

A tempestuous noise of thunder and lightning heard. Enter a SHIPMASTER *and a* BOATSWAIN.

MASTER: Boatswain!

BOATSWAIN: Here, master. What cheer?

MASTER: Good,[1] speak to th' mariners! Fall to't yarely,[2] or we run ourselves aground. Bestir, bestir! *Exit.*

Enter MARINERS.

BOATSWAIN: Heigh, my hearts! Cheerly, cheerly, my hearts! Yare, yare! Take in the topsail! Tend to th' master's whistle! Blow till thou burst thy wind, if room enough![3]

Enter ALONSO, SEBASTIAN, ANTONIO, FERDINAND, GONZALO, *and others.*

ALONSO: Good boatswain, have care. Where's the master? Play the men.[4]

BOATSWAIN: I pray now, keep below.

ANTONIO: Where is the master, bos'n?

BOATSWAIN: Do you not hear him? You mar our labor. Keep your cabins; you do assist the storm.

GONZALO: Nay, good, be patient.

BOATSWAIN: When the sea is. Hence! What cares these roarers for the name of king? To cabin! Silence! Trouble us not!

GONZALO: Good, yet remember whom thou hast aboard.

BOATSWAIN: None that I more love than myself. You are a councilor; if you can command these elements to silence and work the peace of the present,[5] we will not hand[6] a rope more. Use your authority. If you cannot, give thanks you have lived so long, and make yourself ready in your cabin for the mischance of the hour, if it so hap. Cheerly, good hearts! Out of our way, I say. *Exit.*

---

to control him by force. Thus, the play mirrors both the subjugation of nature to the developing instrumentalities of science and the subordination of colonial subjects to European conquest. While Prospero's intentions are comic—to restore himself to his rightful place, to marry his daughter well, and to lead the evildoers to atonement and redemption—his treatment of Ariel and especially of Caliban dramatizes the way the Great Chain of Being became for many a chain of subordination. As a study of power and colonialism, *The Tempest* has become an important play for contemporary writers, such as George Lamming (b. 1927), from Barbados, and Aimé Césaire (b. 1913), from Martinique, whose *Une Tempete* (1969) rewrites the play from Caliban's point of view.

The edition presented here was edited and annotated by Robert Langbaum.

---

[1] **Good:** Good fellow. [All notes in this selection are from editor Robert Langbaum.]

[2] **yarely:** Briskly. [3] **Blow . . . enough!:** The storm can blow and split itself as long as there is open sea without rocks to maneuver in. [4] **Play the men:** Act like men. [5] **work . . . present:** Restore the present to peace (since as a councilor his job is to quell disorder). [6] **hand:** Handle.

GONZALO: I have great comfort from this fellow. Methinks he hath no drowning mark upon him; his complexion is perfect gallows.[7] Stand fast, good Fate, to his hanging! Make the rope of his destiny our cable, for our own doth little advantage.[8] If he be not born to be hanged, our case is miserable.

Exit [*with the rest*].

Enter BOATSWAIN.

BOATSWAIN: Down with the topmast! Yare! Lower, lower! Bring her to try with main course![9] [*A cry within.*] A plague upon this howling! They are louder than the weather or our office.

Enter SEBASTIAN, ANTONIO, *and* GONZALO.

Yet again? What do you here? Shall we give o'er[10] and drown? Have you a mind to sink?

SEBASTIAN: A pox o' your throat, you bawling, blasphemous, incharitable dog!

BOATSWAIN: Work you, then.

ANTONIO: Hang, cur! Hang, you whoreson, insolent noisemaker! We are less afraid to be drowned than thou art.

GONZALO: I'll warrant him for[11] drowning, though the ship were no stronger than a nutshell and as leaky as an unstanched[12] wench.

BOATSWAIN: Lay her ahold, ahold! Set her two courses![13] Off to the sea again! Lay her off![14]

Enter MARINERS *wet.*

MARINERS:

All lost! To prayers, to prayers! All lost! [*Exeunt.*]

BOATSWAIN:

What, must our mouths be cold?

GONZALO:

The King and Prince at prayers! Let's assist them,
For our case is as theirs.

SEBASTIAN:

I am out of patience.

ANTONIO:

We are merely° cheated of our lives by drunkards. — completely
This wide-chopped° rascal—would thou mightst lie drowning — big-mouthed
The washing of ten tides![15]

GONZALO:

He'll be hanged yet,
Though every drop of water swear against it

[7] **drowning . . . gallows:** Alluding to the proverb, "He that's born to be hanged need fear no drowning." [8] **doth . . . advantage:** Gives us little advantage. [9] **Bring . . . course!:** Heave to, under the mainsail. [10] **give o'er:** Give up trying to run the ship. [11] **warrant him for:** Guarantee him against. [12] **unstanched:** Wide-open. [13] **Set . . . courses!:** The ship is still being blown dangerously to shore, so the boatswain orders that the foresail be set in addition to the mainsail; but the ship still moves toward shore. [14] **off:** Away from the shore. [15] **would . . . tides:** Pirates were hanged on the shore and left there until three tides had washed over them.

And gape at wid'st to glut him.

A confused noise within: "Mercy on us!"
"We split, we split!" "Farewell, my wife and children!"
"Farewell, brother!" "We split, we split, we split!"

[*Exit* BOATSWAIN.]

ANTONIO:
Let's all sink wi' th' King.

SEBASTIAN:
Let's take leave of him.

Exit [*with* ANTONIO].

GONZALO: Now would I give a thousand furlongs of sea for an acre of barren ground—long heath,[16] brown furze, anything. The wills above be done, but I would fain die a dry death. *Exit.*

Scene 2

The island. In front of PROSPERO*'s cell.*

Enter PROSPERO *and* MIRANDA.

MIRANDA:
If by your art, my dearest father, you have
Put the wild waters in this roar, allay them.
The sky, it seems, would pour down stinking pitch
But that the sea, mounting to th' welkin's cheek,[17]
Dashes the fire out. O, I have suffered
With those that I saw suffer! A brave[18] vessel
(Who had no doubt some noble creature in her)
Dashed all to pieces! O, the cry did knock
Against my very heart! Poor souls, they perished!
Had I been any god of power, I would
Have sunk the sea within the earth or ere
It should the good ship so have swallowed and
The fraughting[19] souls within her.

PROSPERO:
Be collected.
No more amazement. Tell your piteous heart
There's no harm done.

MIRANDA:
O, woe the day!

PROSPERO:
No harm.
I have done nothing but in care of thee,

[16] **heath:** Heather. [17] **welkin's cheek:** Face of the sky. [18] **brave:** Fine, gallant (the word often has this meaning in the play). [19] **fraughting:** Forming her freight.

Of thee my dear one, thee my daughter, who
Art ignorant of what thou art, naught knowing
Of whence I am, nor that I am more better
Than Prospero, master of a full poor cell,
And thy no greater father.[20]

MIRANDA:

More to know
Did never meddle° with my thoughts. — mingle

PROSPERO:

'Tis time
I should inform thee farther. Lend thy hand
And pluck my magic garment from me. So.

[*Lays down his robe.*]

Lie there, my art. Wipe thou thine eyes; have comfort.
The direful spectacle of the wrack, which touched
The very virtue of compassion in thee,
I have with such provision° in mine art — foresight
So safely ordered that there is no soul—
No, not so much perdition° as an hair — loss
Betid° to any creature in the vessel — happened
Which thou heard'st cry, which thou saw'st sink. Sit down;
For thou must now know farther.

MIRANDA:

You have often
Begun to tell me what I am; but stopped
And left me to a bootless inquisition,
Concluding, "Stay; not yet."

PROSPERO:

The hour's now come;
The very minute bids thee ope thine ear.
Obey, and be attentive. Canst thou remember
A time before we came unto this cell?
I do not think thou canst, for then thou wast not
Out° three years old. — fully

MIRANDA:

Certainly, sir, I can.

PROSPERO:

By what? By any other house or person?
Of anything the image tell me that
Hath kept with thy remembrance.

MIRANDA:

'Tis far off,

[20] **thy . . . father:** Thy father, no greater than the Prospero just described.

And rather like a dream than an assurance
That my remembrance warrants.[21] Had I not
Four or five women once that tended me?

PROSPERO:

Thou hadst, and more, Miranda. But how is it
That this lives in thy mind? What seest thou else
In the dark backward and abysm of time?
If thou rememb'rest aught ere thou cam'st here,
How thou cam'st here thou mayst.

MIRANDA:

But that I do not.

PROSPERO:

Twelve year since, Miranda, twelve year since,
Thy father was the Duke of Milan and
A prince of power.

MIRANDA:

Sir, are not you my father?

PROSPERO:

Thy mother was a piece° of virtue, and — masterpiece
She said thou wast my daughter; and thy father
Was Duke of Milan; and his only heir
And princess, no worse issued.[22]

MIRANDA:

O the heavens!
What foul play had we that we came from thence?
Or blessèd was't we did?

PROSPERO:

Both, both, my girl!
By foul play, as thou say'st, were we heaved thence,
But blessedly holp° hither. — helped

MIRANDA:

O, my heart bleeds
To think o' th' teen that I have turned you to,[23]
Which is from my remembrance! Please you, farther.

PROSPERO:

My brother and thy uncle, called Antonio—
I pray thee mark me—that a brother should
Be so perfidious!—he whom next thyself
Of all the world I loved, and to him put
The manage of my state,[24] as at that time
Through all the signories[25] it was the first,

---

[21] **remembrance warrants:** Memory guarantees. [22] **no worse issued:** Of no meaner lineage than he.
[23] **teen . . . to:** Sorrow I have caused you to remember. [24] **manage . . . state:** Management of my domain.
[25] **signories:** Lordships (of Italy).

And Prospero the prime duke, being so reputed
In dignity, and for the liberal arts
Without a parallel. Those being all my study,
The government I cast upon my brother
And to my state grew stranger, being transported
And rapt in secret studies. Thy false uncle—
Dost thou attend me?

MIRANDA:

Sir, most heedfully.

PROSPERO:

Being once perfected° how to grant suits, grown skillful
How to deny them, who t' advance, and who
To trash for overtopping,[26] new-created
The creatures that were mine, I say—or changed 'em,
Or else new-formed 'em[27]—having both the key[28]
Of officer and office, set all hearts i' th' state
To what tune pleased his ear, that now he was
The ivy which had hid my princely trunk
And sucked my verdure out on't. Thou attend'st not?

MIRANDA:

O, good sir, I do.

PROSPERO:

I pray thee mark me.
I thus neglecting worldly ends, all dedicated
To closeness° and the bettering of my mind— seclusion
With that which, but by being so retired,
O'erprized all popular rate, in my false brother
Awaked an evil nature,[29] and my trust,
Like a good parent,[30] did beget of him
A falsehood in its contrary as great
As my trust was, which had indeed no limit,
A confidence sans bound. He being thus lorded—
Not only with what my revenue yielded
But what my power might else exact, like one
Who having into truth—by telling of it,[31]

[26] **trash for overtopping:** (1) Check the speed of (as of hounds); (2) cut down to size (as of overtall trees) the aspirants for political favor who are growing too bold.

[27] **new-created . . . 'em:** He re-created my following—either exchanging my adherents for his own, or else transforming my adherents into different people.

[28] **key:** A pun leading to the musical metaphor.

[29] **With . . . nature:** With that dedication to the mind which, were it not that it kept me from exercising the duties of my office, would surpass in value all ordinary estimate, I awakened evil in my brother's nature.

[30] **good parent:** Alluding to the proverb cited by Miranda in line 120.

[31] **like . . . it:** Like one who really had these things—by repeatedly saying he had them (*into* = unto).

Made such a sinner of his memory
To credit his own lie, he did believe
He was indeed the Duke, out o' th' substitution
And executing th' outward face of royalty
With all prerogative.[32] Hence his ambition growing—
Dost thou hear?

MIRANDA:
Your tale, sir, would cure deafness.

PROSPERO:
To have no screen between this part he played
And him he played it for, he needs will be
Absolute Milan.[33] Me (poor man) my library
Was dukedom large enough. Of temporal royalties
He thinks me now incapable; confederates
(So dry° he was for sway) wi' th' King of Naples thirsty
To give him annual tribute, do him homage,
Subject his coronet to his crown, and bend
The dukedom, yet unbowed (alas, poor Milan!),
To most ignoble stooping.

MIRANDA:
O the heavens!

PROSPERO:
Mark his condition,[34] and th' event;° then tell me outcome
If this might be a brother.

MIRANDA:
I should sin
To think but nobly of my grandmother.
Good wombs have borne bad sons.

PROSPERO:
Now the condition.
This King of Naples, being an enemy
To me inveterate, hearkens my brother's suit;
Which was, that he, in lieu o' th' premises[35]
Of homage and I know not how much tribute,
Should presently extirpate me and mine
Out of the dukedom and confer fair Milan,
With all the honors, on my brother. Whereon,
A treacherous army levied, one midnight
Fated to th' purpose, did Antonio open
The gates of Milan; and, i' th' dead of darkness,

[32] **out . . . prerogative:** As a result of his acting as my substitute and performing the outward functions of royalty with all its prerogatives. [33] **Absolute Milan:** Duke of Milan in fact. [34] **condition:** Terms of his pact with Naples. [35] **in . . . premises:** In return for the guarantees.

The ministers° for th' purpose hurried thence agents
Me and thy crying self.

MIRANDA:

Alack, for pity!
I, not rememb'ring how I cried out then,
Will cry it o'er again; it is a hint° occasion
That wrings mine eyes to 't.

PROSPERO:

Hear a little further,
And then I'll bring thee to the present business
Which now's upon's; without the which this story
Were most impertinent.

MIRANDA:

Wherefore did they not
That hour destroy us?

PROSPERO:

Well demanded, wench.
My tale provokes that question. Dear, they durst not,
So dear the love my people bore me; nor set
A mark so bloody on the business; but,
With colors fairer, painted their foul ends.
In few,° they hurried us aboard a bark; few words
Bore us some leagues to sea, where they prepared
A rotten carcass of a butt,° not rigged, tub
Nor tackle, sail, nor mast; the very rats
Instinctively have quit it. There they hoist us,
To cry to th' sea that roared to us; to sigh
To th' winds, whose pity, sighing back again,
Did us but loving wrong.

MIRANDA:

Alack, what trouble
Was I then to you!

PROSPERO:

O, a cherubin
Thou wast that did preserve me! Thou didst smile,
Infusèd with a fortitude from heaven,
When I have decked[36] the sea with drops full salt,
Under my burden groaned; which[37] raised in me
An undergoing stomach,° to bear up spirit of endurance
Against what should ensue.

MIRANDA:

How came we ashore?

---

[36] **decked:** Covered (wept salt tears into the sea). [37] **which:** That is, Miranda's smile.

PROSPERO:
By providence divine.
Some food we had, and some fresh water, that
A noble Neapolitan, Gonzalo,
Out of his charity, who being then appointed
Master of this design, did give us, with
Rich garments, linens, stuffs, and necessaries
Which since have steaded° much. So, of his gentleness, been of use
Knowing I loved my books, he furnished me
From mine own library with volumes that
I prize above my dukedom.

MIRANDA:
Would I might
But ever see that man!

PROSPERO:
Now I arise.
Sit still, and hear the last of our sea sorrow.
Here in this island we arrived; and here
Have I, thy schoolmaster, made thee more profit
Than other princess' can,° that have more time princesses can have
For vainer hours, and tutors not so careful.

MIRANDA:
Heavens thank you for't! And now I pray you, sir—
For still 'tis beating in my mind—your reason
For raising this sea storm?

PROSPERO:
Know thus far forth.
By accident most strange, bountiful Fortune
(Now my dear lady)[38] hath mine enemies
Brought to this shore; and by my prescience
I find my zenith° doth depend upon apex of fortune
A most auspicious star, whose influence
If now I court not, but omit,° my fortunes neglect
Will ever after droop. Here cease more questions.
Thou art inclined to sleep. 'Tis a good dullness,
And give it way. I know thou canst not choose.

[MIRANDA *sleeps*.]

Come away, servant, come! I am ready now.
Approach, my Ariel! Come!

Enter ARIEL.

ARIEL:
All hail, great master! Grave sir, hail! I come

[38] **(Now . . . lady):** Formerly my foe, now my patroness.

To answer thy best pleasure; be't to fly,
To swim, to dive into the fire, to ride
On the curled clouds. To thy strong bidding task° — tax to the utmost
Ariel and all his quality.[39]

PROSPERO:

Hast thou, spirit,
Performed, to point,° the tempest that I bade thee? — in every detail

ARIEL:

To every article.
I boarded the King's ship. Now on the beak,° — prow
Now in the waist,° the deck,° in every cabin, — amid ships, poop
I flamed amazement.[40] Sometimes I'd divide
And burn in many places; on the topmast,
The yards, and boresprit° would I flame distinctly,° — bowsprit, in different places
Then meet and join. Jove's lightnings, the precursors
O' th' dreadful thunderclaps, more momentary
And sight-outrunning were not. The fire and cracks
Of sulfurous roaring the most mighty Neptune
Seem to besiege, and make his bold waves tremble;
Yea, his dread trident shake.

PROSPERO:

My brave spirit!
Who was so firm, so constant, that this coil° — uproar
Would not infect his reason?

ARIEL:

Not a soul
But felt a fever of the mad and played
Some tricks of desperation. All but mariners
Plunged in the foaming brine and quit the vessel,
Then all afire with me. The King's son Ferdinand,
With hair up-staring° (then like reeds, not hair), — standing on end
Was the first man that leapt; cried "Hell is empty,
And all the devils are here!"

PROSPERO:

Why, that's my spirit!
But was not this nigh shore?

ARIEL:

Close by, my master.

PROSPERO:

But are they, Ariel, safe?

ARIEL:

Not a hair perished.

[39] **quality:** Cohorts (Ariel is leader of a band of spirits). [40] **flamed amazement:** Struck terror by appearing as (St. Elmo's) fire.

On their sustaining° garments not a blemish,   buoying them up
But fresher than before; and as thou bad'st me,
In troops I have dispersed them 'bout the isle.
The King's son have I landed by himself,
Whom I left cooling of the air with sighs
In an odd angle of the isle, and sitting,
His arms in this sad knot.

[*Illustrates with a gesture.*]

PROSPERO:

Of the King's ship,
The mariners, say how thou hast disposed,
And all the rest o' th' fleet.

ARIEL:

Safely in harbor
Is the King's ship; in the deep nook where once
Thou call'dst me up at midnight to fetch dew
From the still-vexed Bermoothes,° there she's hid;   Bermudas
The mariners all under hatches stowed,
Who, with a charm joined to their suff'red° labor,   undergone
I have left asleep. And for the rest o' th' fleet,
Which I dispersed, they all have met again,
And are upon the Mediterranean flote°   sea
Bound sadly home for Naples,
Supposing that they saw the King's ship wracked
And his great person perish.

PROSPERO:

Ariel, thy charge
Exactly is performed; but there's more work.
What is the time o' th' day?

ARIEL:

Past the mid season.°   noon

PROSPERO:

At least two glasses.° The time 'twixt six and now   two o'clock
Must by us both be spent most preciously.

ARIEL:

Is there more toil? Since thou dost give me pains,°   hard tasks
Let me remember° thee what thou hast promised,   remind
Which is not yet performed me.

PROSPERO:

How now? Moody?
What is't thou canst demand?

ARIEL:

My liberty.

PROSPERO:
Before the time be out? No more!

ARIEL:
I prithee,
Remember I have done thee worthy service,
Told thee no lies, made thee no mistakings, served
Without or grudge or grumblings. Thou did promise
To bate me[41] a full year.

PROSPERO:
Dost thou forget
From what a torment I did free thee?

ARIEL:
No.

PROSPERO:
Thou dost; and think'st it much to tread the ooze
Of the salt deep,
To run upon the sharp wind of the North,
To do me business in the veins° o' th' earth — streams
When it is baked° with frost. — caked

ARIEL:
I do not, sir.

PROSPERO:
Thou liest, malignant thing! Hast thou forgot
The foul witch Sycorax[42] who with age and envy
Was grown into a hoop? Hast thou forgot her?

ARIEL:
No, sir.

PROSPERO:
Thou hast. Where was she born? Speak! Tell me!

ARIEL:
Sir, in Argier.° — Algiers

PROSPERO:
O, was she so? I must
Once in a month recount what thou hast been,
Which thou forget'st. This damned witch Sycorax,
For mischiefs manifold, and sorceries terrible
To enter human hearing, from Argier,
Thou know'st, was banished. For one thing she did
They would not take her life. Is not this true?

---

[41] **bate me:** Reduce my term of service.

[42] **Sycorax:** Name not found elsewhere; probably derived from Greek *sys,* "sow," and *korax,* which means both "raven"—see line 322—and "hook"—hence perhaps "hoop."

ARIEL:
Ay, sir.

PROSPERO:
This blue-eyed[43] hag was hither brought with child
And here was left by th' sailors. Thou, my slave,
As thou report'st thyself, wast then her servant.
And, for thou wast a spirit too delicate
To act her earthy and abhorred commands,
Refusing her grand hests,° she did confine thee, commands
By help of her more potent ministers,
And in her most unmitigable rage,
Into a cloven pine; within which rift
Imprisoned thou didst painfully remain
A dozen years; within which space she died
And left thee there, where thou didst vent thy groans
As fast as millwheels strike. Then was this island
(Save for the son that she did litter here,
A freckled whelp, hagborn) not honored with
A human shape.

ARIEL:
Yes, Caliban her son.

PROSPERO:
Dull thing, I say so! He, that Caliban
Whom now I keep in service. Thou best know'st
What torment I did find thee in; thy groans
Did make wolves howl and penetrate the breasts
Of ever-angry bears. It was a torment
To lay upon the damned, which Sycorax
Could not again undo. It was mine art,
When I arrived and heard thee, that made gape
The pine, and let thee out.

ARIEL:
I thank thee, master.

PROSPERO:
If thou more murmur'st, I will rend an oak
And peg thee in his knotty entrails till
Thou hast howled away twelve winters.

ARIEL:
Pardon, master.
I will be correspondent° to command obedient
And do my spriting gently.[44]

[43] **blue-eyed:** Referring to the livid color of the eyelid, a sign of pregnancy. [44] **do . . . gently:** Render graciously my services as a spirit.

PROSPERO:

Do so; and after two days
I will discharge thee.

ARIEL:

That's my noble master!
What shall I do? Say what? What shall I do?

PROSPERO:

Go make thyself like a nymph o' th' sea. Be subject
To no sight but thine and mine, invisible
To every eyeball else.[45] Go take this shape
And hither come in't. Go! Hence with diligence! *Exit* [ARIEL].
Awake, dear heart, awake! Thou hast slept well.
Awake!

MIRANDA:

The strangeness of your story put
Heaviness in me.

PROSPERO:

Shake it off. Come on.
We'll visit Caliban, my slave, who never
Yields us kind answer.

MIRANDA:

'Tis a villain, sir,
I do not love to look on.

PROSPERO:

But as 'tis,
We cannot miss° him. He does make our fire, — do without
Fetch in our wood, and serves in offices
That profit us. What, ho! Slave! Caliban!
Thou earth, thou! Speak!

CALIBAN [*Within*]:

There's wood enough within.

PROSPERO:

Come forth, I say! There's other business for thee.
Come, thou tortoise! When?[46]

Enter ARIEL *like a water nymph.*

Fine apparition! My quaint° Ariel, — ingenious
Hark in thine ear.

[*Whispers.*]

ARIEL:

My lord, it shall be done. *Exit.*

---

[45] **invisible . . . else:** Ariel is invisible to everyone in the play except Prospero; Henslowe's *Diary,* an Elizabethan stage account, lists "a robe for to go invisible." [46] **When?:** Expression of impatience.

PROSPERO:

Thou poisonous slave, got by the devil himself
Upon thy wicked dam, come forth!

Enter CALIBAN.

CALIBAN:

As wicked dew as e'er my mother brushed
With raven's feather from unwholesome fen
Drop on you both! A southwest blow on ye
And blister you all o'er!

PROSPERO:

For this, be sure, tonight thou shalt have cramps,
Side-stitches that shall pen thy breath up. Urchins[47]
Shall, for that vast of night that they may work,[48]
All exercise on thee; thou shalt be pinched
As thick as honeycomb, each pinch more stinging
Than bees that made 'em.

CALIBAN:

I must eat my dinner.
This island's mine by Sycorax my mother,
Which thou tak'st from me. When thou cam'st first,
Thou strok'st me and made much of me; wouldst give me
Water with berries in't; and teach me how
To name the bigger light, and how the less,
That burn by day and night. And then I loved thee
And showed thee all the qualities o' th' isle,
The fresh springs, brine pits, barren place and fertile.
Cursed be I that did so! All the charms
Of Sycorax—toads, beetles, bats, light on you!
For I am all the subjects that you have,
Which first was mine own king; and here you sty me
In this hard rock, whiles you do keep from me
The rest o' th' island.

PROSPERO:

Thou most lying slave,
Whom stripes° may move, not kindness! I have used thee — lashes
(Filth as thou art) with humane care, and lodged thee
In mine own cell till thou didst seek to violate
The honor of my child.

CALIBAN:

O ho, O ho! Would't had been done!
Thou didst prevent me; I had peopled else
This isle with Calibans.

---

[47] **Urchins:** Goblins in the shape of hedgehogs. [48] **vast . . . work:** The long, empty stretch of night during which malignant spirits are allowed to be active.

MIRANDA:[49]

Abhorrèd slave,
Which any print of goodness wilt not take,
Being capable of all ill![50] I pitied thee,
Took pains to make thee speak, taught thee each hour
One thing or other. When thou didst not, savage,
Know thine own meaning, but wouldst gabble like
A thing most brutish, I endowed thy purposes
With words that made them known. But thy vile race,
Though thou didst learn, had that in't which good natures
Could not abide to be with. Therefore wast thou
Deservedly confined into this rock, who hadst
Deserved more than a prison.

CALIBAN:

You taught me language, and my profit on't
Is, I know how to curse. The red plague rid you
For learning me your language!

PROSPERO:

Hagseed, hence!
Fetch us in fuel. And be quick, thou'rt best,° — you'd better
To answer other business. Shrug'st thou, malice?
If thou neglect'st or dost unwillingly
What I command, I'll rack thee with old[51] cramps,
Fill all thy bones with aches, make thee roar
That beasts shall tremble at thy din.

CALIBAN:

No, pray thee.
[*Aside*] I must obey. His art is of such pow'r
It would control my dam's god, Setebos,
And make a vassal of him.

PROSPERO:

So, slave, hence! *Exit* CALIBAN.

Enter FERDINAND; *and* ARIEL *(invisible), playing and singing.*

Ariel's song.
Come unto these yellow sands,
And then take hands.
Curtsied when you have and kissed
The wild waves whist,[52]
Foot it featly° here and there; — nimbly

---

[49] MIRANDA: Many editors transfer this speech to Prospero as inappropriate to Miranda. [50] **capable . . . ill:** Susceptible only to evil impressions. [51] **old:** Plenty of (with an additional suggestion, "such as old people have"). [52] **when . . . whist:** When you have, through the harmony of kissing in the dance, kissed the wild waves into silence (?); when you have kissed in the dance, the wild waves being silenced (?).

And, sweet sprites, the burden bear.
Hark, hark!
[Burden, dispersedly.][53] *Bow, wow!*
The watchdogs bark.
[Burden, dispersedly.] *Bow, wow!*
Hark, hark! I hear
The strain of strutting chanticleer
Cry cock-a-diddle-dow.

FERDINAND:
Where should this music be? I' th' air or th' earth?
It sounds no more; and sure it waits upon
Some god o' th' island. Sitting on a bank,
Weeping again the King my father's wrack,
This music crept by me upon the waters
Allaying both their fury and my passion° — grief
With its sweet air. Thence I have followed it,
Or it hath drawn me rather; but 'tis gone.
No, it begins again.

Ariel's song.

Full fathom five thy father lies;
Of his bones are coral made;
Those are pearls that were his eyes;
Nothing of him that doth fade
But doth suffer a sea change
Into something rich and strange.
Sea nymphs hourly ring his knell:
[Burden.] *Ding-dong.*
Hark! Now I hear them—ding-dong bell.

FERDINAND:
The ditty does remember my drowned father.
This is no mortal business, nor no sound
That the earth owes.° I hear it now above me. — owns

PROSPERO:
The fringèd curtains of thine eye advance° — raise
And say what thou seest yond.

MIRANDA:
What is't? A spirit?
Lord, how it looks about! Believe me, sir,
It carries a brave form. But 'tis a spirit.

[53] **Burden, dispersedly:** An undersong, coming from all parts of the stage; it imitates the barking of dogs and perhaps in the end the crowing of a cock.

PROSPERO:

No, wench; it eats, and sleeps, and hath such senses
As we have, such. This gallant which thou seest
Was in the wrack; and, but he's something stained
With grief (that's beauty's canker), thou mightst call him
A goodly person. He hath lost his fellows
And strays about to find 'em.

MIRANDA:

I might call him
A thing divine; for nothing natural
I ever saw so noble.

PROSPERO:

[*Aside*] It goes on, I see,
As my soul prompts it. Spirit, fine spirit, I'll free thee
Within two days for this.

FERDINAND:

Most sure, the goddess
On whom these airs attend! Vouchsafe my prayer
May know if you remain[54] upon this island,
And that you will some good instruction give
How I may bear me° here. My prime request, — conduct myself
Which do I last pronounce, is (O you wonder!)
If you be maid or no?

MIRANDA:

No wonder, sir,
But certainly a maid.

FERDINAND:

My language? Heavens!
I am the best of them that speak this speech,
Were I but where 'tis spoken.

PROSPERO:

How? The best?
What wert thou if the King of Naples heard thee?

FERDINAND:

A single[55] thing, as I am now, that wonders
To hear thee speak of Naples. He does hear me;
And that he does I weep. Myself am Naples,
Who with mine eyes, never since at ebb, beheld
The King my father wracked.

MIRANDA:

Alack, for mercy!

---

[54] **Vouchsafe . . . remain:** May my prayer induce you to inform me whether you dwell. [55] **single:** (1) Solitary; (2) helpless.

FERDINAND:
Yes, faith, and all his lords, the Duke of Milan
And his brave son[56] being twain.[57]
PROSPERO:
[*Aside*] The Duke of Milan
And his more braver daughter could control° thee, refute
If now 'twere fit to do't. At the first sight
They have changed eyes.° Delicate Ariel, fallen in love
I'll set thee free for this. [*To* FERDINAND] A word, good sir.
I fear you have done yourself some wrong.[58] A word!
MIRANDA:
Why speaks my father so ungently? This
Is the third man that e'er I saw; the first
That e'er I sighed for. Pity move my father
To be inclined my way!
FERDINAND:
O, if a virgin,
And your affection not gone forth, I'll make you
The Queen of Naples.
PROSPERO:
Soft, sir! One word more.
[*Aside*] They are both in either's pow'rs. But this swift business
I must uneasy make, lest too light winning
Make the prize light. [*To* FERDINAND] One word more! I charge thee
That thou attend me. Thou dost here usurp
The name thou ow'st not, and hast put thyself
Upon this island as a spy, to win it
From me, the lord on't.
FERDINAND:
No, as I am a man!
MIRANDA:
There's nothing ill can dwell in such a temple.
If the ill spirit have so fair a house,
Good things will strive to dwell with't.
PROSPERO:
Follow me.
[*To* MIRANDA] Speak not you for him; he's a traitor. [*To* FERDINAND] Come!
I'll manacle thy neck and feet together;
Sea water shalt thou drink; thy food shall be
The fresh-brook mussels, withered roots, and husks
Wherein the acorn cradled. Follow!

[56] **son:** The only time Antonio's son is mentioned. [57] **twain:** Two (of these lords). [58] **done . . . wrong:** Said what is not so.

FERDINAND:

No.
I will resist such entertainment till
Mine enemy has more pow'r.

He draws, and is charmed from moving.

MIRANDA:

O dear father,
Make not too rash a trial of him, for
He's gentle and not fearful.[59]

PROSPERO:

What, I say,
My foot my tutor?[60] [*To* FERDINAND] Put thy sword up, traitor—
Who mak'st a show but dar'st not strike, thy conscience
Is so possessed with guilt! Come, from thy ward!° fighting posture
For I can here disarm thee with this stick° his wand
And make thy weapon drop.

MIRANDA:

Beseech you, father!

PROSPERO:

Hence! Hang not on my garments.

MIRANDA:

Sir, have pity.
I'll be his surety.

PROSPERO:

Silence! One word more
Shall make me chide thee, if not hate thee. What,
An advocate for an impostor? Hush!
Thou think'st there is no more such shapes as he,
Having seen but him and Caliban. Foolish wench!
To th' most of men this is a Caliban,
And they to him are angels.

MIRANDA:

My affections
Are then most humble. I have no ambition
To see a goodlier man.

PROSPERO:

[*To* FERDINAND] Come on, obey!
Thy nerves° are in their infancy again sinews
And have no vigor in them.

FERDINAND:

So they are.
My spirits, as in a dream, are all bound up.

[59] **gentle . . . fearful:** Of noble birth and no coward. [60] **My . . . tutor?:** Am I to be instructed by my inferior?

My father's loss, the weakness which I feel,
The wrack of all my friends, nor this man's threats
To whom I am subdued, are but light to me,
Might I but through my prison once a day
Behold this maid. All corners else o' th' earth
Let liberty make use of. Space enough
Have I in such a prison.

PROSPERO:
[*Aside*] It works. [*To* FERDINAND] Come on.
[*To* ARIEL] Thou hast done well, fine Ariel! [*To* FERDINAND] Follow me.
[*To* ARIEL] Hark what thou else shalt do me.

MIRANDA:
Be of comfort.
My father's of a better nature, sir,
Than he appears by speech. This is unwonted
Which now came from him.

PROSPERO:
Thou shalt be as free
As mountain winds; but then° exactly do — until then
All points of my command.

ARIEL:
To th' syllable.

PROSPERO:
[*To* FERDINAND] Come, follow. [*To* MIRANDA] Speak not for him. *Exeunt.*

ACT II

Scene 1

Another part of the island.

Enter ALONSO, SEBASTIAN, ANTONIO, GONZALO, ADRIAN, FRANCISCO, *and others.*

GONZALO:
Beseech you, sir, be merry. You have cause
(So have we all) of joy; for our escape
Is much beyond our loss. Our hint of° woe — occasion for
Is common; every day some sailor's wife,
The master of some merchant,[61] and the merchant,
Have just our theme of woe. But for the miracle,
I mean our preservation, few in millions
Can speak like us. Then wisely, good sir, weigh
Our sorrow with our comfort.

ALONSO:
Prithee, peace.

---

[61] **master . . . merchant:** Captain of some merchant ship.

SEBASTIAN [*Aside to* ANTONIO]: He receives comfort like cold porridge.[62]
ANTONIO [*Aside to* SEBASTIAN]: The visitor[63] will not give him o'er so.[64]
SEBASTIAN:
Look, he's winding up the watch of his wit;
by and by it will strike.
GONZALO: Sir—
SEBASTIAN [*Aside to* ANTONIO]: One. Tell.[65]
GONZALO:
When every grief is entertained, that's[66] offered
Comes to th' entertainer—
SEBASTIAN: A dollar.
GONZALO: Dolor comes to him, indeed. You have spoken truer than you purposed.
SEBASTIAN: You have taken it wiselier[67] than I meant you should.
GONZALO: Therefore, my lord—
ANTONIO: Fie, what a spendthrift is he of his tongue!
ALONSO: I prithee, spare.[68]
GONZALO: Well, I have done. But yet—
SEBASTIAN: He will be talking.
ANTONIO: Which, of he or Adrian, for a good wager, first begins to crow?
SEBASTIAN: The old cock.[69]
ANTONIO: The cock'rel.[70]
SEBASTIAN: Done! The wager?
ANTONIO: A laughter.[71]
SEBASTIAN: A match!
ADRIAN: Though this island seem to be desert—
ANTONIO: Ha, ha, ha!
SEBASTIAN: So, you're paid.
ADRIAN: Uninhabitable and almost inaccessible—
SEBASTIAN: Yet—
ADRIAN: Yet—
ANTONIO: He could not miss't.
ADRIAN: It must needs be of subtle, tender, and delicate temperance.[72]
ANTONIO: Temperance was a delicate wench.
SEBASTIAN: Ay, and a subtle, as he mostly learnedly delivered.
ADRIAN: The air breathes upon us here most sweetly.
SEBASTIAN: As if it had lungs, and rotten ones.
ANTONIO: Or as 'twere perfumed by a fen.
GONZALO: Here is everything advantageous to life.
ANTONIO: True; save means to live.

---

[62] **He . . . porridge:** "He" is Alonso; a pun on "peace," since porridge contained peas. [63] **visitor:** Spiritual comforter. [64] **give . . . so:** Release him so easily. [65] **One. Tell:** He has struck one; keep count. [66] **that's:** That which is. [67] **taken it wiselier:** Understood my pun. [68] **spare:** Spare your words. [69] **old cock:** Gonzalo. [70] **cock'rel:** Young cock; Adrian. [71] **A laughter:** The winner will have the laugh on the loser. [72] **temperance:** Climate (in the next line, a girl's name).

SEBASTIAN: Of that there's none, or little.
GONZALO: How lush and lusty the grass looks! How green!
ANTONIO: The ground indeed is tawny.
SEBASTIAN: With an eye[73] of green in't.
ANTONIO: He misses not much.
SEBASTIAN: No; he doth but mistake the truth totally.
GONZALO: But the rarity of it is—which is indeed almost beyond credit—
SEBASTIAN: As many vouched rarities are.
GONZALO: That our garments, being, as they were, drenched in the sea, hold, notwithstanding, their freshness and glosses, being rather new-dyed than stained with salt water.
ANTONIO: If but one of his pockets could speak, would it not say he lies?[74]
SEBASTIAN: Ay, or very falsely pocket up his report.[75]
GONZALO: Methinks our garments are now as fresh as when we put them on first in Afric, at the marriage of the King's fair daughter Claribel to the King of Tunis.
SEBASTIAN: 'Twas a sweet marriage, and we prosper well in our return.
ADRIAN: Tunis was never graced before with such a paragon to their queen.
GONZALO: Not since widow Dido's time.
ANTONIO: Widow? A pox o' that! How came that "widow" in? Widow Dido!
SEBASTIAN: What if he had said "widower Aeneas"[76] too? Good Lord, how you take it!
ADRIAN: "Widow Dido," said you? You make me study of that. She was of Carthage, not of Tunis.
GONZALO: This Tunis, sir, was Carthage.
ADRIAN: Carthage?
GONZALO: I assure you, Carthage.
ANTONIO: His word is more than the miraculous harp.[77]
SEBASTIAN: He hath raised the wall and houses too.
ANTONIO: What impossible matter will he make easy next?
SEBASTIAN: I think he will carry this island home in his pocket and give it his son for an apple.
ANTONIO: And, sowing the kernels of it in the sea, bring forth more islands.
GONZALO: Ay!
ANTONIO: Why, in good time.[78]
GONZALO [*To* ALONSO]: Sir, we were talking that our garments seem now as fresh as when we were at Tunis at the marriage of your daughter, who is now Queen.
ANTONIO: And the rarest that e'er came there.

---

[73] **eye:** Spot (also perhaps Gonzalo's eye). [74] **pockets . . . lies:** The inside of Gonzalo's pockets are stained. [75] **or . . . report:** Unless the pocket were, like a false knave, to receive without resentment the imputation that it is unstained. [76] **"widower Aeneas":** The point of the joke is that Dido was a widow, but one doesn't ordinarily think of her that way; and the same with Aeneas. [77] **harp:** Of Amphion, which only raised the *walls* of Thebes; whereas Gonzalo has rebuilt the whole ancient city of Carthage by identifying it mistakenly with modern Tunis. [78] **in good time:** Hearing Gonzalo reaffirm his false statement about Tunis and Carthage, Antonio suggests that Gonzalo will indeed, at the first opportunity, carry this island home in his pocket.

SEBASTIAN: Bate,[79] I beseech you, widow Dido.
ANTONIO: O, widow Dido? Ay, widow Dido!
GONZALO: Is not, sir, my doublet as fresh as the first day I wore it? I mean, in a sort.
ANTONIO: That "sort" was well fished for.
GONZALO: When I wore it at your daughter's marriage.
ALONSO:
You cram these words into mine ears against
The stomach of my sense.[80] Would I had never
Married my daughter there! For, coming thence,
My son is lost; and, in my rate,° she too, opinion
Who is so far from Italy removed
I ne'er again shall see her. O thou mine heir
Of Naples and of Milan, what strange fish
Hath made his meal on thee?
FRANCISCO:
Sir, he may live.
I saw him beat the surges under him
And ride upon their backs. He trod the water,
Whose enmity he flung aside, and breasted
The surge most swol'n that met him. His bold head
'Bove the contentious waves he kept, and oared
Himself with his good arms in lusty stroke
To th' shore, that o'er his wave-worn basis bowed,[81]
As stooping to relieve him. I not doubt
He came alive to land.
ALONSO:
No, no, he's gone.
SEBASTIAN [*To* ALONSO]:
Sir, you may thank yourself for this great loss,
That would not bless our Europe with your daughter,
But rather loose her to an African,
Where she, at least, is banished from your eye
Who hath cause to wet the grief on't.
ALONSO:
Prithee, peace.
SEBASTIAN:
You were kneeled to and importuned otherwise
By all of us; and the fair soul herself
Weighed, between loathness and obedience, at
Which end o' th' beam should bow.[82] We have lost your son,

---

[79] **Bate:** Except. [80] **against . . . sense:** Though my mind (or feelings) have no appetite for them. [81] **o'er . . . bowed:** The image is of a guardian cliff on the shore. [82] **fair . . . bow:** Claribel's unwillingness to marry was outweighed by her obedience to her father.

I fear, forever. Milan and Naples have
Moe widows in them of this business' making
Than we bring men to comfort them.
The fault's your own.

ALONSO:
So is the dear'st o' th' loss.

GONZALO:
My Lord Sebastian,
The truth you speak doth lack some gentleness,
And time to speak it in. You rub the sore
When you should bring the plaster.

SEBASTIAN:
Very well.

ANTONIO:
And most chirurgeonly.° — like a surgeon

GONZALO [*To* ALONSO]:
It is foul weather in us all, good sir,
When you are cloudy.

SEBASTIAN [*Aside to* ANTONIO]:
Foul weather?

ANTONIO [*Aside to* SEBASTIAN]:
Very foul.

GONZALO:
Had I plantation[83] of this isle, my lord—

ANTONIO:
He'd sow't with nettle seed.

SEBASTIAN:
Or docks, or mallows.

GONZALO:
And were the king on't, what would I do?

SEBASTIAN:
Scape being drunk for want of wine.

GONZALO:
I' th' commonwealth I would by contraries[84]
Execute all things. For no kind of traffic° — trade
Would I admit; no name of magistrate;
Letters° should not be known; riches, poverty, — learning
And use of service,° none; contract, succession,° — servants, inheritance
Bourn,° bound of land, tilth,° vineyard, none; — boundary, agriculture
No use of metal, corn, or wine, or oil;
No occupation; all men idle, all;

[83] **plantation:** Colonization (Antonio then puns by taking the word in its other sense). [84] **by contraries:** In contrast to the usual customs.

And women too, but innocent and pure;
No sovereignty.

SEBASTIAN:
Yet he would be king on't.

ANTONIO:
The latter end of his commonwealth forgets the beginning.

GONZALO:
All things in common nature should produce
Without sweat or endeavor. Treason, felony,
Sword, pike, knife, gun, or need of any engine° — weapon
Would I not have; but nature should bring forth,
Of it own kind, all foison,° all abundance, — abundance
To feed my innocent people.

SEBASTIAN:
No marrying 'mong his subjects?

ANTONIO:
None, man, all idle — whores and knaves.

GONZALO:
I would with such perfection govern, sir,
T' excel the Golden Age.

SEBASTIAN [*Loudly*]:
Save his Majesty!

ANTONIO [*Loudly*]:
Long live Gonzalo!

GONZALO:
And — do you mark me, sir?

ALONSO:
Prithee, no more. Thou dost talk nothing to me.

GONZALO: I do well believe your Highness; and did it to minister occasion[85] to these gentlemen, who are of such sensible[86] and nimble lungs that they always use to laugh at nothing.

ANTONIO: 'Twas you we laughed at.

GONZALO: Who in this kind of merry fooling am nothing to you; so you may continue, and laugh at nothing still.

ANTONIO: What a blow was there given!

SEBASTIAN: And it had not fall'n flatlong.[87]

GONZALO: You are gentlemen of brave mettle; you would lift the moon out of her sphere if she would continue in it five weeks without changing.

Enter ARIEL *(invisible) playing solemn music.*

SEBASTIAN: We would so, and then go a-batfowling.[88]

---

[85] **minister occasion:** Afford opportunity. [86] **sensible:** Sensitive. [87] **flatlong:** With the flat of the sword. [88] **We . . . a-batfowling:** We would use the moon for a lantern in order to hunt birds at night by attracting them with a light and beating them down with bats; i.e., in order to gull simpletons like you (?).

ANTONIO: Nay, good my lord, be not angry.

GONZALO: No, I warrant you; I will not adventure my discretion so weakly.[89] Will you laugh me asleep? For I am very heavy.

ANTONIO: Go sleep, and hear us.

[*All sleep except* ALONSO, SEBASTIAN, *and* ANTONIO.]

ALONSO:
What, all so soon asleep? I wish mine eyes
Would, with themselves, shut up my thoughts. I find
They are inclined to do so.

SEBASTIAN:
Please you, sir,
Do not omit the heavy offer of it.
It seldom visits sorrow; when it doth,
It is a comforter.

ANTONIO:
We two, my lord,
Will guard your person while you take your rest,
And watch your safety.

ALONSO:
Thank you. Wondrous heavy.

[ALONSO *sleeps. Exit* ARIEL.]

SEBASTIAN:
What a strange drowsiness possesses them!

ANTONIO:
It is the quality o' th' climate.

SEBASTIAN:
Why
Doth it not then our eyelids sink? I find not
Myself disposed to sleep.

ANTONIO:
Nor I: my spirits are nimble.
They fell together all, as by consent.
They dropped as by a thunderstroke. What might,
Worthy Sebastian—O, what might?—No more!
And yet methinks I see it in thy face,
What thou shouldst be. Th' occasion speaks thee, and
My strong imagination sees a crown
Dropping upon thy head.

SEBASTIAN:
What? Art thou waking?

---

[89] **adventure . . . weakly:** Risk my reputation for good sense because of your weak wit.

ANTONIO:

Do you not hear me speak?

SEBASTIAN:

I do; and surely
It is a sleepy language, and thou speak'st
Out of thy sleep. What is it thou didst say?
This is a strange repose, to be asleep
With eyes wide open; standing, speaking, moving,
And yet so fast asleep.

ANTONIO:

Noble Sebastian,
Thou let'st thy fortune sleep—die, rather; wink'st
Whiles thou art waking.

SEBASTIAN:

Thou dost snore distinctly;
There's meaning in thy snores.

ANTONIO:

I am more serious than my custom. You
Must be so too, if heed me; which to do
Trebles thee o'er.[90]

SEBASTIAN:

Well, I am standing water.

ANTONIO:

I'll teach you how to flow.

SEBASTIAN:

Do so. To ebb
Hereditary sloth instructs me.

ANTONIO:

O,
If you but knew how you the purpose cherish
Whiles thus you mock it; how, in stripping it,
You more invest it![91] Ebbing men, indeed,
Most often do so near the bottom run
By their own fear or sloth.

SEBASTIAN:

Prithee, say on.
The setting of thine eye and cheek proclaim
A matter from thee; and a birth, indeed,
Which throes thee much[92] to yield.

---

[90] **Trebles thee o'er:** Makes thee three times what thou now art. [91] **You . . . it!:** In stripping the purpose off you, you clothe yourself with it all the more. [92] **throes thee much:** Causes you much pain.

ANTONIO:

Thus, sir:
Although this lord of weak remembrance, this
Who shall be of as little memory
When he is earthed, hath here almost persuaded
(For he's a spirit of persuasion, only
Professes to persuade[93]) the King his son's alive,
'Tis as impossible that he's undrowned
As he that sleeps here swims.

SEBASTIAN:

I have no hope
That he's undrowned.

ANTONIO:

O, out of that no hope
What great hope have you! No hope that way is
Another way so high a hope that even
Ambition cannot pierce a wink beyond,
But doubt discovery there.[94] Will you grant with me
That Ferdinand is drowned?

SEBASTIAN:

He's gone.

ANTONIO:

Then tell me.
Who's the next heir of Naples?

SEBASTIAN:

Claribel.

ANTONIO:

She that is Queen of Tunis; she that dwells
Ten leagues beyond man's life;[95] she that from Naples
Can have no note—unless the sun were post;° messenger
The man i' th' moon's too slow—till newborn chins
Be rough and razorable; she that from whom
We all were sea-swallowed,[96] though some cast[97] again,
And, by that destiny, to perform an act
Whereof what's past is prologue, what to come,
In yours and my discharge.

SEBASTIAN:

What stuff is this? How say you?
'Tis true my brother's daughter's Queen of Tunis;

---

[93] **only . . . persuade:** His only profession is to persuade. [94] **Ambition . . . there:** The eye of ambition can reach no farther, but must even doubt the reality of what it discerns thus far. [95] **Ten . . . life:** It would take a lifetime to get within ten leagues of the place. [96] **she . . . sea-swallowed:** She who is separated from Naples by so dangerous a sea that we were ourselves swallowed up by it. [97] **cast:** Cast upon the shore (with a suggestion of its theatrical meaning, which leads to the next metaphor).

So is she heir of Naples; 'twixt which regions
There is some space.

ANTONIO:

A space whose ev'ry cubit
Seems to cry out "How shall that Claribel
Measure us back to Naples? Keep in Tunis,
And let Sebastian wake!" Say this were death
That now hath seized them, why, they were no worse
Than now they are. There be that can rule Naples
As well as he that sleeps; lords that can prate
As amply and unnecessarily
As this Gonzalo; I myself could make
A chough[98] of as deep chat. O, that you bore
The mind that I do! What a sleep were this
For your advancement! Do you understand me?

SEBASTIAN:

Methinks I do.

ANTONIO:

And how does your content
Tender[99] your own good fortune?

SEBASTIAN:

I remember
You did supplant your brother Prospero.

ANTONIO:

True.
And look how well my garments sit upon me,
Much feater° than before. My brother's servants   more becomingly
Were then my fellows; now they are my men.

SEBASTIAN:

But, for your conscience—

ANTONIO:

Ay, sir, where lies that? If 'twere a kibe,[100]
'Twould put me to my slipper; but I feel not
This deity in my bosom. Twenty consciences
That stand 'twixt me and Milan, candied be they
And melt, ere they molest! Here lies your brother,
No better than the earth he lies upon—
If he were that which now he's like, that's dead—
Whom I with this obedient steel (three inches of it)
Can lay to bed forever; whiles you, doing thus,

---

[98] **chough:** Jackdaw (a bird that can be taught to speak a few words). [99] **Tender:** Regard (i.e., do you like your good fortune). [100] **kibe:** Chilblain on the heel.

To the perpetual wink for aye might put
This ancient morsel, this Sir Prudence, who
Should not upbraid our course. For all the rest,
They'll take suggestion as a cat laps milk;
They'll tell the clock° to any business that say yes
We say befits the hour.

SEBASTIAN:

Thy case, dear friend,
Shall be my precedent. As thou got'st Milan,
I'll come by Naples. Draw thy sword. One stroke
Shall free thee from the tribute which thou payest,
And I the King shall love thee.

ANTONIO:

Draw together;
And when I rear my hand, do you the like,
To fall it on Gonzalo.

[*They draw.*]

SEBASTIAN:

O, but one word!

Enter ARIEL *(invisible) with music and song.*

ARIEL:

My master through his art foresees the danger
That you, his friend, are in, and sends me forth
(For else his project dies) to keep them living.

Sings in GONZALO*'s ear.*

While you here do snoring lie,
Opened-eye conspiracy
His time doth take.
If of life you keep a care,
Shake off slumber and beware.
Awake, awake!

ANTONIO:

Then let us both be sudden.

GONZALO [*Wakes*]:

Now good angels
Preserve the King!

[*The others wake.*]

ALONSO:

Why, how now? Ho, awake! Why are you drawn?
Wherefore this ghastly looking?

GONZALO:

What's the matter?

SEBASTIAN:

Whiles we stood here securing your repose,
Even now, we heard a hollow burst of bellowing
Like bulls, or rather lions. Did't not wake you?
It struck mine ear most terribly.

ALONSO:

I heard nothing.

ANTONIO:

O, 'twas a din to fright a monster's ear,
To make an earthquake! Sure it was the roar
Of a whole herd of lions.

ALONSO:

Heard you this, Gonzalo?

GONZALO:

Upon mine honor, sir, I heard a humming,
And that a strange one too, which did awake me.
I shaked you, sir, and cried. As mine eyes opened,
I saw their weapons drawn. There was a noise,
That's verily.° 'Tis best we stand upon our guard, — the truth
Or that we quit this place. Let's draw our weapons.

ALONSO:

Lead off this ground, and let's make further search
For my poor son.

GONZALO:

Heavens keep him from these beasts!
For he is, sure, i' th' island.

ALONSO:

Lead away.

ARIEL:

Prospero my lord shall know what I have done.
So, King, go safely on to seek thy son. *Exeunt.*

Scene 2

Another part of the island.

Enter CALIBAN *with a burden of wood. A noise of thunder heard.*

CALIBAN:

All the infections that the sun sucks up
From bogs, fens, flats, on Prosper fall, and make him
By inchmeal° a disease! His spirits hear me, — inch by inch
And yet I needs must curse. But they'll nor pinch,
Fright me with urchin shows,° pitch me i' th' mire, — impish apparitions
Nor lead me, like a firebrand,[101] in the dark

[101] **like a firebrand:** In the form of a will-o'-the-wisp.

Out of my way, unless he bid 'em. But
For every trifle are they set upon me;
Sometime like apes that mow° and chatter at me, make faces
And after bite me; then like hedgehogs which
Lie tumbling in my barefoot way and mount
Their pricks at my footfall; sometime am I
All wound with adders, who with cloven tongues
Do hiss me into madness.

Enter TRINCULO.

Lo, now, lo!
Here comes a spirit of his, and to torment me
For bringing wood in slowly. I'll fall flat.
Perchance he will not mind me.

[*Lies down.*]

TRINCULO: Here's neither bush nor shrub to bear off[102] any weather at all, and another storm brewing; I hear it sing i' th' wind. Yond same black cloud, yond huge one, looks like a foul bombard[103] that would shed his liquor. If it should thunder as it did before, I know not where to hide my head. Yond same cloud cannot choose but fall by pailfuls. What have we here? A man or a fish? Dead or alive? A fish! He smells like a fish; a very ancient and fishlike smell, a kind of not of the newest Poor John.[104] A strange fish! Were I in England now, as once I was, and had but this fish painted,[105] not a holiday fool there but would give a piece of silver. There would this monster make a man;[106] any strange beast there makes a man. When they will not give a doit[107] to relieve a lame beggar, they will lay out ten to see a dead Indian. Legged like a man! And his fins like arms! Warm, o' my troth! I do now let loose my opinion, hold it no longer. This is no fish, but an islander, that hath lately suffered by a thunderbolt. [*Thunder.*] Alas, the storm is come again! My best way is to creep under his gaberdine; there is no other shelter hereabout. Misery acquaints a man with strange bedfellows. I will here shroud till the dregs of the storm be past.

[*Creeps under* CALIBAN*'s garment.*]
Enter STEPHANO *singing, a bottle in his hand.*
STEPHANO:

I shall no more to sea, to sea;
Here shall I die ashore.

This is a very scurvy tune to sing at a man's funeral. Well, here's my comfort. *Drinks.*

[102] **bear off:** Ward off. [103] **bombard:** Large leather jug. [104] **Poor John:** Dried hake (a type of fish). [105] **painted:** As a sign hung outside a booth at a fair. [106] **make a man:** Pun: make a man's fortune. [107] **doit:** Smallest coin.

The master, the swabber, the boatswain, and I,
The gunner, and his mate,
Loved Mall, Meg, and Marian, and Margery,
But none of us cared for Kate.
For she had a tongue with a tang,
Would cry to a sailor "Go hang!"
She loved not the savor of tar nor of pitch;
Yet a tailor might scratch her where'er she did itch.
Then to sea, boys, and let her go hang!

This is a scurvy tune too; but here's my comfort. *Drinks.*

CALIBAN: Do not torment me! O!

STEPHANO: What's the matter? Have we devils here? Do you put tricks upon 's with savages and men of Inde, ha? I have not scaped drowning to be afeared now of your four legs. For it hath been said, "As proper a man as ever went on four legs cannot make him give ground"; and it shall be said so again, while Stephano breathes at' nostrils.

CALIBAN: The spirit torments me. O!

STEPHANO: This is some monster of the isle, with four legs, who hath got, as I take it, an ague. Where the devil should he learn our language? I will give him some relief, if it be but for that. If I can recover him, and keep him tame, and get to Naples with him, he's a present for any emperor that ever trod on neat's leather.[108]

CALIBAN: Do not torment me, prithee; I'll bring my wood home faster.

STEPHANO: He's in his fit now and does not talk after the wisest. He shall taste of my bottle; if he have never drunk wine afore, it will go near to remove his fit. If I can recover him and keep him tame, I will not take too much[109] for him. He shall pay for him that hath him, and that soundly.

CALIBAN: Thou dost me yet but little hurt. Thou wilt anon; I know it by thy trembling.[110] Now Prosper works upon thee.

STEPHANO: Come on your ways, open your mouth; here is that which will give language to you, cat.[111] Open your mouth. This will shake your shaking, I can tell you, and that soundly. [*Gives* CALIBAN *drink.*] You cannot tell who's your friend. Open your chaps[112] again.

TRINCULO: I should know that voice. It should be—but he is drowned; and these are devils. O, defend me!

STEPHANO: Four legs and two voices—a most delicate monster! His forward voice now is to speak well of his friend; his backward voice is to utter foul speeches and to detract. If all the wine in my bottle will recover him, I will help his ague. Come! [*Gives drink.*] Amen! I will pour some in thy other mouth.

TRINCULO: Stephano!

---

[108] **neat's leather:** Cowhide. [109] **I . . . much:** Too much will not be enough. [110] **trembling:** Trinculo is shaking with fear. [111] **here . . . cat:** Alluding to the proverb "Liquor will make a cat talk." [112] **chaps:** Jaws.

STEPHANO: Doth thy other mouth call me? Mercy, mercy! This is a devil, and no monster. I will leave him; I have no long spoon.[113]

TRINCULO: Stephano! If thou beest Stephano, touch me and speak to me; for I am Trinculo—be not afeared—thy good friend Trinculo.

STEPHANO: If thou beest Trinculo, come forth. I'll pull thee by the lesser legs. If any be Trinculo's legs, these are they. [*Draws him out from under* CALIBAN*'s garment.*] Thou art very Trinculo indeed! How cam'st thou to be the siege[114] of this mooncalf?[115] Can he vent Trinculos?

TRINCULO: I took him to be killed with a thunderstroke. But art thou not drowned, Stephano? I hope now thou art not drowned. Is the storm overblown? I hid me under the dead mooncalf's gaberdine for fear of the storm. And art thou living, Stephano? O Stephano, two Neapolitans scaped!

STEPHANO: Prithee do not turn me about; my stomach is not constant.

CALIBAN:
[*Aside*] These be fine things, and if they be not sprites.
That's a brave god and bears celestial liquor.
I will kneel to him.

STEPHANO: How didst thou scape? How cam'st thou hither? Swear by this bottle how thou cam'st hither. I escaped upon a butt of sack which the sailors heaved o'erboard—by this bottle which I made of the bark of a tree with mine own hands since I was cast ashore.

CALIBAN: I'll swear upon that bottle to be thy true subject, for the liquor is not earthly.

STEPHANO: Here! Swear then how thou escap'dst.

TRINCULO: Swum ashore, man, like a duck. I can swim like a duck, I'll be sworn.

STEPHANO: Here, kiss the book. [*Gives him drink.*] Though thou canst swim like a duck, thou art made like a goose.

TRINCULO: O Stephano, hast any more of this?

STEPHANO: The whole butt, man. My cellar is in a rock by th' seaside, where my wine is hid. How now, mooncalf? How does thine ague?

CALIBAN: Hast thou not dropped from heaven?

STEPHANO: Out o' th' moon, I do assure thee. I was the Man i' th' Moon when time was.

CALIBAN: I have seen thee in her, and I do adore thee. My mistress showed me thee, and thy dog, and thy bush.[116]

STEPHANO: Come, swear to that; kiss the book. [*Gives him drink.*] I will furnish it anon with new contents. Swear. [CALIBAN *drinks.*]

TRINCULO: By this good light, this is a very shallow monster! I afeard of him? A very weak monster! The Man i' th' Moon? A most poor credulous monster! Well drawn,[117] monster, in good sooth!

---

[113] **long spoon:** Alluding to the proverb "He who sups with (i.e., from the same dish as) the devil must have a long spoon." [114] **siege:** Excrement. [115] **mooncalf:** Monstrosity. [116] **My . . . bush:** The Man in the Moon was banished there, according to legend, for gathering brushwood with his dog on Sunday. [117] **Well drawn:** A good pull at the bottle.

CALIBAN: I'll show thee every fertile inch o' th' island; and I will kiss thy foot. I prithee, be my god.

TRINCULO: By this light, a most perfidious and drunken monster! When's god's asleep, he'll rob his bottle.

CALIBAN: I'll kiss thy foot. I'll swear myself thy subject.

STEPHANO: Come on then. Down, and swear!

TRINCULO: I shall laugh myself to death at this puppy-headed monster. A most scurvy monster! I could find in my heart to beat him—

STEPHANO: Come, kiss.

TRINCULO: But that the poor monster's in drink. An abominable monster!

CALIBAN:

I'll show thee the best springs; I'll pluck thee berries;
I'll fish for thee, and get thee wood enough.
A plague upon the tyrant that I serve!
I'll bear him no more sticks, but follow thee,
Thou wondrous man.

TRINCULO: A most ridiculous monster, to make a wonder of a poor drunkard!

CALIBAN:

I prithee let me bring thee where crabs° grow; *crab apples*
And I with my long nails will dig thee pignuts,° *earthnuts*
Show thee a jay's nest, and instruct thee how
To snare the nimble marmoset. I'll bring thee
To clust'ring filberts, and sometimes I'll get thee
Young scamels[118] from the rock. Wilt thou go with me?

STEPHANO: I prithee now, lead the way without any more talking. Trinculo, the King and all our company else being drowned, we will inherit here. Here, bear my bottle. Fellow Trinculo, we'll fill him by and by again.

CALIBAN *sings drunkenly.*

CALIBAN: Farewell, master; farewell, farewell!

TRINCULO: A howling monster! A drunken monster!

CALIBAN:

No more dams I'll make for fish,
Nor fetch in firing
At requiring,
Nor scrape trenchering,[119] *nor wash dish.*
'Ban, 'Ban, Ca—Caliban
Has a new master. Get a new man!

Freedom, high day! High day, freedom! Freedom, high day, freedom!

STEPHANO: O brave monster! Lead the way. *Exeunt.*

[118] **scamels:** Perhaps a misprint for "seamels" or "seamews," a kind of sea bird. [119] ***trenchering:*** Trenchers, wooden plates.

Act III

Scene 1

In front of PROSPERO*'s cell.*

Enter FERDINAND, *bearing a log.*

FERDINAND:

There be some sports are painful, and their labor
Delight in them sets off;° some kinds of baseness — cancels
Are nobly undergone, and most poor matters
Point to rich ends. This my mean task
Would be as heavy to me as odious, but
The mistress which I serve quickens what's dead
And makes my labors pleasures. O, she is
Ten times more gentle than her father's crabbed;
And he's composed of harshness. I must remove
Some thousands of these logs and pile them up,
Upon a sore injunction. My sweet mistress
Weeps when she sees me work, and says such baseness
Had never like executor. I forget;[120]
But these sweet thoughts do even refresh my labors,
Most busiest when I do it.[121]

Enter MIRANDA; *and* PROSPERO *(behind, unseen).*

MIRANDA:

Alas, now pray you,
Work not so hard! I would the lightning had
Burnt up those logs that you are enjoined to pile!
Pray set it down and rest you. When this burns,
'Twill weep for having wearied you. My father
Is hard at study; pray now rest yourself;
He's safe for these three hours.

FERDINAND:

O most dear mistress,
The sun will set before I shall discharge
What I must strive to do.

MIRANDA:

If you'll sit down,
I'll bear your logs the while. Pray give me that;
I'll carry it to the pile.

FERDINAND:

No, precious creature,
I had rather crack my sinews, break my back,

---

[120] **forget:** Forget my task. [121] **Most . . . it:** My thoughts are busiest when I am (the Folio's *busie lest* has been variously emended; *it* may refer to "task," line 4, the understood object in line 13).

Than you should such dishonor undergo
While I sit lazy by.

MIRANDA:

It would become me
As well as it does you; and I should do it
With much more ease; for my good will is to it,
And yours it is against.

PROSPERO [*Aside*]:

Poor worm, thou art infected!
This visitation[122] shows it.

MIRANDA:

You look wearily.

FERDINAND:

No, noble mistress, 'tis fresh morning with me
When you are by at night. I do beseech you,
Chiefly that I might set it in my prayers,
What is your name?

MIRANDA:

Miranda. O my father,
I have broke your hest to say so!

FERDINAND:

Admired Miranda![123]
Indeed the top of admiration, worth
What's dearest to the world! Full many a lady
I have eyed with best regard, and many a time
Th' harmony of their tongues hath into bondage
Brought my too diligent ear. For several virtues
Have I liked several women; never any
With so full soul but some defect in her
Did quarrel with the noblest grace she owed,
And put it to the foil.° But you, O you, — defeated it
So perfect and so peerless, are created
Of every creature's best.

MIRANDA:

I do not know
One of my sex; no woman's face remember,
Save, from my glass, mine own. Nor have I seen
More that I may call men than you, good friend,
And my dear father. How features are abroad
I am skilless of; but, by my modesty
(The jewel in my dower), I would not wish

[122] **visitation:** (1) Visit; (2) attack of plague (referring to metaphor of "infected"). [123] **Admired Miranda!:** *Admired* means "to be wondered at"; the Latin *Miranda* means "wonderful."

Any companion in the world but you;
Nor can imagination form a shape,
Besides yourself, to like of. But I prattle
Something too wildly, and my father's precepts
I therein do forget.

FERDINAND:

I am, in my condition,
A prince, Miranda; I do think, a king
(I would not so), and would no more endure
This wooden slavery than to suffer
The fleshfly blow my mouth. Hear my soul speak!
The very instant that I saw you, did
My heart fly to your service; there resides,
To make me slave to it; and for your sake
Am I this patient log-man.

MIRANDA:

Do you love me?

FERDINAND:

O heaven, O earth, bear witness to this sound,
And crown what I profess with kind event
If I speak true! If hollowly, invert
What best is boded me[124] to mischief! I,
Beyond all limit of what else i' th' world,
Do love, prize, honor you.

MIRANDA:

I am a fool
To weep at what I am glad of.

PROSPERO:

[*Aside*] Fair encounter
Of two most rare affections! Heavens rain grace
On that which breeds between 'em!

FERDINAND:

Wherefore weep you?

MIRANDA:

At mine unworthiness, that dare not offer
What I desire to give, and much less take
What I shall die to want. But this is trifling;[125]
And all the more it seeks to hide itself,
The bigger bulk it shows. Hence, bashful cunning,
And prompt me, plain and holy innocence!
I am your wife, if you will marry me;

---

[124] **What . . . me:** Whatever good fortune fate has in store for me. [125] **this is trifling:** To speak in riddles like this.

If not, I'll die your maid. To be your fellow
You may deny me; but I'll be your servant,
Whether you will or no.

FERDINAND:

My mistress, dearest,
And I thus humble ever.

MIRANDA:

My husband then?

FERDINAND:

Ay, with a heart as willing
As bondage e'er of freedom.° Here's my hand. to win freedom

MIRANDA:

And mine, with my heart in't; and now farewell
Till half an hour hence.

FERDINAND:

A thousand thousand!

Exeunt FERDINAND *and* MIRANDA *in different directions.*

PROSPERO:

So glad of this as they I cannot be,
Who are surprised withal; but my rejoicing
At nothing can be more. I'll to my book;
For yet ere suppertime must I perform
Much business appertaining. *Exit.*

Scene 2

Another part of the island.

Enter CALIBAN, STEPHANO, *and* TRINCULO.

STEPHANO: Tell not me! When the butt is out, we will drink water; not a drop before. Therefore bear up and board 'em![126] Servant monster, drink to me.

TRINCULO: Servant monster? The folly of this island! They say there's but five upon this isle; we are three of them. If th' other two be brained like us, the state totters.

STEPHANO: Drink, servant monster, when I bid thee; thy eyes are almost set in thy head.

TRINCULO: Where should they be set else? He were a brave monster indeed if they were set in his tail.

STEPHANO: My man-monster hath drowned his tongue in sack. For my part, the sea cannot drown me. I swam, ere I could recover the shore, five-and-thirty leagues off and on, by this light. Thou shalt be my lieutenant, monster, or my standard.[127]

TRINCULO: Your lieutenant, if you list;[128] he's no standard.

[126] **board 'em:** Drink up. [127] **standard:** Standard-bearer, ensign (pun since Caliban is so drunk he cannot stand). [128] **if you list:** If it please you (with pun on "list" as pertaining to a ship that leans over to one side).

STEPHANO: We'll not run, Monsieur Monster.

TRINCULO: Nor go[129] neither; but you'll lie like dogs, and yet say nothing neither.

STEPHANO: Mooncalf, speak once in thy life, if thou beest a good mooncalf.

CALIBAN: How does thy honor? Let me lick thy shoe. I'll not serve him; he is not valiant.

TRINCULO: Thou liest, most ignorant monster; I am in case[130] to justle[131] a constable. Why, thou deboshed[132] fish thou, was there ever man a coward that hath drunk so much sack as I today? Wilt thou tell a monstrous lie, being but half a fish and half a monster?

CALIBAN: Lo, how he mocks me! Wilt thou let him, my lord?

TRINCULO: "Lord" quoth he? That a monster should be such a natural![133]

CALIBAN: Lo, lo, again! Bite him to death, I prithee.

STEPHANO: Trinculo, keep a good tongue in your head. If you prove a mutineer—the next tree![134] The poor monster's my subject, and he shall not suffer indignity.

CALIBAN: I thank my noble lord. Wilt thou be pleased to hearken once again to the suit I made to thee?

STEPHANO: Marry,[135] will I. Kneel and repeat it; I will stand, and so shall Trinculo.

Enter ARIEL, *invisible.*

CALIBAN:

As I told thee before, I am subject to a tyrant,
A sorcerer, that by his cunning hath
Cheated me of the island.

ARIEL:

Thou liest.

CALIBAN:

Thou liest, thou jesting monkey thou!
I would my valiant master would destroy thee.
I do not lie.

STEPHANO: Trinculo, if you trouble him any more in's tale, by this hand, I will supplant some of your teeth.

TRINCULO: Why, I said nothing.

STEPHANO: Mum then, and no more. Proceed.

CALIBAN:

I say by sorcery he got this isle;
From me he got it. If thy greatness will
Revenge it on him—for I know thou dar'st,
But this thing[136] dare not—

STEPHANO:

That's most certain.

CALIBAN:

Thou shalt be lord of it, and I'll serve thee.

---

[129] **go:** Walk. [130] **case:** Fit condition. [131] **justle:** Jostle. [132] **deboshed:** Debauched. [133] **natural:** Idiot. [134] **the next tree:** You will be hanged. [135] **Marry:** An expletive, from "By the Virgin Mary." [136] **thing:** That is, Trinculo.

STEPHANO:
How now shall this be compassed?
Canst thou bring me to the party?

CALIBAN:
Yea, yea, my lord! I'll yield him thee asleep,
Where thou mayst knock a nail into his head.

ARIEL:
Thou liest; thou canst not.

CALIBAN:
What a pied[137] ninny's this! Thou scurvy patch!° *clown*
I do beseech thy greatness, give him blows
And take his bottle from him. When that's gone,
He shall drink naught but brine, for I'll not show him
Where the quick freshes[138] are.

STEPHANO: Trinculo, run into no further danger! Interrupt the monster one word further and, by this hand, I'll turn my mercy out o' doors and make a stockfish[139] of thee.

TRINCULO: Why, what did I? I did nothing. I'll go farther off.

STEPHANO: Didst thou not say he lied?

ARIEL: Thou liest.

STEPHANO: Do I so? Take thou that! [*Strikes* TRINCULO.] As you like this, give me the lie another time.

TRINCULO: I did not give the lie. Out o' your wits, and hearing too? A pox o' your bottle! This can sack and drinking do. A murrain[140] on your monster, and the devil take your fingers!

CALIBAN: Ha, ha, ha!

STEPHANO: Now forward with your tale. [*To* TRINCULO] Prithee, stand further off.

CALIBAN:
Beat him enough. After a little time
I'll beat him too.

STEPHANO:
Stand farther. Come, proceed.

CALIBAN:
Why, as I told thee, 'tis a custom with him
I' th' afternoon to sleep. There thou mayst brain him,
Having first seized his books, or with a log
Batter his skull, or paunch° him with a stake, *stab in the belly*
Or cut his wezand° with thy knife. Remember *windpipe*
First to possess his books; for without them
He's but a sot, as I am, nor hath not
One spirit to command. They all do hate him

---

[137] **pied:** Referring to Trinculo's parti-colored jester's costume. [138] **quick freshes:** Living springs of fresh water. [139] **stockfish:** Dried cod, softened by beating. [140] **murrain:** Plague (that infects cattle).

As rootedly as I. Burn but his books.
He has brave utensils° (for so he calls them) — fine furnishings
Which, when he has a house, he'll deck withal.
And that most deeply to consider is
The beauty of his daughter. He himself
Calls her a nonpareil. I never saw a woman
But only Sycorax my dam and she;
But she as far surpasseth Sycorax
As great'st does least.

STEPHANO:
Is it so brave a lass?

CALIBAN:
Ay, lord. She will become thy bed, I warrant,
And bring thee forth brave brood.

STEPHANO: Monster, I will kill this man. His daughter and I will be King and Queen—save our Graces!—and Trinculo and thyself shall be viceroys. Dost thou like the plot, Trinculo?

TRINCULO: Excellent.

STEPHANO: Give me thy hand. I am sorry I beat thee; but while thou liv'st, keep a good tongue in thy head.

CALIBAN:
Within this half hour will he be asleep.
Wilt thou destroy him then?

STEPHANO:
Ay, on mine honor.

ARIEL:
This will I tell my master.

CALIBAN:
Thou mak'st me merry; I am full of pleasure.
Let us be jocund. Will you troll the catch° — sing the round
You taught me but whilere?° — just now

STEPHANO: At thy request, monster, I will do reason, any reason.[141] Come on, Trinculo, let us sing. *Sings.*

Flout 'em and scout° 'em — jeer at
And scout 'em and flout 'em!
Thought is free.

CALIBAN: That's not the tune.

ARIEL *plays the tune on a tabor*[142] *and pipe.*

STEPHANO: What is this same?

---

[141] **any reason:** Anything within reason. [142] ***tabor:*** Small drum worn at the side.

TRINCULO: This is the tune of our catch, played by the picture of Nobody.[143]

STEPHANO: If thou beest a man, show thyself in thy likeness. If thou beest a devil, take't as thou list.

TRINCULO: O, forgive me my sins!

STEPHANO: He that dies pays all debts. I defy thee. Mercy upon us!

CALIBAN: Art thou afeard?

STEPHANO: No, monster, not I.

CALIBAN:

Be not afeard; the isle is full of noises,
Sounds and sweet airs that give delight and hurt not.
Sometimes a thousand twangling instruments
Will hum about mine ears; and sometime voices
That, if I then had waked after long sleep,
Will make me sleep again; and then, in dreaming,
The clouds methought would open and show riches
Ready to drop upon me, that, when I waked,
I cried to dream again.

STEPHANO: This will prove a brave kingdom to me, where I shall have my music for nothing.

CALIBAN: When Prospero is destroyed.

STEPHANO: That shall be by and by; I remember the story.

TRINCULO: The sound is going away; let's follow it, and after do our work.

STEPHANO: Lead, monster; we'll follow. I would I could see this taborer; he lays it on.

TRINCULO [*To* CALIBAN]: Wilt come?[144] I'll follow Stephano. *Exeunt.*

Scene 3

Another part of the island.

Enter ALONSO, SEBASTIAN, ANTONIO, GONZALO, ADRIAN, FRANCISCO, *etc.*

GONZALO:

By'r Lakin,° I can go no further, sir; — By our Lady
My old bones ache. Here's a maze trod indeed
Through forthrights and meanders.[145] By your patience,
I needs must rest me.

ALONSO:

Old lord, I cannot blame thee,
Who am myself attached° with weariness — seized
To th' dulling of my spirits. Sit down and rest.
Even here I will put off my hope, and keep it

[143] **picture of Nobody:** Alluding to the picture of No-body—a man all head, legs, and arms, but without trunk—on the title page of the anonymous comedy *No-body and Some-body.* [144] **Wilt come?:** Caliban lingers because the other two are being distracted from his purpose by the music. [145] **forthrights and meanders:** Straight and winding paths.

No longer for my flatterer. He is drowned
Whom thus we stray to find; and the sea mocks
Our frustrate search on land. Well, let him go.

ANTONIO:
[*Aside to* SEBASTIAN] I am right glad that he's so out of hope.
Do not for one repulse forgo the purpose
That you resolved t' effect.

SEBASTIAN:
[*Aside to* ANTONIO] The next advantage
Will we take throughly.

ANTONIO:
[*Aside to* SEBASTIAN] Let it be tonight;
For, now they are oppressed with travel, they
Will not nor cannot use such vigilance
As when they are fresh.

SEBASTIAN:
[*Aside to* ANTONIO] I say tonight. No more.

Solemn and strange music; and PROSPERO *on the top*[146] *(invisible). Enter several strange Shapes, bringing in a banquet; and dance about it with gentle actions of salutations; and, inviting the King etc. to eat, they depart.*

ALONSO:
What harmony is this? My good friends, hark!

GONZALO:
Marvelous sweet music!

ALONSO:
Give us kind keepers,° heavens! What were these? — guardian angels

SEBASTIAN:
A living drollery.° Now I will believe — puppet show
That there are unicorns; that in Arabia
There is one tree, the phoenix' throne; one phoenix
At this hour reigning there.

ANTONIO:
I'll believe both;
And what does else want credit, come to me,
And I'll be sworn 'tis true. Travelers ne'er did lie,
Though fools at home condemn 'em.

GONZALO:
If in Naples
I should report this now, would they believe me
If I should say I saw such islanders?

[146] ***top:*** Upper stage (or perhaps a playing area above it).

(For certes these are people of the island)
Who, though they are of monstrous shape, yet note,
Their manners are more gentle, kind, than of
Our human generation you shall find
Many—nay, almost any.

PROSPERO:

[*Aside*] Honest lord,
Thou hast said well; for some of you there present
Are worse than devils.

ALONSO:

I cannot too much muse
Such shapes, such gesture, and such sound, expressing
(Although they want the use of tongue) a kind
Of excellent dumb discourse.

PROSPERO:

[*Aside*] Praise in departing.[147]

FRANCISCO:

They vanished strangely.

SEBASTIAN:

No matter, since
They have left their viands behind; for we have stomachs.
Will't please you taste of what is here?

ALONSO:

Not I.

GONZALO:

Faith, sir, you need not fear. When we were boys,
Who would believe that there were mountaineers
Dewlapped[148] like bulls, whose throats had hanging at 'em
Wallets of flesh? Or that there were such men
Whose heads stood in their breasts? Which now we find
Each putter-out of five for one[149] will bring us
Good warrant of.

ALONSO:

I will stand to, and feed;
Although my last, no matter, since I feel
The best is past. Brother, my lord the Duke,
Stand to, and do as we.

Thunder and lightning. Enter ARIEL, *like a harpy; claps his wings upon the table; and with a quaint device the banquet vanishes.*

---

[147] **Praise in departing:** Save your praise for the end. [148] **Dewlapped:** With skin hanging from the neck (like mountaineers with goiter). [149] **putter-out . . . one:** Traveler who insures himself by depositing a sum of money to be repaid fivefold if he returns safely.

ARIEL:
You are three men of sin, whom destiny—
That hath to instrument this lower world
And what is in't—the never-surfeited sea
Hath caused to belch up you and on this island,
Where man doth not inhabit, you 'mongst men
Being most unfit to live. I have made you mad;
And even with suchlike valor[150] men hang and drown
Their proper selves.

[ALONSO, SEBASTIAN, *etc. draw their swords.*]

You fools! I and my fellows
Are ministers of Fate. The elements,
Of whom your swords are tempered, may as well
Wound the loud winds, or with bemocked-at stabs
Kill the still-closing[151] waters, as diminish
One dowle° that's in my plume. My fellow ministers — bit of down
Are like invulnerable. If you could hurt,[152]
Your swords are now too massy for your strengths
And will not be uplifted. But remember
(For that's my business to you) that you three
From Milan did supplant good Prospero;
Exposed unto the sea, which hath requit it,[153]
Him and his innocent child; for which foul deed
The pow'rs, delaying, not forgetting, have
Incensed the seas and shores, yea, all the creatures,
Against your peace. Thee of thy son, Alonso,
They have bereft; and do pronounce by me
Ling'ring perdition (worse than any death
Can be at once) shall step by step attend
You and your ways; whose wraths to guard you from,
Which here, in this most desolate isle, else falls
Upon your heads, is nothing but heart's sorrow[154]
And a clear life ensuing.

He vanishes in thunder; then, to soft music, enter the Shapes again, and dance with mocks and mows,[155] *and carrying out the table.*

PROSPERO:
Bravely the figure of this harpy hast thou
Performed, my Ariel; a grace it had, devouring.[156]

---

[150] **suchlike valor:** The courage that comes of madness. [151] **still-closing:** Ever closing again (as soon as wounded). [152] **If . . . hurt:** Even if you could hurt us. [153] **requit it:** Avenged that crime. [154] **nothing . . . sorrow:** Only repentance (will protect you from the wrath of these powers). [155] ***mocks and mows:*** Mocking gestures and grimaces. [156] **devouring:** In making the banquet disappear.

Of my instruction hast thou nothing bated
In what thou hadst to say. So, with good life[157]
And observation strange,[158] my meaner ministers[159]
Their several kinds have done.[160] My high charms work,
And these, mine enemies, are all knit up
In their distractions. They now are in my pow'r;
And in these fits I leave them, while I visit
Young Ferdinand, whom they suppose is drowned,
And his and mine loved darling. [*Exit above.*]

GONZALO:
I' th' name of something holy, sir, why stand you
In this strange stare?

ALONSO:
O, it is monstrous, monstrous!
Methought the billows spoke and told me of it;
The winds did sing it to me; and the thunder,
That deep and dreadful organ pipe, pronounced
The name of Prosper; it did bass my trespass.[161]
Therefore my son i' th' ooze is bedded; and
I'll seek him deeper than e'er plummet sounded
And with him there lie mudded. *Exit.*

SEBASTIAN:
But one fiend at a time,
I'll fight their legions o'er![162]

ANTONIO:
I'll be thy second.
Exeunt [SEBASTIAN *and* ANTONIO].

GONZALO:
All three of them are desperate; their great guilt,
Like poison given to work a great time after,
Now 'gins to bite the spirits. I do beseech you,
That are of suppler joints, follow them swiftly
And hinder them from what this ecstasy° May now provoke them to. — madness
May now provoke them to.

ADRIAN:
Follow, I pray you.
Exeunt omnes.

[157] **good life:** Good lifelike acting. [158] **observation strange:** Remarkable attention to my wishes. [159] **meaner ministers:** Inferior to Ariel. [160] **Their . . . done:** Have acted the parts their natures suited them for. [161] **bass my trespass:** Made me understand my trespass by turning it into music for which the thunder provided the bass part. [162] **their legions o'er:** One after another to the last.

ACT IV

Scene 1

In front of PROSPERO*'s cell.*

Enter PROSPERO, FERDINAND, *and* MIRANDA.

PROSPERO:

If I have too austerely punished you,
Your compensation makes amends; for I
Have given you here a third of mine own life,
Or that for which I live; who once again
I tender to thy hand. All thy vexations
Were but my trials of thy love, and thou
Hast strangely° stood the test. Here, afore heaven, wonderfully
I ratify this my rich gift. O Ferdinand,
Do not smile at me that I boast her off,[163]
For thou shalt find she will outstrip all praise
And make it halt° behind her. limp

FERDINAND:

I do believe it
Against an oracle.[164]

PROSPERO:

Then, as my gift, and thine own acquisition
Worthily purchased, take my daughter. But
If thou dost break her virgin-knot before
All sanctimonious ceremonies may
With full and holy rite be minist'red,
No sweet aspersion[165] shall the heavens let fall
To make this contract grow; but barren hate,
Sour-eyed disdain, and discord shall bestrew
The union of your bed with weeds so loathly
That you shall hate it both. Therefore take heed,
As Hymen's lamps shall light you.[166]

FERDINAND:

As I hope
For quiet days, fair issue, and long life,
With such love as 'tis now, the murkiest den,
The most opportune place, the strong'st suggestion
Our worser genius can,[167] shall never melt
Mine honor into lust, to take away

---

[163] **boast her off:** Includes perhaps the idea of showing her off. [164] **Against an oracle:** Though an oracle should declare otherwise. [165] **aspersion:** Blessing (like rain on crops). [166] **As . . . you:** As earnestly as you pray that the torch of the god of marriage shall burn without smoke (a good omen for wedded happiness). [167] **Our . . . can:** Our evil spirit can offer.

The edge° of that day's celebration
When I shall think or Phoebus' steeds are foundered°
Or Night kept chained below.[168]

keen enjoyment
lamed

PROSPERO:

Fairly spoke.
Sit then and talk with her; she is thine own.
What, Ariel! My industrious servant, Ariel!

Enter ARIEL.

ARIEL:

What would my potent master? Here I am.

PROSPERO:

Thou and thy meaner fellows your last service
Did worthily perform; and I must use you
In such another trick. Go bring the rabble,[169]
O'er whom I give thee pow'r, here to this place.
Incite them to quick motion; for I must
Bestow upon the eyes of this young couple
Some vanity of[170] mine art. It is my promise,
And they expect it from me.

ARIEL:

Presently?

PROSPERO:

Ay, with a twink.

ARIEL:

Before you can say "Come" and "Go,"
And breathe twice and cry, "So, so,"
Each one, tripping on his toe,
Will be here with mop and mow.
Do you love me, master? No?

PROSPERO:

Dearly, my delicate Ariel. Do not approach
Till thou dost hear me call.

ARIEL:

Well; I conceive.°

understand

Exit.

PROSPERO:

Look thou be true.[171] Do not give dalliance
Too much the rein; the strongest oaths are straw
To th' fire i' th' blood. Be more abstemious,
Or else good night your vow!

[168] **Or . . . below:** That either day will never end or night will never come. [169] **rabble:** "Thy meaner fellows." [170] **vanity of:** Illusion conjured up by. [171] **Look . . . true:** Prospero appears to have caught the lovers in an embrace.

FERDINAND:

I warrant you, sir.
The white cold virgin snow upon my heart[172]
Abates the ardor of my liver.[173]

PROSPERO:

Well.
Now come, my Ariel; bring a corollary[174]
Rather than want a spirit. Appear, and pertly!
No tongue! All eyes! Be silent. *Soft music.*

Enter IRIS.[175]

IRIS:

Ceres, most bounteous lady, thy rich leas
Of wheat, rye, barley, fetches,[176] oats, and peas;
Thy turfy mountains, where live nibbling sheep,
And flat meads thatched with stover,[177] them to keep;
Thy banks with pionèd and twillèd brims,[178]
Which spongy April at thy hest betrims
To make cold nymphs chaste crowns; and thy broom groves,
Whose shadow the dismissèd bachelor loves,
Being lasslorn; thy pole-clipt vineyard;[179]
And thy sea-marge, sterile and rocky-hard,
Where thou thyself dost air° — the queen o' th' sky,[180] take the air
Whose wat'ry arch and messenger am I,
Bids thee leave these, and with her sovereign grace,

JUNO *descends.*[181]

Here on this grass plot, in this very place,
To come and sport; her peacocks fly amain.[182]
Approach, rich Ceres, her to entertain.

Enter CERES.

CERES:

Hail, many-colored messenger, that ne'er
Dost disobey the wife of Jupiter,
Who, with thy saffron wings, upon my flow'rs
Diffusest honey drops, refreshing show'rs,
And with each end of thy blue bow dost crown

[172] **The . . . heart:** Her pure white breast on mine (?). [173] **liver:** Supposed seat of sexual passion. [174] **corollary:** Surplus (of spirits). [175] IRIS: Goddess of the rainbow and Juno's messenger. [176] **fetches:** Vetch (a kind of forage). [177] **flat . . . stover:** Meadows covered with a kind of grass used for winter fodder. [178] **banks . . . brims:** Obscure; may refer to the trenched and ridged edges of banks that have been repaired after the erosions of winter. [179] **pole-clipt vineyard:** Vineyard whose vines grow neatly around (embrace) poles (though possibly the word is "poll-clipped," i.e., pruned). [180] **queen . . . sky:** Juno. [181] JUNO ***descends:*** This direction seems to come too soon, but the machine may have lowered her very slowly. [182] **amain:** Swiftly (peacocks, sacred to Juno, drew her chariot).

My bosky° acres and my unshrubbed down, shrubbed
Rich scarf to my proud earth. Why hath thy queen
Summoned me hither to this short-grassed green?

IRIS:

A contract of true love to celebrate
And some donation freely to estate° bestow
On the blessed lovers.

CERES:

Tell me, heavenly bow,
If Venus or her son, as thou dost know,
Do now attend the Queen? Since they did plot
The means that dusky Dis my daughter got,[183]
Her and her blind boy's scandaled company
I have forsworn.

IRIS:

Of her society
Be not afraid, I met her Deity
Cutting the clouds towards Paphos,[184] and her son
Dove-drawn with her. Here thought they to have done
Some wanton charm upon this man and maid,
Whose vows are, that no bed-right shall be paid
Till Hymen's torch be lighted. But in vain;
Mars's hot minion is returned again;[185]
Her waspish-headed son[186] has broke his arrows,
Swears he will shoot no more, but play with sparrows
And be a boy right out.[187]

[JUNO *alights.*]

CERES:

Highest queen of state,
Great Juno, comes; I know her by her gait.

JUNO:

How does my bounteous sister? Go with me
To bless this twain, that they may prosperous be
And honored in their issue.

They sing.

JUNO:

Honor, riches, marriage blessing,
Long continuance, and increasing,

[183] **Since . . . got:** Alluding to the abduction of Proserpine by Pluto (Dis), god of the underworld. [184] **Paphos:** In Cyprus, center of Venus's cult. [185] **Mars's . . . again:** Mars's lustful mistress (Venus) is on her way back to Paphos. [186] **waspish-headed son:** Cupid is irritable and stings with his arrows. [187] **a boy right out:** An ordinary boy.

Hourly joys be still upon you!
Juno sings her blessings on you.
[CERES:] *Earth's increase, foison plenty,*
Barns and garners never empty,
Vines with clust'ring bunches growing,
Plants with goodly burden bowing;
Spring come to you at the farthest
In the very end of harvest.[188]
Scarcity and want shall shun you,
Ceres' blessing so is on you.

FERDINAND:
This is a most majestic vision, and
Harmonious charmingly. May I be bold
To think these spirits?

PROSPERO:
Spirits, which by mine art
I have from their confines called to enact
My present fancies.

FERDINAND:
Let me live here ever!
So rare a wond'red[189] father and a wise
Makes this place Paradise.

JUNO *and* CERES *whisper, and send* IRIS *on employment.*

PROSPERO:
Sweet now, silence!
Juno and Ceres whisper seriously.
There's something else to do. Hush and be mute,
Or else our spell is marred.

IRIS:
You nymphs, called Naiades, of the windring[190] brooks,
With your sedged crowns and ever-harmless looks,
Leave your crisp° channels, and on this green land rippling
Answer your summons; Juno does command.
Come, temperate nymphs, and help to celebrate
A contract of true love; be not too late.

Enter certain NYMPHS.

You sunburned sicklemen, of August weary,
Come hither from the furrow and be merry.

[188] ***Spring . . . harvest:*** May there be no winter in your lives. [189] **wond'red:** Possessed of wonders; i.e., both wonderful and wonder-working, and therefore to be wondered at. [190] **windring:** Winding and wandering (?).

Make holiday; your rye-straw hats put on,
And these fresh nymphs encounter everyone
In country footing.° dance

Enter certain REAPERS, *properly habited. They join with the* NYMPHS *in a graceful dance; towards the end whereof* PROSPERO *starts suddenly and speaks;*[191] *after which, to a strange, hollow, and confused noise, they heavily*[192] *vanish.*

PROSPERO:
[*Aside*] I had forgot that foul conspiracy
Of the beast Caliban and his confederates
Against my life. The minute of their plot
Is almost come. [*To the* SPIRITS] Well done!
Avoid!° No more! Begone!

FERDINAND:
This is strange. Your father's in some passion
That works him strongly.

MIRANDA:
Never till this day
Saw I him touched with anger so distempered.

PROSPERO:
You do look, my son, in a movèd sort,° troubled state
As if you were dismayed; be cheerful, sir.
Our revels now are ended. These our actors,
As I foretold you, were all spirits and
Are melted into air, into thin air;
And, like the baseless fabric of this vision,
The cloud-capped towers, the gorgeous palaces,
The solemn temples, the great globe itself,
Yea, all which it inherit, shall dissolve,
And, like this insubstantial pageant faded,
Leave not a rack° behind. We are such stuff wisp of cloud
As dreams are made on, and our little life
Is rounded with a sleep. Sir, I am vexed.
Bear with my weakness; my old brain is troubled.
Be not disturbed with my infirmity.
If you be pleased, retire into my cell
And there repose. A turn or two I'll walk
To still my beating mind.

FERDINAND, MIRANDA:
We wish your peace.

Exit [FERDINAND *with* MIRANDA].

[191] ***speaks:*** Breaking the spell, which depends on silence. [192] ***heavily:*** Reluctantly.

PROSPERO:
Come with a thought! I thank thee, Ariel.[193] Come.

Enter ARIEL.

ARIEL:
Thy thoughts I cleave to. What's thy pleasure?
PROSPERO:
Spirit,
We must prepare to meet with Caliban.
ARIEL:
Ay, my commander. When I presented[194] Ceres,
I thought to have told thee of it, but I feared
Lest I might anger thee.
PROSPERO:
Say again, where didst thou leave these varlets?° ruffians
ARIEL:
I told you, sir, they were red-hot with drinking;
So full of valor that they smote the air
For breathing in their faces, beat the ground
For kissing of their feet; yet always bending
Towards their project. Then I beat my tabor;
At which like unbacked° colts they pricked their ears, unbroken
Advanced° their eyelids, lifted up their noses lifted up
As they smelt music. So I charmed their ears
That calflike they my lowing followed through
Toothed briers, sharp furzes, pricking goss,° and thorns, gorse
Which ent'red their frail shins. At last I left them
I' th' filthy mantled[195] pool beyond your cell,
There dancing up to th' chins, that the foul lake
O'erstunk their feet.
PROSPERO:
This was well done, my bird.
Thy shape invisible retain thou still.
The trumpery[196] in my house, go bring it hither
For stale° to catch these thieves. decoy
ARIEL:
I go, I go. *Exit.*
PROSPERO:
A devil, a born devil, on whose nature
Nurture can never stick; on whom my pains,

---

[193]**thank thee, Ariel:** For the masque (?). [194]**presented:** Acted the part of (?); introduced (?). [195]**filthy mantled:** Covered with filthy scum. [196]**trumpery:** The "glistering apparel" mentioned in the next stage direction.

Humanely taken, all, all lost, quite lost!
And as with age his body uglier grows,
So his mind cankers. I will plague them all,
Even to roaring. *Enter* ARIEL, *loaden with glistering apparel, etc.*
Come, hang them on this line.[197]

[PROSPERO *and* ARIEL *remain, invisible.*] *Enter* CALIBAN, STEPHANO, *and* TRINCULO, *all wet.*

CALIBAN:
Pray you tread softly, that the blind mole may not
Hear a foot fall. We now are near his cell.

STEPHANO:
Monster, your fairy, which you say is a harmless fairy,
has done little better than played the Jack[198] with us.

TRINCULO: Monster, I do smell all horse piss, at which my nose is in great indignation.

STEPHANO: So is mine. Do you hear, monster? If I should take a displeasure against you, look you—

TRINCULO: Thou wert but a lost monster.

CALIBAN:
Good my lord, give me thy favor still.
Be patient, for the prize I'll bring thee to
Shall hoodwink[199] this mischance. Therefore speak softly.
All's hushed as midnight yet.

TRINCULO: Ay, but to lose our bottles in the pool—

STEPHANO: There is not only disgrace and dishonor in that, monster, but an infinite loss.

TRINCULO: That's more to me than my wetting. Yet this is your harmless fairy, monster.

STEPHANO: I will fetch off my bottle, though I be o'er ears[200] for my labor.

CALIBAN:
Prithee, my king, be quiet. Seest thou here?
This is the mouth o' th' cell. No noise, and enter.
Do that good mischief which may make this island
Thine own forever, and I, thy Caliban,
For aye thy footlicker.

STEPHANO: Give me thy hand. I do begin to have bloody thoughts.

TRINCULO: O King Stephano! O peer![201] O worthy Stephano, look what a wardrobe here is for thee!

CALIBAN: Let it alone, thou fool! It is but trash.

TRINCULO: O, ho, monster! We know what belongs to a frippery.[202] O King Stephano!

STEPHANO: Put off that gown, Trinculo! By this hand, I'll have that gown!

---

[197] **line:** Lime tree (linden). [198] **Jack:** (1) Knave; (2) jack-o'-lantern, will-o'-the-wisp. [199] **hoodwink:** Put out of sight. [200] **o'er ears:** Over my ears in water. [201] **O King . . . peer!:** Alluding to the song "King Stephen was and a worthy peer; / His breeches cost him but a crown," quoted in *Othello* II, iii. [202] **frippery:** Old-clothes shop; i.e., we are good judges of castoff clothes.

TRINCULO: Thy Grace shall have it.

CALIBAN:

The dropsy drown this fool! What do you mean
To dote thus on such luggage?[203] Let't alone,
And do the murder first. If he awake,
From toe to crown he'll fill our skins with pinches,
Make us strange stuff.

STEPHANO: Be you quiet, monster. Mistress line, is not this my jerkin?[204] [*Takes it down.*] Now is the jerkin under the line.[205] Now, jerkin, you are like to lose your hair and prove a bald jerkin.[206]

TRINCULO: Do, do! We steal by line and level,[207] and't like[208] your Grace.

STEPHANO: I thank thee for that jest. Here's a garment for't. Wit shall not go unrewarded while I am king of this country. "Steal by line and level" is an excellent pass of pate.[209] There's another garment for't.

TRINCULO: Monster, come put some lime[210] upon your fingers, and away with the rest.

CALIBAN:

I will have none on't. We shall lose our time
And all be turned to barnacles,[211] or to apes
With foreheads villainous low.

STEPHANO: Monster, lay-to your fingers; help to bear this away where my hogshead of wine is, or I'll turn you out of my kingdom. Go to, carry this.

TRINCULO: And this.

STEPHANO: Ay, and this.

A noise of hunters heard. Enter divers SPIRITS *in shape of dogs and hounds, hunting them about;* PROSPERO *and* ARIEL *setting them on.*

PROSPERO: Hey, Mountain, hey!

ARIEL: Silver! There it goes, Silver!

PROSPERO:

Fury, Fury! There, Tyrant, there! Hark, hark!

[CALIBAN, STEPHANO, *and* TRINCULO *are driven out.*]

Go, charge my goblins that they grind their joints
With dry convulsions,[212] shorten up their sinews
With agèd cramps, and more pinch-spotted make them
Than pard or cat o' mountain.[213]

---

[203] **luggage:** Useless encumbrances. [204] **jerkin:** Kind of jacket. [205] **under the line:** Pun: (1) under the lime tree; (2) under the equator. [206] **bald jerkin:** Sailors proverbially lost their hair from fevers contracted while crossing the equator. [207] **line and level:** By plumb line and carpenter's level; i.e., according to rule (with pun on "line"). [208] **and't like:** If it please. [209] **pass of pate:** Sally of wit. [210] **lime:** Birdlime (which is sticky; thieves have sticky fingers). [211] **barnacles:** Kind of geese supposed to have developed from shellfish. [212] **dry convulsions:** Such as come when the joints are dry from old age. [213] **pard . . . mountain:** Leopard or catamount.

ARIEL:

Hark, they roar!

PROSPERO:

Let them be hunted soundly. At this hour
Lies at my mercy all mine enemies.
Shortly shall all my labors end, and thou
Shalt have the air at freedom. For a little,
Follow, and do me service. *Exeunt.*

Act V

Scene 1

In front of PROSPERO*'s cell.*

Enter PROSPERO *in his magic robes, and* ARIEL.

PROSPERO:

Now does my project gather to a head.
My charms crack not, my spirits obey, and time
Goes upright with his carriage.[214] How's the day?

ARIEL:

On the sixth hour, at which time, my lord,
You said our work should cease.

PROSPERO:

I did say so
When first I raised the tempest. Say, my spirit,
How fares the King and 's followers?

ARIEL:

Confined together
In the same fashion as you gave in charge,
Just as you left them—all prisoners, sir,
In the line grove which weather-fends[215] your cell.
They cannot budge till your release. The King,
His brother, and yours abide all three distracted,
And the remainder mourning over them,
Brimful of sorrow and dismay; but chiefly
Him that you termed, sir, the good old Lord Gonzalo.
His tears runs down his beard like winter's drops
From eaves of reeds.[216] Your charm so strongly works 'em,
That if you now beheld them, your affections
Would become tender.

---

[214] **time . . . carriage:** Time does not stoop under his burden (because there is so little left to do). [215] **weather-fends:** Protects from the weather. [216] **eaves of reeds:** A thatched roof.

PROSPERO:

Dost thou think so, spirit?

ARIEL:

Mine would, sir, were I human.

PROSPERO:

And mine shall.
Hast thou, which art but air, a touch, a feeling
Of their afflictions, and shall not myself,
One of their kind, that relish all as sharply,
Passion as they, be kindlier moved than thou art?
Though with their high wrongs I am struck to th' quick,
Yet with my nobler reason 'gainst my fury
Do I take part. The rarer action is
In virtue than in vengeance. They being penitent,
The sole drift of my purpose doth extend
Not a frown further. Go, release them, Ariel.
My charms I'll break, their senses I'll restore,
And they shall be themselves.

ARIEL:

I'll fetch them, sir. *Exit.*

PROSPERO:

Ye elves of hills, brooks, standing lakes, and groves,
And ye that on the sands with printless foot
Do chase the ebbing Neptune, and do fly him° — fly with him
When he comes back, you demi-puppets that
By moonshine do the green sour ringlets[217] make,
Whereof the ewe not bites; and you whose pastime
Is to make midnight mushrumps,° that rejoice — mushrooms
To hear the solemn curfew; by whose aid
(Weak masters[218] though ye be) I have bedimmed
The noontide sun, called forth the mutinous winds,
And 'twixt the green sea and the azured vault
Set roaring war; to the dread rattling thunder
Have I given fire and rifted Jove's stout oak
With his own bolt; the strong-based promontory
Have I made shake and by the spurs° plucked up — roots
The pine and cedar; graves at my command
Have waked their sleepers, oped, and let 'em forth
By my so potent art. But this rough magic
I here abjure; and when I have required
Some heavenly music (which even now I do)

[217] **ringlets:** "Fairy rings," little circles of rank grass supposed to be formed by the dancing of fairies.

[218] **masters:** That is, masters of supernatural power.

To work mine end upon their senses that
This airy charm is for, I'll break my staff,
Bury it certain fathoms in the earth,
And deeper than did ever plummet sound
I'll drown my book.

[*Solemn music.*]
Here enters ARIEL *before; then* ALONSO, *with a frantic gesture, attended by* GONZALO; SEBASTIAN *and* ANTONIO *in like manner, attended by* ADRIAN *and* FRANCISCO. *They all enter the circle which* PROSPERO *had made, and there stand charmed; which* PROSPERO *observing, speaks.*

A solemn air, and the best comforter
To an unsettled fancy, cure thy brains,
Now useless, boiled within thy skull! There stand,
For you are spell-stopped.
Holy Gonzalo, honorable man,
Mine eyes, ev'n sociable to the show of thine,
Fall fellowly drops.[219] The charm dissolves apace;
And as the morning steals upon the night,
Melting the darkness, so their rising senses
Begin to chase the ignorant fumes that mantle
Their clearer reason. O good Gonzalo,
My true preserver, and a loyal sir
To him thou follow'st, I will pay thy graces
Home[220] both in word and deed. Most cruelly
Didst thou, Alonso, use me and my daughter.
Thy brother was a furtherer in the act.
Thou art pinched for't now, Sebastian. Flesh and blood,
You, brother mine, that entertained ambition,
Expelled remorse and nature;° whom, with Sebastian — natural feeling
(Whose inward pinches therefore are most strong),
Would here have killed your king, I do forgive thee,
Unnatural though thou art. Their understanding
Begins to swell, and the approaching tide
Will shortly fill the reasonable shore,
That now lies foul and muddy. Not one of them
That yet looks on me or would know me. Ariel,
Fetch me the hat and rapier in my cell.
I will discase me,° and myself present — disrobe
As I was sometime Milan. Quickly, spirit!
Thou shalt ere long be free.

[*Exit* ARIEL *and returns immediately.*]

[219] **ev'n . . . drops:** Associating themselves with the (tearful) appearance of your eyes, shed tears in sympathy.
[220] **pay . . . Home:** Repay thy favors thoroughly.

ARIEL *sings and helps to attire him.*

Where the bee sucks, there suck I;
In a cowslip's bell I lie;
There I couch when owls do cry.
On the bat's back I do fly
After summer merrily.
Merrily, merrily shall I live now
Under the blossom that hangs on the bough.

PROSPERO:
Why, that's my dainty Ariel! I shall miss thee,
But yet thou shalt have freedom; so, so, so.
To the King's ship, invisible as thou art!
There shalt thou find the mariners asleep
Under the hatches. The master and the boatswain
Being awake, enforce them to this place,
And presently, I prithee.

ARIEL:
I drink the air before me, and return
Or ere your pulse twice beat. *Exit.*

GONZALO:
All torment, trouble, wonder, and amazement
Inhabits here. Some heavenly power guide us
Out of this fearful country!

PROSPERO:
Behold, sir King,
The wrongèd Duke of Milan, Prospero.
For more assurance that a living prince
Does now speak to thee, I embrace thy body,
And to thee and thy company I bid
A hearty welcome.

ALONSO:
Whe'r thou be'st he or no,
Or some enchanted trifle° to abuse me, apparition
As late I have been, I not know. Thy pulse
Beats, as of flesh and blood; and, since I saw thee,
Th' affliction of my mind amends, with which,
I fear, a madness held me. This must crave[221]
(And if this be at all) a most strange story.
Thy dukedom I resign and do entreat
Thou pardon me my wrongs. But how should Prospero
Be living and be here?

[221] **crave:** Require (to account for it).

PROSPERO:

First, noble friend,
Let me embrace thine age, whose honor cannot
Be measured or confined.

GONZALO:

Whether this be
Or be not, I'll not swear.

PROSPERO:

You do yet taste
Some subtleties[222] o' th' isle, that will not let you
Believe things certain. Welcome, my friends all.
[*Aside to* SEBASTIAN *and* ANTONIO] But you, my brace of lords, were I so minded,
I here could pluck his Highness' frown upon you,
And justify° you traitors. At this time prove
I will tell no tales.

SEBASTIAN:

[*Aside*] The devil speaks in him.

PROSPERO:

No.
For you, most wicked sir, whom to call brother
Would even infect my mouth, I do forgive
Thy rankest fault—all of them; and require
My dukedom of thee, which perforce I know
Thou must restore.

ALONSO:

If thou beest Prospero,
Give us particulars of thy preservation;
How thou hast met us here, whom three hours since
Were wracked upon this shore; where I have lost
(How sharp the point of this remembrance is!)
My dear son Ferdinand.

PROSPERO:

I am woe for't, sir.

ALONSO:

Irreparable is the loss, and patience
Says it is past her cure.

PROSPERO:

I rather think
You have not sought her help, of whose soft grace
For the like loss I have her sovereign aid
And rest myself content.

[222] **subtleties:** Deceptions (referring to pastries made to look like something else, e.g., castles made out of sugar).

ALONSO:

You the like loss?

PROSPERO:

As great to me, as late,[223] and supportable
To make the dear loss, have I means much weaker
Than you may call to comfort you; for I
Have lost my daughter.

ALONSO:

A daughter?
O heavens, that they were living both in Naples,
The King and Queen there! That they were, I wish
Myself were mudded in that oozy bed
Where my son lies. When did you lose your daughter?

PROSPERO:

In this last tempest. I perceive these lords
At this encounter do so much admire° — wonder
That they devour their reason, and scarce think
Their eyes do offices° of truth, their words — perform services
Are natural breath. But, howsoev'r you have
Been justled from your senses, know for certain
That I am Prospero, and that very duke
Which was thrust forth of Milan, who most strangely
Upon this shore, where you were wracked, was landed
To be the lord on't. No more yet of this;
For 'tis a chronicle of day by day,
Not a relation for a breakfast, nor
Befitting this first meeting. Welcome, sir;
This cell's my court. Here have I few attendants,
And subjects none abroad.[224] Pray you look in.
My dukedom since you have given me again,
I will requite you with as good a thing,
At least bring forth a wonder to content ye
As much as me my dukedom.

Here PROSPERO *discovers*[225] FERDINAND *and* MIRANDA *playing at chess.*

MIRANDA:

Sweet lord, you play me false.

FERDINAND:

No, my dearest love,
I would not for the world.

---

[223] **As . . . late:** As great to me as your loss, and as recent. [224] **abroad:** On the island. [225] ***discovers:*** Reveals (by opening a curtain at the back of the stage).

MIRANDA:

Yes, for a score of kingdoms you should wrangle,
And I would call it fair play.[226]

ALONSO:

If this prove
A vision of the island, one dear son
Shall I twice lose.

SEBASTIAN:

A most high miracle!

FERDINAND:

Though the seas threaten, they are merciful.
I have cursed them without cause.

[*Kneels.*]

ALONSO:

Now all the blessings
Of a glad father compass thee about!
Arise, and say how thou cam'st here.

MIRANDA:

O, wonder!
How many goodly creatures are there here!
How beauteous mankind is! O brave new world
That has such people in't!

PROSPERO:

'Tis new to thee.

ALONSO:

What is this maid with whom thou wast at play?
Your eld'st acquaintance cannot be three hours.
Is she the goddess that hath severed us
And brought us thus together?

FERDINAND:

Sir, she is mortal;
But by immortal providence she's mine.
I chose her when I could not ask my father
For his advice, nor thought I had one. She
Is daughter to this famous Duke of Milan,
Of whom so often I have heard renown
But never saw before; of whom I have
Received a second life; and second father
This lady makes him to me.

[226] **for . . . play:** If we were playing for stakes just short of the world, you would protest as now; but then, the issue being important, I would call it fair play so much do I love you (?).

ALONSO:

I am hers.
But, O, how oddly will it sound that I
Must ask my child forgiveness!

PROSPERO:

There, sir, stop.
Let us not burden our remembrance with
A heaviness that's gone.

GONZALO:

I have inly wept,
Or should have spoke ere this. Look down, you gods,
And on this couple drop a blessèd crown!
For it is you that have chalked forth the way
Which brought us hither.

ALONSO:

I say amen, Gonzalo.

GONZALO:

Was Milan thrust from Milan that his issue
Should become kings of Naples? O, rejoice
Beyond a common joy, and set it down
With gold on lasting pillars. In one voyage
Did Claribel her husband find at Tunis,
And Ferdinand her brother found a wife
Where he himself was lost; Prospero his dukedom
In a poor isle; and all of us ourselves
When no man was his own.

ALONSO:

[*To* FERDINAND *and* MIRANDA] Give me your hands.
Let grief and sorrow still embrace his heart
That doth not wish you joy.

GONZALO:

Be it so! Amen!

Enter ARIEL, *with the* MASTER *and* BOATSWAIN *amazedly following.*

O, look, sir; look, sir! Here is more of us!
I prophesied if a gallows were on land,
This fellow could not drown. Now, blasphemy,
That swear'st grace o'erboard,[227] not an oath on shore?
Hast thou no mouth by land? What is the news?

BOATSWAIN:

The best news is that we have safely found
Our king and company; the next, our ship,
Which, but three glasses since, we gave out split,

[227] **That . . . o'erboard:** That (at sea) swearest enough to cause grace to be withdrawn from the ship.

Is tight and yare° and bravely rigged as when
We first put out to sea. — shipshape

ARIEL:

[*Aside to* PROSPERO] Sir, all this service
Have I done since I went.

PROSPERO:

[*Aside to* ARIEL] My tricksy spirit!

ALONSO:

These are not natural events; they strengthen
From strange to stranger. Say, how came you hither?

BOATSWAIN:

If I did think, sir, I were well awake,
I'd strive to tell you. We were dead of sleep
And (how we know not) all clapped under hatches;
Where, but even now, with strange and several noises
Of roaring, shrieking, howling, jingling chains,
And moe diversity of sounds, all horrible,
We were awaked; straightway at liberty;
Where we, in all our trim, freshly beheld
Our royal, good, and gallant ship, our master
Cap'ring to eye° her. On a trice, so please you, — dancing to see
Even in a dream, were we divided from them
And were brought moping° hither. — in a daze

ARIEL:

[*Aside to* PROSPERO] Was't well done?

PROSPERO:

[*Aside to* ARIEL] Bravely, my diligence. Thou shalt be free.

ALONSO:

This is as strange a maze as e'er men trod,
And there is in this business more than nature
Was ever conduct° of. Some oracle — conductor
Must rectify our knowledge.

PROSPERO:

Sir, my liege,
Do not infest your mind with beating on
The strangeness of this business. At picked leisure,
Which shall be shortly, single I'll resolve you
(Which to you shall seem probable) of every
These happened accidents;[228] till when, be cheerful
And think of each thing well. [*Aside to* ARIEL] Come hither, spirit.
Set Caliban and his companions free.

[228] **single . . . accidents:** I myself will solve the problems (and my story will make sense to you) concerning each and every incident that has happened.

Untie the spell. [*Exit* ARIEL.] How fares my gracious sir?
There are yet missing of your company
Some few odd lads that you remember not.

Enter ARIEL, *driving in* CALIBAN, STEPHANO, *and* TRINCULO, *in their stolen apparel.*

STEPHANO: Every man shift for all the rest, and let no man take care for himself; for all is but fortune. *Coragio,*[229] bully-monster, *coragio!*

TRINCULO: If these be true spies which I wear in my head, here's a goodly sight.

CALIBAN:
O Setebos,[230] there be brave spirits indeed!
How fine my master is! I am afraid
He will chastise me.

SEBASTIAN:
Ha, ha!
What things are these, my Lord Antonio?
Will money buy 'em?

ANTONIO:
Very like. One of them
Is a plain fish and no doubt marketable.

PROSPERO:
Mark but the badges[231] of these men, my lords,
Then say if they be true. This misshapen knave,
His mother was a witch, and one so strong
That could control the moon, make flows and ebbs,
And deal in her command without her power.[232]
These three have robbed me, and this demi-devil
(For he's a bastard one) had plotted with them
To take my life. Two of these fellows you
Must know and own; this thing of darkness I
Acknowledge mine.

CALIBAN:
I shall be pinched to death.

ALONSO:
Is not this Stephano, my drunken butler?

SEBASTIAN:
He is drunk now. Where had he wine?

ALONSO:
And Trinculo is reeling ripe. Where should they
Find this grand liquor that hath gilded 'em?
How cam'st thou in this pickle?

---

[229] ***Coragio:*** Courage (Italian). [230] **Setebos:** The god of Caliban's mother. [231] **badges:** Worn by servants to indicate to whose service they belong; in this case, the stolen clothes are badges of their rascality. [232] **control . . . power:** Dabble in the moon's realm without the moon's legitimate authority.

TRINCULO: I have been in such a pickle, since I saw you last, that I fear me will never out of my bones. I shall not fear flyblowing.[233]

SEBASTIAN: Why, how now, Stephano?

STEPHANO: O, touch me not! I am not Stephano, but a cramp.

PROSPERO: You'd be king o' the isle, sirrah?

STEPHANO: I should have been a sore[234] one then.

ALONSO: This is a strange thing as e'er I looked on.

PROSPERO:

He is as disproportioned in his manners
As in his shape. Go, sirrah, to my cell;
Take with you your companions. As you look
To have my pardon, trim it handsomely.

CALIBAN:

Ay, that I will; and I'll be wise hereafter,
And seek for grace. What a thrice-double ass
Was I to take this drunkard for a god
And worship this dull fool!

PROSPERO:

Go to! Away!

ALONSO:

Hence, and bestow your luggage where you found it.

SEBASTIAN:

Or stole it rather.

[*Exeunt* CALIBAN, STEPHANO, *and* TRINCULO.]

PROSPERO:

Sir, I invite your Highness and your train
To my poor cell, where you shall take your rest
For this one night; which, part of it, I'll waste
With such discourse as, I not doubt, shall make it
Go quick away—the story of my life,
And the particular accidents gone by
Since I came to this isle. And in the morn
I'll bring you to your ship, and so to Naples,
Where I have hope to see the nuptial
Of these our dear-beloved solemnizèd;
And thence retire me to my Milan, where
Every third thought shall be my grave.

ALONSO:

I long
To hear the story of your life, which must
Take° the ear strangely. captivate

[233] **pickle . . . flyblowing:** Pickling preserves meat from flies. [234] **sore:** (1) Tyrannical; (2) aching.

PROSPERO:

I'll deliver° all; — tell
And promise you calm seas, auspicious gales,
And sail so expeditious that shall catch
Your royal fleet far off. [*Aside to* ARIEL] My Ariel, chick,
That is thy charge. Then to the elements
Be free, and fare thou well! [*To the others*] Please you, draw near.

Exeunt omnes.

EPILOGUE

Spoken by PROSPERO.

Now my charms are all o'erthrown,
And what strength I have's mine own,
Which is most faint. Now 'tis true
I must be here confined by you,
Or sent to Naples. Let me not,
Since I have my dukedom got
And pardoned the deceiver, dwell
In this bare island by your spell;
But release me from my bands° — bonds
With the help of your good hands.[235]
Gentle breath° of yours my sails — favorable comment
Must fill, or else my project fails,
Which was to please. Now I want° — lack
Spirits to enforce, art to enchant;
And my ending is despair
Unless I be relieved by prayer,° — this petition
Which pierces so that it assaults
Mercy itself and frees all faults.
As you from crimes would pardoned be,
Let your indulgence set me free.

Exit.

[235] ***good hands:*** Applause to break the spell.

JOHN MILTON
1608–1674

John Milton may be considered one of the world's great writers. An English Protestant and courageous defender of political liberty, Milton defied both pope and king and was therefore in many respects a prophetic voice for the European opposition to established authority in the late **RENAISSANCE**. He was also an inspiration for political and religious reformers and advocates of civil liberties in subsequent generations. His service to the Puritan cause during the **ENGLISH CIVIL WAR**,[1] including the writing of pamphlets containing strong views on such matters as divorce, freedom of the press, and civil liberties, made him a compelling figure in his own time, but he is best remembered today for his poetry, including his pastoral lyrics "L'Allegro" and "Il Penseroso"; his pastoral elegy "Lycidas"; his drama *Samson Agonistes;* and particularly his great epic, *Paradise Lost.* Modeled in part on the epic poems of Homer and Virgil, *Paradise Lost* aims to transcend the martial and nationalist themes of his precursors and take up what he believes to be the universal theme of the fall of Adam and Eve from paradise. Invoking no less a figure than the Holy Spirit as his muse, Milton set out to write a great Christian epic that would "justify the ways of God to men."

WWW For links to more information about Milton and a quiz on *Paradise Lost,* see *World Literature Online* at bedfordstmartins .com/worldlit.

Education and "Studious Retirement." John Milton was born on December 8, 1608, in Cheapside, London, where his Protestant father was a successful businessman with substantial earnings from real-estate investments and moneylending. In his early years, Milton received a superb classical education from private tutors and at St. Paul's School. Before entering Christ's College, Cambridge, in 1625, Milton was already a master of Latin, Greek, and Hebrew, and he focused his studies on the ministry, earning his bachelor's degree in 1629 and his master of arts in 1632. Disenchanted with the Church of England, Milton after graduation decided not to take orders and went instead into a six-year period of what he called "studious retirement" at the family estate at Horton in Buckinghamshire. There he read extensively in the Greek and Roman classics, Italian literature, science and mathematics, history, and English literature. He also wrote poetry, producing in 1634 the elaborate masque *Comus* and in 1637 one of the greatest pastoral elegies in English, "Lycidas." Milton sensed that he was preparing himself for some great work of serious moral purpose, and he suggests that he was moved by "an inward prompting . . . that by labor and intent study (which I take to be my portion in this life), joined with a strong propensity of nature, I might perhaps leave something so

[1] **English Civil War:** The armed conflict between Charles I (r. 1625–49) and the Parliamentarians that began in 1642, when the king attempted to arrest five members of the House of Commons, and lasted until his surrender in 1646. Hostilities broke out again in 1648, and the war finally ended with the beheading of the king in January 1649. The English Civil War was drawn along religious and political lines: Catholic royalists who supported divine-right monarchy against Protestant republicans who supported Parliamentary rule.

written to aftertimes, as they should not willingly let it die." That he succeeded in his aim to write a poem that would be long remembered is evidenced by the profound influence his epic—its style, its theme, and its controversies—had on later generations of English poets and writers.

Italian Journey and Troubles at Home. After his mother died in 1637, Milton spent nearly two years touring France and Italy, where he visited important writers, scholars, public officials, and scientists, including Galileo, the famous astronomer who was then under the watchful eye of the Vatican. In July of 1639 Milton returned home to face the beginning of the Protestant revolution in England. He moved to St. Bride's churchyard and began tutoring his nephews and other students, and in 1642, at age thirty-three, he married Mary Powell, a sixteen-year-old girl from a Royalist family, who returned home to her parents shortly after the marriage. During this time Milton was writing poetry, as well as occasional essays on politics, education, and religion. The essays included his notorious defense of divorce, *The Doctrine and Discipline of Divorce* (1643; revised 1644 and 1645), which argues that incompatibility should be sufficient grounds for divorce, and his defense of educational reform, *Of Education* (1644), which sketches out a rigorous program of liberal arts, science, and physical education as a means to attain the knowledge, virtue, and skill necessary for responsible citizenship. Looking forward to *Paradise Lost,* Milton claims that the goal of education is to redeem the sins of Adam and Eve by learning again "to know God aright, and out of that knowledge to love him, to imitate him, to be like him" by learning and following the true virtue of the "grace of faith." In 1644 Milton also published *Areopagitica,* an elegant and forceful defense of freedom of the press and the free circulation of ideas. These treatises marked Milton as a radical even in a time when Parliament was demanding more rights from the king and more openly criticizing abuses of power in both the Anglican Church and the monarchy. He was criticized for supporting positions that appeared to advocate the unhinging of an already precarious society. Nonetheless, Milton held out hope that freedom of speech would ensure that civic and religious leaders would be held accountable to the people.

Upholding the principle of reasoned liberty against arbitrary authority, Milton produced a series of pamphlets in English and in Latin, including *The Tenure of Kings and Magistrates,* which defended the right of the people to overthrow and even to execute their king. This pamphlet was published in 1649, the year in which Charles I[2] was executed and a decade of military rule began under the leadership of Oliver Cromwell.[3]

---

[2] **Charles I** (r. 1625–49): the second of the Stuart kings of England; his Catholicism, tyranny, and arrogance riled the Protestants and oppositional members of Parliament in England. The conflict broke out into civil war in 1642 (see note 1).

[3] **Oliver Cromwell** (1599–1658): an Independent (Protestant Separatist) Member of Parliament who led the revolt against Charles I (see notes 1 and 2). After Charles's execution in 1649, Cromwell served as a leading member of the Council of State, the governing body of the newly proclaimed Commonwealth. With the dissolution of the Parliament and establishment of the Protectorate—a constitutional dictatorship—in 1653, Cromwell became Lord Protector until his death in 1658.

Masaccio, *The Expulsion*, 1427
This Renaissance vision of Adam and Eve's expulsion from the Garden of Eden (a paradise lost) is part of a fresco in the Brancacci Chapel in Florence. (The Art Archive / Sta Maria del Carmine Florence / Dagli Orti)

Blindness and Insight. Though he fancied marrying another woman, Milton reconciled with his wife, Mary, when she returned in 1645, the year his first collection of poetry appeared; together they had three daughters. About this time Milton began losing his eyesight, becoming completely blind early in 1652. Milton accepted his blindness—or at least rationalized it—as an exchange of outward for inner vision. In the moving meditation on light at the beginning of Book III of *Paradise Lost,* Milton reflects on the gift of a light that enables him to "see and tell / Of things invisible to mortal sight" (54–55), for which he has had to pay the price of "ever-during dark" (45). In giving up the visible world, Milton suggests, he acquired a visionary one; and it is significant that his major poetic works—*Paradise Lost* (1667; 1674), *Samson Agonistes* (1671), and *Paradise Regained* (1671)—were composed after his blindness. During this time too, Milton continued in his official service to Oliver Cromwell's Commonwealth, serving as Latin Secretary to the Council of State from 1649 to 1660; in this position Milton served as a kind of assistant secretary of state charged with handling foreign correspondence, most of which was written in Latin, but he was also charged with answering some popular books defending Charles's monarchy. Among his answers were the *Pro Populo Anglicano Defensio* (Defense of the English People (1651) and his last defense of the rights of the people against arbitrary monarchy, the *Ready and Easy Way to Establish a New Commonwealth* (1660). He also wrote a major study of the Bible, *De Doctrina Christiana* (On Christian Doctrine), a work that was not published during his lifetime.

In 1658, six years after Mary's death, Milton married again, only to lose his second wife, Katherine Woodcock, two years later. Further misfortune followed quickly when in 1660 he was arrested and held in prison after the restoration of Charles II. Although friends, including the poet and Member of Parliament Andrew Marvell (1621–1678), interceded on Milton's behalf, he just escaped being hanged for treason. Nonetheless, the heavy fines he was forced to pay and the forfeiture of some of his property left him relatively poor for the rest of his life.

In 1663, now fifty-five years old, he married for a third time and moved to Bunhill Fields, where he and his wife, the twenty-four-year-old Elizabeth Munshill, lived in relative comfort and quiet. Despite his blindness and his losses, Milton persevered with his goal to leave behind a great work. He saw to press *Paradise Lost, Samson Agonistes,* and *Paradise Regained,* as well as *The History of Britain* (1670), and a final prose treatise *Of True Religion, Heresy, Toleration, and the Growth of Popery* (1673), arguing that if Protestants were to succeed in defeating Catholic power, they needed to put aside their sectarian conflicts and work together. On November 8, 1674, Milton died at the age of sixty-five. He left behind the greatest of all English epic poems, for which he had received a total of ten pounds.

Poems 1645 to *Samson Agonistes*. *Poems of Mr. John Milton,* a collection of Milton's early poems in English and Latin, was published in 1645. It included several sonnets in English and Italian; "On the Morning of

Christ's Nativity," a celebration of the birth of Christ that Milton had written in 1629; *Comus,* a masque written and performed in 1634 at Ludlow Castle; the celebrated pastoral lyrics "L'Allegro" and "Il Penseroso"; and Milton's great pastoral elegy "Lycidas," which had previously been printed in a 1638 collection of poems dedicated to the memory of Edward King, a Cambridge student who had drowned in the Irish Sea the year before. Successfully adapting the conventions of Greek and Roman pastoral elegies to the English language, "Lycidas" set the standard for the genre in English, leading to some impressive imitations in the nineteenth century, including Percy Bysshe Shelley's "Adonais" (1821) and Matthew Arnold's "Thyrsis" (1866). For many critics, "Lycidas" marks the advent of Milton's maturity as a poet in full command of his language and style, anticipating the mastery that would be fully displayed in *Paradise Lost.* In 1673, the year before his death, Milton published a second edition of his *Poems,* adding some new works written between 1645 and 1673.

In his early poetry and prose Milton anticipates writing a grand poem on an elevated theme, and scholars speculate that Milton began thinking about and writing parts of the poem, originally conceived as a drama, as early as the 1640s. Sometime in the next decade, after his blindness, Milton returned to the project, now reconceived as an epic poem. Completed in 1665, *Paradise Lost* was first published in 1667 as a poem in ten books; a revised edition in twelve books appeared in 1674, printed with a dedicatory poem by Andrew Marvell, who had been Milton's assistant when Milton was Latin Secretary for the Commonwealth. Three years before, Milton had published *Paradise Regained,* a four-book mini-epic about Satan's temptation of Christ in the wilderness, and *Samson Agonistes,* a dramatic poem focusing on how the blind hero triumphed over the Philistines[4]—both psychologically and physically—as they held him captive at Gaza. Many readers and critics, including the great German writer Goethe (1749–1832), have suggested that *Samson Agonistes* comes closer than any other work of European literature to the sparing but powerful dramatic form of Greek tragedy. Both of these poems use the unrhymed BLANK VERSE[5] that Milton perfected in *Paradise Lost.*

Paradise Lost. Milton's *Paradise Lost* is the greatest epic in the English language. A poem in blank verse (unrhymed iambic pentameter) of more

[4] **Philistines:** The Philistines, descendants of a seafaring people from the Aegean, possibly Crete, who settled into the area known as Philistia or Palestine sometime in the Bronze Age, were at war with the Israelites. Samson, prophesied to deliver the Israelites from the Philistines, wreaked havoc among the Philistines until he was finally betrayed into the hands of his enemies by his lover Delilah. Stripped of his strength by having his hair shorn, Samson was blinded and imprisoned by the Philistines, but at the feast of Dagon, his strength returned and he collapsed a temple upon himself and his captors, thereby liberating the Israelites. (See Judges 13–16.)

[5] **blank verse:** Lines of unrhymed iambic pentameter—that is, lines of five feet, each foot consisting of an unaccented syllable followed by an accented syllable. While blank verse (which Milton called "English heroic verse without rhyme") had been used in drama before Milton, after his *Paradise Lost* it became a standard form for long poems in English.

Milton is not an author amongst authors, not a poet amongst poets, but a power amongst powers, and the *Paradise Lost* is not a book amongst books, not a poem amongst poems, but a central force amongst forces.

–Thomas De Quincey, "Life of Milton," 1838

than ten thousand lines, it marks the culmination of Milton's poetic career, which, like Virgil's before him, followed a systematic development from lyric poetry to the epic. Recognized for its grandeur and sublimity, its cosmic scope and dramatic intensity, *Paradise Lost* recounts the heroic story of Satan's rebellion against God and the tragic story of Adam and Eve's fall from Paradise, a fall that opens up the possibility for redemption through faith in Christ and God's grace. A work of Christian HUMANISM, Milton's heady mixture of Greco-Roman and Christian mythology and history fully displays the depth and breadth of his prodigious knowledge of classical and biblical literature.

As announced in the opening verse paragraph, *Paradise Lost* sets out "to assert Eternal Providence / And justify the ways of God to men" (ll. 25–26), taking into account both God's foreknowledge and humans' freedom to choose between good and evil, right and wrong. Within the framework of Milton's Protestant beliefs, the fall from the Garden of Eden—a fall from a state of innocence to a state of self-conscious knowledge—was a fortunate fall, because it imposed on human beings the responsibility to exercise their free will and reason to choose goodness and righteousness over evil in the face of temptation, suffering, and doubt. Milton explains his position in his essay *De Doctrina Christiana:* Since Adam tasted of the tree of knowledge, "we not only know evil, but we know good only by means of evil. For it is by evil that virtue is chiefly exercised, and shines with greater brightness."

Books I–III: Satan Defiant. The first two books of *Paradise Lost* focus on Satan and his defeated forces in hell, where they debate about their best course of action: to engage in another battle against God or to accept their defeat. The proud and defiant Satan offers a third, more sinister and satisfactory, possibility: to find the newly created Adam and Eve and ruin their perfect world in the Garden of Eden. In Book III, God calls upon his Son to observe Satan flying toward earth and explains how Satan will pervert mankind by seducing them into transgressing God's law. In this important book, God further explains that although he can foresee these events, he has not predestined them; because God made human beings free to choose, Adam and Eve alone are responsible for succumbing to Satan's temptations and so they must be punished for their transgression. In *De Doctrina Christiana,* Milton explains that nothing happens *necessarily* because God has foreseen it, but what he foresees will happen *certainly* because "the divine prescience cannot be deceived." In other words, God does not cause Adam and Eve's fall, but he knows for sure it is going to take place. Therefore, God's omnipotence and omniscience do not relieve Adam and Eve from taking responsibility for their choices. Human beings choose to do good or evil, and thus seal their own fate. Once they have sinned, nothing can keep them from eternal punishment except for a savior, one willing to sacrifice and answer for their offense. As God unfolds the story of man's inevitable fall, Jesus offers himself as that savior, the "Ransom for Man," and as the angels celebrate this offer of sacrifice Satan begins to close in on Paradise.

> **Milton stood alone illuminating an age unworthy of him.**
> – Percy Bysshe Shelley, *A Defense of Poetry*, 1821

Book IV: Paradise. In Book IV, the somewhat forlorn, even desperate, but still dangerous Satan arrives in Paradise, which is described in splendid detail as a pastoral garden modeled on the unspoiled landscapes of classical antiquity. Here Milton describes Adam and Eve living in marital bliss and in perfect harmony with the plants and animals over which they exercise a benevolent dominion. Here, as Satan looks on unnoticed, Adam points out to Eve the Tree of Knowledge and warns her that the fruit of the tree is forbidden them. Jealous of the innocence and bliss, the "mutual help / And mutual love" enjoyed by Adam and Eve, Satan determines more than ever to bring about their ruin, and when they go to sleep, he whispers temptations in Eve's ear, sending her a dream to transgress God's law. As the book ends, the angel Gabriel drives Satan from the Garden, where he leaves the couple "emparadis'd in one another's arms."

The relationship between Adam and Eve in Book IV invites readers to consider the relationship between men and women in Milton's world—both that in which he lived and that which he imagined to exist in Paradise. Described in the splendor of their nakedness—"Godlike erect, with native honor clad / In naked Majesty"—both Adam and Eve seem to be "Lords of all." Yet Milton's ideal man and wife, however equal in their majesty and mastery over nature, are not equals. While many readers of Milton have tried to temper his views on gender inequality by emphasizing Adam's admiration and respect for the prelapsarian Eve, Milton's position in *Paradise Lost* on the subordination of women is clear and reflects the patriarchal standards of the time:

> though both
> Not equal, as their sex not equal seem'd;
> For contemplation he and valor form'd;
> For softness she and sweet attractive Grace,
> He for God only, she for God in him: [. . .] (IV 295–99)

Adam has "Absolute rule" in Eden, and Eve acknowledges that it was he "for whom / And from whom I was form'd" (IV 440–41). Nonetheless, before their act of disobedience Eve enjoys a kind of mutual partnership with Adam, and within the idealized view of marriage offered in Book IV both Adam and Eve claim a kind of independence that leads to interdependence. Milton's metaphor for the mutuality of their relationship is "conversation," which encompasses both sexual and intellectual intercourse between man and wife in the "cheerful society of wedlock." While the subordination of women is undeniable, some critics suggest that in his depiction of Eve's independence and the ideal marriage, Milton was ahead of his time in reevaluating sexuality as a positive human attribute and even in anticipating protofeminist ideas about marriage as an institution depending on friendship rather than sexual desire or financial opportunity.

Books V–VIII: The Creation Story. The plot of the fall is interrupted in Books V through VIII, which present a retrospective interlude in the form of a long conversation between Adam and the angel Raphael. Like

Has any great poem ever let in so little light upon one's own joys and sorrows? I get no help in judging life; . . . But how smooth, strong and elaborate it all is! What poetry! . . . though there is nothing like lady Macbeth's terror or Hamlet's cry, no pity or sympathy or intuition, the figures are majestic; in them is summed up much of what men thought of our place in the universe, of our duty to God, our religion.
– Virginia Woolf, 1918 diary entry

Mercury admonishing Aeneas[6] when he begins to forget his purpose, Raphael warns Adam about Satan's presence and reminds him of the responsibility Adam's free will imposes on him to obey God's law. In the course of their dialogue, Raphael describes at length the great war in heaven and the creation of the earth; Adam, in his turn, describes his waking in the garden and the creation of Eve. The stage is now set for the critical action of the poem, the subject of Book IX. Moving from the wonders of creation and the bliss of Eden to the fall into sin, Milton signals his intent: "I now must change / These notes to tragic."

Book IX: The Fall. In Book IX Satan returns to Eden and, entering the body of a serpent, addresses Eve. Appealing first to her vanity and curiosity, then to her pride, he convinces her to eat the forbidden fruit. When she does, all of nature feels the shock:

> Earth felt the wound, and nature from her seat
> Sighing through all her works gave signs of woe
> That all was lost. (IX 782–84)

Sensing her difference now from Adam, Eve tempts him to join her in the act of transgression. Deluded by Satan, who has told her that by eating the fruit he has learned to think and speak, thereby raising himself up along the Great Chain of Being, Eve explains that the fruit of the tree has had a similar effect on her, dilating her spirit and giving her Godlike knowledge. Believing that she differs in degree from Adam, she wants Adam to share equally her newfound powers; otherwise their relationship may be compromised. Though he initially recognizes the flaws of Eve's argument, Adam—through some spurious reasoning of his own—finally allows Eve to persuade him to eat the fruit of the Tree of Knowledge. The couple at first relish the pleasures of their newly acquired knowledge, initially expressed as bodily lust, a sign of fallen sexuality that contrasts to the beauty and bliss of lovemaking described in Book IV, but they soon turn to mutual recrimination. For the first time they feel shame, and in place of love and trust arise the "high passions" of anger, hatred, distrust, and suspicion. Both outer and inner worlds are shot through with the tragic consequences of the fall. Adam's degradation in many ways parallels Satan's downward spiral into absolute sin—that is, the complete absence of good—but unlike Satan, Adam receives the possibility of redemption by means of God's grace.

Books X–XI: The Postlapsarian World. Book X describes more fully the changes that take place after the fall. The guardian angels leave Paradise, while Satan's progeny, Sin and Death, abandon their posts at the gates of hell and take up residence on earth. In a stunning passage in Book X, the proud Satan returns triumphantly to hell to brag about his

[6] **Aeneas:** In Book Four of *The Aeneid,* the great Roman epic recounting the legendary founding of Rome, written by the poet Virgil (70–19 B.C.E.), the messenger god Mercury, sent by Jove, exhorts Aeneas to abandon Carthage and his lover Dido and to fulfill his destiny as the founder of Rome.

perversion of Adam and Eve, whom he has left forlorn and fallen in Paradise. When Satan addresses his force of fallen angels, instead of hearing the "universal shout and high applause" he was expecting, he hears the assembly, now all changed into serpents, reply only with a "dismal universal hiss" (X 507–08). Satan too at that very moment finds himself changed into a gigantic serpent, transformed by the greater power of God. Meanwhile, Adam and Eve fill the Garden of Eden with their lamentations, cursing themselves for their sins and fearing their certain death, having forfeited their immortality. By the close of Book X, however, Adam and Eve, though contrite and sorrowful, are reconciled to each other and to their fate, finding hope and reason to live in the knowledge that from their seed shall come the avenger of their foe and the savior of the human race.

[Milton's] great epic, *Paradise Lost,* is preeminently a poem about knowing and choosing – for the Miltonic Bard, for the characters, for the reader.

– Barbara Kiefer Lewalski, critic, 1999

Books XI and XII show the first couple thinking about death and their imminent exile. Recalling Virgil's and Beatrice's roles as guides for the pilgrim Dante in *The Divine Comedy,*[7] as well as Anchises' role as a prophet when Aeneas meets his ghost in *The Aeneid,*[8] God sends the angel Michael to give Adam a vision of the future of humankind under the jurisdiction of God's grace—a future that culminates in Christ's redemption of Adam's sin and the promise of the second coming. Sadder but wiser, armed with understanding and faith, and filled with trepidation and hope, Adam and Eve leave Paradise hand in hand, the "World . . . all before them" and with Providence as their guide. Although the tragedy of their fall has been mitigated by the promise of Christ's salvation, they leave the garden conscious that their union will last only until death and that they must live their lives on different terms. Moreover, they know that their tragedy, and the labor, suffering, and death that are its consequences, will be passed on to their descendants.

The Power of *Paradise Lost*. Modern readers may be less interested in the theology of *Paradise Lost* than in its literary power. While the elevated diction, Latinisms, inverted word order, and elaborate and highly allusive imagery make reading the poem difficult, its grandeur and sweeping breadth, its vigorous language and style cannot be denied. Its astonishing sound effects and stately metrical quality convey a unique richness in English verse, and Milton's choice of blank verse was so revolutionary in its own time that Milton was compelled to append a defense of it after the first printing. After Milton, blank verse became a standard measure for many English poets aiming for an elevated style. In addition to his style, the psychological depth of Milton's characters, especially the heroic but self-conflicted Satan, give the poem a dramatic quality equal to that of Shakespeare's plays. Satan, who by many accounts comes close to being

[7] ***The Divine Comedy:*** In *The Divine Comedy,* by the Italian poet Dante (1265–1321), the character Virgil, symbolizing right reason, and the character Beatrice, symbolizing God's grace, guide the pilgrim Dante from Hades, through Purgatory, and into Paradise, where he receives a beatific vision of God.

[8] ***The Aeneid:*** In Book Six of *The Aeneid* (see note 6), the hero Aeneas visits the Underworld, where he meets the ghost of his father, Anchises, who shows him a vision of Rome's future.

[Milton] broke the stereotypical scape-goating of Eve as essentially a temptress and uniquely gave her responsible motives for her independent movements on the morning of the Fall. . . .
– Diane K. McColley, critic, 1999

an epic hero—a proud and defiant warrior who casts himself in the Promethean role of overthrowing a tyrannical God—is afflicted with self-torment and self-doubt until his corruption of Adam and Eve leads him to complete degradation, symbolized by his becoming a serpent. Satan's intelligence (or cunning), rhetorical skill (or power of deception), and liberal sentiments, courage, and defiance have tantalized and perplexed Milton's readers, leading the English Romantic poet William Blake (1757–1827) to suggest that Milton was of "the Devil's party without knowing it." Some have debated whether Satan is not the true hero of the poem, overshadowing Adam, the Son, and God. Nonetheless, Satan becomes less appealing as he gradually becomes further corrupted by his own actions, and by Book IX the action centers on Adam and Eve, whose weakness before temptation is paradigmatic of the failings of all men and women.

If Adam and Eve before the fall appear as the perfect husband and wife, they are nonetheless larger-than-life characters who reveal certain weaknesses. Adam's Faustian thirst for knowledge, for example, shows in Book VIII where Raphael reminds Adam that the secrets of the heavens are not within his ken; similarly, Eve is shown in Book IV to be prone to narcissism, having fallen in love with her own reflection in the "clear / Smooth lake" after first waking in Paradise. After the fall, Adam and Eve, like tragic heroes in a Greek drama, confront their sins and must accept the consequences of their actions. Their fate, this great poem implies, is our own; their pride and weakness, as well as their hope and faith, should also, the poem suggests, reflect our own. Thus Milton's *Paradise Lost* gave England and the world a great Renaissance tragedy and epic in one, a grand poem defining the limits of human knowledge and ambition, the responsibility that accompanies human freedom, and, for Milton's time at least, the truth that providence ultimately leads to good, despite the failings of individual men and women.

■ CONNECTIONS

***Ramayana,* Book 1.** Before their fall, Adam and Eve—especially as we see them in Book IV—represent the perfect married couple, at least in Milton's view of marriage. Similarly, through the great Indian epic *Ramayana,* Rama and his wife, Sita, serve as exemplary models of the ideal husband and wife, dedicated to fulfillment of their duties as they understand them. What are the sexual politics of these two poems? How do the ideals of marriage in Milton's poem compare to those in the *Ramayana*? In what ways are the duties of man and wife as depicted in these poems culturally specific? In what ways do they seem to overlap?

Virgil, *Aeneid,* Book 1; Dante, *The Divine Comedy,* Book 1. Milton's *Paradise Lost* is a literary epic, a long poem written in a self-consciously elevated and allusive style that deals with a grand theme—in this case the fall from Paradise. Milton's poem owes much to two precursors in particular, Virgil's *Aeneid* and Dante's *Divine Comedy,* a lyric poem of epic scope and breadth that also deals with a Christian subject. What makes Milton's epic different from these precursor poems? How does he set the scope and themes of *Paradise Lost* apart from those of Virgil and even Dante? In what ways are the poems similar?

Genesis 1–2, Book 1; Machado de Assis, *Adam and Eve,* Book 5; Emilia Pardo Bazan, *The Oldest Story,* Book 5; Elizabeth Cady Stanton, *The Woman's Bible,* Book 5. In the nineteenth century, feminists challenged the story of the fall as described in Genesis because it portrayed Eve as responsible for Adam's sin. Consider the various versions of the story that appear in the selections listed here, from Genesis through *Paradise Lost,* to the stories of Machada, Pardo Bazan, and Cady Stanton. How does each story handle the question of who is responsible for the fall into sin?

■ FURTHER RESEARCH

Biography

Brown, Cedric C. *John Milton: A Literary Life.* 1995.
Lewalski, Barbara Kiefer. *The Life of John Milton: A Critical Biography.* 2001.
Parker, William Riley. *Milton: A Biography.* 2 vols. 2nd Edition. 1996.
Shawcross, John T. *John Milton.* 1993.

Background

Hill, Christopher. *Milton and the English Revolution.* 1977.

Criticism

Belsey, Catherine. *John Milton: Language, Gender, Power.* 1988.
Corns, Thomas. *Regaining* Paradise Lost. 1994.
Crosman, Robert. *Reading* Paradise Lost. 1980.
Fish, Stanley. *Surprised by Sin: The Reader in* Paradise Lost. 1967.
Lewalski, Barbara Kiefer. Paradise Lost *and the Rhetoric of Literary Forms.* 1985.
Nyquist, Mary, and Margaret W. Ferguson, eds. *Re-Membering Milton: Essays on the Texts and Traditions.* 1987.
Patterson, Annabel, ed. *John Milton.* 1992.
Zunder, William, ed. *Paradise Lost.* 1999.

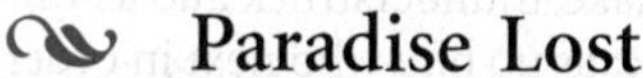

Paradise Lost

The Verse

The measure is English heroic verse without rhyme,[1] as that of Homer in Greek, and of Virgil in Latin; rhyme being no necessary adjunct or true ornament of poem or good verse, in longer works especially, but the invention of a barbarous age, to set off wretched matter and lame metre; graced indeed since by the use of some famous modern poets, carried away by custom, but much to their own vexation, hindrance, and constraint to express many things otherwise, and for the most part worse than

---

Paradise Lost. *Paradise Lost* is one of the great epic poems of world literature, modeled on Greco-Roman epics by Homer and Virgil, and inviting comparison with the great epics of India, the *Ramayana* and the *Mahabharata,* as well as to Dante's *Divine Comedy,* a poem of epic proportion that also influenced Milton's work. Like its precursors, *Paradise Lost* tells a grand tale of serious purport, whose heroic figures engage in almost superhuman feats of courage, suffering, and valor. Unlike the earlier poems, however, Milton's epic takes on a cosmic scope, promising, within its

---

[1] **English . . . rhyme:** Blank verse, that is, unrhymed iambic pentameter—lines of five feet, each foot consisting of an unaccented followed by an accented syllable.

else they would have expressed them. Not without cause therefore some both Italian and Spanish poets of prime note have rejected rhyme both in longer and shorter works, as have also long since our best English tragedies, as a thing of itself, to all judicious ears, trivial and of no true musical delight; which consists only in apt numbers, fit quantity of syllables, and the sense variously drawn out from one verse into another, not in the jingling sound of like endings, a fault avoided by the learned ancients both in poetry and all good oratory. This neglect then of rhyme so little is to be taken for a defect, though it may seem so perhaps to vulgar readers, that it rather is to be esteemed an example set, the first in English, of ancient liberty recovered to heroic poem from the troublesome and modern bondage of rhyming.

Book I
[Satan Awakens All His Legions]

The Argument

This first book proposes, first in brief, the whole subject, man's disobedience, and the loss thereupon of Paradise wherein he was placed; then touches the prime cause of his fall, the serpent, or rather Satan in the serpent; who revolting from God, and drawing to his side many legions of angels, was by the command of God driven out of heaven with all his crew into the great deep. Which action passed over, the poem hastes into the midst of things, presenting Satan with his angels now fallen into hell, described here, not in the centre (for heaven and earth may be supposed as yet not made, certainly not yet accursed) but in a place of utter[2] darkness, fitliest called Chaos: here Satan with his angels lying on the burning lake, thunderstruck and astonished, after a certain space recovers, as from confusion, calls up him who next in order and dignity lay by him; they confer of their miserable fall. Satan awakens all his legions, who lay till then in the same manner confounded; they rise, their numbers, array of battle, their chief leaders named, according to the idols known afterwards in Canaan and the countries adjoining. To these Satan directs his speech, comforts them with hope yet of regaining heaven, but tells them lastly of a new world and new kind of creature to be created, according to an ancient prophecy or report in heaven; for that

---

Christian framework, to be nothing less than a universal story of man's fall from Paradise and of the benevolent design of God's providence. The selections here from Books I, III through IV, IX, X, and XII present the character of Satan, the proud but anguished fallen angel, and his counsel to the Parliament of hell; God's defense of human freedom and His explanation of how the fall will ultimately lead to greater good; the story of Adam and Eve in the Garden of Eden before the fall; the critical action of the fall itself; and the consequences of death and exile. The text is a modernized version of the poem, edited by Jonathan Goldberg and Stephen Orgel, who have updated Milton's spellings and modified the punctuation. Transitions between the selected books are provided by Milton's "Arguments," which along with the defense of heroic verse were added in 1668 to printings of the first edition. The notes are the editors', unless otherwise indicated.

---

[2] **utter:** Both "outer" and "utter."

angels were long before this visible creation, was the opinion of many ancient Fathers. To find out the truth of this prophecy, and what to determine thereon he refers to a full council. What his associates thence attempt. Pandaemonium[3] the palace of Satan rises, suddenly built out of the deep: the infernal peers there sit in council.

Of man's first disobedience, and the fruit[4]
Of that forbidden tree, whose mortal taste
Brought death into the world, and all our woe,
With loss of Eden, till one greater man[5]
Restore us, and regain the blissful seat,
Sing heavenly muse,[6] that on the secret top
Of Oreb, or of Sinai,[7] didst inspire
That shepherd, who first taught the chosen seed,
In the beginning how the heavens and earth
Rose out of chaos: or if Sion hill[8]
Delight thee more, and Siloa's brook that flowed
Fast by the oracle of God; I thence
Invoke thy aid to my adventurous song,
That with no middle flight intends to soar
Above the Aonian mount, while it pursues
Things unattempted yet in prose or rhyme.
And chiefly thou O Spirit,[9] that dost prefer
Before all temples the upright heart and pure,
Instruct me, for thou know'st; thou from the first
Wast present, and with mighty wings outspread

[3] **Pandaemonium:** Milton coined this term, which means "all demons," to designate the palace of the fallen angels in hell.

[4] **fruit:** Both the fruit of the tree and the consequences of transgressing God's law by eating of the fruit; one of the consequences was to bring death into the world, hence the "mortal taste" of the next line.

[5] **one greater man:** Jesus, who, being both man and God, is the greater Adam (*Adam* in Hebrew means "man" or "human").

[6] **heavenly muse:** In the tradition of classical epics, Milton begins his poem with an invocation to the muse, later in the poem identified as Urania, the muse of astronomy, here given a Judeo-Christian significance as the muse of Moses, who is portrayed as a lawgiver, shepherd, and prophetic bard.

[7] **Oreb . . . Sinai:** Both are said to be the mountain on which Moses, the "shepherd" of the next line, was said to have delivered the Ten Commandments to the Israelites, the "chosen seed." Deuteronomy 4:10 identifies the mountain as Oreb; Exodus 19:20, as Sinai.

[8] **Sion hill:** Mt. Zion, the site of Solomon's temple, the Temple of Jerusalem, near which flowed the brook of Siloam, where Jesus cured a man of his blindness (John 9:7). Milton is setting up a Christian topography of inspiration for the Christian poet, to contrast with Mt. Helicon, "the Aonian mount" of line 15, the haunt of the classical muses.

[9] **Spirit:** The Holy Spirit, which Milton describes in *De Doctrina Christiana* as "that impulse or voice of God by which the prophets were inspired." The Spirit is associated in with the creation in Genesis 1:2—"And the spirit of God moved upon the face of the Waters"—and, as it takes the form of a dove to visit Christ, with the advent of Jesus's ministry in the New Testament (see, e.g., John 1:32 and Luke 3:22).

Dove-like sat'st brooding on the vast abyss
And mad'st it pregnant: what in me is dark
Illumine, what is low raise and support;
That to the height of this great argument° — subject
I may assert eternal providence,
And justify the ways of God to men.
Say first, for heaven hides nothing from thy view
Nor the deep tract of hell, say first what cause
Moved our grand parents in that happy state,
Favoured of heaven so highly, to fall off
From their creator, and transgress his will
For one restraint,[10] lords of the world besides?
Who first seduced them to that foul revolt?
The infernal serpent;[11] he it was, whose guile
Stirred up with envy and revenge, deceived
The mother of mankind, what time his pride
Had cast him out from heaven, with all his host
Of rebel angels, by whose aid aspiring
To set himself in glory above his peers,
He trusted to have equalled the most high,
If he opposed; and with ambitious aim
Against the throne and monarchy of God
Raised impious war in heaven and battle proud
With vain attempt. Him the almighty power
Hurled headlong flaming from the ethereal sky
With hideous ruin and combustion down
To bottomless perdition, there to dwell
In adamantine chains and penal fire,
Who durst defy the omnipotent to arms.
Nine times the space that measures day and night[12]
To mortal men, he with his horrid crew
Lay vanquished, rolling in the fiery gulf
Confounded though immortal: but his doom
Reserved him to more wrath; for now the thought
Both of lost happiness and lasting pain
Torments him; round he throws his baleful eyes
That witnessed huge affliction and dismay

[10] **one restraint:** In *De Doctrina Christiana,* Milton explains that it was necessary for one thing to be prohibited to Adam and Eve "and that an act of its own nature indifferent," as a "test of fidelity" and as a means to make possible human obedience.

[11] **infernal serpent:** That is, Satan, whose guile and deceit leads to the fall of both Adam and Eve, "the mother of mankind" of line 36.

[12] **Nine . . . night:** An allusion to Hesiod's *Theogony* (720–25), where the fall of the Titans from heaven to earth took nine days, and from earth to hell another nine days.

Mixed with obdurate pride and steadfast hate:
At once as far as angels' ken[13] he views
The dismal situation waste and wild,
A dungeon horrible, on all sides round
As one great furnace flamed, yet from those flames
No light, but rather darkness visible
Served only to discover sights of woe,
Regions of sorrow, doleful shades, where peace
And rest can never dwell, hope never comes[14]
That comes to all; but torture without end
Still urges, and a fiery deluge, fed
With ever-burning sulphur unconsumed:
Such place eternal justice had prepared
For those rebellious, here their prison ordained
In utter darkness, and their portion set
As far removed from God and light of heaven
As from the centre thrice to the utmost pole.[15]
O how unlike the place from whence they fell!
There the companions of his fall, o'erwhelmed
With floods and whirlwinds of tempestuous fire,
He soon discerns, and weltering by his side
One next himself in power, and next in crime,
Long after known in Palestine, and named
Beelzebub.[16] To whom the arch-enemy,
And thence in heaven called Satan, with bold words
Breaking the horrid silence thus began.
If thou beest he; but O how fallen! how changed[17]
From him, who in the happy realms of light
Clothed with transcendent brightness didst outshine
Myriads though bright: if he whom mutual league,

[13] **as . . . ken:** As far as angels can know as well as see.

[14] **hope never comes:** An allusion to Dante's *Inferno,* in which the gates of hell are inscribed with the warning "Abandon all hope, ye who enter here" (Canto 3, line 9).

[15] **As . . . pole:** Milton describes a Ptolemaic universe with earth at the center, in which heaven lies at the outermost point of the nine circles that comprise our universe. Hell is twice again as far from earth as earth is from heaven.

[16] **Beelzebub:** Satan's second in command, described in Matthew 12:24 as the "prince of devils"; his name means "Lord of the Flies" in Hebrew. Satan, whose name means "adversary" or "enemy" was in heaven called Lucifer, meaning "light bringer."

[17] **how changed:** After their rebellion against God, the fallen angels visibly show their degradation and despair, reflecting in part their awareness that, unlike Adam, they have no hope for redemption. This line is a fine example of the density and economy of Milton's poetry, alluding as it does simultaneously to Aeneas first seeing a vision of the dead Hector—"how changed from that other Hector" (*Aeneid* II 275–74)—and to Isaiah 14:12: "How art thou fallen, O Lucifer, son of the morning!"

United thoughts and counsels, equal hope
And hazard in the glorious enterprise,
Joined with me once, now misery hath joined
In equal ruin: into what pit thou seest
From what height fallen, so much the stronger proved
He[18] with his thunder: and till then who knew
The force of those dire arms? yet not for those,
Nor what the potent victor in his rage
Can else inflict, do I repent or change,
Though changed in outward lustre; that fixed mind
And high disdain, from sense of injured merit,
That with the mightiest raised me to contend,
And to the fierce contention brought along
Innumerable force of spirits armed
That durst dislike his reign, and me preferring,
His utmost power with adverse power opposed
In dubious battle on the plains of heaven,
And shook his throne. What though the field be lost?
All is not lost; the unconquerable will,
And study of revenge, immortal hate,
And courage never to submit or yield:
And what is else not to be overcome?
That glory never shall his wrath or might
Extort from me. To bow and sue for grace
With suppliant knee, and deify his power,
Who from the terror of this arm so late
Doubted his empire,[19] that were low indeed,
That were an ignominy and shame beneath
This downfall; since by fate the strength of gods
And this empyreal substance[20] cannot fail,
Since through experience of this great event
In arms not worse, in foresight much advanced,
We may with more successful hope resolve
To wage by force or guile eternal war
Irreconcilable, to our grand foe,
Who now triumphs, and in the excess of joy
Sole reigning holds the tyranny of heaven.

---

[18] **He:** That is, God and his forces of good angels, led by the Son. In his speech, Satan is attempting to recuperate something positive from his defeat.

[19] **Doubted his empire:** That is, feared for the loss of his empire; Satan is, of course, mistaken in that God does not doubt.

[20] **empyreal substance:** Satan asserts that since they are made of ether, the purest substance of the highest heaven (the Empyrean), the angels—the "gods" of the previous line—cannot be destroyed. His emphasis on "fate" may suggest an affinity to a pagan, rather than a Christian, universe.

So spake the apostate angel, though in pain,
Vaunting aloud, but racked with deep despair:
And him thus answered soon his bold compeer.
O prince, O chief of many thronèd powers,
That led the embattled seraphim[21] to war
Under thy conduct, and in dreadful deeds
Fearless, endangered heaven's perpetual king;
And put to proof° his high supremacy, put to the test
Whether upheld by strength, or chance, or fate,
Too well I see and rue the dire event,
That with sad overthrow and foul defeat
Hath lost us heaven, and all this mighty host
In horrible destruction laid thus low,
As far as gods and heavenly essences
Can perish: for the mind and spirit remains
Invincible, and vigour soon returns,
Though all our glory extinct, and happy state
Here swallowed up in endless misery.
But what if he our conqueror (whom I now
Of force believe almighty, since no less
Than such could have o'erpowered such force as ours)
Have left us this our spirit and strength entire
Strongly to suffer and support our pains,
That we may so suffice° his vengeful ire, satisfy
Or do him mightier service as his thralls
By right of war, whate'er his business be
Here in the heart of hell to work in fire,
Or do his errands in the gloomy deep;
What can it then avail though yet we feel
Strength undiminished, or eternal being
To undergo eternal punishment?
Whereto with speedy words the arch-fiend replied.
Fallen cherub,[22] to be weak is miserable
Doing or suffering: but of this be sure,
To do aught good never will be our task,
But ever to do ill our sole delight,
As being the contrary to his high will
Whom we resist. If then his providence
Out of our evil seek to bring forth good,

---

[21] **seraphim:** In the early Christian commentaries on angels, the seraphim are the highest of the nine orders of angels, followed, in descending order, by the cherubim, thrones, dominions, virtues, powers, principalities, archangels, and angels. Milton largely rejected this hierarchy and uses the terms more loosely. The important angels in the text—Michael, Gabriel, and Raphael—are consistently called archangels.

[22] **Fallen cherub:** See note 21.

Our labour must be to pervert that end,
And out of good still to find means of evil;
Which oft-times may succeed, so as perhaps
Shall grieve him, if I fail° not, and disturb — err, mistake
His inmost counsels from their destined aim.
But see the angry victor hath recalled
His ministers of vengeance and pursuit
Back to the gates of heaven: the sulphurous hail
Shot after us in storm, o'erblown hath laid° — becalmed
The fiery surge, that from the precipice
Of heaven received us falling, and the thunder,
Winged with red lightning and impetuous rage,
Perhaps hath spent his shafts, and ceases now
To bellow through the vast and boundless deep.
Let us not slip[23] the occasion, whether scorn,
Or satiate fury yield it from our foe.
Seest thou yon dreary plain, forlorn and wild,
The seat of desolation, void of light,
Save what the glimmering of these livid flames
Casts pale and dreadful? Thither let us tend
From off the tossing of these fiery waves,
There rest, if any rest can harbour there,
And reassembling our afflicted powers,
Consult how we may henceforth most offend
Our enemy, our own loss how repair,
How overcome this dire calamity,
What reinforcement we may gain from hope,
If not what resolution from despair.
Thus Satan talking to his nearest mate
With head uplift above the wave, and eyes
That sparkling blazed, his other parts besides
Prone on the flood, extended long and large
Lay floating many a rood,[24] in bulk as huge
As whom the fables name of monstrous size,
Titanian, or Earth-born, that warred on Jove,
Briareos or Typhon,[25] whom the den
By ancient Tarsus held, or that sea-beast

---

[23] **slip:** Let pass; i.e., lose the opportunity.

[24] **rood:** Rod, a measure of six to eight yards, or an area of land roughly one quarter of an acre.

[25] **Briareos or Typhon:** Milton compares Satan's fallen form to two rebellious giants of mythology: Briareos, one of the Titans, and Typhon, one of the Giants; both Briareos and Typhon fought against the Olympian gods, who condemned them to eternal punishment in Tartarus, the deepest hell of the classical Underworld.

Leviathan,[26] which God of all his works
Created hugest that swim the ocean stream:
Him haply slumbering on the Norway foam
The pilot of some small night-foundered skiff,
Deeming some island, oft, as seamen tell,
With fixèd anchor in his scaly rind
Moors by his side under the lee, while night
Invests° the sea, and wishèd morn delays: envelops, covers over
So stretched out huge in length the arch-fiend lay
Chained on the burning lake, nor ever thence
Had risen or heaved his head, but that the will
And high permission of all-ruling heaven
Left him at large to his own dark designs,
That with reiterated crimes he might
Heap on himself damnation, while he sought
Evil to others, and enraged might see
How all his malice served but to bring forth
Infinite goodness, grace and mercy shown
On man by him seduced, but on himself
Treble confusion, wrath and vengeance poured.
Forthwith upright he rears from off the pool
His mighty stature; on each hand the flames
Driven backward slope their pointing spires, and rolled
In billows, leave i' the midst a horrid vale.
Then with expanded wings he steers his flight
Aloft, incumbent° on the dusky air lying on
That felt unusual weight, till on dry land
He lights, if it were land that ever burned
With solid, as the lake with liquid fire;
And such appeared in hue, as when the force
Of subterranean wind transports a hill
Torn from Pelorus,[27] or the shattered side
Of thundering Aetna, whose combustible
And fuelled entrails thence conceiving fire,
Sublimed° with mineral fury, aid the winds, vaporized
And leave a singèd bottom all involved
With stench and smoke: such resting found the sole
Of unblessed feet. Him followed his next mate,

[26] **Leviathan:** A great sea beast described in Job 41, often identified with Satan. Here Milton associates Leviathan with a familiar story of a huge whale luring sailors to their death, as they mistake the whale's body for a small island. The passage emphasizes Satan's treachery and deception.

[27] **Pelorus:** Cape Faro, which is near the volcanic Mt. Aetna in Sicily.

Both glorying to have scaped the Stygian flood[28]
As gods, and by their own recovered strength,
Not by the sufferance of supernal power.
    Is this the region, this the soil, the clime,
Said then the lost archangel, this the seat
That we must change for heaven, this mournful gloom
For that celestial light? Be it so, since he
Who now is sovereign can dispose and bid
What shall be right: furthest from him is best
Whom reason hath equalled, force hath made supreme
Above his equals. Farewell, happy fields
Where joy forever dwells: hail horrors, hail
Infernal world, and thou profoundest hell
Receive thy new possessor: one who brings
A mind not to be changed by place or time.
The mind is its own place, and in itself
Can make a heaven of hell, a hell of heaven.
What matter where, if I be still the same,
And what I should be, all but less than he
Whom thunder hath made greater? Here at least
We shall be free; the almighty hath not built
Here for his envy, will not drive us hence:
Here we may reign secure, and in my choice
To reign is worth ambition though in hell:
Better to reign in hell, than serve in heaven.
But wherefore let we then our faithful friends,
The associates and copartners of our loss
Lie thus astonished on the oblivious pool,[29]
And call them not to share with us their part
In this unhappy mansion, or once more
With rallied arms to try what may be yet
Regained in heaven, or what more lost in hell?
    So Satan spake, and him Beelzebub
Thus answered. Leader of those armies bright,
Which but the omnipotent none could have foiled,
If once they hear that voice, their liveliest pledge
Of hope in fears and dangers, heard so oft
In worst extremes, and on the perilous edge
Of battle when it raged, in all assaults
Their surest signal, they will soon resume

[28] **Stygian flood:** That is, the river Styx, one of the main rivers of the classical Underworld.

[29] **oblivious pool:** A pool causing forgetfulness.

New courage and revive, though now they lie
Grovelling and prostrate on yon lake of fire,
As we erewhile, astounded and amazed,
No wonder, fallen such a pernicious height.
He scarce had ceased when the superior fiend
Was moving toward the shore; his ponderous shield
Ethereal temper, massy, large, and round,
Behind him cast; the broad circumference
Hung on his shoulders like the moon, whose orb
Through optic glass the Tuscan artist[30] views
At evening from the top of Fesole,
Or in Valdarno, to descry new lands,
Rivers or mountains in her spotty globe.
His spear, to equal which the tallest pine
Hewn on Norwegian hills, to be the mast
Of some great admiral,° were but a wand, flagship
He walked with to support uneasy steps
Over the burning marl,[31] not like those steps
On heaven's azure, and the torrid clime
Smote on him sore besides, vaulted with fire;
Natheless he so endured, till on the beach
Of that inflamèd sea, he stood and called
His legions, angel forms, who lay entranced
Thick as autumnal leaves that strew the brooks
In Vallombrosa.[32] [. . .]

[. . .] He above the rest
In shape and gesture proudly eminent
Stood like a tower; his form had yet not lost
All her original brightness, nor appeared
Less than archangel ruined, and the excess
Of glory obscured: as when the sun new risen
Looks through the horizontal misty air
Shorn of his beams, or from behind the moon
In dim eclipse disastrous twilight sheds
On half the nations, and with fear of change
Perplexes monarchs. Darkened so, yet shone

[30] **Tuscan artist:** Galileo, who designed a telescope—the "optic glass"—powerful enough to distinguish features on the moon's surface. Fesole (Fiesole), l. 289, is a town near Florence, located in the Valdorno, or valley of the Arno River, where Galileo was living when Milton visited him in 1638.

[31] **burning marl:** The fiery soil, or brimstone, of Hell.

[32] **Vallombrosa:** A vale near Florence; its name means "shady valley"; a valley of shades conjures up images of the dead—known as shades—in the classical Underworld.

Above them all the archangel: but his face
Deep scars of thunder had intrenched, and care
Sat on his faded cheek, but under brows
Of dauntless courage, and considerate° pride — considered, deliberate
Waiting revenge: cruel his eye, but cast
Signs of remorse and passion to behold
The fellows of his crime, the followers rather
(Far other once beheld in bliss) condemned
Forever now to have their lot in pain,
Millions of spirits for his fault amerced° — punished (literally, fined)
Of heaven, and from eternal splendours flung
For his revolt, yet faithful how they stood,
Their glory withered. As when heaven's fire
Hath scathed the forest oaks, or mountain pines,
With singèd top their stately growth though bare
Stands on the blasted heath. He now prepared
To speak; whereat their doubled ranks they bend
From wing to wing, and half enclose him round
With all his peers: attention held them mute.
Thrice he essayed, and thrice in spite of scorn,
Tears such as angels weep burst forth: at last
Words interwove with sighs found out their way.
O myriads of immortal spirits, O powers
Matchless, but with almighty, and that strife
Was not inglorious, though the event° was dire, — outcome
As this place testifies, and this dire change
Hateful to utter: but what power of mind
Foreseeing or presaging, from the depth
Of knowledge past or present, could have feared,
How such united force of gods, how such
As stood like these, could ever know repulse?
For who can yet believe, though after loss,
That all these puissant legions, whose exile
Hath emptied heaven, shall fail to reascend
Self-raised, and repossess their native seat?
For me be witness all the host of heaven,
If counsels different, or danger shunned
By me, have lost our hopes. But he who reigns
Monarch in heaven, till then as one secure
Sat on his throne, upheld by old repute,
Consent or custom, and his regal state
Put forth at full, but still his strength concealed,
Which tempted our attempt, and wrought our fall.
Henceforth his might we know, and know our own

So as not either to provoke, or dread
New war, provoked; our better part remains
To work in close° design, by fraud or guile secret
What force effected not: that he no less
At length from us may find, who overcomes
By force, hath overcome but half his foe.
Space may produce new worlds; whereof so rife
There went a fame in heaven that he ere long
Intended to create, and therein plant
A generation, whom his choice regard
Should favour equal to the sons of heaven:
Thither, if but to pry, shall be perhaps
Our first eruption, thither or elsewhere:
For this infernal pit shall never hold
Celestial spirits in bondage, nor the abyss
Long under darkness cover. But these thoughts
Full counsel must mature: peace is despaired,
For who can think submission? War then, war
Open or understood must be resolved.
    He spake: and to confirm his words, outflew
Millions of flaming swords, drawn from the thighs
Of mighty cherubim; the sudden blaze
Far round illumined hell: highly they raged
Against the highest, and fierce with graspèd arms
Clashed on their sounding shields the din of war,
Hurling defiance toward the vault of heaven. [. . .]

Book II

The Argument

The consultation begun, Satan debates whether another battle be to be hazarded for the recovery of heaven; some advise it, others dissuade: a third proposal is preferred, mentioned before by Satan, to search the truth of that prophecy or tradition in heaven concerning another world, and another kind of creature equal or not much inferior to themselves, about this time to be created: their doubt who shall be sent on this difficult search: Satan their chief undertakes alone the voyage, is honoured and applauded. The council thus ended, the rest betake them several ways and to several employments, as their inclinations lead them, to entertain the time till Satan return. He passes on his journey to hell gates, finds them shut, and who sat there to guard them, by whom at length they are opened, and discover to him the great gulf between hell and heaven; with what difficulty he passes through, directed by Chaos, the power of that place, to the sight of this new world which he sought.

BOOK III
[HYMN TO THE LIGHT AND GOD'S COUNCIL IN HEAVEN]

The Argument

God sitting on his throne sees Satan flying towards this world, then newly created; shows him to the Son who sat at his right hand; foretells the success of Satan in perverting mankind; clears his own justice and wisdom from all imputation, having created man free and able enough to have withstood his tempter; yet declares his purpose of grace towards him, in regard he fell not of his own malice, as did Satan, but by him seduced. The Son of God renders praises to his father for the manifestation of his gracious purpose towards man; but God again declares, that grace cannot be extended toward man without the satisfaction of divine justice; man hath offended the majesty of God by aspiring to Godhead, and therefore with all his progeny devoted to death must die, unless someone can be found sufficient to answer for his offence, and undergo his punishment. The Son of God freely offers himself a ransom for man: the Father accepts him, ordains his incarnation, pronounces his exaltation above all names in heaven and earth; commands all the angels to adore him; they obey, and hymning to their harps in full choir, celebrate the Father and the Son. Meanwhile Satan alights upon the bare convex of this world's outermost orb; where wandering he first finds a place since called the Limbo of Vanity; what persons and things fly up thither; thence comes to the gate of heaven, described ascending by stairs, and the waters above the firmament that flow about it: his passage thence to the orb of the sun; he finds there Uriel the regent of that orb, but first changes himself into the shape of a meaner angel; and pretending a zealous desire to behold the new creation and man whom God had placed here, inquires of him the place of his habitation, and is directed; alights first on Mount Niphates.

Hail holy light, offspring of heaven first-born,
Or of the eternal co-eternal beam
May I express thee unblamed?[33] since God is light,
And never but in unapproachèd light
Dwelt from eternity, dwelt then in thee,
Bright effluence of bright essence increate.° uncreated
Or hear'st thou rather[34] pure ethereal stream,
Whose fountain[35] who shall tell? before the sun,
Before the heavens thou wert, and at the voice
Of God, as with a mantle didst invest

[33] **May . . . unblamed?:** Milton, who had been blind since 1652, asks whether, without blaspheming, he may consider light, since God is light, also to be eternal like God. Light takes on many resonances in this passage, referring to physical and spiritual, that is outer and inner vision, as well as the light of God, the Son, and the Holy Spirit. Many readers find this Milton's most moving meditation on his own physical blindness. "God is Light" appears in 1 John 1:5.

[34] **hear'st thou rather:** That is, would you rather hear.

[35] **fountain:** In Book III, lines 374–75, Milton identifies God as the "author of all being, / Fountain of light."

The rising world of waters dark and deep,
Won from the void and formless infinite.
Thee I revisit now with bolder wing,
Escaped the Stygian pool,[36] though long detained
In that obscure sojourn, while in my flight
Through utter and through middle darkness borne
With other notes than to the Orphean lyre[37]
I sung of Chaos and eternal Night,
Taught by the heavenly Muse[38] to venture down
The dark descent, and up to reascend,
Though hard and rare: thee I revisit safe,
And feel thy sovereign vital lamp; but thou
Revisit'st not these eyes, that roll in vain
To find thy piercing ray, and find no dawn;
So thick a drop serene hath quenched their orbs,
Or dim suffusion[39] veiled. Yet not the more
Cease I to wander where the muses haunt
Clear spring, or shady grove, or sunny hill,
Smit with the love of sacred song; but chief
Thee Sion[40] and the flowery brooks beneath
That wash thy hallowed feet, and warbling flow,
Nightly I visit: nor sometimes forget
Those other two equalled with me in fate,
So were I equalled with them in renown,
Blind Thamyris, and blind Maeonides,
And Tiresias and Phineus prophets old.[41]
Then feed on thoughts, that voluntary move
Harmonious numbers; as the wakeful bird° nightingale
Sings darkling, and in shadiest covert hid
Tunes her nocturnal note. Thus with the year
Seasons return, but not to me returns

---

[36] **Stygian pool:** The pool formed from waters like those of the river Styx, the river of the classical Underworld (see note 28).

[37] **Orphean lyre:** Referring to the myth of Orpheus, the poet-singer whose beautiful music enabled him to enter hell in a failed attempt to bring his wife, Eurydice, back from the dead. Orpheus was said to have composed a "Hymn to Night," a lyric poem, against which Milton sets his epic here.

[38] **heavenly Muse:** Urania; see note 6.

[39] **dim suffusion:** A translation of *suffusio nigra,* the Latin term for cataract; the "drop serene" of the previous line translates *gutta serena,* a medical term for blindness that occurs without a clouding of the eye.

[40] **Sion:** Mt. Zion, the sacred mountain that harbors the Christian muse, in contrast to Mt. Helicon or Mt. Parnassus, the homes of the classical muses; see note 8.

[41] **Blind . . . prophets old:** Milton offers a brief list of bards and prophets who, like him, were afflicted with blindness: Thamyris, a Thracian poet blinded because he proclaimed he could outperform the Muses; Maeonides, another name for Homer; Tiresias, the blind prophet from Thebes; and Phineus, a blind prophet from Thrace.

Day, or the sweet approach of even or morn,
Or sight of vernal bloom, or summer's rose,
Or flocks, or herds, or human face divine;
But cloud instead, and ever-during dark
Surrounds me, from the cheerful ways of men
Cut off, and for the book of knowledge fair
Presented with a universal blank
Of nature's works to me expunged and razed,
And wisdom at one entrance quite shut out.
So much the rather thou celestial light
Shine inward, and the mind through all her powers
Irradiate, there plant eyes, all mist from thence
Purge and disperse, that I may see and tell
Of things invisible to mortal sight.
 Now had the almighty Father from above,
From the pure empyrean where he sits
High throned above all height, bent down his eye,
His own works and their works at once to view:
About him all the sanctities[42] of heaven
Stood thick as stars, and from his sight received
Beatitude past utterance; on his right
The radiant image of his glory sat,
His only son; on earth he first beheld
Our two first parents, yet the only two
Of mankind, in the happy garden placed,
Reaping immortal fruits of joy and love,
Uninterrupted joy, unrivalled love
In blissful solitude; he then surveyed
Hell and the gulf between, and Satan there
Coasting the wall of heaven on this side night
In the dun air sublime, and ready now
To stoop with wearied wings, and willing feet
On the bare outside of this world,[43] that seemed
Firm land embosomed without firmament,
Uncertain which, in ocean or in air.
Him God beholding from his prospect high,
Wherein past, present, future he beholds,
Thus to his only son foreseeing spake.
 Only begotten Son, seest thou what rage
Transports our adversary, whom no bounds

---

[42] **sanctities:** The good angels who remain in Heaven.

[43] **bare . . . world:** Satan is poised at the threshold of the *primum mobile,* the outermost shell of the universe; he has not yet arrived near earth.

Prescribed, no bars of hell, nor all the chains
Heaped on him there, nor yet the main abyss
Wide interrupt can hold; so bent he seems
On desperate revenge, that shall redound
Upon his own rebellious head. And now
Through all restraint broke loose he wings his way
Not far off heaven, in the precincts of light,
Directly towards the new created world,
And man there placed, with purpose to assay
If him by force he can destroy, or worse,
By some false guile pervert; and shall pervert
For man will hearken to his glozing° lies, flattering
And easily transgress the sole command,
Sole pledge of his obedience: so will fall,
He and his faithless progeny: whose fault?
Whose but his own? ingrate, he had of me
All he could have; I made him just and right,
Sufficient to have stood, though free to fall.
Such I created all the ethereal powers
And spirits, both them who stood and them who failed;
Freely they stood who stood, and fell who fell.
Not free, what proof could they have given sincere
Of true allegiance, constant faith or love,
Where only what they needs must do, appeared,
Not what they would? what praise could they receive?[44]
What pleasure I from such obedience paid,
When will and reason (reason also is choice)
Useless and vain, of freedom both despoiled,
Made passive both, had served necessity,
Not me. They therefore as to right belonged,
So were created, nor can justly accuse
Their maker, or their making, or their fate,
As if predestination overruled
Their will, disposed by absolute decree
Or high foreknowledge; they themselves decreed
Their own revolt, not I: if I foreknew,
Foreknowledge had no influence on their fault,
Which had no less proved certain unforeknown.[45]

---

[44] **what . . . receive?:** Milton expresses poetically here his point in *De Doctrina Christiana* that without freedom and without a law to test that freedom, there can be no virtue. As he puts it perhaps most famously in *Areopagitica,* "I cannot praise a fugitive and cloistered virtue, unexercised and unbrathed, that never sallies out and sees her adversary."

[45] **Which . . . unforeknown:** Here God expresses Milton's belief that God's omniscience does not predetermine the fall even though it enables him to know for certain that it will take place.

So without least impulse[46] or shadow of fate,
Or aught by me immutably foreseen,
They trespass, authors to themselves in all
Both what they judge and what they choose; for so
I formed them free, and free they must remain,
Till they enthrall themselves: I else must change
Their nature, and revoke the high decree
Unchangeable, eternal, which ordained
Their freedom, they themselves ordained their fall.
The first sort by their own suggestion fell,
Self-tempted, self-depraved: man falls deceived
By the other first: man therefore shall find grace,
The other none: in mercy and justice both,
Through heaven and earth, so shall my glory excel,
But mercy first and last shall brightest shine.
 Thus while God spake, ambrosial fragrance filled
All heaven, and in the blessèd spirits elect
Sense of new joy ineffable diffused:
Beyond compare the Son of God was seen
Most glorious, in him all his father shone
Substantially expressed, and in his face
Divine compassion visibly appeared,
Love without end, and without measure grace,
Which uttering thus he to his father spake.
 O Father, gracious was that word which closed
Thy sovereign sentence, that man should find grace;
For which both heaven and earth shall high extol
Thy praises, with the innumerable sound
Of hymns and sacred songs, wherewith thy throne
Encompassed shall resound thee ever blessed.
For should man finally be lost, should man
Thy creature late so loved, thy youngest son
Fall circumvented thus by fraud, though joined
With his own folly? that be from thee far,
That far be from thee, Father, who art judge
Of all things made, and judgest only right.
Or shall the adversary thus obtain
His end, and frustrate thine, shall he fulfil
His malice, and thy goodness bring to naught,
Or proud return though to his heavier doom,
Yet with revenge accomplished and to hell
Draw after him the whole race of mankind,

[46] **without least impulse:** That is, without any instigation from God.

By him corrupted? or wilt thou thyself
Abolish thy creation, and unmake,
For him, what for thy glory thou hast made?
So should thy goodness and thy greatness both
Be questioned and blasphemed without defence.
To whom the great creator thus replied.
O Son, in whom my soul hath chief delight,
Son of my bosom, Son who art alone
My word, my wisdom, and effectual might,[47]
All hast thou spoken as my thoughts are, all
As my eternal purpose hath decreed:
Man shall not quite be lost, but saved who will,
Yet not of will in him, but grace in me
Freely vouchsafed; once more I will renew
His lapsèd powers, though forfeit and enthralled
By sin to foul exorbitant desires;
Upheld by me, yet once more he shall stand
On even ground against his mortal foe
By me upheld, that he may know how frail
His fallen condition is, and to me owe
All his deliverance, and to none but me.
Some I have chosen of peculiar grace
Elect above the rest; so is my will:
The rest shall hear me call, and oft be warned
Their sinful state, and to appease betimes
The incensèd deity, while offered grace
Invites; for I will clear their senses dark,
What may suffice, and soften stony hearts
To pray, repent, and bring obedience due.
To prayer, repentance, and obedience due,
Though but endeavoured with sincere intent,
Mine ear shall not be slow, mine eye not shut.
And I will place within them as a guide
My umpire conscience, whom if they will hear,
Light after light well used they shall attain,
And to the end persisting, safe arrive.
This my long sufferance and my day of grace
They who neglect and scorn, shall never taste;
But hard be hardened, blind be blinded more,
That they may stumble on, and deeper fall;
And none but such from mercy I exclude.
But yet all is not done; man disobeying,

[47] **effectual might:** That is, effective power; as the next lines indicate, Christ is the active agency of God's grace.

Disloyal breaks his fealty,[48] and sins
Against the high supremacy of heaven,
Affecting godhead, and so losing all,
To expiate his treason hath naught left,
But to destruction sacred and devote,
He with his whole posterity must die,
Die he or justice must; unless for him
Some other able, and as willing, pay
The rigid satisfaction, death for death.
Say heavenly powers, where shall we find such love,
Which of ye will be mortal to redeem
Man's mortal crime, and just the unjust to save,
Dwells in all heaven charity so dear?[49]

He asked, but all the heavenly choir stood mute,
And silence was in heaven: on man's behalf
Patron or intercessor none appeared,
Much less that durst upon his own head draw
The deadly forfeiture, and ransom set.
And now without redemption all mankind
Must have been lost, adjudged to death and hell
By doom severe, had not the Son of God,
In whom the fulness dwells of love divine,
His dearest mediation thus renewed.

Father, thy word is past, man shall find grace;
And shall grace not find means, that finds her way,
The speediest of thy wingèd messengers,
To visit all thy creatures, and to all
Comes unprevented,° unimplored, unsought, unanticipated
Happy for man, so coming; he her aid
Can never seek, once dead in sins and lost;
Atonement for himself or offering meet,
Indebted and undone, hath none to bring:
Behold me then, me for him, life for life
I offer, on me let thine anger fall;
Account me man; I for his sake will leave
Thy bosom, and this glory next to thee
Freely put off, and for him lastly die
Well pleased, on me let Death wreak all his rage;
Under his gloomy power I shall not long
Lie vanquished; thou hast given me to possess

[48] **fealty:** A term referring to the duty owed to a lord within a feudal system.

[49] **Say . . . dear:** This parallels a speech in Book II, 402–16, in which Beelzebub asks who there could be among the fallen angels to embark on the mission to pervert humankind.

Life in myself forever, by thee I live,
Though now to Death I yield, and am his due
All that of me can die, yet that debt paid,
Thou wilt not leave me in the loathsome grave
His prey, nor suffer my unspotted soul
Forever with corruption there to dwell;
But I shall rise victorious, and subdue
My vanquisher, spoiled of his vaunted spoil;
Death his death's wound shall then receive, and stoop
Inglorious, of his mortal sting disarmed.
I through the ample air in triumph high
Shall lead hell captive maugre° hell, and show despite
The powers of darkness bound. Thou at the sight
Pleased, out of heaven shalt look down and smile,
While by thee raised I ruin all my foes,
Death last, and with his carcass glut the grave:
Then with the multitude of my redeemed
Shall enter heaven long absent, and return,
Father, to see thy face, wherein no cloud
Of anger shall remain, but peace assured,
And reconcilement; wrath shall be no more
Thenceforth, but in thy presence joy entire.
　　His words here ended, but his meek aspect
Silent yet spake, and breathed immortal love
To mortal men, above which only shone
Filial obedience: as a sacrifice
Glad to be offered, he attends the will
Of his great father. Admiration seized
All heaven, what this might mean, and whither tend
Wondering; but soon the almighty thus replied:
　　O thou in heaven and earth the only peace
Found out for mankind under wrath, O thou
My sole complacence! well thou know'st how dear
To me are all my works, nor man the least
Though last created, that for him I spare
Thee from my bosom and right hand, to save,
By losing thee awhile, the whole race lost.
Thou therefore whom thou only canst redeem,
Their nature also to thy nature join;
And be thyself man among men on earth,
Made flesh, when time shall be, of virgin seed,
By wondrous birth: be thou in Adam's room
The head of all mankind, though Adam's son.
As in him perish all men, so in thee
As from a second root shall be restored,

As many as are restored, without thee none.
His crime makes guilty all his sons, thy merit
Imputed shall absolve them who renounce
Their own both righteous and unrighteous deeds,
And live in thee transplanted, and from thee
Receive new life. So man, as is most just,
Shall satisfy for man, be judged and die,
And dying rise, and rising with him raise
His brethren, ransomed with his own dear life.
So heavenly love shall outdo hellish hate
Giving to death, and dying to redeem,
So dearly to redeem what hellish hate
So easily destroyed, and still destroys
In those who, when they may, accept not grace.
Nor shalt thou by descending to assume
Man's nature, lessen or degrade thine own.
Because thou hast, though throned in highest bliss
Equal to God, and equally enjoying
Godlike fruition, quitted all to save
A world from utter loss, and hast been found
By merit more than birthright Son of God,
Found worthiest to be so by being good,
Far more than great or high; because in thee
Love hath abounded more than glory abounds,
Therefore thy humiliation shall exalt
With thee thy manhood also to this throne;
Here shalt thou sit incarnate, here shalt reign
Both God and man, Son both of God and man,
Anointed universal king; all power
I give thee, reign for ever, and assume
Thy merits; under thee as head supreme
Thrones, princedoms, powers, dominions I reduce:
All knees to thee shall bow, of them that bide
In heaven, or earth, or under earth in hell,
When thou attended gloriously from heaven
Shalt in the sky appear, and from thee send
The summoning archangels to proclaim
Thy dread tribunal: forthwith from all winds
The living, and forthwith the cited° dead — summoned
Of all past ages to the general doom
Shall hasten, such a peal shall rouse their sleep.
Then all thy saints assembled, thou shalt judge
Bad men and angels, they arraigned shall sink
Beneath thy sentence; hell her numbers full,

Thenceforth shall be forever shut. Meanwhile
The world shall burn, and from her ashes spring
New heaven and earth, wherein the just shall dwell,
And after all their tribulations long
See golden days, fruitful of golden deeds,
With joy and love triumphing, and fair truth.
Then thou thy regal sceptre shalt lay by,
For regal sceptre then no more shall need,
God shall be all in all. But all ye gods,
Adore him, who to compass all this dies,
Adore the Son, and honour him as me.
  No sooner had the almighty ceased, but all
The multitude of angels with a shout
Loud as from numbers without number, sweet
As from blest voices, uttering joy, heaven rung
With jubilee, and loud hosannas filled
The eternal regions: [. . .]

Book IV
[Adam and Eve in the Garden of Eden]

The Argument

Satan now in prospect of Eden, and nigh the place where he must now attempt the bold enterprise which he undertook alone against God and man, falls into many doubts with himself, and many passions, fear, envy, and despair; but at length confirms himself in evil, journeys on to Paradise, whose outward prospect and situation is described, overleaps the bounds, sits in the shape of a cormorant on the tree of life, as highest in the garden to look about him. The garden described; Satan's first sight of Adam and Eve; his wonder at their excellent form and happy state, but with resolution to work their fall; overhears their discourse, thence gathers that the tree of knowledge was forbidden them to eat of, under penalty of death; and thereon intends to found his temptation, by seducing them to transgress: then leaves them awhile, to know further of their state by some other means. Meanwhile Uriel descending on a sunbeam warns Gabriel, who had in charge the gate of Paradise, that some evil spirit had escaped the deep, and passed at noon by his sphere in the shape of a good angel down to Paradise, discovered after by his furious gestures in the mount. Gabriel promises to find him ere morning. Night coming on, Adam and Eve discourse of going to their rest: their bower described; their evening worship. Gabriel drawing forth his bands of night-watch to walk the round of Paradise, appoints two strong angels to Adam's bower, lest the evil spirit should be there doing some harm to Adam or Eve sleeping; there they find him at the ear of Eve tempting her in a dream, and bring him, though unwilling, to Gabriel; by whom questioned, he scornfully answers, prepares resistance, but hindered by a sign from heaven, flies out of Paradise.

O for that warning voice, which he who saw
The Apocalypse[50] heard cry in heaven aloud,
Then when the dragon, put to second rout,
Came furious down to be revenged on men,
Woe to the inhabitants on earth! that now,
While time was,[51] our first-parents had been warned
The coming of their secret foe, and scaped,
Haply so scaped his mortal snare; for now
Satan, now first inflamed with rage, came down,
The tempter ere the accuser of mankind,[52]
To wreak on innocent frail man his loss
Of that first battle, and his flight to hell:
Yet not rejoicing in his speed, though bold,
Far off and fearless, nor with cause to boast,
Begins his dire attempt, which nigh the birth
Now rolling, boils in his tumultuous breast,
And like a devilish engine[53] back recoils
Upon himself; horror and doubt distract
His troubled thoughts, and from the bottom stir
The hell within him, for within him hell
He brings,[54] and round about him, nor from hell
One step no more than from himself can fly
By change of place: now conscience wakes despair
That slumbered, wakes the bitter memory
Of what he was, what is, and what must be
Worse; of worse deeds worse sufferings must ensue.
Sometimes towards Eden which now in his view
Lay pleasant, his grieved look he fixes sad,
Sometimes towards heaven and the full-blazing sun,
Which now sat high in his meridian tower:
Then much revolving, thus in sighs began.
    O thou that with surpassing glory crowned,
Look'st from thy sole dominion like the god
Of this new world; at whose sight all the stars
Hide their diminished heads; to thee I call,

[50] **he . . . Apocalypse:** St. John, who saw a vision of the battle in heaven against Satan the dragon; see Revelation 12:3–12.

[51] **While time was:** That is, while time yet remained.

[52] **tempter . . . mankind:** Satan came to earth first as the tempter of Eve, and later as the accuser of Job; devil, from the Greek *diabolos,* means "accuser."

[53] **devilish engine:** A weapon; here a cannon.

[54] **within . . . brings:** Compare Christopher Marlowe's *Dr. Faustus,* where Faust says "where we are is hell, / And where hell is, there must we ever be" (II.i.122–23).

But with no friendly voice, and add thy name
O sun, to tell thee how I hate thy beams
That bring to my remembrance from what state
I fell, how glorious once above thy sphere;
Till pride and worse ambition threw me down
Warring in heaven against heaven's matchless king:
Ah wherefore! he deserved no such return
From me, whom he created what I was
In that bright eminence, and with his good
Upbraided none; nor was his service hard.
What could be less than to afford him praise,
The easiest recompense, and pay him thanks,
How due! Yet all his good proved ill in me,
And wrought but malice; lifted up so high
I 'sdained[55] subjection, and thought one step higher
Would set me highest, and in a moment quit
The debt immense of endless gratitude,
So burdensome still paying, still to owe;
Forgetful what from him I still received,
And understood not that a grateful mind
By owing[56] owes not, but still pays, at once
Indebted and discharged; what burden then?
O had his powerful destiny ordained
Me some inferior angel, I had stood
Then happy; no unbounded hope had raised
Ambition. Yet why not? Some other power
As great might have aspired, and me though mean
Drawn to his part; but other powers as great
Fell not, but stand unshaken, from within
Or from without, to all temptations armed.
Hadst thou the same free will and power to stand?
Thou hadst: whom hast thou then or what to accuse,
But heaven's free love dealt equally to all?
Be then his love accursed, since love or hate,
To me alike, it deals eternal woe.
Nay cursed be thou; since against his thy will
Chose freely what it now so justly rues.
Me miserable! which way shall I fly

[55] **'sdained:** Disdained. Satan here thought to rise up one step higher in the Great Chain of Being; when he tempts Eve to eat from the fruit of the Tree of Knowledge, he will promise her a similar advance of degree. See Book IX, 705–12.

[56] **owing:** Both in the sense of "owing" and "owning up to a debt"; the passage suggests that acknowledging one's debt with gratitude provides a kind of payment.

Infinite wrath, and infinite despair?
Which way I fly is hell; myself am hell;
And in the lowest deep a lower deep
Still threatening to devour me opens wide,
To which the hell I suffer seems a heaven.
O then at last relent: is there no place
Left for repentance, none for pardon left?
None left but by submission; and that word
Disdain forbids me, and my dread of shame
Among the spirits beneath, whom I seduced
With other promises and other vaunts
Than to submit, boasting I could subdue
The omnipotent. Ay me, they little know
How dearly I abide° that boast so vain, suffer for
Under what torments inwardly I groan:
While they adore me on the throne of hell,
With diadem and sceptre high advanced
The lower still I fall, only supreme
In misery; such joy ambition finds.
But say I could repent and could obtain
By act of grace my former state; how soon
Would height recall high thoughts, how soon unsay
What feigned submission swore: ease would recant
Vows made in pain, as violent and void.
For never can true reconcilement grow
Where wounds of deadly hate have pierced so deep:
Which would but lead me to a worse relapse,
And heavier fall: so should I purchase dear
Short intermission bought with double smart.
This knows my punisher; therefore as far
From granting he, as I from begging peace:
All hope excluded thus, behold instead
Of us outcast, exiled, his new delight,
Mankind created, and for him this world.
So farewell hope, and with hope farewell fear,
Farewell remorse: all good to me is lost;
Evil be thou my good;[57] by thee at least
Divided empire with heaven's king I hold
By thee, and more than half perhaps will reign;
As man ere long, and this new world shall know.

[57] **So . . . good:** These famous lines symbolizing Satan's utter despair allude to Isaiah 5:20: "Woe unto them that call evil good, and good evil; that put darkness for light, and light for darkness; that put bitter for sweet, and sweet for bitter."

Thus while he spake, each passion dimmed his face
Thrice changed with pale, ire, envy and despair,
Which marred his borrowed visage, and betrayed
Him counterfeit, if any eye beheld.
For heavenly minds from such distempers foul
Are ever clear. Whereof he soon aware,
Each perturbation smoothed with outward calm,
Artificer of fraud; and was the first
That practised falsehood under saintly show,
Deep malice to conceal, couched with revenge:
Yet not enough had practised to deceive
Uriel once warned; whose eye pursued him down
The way he went, and on the Assyrian mount[58]
Saw him disfigured, more than could befall
Spirit of happy sort: his gestures fierce
He marked, and mad demeanour, then alone,
As he supposed, all unobserved, unseen.
So on he fares, and to the border comes,
Of Eden,[59] where delicious Paradise,
Now nearer, crowns with her enclosure green,
As with a rural mound the champaign head[60]
Of a steep wilderness, whose hairy sides
With thicket overgrown, grotesque and wild,
Access denied; and overhead up grew
Insuperable height of loftiest shade,
Cedar, and pine, and fir, and branching palm,
A sylvan scene, and as the ranks ascend
Shade above shade, a woody theatre
Of stateliest view. Yet higher than their tops
The verdurous wall of Paradise up sprung:
Which to our general sire gave prospect large
Into his nether empire neighbouring round.
And higher than that wall a circling row
Of goodliest trees loaden with fairest fruit,
Blossoms and fruits at once of golden hue
Appeared, with gay enamelled° colours mixed: bright
On which the sun more glad impressed his beams
Than in fair evening cloud, or humid bow,
When God hath showered the earth; so lovely seemed

[58] **Assyrian mount:** At the conclusion of Book III, Satan lands on earth on Mt. Niphates, the "Assyrian mount," which is in the Taurus Mountains bordering Armenia and Assyria. The angel Uriel has spied him there.

[59] **Eden:** The word means "delight" or "pleasure" in Hebrew.

[60] **champaign head:** Level surface of a summit or plateau.

That landscape: and of pure now purer air
Meets his approach, and to the heart inspires
Vernal delight and joy, able to drive
All sadness but despair: now gentle gales
Fanning their odoriferous wings dispense
Native perfumes, and whisper whence they stole
Those balmy spoils. As when to them who sail
Beyond the Cape of Hope, and now are past
Mozambique, off at sea north-east winds blow
Sabean odours from the spicy shore
Of Araby[61] the blest, with such delay
Well pleased they slack their course, and many a league
Cheered with the grateful smell old Ocean[62] smiles.
So entertained those odorous sweets the fiend
Who came their bane, though with them better pleased
Than Asmodeus with the fishy fume,
That drove him, though enamoured, from the spouse
Of Tobit's son, and with a vengeance sent
From Media post to Egypt, there fast bound.[63]
    Now to the ascent of that steep savage hill
Satan had journeyed on, pensive and slow;
But further way found none, so thick entwined,
As one continued brake, the undergrowth
Of shrubs and tangling bushes had perplexed
All path of man or beast that passed that way:
One gate there only was, and that looked east
On the other side: which when the arch-felon saw
Due entrance he disdained, and in contempt,
At one slight bound high overleaped all bound
Of hill or highest wall, and sheer within
Lights on his feet. As when a prowling wolf,
Whom hunger drives to seek new haunt for prey,
Watching where shepherds pen their flocks at eve
In hurdled cotes amid the field secure,
Leaps o'er the fence with ease into the fold:
Or as a thief bent to unhoard the cash

[61] **Araby:** Milton's simile here refers to ships in the spice trade approaching Sheba (today's Yemen), after having rounded the Cape of Good Hope and sailing north along the eastern coast of Africa.

[62] **old Ocean:** Oceanus, a Titan, the god of rivers and oceans.

[63] **there fast bound:** The Book of Tobit in the Apocrypha recounts the story of Tobias, the eighth husband of Sara, whose previous husbands have been murdered by the evil spirit Asmodeus, who is in love with the unlucky bride. Following the advice of the angel Raphael, his guardian, Tobias saves himself from the same fate by burning the heart and liver of a fish, and so driving Asmodeus from Media, where they are located in Persia, into the "utmost parts of Egypt." (See Tobit 8:3.)

Of some rich burgher, whose substantial doors,
Cross-barred and bolted fast, fear no assault,
In at the window climbs, or o'er the tiles;
So clomb this first grand thief into God's fold:
So since into his church lewd hirelings[64] climb.
Thence up he flew, and on the tree of life,
The middle tree and highest there that grew,
Sat like a cormorant;[65] yet not true life
Thereby regained, but sat devising death
To them who lived; nor on the virtue thought
Of that life-giving plant, but only used
For prospect, what well used had been the pledge
Of immortality. So little knows
Any, but God alone, to value right
The good before him, but perverts best things
To worst abuse, or to their meanest use.
Beneath him with new wonder now he views
To all delight of human sense exposed
In narrow room nature's whole wealth, yea more,
A heaven on earth, for blissful Paradise
Of God the garden was, by him in the east
Of Eden planted; Eden stretched her line
From Auran eastward to the royal towers
Of great Seleucia, built by Grecian kings,
Or where the sons of Eden long before
Dwelt in Telassar:[66] in this pleasant soil
His far more pleasant garden God ordained;
Out of the fertile ground he caused to grow
All trees of noblest kind for sight, smell, taste;
And all amid them stood the tree of life,
High eminent, blooming ambrosial fruit
Of vegetable gold; and next to life
Our death the tree of knowledge grew fast by,
Knowledge of good bought dear by knowing ill.
Southward through Eden went a river large,
Nor changed his course, but through the shaggy hill
Passed underneath engulfed, for God had thrown
That mountain as his garden mould high raised

[64] **lewd hirelings:** Milton has in mind ministers who only work for pay, not to be of service as did some Puritan ministers; *lewd* means both "vicious" or "vile" and "lay," as in laymen.

[65] **cormorant:** A diving sea bird associated with gluttony and greed.

[66] **in Telassar:** Milton describes Eden as extending from Huaran at the astern border of what is now Israel all the way to Seleucia, a city on the Tigris River in what is now Iraq. Telassar is an ancient city in Mesopotamia, said to be the place where the Assyrians wiped out the "children of Eden." (See Isaiah 37:12.)

Upon the rapid current, which through veins
Of porous earth with kindly° thirst up drawn, natural
Rose a fresh fountain, and with many a rill
Watered the garden; thence united fell
Down the steep glade, and met the nether flood,
Which from his darksome passage now appears,
And now divided into four main streams,
Runs diverse, wandering many a famous realm
And country whereof here needs no account,
But rather to tell how, if art could tell,
How from that sapphire fount the crispèd° brooks, curly or rippling
Rolling on orient pearl and sands of gold,
With mazy error under pendant shades
Ran nectar, visiting each plant, and fed
Flowers worthy of Paradise which not nice art
In beds and curious knots, but nature boon
Poured forth profuse on hill and dale and plain,
Both where the morning sun first warmly smote
The open field, and where the unpiercèd shade
Embrowned the noontide bowers: thus was this place,
A happy rural seat of various view;
Groves whose rich trees wept odorous gums and balm,
Others whose fruit burnished with golden rind
Hung amiable, Hesperian fables[67] true,
If true, here only, and of delicious taste:
Betwixt them lawns, or level downs, and flocks
Grazing the tender herb, were interposed,
Or palmy hillock, or the flowery lap
Of some irriguous° valley spread her store, irrigated, well-watered
Flowers of all hue, and without thorn the rose:
Another side, umbrageous grots and caves
Of cool recess, o'er which the mantling vine
Lays forth her purple grape, and gently creeps
Luxuriant; meanwhile murmuring waters fall
Down the slope hills, dispersed, or in a lake,
That to the fringèd bank with myrtle crowned,
Her crystal mirror holds, unite their streams.
The birds their choir apply; airs, vernal airs,
Breathing the smell of field and grove, attune

[67] **Hesperian fables:** Alludes to the fabled gardens of the Hesperides, the nymphs charged with guarding three golden apples that were said to give eternal life; a serpent helped them watch over their treasure. Hercules managed to steal the apples and kill the serpent.

The trembling leaves, while universal Pan[68]
Knit with the Graces and the Hours in dance
Led on the eternal spring. Not that fair field
Of Enna, where Prosperin' gathering flowers
Herself a fairer flower by gloomy Dis
Was gathered, which cost Ceres[69] all that pain
To seek her through the world; nor that sweet grove
Of Daphne[70] by Orontes, and the inspired
Castalian spring, might with this Paradise
Of Eden strive; nor that Nyseian isle
Girt with the river Triton, where old Cham,
Whom Gentiles Ammon call and Lybian Jove,
His Amalthea and her florid son
Young Bacchus from his stepdame Rhea's eye;[71]
Nor where Abassin kings their issue guard,
Mount Amara,[72] though this by some supposed
True Paradise under the Ethiop line
By Nilus' head, enclosed with shining rock,
A whole day's journey high, but wide remote
From this Assyrian garden,[73] where the fiend
Saw undelighted all delight, all kind
Of living creatures new to sight and strange:
Two of far nobler shape erect and tall,
Godlike erect, with native honour clad
In naked majesty seemed lords of all,
And worthy seemed, for in their looks divine
The image of their glorious maker shone,
Truth, wisdom, sanctitude severe and pure,

---

[68] **Pan:** The Greek god of nature, here associated with universal nature; he is depicted here dancing with the Graces—the attendants of Venus, the goddess of beauty—and the Hours, or Horae—the goddesses who govern the seasons.

[69] **Ceres:** According to Greek myth, Dis, the god of the Underworld, abducted Proserpine from her garden Enna in Sicily. Her mother Ceres, the goddess of grain and agriculture, found Proserpine in the Underworld and arranged that they would alternate living there and on the earth for half the year, thus establishing the seasons, for no crops could grow when Ceres was in Hades.

[70] **sweet . . . Daphne:** A grove on the river Orontes, near Antioch in Syria, which had a spring named after the Castalian spring at Delphi, the site of the oracle of Apollo.

[71] **Rhea's eye:** Ammon, a Libyan king—here identified with Cham (Ham), the son of Noah—had Bacchus, the god of wine, with the nymph Amalthea. To protect Amalthea and Bacchus from his jealous wife Rhea, Ammon hid them away on the island of Nysa.

[72] **Mount Amara:** A high hill in Ethiopia, thought to be near the source of the Nile—"Nilus' head"—where Abyssinian ("Abassin") kings sent their children to be raised in seclusion.

[73] **Assyrian garden:** That is, the Garden of Eden.

Severe but in true filial freedom placed;
Whence true authority in men; though both
Not equal, as their sex not equal seemed;
For contemplation he and valour formed,
For softness she and sweet attractive grace,
He for God only, she for God in him:
His fair large front and eye sublime declared
Absolute rule; and hyacinthine[74] locks
Round from his parted forelock manly hung
Clustering, but not beneath his shoulders broad:
She as a veil down to the slender waist
Her unadornèd golden tresses wore
Dishevelled, but in wanton[75] ringlets waved
As the vine curls her tendrils, which implied
Subjection, but required with gentle sway,
And by her yielded, by him best received,
Yielded with coy submission, modest pride,
And sweet reluctant amorous delay.
Nor those mysterious parts were then concealed,
Then was not guilty shame, dishonest shame
Of nature's works, honour dishonourable,
Sin-bred, how have ye troubled all mankind
With shows instead, mere shows of seeming pure,
And banished from man's life his happiest life,
Simplicity and spotless innocence.
So passed they naked on, nor shunned the sight
Of God or angel, for they thought no ill:
So hand in hand they passed, the loveliest pair
That ever since in love's embraces met,
Adam the goodliest man of men since born
His sons, the fairest of her daughters Eve.
Under a tuft of shade that on a green
Stood whispering soft, by a fresh fountain side
They sat them down, and after no more toil
Of their sweet gardening labour than sufficed
To recommend cool zephyr,[76] and made ease
More easy, wholesome thirst and appetite

[74] **hyacinthine:** Like those of Hyacinth, a beautiful youth and the favorite of Apollo, whom Apollo inadvertently killed; from the youth's blood grew the hyacinth flower impressed with the letters *AI AI,* an expression of grief. Milton alludes to Homer's *Odyssey* here, where Odysseus's hair is described as hyacinthine (VI 231–32).

[75] **wanton:** Here the word means "unrestrained" or "luxuriant," not "lacking moral restraint." Nonetheless, it anticipates what is to come. The same is true of *coy,* which means "shy" rather than "coquettish" in line 310 below.

[76] **zephyr:** The west wind, associated with spring.

More grateful, to their supper fruits they fell,
Nectarine fruits which the compliant boughs
Yielded them, sidelong as they sat recline
On the soft downy bank damasked with flowers:
The savoury pulp they chew, and in the rind
Still as they thirsted scoop the brimming stream;
Nor gentle purpose, nor endearing smiles
Wanted, nor youthful dalliance as beseems
Fair couple, linked in happy nuptial league,
Alone as they. About them frisking played
All beasts of the earth, since wild, and of all chase
In wood or wilderness, forest or den;
Sporting the lion ramped, and in his paw
Dandled the kid; bears, tigers, ounces, pards,
Gambolled before them, the unwieldy elephant
To make them mirth used all his might, and wreathed
His lithe proboscis; close the serpent sly
Insinuating, wove with Gordian twine[77]
His braided train, and of his fatal guile
Gave proof unheeded; others on the grass
Couched, and now filled with pasture gazing sat,
Or bedward ruminating: for the sun
Declined was hasting now with prone career
To the Ocean Isles,[78] and in the ascending scale
Of heaven the stars that usher evening rose:
When Satan still in gaze, as first he stood,
Scarce thus at length failed speech recovered sad.
O hell! what do mine eyes with grief behold,
Into our room of bliss thus high advanced
Creatures of other mould, earth-born perhaps,
Not spirits, yet to heavenly spirits bright
Little inferior;[79] whom my thoughts pursue
With wonder, and could love, so lively shines
In them divine resemblance, and such grace
The hand that formed them on their shape hath poured.
Ah gentle pair, ye little think how nigh
Your change approaches, when all these delights
Will vanish and deliver ye to woe,

[77] **Gordian twine:** As tangled as the Gordian knot, which Alexander undid by cutting it with his sword after others failed to untie it.

[78] **Ocean Isles:** These are identified as the Azores, to the far west, in line 592.

[79] **Little inferior:** Satan's speech alludes to Psalms 8:5, which says of man, "For though has made him a little lower than the angels, and hast crowned him with glory and honour." Satan's admiration and pity indicate that he still has traces of the divine nature and nobility, though they have become corrupt.

More woe, the more your taste is now of joy;
Happy, but for so happy ill secured
Long to continue, and this high seat your heaven
Ill fenced for heaven to keep out such a foe
As now is entered; yet no purposed foe
To you whom I could pity thus forlorn
Though I unpitied: league with you I seek,
And mutual amity so strait, so close,
That I with you must dwell, or you with me
Henceforth; my dwelling haply may not please
Like this fair Paradise, your sense, yet such
Accept your maker's work; he gave it me,
Which I as freely give; hell shall unfold,
To entertain you two, her widest gates,
And send forth all her kings; there will be room,
Not like these narrow limits, to receive,
Your numerous offspring; if no better place,
Thank him who puts me loath to this revenge
On you who wrong me not for him who wronged.
And should I at your harmless innocence
Melt, as I do, yet public reason just,
Honour and empire with revenge enlarged,
By conquering this new world, compels me now
To do what else though damned I should abhor.
So spake the fiend, and with necessity,
The tyrant's plea, excused his devilish deeds.
Then from his lofty stand on that high tree
Down he alights among the sportful herd
Of those four-footed kinds, himself now one,
Now other, as their shape served best his end
Nearer to view his prey, and unespied
To mark what of their state he more might learn
By word or action marked: about them round
A lion now he stalks with fiery glare,
Then as a tiger, who by chance hath spied
In some purlieu[80] two gentle fawns at play,
Straight couches close, then rising changes oft
His couchant watch, as one who chose his ground
Whence rushing he might surest seize them both
Gripped in each paw: when Adam first of men
To first of women Eve thus moving speech,
Turned him all ear to hear new utterance flow.

[80] **purlieu:** An outlying area of a forest, or a haunt.

Sole partner and sole part of all these joys,
Dearer thyself than all; needs must the power
That made us, and for us this ample world
Be infinitely good, and of his good
As liberal and free as infinite,
That raised us from the dust and placed us here
In all this happiness, who at his hand
Have nothing merited, nor can perform
Aught whereof he hath need, he who requires
From us no other service than to keep
This one, this easy charge, of all the trees
In Paradise that bear delicious fruit
So various, not to taste that only tree
Of knowledge, planted by the tree of life,
So near grows death to life, what e'er death is,
Some dreadful thing no doubt; for well thou know'st
God hath pronounced it death to taste that tree,
The only sign of our obedience left
Among so many signs of power and rule
Conferred upon us, and dominion given
Over all other creatures that possess
Earth, air, and sea. Then let us not think hard
One easy prohibition, who enjoy
Free leave so large to all things else, and choice
Unlimited of manifold delights:
But let us ever praise him, and extol
His bounty, following our delightful task
To prune these growing plants, and tend these flowers,
Which were it toilsome, yet with thee were sweet.
To whom thus Eve replied. O thou for whom
And from whom I was formed flesh of thy flesh,
And without whom am to no end, my guide
And head, what thou hast said is just and right.
For we to him indeed all praises owe,
And daily thanks, I chiefly who enjoy
So far the happier lot, enjoying thee
Pre-eminent by so much odds, while thou
Like consort to thyself canst nowhere find.
That day I oft remember, when from sleep
I first awaked, and found myself reposed
Under a shade of flowers, much wondering where
And what I was, whence thither brought, and how.
Not distant far from thence a murmuring sound
Of waters issued from a cave and spread
Into a liquid plain, then stood unmoved

Pure as the expanse of heaven; I thither went
With unexperienced thought, and laid me down
On the green bank, to look into the clear
Smooth lake, that to me seemed another sky.
As I bent down to look, just opposite,
A shape within the watery gleam appeared
Bending to look on me, I started back,
It started back, but pleased I soon returned,
Pleased it returned as soon with answering looks
Of sympathy and love;[81] there I had fixed
Mine eyes till now, and pined with vain desire,
Had not a voice thus warned me, What thou seest,
What there thou seest fair creature is thyself,
With thee it came and goes: but follow me,
And I will bring thee where no shadow stays
Thy coming, and thy soft embraces, he
Whose image thou art, him thou shall enjoy
Inseparably thine, to him shalt bear
Multitudes like thyself, and thence be called
Mother of human race:[82] what could I do,
But follow straight, invisibly thus led?
Till I espied thee, fair indeed and tall,
Under a platan,° yet methought less fair, plane tree
Less winning soft, less amiably mild,
Than that smooth watery image; back I turned,
Thou following cried'st aloud, Return fair Eve,
Whom fly'st thou? Whom thou fly'st, of him thou art,
His flesh, his bone; to give thee being I lent
Out of my side to thee, nearest my heart
Substantial life, to have thee by my side
Henceforth an individual solace dear;
Part of my soul I seek thee, and thee claim
My other half: with that thy gentle hand
Seized mine, I yielded, and from that time see
How beauty is excelled by manly grace
And wisdom, which alone is truly fair.
So spake our general mother, and with eyes
Of conjugal attraction unreproved,
And meek surrender, half embracing leaned

[81] **answering . . . love:** Compare Ovid's *Metamorphoses* 3:339–510, where Narcissus falls in love with his own reflection. In the following lines, the voice of God leads Eve, who is described as Adam's image, away from her reflection and to her husband, the true object of her love.

[82] **Mother . . . race:** Milton alludes to Genesis 3:20: "And Adam called his wife's name Eve; because she was the mother of all living." Her name, which Adam assigns her, means "life."

On our first father, half her swelling breast
Naked met his under the flowing gold
Of her loose tresses hid: he in delight
Both of her beauty and submissive charms
Smiled with superior love, as Jupiter
On Juno[83] smiles, when he impregns the clouds
That shed May flowers; and pressed her matron lip
With kisses pure: aside the devil turned
For envy, yet with jealous leer malign
Eyed them askance, and to himself thus plained.
    Sight hateful, sight tormenting! thus these two
Emparadised in one another's arms
The happier Eden, shall enjoy their fill
Of bliss on bliss, while I to hell am thrust,
Where neither joy nor love, but fierce desire,
Among our other torments not the least,
Still unfulfilled with pain of longing pines;
Yet let me not forget what I have gained
From their own mouths; all is not theirs it seems:
One fatal tree there stands of knowledge called,
Forbidden them to taste: knowledge forbidden?
Suspicious, reasonless. Why should their Lord
Envy them that? can it be sin to know,
Can it be death? and do they only stand
By ignorance, is that their happy state,
The proof of their obedience and their faith?
O fair foundation laid whereon to build
Their ruin! Hence I will excite their minds
With more desire to know, and to reject
Envious commands, invented with design
To keep them low whom knowledge might exalt
Equal with gods; aspiring to be such,
They taste and die: what likelier can ensue?
But first with narrow search I must walk round
This garden, and no corner leave unspied;
A chance but chance may lead where I may meet
Some wandering spirit of heaven, by fountain side,
Or in thick shade retired, from him to draw
What further would be learned. Live while ye may,
Yet happy pair; enjoy, till I return,
Short pleasures, for long woes are to succeed.

[83] **Jupiter . . . Juno:** Jupiter, a sky god and the chief of the Olympian gods, and his wife, Juno, a goddess of the lower air.

So saying, his proud step he scornful turned,
But with sly circumspection, and began
Through wood, through waste, o'er hill, o'er dale his roam. [. . .]

Now came still evening on, and twilight grey
Had in her sober livery all things clad;
Silence accompanied, for beast and bird,
They to their grassy couch, these to their nests
Were slunk, all but the wakeful nightingale;
She all night long her amorous descant° sung; warbling song
Silence was pleased: now glowed the firmament
With living sapphires: Hesperus° that led the evening star
The starry host, rode brightest, till the moon
Rising in clouded majesty, at length
Apparent queen unveiled her peerless light,
And o'er the dark her silver mantle threw.
When Adam thus to Eve: Fair consort, the hour
Of night, and all things now retired to rest
Mind us of like repose, since God hath set
Labour and rest, as day and night to men
Successive, and the timely dew of sleep
Now falling with soft slumbrous weight inclines
Our eyelids; other creatures all day long
Rove idle unemployed, and less need rest;
Man hath his daily work of body or mind
Appointed, which declares his dignity,
And the regard of heaven on all his ways;
While other animals unactive range,
And of their doings God takes no account.
Tomorrow ere fresh morning streak the east
With first approach of light, we must be risen,
And at our pleasant labour, to reform
Yon flowery arbours, yonder alleys green,
Our walk at noon, with branches overgrown,
That mock our scant manuring,[84] and require
More hands than ours to lop their wanton growth:
Those blossoms also, and those dropping gums,
That lie bestrewn unsightly and unsmooth,
Ask riddance, if we mean to tread with ease;
Meanwhile, as nature wills, night bids us rest.
To whom thus Eve with perfect beauty adorned.
My author and disposer, what thou bid'st
Unargued I obey; so God ordains,

[84] **scant manuring:** Light hand labor (i.e., cultivation).

God is thy law, thou mine: to know no more
Is woman's happiest knowledge and her praise.
With thee conversing I forget all time,
All seasons and their change, all please alike.
Sweet is the breath of morn, her rising sweet,
With charm of earliest birds; pleasant the sun
When first on this delightful land he spreads
His orient beams, on herb, tree, fruit, and flower,
Glistering with dew; fragrant the fertile earth
After soft showers; and sweet the coming on
Of grateful evening mild, then silent night
With this her solemn bird and this fair moon,
And these the gems of heaven, her starry train:
But neither breath of morn when she ascends
With charm of earliest birds, nor rising sun
On this delightful land, nor herb, fruit, flower,
Glistering with dew, nor fragrance after showers,
Nor grateful evening mild, nor silent night
With this her solemn bird, nor walk by moon,
Or glittering starlight without thee is sweet.
But wherefore all night long shine these, for whom
This glorious sight, when sleep hath shut all eyes?
To whom our general ancestor replied.
Daughter of God and man, accomplished Eve,
Those have their course to finish, round the earth,
By morrow evening, and from land to land
In order, though to nations yet unborn,
Ministering light prepared, they set and rise;
Lest total darkness should by night regain
Her old possession, and extinguish life
In nature and all things, which these soft fires
Not only enlighten, but with kindly heat
Of various influence foment and warm,
Temper or nourish, or in part shed down
Their stellar virtue on all kinds that grow
On earth, made hereby apter to receive
Perfection from the sun's more potent ray.
These then, though unbeheld in deep of night,
Shine not in vain, nor think, though men were none,
That heaven would want spectators, God want praise;
Millions of spiritual creatures walk the earth
Unseen, both when we wake, and when we sleep:
All these with ceaseless praise his works behold
Both day and night: how often from the steep
Of echoing hill or thicket have we heard
Celestial voices to the midnight air,

Sole, or responsive each to other's note
Singing their great creator: oft in bands
While they keep watch, or nightly rounding walk
With heavenly touch of instrumental sounds
In full harmonic number joined, their songs
Divide the night, and lift our thoughts to heaven.
Thus talking hand in hand alone they passed

On to their blissful bower; [. . .]
Thus at their shady lodge arrived, both stood,
Both turned, and under open sky adored
The God that made both sky, air, earth and heaven
Which they beheld, the moon's resplendent globe
And starry pole.° Thou also mad'st the night, the heavens, the sky
Maker omnipotent, and thou the day,
Which we in our appointed work employed
Have finished happy in our mutual help
And mutual love, the crown of all our bliss
Ordained by thee, and this delicious place
For us too large, where thy abundance wants
Partakers, and uncropped falls to the ground.
But thou hast promised from us two a race
To fill the earth, who shall with us extol
Thy goodness infinite, both when we wake,
And when we seek, as now, thy gift of sleep.
This said unanimous, and other rites
Observing none, but adoration pure
Which God likes best, into their inmost bower
Handed they went; and eased the putting off
These troublesome disguises which we wear,
Straight side by side were laid, nor turned I ween
Adam from his fair spouse, nor Eve the rites
Mysterious of connubial love refused:
Whatever hypocrites austerely talk
Of purity and place and innocence,
Defaming as impure what God declares
Pure, and commands to some, leaves free to all.
Our maker bids increase, who bids abstain
But our destroyer, foe to God and man?
Hail wedded love, mysterious law, true source
Of human offspring, sole propriety
In Paradise of all things common else.
By thee adulterous lust was driven from men
Among the bestial herds to range, by thee
Founded in reason, loyal, just, and pure,

Relations dear, and all the charities
Of father, son, and brother first were known.
Far be it, that I should write thee sin or blame,
Or think thee unbefitting holiest place,
Perpetual fountain of domestic sweets,
Whose bed is undefiled and chaste pronounced,
Present, or past, as saints and patriarchs used.
Here Love his golden shafts employs, here lights
His constant lamp, and waves his purple wings,
Reigns here and revels; not in the bought smile
Of harlots, loveless, joyless, unendeared,
Casual fruition, nor in court amours
Mixed dance, or wanton masque, or midnight ball,
Or serenade, which the starved lover sings
To his proud fair, best quitted with disdain.
These lulled by nightingales embracing slept,
And on their naked limbs the flowery roof
Showered roses, which the morn repaired. Sleep on
Blest pair; and O yet happiest if ye seek
No happier state, and know to know no more. [. . .]

Book V

The Argument

Morning approached, Eve relates to Adam her troublesome dream; he likes it not, yet comforts her: they come forth to their day labours: their morning hymn at the door of their bower. God to render man inexcusable sends Raphael to admonish him of his obedience, of his free estate, of his enemy near at hand; who he is, and why his enemy, and whatever else may avail Adam to know. Raphael comes down to Paradise, his appearance described, his coming discerned by Adam afar off sitting at the door of his bower; he goes out to meet him, brings him to his lodge, entertains him with the choicest fruits of Paradise got together by Eve; their discourse at table: Raphael performs his message, minds Adam of his state and of his enemy; relates at Adam's request who that enemy is, and how he came to be so, beginning from his first revolt in heaven, and the occasion thereof; how he drew his legions after him to the parts of the north, and there incited them to rebel with him, persuading all but only Abdiel a seraph, who in argument dissuades and opposes him, then forsakes him.

Book VI

The Argument

Raphael continues to relate how Michael and Gabriel were sent forth to battle against Satan and his angels. The first fight described: Satan and his powers retire under night: he calls a council, invents devilish engines, which in the second day's fight put Michael and his angels to some disorder; but they at length pulling up mountains overwhelmed both the force and machines of Satan: yet the tumult not so ending, God on the third day sends Messiah his son, for whom he had reserved the glory of that victory: he in the power of his father coming to the place, and causing all his legions to stand still on either side, with his chariot and thunder driving into the midst of his enemies, pursues them unable to resist towards the wall of heaven; which opening, they leap down with horror and confusion into the place of punishment prepared for them in the deep: Messiah returns with triumph to his father.

Book VII

The Argument

Raphael at the request of Adam relates how and wherefore this world was first created; that God, after the expelling of Satan and his angels out of heaven, declared his pleasure to create another world and other creatures to dwell therein; sends his son with glory and attendance of angels to perform the work of creation in six days: the angels celebrate with hymns the performance thereof, and his re-ascension into heaven.

Book VIII

The Argument

Adam inquires concerning celestial motions, is doubtfully answered, and exhorted to search rather things more worthy of knowledge: Adam assents, and still desirous to detain Raphael, relates to him what he remembered since his own creation, his placing in Paradise, his talk with God concerning solitude and fit society, his first meeting and nuptials with Eve, his discourse with the angel thereupon; who after admonitions repeated departs.

Book IX
[The Temptation and Fall]

The Argument

Satan having compassed the earth, with meditated guile returns as a mist by night into Paradise, enters into the serpent sleeping. Adam and Eve in the morning go forth to their labours, which Eve proposes to divide in several places, each labouring apart: Adam consents not, alleging the danger, lest that enemy, of whom they were forewarned, should attempt her found alone: Eve loath to be thought not circumspect or firm enough, urges her going apart, the rather desirous to make trial of her strength; Adam at last yields: the serpent finds her alone; his subtle approach, first gazing, then speaking, with much flattery extolling Eve above all other creatures. Eve wondering to hear the serpent speak, asks how he attained to human speech and such understanding not till now; the serpent answers, that by tasting of a certain tree in the garden he attained both to speech and reason, till then void of both: Eve requires him to bring her to that tree, and finds it to be the tree of knowledge forbidden: the serpent now grown bolder, with many wiles and arguments induces her at length to eat; she pleased with the taste deliberates awhile whether to impart thereof to Adam or not, at last brings him of the fruit, relates what persuaded her to eat thereof: Adam at first amazed, but perceiving her lost, resolves through vehemence of love to perish with her; and extenuating the trespass eats also of the fruit: the effects thereof in them both; they seek to cover their nakedness; then fall to variance and accusation of one another.

No more of talk where God or angel guest
With man, as with his friend, familiar used
To sit indulgent, and with him partake
Rural repast, permitting him the while
Venial discourse unblamed:[85] I now must change
Those notes to tragic; foul distrust, and breach
Disloyal on the part of man, revolt,
And disobedience: on the part of heaven
Now alienated, distance and distaste,
Anger and just rebuke, and judgment given,
That brought into this world a world of woe,
Sin and her shadow Death, and Misery
Death's harbinger: sad task, yet argument
Not less but more heroic than the wrath
Of stern Achilles on his foe pursued
Thrice fugitive about Troy wall; or rage
Of Turnus for Lavinia disespoused,
Or Neptune's ire or Juno's, that so long
Perplexed the Greek and Cytherea's son;[86]
If answerable style I can obtain
Of my celestial patroness, who deigns
Her nightly visitation unimplored,
And dictates to me slumbering, or inspires
Easy my unpremeditated verse:
Since first this subject for heroic song

[85] **Venial . . . unblamed:** Milton refers here to the genial conversation God permitted between the angel Raphael and Adam. He announces that he must turn from this congenial interlude to the tragic action of the fall.

[86] **Cytherea's son:** In these lines Milton elevates his Christian story of the fall above the epic themes of Homer and Virgil. Homer's *Iliad* recounts the wrath of Achilles (who chased his foe Hector around the walls of Troy), and his *Odyssey* tells of Neptune's anger against Odysseus; Virgil's *Aeneid* tells of Juno's wrath against Cytherea's son Aeneas—hence his hope in lines 20–21 to receive an "answerable style" (that is, a dignified style fitted to his serious subject) from his muse, Urania.

Pleased me long choosing, and beginning late;[87]
Not sedulous by nature to indite
Wars, hitherto the only argument
Heroic deemed, chief mastery to dissect° analyze
With long and tedious havoc fabled knights
In battles feigned; the better fortitude
Of patience and heroic martyrdom
Unsung; or to describe races and games,
Or tilting furniture,[88] emblazoned shields,
Impresas quaint, caparisons and steeds;
Bases and tinsel trappings, gorgeous knights
At joust and tournament; then marshalled feast
Served up in hall with sewers, and seneschals;[89]
The skill of artifice or office mean,
Not that which justly gives heroic name
To person or to poem. Me of these
Nor skilled nor studious, higher argument
Remains, sufficient of itself to raise
That name,[90] unless an age too late, or cold
Climate, or years damp my intended wing
Depressed, and much they may, if all be mine,
Not hers who brings it nightly to my ear.
    The sun was sunk, and after him the star
Of Hesperus, whose office is to bring
Twilight upon the earth, short arbiter
Twixt day and night, and now from end to end
Night's hemisphere had veiled the horizon round:
When Satan who late fled before the threats
Of Gabriel out of Eden,[91] now improved

---

[87] **beginning late:** As explained in the introduction to *Paradise Lost,* Milton had long planned to write a great poem on a serious subject, but he did not devote his full attention to the project until after his blindness. In the following lines, he points out that his theme of the fall differs from previous epics and romances, which focused on the heroic deeds of martial heroes and knights. His subject, he believes, is far more important than those; hence, he chose not to devote time writing—"sedulous to indite" (l. 27)—stories about war. Of course, Milton does describe in Book VI the war between the fallen angels and God's forces, but the war theme is subordinated to the story of the fall.

[88] **tilting furniture:** The weapons and accoutrements of the jousting tournament.

[89] **sewers . . . seneschals:** Servants; the sewer attended to guests at banquets, while the seneschal was a kind of steward, overseeing the affairs of the house.

[90] **That name:** That is, the name of heroic verse, or epic. Milton goes on to suggest here that the epic form may be outdated, or his muse may be inhibited by the climate, or his age. "Damp" means to inhibit or depress, but it also suggests the cold, humid climate of Milton's England.

[91] **out of Eden:** At the end of Book IV, Gabriel drives Satan out of Eden; in his exile he has perfected his plan to defraud Adam and Eve.

In meditated fraud and malice, bent
On man's destruction, maugre what might hap
Of heavier on himself, fearless returned.
By night he fled, and at midnight returned
From compassing the earth, cautious of day,
Since Uriel regent of the sun descried
His entrance,[92] and forewarned the cherubim
That kept their watch; thence full of anguish driven,
The space of seven continued nights he rode
With darkness, thrice the equinoctial line
He circled, four times crossed the car of Night
From pole to pole, traversing each colure;[93]
On the eighth returned, and on the coast averse
From entrance or cherubic watch,[94] by stealth
Found unsuspected way. There was a place,
Now not, though sin, not time, first wrought the change,
Where Tigris at the foot of Paradise
Into a gulf shot underground, till part
Rose up a fountain by the tree of life;
In with the river sunk, and with it rose
Satan involved in rising mist, then sought
Where to lie hid; sea he had searched and land
From Eden over Pontus, and the pool
Maeotis, up beyond the river Ob;
Downward as far antarctic; and in length
West from Orontes to the ocean barred
At Darien, thence to the land where flows
Ganges and Indus:[95] thus the orb he roamed
With narrow search; and with inspection deep
Considered every creature, which of all

---

[92] **Since . . . entrance:** Upon Satan's first attempt to slip into Paradise, the angel Uriel spied him alighting on Mt. Niphates; see Book IV 119–30.

[93] **colure:** The colures are two imaginary celestial circles drawn from pole to pole and intersecting at right angles; one passes through the ecliptic of the solstices, the other through the ecliptic of the equinox. Milton describes Satan as traveling for seven days in the shadow of the earth, circling the earth three times along the equator, and then two times each crossing the "car of Night"—the chariot of the Goddess Nyx—along the lines of the two colures.

[94] **averse . . . watch:** Satan enters Eden from the north, a side turned away from and out of sight of the angels guarding the eastern entrance.

[95] **There . . . Indus:** Satan traverses the earth looking for a creature most suitable to carry out his plan of deception. From Eden, in the Tigris–Euphrates area, he goes north over the Black Sea (Pontus) and the Sea of Azof (Maeotis), along the river Ob in Siberia to the Arctic Ocean, and then down to the Antarctic. From there he goes back up to Syria, through which the Orontes flows, then west to Panama (Darien) and to India, where the Ganges and Indus Rivers flow. Milton identifies the Tigris as the river that, according to Genesis 2:10, "went out of Eden to water the garden."

Most opportune might serve his wiles, and found
The serpent subtlest beast of all the field.
Him after long debate, irresolute
Of thoughts revolved, his final sentence chose
Fit vessel, fittest imp of fraud, in whom
To enter, and his dark suggestions hide
From sharpest sight: for in the wily snake,[96]
Whatever sleights none would suspicious mark,
As from his wit and native subtlety
Proceeding, which in other beasts observed
Doubt° might beget of diabolic power — suspicion
Active within beyond the sense of brute.
Thus he resolved, but first from inward grief
His bursting passion into plaints thus poured:
    O earth, how like to heaven, if not preferred
More justly, seat worthier of gods, as built
With second thoughts, reforming what was old!
For what god after better worse would build?
Terrestrial heaven, danced round by other heavens
That shine, yet bear their bright officious lamps,
Light above light, for thee alone, as seems,
In thee concentring all their precious beams
Of sacred influence: as God in heaven
Is centre, yet extends to all, so thou
Centring receiv'st from all those orbs; in thee,
Not in themselves, all their known virtue appears
Productive in herb, plant, and nobler birth
Of creatures animate with gradual life[97]
Of growth, sense, reason, all summed up in man.
With what delight could I have walked thee round,
If I could joy in aught, sweet interchange
Of hill, and valley, rivers, woods and plains,
Now land, now sea, and shores with forest crowned,
Rocks, dens, and caves; but I in none of these
Find place or refuge; and the more I see
Pleasures about me, so much more I feel
Torment within me, as from the hateful siege

[96] **wily snake:** According to Genesis 3:1, "the serpent was more subtil than any beast of the field which the Lord God had made."

[97] **gradual life:** Graduated by degrees; Milton has in mind the Great Chain of Being, where life is arranged in a hierarchy ascending from the vegetable, to the animal, to the human. The human combines the growth and sensation of the first two orders with its own reason. The Great Chain of Being is a critical metaphor in *Paradise Lost,* for Satan had hoped to advance in degree from angel to god, and he will seduce Eve by convincing her that eating from the Tree of Knowledge will advance her and Adam to become Godlike.

Of contraries;[98] all good to me becomes
Bane, and in heaven much worse would by my state,
But neither here seek I, no nor in heaven
To dwell, unless by mastering heaven's supreme;
Nor hope to be myself less miserable
By what I seek, but others to make such
As I, though thereby worse to me redound:
For only in destroying I find ease
To my relentless thoughts; and him destroyed,
Or won to what may work his utter loss,
For whom all this was made, all this will soon
Follow, as to him linked in weal or woe,
In woe then; that destruction wide may range:
To me shall be the glory sole among
The infernal powers, in one day to have marred
What he almighty styled, six nights and days
Continued making, and who knows how long
Before had been contriving, though perhaps
Not longer than since I in one night freed
From servitude inglorious well-nigh half
The angelic name, and thinner left the throng
Of his adorers: he to be avenged
And to repair his numbers thus impaired,
Whether such virtue° spent of old now failed — power
More angels to create, if they at least
Are his created, or to spite us more,
Determined to advance into our room
A creature formed of earth, and him endow,
Exalted from so base original,[99]
With heavenly spoils, our spoils: what he decreed
He effected; man he made, and for him built
Magnificent this world, and earth his seat,
Him lord pronounced, and, O indignity!
Subjected to his service angel wings,
And flaming ministers to watch and tend
Their earthy charge: of these the vigilance
I dread, and to elude, thus wrapped in mist
Of midnight vapour glide obscure, and pry
In every bush and brake, where hap may find

[98] **siege . . . Of contraries:** That is, the conflict between good and evil, pleasure and pain that Satan experiences; he also suggests that he is the seat ("siege") of such conflict.

[99] **base original:** Low or common origin, referring to God creating Adam from dust or clay. Satan, who is made of a purer essence, is jealous that God would grant Adam favors denied to himself.

The serpent sleeping, in whose mazy folds
To hide me, and the dark intent I bring.
O foul descent! that I who erst contended
With gods to sit the highest, am now constrained
Into a beast, and mixed with bestial slime,
This essence to incarnate and imbrute,
That to the height of deity aspired;
But what will not ambition and revenge
Descend to? Who aspires must down as low
As high he soared, obnoxious first or last
To basest things. Revenge, at first though sweet,
Bitter ere long back on itself recoils;
Let it; I reck not,[100] so it light well aimed,
Since higher I fall short, on him who next
Provokes my envy, this new favourite
Of heaven, this man of clay, son of despite,
Whom us the more to spite his maker raised
From dust: spite then with spite is best repaid.
　　So saying, through each thicket dank or dry,
Like a black mist low creeping, he held on
His midnight search, where soonest he might find
The serpent: him fast sleeping soon he found
In labyrinth of many a round self-rolled,
His head the midst, well stored with subtle wiles:
Not yet in horrid shade or dismal den,
Nor nocent[101] yet, but on the grassy herb
Fearless unfeared he slept: in at his mouth
The devil entered, and his brutal sense,
In heart or head, possessing soon inspired
With act intelligential; but his sleep
Disturbed not, waiting close° the approach of morn. in secret, in concealment
Now whenas sacred light began to dawn
In Eden on the humid flowers, that breathed
Their morning incense, when all things that breathe,
From the earth's great altar send up silent praise
To the creator, and his nostrils fill
With grateful smell, forth came the human pair
And joined their vocal worship to the choir
Of creatures wanting° voice, that done, partake lacking
The season, prime for sweetest scents and airs:

[100] **I reck not:** I don't care. Satan goes on to say that if he were to aim his ruin at God himself, he would once again fall short, so he will go after God's favorite, man.

[101] **nocent:** Harmful. The serpent at this point is still innocent.

Then commune how that day they best may ply
Their growing work: for much their work outgrew
The hands' dispatch of two, gardening so wide.
And Eve first to her husband thus began.
Adam, well may we labour still to dress
This garden, still to tend plant, herb and flower,
Our pleasant task enjoined, but till more hands
Aid us, the work under our labour grows,
Luxurious[102] by restraint; what we by day
Lop overgrown, or prune, or prop, or bind,
One night or two with wanton growth derides
Tending to wild. Thou therefore now advise
Or hear what to my mind first thoughts present,
Let us divide our labours, thou where choice
Leads thee, or where most needs, whether to wind
The woodbine round this arbour, or direct
The clasping ivy where to climb, while I
In yonder spring° of roses intermixed — grove
With myrtle, find what to redress till noon:
For while so near each other thus all day
Our task we choose, what wonder if so near
Looks intervene and smiles, or object new
Casual discourse draw on, which intermits
Our day's work brought to little, though begun
Early, and the hour of supper comes unearned.
To whom mild answer Adam thus returned.
Sole Eve, associate sole, to me beyond
Compare above all living creatures dear,
Well hast thou motioned,° well thy thoughts employed — suggested, proposed
How we might best fulfil the work which here
God hath assigned us, nor of me shalt pass
Unpraised: for nothing lovelier can be found
In woman, than to study household good,
And good works in her husband to promote.
Yet not so strictly hath our Lord imposed
Labour, as to debar us when we need
Refreshment, whether food, or talk between,
Food of the mind, or this sweet intercourse
Of looks and smiles, for smiles from reason flow,
To brute denied, and are of love the food,
Love not the lowest end of human life.

[102] **Luxurious:** Luxuriant. Even in the Garden of Eden before the fall, labor is necessary to keep nature's "wanton"—that is, unrestrained and wild—growth within bounds.

For not to irksome toil, but to delight
He made us, and delight to reason joined.
These paths and bowers doubt not but our joint hands
Will keep from wilderness° with ease, as wide — being overgrown, wild
As we need walk, till younger hands ere long
Assist us: but if much converse perhaps
Thee satiate, to short absence I could yield.
For solitude sometimes is best society,
And short retirement urges sweet return.
But other doubt possesses me, lest harm
Befall thee severed from me; for thou know'st
What hath been warned us, what malicious foe
Envying our happiness, and of his own
Despairing, seeks to work us woe and shame
By sly assault; and somewhere nigh at hand
Watches, no doubt, with greedy hope to find
His wish and best advantage, us asunder,
Hopeless to circumvent us joined, where each
To other speedy aid might lend at need;
Whether his first design be to withdraw
Our fealty from God, or to disturb
Conjugal love, than which perhaps no bliss
Enjoyed by us excites his envy more;
Or this, or worse,[103] leave not the faithful side
That gave thee being, still shades thee and protects.
The wife, where danger or dishonour lurks,
Safest and seemliest by her husband stays,
Who guards her, or with her the worst endures.
To whom the virgin[104] majesty of Eve,
As one who loves, and some unkindness meets,
With sweet austere composure thus replied.
Offspring of heaven and earth, and all earth's lord,
That such an enemy we have, who seeks
Our ruin, both by thee informed I learn,
And from the parting angel overheard
As in a shady nook I stood behind,
Just then returned at shut of evening flowers.
But that thou shouldst my firmness therefore doubt
To God or thee, because we have a foe
May tempt it, I expected not to hear.

[103] **Or this, or worse:** Whether [he intends] this or something worse.

[104] **virgin:** Innocent, without sin; with a suggestion of the unfallen or innocent sexuality of the wedded pair in Paradise.

His violence thou fear'st not, being such,
As we, not capable of death or pain,
Can either not receive, or can repel.
His fraud is then thy fear, which plain infers
Thy equal fear that my firm faith and love
Can by his fraud be shaken or seduced;
Thoughts, which how found they harbour in thy breast
Adam, misthought of her to thee so dear?
To whom with healing words Adam replied.
Daughter of God and man, immortal Eve,
For such thou art, from sin and blame entire:° blameless, untouched
Not diffident of thee do I dissuade
Thy absence from my sight, but to avoid
The attempt itself, intended by our foe.
For he who tempts, though in vain, at least asperses° spatters, falsely charges
The tempted with dishonour foul, supposed
Not incorruptible of faith, not proof
Against temptation: thou thyself with scorn
And anger wouldst resent the offered wrong,
Though ineffectual found: misdeem not then,
If such affront I labour to avert
From thee alone, which on us both at once
The enemy, though bold, will hardly dare,
Or daring, first on me the assault shall light.
Nor thou his malice and false guile contemn;
Subtle he needs must be, who could seduce
Angels, nor think superfluous others' aid.
I from the influence of thy looks receive
Access in every virtue, in thy sight
More wise, more watchful, stronger, if need were
Of outward strength; while shame, thou looking on,
Shame to be overcome or over-reached
Would utmost vigour raise, and raised unite.
Why shouldst not thou like sense within thee feel
When I am present, and thy trial choose
With me, best witness of thy virtue tried.
So spake domestic Adam in his care
And matrimonial love; but Eve, who thought
Less attributed to her faith sincere,
Thus her reply with accent sweet renewed.
If this be our condition, thus to dwell
In narrow circuit straitened by a foe,
Subtle or violent, we not endued° endowed
Single with like defence, wherever met,
How are we happy, still in fear of harm?

But harm precedes not sin: only our foe
Tempting affronts us with his foul esteem
Of our integrity: his foul esteem
Sticks no dishonour on our front,° but turns — brow, face
Foul on himself; then wherefore shunned or feared
By us? who rather double honour gain
From his surmise proved false, find peace within,
Favour from heaven, our witness from the event.
And what is faith, love, virtue unassayed
Alone, without exterior help sustained?[105]
Let us not then suspect our happy state
Left so imperfect by the maker wise,
As not secure to single or combined.
Frail is our happiness, if this be so,
And Eden were no Eden thus exposed.
To whom thus Adam fervently replied.
O woman, best are all things as the will
Of God ordained them, his creating hand
Nothing imperfect or deficient left
Of all that he created, much less man,
Or aught that might his happy state secure,
Secure from outward force; within himself
The danger lies, yet lies within his power:
Against his will he can receive no harm.
But God left free the will, for what obeys
Reason, is free, and reason he made right,
But bid her well beware, and still erect,° — ever aware, always alert
Lest by some fair-appearing good surprised
She dictate false, and misinform the will
To do what God expressly hath forbid.
Not then mistrust, but tender love enjoins,
That I should mind° thee oft, and mind thou me. — remind
Firm we subsist, yet possible to swerve,
Since reason not impossibly may meet
Some specious object by the foe suborned,[106]
And fall into deception unaware,
Not keeping strictest watch, as she was warned.
Seek not temptation then, which to avoid
Were better, and most likely if from me
Thou sever not: trial will come unsought.

[105] **without . . . sustained:** Eve's thoughts reflect Milton's belief that an untried virtue is not praiseworthy; see note 44.

[106] **Some . . . suborned:** Some deceptively alluring object secretly procured by the enemy (i.e., Satan).

Wouldst thou approve° thy constancy, approve — test
First thy obedience; the other who can know,
Not seeing thee attempted, who attest?
But if thou think, trial unsought may find
Us both securer° than thus warned thou seem'st, — less careful, overconfident
Go; for thy stay, not free, absents thee more;
Go in thy native innocence, rely
On what thou hast of virtue, summon all,
For God towards thee hath done his part, do thine.
So spake the patriarch of mankind, but Eve
Persisted, yet submiss, though last, replied.
With thy permission then, and thus forewarned
Chiefly by what thy own last reasoning words
Touched only, that our trial, when least sought,
May find us both perhaps far less prepared,
The willinger I go, nor much expect
A foe so proud will first the weaker seek;
So bent, the more shall shame him his repulse.
Thus saying, from her husband's hand her hand
Soft she withdrew, and like a wood-nymph light
Oread or dryad, or of Delia's train,[107]
Betook her to the groves, but Delia's self
In gait surpassed and goddess-like deport,
Though not as she with bow and quiver armed,
But with such gardening tools as art yet rude,
Guiltless of fire[108] had formed, or angels brought.
To Pales, or Pomona[109] thus adorned,
Likeliest she seemed, Pomona when she fled
Vertumnus, or to Ceres[110] in her prime,
Yet virgin of Proserpina from Jove.
Her long with ardent look his eye pursued
Delighted, but desiring more her stay.
Oft he to her his charge of quick return
Repeated, she to him as oft engaged
To be returned by noon amid the bower,

---

[107] **Delia's train:** Diana (Greek Artemis), the goddess of the hunt, who was born on the island of Delos; she is accompanied by a band ("train") of mountain and wood nymphs, the Oreads and dryads.

[108] **Guiltless of fire:** In Paradise before the fall, there is no need for fire, either for cooking or for making tools, as God has provided for all of Adam and Eve's needs.

[109] **Pales, or Pomona:** Pales was the goddess of husbandry and pastures; Pomona, of orchards.

[110] **Vertumnus . . . Ceres:** Vertumus, a nature god, pursued Pomona in various disguises before she finally married him. Ceres, the goddess of agriculture and grain, was the mother of Proserpina, fathered by Jove (Jupiter), the chief of gods.

And all things in best order to invite
Noontide repast, or afternoon's repose.
O much deceived, much failing, hapless Eve,
Of° thy presumed return! event perverse! about
Thou never from that hour in Paradise
Found'st either sweet repast, or sound repose;
Such ambush hid among sweet flowers and shades
Waited with hellish rancour imminent
To intercept thy way, or send thee back
Despoiled of innocence, of faith, of bliss.
For now, and since first break of dawn the fiend,
Mere serpent in appearance, forth was come,
And on his quest, where likeliest he might find
The only two of mankind, but in them
The whole included race, his purposed prey.
In bower and field he sought, where any tuft
Of grove or garden-plot more pleasant lay,
Their tendance or plantation for delight,[111]
By fountain or by shady rivulet
He sought them both, but wished his hap might find
Eve separate, he wished, but not with hope
Of what so seldom chanced, when to his wish,
Beyond his hope, Eve separate he spies,
Veiled in a cloud of fragrance, where she stood,
Half spied, so thick the roses bushing round
About her glowed, oft stooping to support
Each flower of slender stalk, whose head though gay
Carnation, purple, azure, or specked with gold,
Hung drooping unsustained, them she upstays
Gently with myrtle band, mindless the while,
Herself, though fairest unsupported flower,
From her best prop so far, and storm so nigh.
Nearer he drew, and many a walk traversed
Of stateliest covert, cedar, pine, or palm,
Then voluble° and bold, now hid, now seen rolling
Among thick-woven arborets and flowers
Embordered on each bank, the hand° of Eve: handiwork
Spot more delicious than those gardens feigned
Or of revived Adonis,[112] or renowned

[111] **more . . . delight:** That is, particularly any spot they had tended or planted for their delight.

[112] **Adonis:** A beautiful youth beloved by Venus (Greek Aphrodite), the goddess of love; when, somewhat like Eve, Adonis ignored Venus's pleas to stay by her side in their bower, Adonis was killed by a boar; from his blood sprung the red anemone flower. Venus persuaded Jove to revive Adonis for half the year. Beds of short-lived flowers were known as "gardens of Adonis."

Alcinous,[113] host of old Laertes' son,
Or that, not mystic, where the sapient king[114]
Held dalliance with his fair Egyptian spouse.
Much he the place admired, the person more.
As one who long in populous city pent,
Where houses thick and sewers annoy the air,
Forth issuing on a summer's morn to breathe
Among the pleasant villages and farms
Adjoined, from each thing met conceives delight,
The smell of grain, or tedded grass,[115] or kine,° cattle
Or dairy, each rural sight, each rural sound;
If chance with nymph-like step fair virgin pass,
What pleasing seemed, for° her now pleases more, because of
She most, and in her look sums all delight.
Such pleasure took the serpent to behold
This flowery plat,° the sweet recess° of Eve plot / pleasant retreat
Thus early, thus alone; her heavenly form
Angelic, but more soft, and feminine,
Her graceful innocence, her every air
Of gesture or least action overawed
His malice, and with rapine sweet bereaved
His fierceness of the fierce intent it brought:
That space the evil one abstracted stood
From his own evil,[116] and for the time remained
Stupidly good, of enmity disarmed,
Of guile, of hate, of envy, of revenge;
But the hot hell that always in him burns,
Though in mid-heaven, soon ended his delight,
And tortures him now more, the more he sees
Of pleasure not for him ordained: then soon
Fierce hate he recollects, and all his thoughts
Of mischief, gratulating, thus excites.
Thoughts, whither have ye led me, with what sweet
Compulsion thus transported to forget
What hither brought us, hate, not love, nor hope
Of Paradise for hell, hope here to taste
Of pleasure, but all pleasure to destroy,

[113] **Alcinous:** The king of the Phaeacians, described in Book Seven of Homer's *Odyssey,* who entertained Odysseus, Laertes' son; Homer describes his extraordinary gardens.

[114] **sapient king:** Solomon, who married the Pharaoh's daughter; his gardens are described in the Song of Solomon.

[115] **tedded grass:** Fresh-cut grass spread out to dry.

[116] **abstracted . . . evil:** Satan has been so moved by Eve's grace and beauty that he momentarily is separated or distracted from his evil intent.

Save what is in destroying, other joy
To me is lost. Then let me not let pass
Occasion which now smiles, behold alone
The woman, opportune° to all attempts,   open, vulnerable
Her husband, for I view far round, not nigh,
Whose higher intellectual more I shun,
And strength, of courage haughty, and of limb
Heroic built, though of terrestrial mould,
Foe not informidable, exempt from wound,
I not; so much hath hell debased, and pain
Enfeebled me, to what I was in heaven.
She fair, divinely fair, fit love for gods,
Not terrible, though terror be in love
And beauty, not approached by stronger hate,
Hate stronger, under show of love well feigned,
The way which to her ruin now I tend.
    So spake the enemy of mankind, enclosed
In serpent, inmate bad, and toward Eve
Addressed his way, not with indented wave,
Prone on the ground, as since, but on his rear,
Circular base of rising folds, that towered
Fold above fold a surging maze, his head
Crested aloft, and carbuncle° his eyes;   shining red
With burnished neck of verdant gold, erect
Amidst his circling spires, that on the grass
Floated redundant:° pleasing was his shape,   abundantly, in waves
And lovely, never since of serpent kind
Lovelier, not those that in Illyria changed
Hermione and Cadmus,[117] or the god
In Epidaurus;[118] nor to which transformed
Ammonian Jove, or Capitoline[119] was seen,
He with Olympias, this with her who bore
Scipio the height of Rome. With tract oblique
At first, as one who sought access, but feared
To interrupt, sidelong he works his way.
As when a ship by skilful steersman wrought

---

[117] **Hermione and Cadmus:** Ares, the god of war, changed the founder of Thebes Cadmus and his wife Hermione (Harmonia) into serpents and sent them to live in the Elysian Fields (see Ovid's *Metamorphoses,* Book IV).

[118] **the god / In Epidaurus:** Aesculepius, the god of healing, appeared at his shrine in Epidaurus as a fiery-eyed serpent.

[119] **Ammonian Jove, or Capitoline:** Two epithets applied to Jove (Greek Jupiter). In the form of a serpent, he fathered Alexander the Great, with Princess Olympias; in the same form, he was said to have fathered Scipio Africanus, the Roman hero who defeated Hannibal in the Punic Wars.

Nigh river's mouth or foreland, where the wind
Veers oft, as oft so steers, and shifts her sail;
So varied he, and of his tortuous train
Curled many a wanton wreath in sight of Eve,
To lure her eye; she busied heard the sound
Of rustling leaves, but minded not, as used
To such disport before her through the field,
From every beast, more duteous at her call,
Than at Circean call[120] the herd disguised.
He bolder now, uncalled before her stood;
But as in gaze admiring: oft he bowed
His turret crest, and sleek enamelled neck,
Fawning, and licked the ground whereon she trod.
His gentle dumb expression turned at length
The eye of Eve to mark his play; he glad
Of her attention gained, with serpent tongue
Organic, or impulse of vocal air,[121]
His fraudulent temptation thus began.
    Wonder not, sovereign mistress, if perhaps
Thou canst, who art sole wonder, much less arm
Thy looks, the heaven of mildness, with disdain,
Displeased that I approach thee thus, and gaze
Insatiate, I thus single, nor have feared
Thy awful brow, more awful thus retired.
Fairest resemblance of thy maker fair,
Thee all things living gaze on, all things thine
By gift, and thy celestial beauty adore
With ravishment beheld, there best beheld
Where universally admired; but here
In this enclosure wild, these beasts among,
Beholders rude, and shallow to discern
Half what in thee is fair, one man except,
Who sees thee? (and what is one?) who shouldst be seen
A goddess among gods, adored and served
By angels numberless, thy daily train.
    So glozed° the tempter, and his proem tuned; flattered
Into the heart of Eve his words made way,
Though at the voice much marvelling; at length

[120] **Circean call:** Circe, the sorceress who lived on the island of Aeaea, transformed some of Odysseus's men into beasts and tried to seduce Odysseus into remaining with her instead of returning to Ithaca (see *Odyssey,* Book Ten: 133–574).

[121] **Organic . . . air:** Since a serpent has no vocal cords, Satan must use his tongue as an instrument or organ of speech, or produce the appearance of speech by agitating the air.

Not unamazed she thus in answer spake.
What may this mean? Language of man pronounced
By tongue of brute, and human sense expressed?
The first at least of these I thought denied
To beasts, whom God on their creation-day
Created mute to all articulate sound;
The latter I demur,[122] for in their looks
Much reason, and in their actions oft appears.
Thee, serpent, subtlest beast of all the field
I knew, but not with human voice endued;
Redouble then this miracle, and say,
How cam'st thou speakable of mute, and how
To me so friendly grown above the rest
Of brutal kind, that daily are in sight?
Say, for such wonder claims attention due.
　　To whom the guileful tempter thus replied.
Empress of this fair world, resplendent Eve,
Easy to me it is to tell thee all
What thou command'st, and right thou shouldst be obeyed:
I was at first as other beasts that graze
The trodden herb, of abject thoughts and low,
As was my food, nor aught but food discerned
Or sex, and apprehended nothing high:
Till on a day roving the field, I chanced
A goodly tree far distant to behold
Loaden with fruit of fairest colours mixed,
Ruddy and gold: I nearer drew to gaze;
When from the boughs a savoury odour blown,
Grateful° to appetite, more pleased my sense　　pleasing
Than smell of sweetest fennel, or the teats
Of ewe or goat dropping with milk at even,
Unsucked of lamb or kid, that tend their play.
To satisfy the sharp desire I had
Of tasting those fair apples, I resolved
Not to defer; hunger and thirst at once,
Powerful persuaders, quickened at the scent
Of that alluring fruit, urged me so keen.
About the mossy trunk I wound me soon,
For high from ground the branches would require
Thy utmost reach or Adam's: round the tree

[122] **demur:** Doubt; Eve hesitates to believe that animals lack any sense and reason similar to that of human beings.

All other beasts that saw, with like desire
Longing and envying stood, but could not reach.
Amid the tree now got, where plenty hung
Tempting so nigh, to pluck and eat my fill
I spared not, for such pleasure till that hour
At feed or fountain never had I found.
Sated at length, ere long I might perceive
Strange alteration in me, to degree
Of reason in my inward powers, and speech
Wanted not long,[123] though to this shape retained.
Thenceforth to speculations high or deep
I turned my thoughts, and with capacious mind
Considered all things visible in heaven,
Or earth, or middle,° all things fair and good; the air
But all that fair and good in thy divine
Semblance, and in thy beauty's heavenly ray
United I beheld; no fair to thine
Equivalent or second, which compelled
Me thus, though importune perhaps, to come
And gaze, and worship thee of right declared
Sovereign of creatures, universal dame.
    So talked the spirited° sly snake; and Eve possessed, inspirited
Yet more amazed unwary thus replied.
    Serpent, thy overpraising leaves in doubt
The virtue of that fruit, in thee first proved:
But say, where grows the tree, from hence how far?
For many are the trees of God that grow
In Paradise, and various, yet unknown
To us, in such abundance lies our choice,
As leaves a greater store of fruit untouched,
Still hanging incorruptible, till men
Grow up to their provision, and more hands
Help to disburden nature of her birth.[124]
    To whom the wily adder, blithe and glad.
Empress, the way is ready, and not long,
Beyond a row of myrtles, on a flat,
Fast by a fountain, one small thicket past
Of blowing° myrrh and balm; if thou accept blooming
My conduct, I can bring thee thither soon.

---

[123] **Wanted not long:** Lacked not much longer; Satan, appearing before Eve as a serpent, tells Eve that he acquired reason and speech, though retaining his original shape.

[124] **birth:** Milton's original spelling is "bearth," to emphasize the produce of the earth.

Lead then, said Eve. He leading swiftly rolled
In tangles, and made intricate seem straight,
To mischief swift. Hope elevates, and joy
Brightens his crest, as when a wandering fire,
Compact of unctuous vapour, which the night
Condenses, and the cold environs round,
Kindled through agitation to a flame,
Which oft, they say, some evil spirit attends
Hovering and blazing with delusive light,
Misleads the amazed night-wanderer from his way
To bogs and mires, and oft through pond or pool,
There swallowed up and lost, from succour far.
So glistered the dire snake, and into fraud
Led Eve our credulous mother, to the tree
Of prohibition, root of all our woe;
Which when she saw, thus to her guide she spake.
Serpent, we might have spared our coming hither,
Fruitless to me, though fruit be here to excess,
The credit of whose virtue rest with thee,
Wondrous indeed, if cause of such effects.
But of this tree we may not taste nor touch;
God so commanded, and left that command
Sole daughter of his voice; the rest, we live
Law to our selves, our reason is our law.
To whom the tempter guilefully replied.
Indeed? hath God then said that of the fruit
Of all these garden trees ye shall not eat,
Yet lords declared of all in earth or air?
To whom thus Eve yet sinless. Of the fruit
Of each tree in the garden we may eat,
But of the fruit of this fair tree amidst
The garden, God hath said, Ye shall not eat
Thereof, nor shall ye touch it, lest ye die.
She scarce had said, though brief, when now more bold
The tempter, but with show of zeal and love
To man, and indignation at his wrong,
New part puts on, and as to passion moved,
Fluctuates disturbed, yet comely and in act
Raised, as of some great matter to begin.
As when of old some orator renowned
In Athens or free Rome, where eloquence
Flourished, since mute, to some great cause addressed,
Stood in himself collected, while each part,
Motion, each act won audience ere the tongue,
Sometimes in height began, as no delay

Of preface brooking through his zeal of right.[125]
So standing, moving, or to height upgrown
The tempter all impassioned thus began.
O sacred, wise, and wisdom-giving plant,
Mother of science,° now I feel thy power — knowledge
Within me clear, not only to discern
Things in their causes, but to trace the ways
Of highest agents, deemed however wise.
Queen of this universe, do not believe
Those rigid threats of death; ye shall not die:
How should ye? by the fruit? it gives you life
To knowledge: by the threatener? look on me,
Me who have touched and tasted, yet both live,
And life more perfect have attained than fate
Meant me, by venturing higher than my lot.
Shall that be shut to man, which to the beast
Is open? or will God incense his ire
For such a petty trespass, and not praise
Rather your dauntless virtue, whom the pain
Of death denounced,[126] whatever thing death be,
Deterred not from achieving what might lead
To happier life, knowledge of good and evil;
Of good, how just? of evil, if what is evil
Be real, why not known, since easier shunned?
God therefore cannot hurt ye, and be just;
Not just, not God; not feared then, nor obeyed:
Your fear itself of death removes the fear.
Why then was this forbid? Why but to awe,
Why but to keep ye low and ignorant,
His worshipper; he knows that in the day
Ye eat thereof, your eyes that seem so clear,
Yet are but dim, shall perfectly be then
Opened and cleared, and ye shall be as gods,
Knowing both good and evil as they know.
That ye should be as gods, since I as man,
Internal man, is but proportion meet,
I of brute human, ye of human gods.
So ye shall die perhaps, by putting off
Human, to put on gods, death to be wished,
Though threatened, which no worse than this can bring.
And what are gods that man may not become

---

[125] **Sometimes . . . right:** I.e., began at the critical part of his speech, being too impatient to begin with a preface.

[126] **the pain . . . denounced:** That is, under the pain of death, the announced punishment.

As they, participating godlike food?
The gods are first, and that advantage use
On our belief, that all from them proceeds;
I question it, for this fair earth I see,
Warmed by the sun, producing every kind,
Them nothing: if they, all things,[127] who enclosed
Knowledge of good and evil in this tree,
That whoso eats thereof, forthwith attains
Wisdom without their leave? and wherein lies
The offence, that man should thus attain to know?
What can your knowledge hurt him, or this tree
Impart against his will if all be his?
Or is it envy, and can envy dwell
In heavenly breasts? these, these and many more
Causes import your need of this fair fruit.
Goddess humane, reach then, and freely taste.
He ended, and his words replete with guile
Into her heart too easy entrance won:
Fixed on the fruit she gazed, which to behold
Might tempt alone, and in her ears the sound
Yet rung of his persuasive words, impregned
With reason, to her seeming, and with truth;
Meanwhile the hour of noon drew on, and waked
An eager appetite, raised by the smell
So savoury of that fruit, which with desire,
Inclinable° now grown to touch or taste, favorably inclined
Solicited her longing eye; yet first
Pausing a while, thus to her self she mused.
Great are thy virtues, doubtless, best of fruits,
Though kept from man, and worthy to be admired,
Whose taste, too long forborne, at first assay
Gave elocution to the mute, and taught
The tongue not made for speech to speak thy praise:
Thy praise he also who forbids thy use,
Conceals not from us, naming thee the tree
Of knowledge, knowledge both of good and evil;
Forbids us then to taste, but his forbidding
Commends thee more, while it infers the good
By thee communicated, and our want:
For good unknown, sure is not had, or had
And yet unknown, is as not had at all.
In plain then, what forbids he but to know,

[127] **if . . . things:** That is, if they produced all things.

Forbids us good, forbids us to be wise?
Such prohibitions bind not.[128] But if death
Bind us with after-bands, what profits then
Our inward freedom? In the day we eat
Of this fair fruit, our doom is, we shall die.
How dies the serpent? he hath eaten and lives,
And knows, and speaks, and reasons, and discerns,
Irrational till then. For us alone
Was death invented? or to us denied
This intellectual food, for beasts reserved?
For beasts it seems: yet that one beast which first
Hath tasted, envies not, but brings with joy
The good befallen him, author unsuspect,° reliable authority
Friendly to man, far from deceit or guile.
What fear I then, rather what know to fear
Under this ignorance of good and evil,
Of God or death, of law or penalty?
Here grows the cure of all, this fruit divine,
Fair to the eye, inviting to the taste,
Of virtue to make wise: what hinders then
To reach, and feed at once both body and mind?
So saying, her rash hand in evil hour
Forth reaching to the fruit, she plucked, she ate:
Earth felt the wound, and nature from her seat
Sighing through all her works gave signs of woe,
That all was lost. Back to the thicket slunk
The guilty serpent, and well might, for Eve
Intent now wholly on her taste, naught else
Regarded, such delight till then, as seemed,
In fruit she never tasted, whether true
Or fancied so, through expectation high
Of knowledge, nor was godhead from her thought.
Greedily she engorged without restraint,
And knew not eating death: satiate at length,
And heightened as with wine, jocund and boon,
Thus to herself she pleasingly began.
O sovereign, virtuous, precious of all trees
In Paradise, of operation blessed
To sapience,[129] hitherto obscured, infamed,° slandered

[128] **prohibitions bind not:** Following Satan's example and anticipating the sophistry of Adam's later rationalization to eat the fruit, Eve argues that because God's prohibition prevents them from acquiring wisdom, it must be void. She also claims that in order to know the good of the tree, it must be tasted; otherwise it is for naught.
[129] **blessed . . . To sapience:** Endowed with the power to give knowledge.

And thy fair fruit let hang, as to no end
Created; but henceforth my early care,
Not without song, each morning, and due praise
Shall tend thee, and the fertile burden ease
Of thy full branches offered free to all;
Till dieted by thee I grow mature
In knowledge, as the gods who all things know;
Though others envy what they cannot give;
For had the gift been theirs, it had not here
Thus grown. Experience, next to thee I owe,
Best guide; not following thee, I had remained
In ignorance, thou open'st wisdom's way,
And giv'st access, though secret she retire.
And I perhaps am secret; heaven is high,
High and remote to see from thence distinct
Each thing on earth; and other care perhaps
May have diverted from continual watch
Our great forbidder, safe with all his spies
About him. But to Adam in what sort
Shall I appear?[130] shall I to him make known
As yet my change, and give him to partake
Full happiness with me, or rather not,
But keep the odds of knowledge in my power
Without copartner? so to add what wants
In female sex, the more to draw his love,
And render me more equal, and perhaps,
A thing not undesirable, sometime
Superior; for inferior who is free?
This may be well: but what if God have seen,
And death ensue? then I shall be no more,
And Adam wedded to another Eve,
Shall live with her enjoying, I extinct;
A death to think. Confirmed then I resolve,
Adam shall share with me in bliss or woe:
So dear I love him, that with him all deaths
I could endure, without him live no life.
  So saying, from the tree her step she turned,
But first low reverence done, as to the power
That dwelt within, whose presence had infused
Into the plant sciential° sap, derived

knowledge-giving

[130] **in . . . appear:** Eve's unbecoming speech is filled with self-deceptive sophistry as well as guile. She moves from pride, imagining that she might use her new knowledge to set herself above Adam; to jealousy, imagining Adam with another Eve; to selfish love, deciding that Adam should join her in death.

From nectar, drink of gods. Adam the while
Waiting desirous her return, had wove
Of choicest flowers a garland to adorn
Her tresses, and her rural labours crown,
As reapers oft are wont their harvest queen.
Great joy he promised to his thoughts, and new
Solace in her return, so long delayed;
Yet oft his heart, divine of° something ill, — divining, prescient of
Misgave him; he the faltering measure[131] felt;
And forth to meet her went, the way she took
That morn when first they parted; by the tree
Of knowledge he must pass, there he her met,
Scarce from the tree returning; in her hand
A bough of fairest fruit that downy smiled,
New gathered, and ambrosial smell diffused.
To him she hasted, in her face excuse
Came prologue, and apology to prompt,[132]
Which with bland words at will she thus addressed.
Hast thou not wondered, Adam, at my stay?
Thee I have missed, and thought it long, deprived
Thy presence, agony of love till now
Not felt, nor shall be twice, for never more
Mean I to try, what rash untried I sought,
The pain of absence from thy sight. But strange
Hath been the cause, and wonderful to hear:
This tree is not as we are told, a tree
Of danger tasted,° nor to evil unknown — when tasted
Opening the way, but of divine effect
To open eyes, and make them gods who taste;
And hath been tasted such: the serpent wise,
Or not restrained as we, or not obeying,
Hath eaten of the fruit, and is become,
Not dead, as we are threatened, but thenceforth
Endued with human voice and human sense,
Reasoning to admiration, and with me
Persuasively hath so prevailed, that I
Have also tasted, and have also found
The effects to correspond, opener mine eyes,
Dim erst, dilated spirits, ampler heart,

[131] **faltering measure:** The irregular beating of his heart. Adam feels as well as foresees that something is wrong for the first time.

[132] **in . . . prompt:** The expression on Eve's face serves as an introduction, and as an actor's prompt, to her apology, here meaning a justification of her actions, not regret for them.

And growing up to godhead; which for thee
Chiefly I sought, without thee can despise.
For bliss, as thou hast part, to me is bliss,
Tedious, unshared with thee, and odious soon.
Thou therefore also taste, that equal lot
May join us, equal joy, as equal love;
Lest thou not tasting, different degree
Disjoin us, and I then too late renounce
Deity for thee, when fate will not permit.
    Thus Eve with countenance blithe her story told;
But in her cheek distemper° flushing glowed. — disorder, imbalance of spirit
On the other side, Adam, soon as he heard
The fatal trespass done by Eve, amazed,
Astonied° stood and blank, while horror chill — astonished, shocked
Ran through his veins, and all his joints relaxed;
From his slack hand the garland wreathed for Eve
Down dropped, and all the faded roses shed:
Speechless he stood and pale, till thus at length
First to himself he inward silence broke.
    O fairest of creation, last and best
Of all God's works, creature in whom excelled
Whatever can to sight or thought be formed,
Holy, divine, good, amiable or sweet!
How art thou lost, how on a sudden lost,
Defaced, deflowered, and now to death devote?
Rather how hast thou yielded to transgress
The strict forbiddance, how to violate
The sacred fruit forbidden! some cursed fraud
Of enemy hath beguiled thee, yet unknown,
And me with thee hath ruined, for with thee
Certain my resolution is to die;
How can I live without thee, how forgo
Thy sweet converse and love so dearly joined,
To live again in these wild woods forlorn?
Should God create another Eve, and I
Another rib afford, yet loss of thee
Would never from my heart; no no, I feel
The link of nature draw me: flesh of flesh,
Bone of my bone thou art, and from thy state
Mine never shall be parted, bliss or woe.
    So having said, as one from sad dismay
Recomforted, and after thoughts disturbed
Submitting to what seemed remediless,
Thus in calm mood his words to Eve he turned.
    Bold deed thou hast presumed, adventurous Eve,

And peril great provoked, who thus hath dared
Had it been only coveting to eye
That sacred fruit, sacred to abstinence,
Much more to taste it under ban to touch.
But past who can recall, or done undo?
Not God omnipotent, nor fate, yet so
Perhaps thou shalt not die, perhaps the fact
Is not so heinous now, foretasted fruit,
Profaned first by the serpent, by him first
Made common and unhallowed ere our taste;
Nor yet on him found deadly, he yet lives,
Lives, as thou saidst, and gains to live as man
Higher degree of life, inducement strong
To us, as likely tasting to attain
Proportional ascent, which cannot be
But to be gods, or angels demigods.
Nor can I think that God, creator wise,
Though threatening, will in earnest so destroy
Us his prime creatures, dignified so high,
Set over all his works, which in our fall,
For us created, needs with us must fail,
Dependent made; so God shall uncreate,
Be frustrate, do, undo, and labour lose,
Not well conceived of God, who though his power
Creation could repeat, yet would be loath
Us to abolish, lest the adversary
Triumph and say, Fickle their state whom God
Most favours, who can please him long; me first
He ruined, now mankind; whom will he next?
Matter of scorn, not to be given the foe,
However I with thee have fixed my lot,
Certain° to undergo like doom, if death resolved
Consort with thee, death is to me as life;
So forcible within my heart I feel
The bond of nature draw me to my own,
My own in thee, for what thou art is mine;
Our state cannot be severed, we are one,
One flesh; to lose thee were to lose my self.
So Adam, and thus Eve to him replied.
O glorious trial of exceeding love,
Illustrious evidence, example high!
Engaging me to emulate, but short
Of thy perfection, how shall I attain,
Adam, from whose dear side I boast me sprung,
And gladly of our union hear thee speak,

One heart, one soul in both; whereof good proof
This day affords, declaring thee resolved,
Rather than death or aught than death more dread
Shall separate us, linked in love so dear,
To undergo with me one guilt, one crime,
If any be, of tasting this fair fruit,
Whose virtue, for of good still good proceeds,
Direct, or by occasion hath presented
This happy trial of thy love, which else
So eminently never had been known.
Were it I thought death menaced would ensue
This my attempt, I would sustain alone
The worst, and not persuade thee rather die
Deserted, than oblige thee with a fact[133]
Pernicious to thy peace, chiefly assured
Remarkably so late of thy so true,
So faithful love unequalled; but I feel
Far otherwise the event,[134] not death, but life
Augmented, opened eyes, new hopes, new joys,
Taste so divine, that what of sweet before
Hath touched my sense, flat seems to this, and harsh.
On my experience, Adam, freely taste,
And fear of death deliver to the winds.
    So saying, she embraced him, and for joy
Tenderly wept, much won that he his love
Had so ennobled, as of choice to incur
Divine displeasure for her sake, or death.
In recompense (for such compliance bad
Such recompense best merits) from the bough
She gave him of that fair enticing fruit
With liberal hand: he scrupled not to eat
Against his better knowledge, not deceived,[135]
But fondly overcome with female charm.
Earth trembled from her entrails, as again
In pangs, and nature gave a second groan,
Sky loured and muttering thunder, some sad drops
Wept at completing of the mortal sin
Original; while Adam took no thought,

---

[133] **oblige . . . fact:** Make you liable to an act (i.e., a punishment).

[134] **event:** Eventuality (i.e., the consequences, outcome).

[135] **not deceived:** In contrast to Eve, who was deceived by Satan, Adam transgresses God's law fully aware that he is doing wrong and, despite his casuistic reasoning, in full knowledge that there will be consequences to his action.

Eating his fill, nor Eve to iterate
Her former trespass feared, the more to soothe
Him with her loved society, that now
As with new wine intoxicated both
They swim in mirth, and fancy that they feel
Divinity within them breeding wings
Wherewith to scorn the earth: but that false fruit
Far other operation first displayed,
Carnal desire inflaming, he on Eve
Began to cast lascivious eyes, she him
As wantonly repaid; in lust they burn:
Till Adam thus gan Eve to dalliance move.

Eve, now I see thou art exact of taste,
And elegant, of sapience no small part,
Since to each meaning savour we apply,
And palate call judicious; I the praise
Yield thee, so well this day thou hast purveyed.
Much pleasure we have lost, while we abstained
From this delightful fruit, nor known till now
True relish, tasting; if such pleasure be
In things to us forbidden, it might be wished,
For this one tree had been forbidden ten.
But come, so well refreshed, now let us play,
As meet is, after such delicious fare;
For never did thy beauty since the day
I saw thee first and wedded thee, adorned
With all perfections, so inflame my sense
With ardour to enjoy thee, fairer now
Than ever, bounty of this virtuous tree.

So said he, and forbore not glance or toy°
caress
Of amorous intent, well understood
Of Eve, whose eye darted contagious fire.
Her hand he seized, and to a shady bank,
Thick overhead with verdant roof embowered
He led her nothing loath; flowers were the couch,
Pansies, and violets, and asphodel,
And hyacinth, earth's freshest softest lap.
There they their fill of love and love's disport
Took largely, of their mutual guilt the seal,
The solace of their sin, till dewy sleep
Oppressed them, wearied with their amorous play.
Soon as the force of that fallacious fruit,
That with exhilarating vapour bland

About their spirits had played, and inmost powers
Made err, was now exhaled, and grosser sleep
Bred of unkindly fumes, with conscious dreams
Encumbered, now had left them, up they rose
As from unrest, and each the other viewing,
Soon found their eyes how opened, and their minds
How darkened; innocence, that as a veil
Had shadowed them from knowing ill, was gone,
Just confidence, and native righteousness
And honour from about them, naked left
To guilty shame he covered, but his robe
Uncovered more, so rose the Danite strong[136]
Herculean Samson from the harlot-lap
Of Philistean Dalilah, and waked
Shorn of his strength, they destitute and bare
Of all their virtue: silent, and in face
Confounded long they sat, as stricken mute,
Till Adam, though not less than Eve abashed,
At length gave utterance to these words constrained.
O Eve, in evil hour thou didst give ear
To that false worm, of whomsoever taught
To counterfeit man's voice, true in our fall,
False in our promised rising; since our eyes
Opened we find indeed, and find we know
Both good and evil, good lost, and evil got,
Bad fruit of knowledge, if this be to know,
Which leaves us naked thus, of honour void,
Of innocence, of faith, of purity,
Our wonted ornaments now soiled and stained,
And in our faces evident the signs
Of foul concupiscence; whence evil store;° abundance of evil
Even shame, the last of evils; of the first
Be sure then. How shall I behold the face
Henceforth of God or angel, erst with joy
And rapture so oft beheld? those heavenly shapes
Will dazzle now this earthly, with their blaze
Insufferably bright. O might I here
In solitude live savage, in some glade
Obscured, where highest woods impenetrable
To star or sunlight, spread their umbrage broad
And brown as evening: cover me ye pines,

[136] **Danite strong:** Samson, from the tribe of Dan, who awoke from sleep after having been betrayed by his lover Dalilah, a Philistine, who deprived him of his strength by cutting off his hair. See Judges 16:4–20.

Ye cedars, with innumerable boughs
Hide me, where I may never see them more.
But let us now, as in bad plight, devise
What best may for the present serve to hide
The parts of each from other, that seem most
To shame obnoxious, and unseemliest seen,
Some tree whose broad smooth leaves together sewed,
And girded on our loins, may cover round
Those middle parts, that this newcomer, shame,
There sit not, and reproach us as unclean.
So counselled he, and both together went
Into the thickest wood, there soon they chose
The fig-tree, not that kind for fruit renowned,
But such as at this day to Indians known
In Malabar or Deccan[137] spreads her arms
Branching so broad and long, that in the ground
The bended twigs take root, and daughters grow
About the mother tree, a pillared shade
High overarched, and echoing walks between;
There oft the Indian herdsman shunning heat
Shelters in cool, and tends his pasturing herds
At loopholes cut through thickest shade: those leaves
They gathered, broad as Amazonian targe,[138]
And with what skill they had, together sewed,
To gird their waist, vain covering if to hide
Their guilt and dreaded shame; O how unlike
To that first naked glory. Such of late
Columbus found the American so girt
With feathered cincture,[139] naked else and wild
Among the trees on isles and woody shores.
Thus fenced, and as they thought, their shame in part
Covered, but not at rest or ease of mind,
They sat them down to weep, nor only tears
Rained at their eyes, but high winds worse within
Began to rise, high passions, anger, hate,
Mistrust, suspicion, discord, and shook sore
Their inward state of mind, calm region once
And full of peace, now tossed and turbulent:

[137] **Malabar or Deccan:** That is, India. The "fig-tree" described by Milton is the banyan tree, though it has small leaves rather than broad ones.

[138] **Amazonian targe:** The shields of Amazons, legendary women warriors who fought against Athens.

[139] **feathered cincture:** Feathered belts. Christopher Columbus described the Taino, the "Americans," in his *Diario* (see p. 773).

For understanding ruled not, and the will
Heard not her lore, both in subjection now
To sensual appetite, who from beneath
Usurping over sovereign reason claimed
Superior sway:[140] from thus distempered breast,
Adam, estranged in look and altered style,
Speech intermitted thus to Eve renewed.
    Would thou hadst hearkened to my words, and stayed
With me, as I besought thee, when that strange
Desire of wandering this unhappy morn,
I know not whence possessed thee; we had then
Remained still happy, not as now, despoiled
Of all our good, shamed, naked, miserable.
Let none henceforth seek needless cause to approve° test
The faith they owe;[141] when earnestly they seek
Such proof, conclude, they then begin to fail.
    To whom soon moved with touch of blame thus Eve.
What words have passed thy lips, Adam severe,
Imput'st thou that to my default, or will
Of wandering, as thou call'st it, which who knows
But might as ill have happened thou being by,
Or to thy self perhaps: hadst thou been there,
Or here the attempt, thou couldst not have discerned
Fraud in the serpent, speaking as he spake;
No ground of enmity between us known,
Why he should mean me ill, or seek to harm.
Was I to have never parted from thy side?
As good have grown there still a lifeless rib.
Being as I am, why didst not thou the head
Command me absolutely not to go,
Going into such danger as thou saidst?
Too facile[142] then thou didst not much gainsay,
Nay didst permit, approve, and fair dismiss.
Hadst thou been firm and fixed in thy dissent,
Neither had I transgressed, nor thou with me.
    To whom then first incensed Adam replied,
Is this the love, is this the recompense
Of mine to thee, ingrateful Eve, expressed
Immutable[143] when thou wert lost, not I,

[140] **Superior sway:** That is, sensual appetite has subordinated reason, will, and understanding.

[141] **The . . . owe:** Both the faith they own and the faith they must give.

[142] **Too facile:** Too easily persuaded. Eve now casts the blame on Adam.

[143] **expressed . . . Immutable:** Shown to be or declared to be enduring, permanent.

Who might have lived and joyed immortal bliss,
Yet willingly chose rather death with thee:
And am I now upbraided, as the cause
Of thy transgressing? not enough severe,
It seems, in thy restraint: what could I more?
I warned thee, I admonished thee, foretold
The danger, and the lurking enemy
That lay in wait; beyond this had been force,
And force upon free will hath here no place.
But confidence then bore thee on, secure
Either to meet no danger, or to find
Matter of glorious trial; and perhaps
I also erred in overmuch admiring
What seemed in thee so perfect, that I thought
No evil durst attempt thee, but I rue
That error now, which is become my crime,
And thou the accuser. Thus it shall befall
Him who to worth in women overtrusting
Lets her will rule; restraint she will not brook,
And left to herself, if evil thence ensue,
She first his weak indulgence will accuse.
    Thus they in mutual accusation spent
The fruitless hours, but neither self-condemning,
And of their vain contest appeared no end.

Book X
[Recrimination and Reconciliation of Adam and Eve]
The Argument

Man's transgression known, the guardian angels forsake Paradise, and return up to heaven to approve their vigilance, and are approved, God declaring that the entrance of Satan could not be by them prevented. He sends his son to judge the transgressors, who descends and gives sentence accordingly; then in pity clothes them both, and re-ascends. Sin and Death sitting till then at the gates of hell, by wondrous sympathy feeling the success of Satan in this new world, and the sin by man there committed, resolve to sit no longer confined in hell, but to follow Satan their sire up to the place of man: to make the way easier from hell to this world to and fro, they pave a broad highway or bridge over Chaos, according to the track that Satan first made; then preparing for earth, they meet him proud of his success returning to hell; their mutual gratulation. Satan arrives at Pandemonium, in full assembly relates with boasting his success against man; instead of applause is entertained with a general hiss by all his audience, transformed with himself also suddenly into serpents, according to his doom given in Paradise; then deluded with a show of the forbidden tree springing up before them, they greedily reaching to take of the fruit, chew dust and bitter ashes. The proceedings of Sin and Death; God foretells the final victory of his son over them, and the renewing of all things; but for the present commands his angels to make several alterations in the heavens and elements. Adam more and more perceiving his fallen condition heavily bewails, rejects the condolement of Eve; she persists and at length appeases him: then to evade the curse likely to fall on their offspring, proposes to Adam violent ways which he approves not, but conceiving better hope, puts her in mind of the late promise made them, that her seed should be revenged on the serpent, and exhorts her with him to seek peace of the offended Deity, by repentance and supplication.

[. . .] [T]hus began[144]
Outrage from lifeless things; but Discord first
Daughter of Sin, among the irrational,
Death introduced through fierce antipathy:
Beast now with beast gan war, and fowl with fowl,
And fish with fish; to graze the herb all leaving,
Devoured each other; nor stood much in awe
Of man but fled him, or with countenance grim
Glared on him passing: these were from without
The growing miseries, which Adam saw
Already in part, though hid in gloomiest shade,
To sorrow abandoned, but worse felt within,
And in a troubled sea of passion tossed,
Thus to disburden sought with sad complaint.
O miserable of happy! is this the end
Of this new glorious world, and me so late
The glory of that glory, who now become
Accursed of blessed, hide me from the face
Of God, whom to behold was then my height
Of happiness: yet well, if here would end
The misery, I deserved it, and would bear
My own deservings; but this will not serve;
All that I eat or drink, or shall beget,
Is propagated curse.[145] O voice once heard
Delightfully, *Increase and multiply*,[146]
Now death to hear! for what can I increase
Or multiply, but curses on my head?
Who of all ages to succeed, but feeling

[144] **Thus began:** The narrator here recounts some of the consequences of the fall, briefly interrupting Adam's lamentation, which he takes up again at line 720.

[145] **propagated curse:** Sustained curse. Whatever Adam does to sustain his life and to have children only extends and distributes the curse he has brought down upon himself and his progeny.

[146] ***Increase and multiply:*** Genesis 1:28: "And God blessed them, and God said unto them, Be fruitful, and multiply, and replenish the earth and subdue it."

The evil on him brought by me, will curse
My head, Ill fare our ancestor impure,
For this we may thank Adam; but his thanks
Shall be the execration; so besides
Mine own that bide upon me, all from me
Shall with a fierce reflux on me redound,
On me as on their natural centre light
Heavy, though in their place. O fleeting joys
Of Paradise, dear bought with lasting woes!
Did I request thee, maker, from my clay
To mould me man, did I solicit thee
From darkness to promote me, or here place
In this delicious garden? as my will
Concurred not to my being, it were but right
And equal° to reduce me to my dust, just, fair
Desirous to resign, and render back
All I received, unable to perform
Thy terms too hard, by which I was to hold
The good I sought not. To the loss of that,
Sufficient penalty, why hast thou added
The sense of endless woes? inexplicable
Thy justice seems; yet to say truth, too late,
I thus contest; then should have been refused
Those terms whatever, when they were proposed:
Thou[147] didst accept them; wilt thou enjoy the good,
Then cavil the conditions? and though God
Made thee without thy leave, what if thy son
Prove disobedient, and reproved, retort,
Wherefore didst thou beget me? I sought it not:
Wouldst thou admit for his contempt of thee
That proud excuse? yet him not thy election,° choice
But natural necessity begot.
God made thee of choice his own, and of his own
To serve him, thy reward was of his grace,
Thy punishment then justly is at his will.
Be it so, for I submit, his doom° is fair, God's justice
That dust I am, and shall to dust return:
O welcome hour whenever! why delays
His hand to execute what his decree
Fixed on this day? why do I overlive,
Why am I mocked with death, and lengthened out

[147] **Thou:** Adam addresses himself here in the second person, arguing that if he accepted the good portions of God's provisions, he should not quibble ("cavil") about the conditions.

To deathless pain? how gladly would I meet
Mortality my sentence, and be earth
Insensible, how glad would lay me down
As in my mother's lap? there I should rest
And sleep secure; his dreadful voice no more
Would thunder in my ears, no fear of worse
To me and to my offspring would torment me
With cruel expectation. Yet one doubt
Pursues me still, lest all I cannot die,[148]
Lest that pure breath of life, the spirit of man
Which God inspired, cannot together perish
With this corporeal clod; then in the grave,
Or in some other dismal place who knows
But I shall die a living death? O thought
Horrid, if true! yet why? it was but breath
Of life that sinned; what dies but what had life
And sin? the body properly hath neither.
All of me then shall die: let this appease
The doubt, since human reach no further knows.
For though the Lord of all be infinite,
Is his wrath also? be it, man is not so,
But mortal doomed. How can he exercise
Wrath without end on man whom death must end?
Can he make deathless death? that were to make
Strange contradiction, which to God himself
Impossible is held, as argument
Of weakness, not of power. Will he draw out,
For anger's sake, finite to infinite
In punished man, to satisfy his rigour
Satisfied never; that were to extend
His sentence beyond dust and nature's law,
By which all causes else according still
To the reception of their matter act,
Not to the extent of their own sphere.[149] But say
That death be not one stroke, as I supposed,
Bereaving sense, but endless misery
From this day onward, which I feel begun

[148] **lest . . . die:** All of me. Adam fears that the spirit will live on in the dead body. He goes on to propose two other possibilities: that "All of me . . . will die" (l. 92)—that is, both body and soul will die at death—and that death is "but endless misery" (l. 180).

[149] **extent . . . sphere:** Adam has been arguing that infinite punishment is impossible, because by "nature's law" the finite body, once dead, would be out of the reach of punishment. Merrit Hughes cites Newton as a clear explanation of this axiom, which ultimately goes back to Aristotle: "Every efficient [cause] acts according to the powers of what receives its action, not according to its own powers" (*John Milton*, 1957).

Both in me, and without me, and so last
To perpetuity; ay me, that fear
Comes thundering back with dreadful revolution
On my defenceless head; both death and I
Am found eternal, and incorporate both,[150]
Nor I on my part single, in me all
Posterity stands cursed: fair patrimony
That I must leave ye, sons; O were I able
To waste it all my self, and leave ye none!
So disinherited how would ye bless
Me now your curse! Ah, why should all mankind
For one man's fault thus guiltless be condemned,
If guiltless? But from me what can proceed,
But all corrupt, both mind and will depraved,
Not to do only, but to will the same
With me? how can they then acquitted stand
In sight of God? Him after all disputes
Forced I absolve: all my evasions vain,
And reasonings, though through mazes, lead me still
But to my own conviction:[151] first and last
On me, me only, as the source and spring
Of all corruption, all the blame lights due;
So might the wrath. Fond wish! couldst thou support
That burden heavier than the earth to bear,
Than all the world much heavier, though divided
With that bad woman? Thus what thou desir'st
And what thou fear'st, alike destroys all hope
Of refuge, and concludes thee miserable
Beyond all past example and future,
To Satan only like both crime and doom.
O conscience, into what abyss of fears
And horrors hast thou driven me; out of which
I find no way, from deep to deeper plunged!
    Thus Adam to himself lamented loud
Through the still night, not now, as ere man fell,
Wholesome and cool, and mild, but with black air
Accompanied, with damps and dreadful gloom,
Which to his evil conscience represented
All things with double terror: on the ground

[150] **incorporate both:** Adam now embodies death, so death and Adam are united in one body.

[151] **my own conviction:** According to the principles of Milton's *De Doctrina Christiana,* by acknowledging his guilt Adam is taking the first step toward redemption: "Conviction of sin, contrition, confession, departure from evil and conversation to good" are the four steps of regeneration.

Outstretched he lay, on the cold ground, and oft
Cursed his creation, death as oft accused
Of tardy execution, since denounced
The day of his offence. Why comes not death,
Said he, with one thrice acceptable stroke
To end me? Shall truth fail to keep her word,
Justice divine not hasten to be just?
But death comes not at call, justice divine
Mends not her slowest pace for prayers or cries.
O woods, O fountains, hillocks, dales and bowers,
With other echo late I taught your shades
To answer, and resound far other song.
Whom thus afflicted when sad Eve beheld,
Desolate where she sat, approaching nigh
Soft words to his fierce passion she assayed:
But her with stern regard he thus repelled.
    Out of my sight, thou serpent, that name best
Befits thee with him leagued, thyself as false
And hateful; nothing wants, but that thy shape,
Like his, and colour serpentine may show
Thy inward fraud, to warn all creatures from thee
Henceforth; lest that too heavenly form, pretended
To[152] hellish falsehood, snare them. But for thee
I had persisted happy, had not thy pride
And wand'ring vanity, when least was safe,
Rejected my forewarning, and disdained
Not to be trusted, longing to be seen
Though by the devil himself, him overweening
To over-reach,[153] but with the serpent meeting
Fooled and beguiled, by him thou, I by thee,
To trust thee from my side, imagined wise,
Constant, mature, proof against all assaults,
And understood not all was but a show
Rather than solid virtue, all but a rib
Crooked by nature, bent, as now appears,
More to the part sinister[154] from me drawn,
Well if thrown out, as supernumerary
To my just number found. O why did God,
Creator wise, that peopled highest heaven
With spirits masculine, create at last

[152] **pretended . . . To:** Held out as a screen.

[153] **him . . . over-reach:** Having an exaggerated sense that you could outsmart Satan.

[154] **sinister:** Literally, on the left side, but with the ominous overtones.

This novelty on earth, this fair defect
Of nature, and not fill the world at once
With men as angels without feminine,
Or find some other way to generate
Mankind? this mischief had not then befallen,
And more that shall befall, innumerable
Disturbances on earth through female snares,
And strait conjunction with this sex: for either
He never shall find out fit mate, but such
As some misfortune brings him, or mistake,
Or whom he wishes most shall seldom gain
Through her perverseness, but shall see her gained
By a far worse, or if she love, withheld
By parents, or his happiest choice too late
Shall meet, already linked and wedlock-bound
To a fell adversary, his hate or shame:
Which infinite calamity shall cause
To human life, and household peace confound.
He added not, and from her turned, but Eve
Not so repulsed, with tears that ceased not flowing,
And tresses all disordered, at his feet
Fell humble, and embracing them, besought
His peace, and thus proceeded in her plaint.
Forsake me not thus, Adam, witness heaven
What love sincere, and reverence in my heart
I bear thee, and unweeting have offended,
Unhappily deceived; thy suppliant
I beg, and clasp thy knees; bereave me not,
Whereon I live, thy gentle looks, thy aid,
Thy counsel in this uttermost distress,
My only strength and stay: forlorn of thee,
Whither shall I betake me, where subsist?
While yet we live, scarce one short hour perhaps,
Between us two let there be peace, both joining,
As joined in injuries, one enmity
Against a foe by doom express assigned us,
That cruel serpent: on me exercise not
Thy hatred for this misery befallen,
On me already lost, me than thyself
More miserable; both have sinned, but thou
Against God only, I against God and thee,
And to the place of judgment will return,
There with my cries importune heaven, that all
The sentence from thy head removed may light
On me, sole cause to thee of all this woe,

Me me only just object of his ire.
    She ended weeping, and her lowly plight,
Immovable till peace obtained from fault
Acknowledged and deplored, in Adam wrought
Commiseration; soon his heart relented
Towards her, his life so late and sole delight,
Now at his feet submissive in distress,
Creature so fair his reconcilement seeking,
His counsel whom she had displeased, his aid;
As one disarmed, his anger all he lost,
And thus with peaceful words upraised her soon.
    Unwary, and too desirous, as before,
So now of what thou know'st not, who desir'st
The punishment all on thyself; alas,
Bear thine own first, ill able to sustain
His full wrath whose thou feel'st as yet least part,
And my displeasure bear'st so ill. If prayers
Could alter high decrees, I to that place
Would speed before thee, and be louder heard,
That on my head all might be visited,
Thy frailty and infirmer sex forgiven,
To me committed and by me exposed.
But rise, let us no more contend, nor blame
Each other, blamed enough elsewhere, but strive
In offices of love, how we may lighten
Each other's burden in our share of woe;
Since this day's death denounced, if aught I see,
Will prove no sudden, but a slow-paced evil,
A long day's dying to augment our pain,
And to our seed (O hapless seed!) derived.° handed down
    To whom thus Eve, recovering heart, replied.
Adam, by sad experiment I know
How little weight my words with thee can find,
Found so erroneous, thence by just event
Found so unfortunate; nevertheless,
Restored by thee, vile as I am, to place
Of new acceptance, hopeful to regain
Thy love, the sole contentment of my heart
Living or dying, from thee I will not hide
What thoughts in my unquiet breast are risen,
Tending to some relief of our extremes,
Or end, though sharp and sad, yet tolerable
As in our evils,[155] and of easier choice.

[155] **As in our evils:** In our evils (i.e., in such evil conditions).

If care of our descent perplex us most,
Which must be born to certain woe, devoured
By death at last, and miserable it is
To be to others cause of misery,
Our own begotten, and of our loins to bring
Into this cursèd world a woeful race,
That after wretched life must be at last
Food for so foul a monster, in thy power
It lies, yet ere conception to prevent
The race unblest, to being yet unbegot.
Childless thou art, childless remain: so death
Shall be deceived his glut, and with us two
Be forced to satisfy his ravenous maw.
But if thou judge it hard and difficult,
Conversing, looking, loving, to abstain
From love's due rights, nuptial embraces sweet,
And with desire to languish without hope,
Before the present object languishing
With like desire, which would be misery
And torment less than none of what we dread,
Then both ourselves and seed at once to free
From what we fear for both, let us make short,
Let us seek death, or he not found, supply
With our own hands his office on ourselves;
Why stand we longer shivering under fears,
That show no end but death, and have the power,
Of many ways to die the shortest choosing,
Destruction with destruction to destroy.
    She ended here, or vehement despair
Broke off the rest; so much of death her thoughts
Had entertained, as dyed her cheeks with pale.
But Adam with such counsel nothing swayed,
To better hopes his more attentive mind
Labouring had raised, and thus to Eve replied.
    Eve, thy contempt of life and pleasures seems
To argue in thee something more sublime
And excellent than what thy mind contemns;
But self-destruction therefore sought, refutes
That excellence thought in thee, and implies,
Not thy contempt, but anguish and regret
For loss of life and pleasure overloved.
Or if thou covet death, as utmost end
Of misery, so thinking to evade
The penalty pronounced, doubt not but God
Hath wiselier armed his vengeful ire than so
To be forestalled; much more I fear lest death

So snatched will not exempt us from the pain
We are by doom to pay; rather such acts
Of contumacy° will provoke the highest — disobedience
To make death in us live: then let us seek
Some safer resolution, which methinks
I have in view, calling to mind with heed
Part of our sentence, that thy seed shall bruise
The serpent's head;[156] piteous amends, unless
Be meant, whom I conjecture, our grand foe
Satan, who in the serpent hath contrived
Against us this deceit: to crush his head
Would be revenge indeed; which will be lost
By death brought on ourselves, or childless days
Resolved, as thou proposest; so our foe
Shall scape his punishment ordained, and we
Instead shall double ours upon our heads.
No more be mentioned then of violence
Against ourselves, and wilful barrenness,
That cuts us off from hope, and savours only
Rancour and pride, impatience and despite,
Reluctance against God and his just yoke
Laid on our necks. Remember with what mild
And gracious temper he both heard and judged
Without wrath or reviling; we expected
Immediate dissolution, which we thought
Was meant by death that day, when lo, to thee
Pains only in child-bearing were foretold,
And bringing forth, soon recompensed with joy,
Fruit of thy womb: on me the curse aslope° — falling to the side
Glanced on the ground, with labour I must earn
My bread; what harm? Idleness had been worse;
My labour will sustain me; and lest cold
Or heat should injure us, his timely care
Hath unbesought provided, and his hands
Clothed us unworthy, pitying while he judged;
How much more, if we pray him, will his ear
Be open, and his heart to pity incline,
And teach us further by what means to shun
The inclement seasons, rain, ice, hail and snow,
Which now the sky with various face begins

[156] **shall . . . head:** Christ, sent to Eden to judge the transgressing Adam and Eve, made this declaration in Book X: 179–81: "Between Thee and the Woman I will put / Enmity, and between thine and her Seed; / Her Seed shall bruise thy head, thou bruise his heel." Milton here includes Genesis 3:15 almost verbatim.

To show us in this mountain,[157] while the winds
Blow moist and keen, shattering the graceful locks
Of these fair spreading trees; which bids us seek
Some better shroud, some better warmth to cherish
Our limbs benumbed, ere this diurnal star° — the sun
Leave cold the night, how we his gathered beams
Reflected, may with matter sere[158] foment,
Or by collision of two bodies grind
The air attrite to fire, as late the clouds
Jostling or pushed with winds rude in their shock
Tine° the slant lightning, whose thwart flame driven down — ignite, kindle
Kindles the gummy bark of fir or pine,
And sends a comfortable heat from far,
Which might supply° the sun: such fire to use — take the place of
And what may else be remedy or cure
To evils which our own misdeeds have wrought,
He will instruct us praying, and of grace
Beseeching him, so as we need not fear
To pass commodiously this life, sustained
By him with many comforts, till we end
In dust, our final rest and native home.
What better can we do, than to the place
Repairing where he judged us, prostrate fall
Before him reverent, and there confess
Humbly our faults, and pardon beg, with tears
Watering the ground, and with our sighs the air
Frequenting,° sent from hearts contrite, in sign — filling the air
Of sorrow unfeigned, and humiliation meek.
Undoubtedly he will relent and turn
From his displeasure; in whose look serene,
When angry most he seemed and most severe,
What else but favour, grace, and mercy shone?
　　So spake our father penitent, nor Eve
Felt less remorse: they forthwith to the place
Repairing where he judged them prostrate fell
Before him reverent, and both confessed
Humbly their faults, and pardon begged, with tears
Watering the ground, and with their sighs the air
Frequenting, sent from hearts contrite, in sign
Of sorrow unfeigned, and humiliation meek.

---

[157] **this mountain:** That is, Paradise; see Book IV: 132–58.

[158] **sere:** Dry. Adam and Eve must now learn to make fire by rubbing stones together to create friction ("air attrite").

Book XI

The Argument

The Son of God presents to his father the prayers of our first parents now repenting, and intercedes for them: God accepts them, but declares that they must no longer abide in Paradise; sends Michael with a band of cherubim to dispossess them; but first to reveal to Adam future things: Michael's coming down. Adam shows to Eve certain ominous signs; he discerns Michael's approach, goes out to meet him: the angel denounces their departure. Eve's lamentation. Adam pleads, but submits: the angel leads him up to a high hill, sets before him in vision what shall happen till the flood.

Book XII
[The Promise of Exile]

The Argument

The angel Michael continues from the flood to relate what shall succeed; then, in the mention of Abraham, comes by degrees to explain, who that seed of the woman shall be, which was promised Adam and Eve in the Fall; his incarnation, death, resurrection, and ascension; the state of the church till his second coming. Adam greatly satisfied and recomforted by these relations and promises descends the hill with Michael; wakens Eve, who all this while had slept, but with gentle dreams composed to quietness of mind and submission. Michael in either hand leads them out of Paradise, the fiery sword waving behind them, and the cherubim taking their stations to guard the place.

[. . .]He ended;[159] and thus Adam last replied.
How soon hath thy prediction, seer blessed,
Measured this transient world, the race of time,
Till time stand fixed: beyond is all abyss,
Eternity, whose end no eye can reach.
Greatly instructed I shall hence depart,
Greatly in peace of thought, and have my fill
Of knowledge, what this vessel can contain;
Beyond which was my folly to aspire.
Henceforth I learn, that to obey is best,
And love with fear the only God, to walk
As in presence, ever to observe
His providence, and on him sole depend,
Merciful over all his works, with good
Still overcoming evil, and by small
Accomplishing great things, by things deemed weak

[159] **He ended:** Adam is speaking with the angel Michael, whom God has sent to deliver a final vision of the future and the coming of Christ to Adam.

Subverting worldly strong, and worldly wise
By simply meek; that suffering for truth's sake
Is fortitude to highest victory,
And to the faithful death the gate of life;
Taught this by his example whom I now
Acknowledge my redeemer ever blessed.
    To whom thus also the angel last replied:
This having learned, thou hast attained the sum
Of wisdom; hope no higher, though all the stars
Thou knew'st by name, and all the ethereal powers,
All secrets of the deep, all nature's works,
Or works of God in heaven, air, earth, or sea,
And all the riches of this world enjoyed'st,
And all the rule, one empire; only add
Deeds to thy knowledge answerable, add faith,
Add virtue, patience, temperance, add love,
By name to come called Charity, the soul
Of all the rest: then wilt thou not be loath
To leave this Paradise, but shalt possess
A paradise within thee, happier far.
Let us descend now therefore from this top
Of speculation; for the hour precise
Exacts our parting hence; and see the guards,
By me encamped on yonder hill, expect
Their motion, at whose front a flaming sword,
In signal of remove, waves fiercely round;
We may no longer stay: go, waken Eve;
Her also I with gentle dreams have calmed
Portending good, and all her spirits composed
To meek submission: thou at season fit
Let her with thee partake what thou has heard,
Chiefly what may concern her faith to know,
The great deliverance by her seed to come
(For by the woman's seed) on all mankind.
That ye may live, which will be many days,
Both in one faith unanimous though sad,
With cause for evils past, yet much more cheered
With meditation on the happy end.
    He ended, and they both descend the hill;
Descended, Adam to the bower where Eve
Lay sleeping ran before, but found her waked;
And thus with words not sad she him received.
    Whence thou return'st, and whither went'st, I know;
For God is also in sleep, and dreams advise,
Which he hath sent propitious, some great good

Presaging, since with sorrow and heart's distress
Wearied I fell asleep: but now lead on;
In me is no delay; with thee to go,
Is to stay here; without thee here to stay,
Is to go hence unwilling; thou to me
Art all things under heaven, all places thou,
Who for my wilful crime art banished hence.
This further consolation yet secure
I carry hence; though all by me is lost,
Such favour I unworthy am vouchsafed,
By me the promised seed shall all restore.
So spake our mother Eve, and Adam heard
Well pleased, but answered not; for now too nigh
The archangel stood, and from the other hill
To their fixed station, all in bright array
The cherubim descended; on the ground
Gliding meteorous, as evening mist
Risen from a river o'er the marish° glides,   marsh
And gathers ground fast at the labourer's heel
Homeward returning. High in front advanced,
The brandished sword of God before them blazed
Fierce as a comet; which with torrid heat,
And vapour as the Lybian air adust,°   scorched, burned
Began to parch that temperate clime; whereat
In either hand the hastening angel caught
Our lingering parents, and to the eastern gate
Led them direct, and down the cliff as fast
To the subjected plain;° then disappeared.   plain below
They looking back, all the eastern side beheld
Of Paradise, so late their happy seat,
Waved over by that flaming brand, the gate
With dreadful faces thronged and fiery arms:
Some natural tears they dropped, but wiped them soon;
The world was all before them, where to choose
Their place of rest, and providence their guide:
They hand in hand with wandering steps and slow,
Through Eden took their solitary way.

Challenging Orthodoxy

The fifth-century B.C.E. Greek philosopher Protagoras is credited with the statement "Man is the measure of all things"; Plato wrote that "Know thyself" was the inscription over the entrance to the ancient oracle at Delphi. Together these two ideas gradually became central themes for the European **Renaissance** and the new **humanism** based on studying Greek art and philosophy, which were carried over into the European enlightenment of the seventeenth and eighteenth centuries. The shift to an emphasis on the individual and this world as conceived and measured by human beings ultimately constituted a challenge to the prevailing orthodoxies of the period: the established doctrines of religion, social traditions, knowledge, and government. Over time, powerful institutions tend to lose their ability or willingness to adjust to changing times. In Europe, the revolution in thought began by focusing on the apparent rigidity of the Roman Catholic hierarchy and the corruption of its priesthood, but in England dissent was extended to parliamentary and class privilege. In India, the dominant orthodoxy was traditional Hinduism with the vested powers of the Brahmin priests and the caste system. In China, intellectuals revolted against the dominance of the Confucian orthodoxy and the rigidity of social roles.

Although some religious dissidents prior to the sixteenth century had cried out against the abuses of the Catholic Church and the immorality of its clergy, the dramatic inauguration of the **Protestant Reformation** took place when a German monk named Martin Luther (1483–1546) nailed ninety-five theses about the corrupt practices of selling indulgences for saving souls on the church door at Wittenberg on October 31, 1517. On April 18, 1521,

To the Greeks, experimentation seemed irrelevant. . . . Experimentation began to become philosophically respectable in Europe with the support of such philosophers as Roger Bacon . . . and his later namesake Francis Bacon. But it was Galileo who overthrew the Greek view and effected the revolution. He was a convincing logician and a genius as a publicist. He described his experiments and his point of view so clearly and so dramatically that he won over the European learned community.

– Isaac Asimov, *The New Intelligent Man's Guide to Science*, writer, 1965

Stefano della Bella, Frontispiece 1632
This frontispiece to Galileo's Dialogue Concerning the Two Chief World Systems *shows an imaginary conversation among Aristotle, Ptolemy, and Copernicus, three great astronomer-scientists of history, discussing matters of astronomy.*

Luther appeared before the formal assembly known as the Diet of Worms (a town in southwestern Germany), presided over by the Holy Roman Emperor Charles V (r. 1519–58), to give a speech (p. 667) in defense of his criticisms of the Catholic Church. Luther argued that instead of performing good works, Christian souls could be saved by faith alone. His stand against the Catholic authorities clinched the schism between them, and Luther was excommunicated. His many followers in Germany grew into the Lutheran Church.

> **The Copernican Revolution was a distinct scientific revolution because it came out of a crisis: technical breakdown of the Ptolemaic system. It removed the world from the centre of the university and put the sun at the centre of the planetary system.**
>
> **– Ritchie Calder, *Man and the Cosmos*, scientist, 1968**

Similar to the Protestant criticisms of the worship of Mary and the proliferation of saints in the Roman Catholic Church, a movement in India promoted a new kind of monotheism. In his revolt against the rigidities of the Hindu priesthood and the caste system, Nanak (1469–1539), the founder of **Sikhism**, blended the mystical traditions of bhakti Hinduism (based on the worship of Shiva and Krishna, among other gods) and Islamic Sufism (with its goals of

Martin Luther at Wittenberg, Sixteenth Century
A woodcut depicts the famous moment when Martin Luther nailed his ninety-five theses to the church door in Wittenberg, setting off a religious schism that grew into the Protestant Reformation, forever changing the formerly unified Catholic Church. (Bridgeman)

ecstasy and union with the divine). Nanak created a religion whereby, through meditation and other religious practices, an individual could experience God directly, without the intervention of priest or institution. His devotional poems were included in the **Adi Granth**, the Sikh scriptures. p. 671

During this same time period, orthodox **Confucianism** was being challenged in China by those who sought room for individual experience and choice. More so than in either India or Europe, China had built its social, political, and cultural institutions around a monolithic orthodox system of thought, Confucianism. This orthodoxy was sustained and protected by scholar-officials, an intellectual class that ran the highly structured civil service, at the heart of which were civil service examinations that tested individuals on their knowledge of Confucian doctrines. Those who passed were assigned to an appropriate, bureaucratic rung on the imperial ladder. Neo-Confucian reformers, influenced by the individualism of Chinese Buddhism, questioned the hierarchical rule of the emperor and the rigidity of the civil system. The reformer **Li Zhi** (Li Chih; 1527–1602), in his essay **"On the Child-Mind"** went even further in his own challenge to Confucianism by stressing the importance of each individual's inherent knowledge. For Li Zhi, the natural endowment of each individual becomes an argument for personal knowledge and choice.

lee-JUR

p. 677

During what is termed the English Puritan Revolution of 1640 to 1688, all manner of issues involving government and church were brought up and disputed: religious doctrines and the hierarchy of the Anglican clergy, parliamentary responsibilities and class privilege, foreign policy and the rights of individuals. Although John Milton (1608–1674) was at the center of several of these disputes, he was not easy to categorize: He was both a Renaissance writer and a Puritan, a man given to solitude who was nevertheless devoted to public service. He was a sincere Christian who nevertheless chose not to participate in religious services during the last part of his life. In his lengthy essay ***Areopagitica*** (1644), Milton argues for freedom of the press based on the necessity for individuals to have freedom of choice over their reading materials in order that they might freely choose a virtuous life.

eh-ree-ah-pah-JIT-ih-kuh

p. 680

The challenge to orthodoxy also came from scientists who were formulating new ways of conceiving the world from their direct observations and measurements of nature and the cosmos. Ultimately, the new scientists of the sixteenth and seventeenth centuries began to seriously question the intellectual heritage of Greece and Rome—particularly the works of Aristotle and Ptolemy. Initially it was Nicolas Copernicus (1473–1543), a Polish astronomer, who challenged the worldview proposed by Ptolemy of an earth-centered universe and literally turned the cosmos on its head. Copernicus's theory is set forth in ***On the Revolutions of Heavenly Bodies.*** The idea of a heliocentric (sun-centered) system is commonplace today, but it was momentous in Copernicus's day, especially since it implied a shift away from the Judeo-Christian tradition, which held that the earth and human beings were at the center of the universe.

p. 685

The confrontation between the Catholic Church and Galileo Galilei (1564–1642) in the mid-seventeenth century provides perhaps the most familiar example of the confrontation between religious orthodoxy and the innovations of science. Galileo, like Francis Bacon (1567–1626), believed that scientific observations need not interfere with revealed "truths," since Holy Scripture and physical phenomena were both works of God. Discrepancies between religious truth and scientific truth drawn from strict observations of nature, he believed, lay in the ambiguities of scripture, which was allegorical and subject to wide interpretation. In a **letter** to Galileo, the astronomer Johannes Kepler (1571–1630) recommends that Galileo should go public with his defense of Copernicus's views since truth is so powerful. Galileo's defense of Copernicus in *A Dialogue Concerning the Two Chief World Systems* (1632) led to his trial and condemnation by the Catholic Church in 1633.

p. 692

European thought thrived in the struggles between science and faith, reason and revelation. Christianity grew stronger as it was forced to answer the claims of Greek philosophy. In the confirmation of the two traditions, European thought became more secularized, subtle, and varied. The situation in China was actually similar. While there was a Confucian orthodoxy, there was also an opposing tradition that Confucians had to confront: Buddhism, imported from India.

– Kevin Reilly, *The West and the World*, historian, 1989

■ CONNECTIONS

Niccolò Machiavelli, *The Prince*, p. 124. The European Renaissance promoted the idea of direct observation, of realistically appraising social and religious conventions and institutions. Machiavelli promoted this kind of realism; rather than writing about some theoretical or ideal political system, he believed making political judgments based on the actual interaction between prince and populace. How do the ideas of reformers like Machiavelli, Luther, Nanak, and Galileo reflect the conflict between ideal and real?

"In the World: Changing Gods: From Religion to Philosophy," Book 1. The history of ideas and institutions is continually subject to change and evolution, but there are certain periods of history in which the changes are so dramatic that the paradigm shift reverberates throughout the society. In the ancient world, such a period involved the discovery of philosophy and the idea that human beings might investigate for themselves (apart from religious authority) the dimensions of the world, and indeed the nature of the gods themselves. How might ordinary people and their values have been affected by the religious reformers and scientists of the sixteenth and seventeenth centuries?

"In the Tradition: Indian Devotional Poetry," p. 929. In India, devotional saints and poets of the bhakti movement promoted a more direct, unmediated experience of the divine than what they found in the hierarchy of Hinduism and the authority of Brahmin priests. Bhakti songs, still popular today, provided an important expression of religious change, as did the hymns written by Luther and other Protestant reformers who protested the role of Catholic priests as mediators. How do the ideas in bhakti poems compare to those of Luther or Nanak?

■ PRONUNCIATION

Areopagitica: eh-ree-ah-puh-JIT-ih-kuh
Li Zhi: lee-JUR

Martin Luther
1483–1546

Under the guidance of Martin Luther, one of the most fascinating, complex, and contradictory figures of the Renaissance, the Protestant Reformation was more a revolution than a reformation, for it created a major break from the medieval authority of the Catholic Church. Luther's roots were in the Middle Ages. Son of a peasant miner, he grew up in a religious household. Intending to study law at the University of Erfurt, he had a conversion experience in 1505 and instead of Erfurt entered an Augustinian monastery. During his assignment to the new University of Wittenberg, where he taught theology, Luther discovered the foundation of his theology in the biblical book of Romans, written by the apostle Paul, which contains the doctrine that humans are justified by faith alone—not by works, not by priestly mediation, not by sacraments, not by church membership. Faith was the answer, in Luther's belief, to the uncompromising judgments of a terrifying Father-God. He focused on the individual's direct relationship with God, as guided by the authority of God's word in the Bible.

In 1510 on a mission to Rome, Luther was shocked at the secular excesses of the Church hierarchy—the sale of indulgences, the worship of relics, and the proliferation of saints. Initially supported by humanists such as Desidarius Erasmus (1466–1536), Luther began to formulate plans for reforming the Church and curbing its excesses. Luther's ninety-five theses and his defiance of the pope and his Church led inevitably to open confrontations with the Catholic hierarchy. The first hearing on his writings and ideas was held at Augsburg in 1518 before Cardinal Cajetan; Luther refused to recant. When the Church issued a papal bull of condemnation to Luther in 1520, he publicly burned it. Excommunication did not immediately follow because Frederick the Wise (1463–1525) of Saxony, Luther's own prince, came up with a plan that Luther should first have a hearing before the 1521 Diet of Worms (the assembly of Holy Roman Empire princes), and Charles V (r. 1519–58), its Hapsburg leader.

One can only imagine the drama surrounding this meeting. Luther, a simple monk, armed with biblical theology, stood before the extraordinary wealth and power of Charles V, newly elected Holy Roman Emperor, Lord of Austria, Burgundy, the Low Countries, Spain, and Naples. Luther was asked whether he defended his writings or rejected them—of special concern was a tract, *The Babylonian Captivity of the Church* (1520), in which Luther recommended two rather than seven sacraments and denied the mediating role of the priesthood between laity and God. Surprisingly, Luther asked for time to think, and the hearing was postponed. The next day, Luther defended his writings to a crowded hall, giving his famous answers documented in the piece included here. Following the direction of Charles, four out of six electors declared Luther a heretic. Charles returned the next day to affirm his Catholicism and to denounce Luther.

Lucas Cranach the Elder, *Martin Luther,* 1529
This painting of the religious reformer Martin Luther was done by the great German portraitist of the Reformation, Lucas Cranach. (Erich Lessing / Art Resource, NY)

The Diet of Worms failed to heal the breach that continued to widen as Luther's movement gained support from laity as well as princes. Luther married, had children, and spent the rest of his life writing and formulating the direction for the new Lutheran Church. Luther introduced hymn singing and German-language (rather than Latin) church services. He also reformed the liturgy. His greatest literary and religious contribution to the Reformation, however, was his translation of the Bible into a vernacular German, making it accessible to ordinary people.

Speech at the Diet of Worms

Translated by Roger A. Hornsby

[Here I Stand]

"Most serene emperor, most illustrious princes, most clement lords, obedient to the time set for me yesterday evening, I appear before you, beseeching you, by the mercy of God, that your most serene majesty and your most illustrious lordships may deign to listen graciously to this my cause—which is, as I hope, a cause of justice and of truth. If through my inexperience I have either not given the proper titles to some, or have offended in some manner against court customs and etiquette, I beseech you to kindly pardon me, as a man accustomed not to courts but to the cells of monks. I can bear no other witness about myself but that I have taught and written up to this time with simplicity of heart, as I had in view only the glory of God and the sound instruction of Christ's faithful.

"Most serene emperor, most illustrious princes, concerning those questions proposed to me yesterday on behalf of your serene majesty, whether I acknowledged as mine the books enumerated and published in my name and whether I wished to persevere in their defense or to retract them, I have given to the first question my full and complete answer, in which I still persist and shall persist forever. These books are mine and they have been published in my name by me, unless in the meantime, either through the craft or the mistaken wisdom of my emulators, something in them has been changed or wrongly cut out. For plainly I cannot acknowledge anything except what is mine alone and what has been written by me alone, to the exclusion of all interpretations of anyone at all.

"In replying to the second question, I ask that your most serene majesty and your lordships may deign to note that my books are not all of the same kind.

"For there are some in which I have discussed religious faith and morals simply and evangelically, so that even my enemies themselves are compelled to admit that these are useful, harmless, and clearly worthy to be read by Christians. Even the bull, although harsh and cruel, admits that some of my books are inoffensive, and yet allows these also to be condemned with a judgment which is utterly monstrous. Thus, if I should begin to disavow them, I ask you, what would I be doing? Would not I, alone of all men, be condemning the very truth upon which friends and enemies equally agree, striving alone against the harmonious confession of all?

"Another group of my books attacks the papacy and the affairs of the papists as those who both by their doctrines and very wicked examples have laid waste the Christian world with evil that affects the spirit and the body. For no one can deny or conceal this fact, when the experience of all and the complaints of everyone witness that through the decrees of the pope and the doctrines of men the consciences of the faithful have been most miserably entangled, tortured, and torn to pieces. Also, property and possessions, especially in this illustrious nation of Germany, have been devoured by an unbelievable tyranny and are being devoured to this time without letup and by unworthy means. [Yet the papists] by their own decrees (as in dist. 9 and 25; ques. 1 and 2) warn that the papal laws and doctrines which are contrary to the gospel or the opinions of the fathers are to be regarded as erroneous and reprehensible. If, therefore, I should have retracted these writings, I should have done nothing other than to have added strength to this [papal] tyranny and I should have opened not only windows but doors to such great godlessness. It would rage farther and more freely than ever it has dared up to this time. Yes, from the proof of such a revocation on my part, their wholly lawless and unrestrained kingdom of wickedness would become still more intolerable for the already wretched people; and their rule would be further strengthened and established, especially if it should be reported that this evil deed had been done by me by virtue of the authority of your most serene majesty and of the whole Roman Empire. Good God! What a cover for wickedness and tyranny I should have then become.

"I have written a third sort of book against some private and (as they say) distinguished individuals—those, namely, who strive to preserve the Roman tyranny and to destroy the godliness taught by me. Against these I confess I have been more violent than my religion or profession demands. But then, I do not set myself up as a saint; neither am I disputing about my life, but about the teaching of Christ. It is not proper for me to retract these works, because by this retraction it would again happen that tyranny and godlessness would, with my patronage, rule and rage among the people of God more violently than ever before.

"However, because I am a man and not God, I am not able to shield my books with any other protection than that which my Lord Jesus Christ himself offered for his teaching. When questioned before Annas about his teaching and struck by a servant, he said: 'If I have spoken wrongly, bear witness to the wrong' [John 18:19–23]. If the Lord himself who knew that he could not err, did not refuse to hear testimony against his teaching, even from the lowliest servant, how much more ought I, who am the lowest scum and able to do nothing except err, desire and expect that somebody should want to offer testimony against my teaching! Therefore, I ask by the mercy of God, may your most serene majesty, most illustrious lordships, or anyone at all who is able, either high or low, bear witness, expose my errors, overthrowing them by the writings of the prophets and the evangelists. Once I have been taught I shall be quite ready to renounce every error, and I shall be the first to cast my books into the fire.

"From these remarks I think it is clear that I have sufficiently considered and weighed the hazards and dangers, as well as the excitement and dissensions aroused in the world as a result of my teachings, things about which I was gravely and forcefully warned yesterday. To see excitement and dissension arise because of the Word of God is to me clearly the most joyful aspect of all in these matters. For this is the way, the opportunity, and the result of the Word of God, just as He [Christ] said, 'I have not come to bring peace but a sword. For I have come to set a man against his father,' etc. [Matt. 10:34–35]. Therefore, we ought to think how marvelous and terrible is our God in his counsels, lest by chance what is attempted for settling strife grows rather into an intolerable deluge of evils, if we begin by condemning the Word of God. And concern must be shown lest the reign of this most noble youth, Prince Charles (in whom after God is our great hope), become unhappy and inauspicious. I could illustrate this with abundant examples from Scripture—like Pharaoh, the king of Babylon, and the kings of Israel who, when they endeavored to pacify and strengthen their kingdoms by the wisest counsels, most surely destroyed themselves. For it is He who takes the wise in their own craftiness [Job 5:13] and overturns mountains before they know it [Job 9:5]. Therefore we must fear God. I do not say these things because there is a need of either my teachings or my warnings for such leaders as you, but because I must not withhold the allegiance which I owe my Germany. With these words I commend myself to your most serene majesty and to your lordships, humbly asking that I not be allowed through the agitation of my enemies, without cause, to be made hateful to you. I have finished."

When I had finished, the speaker for the emperor said, as if in reproach, that I had not answered the question, that I ought not call into question those things which had been condemned and defined in councils; therefore what was sought from me was not a horned response, but a simple one, whether or not I wished to retract.

Here I answered:

"Since then your serene majesty and your lordships seek a simple answer, I will give it in this manner, neither horned nor toothed: Unless I am convinced by the testimony of the Scriptures or by clear reason (for I do not trust either in the pope or in councils alone, since it is well known that they have often erred and contradicted themselves), I am bound by the Scriptures I have quoted and my conscience is captive to the Word of God. I cannot and I will not retract anything, since it is neither safe nor right to go against conscience.

"I cannot do otherwise, here I stand, may God help me, Amen."

Nanak
1469–?1539

Very few details are known about Nanak's life. Born into a Hindu family in Punjab and raised within Islamic political traditions, the religious poet and founder of **Sikhism** offered a syncretic compromise between Muslim and Hindu religions. Somewhat like the Sufi mystics and Hindu saints, Nanak rejected the asceticism and hierarchical **caste** system of Hinduism but incorporated the doctrines of **karma**, the transmigration of souls, and **nirvana**. His advocacy of a direct spiritual relationship of selfless devotion to one god had more in common with Islam than with the Hindu system that relied on priests and ritual ceremony. Nanak's deity, however, was not the stern Allah, but a compassionate figure sometimes called the "Destroyer of Sorrow" and the "Friend of Sinners." Rather than achieve a synthesis between the two religions, however, Sikhism developed into an independent alternative that drew followers from the working classes of Hindu and Muslim origin. Under the leadership of Gobind Rai (r. 1675–1708), Sikhs ("disciples") were called *singhs* ("lions"). Gobind Rai, who became Gobind Singh, founded a martial brotherhood called the Khalsa, whose members were identified by five items whose names all begin with a *k* in Punjabi: *kangha,* a steel comb for beard and hair; *kara,* a steel bracelet; *kesh,* long hair; *kirpan,* a short knife; and *kuch,* shorts. Under Mughal rule in the seventeenth and early eighteenth centuries, the militant wing of the Sikhs took up arms against the Mughal rulers who persecuted their leaders.

The Adi Granth, in which Nanak's writings appear, is a compendium of devotional literature of the Sikhs and serves as a Sikh equivalent to the Bible or Qur'an. It was compiled by the fifth of the great Sikh gurus, or teachers, Guru Arjan (1563–1606). The selected poems stress the unity of God, that is, how all of creation is a reflection of the ultimate reality.

FROM

Adi Granth

Translated by Dr. Trilochan Singh, Bhai Johd Singh, Kapur Singh, Bawa Harkishen Singh, and Khushwant Singh

1

It is not through thought that He is to be comprehended
Though we strive to grasp Him a hundred thousand times;
Nor by outer silence and long deep meditation
Can the inner silence be reached;
Nor is man's hunger for God appeasable
By piling up world-loads of wealth.
All the innumerable devices of worldly wisdom
Leave a man disappointed; not one avails.

How then shall we know the Truth?
How shall we rend the veils of untruth away?
Abide thou by His Will, and make thine own,
His will, O Nānak, that is written in thy heart.

2

Through His Will He creates all the forms of things,
But what the form of His Will is, who can express?
All life is shaped by His ordering,
By His ordering some are high, some of low estate,
Pleasure and pain are bestowed as His Writ ordaineth.

Some through His Will are graciously rewarded,
Others must grope through births and deaths;
Nothing at all, outside His Will, is abiding.
O Nānak, he who is aware of the Supreme Will
Never in his selfhood utters the boast: "It is I."

3

Those who believe in power,
Sing of His power;
Others chant of His gifts
As His messages and emblems;
Some sing of His greatness,
And His gracious acts;
Some sing of His wisdom

Hard to understand;
Some sing of Him as the fashioner of the body.
Destroying what He has fashioned;
Others praise Him for taking away life
And restoring it anew.

Some proclaim His Existence
To be far, desperately far, from us;
Others sing of Him
As here and there a Presence
Meeting us face to face.

To sing truly of the transcendent Lord
Would exhaust all vocabularies, all human powers of expression,
Myriads have sung of Him in innumerable strains.
His gifts to us flow in such plentitude
That man wearies of receiving what God bestows;
Age on unending age, man lives on His bounty;
Carefree, O Nānak, the Glorious Lord smiles.

4

The Lord is the Truth Absolute,
True is His Name.
His language is love infinite;
His creatures ever cry to Him;
"Give us more, O Lord, give more";
The Bounteous One gives unwearyingly,
What then should we offer
That we might see His Kingdom?
With what language
Might we His love attain?

In the ambrosial hours of fragrant dawn
Think upon and glorify
His Name and greatness.
Our own past actions
Have put this garment on us,
But salvation comes only through His Grace.

O Nānak, this alone need we know,
That God, being Truth, is the one Light of all.

5

He cannot be installed like an idol,
Nor can man shape His likeness.
He made Himself and maintains Himself
On His heights unstained for ever;
Honoured are they in His shrine
Who meditate upon Him.

Sing thou, O Nānak, the psalms
Of God as the treasury
Of sublime virtues.
If a man sings of God and hears of Him,
And lets love of God sprout within him,
All sorrow shall depart;
In the soul, God will create abiding peace.

The Word of the Guru is the inner Music;
The Word of the Guru is the highest Scripture;
The Word of the Guru is all pervading.
The Guru is Śiva, the Guru is Vishṇu and Brahma,
The Guru is the Mother goddess.[1]
If I knew Him as He truly is
What words could utter my knowledge?
Enlightened by God, the Guru has unravelled one mystery
"There is but one Truth, one Bestower of life;
May I never forget Him."

6

I would bathe in the holy rivers
If so I could win His love and grace;
But of what use is the pilgrimage
If it pleaseth Him not that way?

What creature obtains anything here
Except through previous good acts?
Yet hearken to the Word of the Guru

[1] **Siva . . . Mother goddess:** Probably a reference to Kali, although the Mother goddess appears under various names. Shiva, Vishnu, and Brahma represent three manifestations of the divine: destroyer, preserver, and creator, respectively. A guru is a spiritual teacher.

And his counsel within thy spirit
Shall shine like precious stone.

The Guru's divine illumination
Has unravelled one mystery;
There is but one Bestower of life
May I forget Him never.

7

Were a man to live through the four ages,
Or even ten times longer,
Though his reputation were to spread over the nine shores,
Though the whole world were to follow in his train,
Though he were to be universally famous,
Yet lacking God's grace, in God's presence
Such a man would be disowned;
Such a man would be merely a worm among vermin
And his sins will be laid at his door.

21

Pilgrimages, penances, compassion and almsgiving
Bring a little merit, the size of sesame seed.
But he who hears and believes and loves the Name
Shall bathe and be made clean
In a place of pilgrimage within him.

All goodness is Thine, O Lord, I have none;
Though without performing good deeds
None can aspire to adore Thee.
Blessed Thou the Creator and the Manifestation,
Thou art the word, Thou art the primal Truth and Beauty,
And Thou the heart's joy and desire.

When in time, in what age, in what day of the month or week
In what season and in what month did'st Thou create the world?
The Pundits do not know or they would have written it in the Purāṇas;
The Qazis do not know, or they would have recorded it in the Koran;
Nor do the Yogis[2] know the moment of the day,

[2] **Pundits . . . Yogis:** This list includes the sages of several traditions; the Puranas are ancient Hindu scriptures. Yogis typically use ascetic practices to reach enlightenment.

Nor the day of the month or the week, nor the month nor the season.
Only God Who made the world knows when He made it.

Then how shall I approach Thee, Lord?
In what words shall I praise Thee?
In what words shall I speak of Thee?
How shall I know Thee?
O Nānak, all men speak of Him, and each would be wiser than the next man;
Great is the Lord, great is His Name,
What He ordaineth, that cometh to pass,
Nānak, the man puffed up with his own wisdom
Will get no honour from God in the life to come.

22

There are hundreds of thousands of worlds below and above ours,
And scholars grow weary of seeking for God's bounds.
The Vedas proclaim with one voice that He is boundless.
The Semitic Books mention eighteen hundred worlds;
But the Reality behind all is the One Principle.

If it could be written, it would have been,
But men have exhausted themselves in the effort;
O Nānak, call the Lord Great;
None but He knoweth, how great He is.

Li Zhi (Lhi Chih)

1527–1602

The history of Chinese religious thought during the Early Modern Period might be described as an ongoing dialogue between various forms of Confucianism, Daoism, and Buddhism. The first two are indigenous traditions that date back to the fifth and second centuries B.C.E., and the third entered China from India sometime around the first century C.E. By the end of the Tang dynasty (618–907), Chinese Buddhism was divided into several sects, including the Chan (Zen), Pure Land, and Tantric. As in the antagonism between Islam and Hinduism, Buddhism and Confucianism preached strikingly incompatible doctrines — the first emphasizing other-worldliness and spiritual enlightenment, the second this-worldliness and practical ethics, doctrines suitable for administering the affairs of state.

Yin and Yang, seventeenth century
The yin-yang symbol is held up for study in this seventeenth-century Chinese painting. (The Art Archive/British Museum)

As Nanak had attempted to reconcile Islamic and Hindu doctrines, neo-Confucianists attempted to reconcile Confucianism with the spiritual aspects of Buddhism. One of the most influential of these thinkers was Zhu Xi (Chu Hsi, 1130–1200), whose elegant synthesis of competing doctrines eventually became known as the True Way, in part because he integrated the concept of the Dao (Tao) into Confucianism, thereby enriching the ethical teachings with an inward focus on the mind. True Way neo-Confucianism became the official state doctrine and exerted considerable influence on subsequent generations of neo-Confucian scholars during the Ming period (1368–1644). A growing number of intellectuals viewed education as the road to positions in the governmental bureaucracy, but formal study also fostered individualistic thought and challenges to Confucian orthodoxy. Li Zhi has the reputation of being one of the most independent thinkers in Chinese history.

Li Zhi was born in the southern port city of Chuanzhou, across the straits from Taiwan. It is possible that his family was part of the Chinese Muslim community. Although he was provided with a Confucian education as preparation for official examinations and a public post, Li Zhi resisted identification with any organized creed, whether it was Confucian, Daoist, or Buddhist. He passed the provincial exams in 1552, but he didn't take the national exams in the capital, which affected his qualifications for an appointment. For fifteen years he worked as a minor government official in various capacities, and then at the age of forty he experienced a turning point in his thinking. He left government service permanently in order to study and write full-time, and, as he said, "to become an individual." He eventually became a Buddhist monk.

At the foundation of Li Zhi's thought is the belief that humans are born with a pure mind with innate knowledge that the individual should spontaneously pursue. When Li Zhi attacks the state of orthodoxy in "On the Child-Mind," he singles out the doctrine that establishes a parallel relationship between the *dao* and the *li,* the way and the innate pattern, which previous neo-Confucianists claimed to be operating in the mind and in the universe. Like René Descartes (1596–1650) and later Jean-Jacques Rousseau (1712–1778) in the West, Li Zhi argues that what we think of as truth is in fact learned from experience and education; he thus suggests that the basic premises of neo-Confucianism are founded on a corrupt understanding of the relationship between innate ideas and the external world. In fact, the "child-mind" can be corrupted by experience.

On the Child-Mind

Translated by Stephen Owen

When I (using the pseudonym "Mountain Farmer of Dragon Cave") wrote on the play *Western Parlor,* I commented at the end: "Those who judge such matters may not think it is all right that I still have a child-mind." The child-mind is the genuine mind; and if having the child-mind is taken as not being all right, then having a genuine mind is also taken as not being all right. Free of all falseness and entirely genuine, the child-mind is the original mind of one's very first thought. Loss of the child-mind means loss of the genuine mind, and a loss of the genuine mind means loss of the genuine person. One who is a person and not genuine will never again have beginnings.

As the child is the beginning of the person, so the child-mind is beginning of mind. How could mind's beginnings ever be lost — but then how does it happen that the child-mind is indeed lost so abruptly? Initially, things seen and heard come in through eyes and ears. And when we take these as a governing factor from without, the child-mind is lost. As we grow older, the Way and Inherent Pattern come in through what we see and hear. And when we take these as the governing factor from within, the child-mind is lost. After a long time, as what we see and hear of the Way and Inherent Pattern steadily increases, what we know and what we are aware of also steadily broadens. At that point we further learn that to be praised is desirable; we endeavor to enhance opinion of ourselves, and the child-mind is lost. We learn that to be criticized by others is undesirable; we endeavor to avoid that, and the child-mind is lost.

Everything we see and hear of the Way and Inherent Pattern comes from extensive reading and judgments about what is morally right. Of course the ancient Sages read and studied; however, even if they hadn't read and studied, the child-mind would have remained secure within them all by itself. Even though they read and studied extensively, they also guarded their child-mind and kept it from being lost. They were not like scholars of our time, who repress the child-mind by extensive reading and moral judgments. And since scholars have indeed repressed their child-minds by extensive reading and moral judgments, what use was there in the Sages writing so extensively and instituting their words if it only served to make scholars repress their child-minds?

Once the child-mind is repressed, when words are uttered, those words do not come from what lies deep within; when they reveal themselves in questions of governing, what they do lacks any core; and when they write, their writing cannot reach others and accomplish its ends. In such people there is none of the inner reserve that reveals itself as beauty; there is none of the frankness and real substance that gives off its own aura. And if such people try to write even one line with moral force in the words, they ultimately fail. What is the reason for this? Their child-minds have been repressed, and their minds are constituted of things external to themselves; that is, what they have seen and heard, questions of the Way and Innate Pattern.

Since their minds are constituted of things they have seen and heard, the Way and Innate Pattern, then their words come from those external things and are not the words that the child-mind would say on its own. However artful such words may be, what do they have to do with the self? Can an inauthentic person do otherwise than to speak inauthentic words, to act inauthentically, and to write inauthentically? In fact, once a person becomes inauthentic, then he is inauthentic in every way. It follows from this that if you speak inauthentically to an inauthentic person, the inauthentic person will be pleased; if you tell an inauthentic person about inauthentic action, the inauthentic person will be pleased; and if you talk over inauthentic writing with an inauthentic person, the inauthentic person will be pleased. Being inauthentic in every way, it becomes pleasing in every way. When the whole stage is filled with inauthenticity, how can the short person standing in the audience tell the difference? In this case, even if we have the most perfect works of writing in the whole world, it is not uncommon that they are destroyed by inauthentic people and do not survive to be seen by later generations. The reason for this is that the most perfect works of writing in the whole world always come from the child-mind. If the child-mind were permanently preserved, then the Way and Inherent Pattern would not be practiced and external things seen and heard would not take over. If the child-mind were preserved, then literary quality would never be missing from writing and no person would lack literary ability. It wouldn't be at all like the kind of writing constructed to fit formal models, writing that is not literature!

Why should poems have to be like those in the ancient *Anthology*?[1] Why should prose have to be like that of the pre-Qin period? Writing continued to change after those periods, turning into the Six Dynasties style and then turning into regulated poetry. It changed again and turned into classical tales; it changed and turned into the early play-scripts and variety plays.[2] It turned into *The Western Parlor;* it turned into the novel *Water Margin;* it turned into the formal essays that people practice today for the examination. Every time a person of great virtue speaks of the Way of the Sages, it is perfect writing, in times gone by as well as now—it cannot be judged in its historical relation to the tendencies of the age. This is the reason I feel moved by the inherent literary quality of anyone who has the child-mind—who cares about the Six Classics or the *Analects* or the *Mencius*![3]

But let's consider what we find in the Six Classics, the *Analects,* and the *Mencius*—if they're not passages of excessive adoration by some official historian, then they're inordinate praise by some official. If neither of the above, then it was inexperienced followers and dimwitted disciples writing down from memory what their teacher had said. They gave the first part without the last, or got the conclusion but left out the beginning. They wrote it in books according to what they had personally witnessed. Later scholars did not reflect critically, so they claimed that these had come from the Sages' own mouths and decided to view them as "Classics." Who realizes that for the most part these are not the words of the Sages? Even if they did come from the Sages, they were uttered for some particular purpose, nothing more than matching the treatment to the disease, applying a remedy at the proper moment to save this very same dimwitted disciple or inexperienced follower. If the medicine worked for the disease in question, that doesn't mean we should cling fast to it—we certainly shouldn't right away make it the perfect doctrine for thousands of generations!

Be that as it may, the Six Classics, the *Analects,* and the *Mencius* have in fact become the stock excuses for Neo-Confucians and an abundant resource for inauthentic people. It is perfectly obvious that they cannot speak in words that come from the child-mind. This is a sorry state of things indeed! If only I could find someone who had never lost the child-mind of an authentic Sage and have a word with him about writing!

---

[1] ***Anthology:*** The *Shi jing* (*Book of Songs* or *Book of Odes*).

[2] **plays:** "'Play-scripts' (yuan-ben) were a Northern form of drama, no longer extant, that preceded the variety play." [Translator's note.]

[3] ***Mencius:*** A fourth-century-B.C.E. philosopher; Confucius wrote *The Analects.* The classics include: *Yi jing* or *I Ching* (*The Book of Changes*); the *Shu jing* (*The Book of History* or *Book of Documents*); the *Shi jing* (*Book of Songs* or *Book of Odes*); the *Li ji (The Book of Rites);* and the *Chun qiu (The Spring and Autumn Annals).*

JOHN MILTON
1608–1674

In 1641, and for the next twenty years, John Milton took an active part in the public affairs of England. Insofar as he felt that God had called him to proclaim the truth, Milton became an outspoken propagandist. For Milton, religion was at the heart of all civil or political questions. In 1644 he wrote two famous pamphlets, a *Tractate on Education* and *Areopagitica: A Speech of Mr. John Milton for the Liberty of Unlicensed Printing to the Parliament of England.* The title *Areopagitica* means "a presentation to the Areopagus," the ancient tribunal in Athens that convened on the Hill of Ares. By implication, the Areopagus in this instance is the English Parliament, which had passed a severe ordinance for controlling printing on June 14, 1643. In *Areopagitica,* Milton argues against the requirement that a work had to be licensed before it could be published; in fact, *Areopagitica* itself was unlicensed when it appeared November 24, 1644.

After stating that, historically, only inferior cultures had practiced censorship, Milton proceeds to the heart of his argument: Human dignity rests in the freedom to make choices; without choice, there is no basis either for virtue or for punishment of wrongdoing. The text contains one of Milton's most famous statements: "I cannot praise a fugitive and cloistered virtue, unexercised and unbreathed, that never sallies out and sees her adversary, but slinks out of the race where that immortal garland is to be run for, not without dust and heat." To test virtue in the arena of conflicting loyalties, Milton says, it is necessary to be exposed to all manner of books. Since freedom of thought is the basis of morality, an individual only becomes free when mind and spirit are free from falsehood and superstition. The selection here concludes with an impassioned plea: "Give me the liberty to know, to utter, and to argue freely according to conscience, above all liberties."

FROM

Areopagitica

I deny not but that it is of greatest concernment in the church and commonwealth to have a vigilant eye how books demean themselves as well as men; and thereafter to confine, imprison, and do sharpest justice on them as malefactors. For books are not absolutely dead things, but do contain a potency of life in them to be as active as that soul was whose progeny they are; nay, they do preserve as in a vial the purest efficacy and extraction of that living intellect that bred them. I know they are as lively and as vigorously productive as those fabulous dragon's teeth; and being sown up and down, may chance to spring up armed men.[1] And yet, on the other hand, unless wariness be used, as good almost kill a man as kill a good book: who kills a man kills a reasonable creature, God's image; but he who destroys a good book, kills reason itself, kills the image of God, as it were, in the eye. Many a man lives a burden to the earth; but a good book is the precious lifeblood of a master spirit, embalmed and treasured up on purpose to a life beyond life. 'Tis true, no age can restore a life, whereof perhaps there is no great loss; and revolutions of ages do not oft recover the loss of a rejected truth, for the want of which whole nations fare the worse. We should be wary, therefore, what persecution we raise against the living labors of public men, how we spill that seasoned life of man preserved and stored up in books; since we see a kind of homicide may be thus committed, sometimes a martyrdom; and if it extend to the whole impression, a kind of massacre, whereof the execution ends not in the slaying of an elemental life, but strikes at that ethereal and fifth essence, the breath of reason itself, slays an immortality rather than a life. But lest I should be condemned of introducing license, while I oppose licensing, I refuse not the pains to be so much historical as will serve to show what hath been done by ancient and famous commonwealths against this disorder, till the very time that this project of licensing crept out of the Inquisition, was caught up by our prelates, and hath caught some of our presbyters. [. . .]

Good and evil we know in the field of this world grow up together almost inseparably; and the knowledge of good is so involved and interwoven with the knowledge of evil, and in so many cunning resemblances hardly to be discerned, that those confused seeds which were imposed on Psyche[2] as an incessant labor to cull out and sort asunder, were not more intermixed. It was from out the rind of one apple tasted, that the knowledge of good and evil, as two twins cleaving together, leaped forth into the world. And perhaps this is that doom which Adam fell into of knowing good and evil, that is to say, of knowing good by evil.

As therefore the state of man now is, what wisdom can there be to choose, what continence to forbear without the knowledge of evil? He that can apprehend and consider vice with all her baits and seeming pleasures, and yet abstain, and yet distinguish, and yet prefer that which is truly better, he is the true warfaring Christian. I cannot praise a fugitive and cloistered virtue, unexercised and unbreathed, that never sallies out and sees her adversary, but slinks out of the race where that immortal garland is to be run for, not without dust and heat. Assuredly we bring not innocence into the world, we bring impurity much rather: that which purifies us is trial, and trial is by what is contrary. That virtue therefore which is but a youngling in the contemplation of evil, and knows not the utmost that vice promises to her followers, and rejects it, is but a blank virtue, not a pure; her whiteness is but an excremental whiteness; which was the reason why our sage and serious poet Spenser, whom I

[1] **armed men:** In the *Metamorphoses,* Ovid (43 B.C.E.–17 C.E.) tells the story of Cadmus, who sows the teeth of a slain dragon and watches warriors spring up.

[2] **Psyche:** In classical mythology, Venus, the mother of Cupid, tests Psyche by presenting her with a bewildering assortment of seeds to sort; fortunately, Psyche is assisted by a group of ants.

dare be known to think a better teacher than Scotus or Aquinas, describing true temperance under the person of Guyon, brings him in with his palmer through the cave of Mammon and the bower of earthly bliss, that he might see and know, and yet abstain.[3]

Since therefore, the knowledge and survey of vice is in this world so necessary to the constituting of human virtue, and the scanning of error to the confirmation of truth, how can we more safely and with less danger scout into the regions of sin and falsity than by reading all manner of tractates and hearing all manner of reason? And this is the benefit which may be had of books promiscuously read. [. . .]

We boast our light; but if we look not wisely on the sun itself, it smites us into darkness. Who can discern those planets that are oft combust, and those stars of brightest magnitude that rise and set with the sun, until the opposite motion of their orbs bring them to such a place in the firmament, where they may be seen evening or morning. The light which we have gained, was given us, not to be ever staring on, but by it to discover onward things more remote from our knowledge. It is not the unfrocking of a priest, the unmitering of a bishop, and the removing him from off the Presbyterian shoulders that will make us a happy nation; no, if other things as great in the church, and in the rule of life both economical and political, be not looked into and reformed, we have looked so long upon the blaze that Zwinglius and Calvin[4] hath beaconed up to us, that we are stark blind.

There be who perpetually complain of schisms and sects, and make it such a calamity that any man dissents from their maxims. It is their own pride and ignorance which causes the disturbing, who neither will hear with meekness, nor can convince, yet all must be suppressed which is not found in their syntagma. They are the troublers, they are the dividers of unity, who neglect and permit not others to unite those dissevered pieces which are yet wanting to the body of Truth. To be still searching what we know not by what we know, still closing up truth to truth as we find it (for all her body is homogeneal and proportional), this is the golden rule in theology as well as in arithmetic, and makes up the best harmony in a church; not the forced and outward union of cold and neutral and inwardly divided minds.

Lords and Commons of England, consider what nation it is whereof ye are, and whereof ye are the governors; a nation not slow and dull, but of a quick, ingenious, and piercing spirit, acute to invent, subtle and sinewy to discourse, not beneath the reach of any point the highest that human capacity can soar to. Therefore the studies of learning in her deepest sciences have been so ancient and so eminent among us that writers of good antiquity and ablest judgment have been persuaded that even the school of Pythagoras and the Persian wisdom took beginning from the old phi-

---

[3] **Spenser . . . abstain:** The passage referred to comes from the *Faerie Queene* (II:vii) of Edmund Spenser (1552?–1599). A palmer was a pilgrim who carried a palm as a sign of having been to the Holy Land. Mammon represents money as an evil pursuit. Duns Scotus and Thomas Aquinas were medieval theologians.

[4] **Zwinglius . . . Calvin:** John Calvin (1509–1564), a stern Protestant reformer and theologian, had a large influence on the Puritans in England. Ulrich Zwingli (1484–1531) renounced the Catholic Church and led the Protestant Reformation in Switzerland.

losophy of this island.[5] And that wise and civil Roman, Julius Agricola, who governed once here for Cæsar, preferred the natural wits of Britain before the labored studies of the French.[6] Nor is it for nothing that the grave and frugal Transylvanian[7] sends out yearly from as far as the mountainous borders of Russia and beyond the Hercynian wilderness, not their youth, but their staid men to learn our language and our theologic arts.

Yet that which is above all this, the favor and the love of Heaven, we have great argument to think in a peculiar manner propitious and propending towards us. Why else was this nation chosen before any other, that out of her as out of Sion[8] should be proclaimed and sounded forth the first tidings and trumpet of reformation to all Europe? And had it not been the obstinate perverseness of our prelates against the divine and admirable spirit of Wycliffe to suppress him as a schismatic and innovator, perhaps neither the Bohemian Huss and Jerome, no, nor the name of Luther,[9] or of Calvin, had been ever known; the glory of reforming all our neighbors had been completely ours. But now, as our obdurate clergy have with violence demeaned the matter, we are become hitherto the latest and the backwardest scholars of whom God offered to have made us the teachers.

Now once again by all concurrence of signs, and by the general instinct of holy and devout men, as they daily and solemnly express their thoughts, God is decreeing to begin some new and great period in his Church, even to the reforming of reformation itself. What does he then but reveal himself to his servants, and, as his manner is, first to his Englishmen? [. . .]

Methinks I see in my mind a noble and puissant nation rousing herself like a strong man after sleep, and shaking her invincible locks. Methinks I see her as an eagle muing her mighty youth, and kindling her undazzled eyes at the full midday beam; purging and unscaling her long-abused sight at the fountain itself of heavenly radiance; while the whole noise of timorous and flocking birds, with those also that love the twilight, flutter about, amazed at what she means, and in their envious gabble would prognosticate a year of sects and schisms.

What should ye do then, should ye suppress all this flowery crop of knowledge and new light sprung up and yet springing daily in this city? Should ye set an oligarchy of twenty engrossers over it, to bring a famine upon our minds again, when we shall know nothing but what is measured to us by their bushel? Believe it, Lords

---

[5] **studies . . . island:** Milton alludes to an erroneous assumption that the Greek philosopher Pythagoras (sixth century B.C.E.) and the Persian Zoroaster (fl. c. 1000 B.C.E.) were influenced by English thinkers.

[6] **Roman . . . French:** Julius Agricola was the Roman proconsul in Britain (78–85 C.E.). Tacitus, in his *Life of Agricola* (c. 100 C.E.), says that Agricola educated the local chiefs.

[7] **Transylvanian:** Transylvanians were Protestants and probably came to England to study from beyond the Harz Mountains of Germany.

[8] **Sion:** Mt. Zion in Jerusalem, former site of the temple, now known as Temple Mount.

[9] **And . . . Luther:** Although Martin Luther was the moving force behind the Reformation, he was preceded by John Wycliffe (1324?–1384), who translated the Bible into English. Jan Hus (1372 or 1373–1415) was burned at the stake as a heretic; Jerome of Prague (c. 1365–1416), a follower of Hus, was martyred in 1416.

and Commons, they who counsel ye to such a suppressing, do as good as bid ye suppress yourselves; and I will soon show how.

If it be desired to know the immediate cause of all this free writing and free speaking, there cannot be assigned a truer than your own mild and free and humane government. It is the liberty, Lords and Commons, which your own valorous and happy counsels have purchased us, liberty which is the nurse of all great wits. This is that which hath rarefied and enlighten our spirits like the influence of heaven; this is that which hath enfranchised, enlarged, and lifted up our apprehensions degrees above themselves. Ye cannot make us now less capable, less knowing, less eagerly pursuing of the truth, unless ye first make yourselves, that made us so, less the lovers, less the founders of our true liberty. We can grow ignorant again, brutish, formal, and slavish, as ye found us; but you then must first become that which ye cannot be, oppressive, arbitrary, and tyrannous, as they were from whom ye have freed us. That our hearts are now more capacious, our thoughts more erected to the search and expectation of greatest and exactest things, is the issue of your own virtue propagated in us. Ye cannot suppress that unless ye reinforce an abrogated and merciless law, that fathers may despatch at will their own children. And who shall then stick closest to ye, and excite others? not he who takes up arms for coat and conduct, and his four nobles of Danegelt.[10] Although I dispraise not the defense of just immunities, yet love my peace better, if that were all. Give me the liberty to know, to utter, and to argue freely according to conscience, above all liberties.

[10] **Danegelt:** Originally a tax used to buy off the Danish Vikings, Danegelt became simply the name for taxes levied by English kings.

NICOLAS COPERNICUS
1473–1543

Nicolas Copernicus studied astronomy at the University of Krakow, but he spent several years in Italy studying medicine and law. In 1512 he accepted a position as canon, a type of clergyman, of the cathedral in Frauenburg, Prussia. In addition to his duties as a canon, he practiced medicine and made scientific observations. Copernicus's *On the Revolutions of Heavenly Bodies,* which explains his heliocentric theory, was probably completed in 1530 but not published until 1543, just before his death. The Preface, addressed to Pope Paul III (r. 1534–49), provides us with a good example of what it means to negotiate the line between orthodoxy and innovation—innovation that some might see as heresy. With a mixed sense of pride and humility, Copernicus claims that he has set aside his work for at least thirty-six years, withholding publication for fear of offending the Church. Intellectually confident in his proofs and sure of his labors, he makes a humble appeal for a tolerant hearing. His cautious justification for bringing forward his work embodies the ambivalence between humanistic exploration and received doctrine during the Early Modern Period.

FROM

On the Revolutions of Heavenly Bodies

Translated by Edward Rosen

To His Holiness, Pope Paul III, Nicholas Copernicus' Preface to His Books on the Revolutions

I can readily imagine, Holy Father, that as soon as some people hear that in this volume, which I have written about the revolutions of the spheres of the universe, I ascribe certain motions to the terrestrial globe, they will shout that I must be immediately repudiated together with this belief. For I am not so enamored of my own opinions that I disregard what others may think of them. I am aware that a philosopher's ideas are not subject to the judgement of ordinary persons, because it is his endeavor to seek the truth in all things, to the extent permitted to human reason by God. Yet I hold that completely erroneous views should be shunned. Those who know that the consensus of many centuries has sanctioned the conception that the earth remains at rest in the middle of the heaven as its center would, I reflected, regard it as an insane pronouncement if I made the opposite assertion that the earth moves. Therefore I debated with myself for a long time whether to publish the volume which I wrote to prove the earth's motion or rather to follow the example of the Pythagoreans and certain others, who used to transmit philosophy's secrets only to kinsmen and friends, not in writing but by word of mouth, as is shown by Lysis' letter to Hipparchus.[1] And they did so, it seems to me, not, as some suppose, because they were in some way jealous about their teachings, which would be spread around; on the contrary, they wanted the very beautiful thoughts attained by great men of deep devotion not to be ridiculed by those who are reluctant to exert themselves vigorously in any literary pursuit unless it is lucrative; or if they are stimulated to the nonacquisitive study of philosophy by the exhortation and example of others, yet because of their dullness of mind they play the same part among philosophers as drones among bees. When I weighed these considerations, the scorn which I had reason to fear on account of the novelty and unconventionality of my opinion almost induced me to abandon completely the work which I had undertaken.

But while I hesitated for a long time and even resisted, my friends drew me back. Foremost among them was the cardinal of Capua, Nicholas Schönberg, renowned in every field of learning. Next to him was a man who loves me dearly, Tiedemann

---

[1] **Hipparchus:** A Greek astronomer (fl. second century B.C.E.).

The Earth, 1543
In this diagram from Copernicus's On the Revolutions of Heavenly Bodies, *the earth, "Telluris," is shown in the fifth orbit, and the orbits are depicted as circular and uniform.*

NICOLAI COPERNICI

net, in quo terram cum orbe lunari tanquam epicyclo contineri diximus. Quinto loco Venus nono menſe reducitur. Sextum deniq; locum Mercurius tenet, octuaginta dierum ſpacio circũ currens. In medio uero omnium reſidet Sol. Quis enim in hoc

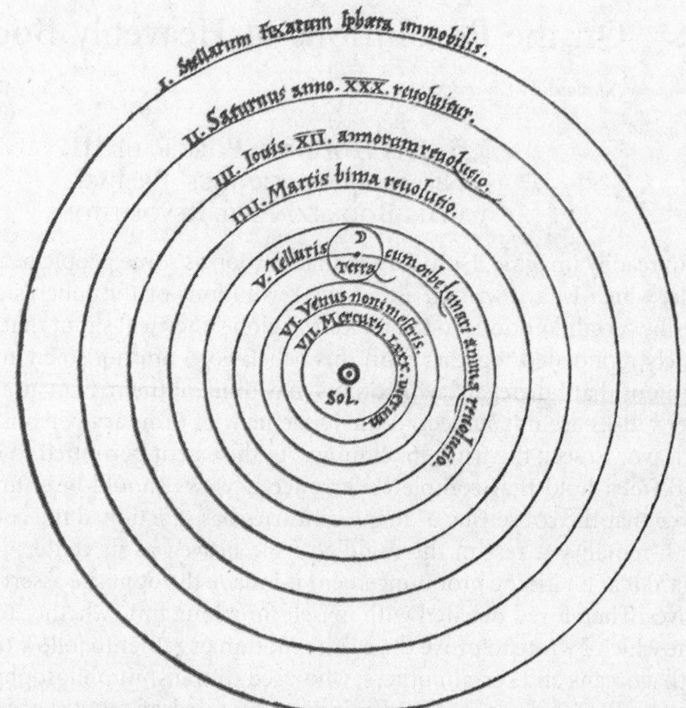

pulcherimo templo lampadem hanc in alio uel meliori loco po neret, quàm unde totum ſimul poſsit illuminare? Siquidem non inepte quidam lucernam mundi, alij mentem, alij rectorem uocant. Trimegiſtus uiſibilem Deum, Sophoclis Electra intuentẽ omnia. Ita profecto tanquam in ſolio re gali Sol reſidens circum agentem gubernat Aſtrorum familiam. Tellus quoq; minime fraudatur lunari miniſterio, ſed ut Ariſtoteles de animalibus ait, maximã Luna cũ terra cognatio nẽ habet. Concipit interea à Sole terra, & impregnatur annuo partu. Inuenimus igitur ſub hac

Giese, bishop of Chełmno, a close student of sacred letters as well as of all good literature. For he repeatedly encouraged me and, sometimes adding reproaches, urgently requested me to publish this volume and finally permit it to appear after being buried among my papers and lying concealed not merely until the ninth year but by now the fourth period of nine years. The same conduct was recommended to me by not a few other very eminent scholars. They exhorted me no longer to refuse, on account of the fear which I felt, to make my work available for the general use of students of astronomy. The crazier my doctrine of the earth's motion now appeared to most people, the argument ran, so much the more admiration and thanks would it gain after they saw the publication of my writings dispel the fog of absurdity by most luminous proofs. Influenced therefore by these persuasive men and by this hope, in the end I allowed my friends to bring out an edition of the volume, as they had long besought me to do.

However, Your Holiness will perhaps not be greatly surprised that I have dared to publish my studies after devoting so much effort to working them out that I did not hesitate to put down my thoughts about the earth's motion in written form too. But you are rather waiting to hear from me how it occurred to me to venture to conceive any motion of the earth, against the traditional opinion of astronomers and almost against common sense. I have accordingly no desire to conceal from Your Holiness that I was impelled to consider a different system of deducing the motions of the universe's spheres for no other reason than the realization that astronomers do not agree among themselves in their investigations of this subject. For, in the first place, they are so uncertain about the motion of the sun and moon that they cannot establish and observe a constant length even for the tropical year. Secondly, in determining the motions not only of these bodies but also of the other five planets, they do not use the same principles, assumptions, and explanations of the apparent revolutions and motions. For while some employ only homocentrics, others utilize eccentrics and epicycles, and yet they do not quite reach their goal. For although those who put their faith in homocentrics showed that some nonuniform motions could be compounded in this way, nevertheless by this means they were unable to obtain any incontrovertible result in absolute agreement with the phenomena. On the other hand, those who devised the eccentrics seem thereby in large measure to have solved the problem of the apparent motions with appropriate calculations. But meanwhile they introduced a good many ideas which apparently contradict the first principles of uniform motion. Nor could they elicit or deduce from the eccentrics the principal consideration, that is, the structure of the universe and the true symmetry of its parts. On the contrary, their experience was just like some one taking from various places hands, feet, a head, and other pieces, very well depicted, it may be, but not for the representation of a single person; since these fragments would not belong to one another at all, a monster rather than a man would be put together from them. Hence in the process of demonstration or "method," as it is called, those who employed eccentrics are found either to have omitted something essential or to have admitted something extraneous and wholly irrelevant. This would not have happened to them, had they followed sound principles. For if the hypotheses assumed by them were not false, everything which follows from their hypotheses would be confirmed beyond any doubt. Even though what I am now saying may be obscure, it will nevertheless become clearer in the proper place.

For a long time, then, I reflected on this confusion in the astronomical traditions concerning the derivation of the motions of the universe's spheres. I began to be annoyed that the movements of the world machine, created for our sake by the best and most systematic Artisan of all, were not understood with greater certainty by the philosophers, who otherwise examined so precisely the most insignificant trifles of this world. For this reason I undertook the task of rereading the works of all the philosophers which I could obtain to learn whether anyone had ever proposed other motions of the universe's spheres than those expounded by the teachers of astronomy in the schools. And in fact first I found in Cicero[2] that Hicetas supposed the earth to move. Later I also discovered in Plutarch[3] that certain others were of this opinion. I have decided to set his words down here, so that they may be available to everybody:

> Some think that the earth remains at rest. But Philolaus the Pythagorean believes that, like the sun and moon, it revolves around the fire in an oblique circle. Heraclides of Pontus and Ecphantus the Pythagorean make the earth move, not in a progressive motion, but like a wheel in a rotation from west to east about its own center.

Therefore, having obtained the opportunity from these sources, I too began to consider the mobility of the earth. And even though the idea seemed absurd, nevertheless I knew that others before me had been granted the freedom to imagine any circles whatever for the purpose of explaining the heavenly phenomena. Hence I thought that I too would be readily permitted to ascertain whether explanations sounder than those of my predecessors could be found for the revolution of the celestial spheres on the assumption of some motion of the earth.

Having thus assumed the motions which I ascribe to the earth later on in the volume, by long and intense study I finally found that if the motions of the other planets are correlated with the orbiting of the earth, and are computed for the revolution of each planet, not only do their phenomena follow therefrom but also the order and size of all the planets and spheres, and heaven itself is so linked together that in no portion of it can anything be shifted without disrupting the remaining parts and the universe as a whole. Accordingly in the arrangement of the volume too I have adopted the following order. In the first book I set forth the entire distribution of the spheres together with the motions which I attribute to the earth, so that this book contains, as it were, the general structure of the universe. Then in the remaining books I correlate the motions of the other planets and of all the spheres with the movement of the earth so that I may thereby determine to what extent the motions and appearances of the other planets and spheres can be saved if they are correlated with the earth's motions. I have no doubt that acute and learned astronomers will agree with me if, as this discipline especially requires, they are willing to examine and consider, not superficially but thoroughly, what I adduce in this volume in proof

---

[2] **Cicero:** Roman orator and philosopher (106–43 B.C.E.).

[3] **Plutarch:** Greek historian (46?–120? C.E.).

of these matters. However, in order that the educated and uneducated alike may see that I do not run away from the judgement of anybody at all, I have preferred dedicating my studies to Your Holiness rather than to anyone else. For even in this very remote corner of the earth where I live you are considered the highest authority by virtue of the loftiness of your office and your love for all literature and astronomy too. Hence by your prestige and judgement you can easily suppress calumnious attacks although, as the proverb has it, there is no remedy for a backbite.

Perhaps there will be babblers who claim to be judges of astronomy although completely ignorant of the subject and, badly distorting some passage of Scripture to their purpose, will dare to find fault with my undertaking and censure it. I disregard them even to the extent of despising their criticism as unfounded. For it is not unknown that Lactantius, otherwise an illustrious writer but hardly an astronomer, speaks quite childishly about the earth's shape, when he mocks those who declared that the earth has the form of a globe. Hence scholars need not be surprised if any such persons will likewise ridicule me. Astronomy is written for astronomers. To them my work too will seem, unless I am mistaken, to make some contribution also to the Church, at the head of which Your Holiness now stands. For not so long ago under Leo X the Lateran Council considered the problem of reforming the ecclesiastical calendar. The issue remained undecided then only because the lengths of the year and month and the motions of the sun and moon were regarded as not yet adequately measured. From that time on, at the suggestion of that most distinguished man, Paul, bishop of Fossombrone, who was then in charge of this matter, I have directed my attention to a more precise study of these topics. But what I have accomplished in this regard, I leave to the judgement of Your Holiness in particular and of all other learned astronomers. And lest I appear to Your Holiness to promise more about the usefulness of this volume than I can fulfill, I now turn to the work itself.

Galileo Galilei
1564–1642

Johannes Kepler
1571–1630

Galileo Galilei and Johannes Kepler, two pioneering astronomers eager to prove that Copernicus was correct in saying that the earth revolved around the sun, were very different men, and Galileo's stubborn refusal to acknowledge the work of his German colleague or to aid Kepler in his research is a sour note in the history of science. In Galileo's insistence on individual glory and personal authority we glimpse a quintessentially Renaissance personality; the self-effacing Kepler may have been the more pleasant man, and in some ways the better scientist of the two. Both however—the proud man and the humble one—exemplify the Renaissance passion for discovery.

Urbane, vain, close to court figures, and good at promoting himself and his ideas, Galileo was a brilliant scientist. At age nineteen, using his pulse for a timer, he observed that a pendulum accomplished each swing in the same amount of time, whether its arc was wide or narrow. He did not invent the telescope, as he liked to say he had, but he was the first to point one heavenward. He found that the moon is a rugged, rocky orb instead of a glowing disc; he discovered the four largest satellites of Jupiter and observed that Venus has phases like the moon.

After his trial by the **Inquisition** for defending Copernicus's views in 1633, Galileo recanted and was confined to a house outside of Florence, where he wrote his last book, *Dialogues Concerning the Two New Sciences* (1638), a treatise on dynamics and motion that prepared the way for what would be one of the most important new paradigms in Western history: mechanism. In his last year, spent under house arrest, he was visited by the English poet John Milton (1608–1674); it is fascinating to think that some of Galileo's ideas may have influenced not only the scientists who came after him but also Milton, in his grand visions of the cosmos "revolv'd on Heaven's great axle."

The deep and mystical love Johannes Kepler felt for the stars was given to him by his eccentric mother, later accused of witchcraft, who carried her little son outside to view the comet of 1577. The adult Kepler was a poor man, a sloppy dresser, and a rather bumbling, gentle soul who mainly made his living by casting horoscopes. He was also a man on fire to understand the secret motions of the universe he found so beautiful. He made plenty of mistakes, but he was an acute observer who, with the help of painstaking measurements recorded by the Danish astronomer Tycho Brahe (1546–1601), formulated three mathematical statements about planetary motion known as Kepler's laws, which he published in two books, *Commentaries on the Motions of Mars* (1609) and *Harmony of the Worlds* (1619). Among other things, these laws postulated that each planet's orbit is an ellipse with the sun at one focus and that planets pick

Noel-Thomas-Joseph Clerian, 1796–1843, *Galileo*
This dramatic painting depicts Galileo, illuminated by a shaft of sunlight, defending himself before the tribunal of the Inquisition. (The Art Archive/ Musée Granet Aix-en-Provence/ Dagli Orti)

up speed when their orbits bring them close to the sun and slow down when distant from it. Later in the century, Sir Isaac Newton (1642–1727) would provide the physical explanations for Kepler's correct observations. Kepler died at age forty-eight, his family and his affairs scattered in the Thirty Years' War and its accompanying plagues; it is said that, on his deathbed, he kept pointing first to his own head, then upward at the stars.

Despite the initial promise of their first exchange of letters, reprinted here, Galileo largely ignored both Kepler's pleas for help in making astronomical observations and his later request to be sent a telescope or even a lens, "so that at last I too can enjoy, like yourself, the spectacle of the skies." Galileo had a good many of the instruments at his disposal and was in the habit of giving them away to friends at court, but he sent none to Kepler. These two men, both of whom possessed partial answers to the mysteries of gravitation, inertia, and planetary movement, might have indeed become "comrades in the pursuit of truth" had they been able to cooperate. As it is, Galileo's name is the one that has come to be more familiar, thanks in part to his forced recantation, at the hands of the Inquisition, of the Copernican theory set forth in his *Dialogue Concerning the Two Chief World Systems* (1632).

[Galileo–Kepler Correspondence]

Translated by Mary Martin McLaughlin

Galileo to Kepler

Padua, August 4, 1597

I received your book, most learned sir, which you sent me by Paulus Amberger, not some days since, but only a few hours ago. And as this Paulus has notified me of his return to Germany, I would consider myself ungrateful if I did not now send you my thanks in the present letter. I thank you, therefore, and most especially because you have judged me worthy of such a token of your friendship. So far I have read only the introduction of your work, but I have to some extent gathered your plan from it, and I congratulate myself on the exceptional good fortune of having such a man as a comrade in the pursuit of truth. For it is too bad that there are so few who seek the truth and so few who do not follow a mistaken method in philosophy. This is not, however, the place to lament the misery of our century, but to rejoice with you over such beautiful ideas for proving the truth. So I add only, and I promise, that I shall read your book at leisure; for I am certain that I shall find the noblest things in it. And this I shall do the more gladly, because I accepted the view of Copernicus many years ago, and from this standpoint I have discovered from their origins many natural phenomena, which doubtless cannot be explained on the basis of the more commonly accepted hypothesis. I have written many direct and indirect arguments for the Copernican view, but until now I have not dared to publish them, alarmed by the fate of Copernicus himself, our master. He has won for himself undying fame in the eyes of a few, but he has been mocked and hooted at by an infinite multitude (for so large is the number of fools). I would dare to come forward publicly with my ideas if there were more people of your way of thinking. As this is not the case, I shall refrain. The shortness of time and my eager desire to read your book compel me to close, but I assure you of my sympathy, and I shall always gladly be at your service. Farewell and do not neglect to send me further good news of yourself.

Kepler to Galileo

Graz, October 13, 1597

I received your letter of August 4 on September 1. It gave me a twofold pleasure, first, because it sealed my friendship with you, the Italian, and second, because of the agreement in our opinions concerning Copernican cosmography. Since at the end of your letter you invite me in friendly fashion to carry on a correspondence with you, and I myself am impelled to do so, I will not overlook the opportunity of sending you a letter by the present young nobleman. Meanwhile, if your time has permitted, I hope that you have come to study my little book more thoroughly. So a great desire has seized me to hear your judgment of it. For it is my way to urge all those to whom I write to give me their true opinion; believe me, I much prefer the sharpest criticism of a single intelligent man to the thoughtless approval of the great masses.

I could only have wished that you, who have so profound an insight, would choose another way. You advise us, by your personal example, and in discreetly veiled fashion, to retreat before the general ignorance and not to expose ourselves or heedlessly to oppose the violent attacks of the mob of scholars (and in this you follow Plato and Pythagoras, our true preceptors). But after a tremendous task has been begun in our time, first by Copernicus and then by many very learned mathematicians, and when the assertion that the earth moves can no longer be considered something new, would it not be much better to pull the wagon to its goal by our joint efforts, now that we have got it under way, and gradually, with powerful voices, to shout down the common herd, which really does not weigh the arguments very carefully? Thus perhaps by cleverness we may bring it to a knowledge of the truth. With your arguments you would at the same time help your comrades who endure so many unjust judgments, for they would obtain either comfort from your agreement or protection from your influential position. It is not only your Italians who cannot believe that they move if they do not feel it, but we in Germany also do not by any means endear ourselves with this idea. Yet there are ways by which we protect ourselves against these difficulties. [. . .]

Be of good cheer, Galileo, and come out publicly. If I judge correctly, there are only a few of the distinguished mathematicians of Europe who would part company with us, so great is the power of truth. If Italy seems less a favourable place for your publication, and if you look for difficulties there, perhaps Germany will allow us this freedom. But enough of this. Let me know privately at least, if you do not want to do so publicly, what you have discovered in support of Copernicus.

Now I should like to ask you for an observation; since I possess no instruments, I must appeal to others. Do you own a quadrant on which minutes and quarter-minutes can be read? If so, please observe, around the time of December 19, the greatest and smallest altitude, in the same night, of the middle star of the handle of the Great Dipper. Also, observe about December 26 both altitudes of the polar star. Also, watch the first star around March 19, 1598, in its height at midnight, the second about September 28, also around midnight. If, as I wish, there could be shown a difference between the two observations, of one or another minute, or even of 10 to 15 minutes, this would be proof of something of great importance for all of astronomy. If no difference is shown, however, we shall still earn together the fame of exploring a very significant problem not hitherto examined by anyone [the fixed-star parallax]. This is enough for those who are enlightened! [. . .] Farewell, and answer me with a very long letter.

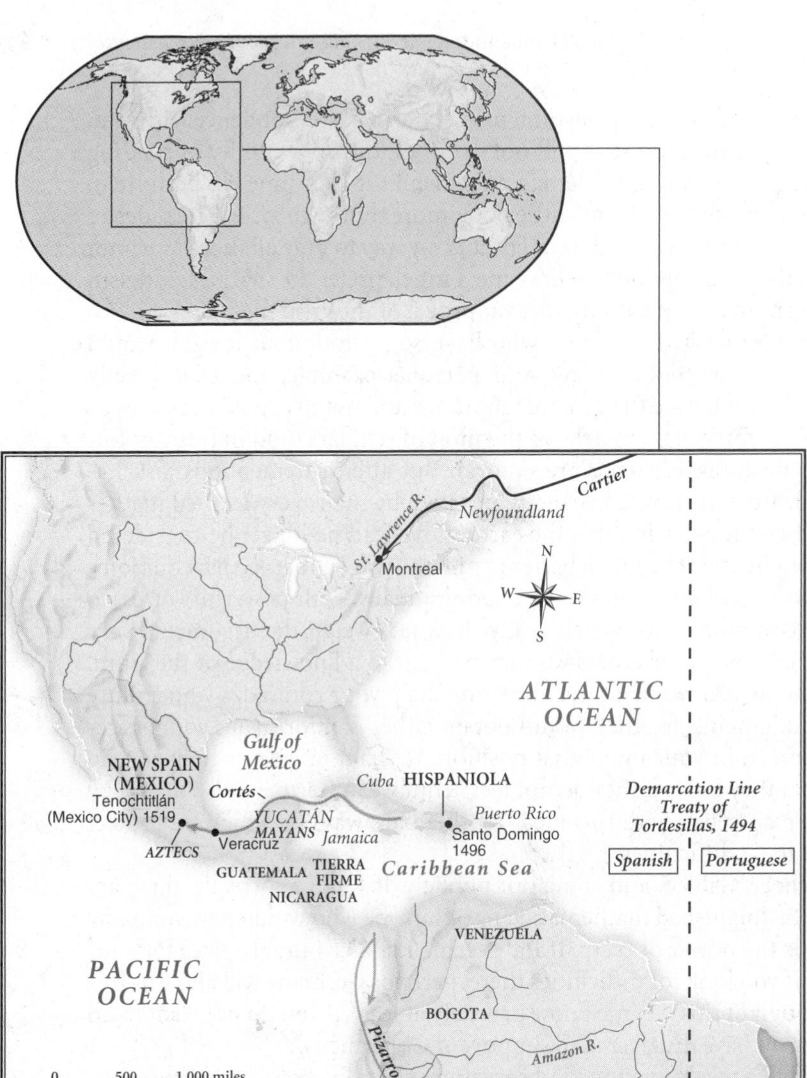

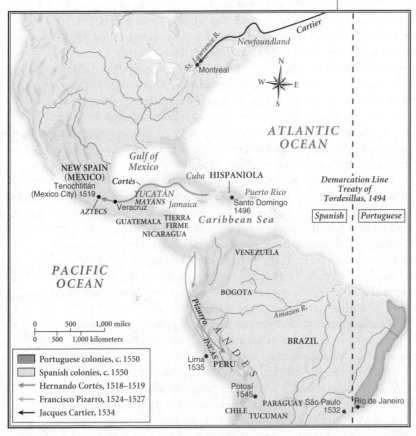

European Colonization of the Americas in the Sixteenth Century

Spanish and Portuguese explorers claimed Central and South America for their respective monarchs, who supported the voyages in part because they desired the precious metals known to be deposited in these regions. There was relatively little exploration of North America at this time, except for the voyage of Jacques Cartier (1491–1557) up the St. Lawrence River; permanent settlement would come later, in the seventeenth century, primarily by the French and English.

THE AMERICAS
Aztec Empire and New Spain

The history of what is today Mexico divides into two distinct parts, the pre-Columbian era — the period of history prior to the arrival of the Europeans in 1519 — and the period after 1519, the year that Hernán Cortés (1485–1547) arrived on the Yucatan Peninsula and began the assault on the Aztec empire. The Aztecs had settled in the Valley of Mexico around Lake Texcoco in the area of today's Mexico City, and they had built an extensive empire of tributary states throughout central Mexico. Their major city, Tenochtitlán, was home to a thriving population of up to two hundred thousand people, and it was the religious and political center of a complex and sophisticated culture that stunned the Spanish who first saw it. After the fall of the Aztecs in 1521, the Spanish took control, gradually extending their influence beyond the former empire and settling a region reaching north into what is now the southwestern part of the United States and south into what are now Colombia, Bolivia, and Peru. By the end of the sixteenth century, the Spanish had built a unique society throughout what was then known as New Spain, with a culture modeled in part on the Old World but inevitably marked with a unique mixture of native and non-native peoples. Among the great literary figures of the Early Modern Period in this part of the world were the Aztecs themselves, who valued skills in rhetoric and the composition of poetry, and the brilliant Sor Juana Inés de la Cruz (1651–1695), the first major writer of Spanish blood to have been born in the New World.

MESOAMERICA BEFORE THE AZTECS

The region of central Mexico and the Yucatan Peninsula — collectively known as Mesoamerica — had been the site of important civilizations dating back to the Olmec, whose culture flourished in the first millennium B.C.E. on the Gulf of Mexico. Urban culture spread quickly throughout Mesoamerica with the remarkable Maya, whose classic period was from 300–900 C.E. Their highly developed skills in mathematics, astronomy, hieroglyphic writing, ceramics, architecture, and warfare made possible the creation of an extensive network of over fifty cities. At the same time, civilization was also taking root on the Mexican highlands: Zapotec Indians created the beautiful Monte Albán near present-day Oaxaca. In the Valley of Mexico, one of the first great cities of the Americas was built at Teotihuacán, the "City of the Gods," beginning in the third century B.C.E., reaching its peak about six hundred years later. Dominated by its great Pyramid of the Sun, a four-tiered structure reaching a height of two hundred feet, the bustling city-state of Teotihuacán had a population of more than two hundred thousand people at its peak in the fifth century and exerted broad economic and political influence over the entire region.

After the demise of Teotihuacán in about 700 C.E., there was a gradual downfall of ceremonial centers throughout the region. Nomadic tribes from the northern plains, called Chichimecs, wandered southward in the ninth century, altering Mexico's history. The Toltecs, who were the descendants of Nahuatl-speaking Chichimecs, inherited the culture of Teotihuacán after its decline and dominated central Mexico until the twelfth century. The name *Toltec* means both a master craftsman and an inhabitant of Tollan. The sixteenth-century Spaniards called the people who built the next great empire in the Valley of Mexico Aztecs, after their mythical home in Aztlán, the Land of Herons.

THE ARRIVAL OF THE AZTECS

Having entered the Valley of Mexico in the early twelfth century from somewhere in the north known as Aztlán, the Aztecs, who spoke a language known as Nahuatl and called themselves *Mexica,* were newcomers to the region. The Aztecs were forced to settle on a swampy island on Lake Texcoco, where in about 1325 they began building Tenochtitlán, meaning Prickly Pear on a Rock. The Aztecs devised ingenious agricultural methods to supply their growing population with food, giving them some measure of self-reliance. In about 1376 Acamapichtli (r. 1376–95), whose mother was a Toltec princess, became the first official ruler of Tenochtitlán. Under the leadership of Acamapichtli and his successors, including Itzcoatl (r. 1427–40), Aztec power, population, and influence grew. With the Texcoco and Tacuba, Itzcoatl formed the so-called Triple Alliance, which went to war against its neighbors in 1428, overthrowing Maxtla, the ruler of Azcapotzalco. This war was followed by a period of empire building under successive rulers including Moctezuma I (r. 1440–69) and Axayacatl (r. 1469–81). Because of their superior skills in warfare and diplomacy, which involved creating a spectacle of terror, by

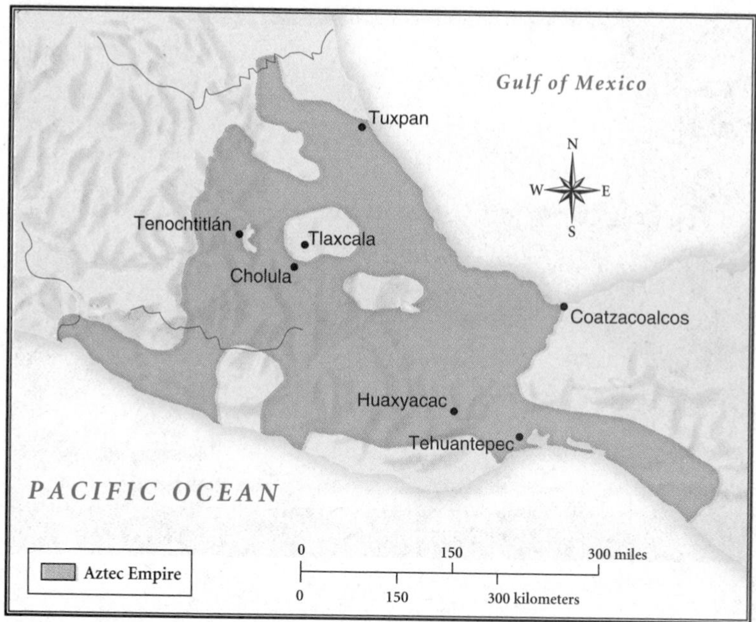

The Aztec Empire, c. 1500
The region of central Mexico and the Yucatan Peninsula has been the site of civilizations dating back to the Olmec, whose culture flourished in the first millennium B.C.E. The Aztecs, who called themselves Mexica, arrived in the Valley of Mexico in the early twelfth century from a mythical area in the north called Aztlán.

the time of Moctezuma II (r. 1502–20) the Aztecs had completed their magnificent capital at Tenochtitlán and created an empire of nearly fifty tributary city-states reaching from the Gulf of Mexico to the Pacific Ocean and southward almost to the border of Guatemala. At the height of its empire, the Aztecs controlled more than a million and a half people in central Mexico and about eleven million throughout the subjugated area. The tributary cities, of course, resented the dominating Aztecs, and the entire region existed in a state of tension and war—a key factor in Cortés's ability to bring down the Aztec empire with only a handful of Spanish soldiers.

AZTEC SOCIETY

Everyday life among the Aztecs was highly ritualistic, and the line between the sacred and the profane was very thin, if there was one at all. At any moment mythic and cosmic forces could, and did, collapse into the temporal march of ordinary

Model of Tenochtitlán

This photo shows a model of the great Aztec capital city showing the temple of Huitzilopochtli at the back center and a painting that reveals its spectacular location. (The Art Archive / National Anthropological Museum Mexico / Dagli Orti)

history. The gods of the Aztecs—whose commands were interpreted by a priest class—demanded strict observance of the rites, including large-scale sacrifice of human beings. The most important god was **Huitzilopochtli** (Blue Hummingbird on the Left), a warlike sun god, who was said to have guided the Aztecs on their trek southward from Aztlán. It was Huitzilopochtli who advised the priests that they should build their city where they saw an eagle with a snake in its mouth sitting atop a cactus—which appeared on the island on Lake Texcoco. It was Huitzilopochtli who demanded the daily blood sacrifices that the Aztecs believed were necessary to sustain the life-giving force of the sun. From the Toltecs the Aztecs had introduced into their pantheon the gods **Quetzalcoatl** (Plumed Serpent) and **Tezcatlipoca** (Smoking Mirror), the god of war. These two gods were said to be locked in an eternal struggle to bring balance between opposing forces in the world—day and night, sky and earth, life and death, peace and war, creation and destruction. One version of the legend of Quetzalcoatl has the peaceful god sailing off into the Gulf of Mexico on a raft of serpents after being defeated by Tezcatlipoca and promising to return. This legend was in part to lead to the demise of the Aztecs, who at first believed (ironically) that the bearded, light-skinned Cortés was the returning god of prosperity, wisdom, and knowledge.

Aztec society followed a rigid class system. The rulers of the Aztec empire, who claimed to be descended from the gods, were elected from among the male members of a royal family. Beneath the rulers, known as *tlatoani,* stood lesser hereditary lords, from whom were drawn the members of the advisory council, the warriors, priests, and government officials. The nobles received a rigorous training in martial arts, religion, social customs, reading, and writing, and there were special schools for both warriors and priests. The commoners, organized into *calpulli,* or wards, similarly were ranked in a hierarchy, with merchants and artisans at the top and agricultural laborers and slaves at the bottom. Each calpulli had a kind of local government, in charge of regulating ordinary affairs and of collecting taxes to be passed upward to the rulers. The artisans and craftspeople of the cities traded their goods with those of other cities and with foodstuffs from farmers outside the city environs by means of a series of canals. All ranks of society received a religious education at the numerous temple schools, and many were prepared to offer themselves for sacrifice in order to avert the total destruction that would occur were the gods to go unappeased. Most of the sacrificial victims, however, were selected from among the captives of the ongoing wars with neighboring cities, prolonged, as some scholars believe, in order to keep a steady supply of victims, whose hearts were torn out and presented to the gods in elaborate daily rituals held in the many temples of Tenochtitlán.

THE SPANISH CONQUEST OF THE AZTEC EMPIRE

With eleven ships, 553 men, and sixteen horses, Hernán Cortés sailed in 1519 from what is now Cuba, then already controlled by the Spanish, to lead a trading expedition to the Valley of Mexico. Shortly after his arrival, he met Malinche (Doña Marina to the Spanish), a Nahuatl-speaking woman, most likely the daughter of an Aztec noble family who had ended up being the slave of the military leader of Tobasco. Malinche, who was familiar with Mayan dialects as well as with Nahuatl and eventually Spanish, served as interpreter and companion to Cortés, providing him with essential information about the local culture and details about the internal dissension spreading through the Aztec empire. With fifteen hundred Totonac warriors who had defected from the empire, Cortés began his march to the highland capital of the Aztecs, Tenochtitlán, gathering support from the Tlascala army and putting down a rebellion in Cholula. Aided by Malinche, Cortés and his men arrived at Tenochtitlán on November 8, 1519, where the first meeting between the Spanish and Aztec leaders, a most extraordinary confrontation, produced confusion and wonderment on both sides. Though Spaniards and Aztecs were similar beings, their concepts of time and history, religion and the place of humans in the cosmic order represented two utterly different worldviews.

After Moctezuma II received them as guests, the Spaniards captured him and held him hostage in his own city. As if giving in to fate, Moctezuma had put up little resistance to the foreigners, though he had observed their movements closely. When Cortés, who had acted in violation of his orders from Governor Diego

Velásquez (1465–1524) in Cuba, was forced to leave Tenochtitlán to repel a Spanish force sent to capture him, Pedro de Alvarado (c. 1485–1541), the Spanish officer left in charge at Tenochtitlán, commanded his soldiers to kill hundreds of Aztec nobles and seize their gold and other valuables. The outraged Aztecs revolted, and Moctezuma was mysteriously killed, either by the Spanish or by his own people, who by now were anxious to resist the violent strangers occupying their city. During what is now called the Noche Triste, the night of sorrow, many Spanish soldiers were killed in battle or, as they fled from the Aztecs, drowned in the waters of Lake Texcoco by the weight of the gold they had plundered. Shortly after vanquishing the Spanish, the Aztecs were hit with a smallpox epidemic that eventually wiped out thousands of men, women, and children, including Cuitlahua (r. 1520), the leader elected after Moctezuma's death. In December, Cortés returned with six hundred well-equipped Spanish soldiers, a hundred thousand disaffected Indian recruits, and thirteen dismantled brigantines that they reassembled on the lake and used to topple the city. Led by the tlatoani Cuauhtemoc (r. 1521–25), the last Aztec emperor and nephew of Moctezuma, the Aztecs defended their city but were defeated on August 13, 1521, when Cuauhtemoc was captured trying to escape across the lake.

SPANISH COLONIALISM

After the Spanish vanquished the Aztec empire in 1521, central Mexico was fast becoming what the conquerors called New Spain, and the Spaniards quickly extended their control over native populations to the north and the south, using their new holdings as a base for exploratory expeditions as far north as what is now New Mexico and as far south as Peru. From his base in Panama, the conquistador Francisco Pizarro (c. 1471–1541) began exploring the coast of Peru in 1524. On his voyage of 1531 to 1533, he ventured inland to the capital of the Inca empire, Cajamarca, which lay midway between the northern city of Quito and the southern city of Cuzco. As in the case of Cortés, Pizarro's success was in part enabled by the untimely death of the Inca emperor in 1527, which led to a civil war between his two surviving sons: Atahualpa in Quito and Huaskar in Cuzco. Just as Atahualpa succeeded in defeating his brother in 1532, Pizarro and his forces arrived and seized Cajamarca. Atahualpa was put on trial and executed. The next year Pizarro overtook Cuzco. Although he founded the colonial capital of Lima in 1535, resistance from the Incas and infighting among Pizarro's men, who killed him in 1541, dragged on for nearly twenty-five years before the Spanish finally took full control over the region.

Spanish rule quickly spread in the sixteenth century throughout Mexico, Central America, and the Pacific seaboard of South America. Moreover, the explor-

Diego Durán, *Totonac Indians Carrying Equipment for the Conquistadors,* 1579
By the late sixteenth century, the encomienda system, whereby the Indians provided "free" labor in return for converting to Christianity, was replaced by a slightly more equitable tributary system called repartimiento. (The Art Archive/Biblioteca Nacional Madrid/Dagli Orti)

ers Juan Ponce de León (1460–1521), Francisco Vásquez de Coronado (c. 1510–1554), Hernando de Soto (c. 1500–1542), Juan de Oñate (1550?–1630), and Sebastián Vizcaíno (1550?–1616), among many others, led expeditions into North America, establishing Catholic missions in and laying claim to territory in what are now Florida, Texas, New Mexico, and Baja California; eventually Spanish explorers reached as far north as Oregon, the Grand Canyon, and Colorado. Meanwhile, the Caribbean Islands, Mexico, and nearly all of South America (with the exception of Portuguese Brazil) were fast becoming Spanish territories, with the indigenous people subject to the rule of their colonial masters.

The Caribbean islands were the first territories to be settled. On his second voyage (1493–96), Columbus founded Santo Domingo on Hispaniola, which he still insisted was a part of India—hence the name Indians for the native peoples of the Americas. Setting a precedent for subsequent Spanish settlement, Columbus divided the territory into parcels and allotted them in various proportions to the settlers; the Indians were compelled to work the land. On Hispaniola, sugarcane production became a profitable agricultural industry, demanding intensive field labor. After the defeat of the Aztecs, Cortés had divvied up the land among his soldiers, reserving a vast extent for his own use. As Spanish settlement spread, the Spanish king gave contracts to men known as *adelantados,* supported in part by private investors, who oversaw the settlement of lands through Mexico and South

America, and who directed the subjugation of the Indians and their conversion to Catholicism.

The vast labor force of Indians was brought under control by the joint means of conversion and of the *encomienda* system, whereby the monarch gave grants of land to a trustee, known as the *encomendero*. Under his contract, the encomendero was obligated to convert the Indians in these lands to Christianity and indoctrinate them in European customs; in exchange for these "benefits," the Indians were obligated to supply free labor. This system was much abused, leading the Spanish kings to issue several decrees in the sixteenth century, first attempting to modify and then to abolish the system. By the end of the sixteenth century the largely defunct encomienda system was replaced first by a tributary system of labor known as the *repartimiento*, or *cuatequil*, and then, by the middle of the seventeenth century, by wage labor. The land grants of the encomienda system were replaced by the great *haciendas*, the privately owned land estates used to grow crops and raise cattle. The haciendas, which sometimes extended to thousands of acres, produced not only food and raw materials for use in New Spain but also crops such as sugar and indigo for export to Spain.

Racial and Cultural Diversity. In the period just after the fall of Tenochtitlán, the encomienda system, as well as other systems of forced and contract labor used in Mexico and Peru, promoted the exploitation of the conquered populations in the Americas. Among those who protested the abuse of the Indians were the Dominican friars, such as Bartolomé de Las Casas (1474–1566), the first bishop of Chiapas and a vocal defender of Indian rights in the Americas. In Brazil, the Jesuits led the call for justice. In a noted debate between Las Casas and the Spanish theologian Juan Ginés de Sepúlveda (1490?–1572), the Catholic bishops argued whether or not the Indians had souls and were human. These debates led to a papal bull of 1537 affirming that the New World natives did indeed have souls, that they were human beings and should enjoy the rights of human beings. Although slavery had been abolished under the "New Laws" handed down in 1542 by King Charles I (r. 1516–56; also Holy Roman Emperor Charles V), abuse of the native population continued. The New Laws were followed by protests and even riots in the colonies, so Charles amended his position to allow Indian slavery for captives of "just wars," providing a loophole for those who chose to continue exploiting the Indians. Thus, in the early seventeenth century King Philip III of Spain (r. 1598–1621) again issued decrees aimed at protecting the Indians from slavery and abuse. The African slaves who increasingly made up the workforce in the Caribbean did not receive the same immunity until the nineteenth century.

By the middle of the sixteenth century, the population of New Spain was a hybridized group of peoples—Spanish, Indian, and African—divided by social rank, race, and ethnicity. The racial distinctions became important in the social hierarchy of New Spain, and the New Spaniards distinguished among themselves. Categories included not only the surviving conquistadors and early settlers but also the *peninsulares,* the new arrivals; the *criollos,* those of Spanish blood born in the New World; and the *mestizos,* mixed-blood peoples born from intermarriages between Spanish and Indians. Mestizos were ranked at the bottom of the social order, along with Indians, Africans, and *mulattoes,* those born of Spanish and African unions. By the middle of the sixteenth century, more women had immigrated from Spain to the New World, and the need for intermarriage was less pressing. Increasingly, the Spanish criollos regarded themselves as superior to all of the other groups. Throughout the colonial period, Indians and mestizos, overrepresented among the poor, rose up from time to time in short-lived but violent rebellions to protest what they saw as discriminatory policies of exploitation and excessive taxation.

Schools and Universities. Soon after the Spanish settlement began in the Americas, missions and missionary schools, primarily run by Franciscan monks, were established to convert the native and mestizo populations. In part because of these institutions, by the end of the sixteenth century hundreds of thousands of Indians had adopted Christianity as their religion, integrating the rituals of the Catholic Church into their own native traditions. In her LOA (prologue) for the play *The Divine Narcissus,* Sor Juana Inés de la Cruz (1651–1695) brilliantly dramatizes this process of syncretism of native religious customs with Catholicism. In 1553, the first European-style university in the New World, the University of Mexico in what is now Mexico City, began holding classes. Admission was open to those of sufficient means and of pure race—whether Indian nobles or Spanish criollos. By the end of the century, many who matriculated in the university had been educated in one of the many primary schools founded throughout New Spain in the sixteenth century, including the prestigious College of San Pedro and San Pablo, founded in 1574 by the Jesuits.

In addition to missions, schools, and universities, the New Spaniards were building churches and cathedrals—such as those in Mexico City, Tlaxcala, Morelia, and Tasco—as well as lavish residences, parks, and civic buildings, such as Alameda Park and the Viceregal Palace in Mexico City. While the earliest cathedrals and churches imitated the Gothic style of Old World cathedrals, architects working with native materials and facing the exigencies of the climate and terrain developed

TIME AND PLACE

The Aztecs and Sacrifice

Before the Aztecs, or Mexica, arrived in the Valley of Mexico and founded the city of Tenochtitlán, they were wandering *Chichimecs,* a Nahuatl word meaning "Sons of Dogs," referring to their status as nomads from the northern deserts. The Chichimecs were similar to the Gothic tribes who invaded Rome in the fifth century: They had strong military skills, but limited abilities for creating and administering cities. When, through a series of alliances, intrigues, and conquests, the Aztecs gained ascendancy in the region in 1432 under the leadership of Itzcoatl, they took steps to alleviate their feelings of illegitimacy, common to uncivilized newcomers. In order to elevate the god Huitzilopochtli from tribal status to a prominence comparable to Quetzalcoatl and Tezcatlipoca, the ruler Itzcoatl's nephew, Tlacaélel, ordered that the ancient codices be burned so that a new cosmogony could be written that would locate Huitzilopochtli at the center of the Aztec solar cult and make the Aztecs the official descendants of the Toltecs. Aztec priests performed sacrifices each morning to provide for Huitzilopochtli's struggle against the stars and moon. Born in the east, the sun was fed by the souls of fallen warriors until it reached the center of the sky at noon; its descent into the west was fed by the souls of women who died in childbirth.

The idea of sacrifice and penance was modeled by Quetzalcoatl, who bled himself to create the first humans, and by the two gods who sacrificed themselves to birth the sun and the moon. While rabbits, snakes, quail, and incense were commonly used for sacrifice, it is thought that Tlacaélel made human sacrifice the center of cult practice. The Aztecs believed that a divine "life force," called *teyolia,* resided in the heart. Every human heart had some, but stronger amounts existed in priests, artists, and warriors who impersonated deities during festivals. When a person died, the teyolia ascended into the sky to become birds or energy for the sun. *Teyolia* is similar to what other peoples have called "mana," which is typically most powerful in blood.

Tlacaélel promoted the building of Huitzilopochtli's main temple at the center of Tenochtitlán; called Coatepec (Serpent Mountain), the pyramid temple was fifteen stories high. At the top was a shrine to Tlaloc, the god of rain and agriculture, and to Huitzilopochtli. In front of an image of Huitzilopochtli was a green sacrificial stone, on which the cosmic drama took place each morning: Four attendants held down the victim or victims while a priest quickly cut into

a style known as the Puebla, as well as a unique form of the Baroque, known as Ultra Baroque. Some churches were also designed simply, reflecting the preference and character of the monastic orders for whom they were built. All of these styles were inflected to some degree with the signature of native craftsmen, carpenters, and masonworkers, particularly the Ultra Baroque, which relied heavily on elaborate designs and ornamentation. Moreover, the cathedrals were adorned

TIME AND PLACE

The Aztecs and Sacrifice continued

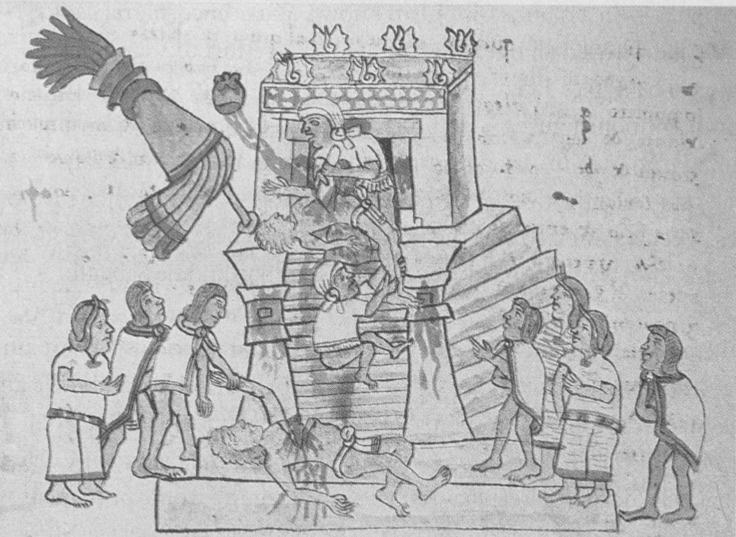

Human Sacrifice *From an Aztec manuscript, the Codex "Magliabecchiano," this illustration shows the ritual sacrifice of two humans by Aztec priests. (Scala / Art Resource, NY)*

the chest with an obsidian knife, withdrew the beating heart—still filled with teyolia—and offered it to the sun. The victims were drawn from prisoners of war and from Aztec warriors who considered it an honor to participate in religious ceremony.

Some scholars suggest that human sacrifice became an obsession in Aztec society with the dedication of Huitzilopochtli's temple in 1487. The temple was completed by the Aztec ruler Ahuitzotl (r. 1486–1503), who had gone on long campaigns to capture victims for the ceremony. Estimates of the number of sacrifices during the four-day dedication ceremony range from twenty thousand to as high as eighty thousand—an astonishing figure. It is said that there were four rows of victims, each over three miles long; when one series of priests became exhausted by the ritual, they were replaced by others. Blood flowed down the sides of the temple, congealing under the steps.

with paintings and sculptures, which, especially in the earlier years, still retained traces of indigenous craftsmanship. Eventually, in sculpture and painting, European styles exerted a strong influence, and the art of the colonial period had its finest painters in the seventeenth century in the work of Cristóbal de Villalpando (c. 1649–1714), whose work focuses on religious themes, and Juan Correa (1646–1739).

THE LITERATURE OF MEXICO AND NEW SPAIN

Much of the work of learning about the language, religion, and culture of the native populations fell to the missionaries and clergymen, some of whom accompanied the explorers and conquistadors. While the Aztecs and Maya had produced thousands of books—in a manuscript form known as a **CODEX** (plural *codices*)—the conquistadors destroyed all but a few of them in an effort to stamp out the "pagan" religion. The Aztecs' language, Nahuatl, was written in the form of glyphs—that is, symbolic figures—and their codices concerned a wide range of subjects, ranging from day-to-day government to hymns and poems. Only sixteen of these codices survived the destruction; three are Mayan and the rest are from the city-states of central Mexico and the Oaxaca region. These works were saved in part due to the efforts of Spanish priests such as Bernardino de Sahagún (1499–1590).

One of the most important works of the early colonial period in New Spain is Sahagún's *General History of the Things of New Spain,* which describes the life and culture of the Aztecs, as well as the Spanish conquest of Mexico. The letters of Hernán Cortés; *The True History of the Conquest of New Spain,* by one of Cortés's soldiers, Bernal Díaz del Castillo (1492–?1581); and Sahagún's works provide us with three very distinctive perspectives on the Spanish Conquest. Díaz del Castillo's episodic eyewitness account of the conquest from the point of view of a soldier, not written until almost thirty years after he took part in the venture, still provides engaging reading.

In addition to these important historical works, throughout the sixteenth and seventeenth centuries, writers of New Spain, many of them criollos, wrote in a variety of genres, including epic and lyric poetry, ballads and songs known as *cancioneros,* fiction, and religious dramas and *comedias,* or plays. The first Mexican-born poet writing in Spanish was Francisco de Terrazas (c. 1540–c. 1584), who wrote a panegyric epic on the conquest of the New World. Other epics celebrating Cortés's vanquishing of the Aztecs appeared, as did satires criticizing the administration of the colonial government. The greatest satirist of the early era is Mateo Rosas de Oquendo (1559?–1612?), whose work targets the preferential treatment of the peninsulares—the Spanish-born officials sent to serve in the colonies. The early colonial theater consisted primarily of short one-act plays known as *autos,* which were designed, like European drama of the Middle Ages, to present important biblical events or rituals, such as the Eucharist, in a simple form of spectacle to aid in the conversion of the native populations, but they were also performed at festivals—both religious and secular. By the seventeenth century, these had given way to the bona fide plays known as comedias.

One of the most important intellectuals of the seventeenth century in New Spain was the scientist, theologian, mathematician, and astronomer Carlos de Sigüenza Góngora (1645–1700). Well versed in Indian languages, as well as in Latin, this humanist of New Spain amassed an extraordinary library of codices, books, and manuscripts on the history and culture of the Indians as well as on the colonial history of Spain. His *Phoenix of the West* reinforced the idea, first broached in the *History of the Indies of New Spain and the Islands of Terra Firma* (c. 1580) by the Dominican friar Diego Durán (c. 1537–1588), that the Quetzalcoatl legend might be linked to the mysterious travels of St. Thomas, who might have visited the Americas.

The most important writer of the seventeenth century and the one who has survived unquestionably as a writer of world literary status is Sor Juana Inés de la Cruz (c. 1648–1695). Although she did not attend the University of Mexico, Sor Juana was a gifted child who studied Latin as a young girl in Mexico City before eventually becoming a nun in order to pursue her studies and writing. The most important writer of colonial Mexico, Sor Juana was a brilliant scholar, a prolific poet and playwright, and an ardent defender of women's right to a liberal education. She wrote hundreds of occasional poems, more than sixty sonnets, several religious dramas, and two comedias; she also wrote longer verse forms and scholarly treatises. Inviting comparison with those of the English poet John Donne, many of her poems explore sophisticated philosophical and religious questions, while others deal with themes of love.

WWW For more information about the culture and context of the Americas in the Early Modern World, see *World Literature Online* at bedfordstmartins.com/worldlit.

THE ANCIENT MEXICANS
SIXTEENTH CENTURY

WWW For quizzes on the Ancient Mexicans, see *World Literature Online* at bedfordstmartins .com/worldlit.

In his remarkable book, *The True History of the Conquest of New Spain,* Bernal Díaz del Castillo, one of Hernán Cortés's soldiers, describes the arrival of the Spanish conquistadors on the Mexican coast in 1519, the long march to the highland plateau of Mexico, and their impressions of seeing for the first time the magnificent capital of the Aztecs, Tenochtitlán, situated on an island in the middle of a large lake. Díaz exclaims, "We did not know what to say, or if this was real that we saw before our eyes." He was looking at one of the most beautiful cities in the world. With about two hundred thousand inhabitants, about five times larger than London, Tenochtitlán was intersected by canals, much like Venice. It contained magnificent buildings, schools, temples, and a huge central marketplace filled with embroidered goods, foods, animals, precious metals and stones, pottery, furniture, flowers, paper, tobacco, and much more. The rich and complex culture of ancient Mexico centered on its ornate ceremonial cities, where scholar-priests made elaborate picture books of omens and heavenly visions, where artists created beautiful murals and jewelry. Poets told amazing stories about gods and goddesses such as Huitzilopochtli and Quetzalcoatl.

In this section the literature of ancient Mexico is divided into two general categories. The first includes fundamental stories of creation and the gods, the kind of stories that form the foundation of all ancient civilizations. Included in this category is the story of the most important messianic hero of the Americas, "The Myth of Quetzalcoatl," and a selection of poems by the most famous poet-king of that period, Nezahualcoyotl. The second category includes a native account of the Spanish conquest of ancient Mexico in 1521 and a defense of Aztec religion by Aztec priests.

The well-documented encounter between the Spanish and the Aztecs provides important information about the historic meeting of two different cultures—Europe and indigenous America. The eventual destruction of the Aztec empire by the Spanish completely changed the face of Mesoamerica, affecting all the peoples who have since lived there.

Calling themselves Mexica and speaking Nahuatl, the original Aztecs followed a fiercely warlike deity, Huitzilopochtli (Blue Hummingbird on the Left) southward in the twelfth century. This deity promised the Aztecs a great destiny and instructed them to build a city where they found an eagle sitting on a cactus with a snake in its mouth. That place was Lake Texcoco, today's Mexico City. Through a series of alliances, intrigues, and conquests, the Aztecs gained ascendancy in the region, and then built an empire. Believing that their destiny was to sustain the life of the sun with blood, they willingly gave their lives for their city and their patron god, Huitzilopochtli. The Aztecs were not particularly good administrators of their empire, having alienated surrounding tribes, and they were strangely vulnerable to the incursion of Europeans with their different values and mindset. In addition to being fierce fighters, the Aztecs were fine poets, having unusually high ideals for the artist and the sage. They revered the Toltecs, who had preceded them on the Mexican plateau, and adopted Toltec mythology and industry. Long after they had disappeared, the Toltecs served as spiritual models for the Aztecs and were celebrated in their poetry: "The Toltecs were truly wise; / they conversed with their own hearts."

The contradictions in Aztec civilization, the cleavage in the Aztec soul, sharpened Western interest in Aztec culture. . . . The "Assyrians of America," whose great plunder empire rested on foundations of war and human sacrifice, were refined lovers of beauty. The poets composed delicate verse filled with allusions to the scent and loveliness of flowers, to the brilliance of fine gems, to the brevity of life and its uncertain joys.

– Benjamin Keen, *The Aztecs in Western Thought*, 1971

Myth and Literature. Although the peoples of Mesoamerica valued art and education, producing thousands of books, Spanish friars immediately following the conquest attempted to eradicate the native, "pagan" religion by destroying the written books, or codices, of the Aztecs and Mayas. Only sixteen of these documents still exist: Three of them are Mayan and the rest are from the Oaxaca region and central Mexico. Ironically, Spanish priests such as Fray Bernardino de Sahagún also became the primary collectors of whatever native materials survived. The priest-ethnographers enlisted native wise men who apparently had access to extant preconquest books and who used the Latin alphabet to record in Nahuatl the ancient myths, sagas, prayers, chronicles, songs, and speeches. It is from these materials that the selections here have come.

The sampling of creation myths included here provide a kind of blueprint of the cosmos: the beginnings of the world and the origins of human beings, fire, suffering, and death—much that is essential for material and spiritual survival. A similar function is provided by the earliest creation stories by the ancient Mesopotamians, Hebrews, Egyptians, and Indians. The principle of opposition, which produced the Aztec cosmos, originated in the androgynous, supreme god of duality Ometeotl (*Ome* = two; *teotl* = god), whose four sons, as the four quarters of space, were transformed into the four ages that preceded this one. The ancient Mexicans, like the Native Americans of the Southwest and analogous to the Hindus of India, believed that there had been different worlds, ages, or suns before this one, roughly corresponding to the four basic elements of the cosmos: earth, air, fire, and water.

Each age was sustained by a delicate balance between opposing forces, dramatized in the myths as a titanic struggle between the gods Quetzalcoatl and Tezcatlipoca. It was not, however, a struggle between good and evil, such as we might find in a Zoroastrian[1] or a Christian version of history, but a question of harmonizing or balancing the antithetical powers of day and night, sky and earth, spirit and matter, as in the Asian conception of yin and yang. Disharmony brought destruction and the end of an age. The ancient Mexicans were concerned with time, perhaps obsessed with it. The inevitable destruction of the present age, the Fifth Sun, by earthquakes is reflected in the profound fatalism of Aztec and other

[1] **Zoroastrian:** Zoroaster (the Western form of the Persian Zarathustra, born c. 650 B.C.E., possibly as early as 1200 B.C.E.) was a Persian prophet who envisioned history as a dualistic struggle between Ahura Mazda (lord of light) and Angra Mainyu (lord of darkness), similar to the Christian belief in Satan.

Creation Myth Pre-Conquest
The god Texcatlipoca is shown here in an illustration of the Aztec creation myth from the Codex Fejérváry-Mayer. (Werner Forman/Art Resource, NY)

Nahuatl-speaking poets. Nevertheless, the end could be postponed if, with sacrifice and penance, the sun were kept alive and healthy in its passage through the sky. This belief provided a divine mission for the Aztecs as "Warriors of the Sun."

p. 715 The myth "**The Creation of the Earth**" tells how Quetzalcoatl and Tezcatlipoca created the heavens and the earth by tearing in two a monstrous earth goddess. Afterward, feeling bad about the harm they had brought her, they gave her gifts and created the mountains, caves, trees, and flowers from parts of her body. The origin of light is related in the p. 716 myth "**How the Sun and Moon Were Created.**" After the gods gather at the ancient site of Teotihuacán, one of them must sacrifice himself to produce the births of the sun and the moon; two gods finally are chosen, but their sacrifice is not sufficient to get the sun and the moon to move in their orbits. The central motif of sacrifice becomes a lesson for later mortals p. 719 in "**The Creation of Man and Woman.**" Quetzalcoatl must descend into the underworld to retrieve the necessary bones for creating human beings. Like the descent myths in ancient Greece and Babylonia, his archetypal journey into the earth suggests the analogy of human life to the vegetation cycle, pointing to the primordial idea that the source of both life and death is in the underworld—a place not to be confused with the Christian hell.

The Myth of Quetzalcoatl. The stories and traditions surrounding Quetzalcoatl form one of the most important spiritual legacies of ancient Mexico. At one time, his influence stretched from what is now Guatemala to northern Mexico. The *quetzal* referred to in the first half of his name is a rare and precious bird with long tail feathers used for ceremonial dress, symbolic of the powers of the sky and the aspirations of the spirit. *Coatl* means "snake" or "serpent" and is tied to the energies of the earth, the mysteries behind fertility and cyclic renewal. Thus in Quetzalcoatl ancient Mexicans had discovered a deity that combined spirit and matter, or mediated between them, reconciling the two realms of heaven and earth. The winged serpent can also be found in European folklore, but its closest kin are found in Asia with the dragons in Chinese and Japanese symbolism.

A merging of mythology with history occurred in the tenth century when the cult of the god Quetzalcoatl became associated with a Toltec ruler and priest, Ce Acatl (One Reed) Topiltzin, who is perhaps Mexico's first historical figure of record. "**The Myth of Quetzalcoatl**" begins with p. 721 the birth of Ce Acatl, whose father was Mixcoatl, the legendary leader of the Toltec-Chichimec tribe. Very little is known about Topiltzin's childhood except that he trains as a warrior and defeats his uncles, who had earlier killed his father. Ultimately Topiltzin becomes a priest of Quetzalcoatl and is made ruler and spiritual model of the Toltecs, respected for his penitential life of self-discipline and piety. He sacrifices snakes, birds, and butterflies, a practice that later draws the anger of those who favor human sacrifice. As a legendary culture-bringer, Topiltzin-Quetzalcoatl, like the Greek Prometheus, invents all the arts necessary for a prosperous life. But the dramatic core of this myth involves Topiltzin's fall from power, his pilgrimage to the sea, and his death and resurrection.

At the height of Toltec fame and prosperity, Topiltzin-Quetzalcoatl withdraws from society into the privacy of his temple. Led by Tezcatlipoca, Quetzalcoatl's mythic adversary, militaristic sorcerers lure Topiltzin out of seclusion and force him to break his ascetic vows by getting him drunk so that he sleeps with his sister, Quetzalpetlatl. Disgraced, Topiltzin-Quetzalcoatl goes into exile, traveling to Tlillan Tlapallan, the "land of black and red" at the eastern horizon, where the morning star announces the rebirth of the sun. Symbolically, it is the place of spiritual fulfillment and enlightenment. There are two different conclusions to this story. Sahagún tells one version that is related to Quetzalcoatl's messianic promise: Quetzalcoatl flies off on a raft of serpents, promising to return one day from over the water. The second version, which is included here, describes Quetzalcoatl's phoenixlike death and resurrection as the

> **In so far as [Quetzalcoatl] was a man, he was of the breed of heroes from whom myths are created. In so far as he is a symbol, he presides like the wind over all space. He is the soul taking wings to heaven, and he is matter descending to earth as the crawling snake; he is virtue rising, and he is the blind force pulling man down; he is waking and dream.**
>
> – IRENE NICHOLSON, *Mexican and Central American Mythology*, 1967

morning star, reflecting in its periodic cycles Quetzalcoatl's own death, resurrection, and promise to return. In addition to his reconciling role between heaven and earth, between matter and spirit, the transformation of his spiritual pilgrimage from despair into beauty marks Topiltzin-Quetzalcoatl as a special hero.

The Poetry of Nezahualcoyotl. Nezahualcoyotl (1402–1472), who lived a generation before the arrival of the Conquistadors, was the ruler of Texcoco for more than forty years and a remarkable poet-philosopher and sage with numerous talents. When Nezahualcoyotl was a boy, his father was murdered; nevertheless, he received an excellent education and with the assistance of the Aztecs was able to defeat his father's enemies and gain the throne of Texcoco. Nezahualcoyotl, whose name means "hungry coyote," then created a golden age for his followers by codifying laws and assembling what was probably the first library in the Americas. As an engineer, he assisted the Aztecs in building their aqueduct and the dikes that separated brackish from sweet water on Lake Texcoco. He worshiped a god called Tloque Nahuaque (Lord of Everywhere), an invisible deity not to be identified with images or statues—an early Mexican version of monotheism. In his poems, of which over thirty still exist, Nezahualcoyotl addresses issues of mortality, political power, and the mystery of death.

The Conquest of the Aztecs. Because of Bernardino de Sahagún, a Franciscan who arrived in New Spain in 1529, we have an account of the Conquest from the point of view of the Aztecs. Considered to be the originator of Mexican ethnography, Sahagún assembled native informants who wrote and illustrated materials, which Sahagún collected into twelve volumes covering a broad spectrum of Aztec life: religion, history, customs, medicine, and literature. The Nahuatl and Spanish version is called *General History of the Things of New Spain.* The historical account we include was excerpted from the *Codex Florentino,* a copy of the *History* sent by Sahagún to Europe in 1580. The excerpts follow generally the chronology of the conquest but include important observations and reflections on the events.

Moctezuma II, the Aztec ruler, was extremely apprehensive about the arrival of the Spanish. Several years before Cortés's actual arrival, the Aztecs had witnessed bad omens in the sky and on earth. The myth of the god Quetzalcoatl was also revived; he had promised to return in the year Ce-Acatl of the Aztec calendar, which happened to coincide with the year 1519. Such was the power of the omens and the myth that the Aztec rulers believed initially that the Spanish were Quetzalcoatl and his retinue returning to claim the throne. Cortés's ships were reported to Moctezuma II as floating mountains or perhaps Quetzalcoatl's four mythic temples, which had been built for penance and symbolized the four directions. This mistake probably contributed to Moctezuma's strange passivity and his indecision about defending the Aztec capital against the outsiders.

On November 8, 1519, Cortés and his band of conquistadors arrived at the magnificent Tenochtitlán, where the first meeting between Cortés and Moctezuma, an unusual, historical confrontation, produced confusion and wonderment on both sides. Certainly as human beings, Spaniard and Aztec were similar; but in their attitudes and values, they represented two radically different worldviews, two kinds of consciousness. The Spaniards carried with them the Renaissance idea that individuals could make and shape history. As Christians, they lived with a linear concept of time and history, guided by a god whose dominion extended to the entire earth; this god granted them a mandate to conquer and exploit "pagan" lands and peoples, who were, in their view, imprisoned by superstition and ignorance. Tenochtitlán was a stepping stone to larger plans. For Moctezuma and his followers, however, the encounter was initially and fundamentally a religious or mythological event. Their lives were shaped by the precarious, reciprocal relationship between human, natural, and divine worlds. Each day was clothed with references to divine favor or disfavor. Nothing—no tree or bird—was simply itself; everything vibrated within a web of sacred meaning and divine implication. As a result, there was no easy or quick way to untangle the Spaniards from the myth of Quetzalcoatl if omens and signs—plus the exotic physical appearance of the Spaniards—had initially intertwined them.

A Defense of Aztec Religion. In 1524, three years after the destruction of the Aztec empire, Pope Adrian VI and Emperor Carlos V of Spain sent twelve Franciscan friars to convert the Indians of Mexico. After the friars had become briefly acquainted with the native culture, they called a conference with native leaders to explain the basic tenets of Christianity and why the Indians should convert. Many ordinary people converted; one Franciscan friar claimed that he baptized fourteen thousand Indians in one day, and another friar baptized four hundred thousand over a lifetime. A few native religious leaders, or sages, however, nobly resisted the efforts at conversion. They were allowed to reply to the friars in defense of their beliefs. "**A Defense of Aztec Religion**" is an eloquent statement revealing the strength of their character, their refinement as human beings, and the depth of their religious faith. p. 765

The Ongoing Debate. The debate has continued to the present time about what appear to be contradictions in the Aztec way of life, between the light and the dark side, the humanism and the barbarism. In his letters, Cortés described the Aztecs as an advanced civilization, equal to Europeans in intelligence and creativity. Other scholars concluded that the Aztecs were simply primitive despots. The reputation of Quetzalcoatl continued to grow over the next centuries. Although his religious influence diminished in the nineteenth century, the figure of Quetzalcoatl remains an exemplary hero from ancient Mexico, a model of all that is admirable in Nahua culture, in contrast to the sometimes oppressive picture of Aztec society found in the statistics of human sacrifice.

The sense of tragedy that pervades the demise of both the Aztecs and the Maya continues to intrigue artists, philosophers, novelists, and poets. The fall of these indigenous peoples reflects the fate of native peoples throughout the Americas and is intertwined with the destiny of the peoples who came later to negotiate a future that recognizes both the sufferings and accomplishments of the past.

■ CONNECTIONS

Epic of Creation, Book 1. It is common for creation stories to depict the transition from chaos to creation, from disorder to order, as overcoming a serpent or dragon. In the Mesopotamian myth of creation, the struggle is between a cosmic hero and the serpentine Tiamat. What are the similarities between the Mexican and the Mesopotamian versions of creation and the role of violence in the transition from chaos to order? How do the twin deities of the Aztec myth transform the feminine into the inhabitable earth?

Christopher Marlowe, *Doctor Faustus,* p. 389. Tragic heroes are often caught between conflicting demands, conflicting value systems, that force a choice leading to tragic consequences. Marlowe's Faustus is caught between a medieval, Christian world and the emerging world of secularism and free thought. Consider how the hero Quetzalcoatl is caught between an ethic of kindness and a worldview represented by Tezcatlipoca. What are the tragic consequences of Quetzalcoatl's plight?

Black Elk, "The Ghost Dance and Wounded Knee," Book 6. The European version of the conquest and dominance of the New World from the sixteenth century onward is well represented in diaries, letters, essays, and books. We do not, however, have many eyewitness accounts from the point of view of native or indigenous peoples. Consider the reasons for the scarcity of native accounts. How do Black Elk's account of the massacre at Wounded Knee and the Aztec account of the Spanish conquest represent turning points in their respective histories?

■ FURTHER RESEARCH

Historical Background

Burland, Cottie A. *Montezuma: Lord of the Aztecs.* 1973.
Carrasco, David. *Religions of Mesoamerica.* 1990.
Clendinnen, Inga. *Aztecs: An Interpretation.* 1991.
Diaz, Bernal. *The Conquest of New Spain.* 1963.
Davies, Nigel. *The Ancient Kingdoms of Mexico.* 1982.
———. *The Aztecs: A History.* 1973.
Keen, Benjamin. *The Aztec Image in Western Thought.* 1971.
León-Portilla, Miguel. *Aztec Thought and Culture: A Study of the Ancient Nahuatl Mind.* 1963.
Séjourné, Laurette. *Burning Water: Thought and Religion in Ancient Mexico.* 1956.
Vaillant, George C. *Aztecs of Mexico.* 1950.

Literary Texts and Criticism

Anderson, Arthur J. O., and Charles E. Dibble, trans. *Florentine Codex: General History of the Things of New Spain.* 1950–81. A bilingual Nahuatl and English edition of Bernardino de Sahagún's history.
Bierhorst, John, trans. *The Codex Chimalpopoca: History and Mythology of the Aztecs.* 1992.
Bierhorst, John, trans. and ed. *Four Masterworks of American Indian Literature: Quetzalcoatl, The Ritual of Condolence, Cuceb, The Night Chant.* 1974.
Brotherston, Gordon. *Book of the Fourth World: Reading the Native Americas through Their Literature.* 1992.
Kissam, Edward, and Michael Schmidt, trans. *Poems of the Aztec Peoples.* 1977.
León-Portilla, Miguel, ed. *Native Mesoamerican Spirituality: Ancient Myths, Discourses, Stories, Doctrines, Hymns, Poems from the Aztec, Yucatec, Quiche-Maya and Other Sacred Traditions.* 1980.

León-Portilla, Miguel, ed. *Pre-Columbian Literatures of Mexico.* 1975.
Nicholson, Irene. *Firefly in the Night: A Study of Ancient Mexican Poetry and Symbolism.* 1959.

■ **PRONUNCIATION**

Cuauhtemoc: kwow-TAY-moke
Huizilopochtli: weet-sih-loh-POHCH-tlee
Malinche: mah-LEEN-chay
Nahuatl: NAH-waht-ul
Quetzalcoatl: ket-sahl-koh-AHT-ul
Tenochtitlán: tay-nohch-teet-LAHN
Teotihuacán: tay-oh-tee-wah-KAHN
Texcoco: tes-KOH-koh
Tezcatlipoca: tes-kah-tlee-POH-kah
Tlaxcalans: tlahs-KAH-lahns

Myths of Creation

Translated by David M. Johnson

The Creation of the Earth

The great gods, Tezcatlipoca and Quetzalcoatl,[1] brought the Earth Goddess[2] down from the heavens. She was an enormous monster full of eyes and mouths. Each of the joints in her body contained a mouth, and these innumerable mouths bit like wild beasts. The world was already full of water, although no one knows its origin.

When the gods saw the huge monster moving back and forth across the water, they said to each other: "We must create the earth." So they transformed themselves into two large serpents. One of them gripped the goddess from her right hand down to her left foot, while the other took her left hand and right foot. Holding on to her, they turned and twisted with such force that she finally tore in two. They lifted her

Myths of Creation. Like creation accounts from the Mediterranean and the ancient Near East, the Aztec creation myths deal with fundamental questions: Where did the world come from? How does it work and who is in control? How did humans arise and what did they eat? A primordial step is taken when order is wrested from chaos, often depicted as a god or gods taking control of a water monster. The basic cosmological picture usually provides a role for religion and an explanation for the participation of humans in the maintenance and harmonious functioning of the world. It was

[1] **Tezcatlipoca and Quetzalcoatl:** Tezcatlipoca, whose name means "smoking mirror," was a powerful deity associated with war, disease, and the material world. A sometimes brother of Quetzalcoatl, he was always his adversary and antithesis. Quetzalcoatl, whose name means "Plumed Serpent" or "precious twin," was the god of light and spirituality, as well as the giver of life.

[2] **Earth Goddess:** Not given a name in the text, she is a primeval, water serpent probably related to Cihuacoatl ("Serpent Woman") and similar to the female serpents of chaos found in other mythological traditions such as in the Mesopotamian *Epic of Creation.*

lower half and made the sky. From the upper part they formed the earth. The rest of the gods looked on and felt ashamed that they had not made anything comparable to this.

Then, in order to make amends for the immense damage inflicted on the Earth Goddess, the other gods came down to console her and give her gifts. As a compensation they declared that out of her body would come all that humans need to sustain themselves and live on the earth. From her hair they made wild grasses, trees and flowers. Her skin was changed into delicate greens and ornamental plants. Her eyes were transformed into small hollows, wells and fountains, her mouth into large caves, her nose into mountains and valleys.

This is the same goddess who sometimes weeps in the night,[3] longing to eat human hearts. She refuses to be silent if she is denied them, and she won't produce fruit unless she is watered with human blood.

How the Sun and Moon Were Created

It is said that before there was day in the world, when all was in darkness, the gods gathered together in Teotihuacán.[4] They counseled together and said: "O gods, who will accept the burden of lighting the world? Who will be the sun and the moon?"

Then a god named Tecuciztecatl[5] responded to these words and said: "I will take on the burden of lighting the world."

The gods spoke once again and said: "Who will be the other?" So they looked at each other and discussed who would be the other. None of them dared to offer himself for that task. All of them were afraid and made excuses.

One of the gods, Nanahuatzin,[6] who was covered with sores, went unnoticed. He did not speak, but listened to what the other gods were saying. And the other gods spoke to him and said: "O Nanahuatzin, you be the one who gives light." Willingly he consented to their commands, and replied: "Gratefully, I accept what you have asked of me. So be it!"

---

important for the Aztecs to understand the origins of sacrifice and penance, since the gods were role models for these functions and the very existence of the cosmos depended on them.

A note on the translation: The five creation myths included here were translated by David M. Johnson from various Spanish sources. "The Creation of the Earth" was translated from Angel María Garibay K.'s *Epica Náhuatl* (1945); "How the Sun and Moon Were Created" was translated from Bernardino de Sahagún's *Historia General de las Cosas de Nueva España* (1946) and Angel María Garibay K.'s *Llave del Náhuatl* (1961); and "The Creation of Man and Woman" was translated from *Leyenda de los Soles* in the *Códice Chimalpopoca* (1945).

---

[3] **This is the . . . night:** It is thought that Cihuacoatl is an ancestor of La Llorona, one of the most famous figures in Southwestern folklore, a woman who weeps in the night searching for her dead children.

[4] **Teotihuacán:** Means "Place of the Gods," an important cultural center northeast of Mexico City, famed for its large Pyramids of the Sun and Moon, and the Pyramid of Quetzalcoatl.

[5] **Tecuciztecatl:** God of the Moon, his name means a person from Tecuciztlan ("near conch shells").

[6] **Nanahuatzin:** A lowly god associated with syphilis, leprosy, or sores.

Then the two of them began to do penance lasting four days.[7] A fire was lit in a hearth which was built on a precipice—a place now called *Teotexcalli.*[8]

The god Tecuciztecatl's offerings—all of them—were expensive. Instead of branches he offered precious feathers called *quetzalli,*[9] and instead of balls of hay, he offered balls of gold. And instead of maguey spines, he offered spines made from precious stones. In place of spines stained with blood, he offered spines made from red coral. And the copal incense which he offered was excellent.

Instead of branches, the god of pustules, Nanahuatzin, offered green reeds, which were tied in bundles of three, with a total of nine. He offered balls of hay and maguey spines stained with his own blood. And for incense, instead of copal, he offered scabs from his sores.

For each of these gods a tower was erected, like a mountain. On these same mountains they did penance for four nights. Today these mountains are called *tzaqualli* and are the Pyramids of the Sun and the Moon at Teotihuacán.

After they finished the four nights of their penance, they threw away the branches and everything else that they used in the performance of the penance.

This was done at the conclusion of their penance, since on the following night they began to perform the rites of office. Just before midnight the other gods gave their adornments to the one called Tecuciztecatl; they gave him a feather headdress and a linen jacket. As for Nanahuatzin, they covered his head with a paper headdress and dressed him in a paper stole and a paper loincloth. With the approach of midnight, all the gods took their places around the hearth called *Teotexcalli,* where the fire had burned for four days.

The gods arranged themselves in two rows, some on one side of the fire and some on the other. And then the two, Tecuciztecatl and Nanahuatzin, took their places in front of the fire, facing the hearth, in between the two rows of gods.

All of them were standing when the gods spoke and said to Tecuciztecatl: "Now then, Tecuciztecatl! Cast yourself into the fire!" And he readied himself to leap into the fire. But the flames were so fierce that when he felt the unbearable heat he became terrified, and was afraid to throw himself into the fire. So he turned back.

Again he turned to cast himself into the flames which leaped even higher, but he stopped, not daring to cast himself into the fire. Four times he tried, but each time he lost his nerve. It was tradition that no one could try more than four times.

Since Tecuciztecatl had tried four times the gods then spoke to Nanahuatzin and said to him: "Now then, Nanahuatzin! You try!" When the gods had spoken to him, he gathered his courage and, closing his eyes, rushed forth and cast himself into the fire, where he began to crackle and sizzle like someone being roasted. When Tecuciztecatl saw that he had leaped into the flames, he gathered his nerve, rushed forward and threw himself into the fire.

They say that an eagle then flew into the fire and also burned; for this reason it

[7] **penance . . . four days:** Penance typically involves prayer, physical pain, sacrifices, and offerings.

[8] ***Teotexcalli:*** "God's Oven or Hearth."

[9] ***quetzalli:*** From the brilliant green tail feathers of the quetzal bird.

has dark or blackish feathers. Finally a jaguar entered. He wasn't burned, but only singed; and for this reason he continued to be stained black and white. From this came the custom of calling men who are skilled in war *cuauhtlocelotl:*[10] *cuauhtli* is said first because the eagle entered the fire first; *ocelotl* is said last because the jaguar entered the fire after the eagle.

After these two gods had flung themselves into the fire, and after both had burned, the remaining gods seated themselves, waiting to see from which direction Nanahuatzin would begin to rise. After they had waited a long time, the sky began to redden, and the light of dawn appeared all around them. And they say that after this the gods knelt down, waiting to see where on the horizon the Sun Nanahuatzin would rise.

As they looked in each direction they turned in a circle, but not one could guess or say the place where he would appear. They could not make up their minds about a single thing. Some thought he would appear in the north, and they fixed their attention there. Others fixed on the south. Some suspected that he would emerge in all directions at once, because the radiance of dawn was everywhere. Others got in a position to look east and said: "Here, in this direction, the sun is to rise." The word of these gods was true.

They say that those who looked east were Quetzalcoatl, who is also called Ehecatl;[11] and another called Totec, and by another name Anahuatlitecu, and by another name Tlatlahuic Tezcatlipoca.[12] And others called Mimixcoa,[13] who are innumerable. And four women: one named Tiacapan, the other Teicu, the third Tlacoyehua, the fourth Xocoyotl.[14]

When the sun began to rise, he looked very red and appeared to sway from side to side. No one could look directly at him because his powerful light would blind them. His rays streamed out in a magnificent way and were scattered in all directions.

Afterwards the moon appeared in the east, in the same direction as the sun. First the sun arose, and afterwards the moon. The order that they entered the fire was the order in which they appeared, and were made sun and moon.

And the storytellers say that the light coming from them was of equal intensity. And when the gods saw that they shone equally they discussed it among themselves again and said: "O gods, what shall come of this? Will it actually work if both are alike and move together? Will it be good that they shine with the same intensity?"

The gods made a judgement and said: "Let it be this way, let it thus be done."

---

[10] ***cuauhtlocelotl:*** A name combining *cuauhtli,* "eagle," and *ocelotl,* "jaguar," two figures that represent the eternal struggle between sky and earth forces in the creation and destruction of the world; the name represents the two classes of Aztec warriors: Eagle-knights and Jaguar-knights.

[11] **Ehecatl:** God of the Wind, a manifestation of Quetzalcoatl.

[12] **Totec, Anahuatlitecu, Tlatlahuic Tezcatlipoca:** Gods representing the various directions.

[13] **Mimixcoa:** Deities representing the stars.

[14] **Tiacapan, Teicu, Tlacoyehua, Xocoyotl:** Four goddesses who match the gods of the four directions present at the creation of the Fifth Sun.

Then one of them ran up and threw a rabbit[15] into the face of Tecuciztecatl, darkening his face and obscuring the light. And his face remained as it is today.

After both had risen over the earth, the sun and moon stayed in one place without moving. And the gods once more spoke and said: "How are we going to live when the sun doesn't move? Are we to live among the peons? Let us all die and give him vitality with our deaths."

And immediately Ehecatl, the Wind, took charge of slaying all the gods, and he killed them. It is said that one named Xolotl[16] refused to die and said to the gods: "O gods, don't kill me!" He wept so intensely that his eyes swelled from crying.

When the executioner arrived, he ran away and hid in the maize fields, and changed himself into the base of the maize plant with two stalks, which field hands call *xolotl.* He was discovered among the bottoms of the maize plant. Again he ran away and hid among the maguey, turning into a maguey with two bodies, which is called *mexolotl.* Again he was spotted. He ran away and hid in the water, changing himself into a fish, which is named *axolotl.* There they took him and killed him.

And they say that even though the gods were dead, the sun still did not move. And then Ehecatl, the Wind, began to blow. Blowing like a monsoon, he caused him to move and get on his way. After the sun began to travel, the moon remained in the place where he was.

After the sun had set, the moon began to move. In this manner they have their separate ways, coming forth at different times. The sun carries on during the day, and the moon works or illuminates the night. And from this comes the saying: that Tecuciztecatl would have been the sun if he had been the first to leap into the fire, because he was named first and he offered precious things in his penance.

The Creation of Man and Woman

The gods consulted with each other and said: "Who will live here, now that the sky has been dammed up and the earth is secure?[17] Who will live here, O gods?" The ones who were negotiating in this manner were Citlallinicue, Citlallatonac, Apantecuhtli, Tepanquizqui, Tlallamanqui, Huictlollinqui, Quetzalcoatl and Titlacahuan.[18]

Then Quetzalcoatl went down to Mictlan,[19] the land of the Dead. He approached the rulers, Mictlantecuhtli and Mictlancihuatl, and said: "I have come for the precious bones which are under your protection." They asked him: "What are you going

[15] **rabbit:** Rather than seeing a man in the moon, the ancient Mexicans saw the figure of a rabbit in the full moon.

[16] **Xolotl:** God of the planet Venus as evening star; twin brother of Quetzalcoatl and a clever sorcerer.

[17] **earth is secure:** The fourth age, the previous age, was destroyed by floods; the rains must be dammed up for the fifth age or Fifth Sun to begin.

[18] **Citlallinicue . . . Titlacahuan:** Citlallinicue and Citlallatonac, sometimes translated as "Skirt-of-the-Stars" and "Light-of-Day," are goddess and god of the heavens. Apantecuhtli, Tepanquizqui, Tlallamanqui, Huictlollinqui, and Titlacahuan are minor sky deities.

[19] **Mictlan:** The underground, the underworld, the land of the dead; similar to the Greek Hades.

to make, Quetzalcoatl?" He answered them by saying: "The gods have discussed using the bones to create the new inhabitants for earth."

Once more the Lord of the Dead spoke: "Very well. Blow my conch shell and circle four times around my throne of jade." But his conch shell had no holes in it, so Quetzalcoatl called for worms who made holes in it. Then large bees and hornets went inside and made it hum with sound. Mictlantecuhtli heard the noise and said: "Very well. Take the bones."

Mictlantecuhtli, however, said to his servants, the Mictecas: "Go after Quetzalcoatl and tell him he must not take them." Quetzalcoatl, planning to carry them away, nevertheless told his *nahual*:[20] "Go and report that I won't be taking them." His *nahual* went and shouted: "I won't be taking them."

Then Quetzalcoatl gathered up the precious bones and quickly began to ascend with them. Gathered together on one side were the man bones, and on the other were the woman bones. Thus he made two bundles and carried them away.

Again Mictlantecuhtli spoke, saying to his servants: "O gods, can it be true that Quetzalcoatl is escaping with the precious bones? Go and dig a deep pit." They went and dug it, and Quetzalcoatl, frightened by some quail, tripped and fell into the pit. He fell like someone who was dead, and at the bottom the precious bones were scattered. Then the quail bit into the bones and chewed on them.

After a time Quetzalcoatl revived. Weeping, he said to his *nahual*: "What will become of this?" His *nahual* replied: "What has come of this? It appears that the negotiations went against us, but all is not lost." Quetzalcoatl again gathered the bones together and made a bundle which he promptly carried to Tamoanchan.[21]

After he arrived with them, the one called Quilaztli[22] (who is also Cihuacoatl) ground them into powder and placed them in a large jade bowl. Unto this powder Quetzalcoatl bled his penis. And immediately all of the gods did penance—Apantecuhtli, Huictlollinqui, Tepanquizqui, Tlallamanac, Tzontemoc, and the sixth, Quetzalcoatl.

Afterwards they made the announcement: "Human beings, servants of the gods, have been born!" Thus it was that for all of us humans the gods did penance.

[20] ***nahual:*** Also *nagual;* a person's soul, alter ego or double, sometimes residing in an animal or bird.

[21] **Tamoanchan:** Meaning "land of the bird-snake," Tamoanchan is the mythic place of origins, similar to Eden in the Judeo-Christian tradition.

[22] **Quilaztli:** An aspect of Chihuacoatl, Quilaztli is an earth goddess associated with childbirth.

The Myth of Quetzalcoatl

Translated by David M. Johnson

The Birth of Ce Acatl

The great warrior, Mixcoatl,[1] marched over the earth conquering towns in the North, the East, and the West. Then Mixcoatl went south to conquer the town of Huitznahuac.[2]

As he approached the battle, the woman Chimalman[3] came out to meet him. He put down his shield on the ground before him, he put down his spear-thrower[4] and his spears. She stood naked before him, without skirt or blouse.

Seeing her, Mixcoatl shot at her with his arrows. The first arrow that he shot at her went above her and she barely had to duck her head. The second one passed by her side, and she twisted away from it. The third one she caught in her hand. And the fourth one that he shot went right between her thighs.

After having shot at her four times, Mixcoatl turned and went away. The woman immediately ran off to hide in the cave of a large canyon.

Once again, Mixcoatl equipped himself, he replenished his arrows, and once

---

The Myth of Quetzalcoatl. Quetzalcoatl was a very old god from the Gulf Coast who was originally associated with the symbolism of shells and the powers of sea and wind. For the Toltecs, the spiritual ancestors of the Aztecs, Quetzalcoatl was a culture-bringer who taught the Toltecs about the mysteries of agriculture and the arts of metalworking and architecture. Quetzalcoatl was also a spiritual leader, since the Toltecs believed that the original Plumed Serpent had come to earth in the figure of a priest-king Topiltzin. He was famous for his higher spirituality, his piety and penitential practices, and, above all, his antipathy toward human sacrifices, preferring instead offerings of snakes, incense, and butterflies. Quetzalcoatl's example and teachings evidently antagonized a militant segment of society who sought his downfall and exile. His death and resurrection elevated him once again to a cosmic status where, as the morning star Venus, he symbolized periodic rebirth and the resolution of spirit and matter.

A note on the translation: "The Myth of Quetzalcoatl" was translated by David M. Johnson from the *Anales de Cuauhtitlán* in the *Códice Chimalpopoca* (1945) and Bernardino de Sahagún's *Historia General de las Cosas de Nueva España* (1946).

---

[1] **Mixcoatl:** Leader of a Chichimec tribe that migrated into the Valley of Mexico around the year 1000 and settled in Colhuacan. His history becomes legendary when he is elevated to a deity. Father of Ce Acatl-Topiltzin, the legendary priest-king linked to Quetzalcoatl, his name means "Cloud Serpent," referring to a tornado, or perhaps to the Milky Way.

[2] **Huitznahuac:** From the Nahuatl *huitz,* "thorn," and *nahuac,* "place or vicinity," Huitznahuac or "Land of the thorns" is in the south of Mexico.

[3] **Chimalman:** From *chimalli,* meaning "shield," Chimalman is the earth-goddess mother of Ce Acatl-Topiltzin (Quetzalcoatl).

[4] **spear-thrower:** Called an *atlatl,* the spear-thrower is a grooved stick to hold the spear; finger loops at one end of the stick are used to propel the spear towards a target.

Quetzalcoatl
This relief sculpture shows a feathered serpent, the major symbol of the Aztec god Quetzalcoatl, between two symbols of years. (Werner Forman/Art Resource, NY)

more he went looking for the woman, but he saw no one. So he abused the other women of Huitznahuac, and they said, "Let us go look for her!"

They went to bring her back, saying to her, "Because of you, he is violating your younger sisters." They were determined to bring Chimalman back, so she returned to Huitznahuac.

Again Mixcoatl went to her, and she came out to meet him. As before, she stood in front of him with nothing covering her crotch. As before, he put his shield and spears on the ground. Again he shot arrows at her and the same thing happened: one went above her, one went by her side, she caught one in her hand, and one went between her thighs.

After all this happened, he took her. He lay with the woman of Huitznahuac, who was Chimalman. And afterwards she was pregnant.

The birth of Ce Acatl took four days and during this time his mother suffered a great deal. And just when he was born, his mother died.

The year was 1-Reed.[5] Thus it is said that in this year Quetzalcoatl was born, he who was called Topiltzin Priest Ce Acatl-Quetzalcoatl.[6] It is said that his mother had the name Chimalman. And some say that she became pregnant when she swallowed a piece of jade.

Ce Acatl Avenges His Father's Murder

Ce Acatl was raised by Quilaztli, who was also called Cihuacoatl.[7]

The years passed; 2-Flint, 3-House, 4-Rabbit, 5-Reed, 6-Flint, 7-House, 8-Rabbit.

9-Reed. When Ce Acatl was a young man he accompanied his father on military

---

[5] ***The year was 1-Reed:*** In the Aztec calendar, each year was given one of four names (Reed, Flint, House, or Rabbit) and a number from one to thirteen; when either the series of names or numbers ended, it was repeated. Thus the year 1-Reed could occur once in fifty-two years.

[6] **Topiltzin Priest Ce Acatl-Quetzalcoatl:** In Nahuatl Ce Acatl means "one reed," and refers to the calendar day (1-Reed) on which Ce Acatl-Topiltzin, the legendary ruler-priest of the Toltecs, was born. Quetzalcoatl was added to his name to indicate he was a priest of Quetzalcoatl.

[7] **Cihuacoatl:** "Serpent Woman," a goddess of childbirth; also called Quilaztli.

expeditions. He learned about being a warrior in a place called Xiuhuacan,[8] where he took several captives.

In that place were Ce Acatl's uncles, the four hundred Mimixcoa[9] who hated his father and eventually killed him. After they killed him, they went and buried him in the sand.

In the Year 9-Reed, Ce Acatl looked for his father and asked about him, "What has become of my father? I want to know my father, I want to see his face." Hearing him, a vulture answered and said, "They killed your father. He lies over there where they buried him."

Without any delay, Ce Acatl went there to dig in the earth, he searched for the bones of his father. After he had gathered up the bones, he took them and buried them in his temple, Mixcoatepetl.[10]

Three of the uncles who had killed his father were named Apanecatl, Zolton, and Cuilton.[11] And Ce Acatl asked them, "What should I sacrifice in order to dedicate this temple? Perhaps only a rabbit, or simply a snake."

And they answered him, "Indeed, that would make us very angry. It is better to use a jaguar, an eagle, and a wolf." Ce Acatl replied to them, "Very well—that's what it will be!"

He called a jaguar, an eagle, and a wolf, and said to them, "Come here my uncles. They say I should use you three to dedicate my temple, but you will not die. Instead, you shall devour my father's brothers when I consecrate my temple." For the sake of deception, he tied the animals' necks together.

Then Ce Acatl called to the moles and he told them, "Come, my uncles, dig a tunnel into our temple." Immediately, the moles began to dig, and soon they had made a tunnel. And that is how Ce Acatl got inside and climbed to the summit of his temple where he emerged.

The brother uncles had said, "We will light the fire on the summit." Happily they watched the howling of the jaguar, eagle and wolf, who pretended to be in pain. And while they were thus distracted, Ce Acatl was already lighting the fire.

His uncles were furious and they prepared to fight. Apanecatl went ahead and hurriedly climbed upward. But Ce Acatl stood tall and hit him in the head with a shiny pot, causing him to fall to the base of the temple.

Next he took hold of Zolton and Cuilton and, as the animals blew on the fire, he put them to death in this manner: he spread chili over them and cut off pieces of their flesh. After he had tortured them, he cut open their chests.

Once again Ce Acatl set out to make further conquests.

---

[8] **Xiuhuacan:** "Place of the Turquoise," perhaps on the Pacific Coast.

[9] **Mimixcoa:** Followers of Mixcoatl who are compared to the stars.

[10] **Mixcoatepetl:** "Mixcoatl's Mountain," or pyramid.

[11] **Apanecatl, Zolton, and Cuilton:** Three leaders of the Mimixcoa, Mixcoatl's brothers. Apanecatl was part of the divine retinue following Huitzilopochtli, the god of war who led the Aztecs from their origins in Aztlan, northern Mexico, to the Valley of Mexico.

Becoming a Priest and Ruler of the Toltecs

The years passed: 10-Flint, 11-House, 12-Rabbit, 13-Reed, 1-Flint, 2-House, 3-Rabbit, 4-Reed, 5-Flint, 6-House, 7-Rabbit, 8-Reed, 9-Flint.

10-House. In this year Huactli died, who had been the ruler of Cuauhtitlán[12] for sixty-two years. This was the ruler who did not know how to cultivate edible corn, and whose followers did not know how to weave blankets. So they dressed only in skins. Their food was nothing more than birds, small snakes, rabbits, and deer. Furthermore, they had no houses, since they wandered from place to place.

The year was 11-Rabbit. In this year the Lady Xiuhtlacuilolxochitzin took the throne. Her thatched house, which is still there today, was at the edge of the plaza, beside a rocky ledge. It is said that they gave her the city because she was Huactli's wife, and she could invoke the demon Itzpapalotl.[13]

The years passed: 12-Reed, 13-Flint, 1-House.

2-Rabbit. It was in this year that Quetzalcoatl arrived in Tollan,[14] where he stayed four years. He built his house of penance, which was supported by cross beams made of turquoise. From there he went to Cuextlan.[15] In that place he crossed the river and there he built a sturdy bridge. They say it still exists today.

The years passed: 3-Reed, 4-Flint.

5-House. In this year the Toltecs[16] went to find Quetzalcoatl in order to make him the ruler in Tollan. He was also their priest. This is part of the written record, and can be found elsewhere.

The years passed: 6-Rabbit.

7-Reed. During this year Lady Xiuhtlacuilolxochitzin died. She had ruled in Cuauhtitlán for twelve years.

8-Flint. In this year Ayauhcoyotzin[17] was enthroned as ruler of Cuauhtitlan, in a place called Tecpancuauhtla (Palace of the Woods).

The years passed: 9-House, 10-Rabbit, 11-Reed, 12-Flint, 13-House, 1-Rabbit.

2-Reed. In the annals of Tezcoco,[18] this was the year Topiltzin Quetzalcoatl of Tollan and Colhuacan[19] died. In the year 2-Reed Ce Acatl-Topiltzin Quetzalcoatl built his house of penance, a place for fasting and prayer.

---

[12] **Cuauhtitlán:** Nahuatl for "Tree side," Cuauhtitlan was a city located on the northwestern shore of Lake Texcoco, the lake forming the center of numerous settlements in the Valley of Mexico. Nothing more is known about Huactli.

[13] **Itzpapalotl:** "Obsidian Butterfly," Itzpapalotl was the earth-goddess consort of Mixcoatl.

[14] **Tollan:** Meaning "Near the Rushes," Tollan was the legendary capital of the Toltecs under the leadership of Topiltzin. Tollan was located at the present-day Tula, north of Mexico City.

[15] **Cuextlan:** Unknown location.

[16] **Toltecs:** A dominant culture in the Valley of Mexico between the ninth and eleventh centuries with their capital at Tollan.

[17] **Ayauhcoyotzin:** Nothing more is known about this ruler or Xiuhtlacuilolxochitzin.

[18] **Tezcoco:** A city-state across the lake from Tenochtitlán; was the intellectual center of the area during the reign of Nezahualcoyotl (1430–1472).

[19] **Colhuacan:** A city-state on the southern portion of the lake in the Valley of Mexico.

He built his house with four chambers: one with turquoise beams, one with coral, one with white shell, one with quetzal feathers. There he performed his penance, he prayed there and he fasted.

Close to midnight he went down to the stream, to a place called Atecpanamochco (Palace of Water). He inflicted himself with spines on the heights of Xicocotl, on Huitzcoc, on Tzincoc, and also on Mount Nonoalco.[20]

He made his spines from precious stones, and he made laurel boughs from quetzal feathers. With the smoke of incense he sanctified the turquoise, jade, and coral. And for his sacrifices he offered snakes, birds, and butterflies.

And it is said that he reverently sent up his prayers to the center of the heavens. He prayed to Ometeotl,[21] god and goddess in one:

She, Skirt-of-Stars and He, Maker-of-Daylight
Lady-of-Our-Flesh and Lord-of-Our-Flesh
Wrapped-in-Blackness and Wrapped-in-Red
Supports-the-Earth and Moves-Clouds-in-the-Sky

It was known that he cried out to Omeyocan,[22] which exists above the nine levels of heaven. Thus it was known that he prayed to those who lived there, and he made petitions to them. And he practiced a life of piety and wisdom, becoming a model for other priests. They followed the example of Quetzalcoatl in the city of Tollan.

Furthermore, in his time, he discovered great treasures of jade, fine turquoise, gold, silver, coral, and shells. And the feathers of beautiful birds: the quetzal, the lovely cotinga, the roseate spoonbill, the trogan, and the blue heron. He also discovered various colors of cocoa and several colors of cotton.

It is said that the Toltecs were very wealthy, and that they had all they needed for eating and drinking. The squash were huge, two meters in circumference. And the ears of maize were so big that a single pair of arms could not stretch around them. The amaranth plants were so tall and thick that people could climb them like trees.

He was a very great artist in all his works. Pieces of earthenware for eating and drinking were painted blue, green, yellow, and red. He taught the Toltecs how to work with jade and gold and feathers.

There was a mountain called Tzatzitepetl,[23] and that is its name today. From the top of it a public crier shouted announcements, and his messages spread over Anahuac.[24] He was heard and the laws were communicated. People came to learn and listen to what Quetzalcoatl had commanded.

---

[20] **Xicocotl, Huitzcoc, Tzincoc, Nonoalco:** The first three are apparently places in mountains outside of Mexico City; Nonoalco is on the Gulf Coast to the south of Mexico City.

[21] **Ometeotl:** The primordial dual-god of the Mexicas, from the Nahuatl *ome,* meaning "two," and *teotl,* meaning "god." As both a male and female god, Ometeotl was a convenient explanation for how the rest of creation came into being.

[22] **Omeyocan:** "Place of Duality."

[23] **Tzatzitepetl:** "Mountain for Shouting."

[24] **Anahuac:** Referring to the "edge of the water," Anahuac meant the Valley of Mexico, as well as the earth itself surrounded by water.

During the period of his rule Quetzalcoatl began to build his temple. He put up columns in the shape of serpents, but he did not finish the entire project.

While he lived there he did not show himself in public. He stayed inside a very dark, well protected chamber. His personal servants protected him on all sides. His own chamber was the most remote; in each of the others were his servants. In the rooms were mats of precious stones, quetzal plumes, and gold.

Thus it was said that he erected his fourfold house of penance.

The Temptation and Fall of Quetzalcoatl

They say that during Quetzalcoatl's lifetime sorcerers repeatedly tried to trick him into making human sacrifices, into killing human beings. But he never wanted this, nor did he give in to this, because he deeply loved his followers, who were the Toltecs.

It can be said that always he used only small snakes, birds, and butterflies for his sacrifices.

They say that because of this the sorcerers were angry. When they made demands they would use ridicule and insults in order to dishonor him, and drive him away.

And so it happened.

The years passed: 3-Flint, 4-House, 5-Rabbit, 6-Reed, 7-Flint, 8-House, 9-Rabbit, 10-Reed, 11-Flint, 12-House, 13-Rabbit.

1-Reed. In this year Quetzalcoatl died. They say that he went to Tlillan Tlapallan[25] to die there. In succession, Matlacxochitl took the throne and ruled in Tollan.

This is what is said about why Quetzalcoatl went away.

When he disobeyed the sorcerers and refused to make human sacrifices, they consulted with each other. Their names were Tezcatlipoca, Ihuimecatl, and Toltecatl.[26] They said, "It is necessary that he leave his city, here where we have to live."

They went on to say, "Let us make pulque.[27] We will get him to drink some. And then he will lose his judgement and give up his life of penance."

Tezcatlipoca then spoke, "I say that we should present him with his body, let him really see it." They schemed together in order to accomplish this.

Tezcatlipoca went first. He took a two-sided mirror, about the size of a person's hand, and wrapped it up. When he arrived at the place where Quetzalcoatl was living, he said to the servants who personally cared for him, "Give this message to the priest: 'Lord, a commoner has arrived to present you with your body, to show it to you.' "

---

[25] **Tlillan Tlapallan:** The mythic destination of Quetzalcoatl after leaving Tollan. The two names in Nahuatl mean "The Black and Red Land" or "Land of Black and Red Ink." Metaphorically, the inks indicate a place of writing (painting books), and therefore Tlillan Tlapallan is the place of wisdom, learning, and enlightenment. From there, Quetzalcoatl announced that he would return in the year Ce Acat (1-Reed).

[26] **Tezcatlipoca, Ihuimecatl, and Toltecatl:** Tezcatlipoca, god of warfare, whose name means "smoking mirror." Ihuimecatl, "a cord of feathers," is related to Huitzilopochtli, the patron god of the Aztecs who promoted war and human sacrifice. Toltecatl's name indicates his origin in Tollan; he was a god of drunkenness.

[27] **pulque:** A fermented drink made from the juice of the maguey.

The servants went inside to report to Quetzalcoatl, who replied to them: "What is this, grandfather servant? What kind of thing is my *body*? First, you inspect what he has brought, and then he may enter."

Tezcatlipoca did not want it to be seen, however, and told them, "Go tell the priest that I must personally show it to him."

So they went and said to him, "Lord, he won't give in. He insists that he must show it to you." Quetzalcoatl said, "Then let him come in, grandfather."

They went to call Tezcatlipoca, who entered and greeted him, saying: "My son, Priest Ce Acatl-Quetzalcoatl. I salute you, my Lord, and have come to let you see your body."

Quetzalcoatl replied, "You are welcome here, grandfather. Where did you come from? What is this concerning my body? Let me see it!"

And the sorcerer answered, "My son, priest, I am your servant, who has come from the foothills of Mount Nonoalco. My Lord, may you look at your body."

Then he gave him the mirror and said, "Look at yourself and know yourself, my son. See how you appear in the mirror."

At once, Quetzalcoatl saw himself and was filled with fear. He said, "If my subjects were to see me they would probably run away." For his eyelids were puffy, his eye sockets were deeply sunk in a face which was swollen and deformed all over.

After looking into the mirror he said, "Never shall my subjects see me, because I shall remain here, in this place."

Dismissing himself, Tezcatlipoca left. In order to ridicule Quetzalcoatl and make fun of him, he consulted with Ihuimecatl, who said, "Coyotlinahual,[28] the feather artist, must now be the one to go."

They contacted Coyotlinahual, the feather artist, and told him that he was to go, and he said: "So be it! I will go to see Quetzalcoatl."

So he went and said to Quetzalcoatl, "My son, I say that you should come out of hiding so that your subjects can see you. I will prepare you so that they may see you."

Quetzalcoatl replied, "Let's see it! Go ahead, grandfather."

Coyotlinahual, the feather artist, began at once. First, he made Quetzalcoatl's plumed headdress. Then he made a turquoise mask for him. With red coloring he brightened the lips, with yellow he colored the forehead. He made a set of fangs for him. From the feathers of the cotinga and spoonbill, he made his beard which was swept back.

After he had dressed and adorned Quetzalcoatl in this manner, he gave him the mirror. When Quetzalcoatl saw himself he was very pleased, and immediately left the place where he was hiding.

Then the artist Coyotlinahual went to tell Ihuimecatl, "I have forced Quetzalcoatl into the open. Now you go!"

He replied, "All right." And he made friends with Toltecatl, an expert with pulque.

[28] **Coyotlinahual:** A sorcerer, whose name is formed from *coyotl,* "coyote," and *nahual,* meaning "cunning" or "deceitful." Used alone, *nahual* means "animal double" or "alter ego."

Together they set out and journeyed to Xonacapacoyan.[29] They stayed with the farmer Maxtli, who was guardian of Toltec Mountain.

They began to make a savory stew from herbs, tomatoes, chili, green corn, and string beans. This was made in a few days.

In this area there were also maguey plants, and they asked Maxtli for some. In only four days they made pulque. They harvested the raw pulque, which was then brewed. Discovering some jugs of honey, they added this to the pulque.

Afterwards they went to Tollan, to the house of Quetzalcoatl. And they carried everything: the stew of herbs, chili, and other things. And the pulque.

They arrived for the showdown, but those who guarded Quetzalcoatl did not permit them to enter. Two or three times they returned without being received. Finally, they were asked where they came from. They answered, "From Priests' Mountain, Toltec Mountain." When Quetzalcoatl heard that, he said, "Let them enter."

They entered and greeted him. And at last they gave him the savory stew. After he ate, they pleaded with him again, trying to give him the pulque. But he told them "No, I will not drink it, because I am fasting. It might be intoxicating or deadly."

They said to him, "Try it with your little finger, because this brew is angry, it has power!"

Quetzalcoatl tried it with his finger and liked it. He said, "Grandfather, I am going to have three drinks more." He did this because the sorcerers had told him: "You have to drink at least four."

When they gave him a fifth drink, they said to him, "This is your *libation.*"[30]

After he had his drinks, they served all his personal servants, five rounds of drinks to each of them. They drank them and became thoroughly drunk.

Again the sorcerers spoke to Quetzalcoatl: "My son, sing. Here is the song you are to sing." And Ihuimecatl sang:

My green house of quetzal plumes
My yellow house of oriole plumes
My red house of coral
I am leaving you *an ya.*[31]

Feeling now so joyful, Quetzalcoatl said, "Go! Bring me my older sister, Quetzalpetlatl,[32] that we might get drunk together."

His servants went to Mount Nonoalco, where she was doing penance, and said to her, "Lady, my daughter, the fasting Quetzalpetlatl, we have come to deliver you. The Priest Quetzalcoatl waits for you. Go and be with him!"

She replied, "Very well. Let us go, grandfather-servant."

[29] **Xonacapacoyan:** "Place Where Onions are Washed."

[30] ***libation:*** Four drinks were allowed; five drinks were a sign of drunkenness; the word "libation" is therefore used ironically.

[31] ***an ya:*** "An ya," and the variants in later stanzas, are meaningless syllables used for rhythmic purposes.

[32] **Quetzalpetlatl:** The sister of Quetzalcoatl, her name combines *quetzal,* "quetzal or precious feathers" and *petlatl,* "mat," perhaps referring to a mat of quetzal feathers used for religious or ceremonial purposes.

When she arrived, she was seated next to Quetzalcoatl. Then they gave her four drinks of pulque, and one more, her *libation*—the fifth.

Having gotten them drunk, Ihuimecatl and Toltecatl performed a musical piece for Quetzalcoatl's older sister. They sang:

Oh Quetzalpetlatl
My sister
Where now do you dwell?
Here, where we drink too much.
Ayn ya ynya ynne an!

After getting intoxicated they no longer said, "But we are still penitents." No more did they go down to the stream. No more did they pierce themselves with spines. No more did they celebrate the dawn.

When they woke up they were filled with remorse, their hearts were broken.

Then Quetzalcoatl said, "My life is ruined!" And he sang the melancholy song which he had composed for his departure.

It is all over
A hard life begins in strange lands
No one wants to stay here now.
If only we could return to the old ways
If only I had the strength for a new kingdom
Never will I be afraid again.

And he sang the second verse of his song:

No more
Shall my mother support me *anya*!
She-of-the-Serpent-Skirt *an*!
A priestess *y yoa*
And her child *yyaa*!
I weep *yya yean*!

While Quetzalcoatl sang, all of his servants were filled with sadness and wept. In turn, they also sang:

In this fallen house
No more will my lords be rich
Quetzalcoatl, no more
With the crown of precious jewels
The beams have been stripped
We are miserable
We weep.

The Journey to the Black and Red Land

After his servants had finished singing, Quetzalcoatl said to them, "Grandfather-servants, that's enough! I am leaving the city. I am leaving. Order a coffin of stone for me."

Quickly a stone coffin was made. And when it was finished, they laid Quetzalcoatl in it.

For a period of four days[33] he lay in the stone coffin. When he no longer felt well, he said to his servants: "That's enough, grandfather-servants! Let us go. Close off everything and hide the riches, the delightful things we discovered—all the beautiful things."

His servants obeyed his wishes. They hid the things where Quetzalcoatl bathed, the place called Atecpanamochco (Palace of Water). Other works were buried in mountains or in canyons.

It is said that Quetzalcoatl ordered that his houses be burned—his house of gold, his house of coral. He changed the cocoa trees into mesquites.

He ordered the birds with the beautiful feathers—the quetzal, the blue cotinga, the roseate spoonbill—to go ahead of him. And they departed for Anahuac.[34]

And then Quetzalcoatl departed. He went on foot. He called all his servants together and wept with them. Then they departed for Tlillan Tlapallan (the Black and Red Land), the burning land.[35]

Quetzalcoatl went down the road and arrived at a place called Cuauhtitlán. A very large tree grew there, broad and tall. He stood close to the tree, and asked his servants for a mirror. Looking at his face in the mirror, he said: "Truly I am old!" So named the place Huehuecuauhtitlán (Beside the Tree of Old Men).

Then he picked up stones and threw them at the tree. All the stones that Quetzalcoatl threw stuck in the tree. For a long time people could see them there. Everyone could see them, from the base of the tree to the top.

So Quetzalcoatl traveled down the road with flute players playing in front of him.

He arrived at another place where he rested placing his hands on a big rock; he then sat down on his hands. Looking back he saw Tollan in the distance, and began to weep with great sadness. The tears which he shed fell to the rock on which he was resting and made holes in it.

As he sat on his hands placed on the rock, he left imprints of his palms, as if they had been placed in mud. He also left the impression of his buttocks on the rock. These marks can be clearly seen today. So he named this place Temacpalco (Rock with Handprints).

Standing up, he then went on further, and arrived at a place called Tepanoayan (Stone Bridge), where a big, wide river flows by. Quetzalcoatl ordered a stone bridge,

[33] **four days:** The ancient Mexicans were fascinated with the death and rebirth cycle of the planet Venus; after Venus, the morning star, is born in the east, it disappears for a time and then is reborn as the evening star in the west. Scholars believe that the four days of Quetzalcoatl's symbolic death represents the period of disappearance and possibly a descent by Quetzalcoatl into the underworld.

[34] **Anahuac:** This use of Anahuac refers to the Gulf Coast. Quetzalcoatl's journey represents the creation of sacred sites and places of worship, reminiscent of other sacred journeys such as the one made by Joseph, Mary, and Jesus along the Nile River which is revered by the Coptic Christian Church.

[35] **burning land:** The south, as well as the place of his cremation.

and it was built across the river. Quetzalcoatl then walked over the bridge, and so the place was called Tepanoayan.

Quetzalcoatl continued on his way and arrived at a place called Coaapan (Serpent's Water). Sorcerers met him there and tried to turn him back, to keep him from going further. They said, "Where are you going? Why did you leave your city? Who is your successor? Who is going to do penance?"

Quetzalcoatl replied to the sorcerers, "You cannot prevent me from going. I must go on."

So the sorcerers asked Quetzalcoatl, "Where are you going?" And Quetzalcoatl replied, "I am going to Tlapallan."

And they asked, "What will you do there?" And Quetzalcoatl answered, "I am called there, the sun has called me."

Thus they said to him, "Very well. Go then. But you must leave behind all the arts and crafts, the creations of the Toltecs." So he left behind all the arts: the casting of gold, the cutting of fine stones, the carving of wood, the painting of books, and the art of feather working.

The sorcerers took everything away from him, and Quetzalcoatl began to throw all of the lovely jewels that he had with him into a spring. And so he named this spring Cozcaapan (Jewels in the Water), the place that is now called Coaapan.

Then he continued on his way down the road. He arrived at a place called Cochtocan (Lying Down to Sleep). A sorcerer came out to meet him and said, "Where are you going?" And he answered, "I am going to Tlapallan."

So the sorcerer said, "Very well. Drink this wine which I brought for you." And Quetzalcoatl said, "No, I cannot drink it, not even a very small taste of it."

But the sorcerer demanded, "You must drink, or at least taste it. No one passes through here without drinking, and getting drunk. So, come! Drink it!"

Quetzalcoatl took the wine and drank it through a reed. Having finished it, he was drunk and fell asleep in the road. His snoring could be heard far and wide.

When he awoke he looked from one side to the other, and arranged his hair with his hand. After that he named this place Cochtocan (Place Where He Slept).

Quetzalcoatl continued on his way, climbing up to a pass between two mountains, Popocatepetl and Iztactepetl.[36] His servants, which were dwarfs and hunchbacks, accompanied him. It snowed, and they died from the cold. Quetzalcoatl felt very sad about the loss of his servants. He wept for them and sang a song of mourning and sighing.

In the distance he saw another white mountain named Poyauhtecatl.[37] Then he visited many places and villages. They say that he left behind many signs of his passing, on the ground and along the roads.

They say that he played on a mountain, sliding down it from the top to the

[36] **Popocatepetl and Iztactepetl:** Popocatepetl is a volcanic mountain 17,887 feet high. Iztactepetl is probably the volcanic mountain Iztacihuatl, 17,343 feet high.

[37] **Poyauhtecatl:** Mount Orizaba, Mexico's highest mountain, 18,700 feet high.

bottom. Maguey grows there now. He ordered a ball court, to be made from square stones. Through the middle of the court he made a line which opened deep into the earth.

At another place he used a silk-cotton tree as an arrow, and he shot it through another silk-cotton tree. In this manner he made a cross. They say he built underground houses at a place called Mictlan.

And furthermore, he erected a large phallic rock, which could be moved with the little finger. But it is said that when several men wanted to move and tilt the rock, they couldn't budge it, even though they were several.

There were many other famous things that Quetzalcoatl did in many villages. He gave names to all the mountains and to all the other places.

Quetzalcoatl's Death and Resurrection

He went seeking and exploring here and there, but no place really suited him. And yet, he arrived at the place for which he was searching. Again he was filled with sorrow, and there he wept.

They say that in the year 1-Reed,[38] having arrived at the sacred shores of the holy sea, he stopped and wept. Then he gathered up his vestments and dressed himself for a ceremony, putting on his robes of quetzal feathers and his turquoise mask.

When he was finished dressing, he immediately set himself on fire, and was consumed by the flames. For this reason the place where Quetzalcoatl was burned is called Tlatlayan (Burning Place).

And it is said that as he burned, his ashes rose, and all the precious birds appeared, rising and circling in the sky: the scarlet guacamaya, the blue jay, the lovely thrush, the shining white bird, the parrots with their yellow feathers, and all the other precious birds.

When the ashes were gone, at that moment, the heart of Quetzalcoatl rose upward. They knew he had risen into the sky and entered the heavens.

The old ones say that he became the star that appears at dawn.[39] They say that it appeared when Quetzalcoatl died, and because of this they named him Lord of the Dawn.

And they say that when he died he was not seen for four days. Thus he went to dwell among the dead in Mictlan. For four days he equipped himself with arrows. And that is why in eight days[40] he appeared as the great star whose name is Quetzalcoatl.

And so it was that he then ascended his heavenly throne and became Lord.

---

[38] **1-Reed:** By an incredible coincidence, Cortés and the conquistadors landed on the Gulf Coast in a year 1-Reed, the year 1519.

[39] **dawn:** Venus.

[40] **eight days:** The planet we call Venus disappears for a period of eight days when it moves from morning star to evening star; the myth of Quetzalcoatl divides this period into two four-day periods, perhaps reflecting periods of death and resurrection or rebirth.

The Poetry of Nezahualcoyotl

Translated by Miguel León-Portilla

I, Nezahualcoyotl, ask this

I, Nezahualcoyotl, ask this:
Is it true one really lives on the earth?
Not forever on earth,
only a little while here.
Though it be jade it falls apart,
though it be gold it wears away,
though it be quetzal plumage[1] it is torn asunder.
Not forever on earth,
only a little while here.

Are You real, are You rooted?

Are You real, are You rooted?
Only You dominate all things,
the Giver of Life.[2]
Is this true?
Perhaps, as they say, it is not true?

May our hearts
be not tormented;
All that is real
all that is rooted,

The Poetry of Nezahualcoyotl. The first two poems describe the fragility of human life and affirm that permanence resides only with Tloque Nahuaque, translated as Giver of Life. The next poems pick up themes common to Nahuatl poetry; the Nahuas believed that flowers and songs were meeting grounds between gods and humans. The gods speak through the natural world and through art. The books that contain poems and songs on earth are mirrored by the Giver of Life, who uses the book of paintings to direct life on earth. The last poems are speculations about life after death.

These poems were translated by Miguel León-Portilla from *Romances de los Señores de Nueva España* and *Colección de Cantares Mexicanos* (1904) and collected in *Native Mesoamerican Spirituality* (1980).

[1] **quetzal plumage:** The quetzal, a resident of Central America, is a bird with long, brilliant green feathers highly prized by the early Mexicans.

[2] **Giver of Life:** Refers to Tloque Nahuaque, "Lord of the Near and the Far." Nezahuacoyotl conceived of this supreme deity who cannot be represented visually and is to be worshiped without idols. Nezahuacoyotl's monotheism was not widely shared in ancient Mexico.

they say that it is not real,
that it is not rooted.
The Giver of Life
only appears absolute.

May our hearts
be not tormented,
because He is the Giver of Life.

With flowers You write

With flowers You write,
O Giver of Life;
With songs You give color,[3]
with songs You shade
those who must live on the earth.

Later You will destroy eagles and ocelots;
we live only in Your book of paintings,[4]
here, on the earth.

With black ink You will blot out
all that was friendship,
brotherhood, nobility.

You give shading
to those who must live on the earth.
We live only in Your book of paintings,
here on the earth.

I comprehend the secret, the hidden

I comprehend the secret, the hidden:
O my lords!

Thus we are,
we are mortal,
men through and through,
we all will have to go away,
we all will have to die on earth.
Like a painting,
we will be erased.

[3] **color:** Tloque Nahuaque is manifested in flowers and songs.

[4] **book of paintings:** Humans live in the created world, which is analogous to the Giver of Life's book of paintings; this book is similar to the Book of Life in the Christian tradition.

Like a flower,
we will dry up
here on earth.
Like plumed vestments of the precious bird,
that precious bird with the agile neck,
we will come to an end . . .
Think on this, my lords,
eagles and ocelots,
though you be of jade,
though you be of gold
you also will go there,
to the place of the fleshless.[5]
We will have to disappear,
no one can remain.

I AM INTOXICATED, I WEEP, I GRIEVE

I am intoxicated, I weep, I grieve,
I think, I speak,
within myself I discover this:
indeed, I shall never die,
indeed, I shall never disappear.
There where there is no death,
there where death is overcome,
let me go there.
Indeed I shall never die,
indeed, I shall never disappear.

THERE, ALONE, IN THE INTERIOR OF HEAVEN

There, alone, in the interior of heaven
You invent Your word,
Giver of Life!
What will You decide?

Do You disdain us here?
Do You conceal Your fame
and Your glory on the earth?
What will You decide?
No one can be intimate
with the Giver of Life . . .
Then, where shall we go?
Direct yourselves,
We all go to the place of mystery.

[5] **place of the fleshless:** The next world after death.

The Conquest of Mexico

Translated by Angel María Garibay K., Lysander Kemp, and David M. Johnson
Edited by Miguel León-Portilla

THE OMENS AS DESCRIBED BY SAHAGÚN'S INFORMANTS

The first bad omen: Ten years before the Spaniards first came here, a bad omen appeared in the sky. It was like a flaming ear of corn, or a fiery signal, or the blaze of daybreak; it seemed to bleed fire, drop by drop, like a wound in the sky. It was wide at the base and narrow at the peak, and it shone in the very heart of the heavens.

This is how it appeared: it shone in the eastern sky in the middle of the night. It appeared at midnight and burned till the break of day, but it vanished at the rising of the sun. The time during which it appeared to us was a full year, beginning in the year 12-House.[1]

When it first appeared, there was great outcry and confusion. The people clapped their hands against their mouths; they were amazed and frightened, and asked themselves what it could mean.

The second bad omen: The temple of Huitzilopochtli[2] burst into flames. It is thought that no one set it afire, that it burned down of its own accord. The name of its divine site was Tlacateccan [House of Authority].

And now it is burning, the wooden columns are burning! The flames, the tongues of fire shoot out, the bursts of fire shoot up into the sky!

The flames swiftly destroyed all the woodwork of the temple. When the fire was first seen, the people shouted: "Mexicanos, come running! We can put it out! Bring your water jars . . . !" But when they threw water on the blaze it only flamed higher. They could not put it out, and the temple burned to the ground.

The third bad omen: A temple was damaged by a lightning-bolt. This was the temple of Xiuhtecuhtli,[3] which was built of straw, in the place known as Tzonmolco.[4] It was raining that day, but it was only a light rain or a drizzle, and no thunder was

---

"The Conquest of Mexico." The primary sources of "The Conquest of Mexico" are the Nahuatl and Spanish texts of Bernardino de Sahagún's *Historia General de las Cosas de Nueva España* (1946); translated and edited by Angel María Garibay K.; translated into English by Lysander Kemp; and edited by Miguel León-Portilla for *The Broken Spears: The Aztec Account of the Conquest of Mexico* (1992). The selection here includes two chapters from the *Historia General* not included in *The Broken Spears* and translated by David M. Johnson. All notes are the editors'.

---

[1] **12-House:** In the Aztec calendar, each year was given one of four names (Reed, Flint, House, or Rabbit) and a number from one to thirteen; when either the series of names or numbers ended, it was repeated. Thus the year 12-House could occur once in fifty-two years.

[2] **Huitzilopochtli:** The sun god and god of war, patron deity of the Aztecs.

[3] **Xiuhtecuhtli:** Fire god.

[4] **Tzonmolco:** Part of Tenochtitlan's main temple.

Cortés's Route, Sixteenth Century

This map shows the route of the Spanish conquistador Hernán Cortés from the East Coast to the Aztec capital, Tenochtitlán, in central Mexico. (The Art Archive / Museo Ciudad Mexico / Dagli Orti)

heard. Therefore the lightning-bolt was taken as an omen. The people said: "The temple was struck by a blow from the sun."

The fourth bad omen: Fire streamed through the sky while the sun was still shining. It was divided into three parts. It flashed out from where the sun sets and raced straight to where the sun rises, giving off a shower of sparks like a red-hot coal. When the people saw its long train streaming through the heavens, there was a great outcry and confusion, as if they were shaking a thousand little bells.

The fifth bad omen: The wind lashed the water until it boiled. It was as if it were boiling with rage, as if it were shattering itself in its frenzy. It began from far off, rose high in the air and dashed against the walls of the houses. The flooded houses collapsed into the water. This was in the lake that is next to us.

The sixth bad omen: The people heard a weeping woman night after night. She passed by in the middle of the night, wailing and crying out in a loud voice: "My children, we must flee far away from this city!" At other times she cried: "My children, where shall I take you?"[5]

The seventh bad omen: A strange creature was captured in the nets. The men who fish the lakes caught a bird the color of ashes, a bird resembling a crane. They brought it to Motecuhzoma[6] in the Black House.[7]

This bird wore a strange mirror in the crown of its head. The mirror was pierced in the center like a spindle whorl, and the night sky could be seen in its face. The hour was noon, but the stars and the *mamalhuaztli*[8] could be seen in the face of that mirror. Motecuhzoma took it as a great and bad omen when he saw the stars and the *mamalhuaztli.*

But when he looked at the mirror a second time, he saw a distant plain. People were moving across it, spread out in ranks and coming forward in great haste. They made war against each other and rode on the backs of animals resembling deer.

Motecuhzoma called for his magicians and wise men and asked them: "Can you explain what I have seen? Creatures like human beings, running and fighting . . . !" But when they looked into the mirror to answer him, all had vanished away, and they saw nothing.

The eighth bad omen: Monstrous beings appeared in the streets of the city: deformed men with two heads but only one body. They were taken to the Black House and shown to Motecuhzoma; but the moment he saw them, they all vanished away.

Motecuhzoma Instructs His Messengers

Motecuhzoma then gave orders to Pinotl of Cuetlaxtlan and to other officials. He said to them: "Give out this order: a watch is to be kept along all the shores at Nauhtla, Tuztlan, Mictlancuauhtla,[9] wherever the strangers appear." The officials left at once and gave orders for the watch to be kept.

---

[5] **you:** A reference to Cihuacoatl, an earth goddess, and an antecedent to the legend of La Llorona ("Weeping Woman") found in the Southwestern United States and Mexico. [6] **Motecuhzoma:** Moctezuma II. [7] **Black House:** The house of magical studies. [8] ***mamalhuaztli:*** The three stars in the constellation Taurus; priests offered copal incense to them three times nightly. [9] **Nauhtla . . . Mictlancuauhtla:** Places along the Gulf of Mexico.

Motecuhzoma now called his chiefs together: Tlilpotonque, the serpent woman,[10] Cuappiatzin, the chief of the house of arrows,[11] Quetzalaztatzin, the keeper of the chalk,[12] and Hecateupatiltzin, the chief of the refugees from the south. He told them the news that had been brought to him and showed them the objects he had ordered made. He said: "We all admire these blue turquoises, and they must be guarded well. The whole treasure must be guarded well. If anything is lost, your houses will be destroyed and your children killed, even those who are still in the womb."

The year 13-Rabbit now approached its end. And when it was about to end, they appeared, they were seen again. The report of their coming was brought to Motecuhzoma, who immediately sent out messengers. It was as if he thought the new arrival was our prince Quetzalcoatl.

This is what he felt in his heart: *He has appeared! He has come back! He will come here, to the place of his throne and canopy, for that is what he promised when he departed!*

Motecuhzoma sent five messengers to greet the strangers and to bring them gifts. They were led by the priest in charge of the sanctuary of Yohualichan. The second was from Tepoztlan; the third from Tizatlan; the fourth, from Huehuetlan; and the fifth, from Mictlan the Great.[13] He said to them: "Come forward, my Jaguar Knights, come forward. It is said that our lord has returned to this land. Go to meet him. Go to hear him. Listen well to what he tells you; listen and remember."

The Gifts Sent to the New Arrivals

Motecuhzoma also said to the messengers: "Here is what you are to bring our lord. This is the treasure of Quetzalcoatl." This treasure was the god's finery: a serpent mask inlaid with turquoise, a decoration for the breast made of quetzal[14] feathers, a collar woven in the petatillo style[15] with a gold disk in the center, and a shield decorated with gold and mother-of-pearl and bordered with quetzal feathers with a pendant of the same feathers.

There was also a mirror like those which the ritual dancers wore on their buttocks. The reverse of this mirror was a turquoise mosaic: it was encrusted and adorned with turquoises. And there was a spear-thrower inlaid with turquoise, a bracelet of *chalchihuites*[16] hung with little gold bells and a pair of sandals as black as obsidian.

Motecuhzoma also gave them the finery of Tezcatlipoca.[17] This finery was: a helmet in the shape of a cone, yellow with gold and set with many stars, a number of earrings adorned with little gold bells, a fringed and painted vest with feathers as

[10] **the serpent woman:** The ruler's chief counselor was traditionally given this title; the earth goddess had both masculine and feminine qualities. [11] **arrows:** The suffix *-tzin* indicates a high rank. [12] **chalk:** Official in charge of ceremonial colors used by the priests. [13] **Yohualichan . . . Mictlan the Great:** The first four places are in the Lake Texcoco region; the fifth is Mitla in the Oaxaca region. [14] **quetzal:** A precious bird with long, green tail feathers; as part of the name *Quetzalcoatl,* quetzal means "feathered" or "sky," and *coatl* means "serpent." [15] **petatillo style:** Like a rush mat, but a finer weave. [16] ***chalchihuites:*** Green stones like jade or emerald. [17] **Tezcatlipoca:** God of war and disease.

delicate as foam and a blue cloak known as "the ringing bell," which reached to the ears and was fastened with a knot.

There was also a collar of fine shells to cover the breast. This collar was adorned with the finest snail shells, which seemed to escape from the edges. And there was a mirror to be hung in back, a set of little gold bells and a pair of white sandals.

Then Motecuhzoma gave them the finery of Tlaloc.[18] This finery was: a headdress made of quetzal feathers, as green as if it were growing, with an ornament of gold and mother-of-pearl, earrings in the form of serpents, made of *chalchihuites,* a vest adorned with *chalchihuites* and a collar also of *chalchihuites,* woven in the petatillo style, with a disk of gold.

There was also a serpent wand inlaid with turquoise, a mirror to be hung in back, with little bells, and a cloak bordered with red rings.

Then Motecuhzoma gave them the finery of Quetzalcoatl. This finery was: a diadem made of jaguar skin and pheasant feathers and adorned with a large green stone, round turquoise earrings with curved pendants of shell and gold, a collar of *chalchihuites* in the petatillo style with a disk of gold in the center, a cloak with red borders, and little gold bells for the feet.

There was also a golden shield, pierced in the middle, with quetzal feathers around the rim and a pendant of the same feathers, the crooked staff of Ehecatl[19] with a cluster of white stones at the crook, and his sandals of fine soft rubber.

These were the many kinds of adornments that were known as "divine adornments." They were placed in the possession of the messengers to be taken as gifts of welcome along with many other objects, such as a golden snail shell and a golden diadem. All these objects were packed into great baskets; they were loaded into panniers for the long journey.

Then Motecuhzoma gave the messengers his final orders. He said to them: "Go now, without delay. Do reverence to our lord the god. Say to him: 'Your deputy, Motecuhzoma, has sent us to you. Here are the presents with which he welcomes you home to Mexico.'"

The Messengers Contact the Spaniards

When they arrived at the shore of the sea, they were taken in canoes to Xicalanco. They placed the baskets in the same canoes in which they rode, in order to keep them under their personal vigilance. From Xicalanco they followed the coast until they sighted the ships of the strangers.

When they came up to the ships, the strangers asked them: "Who are you? Where are you from?"

"We have come from the City of Mexico."[20]

---

[18] **Tlaloc:** God of rain and fertility. [19] **Ehecatl:** God of wind, a manifestation of Quetzalcoatl. [20] **City of Mexico:** The Spaniards and messengers could communicate because of La Malinche (called Doña Marina by the Spanish), an Indian from the Gulf Coast, who spoke Mayan and Nahuatl and Jeronimo de Aguilar, who had spent eight years with Maya in Yucatan and spoke Mayan and Spanish.

The strangers said: "You may have come from there, or you may not have. Perhaps you are only inventing it. Perhaps you are mocking us." But their hearts were convinced; they were satisfied in their hearts. They lowered a hook from the bow of the ship, and then a ladder, and the messengers came aboard.

One by one they did reverence to Cortés by touching the ground before him with their lips. They said to him: "If the god will deign to hear us, your deputy Motecuhzoma has sent us to render you homage. He has the City of Mexico in his care. He says: 'The god is weary.'"

Then they arrayed the Captain in the finery they had brought him as presents. With great care they fastened the turquoise mask in place, the mask of the god with its crossband of quetzal feathers. A golden earring hung down on either side of this mask. They dressed him in the decorated vest and the collar woven in the petatillo style—the collar of *chalchihuites*, with a disk of gold in the center.

Next they fastened the mirror to his hips, dressed him in the cloak known as "the ringing bell" and adorned his feet with the greaves used by the Huastecas,[21] which were set with *chalchihuites* and hung with little gold bells. In his hand they placed the shield with its fringe and pendant of quetzal feathers, its ornaments of gold and mother-of-pearl. Finally they set before him the pair of black sandals. As for the other objects of divine finery, they only laid them out for him to see.

The Captain then asked them: "And is this all? Is this your gift of welcome? Is this how you greet people?"

They replied: "This is all, our lord. This is what we have brought you."

Cortés Frightens the Messengers

Then the Captain gave orders, and the messengers were chained by the feet and by the neck. When this had been done, the great cannon was fired off. The messengers lost their senses and fainted away. They fell down side by side and lay where they had fallen. But the Spaniards quickly revived them: they lifted them up, gave them wine to drink and then offered them food.

The Captain said to them: "I have heard that the Mexicans are very great warriors, very brave and terrible. If a Mexican is fighting alone, he knows how to retreat, turn back, rush forward and conquer, even if his opponents are ten or even twenty. But my heart is not convinced. I want to see it for myself. I want to find out if you are truly that strong and brave."

Then he gave them swords, spears and leather shields. He said: "It will take place very early, at daybreak. We are going to fight each other in pairs, and in this way we will learn the truth. We will see who falls to the ground!"

They said to the Captain: "Our lord, we were not sent here for this by your deputy Motecuhzoma! We have come on an exclusive mission, to offer you rest and repose and to bring you presents. What the lord desires is not within our warrant. If

[21] **Huastecas:** Indians of eastern Mexico.

we were to do this, it might anger Motecuhzoma, and he would surely put us to death."

The Captain replied: "No, it must take place. I want to see for myself, because even in Castile they say you are famous as brave warriors. Therefore, eat an early meal. I will eat too. Good cheer!"

With these words he sent them away from the ship. They were scarcely into their canoes when they began to paddle furiously. Some of them even paddled with their hands, so fierce was the anxiety burning in their souls. They said to each other: "My captains, paddle with all your might! Faster, faster! Nothing must happen to us here! Nothing must happen . . . !"

They arrived in great haste at Xicalanco, took a hurried meal there, and then pressed on until they came to Tecpantlayacac. From there they rushed ahead and arrived in Cuetlaxtlan. As on the previous journey, they stopped there to rest. When they were about to depart, the village official said to them: "Rest for at least a day! At least catch your breath!"

They said: "No, we must keep on! We must report to our king, Motecuhzoma. We will tell him what we have seen, and it is a terrifying thing. Nothing like it has ever been seen before!" Then they left in great haste and continued to the City of Mexico. They entered the city at night, in the middle of the night.

[Motecuhzoma is very anxious about the arrival of the Spaniards. When the messengers return to Tenochtitlán, they are purified by a sacrifice since they are thought to have seen gods.]

The Messengers' Report

When the sacrifice was finished, the messengers reported to the king. They told him how they had made the journey, and what they had seen, and what food the strangers ate. Motecuhzoma was astonished and terrified by their report, and the description of the strangers' food astonished him above all else.

He was also terrified to learn how the cannon roared, how its noise resounded, how it caused one to faint and grow deaf. The messengers told him: "A thing like a ball of stone comes out of its entrails: it comes out shooting sparks and raining fire. The smoke that comes out with it has a pestilent odor, like that of rotten mud. This odor penetrates even to the brain and causes the greatest discomfort. If the cannon is aimed against a mountain, the mountain splits and cracks open. If the cannon is aimed against a tree, it shatters the tree into splinters. This is a most unnatural sight, as if the tree had exploded from within."

The messengers also said: "Their trappings and arms are all made of iron. They dress in iron and wear iron casques on their heads. Their swords are iron; their bows are iron; their shields are iron; their spears are iron. Their deer carry them on their backs wherever they wish to go. These deer, our lord, are as tall as the roof of a house.

"The strangers' bodies are completely covered, so that only their faces can be seen. Their skin is white, as if it were made of lime. They have yellow hair, though some of them have black. Their beards are long and yellow, and their moustaches are also yellow. Their hair is curly, with very fine strands.

"As for their food, it is like human food. It is large and white, and not heavy. It is something like straw, but with the taste of a cornstalk, of the pith of a cornstalk. It is a little sweet, as if it were flavored with honey; it tastes of honey, it is sweet-tasting food.

"Their dogs are enormous, with flat ears and long, dangling tongues. The color of their eyes is a burning yellow; their eyes flash fire and shoot off sparks. Their bellies are hollow, their flanks long and narrow. They are tireless and very powerful. They bound here and there, panting, with their tongues hanging out. And they are spotted like an ocelot."

When Motecuhzoma heard this report, he was filled with terror. It was as if his heart had fainted, as if it had shriveled. It was as if he were conquered by despair.

[Motecuhzoma sent out wizards and magicians to stop the advance of the Spaniards, but they failed. The Spaniards began their march from the coast to Tenochtitlán, the capital of the Aztec Empire on the high central plateau of Mexico.]

The Spaniards March Inland

At last they came. At last they began to march toward us.

A man from Cempoala, who was known as the Tlacochcalcatl [Chief of the House of Arrows], was the first official to welcome them as they entered our lands and cities. This man spoke Nahuatl. He showed them the best routes and the shortest ways; he guided and advised them, traveling at the head of the party.

When they came to Tecoac, in the land of the Tlaxcaltecas, they found it was inhabited by Otomies.[22] The Otomies came out to meet them in battle array; they greeted the strangers with their shields.

But the strangers conquered the Otomies of Tecoac; they utterly destroyed them. They divided their ranks, fired the cannons at them, attacked them with their swords and shot them with their crossbows. Not just a few, but all of them, perished in the battle.

And when Tecoac had been defeated, the Tlaxcaltecas soon heard the news; they learned what had taken place there. They felt premonitions of death: terror overwhelmed them, and they were filled with foreboding.

Therefore the chiefs assembled; the captains met together in a council. They talked about what had happened, and said: "What shall we do? Shall we go out to meet them? The Otomi is a brave warrior, but he was helpless against them: they scorned him as a mere nothing! They destroyed the poor *macehual*[23] with a look, with a glance of their eyes! We should go over to their side: we should make friends with them and be their allies. If not, they will destroy us too. . . ."

[22] **Otomies:** One of the tribes that had settled in the Valley of Mexico before the arrival of the Aztecs.

[23] ***macehual:*** A common, ordinary person in Aztec society.

The Arrival at Tlaxcala

Therefore the lords of Tlaxcala went out to meet them, bringing many things to eat: hens and hens' eggs and the finest tortillas. They said to the strangers: "Our lords, you are weary."

The strangers replied: "Where do you live? Where are you from?"

They said: "We are from Tlaxcala. You have come here, you have entered our land. We are from Tlaxcala; our city is the City of the Eagle, Tlaxcala." (For in ancient times it was called Texcala,[24] and its people were known as Texcaltecas.)

Then they guided them to the city; they brought them there and invited them to enter. They paid them great honors, attended to their every want, joined with them as allies and even gave them their daughters.

The Spaniards asked: "Where is the City of Mexico? Is it far from here?"

They said: "No, it is not far, it is only a three-day march. And it is a great city. The Aztecs are very brave. They are great warriors and conquerors and have defeated their neighbors on every side."

Intrigues against Cholula

At this time the Tlaxcaltecas were enemies of Cholula. They feared the Cholultecas; they envied and cursed them; their souls burned with hatred for the people of Cholula. This is why they brought certain rumors to Cortés, so that he would destroy them. They said to him: "Cholula is our enemy. It is an evil city. The people are as brave as the Aztecs and they are the Aztecs' friends."

When the Spaniards heard this, they marched against Cholula. They were guided and accompanied by the Tlaxcaltecas and the chiefs from Cempoala, and they all marched in battle array.[25]

The Massacre at Cholula

When they arrived, the Tlaxcaltecas and the men of Cholula called to each other and shouted greetings. An assembly was held in the courtyard of the god, but when they had all gathered together, the entrances were closed, so that there was no way of escaping.

Then the sudden slaughter began: knife strokes, and sword strokes, and death. The people of Cholula had not foreseen it, had not suspected it. They faced the Spaniards without weapons, without their swords or their shields. The cause of the slaughter was treachery. They died blindly, without knowing why, because of the lies of the Tlaxcaltecas.

And when this had taken place, word of it was brought to Motecuhzoma. The

[24] **Texcala:** "Where there are many rocks."

[25] **array:** This was customary, so the Cholultecas were not suspicious.

messengers came and departed, journeying back and forth between Tenochtitlán and Cholula. The common people were terrified by the news; they could do nothing but tremble with fright. It was as if the earth trembled beneath them, or as if the world were spinning before their eyes, as it spins during a fit of vertigo. . . .

When the massacre at Cholula was complete, the strangers set out again toward the City of Mexico. They came in battle array, as conquerors, and the dust rose in whirlwinds on the roads. Their spears glinted in the sun, and their pennons fluttered like bats. They made a loud clamour as they marched, for their coats of mail and their weapons clashed and rattled. Some of them were dressed in glistening iron from head to foot; they terrified everyone who saw them.

Their dogs came with them, running ahead of the column. They raised their muzzles high; they lifted their muzzles to the wind. They raced on before with saliva dripping from their jaws.

The Spaniards See the Objects of Gold

Then Motecuhzoma dispatched various chiefs. Tzihuacpopocatzin was at their head, and he took with him a great many of his representatives. They went out to meet the Spaniards in the vicinity of Popocatepetl and Iztactepetl,[26] there in the Eagle Pass.

They gave the "gods" ensigns of gold, and ensigns of quetzal feathers, and golden necklaces. And when they were given these presents, the Spaniards burst into smiles; their eyes shone with pleasure; they were delighted by them. They picked up the gold and fingered it like monkeys; they seemed to be transported by joy, as if their hearts were illumined and made new.

The truth is that they longed and lusted for gold. Their bodies swelled with greed, and their hunger was ravenous; they hungered like pigs for that gold. They snatched at the golden ensigns, waved them from side to side and examined every inch of them. They were like one who speaks a barbarous tongue: everything they said was in a barbarous tongue.

[Envoys were sent out by Motecuhzoma to try to convince the Spaniards to turn back; one of the envoys tried to impersonate Motecuhzoma, but failed in his disguise.]

The Apparition of Tezcatlipoca

But then there was another series of envoys: magicians, wizards and priests. They also left the city and went out to meet the strangers, but they were completely helpless: they could not blind their eyes or overcome them in any way.

They even failed to meet and speak with the "gods," because a certain drunkard blundered across their path. He used gestures that are used by the people of

[26] **Popocatepetl and Iztactepetl:** Two high mountains in the vicinity of the Valley of Mexico.

Chalco, and he was dressed like a Chalca, with eight cords of couch-grass across his breast. He seemed to be very drunk; he feigned drunkenness; he pretended to be a drunkard.

He came up to them while they were about to meet the Spaniards. He rushed up to the Mexicanos and cried: "Why have you come here? For what purpose? What is it you want? What is Motecuhzoma trying to do? Has he still not recovered his wits? Does he still tremble and beg? He has committed many errors and destroyed a multitude of people. Some have been beaten and others wrapped in shrouds; some have been betrayed and others mocked and derided."

When the magicians heard these words, they tried in vain to approach him. They wanted to ask his help, and they hurriedly built him a small temple and altar and a seat made of couch-grass. But for a while they could not see him.

They labored in vain, they prepared his temple in vain, for he spoke to them only in oracles. He terrified them with his harsh reproofs and spoke to them as if from a great distance: "Why have you come here? It is useless. Mexico will be destroyed! Mexico will be left in ruins!" He said: "Go back, go back! Turn your eyes toward the city. What was fated to happen has already taken place!"

They looked in the direction of Tenochtitlán. The temples were in flames, and so were the communal halls, the religious schools and all the houses. It was as if a great battle were raging in the city.

When the magicians saw this, they lost heart. They could not speak clearly, but talked as if they were drunk: "It was not proper for us to have seen this vision. Motecuhzoma himself should have beheld it! This was not a mere mortal. This was the young Tezcatlipoca!"

Suddenly the god disappeared, and they saw him no longer. The envoys did not go forward to meet the Spaniards; they did not speak with them. The priests and magicians turned and went back to report to Motecuhzoma.

Motecuhzoma's Despair

When the envoys arrived in the city, they told Motecuhzoma what had happened and what they had seen. Motecuhzoma listened to their report and then bowed his head without speaking a word. For a long time he remained thus, with his head bent down. And when he spoke at last, it was only to say: "What help is there now, my friends? Is there a mountain for us to climb? Should we run away? We are Mexicanos: would this bring any glory to the Mexican nation?

"Pity the old men, and the old women, and the innocent little children. How can they save themselves? But there is no help. What can we do? Is there nothing left us?

"We will be judged and punished. And however it may be, and whenever it may be, we can do nothing but wait."

[The center of the Valley of Mexico was covered by five interconnected lakes; Tenochtitlan was located on an island in the middle of Lake Texcoco, the largest lake in the middle of the five lakes. The Spaniards arrived at the southwestern corner of the Valley and Lakes Chalco and Xochimilco, famous for their floating gardens. As they moved closer to Tenochtitlán they enlisted the aid of cities at the edge of the lakes.]

Motecuhzoma Commands That the Road Be Closed

Motecuhzoma in vain commanded that the road be closed off. They planted the one to Mexico with a wall of maguey plants. The Spaniards saw through this plan of blocking the road. They tore up the maguey plants and threw them away.

They slept at Amaquemecan. The next day they left there and traveled to Cuitlauac and spent the night.

They assembled the rulers who were responsible for the people of the floating gardens—Xochimilco, Cuitlauac, Mizquic. They spoke to them in the same way that they had spoken to the Chalcan rulers. And these rulers of the people of the floating gardens at once also submitted to them.

When the Spaniards were satisfied, they moved on, resting at Itztapalapan. They summoned the local rulers who were known as the Four Lords: of Itztapalapan, of Mexicatzinco, of Colhuacan, of Uitzilopochco. In the same manner as they had spoken to others, they spoke to these rulers, who peacefully submitted to the Spaniards.

Motecuhzoma did not command that war should be made against them. No one was to fight them. He commanded only that they not be ignored.

When this happened, it was as if Mexico lay silent. No one went outside. Mothers kept their children in. The roads were empty, wide open as in early morning. People stayed in their houses with their fears. They spoke to each other: "Let happen what will happen. We are ready to die. The time comes when we will be destroyed. Here we await our death."

The Spaniards Travel from Itztapalapan to Mexico

On the last stage of the journey to Mexico, the Spaniards put on their battle dress. They arranged their horses into neat and orderly rows.

Four horsemen went in front as the vanguard. And as they went they continually turned around facing the people, looking here and there. They looked at all the houses, they looked up at the roof terraces. They also had their dogs in the procession, which panted and sniffed at things.

A lone standard bearer marched along holding the standard on his shoulders and shaking it from side to side in the breeze. Bobbing up and down it looked like a warrior.

Following him came the bearers of iron swords, which flashed in the sun. They carried their wooden and leather shields on their shoulders.

In a second group came the soldiers on horses wearing their cotton breast protectors. They carried leather shields, iron swords and lances hanging at the horses' necks. Each horse had bells which loudly rang. The horses which were thought to be deer, neighed and sweat. They sweat so much it looked as if water flowed from them.

Motecuhzoma Commands . . . and **The Spaniards Travel. . . .** These two sections were translated by David M. Johnson.

Flecks of foam bubbled from their mouths like soapsuds. Their hooves beat on the ground with the sound of pounding stones. Each hoof left its mark in the ground, both the forelegs and the hind legs.

In the third group came the men with the iron crossbows, which were carried in their arms. Some pointed the crossbows here and there, while others rested them on their shoulders. Their quivers hung at their sides filled with iron tipped arrows. Their dense, close-woven cotton armor reached to their knees. Their heads were covered in the same way with cotton armor, which had precious feathers sticking out on top.

The fourth group had horsemen dressed like the second.

The fifth group carried arquebuses[27] on their shoulders. Some had them pointed upwards and fired them when they entered the great palace, the residence of the rulers. The shots were like explosions of thunder with large clouds of smoke spreading around. It smelled awful and some people fainted.

At the very rear came the commander, who was the same as the *tlacateccatl,*[28] the battle chief. Surrounding him were his personal attendants and his insignia bearers, who were like the brave Otomi warriors attending the Mexica rulers.

Following behind were warriors from distant cities—the Tlaxcallan, the Tliliuhquitepecan, the Huexotzincan. They were dressed for war, each in his cotton armor, each with his shield, each with his bow. Each one's quiver was filled with feathered arrows, some with barbed points, some blunted, some obsidian-pointed. They walked in a crouch, yelling and striking their mouths with their hands. They sang the Tocuillan[29] song while whistling and shaking their heads. Some carried supplies on their backs with a tump line around their foreheads or a band around their chests. Some used frames or deep baskets for their loads. Other men dragged the great lombard guns[30] which rested on wooden wheels. They sang as they moved them along.

Motecuhzoma Goes Out to Meet Cortés

The Spaniards arrived in Xoloco,[31] near the entrance to Tenochtitlán. That was the end of the march, for they had reached their goal.

Motecuhzoma now arrayed himself in his finery, preparing to go out to meet them. The other great princes also adorned their persons, as did the nobles and their chieftains and knights. They all went out together to meet the strangers.

They brought trays heaped with the finest flowers—the flower that resembles a shield; the flower shaped like a heart; in the center, the flower with the sweetest aroma; and the fragrant yellow flower, the most precious of all. They also brought garlands of flowers, and ornaments for the breast, and necklaces of gold, necklaces hung with rich stones, necklaces fashioned in the petatillo style.

---

[27] **arquebuses:** An early type of gun. [28] ***tlacateccatl:*** A commander in charge of eight thousand warriors from the Tlacatecco, a temple consecrated to Huitzilopochtli. [29] **Tocuillan:** An unknown warrior song, perhaps named after the crane. [30] **lombard guns:** A type of cannon. [31] **Xoloco:** The region on the south end of Tenochtitlán, next to the bridge, over the canal.

Thus Motecuhzoma went out to meet them, there in Huitzillan.[32] He presented many gifts to the Captain and his commanders, those who had come to make war. He showered gifts upon them and hung flowers around their necks; he gave them necklaces of flowers and bands of flowers to adorn their breasts; he set garlands of flowers upon their heads. Then he hung the gold necklaces around their necks and gave them presents of every sort as gifts of welcome.

Speeches of Motecuhzoma and Cortés

When Motecuhzoma had given necklaces to each one, Cortés asked him: "Are you Motecuhzoma? Are you the king? Is it true that you are the king Motecuhzoma?"

And the king said: "Yes, I am Motecuhzoma." Then he stood up to welcome Cortés; he came forward, bowed his head low and addressed him in these words: "Our lord, you are weary. The journey has tired you, but now you have arrived on the earth. You have come to your city, Mexico. You have come here to sit on your throne, to sit under its canopy.[33]

"The kings who have gone before, your representatives, guarded it and preserved it for your coming. The kings Itzcoatl, Motecuhzoma the Elder, Axayacatl, Tizoc and Ahuitzol[34] ruled for you in the City of Mexico. The people were protected by their swords and sheltered by their shields.

"Do the kings know the destiny of those they left behind, their posterity? If only they are watching! If only they can see what I see!

"No, it is not a dream. I am not walking in my sleep. I am not seeing you in my dreams. . . . I have seen you at last! I have met you face to face! I was in agony for five days, for ten days, with my eyes fixed on the Region of the Mystery.[35] And now you have come out of the clouds and mists to sit on your throne again.

"This was foretold by the kings who governed your city, and now it has taken place. You have come back to us; you have come down from the sky. Rest now, and take possession of your royal houses. Welcome to your land, my lords!"

When Motecuhzoma had finished, La Malinche translated his address into Spanish so that the Captain could understand it. Cortés replied in his strange and savage tongue, speaking first to La Malinche: "Tell Motecuhzoma that we are his friends. There is nothing to fear. We have wanted to see him for a long time, and now we have seen his face and heard his words. Tell him that we love him well and that our hearts are contented."

Then he said to Motecuhzoma: "We have come to your house in Mexico as friends. There is nothing to fear."

La Malinche translated this speech and the Spaniards grasped Motecuhzoma's hands and patted his back to show their affection for him.

---

[32] **Huitzillan:** A region of Tenochtitlán north of Xoloco. [33] **canopy:** An extraordinary speech in which Motecuhzoma speaks to Cortés as if he were a deity returning to claim his earthly throne. [34] **Itzcoatl . . . Ahuitzol:** Previous Aztec rulers; Itzcoatl began his rule in 1428 and Motecuhzoma II began to rule in 1502. [35] **Region of the Mystery:** The heavens, which were divided into thirteen different heavens, the most important of which is Omeyocan, the home of Ometeotl and the source of life.

The Spaniards Take Possession of the City

When the Spaniards entered the Royal House, they placed Motecuhzoma under guard and kept him under their vigilance. They also placed a guard over Itzcuauhtzin,[36] but the other lords were permitted to depart.

Then the Spaniards fired one of their cannons, and this caused great confusion in the city. The people scattered in every direction; they fled without rhyme or reason; they ran off as if they were being pursued. It was as if they had eaten the mushrooms that confuse the mind, or had seen some dreadful apparition. They were all overcome by terror, as if their hearts had fainted. And when night fell, the panic spread through the city and their fears would not let them sleep.

In the morning the Spaniards told Motecuhzoma what they needed in the way of supplies: tortillas, fried chickens, hens' eggs, pure water, firewood and charcoal. Also: large, clean cooking pots, water jars, pitchers, dishes and other pottery. Motecuhzoma ordered that it be sent to them. The chiefs who received this order were angry with the king and no longer revered or respected him. But they furnished the Spaniards with all the provisions they needed—food, beverages and water, and fodder for the horses.

The Spaniards Reveal Their Greed

When the Spaniards were installed in the palace, they asked Motecuhzoma about the city's resources and reserves and about the warriors' ensigns and shields. They questioned him closely and then demanded gold.

Motecuhzoma guided them to it. They surrounded him and crowded close with their weapons. He walked in the center, while they formed a circle around him.

When they arrived at the treasure house called Teucalco, the riches of gold and feathers were brought out to them: ornaments made of quetzal feathers, richly worked shields, disks of gold, the necklaces of the idols, gold nose plugs, gold greaves and bracelets and crowns.

The Spaniards immediately stripped the feathers from the gold shields and ensigns. They gathered all the gold into a great mound and set fire to everything else, regardless of its value. Then they melted down the gold into ingots. As for the precious green stones, they took only the best of them; the rest were snatched up by the Tlaxcaltecas. The Spaniards searched through the whole treasure house, questioning and quarreling, and seized every object they thought was beautiful.

The Seizure of Motecuhzoma's Treasures

Next they went to Motecuhzoma's storehouse, in the place called Totocalco [Place of the Palace of the Birds],[37] where his personal treasures were kept. The Spaniards grinned like little beasts and patted each other with delight.

---

[36] **Itzcuauhtzin:** Ruler of Tlatloloco. [37] **Palace of the Birds:** The zoo attached to the royal palaces.

When they entered the hall of treasures, it was as if they had arrived in Paradise. They searched everywhere and coveted everything; they were slaves to their own greed. All of Motecuhzoma's possessions were brought out: fine bracelets, necklaces with large stones, ankle rings with little gold bells, the royal crowns and all the royal finery—everything that belonged to the king and was reserved to him only. They seized these treasures as if they were their own, as if this plunder were merely a stroke of good luck. And when they had taken all the gold, they heaped up everything else in the middle of the patio.

La Malinche called the nobles together. She climbed up to the palace roof and cried: "Mexicanos, come forward! The Spaniards need your help! Bring them food and pure water. They are tired and hungry; they are almost fainting from exhaustion! Why do you not come forward? Are you angry with them?"

The Mexicans were too frightened to approach. They were crushed by terror and would not risk coming forward. They shied away as if the Spaniards were wild beasts, as if the hour were midnight on the blackest night of the year. Yet they did not abandon the Spaniards to hunger and thirst. They brought them whatever they needed, but shook with fear as they did so. They delivered the supplies to the Spaniards with trembling hands, then turned and hurried away.

[The fiesta of Huitzilopochtli, which, according to Sahagun, "was the most important of their fiestas. It is like our Easter and fell at almost the same time." Cortés left Tenochtitlan twenty days before the fiesta to fight Panfilo de Narvaez who had been sent by Diego Velazques, governor of Cuba, to arrest Cortés. His deputy, Pedro de Alvarado, murdered the Aztec celebrants at the height of the fiesta.]

The Preparations for the Fiesta

The Aztecs begged permission of their king to hold the fiesta of Huitzilopochtli. The Spaniards wanted to see this fiesta to learn how it was celebrated. A delegation of the celebrants came to the palace where Motecuhzoma was a prisoner, and when their spokesman asked his permission, he granted it to them.

As soon as the delegation returned, the women began to grind seeds of the chicalote.[38] These women had fasted for a whole year. They ground the seeds in the patio of the temple.

The Spaniards came out of the palace together, dressed in armor and carrying their weapons with them. They stalked among the women and looked at them one by one; they stared into the faces of the women who were grinding seeds. After this cold inspection, they went back into the palace. It is said that they planned to kill the celebrants if the men entered the patio.

The Statue of Huitzilopochtli

On the evening before the fiesta of Toxcatl, the celebrants began to model a statue of Huitzilopochtli. They gave it such a human appearance that it seemed the body of a

[38] **chicalote:** Prickly poppy; other texts say they used amaranth seeds.

living man. Yet they made the statue with nothing but a paste made of the ground seeds of the chicalote, which they shaped over an armature of sticks.

When the statue was finished, they dressed it in rich feathers, and they painted crosses over and under its eyes. They also clipped on its earrings of turquoise mosaic; these were in the shape of serpents, with gold rings hanging from them. Its nose plug, in the shape of an arrow, was made of gold and was inlaid with fine stones.

They placed the magic headdress of hummingbird feathers on its head. They also adorned it with an *anecuyotl,* which was a belt made of feathers, with a cone at the back. Then they hung around its neck an ornament of yellow parrot feathers, fringed like the locks of a young boy. Over this they put its nettle-leaf cape, which was painted black and decorated with five clusters of eagle feathers.

Next they wrapped it in its cloak, which was painted with skulls and bones, and over this they fastened its vest. The vest was painted with dismembered human parts: skulls, ears, hearts, intestines, torsos, breasts, hands and feet. They also put on its *maxtlatl,* or loincloth, which was decorated with images of dissevered limbs and fringed with amate paper. This *maxtlatl* was painted with vertical stripes of bright blue.

They fastened a red paper flag at its shoulder and placed on its head what looked like a sacrificial flint knife. This too was made of red paper; it seemed to have been steeped in blood.

The statue carried a *tehuehuelli,* a bamboo shield decorated with four clusters of fine eagle feathers. The pendant of this shield was blood-red, like the knife and the shoulder flag. The statue also carried four arrows.

Finally, they put the wristbands on its arms. These bands, made of coyote skin, were fringed with paper cut into little strips.

The Beginning of the Fiesta

Early the next morning, the statue's face was uncovered by those who had been chosen for that ceremony. They gathered in front of the idol in single file and offered it gifts of food, such as round seedcakes or perhaps human flesh. But they did not carry it up to its temple on top of the pyramid.

All the young warriors were eager for the fiesta to begin. They had sworn to dance and sing with all their hearts, so that the Spaniards would marvel at the beauty of the rituals.

The procession began, and the celebrants filed into the temple patio to dance the Dance of the Serpent. When they were all together in the patio, the songs and the dance began. Those who had fasted for twenty days and those who had fasted for a year were in command of the others; they kept the dancers in file with their pine wands. (If anyone wished to urinate, he did not stop dancing, but simply opened his clothing at the hips and separated his clusters of heron feathers.) . . .

The great captains, the bravest warriors, danced at the head of the files to guide the others. The youths followed at a slight distance. Some of the youths wore their hair gathered into large locks, a sign that they had never taken any captives. Others carried their headdresses on their shoulders; they had taken captives, but only with help.

Then came the recruits, who were called "the young warriors." They had each captured an enemy or two. The others called to them: "Come, comrades, show us how brave you are! Dance with all your hearts!"

The Spaniards Attack the Celebrants

At this moment in the fiesta, when the dance was loveliest and when song was linked to song, the Spaniards were seized with an urge to kill the celebrants. They all ran forward, armed as if for battle. They closed the entrances and passageways, all the gates of the patio: the Eagle Gate in the lesser palace, the Gate of the Canestalk and the Gate of the Serpent of Mirrors. They posted guards so that no one could escape, and then rushed into the Sacred Patio to slaughter the celebrants. They came on foot, carrying their swords and their wooden or metal shields.

They ran in among the dancers, forcing their way to the place where the drums were played. They attacked the man who was drumming and cut off his arms. Then they cut off his head, and it rolled across the floor.

They attacked all the celebrants, stabbing them, spearing them, striking them with their swords. They attacked some of them from behind, and these fell instantly to the ground with their entrails hanging out. Others they beheaded: they cut off their heads, or split their heads to pieces.

They struck others in the shoulders, and their arms were torn from their bodies. They wounded some in the thigh and some in the calf. They slashed others in the abdomen, and their entrails all spilled to the ground. Some attempted to run away, but their intestines dragged as they ran; they seemed to tangle their feet in their own entrails. No matter how they tried to save themselves, they could find no escape.

Some attempted to force their way out, but the Spaniards murdered them at the gates. Others climbed the walls, but they could not save themselves. Those who ran into the communal houses were safe there for a while; so were those who lay down among the victims and pretended to be dead. But if they stood up again, the Spaniards saw them and killed them.

The blood of the warriors flowed like water and gathered into pools. The pools widened, and the stench of blood and entrails filled the air. The Spaniards ran into the communal houses to kill those who were hiding. They ran everywhere and searched everywhere; they invaded every room, hunting and killing.

The Aztecs Retaliate

When the news of this massacre was heard outside the Sacred Patio, a great cry went up: "Mexicanos, come running! Bring your spears and shields! The strangers have murdered our warriors!"

This cry was answered with a roar of grief and anger: the people shouted and wailed and beat their palms against their mouths. The captains assembled at once, as if the hour had been determined in advance. They all carried their spears and shields.

Then the battle began. The Aztecs attacked with javelins and arrows, even with the light spears that are used for hunting birds. They hurled their javelins with all their strength, and the cloud of missiles spread out over the Spaniards like a yellow cloak.

The Spaniards immediately took refuge in the palace. They began to shoot at the Mexicans with their iron arrows and to fire their cannons and arquebuses. And they shackled Motecuhzoma in chains.

The Lament for the Dead

The Mexicans who had died in the massacre were taken out of the patio one by one and inquiries were made to discover their names. The fathers and mothers of the dead wept and lamented.

Each victim was taken first to his own home and then to the Sacred Patio, where all the dead were brought together. Some of the bodies were later burned in the place called the Eagle Urn, and others in the House of the Young Men.

Motecuhzoma's Message

At sunset, Itzcuauhtzin climbed onto the roof of the palace and shouted this proclamation: "Mexicanos! Tlatelolcas! Your king, the lord Motecuhzoma, has sent me to speak for him. Mexicanos, hear me, for these are his words to you: 'We must not fight them. We are not their equals in battle. Put down your shields and arrows.'

"He tells you this because it is the aged who will suffer most, and they deserve your pity. The humblest classes will also suffer, and so will the innocent children who still crawl on all fours, who still sleep in their cradles.

"Therefore your king says: 'We are not strong enough to defeat them. Stop fighting, and return to your homes.' Mexicanos, they have put your king in chains; his feet are bound with chains."

When Itzcuauhtzin had finished speaking, there was a great uproar among the people. They shouted insults at him in their fury, and cried: "Who is Motecuhzoma to give us orders? We are no longer his slaves!" They shouted war cries and fired arrows at the rooftop. The Spaniards quickly hid Motecuhzoma and Itzcuauhtzin behind their shields so that the arrows would not find them.

The Mexicans were enraged because the attack on the captains had been so treacherous: their warriors had been killed without the slightest warning. Now they refused to go away or to put down their arms.

The Spaniards Are Besieged

The royal palace was placed under siege. The Mexicans kept a close watch to prevent anyone from stealing in with food for the Spaniards. They also stopped delivering supplies: they brought them absolutely nothing, and waited for them to die of hunger.

A few people attempted to communicate with the Spaniards. They hoped to win their favor by giving them advice and information or by secretly bringing them food. But the guards found them and killed them on the spot: they broke their necks or stoned them to death. [. . .]

After they had trapped the Spaniards in the palace, the Mexicans kept them under attack for seven days, and for twenty-three days they foiled all their attempts to break out. During this time all the causeways were closed off. The Mexicans tore up the bridges, opened great gaps in the pavement and built a whole series of barricades; they did everything they could to make the causeways impassable. They also closed off the roads by building walls and roadblocks; they obstructed all the roads and streets of the city.

[After Cortés defeated Panfilo de Narvaez, he returned to Tenochtitlán to defend against the Aztecs. Both Motecuhzoma and Itzcuauhtzin were killed, but the details of their deaths are unknown. The massacre of the escaping Spaniards has come to be known as "La Noche Triste," the Night of Sorrows.]

The Spaniards Abandon the City

At midnight the Spaniards and Tlaxcaltecas came out in closed ranks, the Spaniards going first and the Tlaxcaltecas following. The allies kept very close behind, as if they were crowding up against a wall. The sky was overcast and rain fell all night in the darkness, but it was gentle rain, more like drizzle or a heavy dew.

The Spaniards carried portable wooden bridges to cross the canals. They set them in place, crossed over and raised them again. They were able to pass the first three canals—the Tecpantzinco, the Tzapotlan, and the Atenchicalco—without being seen. But when they reached the fourth, the Mixcoatechialtitlan, their retreat was discovered.

The Battle Begins

The first alarm was raised by a woman who was drawing water at the edge of the canal. She cried: "Mexicanos, come running! They are crossing the canal! Our enemies are escaping!"

Then a priest of Huitzilopochtli shouted the call to arms from the temple pyramid. His voice rang out over the city: "Captains, warriors, Mexicanos! Our enemies are escaping! Follow them in your boats. Cut them off, and destroy them!"

When they heard this cry, the warriors leaped into the boats and set out in pursuit. These boats were from the garrisons of Tenochtitlán and Tlatelolco, and were protected by the warriors' shields. The boatmen paddled with all their might; they lashed the water of the lake until it boiled.

Other warriors set out on foot, racing to Nonohualco and then to Tlacopan to cut off the retreat.

The boats converged on the Spaniards from both sides of the causeway, and the warriors loosed a storm of arrows at the fleeing army. But the Spaniards also turned to shoot at the Aztecs; they fired their crossbows and their arquebuses. The

Spaniards and Tlaxcaltecas suffered many casualties, but many of the Aztec warriors were also killed or wounded.

The Massacre at the Canal of the Toltecs

When the Spaniards reached the Canal of the Toltecs, in Tlaltecayohuacan, they hurled themselves headlong into the water, as if they were leaping from a cliff. The Tlaxcaltecas, the allies from Tliliuhquitepec, the Spanish foot soldiers and horsemen, the few women who accompanied the army—all came to the brink and plunged over it.

The canal was soon choked with the bodies of men and horses; they filled the gap in the causeway with their own drowned bodies. Those who followed crossed to the other side by walking on the corpses.

When they reached Petlalco, where there was another canal, they crossed over on their portable bridge without being attacked by the Aztecs.[39] They stopped and rested there for a short while, and began to feel more like men again. Then they marched on to Popotla.

Dawn was breaking as they entered the village. Their hearts were cheered by the brightening light of this new day: they thought the horrors of the retreat by night were all behind them. But suddenly they heard war cries and the Aztecs swarmed through the streets and surrounded them. They had come to capture Tlaxcaltecas for their sacrifices. They also wanted to complete their revenge against the Spaniards.

The Aztecs harried the army all the way to Tlacopan. Chimalpopoca, the son of Motecuhzoma, was killed in the action at Tlilyuhcan by an arrow from the crossbows. Tlaltecatzin, the Tepanec prince, was wounded in the same action and died shortly after. He had served the Spaniards as a guide and advisor, pointing out the best roads and short cuts.

The Aztecs Recover the Spoils

As soon as it was daylight, the Aztecs cleared the dead Spaniards and Tlaxcaltecas out of the canals and stripped them of everything they wore. They loaded the bodies of the Tlaxcaltecas into canoes and took them out to where the rushes grow; they threw them among the rushes without burying them, without giving them another glance.

They also threw out the corpses of the women who had been killed in the retreat. The naked bodies of these women were the color of ripe corn, for they had painted themselves with yellow paint.

But they laid out the corpses of the Spaniards apart from the others; they lined them up in rows in a separate place. Their bodies were as white as the new buds of the canestalk, as white as the buds of the maguey. They also removed the dead "stags" that had carried the "gods" on their shoulders.

[39] **Aztecs:** A contradiction; the portable bridge was abandoned before the Spaniards reached the Canal of the Toltecs.

Then they gathered up everything the Spaniards had abandoned in their terror. When a man saw something he wanted, he took it, and it became his property; he hefted it onto his shoulders and carried it home. They also collected all the weapons that had been left behind or had fallen into the canal—the cannons, arquebuses, swords, spears, bows and arrows—along with all the steel helmets, coats of mail and breastplates, and the shields of metal, wood and hide. They recovered the gold ingots, the gold disks, the tubes of gold dust and the *chalchihuite* collars with their gold pendants.

They gathered up everything they could find and searched the waters of the canal with the greatest care. Some of them groped with their hands and others felt about with their feet. Those who went first were able to keep their balance but those who came along behind them all fell into the water.

Tenochtitlán after the Departure of Cortés

When the Spaniards left Tenochtitlán, the Aztecs thought they had departed for good and would never return. Therefore they repaired and decorated the temple of their god, sweeping it clean and throwing out all the dirt and wreckage.

Then the eighth month arrived, and the Aztecs celebrated it as always.[40] They adorned the impersonators of the gods, all those who played the part of gods in the ceremonies, decking them with necklaces and turquoise masks and dressing them in the sacred clothing. This clothing was made of quetzal feathers, eagle feathers and yellow parrot feathers. The finery of the gods was in the care of the great princes.

The Plague Ravages the City

While the Spaniards were in Tlaxcala, a great plague[41] broke out here in Tenochtitlán. It began to spread during the thirteenth month and lasted for seventy days, striking everywhere in the city and killing a vast number of our people. Sores erupted on our faces, our breasts, our bellies; we were covered with agonizing sores from head to foot.

The illness was so dreadful that no one could walk or move. The sick were so utterly helpless that they could only lie on their beds like corpses, unable to move their limbs or even their heads. They could not lie face down or roll from one side to the other. If they did move their bodies, they screamed with pain.

A great many died from this plague, and many others died of hunger. They could not get up to search for food, and everyone else was too sick to care for them, so they starved to death in their beds.

[40] **the eighth month . . . always:** The eighth month corresponds to June 22–July 11, and the fiesta celebrated Huixtocihuatl, goddess of salt.

[41] **plague:** Starting in Veracruz, smallpox ravaged the Mexican population, killing hundreds of thousands of people, perhaps millions. Motecuhzoma's successor Cuitlahua, died from smallpox.

Some people came down with a milder form of the disease; they suffered less than the others and made a good recovery. But they could not escape entirely. Their looks were ravaged, for wherever a sore broke out, it gouged an ugly pockmark in the skin. And a few of the survivors were left completely blind.

The first cases were reported in Cuatlan. By the time the danger was recognized, the plague was so well established that nothing could halt it, and eventually it spread all the way to Chalco. Then its virulence diminished considerably, though there were isolated cases for many months after. The first victims were stricken during the fiesta of Teotlecco,[42] and the faces of our warriors were not clean and free of sores until the fiesta of Panquetzaliztli.[43]

The Spaniards Return

And now the Spaniards came back again. They marched here by way of Tezcoco, set up headquarters in Tlacopan and then divided their forces. Pedro de Alvarado was assigned the road to the Tlatelolco quarter as his personal responsibility, while Cortés himself took charge of the Coyoacan area and the road from Acachinanco to Tenochtitlán proper. Cortés knew that the captain of Tenochtitlán was extremely brave.

The first battle began outside Tlatelolco, either at the ash pits or at the place called the Point of the Alders, and then shifted to Nonohualco. Our warriors put the enemy to flight and not a single Aztec was killed. The Spaniards tried a second advance but our warriors attacked them from their boats, loosing such a storm of arrows that the Spaniards were forced to retreat again.

Cortés, however, set out for Acachinanco and reached his goal. He moved his headquarters there, just outside the city. Heavy fighting ensued, but the Aztecs could not dislodge him.

The Spaniards Launch Their Brigantines

Finally the ships, a dozen in all, came from Tezcoco and anchored near Acachinanco. Cortés went out to inspect the canals that traversed the causeways, to discover the best passages for his fleet. He wanted to know which were the nearest, the shortest, the deepest, the straightest, so that none of his ships would run aground or be trapped inside. One of the canals across the Xoloco thoroughfare was so twisted and narrow that only two of the smaller ships were able to pass through it.

The Spaniards now decided to attack Tenochtitlán and destroy its people. The cannons were mounted in the ships, the sails were raised and the fleet moved out onto the lake. The flagship led the way, flying a great linen standard with Cortés's coat of arms. The soldiers beat their drums and blew their trumpets; they played their flutes and chirimias[44] and whistles.

---

[42] **Teotlecco:** September 10–29. [43] **Panquetzaliztli:** November 9–28. [44] **chirimias:** Similar to shepherd's pipes.

When the ships approached the Zoquiapan quarter,[45] the common people were terrified at the sight. They gathered their children into the canoes and fled helter-skelter across the lake, moaning with fear and paddling as swiftly as they could. They left all their possessions behind them and abandoned their little farms without looking back.

Our enemies seized all our possessions. They gathered up everything they could find and loaded it into the ships in great bundles. They stole our cloaks and blankets, our battle dress, our tabors and drums, and carried them all away. The Tlatelolcas followed and attacked the Spaniards from their boats but could not save any of the plunder.

When the Spaniards reached Xoloco, near the entrance to Tenochtitlán, they found that the Indians had built a wall across the road to block their progress. They destroyed it with four shots from the largest cannon. The first shot did little harm, but the second split it and the third opened a great hole. With the fourth shot, the wall lay in ruins on the ground.

Two of the brigantines, both with cannons mounted in their bows, attacked a flotilla of our shielded canoes. The cannons were fired into the thick of the flotilla, wherever the canoes were crowded closest together. Many of our warriors were killed outright; others drowned because they were too crippled by their wounds to swim away. The water was red with the blood of the dead and dying. Those who were hit by the steel arrows were also doomed; they died instantly and sank to the bottom of the lake.

Defensive Tactics of the Aztecs

When the Aztecs discovered that the shots from the arquebuses and cannons always flew in a straight line, they no longer ran away in the line of fire. They ran to the right or left or in zigzags, not in front of the guns. If they saw that a cannon was about to be fired and they could not escape by running, they threw themselves to the ground and lay flat until the shot had passed over them. The warriors also took cover among the houses, darting into the spaces between them. The road was suddenly as empty as if it passed through a desert.

Then the Spaniards arrived in Huitzillan, where they found another wall blocking the road. A great crowd of our warriors was hiding behind it to escape the gunfire.

The Spaniards Debark

The brigantines came up and anchored nearby. They had been pursuing our war canoes in the open lake, but when they had almost run them down, they suddenly turned and sailed toward the causeway. Now they anchored a short distance from

[45] **Zoquiapan quarter:** Southwestern Tenochtitlán.

the houses. As soon as the cannons in their bows were loaded again, the soldiers aimed and fired them at the new wall.

The first shot cracked it in a dozen places, but it remained standing. They fired again: this time it cracked from one end to the other and crumpled to the ground. A moment later the road was completely empty. The warriors had all fled when they saw the wall collapsing; they ran blindly, this way and that, howling with fear. [. . .]

The Spaniards now joined all their forces into one unit and marched together as far as the Eagle Gate, where they set up the cannons they had brought with them. It was called the Eagle Gate because it was decorated with an enormous eagle carved of stone. The eagle was flanked on one side by a stone jaguar; on the other side there was a large honey bear, also of carved stone. [. . .]

The Last Stand

Then the great captain Tzilacatzin arrived, bringing with him three large, round stones of the kind used for building walls. He carried one of them in his hand; the other two hung from his shield. When he hurled these stones at the Spaniards, they turned and fled the city.

Tzilacatzin's military rank was that of Otomi, and he clipped his hair in the style of the Otomies. He scorned his enemies, Spaniards as well as Indians; they all shook with terror at the mere sight of him.

When the Spaniards found out how dangerous he was, they tried desperately to kill him. They attacked him with their swords and spears, fired at him with their crossbows and arquebuses, and tried every other means they could think of to kill or cripple him. Therefore he wore various disguises to prevent them from recognizing him.

Sometimes he wore his lip plug, his gold earrings and all the rest of his full regalia, but left his head uncovered to show that he was an Otomi. At other times he wore only his cotton armor, with a thin kerchief wrapped around his head. At still other times, he put on the finery of the priests who cast the victims into the fire: a plumed headdress with the eagle symbol on its crest, and gleaming gold bracelets on both arms, and circular bands of gleaming gold on both ankles.

The Spaniards came back again the next day. They brought their ships to a point just off Nonohualco, close to the place called the House of Mist. Their other troops arrived on foot, along with the Tlaxcaltecas. As soon as they had formed ranks, they charged the Aztec warriors.

The heaviest fighting began when they entered Nonohualco. None of our enemies and none of our own warriors escaped harm. Everyone was wounded, and the toll of the dead was grievous on both sides. The struggle continued all day and all night.

[The Aztec forces slowly lose ground, but at one point they capture fifty-three Spaniards and four horses and sacrifice them; their heads are placed on poles. The Spaniards blockade the city.]

The Sufferings of the Inhabitants

The Spanish blockade caused great anguish in the city. The people were tormented by hunger, and many starved to death. There was no fresh water to drink, only stagnant water and the brine of the lake, and many people died of dysentery.

The only food was lizards, swallows, corncobs and the salt grasses of the lake. The people also ate water lilies and the seeds of the colorin, and chewed on deerhides and pieces of leather. They roasted and seared and scorched whatever they could find and then ate it. They ate the bitterest weeds and even dirt.

Nothing can compare with the horrors of that siege and the agonies of the starving. We were so weakened by hunger that, little by little, the enemy forced us to retreat. Little by little they forced us to the wall.

The Battle in the Market Place

On one occasion, four Spanish cavalrymen entered the market place. They rode through it in a great circle, stabbing and killing many of our warriors and trampling everything under their horses' hooves. This was the first time the Spaniards had entered the market place, and our warriors were taken by surprise. But when the horsemen withdrew, the warriors recovered their wits and ran in pursuit.

It was at this same time that the Spaniards set fire to the temple and burned it to the ground. The flames and smoke leaped high into the air with a terrible roar. The people wept when they saw their temple on fire; they wept and cried out, fearing that afterward it would be plundered.

The battle lasted for many hours and extended to almost every corner of the market place. There was no action along the wall where the vendors sold lime, but the fighting raged among the flower stalls, and the stalls offering snails, and all the passageways between them.

Some of our warriors stationed themselves on the rooftops of the Quecholan district, which is near the entrance to the market place, and from there they hurled stones and fired arrows at the enemy. Others broke holes in the rear walls of all the houses of Quecholan, holes just big enough for a man's body to pass through. When the cavalry attacked and were about to spear our warriors, or trample them, or cut off their retreat, they slipped through the holes and the mounted men could not follow.

The Aztec Defense

Our warriors rallied to defend the city. Their spirits and courage were high; not one of them showed any fear or behaved like a woman. They cried: "Mexicanos, come here and join us! Who are these savages? A mere rabble from the south!"[46] They did not move in a direct line; they moved in a zigzag course, never in a straight line.

[46] **south:** In terms of religious geography, the south was a region of disorder or chaos.

The Spanish soldiers often disguised themselves so that they would not be recognized. They wore cloaks like those of the Aztecs and put on the same battle dress and adornments, hoping to deceive our warriors into thinking they were not Spaniards.

Whenever the Aztecs saw the enemy notching their arrows, they either dispersed or flattened themselves on the ground. The warriors of Tlatelolco were very alert; they were very cautious and vigilant, and watched intently to see where the shots were coming from.

But step by step the Spaniards gained more ground and captured more houses. They forced us backward along the Amaxac road with their spears and shields.

The Quetzal-Owl

Cuauhtemoc[47] consulted with a group of his captains and then called in a great captain named Opochtzin, who was a dyer by trade. They dressed him in the finery of the Quetzal-Owl, which had belonged to King Ahuitzotl. Then Cuauhtemoc said to him: "This regalia belonged to my father, the great warrior Ahuitzotl. Terrify our enemies with it. Annihilate our enemies with it. Let them behold it and tremble."

The king ordered four captains to go with Opochtzin as a rear guard. He placed in the captain's hands the magic object that was the most important part of the regalia. This was an arrow with a long shaft and an obsidian tip.

The captain Tlacotzin said: "Mexicanos, the power of Huitzilopochtli resides in this finery. Loose the sacred arrow at our enemies, for it is the Serpent of Fire, the Arrow that Pierces the Fire. Loose it at the invaders; drive them away with the power of Huitzilopochtli. But shoot it straight and well, for it must not fall to earth. And if it should wound one or two of our foes, then we shall still have a little time left and a chance to conquer them. Now, let us see what the god's will may be!"

The Quetzal-Owl departed with the four captains, and the quetzal feathers seemed to open out, making him appear even greater and more terrifying. When our enemies saw him approach, they quaked as if they thought a mountain were about to fall on them. They trembled with dread, as if they knew the finery could work magic.

The Quetzal-Owl climbed up onto a rooftop. When our enemies saw him, they came forward and prepared to attack him, but he succeeded in driving them away. Then he came down from the rooftop with his quetzal feathers and his gold ornaments. He was not killed in this action and our enemies could not capture the feathers or the gold. Three of the enemy soldiers were taken prisoner.

Suddenly the battle ended. Neither side moved against the other; the night was calm and silent, with no incidents of any kind. On the following day, absolutely nothing took place, and neither the Spaniards nor the Indians spoke a word. The

[47] **Cuauhtemoc:** A nephew of Motecuhzoma, Cuauhtemoc was the last of the Aztec rulers (1520–1524); his courage became legendary throughout Mexico.

Indians waited in their defense works, and the Spaniards waited in their positions. Each side watched the other closely but made no plans for launching an attack. Both sides passed the whole day in this fashion, merely watching and waiting.

The Final Omen

At nightfall it began to rain, but it was more like a heavy dew than a rain. Suddenly the omen appeared, blazing like a great bonfire in the sky. It wheeled in enormous spirals like a whirlwind and gave off a shower of sparks and red-hot coals, some great and some little. It also made loud noises, rumbling and hissing like a metal tube placed over a fire. It circled the wall nearest the lakeshore and then hovered for a while above Coyonacazco. From there it moved out into the middle of the lake, where it suddenly disappeared. No one cried out when this omen came into view: the people knew what it meant and they watched it in silence.

Nothing whatever occurred on the following day. Our warriors and the Spanish soldiers merely waited in their positions. Cortés kept a constant watch, standing under a many-colored canopy on the roof of the lord Aztautzin's house, which is near Amaxac. His officers stood around him, talking among themselves.

Cuauhtemoc's Surrender

The Aztec leaders gathered in Tolmayecan to discuss what they should do. Cuauhtemoc and the other nobles tried to determine how much tribute they would have to pay and how best to surrender to the strangers. Then the nobles put Cuauhtemoc into a war canoe, with only three men to accompany him: a captain named Teputztitloloc, a servant named Iaztachimal and a boatman named Cenyautl. When the people saw their chief departing, they wept and cried out: "Our youngest prince is leaving us! He is going to surrender to the Spaniards! He is going to surrender to the 'gods'!"

The Spaniards came out to meet him. They took him by the hand, led him up to the rooftop and brought him into the presence of Cortés. The Captain stared at him for a moment and then patted him on the head. Then he gestured toward a chair and the two leaders sat down side by side.

The Spaniards began to shoot off their cannons, but they were not trying to hit anyone. They merely loaded and fired, and the cannonballs flew over the Indians' heads. Later they put one of the cannons into a boat and took it to the house of Coyohuehuetzin, where they hoisted it to the rooftop.

The Flight from the City

Once again the Spaniards started killing and a great many Indians died. The flight from the city began and with this the war came to an end. The people cried: "We have suffered enough! Let us leave the city! Let us go live on weeds!" Some fled across the lake, others along the causeways, and even then there were many killings. The Spaniards were angry because our warriors still carried their shields and *macanas*.[48]

Those who lived in the center of the city went straight toward Amaxac, to the fork in the road. From there they fled in various directions, some toward Tepeyacac, others toward Xoxohuiltitlan and Nonohualco; but no one went toward Xoloco or Mazatzintamalco. Those who lived in boats or on the wooden rafts anchored in the lake fled by water, as did the inhabitants of Tolmayecan. Some of them waded in water up to their chests and even up to their necks. Others drowned when they reached water above their heads.

The grownups carried their young children on their shoulders. Many of the children were weeping with terror, but a few of them laughed and smiled, thinking it was great sport to be carried like that along the road.

Some of the people who owned canoes departed in the daytime, but the others, the majority, left by night. They almost crashed into each other in their haste as they paddled away from the city.

The Spaniards Humiliate the Refugees

The Spanish soldiers were stationed along the roads to search the fleeing inhabitants. They were looking only for gold and paid no attention to jade, turquoise or quetzal feathers. The women carried their gold under their skirts and the men carried it in their mouths or under their loincloths. Some of the women, knowing they would be searched if they looked prosperous, covered their faces with mud and dressed themselves in rags. They put on rags for skirts and rags for blouses; everything they wore was in tatters. But the Spaniards searched all the women without exception: those with light skins, those with dark skins, those with dark bodies.

A few of the men were separated from the others. These men were the bravest and strongest warriors, the warriors with manly hearts. The youths who served them were also told to stand apart. The Spaniards immediately branded them with hot irons, either on the cheek or the lips.

The day on which we laid down our shields and admitted defeat was the day 1-Serpent in the year 3-House. [. . .][49]

[48] ***macanas:*** Flattened clubs. [49] **3-House:** August 13, 1521.

A Defense of Aztec Religion

Translated by David M. Johnson and Armando Jimarez

Our Lords, esteemed Lords.

We welcome you to our lands and cities. We who are so unworthy are reluctant to look on the faces of such valiant persons.

You brought a lord, our Prince, to govern us. We are ignorant about where you came from, where your gods and lords live, because you came by sea, between clouds and fog. A road we do not know.

Via your ears, eyes and mouth, your god was sent among us. That which is invisible and spiritual was made visible. With our ears we heard the words about living and being which you brought us. With admiration we have heard the words of the Lord of the World whose love brought you to us, and brought also the book of heavenly words.

And now, what can we say about ourselves? What words can we lift to your ears that would be worthy of your status? We are nothing, common people of low status. By the rule of iron your king forced us into the corners of his dais.

Nevertheless, with two or three reasons, we will contradict the words of the Giver of Life, the Lord of the World.

Perhaps we will provoke his anger against us, and cause our downfall, cause our ultimate ruin. Perhaps we are already doomed. What can we do, we who are ordinary people, and mortal besides?

If we die, we die. Leave us then to perish. The truth is, gods also die.

Do not be sad of heart, dear lords, because with delicacy and care we want to examine the divine secrets, like a thief who opens a coffer of riches to see what is inside.

You have told us that we don't know the Lord and Giver of Life, the Lord of sky and earth. You have said that the ones we worship are not true gods.

This way of talking is new to us and very disturbing. We are troubled with statements like these, because our forefathers, those who begot us and ruled over us, didn't tell us these things.

Long ago they left us the customs that we have for worshipping our gods. They believed in them and worshipped them all the time that they lived on the earth. They taught us the way that we should honor them: we kneel on the earth for ritual meals; we do penance by bleeding ourselves; we keep our words; we burn incense; and we offer sacrifices.

They told us that because of the gods' sacrifices we have life. We deserved life because we belonged to them and served them. And this was customary during the time before the sun began to shine.

A Defense of Aztec Religion. This selection was translated from Bernardino de Sahagún's *Colloguies y Doctrina Christiana* (1944) by David M. Johnson, with Armando Jimarez.

They said that these gods whom we worship gave us all the things necessary for our physical life: maize, beans, sage and amaranth. To them we pray for rain, so things on this earth can grow.

These our gods are very rich. All delights and riches are theirs. They live in a wonderful place, where there are always flowers and vegetables. A refreshing place not seen or known by mortals, called Tlalocan.[1] A place where there is never hunger, poverty or sickness.

These gods give us the honors, our capacity to fight and to rule, gold and silver, precious feathers and precious stones.

There is no record of when our gods were first honored, invoked and adored. Fortunately, for several centuries, there have been places where they were celebrated, places where sacred events occurred and answers given. Places like Tula, Huapalcalco, Xuchatlapan, Tlamohuanchan, Yohuallichan, Teotihuacán.

The inhabitants of these places took possession of the earth and governed our world. They give us order, fame, glory and majesty.

It would be foolish of us to destroy the ancient laws and customs left to us by the Chichimecs, the Toltecs, the Acolhuas, the Tepanecs.[2] Into the service of our gods we were born and we were raised. We have it imprinted on our hearts.

Oh Lords. Listen to us.

Do not disturb and harm our people. How could poor old men and old women leave a way of life which they have believed in for their whole lives?

Do not make us invite the anger of our gods. Do not make the people rebel against us by having us tell them that the gods they believed in are not gods at all.

It has been necessary, dear lords, to look into this matter with patience and unity. We are not satisfied nor are we persuaded by what you have said. We do not agree with what you have said about our gods.

It saddens us, lords and priests, to speak in this way. In attendance are the lords who have the responsibility to rule the kingdoms of this world. But we all feel the same way about this.

It is enough for us to have lost, to have the power and rule taken from us. When it comes to our gods, first we will die rather than leave their worship and service.

This is our determination. Do with us what you want. Our answer to you is sufficient. We have nothing more to say.

[1] **Tlalocan:** "Place of Tlaloc" is a paradise of abundance for all those associated with the rain-god Tlaloc, such as those who died by drowning and leprosy.

[2] **Chichimecs . . . Tepanecs:** Predecessors of the Aztecs, Chichimecs were the nomadic peoples who migrated south into the Valley of Mexico and included seven tribes whose legendary origin was Chicomoztoc ("seven caves"); three of those tribes were the Acolhuas, Tepanecs, and Mexicas (Aztecs). The Toltecs were a dominant culture in the Valley of Mexico between the ninth and eleventh centuries, with their capital at Tollan.

Europe Meets America

The encounter between European adventurers and the indigenous peoples of the Americas was so momentous that cultural differences and misunderstandings among inhabitants on both sides of the Atlantic continue to the present day. The selection of writings for the ancient Mexicans represents Mesoamerican beliefs, values, prophecies, and history; this section provides a sampling of contrasting European attitudes toward the peoples of America, plus a final piece by a woman writer who attempted to reconcile the Old and New Worlds, Christianity and native religion.

Historians have recorded in detail the events of the conquest of the Americas from the European point of view; only bits and pieces remain of what the indigenous people thought of the overwhelming forces against them. Whether it was prompted by the desire for commercial gain or religious conversion, the Europeans' arrival in the New World resulted in mass slaughter, epidemics, slavery, and genocide. Although the focus of this section is on Spain's conquest of ancient Mexico, the actions of the English, French, and Dutch north of the border were equally destructive. What might European Americans have learned about living on this continent from native peoples? How much knowledge was lost when the Catholic priests of Mexico burned almost all the written records of the Maya and the Mexica? The Europeans' initial spirit of dominance long influenced the world's view of the Native Americans, and it continues to overshadow historical accounts of the magnificent civilizations of Mesoamerica.

No one knows how many people crossed both oceans to leave

[W]hen we saw all those cities and villages built in the water, and other great towns on dry land, and that straight and level causeway leading to Mexico, we were astounded. These great towns . . . and buildings rising from the water, all made of stone, seemed like an enchanted vision from the tale of Amadis. Indeed, some of our soldiers asked whether it was not all a dream.

– Bernal Díaz del Castillo, *The Conquest of New Spain*, c. 1568

Cortés Arriving in the New World, 1519–22
A drawing by an Indian artist of the sixteenth century depicts the Spanish conquistador Hernán Cortés with his sword drawn and flag flying as he approaches a plant-carrying native. (Vatican Museum, Rome)

Whereas [Bartolomé de Las Casas] had once pitied the Indians in their gentleness and simplicity, increasingly he was drawn to an admiration for the *rightness* of their cultures. At last he would venture that it would have been better for their souls never to have been touched by the Christians — surely a blasphemous judgment for one of his position and time. God, he wrote, did not want the extension of Christianity at such a cost.

– Frederick Turner, ***Beyond Geography***, 1983

their imprint on the Americas before Christopher Columbus's voyage of 1492. Given the wind patterns and currents, the sophisticated sea vessels of many ancient peoples, and the human spirit of adventure, it would actually be rather strange if there had not been occasional landfalls, both deliberate and accidental, over the millennia. Old stories suggest that Phoenicians, Chinese, Portuguese, Basques, West Africans from Guiana, and others may have preceded Columbus in the Americas. Norse explorers definitely tried to colonize North America by the tenth century C.E., but they were simply too far from European support to survive, and the stories of their discoveries passed into the folk history of the sagas, an oral literature not known to most of Europe.

There were monetary reasons for adventure in the Early Modern Period. Granada, the last Moorish stronghold in Spain, fell to the Christians in 1492. Also in that year, the monarchs signed a decree expelling all Jews; although many estates had been confiscated, much capital left the country with the exiled Jewish families, leaving Spain gold-poor. Columbus presented his plan to reach Asian sources of gold and spice at a most opportune time. Legends about vast stores of gold on islands in the Atlantic fed the fantasies of ship captains and stimulated the financing of expeditions. The fervor behind Christian missionary societies and the desire to convert "heathen natives" also drove the European settlement of the Americas. It became Europe's greatest religious campaign since the Crusades.

In many respects, Christopher Columbus (1451–1506) set a pattern for his successors. His ***Diario***, or log, records the encounter between Europe and the Americas that was to alter radically almost every significant natural and social feature of the planet: its flora, fauna, genetic pools and populations, economics, politics, and arts. The only text that survives is a condensation of the original log made by Bartolomé de Las Casas (1474–1566). It was fortunate that Columbus kept a journal of his voyage, since daily ship's logs were not common until the sixteenth century and Columbus seems not to have kept one on subsequent voyages. In its mixture of dogged detail, shrewd observation, self-revelation, idealism, poetry, and real-estate promotion, the *Diario* suggests the shimmer of expectations through which Columbus beheld American lands and peoples. The *Diario* can almost be seen as a working script for the subsequent history of American colonization. From the moment of Columbus's first landfall, the Americas were never again empty of Europeans. His voyage took place at a time when Spain, under the joint rule of Ferdinand and Isabella, had newly become a unified and homogeneously Catholic nation, eager to extend its enterprises and to compete with Portugal, France, and England in the business of foreign trade and colonization. Columbus the man and his explorations have left a complicated heritage. At one extreme are the cruelties inflicted on largely defenseless indigenous peoples. On the other extreme, however, are the knowledge and the courage requisite for opening up the Americas to European settlement.

p. 773

The letters of Hernán Cortés (1485–1547) reveal an intelligent, observant, and calculating man. Each step along the pathway of his conquest of Mexico demanded shrewdness, courage, sacrifice, and risk. As is evident from his letters, overpowering weaponry was the key to his successes. The "**second letter**," presented here, is valuable in providing information about one of the first encounters with the very different world of the ancient Mexicans. With a strange mixture

p. 783

When Las Casas spoke at Valladolid for the American Indians, one more painful and faltering step was . . . taken along the road of justice for all races.

– Lewis Hanke, historian, 1949

of admiration and revulsion, Cortés pursued a plan to reduce the Aztec capital to ashes. It did not seem to occur to him that he and his crew might learn valuable lessons about the Americas from its original inhabitants. With his portraits of the exploitation and suffering of the Indians, Las Casas presents an entirely different point of view of the conquest. While his sympathies for the plight of the natives and his campaign for Indian rights were commendable, he is sometimes criticized today for fathering the Black Legend, a one-sided picture of the Spanish colonization of the Americas as only brutal and sadistic. Nevertheless, his writings raised the consciousness, and occasionally pricked the consciences, of Spanish leaders.

mone-TEN

The excerpt from the essay "Of Coaches," by Michel Eyquem de **Montaigne** (1533–1592), provides another sympathetic, tolerant voice, and this time from a well-respected European intellectual. Montaigne was writing somewhat later in the sixteenth century than Las Casas, and his views suggest how an educated man of the European **Renaissance** might assess the expanding frontiers of commerce and communication. Although Montaigne never visited the New World, he nevertheless had a broad appreciation for what Europeans might learn from its peoples. The last piece in this section is a prologue, called a *loa,* to an unusual play, *The Divine Narcissus,* by an even more remarkable writer—a Mexican nun whose writing career was situated in a convent in Mexico City. **Sor Juana Inés de la Cruz** (1648–1695) felt a sympathy for the preconquest beliefs of native Americans that eventually brought her into direct confrontation with the Catholic hierarchy in Mexico City. Unlike Las Casas, whose views were heard by a special commission of priests appointed by the Spanish crown, Sor Juana was silenced and isolated by a fearful archbishop. Nevertheless, her discourses on such unorthodox topics as the dignity and equality of women and the validity of the Mexican Indians' religious beliefs became an inspiration for later Latin American writers and defenders of native culture.

sore-WAH-nah ee-NES deh-lah-KROOTH

There have been men with deeper insight; but, one would say, never a man with such abundance of thoughts [as Montaigne]: he is never dull, never insincere, and has the genius to make the reader care for all that he cares for.

– Ralph Waldo Emerson, 1850

■ CONNECTIONS

"In the World: Pilgrimage and Travel," Book 2; "In the World: Travel Narratives," Book 4. Travel is broadening, goes the old saying. These two "In the World" sections, from the Middle Period and the Eighteenth Century, are filled with experiences and observations of travelers in lands where they were confronted with cultures very different from their own. What did these travelers notice on their travels? What impressed them? Consider what Columbus chose to set down in his diaries and what Cortés reported in his letters. Were these two explorers thoughtful observers? Can their writings be trusted for accuracy?

William Shakespeare, *The Tempest*, p. 495. Through voyages of discovery Europeans encountered cultures, values, and worldviews that were radically different from their own. How does Shakespeare's treatment of Caliban raise questions about the relationship between Europeans and native peoples? What European values made it difficult for the Spanish to understand the indigenous cultures of Mexico?

■ PRONUNCIATION

Montaigne: mone-TEN
Sor Juana Inés de la Cruz: sore-WAH-na ee-NES deh-lah-KROO*TH*

CHRISTOPHER COLUMBUS
1451–1506

Christopher Columbus, or Cristóbal Colón as he is called in Spanish, the man whose name means "Christ-bearing dove," was born in the republic of Genoa, Italy, the son of a weaver. "At a tender age," as he says, he went to sea for the first time, probably on short voyages along the coastlines. His first long voyage was to the island of Chios in 1474, a Genoese colony in the Aegean renowned for its gum mastic, the sap of an evergreen tree used as a painkiller; Columbus later would mistakenly believe he had found a new source for this raw material in the Caribbean. In 1476, when a merchant ship on which he was serving was attacked and sunk off the coast of Portugal, Columbus swam ashore and made his way to Lisbon, Portugal, the European center of navigational study, where he lived in the Genoese community. Sometime between his coming to Lisbon and 1484, when he began his quest to finance an expedition, he became obsessed with the idea that it would be possible to reach the Indies by sailing westward. Contrary to popular myth, Columbus did not set out to prove that the earth was round; by his time, the idea of a spherical earth was fairly widely accepted, and the real difficulty people found with his proposal lay in his estimate of the distance between Europe and the Indies; many thought—rightly so—that Columbus underestimated, and that ships of the time could not carry enough provisions to cross the open ocean presumed to lie between Europe and Asia.

Failing to interest Portugal in his plan, Columbus finally convinced the Spanish monarchs Ferdinand V (1452–1516) and Isabella I (1451–1504) to finance the expedition. The three caravels, the *Pinta,* the *Niña,* and the *Santa Maria,* left Spain on August 3, 1492, heading for the Canary Islands; from there, the trip was remarkably uneventful except for the growing anxiety and surliness of the crew, whom Columbus tried to calm

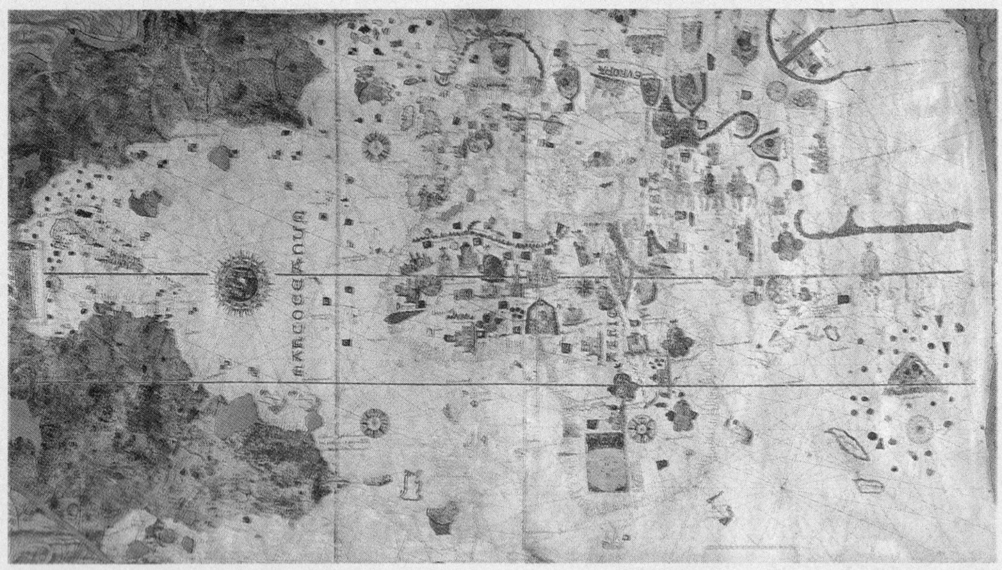

Juan de la Cosa, *Map of the New World,* 1500
Drawn by Columbus's pilot and cartographer, this is the first European map of the Caribbean and the coast of the New World. (Museo Naval, Madrid)

by falsifying the log, telling them each day that they had sailed fewer miles than was actually the case. The ships made landfall on the sunny morning of October 12, 1492, on the island of San Salvador in the Bahamas, where Taino people, who called the island Guanahani, ran down the beach and swam out to greet the ships. The exact landing spot, however, is still disputed.

On this first voyage Columbus explored not only the island where he landed but also the shores of Hispaniola and Cuba, which he believed to be Japan. The *Santa Maria* ran aground off Hispaniola on Christmas Day, and a fort called *La Navidad* was built from its shattered timbers; thirty-nine men stayed behind to run it. The *Pinta* and *Niña* set sail for home with a number of Indian prisoners, most of whom died on the passage or soon after landing on European soil in the spring of 1493. Christopher Columbus, along with his brothers Bartolomé and Diego, immediately readied a second voyage to establish a colony on Hispaniola. When his seventeen ships arrived in the Lesser Antilles on November 3, 1493, word had obviously traveled around the Caribbean about the prisoners who had been snatched on the earlier expedition; this time, villages stood empty everywhere Columbus and his crew passed. The thirty-nine sailors who had been left behind had been killed by the natives.

Columbus was under a great deal of pressure from the Spanish Crown to produce some kind of wealth from his discoveries. Columbus loaded his ships with five hundred slaves, three hundred of whom survived the journey to Spain. That, however, was not sufficient payment on his debt. So Columbus instituted a tax system requiring certain amounts of gold from individual Indians; any Indian who did not pay had his hands cut off. The Taino population was already dwindling due to the barbaric treatment workers received on plantations and in the mines, and to mass suicides. When Columbus went off to explore Jamaica and the Cuban coastline, some men returned to Spain to entreat the Crown to recall Columbus; the colony was in chaos, and the treatment of the Indians was vicious even by the standards of the times.

In March of 1496, Columbus returned to Spain and was granted one more expedition, which left for the Caribbean in May of 1498. Determined to reach China, Columbus sailed along the coast of Venezuela, discovering for the first time the mainland of a continent. In a long report to Ferdinand and Isabella, Columbus described the area in terms of the original Paradise, the biblical Eden, shaped like a woman's breast. Back on Hispaniola, conditions were chaotic: Indians were dying and the Spanish, some sick with syphilis, were feuding. In 1500 the Spanish court sent a replacement for Columbus, who was returned to Spain in chains to be tried. Columbus was acquitted, and in 1502 he somehow wrangled a fourth voyage from the court, which turned out to be another failure at finding gold. Columbus's letters promised gold fields that were never found. After returning to Spain in 1504, he lived for two more years, depressed and in poor health.

Clearly the accounts of the first European explorers were tainted with their prejudices and expectations. The simple living conditions of the Taino people, for example, did not measure up to the expectations of civilized, Christian society. Later on, Columbus would describe the Indians as vicious and cruel, but in the first entries of his *Diario* he seemed delighted with his discoveries.

FROM

Diario

Translated by Robert H. Fuson

The Outward Voyage 3 August to 10 October 1492

In the Name of Our Lord Jesus Christ

Most Christian, exalted, excellent, and powerful princes, King and Queen of the Spains and of the islands of the sea, our Sovereigns: It was in this year of 1492 that Your Highnesses concluded the war with the Moors who reigned in Europe. On the second day of January, in the great city of Granada, I saw the royal banners of Your Highnesses placed by force of arms on the towers of the Alhambra, which is the fortress of the city. And I saw the Moorish king come to the city gates and kiss the royal hands of Your Highnesses, and those of the Prince, my Lord. Afterwards, in that same month, based on the information that I had given Your Highnesses about the land of India and about a Prince who is called the Great Khan, which in our language means "Kings of Kings," Your Highnesses decided to send me, Christopher Columbus,[1] to the regions of India, to see the Princes there and the peoples and the lands, and to learn of their disposition, and of everything, and the measures which could be taken for their conversion to our Holy Faith.

I informed Your Highnesses how this Great Khan and his predecessors had sent to Rome many times to beg for men learned in our Holy Faith so that his people might be instructed therein, and that the Holy Father had never furnished them, and therefore, many peoples believing in idolatries and receiving among themselves sects of perdition were lost.

Your Highnesses, as Catholic Christians and Princes devoted to the Holy Christian faith and to the spreading of it, and as enemies of the Muslim sect and of all idolatries and heresies, ordered that I should go to the east, but not by land as is customary. I was to go by way of the west, whence until today we do not know with certainty that anyone has gone.

Therefore, after having banished all the Jews from all your Kingdoms and realms, during this same month of January Your Highnesses ordered me to go with a sufficient fleet to the said regions of India. For that purpose I was granted great favors and ennobled; from then henceforward I might entitle myself *Don* and be High Admiral of the Ocean Sea and Viceroy and perpetual Governor of all the islands and continental land that I might discover and acquire, as well as any other future discoveries in the Ocean Sea. Further, my eldest son shall succeed to the same position, and so on from generation to generation for ever after.

I left Granada on Saturday, the 12th day of the month of May in the same year of 1492 and went to the town of Palos, which is a seaport. There I fitted out three vessels, very suited to such an undertaking. I left the said port well supplied with a large quantity of provisions and with many seamen on the third day of the month of August in the said year, on a Friday, half an hour before sunrise. I set my course for the Canary Islands of Your Highnesses, which are in the Ocean Sea, from there to embark on a voyage that will last until I arrive in the Indies and deliver the letter of Your Highnesses to those Princes, and do all that Your Highnesses have commanded me to do.

To this end I decided to write down everything I might do and see and experience on this voyage, from day to day, and very carefully. Also, Sovereign Princes, besides describing each night what takes place during the day, and during the day the sailings of the night, I propose to make a new chart for navigation, on which I will set down all the sea and lands of the Ocean Sea, in their correct locations and with their correct bearings. Further, I shall compile a book and shall map everything by

---

[1] **Your . . . Columbus:** The transcription reads, "*pensarō de embiarme a mi xp̄oual Colon*" ("You thought of sending me, Cristóval Colón"). Inasmuch as Columbus never signed his name in this conventional form, some believe that the entire prologue was written by Las Casas. It is more reasonable to assume that Las Casas inserted the name when he made his abstract. [All notes in this selection are the Translator's.]

latitude and longitude. And above all, it is fitting that I forget about sleeping and devote much attention to navigation in order to accomplish this. And these things will be a great task. [. . .]

The Discovery of the Bahamas
11 October to 27 October 1492

Thursday, 11 October 1492

I sailed to the WSW, and we took more water aboard than at any other time on the voyage. I saw several things that were indications of land. At one time a large flock of sea birds flew overhead, and a green reed was found floating near the ship. The crew of the *Pinta* spotted some of the same reeds and some other plants; they also saw what looked like a small board or plank. A stick was recovered that looks manmade, perhaps carved with an iron tool. Those on the *Niña* saw a little stick covered with barnacles. I am certain that many things were overlooked because of the heavy sea, but even these few made the crew breathe easier; in fact, the men have even become cheerful. I sailed 81 miles from sunset yesterday to sunset today. As is our custom, vespers were said in the late afternoon, and a special thanksgiving was offered to God for giving us renewed hope through the many signs of land He has provided.

After sunset I ordered the pilot to return to my original westerly course, and I urged the crew to be ever-vigilant. I took the added precaution of doubling the number of lookouts, and I reminded the men that the first to sight land would be given a silk doublet as a personal token from me. Further, he would be given an annuity of 10,000 maravedíes from the Sovereigns.

About 10 o'clock at night, while standing on the sterncastle, I thought I saw a light to the west. It looked like a little wax candle bobbing up and down. It had the same appearance as a light or torch belonging to fishermen or travellers who alternately raised and lowered it, or perhaps were going from house to house. I am the first to admit that I was so eager to find land that I did not trust my own senses, so I called for Pedro Gutiérrez, the representative of the King's household, and asked him to watch for the light. After a few moments, he too saw it. I then summoned Rodrigo Sánchez of Segovia, the comptroller of the fleet, and asked him to watch for the light. He saw nothing, nor did any other member of the crew. It was such an uncertain thing that I did not feel it was adequate proof of land.

The moon, in its third quarter, rose in the east shortly before midnight. I estimate that we were making about 9 knots and had gone some 67½ miles between the beginning of night and 2 o'clock in the morning. Then, at two hours after midnight, the *Pinta* fired a cannon, my prearranged signal for the sighting of land.

I now believe that the light I saw earlier was a sign from God and that it was truly the first positive indication of land. When we caught up with the *Pinta,* which was always running ahead because she was a swift sailer, I learned that the first man to sight land was Rodrigo de Triana, a seaman from Lepe.

I hauled in all sails but the mainsail and lay-to till daylight. The land is about six miles to the west.

Friday, 12 October 1492
(Log entry for 12 October is combined with that of 11 October.)

At dawn we saw naked people, and I went ashore in the ship's boat, armed, followed by Martín Alonso Pinzón, captain of the *Pinta*, and his brother, Vincente Yáñez Pinzón, captain of the *Niña.* I unfurled the royal banner and the captains brought the flags which displayed a large green cross with the letters F and Y at the left and right side of the cross. Over each letter was the appropriate crown of that Sovereign. These flags were carried as a standard on all of the ships. After a prayer of thanksgiving I ordered the captains of the *Pinta* and *Niña*, together with Rodrigo de Escobedo (secretary of the fleet), and Rodrigo Sánchez of Segovia (comptroller of the fleet) to bear faith and witness that I was taking possession of this island for the King and Queen. I made all the necessary declarations and had these testimonies carefully written down by the secretary. In addition to those named above, the entire company of the fleet bore witness to this act. To this island I gave the name *San Salvador*, in honor of our Blessed Lord.

No sooner had we concluded the formalities of taking possession of the island than people began to come to the beach, all as naked as their mothers bore them, and the women also, although I did not see more than one very young girl. All those that I saw were young people, none of whom was over 30 years old. They are very well-built people, with handsome bodies and very fine faces, though their appearance is marred somewhat by very broad heads and foreheads, more so than I have ever seen in any other race. Their eyes are large and very pretty, and their skin is the color of Canary Islanders or of sunburned peasants, not at all black, as would be expected because we are on an east–west line with Hierro in the Canaries. These are tall people and their legs, with no exceptions, are quite straight, and none of them has a paunch. They are, in fact, well proportioned. Their hair is not kinky, but straight, and coarse like horsehair. They wear it short over the eyebrows, but they have a long hank in the back that they never cut. Many of the natives paint their faces; others paint their whole bodies; some, only the eyes or nose. Some are painted black, some white, some red; others are of different colors.

The people here called this island *Guanahaní* in their language, and their speech is very fluent, although I do not understand any of it. They are friendly and well-dispositioned people who bear no arms except for small spears, and they have no iron. I showed one my sword, and through ignorance he grabbed it by the blade and cut himself. Their spears are made of wood, to which they attach a fish tooth at one end, or some other sharp thing.

I want the natives to develop a friendly attitude toward us because I know that they are a people who can be made free and converted to our Holy Faith more by love than by force. I therefore gave red caps to some and glass beads to others. They hung the beads around their necks, along with some other things of slight value that I gave them. And they took great pleasure in this and became so friendly that it was a marvel. They traded and gave everything they had with good will, but it seems to me that they have very little and are poor in everything. I warned my men to take nothing from the people without giving something in exchange.

This afternoon the people of San Salvador came swimming to our ships and in boats made from one log. They brought us parrots, balls of cotton thread, spears, and many other things, including a kind of dry leaf[2] that they hold in great esteem. For these things we swapped them little glass beads and hawks' bells.

Many of the men I have seen have scars on their bodies, and when I made signs to them to find out how this happened, they indicated that people from other nearby islands come to San Salvador to capture them; they defend themselves the best they can. I believe that people from the mainland come here to take them as slaves. They ought to make good and skilled servants, for they repeat very quickly whatever we say to them. I think they can easily be made Christians, for they seem to have no religion. If it pleases Our Lord, I will take six of them to Your Highnesses when I depart, in order that they may learn our language.

Saturday, 13 October 1492

After sunrise people from San Salvador again began to come to our ships in boats fashioned in one piece from the trunks of trees. These boats are wonderfully made, considering the country we are in, and every bit as fine as those I have seen in Guinea. They come in all sizes. Some can carry 40 or 50 men; some are so small that only one man rides in it. The men move very swiftly over the water, rowing with a blade that looks like a baker's peel. They do not use oarlocks, but dip the peel in the water and push themselves forward. If a boat capsizes they all begin to swim, and they rock the boat until about half of the water is splashed out. Then they bail out the rest of the water with gourds that they carry for that purpose.

The people brought more balls of spun cotton, spears, and parrots. Other than the parrots, I have seen no beast of any kind on this island.

I have been very attentive and have tried very hard to find out if there is any gold here. I have seen a few natives who wear a little piece of gold hanging from a hole made in the nose. By signs, if I interpret them correctly, I have learned that by going to the south, or rounding the island to the south, I can find a king who possesses a lot of gold and has great containers of it. I have tried to find some natives who will take me to this great king, but none seems inclined to make the journey.

Tomorrow afternoon I intend to go to the SW. The natives have indicated to me that not only is there land to the south and SW, but also to the NW. I shall go to the SW and look for gold and precious stones. Furthermore, if I understand correctly, it is from the NW that strangers come to fight and capture the people here.

The island is fairly large and very flat. It is green, with many trees and several bodies of water. There is a very large lagoon[3] in the middle of the island and there are no mountains. It is a pleasure to gaze upon this place because it is all so green, and

---

[2] **dry leaf:** The "dry leaves" are not actually mentioned until the October 15 entry. At that time Columbus tells us that these highly prized dry leaves were offered to him on October 12. It is reasonable, then, that the tobacco was part of "the many other things" cited in the log entry.

[3] **lagoon:** The Log states: "*. . . y muchas aguas y una laguna en medio muy grande. . . .*" The word is *laguna* (lagoon), not *lago* (lake). Columbus probably meant that the island had many small lakes and ponds *(muchas aguas)* and a saltwater lagoon in the middle ("halfway," "in between") on the coast he was on.

the weather is delightful. In fact, since we left the Canaries, God has not failed to provide one perfect day after the other.

I cannot get over the fact of how docile these people are. They have so little to give but will give it all for whatever we give them, if only broken pieces of glass and crockery. One seaman gave three Portuguese *ceitis* (not even worth a penny!) for about 25 pounds of spun cotton. I probably should have forbidden this exchange, but I wanted to take the cotton to Your Highnesses, and it seems to be in abundance. I think the cotton is grown on San Salvador, but I cannot say for sure because I have not been here that long. Also, the gold they wear hanging from their noses comes from here, but in order not to lose time I want to go to see if I can find the island of Japan.

When night came, all of the people went ashore in their boats.

[. . .] All the people I have seen so far resemble each other. They have the same language and customs, except that these on Fernandina seem to be somewhat more domestic and tractable, and more subtle, because I notice that when they bring cotton and other things to the ship they drive a harder bargain than those of the first islands visited. And also, on Fernandina I saw cotton clothes made like short tunics. The people seem better disposed, and the women wear a small piece of cotton in front of their bodies, though it barely covers their private parts. I do not recognize any religion in the people, and I believe that they would turn Christian quickly, for they seem to understand things quite well.

This is a very green, level, and fertile island, and I have no doubt that the people sow and reap grain, and also many other things, year around. I saw many trees quite different from ours. Many of them have branches of different kinds, all on one trunk;[4] one twig is of one kind and another of another, and so different from each other that it is the greatest wonder of the world. How great is the diversity of one kind from the other. For example, one branch has leaves like cane, another like mastic; thus on one tree five or six kinds, and all so different. Nor are these grafted so that one can say that the graft does it, for these trees are right there in the woods, and the people do not take care of them.

Here the fishes are so unlike ours that it is amazing; there are some like dorados, of the brightest colors in the world—blue, yellow, red, multi-colored, colored in a thousand ways; and the colors are so bright that anyone would marvel and take a great delight at seeing them. Also, there are whales. I have seen no land animals of any sort, except parrots and lizards—although a boy told me that he saw a big snake. I have not seen sheep, goats, or any other beasts, but I have only been here a very short time—half a day—yet if there were any, I could not have failed to have seen some. The circumnavigation of this island I shall write about after I have done it. [. . .]

During this time I walked among the trees, which are the most beautiful I have ever seen. I saw as much greenery, in such density, as I would have seen in Andalucia

[4] **trees . . . trunk:** There is no such tree, but Columbus may have seen a complex community of epiphytes and vines amid the trees.

in May. And all of the trees are so different from ours as day is from night, and so are the fruits, the herbage, the rocks, and everything. It is true that some of the trees are like those in Castile, but most of them are very different. There are so many trees of so many different kinds that no one can say what they are, nor compare them to those of Castile.

The people on Fernandina are the same as the others already mentioned: of the same condition, usually nude, of the same stature, and willing to give what they had for whatever we gave them. Some of the ships' boys traded broken glass and bowls to them for spears. The others that had gone for the water told me that they had been in the houses and found them very simple but clean, with beds and furnishings that were like nets[5] of cotton.

The houses look like Moorish tents, very tall, with good chimneys. But I have not seen a village yet with more than 12 or 15 houses. I also learned that the cotton coverings were worn by married women or women over 18 years of age. Young girls go naked. And I saw dogs: mastiffs and pointers. One man was found who had a piece of gold in his nose, about half the size of a *castellano,*[6] and on which my men say they saw letters. I scolded them because they would not exchange or give what was wanted, for I wished to see what and whose money that was, but they answered me that the man would not barter for it.

After taking on water, I returned to the ship and sailed to the NW until I had explored all that part of the island as far as the coast that runs east–west. The Indians on board began to say that this island was smaller than Samoet, and that it would be a good idea to turn around to get there sooner. The wind went calm, then began to blow from the WNW, which was contrary to the way we had come. I turned and sailed all this night to the ESE, sometimes due east and sometimes to the SE. I had to do this to keep clear of land, for there were heavy clouds and the weather was very threatening. But there was little wind and I was unable to approach land to anchor. Later it rained very hard from midnight to daylight, and it is still cloudy and threatening. We will go to the SE cape of the island, where I hope to anchor until it clears it up. It has rained every day since I have been in these Indies, some times more, some less. Your Highnesses may rest assured that this land is the best and most fertile and temperate and level and good that there is in the world. [. . .]

Sunday, 21 October 1492

At 10 o'clock in the morning I arrived at *Cabo del Isleo*[7] and anchored, as did the other two ships. After having eaten, I went ashore and found no settlement except one house. I found no one; the inhabitants must have fled in fear, for all their housewares were left behind. I did not permit my men to touch a thing, and I went with my captains to see the island. If the other islands are very green and beautiful and fertile, this is much more, with great and green groves of trees. There are some large lakes and above and around them is the most wonderful wooded area. The woods

[5] **nets:** Columbus's first reference to hammocks, although he had almost certainly seen them before on San Salvador. [6] ***castellano:*** Half of a gold ducat, worth about $10. [7] ***Cabo del Isleo:*** Cape of the Island.

and vegetation are as green as in April in Andalucía, and the song of the little birds might make a man wish never to leave here. The flocks of parrots that darken the sun and the large and small birds of so many species are so different from our own that it is a wonder. In addition, there are trees of a thousand kinds, all with fruit according to their kind, and they all give off a marvelous fragrance. I am the saddest man in the world for not knowing what kinds of things these are because I am very sure that they are valuable. I am bringing a sample of everything I can.

While going around one of the lagoons I saw a serpent,[8] which we killed with lances, and I am bringing Your Highnesses the skin. When it saw us, it went into the lagoon, and we followed it in because the water is not very deep. This serpent is about 6 feet long. I think there are many such serpents in these lagoons. The people here eat them and the meat is white and tastes like chicken.

I recognized the aloe[9] here, and tomorrow I am going to have 1,000 pounds of it brought to the ship because they tell me that it is very valuable. Also, while looking for good water, we stumbled onto a settlement about two miles from where we are anchored. When the people sensed our coming, they left their houses and fled, hiding their clothing and other things they had in the woods. I did not allow my men to take anything, not even something the value of one pin. Eventually some of the men came to us, and I gave one of them some hawks' bells and some small glass beads. He left very contented and very happy. And in order that our friendship might grow, and that something be asked of them, I requested water. Later, after I returned to the ship, they came to the beach with their gourds filled and were very delighted to give it to us. I ordered that they be given another string of glass beads, and they said they would return in the morning. I wanted to top off all of the ships' water casks while I had the chance.

If the weather permits, I shall depart this Cabo del Isleo and sail around Isabela until I find the king and see if I can get from him the gold which I hear that he wears. Then I shall sail for another great island which I strongly believe should be Japan, according to the signs made by the San Salvador Indians with me. They call that island *Colba,*[10] where they say there are many great ships and navigators. And from that island I intend to go to another that they call *Bohío,*[11] which is also very large. As to any others that lie in between, I shall see them in passing, and according to what gold or spices I find, I will determine what I must do. But I have already decided to go to the mainland and to the city of Quisay,[12] and give Your Highnesses' letters to the Grand Khan and ask for a reply and return with it.

---

[8] **serpent:** An iguana.

[9] **aloe:** Columbus was probably confusing *Agave americana* (or one of its close relatives) with either *Aloe vera* or *lignum aloe.* The former is grown as an ornamental indoor plant that serves as a readily accessible burn remedy. It is native to the Mediterranean area and was certainly known to Columbus. *Lignum aloe* is mentioned by Marco Polo. It is a fragrant, resinous wood used as incense. Columbus used the term *lignaloe,* which is a common name for this wood today.

[10] ***Colba:*** The reference is the first to Cuba, but the name *Cuba* is not used until October 23.

[11] ***Bohío:*** The Indian name for Hispaniola.

[12] **Quisay:** Quinsay; the modern city of Hangzhou, China.

Monday, 22 October 1492

I was here all last night and today waiting to see if the king on this island, or some other persons, would bring gold or something else substantial. And there came many of these people, similar to the others on the other islands, also naked and also painted. Some are painted white, some red, some black; others are in different colors. They brought spears and balls of cotton which they traded with some sailors for pieces of glass, broken cups, and pieces of clay bowls. A few brought pieces of gold hanging from their noses, which, with good will, they gave for a hawk's bell or small glass beads. It is so little that it is nothing. But it is true that they will trade anything they have for what little thing we may give them.

These people hold our arrival with great wonder and believe that we have come from heaven. We have been getting our water from a lake near the Cabo del Isleo, and in that lagoon Martín Alonso Pinzón, captain of the *Pinta,* killed another serpent like the one that was killed yesterday. It was about the same length. I have taken as much of the aloe as I could find.

Tuesday, 23 October 1492

I want to leave today for the island of Cuba,[13] which I believe to be Japan, according to the signs these people give of its magnificence and wealth. I do not want to tarry here any longer or explore this island looking for a settlement, even though I had originally planned to do this. I am not going to waste any more time looking for this king or lord, since I know there is no gold mine here. Furthermore, to sail around these small islands would require winds from many directions, and it does not blow that way; usually the wind is from the east or NE. And since I must go where there might be great commerce, it is foolish to delay. I must move on and discover many lands, until I come across a very profitable one. This island of Isabela may have many valuable spices, but I do not recognize them, and this causes me a great deal of sorrow, for I see a thousand kinds of fruit trees, each of which is as green now as in Spain during the months of May and June; there are also a thousand kinds of plants and herbs, and the same with flowers. And I know nothing except this aloe which I am carrying to Your Highnesses in great quantity.

[13] **Cuba:** This is the first correct spelling of the Indian name. It is one of the few native place-names that has survived.

HERNÁN CORTÉS

1485–1547

Columbus had opened up and explored the "new" lands of the Americas, but he had not brought riches to the Spanish Crown. When gold fell in short supply during the Middle Ages, legends began to circulate in Spain about cities of gold located somewhere in the west, and conquistadors like Hernán Cortés followed their dreams of discovering a golden paradise. After giving up the study of law, Cortés was encouraged at age nineteen to make his fortune in the Indies. He went to Cuba and, rising up through the ranks, became secretary to Diego Velásquez (1465–1524), the island's governor. He finally got permission at age thirty-three to lead an expedition to the mainland of Mexico to rescue several Spaniards from an earlier expedition and to explore the coastline. Later Velásquez would realize that Cortés had violated the terms of his expedition and was indeed intent on venturing into the interior of Mexico in order to colonize the new territory and become, if possible, its Spanish ruler. At the very least, Cortés sought a major share of the anticipated riches.

Cortés's letters not only provided a record of his encounter with the indigenous peoples of Mexico but also served as political instruments by which Cortés sought to ingratiate himself with King Charles I of Spain,

Diego Durán, *Montezuma*, 1579

This illustration from the Dominican friar Diego Durán's History of the Indies of New Spain *(c. 1579–81) shows the great Aztec king Montezuma sending ambassadors to the Spanish conquistadors. Diego Durán (1537–1588) was born in Spain, but spent most of his life in Texcoco and Mexico City. (The Art Archive / Biblioteca Nacional Madrid / Dagli Orti)*

who in November of 1519 became Charles V of the Holy Roman Empire (r. 1519–58). Cortés's first letter was sent in July of 1519 at a time when his forces had a precarious hold over the Aztec capital city of Tenochtitlán. His second letter, parts of which are presented here, describe the initial encounter with the Aztec rulers and the living conditions in the capital. We cannot entirely trust Cortés's description of the momentous meeting between himself and Moctezuma (whom Cortés called Mutezuma) or the transcription of the conversation. The theme of Moctezuma's speech clearly refers to the legendary return of Quetzalcoatl and the feeling that the Aztecs, or Mexica, were somehow immigrants to the region and temporary rulers. Cortés's detailed descriptions of the beautiful city illustrate the rather high standard of living enjoyed by the Aztecs—at least the ruling classes—and raise the question of why it was necessary to destroy the city and to eradicate the culture after the Aztecs' defeat. Shortly after Cortés, the Spanish colonists became involved in an extended debate about their treatment of indigenous peoples.

Letters from Mexico

Translated by Anthony Pagden

From the Second Letter

On the following day I left this city and after traveling for half a league came to a causeway which runs through the middle of the lake for two leagues until it reaches the great city of Temixtitan, which is built in the middle of the lake. This causeway is as wide as two lances, and well built, so that eight horsemen can ride abreast. In the two leagues from one end to the other there are three towns, and one of them, which is called Misicalcango, is in the main built on the water, and the other two, which are called Niciaca and Huchilohuchico,[1] are built on the shore, but many of their houses are on the water. The first of these cities has three thousand inhabitants, the second more than six thousand, and the third another four or five thousand, and in all of them there are very good houses and towers, especially the houses of the chiefs and persons of high rank, and the temples or oratories where they keep their idols.

In these cities there is much trading in salt, which they extract from the water of the lake and from the shallow area which is covered by the waters of the lake. They bake it in some way to make cakes, which are sold to the inhabitants and also beyond.

Thus I continued along this causeway, and half a league before the main body of the city of Temixtitan, at the entrance to another causeway which meets this one from the shore, there is a very strong fortification with two towers ringed by a wall four yards wide with merloned battlements all around commanding both causeways. There are only two gates, one for entering and one for leaving. Here as many as a thousand men came out to see and speak with me, important persons from that

[1] **Niciaca and Huchilohuchico:** Niciaca might be Coyoacan; Huchilohuchico is now called Churubusco.

city, all dressed very richly after their own fashion. When they reached me, each one performed a ceremony which they practice among themselves; each placed his hand on the ground and kissed it. And so I stood there waiting for nearly an hour until everyone had performed his ceremony. Close to the city there is a wooden bridge ten paces wide across a breach in the causeway to allow the water to flow, as it rises and falls. The bridge is also for the defense of the city, because whenever they so wish they can remove some very long broad beams of which this bridge is made. There are many such bridges throughout the city as later Your Majesty will see in the account I give of it.

After we had crossed this bridge, Mutezuma came to greet us and with him some two hundred lords, all barefoot and dressed in a different costume, but also very rich in their way and more so than the others. They came in two columns, pressed very close to the walls of the street, which is very wide and beautiful and so straight that you can see from one end to the other. It is two-thirds of a league long and has on both sides very good and big houses, both dwellings and temples.

Mutezuma came down the middle of this street with two chiefs, one on his right hand and the other on his left. One of these was that great chief who had come on a litter to speak with me, and the other was Mutezuma's brother, chief of the city of Yztapalapa, which I had left that day. And they were all dressed alike except that Mutezuma wore sandals whereas the others went barefoot; and they held his arm on either side. When we met I dismounted and stepped forward to embrace him, but the two lords who were with him stopped me with their hands so that I should not touch him; and they likewise all performed the ceremony of kissing the earth. When this was over Mutezuma requested his brother to remain with me and to take me by the arm while he went a little way ahead with the other; and after he had spoken to me all the others in the two columns came and spoke with me, one after another, and then each returned to his column.

When at last I came to speak to Mutezuma himself I took off a necklace of pearls and cut glass that I was wearing and placed it round his neck; after we had walked a little way up the street a servant of his came with two necklaces, wrapped in a cloth, made from red snails' shells, which they hold in great esteem; and from each necklace hung eight shrimps of refined gold almost a span in length. When they had been brought he turned to me and placed them about my neck, and then continued up the street in the manner already described until we reached a very large and beautiful house which had been very well prepared to accommodate us. There he took me by the hand and led me to a great room facing the courtyard through which we entered. And he bade me sit on a very rich throne, which he had had built for him and then left saying that I should wait for him. After a short while, when all those of my company had been quartered, he returned with many and various treasures of gold and silver and featherwork, and as many as five or six thousand cotton garments, all very rich and woven and embroidered in various ways. And after he had given me these things he sat on another throne which they placed there next to the one on which I was sitting, and addressed me in the following way:

"For a long time we have known from the writings of our ancestors that neither I, nor any of those who dwell in this land, are natives of it, but foreigners who came from very distant parts; and likewise we know that a chieftain, of whom they were all vassals, brought our people to this region. And he returned to his native land and after many years came again, by which time all those who had remained were married to native women and had built villages and raised children. And when he wished to lead them away again they would not go nor even admit him as their chief; and so he departed. And we have always held that those who descended from him would come and conquer this land and take us as their vassals. So because of the place from which you claim to come, namely, from where the sun rises, and the things you tell us of the great lord or king who sent you here, we believe and are certain that he is our natural lord, especially as you say that he has known of us for some time. So be assured that we shall obey you and hold you as our lord in place of that great sovereign of whom you speak; and in this there shall be no offense or betrayal whatsoever. And in all the land that lies in my domain, you may command as you will, for you shall be obeyed; and all that we own is for you to dispose of as you choose. Thus, as you are in your own country and your own house, rest now from the hardships of your journey and the battles which you have fought, for I know full well of all that has happened to you from Puntunchan[2] to here, and I also know how those of Cempoal and Tascalteca have told you much evil of me; believe only what you see with your eyes, for those are my enemies, and some were my vassals, and have rebelled against me at your coming and said those things to gain favor with you. I also know that they have told you the walls of my houses are made of gold, and that the floor mats in my rooms and other things in my household are likewise of gold, and that I was, and claimed to be, a god; and many other things besides. The houses as you see are of stone and lime and clay."

Then he raised his clothes and showed me his body, saying, as he grasped his arms and trunk with his hands, "See that I am of flesh and blood like you and all other men, and I am mortal and substantial. See how they have lied to you? It is true that I have some pieces of gold left to me by my ancestors; anything I might have shall be given to you whenever you ask. Now I shall go to other houses where I live, but here you shall be provided with all that you and your people require, and you shall receive no hurt, for you are in your own land and your own house."[3]

I replied to all he said as I thought most fitting, especially in making him believe that Your Majesty was he whom they were expecting; and with this he took his leave. When he had gone we were very well provided with chickens, bread, fruit and other requisites, especially for the servicing of our quarters. In this manner I spent six days, very well provisioned with all that was needed and visited by many of those chiefs. [. . .]

Thinking of all the ways and means to capture him without causing a disturbance, I remembered what the captain I had left in Vera Cruz had written to me about the events in the city of Almería, and how all that had happened there had been by order of Mutezuma. I left a careful watch on the crossroads and went to

---

[2] **Puntunchan:** Potonchan. [3] **"See . . . house":** Both this speech and the following one seem to be fabricated by Cortés, perhaps in order to fit native mythology.

Mutezuma's houses, as I had done at other times, and after having joked and exchanged pleasantries with him and after he had given me some gold jewelry and one of his daughters and other chiefs' daughters to some of my company, I told him that I knew of what had happened in the city of Nautecal (or Almería, as we called it), and the Spaniards who had been killed there; and that Qualpopoca excused himself by saying that all had been done by Mutezuma's command, and that as his vassal he could not have done otherwise. [. . .] He immediately sent for certain of his men to whom he gave a small stone figure in the manner of a seal, which he carried fastened to his arm, and he commanded them to go to the city of Almería, which is sixty or seventy leagues from Temixtitan, and to bring Qualpopoca, and to discover who were the others who had been concerned with the death of the Spaniards and to bring them likewise. If they did not come voluntarily, they were to be brought as prisoners, and if they resisted capture, Mutezuma's messengers were to request of certain communities close to the city, which he indicated to them, to send forces to seize them, but on no account to return without them.

These left at once, and after they had gone I thanked Mutezuma for the great care which he had taken in this matter, for it was my responsibility to account to Your Highness for those Spaniards, but asked that he should stay in my quarters until the truth were known and he was shown to be blameless. I begged him not to take this ill, for he was not to be imprisoned but given all his freedom, and I would not impede the service and command of his domains, and he should choose a room in those quarters where I was, whichever he wished. There he would be very much at his ease and would certainly be given no cause for annoyance or discomfort, because as well as those of his service my own men would serve him in all he commanded. In this we spent much time reasoning and discussing, all of which is too lengthy to write down and too tedious and too little pertinent to the issue to give Your Highness an account; so I will say only that at last he said he would agree to go with me. Then he ordered the room where he wished to stay to be prepared, and it was very well prepared. When this was done many chiefs came, and removing their garments they placed them under their arms, and walking barefoot they brought a simple litter, and weeping carried him in it in great silence. Thus we proceeded to my quarters with no disturbance in the city, although there was some agitation which, as soon as Mutezuma knew of it, he ordered to cease; and all was quiet and remained so all the time I held Mutezuma prisoner, for he was very much at his ease and kept all his household—which is very great and wonderful, as I will later relate—with him as before. And I and those of my company satisfied his needs as far as was possible. [. . .]

This great city of Temixtitan[4] is built on the salt lake, and no matter by what road you travel there are two leagues from the main body of the city to the mainland. There are four artificial causeways leading to it, and each is as wide as two cavalry lances. The city itself is as big as Seville or Córdoba. The main streets are very wide

[4] **Temixtitan:** Tenochtitlán.

and very straight; some of these are on the land, but the rest and all the smaller ones are half on land, half canals where they paddle their canoes. All the streets have openings in places so that the water may pass from one canal to another. Over all these openings, and some of them are very wide, there are bridges made of long and wide beams joined together very firmly and so well made that on some of them ten horsemen may ride abreast.

Seeing that if the inhabitants of this city wished to betray us they were very well equipped for it by the design of the city, for once the bridges had been removed they could starve us to death without our being able to reach the mainland, as soon as I entered the city I made great haste to build four brigantines, and completed them in a very short time. They were such as could carry three hundred men to the land and transport the horses whenever we might need them.

This city has many squares where trading is done and markets are held continuously. There is also one square twice as big as that of Salamanca,[5] with arcades all around, where more than sixty thousand people come each day to buy and sell, and where every kind of merchandise produced in these lands is found; provisions as well as ornaments of gold and silver, lead, brass, copper, tin, stones, shells, bones, and feathers. They also sell lime, hewn and unhewn stone, adobe bricks, tiles, and cut and uncut woods of various kinds. There is a street where they sell game and birds of every species found in this land: chickens, partridges and quails, wild ducks, flycatchers, widgeons, turtledoves, pigeons, cane birds, parrots, eagles and eagle owls, falcons, sparrow hawks and kestrels, and they sell the skins of some of these birds of prey with their feathers, heads and claws. They sell rabbits and hares, and stags and small gelded dogs which they breed for eating.

There are streets of herbalists where all the medicinal herbs and roots found in the land are sold. There are shops like apothecaries', where they sell ready-made medicines as well as liquid ointments and plasters. There are shops like barbers' where they have their hair washed and shaved, and shops where they sell food and drink. There are also men like porters to carry loads. There is much firewood and charcoal, earthenware braziers and mats of various kinds like mattresses for beds, and other, finer ones, for seats and for covering rooms and hallways. There is every sort of vegetable, especially onions, leeks, garlic, common cress and watercress, borage, sorrel, teasels and artichokes; and there are many sorts of fruit, among which are cherries and plums like those in Spain.

They sell honey, wax, and a syrup made from maize canes, which is as sweet and syrupy as that made from the sugar cane. They also make syrup from a plant which in the islands is called *maguey*, which is much better than most syrups, and from this plant they also make sugar and wine,[6] which they likewise sell. There are many sorts of spun cotton, in hanks of every color, and it seems like the silk market at Granada, except here there is a much greater quantity. They sell as many colors for painters as

---

[5] **Salamanca:** The marketplace in Tlateloco. [6] ***maguey* . . . wine:** *Maguey* is any of several varieties of agave; the wine made from this plant is called pulque.

may be found in Spain and all of excellent hues. They sell deerskins, with and without the hair, and some are dyed white or in various colors. They sell much earthenware, which for the most part is very good; there are both large and small pitchers, jugs, pots, tiles, and many other sorts of vessel, all of good clay and most of them glazed and painted. They sell maize both as grain and as bread and it is better both in appearance and in taste than any found in the islands or on the mainland. They sell chicken and fish pies, and much fresh and salted fish, as well as raw and cooked fish. They sell hen and goose eggs, and eggs of all the other birds I have mentioned, in great number, and they sell *tortillas* made from eggs.

Finally, besides those things which I have already mentioned, they sell in the market everything else to be found in this land, but they are so many and so varied that because of their great number and because I cannot remember many of them nor do I know what they are called I shall not mention them. Each kind of merchandise is sold in its own street without any mixture whatever; they are very particular in this. Everything is sold by number and size, and until now I have seen nothing sold by weight. There is in this great square a very large building like a courthouse, where ten or twelve persons sit as judges. They preside over all that happens in the markets, and sentence criminals. There are in this square other persons who walk among the people to see what they are selling and the measures they are using; and they have been seen to break some that were false.

There are, in all districts of this great city, many temples or houses for their idols. They are all very beautiful buildings, and in the important ones there are priests of their sect who live there permanently; and, in addition to the houses for the idols, they also have very good lodgings. All these priests dress in black and never comb their hair from the time they enter the priesthood until they leave; and all the sons of the persons of high rank, both the lords and honored citizens also, enter the priesthood and wear the habit from the age of seven or eight years until they are taken away to be married; this occurs more among the first-born sons, who are to inherit, than among the others. They abstain from eating things, and more at some times of the year than at others; and no woman is granted entry nor permitted inside these places of worship.

Amongst these temples there is one, the principal one, whose great size and magnificence no human tongue could describe, for it is so large that within the precincts, which are surrounded by a very high wall, a town of some five hundred inhabitants could easily be built. All round inside this wall there are very elegant quarters with very large rooms and corridors where their priests live. There are as many as forty towers, all of which are so high that in the case of the largest there are fifty steps leading up to the main part of it; and the most important of these towers is higher than that of the cathedral of Seville. They are so well constructed in both their stone and woodwork that there can be none better in any place, for all the stonework inside the chapels where they keep their idols is in high relief, with figures and little houses, and the woodwork is likewise of relief and painted with monsters and other figures and designs. All these towers are burial places of chiefs, and the chapels therein are each dedicated to the idol which he venerated.

There are three rooms within this great temple for the principal idols, which are of remarkable size and stature and decorated with many designs and sculptures, both in stone and in wood. Within these rooms are other chapels, and the doors to them are very small. Inside there is no light whatsoever; there only some of the priests may enter, for inside are the sculptured figures of the idols, although, as I have said, there are also many outside.

The most important of these idols, and the ones in whom they have most faith, I had taken from their places and thrown down the steps; and I had those chapels where they were cleaned, for they were full of the blood of sacrifices; and I had images of Our Lady and of other saints put there, which caused Mutezuma and the other natives some sorrow. First they asked me not to do it, for when the communities learnt of it they would rise against me, for they believed that those idols gave them all their worldly goods, and that if they were allowed to be ill treated, they would become angry and give them nothing and take the fruit from the earth leaving the people to die of hunger. I made them understand through the interpreters how deceived they were in placing their trust in those idols which they had made with their hands from unclean things. They must know that there was only one God, Lord of all things, who had created heaven and earth and all else and who made all of us; and He was without beginning or end, and they must adore and worship only Him, not any other creature or thing. And I told them all I knew about this to dissuade them from their idolatry and bring them to the knowledge of God our Saviour. All of them, especially Mutezuma, replied that they had already told me how they were not natives of this land, and that as it was many years since their forefathers had come here, they well knew that they might have erred somewhat in what they believed, for they had left their native land so long ago; and as I had only recently arrived from there, I would better know the things they should believe, and should explain to them and make them understand, for they would do as I said was best. Mutezuma and many of the chieftains of the city were with me until the idols were removed, the chapel cleaned and the images set up, and I urged them not to sacrifice living creatures to the idols, as they were accustomed, for, as well as being most abhorrent to God, Your Sacred Majesty's laws forbade it and ordered that he who kills shall be killed. And from then on they ceased to do it, and in all the time I stayed in that city I did not see a living creature killed or sacrificed.

The figures of the idols in which these people believe are very much larger than the body of a big man. They are made of dough from all the seeds and vegetables which they eat, ground and mixed together, and bound with the blood of human hearts which those priests tear out while still beating. And also after they are made they offer them more hearts and anoint their faces with the blood. Everything has an idol dedicated to it, in the same manner as the pagans who in antiquity honored their gods. So they have an idol whose favor they ask in war and another for agriculture; and likewise for each thing they wish to be done well they have an idol which they honor and serve.

Bartolomé de Las Casas
1484–1566

Born in Seville, Spain, Bartolomé de Las Casas was only eighteen years old when he first saw Columbus parading through the streets of Seville with seven Taino Indians, a number of parrots, and other exotic items. His father, Pedro, on returning from accompanying Columbus on his second voyage, actually gave Bartolomé a Taino slave; the Taino youth was later returned to the Indies. Bartolomé de Las Casas came to Hispaniola with his father in 1502 as a teacher to impart Christian doctrine to the natives. He was rewarded for helping subdue Indian revolts with an *encomienda,* a tract of land with accompanying Indian workers. He was ordained a Dominican priest in 1512, the first priest ordained in the New World. Shortly thereafter he underwent a shift in attitude; he renounced his encomienda and, deeply troubled by the Europeans' cruel treatment of Indians, gradually became the champion of human rights for them. For the next decades, Las Casas traveled back and forth between Spain and the New World defending the rights of Indians and proposing schemes for coexistence with them.

A most unusual event took place when the king of Spain—who was also the Holy Roman Emperor—questioned Spain's policies in America, in part because of Las Casas's criticism. Charles V scheduled a great debate in 1550, held in Valladolid, Spain, about whether natives had souls, and how that would influence colonizing the New World. Las Casas's opponent was Juan Ginés de Sepúlveda (1490?–1572), who argued that the Indians' inferior natures warranted the inhumane treatment; they were, in Artistotle's terms, "slaves by nature." Las Casas's arguments that Indians were rational beings finally won the day, and the Council of the Indies eventually abolished slavery in the "Ordinances of Discovery and Settlement" of 1573.

Las Casas's most famous writings are the *Apologetic History,* finished around 1559, and the *History of the Indies* (c. 1564). The first selection from the *History of the Indies* shows the ease with which killing could take place; Las Casas was traveling with a friend in Cuba when he observed the slaughter of innocent Indians. The second piece concerns a sermon he heard in Hispaniola in which the priest, Fray Antonio de Montesinos, rebuked the Spanish for their inhumanity; it contains the phrase that vibrates through Las Casas's mission: "Are these not men? Do they not have rational souls?" The authorities asked Montesinos, who was one of the first Spaniards to protest the cruel treatment of natives, to recant in his next sermon, but instead he reinforced his argument with more scripture. The last piece is from Las Casas's best-known work, the *Very Brief Account of the Destruction of the Indies* (c. 1542), in which he points the finger at Spanish excess and immorality.

Bartolomé de Las Casas
This is a portrait of the early Spanish historian and Dominican missionary Bartolomé de Las Casas. (The Art Archive / General Archive of the Indies Seville / Dagli Orti)

The History of the Indies

Translated by George Sanderlin

[Slaughtering Indians in Cuba]

They arrived at the town of Caonao[1] in the evening. Here they found many people, who had prepared a great deal of food consisting of cassava bread and fish, because they had a large river close by and also were near the sea. In a little square were 2,000 Indians, all squatting because they have this custom, all staring, frightened, at the mares. Nearby was a large *bohio,* or large house, in which were more than 500 other Indians, close-packed and fearful, who did not dare come out.

---

[1] **Caonao:** Village in Cuba.

When some of the domestic Indians the Spaniards were taking with them as servants (who were more than 1,000 souls . . .) wished to enter the large house, the Cuban Indians had chickens ready and said to them: "Take these—do not enter here." For they already knew that the Indians who served the Spaniards were not apt to perform any other deeds than those of their masters.

There was a custom among the Spaniards that one person, appointed by the captain, should be in charge of distributing to each Spaniard the food and other things the Indians gave. And while the captain was thus on his mare and the others mounted on theirs, and the father himself was observing how the bread and fish were distributed, a Spaniard, in whom the devil is thought to have clothed himself, suddenly drew his sword. Then the whole hundred drew theirs and began to rip open the bellies, to cut and kill those lambs—men, women, children, and old folk, all of whom were seated, off guard and frightened, watching the mares and the Spaniards. And within two credos, not a man of all of them there remains alive.

The Spaniards enter the large house nearby, for this was happening at its door, and in the same way, with cuts and stabs, begin to kill as many as they found there, so that a stream of blood was running, as if a great number of cows had perished. Some of the Indians who could make haste climbed up the poles and woodwork of the house to the top, and thus escaped.

The cleric had withdrawn shortly before this massacre to where another small square of the town was formed, near where they had lodged him. This was in a large house where all the Spaniards also had to stay, and here about forty of the Indians who had carried the Spaniards' baggage from the provinces farther back were stretched out on the ground, resting. And five Spaniards chanced to be with the cleric. When these heard the blows of the swords and knew that the Spaniards were killing the Indians—without seeing anything, because there were certain houses between—they put hands to their swords and are about to kill the forty Indians . . . to pay them their commission.

The cleric, moved to wrath, opposes and rebukes them harshly to prevent them, and having some respect for him, they stopped what they were going to do, so the forty were left alive. The five go to kill where the others were killing. And as the cleric had been detained in hindering the slaying of the forty carriers, when he went he found a heap of dead, which the Spaniards had made among the Indians, which was certainly a horrible sight.

When Narváez, the captain, saw him he said: "How does Your Honor like what these our Spaniards have done?"

Seeing so many cut to pieces before him, and very upset at such a cruel event, the cleric replied: "That I commend you and them to the devil!"

The heedless Narváez remained, still watching the slaughter as it took place, without speaking, acting, or moving any more than if he had been marble. For if he had wished, being on horseback and with a lance in his hands, he could have prevented the Spaniards from killing even ten persons.

Then the cleric leaves him, and goes elsewhere through some groves seeking Spaniards to stop them from killing. For they were passing through the groves looking for someone to kill, sparing neither boy, child, woman, nor old person. And they did more, in that certain Spaniards went to the road to the river, which was nearby. Then all the Indians who had escaped with wounds, stabs, and cuts—all who could flee to throw themselves into the river to save themselves—met with the Spaniards who finished them.

Another outrage occurred which should not be left untold, so that the deeds of our Christians in these regions may be observed. When the cleric entered the large house where I said there were about 500 souls—or whatever the number, which was great—and saw with horror the dead there and those who had escaped above by the poles or woodwork, he said to them:

"No more, no more. Do not be afraid. There will be no more, there will be no more."

With this assurance, believing that it would be thus, an Indian descended, a well-disposed young man of twenty-five or thirty years, weeping. And as the cleric did not rest but went everywhere to stop the killing, the cleric then left the house. And just as the young man came down, a Spaniard who was there drew a cutlass or half sword and gives him a cut through the loins, so that his intestines fall out. [. . .]

The Indian, moaning, takes his intestines in his hands and comes fleeing out of the house. He encounters the cleric [. . .] and the cleric tells him some things about the faith, as much as the time and anguish permitted, explaining to him that if he wished to be baptized he would go to heaven to live with God. The sad one, weeping and showing pain as if he were burning in flames, said yes, and with this the cleric baptized him. He then fell dead on the ground. [. . .]

Of all that has been said, I am a witness. I was present and saw it; and I omit many other particulars in order to shorten the account.

"Are Not the Indians Men?"

When Sunday and the hour to preach arrived, . . . Father Fray Antonio de Montesinos ascended the pulpit and took as the text and foundation of his sermon, which he carried written out and signed by the other friars: "I am the voice of one crying in the desert." After he completed his introduction and said something concerning the subject of Advent, he began to emphasize the aridity in the desert of Spanish consciences in this island, and the ignorance in which they lived; also, in what danger of eternal damnation they were, from taking no notice of the grave sins in which, with such apathy, they were immersed and dying.

Then he returns to his text, speaking thus: "I have ascended here to cause you to know those sins, I who am the voice of Christ in the desert of this island. Therefore it is fitting that you listen to this voice, not with careless attention, but with all your heart and senses. For this voice will be the strangest you ever heard, the harshest and hardest, most fearful and most dangerous you ever thought to hear."

This voice cried out for some time, with very combative and terrible words, so that it made their flesh tremble, and they seemed already standing before the divine judgment. Then, in a grand manner, the voice . . . declared what it was, or what that divine inspiration consisted of: "This voice," he said, "declares that you are all in mortal sin, and live and die in it, because of the cruelty and tyranny you practice among these innocent peoples.

"Tell me, by what right or justice do you hold these Indians in such a cruel and horrible servitude? On what authority have you waged such detestable wars against these peoples, who dwelt quietly and peacefully on their own land? Wars in which you have destroyed such infinite numbers of them by homicides and slaughters never before heard of? Why do you keep them so oppressed and exhausted, without giving them enough to eat or curing them of the sicknesses they incur from the excessive labor you give them, and they die, or rather, you kill them, in order to extract and acquire gold every day?

"And what care do you take that they should be instructed in religion, so that they may know their God and creator, may be baptized, may hear Mass, and may keep Sundays and feast days? Are these not men? Do they not have rational souls? Are you not bound to love them as you love yourselves? Don't you understand this? Don't you feel this? Why are you sleeping in such a profound and lethargic slumber? Be assured that in your present state you can no more be saved than the Moors or Turks, who lack the faith of Jesus Christ and do not desire it."

In brief, the voice explained what it had emphasized before in such a way that it left them astonished—many numb as if without feeling, others more hardened than before, some somewhat penitent, but none, as I afterward understood, converted.

When the sermon was concluded, Antonio de Montesinos descended from the pulpit with his head not at all low, for he was not a man who would want to show fear—as he felt none—if he displeased his hearers by doing and saying what seemed fitting to him, according to God. With his companion he goes to his thatch house where, perhaps, they had nothing to eat but cabbage broth without olive oil, as sometimes happened. But after he departed, the church remains full of murmurs so that, as I believe, they scarcely permitted the Mass to be finished. One may indeed suppose that a reading from the *Contempt of the World*[2] was not given at everyone's table that day.

After finishing their meal, which must not have been very appetizing, the whole city gathers at the house of the Admiral, Don Diego Columbus . . . , especially the king's officials, the treasurer and auditor, factor and comptroller. They agree to go rebuke and frighten the preacher and the others, if not to punish him as a scandalous man, sower of a new and unheard of doctrine which condemned them all. [. . .]

---

[2] ***Contempt of the World:*** A book about the rigors of a spiritual life written by Diego de Estella (1524–1578), Franciscan friar and mystic, in Spanish and published in 1586. Inspirational works are read during mealtimes for monks.

FROM

Very Brief Account of the Destruction of the Indies

Translated by George Sanderlin

The Destruction of the Indies

The Indies were discovered in the year 1492. The year following, Spanish Christians went to inhabit them, so that it is since forty-nine years that numbers of Spaniards have gone there: and the first land, that they invaded to inhabit, was the large and most delightful isle of Hispaniola, which has a circumference of 600 leagues.

There are numberless other islands, and very large ones . . . that were all—and we have seen it—as inhabited and full of their native Indian peoples as any country in the world. Of the continent . . . more than 10,000 leagues of maritime coast have been discovered, and more is discovered every day; all that has been discovered up to the year 1549 is full of people, like a hive of bees. . . .

God has created all these numberless people to be quite the simplest, without malice or duplicity, most obedient, most faithful to their natural lords, and to the Christians, whom they serve. . . . They are likewise the most delicate people, weak and of feeble constitution, and less than any other can they bear fatigue. . . . They are also a very poor people, who of worldly goods possess little, nor wish to possess; and they are therefore neither proud, nor ambitious, nor avaricious.

Their food is so poor, that it would seem that of the Holy Fathers in the desert was not scantier nor less pleasing. Their way of dressing is usually to go naked, covering the private parts. . . . Their beds are of matting, and they mostly sleep in certain things like hanging nets, called in the language of Hispaniola *hamacas.*

They are likewise of a clean, unspoiled, and vivacious intellect, very capable, and receptive to every good doctrine; most prompt to accept our Holy Catholic Faith, to be endowed with virtuous customs.

Among these gentle sheep . . . the Spaniards entered . . . like wolves, tigers, and lions which had been starving for many days, and since forty years they have done nothing else; nor do they otherwise at the present day, than outrage, slay, afflict, torment, and destroy them. . . . To such extremes has this gone that, whereas there were more than 3 million souls, whom we saw in Hispaniola, there are today, not 200 of the native population left.

The island of Cuba is almost as long as the distance from Valladolid to Rome; it is now almost entirely deserted. The islands of San Juan [Puerto Rico] and Jamaica . . . are both desolate. The Lucaya Isles lie near Hispaniola and Cuba to the north and number more than sixty. . . . The poorest of these . . . contained more than 500,000 souls, but today there remains not even a single creature. All were killed in transporting them to Hispaniola, because it was seen that the native population there was disappearing.

We are assured that our Spaniards, with their cruelty and execrable works, have depopulated and made desolate the great continent, and that more than ten kingdoms, larger than all Spain . . . although formerly full of people, are now deserted.

We give as a real and true reckoning, that in the said forty years, more than 12 million persons, men, and women, and children, have perished unjustly and through tyranny, by the infernal deeds and tyranny of the Christians. [. . .]

Two ordinary and principal methods have the self-styled Christians, who have gone there, employed in extirpating these miserable nations. . . . The one, by unjust, cruel, and tyrannous wars. The other, by slaying all those who might aspire to . . . liberty or to escape from the torments that they suffer, such as all the native lords and adult men. [. . .]

The reason why the Christians have killed and destroyed such infinite numbers of souls is solely because they have made gold their ultimate aim, seeking to load themselves with riches in the shortest time. . . . These lands, being so happy and so rich, and the people so humble, so patient, and so easily subjugated, they have . . . taken no more account of them . . . than—I will not say of animals, for would to God they had considered and treated them as animals—but as even less than the dung in the streets.

In this way have they cared for their lives—and for their souls: and therefore, all the millions above mentioned have died without faith and without sacraments. And it is . . . admitted . . . by all . . . that the Indians throughout the Indies never did any harm to the Christians: they even esteemed them as coming from heaven, until they and their neighbors had suffered the same many evils, thefts, deaths, violence, and visitations at their hands. [. . .]

Michel Eyquem de Montaigne

1533–1592

Born in Montaigne, a town in southwestern France, Montaigne was raised in a prominent family that valued a classical education. After studying law and holding several political positions in the parliament of Bordeaux, he withdrew from public life at the age of thirty-seven in order to devote himself to study and to the publication of his writings, which he called *essais,* or "attempts." While on a trip to Rome, Montaigne found out that he had been elected mayor of Bordeaux, a position he served until 1585 when he again withdrew to pursue his writing.

Montaigne is actually considered the originator of the personal essay, a kind of writing devoted as much to the journey of the mind as to any conclusions about a particular subject or theme. Montaigne's essays about books, sleep, cannibals, women, leisure, clothes, and numerous other topics reflect how he thought and how he arrived at conclusions. It is not surprising that his essays are filled with digressions and detours. The selection here comes from the essay "Of Coaches," which begins with the use of coaches in the past, leading to a discussion of wealth and extravagance. Montaigne addresses the fact that Europe's knowledge of the world, while extensive, is woefully incomplete. He feels that the "discovery" of another world, the Americas, offers an opportunity to greatly expand the body of European learning by drawing on those people of the New World who have built magnificent cities like Cuzco in Peru and Mexico City (Tenochtitlán). Montaigne then provides evidence for believing that the native peoples of the Americas have something to teach Europeans, but that the conquerors are as likely to destroy as to benefit from their experience with New World civilizations. In developing his essay, Montaigne shows a remarkable understanding of the customs and beliefs of the ancient Mexicans.

FROM

Of Coaches

Translated by Donald M. Frame

[. . .] Even if all that has come down to us by report from the past should be true and known by someone, it would be less than nothing compared with what is unknown. And of this very image of the world which glides along while we live on it, how puny and limited is the knowledge of even the most curious! Not only of particular events which fortune often renders exemplary and weighty, but of the state of great governments and nations, there escapes us a hundred times more than comes to our knowledge. We exclaim at the miracle of the invention of our artillery, of our printing; other men in another corner of the world, in China, enjoyed these a thousand years earlier. If we saw as much of the world as we do not see, we would perceive, it is likely, a perpetual multiplication and vicissitude of forms.

There is nothing unique and rare as regards nature, but there certainly is as regards our knowledge, which is a miserable foundation for our rules and which is apt to represent to us a very false picture of things. As vainly as we today infer the decline and decrepitude of the world from the arguments we draw from our own weakness and decay—

> This age is broken down, and broken down the earth
>
> —LUCRETIUS[1]

[1] **Lucretius:** (96?–55? B.C.E.), a Roman philosopher.

—so vainly did this poet infer the world's birth and youth from the vigor he saw in the minds of his time, abounding in novelties and inventions in various arts:

> The universe, I think, is very new,
> The world is young, its birth not far behind;
> Hence certain arts grow more and more refined
> Even today; the naval art is one.
>
> —LUCRETIUS

Our world has just discovered another world (and who will guarantee us that it is the last of its brothers, since the daemons, the Sibyls, and we ourselves have up to now been ignorant of this one?) no less great, full, and well-limbed than itself, yet so new and so infantile that it is still being taught its A B C; not fifty years ago it knew neither letters, nor weights and measures, nor clothes, nor wheat, nor vines. It was still quite naked at the breast, and lived only on what its nursing mother provided. If we are right to infer the end of our world, and that poet is right about the youth of his own age, this other world will only be coming into the light when ours is leaving it. The universe will fall into paralysis; one member will be crippled, the other in full vigor.

I am much afraid that we shall have very greatly hastened the decline and ruin of this new world by our contagion, and that we will have sold it our opinions and our arts very dear. It was an infant world; yet we have not whipped it and subjected it to our discipline by the advantage of our natural valor and strength, nor won it over by our justice and goodness, nor subjugated it by our magnanimity. Most of the responses of these people and most of our dealings with them show that they were not at all behind us in natural brightness of mind and pertinence.

The awesome magnificence of the cities of Cuzco and Mexico[2] (and, among many similar things, the garden of that king in which all the trees, the fruits, and all the herbs were excellently fashioned in gold, and of such size and so arranged as they might be in an ordinary garden; and in his curio room were gold replicas of all the living creatures native to his country and its waters), and the beauty of their workmanship in jewelry, feathers, cotton, and painting, show that they were not behind us in industry either. But as for devoutness, observance of the laws, goodness, liberality, loyalty, and frankness, it served us well not to have as much as they: by their advantage in this they lost, sold, and betrayed themselves.

As for boldness and courage, as for firmness, constancy, resoluteness against pains and hunger and death, I would not fear to oppose the examples I could find among them to the most famous ancient examples that we have in the memories of our world on this side of the ocean. For as regards the men who subjugated them, take away the ruses and tricks that they used to deceive them, and the people's natural astonishment at seeing the unexpected arrival of bearded men, different in language, religion, shape, and countenance, from a part of the world so remote, where

---

[2] **Cuzco and Mexico:** Cuzco was the capital of the Inca empire, plundered by Spanish conqueror Francisco Pizarro in 1533; Mexico was the capital city of the Aztec empire, captured and plundered by the Spanish conqueror Hernán Cortés in 1521.

they had never imagined there was any sort of human habitation, mounted on great unknown monsters, opposed to men who had never seen not only a horse, but any sort of animal trained to carry and endure a man or any other burden; men equipped with a hard and shiny skin and a sharp and glittering weapon, against men who, for the miracle of a mirror or a knife, would exchange a great treasure in gold and pearls, and who had neither the knowledge nor the material by which, even in full leisure, they could pierce our steel; add to this the lightning and thunder of our cannon and harquebuses—capable of disturbing Caesar himself, if he had been surprised by them with as little experience and in his time—against people who were naked (except in some regions where the invention of some cotton fabric had reached them), without other arms at the most than bows, stones, sticks, and wooden bucklers; people taken by surprise, under color of friendship and good faith, by curiosity to see strange and unknown things: eliminate this disparity, I say, and you take from the conquerors the whole basis of so many victories.

When I consider that indomitable ardor with which so many thousands of men, women, and children came forth and hurled themselves so many times into inevitable dangers for the defense of their gods and of their liberty, and that noble, stubborn readiness to suffer all extremities and hardships, even death, rather than submit to the domination of those by whom they had been so shamefully deceived (for some of them when captured chose rather to let themselves perish of hunger and fasting than to accept food from the hands of such basely victorious enemies), I conclude that if anyone had attacked them on equal terms, with equal arms, experience, and numbers, it would have been just as dangerous for him as in any other war we know of, and more so.

Why did not such a noble conquest fall to Alexander[3] or to those ancient Greeks and Romans? Why did not such a great change and alteration of so many empires and peoples fall into hands that would have gently polished and cleared away whatever was barbarous in them, and would have strengthened and fostered the good seeds that nature had produced in them, not only adding to the cultivation of the earth and the adornment of cities the arts of our side of the ocean, in so far as they would have been necessary, but also adding the Greek and Roman virtues to those originally in that region? What an improvement that would have been, and what an amelioration for the entire globe, if the first examples of our conduct that were offered over there had called those peoples to the admiration and imitation of virtue and had set up between them and us a brotherly fellowship and understanding! How easy it would have been to make good use of souls so fresh, so famished to learn, and having, for the most part, such fine natural beginnings! On the contrary, we took advantage of their ignorance and inexperience to incline them the more easily toward treachery, lewdness, avarice, and every sort of inhumanity and cruelty, after the example and pattern of our ways. Who ever set the utility of commerce and trading at such a price? So many cities razed, so many nations exterminated, so many millions of people put to the sword, and the richest and most beautiful part of the

[3] **Alexander:** Alexander the Great (356–323 B.C.E.), a student of Aristotle, was king of Macedon and eventually gained control over all of Greece by defeating the Persian Empire of Darius III.

world turned upside down, for the traffic in pearls and pepper! Base and mechanical victories! Never did ambition, never did public enmities, drive men against one another to such horrible hostilities and such miserable calamities.

Coasting the sea in quest of their mines, certain Spaniards landed in a fertile, pleasant, well-populated country, and made their usual declarations to its people: that they were peaceable men, coming from distant voyages, sent on behalf of the king of Castile, the greatest prince of the habitable world, to whom the Pope, representing God on earth, had given the principality of all the Indies; that if these people would be tributaries to him, they would be very kindly treated. They demanded of them food to eat and gold to be used in a certain medicine, and expounded to them the belief in one single God and the truth of our religion, which they advised them to accept, adding a few threats.

The answer was this: As for being peaceable, they did not look like it, if they were. As for their king, since he was begging, he must be indigent and needy; and he who had awarded their country to him must be a man fond of dissension, to go and give another person something that was not his and thus set him at strife with its ancient possessors. As for food, they would supply them. Gold they had little of, and it was a thing they held in no esteem, since it was useless to the service of their life, their sole concern being with passing life happily and pleasantly; however, they might boldly take any they could find, except what was employed in the service of their gods. As for one single God, the account had pleased them, but they did not want to change their religion, having followed it so advantageously for so long, and they were not accustomed to take counsel except of their friends and acquaintances. As for the threats, it was a sign of lack of judgment to threaten people whose nature and means were unknown to them. Thus they should promptly hurry up and vacate their land, for they were not accustomed to take in good part the civilities and declarations of armed strangers; otherwise they would do to them as they had done to these others—showing them the heads of some executed men around their city.

There we have an example of the babbling of this infancy. But at all events, neither in that place nor in several others where the Spaniards did not find the merchandise they were looking for, did they make any stay or any attack, whatever other advantages there might be; witness my Cannibals.[4]

Of the two most powerful monarchs of that world, and perhaps of this as well, kings of so many kings, the last two that they drove out, one, the king of Peru,[5] was taken in a battle and put to so excessive a ransom that it surpasses all belief; and when this had been faithfully paid, and the king in his dealings had given signs of a frank, liberal, and steadfast spirit and a clear and well-ordered understanding, the conquerors, after having extracted from him one million three hundred and twenty-five thousand five hundred ounces of gold, besides silver and other things that amounted to no less, so that their horses thenceforth went shod with solid gold, were seized with the desire to see also, at the price of whatever treachery, what could be

[4] **Cannibals:** See p. 214.

[5] **king of Peru:** Atahualpa, leader of the Incas, was executed by Pizarro in 1532.

the remainder of this king's treasures, and to enjoy freely what he had reserved. They trumped up against him a false accusation and false evidence that he was planning to rouse his provinces in order to regain his freedom. Whereupon, in a beautiful sentence pronounced by those very men who had set afoot this treachery against him, he was condemned to be publicly hanged and strangled, after being permitted to buy his way out of the torment of being burned alive by submitting to baptism at the moment of the execution. A horrible and unheard-of calamity, which nevertheless he bore without belying himself either by look or word, with a truly royal bearing and gravity. And then, to lull the people, stunned and dazed by such a strange thing, they counterfeited great mourning over his death and ordered a sumptuous funeral for him.

The other one, the king of Mexico,[6] had long defended his besieged city and shown in this siege all that endurance and perseverance can do, if ever prince and people did so, when his bad fortune put him in his enemies' hands alive, on their promise that they would treat him as a king; nor did he in his captivity show anything unworthy of this title. After this victory, his enemies, not finding all the gold they had promised themselves, first ransacked and searched everything, and then set about seeking information by inflicting the cruelest tortures they could think up on the prisoners they held. But having gained nothing by this, and finding their prisoners' courage stronger than their torments, they finally flew into such a rage that, against their word and against all law of nations, they condemned the king himself and one of the principal lords of his court to the torture in each other's presence. This lord, finding himself overcome with the pain, surrounded with burning braziers, in the end turned his gaze piteously toward his master, as if to ask his pardon because he could hold out no longer. The king, fixing his eyes proudly and severely on him in reproach for his cowardice and pusillanimity, said to him only these words, in a stern, firm voice: "And I, am I in a bath? Am I more comfortable than you?" The other immediately after succumbed to the pain and died on the spot. The king, half roasted, was carried away from there, not so much out of pity (for what pity ever touched souls who, for dubious information about some gold vase to pillage, had a man grilled before their eyes, and what is more, a king so great in fortune and merit?), but because his fortitude made their cruelty more and more shameful. They hanged him later for having courageously attempted to deliver himself by arms from such a long captivity and subjection, and he made an end worthy of a great-souled prince.

Another time they burned alive, all at once and in the same fire, four hundred and sixty men, the four hundred being of the common people, the sixty from among the chief lords of a province, all merely prisoners of war.

We have these narrations from themselves, for they not only admit them but boast of them and preach them. Would it be as a testimonial to their justice or their zeal for religion? Truly, those are ways too contrary and hostile to so holy an end. If they had proposed to extend our faith, they would have reflected that faith is not

[6] **king of Mexico:** Montezuma, ruler of the Aztec empire, was captured by Cortés and eventually killed in 1520.

spread by possession of territory but by possession of men, and they would have been more than satisfied with the murders brought about by the necessity of war, without adding to these an indiscriminate butchery, as of wild animals, as universal as fire and sword could make it, after purposely sparing only as many as they wanted to make into miserable slaves for the working and service of their mines: with the result that many of the leaders were punished with death by order of the kings of Castile, who were justly shocked by the horror of their conduct; and almost all were disesteemed and loathed. God deservedly allowed this great plunder to be swallowed up by the sea in transit, or by the intestine wars in which they devoured one another; and most of them were buried on the spot without any profit from their victory.

As for the fact that the revenue from this, even in the hands of a thrifty and prudent prince,[7] corresponds so little to the expectation of it given to his predecessors and to the abundance of riches that was first encountered in these new lands (for although much is being gotten out, we see that it is nothing compared with what was to be expected), the reason is that the use of money was entirely unknown, and that consequently their gold was found all collected together, being of no other use than for show and parade, like a chattel preserved from father to son by many powerful kings who were constantly exhausting their mines to make that great heap of vases and statues for the adornment of their palaces and their temples; whereas our gold is all in circulation and in trade. We cut it up small and change it into a thousand forms; we scatter and disperse it. Imagine it if our kings thus accumulated all the gold they could find for many centuries and kept it idle.

The people of the kingdom of Mexico were somewhat more civilized and skilled in the arts than the other nations over there. Thus they judged, as we do, that the universe was near its end, and they took as a sign of this the desolation that we brought upon them. They believed that the existence of the world was divided into five ages and into the life of five successive suns, of which four had already run their time, and that the one which gave them light was the fifth. The first perished with all other creatures by a universal flood of water. The second, by the heavens falling on us, which suffocated every living thing; to which age they assign the giants, and they showed the Spaniards some of their bones, judging by the size of which these men must have stood twenty hands high. The third, by fire, which burned and consumed everything. The fourth, by a turbulence of air and wind which beat down even many mountains; the men did not die, but they were changed into baboons (to what notions will the laxness of human credulity not submit!). After the death of this fourth sun, the world was twenty-five years in perpetual darkness, in the fifteenth of which a man and a woman were created who remade the human race; ten years later, on a certain day of their calendar, the sun appeared newly created, and since then they reckon their years from that day. The third day after its creation the old gods died; the new ones have been born since little by little. What they think about the manner in which this last sun will perish, my author[8] did not learn. But their calcula-

[7] **prince:** King Philip II of Spain.

[8] **my author:** Lopez de Gómara, a contemporary of Montaigne, who read his histories of Cortés and the West Indies.

tion of this fourth change coincides with that great conjunction of stars which produced, some eight hundred years ago, according to the reckoning of the astrologers, many great alterations and innovations in the world.

As for pomp and magnificence, whereby I entered upon this subject, neither Greece nor Rome nor Egypt can compare any of its works, whether in utility or difficulty or nobility, with the road which is seen in Peru, laid out by the kings of the country, from the city of Quito as far as Cuzco (a distance of three hundred leagues), straight, even, twenty-five paces wide, paved, lined on both sides with fine high walls, and along these, on the inside, two ever-flowing streams, bordered by beautiful trees, which they call *molly.* Wherever they encountered mountains and rocks, they cut through and leveled them, and filled the hollows with stone and lime. At the end of each day's journey there are fine palaces furnished with provisions, clothes, and arms, for travelers as well as for the armies that have to pass that way.

In my estimate of this work I have counted the difficulty, which is particularly considerable in that place. They did not build with any stones less than ten feet square; they had no other means of carrying than by strength of arm, dragging their load along; and they had not even the art of scaffolding, knowing no other device than to raise an equal height of earth against their building as it rose, and remove it afterward.

Let us fall back to our coaches. Instead of these or any other form of transport, they had themselves carried by men, and on their shoulders. That last king of Peru, the day that he was taken, was thus carried on shafts of gold, seated in a chair of gold, in the midst of his army. As many of these carriers as they killed to make him fall—for they wanted to take him alive—so many others vied to take the place of the dead ones, so that they never could bring him down, however great a slaughter they made of those people, until a horseman seized him around the body and pulled him to the ground.

Sor Juana Inés de la Cruz
1651–1695

Latin American writers honor as their forerunner a seventeenth-century woman who became a poet despite her unpromising circumstances. Juana Inés de la Cruz was born out of wedlock into a rural Mexican family. At twenty, she became a nun. Within her convent she wrote plays, poems, and comic verse, as well as theological and philosophical discourses on such unorthodox topics as the dignity and equality of women and the validity of the religious beliefs of Mexican Indian peoples. As an independent-minded visionary whose work called attention to herself and her views, she was always in danger of being censured; indeed, she spent the last four years of her life in a silence imposed by Roman Catholic authorities who found it necessary to repress her liberal views. Her writings fell from notice after her death, but in the twentieth century, when writers in many Latin American countries faced censorship for voicing their ideas, Sor Juana and her work became a model of courage and honesty.

The selection presented here is the LOA for the play *The Divine Narcissus,* probably written between 1686 and 1688. *Loa* is a Spanish word for the short theatrical prologues that sometimes preceded early plays. Though the play was first printed in Mexico in 1690 and was staged in Madrid before the Spanish court, it was never performed in Mexico. The subject was certain to anger the archbishop of Mexico since it merges the classical figure of Narcissus, famous for falling in love with his own image in a pool of water, with the figure of Jesus. In the loa, Sor Juana makes use of the idea put forth by many Christian humanists that pagan peoples were capable of experiencing partial, nonbiblical revelations of divine truth. A number of Christian intellectuals during this time were attempting to reconcile the discovery of Christian symbols among ancient Mexican and Mayan shrines: A magnificent cross, for example, was discovered at Palenque, a Mayan ruin, and the messianic Quetzalcoatl was typically pictured with what seems to be a bishop's miter and a bishop's staff.

In the loa Sor Juana maintains that the Indians of the Americas have the beginnings of an authentic spirituality. She draws from an account of Juan de Torquemada (c. 1563–1624), an early historian of Mexico, who described an Aztec rite called *teocualo,* "God is eaten." In this rite, once celebrated each December third, seeds and grain were kneaded together with the blood of sacrificed children and shaped into an edible effigy of Huitzilopochtli, the principal god of Mexico. (In his second letter, Hernán Cortés includes human blood in the dough, but the Dominican friar Diego Durán [1537–1588], who wrote several chronicles of New Spain, makes no mention of sacrificial blood in the mixture, but lists only *tzoalli,* or amaranth-seed, for the dough.) The priests then shattered the figure with arrows and shared the pieces among the celebrants. Sor Juana takes note of the resemblance of the rite to the Christian sacrament of the Eucharist and at one point in the play suggests that the differences between Indian and Christian rituals can be bridged through metaphor. In the loa the female figure standing for Christian Religion argues with the military-minded male Zeal, urging that the Indians can be won over gently, through persuasion, because they are already receptive to certain elements of Christianity. Indeed, when she patiently points out to the native couple, Occident and America, the similarities of their own religion to Christianity, they are joyously converted. What is extraordinary for a writer of the seventeenth century in Mexico is the honesty and openness with which Sor Juana pays tribute to the beliefs and rituals of native America.

Loa for The Divine Narcissus

Translated by Margaret Peden

CAST OF CHARACTERS:

OCCIDENT
AMERICA
ZEAL
RELIGION
MUSICIANS
SOLDIERS

Scene 1

Enter OCCIDENT, *a stately Indian wearing a crown, and* AMERICA *beside him, a noble Indian woman, in the* mantas *and* huipiles *worn when singing a* tocotín.[1] *They sit in two chairs; several Indian men and women dance holding feathers and rattles in their hands, as is traditional during this celebration; as they dance,* MUSIC *sings:*

MUSIC:

Most noble Mexicans,
whose ancient origin
is found in the brilliant rays
cast like arrows by the Sun,
mark well the time of year,
this day is given to laud
and honor in our way
the highest of our gods.
Come clad in ornaments
of your station the sign,
and to your piety
let happiness be joined:
with festive pageantry
worship the all-powerful God of Seeds![2]

MUSIC:

The riches of our lands
in copious plenteousness
are owing to the one
who makes them bounteous.
So bring your fervent thanks,
and at the harvest time,
give unto Him his due,

---

[1] ***tocotín:*** A poem written in Nahuatl that accompanies a Mexican folk dance.

[2] **God of Seeds:** Sor Juana appears to be combining two important Aztec deities in the God of Seeds: the central Aztec deity before the conquest was Huitzilopochtli, the god of war and the sun. Sacrifices of blood, the life substance, sustained Huitzilopochtli's journey across the sky. The god of agriculture and water was Tlaloc, who was often pictured as raining seeds on the world.

the first fruit of the vine.
Let flow the purest blood,
give from your own veins,
to blend with many bloods
and thus His cult sustain.
With festive pageantry
worship the all-powerful God of Seeds!

[OCCIDENT *and* AMERICA *sit, as* MUSIC *ceases.*]

OCCIDENT:

So great in number are the Gods
that our religion sanctifies,
so many in this place alone
the many rites we solemnize,
that this our Royal City is
the scene of cruelest sacrifice:
two thousand gods are satisfied,
but human blood must be the price;
now see the entrails that still throb,
now see hearts that redly beat,
and though the gods are myriad,
our gods so many (I repeat),
the greatest God among them all
is our Great God, the God of Seeds!

AMERICA:

And rightly so, for He alone
has long sustained our monarchy,
for all the riches of the field
we owe to Him our fealty,
and as the greatest benefice,
in which all others are contained,
is that abundance of the land,
our life and breath by it maintained,
we name Him greatest of the Gods.
What matters all the glittering gold
in which America abounds,
what value precious ores untold,
if their excrescences befoul
and sterilize a fertile earth,
if no fruits ripen, no maize grows,
and no tender buds spring forth?
But the protection of this God
is broader than continuance,
with the provision of our food,
of our daily sustenance,

He makes a paste of His own flesh,
and we partake with veneration[3]
(though first the paste is purified
of bodily contamination),
and so our Soul he purifies
of all its blemishes and stains.
And thus in homage to His cult,
may everyone with me proclaim:

ALL *and* MUSIC:

In festive pageantry,
worship the all-powerful God of Seeds!

Scene 2

[*They exit, dancing, and then enter* CHRISTIAN RELIGION, *as a Spanish Lady, and* ZEAL, *as a Captain General, armed; behind them, Spanish* SOLDIERS.]

RELIGION:

How is it, then, as you are Zeal,
your Christian wrath can tolerate
that here with blind conformity
they bow before Idolatry,
and, superstitious, elevate
an Idol, with effrontery,
above our Christianity?

ZEAL:

Religion, do not be dismayed:
my compassion you upbraid,
my tolerance you disavow,
but see, I stand before you now
with arm upraised, unsheathed my blade,
which I address to your revenge
And now, retire, your cares allayed,
as their transgressions I avenge.

[*Enter, dancing,* OCCIDENT *and* AMERICA, *and from the other side,* MUSIC, *with accompaniment*]

MUSIC:

And with festive pageantry,
worship the all-powerful God of Seeds!

ZEAL:

They are here. I will approach.

---

[3] **veneration:** Sor Juana is referring to a rite in which a dough is shaped into the image of Huitzilopochtli and then eaten by the celebrants. She later compares this ritual to the Christian Eucharist, in which bread and wine are transformed into Jesus' body and blood and then are eaten and drunk.

RELIGION:
And I as well, with all compassion,
for I would go with tones of peace
(before unleashing your aggression)
to urge them to accept my word,
and in the faith be sanctified.

ZEAL:
Then let us go, for even now
they practice their revolting rite.

MUSIC:
And with festive pageantry,
worship the great God of Seeds!

[ZEAL *and* RELIGION *approach*]

RELIGION:
Hear me, mighty Occident,
America, so beautiful,
your lives are led in misery
though your land is bountiful.
Abandon this unholy cult
which the Devil doth incite.
Open your eyes. Accept my word
and follow in the Path of Light,
fully persuaded by my love.

OCCIDENT:
These unknown persons, who are they
who now before my presence stand?
Oh gods, who ventures thus to stay
the festive moment's rightful course?

AMERICA:
What Nations these, which none has seen?
Do they come here to interfere,
my ancient power contravene?

OCCIDENT:
Oh, Lovely Beauty, who are you,
fair Pilgrim from another nation?
I ask you now, why have you come
to interrupt my celebration?

RELIGION:
Christian Religion is my name,
and I propose that all will bend
before the power of my word.

OCCIDENT:
A great endeavor you intend!

AMERICA:
A great madness you display!
OCCIDENT:
The inconceivable you scheme!
AMERICA:
She must be mad, ignore her now,
let them continue with our theme!
ALL *and* MUSIC:
With festive pageantry,
worship the all-powerful God of Seeds!
ZEAL:
How, barbaric Occident,
and you, oh blind Idolatry,
Can you presume to scorn my Wife,
beloved Christianity?
For brimming to the vessel's lip
we see your sinful degradation;
the Lord our God will not allow
That you continue in transgression,
and He sends me to punish you.
OCCIDENT:
And who are you, who terrorize
all those who gaze upon your face?
ZEAL:
I am Zeal. Whence your surprise?
For when Religion you would scorn
with practices of vile excess,
then Zeal must enter on the scene
to castigate your wickedness.
I am a Minister from God
Who, witnessing your tyranny,
the error of these many years
of lives lived in barbarity,
has reached the limits of His grace
and sends His punishment through me.
And thus these armed and mighty Hosts
whose gleaming blades of steel you see
are His ministers of wrath,
the instruments of Holy rage.
OCCIDENT:
What god, what error, what offense,
what punishment do you presage?
I do not understand your words,
nor does your argument persuade;

I know you not, who, brazenly,
would thus our rituals invade
and with such zeal that you prevent
that in just worship people say:

MUSIC:
With festive pageantry,
worship the great God of Seeds!

AMERICA:
Oh mad, blind, barbaric man,
disturbing our serenity,
you bring confusing arguments
to counter our tranquillity;
you must immediately cease,
unless it is your wish to find
all here assembled turned to ash
with no trace even on the wind!
And you, Husband, and your vassals,

[*to* OCCIDENT]

you must close your ears and eyes,
do not heed their fantasies,
do not listen to their lies;
proceed, continue with your rites!
Our rituals shall not be banned
by these Nations, still unknown,
so newly come unto our land.

MUSIC:
And with festive pageantry,
worship the great God of Seeds!

ZEAL:
As our first offering of peace
you have so haughtily disdained,
accept the second, that of war,
from war we will not be restrained!
War! War! To arms! To arms!

[*Sound of drums and trumpets*]

OCCIDENT:
What is this wrath the gods devise?
What are the weapons here displayed
that so confound my awestruck eyes?
Ho, my Soldiers, ho there, Guards!
Those arrows that you hold prepared
now send against the enemy!

AMERICA:

Why have the gods their lightning bared
to strike me down? What are these spheres
that fall like fiery leaden hail?
What are these Centaurs, man and horse,[4]
that now my followers assail?

[*Off*]

To arms! To arms! We are at war!

[*Drums and trumpets*]

Long live Spain! Her King we hail!

[*The battle is struck:* INDIANS *enter and flee across the stage, pursued by the* SPANISH; OCCIDENT *and* AMERICA *begin to retreat before* RELIGION *and* ZEAL]

Scene 3

RELIGION:

Surrender, haughty Occident!

OCCIDENT:

Your declarations I defy
and only to your power yield.

ZEAL:

Now bold America must die!

RELIGION:

Hold, Zeal, do not strike them dead,
keep America alive!

ZEAL:

What, you defend America
When she has your faith reviled?

RELIGION:

There is no doubt that her defeat
is owing to your bravery,
but now allowing her to live
is witness to my clemency;
it was your duty, with your force,
to conquer her; but now with reason
I, too, work to vanquish her,
but I shall win with soft persuasion.

---

[4] **man and horse:** In Greek mythology, centaurs were half-man and half-horse; at first the Aztecs thought that the Spaniard on a horse was one creature.

ZEAL:

But their perversion you have seen,
how they abhor and scorn your Word;
they are blind, is it not better
that they die?

RELIGION:

Put up your sword.
Forebear, Zeal, do not attack,
it is my nature to forgive,
I do not want their immolation,
but conversion, let them live.

AMERICA:

If in petitioning for my life,
and in exhibiting compassion,
it is your hope that I will yield,
that you will thus divert my passion,
employing arguments of words
as once before you employed arms,
then you will find yourself deceived,
for though my person come to harm,
and though I weep for liberty,
my liberty of will, will grow,
and I shall still adore my Gods!

OCCIDENT:

I have told you, and all know,
that I have bowed before your might,
but this caution you must heed,
that there is no strength or might
that ever can my will impede
from its just course, free of control;
though captive I may moan in pain,
your will can never conquer mine,
and in my heart I will proclaim:
I worship the great God of Seeds!

Scene 4

RELIGION:

But wait, for what we offer here
is not might, but gentleness.
What God is this that you adore?

OCCIDENT:

The Great Lord of fruitfulness.
He makes fertile all the fields,

all the heavens bow to Him,
it is He the rain obeys,
and finally, of all our sin
He cleanses us, then of His being
makes a feast to nurture us.
Tell me whether there can be,
in a God so bounteous,
any greater benefice
than I give in this summary?

RELIGION [*Aside*]:

May God have mercy! What reflection
do I see, what counterfeit,
thus patterned in their evil lies,
to mock our holy sacred Truths?
Oh, wily Serpent, sly Reptile,[5]
oh, venom from the Viper's tooth!
Oh, Hydra,[6] seven-headed beast
whose seven mouths spew, lethally,
rivers of poison on our heads,
how far, and how maliciously,
can you continue in this way
God's sacred Miracles to mime?
Now if God will grace my tongue,
this same deceit I shall refine
and use your arguments to win.

AMERICA:

What mischief do you fabricate?
Do you not see there is no God,
none other, who corroborates
in benefices all His works?

RELIGION:

Then I shall be like Paul, and speak
from holy doctrine; for when he
had come to preach among the Greeks,
he found in Athens the strict law
that he who sought to introduce
an unfamiliar god, would die,
but as he knew they had the use
of faithful worship in a place

[5] **Reptile:** Satan.

[6] **Hydra:** In Greek mythology, a monster with either seven or nine heads defeated by Heracles; when one head was cut off, two would grow back.

devoted to THE UNKNOWN GOD,[7]
he said: this God I give to you
is not unknown, but One you laud,
you ignorantly worship Him,
now Him declare I unto you.
And thus do I. . . . Hear, Occident,
Idolatry, attend me, too,
for if you listen to my words
you will find salvation there.
Those many wonders you recount,
the miracles to which you swear,
the shimmering light, the flashing gleam
you glimpsed through Superstition's veil,
the prodigies, the prophecies,
the portents we heard you detail,
attributing their consequence
to your mendacious deities,
are but the work of One True God,
His wisdom and His sovereignty.
For if the flowering meadows bloom
and gardens yield their rich supply,
if the fields are fertilized,
and if their fruits do multiply,
if the plants from seedlings grow,
and if the clouds their rain distill,
all must come from His right hand,
and never will the arm that tills,
nor the rains that feed the earth,
nor the warmth that wakes the seeds,
have the power to make plants live
if Providence has not decreed
that they have life: all nature's green,
her verdant soul, is His design.

AMERICA:

And if all this is as you say,
is He, tell me, so benign,
this God of yours, your Deity,
so kind that he will tolerate
that I touch Him with my hands,

[7] THE UNKNOWN GOD: On the road from Athens to the port city of Piraeus, the Greeks erected shrines to all their major deities, and, in case they had omitted an important figure, they erected a separate shrine to the Unknown God (*Agnostos Theos,* which became the root of the word *agnosticism*).

like the Idol I create
from many seeds and from the blood
of innocents, blood that is shed
for this alone, this one intent?

RELIGION:

Although in Essence the Godhead
is both invisible and vast,
as that Essence is combined
And with our Being bound so fast,
thus He is like to Humankind,
and His benevolence allows
that undeserving though they be,
He may be touched by hands of Priests.

AMERICA:

In this much, then, we are agreed.
For of my God the same is true,
and none may touch our Deity
except for those who as His priests
to serve Him have authority;
not only may He not be touched,
but neither may they enter in
His Chapel who are not ordained.

ZEAL:

What reverence, whose origin
were better found in Our True God!

OCCIDENT:

Then tell me, though much more you swear:
is this God formed of elements
that are as exquisite, as rare,
as that of blood shed valiantly
and offered up as sacrifice,
as well as seeds, our sustenance?

RELIGION:

His Majesty, I say this twice
is infinite and without form,
but His divine Humanity,
found in the Sacrament of Mass,
with mercy, not with cruelty,
assuming the white innocence
which in the seeds of wheat resides,
becomes incarnate in these seeds,
in Flesh and Blood is deified;
here in this Chalice is His Blood,
the Blood He sacrificed for us,
which on the Altar of the Cross,

unsullied, pure, in righteousness,
was the Redemption of the World.

AMERICA:

I stand in awe of all you say,
and hearing, I want to believe;
but could this God that you portray
be so loving that as food
He would give Himself to me,
like the God that I adore?

RELIGION:

Yes, for in His Wisdom, He
came down with only this in view,
to lie on earth among mankind.

AMERICA:

So, may I not see this God,
that true persuasion I may find?

OCCIDENT:

And I as well, thus will it be
that my obsession be forgot?

RELIGION:

Oh, you will see, once you are washed
in the crystalline, holy font
of Baptism.

OCCIDENT:

Yes, this I know,
before aspiring to come near
the fruitful table, I must bathe;
that ancient rite is practiced here.

ZEAL:

That bathing for your rituals
will not cleanse you of your stains.

OCCIDENT:

What bathing will?

RELIGION:

The Sacrament,
which in pure waters like the rains
will cleanse you of your every sin.

AMERICA:

The magnitude of this you bring
as notices, as yet I cannot
comprehend, of everything
I would know more, and in detail,
for I am moved by powers divine,
inspired to know all you can tell.

OCCIDENT:

An even greater thirst is mine,
I would know of the Life and Death
of this great God found in the Bread.

RELIGION:

That we shall do. I shall give you
a metaphor, an idea clad
in rhetoric of many colors
and fully visible to view,
this shall I show you, now I know
that you are given to imbue
with meaning what is visible;
it is now clear you value less
what Faith conveys unto your ears,
thus it is better you assess
what you can see, and with your eyes
accept the lessons She conveys.

OCCIDENT:

Yes, it is so, for I would see,
and not rely on what you say.

Scene 5

RELIGION:

Let us begin.

ZEAL:

Religion, speak,
to represent the Mysteries,
what form do you plan to employ?

RELIGION:

An allegory it will be,
the better to instruct the two,
an *Auto*[8] that will clearly show
America and Occident
all that they now beg to know.

ZEAL:

This Allegory as *Auto,*
what title for it do you plan?

RELIGION:

Divine Narcissus, for although
America, unhappy land,

[8] ***Auto:*** An *auto sacramental* is a one-act allegory illustrating a religious truth.

adored an Idol symbolized
by signs of such complexity
that through that Idol Satan tried
to feign the highest Mystery,
that of the Sacred Eucharist,
there was, as well, intelligence
among the Gentiles of this land
of other marvelous events.

ZEAL:

And where will they enact your play?

RELIGION:

In Madrid, the Royal Town,
the Center of our Holy Faith,
the Jewel in the Royal Crown,
the Seat of Catholic Kings and Queens
through whom the Indies have been sent
the blessing of Evangel Light
that shines throughout the Occident.

ZEAL:

But does it not seem ill-advised
that what you write in Mexico
be represented in Madrid?

RELIGION:

Oh, tell me, did you never know
an object fashioned in one place
and subsequently used elsewhere?
As for the act of writing it,
you find no whim or fancy there,
but only due obedience
attempting the impossible.
Therefore this work, though it may be
inelegant, its lustre dull,
is owing to obedience,
and not born of effrontery.

ZEAL:

Religion, tell me, as the play
is your responsibility,
how do you counter the complaint
that in the Indies was begun
what you would carry to Madrid?

RELIGION:

The drama's purpose is but one,
to celebrate the Mystery,
as to the persons introduced,
they are but an abstraction,

symbolic figures who educe
the implication of the work,
and no part need be qualified
though it be taken to Madrid;
for men of reason realize
there is no distance that deters,
nor seas that interchange efface.

ZEAL:

Prostrate, at the Royal Feet
that regally Two Worlds embrace,
we seek permission to proceed,

RELIGION:

and of the Queen, our Sovereign,

AMERICA:

at whose feet the Indies kneel
to pledge obeisance once again,

ZEAL:

and of her Supreme Councillers,

RELIGION:

and Ladies, who illuminate
the Hemisphere;

AMERICA:

and the Erudite
whom I most humbly supplicate
to pardon the poor lack of wit
in wishing with these clumsy lines
to treat so great a Mystery.

OCCIDENT:

My agony is exquisite,
come, show me how in bread and wine
this God gives of Himself to me.

[AMERICA, OCCIDENT, *and* ZEAL *sing*]

Now are the Indies
all agreed,
there is but One
True God of Seeds!
With tender tears
by joy distilled,
raise voices high
with gladness filled:

ALL:

Blessed the day
I came to know the great God of the Seeds!

[*All exit, dancing and singing*]

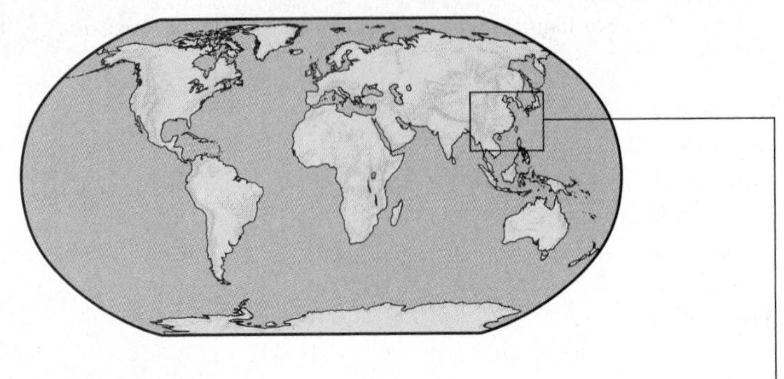

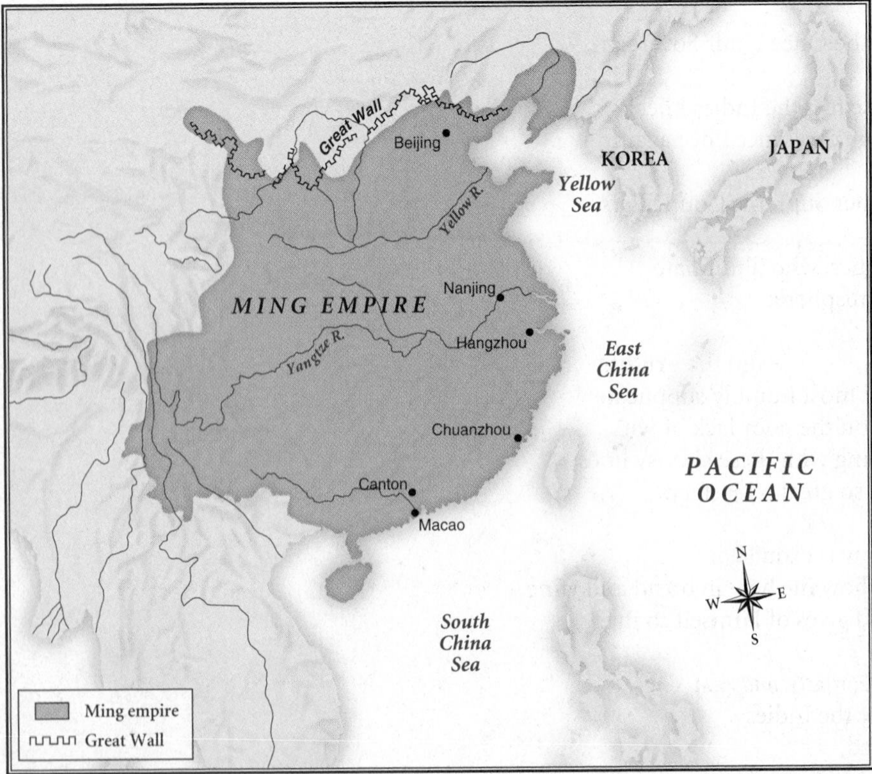

The Ming Empire c. 1600

In 1368, the Chinese regained power over their lands in a successful revolt, led by Zhu Yuanzhang, against the last Mongol emperor. Zhu, taking the title Ming Hongwu, founded the Ming dynasty, which lasted from 1368 until 1644, when it was replaced by the Qing dynasty. During the Ming dynasty, China underwent a period of social and political transformation as agricultural lands were consolidated into the hands of rich farmers, a new urban middle class was formed, and new forms of literature and art were developed.

CHINA
The Glory of the Ming

The Yuan, or Mongol, dynasty, founded in China in 1260 by Kublai Khan (r. 1260–94), came to an end in 1368, when the resourceful Zhu Yuanzhang (Chu Yüan-chang; 1328–1398), a peasant from the Yangtze Valley, led a successful rebellion against the last of the Mongol emperors. Taking the title Ming Hongwu, Zhu founded the Ming dynasty, which lasted from 1368 until it was torn by internal strife and invaded by the Manchus in 1644. The last of the native Chinese dynasties, the Ming (bright) dynasty gradually restored prosperity to China. In the early years of the Ming under emperors Hongwu (r. 1368–98) and Yongle (Yung-lo; r. 1403–24), the Chinese undertook a massive project of rebuilding their economy and infrastructure, expanding their territory, and restoring their dignity and power. China underwent a period of social transformation, involving the consolidation of agricultural lands into the lands of rich farmers, the formation of an urban and commercial middle class in the growing cities, and a proliferation of new forms of literature and art, especially in the sixteenth century. At the same time, economic imbalances—which had a negative impact on the poor, especially in the countryside—ultimately set the conditions for the collapse of the empire in the middle of the seventeenth century.

ORIGINS OF THE MING DYNASTY

As the first emperor of the Ming, Hongwu began the process of stabilizing and reunifying China under his capital at Nanjing (Nanking), preparing the grounds for later expansion. Hongwu implemented a series of agricultural reforms, rebuilding China's infrastructure by means of massive reforestation and reclamation projects, and consolidating imperial power through a series of iron-fisted purges of untrustworthy officials. Though many of the elite literati and scholar-officials were alienated from his government in the process, Hongwu put China back on the track of economic recovery.

After Hongwu' s death, power first passed to his eldest grandson, Jianwen (Chien Wen; r. 1398–1402), before being usurped by Jianwen's uncle Zhu Di, who became the emperor Yongle (Yung-lo; r. 1403–24). China prospered under Yongle, who embarked on an aggressive plan of expansion, conquering Annan (now Vietnam) to the south and pushing into Manchuria to the north and into some territories to the west. Yongle began rebuilding the Great Wall of China, built up along the northern borders, and he began the gradual relocation of the capital from Nanjing in the south to Beijing (Peking) in the north. Here he began building the extensive palace known as the Forbidden City, one of the great architectural accomplishments of the Ming.

Among the most notable achievements of Yongle's expansionist policies were the maritime expeditions of Zheng He (Cheng Ho; c. 1371–c. 1433), who undertook a series of voyages throughout Southeast Asia and into the Indian Ocean. Commanding a spectacular fleet of two hundred or more seafaring junks, the largest and most seaworthy ships of any nation before the Portuguese caravels of the next century, Zheng He expanded China's tributary network from what is now Indonesia to ports along the Indian Ocean, reaching all the way to Malindi, on the coast of East Africa. His feats are still described in heroic terms in the *History of the Ming*, written by Zhang Ting-yu (Chang T'ing-yü; 1672–1755) and his collaborators nearly three centuries later. When Zheng He's voyages ended in 1433, China undertook no further expeditions and limited its official trade to Japan, the Philippines, and parts of Southeast Asia. A reversal of fortunes along the Mongol front to the north, as well as criticism of the high cost of such voyages from the palace eunuchs, led to the decision to withdraw from any maritime ambitions. Hence, the country with the greatest naval power in the world at the time missed out on its chance to share in the age of discovery led by Portugal and Spain at the end of the fifteenth century.

MING POLITICS

After their country had been ruled by outsiders for more than a century, the first Ming emperors aimed to restore its native traditions. Hongwu took extraordinary measures, setting himself at odds with the scholar-officials and literati who feared his repressive policies and despised the secret police he created to sniff out dissent among the court officials. Successive emperors, including Yongle, followed Hongwu's lead in establishing and maintaining a strong central authority. Nonetheless, after Yongle, the palace eunuchs—high-ranking officials entrusted with the innermost private matters of the emperor—began to commandeer more and more influence over imperial policymaking. Leaders of the palace guards, as well as overseers of the tributary networks, the eunuchs eventually became the chief architects of imperial policies and the arbiters of political appointments. Using the Privy Council, created in 1426, as their forum, the eunuchs further alienated the Confucian scholar-officials who were uneasy with the arbitrary measures and central authority of the eunuchs. When the capital was changed from Nanjing (in the commercial and industrial center of China where many scholar-officials and literati were based) to Beijing, some saw the move as a symbol of the distancing of imperial power from Confucian principles. In the seventeenth century, the opposition between scholars and the court came to a head when the imperial authorities, under the direction of the corrupt eunuch Wei Zhongxian (Wei Chung-hsien; r. 1568–1627), shut down Donglin (Tung-lin) University and other private academies for harboring subversive ideas. The last Ming emperor, Chongzhen (Ch'ung-chen; r. 1627–44), denounced the prevailing neo-Confucian philosophy of Wang Yang-ming (1472–1529) because it was seen to reject central authority and promote criticism of the government. As one historian has noted, in contradiction perhaps to its own principles and to the commonplace assumption that it was a state-controlled ideology, Confucianism did serve at times as an intellectual tool against the state.

MING SOCIETY

In the earliest years of the Ming, Hongwu tried to enforce a rigid social hierarchy that some describe as more reminiscent of Mongol than Chinese practices. Under Hongwu's system, occupations were to be determined for life by heredity rather than talent. Beneath the level of the nobles and the elite scholar-officials, society was divided into three major groups—soldiers, artisans, and peasants—each overseen by its own branch of government bureaucracy. For the common people, the base of economic organization was the *li-jia,* a unit of ten families, who were responsible for sharing tax burdens, enforcing domestic order, and looking out for each other's welfare. However, this structure, which proved to be ineffective and subject to abuse, was abandoned before the fifteenth century. As China had increasingly profited from commerce and trade, and as urbanization created the need for new methods of agricultural organization, economic forces proved impossible to suppress. With the increase of people in cities, and the transfer of agricultural lands into the hands of the wealthier farmers, many of China's former tenant farmers or peasants either became itinerant laborers or found their way into more profitable, but illicit, activities, such as illegal mining, piracy, or smuggling—especially in the sixteenth century.

After Zheng He's voyages of the fifteenth century and the arrival of European traders in the sixteenth century, China found itself inextricably linked to the expanding networks of trade involving Africa, the Americas, Europe, India, the

Dragon Teapot, 1465–87
During the Ming dynasty Chinese porcelain production grew to meet increasing foreign demand. This beautifully figured dragon teapot is a good example of the quality of ceramics produced in this period. (The Art Archive / Central Museum Taiwan / Harper Collins Publisher)

Arabic world, and the West Indies. The Portuguese first reached the coast of China in 1514, and though they were soon forced to leave, they were allowed to establish a trading colony at Macao in 1552. It was not long before both the Spanish, from their base in the Philippines, and the Dutch, who were encroaching on the Portuguese trade, had edged their way into the East Asia trade. A thriving urban class of merchants, traders, suppliers, and manufacturers grew up, especially in the port cities. Already by the late fifteenth century but especially throughout the next two centuries, Japanese and European demand for Chinese crafts and goods—including porcelains, lacquerware, luxury silks, tea, paintings, and printed books—expanded dramatically. Foreign demand for porcelains transformed the handicraft production of ceramic objects into modes of industrial production, leading to greater profits. New technologies such as cotton looms, multicolored block printing, and movable type further transformed China's economic and social life. Contact with European traders also brought in yams, tobacco, ground nuts, and corn, leading (as it did in Europe) to a change in Chinese agriculture and diet. Despite China's attempt to control and limit such trade, smuggling and piracy were rife throughout the sixteenth and seventeenth centuries, creating a robust industry in contraband trade. After 1530, when China officially closed its door to trade with Japan, Japanese piracy was so extensive that many areas along the coast were literally under siege; it took many years for the Chinese to restore order.

END OF THE MING

Throughout the fifteenth century China became increasingly vulnerable to attacks along the northern border, not to mention constant harassment along the coast, not only by the Japanese pirates but also by the Dutch traders. Furthermore, Ming rulers after Yongle lost much of their authority as the palace eunuchs came to exercise more and more control over government policies, official appointments, internal affairs, and commerce. Extravagance in the court, as well as the high cost of defense, drained the coffers of the Forbidden City, forcing the royals to impose heavy, unpopular taxes on commerce and agriculture. Moreover, in the rural regions, wealthier landlords began to acquire larger tracts of land at the expense of small farmers. Outside the commercial cities of the port towns and along the Yangtze, exploitation was rife, leading to peasant rebellions as early as 1516. Some of these rebellions, like those in India, were linked to spiritual movements (in this case Buddhist ones), and the government attempts to repress the social unrest only exacerbated the problems. Combined with court intrigue and continuing financial difficulties, the rebellions eventually dragged down the Ming empire. In 1644 the last Ming emperor, Chongzhen, killed himself after Beijing was overrun by rebel forces. Seizing the opportunity, the Manchus to the north allied with the rebels, only to seize Beijing for themselves, inaugurating the Qing dynasty (1644–1911).

FOREIGN INFLUENCES DURING THE MING

Like political life, intellectual and religious life during the Ming was also affected by contact with the outside world. Despite official policy and intentions, even from the beginning the Ming emperors showed significant interest in, and were increasingly influenced by, traditions from outside the borders. During the Yuan dynasty, the Mongol rulers had encouraged the spread of Islam, which took hold especially in the north and in Yunnan, which was governed by a Muslim official from Bukhara. Kublai Khan commissioned a Muslim architect to work on the palace at Khanbalik (the Mongol name for the capital city of Beijing), and mosques appeared in several cities throughout China. The official embassies between Japan and China during the Ming era brought Buddhist monks from Japan to China, and Chinese Buddhist monks to Japan, strengthening intellectual ties between the two countries. Moreover, in both the Yuan and the Ming eras, the Chinese demonstrated a keen interest in Muslim and European sciences, mathematics, and astronomy, a fact that enabled the Italian Jesuit priest Matteo Ricci (1552–1610), with his extensive knowledge of science, to find acceptance among the Chinese.

Ricci was the most important of the Catholic missionaries who arrived in China in the sixteenth century. The first Christian missionaries appeared in East Asia in 1549, when the Spanish priest Francis Xavier (1506–1552) arrived in Japan. In 1583, Ricci arrived at Guangdong (Kwangtung) province, where he and his companion Father Michele Ruggieri (1543–1607) immersed themselves in Chinese culture. Unlike previous Jesuit missionaries, Ricci adopted Chinese dress and customs, gradually winning over the otherwise suspicious Chinese officials. After spending some time in Nanjing, Ricci settled in Beijing, where he was accepted among the court officials and scholars, who were interested in his knowledge of mathematics, astronomy, and other sciences. Ricci also brought along scientific instruments, including a clock, that aroused the curiosity of his hosts.

Ricci was soon followed by other Christian visitors, some of whom were Dominican and Franciscan monks. They had not gone to China simply to share ideas and gather information about the Chinese culture; even Ricci's mission was to convert the Chinese to Christianity. Several missions were founded, especially in the south of China, but the efforts to syncretize Christian beliefs with Chinese traditions met with resistance from Chinese officials and literati, and perhaps especially from the Buddhists in China who were also drawing disciples to their beliefs. Ricci wrote two books defending Christianity, not so much against Confucianism as against Buddhism. While the missionary activities took hold primarily among the less well-educated people, several converts did come from among the scholar-officials, and Ricci himself brought a number of high-ranking officials into the Catholic Church. It is estimated that there were in all about 150,000 converts by the end of the Ming dynasty—a fairly small percentage of the total population of about 130 million people. After Ricci's death, in 1610, the Vatican discouraged "accommodation" to Chinese ways, and what was once a cautious but mutually respectful encounter became increasingly confrontational.

CONFUCIANISM DURING THE MING

As noted above, Confucian scholar-officials had an uneasy relationship with their government leaders during the Ming dynasty. In the early years of the dynasty, Hongwu's distrust of the literati and his frequent purges of dissenting officials led many to avoid government service altogether, putting them at odds with their

Confucian principles of allegiance to the state. Hongwu went so far as to abolish the examination system in order to fill his bureaucracy with officials more to his liking. In 1382 the examinations were revived, but some complained that the new system lowered the bar, reducing the intellectual autonomy of the examinees and focusing on rote memorization of a standard set of texts in an attempt to draw from a wider base of potential civil service officials. The Confucian canon, which had been modified by the Song era philosopher Zhu Xi (Chu Hsi; 1130–1200), was the official doctrine of the state (and would be until the end of the Qing dynasty in the early twentieth century), but it was not without its critics. Zhu Xi's philosophy emphasized the importance of discovering the underlying principles of things, by studying not only the things themselves but also the classics. By the time of the Ming, Zhu Xi's work itself had become part of the standardized canon of required texts, and many Confucian scholars, such as Wang Yang-ming and his more radical student Li Zhi (Li Chih; 1527–1602), believed it was time to wrest themselves free, at least in part, from what had become a standard, overly routine, system of thought. Thus, in an atmosphere of vigorous commentary and debate many scholars reexamined the various tenets and interpretations of Confucianism, exploring its relationship to Buddhism, Daoism (Taoism), and even Christianity. Wang Yang-ming, who criticized Zhu Xi for overemphasizing the value of books, argued for a more inward-looking form of Confucianism; he believed that the cultivation of the simple, essential goodness within the self would do far more good for society than would arcane scholarship. Li Zhi further elaborated his master's ideas in his notion of the "child-mind"—a state of mind achieved only by stripping away all of what we learn and acquire from experience, education, and custom. In a radical move that created controversy among his contemporaries, Li Zhi argued that the basic premises of neo-Confucianism were founded on a corrupt understanding of the relationship between innate ideas and the external world.

The debates over Confucian or neo-Confucian ideas in China had an impact on Japan, which during the fifteenth and sixteenth centuries was under the control of various military leaders known as *shoguns.* Japanese thinkers such as Hayashi Razan (1583–1657) followed Fujiwara Seika (1561–1619), the founder of neo-Confucianism in Japan. The Japanese, especially the shoguns of the later Tokugawa era (1603–1867), were drawn to neo-Confucianism's emphasis on history and tradition, but especially to its call for filial piety and civic loyalty. Hayashi Razan was instrumental in adapting the Chinese philosophy to Japanese needs.

CHINESE LITERATURE OF THE MING

The economic changes that took place during the Ming dynasty led to the rise of a class of wealthy commercial and industrial owners and a working class in the cities,

Mandarins, Fifteenth Century
Two Mandarins of the Ming dynasty court are shown here in a fifteenth-century silk painting. (The Art Archive / Topkapi Museum Istanbul / Dagli Orti)

a group of large landowners and a peasant labor force in the countryside. Prosperity did not necessarily trickle down to the lower ranks of society, but it did spread sufficiently to foster a proliferation of arts, scholarship, and literature that some refer to as a second renaissance in China. With the restoration of Chinese leadership and the rise of an increasingly literate urban middle class who could afford to buy books and go to plays, the impetus for popular vernacular works accelerated, especially in the sixteenth century. Schools and libraries spread throughout the growing cities, and, as in Europe, new technologies in printing, including the development of a metal movable type, brought to the marketplace relatively inexpensive editions of the classics, as well as popular works, such encyclopedias, songs, collections of poetry (especially classical and Tang dynasty poetry), and collections of short stories. In addition, new genres such as the novel developed, and, as in Spain and England, China saw the flowering of theater.

Continuing a trend that began as far back as the Jin (Jurchen) era (1115–1234), the Ming became the great age of popular vernacular literature. Encyclopedias on topics such as mining, agriculture, botany, geography, music, and medicine appeared, as did some of the first dictionaries, some of them aimed at normalizing and reducing the number of signs for Chinese characters. Short-story collections contained satirical, supernatural, romantic, and erotic tales. Among these collections, two from the late Ming stand out: *Stories, Old and New* (1620–27), by Feng Menglong (1574–1646), and *Striking the Table in Amazement at the Wonders* (1628), by Ling Mengchu (1580–1644). Many of the stories in these collections give a realistic picture of the everyday lives of townspeople.

Drama, especially long and elaborate plays using song, music, and dance to highlight emotional states of characters, became very popular during the Ming. Of the great dramas, *The Peony Pavilion,* by Tang Xianzhu (1550–1616), is one of the great masterpieces of the era. With a cast of more than one hundred characters, it begins by telling of Du Li-niang, a young woman who dies of a broken heart when she learns that her marriage to Liu Meng-mei, a student, was only the figment of her imaginary dreams. Then, for his part, Liu Meng-mei, after happening upon a painting of Du Li-niang that she left behind, falls in love with the image in the painting. Because their reciprocal love is so strong, the two young people are united first in spirit and then in reality as Du Li-niang miraculously comes back to life. After overcoming a series of obstacles involving political intrigue and rebellion, the two are married and so fulfill their hearts' desire. One of the most popular of all Chinese plays, *The Peony Pavilion* has inspired numerous stories, operas, woodblock prints, comics, and films.

Among the novels written during the Ming dynasty, *Journey to the West* (1570), by Wu Chengen (c. 1500–c. 1582), stands out as one of the greatest of all Chinese works of fiction. Many of the late Yuan and Ming dynasty novels were drawn from familiar stories that had acquired several layers of invention and ornament over time. Also translated as *Monkey,* Wu Chengen's novel is based on the travels of the seventh-century Buddhist monk Xuanzang (Hsüan Tsang), known as Tripitaka, who undertook a pilgrimage to India. A comic fantasy, the story recounts the Quixote-like adventures of the Xuanzang and his companion pilgrims, including the Monkey king, Sun Wukong, who is endowed with supernatural powers. Other

TIME AND PLACE

The Forbidden City

In 1406, the Ming emperor Yongle decided to move the seat of imperial power from the capital at Nanjing, in the Yangtze River valley in southern China, to the older northern capital of Beijing (Peking). Here, near the site of the Yuan (Mongol) capital of Khanbalak, Yongle ordered the construction of Gu Gong, or "Forbidden City." So named because only those with official duties and invitations could enter there, the Forbidden City reaches to an area of over seventy-four hectares (2.35 million square feet), making it the largest palace compound in the world both then and now. With its various levels of interior buildings and apartments, the Forbidden City became a symbol of the austere power and mystery of the Ming and later Qing emperors, who ruled over China with a "mandate from heaven."

Construction of the imperial palace took nearly fourteen years, and the move of the capital was not completed until 1450. This move had important practical, as well as symbolic, consequences, at once positioning the

Zhu Bang*, The Forbidden City, *1368–1644. *This silk painting depicts the famous city founded by the first Ming emperor that became home to all subsequent Chinese emperors into the twentieth century. (The Art Archive / The Art Archive)*

important novels of the Ming include *The Plum in the Golden Vase,* whose anonymous author is often called the Scoffing Scholar of Lanling, and *The Tale of the Water Margin,* a loosely structured novel recounting the escapades of several bandits. The latter was the most popular novel of its own time. With varying emphasis, these novels show a greater sense of plot development, realistic character portrayal, and psychological exploration than earlier works of Chinese fiction.

TIME AND PLACE

The Forbidden City *continued*

capital closer to the troubled northern border, where the emperor could oversee the empire's defense, but also removing the emperor from the culturally and commercially rich Yangtze Valley. By some reports, the construction involved nearly one million laborers, including a hundred thousand artisans, who worked on the elaborate wood carvings and ornamental designs, sculptures, and inscriptions found everywhere throughout the palace. The palace complex was built according to Yongle's plans and later modified under the emperor Jia Jing (r. 1522–66). Guided by *feng shui,* a system whereby architectural spaces are patterned to reflect the balance and order of the cosmos, the Forbidden City is aligned with the position of the North Star and laid out on a rectangular grid along true north–south, east–west axes, with massive and ornate gates on each side and towers at the four corners. In China, the number nine symbolizes perfection and imperial power, so throughout the palace patterns of nine are repeated, from the number of rooms (9,999) and courtyards (nine) to the nine dragons on each of the three ornate screens and the clusters of nine studs or nails used throughout the wood, marble, and tile construction. Yellow, the color associated with the royal family, is also a dominant feature, with bright yellow tiles on all of the roofs except for the roof of the Imperial Library, which has black tiles, representing water.

The emperor and his imperial household, including concubines, eunuchs, and servants, lived and worked in the Inner Court (the northern section), in such apartments as the Palace of Heavenly Purity and the Hall of Mental Cultivation, where routine business was also conducted. Important official business, ceremonies, and festivals were held in the Outer Court (the southern section), consisting of the three main Halls of State: the Hall of Supreme Harmony, the Hall of Middle Harmony, and the Hall of Preserving Harmony. From the time of Yongle, the Forbidden City was home to fourteen Ming and ten Qing dynasty emperors, serving as the imperial palace until 1924, when the last emperor of the Qing dynasty fell from power. It is now the Palace Museum, itself a monument of Chinese architecture, and the repository of many cultural treasures, paintings, sculptures, carvings, lacquerware, and books from the Ming and Qing dynasties.

WWW For more information about the culture and context of China in the Early Modern Period, see *World Literature Online* at bedfordstmartins.com/worldlit.

~ Wu Chengen

c. 1500–c. 1582

SHEE-yoh JEE

Translated literally, the title of the epic Chinese novel ***Xiyou ji*** (*Hsi Yu Chi*) is *Journey to the West;* it is an imaginative account of a religious pilgrimage to secure the Buddhist scriptures from India and bring them back to China. Translator Arthur Waley's title *Monkey* represents the fantasy side of the story, which concerns the exploits of the monkey-king Sun Wukung, a superhero whose extraordinary powers make the journey possible. *Monkey* combines a serious religious allegory with extravagant adventure stories and comic satire. The historical journey on which it is based took place in the seventh century and inspired numerous legends, folktales, and myths that circulated orally for several centuries until they were turned into a novel, probably by **Wu Chengen**, in the sixteenth century. *Monkey* is as popular and well known in Asia as Homer's *Iliad* and *Odyssey* are in the West. The story has been retold in novels, plays, operas, manga (comic books), and animé (animated films).

woo-chung-EN

Wu Chengen. The folk process that led to the creation of *Monkey* was similar to that which produced Homer's *Iliad* many centuries after the Trojan War. The role of the author in the final text has been similarly controversial. Some consider Wu Chengen to be a convenient name for a committee of writers who collected and assembled the oral materials into a single written text. Others give Wu more credit for shaping the story, giving it a consistent authorial voice, and placing Monkey (rather than Tripitaka, the historical monk who brought the scriptures back to China) as the heroic central figure in the tale.

Little is known of Wu Chengen. A native of Huaian in Jiangsu (Kiangsu) province, about a hundred miles north of Nanjing, Wu seems to have taken up writing after retiring from a career as a district magistrate. Some of his poems survive in anthologies of verse from the Ming period. He also wrote stories that, like the poems, were in the accepted neoclassical style of the time, imitating the work of the Tang poets (618–907 C.E.). Wu turned away from traditional literary conventions to write, in the vernacular, his masterwork *Monkey,* one of three great Chinese novels of the sixteenth century. The other two novels were *Xiyang ji* (*Hsi Yang Chi; Adventures to the Western Ocean*), a tale about a fifteenth-century explorer by Luo Maodeng (Lo Mao-teng), and the anonymous *Jinping Mei* (*Chin Ping Mei; The Golden Lotus*), a novel of contemporary life.

The Pilgrimage. The central story of the novel, the pilgrimage of the monk **Xuanzang** (Hsüan Tsang), is grounded in historical fact. The actual journey from China to India to bring back the Buddhist scriptures took seventeen years, from 629 to 645. In his own account of his travels, Xuanzang described his difficulties starting his journey, when he was forbidden to leave China; his years in India, where he learned Sanskrit and became a Buddhist scholar; and his triumphant return with the scrip-

shwen-DZAHNG

T'ang Yin, *Dreaming of Immortality in a Thatched Cottage* (left side of scroll), 1470–1523
A man contemplates the vastness of the universe in this beautifully rendered misty mountain landscape. (The Art Archive / Freer Gallery of Art / The Art Archive)

tures to become a favorite of the Chinese emperor, who conferred the name Tripitaka (literally, three baskets) on the monk, indicative of the three parts of the Buddhist scriptures. In the popular culture, Tripitaka's story was expanded with folk tales, animal fables, and myths, and many literary works drawing on these materials and describing his journey have been written, both before and after *Xiyou ji*.

Historically, the journey reflects the growing Chinese interest in the territories to the west during the Tang period. The important trade routes to India began at Chang'an, the capital of the dynasty and the largest city in the world at the time. Xuanzang's journey also represents an important period in Chinese Buddhism. After he returned to China, the Tang emperor Taizong (Tai-tsung; r. 646–49), who traced his ancestry back to **Laozi** (Lao Tzu), became a proponent of Buddhism.

low-DZUH

Monkey. Although he is the hero of the pilgrimage story, his disciple, Monkey, has the dominant role in Wu's novel. Monkey's story opens the novel, and he is the one who overcomes the obstacles to make the pilgrimage successful. In the original novel, the first seven chapters describe Monkey's origins, how he achieves his power, and how he misbehaves and ends up imprisoned in a mountain. The next five chapters introduce Xuanzang, giving a mythological account of his birth and childhood not unlike the story of Moses in certain details, and describing how he comes by his mission to secure the scriptures from India. The rest of the novel's one hundred chapters describe the eighty-one tests Tripitaka undergoes on the journey and his final success in obtaining the scriptures. Nearly all

WWW For links to more information about Wu Chengen and a quiz on *Monkey,* see *World Literature Online* at bedfordstmartins.com/worldlit.

of the tests involve overcoming monsters or dragons, and Monkey, with his quick wits and magical needle, is a match for even the most powerful dragons.

The combination of animal fable, physical comedy, superhero romance, political and religious **SATIRE**, and spiritual journey gives rich variety in incident and mood to the story. But *Monkey* is also fairly repetitive. After the first four or five encounters with dragons, all dragons may begin to look alike to a Western reader. To the Chinese reader, however, each of the eighty-one obstacles Tripitaka and Monkey must overcome adds a new allegorical dimension to the spiritual achievement that is unfolding. Although it is hard for a Western reader to distinguish between the dragons, and comprehend the significance of each one, the basic **ALLEGORY**[1] is clear. Tripitaka, mythical hero and potential saint (**bodhisattva**), is a kind of everyman. Naive, even simple-minded, he trusts nearly everyone he meets, and this trust gets him into trouble. He needs the help of his disciples, especially Monkey—a figure related to Hanuman, the Indian monkey-god—who represents human genius in this allegory. Monkey's cleverness is essential for getting the pilgrims out of one scrape after another. But it also occasionally gets them into trouble, for Monkey is proud and impetuous. He will take on anyone, even the gods. Only when his intelligence is disciplined, reined in by the cap given to Tripitaka by the bodhisattva **Kuan-yin**, does Monkey become a useful servant to the monk. The other two disciples, Pigsy, who represents the gross physical appetites, and Sandy, a faithful though sometimes clumsy disciple whose allegorical significance is unclear, make up the unusual group of pilgrims who together manage to secure the scriptures from India.

boh-dih-SAHT-vuh

kwahn-YIN

Monkey, a trickster who challenges all who oppose him, is related to figures such as Coyote in Native American folklore and Prometheus[2] in classical myth. He is not cowed by arbitrary power. He seeks out challenges, for he is, as he boastfully reminds others, "The Great Sage, Equal of Heaven." In his arrogance and self-confidence, he is a soul-brother to such overreaching tricksters of the Renaissance as Don Juan and Faustus. Like them, he enjoys challenges, confrontations, and combats, for in such tests of strength, he can prove his intelligence and power. But his exploits do not end in damnation. Constrained by the cap given to Tripitaka by Kuan-yin, Monkey's exploits serve his master and in the end he is rewarded with sainthood.

In its melding of the spiritual and the worldly, *Monkey* has some of the flavor of **CHIVALRIC ROMANCES** where fabulous adventures take on spiritual significance. But the realm of the gods in *Monkey* is more like

[1] **allegory:** A narrative in which the characters, settings, and episodes are contrived to stand for another order of persons, places, and events. Traditionally, most allegories used such signifying stories to correlate to spiritual concepts, as in Dante's *Divine Comedy* (1321) or John Bunyan's *The Pilgrim's Progress* (1678). Some later allegories, such as George Orwell's *Animal Farm* (1946), an allegory of the Bolshevik revolution in Russia, connect their stories to political, historical, or sociological subjects.

[2] **Prometheus:** In Greek mythology, Prometheus stole fire from the gods and gave it to mankind, thus enabling human knowledge and artistry. Zeus punished Prometheus by chaining him to a rock.

an Olympian bureaucracy than a spiritual ideal; they are forever setting down rules and enforcing trivial decrees. Spiritual enlightenment does not seem to be a result of becoming familiar with this divine bureaucracy or learning its rules. The gods are as much objects of satire as they are spiritual guides. Enlightenment is rather a product of the journey itself. Tripitaka and his disciples all grow spiritually as they help each other overcome the obstacles in their path.

Comic Epic. The task that the pilgrims undertake is an EPIC one, for the story of their journey is a FOUNDING MYTH,[3] describing the establishment of Buddhism in China. Monkey's magical powers of shape-changing and traveling between heaven and earth are also those of the supernatural heroes of the epic. At the same time that he and his companions are fabulous and funny, they are also characters who learn and grow through their experiences. This unusual mixture in *Monkey* of the serious and the comic, of epic and novel, may bring us closer to something that might be described as comic epic[4] than does Henry Fielding's *Joseph Andrews.* For all their superhuman powers, Wu's heroes—Monkey, Pigsy, and Sandy—are less than perfect. To merit their role in the spiritual task they have undertaken and their ultimate rewards, they too must grow during the journey, like their leader, the "everyman" Tripitaka.

Monkey is unique in its combination of beauty with absurdity, of profundity with nonsense. Folk-lore, allegory, religion, history, anti-bureaucratic satire, and pure poetry – such are the diverse elements out of which the book is compounded.

– ARTHUR WALEY, scholar, translator, 1942

■ CONNECTIONS

Homer, *The Odyssey,* Book 1; Miguel de Cervantes Saavedra, *Don Quixote,* p. 262. The quest is one of the most common archetypes in literature, inspiring works as different as epics and road novels. The fabulous adventures encountered by Odysseus – at Circe's island, for example, or with the Cyclops – are tests of his heroism and leadership. In quest novels like *Don Quixote,* the fabulous gets more realistic treatment and Quixote must learn to distinguish between the giants he imagines and the windmills of reality. Consider the relation between the fantastic and realistic in *Monkey.* Is it more like the epic tasks faced by Odysseus or the illusions that Quixote harbors? Is Tripitaka an Odysseus or a Quixote? Is there a Sancho Panza in *Monkey*?

Virgil, *The Aeneid,* Book 1; John Milton, *Paradise Lost,* p. 575. Epic poems often relate founding myths that explain the origins and beliefs of particular cultures. *The Aeneid,* for example, traces Rome back to Troy by describing Aeneas's role in Rome's founding. Milton goes even further back to trace the founding of the human race in the story of Adam and Eve. *Monkey* is also a founding story; it explains how China became a Buddhist nation. What qualities does each of these founding stories celebrate? What differences do the stories suggest between the cultures established in each case?

[3] **founding myth:** A legend that explains how a particular nation or culture came to be, such as Virgil's *Aeneid,* which describes the founding of Rome. Many epic poems, sometimes called national epics, tell such founding stories.

[4] **comic epic:** One of the earliest English novelists, Henry Fielding (1707–1754) characterized the kind of literature he was creating in his novel *Joseph Andrews* (1742) as "a comic epic in prose," thus distinguishing it from serious or tragic epic poems that treated noble characters and elevated subjects. His novel was about common people and everyday events.

***Arabian Nights,* Book 2; Gabriel García Marquez, "The Very Old Man with Enormous Wings," Book 6.** Tales of fantasy, like those in the *Arabian Nights* or in contemporary magical realism, describe improbable, miraculous, or imaginary creatures and events. Compare the jinns from the *Arabian Nights,* García Marquez's angel, and some of the fabulous creatures—perhaps Monkey himself—from *Monkey.* Are they all allegorical or symbolic? How does "reality" differ in the three works?

■ FURTHER RESEARCH

Translations

Waley, Arthur. *Monkey.* 1942.

Yu, Anthony. *Journey to the West.* 1983. A complete English translation.

Commentary

Dudbridge, Glen. *The "Hsi-yu chi": A Study of Antecedents to the Sixteenth-Century Chinese Novel.* 1970.

Hanan, Patrick. *The Chinese Vernacular Story.* 1981.

Hsia, C. T. *The Classic Chinese Novel: A Critical Introduction.* 1968.

Plaks, Andrew H., ed. *Chinese Narrative: Critical and Theoretical Essays.* 1977.

■ PRONUNCIATION

Amitabha: uh-mih-TAH-buh
bodhisattva: boh-dih-SAHT-vuh
Chang Liang: chahng-LYAHNG, -lee-AHNG
Erh-Lang: ar-LAHNG
Hsiao: SHOW
Kasyapa: KUSH-yuh-puh
Kuan-yin: kwahn-YIN
Laozi: low-DZUH
Manjuśrī: mun-joo-SHREE
Sakyamuni: shahk-yuh-MOO-nee
Vaiśravana: vigh-SHRUH-vuh-nuh
Vajrapani: vuj-ruh-PAH-nee
Wu Chengen: woo-chung-EN
Xiyou ji: SHEE-yoh JEE
Xuanzang: shwen-DZAHNG

Monkey

Translated by Arthur Waley

Chapter 8

One day when Buddha had been preaching to the Bodhisattvas and Arhats,[1] he said at the end of his sermon, "I have been noticing that there is a lot of difference in the inhabitants of the Four Continents of the universe. Those in the Eastern Continent are respectful, peaceable and cheerful; those of the Northern are somewhat prone to take life, but they are so dumb, lethargic and stupid that they don't do much harm. In our Western Continent, there is no greed or slaughter; we nurture our humours and hide our magic, and although we have no supreme illuminates everyone is safe against the assaults of age. But in Jumbudvīpa, the Southern Continent, they are greedy, lustful, murderous, and quarrelsome. I wonder whether a knowledge of the True Scriptures would not cause some improvement in them?"

"Do you yourself possess those scriptures?" asked the Bodhisattvas.

"Yes, three baskets of them," said Buddha. "One contains the Vinaya, which speaks of heaven, one contains the Saastras, which tell of Earth, one contains the Sutras, which save the damned. The whole is divided into thirty-five divisions written on 15,144 rolls. These are the path to perfection, the only gate to virtue. I would send it straight to the people of the common world; but they are so stupid that they would only jeer at the truth, misunderstand the meaning of my Law, and scorn the true sect of Yoga. I wish I knew of a holy one who would go to the eastern land and find a believer who could be sent over hill and dale, all the way from China to this

---

Monkey. Although the nominal subject of Wu Chengen's novel is the journey of the monk Xuanzang in the seventh century to secure the Buddhist scriptures and bring them back to China, the figure who centers the novel is not the monk but rather the monkey-king, Sun Wukung, whose magical powers make the mission a success. Arthur Waley, whose very readable translation and abridgment of the novel is the source of the selection presented here, acknowledged Sun Wukung's importance by titling his version *Monkey.* This selection omits the early chapters, which relate the story of Monkey's birth, his challenge to the gods, and his punishment by being imprisoned under a mountain. The focus here is on the pilgrimage itself as the monk Tripitaka and his three disciples—the Monkey-king, a rebellious clever rogue; Pigsy, a self-indulgent glutton enamored of food and women; and Sandy, a faithful but unimaginative follower—confront test after test on the road to India. Included are only a few of the eighty-one challenges that enable the pilgrims to grow and earn their final sanctification as they successfully reach India and return the scriptures to China.

A more literal translation of the whole work is available in Anthony Yu's translation, *Journey to the West* (1983). All notes are the editors'.

---

[1] **Bodhisattvas and Arhats:** Bodhisattvas are Buddhist saints who forgo Nirvana to remain on earth and save others. The Bodhisattva Kuan-yin is one of the most important of these saviors in the pantheon of Chinese Buddhism. An Arhat is one who has reached the end of the fourfold way and attained Nirvana.

place. I would give him the scriptures to take back to China, and he would explain them to the people and change their hearts. That would be an untold blessing. Is any of you willing to go?"

Kuan-yin came up to the lotus platform, bowed three times to the Buddha, and said, "I don't know if I can make a success of it, but I should like to go to the eastern land and find someone to fetch the scriptures."

"You're just the person," said Buddha. "A venerable Bodhisattva with great sanctity and magic powers—we couldn't do better."

"Have you any particular instructions?" asked Kuan-yin.

"I want you," said Buddha, "to make a thorough study of the air at a fairly low altitude, not up among the stars. Keep an eye on the mountains and rivers, and make careful note of the distances and travelling-stages, so that you may assist the scripture-seeker. But it is going to be a very difficult journey for him, and I have five talismans which I should like you to give him." An embroidered cassock and a priest's staff with nine rings were then fetched, and he said to Kuan-yin, "When he feels his courage failing him on the road, let him put on this cassock. If he carries this staff, he will never meet with poison or violence. And here," Buddha continued, "I have three fillets. They are all alike, but their use is different; each has its separate spell. If on his journey the pilgrim meets with any ogre of superlative powers, you must attempt to convert this ogre and make him the scripture-seeker's disciple. If he resists, the pilgrim is to put one of these fillets on his head, reciting the spell that belongs to it. Whereupon the ogre's eyes will swell and his head ache so excruciatingly that he will feel as if his brains were bursting, and he will be only too glad to embrace our Faith."

Kuan-yin bowed and called upon her disciple Hui-yen to follow her. He carried a great iron cudgel, weighing a thousand pounds, and hovered round the Bodhisattva, acting as her bodyguard. Kuan-yin made the cassock into a bundle and put it on his back. She took the fillets herself and held the nine-ringed staff in her hand. When they came to the Weak Waters, which form the boundary of the River of Sand, Kuan-yin said, "My disciple, this place is very difficult going. The scripture-seeker will be a man of common mortal birth. How will he get across?"

"Tell me first," said Hui-yen, "how wide is the River of Sands?"

The Bodhisattva was examining the river, when suddenly there was a great splash, and out jumped the most hideous monster imaginable. Holding a staff in its hand this creature made straight for the Bodhisattva.

"Halt!" cried Hui-yen, fending off the monster with his iron cudgel; and there on the shore of the River of Sands a fearful combat began. Up and down the shore the battle moved, and they had fought twenty or thirty bouts without reaching a decision, when the monster halted with his iron cudgel held up in front of him and said, "What priest are you, and where do you come from, that you dare resist me?"

"I am Prince Moksha, second son of Vaiśravana, now called Hui-yen.[2] I am now

[2] **Hui-yen:** The guardian spirit of the north; his name means "he who has heard everything."

defending my superior on the journey to China, where we hope to find one who will come and fetch scriptures. What creature are you who dare to bar our path?"

"Ah," said the monster, suddenly remembering, "didn't I use to see you in Kuan-yin's bamboo-grove, practising austerities? What have you done with the Bodhisattva?"

"You didn't realize then that it was she on the bank?" said Hui-yen.

The creature was aghast; he lowered his weapon and allowed himself to be brought to Kuan-yin. "Bodhisattva, forgive my crime," he cried, bowing profoundly. "I am not the monster that I seem, but was a marshal of the hosts of Heaven, charged to wait upon the Jade Emperor when he rode in his Phoenix Chariot. But at a heavenly banquet I had the misfortune to break a crystal dish. By the Emperor's orders I received 800 lashes, and was banished to the world below, transformed into my present hideous shape. He sends flying swords that stab my breast and sides one day in every seven. I get nothing to eat, and every few days hunger drives me to come out and look for some traveller, on whose flesh I feed. Little did I think today that the traveller whom I was blindly attacking was none other than the Bodhisattva."

"It was for sinning in Heaven," said Kuan-yin, "that you were banished. Yet here you are adding sin to sin, slaying living creatures. I am on my way to China to look for a scripture-seeker. Why don't you join our sect, reform your ways, become a disciple of the scripture-seeker, and go with him to India to fetch the scriptures? I'll see to it that the flying swords stop piercing you. If the expedition is a success, you will have expiated your crime and be allowed to go back to your old employment in Heaven. Doesn't that idea please you?"

"I would gladly embrace the Faith," said the creature, "but there is something I must first confess. I have since I came here devoured countless human beings. Pilgrims have come this way several times, and I ate them all. The heads I threw into the River of Flowing Sands, and they sank to the bottom (such is the nature of this river that not even a goosefeather will float upon it). But there were nine skulls that remained floating on the water and would not sink. Seeing that these skulls behaved so strangely, I moored them with a rope, and in leisure moments drew them in and sported with them. If this is known, it seems likely that future pilgrims will not care to come this way, and my chances of salvation are lost."

"Not come this way! Nonsense!" said the Bodhisattva. "You can take the skulls and hang them round your neck. When the scripture-seeker arrives, a good use will be found for them." The monster accordingly took his vows and was received into the Faith, receiving the name of Sandy Priest. Having escorted Kuan-yin across the river, he went back and devoted himself to penances and purifications, never again taking life, but watching all the while for the pilgrim who was destined to come.

So the Bodhisattva parted with him and went on with Hui-yen towards China. After a while they came to a high mountain, from which there came an extremely bad smell. They had just decided to ride high over it on their clouds when there came a mad blast of wind, and there suddenly appeared before them a monster of hideous appearance. His lips curled and drooped like withered lotus leaves, his ears flapped like rush-work fans. He had tusks sharp as awls and a snout like the nozzle of a bellows. He rushed straight at Kuan-yin, striking at her with a muck-rake. Hui-yen warded off the blow, crying, "Foul fiend, mend your manners, and look out for my cudgel."

"This priest," cried the monster, "little knows what he is up against. Look out for my rake!"

And at the foot of the mountain the two of them had a great fight. Just when it was at its best, Kuan-yin who was watching in the sky above threw down some lotus flowers which fell just between the cudgel and the rake.

"What sort of a priest are you?" the monster cried, "that you dare play upon me the trick of the 'flower in the eye.'"

"Grovelling, low-born monster," said Hui-yen, "I am a disciple of the Bodhisattva Kuan-yin, and it was she who threw down these flowers. Didn't you recognize her?"

"You don't mean it!" said he. "The great Bodhisattva, the one that saves us from the three calamities and eight disasters?"

"Whom else should I mean?" said Hui-yen.

The monster dropped his rake and bowed low. "Old chap," he said, "where is the Bodhisattva? I wish you'd introduce me."

Hui-yen looked up and pointed. "There she is all right," he said.

The monster kowtowed skyward, crying in a loud voice, "Forgive me, Bodhisattva, forgive me."

Kuan-yin lowered her cloud and came up to him, saying, "How dare a filthy old pig-spirit like you attempt to bar my path?"

"I am not really a pig at all," he said. "I was a marshal of the hosts of Heaven, but one day I got a bit drunk and misbehaved with the Goddess of the Moon. For this the Jade Emperor had me soundly thrashed and banished me to the world below. When the time came for my next incarnation, I lost my way and got by mistake into the belly of an old mother pig, which accounts for what I look like now. I spend my time eating people, that I own. But I never noticed it was you I had run into. Save me, save me!"

"There is a proverb," said the Bodhisattva, "which runs: 'Works of damnation cannot lead to salvation.' Having been banished from Heaven because you broke its laws, you have not repented, but live on human flesh. Are you not inviting a double punishment for both your crimes?"

"Salvation indeed!" cried the monster. "If I followed your advice, what should I live on? On the wind, I suppose. There's another proverb which says, 'If the Government gets hold of you they'll flog you to death; if the Buddhists get hold of you they'll starve you to death.' Go away! I see I shall get on much better by catching a family of travellers now and then, and eating their daughter if she's buxom and tasty, no matter whether that's two crimes, three crimes, or a thousand crimes."

"There is a saying," the Bodhisattva replied, "'Heaven helps those who mean well.' If you give up your evil ways, you may be sure you won't lack nourishment. There are five crops in the world; so there is no need to starve. Why should you feed on human flesh?"

The monster was like one who wakes from a dream. "I should like to reform," he said, "but 'Him no prayer can help who has sinned against Heaven.'"

"Here's a chance for you," said Kuan-yin. "We are on our way to China to look for a seeker of scriptures. If you were to become his disciple and go with him to India, you would wipe out all your old sin."

"I will, I will," blurted out the creature. All that remained now was to tonsure him and administer the vows, and it was agreed that he should be known in religion as Pigsy. He was told to fast, do penance, and keep all the while on the watch for the destined pilgrim.

Proceeding on their way Kuan-yin and Hui-yen were presently accosted by a dragon. "What dragon are you?" asked the Bodhisattva, "and what have you done that you should be cast adrift here?"

"I am a son of the Dragon King of the Western Ocean," the dragon said. "I inadvertently set fire to his palace and some of his Pearls of Wisdom were burnt. My father insisted that I had done it on purpose and accused me in the Courts of Heaven of attempted rebellion. The Jade Emperor hung me up here in the sky, had me given 300 cuts of the lash, and in a few days I am to be executed. Can you do anything to help me?"

Kuan-yin promptly went up to Heaven, secured an interview with the Jade Emperor, and begged that the dragon might be forgiven, on condition that he allowed himself to be ridden upon by the pilgrim who was going to India to bring back the true scriptures. The request was granted, and the Bodhisattva ordered the little dragon to go down into a deep canyon and await the arrival of the pilgrim. It was then to change into a white horse and carry him to India.

Kuan-yin and Hui-yen had not gone far on their way to China when they suddenly saw great shafts of golden light and many wreaths of magic vapour.

"That is the Mountain of the Five Elements," said Hui-yen. "I can see the imprint of Buddha's seal upon it."

"Is not that the mountain," said Kuan-yin, "under which is imprisoned the Sage Equal of Heaven, who upset the Peach Banquet and ran amok in the halls of Heaven?"

"Very true," said Hui-yen.

They alighted on the mountain and examined the seal, which was the six-syllable spell OM MANI PADME HUM. Kuan-yin sighed a deep sigh, and recited the following poem:

"Long ago performed in vain prodigies of valour.
In his blackness of heart he upset the Heavenly Peach Banquet;
In mad rashness he dared to rob the Patriarch of Tao.
A hundred thousand heavenly troops could not overcome him;
He terrorized the realm of Heaven throughout its nine spheres.
At last in Buddha Tathagata Monkey met his match.
Will he ever again be set at large and win back his renown?"

"Who is it," a voice came from inside the mountain, "who recites verses that tell of my misdoings?"

Kuan-yin came down towards the place from which the voice seemed to come, and at the foot of a cliff found the guardian deities of the place, who after welcoming the Bodhisattva, led her to where Monkey was imprisoned. He was pent in a kind of stone box, and though he could speak he could not move hand or foot.

"Monkey," cried the Bodhisattva, "do you know me or not?"

He peered through a chink with his steely, fiery eyes and cried aloud, "How should I not know you? You are she of Potalaka, the Saviour Kuan-yin. To what do I owe this pleasure? Here where days and years are one to me, no friend or acquaintance has ever come to seek me out. Where, pray, do you come from?"

"Buddha sent me," said she, "to China, to look for one who will come to India and fetch the scriptures, and as this place is on the way, I took the opportunity of calling upon you."

"Buddha tricked me," said Monkey, "and imprisoned me under this mountain five hundred years ago, and here I have been ever since. I entreat you to use your powers to rescue me."

"Your sins were very great," she said, "and I am by no means confident that if you get out you would not at once get into trouble again."

"No," said Monkey, "I have repented, and now want only to embrace the Faith and devote myself to good works."

"Very well, then," said the Bodhisattva, delighted. "Wait while I go to the land of T'ang and find my scripture-seeker. He shall deliver you. You shall be his disciple and embrace our Faith."

"With all my heart," said Monkey.

"In that case," said Kuan-yin, "you will have to have a name in religion."

"I've got one," said Monkey. "I am called Aware-of-Vacuity."

"In that case," said Kuan-yin, "there is nothing more I need tell you at present. I must be going."

They left Monkey and went on eastwards. In a few days they reached the land of T'ang, and soon came to the city of Ch'ang-an,[3] where they changed themselves into shabby wandering priests, and coming to the shrine of a local deity in one of the main streets, they went straight in. The deity and his attendant demons recognized Kuan-yin at once, despite her disguise, and welcomed her with a great flurry of bowings and scrapings. Then he sent word to the god of the Municipal Shrine, and all the temples in Ch'ang-an, informing the gods that the Bodhisattva had arrived. Presently they all came tramping along, begging to be excused for not having come to meet her. "This must not get out," she said. "I am here completely incognito. I have come by Buddha's orders to look for someone to bring the scriptures from India. I should like to put up for a day or two in one of your temples, and as soon as I have found my pilgrim I shall leave."

The gods then all retired to their temples, Kuan-yin and Hui-yen putting up for the time being in the shrine of the Municipal God, where they passed for a couple of ordinary priests.

If you do not know whom they found to fetch scriptures, you must listen to what is told in the next chapter. . . .

[3] **Ch'ang-an:** Chang'an, ancient city at the site of the present-day Xian in Shaanxi province. At the time of the Tang dynasty (618–907), it was the cultural capital of East Asia and the largest city in the world.

FROM

Chapter 12

[. . .] Meanwhile the Bodhisattva Kuan-yin had been looking everywhere in Ch'ang-an for a priest to fetch the scriptures from India. Hearing that the Emperor T'ai Tsung[4] was celebrating a great Mass, and that the ceremony was being directed by that River Float with whose birth she had herself been connected, "Who," she asked herself, "could be better fitted for that mission than he?" And she set out into the streets, taking with her Moksha, and the treasures that Buddha had given to her. "What were these treasures?" you ask. They were a magic brocaded cassock, and a priest's staff with nine rings. Apart from these, there were the three magic fillets which she left in safe keeping for future use, only taking with her the cassock and staff. Wandering about the streets of Ch'ang-an was a stupid priest who had failed to be chosen to take part in the Mass. Seeing the Bodhisattva, disguised as a shabby priest, barefoot and in rags, holding up his shining cassock as though for sale, he remembered that he still had a few strings of cash upon him, and coming forward he said, "What would you take for the cassock?"

"The cassock," said Kuan-yin, "is worth five thousand pounds; the staff, two thousand."

"Seven thousand pounds for a couple of coarse, low-class articles like that! You must be mad," he said. "Why, if it were guaranteed that the user of them would be immortal, or that he would become a living Buddha, they wouldn't fetch that price. Be off with you! I don't want them."

The Bodhisattva said not a word more, but signing to Moksha went on her way. They had not gone far before they reached the Eastern Flower Gate, where whom should they meet but the minister Hsiao Yü, just returning from Court. His outriders were clearing the streets, but Kuan-yin, so far from removing herself, stood right in the minister's path, holding up the cassock. He reined in his horse, and seeing this dazzling object held up in front of him, he told a servant to ask the price.

"Five thousand pounds for the cassock and two thousand for the staff," said Kuan-yin.

"What makes them so expensive?" asked Hsiao.

"The cassock," said Kuan-yin, "would be valuable to some people and quite the reverse to others; it would cost some people a lot of money, and others none at all."

"What does that mean?" asked Hsiao.

"The wearer of my cassock," said Kuan-yin, "will not be drowned or poisoned or meet wild beasts upon his way. But that is only if he is a good man; if it gets on to the back of a gluttonous, lustful priest, or one who does not keep his vows, or of a layman who destroys scriptures and speaks evil of Buddha, he will rue the day that he saw this cassock."

"And what do you mean," asked Hsiao, "by saying that it would cost some people a lot of money and others none at all?"

---

[4] **T'ai Tsung:** Taizong, second emperor of the Tang dynasty, who ruled from 626 to 649.

"To a purchaser who does not reverence Buddha's Law and Three Treasures, the price of the cassock and staff together would be seven thousand pounds," said Kuan-yin. "But a pious and reverent man, devoted to our Buddha, could have them both for the asking."

Hearing this, Hsiao dismounted, and bowing respectfully, "Reverend Sir," he said, "the Emperor of this great land is himself a most devout man, and all his ministers vie with one another in carrying out his behests. At present he is celebrating a Great Mass, and this cassock might well be worn by the high priest Hsüan Tsang, who is in charge of the whole ceremony. Let us go to the palace and speak to the Emperor about this."

The Emperor was delighted at this proposal, and at once told Hsüan Tsang to put on the cassock and hold the staff in his hand. Then he appointed a retinue to accompany him, and had him led through the city in triumph, for all the world like a successful candidate at the examinations. In the great city of Ch'ang-an travelling merchants and tradesmen, princes and nobles, writers and scholars, grown men and young girls all fought with one another for good places from which to view the procession. "A noble priest! A Lohan[5] come to earth, a living Bodhisattva!" they cried in admiration when they saw Hsüan Tsang pass. And the priests in his temple when he returned, seeing him thus accoutred, could scarcely believe that it was not the Bodhisattva Kshitigarbha[6] himself who had come to visit them.

Time passed, and now at last came the final ceremonies of the forty-ninth day, at which Hsüan Tsang was to deliver the closing sermon. "The Great Mass closes today," said Kuan-yin to Moksha. "Let us mingle in the throng, so that we may see how the ceremonies are conducted and what blessing there is in our gift, and hear what school of Buddhism he preaches." The great Hsüan Tsang, mounted on a high dais, first read the Sutra on the Salvation of the Dead, then discussed the Collect upon the Security of Kingdoms, and finally expounded the Exhortation to Pious Works. At this point Kuan-yin approached the dais, and cried in a loud voice, "Why can't you give us some Big Vehicle Scriptures?"

So far from being put out by this interruption, Hsüan Tsang was delighted to hear of other scriptures, and scrambling down from the dais he saluted his interrupter and said, "Reverend Sir, forgive me for not knowing that I had one so learned as you in my audience. It is true that we have none of us any knowledge of the Big Vehicle, and have only expounded the Little Vehicle."

"Your Little Vehicle," said Kuan-yin, "cannot save the souls of the dead, and only leads to general misapprehension and confusion. I have three sections of Great Vehicle teaching, called the Tripitaka or Three Baskets. These can carry the souls of the dead to Heaven, can save all those that are in trouble, can add immeasurably to life's span, and can deliver those that trust in it from the comings and goings of Incarnation."

At this point one of the ushers rushed to the Emperor and announced that two shabby priests had interrupted the Master, pulled him down from the dais, and

---

[5] **Lohan:** A Buddhist saint or martyr. [6] **Kshitigarbha:** The savior who delivers souls from the underworld.

started some nonsensical argument with him. The Emperor ordered them to be seized and brought to him. On appearing before the Emperor they did not prostrate themselves or even salute him, but merely asked what he wanted of them.

"Are you not the priest who gave me the cassock the other day?" said the Emperor. "I am," said Kuan-yin.

"You had a perfect right," said the Emperor, "to come here and listen to the preaching, eat with the other priests, and go away quietly. But you have no business to interrupt the preaching and disturb the whole proceedings."

"Your preacher," Kuan-yin said, "knows only about the Little Vehicle, which cannot save souls. We possess the Tripitaka of the Big Vehicle, which saves the souls of the dead and succours those that are in peril."

The Emperor was delighted at this news, and asked at once where it was.

"It is in India," said Kuan-yin, "at the temple of the Great Thunder Clap, where the Buddha Tathagata dwells."

"Do you know these teachings by heart?" asked the Emperor.

"I do," said the Bodhisattva.

"Then Hsüan Tsang shall retire," said the Emperor, "and you shall mount the dais and expound them to us." But instead of doing so Kuan-yin floated up into the sky and revealed herself in all the glory of her true form, holding the willow-spray and the sacred vase, while Moksha stood at her left side, holding his staff.

The Emperor hastened to prostrate himself, and all his ministers knelt down and burned incense, while the audience, priests, nuns, officers, craftsmen and merchants, bowed down, crying, "The Bodhisattva, the Bodhisattva!"

The Emperor's joy was so great that he forgot his rivers and hills, his ministers in their excitement broke every rule of etiquette, and all the multitude murmured again and again "Glory be to the Great Bodhisattva Kuan-yin." His Majesty decided to have a picture of the Bodhisattva painted by a skilful artist, in full colours. His choice fell upon Wu Tao-tzu, that genius of the brush, that prodigy of portraiture, that fabulous embodiment of vision and inspiration. It was this painter who afterwards made the portraits of the heroes of the dynasty in the Tower of Rising Smoke. He now wielded his magic brush and rendered every detail of these sacred forms. Presently the figures began to recede farther and farther into the sky, and finally their golden effulgence could be seen no more.

At this point the Emperor dismissed the assembly, and declared that the next thing to do was to find a traveller who would go to India and fetch the Scriptures. An inquiry was made in the temple, and Hsüan Tsang immediately came forward and bowing low said, "I am a humble cleric, devoid of any capacity; but I am ready to undertake the quest of these Scriptures, be the fatigues and difficulties what they may, if by doing so I may promote the security of your Majesty's streams and hills." The Emperor was delighted, and raising him from his knees with his royal hand, "Reverend Sir," he said, "if indeed you are willing to do me this loyal service, undeterred by the length of the journey and all the mountains and rivers that you will have to cross, I will make you my bond-brother." And true to his word, in front of the Buddha image in that temple, he bowed four times to Hsüan Tsang and addressed him as "Holy Priest, my brother." Hsüan Tsang on his side, burning incense before the Buddha, swore to do all that lay in his power to reach India. "And if I do not reach India and do not bring back the Scriptures, may I fall into the nethermost pit of Hell, rather than return empty-handed to China."

When Hsüan Tsang rejoined the other priests, they pressed round him, asking whether it was indeed true that he had sworn to go to India. "For I have heard," one of them said, "that it is a very long way and that on the road there are many tigers, panthers and evil spirits. I fear you will not come back to us alive." "I have taken my oath," said Hsüan Tsang, "and I must faithfully fulfil it. I know well enough that the hazards of such a journey are great." And presently he said, "My disciples, I may be away for two or three years, or five, or seven. If you see the branches of the pine-tree at the gate turning eastward, you will know I am coming back. If not, it will mean that I shall never return."

Early next day, in the presence of all his ministers, the Emperor signed a rescript authorizing Hsüan Tsang's quest, and stamped it with the seal of free passage. The astrologers announced that the posture of the heavens made the day particularly favourable for the start of a long journey. At this point, Hsüan Tsang himself was announced. "Brother," said the Emperor, "I am told that this would be a lucky day for you to start. Here are your travelling papers, and here is a golden bowl for you to collect alms in during your journey. I have chosen two followers to go with you, and a horse for you to ride. It only remains for you to start." Hsüan Tsang was ready enough, and taking the Emperor's present set out towards the gates of the city, accompanied by the Emperor and a host of officials. When they reached the gates, they found that the priests of the Hung-fu temple were waiting there with a provision of winter and summer clothing. When it had been added to the luggage, the Emperor told a servant to bring wine, and raising the cup he asked Hsüan Tsang if he had a by-name.

"Being a priest," said Hsüan Tsang, "I have not thought it proper to assume a by-name."

"The Bodhisattva mentioned," said the Emperor, "that the Scriptures in India are called the Tripitaka. How would it be if you took 'Tripitaka' as your by-name?"

Hsüan Tsang accepted with thanks, but when he was offered the wine-cup, he declined, saying that abstinence from wine was the first rule of priesthood, and that he never took it. "This is an exceptional occasion," said the Emperor, "and the wine is not at all strong; just drink one cup to speed you on your journey." Tripitaka dared not refuse; but just as he was going to drink, the Emperor stooped down and with his royal fingers scooped up a handful of dust and threw it into the cup. At first Tripitaka could not make out why he had done this, but the Emperor said laughing, "Tell me, brother, how long do you expect to be away?"

"I hope," said Tripitaka, "to be back in three years."

"That's a long time," said the Emperor, "and you have a long way to go. You would do well to drink this cup, for are we not told that a handful of one's country's soil is worth more than ten thousand pounds of foreign gold?"

Then Tripitaka understood why the Emperor had thrown the dust into the cup, drank it down to the last dregs, and set out upon his way. And if you do not know how he fared upon that way, listen to what is told in the next chapter.

FROM

Chapter 13

[...] Tripitaka ... travelled over difficult country for half a day, without seeing any sign of human habitation. He was now very hungry, and the road was extremely precipitous. He was at the height of his difficulties when he heard two tigers roaring just ahead of him and saw behind him several huge serpents twisting and twining. To make matters worse, on his left was some species of deadly scorpion, and on his right a wild beast of unknown species. To cope single-handed with such a situation was clearly impossible, and there was nothing for it but to resign himself to his fate. Soon his horse sank quivering on to its knees and refused to budge. Suddenly a medley of tigers and wolves, with other wild and fearful creatures, set upon him all together. He would have been utterly lost, had there not at this very moment appeared a man with a three-pronged spear in his hand and bow and arrows at his waist. "Save me, save me!" cried Tripitaka. The man rushed forward and throwing aside his spear, raised Tripitaka from his knees. "Do not be afraid," he said, "I am a hunter, and I came out to find a couple of mountain creatures to eat for my supper. You must forgive me for intruding upon you so unceremoniously." Tripitaka thanked the hunter, and explained what brought him to this place. "I live near here," said the hunter, "and spend all my time in dealing with tigers and serpents and the like, so that such creatures are afraid of the sight of me and run away. If you indeed come from the Court of T'ang we are fellow-countrymen, for the frontier of the empire is a little way beyond here."

[...]

Mountain scenery of indescribable beauty stretched out before them. Towards noon they came to a gigantic mountain, up which Tripitaka began to clamber with great pains, while the hunter sprang up it as though he had been walking on flat ground. Halfway up the hunter halted, and turning to Tripitaka, he said, "I fear at this point we must part."

"I entreat you to take me just one stage farther," begged Tripitaka.

"Sir," said the hunter, "you do not know. This mountain is called the Mountain of the Two Frontiers. Its east side belongs to our land of T'ang; on the west side lies the land of the Tartars. The wolves and tigers on the far side I have not subjected, moreover I have not the right to cross the frontier. You must go on alone."

Tripitaka wrung his hands in despair, clutched at the hunter's sleeve and wept copiously. At this point there came from under the mountain a stentorian voice, crying repeatedly, "The Master has come." Both Tripitaka and the hunter started, in great surprise. If you do not know whose voice it was they heard, listen to what is told in the next chapter.

Chapter 14

The hunter and Tripitaka were still wondering who had spoken, when again they heard the voice saying, "The Master has come."

The hunter's servants said, "That is the voice of the old monkey who is shut up in the stone casket of the mountain side."

"Why, to be sure it is!" said the hunter.

"What old monkey is that?" asked Tripitaka.

"This mountain," said the hunter, "was once called the Mountain of the Five Elements. But after our great T'ang Dynasty had carried out its campaigns to the West, its name was changed to Mountain of the Two Frontiers. Years ago a very old man told me that at the time when Wang Mang overthrew the First Han Dynasty, Heaven dropped this mountain in order to imprison a magic monkey under it. He has local spirits as his gaolers, who, when he is hungry, give him iron pills to eat, and when he is thirsty give him copper-juice to drink, so that despite cold and short commons[7] he is still alive. That cry certainly comes from him. You need not be uneasy. We'll go down and have a look."

After going downhill for some way they came to the stone box, in which there was really a monkey. Only his head was visible, and one paw, which he waved violently through the opening, saying, "Welcome, Master! Welcome! Get me out of here, and I will protect you on your journey to the West."

The hunter stepped boldly up, and removing the grasses from Monkey's hair and brushing away the grit from under his chin, "What have you got to say for yourself?" he asked.

"To you, nothing," said Monkey. "But I have something to ask of that priest. Tell him to come here."

"What do you want to ask me?" said Tripitaka.

"Were you sent by the Emperor of T'ang to look for Scriptures in India?" asked Monkey.

"I was," said Tripitaka. "And what of that?"

"I am the Great Sage Equal of Heaven," said Monkey. "Five hundred years ago I made trouble in the Halls of Heaven, and Buddha clamped me down in this place. Not long ago the Bodhisattva Kuan-yin, whom Buddha had ordered to look around for someone to fetch Scriptures from India, came here and promised me that if I would amend my ways and faithfully protect the pilgrim on his way, I was to be released, and afterwards would find salvation. Ever since then I have been waiting impatiently night and day for you to come and let me out. I will protect you while you are going to get Scriptures and follow you as your disciple."

Tripitaka was delighted. "The only trouble is," he said, "that I have no axe or chisel, so how am I to get you out?"

"There is no need for axe or chisel," said Monkey. "You have only to want me to be out, and I shall be out."

"How can that be?" asked Tripitaka.

"On the top of the mountain," said Monkey, "is a seal stamped with golden letters by Buddha himself Take it away, and I shall be out."

Tripitaka was for doing so at once, but the hunter took him aside and said there was no telling whether one could believe the monkey or not. "It's true, it's true!" screamed Monkey from inside the casket. At last the hunter was prevailed upon to

[7] **commons:** Rations.

come with him and, scrambling back again to the very top, they did indeed see innumerable beams of golden light streaming from a great square slab of rock, on which was imprinted in golden letters the inscription OM MANI PADME HUM.[8]

Tripitaka knelt down and did reverence to the inscription, saying, "If this monkey is indeed worthy to be a disciple, may this imprint be removed and may the monkey be released and accompany me to the seat of Buddha. But if he is not fit to be a disciple, but an unruly monster who would discredit my undertaking, may the imprint of this seal remain where it is." At once there came a gust of fragrant wind that carried the six letters of the inscription up into the air, and a voice was heard saying, "I am the Great Sage's gaoler. Today the time of his penance is ended and I am going to ask Buddha to let him loose." Having bowed reverently in the direction from which the voice came, Tripitaka and the hunter went back to the stone casket and said to Monkey, "The inscription is removed. You can come out."

"You must go to a little distance," said Monkey. "I don't want to frighten you."

They withdrew a little way, but heard Monkey calling to them "Farther, farther!" They did as they were bid, and presently heard a tremendous crushing and rending. They were all in great consternation, expecting the mountain to come hurtling on top of them, when suddenly the noise subsided, and Monkey appeared, kneeling in front of Tripitaka's horse, crying, "Master, I am out!" Then he sprang up and called to the hunter, "Brother, I'll trouble you to dust the grass-wisps from my cheek." Then he put together the packs and hoisted them on to the horse, which on seeing him became at once completely obedient. For Monkey had been a groom in Heaven, and it was natural that an ordinary horse should hold him in great awe.

Tripitaka, seeing that he knew how to make himself useful and looked as though he would make a pretty tolerable śramana,[9] said to him, "Disciple, we must give you a name in religion."

"No need for that," said Monkey, "I have one already. My name in religion is 'Aware-of-Vacuity.' "

"Excellent!" said Tripitaka. "That fits in very well with the names of my other disciples. You shall be Monkey Aware-of-Vacuity."

The hunter, seeing that Monkey had got everything ready, said to Tripitaka, "I am very glad you have been fortunate enough to pick up this excellent disciple. As you are so well provided for, I will bid you good-bye and turn back."

"I have brought you a long way from home," said Tripitaka, "and cannot thank you enough. Please also apologize to your mother and wife for all the trouble I gave, and tell them I will thank them in person on my return."

Tripitaka had not been long on the road with Monkey and had only just got clear of the Mountain of the Two Frontiers, when a tiger suddenly appeared, roaring savagely and lashing its tail. Tripitaka was terrified, but Monkey seemed delighted. "Don't be frightened, Master," he said. "He has only come to supply me with an apron." So saying, he took a needle from behind his ear and, turning his face to the

---

[8] **OM MANI PADME HUM:** A magic spell in Sanskrit that keeps Monkey trapped under the mountain.

[9] **śramana:** A monk.

wind, made a few magic passes, and instantly it became a huge iron cudgel. "It is five hundred years since I last used this precious thing," he said, "and today it is going to furnish me with a little much-needed clothing."

Look at him! He strides forward, crying, "Cursed creature, stand your ground!" The tiger crouched in the dust and dared not budge. Down came the cudgel on its head. The earth was spattered with its blood. Tripitaka rolled off his horse as best he could, crying with an awe-struck voice, "Heavens! When the hunter killed that stripy tiger yesterday, he struggled with it for hours on end. But this disciple of mine walked straight up to the tiger and struck it dead. True indeed is the saying 'Strong though he be, there is always a stronger.'"

"Sit down a while," said Monkey, "and wait while I undress him; then when I am dressed, we'll go on."

"How can you undress him?" said Tripitaka. "He hasn't got any clothes."

"Don't worry about me," said Monkey. "I know what I am about."

Dear Monkey! He took a hair from his tail, blew on it with magic breath, and it became a sharp little knife, with which he slit the tiger's skin straight down and ripped it off in one piece. Then he cut off the paws and head, and trimmed the skin into one big square. Holding it out, he measured it with his eye, and said, "A bit too wide. I must divide it in two." He cut it in half, put one half aside and the other round his waist, making it fast with some rattan that he pulled up from the roadside. "Now we can go," he said, "and when we get to the next house, I'll borrow a needle and thread and sew it up properly."

"What has become of your cudgel?" asked Tripitaka, when they were on their way again.

"I must explain to you," said Monkey. "This cudgel is a piece of magic iron that I got in the Dragon King's palace, and it was with it that I made havoc in Heaven. I can make it as large or as small as I please. Just now I made it the size of an embroidery needle and put it away behind my ear, where it is always at hand in case I need it."

"And why," asked Tripitaka, "did that tiger, as soon as it saw you, crouch down motionless and allow you to strike it just as you chose?"

"The fact is," said Monkey, "that not only tigers but dragons too dare not do anything against me. But that is not all. I have such arts as can make rivers turn back in their course, and can raise tempests on the sea. Small wonder, then, that I can filch a tiger's skin. When we get into real difficulties you will see what I am really capable of."

"Master," said Monkey presently, "it is getting late. Over there is a clump of trees, and I think there must be a house. We had better see if we can spend the night there." Tripitaka whipped his horse, and soon they did indeed come to a farm, outside the gates of which he dismounted. Monkey cried "Open the door!" and presently there appeared a very old man, leaning on a staff. Muttering to himself, he began to push open the door, but when he saw Monkey, looking (with the tiger skin at his waist) for all the world like a thunder demon, he was terrified out of his wits and could only murmur "There's a devil at the door, sure enough there's a devil!" Tripitaka came up to him just in time to prevent him hobbling away. "Old patron," he said, "you need not be afraid. This is not a devil; it is my disciple." Seeing that Tripitaka at any rate was a clean-built, comely man, he took comfort a little and said, "I don't know what temple you come from, but you have no right to bring such an evil-looking fellow to my house."

"I come from the Court of T'ang," said Tripitaka, "and I am going to India to get Scriptures. As my way brought me near your house, I have come here in the hope that you would consent to give me a night's lodging. I shall be starting off again tomorrow before daybreak."

"You may be a man of T'ang," said the old man, "but I'll warrant that villainous fellow is no man of T'ang!"

"Have you no eyes in your head," shouted Monkey. "The man of T'ang is my master. I am his disciple, and no man of T'ang or sugar-man[10] or honey-man either. I am the Great Sage Equal of Heaven. You people here know me well enough, and I have seen you before."

"Where have you seen me?" he asked. "Didn't you when you were small cut the brushwood from in front of my face and gather the herbs that grew on my cheek?"

"The stone monkey in the stone casket!" gasped the old man. "I see that you are a little like him. But how did you get out?"

Monkey told the whole story, and the old man at once bowed before him, and asked them both to step inside.

"Great Sage, how old are you?" the old man asked, when they were seated.

"Let us first hear your age," said Monkey.

"A hundred and thirty," said the old man.

"Then you are young enough to be my great-great-grandson at least," said Monkey. "I have no idea when I was born. But I was under that mountain for five hundred years."

"True enough," said the old man. "I remember my grandfather telling me that this mountain was dropped from Heaven in order to trap a monkey divinity, and you say that you have only just got out. When I used to see you in my childhood, there was grass growing out of your head and mud on your cheeks. I was not at all afraid of you then. Now there is no mud on your cheeks and no grass on your head. You look thinner, and with that tiger-skin at your waist, who would know that you weren't a devil?"

"I don't want to give you all a lot of trouble," said Monkey presently, "but it is five hundred years since I last washed. Could you let us have a little hot water? I am sure my Master would be glad to wash too."

When they had both washed, they sat down in front of the lamp. "One more request," said Monkey. "Could you lend me a needle and thread?"

"By all means, by all means," said the old man, and he told his old wife to bring them. Just then Monkey caught sight of a white shirt that Tripitaka had taken off when he washed and not put on again. He snatched it up and put it on. Then he wriggled out of the tiger-skin, sewed it up in one piece, made a "horse-face fold"[11]

---

[10] **sugar-man:** "Sugar" in Chinese is *T'ang.* [11] **"horse-face fold":** Meaning uncertain. The modern edition substitutes "sewed it into a skirt."

and put it round his waist again, fastening the rattan belt. Presenting himself to Tripitaka he said, "How do you like me in this garb? Is it an improvement?"

"Splendid!" said Tripitaka. "Now you really do look like a pilgrim."

"Disciple," added Tripitaka, "if you don't mind accepting an off-cast, you can have that shirt for your own."

They rose early next day, and the old man brought them washing-water and breakfast. Then they set out again on their way, lodging late and starting early for many days. One morning they suddenly heard a cry and six men rushed out at them from the roadside, all armed with pikes and swords. "Halt, priest!" they cried. "We want your horse and your packs, and quickly too, or you will not escape with your life."

Tripitaka, in great alarm, slid down from his horse and stood there speechless.

"Don't worry," said Monkey. "This only means more clothes and travelling-money for us."

"Monkey, are you deaf?" said Tripitaka. "They ordered us to surrender the horse and luggage, and you talk of getting clothes and money from them!"

"You keep an eye on the packs and the horse," said Monkey, "while I settle matters with them! You'll soon see what I mean."

"They are very strong men and there are six of them," said Tripitaka. "How can a little fellow like you hope to stand up against them single-handed?"

Monkey did not stop to argue, but strode forward and, folding his arms across his chest, bowed to the robbers and said, "Sirs, for what reason do you stop poor priests from going on their way?"

"We are robber kings," they said, "mountain lords among the Benevolent.[12] Everyone knows us. How comes it that you are so ignorant? Hand over your things at once, and we will let you pass. But if half the word 'no' leaves your lips, we shall hack you to pieces and grind your bones to powder."

"I, too," said Monkey, "am a great hereditary king, and lord of a mountain for hundreds of years; yet I have never heard your names."

"In that case, let us tell you," they said. "The first of us is called Eye that Sees and Delights; the second, Ear that Hears and is Angry; the third, Nose that Smells and Covets; the fourth, Tongue that Tastes and Desires; the fifth, Mind that Conceives and Lusts; the sixth, Body that Supports and Suffers."

"You're nothing but six hairy ruffians," said Monkey, laughing. "We priests, I would have you know, are your lords and masters, yet you dare block our path. Bring out all the stolen goods you have about you and divide them into seven parts. Then, if you leave me one part, I will spare your lives."

The robbers were so taken aback that they did not know whether to be angry or amused. "You must be mad," they said. "You've just lost all you possess, and you talk of sharing our booty with us!" Brandishing their spears and flourishing their swords they all rushed forward and began to rain blows upon Monkey's head. But he stood stock still and betrayed not the slightest concern.

[12] **Benevolent:** *Benevolent* was thieves' slang for "bandit."

"Priest, your head must be very hard!" they cried.

"That's all right," said Monkey, "I'm not in a hurry. But when your arms are tired, I'll take out my needle and do my turn."

"What does he mean?" they said. "Perhaps he's a doctor turned priest. But we are none of us ill, so why should he talk about using the needle?"

Monkey took his needle from behind his ear, recited a spell which changed it into a huge cudgel, and cried, "Hold your ground and let old Monkey try his hand upon you!" The robbers fled in confusion, but in an instant he was among them and striking right and left he slew them all, stripped off their clothing and seized their baggage. Then he came back to Tripitaka and said laughing, "Master, we can start now; I have killed them all."

"I am very sorry to hear it," said Tripitaka. "One has no right to kill robbers, however violent and wicked they may be. The most one may do is to bring them before a magistrate. It would have been quite enough in this case if you had driven them away. Why kill them? You have behaved with a cruelty that ill becomes one of your sacred calling."

"If I had not killed them," said Monkey, "they would have killed you."

"A priest," said Tripitaka, "should be ready to die rather than commit acts of violence."

"I don't mind telling you," said Monkey, "that five hundred years ago, when I was a king, I killed a pretty fair number of people, and if I had held your view I should certainly never have become the Great Sage Equal of Heaven."

"It was because of your unfortunate performances in Heaven," said Tripitaka, "that you had to do penance for five hundred years. If now that you have repented and become a priest you go on behaving as in old days, you can't come with me to India. You've made a very bad start."

The one thing Monkey had never been able to bear was to be scolded, and when Tripitaka began to lecture him like this, he flared up at once and cried, "All right! I'll give up being a priest, and won't go with you to India. You needn't go on at me any more. I'm off!"

Tripitaka did not answer. His silence enraged Monkey even further. He shook himself and with a last "I'm off!" he bounded away. When Tripitaka looked up, he had completely disappeared. "It's no use trying to teach people like that," said Tripitaka to himself gloomily. "I only said a word or two, and off he goes. Very well then. Evidently it is not my fate to have a disciple; so I must get on as best I can without one."

He collected the luggage, hoisted it on to the horse's back and set out on foot, leading the horse with one hand and carrying his priest's staff with the other, in very low spirits. He had not gone far, when he saw an old woman carrying a brocaded coat and embroidered cap. As she came near, Tripitaka drew his horse to the side of the road to let her pass.

"Where are you off to all alone?" she asked.

"The Emperor of China has sent me to India to fetch Scriptures," said Tripitaka.

"The Temple of the Great Thunder Clap where Buddha lives," said she, "is a hundred and one thousand leagues away. You surely don't expect to get there with only one horse and no disciple to wait upon you?"

"I picked up a disciple a few days ago," said Tripitaka, "but he behaved badly and I was obliged to speak rather severely to him; whereupon he went off in a huff, and I have not seen him since."

"I've got a brocade coat and a cap with a metal band," said the old woman. "They belonged to my son. He entered a monastery, but when he had been a monk for three days, he died. I went and fetched them from the monastery to keep in memory of him. If you had a disciple, I should be very glad to let you have them."

"That is very kind of you," said Tripitaka, "but my disciple has run away, so I cannot accept them."

"Which way did he go?" asked the old woman.

"The last time I heard his voice, it came from the east," said Tripitaka.

"That's the way that my house lies," said the old woman. "I expect he'll turn up there. I've got a spell here which I'll let you learn, if you promise not to teach it to anybody. I'll go and look for him and send him back to you. Make him wear this cap and coat. If he disobeys you, say the spell, and he'll give no more trouble and never dare to leave you."

Suddenly the old woman changed into a shaft of golden light, which disappeared towards the east. Tripitaka at once guessed that she was the Bodhisattva Kuan-yin in disguise. He bowed and burned incense towards the east. Then having stored away the cap and coat he sat at the roadside, practising the spell.

After Monkey left the Master, he somersaulted through the clouds and landed right in the palace of the Dragon King of the Eastern Ocean.

"I heard recently that your penance was over," said the dragon, "and made sure you would have gone back to be king in your fairy cave."

"That's what I am doing," said Monkey. "But to start with I became a priest."

"A priest?" said the dragon. "How did that happen?"

"Kuan-yin persuaded me to accompany a priest of T'ang," said Monkey, "who is going to India to get Scriptures; so I was admitted to the Order."

"That's certainly a step in the right direction," said the dragon. "I am sure I congratulate you. But in that case, what are you doing here in the east?"

"It comes of my master being so unpractical," said Monkey. "We met some brigands, and naturally I killed them. Then he started scolding me. You may imagine I wasn't going to stand that. So I left him at once, and am going back to my kingdom. But I thought I would look you up on the way, and see if you could give me a cup of tea."

When he had been given his cup of tea, he looked round the room, and saw on the wall a picture of Chang Liang[13] offering the slipper. Monkey asked what it was about. "You were in Heaven at the time," said the dragon, "and naturally would not know about it. The immortal in the picture is Huang Shih Kung, and the other figure is Chang Liang. Once when Shih Kung was sitting on a bridge, his shoe came off and fell under the bridge. He called to Chang Liang to pick it up and bring it to him.

---

[13] **Chang Liang:** A warrior who died in 189 B.C.E., famous for his part in assisting the Han dynasty against the Qin Ch'in (221-207 B.C.E.).

Chang Liang did so, whereupon the Immortal at once let it fall again, and Chang Liang again fetched it. This happened three times, without Chang Liang showing the slightest sign of impatience. Huang Shih Kung then gave him a magic treatise, by means of which he defeated all the enemies of the House of Han, and became the greatest hero of the Han dynasty. In his old age he became a disciple of the Immortal Red Pine Seed and achieved Tao.[14] Great Sage, you must learn to have a little more patience, if you hope to accompany the pilgrim to India and gain the Fruits of Illumination." Monkey looked thoughtful. "Great Sage," said the dragon, "you must learn to control yourself and submit to the will of others, if you are not to spoil all your chances."

"Not another word!" said Monkey, "I'll go back at once."

On the way he met the Bodhisattva Kuan-yin. "What are you doing here?" she asked.

"The seal was removed and I got out," said Monkey, "and became Tripitaka's disciple. But he said I didn't know how to behave, and I gave him the slip. But now I am going back to look after him."

"Go as fast as you can," said the Bodhisattva, "and try to do better this time."

"Master," said Monkey, when he came back and found Tripitaka sitting dejectedly by the roadside, "what are you doing still sitting here?"

"And where have you been?" asked Tripitaka. "I hadn't the heart to go on, and was just sitting here waiting for you."

"I only went to the Dragon of the Eastern Ocean," said Monkey, "to drink a cup of tea."

"Now Monkey," said Tripitaka, "priests must always be careful to tell the truth. You know quite well that the Dragon King lives far away in the east, and you have only been gone an hour."

"That's easily explained," said Monkey. "I have the art of somersaulting through the clouds. One bound takes me a hundred and eight thousand leagues."

"It seemed to me that you went off in a huff," said Tripitaka, "because I had to speak rather sharply to you. It's all very well for you to go off and get tea like that, if you are able to. But I think you might remember that I can't go with you. Doesn't it occur to you that I may be thirsty and hungry too?"

"If you are," said Monkey, "I'll take a bowl and go and beg for you."

"There isn't any need to do that," said Tripitaka. "There are some dried provisions in the pack."

When Monkey opened the pack, his eye was caught by something bright. "Did you bring this coat and cap with you from the east?" he asked.

"I used to wear them when I was young," replied Tripitaka, saying the first thing that came into his head. "Anyone who wears this cap can recite scriptures without having to learn them. Anyone who wears this coat can perform ceremonies without having practised them."

"Dear Master," said Monkey, "let me put them on."

---

[14]**Tao (Dao):** Immortality.

"By all means," said Tripitaka.

Monkey put on the coat and cap, and Tripitaka, pretending to be eating the dried provisions, silently mumbled the spell. "My head is hurting!" screamed Monkey. Tripitaka went on reciting, and Monkey rolled over on the ground, frantically trying to break the metal fillet of the cap. Fearing that he would succeed, Tripitaka stopped for a moment. Instantly the pain stopped. Monkey felt his head. The cap seemed to have taken root upon it. He took out his needle and tried to lever it up; but all in vain. Fearing once more that he would break the band, Tripitaka began to recite again. Monkey was soon writhing and turning somersaults. He grew purple in the face and his eyes bulged out of his head. Tripitaka, unable to bear the sight of such agony, stopped reciting, and at once Monkey's head stopped hurting.

"You've been putting a spell upon me," he said.

"Nothing of the kind," said Tripitaka. "I've only been reciting the Scripture of the Tight Fillet."

"Start reciting again," said Monkey. When he did so, the pain began at once.

"Stop, stop!" screamed Monkey. "Directly you begin, the pain starts; you can't pretend it's not you that are causing it."

"In future, will you attend to what I say?" asked Tripitaka.

"Indeed I will," said Monkey.

"And never be troublesome again?" said Tripitaka.

"I shouldn't dare," said Monkey. So he said, but in his heart there was still lurking a very evil intent. He took out his cudgel and rushed at Tripitaka, fully intending to strike. Much alarmed, the Master began to recite again, and Monkey fell writhing upon the ground; the cudgel dropped from his hand.

"I give in, I give in!" he cried.

"Is it possible," said Tripitaka, "that you were going to be so wicked as to strike me?"

"I shouldn't dare, I shouldn't dare," groaned Monkey. "Master, how did you come by this spell?"

"It was taught me by an old woman whom I met just now," said Tripitaka.

"Not another word!" said Monkey. "I know well enough who she was. It was the Bodhisattva Kuan-yin. How dare she plot against me like that? Just wait a minute while I go to the Southern Ocean and give her a taste of my stick."

"As it was she who taught me the spell," said Tripitaka, "she can presumably use it herself. What will become of you then?"

Monkey saw the logic of this, and kneeling down he said contritely, "Master, this spell is too much for me. Let me go with you to India. You won't need to be always saying this spell. I will protect you faithfully to the end."

"Very well then," said Tripitaka. "Help me on to my horse."

Very crestfallen, Monkey put the luggage together, and they started off again towards the west.

If you do not know how the story goes on, you must listen to what is told in the next chapter.

[. . .]

Chapter 16

They had been travelling for several days through very wild country when at last, very late in the evening, they saw a group of houses in the far distance.

"Monkey," said Tripitaka, "I think that is a farm over there. Wouldn't it be a good plan to see if we can't sleep there tonight?"

"Let me go and have a look at it," said Monkey, "to see whether it looks lucky or unlucky, and we can then act accordingly."

"You can proceed," Monkey reported presently. "I am certain that good people live there."

Tripitaka urged on the white horse and soon came to a gate leading into a lane down which came a lad with a cotton wrap round his head, wearing a blue jacket, umbrella in hand and a bundle on his back. He was striding along, with a defiant air. "Where are you off to?" said Monkey stopping him. "There's something I want to ask you. What place is this?"

The man tried to brush him aside, muttering, "Is there no one else on the farm, that you must needs pester me with questions?"

"Now don't be cross," said Monkey laughing. "What harm can it do you to tell me the name of a place? If you're obliging to us, maybe we can do something to oblige you."

Finding he could not get past, for Monkey was holding on to him tightly, he began to dance about in a great rage. "It's enough to put anyone out," he cried. "I've just been insulted by the master of the house, and then I run straight into this wretched bald-pate, and have to swallow his impudence!"

"Unless you're clever enough to shake me off, which I very much doubt," said Monkey, "here you'll stay." The man wriggled this way and that, but all to no purpose. He was caught as though by iron pincers. In the struggle he dropped his bundle, dropped his umbrella, and began to rain blows on Monkey with both fists. Monkey kept one hand free to catch on to the luggage, and with the other held the lad fast.

"Monkey," said Tripitaka, "I think there's someone coming over there. Wouldn't it do just as well if you asked him, and let this lad go?"

"Master," said Monkey, "you don't know what you're talking about. There's no point in asking anyone else. This is the only fellow out of whom we can get what we want."

At last, seeing that he would never get free, the lad said, "This is called old Mr. Kao's farm. Most of the people that live and work here have the surname Kao, so the whole place is called Kao Farm. Now let me go!"

"You look as if you were going on a journey," said Monkey. "Tell me where you are going, and on what business, and I will let you go."

"My name," he said, "is Kao Ts'ai. Old Mr. Kao has a daughter about twenty years old and unmarried. Three years ago she was carried off by a monster, who since has kept her as his wife, and lived with her here on the farm. Old Mr. Kao was not pleased. 'To have a monster as a son-in-law in the house,' he says, 'doesn't work very well. It's definitely discreditable to the house, and unpleasant not to be able to look forward to comings and goings between the two families.' He did everything in his power to drive away the monster, but it was no good; and in the end the creature took the girl and locked her away in that back building, where she has been for six months and no one in the family has seen her.

"Old Mr. Kao gave me two or three pieces of silver and told me to go and find an exorcist, and I spent a long time chasing round all over the countryside. I succeeded at last in getting the names of three or four practitioners, but they all turned out to be unfrocked priests or mouldy Taoists, quite incapable of dealing with such a monster. Mr. Kao only just now gave me a great scolding and accused me of bungling the business. Then he gave me five pieces of silver to pay for my travelling expenses and told me to go on looking till I found a really good exorcist, and I should be looking for one now if I hadn't run into this little scamp who won't let me pass. There! You have forced me to tell you how things are, and now you can let me go."

"You've thrown a lucky number," said Monkey. "This is just my job. You needn't go a step farther or spend an ounce of your silver. I'm no unfrocked priest or mouldy Taoist, I really do know how to catch monsters. You've 'got your stye cured on the way to the doctor's.' I'll trouble you to go to the master of the house, and tell him that a priest and his disciple have come, who are on their way to get scriptures in India, and that they can deal with any monster."

"I hope you're telling me the truth," said the lad. "You'll get me into great trouble if you fail."

"I'll positively guarantee," said Monkey, "that I'm not deceiving you. Make haste and lead us in."

The lad saw nothing for it but to pick up his bundle and go back to the house. "You half-wit," roared old Mr. Kao, "what have you come back for?" But as soon as he had heard the lad's story, he quickly changed into his best clothes and came out to greet the guests, smiling affably. Tripitaka returned his greeting, but Monkey did not bow or say a word. The old man looked him up and down, and not knowing quite what to make of him did not ask him how he did.

"And how about me? Don't you want to know how I am?" said Monkey.

"Isn't it enough to have a monster in the house as son-in-law," grumbled the old man, "without your bringing in this frightful creature to molest me?"

"In all the years you've lived," said Monkey, "you've evidently learnt very little wisdom. If you judge people by their appearances, you'll always be going wrong. I'm not much to look at, I grant; but I have great powers, and if you are having any trouble with bogeys or monsters in the house, that's just where I come in. I'm going to get you back your daughter, so you had better stop grumbling about my appearance."

Mr. Kao, trembling with fear, managed at last to pull himself together sufficiently to invite them both in. Monkey, without so much as by-your-leave, led the horse into the courtyard and tied it to a pillar. Then he drew up an old weather-beaten stool, asked Tripitaka to be seated, and taking another stool for himself calmly sat down at Tripitaka's side.

"The little priest knows how to make himself at home," said Mr. Kao.

"This is nothing," said Monkey. "Keep me here a few months and you'll see me really making myself at home!"

"I don't quite understand," said the old man, "whether you've come for a night's lodging or to drive out the monster."

"We've come for a night's lodging," said Monkey, "but if there are any monsters about I don't mind dealing with them, just to pass the time. But first, I should like to know how many of them there are?"

"Heavens!" cried the old man, "isn't one monster enough to afflict the household, living here as my son-in-law?"

"Just tell me about it from the beginning," said Monkey. "If I know what he's good for, I can deal with him."

"We'd never had any trouble with ghosts or goblins or monsters on this farm before," said the old man. "Unfortunately I have no son, but only three daughters. The eldest is called Fragrant Orchid, the second Jade Orchid, and the third Blue Orchid. The first two were betrothed from childhood into neighbouring families. Our plan for the youngest was to marry her to someone who would come and live with her here and help look after us in our old age. About three years ago a very nice-looking young fellow turned up, saying that he came from Fu-ling, and that his surname was Hog. He said he had no parents or brothers and sisters, and was looking for a family where he would be taken as son-in-law, in return for the work that he did about the place. He sounded just the sort we wanted, and I accepted him. I must say he worked very hard. He pushed the plough himself and never asked to use a bull; he managed to do all his reaping without knife or staff. For some time we were perfectly satisfied, except for one thing—his appearance began to change in a very odd way."

"In what way?" asked Monkey.

"When he first came," said the old man, "he was just a dark, stoutish fellow. But afterwards his nose began to turn into a regular snout, his ears became larger and larger, and great bristles began to grow at the back of his neck. In fact, he began to look more and more like a hog. His appetite is enormous. He eats four or five pounds of rice at each meal, and as a light collation in the morning I've known him to get through over a hundred pasties. He's not at all averse to fruit and vegetables either, and what with this and all the wine he drinks, in the course of the last six months he's pretty well eaten and drunk us out of house and home."

"No doubt," said Tripitaka, "anyone who works so hard as he does needs a lot of nourishment."

"If it were only this business of food," said the old man, "it wouldn't be so bad. But he frightens everybody round by raising magic winds, suddenly vanishing and appearing again, making stones fly through the air and such like tricks. Worst of all, he has locked up Blue Orchid in the back outhouse,[15] and it is six months since we set eyes on her. We don't even know if she is dead or alive. It is evident that he's an ogre of some kind, and that is why we were trying to get hold of an exorcist."

---

[15] **outhouse:** An outbuilding.

"Don't you worry," said Monkey. "This very night I'll catch him and make him sign a Deed of Relinquishment[16] and give you back your daughter."

"The main thing is to catch him," said Mr. Kao. "It doesn't so much matter about documents."

"Perfectly easy," said Monkey. "Tonight as soon as it is dark, you'll see the whole thing settled."

"What weapons do you need, and how many men to help you?" asked Mr. Kao. "We must get on with the preparations."

"I'm armed already," said Monkey.

"So far as I can see, all you've got between you is a priest's staff," said the old man. "That wouldn't be much use against such a fiend as this."

Monkey took his embroidery needle from behind his ear and once more changed it into a great iron cudgel. "Does this satisfy you?" he asked. "I doubt if your house could provide anything tougher."

"How about followers?" said the old man.

"I need no followers," said Monkey. "All I ask for is some decent elderly person to sit with my master and keep him company."

Several respectable friends and relatives were fetched, and having looked them up and down Monkey said to Tripitaka, "Sit here quietly and don't worry. I'm off to do this job."

"Take me to the back building," he said to Mr. Kao, grasping his cudgel. "I'd like to have a look at the monster's lodging-place."

"Give me the key," he said, when they came to the door.

"Think what you're saying," said the old man. "Do you suppose that if a key was all that was wanted, we should be troubling you?"

"What's the use of living so long in the world if you haven't learnt even to recognize a joke when you hear one?" said Monkey laughing. Then he went up to the door and with a terrific blow of his cudgel smashed it down. Within, it was pitch dark. "Call to your daughter and see if she is there," said Monkey. The old man summoned up his courage and cried, "Miss Three!" Recognizing her father's voice, she answered with a faint "Papa, I am here." Monkey peered into the darkness with his steely eyes, and it was a pitiable sight that he saw. Unwashed cheeks, matted hair, bloodless lips, weak and trembling. She tottered towards her father, flung her arms round him and burst into tears. "Don't make that noise," said Monkey, "but tell us where your monster is."

"I don't know," she said. "Nowadays he goes out at dawn and comes back at dusk, I can't keep track of him at all. He knows that you're trying to find someone to exorcise him; that's why he keeps away all day."

"Not a word more!" said Monkey. "Old man, take your darling back to the house and calm her down. I'll wait here for the monster. If he doesn't come, it is not my fault, and if he comes I'll pluck up your trouble by the roots."

Left alone, Monkey used his magic arts to change himself into the exact image of

[16] **Deed of Relinquishment:** Divorce decree.

Blue Orchid, and sat waiting for the monster to return. Presently there was a great gust of wind; stones and gravel hurtled through the air. When the wind subsided there appeared a monster of truly terrible appearance. He had short bristles on his swarthy cheeks, a long snout, and huge ears. He wore a cotton jacket that was green but not green, blue but not blue, and had a spotted handkerchief tied round his head. "That's the article," laughed Monkey to himself.

Dear Monkey! He did not go to meet the monster or ask him how he did, but lay on the bed groaning, as though he were ill. The monster, quite taken in, came up to the bed and grabbing at Monkey tried to kiss him. "None of your lewd tricks on old Monkey!" laughed Monkey to himself, and giving the monster a great clout on the nose sent him reeling.

"Dear sister," said the monster, picking himself up, "why are you cross with me today? Is it because I am so late?"

"I'm not cross," said Monkey.

"If you're not cross," said the monster, "why do you push me away?"

"You've got such a clumsy way of kissing," said Monkey. "You might have known that I'm not feeling well today, when you saw I did not come to the door to meet you. Take off your clothes and get into bed." Still suspecting nothing the monster began to undress. Monkey meanwhile jumped up and sat on the commode. When the monster got into bed he felt everywhere but could not find his bride. "Sister," he called, "what has become of you? Take off your clothes and get into bed."

"You go to sleep first," said Monkey. "I'll follow when I've done my duties." Monkey suddenly began to sigh, murmuring "Was there ever such an unhappy girl as I?"

"What are you grumbling about?" said the monster. "Since I came here, I've cost you something in food and drink, that I own. But I've more than earned what I have got. Haven't I cleaned the ground and drained ditches, carried bricks and tiles, built walls, ploughed fields, planted grain, and improved the farm out of all knowing? You've good clothes to wear and all the food you need. What's all this childish nonsense about being unhappy?"

"That's not it at all," said Monkey. "Today my parents came and made a fearful scene through the partition wall."

"What did they make a scene about?" said the monster.

"They don't like having you here as their son-in-law," said Monkey. "They say you've got an ugly face, and they don't know who your father is and haven't seen any of your relations. They say you come and go no one knows when or where, and it's bad for the credit of the house that we don't know your name or anything at all about you. That's what they said, and it has made me miserable."

"What do looks matter?" said the monster. "It's a strong man they need about the place, and they can't say anything against me on that score. And if they think so ill of me, why did they accept me here at all? As for who I am, there's no mystery about it. I come from the Cloud-Ladder Cave at Fu-ling, and because I look a bit like a pig they call me Pigsy—Pigsy Bristles; next time they ask just tell them that."

"Confiding monster!" thought Monkey. "It needs no tortures to get a confession from him. Now we know where he comes from and who he is. It only remains to catch him."

"They are looking for an exorcist to drive you away," he said to the monster.

"Go to sleep," said Pigsy, "and don't worry about them any more. Am not I strong enough, with my nine-pronged muck-rake, to frighten off any exorcist or priest or what-not? Even if your old man's prayers could bring down the master of all devils from the Ninth Heaven,[17] as a matter of fact he's an old friend of mine and wouldn't do anything against me."

"He's done more than that," said Monkey. "He has called in the Great Sage, who five hundred years ago made turmoil in Heaven."

"If that's so," said Pigsy, "I'm off! There'll be no more kissing tonight!"

"Why are you going?" asked Monkey.

"You don't know," said Pigsy. "That chap is terribly powerful, and I don't know that I could deal with him. I'm frightened of losing my reputation." He dressed hastily, opened the door, and went out. But Monkey caught hold of him and making a magic pass changed himself back into his true form. "Monster, look round," he cried, "and you will see that I am he."

When Pigsy turned and saw Monkey with his sharp little teeth and grinning mouth, his fiery, steely eyes, his flat head and hairy cheeks, for all the world like a veritable thunder-demon, he was so startled that his hands fell limp beside him and his legs gave way. With a scream he tore himself free, leaving part of his coat in Monkey's hand, and was gone like a whirlwind. Monkey struck out with his cudgel; but Pigsy had already begun to make for the cave he came from. Soon Monkey was after him, crying, "Where are you off to? If you go up to Heaven I will follow you to the summit of the Pole Star, and if you go down into the earth I will follow you to the deepest pit of hell."

If you do not know how far he chased him or which of them won the fight, you must listen to what is told in the next chapter.

Chapter 17

The monster fled with Monkey at his heels, till they came at last to a high mountain, and here the monster disappeared into a cave, and a moment later came back brandishing a nine-pronged muck-rake. They set to at once and battled all night long, from the second watch till dawn began to whiten in the sky. At last the monster could hold his ground no longer, and retreating into the cave bolted the door behind him. Standing outside the cave-door, Monkey saw that on a slab of rock was the inscription "Cloud-ladder Cave." As the monster showed no sign of coming out again and it was now broad daylight, Monkey thought to himself, "The Master will be wondering what has happened to me. I had better go and see him and then come back and catch the monster." So tripping from cloud to cloud he made his way back to the farm.

Tripitaka was still sitting with the old man, talking of this and that. He had not slept all night. He was just wondering why Monkey did not return when Monkey

[17] **Ninth Heaven:** The highest level of heaven.

alighted in the courtyard, and suddenly stood before them. "Master, here I am," he said. The old men all bowed down before him, and supposing that he had accomplished his task thanked him for all his trouble.

"You must have had a long way to go, to catch the creature," said Tripitaka.

"Master," said Monkey, "the monster is not a common incubus or elf. I have recognized him as a former inhabitant of Heaven, where he was in command of all the watery hosts. He was expelled to earth after an escapade with the daughter of the Moon Goddess, and though he was here re-incarnated with a pig-like form, he retains all his magic powers. I chased him to his mountain-cave, where he fetched out a nine-pronged muck-rake, and we fought together all night. Just at dawn he gave up the fight, and locked himself up in his cave. I would have beaten down the door and forced him to fight to a decision, but I was afraid the Master might be getting anxious, so I thought I had better come back first and report."

"Reverend Sir," said old Mr. Kao to Monkey, "I am afraid this hasn't helped matters much. True, you have driven him away; but after you have gone he's certain to come back again, and where shall we be then? We shall have to trouble you to catch him for us. That is the only way to pluck out our trouble by the root. I'll see to it that you have no cause to regret the trouble you take. You shall have half of all that is ours, both land and goods. If you like, my friends and relations shall sign a document to this effect. It will be well worth their while, if only we can remove this shame from our home."

"I think you make too much of the whole affair," said Monkey. "The monster himself admits that his appetite is large; but he has done quite a lot of useful work. All the recent improvements in the estate are his work. He claims to be well worth what he costs in keep, and does not see why you should be so anxious to get rid of him. He is a divinity from Heaven, although condemned to live on earth, he helps to keep things going, and so far as I can see he hasn't done any harm to your daughter."

"It may be true," said old Mr. Kao, "that he's had no influence upon her. But I stick to it that it's very bad for our reputation. Wherever I go I hear people saying 'Mr. Kao has taken a monster as his son-in-law.' What is one to say to that?"

"Now, Monkey," said Tripitaka, "don't you think you had better go and have one more fight with him and see if you can't settle the business once and for all?"

"As a matter of fact," said Monkey, "I was only having a little game with him, to see how things would go. This time I shall certainly catch him and bring him back for you to see. Don't you worry! Look after my master," he cried to Mr. Kao, "I'm off!"

So saying, he disappeared into the clouds and soon arrived at the cave. With one blow of his cudgel he beat the doors to bits, and standing at the entrance he cried, "You noisome lout, come out and fight with Old Monkey." Pigsy lay fast asleep within, snoring heavily. But when he heard the door being beaten down and heard himself called a noisome lout, he was so much enraged that he snatched up his rake, pulled himself together, and rushed out, crying, "You wretched stableman, if ever there was a rogue, you're he! What have I to do with you, that you should come and knock down my door? Go and look at the Statute Book. You'll find that 'obtaining entry to premises by forcing a main door' is a Miscellaneous Capital Offence."

"You fool," said Monkey. "Haven't I a perfectly good justification at law for forcing your door? Remember that you laid violent hands on a respectable girl, and lived with her without matchmaker or testimony, tea, scarlet, wine, or any other ceremony. Are you aware that heads are cut off for less than that?"

"Stop that nonsense, and look at Old Pig's rake," cried Pigsy.

He struck out, but Monkey warded off the blow, crying, "I suppose that's the rake you used when you worked on the farm. Why should you expect me to be frightened of it?"

"You are very much mistaken," said Pigsy. "This rake was given to me by the Jade Emperor himself."

"A lie!" cried Monkey. "Here's my head. Hit as hard as you please, and we'll see!"

Pigsy raised the rake and brought it down with such force on Monkey's head that the sparks flew. But there was not a bruise or scratch. Pigsy was so much taken aback, that his hands fell limp at his side. "What a head!" he exclaimed.

"You've still something to learn about me," said Monkey. "After I made havoc in Heaven and was caught by Erh-lang,[18] all the deities of Heaven hacked me with their axes, hammered me with their mallets, slashed me with their swords, set fire to me, hurled thunderbolts at me, but not a hair of my body was hurt. Lao Tzu[19] put me in his alchemic stove and cooked me with holy fire. But all that happened was that my eyes became fiery, my head and shoulders hard as steel. If you don't believe it, try again, and see whether you can hurt me or not."

"I remember," said Pigsy, "that before you made havoc in Heaven, you lived in the Cave of the Water Curtain. Lately nothing has been heard of you. How did you get here? Perhaps my father-in-law asked you to come and deal with me."

"Not at all," said Monkey, "I have been converted and am now a priest, and am going with a Chinese pilgrim called Tripitaka, who has been sent by the Emperor to fetch scriptures from India. On our way we happened to come past Mr. Kao's farm, and we asked for a night's lodging. In the course of conversation Mr. Kao asked for help about his daughter. That's why I'm after you, you noisome lout!"

No sooner did Pigsy hear these words than the rake fell from his hand. "Where is that pilgrim?" he gasped. "Take me to him."

"What do you want to see him for?" asked Monkey.

"I've been converted," said Pigsy. "Didn't you know? The Bodhisattva Kuan-yin converted me and put me here to prepare myself by fasting and abstention for going to India with a pilgrim to fetch scriptures; after which, I am to receive illumination. That all happened some years ago, and since then I have had no news of this pilgrim. If you are his disciple, what on earth possessed you not to mention this scripture-seeking business? Why did you prefer to pick a quarrel and knock me about in front of my own door?"

"I suspect," said Monkey, "that you are just making all this up, in order to get away. If it's really true that you want to escort my Master to India, you must make a

[18] **Erh-lang:** A legendary figure in Chinese mythology, famous for slaying dragons and quelling floods.

[19] **Lao Tzu:** Laozi, the founder of Taoism, was a popular figure in Chinese legends by the time of *Monkey.* He is described as having the powers of a sage, healer, and magician.

solemn vow to Heaven that you're telling the truth. Then I'll take you to him." Pigsy flung himself upon his knees and, kow-towing at the void, up and down like a pestle in the mortar, he cried, "I swear before the Buddha Amitabha,[20] praised be his name, that I am telling the truth; and if I am not, may I be condemned once more by the tribunals of Heaven and sliced into ten thousand pieces."

When Monkey heard him make this solemn vow, "Very well then," he said. "First take a torch and burn down your lair, and then I will take you with me." Pigsy took some reeds and brambles, lit a fire and soon reduced the cave to the state of a burnt-out kiln.

"You've nothing against me now," he said. "Take me along with you."

"You'd better give your rake to me," said Monkey. When Pigsy had handed over the rake, Monkey took a hair, blew on it with magic breath, and changed it into a three-ply hemp cord. Pigsy put his hands behind his back and let himself be bound. Then Monkey caught hold of his ear and dragged him along, crying, "Hurry up! Hurry up!"

"Don't be so rough," begged Pigsy. "You're hurting my ear."

"Rough indeed!" said Monkey. "I shouldn't get far by being gentle with you. The proverb says, 'The better the pig, the harder to hold.' Wait till you have seen the Master and shown that you are in earnest. Then we'll let you go."

When they reached the farm, Monkey twitched Pigsy's ear, saying, "You see that old fellow sitting so solemnly up there? That's my Master." Mr. Kao and the other old men, seeing Monkey leading the monster by the ear, were delighted beyond measure, and came out into the courtyard to meet him. "Reverend Sir," they cried, "that's the creature, sure enough, that married our master's daughter." Pigsy fell upon his knees and with his hands still tied behind his back, kow-towed to Tripitaka, crying, "Master, forgive me for failing to give you a proper reception. If I had known that it was you who were staying with my father-in-law I would have come to pay my respects, and all these unpleasantnesses would never have happened."

"Monkey," said Tripitaka, "how did you manage to bring him to this state of mind?" Monkey let go his ear, and giving him a knock with the handle of the rake, shouted, "Speak, fool!" Pigsy then told how he had been commissioned by Kuan-yin. "Mr. Kao," said Tripitaka, when he heard the story, "this is the occasion for a little incense." Mr. Kao then brought out the incense tray, and Tripitaka washed his hands, and burning incense he turned towards the south and said, "I am much beholden, Bodhisattva!" Then he went up into the hall and resumed his seat, bidding Monkey release Pigsy from his bonds. Monkey shook himself; the rope became a hair again and returned to his body. Pigsy was free. He again did obeisance, and vowed that he would follow Tripitaka to the west. Then he bowed to Monkey, whom as the senior disciple he addressed as "Elder Brother and Teacher."

"Where's my wife?" said Pigsy to Mr. Kao. "I should like her to pay her respects to my Father and Brother in the Law." "Wife indeed!" laughed Monkey. "You haven't got a wife now. There are some sorts of Taoists that are family men; but who ever

---

[20] **Buddha Amitabha:** The Buddha of the Pure Land School of Buddhism, which envisioned an extremely material Paradise.

heard of a Buddhist priest calmly talking about his 'wife'? Sit down and eat your supper, and early tomorrow we'll all start out for India."

After supper Mr. Kao brought out a red lacquer bowl full of broken pieces of silver and gold, and offered the contents to the three priests, as a contribution towards their travelling expenses. He also offered them three pieces of fine silk to make clothes. Tripitaka said, "Travelling priests must beg their way as they go. We cannot accept money or silk." But Monkey came up and plunging his hand into the dish took out a handful of gold and silver, and called to the lad Kao Ts'ai, "You were kind enough yesterday to introduce my Master into the house and we owe it to you that we have found a new disciple. I have no other way of showing my thanks but giving you these broken pieces of gold and silver, which I hope you will use to buy yourself a pair of shoes. If you come across any more monsters, please bespeak them for me, and I shall be even further obliged to you."

"Reverend Sirs," said Mr. Kao, "if I can't persuade you to accept silver or gold, I hope that you will at least let me show my gratitude by giving you these few pieces of coarse stuff, to make into cassocks."

"A priest who accepts so much as a thread of silk," said Tripitaka, "must do penance for a thousand aeons to expiate his crime. All I ask is a few scraps left over from the household meal, to take with us as dry provisions."

"Wait a minute," cried Pigsy. "If I get my due for all I've done on this estate since I married into the family, I should carry away several tons of provisions. That's by the way. But I think my father-in-law might in decency give me a new jacket. My old one was torn by Brother Monkey in the fight last night. And my shoes are all in pieces; I should be glad of a new pair."

Mr. Kao acceded to his request, and Pigsy, delighted by his new finery, strutted up and down in front of the company, calling to Mr. Kao, "Be so kind as to inform my mother-in-law, my sisters-in-law, and all my kinsmen by marriage that I have become a priest and must ask their pardon for going off without saying good-bye to them in person. And father-in-law, I'll trouble you to take good care of my bride. For if we don't bring off this scripture business, I shall turn layman again and live with you as your son-in-law."

"Lout!" cried Monkey. "Don't talk rubbish."

"It's not rubbish," said Pigsy. "Things may go wrong, and then I shall be in a pretty pass! No salvation, and no wife either."

"Kindly stop this silly argument," said Tripitaka. "It is high time we started." So they put together the luggage, which Pigsy was told to carry, and when the white horse was saddled Tripitaka was set astride. Monkey, with his cudgel over his shoulder, led the way. And so, parting from Mr. Kao and all his relations, the three of them set out for the West. And if you do not know what befell them, you must listen to what is told in the next chapter.

Chapter 18

So the three of them travelled on towards the west, and came at last to a great plain. Summer had passed and autumn come. They heard "the cicada singing in the rotten willow," saw "the Fire-Star rolling to the west." At last they came to a huge and turbulent river, racing along with gigantic waves. "That's a very broad river," cried Tripitaka from on horseback. "There does not seem to be a ferry anywhere about. How are we to get across?"

"A boat wouldn't be much use in waters as rough as that," said Pigsy.

Monkey leapt into the air, and shading his eyes with his hand gazed at the waters. "Master," he cried, "this is going to be no easy matter. For me, yes. I should only have to shake my hips, and I should be across at one bound. But for you it's not going to be such easy work."

"I can't even see the other side," said Tripitaka. "How far is it, do you suppose?"

"About eight hundred leagues," said Monkey.

"How do you come to that reckoning?" asked Pigsy.

"I'll tell you frankly," said Monkey. "My sight is so good that I can see everything, lucky or unlucky, a thousand leagues away, and when I looked down on this river from above I could see well enough that it must be a good eight hundred leagues across." Tripitaka was very much depressed, and was just turning his horse when he saw a slab of stone on which was the inscription "River of Flowing Sand." Underneath in small letters was the verse:

> In the Floating Sands, eight hundred wide,
> In the Dead Waters, three thousand deep,
> A goose-feather will not keep afloat,
> A rush-flower sinks straight to the bottom.

They were looking at this inscription when suddenly a monster of horrifying aspect came surging through the mountainous waves. His hair was flaming red, his eyes were like two lanterns; at his neck were strung nine skulls, and he carried a huge priest's staff. Like a whirlwind he rushed straight at the pilgrims. Monkey seized Tripitaka and hurried him up the bank to a safe distance. Pigsy dropped his load and rushed at the monster with his rake. The monster fended off the blow with his priest's staff. The fight that followed was a good one, each displaying his powers on the shores of the River of Flowing Sands. They fought twenty bouts without reaching a decision. Monkey, seeing the grand fight that was in progress, itched to go and join in it. At last he said to Tripitaka, "You sit here and don't worry. I am going off to have a bit of fun with the creature." Tripitaka did his best to dissuade him. But Monkey with a wild whoop leapt into the fray. At this moment the two of them were locked in combat, and it was hard to get between them. But Monkey managed to put in a tremendous blow of the cudgel right on the monster's head. At once the monster broke away, and rushing madly back to the water's edge leapt in and disappeared. Pigsy was furious.

"Heigh, brother," he cried. "Who asked you to interfere? The monster was just beginning to tire. After another three or four rounds he would not have been able to fend off my rake, and I should have had him at my mercy. But as soon as he saw your ugly face he took to his heels. You've spoilt everything!"

"I'll just tell you how it happened," said Monkey. "It's months since I had a chance to use my cudgel, and when I saw you having such a rare time with him my feet itched with longing not to miss the fun, and I couldn't hold myself back. How was I to know that the monster wouldn't play?" So hand in hand, laughing and talking, the two of them went back to Tripitaka.

"Have you caught the monster?" he asked.

"He gave up the fight," said Monkey, "and went back again into the water."

"It wouldn't be a bad thing," said Tripitaka, "if we could persuade him to show us how to get across. He's lived here a long time and must know this river inside out. Otherwise I don't see how we are to get across an enormous river like this without a boat."

"There is something in that," said Monkey. "Does not the proverb say 'You cannot live near cinnabar[21] without becoming red, or near ink without becoming black.' If we succeed in catching him we certainly ought not to kill him, but make him take the Master across this river and then dispose of him."

"You shall have your chance this time," said Pigsy to Monkey. "I'll stay here and look after the Master."

"That's all very well," said Monkey, "but this job is not at all in my line. I'm not at my best in the water. To get along here, I have to change myself into some water creature, such as a fish or crab. If it were a matter of going up into the clouds, I have tricks enough to deal with the ugliest situation. But in the water I confess I am at a disadvantage."

"I used, of course," said Pigsy, "to be Marshal of the River of Heaven, and had the command of eighty thousand watery fellows, so that I certainly ought to know something about that element. My only fear is that if whole broods of water-creatures were to come to the monster's help, I might get myself into a bit of a fix."

"What you must do," said Monkey, "is to lure the monster out, and not get yourself involved in more of a scrap than you can help. Once he is out, I'll come to your assistance."

"That's the best plan," said Pigsy, "I'll go at once."

So saying, he stripped off his blue embroidered jacket and shoes, and brandishing his rake plunged into the river. He found that he had forgotten none of his old water-magic, and lashing through the waves soon reached the bed of the stream and made his way straight ahead. After retiring from the fight, the monster lay down and had a nap. Soon however he was woken by the sound of someone coming through the water, and starting up he saw Pigsy pushing through the waves, rake in hand. Seizing his staff, he came towards him shouting, "Now then, shaven pate, just look where you're going or you'll get a nasty knock with this staff!"

Pigsy struck the staff aside with his rake, crying, "What monster are you, that you dare to bar my path?"

"I'm surprised that you don't recognize me," said the monster. "I am not an ordinary spook, but a divinity with name and surname."

"If that is so," said Pigsy, "what are you doing here, taking human lives? Tell me who you are, and I'll spare you!"

---

[21] **cinnabar:** A red ore of mercury.

"So great was my skill in alchemic arts," said the monster, "that I was summoned to Heaven by the Jade Emperor and became a Marshal of the Hosts of Heaven. One day, at a celestial banquet, my hand slipped and I broke a crystal cup. The Jade Emperor was furious, and I was hurried away to the execution ground. Fortunately for me the Red-legged Immortal begged for my release, and my sentence was changed to one of banishment to the River of Flowing Sands. When I am hungry I go ashore and eat whatever living thing comes my way. Many are the woodmen and fishermen who have fallen to me as my prey, and I don't mind telling you I am very hungry at this moment. Don't imagine that your flesh would be too coarse for me to eat. Chopped up fine and well sauced, you'll suit me nicely!"

"Coarse indeed!" said Pigsy. "I'm a dainty enough morsel to make any mouth water. Mind your manners, and swallow your grandfather's rake!"

The monster ducked and avoided the blow. Then both of them came up to the surface of the water, and treading the waves fought stubbornly for two hours without reaching a decision. It was a case of "the copper bowl meeting the iron broom, the jade gong confronted by the metal bell."

After some thirty rounds Pigsy pretended to give in, and dragging his rake after him made for the shore, with the monster hard on his heels. "Come on!" cried Pigsy. "With firm ground under our feet we'll have a better fight than before."

"I know what you're up to," cried the monster. "You've lured me up here, so that your partner may come and help you. We'll go back into the water and finish the fight there."

The monster was too wily to come any farther up the bank and they soon were fighting again, this time at the very edge of the water. This was too much for Monkey, who was watching them from a distance. "Wait here," he said to Tripitaka, "while I try the trick called 'The ravening eagle pouncing on its prey.'" So saying, he catapulted into the air and swooped down on the monster, who swiftly turning his head and seeing Monkey pouncing down upon him from the clouds, leapt straight into the water and was seen no more.

"He's given us the slip," said Monkey. "He's not likely to come out on the bank again. What are we going to do?"

"It's a tough job," said Pigsy, "I doubt if I can beat him. Even if I sweat till I burst I can't get beyond quits."

"Let's go and see the Master," said Monkey.

They climbed the bank, and finding Tripitaka they told him of their predicament. Tripitaka burst into tears.

"We shall never get across," he sobbed.

"Don't you worry," said Monkey. "It is true that with that creature lying in wait for us, we can't get across. But Pigsy, you stay here by the Master and don't attempt to do any more fighting. I am going off to the Southern Ocean."

"And what are you going to do there?" asked Pigsy.

"This scripture-seeking business," said Monkey, "is an invention of the Bodhisattva, and it was she who converted us. It is surely for her to find some way of getting us over this river. I'll go and ask her. It's a better idea than fighting with the monster."

"Brother," said Pigsy, "when you're there you might say a word to her for me; tell her I'm very much obliged indeed for having been put on the right way."

"If you are going," said Tripitaka, "you had better start at once and get back as soon as you can."

Monkey somersaulted into the clouds, and in less than half an hour he had reached the Southern Ocean and saw Mount Potalaka rise before him. After landing, he went straight to the Purple Bamboo Grove, where he was met by the Spirits of the Twenty-Four Ways.

"Great Sage, what brings you here?" they said.

"My Master is in difficulties," said Monkey, "and I wish to have an interview with the Bodhisattva."

"Sit down," they said, "and we will announce you."

The Bodhisattva was leaning against the parapet of the Lotus Pool, looking at the flowers, with the Dragon King's daughter, bearer of the Magic Pearl, at her side. "Why aren't you looking after your Master?" she said to Monkey, when he was brought in.

"When we came to the River of Flowing Sands," said Monkey, "we found it guarded by a monster formidable in the arts of war. My fellow-disciple Pigsy, whom we picked up on the way, did his best to subdue the creature, but was not successful. That is why I have ventured to come and ask you to take pity on us, and rescue my Master from this predicament."

"You obstinate ape," said the Bodhisattva, "this is the same thing all over again. Why didn't you say that you were in charge of the priest of T'ang?"

"We were both far too busy trying to catch him and make him take the Master across," said Monkey.

"I put him there on purpose to help scripture-seekers," said Kuan-yin. "If only you had mentioned the fact that you had come from China to look for scriptures, you would have found him very helpful."

"At present," said Monkey, "he is skulking at the bottom of the river. How are we to get him to come out and make himself useful? And how is Tripitaka going to get across the river?"

The Bodhisattva summoned her disciple Hui-yen, and taking a red gourd from her sleeve she said to him, "Take this gourd, go with Monkey to the river and shout 'Sandy!' He will come out at once, and you must then bring him to the Master to make his submission. Next string together the nine skulls that he wears at his neck according to the disposition of the Magic Square, with the gourd in the middle, and you will find you have a holy ship that will carry Tripitaka across the River of Flowing Sands."

Soon Hui-yen and Monkey alighted on the river-bank. Seeing who Monkey had brought with him, Pigsy led forward the Master to meet them. After salutations had been exchanged, Hui-yen went to the edge of the water and called, "Sandy, Sandy! The scripture-seekers have been here a long time. Why do you not come out and pay your respects to them?"

The monster Sandy, knowing that this must be a messenger from Kuan-yin, hastened to the surface, and as soon as his head was above water he saw Hui-yen and

Monkey. He put on a polite smile and came towards them bowing and saying to Hui-yen, "Forgive me for not coming to meet you. Where is the Bodhisattva?"

"She has not come," said Hui-yen. "She sent me to tell you to put yourself at Tripitaka's disposal and become his disciple. She also told me to take the skulls that you wear at your neck and this gourd that I have brought, and make a holy ship to carry the Master across."

"Where are the pilgrims?" asked Sandy.

"Sitting there on the eastern bank," said Hui-yen.

"Well," said Sandy, looking at Pigsy, "that filthy creature never said a word about scriptures, though I fought with him for two days." Then seeing Monkey, "What, is that fellow there too?" he cried. "He's the other's partner. I'm not going near them."

"The first is Pigsy," said Hui-yen, "and the second is Monkey. They are both Tripitaka's disciples and both were converted by the Bodhisattva. You have nothing to fear from them. I myself will introduce you to the Master."

Sandy put away his staff, tidied himself and scrambled up the bank. When they reached Tripitaka, Sandy knelt before him, exclaiming, "How can I have been so blind as not to recognize you? Forgive me for all my rudeness!"

"You brazen creature," said Pigsy, "why did you insist on having a row with us, instead of joining our party from the start?"

"Brother," laughed Monkey, "don't scold him. It is we who are to blame, for never having told him that we were going to get scriptures."

"Is it indeed your earnest desire to dedicate yourself to our religion?" asked Tripitaka.

Sandy bowed his assent, and Tripitaka told Monkey to take a knife and shave his head.[22] He then once more did homage to Tripitaka, and in a less degree to Monkey and Pigsy. Tripitaka thought that Sandy shaped very well as a priest, and was thoroughly satisfied with him.

"You had better be quick and get on with your boat-building," said Hui-yen.

Sandy obediently took the skulls from his neck, and tying them in the pattern of the Magic Square he put the Bodhisattva's gourd in the middle, and called to Tripitaka to come down to the water. Tripitaka then ascended the holy ship, which he found as secure as any light craft. Pigsy supported him on the left, Sandy on the right, while Monkey in the stern held the halter of the white horse, which followed as best it could. Hui-yen floated just above them. They soon arrived in perfect safety at the other side.

And if you do not know how long it was before they got Illumination you must listen to what is told in the next chapter.

Chapter 19

Tripitaka sat in the Zen Hall of the Treasure Wood Temple, under the lamp; he recited the Water Litany of the Liang Emperor and read through the True Scripture

---

[22] **shave his head:** A sign of becoming a Buddhist monk.

of the Peacock. It was now the third watch (12 p.m.), and he put his books back into their bag, and was just going to get up and go to bed when he heard a great banging outside the gate and felt a dank blast of ghostly wind. Fearing the lamp would be blown out, he hastened to screen it with his sleeve. But the lamp continued to flicker in the strangest way, and Tripitaka began to tremble. He was, however, very tired, and presently he lay down across the reading-desk and dozed. Although his eyes were closed, he still knew what was going on about him, and in his ears still sounded the dank wind that moaned outside the window. And when the wind had passed by, he heard a voice outside the Zen Hall whispering: "Master!"

Tripitaka raised his head, and in his dream he saw a man standing there, dripping from head to foot, with tears in his eyes, and continually murmuring, "Master, Master." Tripitaka sat up and said, "What can you be but a hobgoblin, evil spirit, monster or foul bogey, that you should come to this place and molest me in the middle of the night? But I must tell you that I am no common scrambler in the greedy world of man. I am a great and illustrious priest who at the bidding of the Emperor of T'ang am going to the west to worship the Buddha and seek scriptures. And I have three disciples, each of whom is adept in quelling dragons and subduing tigers, removing monsters and making away with bogeys. If these disciples were to see you, they would grind you to powder. I tell you this for your own good, in kindness and compassion. You had best hide at once, and not set foot in this place of Meditation."

But the man drew nearer to the room and said, "Master, I am no hobgoblin, evil spirit, monster, nor foul bogey either."

"If you are none of these things," said Tripitaka, "what are you doing here at depth of night?"

"Master," said the man, "rest your eyes upon me and look at me well."

Then Tripitaka looked at him with a fixed gaze and saw that there was a crown upon his head and a sceptre at his waist, and that he was dressed and shod as only a king can be.

When Tripitaka saw this he was much startled and amazed. At once he bowed down and cried out with a loud voice: "Of what court is your majesty the king? I beg of you, be seated." But the hand he stretched to help the king to his seat plunged through empty space. Yet when he was back in his seat and looked up, the man was still there.

"Tell me, your majesty," he cried, "of what are you emperor, of where are you king? Doubtless there were troubles in your land, wicked ministers rebelled against you and at midnight you fled for your life. What is your tale? Tell it for me to hear."

"Master," he said, "my home is due west of here, only forty leagues away. At that place, there is a city moated and walled, and this city is where my kingdom was founded."

"And what is its name?" asked Tripitaka.

"I will not deceive you," he said. "When my dynasty was set up there, a new name was given to it, and it was called Crow-cock."

"But tell me," said Tripitaka, "what brings you here in such consternation?"

"Master," he said, "five years ago there was a great drought. The grass did not grow and my people were all dying of hunger. It was pitiful indeed!"

Tripitaka nodded. "Your majesty," he said, "there is an ancient saying, 'Heaven favours, where virtue rules.' I fear you have no compassion for your people; for now that they are in trouble, you leave your city. Go back and open your store-houses, sustain your people, repent your misdeeds, and do present good twofold to make recompense. Release from captivity any whom you have unjustly condemned, and Heaven will see to it that rain comes and the winds are tempered."

"All the granaries in my kingdom were empty," he said, "I had neither cash nor grain. My officers civil and military were unpaid, and even at my own board no relish could be served. I have shared sweet and bitter with my people no less than Yü the Great[23] when he quelled the floods; I have bathed and done penance; morning and night I have burnt incense and prayed. For three years it was like this, till the rivers were all empty, the wells dry.

"Suddenly, when things were at their worst, there came a magician from the Chung-nan mountains who could call the winds and summon the rain, and make stones into gold. First he obtained audience with my many officers, civil and military, and then with me. At once I begged him to mount the altar and pray for rain. He did so, and was answered; no sooner did his magic tablet resound than floods of rain fell. I told him three feet would be ample. But he said after so long a drought, it took a lot to soak the ground, and he brought down another two inches. And I, seeing him to be of such great powers, prostrated myself before him and treated him henceforth as my elder brother."

"This was a great piece of luck," said Tripitaka.

"Whence should my luck come?" asked he.

"Why," said Tripitaka, "if your magician could make rain when you wanted it, and gold whenever you needed it, what did you lack that you must needs leave your kingdom and come to me here?"

"For two years," he said, "he was my fellow at board and bed. Then at spring time when all the fruit trees were in blossom and young men and girls from every house, gallants from every quarter, went out to enjoy the sights of spring, there came a time when my officers had all returned to their desks and the ladies of the court to their bowers. I with that magician went slowly stepping hand in hand, till we came to the flower-garden and to the eight-cornered crystal well. Here he threw down something, I do not know what, and at once there was a great golden light. He led me to the well-side, wondering what treasure was in the well. Then he conceived an evil intent, and with a great shove pushed me into the well; then took a paving-stone and covered the well-top and sealed it with clay, and planted a banana-plant on top of it . . . Pity me! I have been dead three years; I am the phantom unavenged of one that perished at the bottom of a well."

---

[23] **Yü the Great:** An emperor who ruled from 2205 to 2197 B.C.E., legendary for draining the great floods with nine years of incessant labor.

When the man said that he was a ghost, Tripitaka was terrified; his legs grew flabby beneath him, and his hair stood on end. Controlling himself at last, he asked him saying "Your Majesty's story is hard to reconcile with reason. You say you have been dead for three years. How is it that in all this time none of your officers civil and military, nor of your queens and concubines and chamberlains ever came to look for you?"

"I have told you already," the man said, "of the magician's powers. There can be few others like him in all the world. He had but to give himself a shake, and there and then, in the flower-garden, he changed himself into the exact image of me. And now he holds my rivers and hills, and has stolen away my kingdom. All of my officers, the four hundred gentlemen of my court, my queens and concubines—all, all are his."

"Your Majesty is easily daunted," said Tripitaka.

"Easily daunted?" he asked.

"Yes," said Tripitaka, "that magician may have strange powers, turn himself into your image, steal your lands, your officers knowing nothing, and your ladies unaware. But you that were dead at least knew that you were dead. Why did you not go to Yama, King of Death,[24] and put in a complaint?"

"The magician's power," he said, "is very great, and he is on close terms with the clerks and officers of Death. The Spirit of Wall and Moat is forever drinking with him; all the Dragon Kings of the Sea are his kinsmen. The God of the Eastern Peak is his good friend; the ten kings of Judgement are his cousins. I should be barred in every effort to lay my plaint before the King of Death."

"If your Majesty," said Tripitaka, "is unable to lay your case before the Courts of the Dead, what makes you come to the world of the living with any hope of redress?"

"Master," he said, "how should a wronged ghost dare approach your door? The Spirit that Wanders at Night caught me in a gust of magic wind and blew me along. He said my three years' water-misery was ended and that I was to present myself before you; for at your service, he said, there was a great disciple, the Monkey Sage, most able to conquer demons and subdue impostors. I beg of you to come to my kingdom, lay hands on the magician and make clear the false from the true. Then, Master, I would repay you with all that will be mine to give."

"So then," said Tripitaka, "you have come to ask that my disciple should drive out the false magician?"

"Indeed, indeed," he said.

"My disciple," said Tripitaka, "in other ways is not all that he should be. But subduing monsters and evil spirits just suits his powers. I fear however that the circumstances make it hard for him to deal with this evil power."

"Why so?" asked the king.

"Because," said Tripitaka, "the magician has used his magic powers to change himself into the image of you. All the officers of your court have gone over to him, and all your ladies have accepted him. My disciple could no doubt deal with them;

[24] **Yama, King of Death:** Ruler of the underworld.

but he would hesitate to do violence to them. For should he do so, would not he and I be held guilty of conspiring to destroy your kingdom? And what would this be but to paint the tiger and carve the swan?"[25]

"There is still someone of mine at Court," he said.

"Excellent, excellent," said Tripitaka. "No doubt it is some personal attendant, who is guarding some fastness for you."

"Not at all," he said. "It is my own heir apparent."

"But surely," said Tripitaka, "the false magician has driven him away."

"Not at all," he said. "He is in the Palace of Golden Bells, in the Tower of the Five Phoenixes, studying with his tutor, or on the steps of the magician's throne. But all these three years he has forbidden the prince to go into the inner chambers of the Palace, and he can never see his mother."

"Why is that?" asked Tripitaka.

"It is the magician's scheme," he said. "He fears that if they were to meet, the queen might in the course of conversation let drop some word that would arouse the prince's suspicions. So these two never meet, and he all this long time has lived secure."

"The disaster that has befallen you, no doubt at Heaven's behest, is much like my own misfortune. My own father was killed by brigands, who seized my mother and after three months she gave birth to me. I at length escaped from their hands and by good chance met with kindness from a priest of the Golden Mountain Temple, who brought me up. Remembering my own unhappy state, without father or mother, I can sympathize with your prince, who has lost both his parents. But tell me, granted that this prince is still at Court, how can I manage to see him?"

"What difficulty in that?" he said.

"Because he is kept under strict control," said Tripitaka, "and is not even allowed to see the mother who bore him. How will a stray monk get to him?"

"Tomorrow," the king said, "he leaves the Court at daybreak."

"For what purpose?"

"Tomorrow, early in the morning, with three thousand followers and falcons and dogs, he will go hunting outside the city, and it will certainly be easy for you to see him. You must then tell him what I have told you, and he cannot fail to believe you."

"He is only a common mortal," said Tripitaka, "utterly deceived by the false magician in the palace, and at every turn calling him father and king. Why should he believe what I tell him?"

"If that is what worries you," the king said, "I will give you a token to show to him."

"And what can you give me?"

In his hand the king carried a tablet of white jade, bordered with gold. This he laid before Tripitaka saying, "Here is my token."

---

[25] **to paint . . . swan:** That is, an enterprise that, if successful, does more harm than inaction.

"What thing is this?" asked Tripitaka.

"When the magician disguised himself as me," said the king, "this treasure was the one thing he forgot about. When the queen asked what had become of it, he said that the wonder-worker who came to make rain took it away with him. If my prince sees it, his heart will be stirred towards me and he will avenge me."

"That will do," said Tripitaka. "Wait for me a little, while I tell my disciple to arrange this matter for you. Where shall I find you?"

"I dare not wait," he said. "I must ask the Spirit that wanders at Night to blow me to the inner chambers of the palace, where I will appear to the queen in a dream and tell her how to work with her son, and to conspire with you and your disciple."

Tripitaka nodded and agreed, saying, "Go, if you will."

Then the wronged ghost beat its head on the floor and turned as though to depart. Somehow it stumbled, and went sprawling with a loud noise that woke Tripitaka up. He knew that it had all been a dream, and finding himself sitting with the dying lamp in front of him, he hurriedly cried: "Disciple, disciple!"

"Hey, what's that?" cried Pigsy, waking up and coming across to him. "In the old days when I was a decent chap and had my whack of human flesh whenever I wanted, and all the stinking victuals I needed, that was a happy life indeed. A very different matter from coddling an old cleric on his journey! I thought I was to be an acolyte, but this is more like being a slave. By day I hoist the luggage and lead the horse; by night I run my legs off bringing you your pot. No sleep early or late! What's the matter this time?"

"Disciple," said Tripitaka, "I was dozing just now at my desk, and had a strange dream."

At this point Monkey sat up, and coming across to Tripitaka said, "Master, dreams come from waking thoughts. Each time we come to a hill before we have even begun to climb it, you are in a panic about ogres and demons. And you are always brooding about what a long way it is to India, and wondering if we shall ever get there; and thinking about Ch'ang-an, and wondering if you will ever see it again. All this brooding makes dreams. You should be like me. I think only about seeing Buddha in the west, and not a dream comes near me."

"Disciple," said Tripitaka, "this was not a dream of home-sickness. No sooner had I closed my eyes than there came a wild gust of wind, and there at the door stood an Emperor, who said he was the King of Crow-cock. He was dripping from head to foot, and his eyes were full of tears." Then he told Monkey the whole story.

"You need say no more," said Monkey. "It is clear enough that this dream came to you in order to bring a little business my way. No doubt at all that this magician is an ogre who has usurped the throne. Just let me put him to the test. I don't doubt my stick will make short work of him."

"Disciple," said Tripitaka, "he said the magician was terribly powerful."

"What do I care how powerful he is?" said Monkey. "If he had any inkling that Monkey might arrive on the scene, he would have cleared out long ago."

"Now I come to think of it," said Tripitaka, "he left a token."

Pigsy laughed. "Now, Master," he said, "you must pull yourself together. A dream's a dream. Now it is time to talk sense again."

But Sandy broke in, " 'He who does not believe that straight is straight must guard against the wickedness of good.' Let us light torches, open the gate, and see for ourselves whether the token has been left or not."

Monkey did indeed open the gate, and there, in the light of the stars and moon, with no need for torches, they saw lying on the ramp of the steps a tablet of white jade with gold edges. Pigsy stepped forward and picked it up, saying, "Brother, what's this thing?"

"This," said Monkey, "is the treasure that the king carried in his hand. It is called a jade tablet. Master, now that we have found this thing, there is no more doubt about the matter. Tomorrow it will be my job to catch this fiend."

Dear Monkey! He plucked a hair from his tail, blew on it with magic breath, cried out "Change!," and it became a casket lacquered in red and gold; he laid the tablet in it, and said, "Master, take this in your hand, and when day comes put on your embroidered cassock, and sit reading the scriptures in the great hall. Meanwhile I will inspect that walled city. If I find that an ogre is indeed ruling there, I will slay him, and do a deed by which I shall be remembered here. But if it is not an ogre, we must beware of meddling in the business at all."

"You are right," said Tripitaka.

"If," said Monkey, "the prince does not go out hunting, then there is nothing to be done. But if the dream comes true, I will bring him here to see you."

"And if he comes here, how am I to receive him?"

"When I let you know that he is coming, open the casket and wait while I change myself into a little priest two inches long, and put me in the casket. When the prince comes here, he will go and bow to the Buddha. Don't you take any notice of the prince or kneel down before him. When he sees that you, a commoner, do not bow down to him, he will order his followers to seize you. You will, of course, let yourself be seized, and beaten too, if they choose to beat you, and bound if they choose to bind you. Let them kill you, indeed, if they want to."

"They will be well armed," said Tripitaka. "They might very well kill me. That is not a good idea at all."

"It would not matter," said Monkey. "I could deal with that. I will see to it that nothing really serious happens. If he questions you, say that you were sent by the Emperor of China to worship Buddha and get scriptures, and that you have brought treasures with you. When he asks what treasures, show him your cassock and say it is the least of the three treasures, and that there are two others. Then show him the casket and tell him that there is a treasure within that knows what happened five hundred years ago, and what will happen in five hundred years long hence, and five hundred years between. One thousand five hundred years in all, of things past and present. Then let me out of the casket and I will tell the prince what was revealed in the dream. If he believes, I will go and seize the magician and the prince will be avenged upon his father's murderer and we shall win renown. But if he does not believe, I will show him the jade tablet. Only I fear he is too young, and will not recognize it."

Tripitaka was delighted. "An excellent plan," he said. "But what shall we call the third treasure? The first is the embroidered cassock, the second the white jade tablet. What is your transformation to be called?"

"Call it," said Monkey, "the Baggage that makes Kings." Tripitaka agreed, and committed the name to memory.

Neither disciple nor teacher could sleep. How gladly would they have been able, by a nod, to call up the sun from the Mulberry Tree[26] where it rests, and by a puff of breath blow away the stars that filled the sky!

However, at last it began to grow white in the east, and Monkey got up and gave his orders to Pigsy and Sandy. "Do not," he said, "upset the other priests in the temple by coming out of your cell and rollicking about. Wait till I have done my work, and then we will go on again together."

As soon as he had left them he turned a somersault and leapt into the air. Looking due west with his fiery eyes he soon saw a walled and moated city. You may ask how it was that he could see it. Well, it was only forty leagues away from the temple, and being so high in the air he could see as far as that.

Going on a little way and looking closely, he saw that baleful clouds hung round the city and fumes of discontent surrounded it, and suspended in mid-air Monkey recited:

"Were he a true king seated on the throne,
Then there would be a lucky gleam and fire-coloured clouds.
But as it is, a false fiend has seized the Dragon Seat,[27]
And coiling wreaths of black fume tarnish the Golden Gate."

While he was gazing at this sad sight, Monkey suddenly heard a great clanging, and looking down he saw the eastern gate of the city open, and from it a great throng of men and horses come out; truly a host of huntsmen. Indeed, a brave show; look at them:

At dawn they left the east of the Forbidden City;[28]
They parted and rounded up in the field of low grass,
Their bright banners opened and caught the sun,
Their white palfreys charged abreast the wind.
Their skin drums clatter with a loud roll;
The hurled spears fly each to its mark.

The hunters left the city and proceeded eastwards for twenty leagues towards a high plain. Now Monkey could see that in the midst of them was a little, little general in helmet and breast-plate, in his hand a jewelled sword, riding a bay charger, his bow at his waist. "Don't tell me!" said Monkey in the air, "that is the prince. Let me go and play a trick on him."

Dear Monkey! He lowered himself on his cloud, made his way through the ranks of the huntsmen and, when he came to the prince, changed himself into a white hare and ran in front of the prince's horse. The prince was delighted, took an arrow from his quiver, strung it and shot at the hare, which he hit. But Monkey had

[26] **Mulberry Tree:** The tree where the sun rests before rising. [27] **Dragon Seat:** The throne. The Golden Gate in the next line is the entrance to the palace. [28] **Forbidden City:** The palace.

willed the arrow to find its aim, and with a swift grab, just as it was about to touch him, he caught hold of it and ran on.

The prince, seeing that he had hit his mark, broke away from his companions and set out in pursuit. When the horse galloped fast, Monkey ran like the wind; when it slowed down, Monkey slowed down. The distance between them remained always the same, and so bit by bit he enticed the prince to the gates of the Treasure Wood Temple. The hare had vanished, for Monkey went back to his own form. But in the door-post an arrow was stuck.

"Here we are, Master," said Monkey, and at once changed again into a two-inch priest and hid in the casket.

Now when the prince came to the temple-gate and found no hare, but only his own arrow sticking in the gate-post, "Very strange!" said the prince, "I am certain I hit the hare. How is it that the hare has disappeared, but the arrow is here? I think it was not a common hare, but one that had lived too long and changed at last into a sprite."

He pulled out the arrow, and looking up saw that above the gate of the temple was an inscription which said "Treasure Wood Temple, erected by Royal Command." "Why, of course!" said the prince. "I remember years ago my father the king ordered an officer to take gold and precious stuffs to the priests of this temple, so that they might repair the chapel and images. I little thought that I would come here one day like this! A couplet says:

Chance brought me to a priest's cell
    and I listened to his holy talk;
From the life of the troubled world I got
    Half a day's rest.

I will go in.

The prince leapt from his horse's back and was just going in when three thousand officers who were in attendance upon him came galloping up in a great throng, and were soon pouring into the courtyard. The priests of the temple, much astonished, came out to do homage to the prince, and escort him into the Buddha Hall, to worship the Buddha. The prince was admiring the cloisters, when suddenly he came upon a priest who sat there and did not budge when he came past. "Has this priest no manners?" the prince cried in a rage. "As no warning was given that I was visiting this place, I could not expect to be met at a distance. But so soon as you saw men-at-arms approaching the gate, you ought to have stood up. How comes it that you are still sitting here without budging? Seize him!"

No sooner had he uttered the command than soldiers rushed from the sides, dragged Tripitaka off with them and made ready to bind him hand and foot. But Monkey in the casket soundlessly invoked the guardian spirits, Devas that protect the Law, and Lu Ting and Lu Chia: "I am now on an errand to subdue an evil spirit. But this prince, in his ignorance, has bade his servants bind my master, and you must come at once to his aid. If he is indeed bound, you will be held responsible!"

Thus secretly addressed by Monkey, how could they venture to disobey? They set a magic ring about Tripitaka, so that each time any one tried to lay hands on him, he could not be reached, any more than if he had been hedged in with a stout wall. "Where do you come from," the prince asked at last, "that you can cheat us like this, making yourself unapproachable?"

Tripitaka now came forward and bowed. "I have no such art," he said. "I am only a priest from China, going to the west to worship Buddha and get scriptures."

"China?" said the prince. "Although it is called The Middle Land,[29] it is a most destitute place. Tell me, for example, if you have anything of value upon you."

"There is the cassock on my back," said Tripitaka. "It is only a third-class treasure. But I have treasures of the first and second class, which are far superior."

"A coat like yours," said the prince, "that leaves half the body bare! It seems a queer thing to call that a treasure."

"This cassock," said Tripitaka, "although it covers only half my body, is described in a poem:

'Buddha's coat left one side bare,
But it hid the Absolute from the world's dust.
Its ten thousand threads and thousand stitches fulfilled the fruits of Meditation.
Is it a wonder that when I saw you come I did not rise to greet you?
You who call yourself a man, yet have failed to avenge a father's death!' "

"What wild nonsense this priest is talking!" said the prince in a great rage. "That half-coat, if it has done nothing else for you, has given you the courage to babble ridiculous fustian. How can my father's death be unavenged, since he is not dead? Just tell me that!"

Tripitaka came out one step forward, pressed the palms of his hands together and said: "Your Majesty, to how many things does man, born into the world, owe gratitude?"

"To four things," said the prince.

"To what four things?"

"He is grateful," said the prince, "to Heaven and Earth for covering and supporting him, to the sun and moon for shining upon him, to the king for lending him water and earth, and to his father and mother for rearing him."

Tripitaka laughed. "To the other three he owes gratitude indeed," he said. "But what need has he of a father and mother to rear him?"

"That's all very well for you," said the prince, "who are a shaven-headed, disloyal, food-cadging wanderer. But if a man had no father or mother, how could he come into the world?"

"Your Majesty," said Tripitaka, "I do not know. But in this casket there is a treasure called 'The baggage that makes kings.' It knows everything that happened during the five hundred years long ago, the five hundred years between, and the five hundred years to come, one thousand five hundred years in all. If he can quote a case

[29] **Middle Land:** China, seen as the center of the world.

where there was no gratitude to father and mother, then let me be detained captive here."

"Show him to me," said the prince. Tripitaka took off the cover and out jumped Monkey, and began to skip about this way and that. "A little fellow like that can't know much," said the prince. Hearing himself described as too small, Monkey used his magic power and stretched himself till he was three feet four inches high. The huntsmen were astonished, and said, "If he goes on growing like this, in a few days he will be bumping his head against the sky." But when he reached his usual height, Monkey stopped growing. At this point the prince said to him, "Baggage who makes Kings, the old priest says you know all things good and ill, in past and present. Do you divine by the tortoise or by the milfoil?[30] Or do you decide men's fates by sentences from books?"

"Not a bit of it," said Monkey; "all I rely on is my three inches of tongue, that tells about everything."

"This fellow talks great nonsense," said the prince. "It has always been by the *Book of Changes*[31] that mysteries have been elucidated and the prospects of the world decided, so that people might know what to pursue and what to avoid. Is it not said: 'The tortoise for divination, the milfoil for prognostication'? But so far as I can make out you go on no principle at all. You talk at random about fate and the future exciting and misleading people to no purpose."

"Now don't be in a hurry, Your Highness," said Monkey, "but listen to me. You are the Crown Prince of Crow-cock. Five years ago there was a famine in your land. The king and his ministers prayed and fasted, but they could not get a speck of rain. Then there came a wizard from the Chung-nan mountains who could call the winds, fetch rain, and turn stone into gold. The king was deceived by his wiles and hailed him as elder brother. Is this true?"

"Yes, yes, yes," said the prince. "Go on!"

"For the last three years the magician has not been seen," said Monkey. "Who is it that has been on the throne?"

"It is true about the wizard," said the prince. "My father did make this wizard his brother, and ate with him and slept with him. But three years ago, when they were walking in the flower garden and admiring the view, a gust of magic wind that the magician sent blew the jade tablet that the king carried out of his hand, and the magician went off with it straight to the Chung-nan mountains. My father still misses him and has no heart to walk in the flower garden without him. Indeed, for three years it has been locked up and no one has set foot in it. If the king is not my father, who is he?"

At this Monkey began to laugh, and did not stop laughing when the prince asked him what was the matter, till the prince lost his temper.

---

[30] **the tortoise or by the milfoil:** Two methods of divination in ancient China.

[31] ***Book of Changes:*** The Yijng (*I Ching*), a Chinese classic from the twelfth century B.C.E., which interprets sixty-four hexagrams for their moral, political, and spiritual significance.

"Why don't you say something?" he said, "instead of standing there laughing."

"I have quite a lot to say," said Monkey, "but I cannot say it in front of all these people."

The prince thought this reasonable, and motioned to the huntsmen to retire. The leader gave his orders, and soon the three thousand men and horses were all stationed outside the gates. None of the priests of the temple were about. Monkey stopped laughing and said, "Your Highness, he who vanished was the father that begot you; he who sits on the throne is the magician that brought rain."

"Nonsense," cried the prince. "Since the magician left us, the winds have been favouring, the people have been at peace. But according to you it is not my father who is on the throne. It is all very well to say such things to me who am young and let it pass; but if my father were to hear you uttering this subversive talk, he would have you seized and torn into ten thousand pieces." He began railing at Monkey, who turned to Tripitaka and said, "What is to be done? I have told him and he does not believe me. Let's get to work. Show him your treasure, and then get your papers seen to, and go off to India." Tripitaka handed the lacquer-box to Monkey, and Monkey taking it gave himself a shake, and the box became invisible. For it was in reality one of Monkey's hairs, which he had changed into a box, but now put back again as a hair on his body. But the white jade tablet he presented to the prince.

"A fine sort of priest," the prince exclaimed. "You it was who came five years ago disguised as a magician, and stole the family treasure, and now, disguised as a priest, are offering it back again! Seize him!" This command startled Tripitaka out of his wits and pointing at Monkey, "It's you," he cried, "you wretched horse-groom, who have brought this trouble on us for no reason at all." Monkey rushed forward and checked him. "Hold your tongue," he said, "and don't let out my secrets. I am not called 'the Baggage that makes Kings.' My real name is quite different."

"I shall be glad to know your real name," said the prince, "that I may send you to the magistrate to be dealt with as you deserve."

"My name then," said Monkey, "is the Great Monkey Sage, and I am this old man's chief disciple. I was going with my Master to India to get scriptures, and last night we came to this temple and asked for shelter. My Master was reading scriptures by night, and at the third watch he had a dream. He dreamt that your father came to him and said he had been attacked by that magician, who in the flower garden pushed him into the eight-cornered crystal well. Then the wizard changed himself into your father's likeness. The court and all the officers were completely deceived; you yourself were too young to know. You were forbidden to enter the inner apartments of the Palace and the flower garden was shut up, lest the secret should get out. Tonight your father came and asked me to subdue the false magician. I was not sure that he was an evil spirit, but when I looked down from the sky I was quite certain of it. I was just going to seize him, when I met you and your huntsmen. The white hare you shot was me. It was I who led you here and brought you to my Master. This is the truth, every word of it. You have recognized the white tablet, and all that remains is for you to repay your father's care and revenge yourself on his enemy."

This upset the prince very much. "If I do not believe this story," he said to himself, "it must in any case have an unpleasant amount of truth in it. But if I believe it, how can I any longer look upon the present king as my father?" He was in great perplexity.

"If you are in doubt," said Monkey, "ride home and ask your mother a question that will decide it. Ask whether she and the king, as man and wife, are on changed terms, these last three years."

"That is a good idea," said the prince. "Just wait while I go and ask my mother." He snatched up the jade tablet and was about to make off, when Monkey stopped him, saying, "If all your gentlemen follow you back to the palace, suspicions will be aroused, and how can I succeed in my task? You must go back all alone and attract no attention. Do not go in at the main gate but by the back gate. And when you get to the inner apartments and see your mother, do not speak loudly or clearly, but in a low whisper; for if the magician should hear you, so great is his power that your life and your mother's would be in danger."

The prince did as he was told, and as he left the temple he told his followers to remain there on guard and not to move. "I have some business," he said. "Wait till I have got to the city and then come on yourselves!" Look at him!

> He gives his orders to the men-at-arms,
> Flies on horseback home to the citadel.

If you do not know whether on this occasion he succeeded in seeing his mother, and if so what passed between them, you must listen to the next chapter.

Chapter 20

The Prince was soon back at the city of Crow-cock, and as instructed he made no attempt to go in by the main gate, but without announcing himself went to the back gate, where several eunuchs were on guard. They did not dare to stop him, and (dear prince!) he rode in all alone, and soon reached the Arbour of Brocade Perfume, where he found his mother surrounded by her women, who were fanning her, while she leant weeping over a carven balustrade. Why, you will ask, was she weeping? At the fourth watch she had had a dream, half of which she could remember and half of which had faded; and she was thinking hard. Leaping from his horse, the prince knelt down before her and cried "Mother!" She forced herself to put on a happier countenance, and exclaimed, "Child, this is a joy indeed! For years past you have been so busy in the men's quarters at the Palace, studying with your father, that I have never seen you, which has been a great sorrow to me. How have you managed to find time today? It is an unspeakable pleasure! My child, why is your voice so mournful? Your father is growing old. Soon the time will come when the 'dragon returns to the pearl-grey sea, the phoenix to the pink mists'; you will then become king. Why should you be dispirited?"

The prince struck the floor with his forehead. "Mother, I ask you," he said, "who is it that sits upon the throne?"

"He has gone mad," said the queen. "The ruler is your father and king. Why should you ask?"

"Mother," the prince said, "if you will promise me forgiveness I will speak. But if not, I dare not speak."

"How can there be questions of guilt and pardon between mother and son? Of course, you are free to speak. Be quick and begin."

"Mother," said the prince, "if you compare your life with my father these last three years with your life with him before, should you say that his affection was as great?"

Hearing this question the queen altogether lost her presence of mind, and leaping to her feet ran down from the arbour and flung herself into his arms, saying, "Child, why, when I have not seen you for so long, should you suddenly come and ask me such a question?"

"Mother," said the prince hotly, "do not evade this question. For much hangs upon the answer to it."

Then the queen sent away all the Court ladies, and with tears in her eyes said in a low voice, "Had you not asked me, I would have gone down to the Nine Springs of Death[32] without ever breathing a word about this matter. But since you have asked, hear what I have to say:

> What three years ago was warm and bland,
> These last three years has been cold as ice.
> When at the pillow's side I questioned him,
> He told me age had impaired his strength
> and that things did not work.

When he heard this, the prince shook himself free, gripped the saddle, and mounted his horse. His mother tried to hold him back, saying, "Child, what is it that makes you rush off before our talk is done?"

The prince returned and knelt in front of her. "Mother," he said, "I dare not speak. Today at dawn I received a command to go hunting outside the city with falcon and dog. By chance I met a priest sent by the Emperor of China to fetch scriptures. He has a chief disciple named Monkey, who is very good at subduing evil spirits. According to him my father the king was drowned in the crystal well in the flower garden, and a wizard impersonated him and seized his throne. Last night at the third watch my father appeared in a dream to this priest and asked him to come to the city and seize the impostor. I did not believe all this, and so came to question you. But what you have just told me makes me certain that it is an evil spirit."

"My child," said the queen, "why should you believe strangers, of whom you have no knowledge?"

"I should not," said the prince, "have dared to accept the story as true, had not the king my father left behind a token in the hands of these people." The queen asked what it was, and the prince took out from his sleeve the white jade tablet bordered with gold, and handed it to his mother. When she saw that it was indeed a treasure that had been the king's in old days, she could not stop her tears gushing out like a

[32] **Nine Springs of Death:** The Underworld.

waterspring. "My lord and master," she cried, "why have you been dead three years and never come to me, but went first to a priest and afterwards to the prince?"

"Mother," said the prince, "what do these words mean?"

"My child," she said, "at the fourth watch I too had a dream. I dreamt I saw your father stand in front of me, all dripping wet, saying that he was dead, and that his soul had visited a priest of T'ang and asked him to defeat the false king and rescue his own body from where it had been thrown. That is all I can remember, and it is only half. The other half I cannot get clear, and I was puzzling about it when you came. It is strange that you should just at this moment come with this tale, and bring this tablet with you. I will put it away, and you must go and ask that priest to come at once and do what he promises. If he can drive away the impostor and distinguish the false from the true, you will have repaid the king your father for the pains he bestowed upon your upbringing."

The prince was soon back at the gates of the Treasure Wood Temple, where he was joined by his followers. The sun's red disc was now falling. He told his followers to stay quietly where they were, went into the temple alone, arranged his hat and clothes, and paid his respects to Monkey, who came hopping and skipping from the main hall. The prince knelt down, saying, "Here I am again, Father."

Monkey raised him from his knees. "Did you ask anyone anything when you were in the city?" he said.

"I questioned my mother," said the prince; and he told the whole story.

Monkey smiled. "If it is as cold as that," he said, "he is probably a transformation of some chilly creature. No matter! Just wait while I mop him up for you. But today it is growing late, and I cannot very well start doing anything. You go back now, and I will come early tomorrow."

"Master," said the prince, kneeling before him, "let me wait here till the morning, and then go along with you."

"That will not do," said Monkey. "If I were to come into the city at the same time as you, the suspicions of the impostor would be aroused. He would not believe that I forced myself upon you, but would be sure you had invited me. And in this way the blame would fall on you."

"I shall get into trouble anyhow," said the prince, "if I go into the city now."

"What about?" asked Monkey.

"I was sent out hunting," said the prince, "and I have not got a single piece of game. How dare I face the king? If he accuses me of incompetence and casts me into prison, who will you have to look after you when you arrive tomorrow? There is not one of the officers who knows you."

"What matter?" said Monkey. "You have only to mention that you need some game, and I will procure it for you." Dear Monkey! Watch him while he displays his arts before the prince. He gives himself a shake, jumps up on to the fringe of a cloud, performs a magic pass and murmurs a spell which compels the spirits of the mountain and the local deities to come before him and do obeisance.

"Great Sage," they said, "what orders have you for us little divinities?"

"I guarded a priest of T'ang on his way here," said Monkey. "I want to seize an evil spirit, but this prince here has nothing to show for his hunting, and does not dare return to Court. I have sent for you divinities to ask you to do me a favour. Find some musk deer, wild boar, hares and so on—any wild beasts or birds you can discover, and bring them here."

The divinities dared not disobey. "How many do you require of each?" they asked.

"It does not matter exactly how many," said Monkey. "Just bring some along; that is all."

Then these divinities, using the secret instruments that appertained to them, made a magic wind that drew together wild beasts. Soon there were hundreds and thousands of wild fowl, deer, foxes, hares, tigers, panthers, and wolves collected in front of Monkey. "It is not I who want them!" he cried. "You must get them on the move again, and string them out on each side of the road for forty leagues. The hunters will be able to take them home without use of falcon or dog. That is all that is required of you."

The divinities obeyed, and spread out the game on each side of the road. Monkey then lowered his cloud and said to the prince, "Your Highness may now go back. There is game all along the road; you have only to collect it."

When the prince saw him floating about in the air and exercising magic powers, he was deeply impressed, and bent his head on the ground in prostration before Monkey, from whom he humbly took his leave. He then went out in front of the temple and gave orders to the huntsmen to return to Court. They were astonished to find endless wild game on each side of the road, which they took without use of falcon or dog, merely by laying hands upon it. They all believed that this blessing had been vouchsafed to the prince, and had no idea that it was Monkey's doing. Listen to the songs of triumph that they sing as they throng back to the city!

When the priests of the temple saw on what terms Tripitaka and the rest were with the prince, they began to treat them with a new deference. They invited them to refreshments, and again put the Zen Hall at Tripitaka's disposal. It was near the first watch; but Monkey had something on his mind and could not get to sleep at once. Presently he crept across to Tripitaka's bed and called, "Master!" Tripitaka was not asleep either; but knowing that Monkey liked giving people a start, he pretended to be asleep. Monkey rubbed his tonsure and shaking him violently, he said, "Master, why are you sleeping?"

"The rogue!" cried Tripitaka crossly. "Why can't you go to sleep, instead of pestering me like this?"

"Master," said Monkey, "there is something you must give me your advice about."

"What is that?" said Tripitaka.

"I talked very big to the prince," said Monkey, "giving him to understand that my powers were high as the hills and deep as the sea, and that I could catch the false wizard as easily as one takes things out of a bag—I had only to stretch out my hand and carry him off. But I cannot get to sleep, for it has occurred to me that it may not be so easy."

"If you think it's too difficult, why do it?" said Tripitaka.

"It's not that there's any difficulty about catching him," said Monkey. "The only question is whether it is legal."

"What nonsense this monkey talks," said Tripitaka. "How can it be illegal to arrest a monster that has seized a monarch's throne?"

"You only know how to read scriptures, worship Buddha, and practise Zen, and have never studied the Code of Hsiao Ho.[33] But you must at least know the proverb 'Take robber, take loot.' The magician has been king for three years and not the slightest suspicion has been felt by anyone. All the late king's ladies sleep with him, and the ministers civil and military disport themselves with him. Even if I succeed in catching him, how am I to convince anyone of his guilt?"

"What is the difficulty?" asked Tripitaka.

"Even if he were as dumb as a calabash, he would be able to talk one down. He would say boldly, 'I am the king of Crow-cock. What crime have I committed against Heaven that you should arrest me?' How would one argue with him then?"

"And you," said Tripitaka, "what plan have you got?"

"My plan is already made," said Monkey smiling. "The only obstacle is that you have a partiality."

"A partiality for whom?" said Tripitaka.

"Pigsy," said Monkey; "you have a preference for him because he is so strong."

"What makes you think that?" asked Tripitaka.

"If it were not so," said Monkey, "you would pull yourself together and have the courage to stay here with Sandy to look after you, while I and Pigsy go off to the city of Crow-cock, find the flower garden, uncover the well, and bring up the Emperor's body, which we will wrap in our wrapper, and next day bring to Court. There we will get our papers put in order, confront the Magician, and I will fell him with my cudgel. If he tries to exonerate himself, I will show him the body and say, 'Here is the man you drowned.' And I will make the prince come forward and wail over his father, the queen come out and recognize her husband, the officers civil and military look upon their lord, and then I and my brother will get to work. In this way the whole thing will be on a proper footing."

Tripitaka thought this was a splendid plan, but he was not sure that Pigsy would consent. "Why not?" said Monkey. "Didn't I say you were partial to him and did not want him to go? You think he would refuse to go because you know that when I call you it is often half an hour before you take any notice. You'll see when I start, that I shall only need a turn or two of my three-inch tongue, and no matter if he is Pigsy or Wigsy I am quite capable of making him follow me."

"Very well," said Tripitaka, "call him when you go."

"Pigsy, Pigsy," cried Monkey at Pigsy's bedside. That fool did most of the hard work when they were on the road, and no sooner did his head touch the pillow than he was snoring, and it took a great deal more than a shout to wake him.

Monkey pulled his ears, tweaked his bristles, and dragged him from the pillow, shouting "Pigsy!" That fool pushed him away. Monkey shouted again.

"Go to sleep and don't be so stupid," Pigsy said. "Tomorrow we have got to be on the road again."

[33] **Code of Hsiao Ho:** A legal code from the Han Dynasty devised by Xiao He (Hsiao Ho; b. 193 B.C.E.).

"I am not being stupid," said Monkey, "there is a bit of business I want your help in."

"What business?" asked Pigsy.

"You heard what the prince said?" said Monkey.

"No," said Pigsy, "I did not set eyes on him, or hear anything he said."

"He told me," said Monkey, "that the magician has a treasure worth more than any army of ten thousand men. When we go to the city tomorrow, we are sure to fall foul of him, he will use it to overthrow us. Wouldn't it be much better if we got in first and stole the treasure?"

"Brother," said Pigsy, "are you asking me to commit robbery? If so, that's a business I have experience of and can really be of some help. But there is one thing we must get clear. If I steal a treasure or subdue a magician I expect more than a petty, skunking share. The treasure must be mine."

"What do you want it for?" asked Monkey.

"I am not so clever as you are at talking people into giving me alms. I am strong, but I have a very common way of talking, and I don't know how to recite the scriptures. When we get into a tight place, wouldn't this treasure be good to exchange for something to eat and drink?"

"I only care for fame," said Monkey. "I don't want any treasures. You may have it all to yourself."

That fool, when he heard that it was all to be his, was in high glee. He rolled out of bed, hustled into his clothes, and set out with Monkey.

Clear wine brings a blush to the cheeks;
Yellow gold moves even a philosophic heart.

The two of them opened the temple gate very quietly and, leaving Tripitaka, mounted a wreath of cloud and soon reached the city, where they lowered their cloud, just as the second watch was being sounded on the tower.

"Brother! it's the second watch," said Monkey.

"Couldn't be better," said Pigsy. "Everyone will just be deep in their first sleep."

They did not go to the main gate, but to the back gate, where they heard the sound of the watchman's clappers and bells.

"Brother," said Monkey, "they are on the alert at all the gates. How shall we get in?"

"When did thieves ever go in by a gate?" said Pigsy. "We must scramble over the wall." Monkey did so, and at a bound was over the rampart and wall. Pigsy followed, and the two stealthily made their way in, soon rejoining the road from the gate. They followed this till they came to the flower garden.

In front of them was a gate-tower with three thatched white gables, and high up was an inscription in shining letters, catching the light of the moon and stars. It said "Imperial Flower Garden." When Monkey came close, he saw that the locks were sealed up several layers deep, and he told Pigsy to get to work. That fool wielded his iron rake, which he brought crashing down upon the gate and smashed it to bits. Monkey stepped over the fragments, and once inside could not stop himself jumping and shouting for joy. "Brother," said Pigsy, "you'll be the ruin of us. Who ever heard of a thief making all that noise? You'll wake everyone up, we shall be arrested and taken before the judge, and if we are not condemned to death we shall certainly be sent back to where we came from and drafted into the army."

"Why try to make me nervous?" said Monkey. "Look!

The painted and carven balustrades are scattered and strewn;
The jewel-studded arbours and trees are toppling down.
The sedgy islands and knot-weed banks are buried in dust;
The white peonies and yellow glove-flowers, all dust-destroyed.
Jasmine and rose perfume the night;
The red peony and tiger-lily bloom in vain,
The hibiscus and Syrian mallow are choked with weeds;
Strange plant and rare flower are crushed and die.

"And what does it matter if they do?" said Pigsy. "Let's get on with our business."

Monkey, although deeply affected by the scene, called to mind Tripitaka's dream, in which he was told that the well was underneath a banana-plant, and when they had gone a little further they did indeed discover a most singular banana-plant, which grew very thick and high.

"Now Pigsy," said Monkey. "Are you ready? The treasure is buried under this tree." That fool lifted his rake in both hands, beat down the banana-tree and began to nuzzle with his snout till he had made a hole three or four feet deep. At last he came to a slab of stone. "Brother," he cried, "here's luck. We've found the treasure. It's bound to be under this slab. If it's not in a coffer it will be in a jar."

"Hoist it up and see," said Monkey.

Pigsy went to work again with his snout and raised the slab till they could see underneath. Something sparkled and flashed. "Didn't I say we were in luck," said Pigsy. "That is the treasure glittering." But when they looked closer, it was the light of the stars and moon reflected in a well.

"Brother," said Pigsy, "you should not think so much of the trunk that you forget the root."

"Now, what does that mean?" asked Monkey.

"This is a well," said Pigsy. "If you had told me before we started that the treasure was in a well, I should have brought with me the two ropes we tie up our bundles with, and you could have contrived to let me down. As it is, how are we to get at anything down there and bring it up again?"

"You intend to go down?" said Monkey.

"That's what I should do," said Pigsy, "if I had any rope."

"Take off your clothes," said Monkey, "and I'll manage it for you."

"I don't go in for much in the way of clothes," said Pigsy. "But I'll take off my jerkin, if that's any good."

Dear Monkey! He took out his metal-clasped cudgel, called to it "Stretch!," and when it was some thirty feet long he said to Pigsy, "You catch hold of one end, and I'll let you down."

"Brother," said Pigsy, "let me down as far as you like, so long as you stop when I come to the water."

"Just so," said Monkey.

Pigsy caught hold of one end of the staff, and was very gently raised and let down into the well by Monkey. He soon reached the water. "I'm at the water," he called up. Monkey, hearing this, let him down just a little further. That fool Pigsy, when he felt the water touch him, began to beat out with his trotters, let go of the staff and flopped right into the water. "The rascal!" he cried, spluttering and blowing. "I told him to stop when I came to the water, and instead he let me down further."

Monkey only laughed, and withdrew the staff. "Brother," he said, "have you found the treasure?"

"Treasure indeed!" said Pigsy. "There's nothing but well-water."

"The treasure is under the water," said Monkey. "Just have a look."

Pigsy, it so happened, was thoroughly at home in the water. He took a great plunge straight down into the well. But, oh what a long way it was to the bottom! He dived again with all his might, and suddenly opening his eyes saw in front of him an entrance, above which was written "The Crystal Palace." This astonished him very much. "That finishes it," he cried. "I've come the wrong way and got into the sea! There is a Crystal Palace in the sea; but I never heard of one down a well." For he did not know that the Dragon King of the Well also has a Crystal Palace.

Pigsy was thus debating with himself when a yaksha,[34] on patrol-duty in the waters, opened the door, saw the intruder, and immediately withdrew to the interior, announcing: "Great King, a calamity! A long-snouted, long-eared priest has dropped down into our well, all naked and dripping. He is still alive, and speaks to himself rationally."

The Dragon King of the Well was, however, not at all surprised. "If I am not mistaken," he said, "this is General Pigsy. Last night the Spirit that Wanders by Night received orders to come here and fetch the soul of the king of Crow-cock and bring it to the priest of T'ang to ask the Monkey Sage to subdue the wicked magician. I imagine that Monkey has come, as well as General Pigsy. They must be treated with great consideration. Go at once and ask the General to come in." The Dragon King then tidied his clothes, adjusted his hat, and bringing with him all his watery kinsmen he came to the gate and cried in a loud voice: "General Pigsy, pray come inside and be seated!"

Pigsy was delighted. "Fancy meeting with an old friend!" he said. And without thinking what he was in for, that fool went into the Crystal Palace. Caring nothing for good manners, all dripping as he was, he sat down in the seat of honour.

"General," said the Dragon King, "I heard lately that your life was spared to you on condition you should embrace the faith of Sakyamuni[35] and protect Tripitaka on his journey to India. What then are you doing down here?"

"It's just in that connexion that I come," said Pigsy. "My brother Monkey presents his best compliments and sends me to fetch some treasure or other."

"I am sorry," said the Dragon King, "but what should I be doing with any treasure? You're mixing me up with the dragons of the Yangtze, the Yellow River, the Huai

[34] **yaksha:** A species of demon or genie living in the earth or waters.

[35] **Sakyamuni:** A title sometimes given to Gautama, the Buddha.

and the Chi, who soar about the sky and assume many shapes. They no doubt have treasures. But I stay down here all the time in this wretched hole never catching a glimpse of the sky above. Where should I get a treasure from?"

"Don't make excuses," said Pigsy. "I know you have got it; so bring it out at once."

"The one treasure I have," said the Dragon King, "can't be brought out. I suggest you should go and look at it for yourself."

"Excellent," said Pigsy. "I'll come and have a look."

The Dragon King led him through the Crystal Palace till they came to a cloister in which lay a body six feet long. Pointing at it the Dragon King said, "General, there is your treasure." Pigsy went up to it, and oh! what did he see before him? It was a dead Emperor, on his head a tall crown, dressed in a red gown, on his feet upturned shoes, girded with a belt of jades, who lay stretched full length upon the floor. Pigsy laughed. "You won't kid me like that," he said. "Since when did this count as a treasure? Why, when I was an ogre in the mountains I made my supper on them every day. When one has not only seen a thing time after time, but also eaten it again and again, can one be expected to regard it as a treasure?"

"General," said the Dragon King, "you do not understand. This is the body of the King of Crow-cock. When he fell into the well I preserved him with a magic pearl, and he suffered no decay. If you care to take him up with you, show him to Monkey and succeed in bringing him back to his senses, you need worry no more about 'treasures,' you'll be able to get anything out of him that you choose to ask for."

"Very well then," said Pigsy, "I'll remove him for you, if you'll let me know how much I shall get as my undertaker's fee."

"I haven't got any money," said the Dragon King.

"So you expect to get jobs done for nothing?" said Pigsy. "If you haven't got any money I won't remove him."

"If you won't," said the Dragon King, "I must ask you to go away."

Pigsy at once retired. The Dragon King ordered two powerful yakshas to carry the body to the gate of the Crystal Palace and leave it just outside. They removed from the gate its water-fending pearls, and at once there was a sound of rushing waters! Pigsy looked round. The gate had vanished, and while he was poking about for it, his hand touched the dead king's body, which gave him such a start that his legs gave way under him. He scrambled to the surface of the water, and squeezing against the well-wall, he cried, "Brother, let down your staff and get me out of this."

"Did you find the treasure?" asked Monkey.

"How should I?" said Pigsy. "All I found was a Dragon King at the bottom of the water, who wanted me to remove a corpse. I refused, and he had me put out at the door. Then his palace vanished, and I found myself touching the corpse. It gave me such a turn that I feel quite weak. Brother, you must get me out of this."

"That was your treasure," said Monkey. "Why didn't you bring it up with you?"

"I knew he had been dead a long time," said Pigsy. "What was the sense of bringing him?"

"You'd better," said Monkey, "or I shall go away."

"Go?" said Pigsy. "Where to?"

"I shall go back to the temple," said Monkey, "and go to sleep like Tripitaka."

"And I shall be left down here?" said Pigsy.

"If you can climb out," said Monkey, "there is no reason why you should stay here; but if you can't there's an end of it."

Pigsy was thoroughly frightened; he knew he could not possibly climb out. "Just think," he said, "even a city wall is difficult to get up. But this well-shaft has a big belly and a small mouth. Its walls slope in, and as no water has been drawn from it for several years they have become all covered with slime. It's far too slippery to climb. Brother, just to keep up a nice spirit between friends, I'll carry it up."

"That's right," said Monkey. "And be quick about it, so that we can both of us go home to bed."

That fool Pigsy dived down again, found the corpse, hoisted it on to his back, clambered up to the surface of the water, and propped himself and the body against the wall. "Brother," he called. "I've brought it." Monkey peered down, and seeing that Pigsy had indeed a burden on his back, he lowered his staff into the well.

That fool was a creature of much determination. He opened his mouth wide, bit hard on the staff, and Monkey pulled him gently up. Putting down the corpse, Pigsy pulled himself into his clothes. The Emperor, Monkey found on examining him, was indeed in the most perfect preservation. "Brother," he asked, "how comes it that a man who has been dead for three years can look so fresh?"

"According to the Dragon King of the Well," said Pigsy, "he used a magic pearl which prevented the body from decaying."

"That was a bit of luck," said Monkey. "But it still remains to take vengeance upon his enemy and win glory for ourselves. Make haste and carry him off."

"Where to?" asked Pigsy.

"To the temple," said Monkey, "to show him to Tripitaka."

"What an idea!" grumbled Pigsy to himself "A fellow was having a nice, sound sleep, and along comes this baboon with a wonderful yarn about a job that must be done, and in the end it turns out to be nothing but this silly game of carting about a corpse. Carry that stinking thing! It will dribble filthy water all over me and dirty my clothes; there's no one to wash them for me. There are patches in several places, and if the water gets through I have nothing to change into."

"Don't worry about your clothes," said Monkey. "Get the body to the temple, and I will give you a change of clothes."

"Impudence!" cried Pigsy. "You've none of your own. How can you give me any to change into?"

"Does that twaddle mean that you won't carry it?" asked Monkey.

"I'm not going to carry it," said Pigsy.

"Then hold out your paw and take twenty," said Monkey.

"Brother," said Pigsy, much alarmed, "that cudgel is very heavy; after twenty strokes of it there would not be much to choose between me and this Emperor."

"If you don't want to be beaten," said Monkey, "make haste and carry it off."

Pigsy did indeed fear the cudgel, and sorely against his will he hoisted the corpse on to his back and began to drag himself along towards the garden gate. Dear Monkey! He performed a magic pass, recited a spell, traced a magic square on the ground, and going to it blew a breath that turned into a great gust of wind which blew Pigsy clean out of the palace grounds and clear of the city moat. The wind stopped, and alighting they set out slowly on their way. Pigsy was feeling very ill-used and thought of a plan to revenge himself. "This monkey," he said to himself "has played a dirty trick on me, but I'll get even with him all right when we get back to the temple, I will tell Tripitaka that Monkey can bring the dead to life. If he says he can't, I shall persuade Tripitaka to recite the spell that makes this monkey's head ache, and I shan't be satisfied till his brains are bursting out of his head." But thinking about it as he went along, he said to himself, "That's no good! If he is asked to bring the king to life, he won't have any difficulty; he will go straight to Yama, King of Death, ask for the soul, and so bring the king to life. I must make it clear that he is not to go to the Dark Realm, but must do his cure here in the World of Light. That's the thing to do."

They were now at the temple gate, went straight in, and put down the corpse at the door of the Zen Hall, saying, "Master, get up and look!" Tripitaka was not asleep, but was discussing with Sandy why the others were away so long. Suddenly he heard them calling, and jumping up he said, "Disciples, what is this I see?"

"Monkey's father-in-law," said Pigsy; "he made me carry him."

"You rotten fool," said Monkey, "where have I any father-in-law?"

"Brother, if he isn't your father-in-law," said Pigsy, "why did you make me carry him? It has been tiring work for me, I can tell you that!"

When Tripitaka and Sandy examined the body, and saw that the Emperor looked just like a live man, Tripitaka suddenly burst into lamentation. "Alas, poor Emperor," he cried, "in some forgotten existence you doubtless did great wrong to one that in this incarnation has now confounded you, and brought you to destruction. You were torn from wife and child; none of your generals or counsellors knew, none of your officers were aware. Alas, for the blindness of your queen and prince that offered no incense, no tea to your soul!" Here he broke down, and his tears fell like rain.

"Master," said Pigsy, "what does it matter to you that he is dead? He is not your father or grandfather, why should you wail over him?"

"Disciple," said Tripitaka, "for us who are followers of Buddha compassion is the root, indulgence the gate. Why is your heart so hard?"

"It isn't that my heart is hard," said Pigsy. "But Brother Monkey tells me he can bring him to life. If he fails I am certainly not going to cart him about any more."

Now Tripitaka, being by nature pliable as water, was easily moved by that fool's story. "Monkey," he said, "if you can indeed bring this Emperor back to life, you will be doing what matters more than that we should reach the Holy Mountain and worship the Buddha. They say 'To save one life is better than to build a seven-storeyed pagoda.'"

"Master," said Monkey, "do you really believe this fool's wild talk? When a man is dead, in three times seven, five times seven, or at the end of seven hundred days, when he has done penance for his sins in the World of Light, his turn comes to be born again. This king has been dead for three years. How can he possibly be saved?"

"I expect we had better give up the idea," said Tripitaka, when he heard this.

But Pigsy was not to be cheated of his revenge. "Don't let him put you off," he said to Tripitaka. "Remember, his head is very susceptible. You have only to recite that stuff of yours, and I guarantee that he'll turn the king into a live man."

Tripitaka accordingly did recite the headache spell, and it gripped so tight that Monkey's eyes started out of his head, and he suffered frightful pain.

If you do not know whether in the end this king was brought to life, you must listen to what is unfolded in the next chapter.

Chapter 21

The pain in that great Monkey Sage's head was so severe that at last he could bear it no longer and cried piteously, "Master, stop praying, stop praying! I'll doctor him."

"How will you do it?" asked Tripitaka.

"The only way is to visit Yama, King of Death, in the Land of Darkness, and get him to let me have the king's soul," said Monkey.

"Don't believe him, Master," said Pigsy. "He told me there was no need to go to the Land of Darkness. He said he knew how to cure him here and now, in the World of Light."

Tripitaka believed this wicked lie, and began praying again; and Monkey was so harassed that he soon gave in. "All right, all right," he cried. "I'll cure him in the World of Light."

"Don't stop," said Pigsy. "Go on praying as hard as you can."

"You ill-begotten idiot," cursed Monkey, "I'll pay you out for making the Master put a spell upon me."

Pigsy laughed till he fell over. "Ho, ho, brother," he cried, "you thought it was only on me that tricks could be played. You didn't think that I could play a trick on you."

"Master, stop praying," said Monkey, "and let me cure him in the World of Light."

"How can that be done?" asked Tripitaka.

"I will rise on my cloud trapeze," said Monkey, "and force my way into the southern gate of Heaven. I shall not go to the Palace of the Pole and Ox, nor to the Hall of Holy Mists, but go straight up to the thirty-third heaven, and in the Trayaśimstra Courtyard of the heavenly palace of Quit Grief I shall visit Lao Tzu and ask for a grain of his Nine Times Sublimated Life Restoring Elixir, and with it I shall bring the king back to life."

This suggestion pleased Tripitaka very much. "Lose no time about it," he said.

"It is only the third watch," said Monkey. "I shall be back before it is light. But it would look all wrong if the rest of you went quietly to sleep. It is only decent that someone should watch by the corpse and mourn."

"You need say no more," said Pigsy. "I can see that you expect me to act as mourner."

"I should like to see you refuse!" said Monkey. "If you don't act as mourner, I certainly shan't bring him to life."

"Be off, Brother," said Pigsy, "and I'll do the mourning."

"There are more ways than one of mourning," said Monkey. "Mere bellowing with dry eyes is no good. Nor is it any better just to squeeze out a few tears. What counts is a good hearty howling, with tears as well. That's what is wanted for a real, miserable mourning."

"I'll give you a specimen," said Pigsy. He then from somewhere or other produced a piece of paper which he twisted into a paper-spill and thrust up his nostrils. This soon set him snivelling and his eyes running, and when he began to howl he kept up such a din that anyone would have thought he had indeed lost his dearest relative. The effect was so mournful that Tripitaka too soon began to weep bitterly.

"That's what you've got to keep up the whole time I'm away," said Monkey laughing. "What I am frightened of is that this fool, the moment my back is turned, will stop wailing. I shall creep back and listen, and if he shows any sign of leaving off he will get twenty on the paw."

"Be off with you," laughed Pigsy. "I could easily keep this up for two days on end."

Sandy, seeing that Pigsy had settled down to his job, went off to look for some sticks of incense to burn as an offering. "Excellent!" laughed Monkey. "The whole family is engaged in works of piety! Now's the time for Old Monkey to get to business."

Dear Monkey! Just at midnight he left his teacher and fellow-disciples, mounted his cloud trapeze and flew in at the southern gate of Heaven. He did not indeed call at the Precious Hall of Holy Mists or go on to the Palace of the Pole and Ox, but only along a path of cloudy light went straight to the thirty-third heaven, to the Trayaśimstra Courtyard of the heavenly palace of Quit Grief. Just inside the gate he saw Lao Tzu in his alchemical studio, with a number of fairy boys holding banana-leaf fans, and fanning the fire in which the cinnabar was sublimating.

As soon as Lao Tzu saw him coming, he called to the boys, "Be careful, all of you. Here's the thief who stole the elixir come back again."

Monkey bowed, and said laughing, "Reverend Sir, there is no need to be in such a fret. You need take no precautions against me. I have come on quite different business."

"Monkey," said Lao Tzu, "five hundred years ago you made great trouble in the Palace of Heaven, and stole a great quantity of my holy elixir; for which crime you were arrested and placed in my crucible, where you were smelted for forty-nine days, at the cost of I know not how much charcoal. Now you have been lucky enough to obtain forgiveness, enter the service of Buddha, and go with Tripitaka, the priest of T'ang, to get scriptures in India. Some while ago you quelled a demon in the Flat Topped Mountain and tricked disaster, but did not give me my share in the treasure. What brings you here today?"

"In those old days," said Monkey, "I lost no time in returning to you those five treasures of yours. You have no reason to be suspicious of me."

"But what are you doing here?" asked Lao Tzu, "creeping into my palace instead of getting on with your journey?"

"On our way to the west," said Monkey, "we came to a country called Crowcock. The king of the country employed a wizard, who had disguised himself as a Taoist, to bring rain. This wizard secretly did away with the king, whose form he assumed, and now he is ensconced in the Hall of Golden Bells. My Master was reading the scriptures in the Treasure Wood Temple, when the soul of the king came to him and earnestly requested that I might be sent to subdue the wizard, and expose his imposture. I felt that I had no proof of the crime, and went with my fellow-disciple Pigsy. We broke into the flower garden by night, and looked for the crystal well into which the king had been thrown. We fished him up, and found him still sound and fresh. When we got back to the temple and saw Tripitaka, his compassion was aroused and he ordered me to bring the king to life. But I was not to go to the World of Darkness to recover his soul; I must cure him here in the World of Light. I could think of no way but to ask for your help. Would you be so kind as to lend me a thousand of your nine times sublimated life-restoring pills? Then I shall be able to set him right."

"A thousand pills indeed!" exclaimed Lao Tzu. "Why not two thousand? Is he to have them at every meal instead of rice? Do you think one has only to stoop and pick them up like dirt from the ground? Shoo! Be off with you! I've nothing for you."

"I'd take a hundred," said Monkey laughing.

"I dare say," said Lao Tzu. "But I haven't any."

"I'd take ten," said Monkey.

"A curse on this Monkey!" said Lao Tzu, very angry. "Will he never stop haggling? Be off with you immediately."

"If you really haven't got any," said Monkey, "I shall have to find some other way of bringing him to life."

"Go, go, go!" screamed Lao Tzu.

Very reluctantly Monkey turned away. But suddenly Lao Tzu thought to himself: "This monkey is very crafty. If he really went away and stayed away, it would be all right. But I am afraid he will slip back again and steal some." So he sent a fairy boy to bring Monkey back, and said to him, "If you are really so anxious to have some, I'll spare you just one pill."

"Sir," said Monkey, "if you had an inkling of what I can do if I choose, you would think yourself lucky to go shares in it with me. If you hadn't given in, I should have come with my dredge and fished up the whole lot."

Lao Tzu took a gourd-shaped pot and, tilting it up, emptied one grain of elixir and passed it across to Monkey, saying, "That's all you'll get, so be off with it. And if with this one grain you can bring the king back to life, you are welcome to the credit of it."

"Not so fast," said Monkey. "I must taste it first. I don't want to be put off with a sham." So saying, he tossed it into his mouth. Lao Tzu rushed forward to stop him, and pressing his fists against his skull-cap he cried in despair, "If you swallow it, I shall kill you on the spot!"

"Revolting meanness," said Monkey. "Keep calm; no one is eating anything of yours. And how much is it worth, anyhow? It's pretty wretched stuff, and come to that, I haven't swallowed it; it's here."

For the fact is that monkeys have a pouch under the gullet, and Monkey had stored the grain of elixir in his pouch. Lao Tzu pinched him and said, "Be off with you, be off with you, and don't let me find you hanging round here any more." So Monkey took leave of him, and quitted the Trayaśimstra Heaven. In a moment he had left by the Southern Gate, and turning eastward he saw the great globe of the sun just mounting. Lowering his cloud-seat, he soon reached the Treasure Wood

Temple, where even before he entered the gate he could hear Pigsy still howling. He stepped briskly forward and cried "Master."

"Is that Monkey?" said Tripitaka delightedly. "Have you got your elixir?"

"Certainly," said Monkey.

"What's the use of asking?" said Pigsy. "You can count on a sneak like that to bring back some trifle that doesn't belong to him."

"Brother," laughed Monkey, "you can retire. We don't need you any more. Wipe your eyes, and if you want to do more howling do it elsewhere. And you, Sandy, bring me a little water." Sandy hurried out to the well behind the temple, where there was a bucket of water ready drawn. He dipped his bowl into it and brought half a bowlful of water. Monkey filled his mouth with water, and then spat out the elixir into the Emperor's lips. Next he forced open his jaws, and pouring in some clean water, he floated the elixir down into his belly. In a few moments there was a gurgling sound inside; but the body still did not move. "Master," said Monkey, "what will become of me if my elixir fails? Shall I be beaten to death?"

"I don't see how it can fail," said Tripitaka. "It's already a miracle that a corpse that has been dead so long can swallow water. After the elixir entered his belly, we heard the guts ring. When the guts ring, the veins move in harmony. It only remains to get the breath into circulation. But even a piece of iron gets a bit rusty when it has been under water for three years; it is only natural that something of the same kind should happen to a man. All that's wrong with him is that he needs a supply of breath. If someone puts a mouthful of good breath into him, he would be quite himself again."

Pigsy at once offered himself for this service, but Tripitaka held him back. "You're no use for that," he cried. "Let Monkey do it." Tripitaka knew what he was talking about. For Pigsy had in his early days eaten living things, and even monstrously devoured human flesh, so that all his stock of breath was defiled. Whereas Monkey had always lived on pine-seeds, cypress cones, peaches, and the like, and his breath was pure.

So Monkey stepped forward, and putting his wide mouth against the Emperor's lips he blew hard into his throat. The breath went down to the Two-Storeyed Tower, round the Hall of Light, on to the Cinnabar Field, and from the Jetting Spring went back again into the Mud Wall Palace. Whereupon there was a deep panting sound. The king's humours concentrated, his spirits returned. He rolled over, brandished his fist, and bent his legs. Then with a cry "Master!" he knelt down in the dust and said, "Little did I think, when my soul visited you last night, that today at dawn I should again belong to the World of Light!" Tripitaka quickly raised him from his knees and said, "Your Majesty, this is no doing of mine. You must thank my disciple."

"What talk is that?" said Monkey laughing. "The proverb says 'A household cannot have two masters.' There is no harm in letting him pay his respects to you."

Tripitaka, still feeling somewhat embarrassed, raised the Emperor to his feet and brought him to the Hall of Meditation, where he and his disciples again prostrated themselves, and set him on a seat. The priests of the temple had got ready their breakfast, and invited Tripitaka and his party to join them. Imagine their astonishment when they saw an Emperor, his clothes still dripping. "Don't be surprised," said

Monkey, coming forward. "This is the King of Crow-cock, your rightful lord. Three years ago he was robbed of his life by a fiend, and tonight I brought him back to life. Now we must take him to the city and expose the impostor. If you have anything for us to eat, serve it now, and we will start as soon as we have breakfasted."

The priests brought the Emperor hot water to wash in, and helped him out of his clothes. The almoner brought him a cloth jacket, and instead of his jade belt tied a silk sash round his waist; took off his upturned shoes, and gave him a pair of old priest's sandals. Then they all had breakfast, and saddled the horse.

"Pigsy, is your luggage very heavy?" asked Monkey.

"Brother, I've carried it so many days on end that I don't know whether it's heavy or not."

"Divide the pack into two," said Monkey, "take one half yourself, and give the other to this Emperor to carry. In that way we shall get quicker to the city and dispose of our business."

"That's a bit of luck," said Pigsy. "It was a nuisance getting him here. But now that he's been made alive, he is coming in useful as a partner."

Pigsy then divided the luggage after his own methods. Borrowing a hod from the priests of the temple he put everything light into his own load, and everything heavy into the king's. "I hope your Majesty has no objection," said Monkey laughing, "to being dressed up like this, and carrying the luggage, and following us on foot."

"Master," said the Emperor, instantly flinging himself upon his knees, "I can only regard you as my second progenitor, and let alone carrying luggage for you, my heartfelt desire is to go with you all the way to India, even if I were only to serve you as the lowest menial, running beside you whip in hand as you ride."

"There's no need for you to go to India," said Monkey. "That's our special concern. All you have to do is to carry the luggage forty leagues to the city and then let us seize the fiend. After which you can go on being Emperor again, and we can go on looking for scriptures."

"That's all very well," said Pigsy. "But in that case he gets off with forty leagues, while I shall be on the job all the time."

"Brother," said Monkey, "don't talk nonsense, but be quick and lead the way out." Pigsy and the Emperor accordingly led the way, while Sandy supported Tripitaka on his horse and Monkey followed behind. They were accompanied to the gates by five hundred priests in gorgeous procession, blowing conches as they walked. "Don't come with us any further," said Monkey. "If some official were to notice, our plans might get out, and everything would go wrong. Go back at once, and have the Emperor's clothes well cleaned, and send them to the city tonight or early tomorrow. I will see to it that you are well paid for your pains."

They had not travelled for half a day when the walls and moat of the city of Crow-cock came into view. "Monkey," said Tripitaka, "I think this place in front of us must be the city of Crow-cock."

"It certainly is," said Monkey. "Let us hurry on and do our business."

When they reached the city they found the streets and markets thronging with people, and everywhere a great stir and bustle. Soon they saw rising before them towers and gables of great magnificence. "Disciples," said Tripitaka, "let us go at once to Court and get our papers put in order. Then we shall have no more trouble hanging about in government offices."

"That is a good idea," said Monkey. "We will all come with you; the more the tellers, the better the story."

"Well, if you all come," said Tripitaka, "you must behave nicely, and not say anything till you have done homage as humble subjects of the throne."

"But that means bowing down," said Monkey.

"To be sure," said Tripitaka. "You have to bow down five times and strike your forehead on the ground three times."

"Master," said Monkey, "that's not a good idea. To pay homage to a thing like that is really too silly. Let me go in first, and I will decide what we are to do. If he addresses us, let me answer him. If you see me bow, then you must bow too; if I squat, then you must squat."

Look at him, that Monkey King, maker of many troubles, how he goes straight up to the door and says to the high officer in charge: "We were sent by the Emperor of China to worship Buddha in India, and fetch scriptures. We want to have our papers put in order here, and would trouble you to announce our arrival. By doing so, you will not fail to gain religious merit." The eunuch went in and knelt on the steps of the throne, announcing the visitors and their request. "I did not think it right to let them straight in," he said. "They await your orders outside the door." The false king then summoned them in. Tripitaka entered, accompanied by the true king, who as he went could not stop the tears that coursed down his cheeks.

"Alas," he sighed to himself, "for my dragon-guarded rivers and hills, my iron-girt shrines! Who would have guessed that a creature of darkness would possess you all?"

"Emperor," said Monkey, "you must control your emotion, or we shall be discovered. I can feel the truncheon behind my ear twitching, and I am certain that I shall be successful. Leave it to me to slay the monster and when things are cleaned up, those rivers and hills will soon be yours again."

The true king dared not demur. He wiped away his tears, and followed as best he could. At last they reached the Hall of Golden Bells, where they saw the two rows of officials civil and military, and the four hundred Court officers, all of imposing stature and magnificently apparelled. Monkey led forward Tripitaka to the white jade steps, where they both stood motionless and erect. The officials were in consternation. "Are these priests so utterly bereft of decency and reason?" they exclaimed. "How comes it that, seeing our king, they do not bow down or greet him with any word of blessing? Not even a cry of salutation escaped their lips. Never have we seen such impudent lack of manners!"

"Where do they come from?" interrupted the false king.

"We were sent from the eastern land of T'ang in Southern Jambudvīpa," said Monkey haughtily, "by royal command, to go to India that is in the Western Region, and there to worship the Living Buddha in the Temple of the Great Thunder Clap, and obtain true scriptures. Having arrived here we dare not proceed without coming first to you to have our passports put in order."

The false king was very angry. "What is this eastern land of yours?" he said. "Do I pay tribute to it, that you should appear before me in this rude fashion, without bowing down? I have never had any dealings with your country."

"Our eastern land," said Monkey, "long ago set up a Heavenly Court and became a Great Power. Whereas yours is a Minor Power, a mere frontier land. There is an old saying, 'The king of a Great Country is father and lord; the king of a lesser country is vassal and son.' You admit that you have had no dealings with our country. How dare you contend that we ought to bow down?"

"Remove that uncivil priest," the king called to his officers of war. At this all the officers sprang forward. But Monkey made a magic pass and cried "Halt!" The magic of the pass was such that these officers all suddenly remained rooted to the spot and could not stir. Well might it be said:

> The captains standing round the steps became like figures of wood,
> The generals on the Royal Dais were like figures of clay.

Seeing that Monkey had brought his officers civil and military to a standstill, the false king leapt from his Dragon Couch and made as though to seize him. "Good," said Monkey to himself "That is just what I wanted. Even if his hand is made of iron, this cudgel of mine will make some pretty dents in it!"

But just at this moment a star of rescue arrived. "Who can this have been?" you ask. It was no other than the prince of Crow-cock, who hastened forward and clutched at the false king's sleeve, and kneeling before him cried, "Father and king, stay your anger."

"Little son," asked the king, "why should you say this?"

"I must inform my father and king," said the prince. "Three years ago I heard someone say that a priest had been sent from T'ang to get scriptures in India, and it is he who has now unexpectedly arrived in our country. If my father and king, yielding to the ferocity of his noble nature, now arrests and beheads this priest, I fear that the news will one day reach the Emperor of T'ang, who will be furiously angry. You must know that after Li Shih-min[36] had established this great dynasty of T'ang and united the whole land, his heart was still not content, and he has now begun to conquer far-away lands. If he hears that you have done harm to his favourite priest, he will raise his hosts and come to make war upon you. Our troops are few and our generals feeble. You will, when it is too late, be sorry indeed that you provoked him. If you were to follow your small son's advice, you would question these four priests, and only punish such of them as are proved not to travel at the King of China's bidding."

This was a stratagem of the prince's. For he feared that harm might come to Tripitaka, and therefore tried to check the king, not knowing that Monkey was ready to strike.

The false king believed him, and standing in front of the Dragon Couch, he cried in a loud voice: "Priest, how long ago did you leave China, and why were you sent to get scriptures?"

---

[36] **Li Shih-min:** Another name for Taizong (T'ai-tsung) (r. 626–49), second emperor of the Tang dynasty.

"My Master," said Monkey haughtily, "is called Tripitaka, and is treated by the Emperor of China as his younger brother. The Emperor in a vision went to the Realms of Death, and on his return he ordered a great Mass for all souls in torment. On this occasion my Master recited so well and showed such compassionate piety that the Goddess Kuan-yin chose him to go on a mission to the west. My Master vowed that he would faithfully perform this task in return for his sovereign's bounties, and he was furnished by the Emperor with credentials for the journey. He started in the thirteenth year of the Emperor's reign, in the ninth month, three days before the full moon. After leaving China, he came first to the Land of the Two Frontiers, where he picked up me, and made me his chief disciple. In the hamlet of the Kao family, on the borders of the country of Wu-ssu, he picked up a second disciple, called Pigsy; and at the river of Flowing Sands he picked up a third, whom we call Sandy. Finally a few days ago, at the Temple of the Treasure Wood, he found another recruit—the servant who is carrying the luggage."

The false king thought it unwise to ask any more questions about Tripitaka; but he turned savagely upon Monkey and addressed to him a crafty question. "I can accept," he said, "that one priest set out from China, and picked up three priests on the way. But your story about the fourth member of your party I altogether disbelieve. This servant is certainly someone whom you have kidnapped. What is his name? Has he a passport, or has he none? Bring him before me to make his deposition!"

The true king shook with fright. "Master," he whispered, "what am I to depose?"

"That's all right," said Monkey. "I'll make your deposition for you."

Dear Monkey! He stepped boldly forward and cried to the magician in a loud, clear voice: "Your Majesty, this old man is dumb and rather hard of hearing. But it so happens that when he was young, he travelled in India, and knows the way there. I know all about his career and origins and with your Majesty's permission I will make a deposition on his behalf."

"Make haste," said the false king, "and furnish a true deposition or you will get into trouble."

Monkey then recited as follows:

> The subject of this deposition is far advanced in years; he is deaf and dumb, and has fallen on evil days. His family for generations has lived in these parts; but five years ago disaster overtook his house. Heaven sent no rain; the people perished of drought, the lord king and all his subjects fasted and did penance. They burned incense, purified themselves and called upon the Lord of Heaven; but in all the sky not a wisp of cloud appeared. The hungry peasants dropped by the roadside, when suddenly there came a Taoist magician from the Chung-nan Mountains, a monster in human form. He called to the winds and summoned the rain, displaying godlike power; but soon after secretly destroyed this wretched man's life. In the flower-garden he pushed him down into the crystal well; then set himself on the Dragon Throne, none knowing it was he. Luckily I came and achieved a great success; I raised him from the dead and restored him to life without hurt or harm. He earnestly begged to be admitted to our faith, and act as carrier on the road, to join with us in our quest and journey to the Western Land. The false king who sits on the throne is that foul magician; he that now carries our load is Crow-cock's rightful king!

When the false king in the Palace of Golden Bells heard these words, he was so startled that his heart fluttered like the heart of a small deer. Then clouds of shame suffused his face, and leaping to his feet he was about to flee, when he remembered that he was unarmed. Looking round he saw a captain of the Guard with a dagger at his waist, standing there dumb and foolish as a result of Monkey's spell. The false king rushed at him and snatched the dagger; then leapt upon a cloud and disappeared into space.

Sandy burst into an exclamation of rage, and Pigsy loudly abused Monkey for his slowness. "It's a pity you didn't look sharp and stop him," he said. "Now he has sailed off on a cloud, and we shall never be able to find him."

"Don't shout at me, brothers!" said Monkey laughing. "Let us call to the prince to come and do reverence to his true father, and the queen to her husband." Then undoing by a magic pass the spell that he had put upon the officers, he told them to wake up and do homage to their lord, acknowledging him as their true king. "Give me a few facts to go upon," he said, "and as soon as I have got things clear, I will go and look for him."

Dear Monkey! He instructed Pigsy and Sandy to take good care of the prince, king, ministers, queen, and Tripitaka; but while he was speaking he suddenly vanished from sight. He had already jumped up into the empyrean, and was peering round on every side, looking for the wizard. Presently he saw that monster flying for his life towards the north-east. Monkey caught him up and shouted, "Monster, where are you off to? Monkey has come." The wizard turned swiftly, drew his dagger, and cried, "Monkey, you scamp, what has it got to do with you whether I usurp someone else's throne? Why should you come calling me to account and letting out my secrets?"

"Ho, ho," laughed Monkey. "You impudent rascal! Do you think I am going to allow you to play the emperor? Knowing who I am you would have done well to keep out of my way. Why did you bully my master, demanding depositions and what not? You must admit now that the deposition was not far from the truth. Stand your ground and take old Monkey's cudgel like a man!"

The wizard dodged and parried with a thrust of his dagger at Monkey's face. It was a fine fight! After several bouts the magician could no longer stand up against Monkey, and suddenly turning he fled back the way he had come, leapt into the city, and slipped in among the officers who were assembled before the steps of the throne. Then giving himself a shake, he changed into an absolute counterpart of Tripitaka and stood beside him in front of the steps. Monkey rushed up and was about to strike what he supposed to be the wizard, when this Tripitaka said, "Disciple, do not strike! It is I!" It was impossible to distinguish between them. "If I kill Tripitaka, who is a transformation of the wizard, then I shall have achieved a glorious success; but supposing, on the other hand, it turns out that I have killed the real Tripitaka, that would not be so good . . ." There was nothing for it but to stay his hand, and calling to Pigsy and Sandy he asked, "Which really is the wizard, and which is our master? Just point for me, and I will strike the one you point at."

"We were watching you going for one another up in the air," said Pigsy, "when suddenly we looked round and saw that there were two Tripitakas. We have no idea which is the real one."

When Monkey heard this, he made a single pass and recited a spell to summon the *devas* that protect the Law, the local deities and the spirits of the neighbouring hills, and told them of his predicament. The wizard thought it time to mount the clouds again, and began to make towards the door. Thinking that Tripitaka was clearing the ground for him, Monkey raised his cudgel, and had it not been for the deities he had summoned he would have struck such a big blow at his master as would have made mince-meat of twenty Tripitakas. But in the nick of time the guardian deities stopped him, saying, "Great Sage, the wizard is just going to mount the clouds again." Monkey rushed after him, and was just about to cut off his retreat, when the wizard turned round, slipped back again into the crowd, and was once more indistinguishable from the real Tripitaka.

Much to Monkey's annoyance, Pigsy stood by, laughing at his discomfiture. "You've nothing to laugh at, you hulking brute," he said. "This means you've got two masters to order you about. It's not going to do you much good."

"Brother," said Pigsy, "you call me a fool, but you're a worse fool than I. You can't recognize your own Master, and it's a waste of effort to go on trying. But you would at least recognize your own headache, and if you ask our Master to recite his spell, Sandy and I will stand by and listen. The one who doesn't know the spell will certainly be the wizard. Then all will be easy."

"Brother," said Monkey, "I am much obliged to you. There are only three people who know that spell. It sprouted from the heart of the Lord Buddha himself; it was handed down to the Bodhisattva Kuan-yin, and was then taught to our master by the Bodhisattva herself. No one else knows it. Good, then! Master, recite!"

The real Tripitaka at once began to recite the spell; while the wizard could do nothing but mumble senseless sounds. "That's the wizard," cried Pigsy. "He's only mumbling." And at the same time he raised his rake and was about to strike when the wizard sprang into the air and ran up along the clouds. Dear Pigsy! With a loud cry he set off in pursuit, and Sandy, leaving Tripitaka, hastened to the attack with his priest's staff. Tripitaka stopped reciting, and Monkey, released from his headache, seized his iron cudgel and sped through the air. Heigh, what a fight! Three wild priests beleaguered one foul fiend. With rake and staff Pigsy and Sandy assailed him from right and left. "If I join in," said Monkey, "and attack him in front, I fear he is so frightened of me that he will run away again. Let me get into position above him and give him a real garlic-pounding blow that will finish him off for good and all." He sprang up into the empyrean, and was about to deliver a tremendous blow when, from a many-coloured cloud in the north-east, there came a voice which said, "Monkey, stay your hand!" Monkey looked round and saw it was the Bodhisattva Manjuśrī.[37] He withdrew his cudgel, and coming forward did obeisance, saying "Bodhisattva, where are you going to?"

"I came to take this monster off your hands," said Manjuśrī.

"I am sorry you should have the trouble," said Monkey.

The Bodhisattva then drew from his sleeve a magic mirror that showed demons

---

[37] **Bodhisattva Manjuśrī:** The primary figure in one cult of Tantric Buddhism, centered at Wu-Taishan (Mountain of the Five Terraces) in India.

in their true form. Monkey called to the other two to come and look, and in the mirror they saw the wizard in his true shape. He was Manjuśrī's lion! "Bodhisattva," said Monkey, "this is the blue-maned lion that you sit upon. How comes it that it ran away and turned into an evil spirit? Can't you keep it under control?"

"It did not run away," said Manjuśrī. "It acted under orders from Buddha himself."

"You mean to tell me," said Monkey, "that it was Buddha who told this creature to turn into an evil spirit and seize the Emperor's throne? In that case all the troubles I meet with while escorting Tripitaka are very likely ordered by His Holiness. A nice thought!"

"Monkey," said Manjuśrī, "you don't understand. In the beginning this king of Crow-cock was devoted to good works and the entertaining of priests. Buddha was so pleased that he sent me to fetch him away to the Western Paradise, where he was to assume a golden body and become an Arhat. As it was not proper for me to show myself in my true form I came disguised as a priest and begged for alms. Something I said gave him offence, and not knowing that I was anyone in particular he had me bound and cast into the river, where I remained under water for three nights and three days, till at last a guardian spirit rescued me and brought me back to Paradise. I complained to Buddha, who sent this creature to throw the king into the well, and let him remain there three years as a retaliation for the three days that I was in the river. You know the saying: 'Not a sip, not a sup . . .'[38] But now you have arrived on the scene, the episode is successfully closed."

"That is all very well," said Monkey. "All these 'sips and sups' may have enabled you to get even with your enemy. But what about all the unfortunate people whom this fiend has ruined?"

"He hasn't ruined any one," said Manjuśrī. "During the three years that he was on the throne, rain has fallen, the crops have been good, and the people at perfect peace. How can you speak of his ruining people?"

"That may be," said Monkey. "But how about all the ladies of the Court who have been sleeping with him and unwittingly been led into a heinous and unnatural offence? They would hardly subscribe to the view that he had done no harm."

"He isn't in a position to defile anyone," said Manjuśrī. "He's a gelded lion!"

At this Pigsy came up to the wizard and felt him. "Quite true," he announced, laughing. "This is a 'blotchy nose that never sniffed wine'; 'a bad name and nothing to show for it.'"

"Very well then," said Monkey. "Take him away. If you had not come just in time, he'd have been dead by now."

Manjuśrī then recited a spell and said, "Creature, back to your true shape and look sharp about it!" The wizard at once changed into his real lion form, and Manjuśrī, putting down the lotus that he carried in his hand, harnessed the lion, mounted him, and rode away over the clouds.

If you do not know how Tripitaka and his disciples left the city you must listen while it is explained to you in the next chapter.

[38] **'Not . . . sup . . .':** Everything that happens depends on karma.

FROM

CHAPTER 22

Monkey and the other two disciples lowered the clouds on which they rode and returned to Court, where they received the humble thanks of the king, his ministers, heir and consort, and all the officers. Monkey told them how Manjuśrī had reclaimed the fiend, at which they prostrated themselves with extreme awe and reverence. In the midst of these congratulations and rejoicings a eunuch suddenly arrived, saying, "My lord and master, four more priests have arrived."

"Brother," said Pigsy, in consternation, "what if it should turn out that the fiend, having disguised himself as Manjuśrī and taken us all in, has now turned himself into a priest, in the hope of confounding us?"

"Impossible!" said Monkey, and he ordered them to be shown in. The officers of the Court sent word that they were to be admitted, and when they appeared Monkey saw at once that they were priests from the Treasure Wood Temple, bringing the crown, belt, cloak and upturned shoes of the king. "Just at the right moment!" said Monkey, delighted. He then called to the "porter" to come forward, took off his head-wrap and put on the crown, took off his cloth coat and put on the royal robe, undid the sash and girded him with the belt of jades, slipped off his priest's sandals and put on the upturned shoes. Then he told the prince to bring out the white jade tablet, and put it in the king's hand, bidding him mount the dais and proclaim his sovereignty, in accordance with the old saying "A court must not, even for a day, be without a sovereign."

But the king was very loth to sit upon the throne, and weeping bitterly he knelt on the centre of the steps, saying, "I was dead for three years, and having now by your doing been brought back to life, how can I dare proclaim myself your sovereign? It would be better that one of you priests should be king, and that I should take my wife and child and live like a commoner outside the walls of the city."

Tripitaka of course would not accept, as his heart was set upon going to worship the Buddha and get scriptures. The king then asked Monkey. "Gentlemen," said Monkey laughing, "I will not deceive you. If I had wanted to be an Emperor, I could have had the throne in any of the ten thousand lands and nine continents under heaven. But I have got used to being a priest and leading a lazy, comfortable existence. An Emperor has to wear his hair long; at nightfall he may not doze, at the fifth drum he must be awake. Each time there is news from the frontier his heart jumps; when there are calamities and disasters he is plunged in sorrow and despair; I should never get used to it. You go back to your job as Emperor, and let me go back to mine as priest, doing my deeds and going upon my way."

Seeing that it was useless to refuse, the king at last mounted the dais, turned towards his subjects and proclaimed his sovereignty, announcing a great amnesty throughout his realm. He loaded the priests from the Treasure Wood Temple with presents and sent them home. Then he opened the eastern upper room and held a banquet for Tripitaka. He also sent for a painter to make portraits of the blessed countenances of Tripitaka and his disciples, which were to be hung in the Palace of Golden Bells, and reverenced as objects of worship.

Having put the king upon his throne, Tripitaka and his disciples were anxious to start out again as soon as possible. The king, his ladies, the prince, and all the ministers pressed upon them all the heirlooms of the kingdom, and gold, silver, silks, and satins, to show their deep gratitude. But Tripitaka would not accept so much as a split hair, and when their passports had been put in order, he urged Monkey and the rest to get the horse saddled, so that they might start at once. The king, very loth to part with them, ordered his State Coach to be got ready and made Tripitaka ride in it. He was drawn by officers civil and military, while the prince and ladies of the Court pushed at the sides, till they were beyond the walls of the town. Here Tripitaka alighted, and took leave of them all. [. . .]

FROM
CHAPTER 28

They travelled westward for many months, and at last began to be aware that the country through which they were now passing was different from any that they had seen. Everywhere they came across gem-like flowers and magical grasses, with many ancient cypresses and hoary pines. In the villages through which they passed every family seemed to devote itself to the entertainment of priests and other pious works. On every hill were hermits practising austerities, in every wood pilgrims chanting holy writ. Finding hospitality each night and starting again at dawn, they journeyed for many days, till they came at last within sudden sight of a cluster of high eaves and towers.

"Monkey, that's a fine place," said Tripitaka, pointing to it with his whip.

"Considering," said Monkey, "how often you have insisted upon prostrating yourself at the sight of false magicians' palaces and arch impostors' lairs, it is strange that when at last you see before you Buddha's true citadel, you should not even dismount from your horse."

At this Tripitaka in great excitement sprang from his saddle, and walking beside the horse was soon at the gates of the high building. A young Taoist came out to meet them. "Aren't you the people who have come from the east to fetch scriptures?" he asked. Tripitaka hastily tidied his clothes and looking up saw that the boy was clad in gorgeous brocades and carried a bowl of jade dust in his hand. Monkey knew him at once.

"This," he said to Tripitaka, "is the Golden Crested Great Immortal of the Jade Truth Temple at the foot of the Holy Mountain."

Tripitaka at once advanced bowing. "Well, here you are at last!" said the Immortal. "The Bodhisattva misinformed me. Ten years ago she was told by Buddha to go to China and find someone who would fetch scriptures from India. She told me she had found someone who would arrive here in two or three years. Year after year I waited, but never a sign! This meeting is indeed a surprise."

"I cannot thank you enough, Great Immortal, for your patience," said Tripitaka.

Then they all went into the temple and were shown round by the Immortal; tea and refreshments were served, and perfumed hot water was brought for Tripitaka to wash in. Soon they all turned in for the night. Early next day Tripitaka changed into his brocaded cassock and jewelled cap, and staff in hand presented himself to the Immortal in the hall of the temple, to take his leave. "That's better!" said the Immortal. "Yesterday you were looking a bit shabby; but now you look a true child of Buddha!"

Tripitaka was just going when the Immortal stopped him, saying, "You must let me see you off."

"It's really not necessary," said Tripitaka. "Monkey knows the way."

"He only knows the way by air," said the Immortal. "You have got to go on the ground."

"That's true enough," said Monkey. "We will trouble you just to set us on the right way. My Master is pining to get into the presence of the Buddha, and it would be a pity if there were any delay."

Taking Tripitaka by the hand he led him right through the temple and out at the back. For the road did not go from the front gate, but traversed the courtyards and led on to the hill behind.

"You see that highest point, wreathed in magic rainbow mists," said the Immortal, pointing to the mountain. "That is the Vulture Peak, the sacred precinct of the Buddha."

Tripitaka at once began kow-towing. "Master," said Monkey, "you had better keep that for later on. If you are going to kow-tow all the way up to the top, there won't be much left of your head by the time we get there. It's still a long way off."

"You stand already on Blessed Ground," said the Immortal. "The Holy Mountain is before you. I shall now turn back."

Monkey led them up the hill at a leisurely pace. They had not gone more than five or six leagues when they came to a great water about eight leagues wide. It was exceedingly swift and rough. No one was to be seen in any direction.

"I don't think this can be the right way," said Tripitaka. "Do you think the Immortal can possibly have been mistaken? This water is so wide and so rough that we cannot possibly get across."

"This is the way all right," said Monkey. "Look! Just over there is a bridge. That's the right way to Salvation."

Presently Tripitaka came to a notice-board on which was written Cloud Reach Bridge. But it proved, when they came up to it, that the bridge consisted simply of slim tree trunks laid end on end, and was hardly wider than the palm of a man's hand.

"Monkey," protested Tripitaka in great alarm, "it's not humanly possible to balance on such a bridge as that. We must find some other way to get across."

"This is the right way," said Monkey, grinning.

"It may be the right way," said Pigsy, "but it's so narrow and slippery that no one would ever dare set foot on it. And think how far there is to go, and what it's like underneath."

"All wait where you are, and watch while I show you how," cried Monkey. Dear Monkey! He strode up to the bridge, leapt lightly on to it, and had soon slipped across. "I'm over!" he shouted, waving from the other side. Tripitaka showed no sign of following him, and Pigsy and Sandy bit their fingers murmuring, "Can't be done! Can't be done!" Monkey sprang back again and pulled at Pigsy, saying, "Fool, follow me across."

But Pigsy lay on the ground and would not budge. "It's much too slippery," he said. "Let me off. Why can't I have a wind to carry me?"

"What would be the good of that?" said Monkey. "Unless you go by the bridge you won't turn into a Buddha."

"Buddha or no Buddha," said Pigsy, "I'm not going on to that bridge."

The quarrel was at its height, when Sandy ran between them and at last succeeded in making peace. Suddenly Tripitaka saw someone punting a boat towards the shore and crying, "Ferry, ferry!"

"Stop your quarrelling, disciples," said Tripitaka. "A boat is coming."

They all gazed with one accord at the spot to which he pointed. A boat was coming indeed; but when it was a little nearer they saw to their consternation that it had no bottom. Monkey with his sharp eyes had already recognized the ferryman as the Conductor of Souls, also called Light of the Banner. But he did not tell the others, merely crying "Ahoy, ferry, ahoy!" When the boat was along shore, the ferryman again cried "Ferry, ferry!"

"Your boat is broken and bottomless," said Tripitaka, much perturbed. "How can you take people across?"

"You may well think," said the ferryman, "that in a bottomless boat such a river as this could never be crossed. But since the beginning of time I have carried countless souls to their Salvation."

"Get on board, Master," said Monkey. "You will find that this boat, although it has no bottom, is remarkably steady, however rough the waters may be."

Seeing Tripitaka still hesitate, Monkey took him by the scruff of the neck and pushed him on board. There was nothing for Tripitaka's feet to rest on, and he went straight into the water. The ferryman caught at him and dragged him up to the side of the boat. Sitting miserably there, he wrung out his clothes, shook out his shoes, and grumbled at Monkey for having got him into this scrape. But Monkey, taking no notice, put Pigsy and Sandy, horse and baggage, all on board, ensconcing them as best he could in the gunwale. The ferryman punted them dexterously out from shore. Suddenly they saw a body in the water, drifting rapidly down stream. Tripitaka stared at it in consternation. Monkey laughed.

"Don't be frightened, Master," he said. "That's you."

And Pigsy said, "It's you, it's you."

Sandy clapped his hands. "It's you, it's you," he cried.

The ferryman too joined in the chorus. "There *you* go!" he cried. "My best congratulations." He went on punting, and in a very short while they were all safe and sound at the other side. Tripitaka stepped lightly ashore. He had discarded his earthly body; he was cleansed from the corruption of the senses, from the fleshly inheritance of those bygone years. His was now the transcendent wisdom that leads to the Further Shore, the mastery that knows no bounds.

When they were at the top of the bank, they turned round and found to their astonishment that boat and ferryman had both vanished. Only then did Monkey tell them who the ferryman was. Tripitaka began thanking his disciples for all they had done for him. "Every one of us," said Monkey, "is equally indebted to the other. If the Master had not received our vows and accepted us as his disciples we should not have had the chance to do good works and win salvation. If we had not protected the Master and mounted guard over him, he would never have got rid of his mortal body. Look, Master, at this realm of flowers and happy creatures—of phoenixes, cranes, and deer. Is it not a better place indeed than the haunted deserts through which you and I have passed?" Tripitaka still murmured his thanks, and with a strange feeling of lightness and exhilaration they all set off up the Holy Mountain and were soon in sight of the Temple of the Thunder Clap, with its mighty towers brushing the firmament, its giant foundations rooted in the seams of the Hill of Life.

Near the top of the hill they came upon a party of Upasakas filing through the green pinewoods, and under a clump of emerald cedars they saw bands of the Blessed. Tripitaka hastened to bow down to them. Worshippers male and female, monks and nuns pressed together the palms of their hands, crying. "Holy priest, it is not to us that your homage should be addressed. Wait till you have seen Sakyamuni, and afterwards come and greet us each according to his rank."

"He's always in too much of a hurry," laughed Monkey. "Come along at once and let us pay our respects to the people at the top."

Twitching with excitement Tripitaka followed Monkey to the gates of the Temple. Here they were met by the Vajrapani[39] of the Four Elements.

"So your Reverence has at last arrived!" he exclaimed.

"Your disciple Hsüan Tsang has indeed arrived," said Tripitaka, bowing.

"I must trouble you to wait here a moment, till your arrival has been announced," said the Vajrapani.

He then gave instructions to the porter at the outer gate to tell the porter at the second gate that the Vajrapani wished to report that the priest from China had arrived. The porter at the second gate sent word to the porter at the third gate. At this gate were holy priests with direct access to the Powers Above. They hurried to the Great Hall and informed the Tathagata,[40] the Most Honoured One, even Sakyamuni Buddha himself that the priest from the Court of China had arrived at the Mountain to fetch scriptures.

Father Buddha was delighted. He ordered the Bodhisattva, Vajrapanis, Arhats, Protectors, Planets, and Temple Guardians to form up in two lines. Then he gave orders that the priest of T'ang was to be shown in. Again the word was passed along from gate to gate: "The priest of T'ang is to be shown in." Tripitaka, Monkey, Pigsy, and Sandy, carefully following the rules of etiquette prescribed to them, all went forward, horse and baggage following. When they reached the Great Hall they first prostrated themselves before the Tathagata and then bowed to right and left. This they repeated three times, and then knelt before the Buddha and presented their passports. He looked through them one by one and handed them back to Tripitaka, who bent his head in acknowledgement, saying, "The disciple Hsüan Tsang has come by

---

[39] **Vajrapani:** "The thunderbolt-handed," a personification of force. [40] **Tathagata:** The Buddha.

order of the Emperor of the great land of T'ang, all the way to this Holy Mountain, to fetch the true scriptures which are to be the salvation of all mankind. May the Lord Buddha accord this favour and grant me a quick return to my native land."

Hereupon the Tathagata opened the mouth of compassion and gave vent to the mercy of his heart: "In all the vast and populous bounds of your Eastern Land, greed, slaughter, lust, and lying have long prevailed. There is no respect for Buddha's teaching, no striving towards good works. So full and abundant is the measure of the people's sins that they go down forever into the darkness of Hell, where some are pounded in mortars, some take on animal form, furry and horned. In which guise they are done by as they did on earth, their flesh becoming men's food. Confucius stood by their side teaching them all the virtues, king after king in vain corrected them with fresh penalties and pains. No law could curb their reckless debauches, no ray of wisdom penetrate their blindness.

"But I have three Baskets of Scripture that can save mankind from its torments and afflictions. One contains the Law, which tells of Heaven, one contains the Discourses, which speak of Earth, one contains the Scriptures, which save the dead. They are divided into thirty-five sections and are written upon fifteen thousand one hundred and forty-four scrolls. They are the path to Perfection, the gate that leads to True Good. In them may be learnt all the motions of the stars and divisions of earth, all that appertains to man, bird, beast, flower, tree and implement of use; in short, all that concerns mankind is found therein. In consideration of the fact that you have come so far, I would give you them all to take back. But the people of China are foolish and boisterous; they would mock at my mysteries and, would not understand the hidden meaning of our Order . . . Ānanda, Kaśyapa,"[41] he cried, "take these four to the room under the tower, and when they have refreshed themselves, open the doors of the Treasury, and select from each of the thirty-five sections a few scrolls for these priests to take back to the east, to be a boon there forever."

In the lower room they saw countless rarities and treasures, and were still gazing upon them in wonder when spirits ministrant began to spread the feast. The foods were all fairy fruits and dainties unknown in the common world. Master and disciples bowed acknowledgement of Buddha's favour and set to with a good will. This time it was Pigsy who was in luck and Sandy who scored; for Buddha had provided for their fare such viands as confer long life and health and magically transform the substance of common flesh and bone. When Ānanda and Kaśyapa had seen to it that the four had all they wanted, they went into the Treasury. The moment the door was opened, beams of magic light shot forth, filling the whole air far around. On chests and jewelled boxes were stuck red labels, on which were written the names of the holy books. The two disciples of Buddha led Tripitaka up to the place where the scriptures lay, and inviting him to study the titles said, "Having come here from China you have no doubt brought a few little gifts for us. If you will kindly hand them over, you shall have your scriptures at once."

---

[41] **Ānanda, Kaśyapa:** Ānanda: one of the foremost disciples of the Buddha, his name means "joy." Kaśyapa: a Buddhist sage and writer of hymns.

"During all my long journey," said Tripitaka, "I have never once found it necessary to lay in anything of the kind."

"Splendid," said the disciples. "So we're to spend our days handing over scriptures gratis! Not a very bright outlook for our heirs!"

Thinking by their sarcastic tone that they had no intention of parting with the scriptures, Monkey could not refrain from shouting angrily, "Come along, Master! We'll tell Buddha about this and make him come and give us the scriptures himself."

"Don't shout," said Ānanda. "There's nothing in the situation that demands all this bullying and blustering. Come here and fetch your scriptures."

Pigsy and Sandy, mastering their rage and managing to restrain Monkey, came across to take the books. Scroll by scroll was packed away into the bundle, which was hoisted on to the horse's back. Then the two luggage packs were tied up and given to Pigsy and Sandy to carry. They first went and kow-towed their thanks to Buddha.

"These books," said Ānanda, "written on five thousand and forty-eight scrolls, have all been given to the priests of China to keep forever in their land. They are all now securely packed on their horse's back or in parcels to be carried by hand, and the pilgrims are here to thank you."

Tripitaka and the disciples tethered the horse, put down the burdens and bowed with the palms of their hands pressed together. "The efficacy of these scriptures is boundless," said Buddha. "They are not only the mirror of our Faith, but also the source and origin of all three religions. When you return to the world and show them to common mortals, they must not be lightly handled. No scroll must be opened save by one who has fasted and bathed. Treasure them, value them! For in them is secreted the mystic lore of Immortality, in them is revealed the wondrous receipt for ten thousand transformations."

Tripitaka kow-towed his thanks, doing leal homage, and prostrating himself three times, as he had done before. When they reached the outer gates, they paid their respects to the bands of the faithful, and went on their way.

After dismissing the pilgrims, Buddha broke up the assembly. Presently the Bodhisattva Kuan-yin appeared before the throne, saying, "Long ago I was instructed by you to find someone in China who would come here to fetch scriptures. He has now achieved this task, which has taken him five thousand and forty days. The number of the scrolls delivered to him is five thousand and forty-eight. I suggest that it would be appropriate if he were given eight days in which to complete his mission, so that the two figures may concord."

"A very good idea," said Buddha. "You may have that put into effect."

He then sent for the eight Vajrapanis and said to them, "You are to exert your magic powers and carry back Tripitaka to the east. When he has deposited the scriptures, you are to bring him back here. All this must be done in eight days, that the number of days taken by the journey may concord with the number of scrolls allotted to him." The Vajrapanis at once went after Tripitaka, caught him up and said to him, "Scripture-taker, follow us." A sudden lightness and agility possessed the pilgrims and they were borne aloft upon a magic cloud.

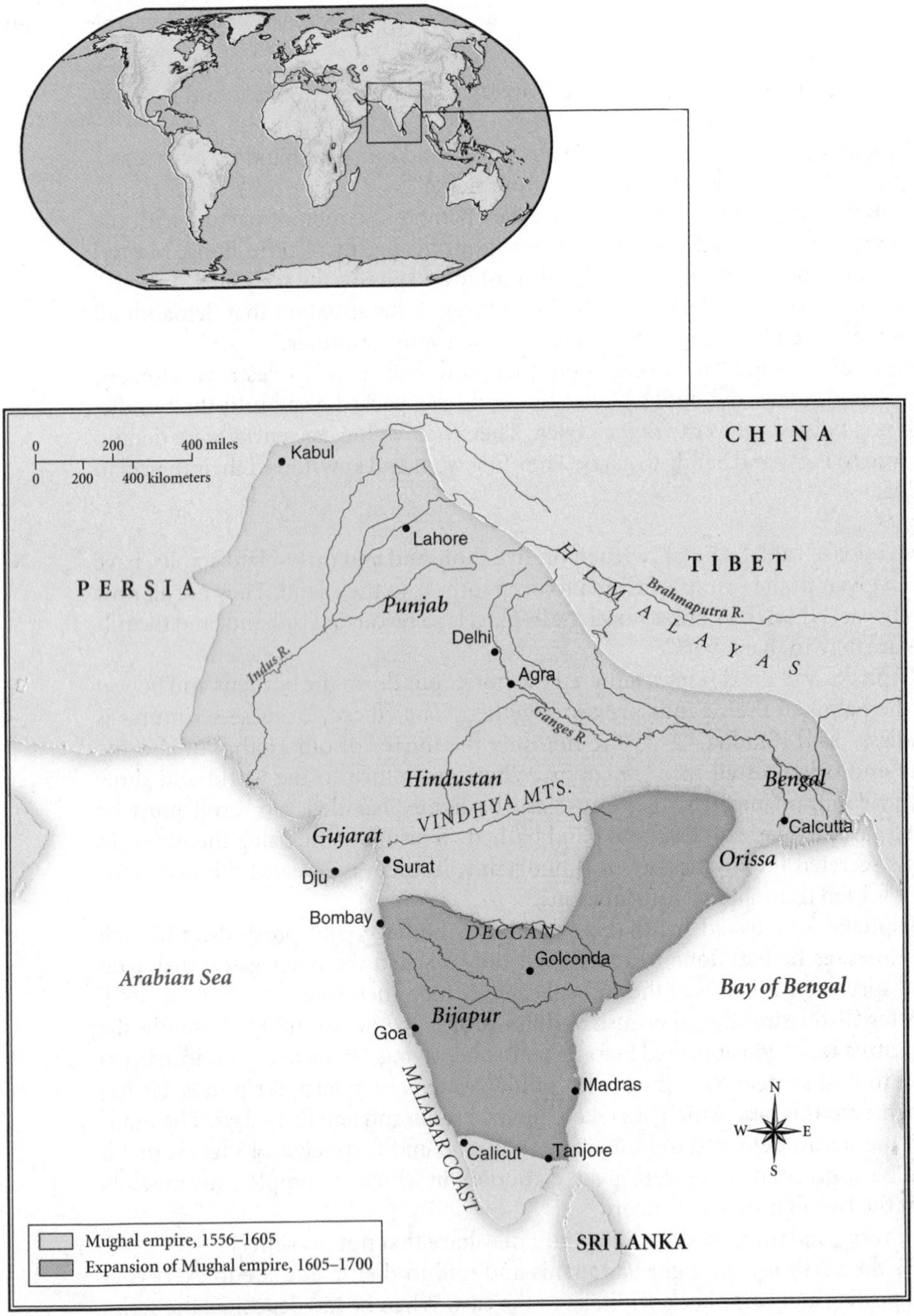

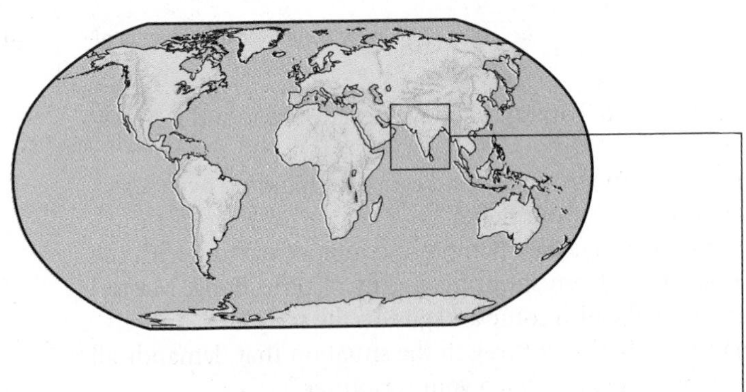

The Mughal Empire, 1526–1757

The Mughal empire began in the north of India in 1526 when Babur (1483–1530), who had begun his invasion from Kabul, took over Delhi. The empire spread steadily southward, reaching its greatest extent during the reign of Aurangzeb (r. 1658–1707), who pushed the empire as far south as Tanjore. Under the reign of Akbar (r. 1556–1605) the empire experienced its cultural and political heyday. Mughal control was never as strong in the south of India, the former site of the Vijayanagar state and, in the Western Ghats along the southwest coast, the seat of armed opposition to the Mughals.

INDIA

Spiritual Devotion and the Coming of the Mughals

After a golden age (which some historians call the Classical Age) and the breakdown of the Gupta empire (c. 320–550 C.E.), the country known today as India was divided into many kingdoms that continually waged war with one another and were given to internal conflict as well. The boundaries of these kingdoms shifted frequently as rival kings competed for territory, resources, and trade. During this period of constant discord and political turmoil, a number of devotional Hindu sects led by charismatic figures known as **BAKHTI** (devotional) saints swept through India, drawing followers away from more traditional forms of Hinduism and from Buddhism, which had begun to splinter and decline. It was not until the arrival of the Mughals, Turko-Mongol invaders from the north who captured Delhi and the northern part of India in the fifteenth century, that India would again be united under a central authority. Because the literature of the Mughal empire did not reach its peak until the seventeenth and eighteenth centuries, we focus in this book on the powerful, still important tradition of the bhakti saints, whose lyric poems and songs play a vital part in Hindu devotion even today.

PRE-MUGHAL INDIA

In a series of invasions from the eighth through the twelfth centuries, Arab Muslims gradually took control over the kingdom of Sind and the Punjab region of the upper Indus Valley, culminating in the founding of the sultanate at Delhi in 1206 by Qutb-ud-Din Aybak (r. 1206–10). After the establishment of the sultanate, India was effectively divided into two parts: a relatively unified Muslim north and a divided Hindu south, which was separated among several decentralized Hindu kingdoms.

Over the next three centuries, successive Muslim dynasties based in Delhi launched attacks on the various Hindu states in the Deccan Plateau (in the central region of India, south of Delhi), Bengal, and kingdoms farther south on the Indian peninsula, including Vijayanagar. In 1399 Mongol troops led by Tamerlane (Timur the Lame; 1336–1405) totally destroyed Delhi, killing and capturing tens of thousands of people and plundering the city's treasures. After Tamerlane withdrew, two more sultanates—the Sayyid and the Lodi—arose before the arrival of the Mughals. The Lodi sultan Sikandar (r. 1489–1517), a poet and patron of the arts and learning, restored Delhi as a major cultural center and built a new capital at Agra. As Sikandar's wars against his neighbors were draining his treasury, in Afghanistan a descendant of Tamerlane and Ghengis Khan named Zahir-ud-Din Muhammad, more famously known as Babur (1483–1530), was coming into power. In 1504, Babur seized Kabul and then set his sights on Delhi.

THE MUGHAL EMPIRE

Babur entered India from Kabul in 1517 and advanced toward Delhi, where in 1526 he brought an end to the reign of the last Lodi sultan, Ibrahim (r. 1517–26). Babur seized both Delhi and Agra, which would serve as capital cities of the Mughal empire for nearly three centuries—until the Battle of Plassey in 1757, when a British victory effectively ended Mughal control over India. The Mughal empire reached its zenith under the rule of Babur's grandson, Akbar (r. 1556–1605), the third emperor. Known as Akbar the Great, he is remembered for his humane and tolerant policies, which were influenced by his shrewd adviser Abu'l Fazl (1551–1602), who wrote the *Institutes of Akbar* as well as the *Akbar-nama,* a chronicle of his leader's accomplishments. According to Abu'l Fazl, Akbar would go out in disguise among his subjects to learn about their concerns, and like the great Mongol khans, to whom he was distantly related, he would invite representatives from all religions, including Hindus, Jains, Sufis, and Christians, to debate the relative merits of their beliefs.

Akbar allowed non-Muslims to serve as minor officials, and he gave Hindus *DHIMMI* status. Under Islamic law, Christians and Jews were known as *dhimmis,* "people of the book"; they could practice their religion but were subject to a hated tax known as the *jizya.* Under Akbar, who had married a Hindu woman from Amber (near today's Jaipur), the jizya was abolished, as was another hated tax levied on Hindu pilgrims. Akbar's leniency toward non-Muslims, as well as his founding of a syncretic religion known as the Divine Faith, led to criticism from more orthodox Muslims—both the *mulla,* the religious leaders, and scholars, such as Abd al-Qadir Bada'uni (1540–c. 1615), the author of a biography critical of the emperor.

In addition to being a humane ruler, Akbar was an astute military leader. He unified nearly all of northern India above the Deccan Plateau under his authority—from what is now Kashmir in the northwest to Bengal in the east.

Govardham, ***Mughal Lovers,*** **1615**

Lovers embrace in this Mughal-era miniature illustration with a wonderfully decorative floral border.

Although Akbar's policies did not survive untarnished under subsequent emperors, the Mughal empire continued to expand under Jahangir (r. 1605–27) and Shah Jahan (r. 1627–58), under whose rule were built the Red Fort at Delhi and the Taj Mahal at Agra. Lavish spending at court, however, led to high taxes and neglect of the less fortunate, particularly peasants, who suffered from famine and drought. When Aurungzeb (r. 1658–1707) seized power from his father, Shah Jahan, he repealed Akbar's reforms, reinstated the jizya, and forbade the construction of new Hindu temples. Inevitably, resentment and hunger among the people led to numerous revolts throughout India, leading the way for Europeans to exploit internal conflicts and play India into their imperial designs.

EUROPEAN CONTACT

During the Mughal era, Europeans began to encroach on India, first as traders and adventurers and eventually as colonizers. Vasco da Gama (c. 1460–1524) reached Calicut, on the Malabar coast, on May 27, 1498, inaugurating a century-long Portuguese presence on the southwestern coast of India. Two years later, six Portuguese ships arrived again at Calicut, forcing the local leader to enter into a trade agreement with Portugal. When da Gama himself returned in 1502, several Portuguese traders had been murdered by Muslims in revenge for the plundering of a Muslim ship. Da Gama used his cannons to pummel the port, and he executed many Muslim sailors. In 1510, Afonso de Albuquerque (1453–1515), under the title of Viceroy of Portugal in the East, occupied the island port city of Goa, from where the Portuguese conducted their trade with India as well as their piracy of Muslim shipping in the Indian Ocean. The first Jesuit missionaries arrived in 1542, led by Francis Xavier (1506–1552), who also undertook the first Jesuit mission to Japan. Intermixing of cultures and intermarriages occurred, but this hybrid culture did not spread beyond the confines of Goa, despite the efforts of the Jesuits who found their way to Akbar's court.

The arrival of the Portuguese went largely unnoticed in Delhi, where the weakened sultanate under Sikandar would have been helpless to intervene anyway. In nearby Vijayanagar, however, the Hindu king Krishna Deva Raya (r. 1509–30) eagerly traded with the Portuguese, until his army was routed and his capital city destroyed by Muslim forces from the Deccan at the Battle of Talikot in 1565. With its major partner in shambles, the Portuguese trade at Goa began to flounder, especially after Portugal was subsumed in 1580 by Spain, whose attention was focused on the Americas. Into the breach came the Dutch and the English, the Dutch arriving in 1595 and the English in 1608. By the turn of the century, the Dutch and English had both established East India Companies and, by 1619, after signing a trade agreement with Jahangir, established a trading factory at Surat. Three years later, the English captured Ormuz from the Portuguese, and by the middle of the seventeenth century they had set up trading factories at Fort William (now Calcutta) and Madras. Though the Dutch and French vied for a share in India's trade, over the next century England stymied their efforts and eventually broke down the Mughal rulers and began to establish their own empire.

SPIRITUAL MOVEMENTS IN THE FOURTEENTH AND FIFTEENTH CENTURIES

The arrival of Islam in India ushered in a long history of an often uneasy balance between Islam, Hinduism, and other religions, such as Buddhism, Jainism, Sikhism, and Christianity. When the Muslims first arrived, they often destroyed Hindu and Buddhist temples and stupas (shrines), and they sometimes built mosques on local holy sites. As a result of the Mughal incursions, many Buddhist monks fled from India into Tibet, Nepal, or Sri Lanka. Once the Muslim rulers were established, however, they, especially Akbar, attempted to accommodate the indigenous traditions of the Indian population; many Hindus converted to Islam, and a general cross-pollination of ideas, beliefs, and practices took place. Because of the rigid hierarchy of Hinduism, which set the **Brahmins** apart from the lower **castes**, many of the converts to Islam were among the lower classes, who found in Islam a measure of equality. Perhaps the greatest cross-pollination occurred among those drawn to the Muslim mystical tradition of the Sufis and the Hindu devotional sects in the bhakti movement.

Originating among speakers of the Dravidian-based languages of southern India after the fifth century, the bhakti movement had by the sixteenth century spread throughout India, often becoming entangled with social, political, and regional struggles for freedom from oppression—whether from the Brahminic caste system or from the hegemony of non-native rulers. Some bhakti saints themselves, however, came from the Brahmin or professional castes. Though the various bhakti sects differed widely, centering on different gods and drawing on different linguistic and poetic traditions, the movement shared a belief that the worship of God and spiritual salvation are open to all people, men and women alike, without regard to social rank, education, or material accomplishment. Intensity of feeling in the act of devotion and dedication to an unmediated union with the god or the divine were the keys to release *(moksha)* from the wheel of suffering and rebirth *(samsara)*. Chief among the gods worshiped by the bhakti saints were Shiva, the destroyer, and Vishnu, the preserver. Bhakti cults also grew up around Krishna and Rama, two of the avatars of Vishnu; the mother goddess Mahadevi; and Kali, the devouring goddess.

Sufism, like some of the Hindu bhakti sects, rejected the rationalist doctrines and institutionalized dogma of Islam and focused instead on a more intuitive,

Vishnu, 1200
The Hindu god Vishnu sits in the center of a lotus flower surrounded by his eight incarnations in this finely wrought bronze sculpture. Krishna and Rama are two of these incarnations, or avatars. (Bridgeman Art Library)

inward-looking spiritual relation to the divine. Sufis, again like some of the bhakti, emphasize those practices—such as meditation, fasting, the utterance of mantras, and physical discipline—that promote a kind of ecstatic union with the divine. As with the bhakti sects, many of the great Sufis were also important lyric poets, including the great thirteenth- and fourteenth-century Persian poets Rumi and Hafiz.

In Bengal, which had become independent from Delhi in 1338 under Shams-ud-Din (r. 1339–59), Sufi and bhakti preachers were free to spread their teachings, and Bengal became an important spiritual center for the Hindu bhakti saints as well. It was here in the fifteenth century that Kabir (1440–1518), a Muslim-born weaver from Benares, vexed both Muslim and Hindu authorities alike by advocating the fraternity between the devotees of both religions. A disciple of the Hindu saint and important bhakti teacher Ramananda (c. 1400–c. 1470), Kabir became an important bhakti teacher himself and authored hundreds of inspirational poems that drew many new followers from among Hindus, Muslims, and Buddhists. Bengal was also home to the bhakti saint Caitanya (1485–1533), who developed what was called Satya-Pur (Truth-Saint) worship. The bhakti movement was by no means limited to Bengal or even to the south of India, and in the Punjab region an important new religion, Sikhism, was founded by Nanak (c. 1469–1538). The Sikhs are devoted to Truth, embodied as a divinity under the name of Satya. Thus, as it entered the sixteenth century, India was a center for a wide variety of spiritual and religious movements.

THE BHAKTI LITERATURE OF INDIA

While the great epics and the plays of India's Classical Age were all written in Sanskrit, the bhakti movement inspired the development of works in the vernacular throughout the many regions of India. This shift was similar to the move from Latin to vernacular languages that took place in Europe during the early modern period. To light the flame of devotion among their followers, some of the bhakti saints composed impromptu lyrics, which were sung, often accompanied by music and dancing, in communal sessions known as *kirtan.* Others, such as the Bengali saint and poet Jayadeva (twelfth century), the author of the dramatic *Gitagovinda,* wrote formal and intricately linked songs, or *ragas,* in Sanskrit. These songs are even today performed to music and dance in the celebrations devoted to the saint and his namesake, the god Krishna. Despite the common goal of union with the divine, the distinctive forms of bhakti poetry, as well as the language and regional differences, led to rivalry and division among the poets, who often criticized each other in their work, pitting their particular god against that of their rivals.

Among the Dravidian dialects spoken in the south of India was Tamil, in which the first bhakti poetry was written. The earliest Tamil poets included Karaikkal Ammaiyar and her followers, including Appar, Campatar, and Cuntarar, all of them active from the sixth to the eighth centuries. The poet-saints called Nayanars were also known as Shaivites, named after their god, the fearsome Shiva, who was known as the "Lord of the Dance." Their poetry set the stage for a flourishing of vernacular traditions in languages such as Tamil, Hindi, Kannada, Marathi, Telugu, and Malayalam, to name only a few. In the twelfth century, for example, the bhakti saints Basavanna and Mahadaviyakka began producing lyrics and songs known as *vacanas* in Kannada, the language spoken in the Karnataka region of southern India. Their works mark the origins of a literary tradition in that language. Vidyapati (fourteenth century), Govindadasa (fifteenth century), and Chandidasa (sixteenth century) composed their works in the dialects of the eastern region of Bengal, while others such as Kabir (1440–1518) and Mirabai (1498–1547), who is perhaps one of the greatest of all the bhakti poets, composed in Hindi. With the exception of Kabir, who represents a strain of bhakti known as *nirgun*—the belief in a divinity without qualities, that is, an unnameable and unembodied spiritual essence—these later poets represent Vaishnava tradition, the

TIME AND PLACE

Shiva

With their devotional practices seeking a personal, intuitive, and immediate relationship with the gods of the divine, the saints and devotees of the bhakti movement in India challenged the rigid hierarchies of orthodox Hinduism. Hymns, songs, dancing, music, and even painting were often the means used to attain an ecstatic, mystical union with the gods, chief among whom were Shiva and Vishnu, as well as Vishnu's avatars Krishna and Rama. Among the Shaivites, the destroyer god Shiva is the chief of the classical Hindu trinity, which also includes Brahma, the creator, and Vishnu, the preserver.

Associated with storms, lightning, and other natural forces of destruction, Shiva is a terrifying god whose earthly dwelling is said to be in the high mountains of the Himalayas. Shiva is sometimes represented as a haggard figure draped with snakes or skulls, riding his mighty bull Nandi, followed by a train of demons. Yet, because in the Hindu view death is an essential part of the cycle of life, death, and rebirth, Shiva embodies aspects of both creation and destruction. Thus, he is best known in his guise as Nataraja, the "Lord of the Dance," as depicted in a famous bronze statue from the southern Hindu state of Vijayanagar. (See illustration.) In this statue, Shiva appears with four arms, dancing in a ring of fire. Under his feet is the demon Apasmara, a symbol of ignorance, and in his hair a figure symbolizing the holy river Ganges. Like a powerful mountain storm precipitating a devastating flood in the valleys below, Shiva's dance brings about destruction; but that destruction, like the Ganges, brings the life-giving waters that lead to renewal.

On the level of the devotee, Shiva's dancing extinguishes the self and releases it into the Brahman, or great soul, achieving *moksha,* or the release from the cycle of rebirth. In his dualism, Shiva also embodies both male and female, and his female aspect, known as Shakti, had her own followers, especially in her guise as the dark, blood-drinking goddess Kali. Shiva worship often involves representations of the *lingam,* or phallus, and the *yoni,* or vulva, symbolizing the gateway to life. Like the other main Hindu deities, Shiva has a *vayana,* a special means of conveyance—Nandi, the sacred white bull. In pre-Aryan times, the bull was also linked to dancing and creation, and it serves to enhance the sense of Shiva's virility and strength as well as his discipline and ability to control natural forces.

Shiva, c. Thirteenth Century. *Shiva Nataraja, the Lord of the Dance, one of the most important and popular images of Shiva, god of creation and destruction. Shiva dances in a ring of fire, symbolizing reincarnation, his raised foot suggesting the possibility of* moksha, *the escape from the cycle of rebirth. Beneath his foot he tramples the demon Apasmara, ignorance. Overall, the image symbolizes the cycles of life and death, creation and destruction, and the promise of enlightenment. (The Art Archive / Museé Guimet Paris)*

name given to those who devote themselves to Krishna. While there exists great variety within the bhakti traditions, as a whole these saints and poets have exerted a tremendous influence on India's religious and political culture, and their lyrics form an integral and vital function in devotional practices even today.

WWW For more information about the culture and context of India in the Early Modern Period, see *World Literature Online* at bedfordstmartins.com/worldlit.

MIRABAI
1498–1547

One of the most interesting aspects of **Mirabai**'s life, and a rich source of material for her poetry, is that though she was born to a noble family and married at an early age to a powerful prince, she rejected courtly life and her husband's family in favor of a life of devotion to Krishna. To the astonishment of many, she reveled in dancing at her god's temples, singing songs of devotion, and seeking the company of wandering holy men. She was persecuted for living her vision of a personal, intimate worship of the divine, but despite the disapproval at home, she became extraordinarily popular among devotees across the country and rose to the status of saint. Her songs—beautifully melodious, defiant in the face of worldly expectations (especially for women), and above all passionate in the quest for union with Krishna—are possibly the most widely known lyrics of the devotional movement in India.

mee-rah-BIGH

Marriage to Krishna. Because her mother died when Mirabai was a young child and her father, a Rajput chieftain, was often away fighting the Muslims, Mirabai was raised in the palace of her grandfather, Rao Dudaji, who reportedly took the city of Merta (which the family ruled) from the Muslims in 1461. Some scholars suggest that the members of this household favored the worship of Krishna, and, according to legend, Mirabai requested and received at a very young age an idol of Krishna from a wandering monk. As a Rajput princess, Mirabai likely received a royal education, including studies in music, dancing, Sanskrit, religion, and politics, but her freedom was severely limited by ancient customs, including the practice of arranging marriages. Through the mediation of her uncle, in 1516 she married Bhoja Raj, a famous warrior and ruler, but reportedly Mirabai had little interest in this marriage and the couple had no children. It is said that at her wedding Mirabai secretly vowed herself to Krishna instead of her husband, and that on entrance into her new home she refused to bow to her mother-in-law. She reportedly aroused

Tefri Garwhal, *Radha and Krishna on the Bed*, c. 1860–1870
This nineteenth-century painting illustrates a scene from the legend of Radha and Lord Krishna, and captures the mix of the corporeal and spiritual embodied in the God Krishna. Though Mirabai wrote her poetry 300 years earlier, she used this legend as an inspiration for much of her verse, in which the poet assumes the role of Radha yearning for union with Krishna, "Lifter of Mountains." (The Art Archive / Victoria and Albert Museum London / Sally Chappell)

the anger of her new family by seeking association with wandering religious folk and was imprisoned for her behavior. One of the most famous stories of her life says that the king tried to kill her while she was in prison, but the poison he sent her was purified by Krishna as she drank it.

The popular legend of Radha, who left her husband to pursue a passionate relationship with the youthful, dark-skinned lord Krishna, provides an interesting backdrop for the life of Mirabai, and, more important, a significant source for her work. Like many poets before her, Mirabai depicts Krishna as the ultimate god, whose love is all-consuming. Separation from the divine causes painful suffering, but union—achieved by realizing Krishna's presence in everything (including the self) and practicing a life of sincere devotion—means release from the everyday world and dissolution of the soul into everlasting bliss. Poets like Jayadeva (twelfth century) and **Vidyapati** (fourteenth century) explore the erotic, sensual love of Radha for Krishna as an allegory of the soul's desire for union with the divine, and some even elevated Radha to the level of a goddess. Mirabai's songs are passionate but not heavily erotic, and in them it is not Radha but the poet herself who longs for and unites with the dark lord. While male devotees had to imagine the perspective of a woman enamored with Krishna, Mirabai could step into the shoes of Radha and express from her own female being the experience of giving oneself over to love of the godhead.

vid-YAH-puh-tee

Songs to Krishna. Directly or indirectly, the songs of devotional saints often call attention to the devotee's transgression of societal expectations. Mirabai, who surprised her noble family by choosing to practice a devotional life, refers repeatedly in her work to the criticism she faced:

> Having beheld Thy beauty
> I am caught and enmeshed.
> My family members repeatedly try to restrain me,
> But attachment to the Dancer with the Peacock Plume
> Has now sunk deep.
> My mind is drowned in the beauty of Shyām,
> And the world says I have gone astray.
> Mīrā has taken refuge with the Lord
> Who knows the contents of every heart.
> (Translated by A. J. Alston.)

In Mirabai's vision, the love of the deity and the desire for union with him can only be inhibited by worldly concerns. No mediator, no formal education, no rule-ridden ritual, no refuge other than an intense devotion, is required. As with much devotional poetry, Mirabai's works are notably musical—rhythmic and alliterative, full of repetition and refrain, and relatively simple in form and style. Illustrating a reverence for the holy name, the utterance of which is a sacred act of worship, many of her songs call directly to the lord Krishna, or to Giridhara—Krishna's role as "mountain lifter." Many also end with a signature announcing the author, her intention in the song, and/or her relation to the god. In addition to expressing the sufferings and joys of her life as a devotee, Mirabai invites her audience to join in the experience of worship and the ultimate form of love.

■ CONNECTIONS

Margery Kempe, *The Book of Margery Kempe,* Book 2. Margery Kempe communicates the struggles of a woman searching to express a personal experience of the divine in a patriarchal society. Like Mirabai, she suffered much criticism because of her spiritual passion and dedication. In what ways are Kempe's relations of personal mystical visions similar to or different from Mirabai's religious expressions?

Laozi, *Dao De Jing,* Book 1; Zhuangzi, *The Writings of Chuang Tzu,* Book 1. The Taoists emphasize eliminating worldly desires and pride in favor of a life of contemplation and harmony with the natural flow of existence. Both Laozi and Zhuangzi emphasize a personal, subjective approach to achieving this spiritual harmony. What attitudes toward earthly life do these authors share with Mirabai? How is Mirabai's focus on union with Krishna similar to or different from the goal of living in harmony with the Tao?

FURTHER RESEARCH

Alston, A. J. *The Devotional Poems of Mirabai.* 1980.
Goetz, Hermann. *Mira Bai: Her Life and Times.* 1966.
Hawley, John Stratton, and Mark Jurgensmeyer. *Songs of the Saints of India.* 1988.
Vaudeville, Charlotte. *Myths, Saints and Legends in Medieval India.* 1996.

PRONUNCIATION

bhakti: BAHK-tee
Kabir: Kuh-BEER
Mirabai: mee-rah-BIGH
Vidyapati: vid-YAH-puh-tee

Life without Hari Is No Life, Friend

This and the following three poems translated by J. S. Hawley and Mark Jurgensmeyer

Life without Hari is no life, friend,
And though my mother-in-law fights,
  my sister-in-law teases,
  the *rana* is angered,
A guard is stationed on a stool outside,
  and a lock is mounted on the door,
How can I abandon the love I have loved
  in life after life?
Mira's Lord is the clever Mountain Lifter:
  Why would I want anyone else?

Selected Poems. Mirabai uses biographical details to contrast the pressure she feels from her family (the guard stationed outside her door on a stool) with her desire for a relationship with her god, alternately referred to as Hari, dark Lord, and Lifter of Mountains.

A note on the translations: The first four poems reprinted here are from J. S. Hawley's and Mark Jurgensmeyer's 1988 collection, *Songs of the Saints of India.* The last four are from A. J. Alston's 1980 translation, *The Devotional Poems of Mirabai,* which uses the diacritical marks, *Mīrā* rather than the romanized spelling *Mira.* The two translators have other interesting distinctions; compare their word choice and the feel of the lines.

Today Your Hari Is Coming

Today your Hari is coming,
my friend,
to play the game of Spring.
The harbinger crow in the courtyard speaks,
my friend,
an omen of good times ahead.
All the cowherds have gathered in the garden,
my friend,
where the basil grows:
I hear the sound of tambourines and drums,
my friend.
Why sleep? Wake up and go!
There's water and betel-leaf, mats and sheets,
my friend.
Go greet him: touch his feet.
Mira's Lord is the clever Mountain Lifter,
my friend,
the best blessing you could have.

The Bhil Woman Tasted Them, Plum after Plum

The Bhil woman tasted them, plum after plum,
and finally found one she could offer him.
What kind of genteel breeding was this?
And hers was no ravishing beauty.
Her family was poor, her caste quite low,
her clothes a matter of rags,
Yet Ram took that fruit—that touched, spoiled fruit—
for he knew that it stood for her love.
This was a woman who loved the taste of love,
and Ram knows no high, no low.
What sort of Veda could she ever have learned?
But quick as a flash she mounted a chariot
And sped to heaven to swing on a swing,
tied by love to God.
You are the Lord who cares for the fallen;
rescue whoever loves as she did:
Let Mira, your servant, safely cross over,
a cowherding Gokul girl.

I Have Talked to You, Talked

I have talked to you, talked,
dark Lifter of Mountains,
About this old love,
from birth after birth.
Don't go, don't,
Lifter of Mountains,
Let me offer a sacrifice—myself—
beloved,
to your beautiful face.
Come, here in the courtyard,
dark Lord,
The women are singing auspicious wedding songs;
My eyes have fashioned
an altar of pearl tears,
And here is my sacrifice:
the body and mind
Of Mira,
the servant who clings to your feet,
through life after life,
a virginal harvest for you to reap.

I Donned Anklets and Danced

This and the following three poems translated by A. J. Alston

I donned anklets and danced.
The people said "Mīrā is mad."
My mother-in-law declared
That I had ruined the family's reputation.
The King sent me a cup of poison
Which I drank with a smile.
I have offered body and mind
To the feet of Hari,
And will drink the nectar of His holy sight.
Mīrā's Lord is the courtly Giridhara:
My Lord, to Thee will I go for refuge.

Who Can Understand the Grief

Who can understand the grief
Of a woman parted from her beloved?
Only one who has felt the pangs of absence,
Or perhaps a devotee.
The physician is present within the patient:
Only the physician knows the remedy.
The dagger of the absence of the Beloved
Has pierced my breast:
Without Hari, all pleasures are as dust.
I am like a mad cow roaming the forest,
Who can think only of her lost calf.
The Chātak dreams of the rain of Swātī,[1]
Crying "Lord, Lord"[2] in great distress.
The world is all thorns,
A veritable garbage-heap,
And no one sees my pain.
Krishna is Mīrā's Lord and Master:
She could not find another if she sought.

---

[1] **Chātak . . . Swātī:** The cātaka bird (Indian cuckoo) is fabled to drink only that water which has fallen when the moon is in the constellation of Svāti and to spurn all other water. [Trans.]

[2] **Crying "Lord, Lord":** The bird's natural call is taken to be a repetition of the word "pīva" meaning "Beloved" or "Darling" as she waits faithfully for her "lover," the rain-cloud that appears at the time when the moon is passing through the constellation of Svāti. This call to the Beloved reminds Mīrā agonizingly of her absent Lord. [Trans.]

Shrī Krishna Has Entered My Heart

Shrī Krishna has entered my heart
And the clouds have filled the sky.
Thunder roars, clouds quake
And the flashes of lightning inspire terror.
Cloud-banks mount as the east wind blows.
Frogs croak, the cuckoo sings,
And the cry of the peacock is heard.
Says Mīrā: O my Master, the courtly Giridhara,
My mind has gone to Thy lotus feet.

Do Not Mention the Name of Love

Do not mention the name of love,
O my simple-minded companion.
Strange is the path
When you offer your love.
Your body is crushed at the first step.
If you want to offer love
Be prepared to cut off your head
And sit on it.
Be like the moth,
Which circles the lamp and offers its body.
Be like the deer, which, on hearing the horn,
Offers its head to the hunter.
Be like the partridge,
Which swallows burning coals[1]
In love of the moon.
Be like the fish,
Which yields up its life
When separated from the sea.
Be like the bee,
Entrapped in the closing petals of the lotus.
Mīrā's Lord is the courtly Giridhara
She says: Offer your mind
To those lotus feet.

[1] **partridge . . . coals:** According to the poetic convention, the partridge is so much in love with the moon that it swallows burning coals, mistaking them for fragments of the moon. [Trans.]

Indian Devotional Poetry

Devotional poetry written in India between the Vedic period (c. 1500 B.C.E.–500 C.E.) and the seventeenth century both reflected and had a profound influence on the evolving religious, political, and social beliefs and practices of a culture in transition. The great literary/religious works of India's ancient history—the Vedas and the **Upanishads**—had imparted into its culture a strictly hierarchical caste system, a definition of the search for spirituality as a highly intellectual exercise, and an emphasis on formal ritual and sacrifice that distanced the common person from immediate worship of the divine. By the fifth and sixth centuries, the everyday rituals drawn from the ancient religious texts, all written in Sanskrit, became increasingly seen as elitist and unjust, even as tools exercised by the powerful to control and dominate the common people. Powerful **Brahmins** (priests), who held the highest position in the caste system and were trained to read and interpret Sanskrit writings, were seen by some as dictating religious practices and dealing out moral judgment based more on hereditary status and educational opportunity than on any deep spiritual sense. Certainly this resentment was not helped by the fact that in the Middle Ages regional rulers sometimes brought in Brahmins to help consolidate their control of the masses.

oo-PAHN-ih-shudz

BRAH-hmuhnz

In many ways, the poetry of this section can be seen as a reaction against the rigid hierarchy of Hinduism and the power of the Brahmins. Posing a direct, personal relationship with God, emphasizing the communal nature of spiritual and social practice, and even mocking intellectual pursuits in favor of an emotional and earthy mysticism, proponents of the devotional movement, known

Krishna, Twelfth Century
The Hindu god Krishna, the eighth incarnation of Vishnu, is shown here dancing on the body of the serpent-king Kaliya. Many strands of Indian devotional poetry took the story of Krishna as a central theme and focus. (Bridgeman Art Library)

BAHK-tee

as the **bhakti** movement, undermined many prevailing notions regarding the autonomy of the individual devotee and the authority of the Brahmin institutions as opposed to the immediate authority of the divine. Inspired by deeply felt religious emotion, their songs led to, and took part in, nothing less than a revolution inspiring a popular redefinition of a person's interaction with the divine. This revolution invited a reexamination of assumptions about the rules governing the interaction of human beings in everyday reality. To this day, writers like **Jayadeva** (twelfth century), **Basavanna** (twelfth century), **Vidyapati** (fourteenth century), **Kabir** (1440–1518), and **Mirabai** (1498–1547) are recognized as key figures in the development of the Hindu religion in India.

jay-yuh-DAY-vuh; BAH-sah-VAH-nah; vid-YAH-puh-tee; kuh-BEER; mee-rah-BIGH

A LITERARY HERITAGE

One cannot fully understand or appreciate the significance of the devotional movement without viewing it in light of a larger context of Indian literature, history, and tradition. Great religious works of the Vedic period in India—the Rig Veda, the **Brahmanas** (providing instructions on rituals and sacrifices), and the Upanishads (a series of mystical speculations)—greatly influenced all aspects of Indian society for centuries after their appearance. The Rig Veda, for example, tells the story of the dismembering of Purusha, the primordial man, in order to explain the divine origins of the caste system. Purusha's mouth became the **BRAHMIN** (priests), his arms became the **Rajanya** (warriors), his thighs became the **Vaishyas** (merchants and farmers), and his feet became the Shudra (laborers). Rigidly hereditary and highly divisive, the caste system affected a person's access to education, social treatment, ascribed religious and social duties, even status in the eyes of the law. The Brahmanas set forth guidelines regarding ritual and sacrifice and defined their spiritual significance. Though the "rules" described therein were not delineated as authoritative or absolute, through the course of time they became just that, and the Brahmins were able to establish such an authoritative stance in the interpretation and practice of these rites that they could present themselves as the gatekeepers or shepherds guiding, or determining, one's connection to the god(s). One of the most influential religious works of India's ancient period, the Upanishads, takes as an important theme the search for a knowledge of **Brahman**, the ultimate reality sought by an individual in order to release the soul from the cycle, or karma, of earthly life. Attainable only through extraordinary, detached intellectual and philosophical contemplation, and therefore not available to the masses, Brahman is eternal and absolute, infinite and illusory, beyond the grasp of the ordinary senses and available only in the world of pure thought. Far less stressed, but still present, in the Upanishads is an alternate approach to spirituality that would inspire the devotional poets of later periods. This approach suggests a personal relationship to a beneficent deity concerned about human needs and deserving of religious devotion.

BRAH-mah-nuhs

RAH-juh-nyuh; VIGH-shuhs

BRAH-hmuhn

People in the West can discover their own myths by reading Indian myths. You have an alternative other than the one dictated by birth and family connections. I find Hindu myths best answer the questions man asks, making it a great mythology. They are rich, enormously full of life—passion, humor, food, animal, and sex.
–Wendy O'Flaherty, religious historian

FROM BRAHMIN TO BHAKTI

All of the texts mentioned here appeared in their first written version in Sanskrit. Much like Latin in the Middle Period in Europe, the language of Sanskrit came to be read in India only by those who had the money and leisure time to study it. It became associated with the elite and powerful classes, particularly with the Brahmins, as a "secret" language holding the mysteries of the nature of human existence and the path to escaping it. As persons able to read and interpret the revered ancient Sanskrit texts, Brahmins were widely respected as spiritual advisers, but eventually their mediation of spiritual matters came under attack as impersonal, erudite, and exclusive. Just as European Protestants criticized Catholic priests, some people in India came to resent and speak out against the Brahmins. Those who sought a more egalitarian and personally empowered relationship with the divine revolted against the formal religious practices, caste distinctions, and intellectualism the Brahmin priesthood had come to represent.

Originating in south India around the fifth century C.E. and spreading rapidly northward, the bhakti movement defined the path of religious devotion as available to everyone (without regard to caste, gender, or occupation); replaced formal knowledge and ritual with the expression of passionate feeling and dedication; and often focused on a communal celebration of the glory of the divine. In this belief system, personal worth is measured not by birth or earthly accomplishment but by the depth and sincerity of one's devotion. Male or female, priest or farmer, prince or potter, the individual holds a personal relationship with a loving god and may, through acts of praise and a life reflecting sincere love of the deity, achieve release from earthly existence. Letting go of earthly desires and connections to worldly concerns, devotees contemplate an ecstatic union of the self and the lord or universe, dedicate themselves to such acts of praise as traveling to sacred sites and shrines, and inspire others by creating and singing songs of devotion. The creation of a song is a religious act practicing an individual's search for communion with the divine, but the singing of it indicates more than a personal act of worship. Sung even now during religious celebrations, bhakti hymns are meant to be performed—to inspire a shared, communal experience of ecstatic love and a vision of the release of the soul into eternal bliss.

HINDU GODS: SHIVA AND KRISHNA

In the practice of Hinduism, the early bhakti poets are to this day regarded by their sects as saints and their poetry is revered as scripture. Historically, the religion of Hinduism is relatively difficult to define as a set of certain beliefs and practices. Flexible and varied in the espousal of spiritual ideologies, Hinduism draws heavily on the sacred texts of its history, some of which are described briefly above. Fundamental to Hindu belief are the concepts of *atman,* a person's soul or universal spirit; ***dharma,*** the religious and ethical duties of the individual; *karma,* the acts of the individual and the ramifications of those acts; and *moksha,* the release of the soul from earthly life and union with Brahman. The bhakti tradition draws from the sacred literary texts and clings to some fundamental concepts of Hinduism but specifies a particular god as the lord of all existence and focuses the worship of its followers on a personal, emotional devotion to this deity.

DAR-muh

Shaivism, worship of the god **Shiva**, and **Virashavism**, heroic or radical worship of Shiva, recognize Shiva as the universal ruler of all existence. With matted red hair, living cobras around his neck and wrists, and bearing the crescent moon on his crown, this god is one of the major deities of the Hindu pantheon. He is the destroyer god in a triad also including Brahma as the creator god and **Vishnu** as the preserver god. Rider of a bull named Nandi, Shiva is often associated with the protection of animals, music, and dance. To Shaivites, he emerges above other gods as the creator, preserver, and destroyer of all existence.

SHEE-vuh; vee-ruh-SHAH-viz-um

VISH-noo

Krishna, the worship of whom is called Vaishnavism, is possibly the most complicated god of Hindu mythology. Descriptions of him in the **Mahabharata** present a hero of cowherds, among whom he was hidden as a child; an amorous and playful youth who grows into a destroyer of demons; and a powerful leader who is a form or incarnation of the god Vishnu. Associated with spring festivals and sexual love, Krishna is a conqueror who absorbs the powers of the conquered. Often a dark, long-haired being with many faces, as is seen in Jayadeva's ***Gitagovinda,*** he is treated in literature sometimes as an amorous lover and sometimes as a divine hero with cosmic powers. In the bhakti movement, his sexual nature and divine superiority are united. The poets **Jayadeva**, Kabir, and Mirabai all treat the passionate and physical love of Krishna as an erotic union with the ultimate universal divine.

muh-huh-BAH-rah-tuh

gee-tah-goh-VIN-duh

jah-yuh-DAY-vuh

Anonymous Kalighat artist, *Krishna as Cowherd*, 1890
Krishna is the most popular of the nine incarnations of Vishnu, and this nineteenth century painting of his youth as a cowherd (where he was hidden from demons who were trying to kill him) captures the charm of this god of the people. Legend has it that the young Krishna was mischievous, beautiful, and beloved by all who encountered him. (The Art Archive, British Library)

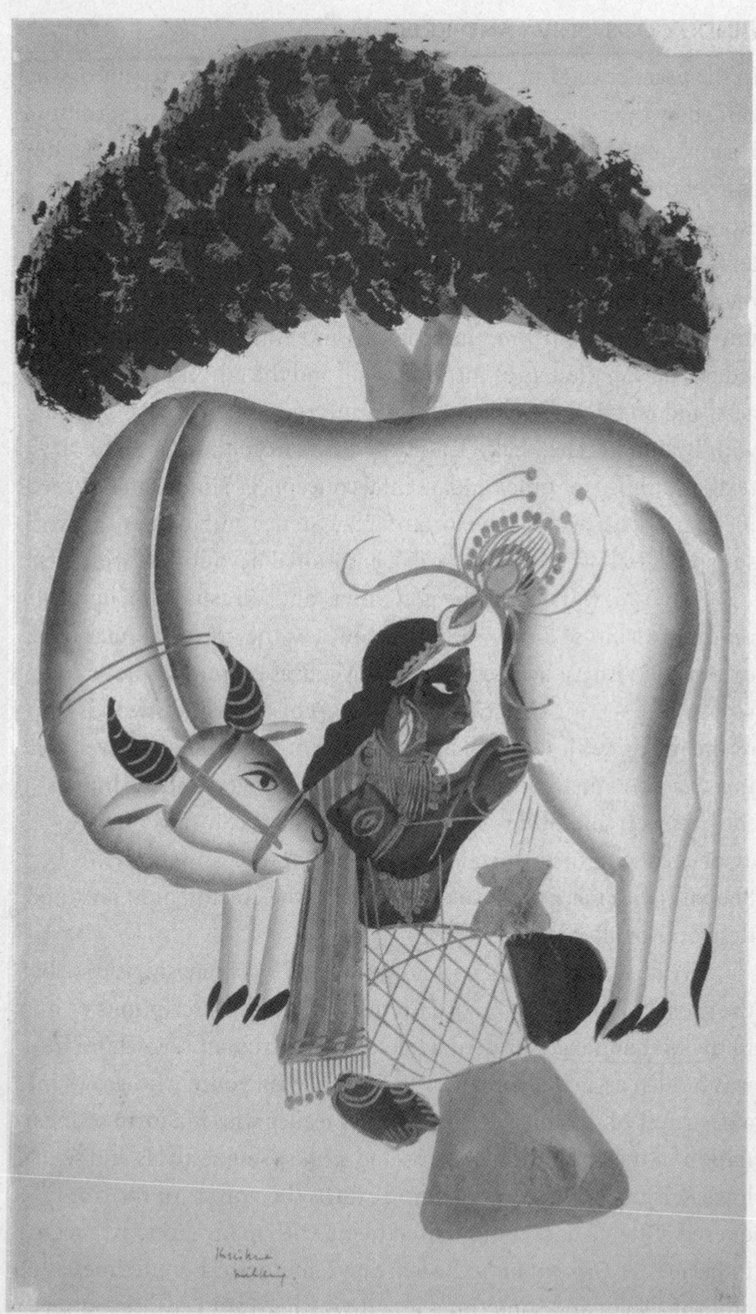

SUFISM

Islam was introduced in India around the eighth century C.E. but did not gain a significant stronghold until the Muslim invasions of northern India between 1000 and 1200. A monotheistic religion with a rigid code of laws, Islam offered a path of devotion very different from the polytheistic practices of Hinduism. Like Hinduism, however, it saw the development among its practitioners of a protest movement toward a more personal and mystical relationship with God. The devotees of this movement, called Sufis, called for the renunciation of worldly concerns and a search within the self for the true nature of God. Sufism came to be widely respected by Hindus in India, and the great saint and bhakti poet Kabir is said to have been heavily influenced by it.

[I]t is the special vocation of the mystical consciousness to mediate between two orders, going out in loving adoration towards God and coming home to tell the secrets of Eternity to other men.

– EVELYN UNDERHILL, *Poems of Kabir*, 1915

SINGERS AND SONGS OF DEVOTIONAL POETRY

Many poets of the bhakti movement practiced their devotion by traveling the countryside to visit sacred sites and temples where they found inspiration. The poet Appar, for example, made long pilgrimages across India, visiting temples of Shiva, in the company of followers who found in his poetry a connection to the divine. Their origin in travel and the memorable beauty and rhythm of their verse turned the hymns sung by the bhakti saints into more than expressions of personal faith—these songs served to unite geographically and religiously dispersed peoples into organized sects of devotion to particular gods. Generally critical of the formal traditions associated with the Vedic tradition, Buddhism, and **Jainism** (a rival of Buddhism that arose in the sixth century), these poets sounded a religion that united a personal, passionate vision of the divine with a dedication to the shared, communal exercise of spiritual practice.

JIGH-niz-um

Devotional poems are generally intimate and emotional, often erotic, and widely accessible. Taking as their topic the glory of, and human relationship to, a single god offering escape from the drudgery of earthly existence, they tend to explore the individual's perspective of physical existence as he or she faces, longs for, or embraces the universal. Love, in its many forms, is the great theme of bhakti hymns. Human relationships—between husband and wife, parent and child, sister and brother, even prostitute and customer—are instruments through which the poets explore and comment on the nature of supernatural love. Most common is the exploration of a "romantic" relationship between man and woman, where the man represents the lord and the woman his human devotee. Brimming with detailed imagery—of lush landscapes, the heroic deeds and mythic characteristics of the deity, even the devotee's physical body and sensual desires—these poems draw the reader into intense, and very human, experiences that move from everyday reality into mystical communion with the divine. Seduction, longing, loss, and union are all a part of the human understanding of love, but they serve also in these poems as allegories of the soul's search for a love beyond the physical. The songs are made memorable by their references to human realities, their musical rhythms and repetitions, and the recitation of familiar myths and legends.

■ CONNECTIONS

St. Augustine, *The Confessions,* Book 2. Though the various devotional sects in India served different gods, each particular community of devotees created and sang songs that defined and celebrated the supremacy of their lord, situated the individual soul in relation to the divine, and worked to create a community of worshipers. How do the goals of the bhakti hymns compare to the writing of St. Augustine, with its function to demonstrate the supremacy of the Christian God, to elaborate the doctrine of grace, and to inspire others to follow his example?

Ibn Hazm, *The Dove's Necklace,* Book 2. The bhakti movement of India between the sixth and seventeenth centuries celebrated an individual's personal relationship with a single god. Poetry inspired by this movement often explored the love between human beings—parent and child, sister and brother, man and woman—as an allegory of the relationship of humanity and the divine. How does the bhakti poets' treatment of various love relationships compare with the definitions of love offered by Ibn Hazm in *The Dove's Necklace*?

John Donne's poems, p. 108; Andrew Marvell, "To His Coy Mistress," p. 115. Reacting against the view that escape from the karma of earthly life required mediation—of a Brahmin, a guru, or a yogi, for example—many devotional groups redefined salvation as dependent on a sincere and intense search for the divine within the self. Religious poets of seventeenth-century England often struggled to identify the place of the individual in the divine plan, explore what it means to live a spiritual life, and communicate the pain or confusion caused by alienation from God. How do these very different traditions share and express similar concerns?

■ FURTHER RESEARCH

Backgrounds

Hawley, John Stratton, and Mark Jurgensmeyer. *Songs of the Saints of India.* 1988.
Tharu, Susie, and K. Lalita. *Women Writing in India.* 1991.
Tulpule, Shankar Gopal. *Mysticism in Medieval India.* 1984.

Tamil Songs to Shiva

Hart, George L. *The Poems of Ancient Tamil: Their Milieu and Their Sanskrit Counterparts.* 1975.

Peterson, Indira Viswanathan. *Poems to Shiva: The Hymns of Tamil Saints.* 1989.
Shulman, David Dean. *Songs of the Harsh Devotee: The Tēvāram of Cuntaramūrttināyanār.* 1990.

Kannada Songs to Shiva

Ramanujan, A. K. *Speaking of Shiva.* 1973.
Zvelebil, K. V. *The Lord of the Meeting Rivers: Devotional Poems of Basavanna.* 1984.

Jayadeva

McGregor, R. S. *The Round Dance of Krishna.* 1973.
Miller, Barbara Stoler. *Love Song of the Dark Lord: Jayadeva's* Gitagovinda. 1977.
Vaudeville, Charlotte. *Myths, Saints and Legends in Medieval India.* 1996.

Bengali Songs to Krishna

Dimock, Edward C. *The Place of the Hidden Moon.* 1966.
Klaiman, M. H. *Singing the Glory of Krishna.* 1984.

Kabir

Bly, Robert. *The Kabir Book: Forty-four of the Ecstatic Poems of Kabir.* 1977.
Hawley, John Stratton, and Mark Jurgensmeyer. *Songs of the Saints of India.* 1988.
Tagore, Rabindranath. *One Hundred Poems of Kabir.* 1915.
Vaudeville, Charlotte. *A Weaver Named Kabir: Selected Verses with a Detailed Biographical and Historical Introduction.* 1993.

■ PRONUNCIATION

Basavanna: BAH-sah-VAH-nah
bhakti: BUK-tee, BAHK-tee
Brahma: BRAH-hmuh
Brahman: BRAH-hmuhn
Brahmana: BRAH-mah-nuh
dharma: DAR-muh
Gitagovinda: gee-tah-goh-VIN-duh
Jainism: JIGH-niz-um
Jayadeva: jah-yuh-DAY-vuh
Kabir: kuh-BEER
Mahabharata: muh-huh-BAH-ruh-tuh
Mirabai: mee-rah-BIGH
Rajanya: RAH-jun-yuh
Shiva: SHEE-vuh, SEE-vuh, SHIH-vuh
Upanishads: oo-PAHN-ih-shudz
Vaishyas: VIGH-shuhs
Vidyapati: vid-YAH-puh-tee
Virashavism: vee-ruh-SHAH-viz-um
Vishnu: VISH-noo

Tamil Songs to Shiva

500–800 C.E.

Between the fifth and the ninth centuries C.E., in the Tamil culture of southern India, the worship of the god Shiva grew enormously in popularity. Partly due to the bhakti poets, Shaivism gained during this period a relatively unified organization of devotees and changed the face of Hinduism and Tamil culture significantly. The devotional followers of Shiva were brought together largely because of the importance of pilgrimages as acts demonstrating spiritual faith. All three of the poets in this section—Appar, Campantar, and Cuntarar—were known to have made several lengthy voyages, traveling to sacred sites and temples to create and sing songs of worship that served to unify their followers. Generally emerging on the spot out of divine inspiration, these hymns were individual expressions of praise and passionate faith, but they were meant as well to inspire in the hearts of listeners a communal, ecstatic love of the deity.

Collected in the eleventh century into a single text called the *Tevaram*, the works of Appar, Campantar, and Cuntarar beautifully illustrate the oral, musical origins of bhakti poetry as well as its emphasis on sacred places, vivid imagery, and myth. Sung as acts of worship and connection to a personal god, the hymns came to be regarded as sacred texts, as scripture, and their singers are the first three saints of the Tamil Saiva sect. References to physical appearance ("O god with matted hair!"), heroic deeds

Temple Lovers, Sixth to Seventh Centuries
An early temple relief sculpture of a couple in an amorous pose. (The Art Archive / Dagli Orti)

("god who became a ball of fire"), and divine status ("First among the gods!") are common and reflect both the ancient mythology of Shiva as well as his evolving status in a hierarchy of godheads. Dual and androgynous, the god assumes an essential and overwhelming presence in people's lives. This presence is seen in the praise of towns and temples devoted to Shaivism, in the practice of rapturous song and dance, and in the physical and emotional suffering of the speaker as it affects his or her ability to function in the world. It is worth noting that the various speakers of these poems, all written by men, may be male or female, confident or worried, subsumed within or feeling separation from the god. In contrast to the bhakti poetry arising in other parts of India, the *Tevaram* writers situated themselves against the Buddhist and Jain monks rather than against the Vedic tradition and the powerful Brahmins. Unlike later devotionalists, they did not protest against Hindu orthodoxy or the practice of ritual; their concern was to revitalize the practice of the Hindu religion with a focus on worship of Shiva as the god whose grace ends karma.

FROM THE TEVARAM

Campantar

"O God with Matted Hair!" She Cries.[1]

This and the following seven poems translated by Indira Viswanathan Peterson

1

"O god with matted hair!" she cries.
"You are my sole refuge!" she cries.
"Bull rider!"[2] she cries, and faints in awe.
O Lord of Marukal[3]

Selected Hymns. The three authors of the Tevaram represented here—Appar, Campantar, and Cuntarar—share rhythm, style, and subject. The eight hymns reprinted here (of the 796 in the *Tevaram*) use alliteration, repetition, and refrains in calling forth praise of the lush landscapes and traditional attributes of the god Shiva.

A note on the translation: The poems reprinted here are taken from Indira Viswanathan Peterson's 1989 translation. All notes are the editors' unless marked [Trans.].

[1] **she cries:** The speaker in this poem is the heroine's (devotee's) girlfriend. The girlfriend pleads with the hero (God) to take pity on her friend (the devotee). At the end of the hymn, Shiva revived the young man, and the lovers were united. [Trans.]

[2] **"Bull rider!":** The powerful bull Nandi, a popular symbol for this god, is Shiva's most recognized method of conveyance.

[3] **Marukal:** Sacred place in southern India.

where the blue lily blooms in field waters,
is it fair
to make this woman waste from love's disease?

2

"Object of my thoughts!" she cries.
"Śiva!" she cries.
"Primal Being!" she cries.
"First among the gods!" she cries.
O our father who dwells in Marukal
where the blue lily blooms in clusters,
is it right
to afflict this woman with longing?

3

God who wears the sounding hero's band,
the flame-tongued snake
and moon-adorned matted hair!
You who delight in Marukal
rich in great scholars of the Veda!
You have taken her noisy bracelets
and with them, her well-being.

7

She never fails to cry upon waking,
"Long live my Lord's feet!"
She thinks of you day and night.
You who bear the axe and the sword,
she worships you, Lord of Marukal,
why torment her?

8

Lord of the strong-walled city of Marukal,
when Laṅkā's king lifted the mountain,
you bore down with your toe,
making him helpless.[4]
You have made this woman,

[4]**lifted . . . helpless:** Possibly referring to a section of the Ramayana describing Ravana's attempt to show his strength by lifting Shiva's sacred mountain. The attempt was foiled when Shiva placed his toe on the mountain and trapped Ravana under its weight.

frail as a flower garland,
the object of slander.

9

Lord of Marukal
where your immortal devotees live,
god who became a ball of fire,
so that the two could not fathom
your flaming hair and feet,[5]
you have made this fine young woman
faint with suffering.

10

The ignorant Jains
and the wandering packs of Buddhists[6]
go about committing crimes.
O Lord of Marukal, you who hold
the fawn in your hand,
you have utterly ruined
the young woman with thick coiled hair.

[5] **ball . . . feet:** Possibly referring to the legend of Vishnu's and Shiva's visit, in disguise, to the Daruka Forest, where their hosts took insult to the deception and attacked them with a tiger, a ball of fire, a serpent, and a monster. Shiva is said to have skinned the tiger, caught and brandished the ball of fire, calmed the serpent, and stood on the monster.

[6] **Jains . . . Buddhists:** Jainism and Buddhism were popular in India during this period and posed challenges to the Hindu belief system.

Campantar

Karma Cannot Touch

Karma cannot touch
those who can cry, "Lord of the gods!
God, bull rider, madman who is
man, woman, and in-between,
moon-crowned god,
our King who lives in Erukkatampuliyūr's
shrine, which we revere!"

Appar

An Earring of Bright New Gold Glows on One Ear

An earring of bright new gold glows on one ear;
a coiled conch shell sways on the other.
On one side he chants the melodies of the ritual Veda,
on the other, he gently smiles.
Matted hair adorned with sweet *koṉṟai* blossoms
on one half of his head,
and a woman's curls[1] on the other, he comes.
The one is the nature of his form,
the other, of hers;
And both are the very essence
of his beauty.
the Supreme Lord
who dwells in the beautiful shrine
of holy Ēkampam in Kacci.

[1] **a woman's curls:** *Kulal,* a way of dressing the hair in tubular coils. [Trans.]

Appar

See the God!

See the god!
See him who is higher than the gods!
See him who is Sanskrit of the North
and southern Tamil and the four Vedas!
See him who bathes in milk and ghee,[1]
see the Lord, see him who dances, holding fire,
in the wilderness of the burning-ground,

[1] **ghee:** Clarified butter—a food of the elite classes.

see him who blessed the hunter-saint![2]
See him who wells up as honey
in the heart-lotus of his lovers!
See him who has the unattainable treasure!
See Śiva! See him who is our treasure
here in Civapuram!

[2] **the hunter-saint:** The hunter-saint Kannapar reportedly tore out one of his eyes in an attempt to heal the wounded eye of Shivalinga.

Appar

The Unholy Town Where No Temple Stands

The unholy town where no temple stands,
the town where men do not wear the holy ash,
the town which does not resound with sacred song,
the town which is not resplendent with many shrines,
the town where the white conch is not reverently blown,
the town where festive canopies and white flags are not seen,
the town where devotees do not gather flowers for the worship
that town is no town, it is a mere wilderness.

Appar

Why Was I Born

1

Why was I born,
I who cared only for my pride,
I who was caught in women's snares,

I who failed to think of my dear kinsman,
my ambrosia, the world's beginning and end,
my Lord whose form bright as the sunset sky
lay buried within my heart?

4

Once, a slave of past karma,
I failed to remember my Lord.
Now, having gone mad,
I babble like a fool.
I cannot hold in my heart
the god who is all the goodness
that dwells in me.
Why was I born?

Cuntarar

Life Is an Illusion

Life is an illusion,
all things end in dust.
The sea of birth is a waste,
the body is a trap made of hunger and disease.
Do good deeds without delay,
say "holy Kētāram,"
place of him whose immense form
sent Viṣṇu with the long eyes
and Brahmā of the lotus seat
searching above and below!

Cuntarar

I Will Think of the Day on Which

I will think of the day on which
I should forget you
as the day of my death,
the day when the senses fail,
the day life leaves the body,
the day when I shall be carried away on the bier.
O poet in glorious Pāṇṭikkoṭumuṭi
washed by the Kaveri's cool, swelling tide,
Even if I should forget you, my tongue
would still say, "Hail Siva!"

Kannada Songs to Shiva

1100–1200

Organized devotion to the god Shiva, called Shaivism, is thought to have originated in Tamil culture and the bhakti poetry of the Tamil saints. It is not surprising, then, that the literary works of Virashavism, which means "heroic devotion to Shiva," recognize those saints as forebears and share many characteristics with their poetry. Among the first great Virashavist bhakti poets of the Kannada region, Basavanna and Mahadeviyakka created songs in their native language expressing a personal, mystical relationship with the divine, an admiration of Shiva as the ultimate god with whom one longs for intimacy, and a feverish desire for rescue from everyday reality. Virashavism cuts across caste, gender, and occupational restrictions; is scornful of Buddhist and Jainist orthodoxy; and upholds a vision of equal access to divine grace. Unlike the Tamil bhakti poets, however, the Kannada bhakti poets held little respect for the Vedic tradition or Brahmin orthodoxy. Theirs was a more radical vision of religious and social revolution. Protesting against any religious mediation—the priests as interpreters of scripture and ritual, the caste system as determinate of spiritual status, even social custom as designating individual spiritual worth—Virashavist bhakti writing opens the opportunity of divine grace to any person dedicated, prepared, and willing to accept it. Rejecting class and gender distinctions, these works often express a defense of

Anonymous, *Kali on Shiva*, c. 1800
Shiva is the third essential god in the Hindu trinity (the other two are Brahma and Vishnu). He is known as the god of destruction of ignorance and impurity, and is often depicted, as here, with his consort Kali. Kali, sometimes called the Black Mother, absorbs the evil of her children—while Shiva is white and often shown lying still at Kali's feet to counteract her constant movement. (The Art Archive / Victoria and Albert Museum London / Eileen Tweedy)

the poor, the outcast, and the downtrodden against the claims of the rich and privileged to religious devotion.

The devotional works of Virashavism are *vacanas*, lyrics written in free verse in the Kannada language. Vacanas are, ultimately, the production of Shiva, who inspires the poet to sing just as a musician might play an instrument. Centrally focused on the state of the worshiper, they embrace the everyday lives and struggles of real people and often express love of the divine in terms of human personal relationships, between friend and friend, parent and child, even a prostitute and a lecher, for example. The songs are bound by no formal rules of poetry; they follow no set metrical pattern or rhyme scheme. To read them is to enjoy the spontaneous act of direct, passionate interaction between a devotee and his or her god.

Basavanna

You Can't Just Do

This and the following five poems translated by K. V. Zvelebi

You can't just do
this thing called bhakti.

Like a saw it cuts when it goes,
it cuts when it comes.
Place your hand in a pitcher
with a hooded snake:
won't it bite,
O Lord of the Meeting Rivers?[1]

[1] **Lord . . . Rivers:** According to legend, at a temple to Shiva located where the rivers Krishna and Malaprabha meet, Shiva appeared to Basavanna and blessed him. The notion of rivers running together also introduces the concept of the union of the soul with the divine. The repetition this phrase illustrates is the bhakti concept that remembering and speaking the name of the divine is a sacred act.

Basavanna

Melt My Mind, O Lord

Melt my mind, O Lord,
and purge its stains.
Test it on the touchstone for its colour
and refine it in fire.

Selected Songs. These songs often end with an *ankita,* a kind of signature with the author's name and/or a statement of purpose. While their musical origins are apparent in melodic rhythms, alliteration, and repetition, the songs are not confined to a certain number of lines per stanza or a number of stanzas per poem.

A note on the translations: The first six songs by Basavanna reprinted here are from K. V. Zvelebi's 1984 translation, *The Lord of Meeting Rivers.* The four by Mahadeviyakka are from A. K. Ramanujan's *Speaking of Siva* (1973). All notes are the editors' unless otherwise indicated.

Cut it and beat it to pure shining gold
  and hammer from it anklets
    for the feet of your devotees.
  O Lord of the Meeting Rivers!

Basavanna

Feet Will Dance

Feet will dance
and tire not
Eyes will see
and tire not
Tongue will sing
and tire not
    What else What else
    shall I do
I worship with full hands
the heart is not content
    What else What else
    shall I do
Listen O Lord
What I desire most
is to burst your belly
and enter you
    O Lord of Confluence

Basavanna

What of It That You Have Read So Much?

What of it that you have read so much?
What of it that you have heard so much?
What of it that you know by heart
all the four Vedas inside out?
    Unless you perform the worship of the Linga,[1]
    great god, should I call you a Brahmin?
    Never!
It is said:
    A man is born a Śūdra;[2]
    he becomes a twice-born by his deeds;
    he becomes a scholar by his lore;
    he becomes a Brahmin who walks the Brahmin way.
It is said:
    The man in whom there is no Brahman is low born.
Therefore, O Lord of the Meeting Rivers,
I say:
    The Brahmin is the ass who carries the Veda as load.

[1] **Linga:** A reference to Shiva and his regenerative role in the cosmos. To this day, some Virashavist devotees, called Lingayats, carry phallic pendants of Shiva as a symbol of their worship.

[2] **Śūdra:** A servile caste near in status to the untouchables.

Basavanna

He'll Grind You into Tiny Shape

He'll grind you into tiny shape.
    He'll rub you till your colour shows.
If, on grinding, you become small,
if, on rubbing, you become gold,
    the Lord of the Meeting Rivers
    will love you
    and treasure you in his heart.

Basavanna

Mother, / What News Shall I Tell

Mother,
what news shall I tell
of the lord of my household?
The body-language he dislikes.
Unless I wipe off the dirt in my eyes
he won't let me see him.
Unless I wash my hands
he won't let me touch him.
    Unless I wash my feet
    he won't sleep with me.

Because I washed my body from head to feet
the Lord of the Meeting Rivers
has made love to me!

Mahadeviyakka

Like a Silkworm Weaving

This and the following three poems translated by A. K. Ramanujan

Like a silkworm weaving
her house with love
from her marrow,
                    and dying
in her body's threads
winding tight, round
and round,
            I burn
desiring what the heart desires.

Cut through, O lord,
my heart's greed,

and show me
your way out,

O lord white as jasmine.

Mahadeviyakka

He Bartered My Heart

He bartered my heart,
looted my flesh,
claimed as tribute
my pleasure,
took over
all of me.

I'm the woman of love
for my lord, white as jasmine.

Mahadeviyakka

Husband Inside

Husband inside,
lover outside.
I can't manage them both.

This world
and that other,
cannot manage them both.

O lord white as jasmine

I cannot hold in one hand
both the round nut
and the long bow.

Mahadeviyakka

I Love the Handsome One

I love the Handsome One:
he has no death
decay nor form
no place or side
no end nor birthmarks.
I love him O mother. Listen.

I love the Beautiful One
with no bond nor fear
no clan no land
no landmarks
for his beauty.

So my lord, white as jasmine, is my husband.

Take these husbands who die,
decay, and feed them
to your kitchen fires!

Songs to Krishna: Jayadeva

1100–1200

A beautiful expression of devotion to the god Krishna, called Vaishnavism, Jayadeva's *Gitagovinda* is important both in its own right and as a source from which bhakti poets would draw for centuries. The overlying story of this dramatic poem tells the tale of Krishna's pursuit, estrangement from, and love of a cowherdess named Radha, but more important is what the work reveals about the nature of human and divine love. Sexual passion, deep emotional longing, fear and disappointment, the bliss of erotic union—all of these very human aspects of the love relationship transcend mundane earthly experience and reveal the experience of true love of the divine. Emphasizing Krishna's association with cowherds, his heroic deeds, and his playfully amorous nature, this text illustrates many facets (some admirably noble, others petty and cruel) of the "lord of all existence." Krishna's relationship with Radha in this text, though it draws

Anonymous, *Krishna and Radha*, Mid-Nineteenth Century
While Krishna is divine, Radha is human; and the story of the love between them embodies human and divine love. The painting here illustrates Krishna's love for Radha. (The Art Archive / Victoria and Albert Museum London / Eileen Tweedy)

from a long tradition of Sanskrit love poetry, is unique in its elevated treatment of this notably heroic female consort. In fact, it is the pairing of this duo and the treatment of Radha that most influenced later bhakti poetry of Vaishnavism.

Born to a Brahmin family during the twelfth century and well educated in classical texts, Jayadeva was a court poet of Sri Lakshman Sena (the king of Bengal) and composed in Sanskrit. Like other bhakti saints, after converting to the devotional worship of one god, Jayadeva traveled the country creating and singing songs of praise. Immediately popular, these songs drew significant numbers of people to the devotional worship of Krishna. Perhaps more important, however, is the fact that the pairing of Krishna and Radha, the glorification of Radha as a strong and worthy partner for the god, and an emphasis on the interplay between longing and union (or reunion) as the very essence of a search for the divine dramatically affected the path of Krishna-worship. Bhakti poetry appearing later—particularly Bengali works and especially the works of Vidyapati, Kabir, and Mirabai—diverges significantly from Jayadeva's work but is nevertheless heavily indebted to it.

Gitagovinda

from Careless Krishna

This and the following poems translated by Barbara Stoler Miller

While Hari roamed in the forest
Making love to all the women,
Rādhā's hold on him loosened,
And envy drove her away.
But anywhere she tried to retreat
In her thicket of wild vines,
Sounds of bees buzzing circles overhead
Depressed her—
She told her friend the secret.
. . .
Vines of his great throbbing arms circle a thousand cowherdesses.
Jewel rays from his hands and feet and chest break the dark night.
    My heart recalls Hari here in his love dance,
    Playing seductively, laughing, mocking me.
. . .
Meeting me under a flowering tree, he calms my fear of dark time,
Delighting me deeply by quickly glancing looks at my heart.
    My heart recalls Hari here in his love dance,
    Playing seductively, laughing, mocking me.

Selected Songs. Reflected in its musical rhythms, alliteration, and repetition, the *Gitadovinda* is meant to be a circle of songs performed in public. These excerpts suggest the many facets of the narrative of the poem, and of Krishna and Radha as both characters and objects of worship.

A note on the translation: The text reprinted here is taken from Barbara Stoler Miller's translation from the Sanskrit, collected in *Love Song of the Dark Lord* (1977). All notes are the editors' unless otherwise indicated.

Jayadeva's song evokes an image of Madhu's[1] beautiful foe
Fit for worthy men who keep the memory of Hari's feet.
My heart recalls Hari here in his love dance,
Playing seductively, laughing, mocking me.

[1] **Madhu:** A demon killed by Krishna.

FROM Bewildered Krishna

Krishna, demon Kaṁsa's foe,[1]
Feeling Rādhā bind his heart with chains
Of memories buried in other wordly lives,
Abandoned the beautiful cowherd girls.

As he searched for Rādhikā[2] in vain,
Arrows of love pierced his weary mind
And Mādhava[3] repented as he suffered
In a thicket on the Jumna riverbank.

The Seventh Song

She saw me surrounded in the crowd of women,
And went away.
I was too ashamed,
Too afraid to stop her.
Damn me! My wanton ways
Made her leave in anger.

What will she do, what will she say to me
For deserting her this long?
I have little use for wealth or people
Or my life or my home.
Damn me! My wanton ways
Made her leave in anger.

I brood on her brow curving
Over her anger-shadowed face,

[1] **Kaṁsa's foe:** Kaṁsa was an evil king who tried to destroy Krishna because it was foretold that Krishna would kill him. Krishna was hidden among the cowherds until he became strong and was able to kill Kamsa.

[2] **Rādhikā:** Radha.

[3] **Mādhava:** A name for Krishna referring to his defeat of the demon Madhu.

Like a red lotus
Shadowed by a bee hovering above.
Damn me! My wanton ways
Made her leave in anger.

In my heart's sleepless state
I wildly enjoy her loving me.
Why do I follow her now in the woods?
Why do I cry in vain?
Damn me! My wanton ways
Made her leave in anger.

Frail Rādhā, I know jealousy
Wastes your heart.
But I can't beg your forgiveness
When I don't know where you are.
Damn me! My wanton ways
Made her leave in anger.

You haunt me,
Appearing, disappearing again.
Why do you deny me
Winding embraces you once gave me?
Damn me! My wanton ways
Made her leave in anger.

Forgive me now!
I won't do this to you again!
Give me a vision, beautiful Rādhā!
I burn with passion of love.
Damn me! My wanton ways
Made her leave in anger.

FROM Ecstatic Krishna

Translated by Barbara Stoler Miller

When her friends had gone,
Smiles spread on Rādhā's lips
While love's deep fantasies
Struggled with her modesty.
Seeing the mood in Rādhā's heart,
Hari spoke to his love;

Her eyes were fixed
On his bed of buds and tender shoots.

The Twenty-third Song

Leave lotus footprints on my bed of tender shoots, loving Rādhā!
Let my place be ravaged by your tender feet!
Nārāyaṇa[1] is faithful now. Love me, Rādhikā!

I stroke your foot with my lotus hand — You have come far.
Set your golden anklet on my bed like the sun.
Nārāyaṇa is faithful now. Love me, Rādhikā!

Consent to my love; let elixir pour from your face!
To end our separation I bare my chest of the silk that bars your breast.
Nārāyaṇa is faithful now. Love me, Rādhikā!

Throbbing breasts aching for loving embrace are hard to touch.
Rest these vessels on my chest! Quench love's burning fire!
Nārāyaṇa is faithful now. Love me, Rādhikā!

Offer your lips' nectar to revive a dying slave, Rādhā!
His obsessed mind and listless body burn in love's desolation.
Nārāyaṇa is faithful now. Love me, Rādhikā!

Rādhā, make your jeweled girdle cords echo the tone of your voice!
Soothe the long torture my ears have suffered from cuckoo's shrill cries!
Nārāyaṇa is faithful now. Love me, Rādhikā!

Your eyes are ashamed now to see me tortured by baseless anger;
Glance at me and end my passion's despair!
Nārāyaṇa is faithful now. Love me, Rādhikā!

Each verse of Jayadeva's song echoes the delight of Madhu's foe.
Let emotion rise to a joyful mood of love in sensitive men!
Nārāyaṇa is faithful now. Love me, Rādhikā!

Displaying her passion
In loveplay as the battle began,
She launched a bold offensive
Above him

[1] **Nārāyaṇa:** A name for Krishna referring to his status as the supreme life force of the universe.

And triumphed over her lover.
Her hips were still,
Her vine-like arm was slack,
Her chest was heaving,
Her eyes were closed.
Why does a mood of manly force
Succeed for women in love?

Bengali Songs to Krishna

1300–1500

Recognizing the wandering devotee Caitanya (1485–1533) as a great religious leader, the cult of Krishna worship spread rapidly in Bengal between the fourteenth and sixteenth centuries. This movement, still strongly influential in India today, is essentially devotional in nature. Welcoming members regardless of caste or gender; calling for a life of dedication to a supreme being existing in everything; treating expressions of love for the divine in song as sacred, communal acts of worship; and using human experience of personal relationships as an allegory for desire for union with God, Vaishnavism in this period worked toward important social and religious reform. Drawing from a long tradition of Sanskrit love poetry, but composing in the language of regional cultures, Vidyapati (fourteenth century), Govindadasa (fifteenth century), and Chandidasa (sixteenth century) take as their primary theme the story of Radha and Krishna. Their works are clearly indebted to others, such as Jayadeva's *Gitagovinda*.

In the Bengali bhakti tradition Krishna is usually described in his youth. He is friend of cowherds and lover of cowherdesses, the dark-skinned embodiment of love and joy, and the powerful supreme lord of all existence, offering escape from earthly life. Most important, he is the suitor of the admirable Radha, who is elevated in some poems to equal status with the god. Drawn by the music of Krishna's lute, Radha leaves her husband, turning her back on the concerns and expectations of earthly life, and enters into a tumultuous relationship with the lord. Her absolute and passionate devotion, feverish desire for union, and acute suffering in the absence of her lord provide rich grounds for the exploration of the human relationship to the divine. Indeed, many of the songs speak from her perspective or honor her as their focus, telling of her shyness and reluctance, her jealousy of Krishna's play with the cowherd girls,

Murshidabad, ***Krishna Dancing in Glade,*** **c. 1760**
This eighteenth-century painting depicts Krishna dancing to the music played by three ladies and suggests the importance of music to Krishna worship. (The Art Archive / Victoria and Albert Museum London / Eileen Tweedy)

and her worthiness as a devotee. In the bhakti tradition, suffering in desire for, and separation from, the divine is an essential counterpart to the promise and joy of union. These poets speak beautifully, in the melodic rhythms of their musical origins and with powerful emotion reflecting their intent—that of inspiring a group of worshipers—to the condition of the human in search of salvation.

Vidyapati

There Was a Shudder in Her Whispering Voice

This and the following two poems translated by Deben Bhattacharya

There was a shudder in her whispering voice.
She was shy to frame her words.
What has happened tonight to lovely Rādhā?
Now she consents, now she is afraid.
When asked for love, she closes up her eyes,
Eager to reach the ocean of desire.
He begs her for a kiss.
She turns her mouth away
And then, like a night lily, the moon[1] seized her.
She felt his touch startling her girdle.
She knew her love treasure was being robbed.
With her dress she covered up her breasts.[2]
The treasure was left uncovered.

Vidyāpati wonders at the neglected bed.
Lovers are busy in each other's arms.

Selected Songs. These love poems by Vidyapati, Govindadasa, and Chandidasa are striking in their deeply felt emotion, eroticism, and lush imagery.

A note on the translations: All of Vidyapati's poems are reprinted from Deben Bhattacharya's *Love Songs of Vidyapati* (1969). Bhattacharya writes, "Love poems, in particular lyrics, do not translate well. . . . I have concentrated on the atmosphere of the originals rather than on scrupulously adhering to tiny detail." The notes for the poems are adapted from Bhattacharya's unless otherwise noted. The poems by Govindadasa and Chandidasa are taken from *In Praise of Krishna,* a 1967 translation by Edward C. Dimock, Jr., and poet Denise Levertov. The notes for those poems are the editor's unless otherwise noted.

[1] **moon:** On account of its dazzling beauty, the moon is an obvious symbol for Krishna the lover.

[2] **breasts:** The breasts were regarded as the prime seat of modesty.

VIDYAPATI

O Friend, I Cannot Tell You

O friend, I cannot tell you
Whether he was near or far, real or a dream.
Like a vine of lightning,
As I chained the dark one,
I felt a river flooding in my heart.
Like a shining moon,
I devoured that liquid face.
I felt stars shooting around me.
The sky fell with my dress,
Leaving my ravished breasts.
I was rocking like the earth.
In my storming breath
I could hear my ankle-bells,
Sounding like bees.
Drowned in the last waters of dissolution,[1]
I knew that this was not the end.

Says Vidyāpati:
How can I possibly believe such nonsense?

---

[1] **last . . . dissolution:** Refers to the deluge which in Hindu thought is supposed to end each world cycle. When one cycle has ended, another commences.

VIDYAPATI

Her Hair, Dishevelled

Her hair, dishevelled,
Veils the beauty of her face
As evil shadows eat the glowing moon.
Strings of blossom in her hair
Wantonly play

As flooded rivers
Twine about their twins.[1]

Exquisite today,
This sport of love,
As Rādhā rides on Krishna.[2]
Beads of sweat glisten on her face
Like pearls on the moon,
A present to her
From the god of love.

With all her force
She kisses her lover's lips,
Like the moon swooping
To drink a lotus bloom.
Her necklace dangles
Below her hanging breasts,
Like streams of milk
Trickling from golden jars.
The jingling bells around her waist
Sang glory to the god of love.

[1] **As . . . twins:** Rivers that normally run parallel to each other get merged together at times of flood.

[2] **Rādhā . . . Krishna:** A reference to Rādhā's active role at the climax of their lovemaking.

Govindadasa

When They Had Made Love

This and the following five poems translated by Edward C. Dimock, Jr., and Denise Levertov

When they had made love
she lay in his arms in the *kunja* grove.[1]
Suddenly she called his name
and wept—as if she burned in the fire of
separation.

[1] ***kunja* grove:** A grove of creeping vines and flowers where Rādhā and Krishna make love.

The gold was in her *anchal*[2]
but she looked afar for it!
—Where has he gone? Where has my love gone?
O why has he left me alone?
And she writhed on the ground in despair,
only her pain kept her from fainting.
Krishna was astonished
and could not speak.

Taking her beloved friend by the hand,
Govinda-dāsa led her softly away.

---

[2] ***anchal:*** The end-piece of a sari that hangs loose on the shoulder, often used for carrying keys or coins.

Govindadasa

The Marks of Fingernails Are on Your Breast

The marks of fingernails are on your breast
and my heart burns.
Kohl[1] of someone's eyes upon your lips
darkens my face.
I am awake all night;
your eyes are red.
So why do you entreat me, Kān,[2]
saying that you and I have but one heart?
You come with choking voice
while I want to weep.
"Only our bodies are apart."
But mine is light,
and yours is dark.
Go home, then,

says Govinda-dāsa.

---

[1] **Kohl:** A fine black powder mixed with almond oil used like eye shadow to make the eyes sparkle.

[2] **Kān:** A name for Krishna, possibly referring to his dark color.

Govindadasa

Let the Earth of My Body Be Mixed with the Earth

She speaks:

Let the earth of my body be mixed with the earth
my beloved walks on.
Let the fire of my body be the brightness
in the mirror that reflects his face.
Let the water of my body join the waters
of the lotus pool he bathes in.
Let the breath of my body be air
lapping his tired limbs.
Let me be sky, and moving through me
that cloud-dark Shyāma,[1] my beloved.

Govinda-dāsa says, O golden one,
Could he of the emerald body let you go?

---

[1] **Shyāma:** Meaning "dusky," Shyāma is a name for Krishna.

Chandidasa

How Can I Describe His Relentless Flute

To her friend:

How can I describe his relentless flute,
which pulls virtuous women from their homes
and drags them by their hair to Shyām
as thirst and hunger pull the doe to the snare?
Chaste ladies forget their lords,
wise men forget their wisdom,

and clinging vines shake loose from their trees,
hearing that music.
Then how shall a simple dairymaid withstand its call?

Chandidāsa says, Kālā[1] *the puppetmaster leads the dance.*

[1] **Kālā:** Meaning "dark-colored," Kālā is a name for Krishna.

Chandidasa

My Mind Is Not on Housework

To her friend:

My mind is not on housework.
Now I weep, now I laugh at the world's
censure.
He draws me — to become
an outcast, a hermit woman in the woods!
He has bereft me of parents, brothers, sisters,
my good name. His flute
took my heart —
his flute, a thin bamboo trap enclosing me —
a cheap bamboo flute was Rādhā's ruin.
That hollow, simple stick —
fed nectar by his lips, but issuing
poison . . .

If you should find
a clump of jointed reeds,
pull off their branches!
Tear them up by the roots!
Throw them
into the sea.

Dvija Chandidāsa says, Why the bamboo?
Not it, but Krishna enthralls you: him you cannot uproot.

Chandidasa

I Brought Honey and Drank It Mixed with Milk

To herself:

I brought honey and drank it mixed with milk—
but where was its sweetness? I tasted gall.
I am steeped in bitterness, as the seed
of a bitter fruit in its juice.
My heart smolders.
A fire without is plain to be seen
but this fire flames within,
it sears my breast.
Desire burns the body—how can it be relieved?

By the touch of Kānu, says Chandidāsa.

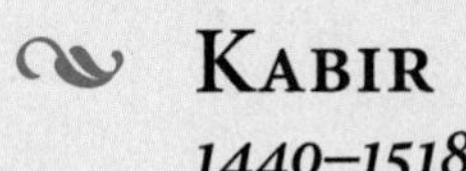

Kabir
1440–1518

Husband and saint, laborer and poet, common man with an uncommon vision, Kabir reveals in his works a devotion to God, whom he refers to by the Hindu name Ram (Rama), that is, direct, personal, and uninhibited (though not uninfluenced) by the popular religious movements of his day. Kabir's origins and life are clouded in mystery, but it is generally agreed that he was born the son of a Muslim weaver in or near Benares. Though the course of his conversion is unclear—one theory holds that he was accepted and taught as a disciple of the Hindu ascetic Ramanada (c. 1400–c. 1470)—it is clear that he came to treat both the Hindu and Muslim religions with indifference. Though it draws from many traditions, Kabir's poetry expresses a strong contempt for institutionalized religions. Defining the path to salvation as an individual, inner search for the divine fraught with suffering but available to all, Kabir vehemently condemns the requirements of intellectual learning, ritual sacrifice, idol worship, and even pilgrimage, all of which were popular in other belief systems of his period. Since God is everywhere, including inside the self, union of the soul with the ultimate reality calls for an emergence from the limited vision of daily reality, an awakening into the practice of vigorous devotion, and a sincere search for the true self that is in union with the universal. This kind of awakening, in the philosophy of Kabir, is more likely to be achieved by the common man performing his or her common duties than by the arrogant and removed holy man. Despite his low caste and probable illiteracy, or near illiteracy, Kabir's inclusiveness, bold and frank urgency, and depth of devotion made him a powerful leader in his own time, and his poems are known widely in India to this day.

The modern Indian writer Rabindranath Tagore notes of Kabir that it is "impossible to say he was Brahmin or Sufi, Vendantist or Vaishnavite—he is, as he says, 'at once the child of Allah and of Rām.'" Praised by many as a great religious reformer, Kabir is particularly noted for his ability to draw on the many religious traditions of his culture while at the same time demonstrating a lack of obligation to them or concern over the objections of more orthodox members of his audience. What fascinates many of his admirers is a confidence of belief and a strength of character evident in what we know of his life and his works. Reputedly imprisoned and threatened with execution for refusing to compromise his beliefs, especially for refusing to bow to the Lodi sultan Sikandar (r. 1489–1517) because the true devotee bows only to God, Kabir miraculously escaped three attempts on his life and eventually saw the sultan bow to him. This kind of conviction is apparent in the straightforward and often brash language of his poetry, which takes as one of its favorite themes the difficulty with which the soul sheds its blindness and comes to sight of the truly divine.

Spoken in the vernacular and written down by his disciples, Kabir's poems embrace a wide range of emotions, celebrate the life of the common folk, and express worship as spontaneous songs of ecstatic love for the divine. In contrast to the misery and suffering inherent in human existence are the presence of the love of Ram, the joy of realization to those who awake to the universal within the self, and the promise of the bliss of union. Full of paradoxes, one function of which is to wake the spiritually asleep audience, these poems use imagery drawn from everyday life—these are the masses existing in ignorance of the supernatural that exists within themselves.

In [*Songs of the Saints of India*] I'm interested in the shape of the poet-saints' life as remembered in the hagiographical literature and the impact these saints have made in the present day. For instance, in the case of Kabir, it's important for a Western reader to know that this is not just a fifteenth-century figure whose poems are held in esteem in the same way that Shakespeare is. . . . He is also today recited in temples and revered, in some cases, as a sort of representation in this world of the Godhead.

–John Stratton Hawley, translator

KABIR

Go Naked If You Want

This and the following poem translated by John Stratton Hawley and Mark Jurgensmeyer

Go naked if you want,
Put on animal skins.
What does it matter till you see the inward Ram?

If the union yogis[1] seek
Came from roaming about in the buff,
every deer in the forest would be saved.

If shaving your head
Spelled spiritual success,
heaven would be filled with sheep.

And brother, if holding back your seed
Earned you a place in paradise,
eunuchs[2] would be the first to arrive.

Kabir says: Listen brother,
Without the name of Ram
who has ever won the spirit's prize?

Selected Poems. Using simple metaphors, Kabir refers often to the activities of everyday people (weaving and other crafts, gambling, even prostitution) and presents Ram as a warm companion, spouse, or teacher. Kabir's language, lacking literary ornamentation and formal figures of speech, can be bawdy, sarcastic, and witty, and always strikes the reader as honest and sincere.

A note on the translations: Three translations of Kabir are represented here, taken from Rabindranath Tagore and Evelyn Underhill's 1988 *Songs of the Saints of India,* Rabindranath Tagore's 1915 *One Hundred Poems of Kabir,* and poet Robert Bly's 1971 *The Fish in the Sea Is Not Thirsty.* Read together, the poems are interesting examples of the different choices made by a translator. Note especially the two translations of the same poem that follow: the Tagore/Underhill version, "I Do Not Know What Manner of God Is Mine" and Bly's "I Don't Know What Sort of a God We Have Been Talking About."

[1] **yogis:** Devotees who practice yoga, a set of physical and mental exercises meant to give one control over the body and mind. Some yogis, viewing strict physical self-denial as the key to spiritual discipline, were known to wear animal skins, go naked, shave their heads, and refrain from sex in order to approach union with the divine.

[2] **eunuchs:** Castrated men.

Kabir

Pundit, How Can You Be So Dumb?

Pundit,[1] how can you be so dumb?
You're going to drown, along with all your kin,
    unless you start speaking of Ram.

Vedas, Puranas[2]—why read them?
    It's like loading an ass with sandalwood!
Unless you catch on and learn how Ram's name goes,
    how will you reach the end of the road?

You slaughter living beings and call it religion:
    hey brother, what would irreligion be?
"Great Saint"—that's how you love to greet each other:
    Who then would you call a murderer?

Your mind is blind. You've no knowledge of yourselves.
    Tell me, brother, how can you teach anyone else?
Wisdom is a thing you sell for worldly gain,
    so there goes your human birth—in vain.

You say: "It's Narad's command."
    "It's what Vyas says to do."
    "Go and ask Sukdev, the sage."[3]
Kabir says: you'd better go and lose yourself in Ram
    for without him, brother, you drown.

---

[1] **Pundit:** A person specializing in a specific field of knowledge and considered an expert therein.

[2] **Vedas, Puranas:** Sacred texts of the Hindu tradition.

[3] **Narad, Vyas, Sukdev:** Various respected writers of works guiding religious conduct.

Kabir

The River and Its Waves Are One Surf

This and the following poem translated by Rabindranath Tagore and Evelyn Underhill

The river and its waves are one surf:
where is the difference between the
river and its waves?
When the wave rises, it is the water;
and when it falls, it is the same
water again. Tell me, Sir, where
is the distinction?
Because it has been named as wave,
shall it no longer be considered as
water?

Within the Supreme Brahma, the
worlds are being told like beads:
Look upon that rosary with the eyes
of wisdom.

Kabir

I Do Not Know What Manner of God Is Mine

I do not know what manner of God is
mine.
The Mullah[1] cries aloud to Him: and
why? Is your Lord deaf? The
subtle anklets that ring on the
feet of an insect when it moves
are heard of Him.

---

[1] **Mullah:** An Islamic religious teacher or leader.

Tell your beads, paint your forehead
with the mark of your God, and
wear matted locks long and showy:
but a deadly weapon is in your heart,
and how shall you have God?

Kabir

I Don't Know What Sort of a God We Have Been Talking About

This and the following poem translated by Robert Bly

I don't know what sort of a God we have been talking about.

The caller calls in a loud voice to the Holy One at dusk.
Why? Surely the Holy One is not deaf.
He hears the delicate anklets that ring on the feet of an insect
as it walks.

Go over and over your beads, paint designs
on your forehead,
wear your hair matted, long, and ostentatious,
but when deep inside you there is a loaded gun,
how can you have God?

Kabir

I Laugh When I Hear That the Fish in the Water Is Thirsty

I laugh when I hear that the fish in the water is thirsty.

You don't grasp the fact that what is most alive of all
    is inside your own house;
and so you walk from one holy city to the next
    with a confused look!

Kabir will tell you the truth: go wherever you like, to Calcutta
    or Tibet;
if you can't find where your soul is hidden,
for you the world will never be real!

GLOSSARY OF LITERARY AND CRITICAL TERMS

Accent The emphasis given to a syllable or word, especially in poetry, that stresses a particular word in a line and may be used to define a poetic foot.

Acropolis The most fortified part of a Greek city, located on a hill; the most famous acropolis is in Athens, the site of the Parthenon.

Act A major division in the action of a play. In many full-length plays, acts are further divided into SCENES, which often mark a point in the action when the location changes or when a new character enters.

Adab An Islamic literary genre distinguished by its humanistic concerns on a variety of subjects that highlights the sensibilities and interests of authors and flourished throughout the tenth and eleventh centuries.

Aeneas The hero of Virgil's *Aeneid,* the Trojan Aeneas wanders for years after the Greek destruction of Troy before reaching the shores of Italy, where his descendants would later found the city of Rome.

The Aeneid The great epic poem of Virgil that tells of the adventures of its hero, Aeneas, after the Trojan War and provides illustrious historical background for the Roman Empire.

Age of Pericles The golden age of Athens in the fifth century B.C.E. when Pericles (c. 495–429 B.C.E.) was the head of the Athenian government. During this period, Athenian democracy was at its apex; the Parthenon was constructed and drama and music flourished.

Ahimsa The Buddhist belief that all life is one and sacred, resulting in the principle of nonviolence toward all living things.

Akam In Indian Tamil poetry, *akam* are "inner" poems, chiefly concerning passion and personal emotions.

Allegory A narrative in which the characters, settings, and episodes stand for something else. Traditionally, most allegories come in the form of stories that correlate to spiritual concepts; examples of these can be found in Dante's *Divine Comedy* (1321). Some later allegories allude to political, historical, and sociological ideas.

Alliteration The repetition of the same consonant sound or sounds in a sequence of words, usually at the beginning of a word or stressed syllable: "*d*escen*d*ing *d*ew *d*rops"; "*l*uscious *l*emons." Alliteration derives from the sounds, not the spelling of words; for example, "*k*een" and "*c*ar" alliterate, but "*c*ar" and "*c*ite" do not. Used sparingly, alliteration can intensify ideas by emphasizing key words.

Allusion A brief reference, sometimes direct, sometimes indirect, to a person, place, thing, event, or idea in history or literature. Such references could be to a scene in one of Shakespeare's plays, a historic figure, a war, a great love story, a biblical authority, or anything else that might enrich an author's work. Allusions, which function as a kind of shorthand, imply that the writer and the reader share similar knowledge.

Ambiguity Allows for two or more simultaneous interpretations of a word, phrase, action, or situation, all of whose meanings are supported by the work. Deliberate ambiguity can contribute to the effectiveness and richness of a piece of writing; unintentional ambiguity obscures meaning and may confuse readers.

Amor imperii Latin for love of power.

Anagnorisis The discovery or recognition that takes place in a tragedy, resulting in the protagonist's *PERIPETEIA*, or reversal of fortune.

Anagram A word or phrase made up of the same letters as another word or phrase; *heart* is an anagram of *earth.* Often considered merely an exercise of one's ingenuity, anagrams are sometimes used by writers to conceal proper names, veil messages, or suggest an important connection between words, such as that between *hated* and *death.*

Antagonist The character, force, or collection of forces in fiction or drama that opposes the PROTAGONIST and gives rise to the conflict in the story; an opponent of the protagonist, such as Caliban in Shakespeare's play *The Tempest.*

Anthropocentric Human-centered. A point of view that considers everything in the world or universe in terms of its relation to or value for human beings.

Apocalypse A prophetic revelation, particularly one that predicts the destruction of the world, as in the final battle between good and evil foreseen in Zoroastrianism and in the Revelation of St. John the Divine; the time when God conquers the powers of evil.

Apostrophe A statement or address made to an implied interlocutor, sometimes a nonhuman figure, or PERSONIFICATION. Apostrophes often provide a speaker with the opportunity to reveal his or her thoughts.

Archetype A universal symbol that evokes deep and sometimes unconscious responses in a reader. In literature, characters, images, and themes that symbolize universal meanings and basic human experiences are considered archetypes. Common literary archetypes include quests, initiations, scapegoats, descents to the underworld, and ascents to heaven.

Archon The chief ruler of Athens during the classical era.

Aryans A people who settled in Iran (Persia) and northern India in prehistoric times. Gradually, they spread through India in the first millennium B.C.E., extending their influence to southern India in the first three centuries C.E. Through their early writings in the Sanskrit language, the VEDAS, they established the basis of Hinduism and Indian culture.

Aside In drama, a speech directed to the audience that supposedly is not audible to the other characters onstage.

Assonance The repetition of vowel sounds in nearby words, as in "asl*ee*p under a tr*ee*" or "*ea*ch *e*vening." When words also share similar endings, as in "asl*eep* in the d*eep*," RHYME occurs. Assonance is an effective means of emphasizing important words.

Autobiography A narrative form of biography in which an author accounts for his or her own life and character to a public audience. As a literary genre, autobiography developed differently in several cultures: the *Confessions* of St. Augustine, written in Latin in the fifth century, served as a model in Europe; Ibn Ishaq's biography of Muhammad, written in Arabic in the eighth century, served as the model for both biographies and autobiographies by later Arabic writers.

Ballad A narrative verse form originally meant to be sung; it generally tells a dramatic tale or a simple story. Ballads are associated with the oral traditions or folklore of common people. The folk ballad stanza usually consists of four lines of alternating tetrameter (four accented syllables) and trimeter (three accented syllables) and follows a rhyme scheme of *abab* or *abcb.*

Ballad stanza A four-line stanza, known as a QUATRAIN, consisting of alternating eight- and six-syllable lines. Usually, only the second and fourth lines rhyme (an *abcb* pattern). Samuel

Taylor Coleridge adapted the ballad stanza in *The Rime of the Ancient Mariner* (1798).

Baroque A style found in architecture, art, and literature from the late sixteenth century through the early eighteenth century, characterized by extravagance of theme, language, and form; striking and abrupt turns of line and logic; and ingenious and dynamic imagery. The English poet John Donne (1572–1631) and the Spanish-American poet Sor Juana Inés de la Cruz (c. 1648–1695) often employ what may be considered baroque styles.

Bhagavad Gita An ancient text of Hindu wisdom from the first century B.C.E. or first century C.E. inserted into the epic poem *Mahabharata.*

Bhakti From the Sanskrit for *devotion,* refers to the popular mystical movement stemming from Hinduism. In contrast to forms of Hinduism that stress knowledge, ritual, and good works, Bhakti cults emphasize that personal salvation may be achieved through the loving devotion and ecstatic surrender of an individual to a chosen deity, such as Shiva, Vishnu, and their consorts, often worshiped as a child, parent, beloved, or master.

Bible A collection of writings sacred to Christianity made up of the Hebrew Scriptures (also known as the Old Testament), containing the history, teachings, and literature of the ancient Hebrews and Jews, and the New Testament, the history, teachings, and literature associated with Jesus of Nazareth and his followers.

Biography A nonfiction literary genre that provides the history of an individual's life, detailing not only the facts of that life but also insights into the individual's personality and character. Biography is distinguished from autobiography in that it is written by someone other than the person who is the subject of the work. Biography became popular as a form beginning in the Renaissance.

Black Death The bubonic plague, a devastating disease that swept through Europe in the fourteenth century, leaving a trail of death in its wake.

Blank verse Unrhymed IAMBIC PENTAMETER. Blank verse is often considered the form closest to the natural rhythms of English speech and is therefore the most common pattern found in traditional English narrative and dramatic poetry, from Shakespeare to the writers of the early twentieth century.

Blazon A catalog of similes or metaphors drawn from nature wherein the fair parts of the lover's body are compared to what eventually came to be a stock set of images drawn from nature, seen in the Song of Songs, and earlier love poems. Shakespeare's "My mistress's eyes are nothing like the sun" parodies this convention.

Bodhisattva In Buddhism, a person who temporarily puts off nirvana in order to assist others on earth; one who has achieved great moral and spiritual enlightenment and is en route to becoming a Buddha.

Book of History An ancient collection of documents on Chinese history and politics written in prose dating back to the early years of the Zhou dynasty (c. 1027–221 B.C.E.), if not earlier. It is one of the oldest works of history and was a foundation for Confucian ideas; among other things it describes history as a process of change, and delineates the important "Mandate of Heaven," which said that emperors ruled by divine right, but if or when an emperor violated his office, the mandate would pass to another.

Book of Songs Also known as the *Poetry Classic, Book of Poems,* or *Book of Odes,* this is the oldest Chinese anthology of poems, dating from the ninth through the sixth centuries B.C.E. Written primarily in four-character verse, these poems treat a variety of subjects and form the foundation of later Chinese verse.

Brahman In the UPANISHADS—sacred Hindu texts—Brahman is the ultimate reality, the single unifying essence of the universe that transcends all names and descriptions. A Brahman, or Brahmin, is also a Hindu priest and thus of the highest caste in the traditional Hindu caste system.

Brahmanic period The period in ancient India (c. 1000–600 B.C.E.), in which VEDIC society was dominated by the Brahmins and every aspect of Aryan life was under the control of religious rituals. Both heroic epics of Indian culture, the

Mahabharata and the *Ramayana,* were originally formulated and told in this period, though transcribed to written form much later, between 400 B.C.E. and 400 C.E.

Brahmin The priestly caste, the highest in the traditional Hindu caste system; a Hindu priest. Also spelled *BRAHMAN.*

Buddhism A religion founded in India in the sixth century B.C.E. by Siddhartha Gautama, the Buddha. While Buddhism has taken different forms in the many areas of the world to which it has spread, its central tenet is that life is suffering caused by desire. In order to obtain salvation, or nirvana, one must transcend desire through following an eightfold path that includes the practice of right action and right mindfulness.

Bunraku New name for *joruri,* traditional Japanese puppet theater.

Bushido The code of honor and conduct of the Japanese SAMURAI class. *Bushido* emphasizes self-discipline and bravery.

Cacophony In literature, language that is discordant and difficult to pronounce. Cacophony (from the Greek for "bad sound") may be unintentional, or it may be used for deliberate dramatic effect; also refers to the combination of loud, jarring sounds.

Caesura A pause within a line of poetry that contributes to the line's RHYTHM. A caesura can occur anywhere within a line and need not be indicated by punctuation. In scansion, caesuras are indicated by two vertical lines.

Caliph The chief civil and religious leader of a Muslim state, as a successor of Muhammad.

Caliphate Both the reign or term of a caliph as well as the area over which he rules.

Calvinists A Protestant denomination whose adherents follow the beliefs originally outlined by French Protestant reformer, John Calvin (1509-1564), especially predestination and salvation of the elect through God's grace alone.

Canon The works generally considered by scholars, critics, and teachers to be the most important to read and study and that collectively constitute the masterpieces of literature. Since the 1960s, the traditional English and American literary canons, consisting mostly of works by white male writers, have been expanding to include many female writers and writers of varying ethnic backgrounds. At the same time the world literature canon, as constructed in the West, has been broadened to include many works from non-Western literatures, especially those of Asia and Africa.

Canzoniere Medieval Italian lyric poetry. Masters of the form included Petrarch, Dante, Tasso, and Cavalcanti.

Carpe diem Latin phrase meaning "seize the day." This is a common literary theme, especially in lyric poetry, conveying that life is short, time is fleeting, and one should make the most of present pleasures. Andrew Marvell's poem "To His Coy Mistress" is a good example.

Caste The hereditary class to which a member of Hindu society belongs; stemming from the teachings of the VEDAS, Hindu society observes a strict hierarchy with the Brahmins, or priests, at the top; followed by the *KSHATRIYAS,* or warriors and rulers; and the Vaishyas, or farmers, merchants, and artisans; and a fourth class, added later than the others, the Shudras, servants. Only members of the first three "twice-born" castes could study the VEDAS and take part in religious rituals. Outside of this system were the outcastes, known as Untouchables.

Catechumen In the early Christian church, an individual officially recognized as a Christian and admitted to religious instruction required for full membership in the church.

Catharsis Meaning "purgation," or the release of the emotions of pity and fear by the audience at the end of a tragedy. In *Poetics,* Aristotle discusses the importance of catharsis. The audience faces the misfortunes of the PROTAGONIST, which elicit pity and compassion. Simultaneously, the audience confronts the protagonist's failure, thus receiving a frightening reminder of human limitations and frailties.

Character, characterization A character is a person presented in a dramatic or narrative work; characterization is the process by which a writer presents a character to the reader.

Chin-Shi Examinations First begun in the Sui dynasty in China (581–618 C.E.) under Yang Jian and formalized during the Tang era, the system of chin-shi examinations brought bright and talented men from all over China into the government bureaucracy.

Chivalric romances Idealized stories from the medieval period that espoused the values of a sophisticated courtly society. These tales centered around the lives of knights who were faithful to God, king, and country and willing to sacrifice themselves for these causes and for the love and protection of women. Chivalric romances were highly moral and fanciful, often pitting knights against dark or supernatural forces.

Choka A Japanese form of an ode associated with Kakinomoto Hitomaro (late seventh century); a long poem often inspired by public occasions but also full of personal sentiment.

Chorus In Greek tragedies, a group of people who serve mainly as commentators on the play's characters and events, adding to the audience's understanding of a play by expressing traditional moral, religious, and social attitudes. Choruses are occasionally used by modern playwrights.

Christianity A world religion founded in Palestine in the first millennium C.E. upon the teachings of Jesus Christ, whose followers believe he is the Messiah prophesied in the Hebrew Scriptures (Old Testament). The central teachings of Christianity are that Jesus of Nazareth was the son of God, that his crucifixion and resurrection from the dead provide atonement for the sins of humanity, and that through faith in Jesus individuals might attain eternal life. Christianity has played a central role in the history of Europe and the Americas.

Chthonic From the Greek *chthonios,* meaning "in the earth," *chthonic* refers to the underworld spirits and deities in ancient religion and mythology.

Cliché An idea or expression that has become tired and trite from overuse.

Closet drama A play that is to be read rather than performed onstage. In closet dramas, literary art outweighs all other considerations.

Colloquial Informal diction that reflects casual, conversational language and often includes slang expressions.

Comedy A work intended to interest, involve, and amuse readers or an audience, in which no terrible disaster occurs and which ends happily for the main characters.

Comic relief A humorous scene or incident that alleviates tension in an otherwise serious work. Often these moments enhance the thematic significance of a story in addition to providing humor.

Comitatus Arrangement whereby young warriors attached themselves to the leader of a group and defended him in return for his economic and legal protection. Also, the bond among warriors attached to such a leader.

Conceit A figure of speech elaborating a surprising parallel between two dissimilar things. It was a favorite poetic device of the Petrarchan sonneteers and the English metaphysical poets of the seventeenth century.

Conflict In a literary work, the struggle between opposing forces. The PROTAGONIST is engaged in a conflict with the antagonist.

Confucianism A religious philosophy that has influenced Chinese and East Asian spirituality and culture for more than two thousand years. Based on the writings of Confucius (Kongfuzi; 551–479 B.C.E.), Confucianism asserts that humans can improve and even perfect themselves through education and moral reform. In its various manifestations, Confucianism has affected the social and political evolution of China and East Asia while providing a spiritual and moral template.

Connotation Implications going beyond the literal meaning of a word that derive from how the word has been commonly used and from ideas or things associated with it. For example, the word *eagle* in the United States connotes ideas of liberty and freedom that have little to do with the term's literal meaning.

Consonance A common type of near-rhyme or half rhyme created when identical consonant sounds are preceded by different vowel sounds: *home, same; worth, breath.*

Convention A characteristic of a literary genre that is understood and accepted by readers and audiences because it has become familiar. For example, the division of a play into acts and scenes is a dramatic convention, as are SOLILOQUIES and ASIDES.

Cosmogony An explanation for the origins of the universe and how the functioning of the heavens is related to the religious, political, and social organization of life on earth. The primary function of creation myths, such as the Hebrew Book of Genesis and the Mesopotamian *Epic of Creation,* is to depict a cosmogonic model of the universe.

Cosmology The metaphysical study of the origin and nature of the universe.

Cosmopolis A large city inhabited by people from many different countries.

Counter-Reformation The period of Catholic revival and reform from the beginning of the pontificate of Pope Pius IV in 1560 to the end of the Thirty Years' War in 1648 in response to the Protestant Reformation. Spearheaded in great part by members of the Society of Jesus (the Jesuits), it was a period in which the Roman Catholic church reaffirmed the veneration of saints and the authority of the pope and initiated many institutional reforms.

Couplet A two-line stanza.

Creation myth A symbolic narrative of the beginning of the world as configured by a particular society or culture. Examples of creation myths range from the Mesopotamian classic *Epic of Creation* to the Book of Genesis in Hebrew Scriptures to the creation myths of the Ancient Mexicans of the Americas.

Crisis The moment in a work of drama or fiction in which the elements of the conflict reach the point of maximum tension. The crisis is is not necessarily the emotional crescendo, or climax.

Cultural criticism An approach to literature that focuses on the historical, social, political, and economic contexts of a work. Cultural critics use widely eclectic strategies, such as anthropology, NEW HISTORICISM, psychology, gender studies, and DECONSTRUCTION, to analyze not only literary texts but everything from radio talk shows to comic strips, calendar art, advertising, travel guides, and baseball cards.

Cuneiform The wedge-shaped writing characters that stood for syllables or sounds and not letters in ancient Akkadian, Assyrian, Persian, and Babylonian inscriptions.

Daoism (Taoism) A religion/philosophy based on the Dao De Jing (Tao Te Ching) of Laozi (Lao Tzu) that emphasizes individual freedom, spontaneity, mystical experience, and self-transformation, and is the antithesis of CONFUCIANISM. In pursuit of the dao, or the Way—the eternal creative reality that is the essence of all things—practitioners embrace simplicity and reject learned wisdom. The Daoist tradition has flourished in China and East Asia for more than two thousand years.

Deconstructionism An approach to literature that suggests that literary works do not yield single, fixed meanings because language can never say exactly what one intends it to mean. Deconstructionism seeks to destabilize meaning by examining the gaps in and ambiguities of a text's language. Deconstructionists pay close attention to language in order to discover and describe how a variety of close readings of any given work can be generated.

Denouement French term meaning "unraveling" or "unknotting" used to describe the resolution of a PLOT following the action's climax.

Deus ex machina Latin for "god from the machine," a phrase originally applied to Greek plays, especially those by Euripides, in which resolution of the conflict was achieved by the intervention of a god who was lowered onto the stage mechanically. In its broader use, the phrase is applied to any plot that is resolved by an improbable or fortuitous device from outside the action.

Dharma Cosmic order or law in the Hindu tradition that includes the natural and moral laws that apply to all beings and things.

Dhimmi See THE PEOPLE OF THE BOOK.

Dialect A type of informal diction. Dialects are spoken by definable groups of people from a particular geographic region, economic group, or social class. Writers use dialect to express and contrast the education, class, and social and regional backgrounds of their characters.

Dialogue Verbal exchange between CHARACTERS. Dialogue reveals firsthand characters' thoughts, responses, and emotional states.

Diaspora From the Greek for "dispersion," this term was initially applied to the Jews exiled to Babylonia after the destruction of the Temple of Jerusalem in 586 B.C.E. and again forced into exile after the Romans defeated Jerusalem in 70 C.E. The term now refers to other peoples who have been forced from their homelands, such as the Africans uprooted by the slave trade.

Diction A writer's choice of words, phrases, sentence structure, and figurative language, which combine to help create meaning.

Didactic Literature intended to teach or convey instruction, especially of a moral, ethical, or religious nature, such as a didactic essay or poem.

Digressions In epics such as *Beowulf,* these are narratives imbedded in the story to illustrate a point or recall another situation. Digressions may consist of conventional wisdom; suggest how one is supposed to behave; or remind the audience of events occurring either before or after those treated in the story.

Dionysiac festival In Athens, plays were performed during two major festivals in honor of the god Dionysus: the Lenaea during January and February, and the Great Dionysia in March and April.

Dionysus The god of wine in Greek mythology whose cult originated in Thrace and Phrygia, north and east of the Greek peninsula. Dionysus was often blamed for people's irrational behavior and for chaotic situations. However, many Greeks also believed that Dionysus taught them good farming skills, especially those related to wine production. Greek tragedy evolved from a ceremony that honored Dionysus, and the theater in Athens was dedicated to him.

Dithyramb Originally a highly passionate, lyrical hymn sung during the rites of Dionysius in Greece, dithyramb now refers to any impassioned sequence of verse or prose, often characterized by irregular or unrestrained rhythms and extravagant imagery.

Divine Comedy Dante Alighieri's fourteenth-century narrative poem that deals with the poet's imaginary journey through hell, purgatory, and paradise.

Doggerel A derogatory term for poetry whose subject is trite and whose rhythm and sounds are monotonously heavy-handed.

Drama Derived from the Greek word *dram,* meaning "to do" or "to perform," *drama* may refer to a single play, a group of plays, or to plays in general. Drama is designed to be performed in a theater: Actors take on the roles of CHARACTERS, perform indicated actions, and deliver the script's DIALOGUE.

Dramatic monologue A type of lyric or narrative poem in which a speaker addresses an imagined and distinct audience in such a way as to reveal a dramatic situation and, often unintentionally, some aspect of his or her temperament or personality.

Dravidians A group of dark-skinned peoples of India who were either ancient occupants of the southern peninsula, refugees of earlier tribes pushed down from the north, or late arrivals to India from the Mediterranean seacoast.

Edo The ancient name for Tokyo. During the Tokugawa period (1600–1868), Edo became the imperial capital of Japan.

Elegiac couplets The conventional strophic form of Latin elegiac love poetry, consisting of one dactylic hexameter line followed by one dactylic pentameter line. A dactylic hexameter line is composed of six feet, each foot comprising one long, or accented, and two short, or unaccented, syllables; the sixth foot may be shortened by one or two syllables; a pentameter line consists of five such feet. The elegiac couplet is also known as a "distich."

Elegy A mournful, contemplative lyric poem often ending in consolation, written to commemorate someone who has died. *Elegy* may also refer to a serious, meditative poem that expresses a speaker's melancholy thoughts.

Elizabethan Of or characteristic of the time when Elizabeth I (1558–1603) was the queen of England. This era was perhaps the most splendid literary period in the history of English literature in that it encompassed the works of Sidney, Spenser, Marlowe, and Shakespeare, among many others, and saw the flourishing of such genres as poetry, especially the SONNET, and was a golden age of drama of all forms.

Elysian Fields In Greek mythology, some fortunate mortals spend their afterlife in the bliss of these Islands of the Blest, rather than in Hades, the underworld.

End-stopped line A line in a poem after which a pause occurs. End-stopped lines reflect normal speech patterns and are often marked by punctuation.

Enjambment In poetry, a line continuing without a pause into the next line for its meaning; also called a run-on line.

Ennead The group of nine primary deities in the religion of ancient Egypt.

Epic A long narrative poem told in a formal, elevated style that focuses on a serious subject and chronicles heroic deeds and events important to a culture or nation. It usually includes a supernatural dimension, like the gods in Homer. Most epics follow established conventions, such as beginning *in medias res* (in the middle of things); employing elaborate comparisons known as epic similes; and identifying characters with repeated epithets, such as "wily Odysseus." Oral or folk epics, recited tales told for many generations before being written down, such as *The Iliad* and *Sunjata,* are sometimes distinguished from literary epics like *The Aeneid* or *Paradise Lost,* whose original creation was the work of a single poet.

Epicureanism The doctrines of Epicurus (341–270 B.C.E.), the Greek philosopher who espoused a life of pleasure and the avoidance of pain; commonly thought of as a license for indulgence, Epicureanism actually stipulates a life of simplicity and morality.

Essays A literary form that is an analytical, interpretive, or critical composition usually shorter and less formal than a dissertation or thesis and more personal in nature. The term was coined in the Renaissance by the master of the form, Montaigne (1533–1592), who chose it to underscore that his writings (from the French word *essai,* literally meaning "trial," or "test") were attempts toward understanding.

Euphony From the Greek for "good sound"; refers to language that is smooth and musically pleasant to the ear.

Exposition A narrative device often used at the beginning of a work to provide necessary background information about characters and their circumstances. Exposition explains such matters as what has gone on before; the relationships between characters; theme; and conflict.

Fabliau Although the *fabliau* originated in France as a comic or satiric tale in verse, by the time of Giovanni Boccaccio (1313–1375) and Geoffrey Chaucer (1340–1400) the term also stood for bawdy and ribald prose tales like "The Miller's Tale" in Chaucer's *Canterbury Tales* or Boccaccio's "Rustico and Alibech."

Farce A form of humor based on exaggerated, improbable incongruities. Farce involves rapid shifts in action and emotion as well as slapstick comedy and extravagant dialogue.

Feminist criticism An approach to literature that seeks to correct or supplement a predominantly male-dominated critical perspective with a feminist consciousness. Feminist criticism places literature in a social context and uses a broad range of disciplines, including history, sociology, psychology, and linguistics, to provide interpretations that are sensitive to feminist issues.

Feudal aristocracy, Feudalism A system of government that existed with some variations in Europe, China, and Japan in the Middle Period. The feudal system refers to a mode of agricultural production in which peasants worked for landowners, or lords, in return for debt forgiveness, food, and military protection.

Fiction Literature created from the imagination and not presented as fact, though it may be based on a true story or real-life situation. Genres of fiction include the short story, the novella, and the novel.

Figures of speech Ways of using language that deviate from the literal, denotative meanings of words, through comparison, exaggeration, or other verbal devices in order to suggest additional meanings or effects.

Fixed form A poem characterized by a fixed pattern of lines, syllables, or METER. A SONNET is a fixed form of poetry because it must have fourteen lines.

Flashback A literary or dramatic device that allows a past occurrence to be inserted into the chronological order of a narrative.

Flying Dutchman The legend of a ghostly ship doomed to sail for eternity. If a vision of it appears to sailors, it signals imminent disaster. Most versions of the story have the captain of the ill-fated ship playing dice or gambling with the devil.

Foil A character in a literary work or drama whose behavior or values contrast with those of another character, typically the PROTAGONIST.

Foot A poetic foot is a poem's unit of measurement, defined by an accented syllable and a varying number of unaccented syllables. In English, the iambic foot, an accented syllable followed by an unaccented syllable, is the most common.

Foreshadowing Providing hints of what is to happen in order to build suspense.

Formalism A type of criticism dominant in the early twentieth century that emphasizes the form of an artwork. Two of its prominent schools are Russian formalism, which favors the form of an artwork over its content and argues that it is necessary for literature to defamiliarize the ordinary objects of the world, and American NEW CRITICISM, which treats a work of art as an object and seeks to understand it through close, careful analysis.

Founding myth A story that explains how a particular nation or culture came to be, such as Virgil's *Aeneid,* which describes the founding of Rome. Many epic poems, sometimes called national epics, are founding myths.

Four classes In Hindu tradition, humans are created as one of four classes, or VARNA: in descending order, the BRAHMINS (priests), the *KSHATRIYA* (warriors), the *Vaisya* (merchants and farmers), and the *Shudra* (laborers and servants).

Framed narration Also called *framed tale.* A story within a story. In Chaucer's *Canterbury Tales,* each pilgrim's story is framed by the story of the pilgrimage itself. This device, used by writers from ancient times to the present, enjoyed particular popularity during the thirteenth, fourteenth, and fifteenth centuries and was most fully developed in *The Arabian Nights,* a work in which the framing is multilayered.

Free verse Highly irregular poetry, typically, free verse employs varying line patterns and rhythms and does not rhyme.

Freudian criticism A method of literary criticism associated with Freud's theories of psychoanalysis. Early Freudian critics sought to illustrate how literature is shaped by the unconscious desires of the author, but the term now more broadly encompasses many schools of thought that link psychoanalysis to the interpretation of literature.

Fu A mixed-genre Chinese literary form developed during the Han dynasty (206 B.C.E.–220 C.E.) that combines elements of prose and poetry; it begins with a prose introduction followed by lines of poetry of various metrical lengths.

Gaia From the Greek *Ge* meaning "earth," Gaia or Gaea was an earth goddess, mother of the Titans in Greek mythology.

Gay and lesbian criticism School of literary criticism that focuses on the representation of homosexuality in literature; also interested in how homosexuals read literature and to what extent sexuality and gender is culturally constructed.

Gender criticism Literary school that analyzes how an author's or a reader's sex affects the writing and reading experiences.

Genre A category of artistic works or literary compositions that have a distinctive style or content. Poetry, fiction, and drama are genres. Different genres have dominated at various times and places. Traditional genres include tragedy, comedy, romance, novel, epic, and lyric.

Georgic poetry Poetry dealing with the practical aspects of agriculture and rural affairs as first seen in the work of the Greek poet Nicander of Colophon (second century B.C.E.) and practiced by later poets such as Virgil (70–19 B.C.E.).

Ghazal A form of lyric poetry composed of three to seven couplets, called *sh'ir,* that follow the strict rhyme scheme of *aa ba ca da,* and so on, known as the *qafiyah.* Strict adherence to the form requires the use of the *radif,* a word that is repeated in a pattern dictated by the first couplet, throughout the poem. Literally meaning "dialogue with the beloved," the *ghazal,* as practiced in Arabia, Persia, Turkey, and India beginning around 1200, became the predominant form for love poetry.

Gnostics Members of an ancient sect in the Middle East who believed that hidden knowledge held the key to the universe. Throughout history there have been Gnostics who have formed secret societies with secret scriptures and who have believed they understood the workings of the cosmos.

Golden Age of Arabic science The period of the Abbassid caliphs, between 750 and 945 C.E., particularly the reigns of Harun al-Rashid (786–809) and al-Ma'mun (813–833). Al-Ma'mun founded a scientific academy in Baghdad, collected and had translated many ancient Greek and Indian manuscripts upon which Arab scholars built, and encouraged scholarship of all kinds, resulting in major advances in mathematics, astronomy, medicine, and geography.

Golden Age of Spain The "Siglo de Oro" period from the early sixteenth century to the end of the seventeenth century that is considered the high point of Spain's literary history. The age began with the political unification of Spain around 1500 and extended through 1681, the year in which Pedro Calderon (1600–1681) died. In addition to Calderon, this period saw the flourishing of such writers as Cervantes (1547–1616) and Lope de Vega (1562–1635).

Gothic A style of literature (especially novels) in the late eighteenth and early nineteenth centuries that reacted against the mannered decorum of earlier literature. Gothic novels explore the darker side of human experience; they are often set in the past and in foreign countries, and they employ elements of horror, mystery, and the supernatural.

Gravitas Formality in bearing and appearance; a reserved dignity of behavior and speech, especially in a leader or a ruler.

Great Chain of Being A conception of the universal order of things derived from Greek philosophy that exerted considerable influence on the European understanding of nature and the universe from the Renaissance through the eighteenth century. The Great Chain of Being posits that God ordered the universe so as to create the greatest possible diversity, continuity, and order, and envisions a hierarchical structure whereby every being, according to its nature, occupies a designated place on a ladder reaching from the basest matter to the highest spiritual entity, or God. This metaphor offered the assurance that degree, proportion, and place would be, or should be, observed in the social and natural order. Human beings occupy the middle position on this ladder or chain, sharing the spiritual potentials of "higher" beings as well as the material limits of the "lower" beings.

Greater Dionysia In ancient Greece, dramas were performed at festivals that honored the god Dionysus: the Lenaea during January and February and the Greater Dionysia in March and April. The best tragedies and comedies were awarded prizes by an Athenian jury.

Griot A storyteller in West Africa who perpetuates the oral traditions of a family or village.

Gupta dynasty The time of the reign of the Gupta emperors (320–550), considered the golden age of classical Indian history. The dynasty, established by Chandragupta I (r. 320–35), disintegrated in the middle of the sixth century. It was during this period that the great poetry of Kalidasa was written.

Gushi In Chinese literature, a verse form that consists of even-numbered, alternately rhymed lines of five syllables each. Referred to as "old-style verse."

Hadith Islamic source of religious law and moral guidance. According to tradition, the Hadith were passed down orally to the prophet Muhammad, and today they are critical to the study of the early development of Islam.

Hajj The pilgrimage to Mecca, Saudi Arabia, one of the five pillars of Islam and the duty of every Muslim at least once in his or her lifetime.

Hamartia A tragic flaw or error that in ancient Greek tragedies leads to the hero's reversal of fortune, known as the *peripeteia*.

Hebrew Scriptures A collection of thirty-nine books sacred to Judaism sometimes called the Hebrew Bible, these writings contain the history, teachings, and literature of the ancient Hebrews and Jews; called the Old Testament by Christians.

Hellene The name for a Greek, dating from the inhabitants of ancient Greece, who took their name from Hellen, the son of the legendary Deucalion and Pyrrha.

Hellenism The language, thought, art, customs, and literature characteristic of classical Greece.

Heroic couplet A rhymed, iambic-pentameter stanza of two lines that completes its thought within the two-line form. Alexander Pope (1688–1744), the most accomplished practitioner of the form in English, included this couplet in his *Essay on Criticism:* "True wit is nature to advantage dressed, / What oft was thought, but ne'er so well expressed."

Heroic poetry Narrative verse that is elevated in mood and uses a dignified, dramatic, and formal style to describe the deeds of aristocratic warriors and rulers. Typically, it was transmitted orally over several generations and written down at a later date. Examples of the form include *The Iliad* and *The Odyssey.*

Hexameter couplets The conventional strophic form of Greek and Latin epic poetry consisting of two dactylic hexameter lines; each line is composed of six feet, and each foot comprises one long (accented) and two short (unaccented) syllables. The final foot is known as a catalectic foot, for it is generally shortened by one or two syllables.

Hieroglyphic writing A writing system using picture symbols to represent sounds, words, or images instead of alphabetical letters. It was used by the ancient Egyptians, Mexicans, and others.

Hieros gamos Literally, "sacred marriage"; a fertility ritual in which the god-king or priest-king is united with the goddess or priestess-queen in order to provide a model for the kingdom and establish the king's right to rule.

Hinduism The major religion of India based on the ancient doctrines found in the SANSKRIT texts known as the VEDAS and the UPANISHADS, dating from 1000 B.C.E.

Historical criticism An approach to literature that uses history as a means of understanding a literary work. Such criticism moves beyond both the facts of an author's life and the text itself to examine the social and intellectual contexts in which the author composed the work.

Homeric Hymns At one time attributed to Homer, the *Homeric Hymns* (seventh through sixth centuries B.C.E.) are now believed to have been created by poets from a Homeric school or simply in the style of Homer. Five of the longer hymns contain important stories about gods such as Demeter, DIONYSUS, Apollo, Aphrodite, and Hermes.

Homo viator Latin for "man the traveler," used by Augustine to signify man's pilgrimage through life toward God.

Hoplite The name used to designate the foot soldiers of ancient Greece.

Hubris Exaggerated pride or arrogance; in Greek tragedies, hubris causes fatal errors.

Huguenots French Protestant members of the Reformed Church established in France by John Calvin in about 1555. Due to religious persecution, many Huguenots fled to other countries in the sixteenth and seventeenth centuries.

Humanism The learning or cultural impulse that flourished during the European Renaissance characterized by a revival of classical letters, an individualistic and critical spirit, and a shift from religious to secular concerns.

Hundred Years' War A series of wars between the English and the French that lasted from 1337 to 1453 in which England lost all of its possessions in France except Calais, also eventually lost in 1565.

Hymn A form of lyric poetry, characterized by solemnity and high religious feeling, intended to be sung in praise of gods or heroic men and women.

Hyperbole A figure of speech; using overstatement or extravagant exaggeration.

Iambic pentameter A poetic line made up of five feet, or iambs, or a ten-syllable line.

Idealism Philosophical Idealism in its various forms holds that objects of perception are in reality mental constructs and not the material objects themselves.

Ideogram A pictorial symbol used in writing that stands for an idea or concept.

Image A verbal representation of a sensory phenomenon—visual, auditory, olfactory, etc. The two types of images are literal and figurative. Literal images are very detailed, almost photographic; figurative images are more abstract and often use symbols.

Imam The leader of prayer in a Muslim mosque; also a title indicating respect for a man of learning.

In medias res Literally, "in the midst of things"; a term used to characterize the beginning of epic poems, which typically start at a crucial point far along in the story. Earlier details are conveyed by means of flashbacks and digressions.

Inquisition A medieval institution established by the Fourth Lateran Council of the Roman Catholic Church, which met in 1215 and was presided over by Pope Innocent III. The Inquisition was formed largely to combat heresy in the aftermath of the Albigensian Crusade in Spain (1209–1229). Punishments included death by burning at the stake and long imprisonment as well as forfeiture of land and property. One of the late and most notorious results of the Inquisition was the trial and execution of Joan of Arc in France in 1456.

Irony A device used in writing and speech to deliberately express ideas so they can be understood in two ways. In drama, irony occurs when a character does not know something that the other characters or the audience knows.

Islam A world religion founded in the seventh century C.E. on the teachings of the prophet Muhammad, whose followers believe that the Qur'an (Koran), the holy book of Islam, contains the revelations of Allah. The Five Pillars of Islam are: to recite the creed, "There is no God but Allah, and Muhammad is his Prophet"; to acknowledge the oneness of Allah in prayer five times each day by reciting the opening verses of the Qur'an; to practice charity and help the needy; to fast in the month of Ramadan; and to make the *hajj,* or pilgrimage to Mecca, at least once in a lifetime if possible. Islam has played a major role in the history of the Middle East and Asia.

Jainism A religion founded in India by Mahavira (d. 469 B.C.E.), a contemporary of the Buddha. In reaction to the rigid and hierarchical structure of traditional Hinduism, Jainism teaches that divinity resides within each individual. Salvation is achieved through the ascetic renunciation of the world and through the practice of *AHIMSA*, nonviolence toward all living beings.

Jen (Ren) As a basic element of CONFUCIANISM, *jen* means "benevolence" or "love for fellow humans"; Mencius (fourth century B.C.E.) argued that all humans are endowed with *jen;* also spelled *ren.*

Jesuits A Roman Catholic religious order founded in 1540 by Ignatius Loyola (1491–1556) under the title the Society of Jesus as part of the wider Counter-Reformation.

Jewish mysticism Like all forms of mysticism, Jewish mysticism focuses on learning and practices that lead to unity with the creator; its teachings are contained in the Cabala (Kabala, Kabbalah).

Jihad From the Arabic *jahada,* meaning "striving," "struggle," or "exertion," this term came to mean a holy war conducted by Muslims against unbelievers or enemies of Islam carried out as a religious duty. After the death of Muhammad in 632, Muslim conquests extended beyond Arabia until early into the next century. *Jihad* also denotes a spiritual struggle for perfection and self-control by practicing Muslims, as well as a struggle for the faith conducted peacefully with unbelievers.

Judgment of Paris In Greek legend, Paris (Alexandros) was selected by the god Zeus to judge which of three goddesses was the most beautiful. He chose Aphrodite, who had bribed him by agreeing to help him seduce Helen, the most beautiful woman in the world. Paris' abduction of Helen and refusal to return her was the cause of the Trojan War.

Ka'ba (ka'bah) The sacred Muslim shrine at Mecca, toward which believers turn when praying.

Kana The portion of the Japanese writing system that represents syllables.

Karma In Hindu and Buddhist philosophy, the totality of a person's actions in any one of the successive states of that person's existence, thought to determine the fate of the next stage. More generally, fate or destiny.

Karma-yoga One of four types of yoga; the practitioner of karma-yoga strives to serve humanity selflessly and without ego, a practice that purifies the heart and prepares the heart and mind for the reception of divine light, or the attainment of knowledge of the self.

Kharja The short, two- or four-line tag ending of an Arabic *muwashshah,* a long, formal beginning to a poem consisting of five or six end-rhymed stanzas. The *Kharja* was often written in MOZARABIC, the spoken language of Andalusia (Spain) that included elements of Arabic, Spanish, and Hebrew. It was often conceived of as a direct, provocative remark made by a servant girl or other uneducated person.

Kshatriya The second highest of the four primary Hindu castes, the military or warrior caste just below the Brahmin class.

Lacunae Spaces where something has been left out; particularly, a gap or missing portion of a text.

Laisses In Medieval poetry, stanzas composed of a variable number of ten-syllable lines; the concluding line of the first stanza is repeated as a refrain at the end of subsequent stanzas.

Lay (Lai) A song or musical interlude; by extension, a poem accompanied by a musical instrument. Marie de France, a popular Anglo-Norman poet of the twelfth century, composed what she called "Breton Lais," short versions of courtly romances suitable for recitation.

Leitmotifs Themes, brief passages, or single words repeated within a work.

Line A sequence of words. In poetry, lines are typically measured by the number of feet they contain.

Lingam The phallic symbol through which Shiva is worshipped in his personification as the creative and reproductive power in the universe.

Literary epic A literary epic—as distinguished from folk epics such as the *Mahabharata* or *The Iliad,* which are made up of somewhat loosely linked episodes and closely follow oral conventions—is written with self-conscious artistry, has a tightly knit organic unity, and is stylistically rooted in a written, literate culture. In actuality, great epics often blur the distinction between the oral or folk epic and the literary epic.

Loa In Spanish and Spanish American drama, a prologue that sets the scene and adumbrates the themes of a play.

Logos In ancient Greece, philosophers such as Aristotle (384–322 B.C.E.) used *logos* to mean reason or thought as opposed to pathos or feeling and emotion. Logos was thought of as the controlling principle of the universe made manifest in speech or rhetoric.

Lushi A highly structured Chinese form of poetry consisting of eight lines of five or seven syllables each. Also referred to as "regulated verse."

Lyric Originally, poetry composed to the accompaniment of a lyre (a stringed musical instrument). By extension, lyric is any poetry that expresses intense personal emotion in a manner suggestive of a song, as opposed to narrative poetry that relates the events of a story. Short poems, often on the subject of love, exist in most of the world's cultures and can fall under the common designation of lyric.

Maat An ancient Egyptian word for the idea of "right order" or justice, the basis of both cosmic order and a civil society. *Maat* was associated with either the sun-god Re or the creator Ptah.

Maghazi Legendary accounts of "the raids of the Prophet" in Islamic literature, examples of which can be found in Ibn Ishaq's *The Biography of the Prophet,* which depicts events of Muhammad's embattled later life.

Mahabharata One of the two great epics of ancient India and the longest poem in world literature, consisting of nearly 100,000 stanzas—more than seven times longer than *The Iliad* and *The Odyssey* combined. Attributed to Vyasa, whose name means the "compiler" or "arranger," the *Mahabharata* was composed between the fifth century B.C.E. and the fourth century C.E.; written in Sanskrit, the epic appeared in its final written form sometime in the fourth century C.E.

Manicheanism A dualistic religion founded by Mani, a Persian philosopher, in the third century C.E. Combining Christian, Buddhist, and Zoroastrian elements, Mani taught that there were two gods, one good and one evil, a school of belief that affected such later church thinkers as Augustine of Hippo, as seen in his *Confessions.*

Manuscript illumination The elaborate illustration of manuscripts (handwritten and handmade books) in the Middle Ages with beautiful images, borders, and letters, embellished with luminous color, especially gold.

Marathi A Sanskritic language of western India spoken by the Marathas, known as the SAMURAI of western India for their defense of Hinduism against the onslaught of the Muslim invaders of India.

Marxist criticism Literary criticism that evolved from Karl Marx's political and economic theories. In the view of Marxist critics, texts must be understood in terms of the social class and the economic and political positions of their characters.

Masque Developed in the Renaissance, masques are highly stylized and structured performances with an often mythological or allegorical plot, combining drama, music, song, and dance in an elaborate display.

Materialism A worldview that explains the nature of reality in terms of physical matter and material conditions rather than by way of ideas, emotions, or the supernatural.

Mathnavi Persian poetic form used for romantic, epic, didactic, and other types of poems whose subjects demand a lengthy treatment; its verse structure is similar to that of the Western heroic couplet, but with two rhyming halves in a single line.

Maurya dynasty The Indian dynasty that existed between 322 and 185 B.C.E. Established by Chandragupta Maurya (r. 322–296 B.C.E.), the dynasty eventually united all of India except for the extreme south under one imperial power. During this period trade flourished, agriculture was regulated, weights and measures were standardized, and money first came into use.

Maya From the Sanskrit for "deception" or "illusion," *maya* is the veil drawn over the ultimate, eternal reality of BRAHMAN and therefore represents the phenomenal world of appearances that humans misinterpret as the only reality.

Me According to Sumerian philosophers, the *me* were the divine laws and rules that governed the universe as well as the cultural elements, like metalworking and the arts, that constituted urban life. In Sumerian mythology, the *me* are the gift of the goddess Inanna to humankind.

Medieval Romances See CHIVALRIC ROMANCES.

Menippian satire Named for its originator, the Greek Cynic philosopher Menippus (first half of the third century B.C.E.), Menippian satire uses a mixture of prose, dialogue, and verse to make ludicrous a whole social class or a broad spectrum of social types. The form is sometimes called an "anatomy" because it catalogs the many social and intellectual types who constitute the social group it satirizes.

Mestizos Peoples in the Americas of mixed ethnic or cultural heritage, usually a combination of Spanish and Native American.

Metaphor A comparison of two things that does not use the words *like* or *as.* For example, "love is a rose."

Metaphysical poetry Poetry written primarily in seventeenth-century England that has as its focus the analysis of feeling. Its chief characteristics are complexity and subtlety of thought, frequent use of paradox, often deliberate harshness or rigidity of expression, and the use of bold and ingenious conceits—sometimes forced comparisons of unlike ideas or things that startle the reader into a closer analysis of the argument of the poem. John Donne and Andrew Marvell are known as metaphysical poets; the term is sometimes also used with other poetry of this type.

Meter The RHYTHM of a poem based on the number of syllables in each line and which syllables are accented. See also FOOT.

Middle Ages A term applied specifically to Europe, dating from the decline of the Roman Empire in the fourth to sixth centuries to the revival of learning and the arts in the Early Modern or Renaissance period in the late fourteenth and fifteenth centuries.

Millenarianism A utopian belief that the end of time is imminent, after which there will be a thousand-year era of perfect peace on earth.

Ming dynasty (1368–1644) Founded by Zhu Yuanzhang, who restored native Chinese rule from the Mongols who had ruled China during the previous Yuan dynasty (1271–1368) established by Kubla Khan. The Ming dynasty saw a flourishing of Chinese culture, the restoration of CONFUCIANISM, and the rise of the arts, including porcelain, architecture, drama, and the novel.

Miyabi A Japanese term denoting a delicate taste for the beautiful—a refined sensibility for subtle nuances of style and form in art, literature, and social conduct.

Moira In Greek mythology, the deity who assigns to every person his or her lot.

Moksha In the Hindu tradition, the *moksha* is the highest goal for all humans; it means the final liberation from all earthly, material existence and complete union with God or the ultimate reality.

Monism A unitary conception of the world in which everything that is—the whole of reality—constitutes an inseparable self-inclusive whole, as opposed to dualism, which sees reality as made up of opposing elements, such as mind and matter, and good and evil.

Monogatari Loosely translated from the Japanese as "tale" or the "telling of things," *monogatari* refers to the genre of fiction; as in the case of *NIKKI*, *monogatari* were written in KANA and often contained poetic passages in the form of *WAKA*. Lady Murasaki's *The Tale of Genji* is perhaps the greatest example of the *monogatari* in Japanese literature.

Monologue A speech of significant length delivered by one person; in drama, speech in which a CHARACTER talks to himself or herself or reveals personal secrets without addressing another character.

Monotheism The doctrine or belief that there is only one deity or God, such as Allah or Yaweh, as opposed to the polytheistic religions of ancient Greece and Rome that involved the worship of numerous gods.

Mozarabic Pertaining to Spanish Christians and Jews who were permitted to practice their religions during the period of Muslim rule in Andalusia. Also refers to the vernacular language spoken in Andalusia, a combination of Arabic, Christian, and Hebrew elements.

Mullah (Mulla) A Muslim teacher or interpreter of Muslim religious law; the more current usage is as a general title of respect for a learned person.

Muse In ancient Greek mythology, any of the nine daughters of Zeus who presided over the arts; current usage denotes a muse as the spirit that inspires a poet or artist to create.

Muwashshah A conventional Andalusian love poem, usually written in Arabic but occasionally in Hebrew, consisting of five or six end-rhymed stanzas followed by a brief "tag" ending called a *KHARJA*, usually written in MOZARABIC.

Mystery religions Mystery cults were very popular in ancient Greece and Rome for at least one thousand years, beginning around 1000 B.C.E. The details of each cult were kept a secret, but all cults shared a rigorous rite of initiation, a concern about death, and a hope for immortality centered on a deity who had personal knowledge of the afterlife. The most popular Greek versions were the Orphic and Eleusinian mysteries. The mysteries of Isis and Mithra were favored in the Roman world.

Mysticism The belief that communion with God can be achieved intuitively through contemplation and meditation on the divine spirit akin to an act of faith rather than through the intellect.

Mythological criticism A type of literary criticism that focuses on the archetypal stories common to all cultures. Initiated by Carl Jung in the early twentieth century, mythological criticism seeks to reveal how the psychological impulses and patterns lodged deep in human consciousness take the form of ARCHETYPAL stories and are the basis for literature.

Narrative poem A poem that tells a story. Ballads, epics, and romances are typically narrative poems.

Narrator The voice that in fiction describes the PLOT or action of a story. The narrator can speak in the first, second, or third person and, depending on the effect the author wishes to create, can be very visible or almost invisible (an explicit or an implicit narrator); he or she also can be involved in the action or be removed from it. See also POINT OF VIEW and SPEAKER.

Nasib The prelude or introductory stanzas of a *qasidah,* the Arabic lyric form comparable to the ode.

Nataka In Sanskrit drama, the heroic romance with an idealized warrior king as its central figure and a comic story concentrating on heroic and erotic themes.

Necropolis Literally meaning "city of the dead," *necropolis* was the name given to a cemetery in the ancient world.

Neo-Confucianism Refers generally to the philosophical tradition in China and Japan based on the thought of Confucius (Kongfuzi, 551–479 B.C.E.) and his commentators, particularly Mencius (Mengzi, 370–290 B.C.E.) and Zhu Xi (Chu Hi, 1130–1200). Neo-Confucianism, which arose during the Sung dynasty (960–1279), asserts that an understanding of things must be based on their underlying principles; in moral and political philosophy, it emphasizes the study of history, loyalty to family and nation, and order.

Neoplatonism Considered the last great Greek philosophy, Neoplatonism was developed by Plotnus (204–270 C.E.), based on his reading of the works of Plato. This school of philosophy espouses a single source from which all forms of existence emanate and with which the soul seeks a mystical union.

New Criticism A type of formalist literary criticism that disregards historical and biographical information to focus on the text. The New Critics perform a close reading of a work and give special attention to technical devices such as irony and ambiguity.

New Historicism A school of literary criticism developed in the 1980s in part as a reaction to NEW CRITICISM and other formalist methods of literary analysis. In contrast to formalism, which focuses strictly on internal relations of form and structure in a text, New Historicism emphasizes the relation of the text to its historical and cultural contexts. New Historicists make a self-conscious attempt to place their own critical practice within the political and historical framework of their own time, and align the language, rhetorical strategies, and other features of the texts they study with those of works not usually considered literary.

New Testament The sacred writings of Christianity, which tell the life of Jesus in the Gospels, the history of the establishment of the early church in Paul's Epistles, and the prophesy of the ultimate fulfillment of Christian history in the Revelation of St. John the Divine. From the Christian perspective, the New Testament fulfills the prophesies of the Hebrew Scriptures, known to Christians as the Old Testament.

Nikki An important genre of Japanese literature, the prose diary, which flourished among women writers in the Heian period; these diaries were written primarily in KANA, the woman's form of writing, which formed the basis of the vernacular literary tradition in Japan, and, like *The Tale of Genji,* contained poetic passages in the form of WAKA.

Nirgun In Indian devotional tradition, or *glakti,* the idea that God is transcendent, having no physical or material attributes.

Nirvana In Buddhism, the state of perfect blessedness achieved by the extinction of individual existence and absorption of the soul into the supreme spirit, or by the extinction of all earthly passions and desires.

Nō The highly elaborate and ritualistic classical theater of Japan, known for its minimalist approach to plot, scenery, and stage effects and the stately performance and Zen-like mastery of its actors; *Nō* means "talent" or "accomplishment."

Novel An extended work of fictional prose narrative. The novel is a modern outgrowth of earlier genres such as the romance. There is considerable debate as to the origins of the novel; some critics trace it to Cervantes' *Don Quixote* (1605), others to Lady Murasaki's *The Tale of Genji* (c. 1022).

Octave A STANZA of eight lines in poetry.

Ode An elevated form of LYRIC generally written on a single theme, using varied metric and rhyme patterns. With the ode, poets working within classical schemes can introduce considerable innovation. There are three major types of odes in English: the Pindaric, or Regular; the Horatian; and the Irregular. The Pindaric ode is structured by three-strophe divisions, modulating between the strophe, antistrophe, and epode, which vary in tone. The Horatian ode uses only one STANZA type; variation is introduced within each stanza. The Irregular ode, sometimes called the English ode, allows wide variety among stanza forms, rhyme schemes, and metrical patterns. Related forms adopted by particular cultures include the Arabic *QASIDAH* as practiced by the pre-Muslim poet Imru al-Qays, and the ancient Japanese *CHOKA* as practiced by Kakinomoto Hitomaro.

Oedipus complex Sigmund Freud's conception of the unconscious male desire to kill one's own father and sleep with one's own mother. The term derives from the Greek myth of Oedipus, who unknowingly murdered his father and married his mother; his self-inflicted punishment was to blind himself. FREUDIAN CRITICS do not take the complex or the story literally, but frequently use the concept to examine in literature the guilt associated with sexual desire and with competition with or hostility toward one's father.

Onomatopoeia The quality of a word that sounds like the thing it refers to: for example, the *buzz* of bees.

Open form Also known as *free verse.* A type of poetry that does not follow established conventions of METER, RHYME, and STANZA.

Opera A musical drama in which the dialogue is sung to orchestral accompaniment. As a form, it has its origins in the liturgical drama of the Middle Ages. In sixteenth-century Italy, opera rose to grand musical productions marked by elaborate costuming, scenery, and choreography.

Organic form The concept that the structure of a literary work develops according to an internal logic. The literary work grows and becomes an organic whole that follows the principles of nature, not mechanics. The created work of art is akin to a growing plant that relies on all of its parts working together.

Ottava rima Italian stanza form composed of eleven-syllable lines, rhyming *ab ab ab cc* that originated in the late thirteenth and early fourteenth centuries in Italy. The early master of the form was Giovanni Boccaccio (1313–1375), who established it as the standard form for epic and narrative verse in his time, but later poets continued to make use of it.

Oxymoron A rhetorical figure of speech in which contradictory terms are combined, such as *jumbo shrimp* and *deafening silence.*

Panegyric An oration or eulogy in praise of some person or achievement. Primarily associated with classical antiquity, panegyrics continued to be written through the Middle Ages and Renaissance, especially in Elizabethan England, the Spanish Golden Age, and in France under Louis XIV.

Pantheism Literally, "God everywhere," the belief that God is immanent throughout the universe—that God is manifest in all things.

Pantheon Generally, all the deities of a particular religion considered collectively; also, a temple dedicated to all the gods; specifically, the temple built in Rome by Agrippa in 27 C.E. and rebuilt by Hadrian in the second century C.E.

Paraphrase To rewrite or say the same thing using different words.

Parataxis Literally, "placing one thing after another." The term refers to linear narrative, often employed in storytelling, consisting of a series of sentences or clauses joined by a coordinator (that happened . . . , then this happened . . .).

Parody A humorous imitation of another, usually serious, work. Parody can be a form of literary criticism that exposes defects in a work, or it can function as an acknowledgement of a work's cultural and literary importance.

Pastoral poetry A poem or a play dealing with the lives of shepherds or rural life in general and usually depicting shepherds as representative of a simple life of innocence and serenity as opposed to the misery and corruption of city or court life. An early example of the form is Virgil's *Eclogues,* which greatly influenced the Renaissance work of such writers as Dante, Petrarch, Boccaccio, and Shakespeare.

Patois A regional dialect of a language.

Patrician Originally, the hereditary aristocracy and nobility of ancient Rome. Later the term referred to any person who by birth or special compensation belonged to the nobility. More current usage denotes a person of high birth or a person of refined upbringing and manners.

Pax Romana Literally meaning "Roman peace," this is the long period of comparative peace enforced on states in the Roman Empire between the years 27 B.C.E. and 180 C.E.

People of the Book (Dhimmi) The Muslim name for Jews and Christians, followers of the teachings of the prophets of Hebrew Scriptures and the New Testament. Under normal conditions Islamic authorities granted Jews and Christians religious tolerance.

Peloponnesian War (431–404 B.C.E.) War between the Athenian and Spartan alliance systems that encompassed most of the Greek world. The war set new standards for warfare—Athens used its navy to support the land offensive, for instance—but the new tactics also prolonged the fighting; instead of there being one decisive battle, the war dragged on for three decades. Eventually, Athens was defeated, and Sparta took over the defeated power's overseas empire.

Peripeteia (Peripety) A character's reversal of fortune in the denouement of a plot. In tragedy, it means the hero's destruction, in comedy his or her happy resolution.

Persian Wars A series of wars between a coalition of Greek city-states and the Persian empire fought between 500 and 449 B.C.E.; the Greek victory set the stage for the flourishing of Greek culture.

Persona Literally, persona means "mask." In literature, a persona is a speaker created by a writer to tell a story or to speak in a poem. A persona is not a character in a story or narrative, nor does it necessarily directly reflect the author's personal voice.

Personification A figure of speech in which abstractions or inanimate objects are given human qualities or form.

Petrarchan conceit From *concept* or *conception,* this was an originally novel form of metaphor in which the speaker of a poem compared his or her beloved to something else, such as a doe, a rose, a summer's day, or even a newly discovered land. Originating with the Italian poet Petrarch, the freshness of this device soon wore off and the Petrarchan conceit became a stale convention, revitalized by only the most ingenious poets.

Petrarchan sonnet A fourteen-line lyric poem. The Petrarchan SONNET was the first basic sonnet form. It is divided into an eight-line octet and a six-line sestet, each with a specific but varied pattern of rhymes, for example *ab ba cd ec de.*

Philistines A powerful non-Semitic tribe that in biblical times inhabited the tract of land between Judea and Egypt; in almost perpetual war with the Israelites, they were ultimately conquered by the Romans.

Phonogram A letter, character, or mark used to represent a sound.

Picaresque A novel loosely structured around an episodic succession of adventures of a rogue hero—a *picaro*—who is on an aimless journey.

The picaresque tale often provides a sweeping and satiric view of society and its customs. Examples include Petronius's *The Satyricon* and Voltaire's *Candide.*

Pictograh A picture used to represent an idea; hieroglyphics are pictographs.

Pieta A representation in painting or sculpture of the Virgin Mary mourning over the dead body of Jesus after the Crucifixion.

Pietas In ancient Roman Stoic philosophy, *pietas* is respect for authority.

Platonic Characteristic of the philosophy of Plato, essentially connoting idealistic or visionary outlooks.

Platonic love A pure, spiritual love between a man and a woman that is based on intellectual appreciation of the other person and is unmixed with sexual desire.

Platonist One who adheres to the philosophy of Plato, especially the doctrine that holds that things exist only as ideas in the mind rather than as material objects independent of the mind.

Plebeians Members of the ancient Roman lower class or common people, as opposed to PATRICIANS.

Plot The pattern of events told in a narrative or drama. Plot has a causal sequence and a unifying theme, in contrast to story, which is the simple narrative of the action.

Point of view The perspective from which the author, SPEAKER, OR NARRATOR presents a story. A point of view might be localized within a CHARACTER, in which case the story is told from a first-person point of view. There is a range of possibilities between first-person point of view and omniscience, wherein a story is told from a perspective unlimited by time, place, or character.

Polis Greek term meaning "city"; designates the Greek city-states, such as Athens and Sparta, that arose in the sixth century B.C.E.

Polytheism The belief in or worship of many gods as opposed to monotheism, which is the doctrine or worship of a single god.

Pragmatism A philosophical approach that evaluates ideas and beliefs in terms of their usefulness and applicability to practical action.

Prologue Text that typically is placed prior to an introduction or that replaces a traditional introduction; often discusses events of importance for the general understanding of the work. See also LOA.

Protagonist A leading figure or the main character in a drama or other literary work.

Protestant Reformation See REFORMATION.

Psychological criticism An approach to literature that draws on psychoanalytic theories, especially those of Sigmund Freud (1856–1939) and Jacques Lacan (1901–1981), to understand more fully a text, its writer, and readers.

Pun A play on words that relies on a word's having more than one meaning or sounding like another word.

Punic Wars The series of wars between Rome and Carthage during the third and second centuries B.C.E.—the first taking place between 264 and 241 B.C.E., the second between 218 and 201, and the third between 149 and 146—which the Romans ultimately won.

Purdah Practice adopted by some Muslims and Hindus that obscures women from public sight by mandating that they wear concealing clothing, especially veils. The custom originated in the seventh century C.E. and is still common in Islamic countries, though it has largely disappeared in Hinduism.

Purim A Jewish holiday, also known as the Feast of Lots, celebrating the deliverance of the Jews by Esther from the planned massacre plotted by Haman.

Qasidah An Arabic form of lyric poetry, comparable to the ode, originally composed orally and consisting of several dozen to some sixty rhymed couplets, expressing reflection and sentiment while evoking scenes of desert life, romantic memories, and a tone of despair or self-glorification. Later literary versions of the *qasidah* often lost their desert setting but retained their reflective, romantic character.

Quatrain A stanza of four lines in a poem.

Quetzalcoatl The most important god of Mesoamerica, whose name means Plumed Serpent or Precious Twin. As a god, he was instrumental in creating the four previous worlds; as a hero-ruler of Tollan, he assumed the mantle of the priesthood of Quetzalcoatl, fell from grace, and delivered a messianic promise to return home.

Quietism Scholars use this term to characterize thinkers in the fourth century B.C.E. who advocated withdrawal from the turbulence of society and concentration on inner peace and harmony.

Quixotic Like Don Quixote, or having the characteristics of being romantic in the extreme, absurdly chivalrous, or foolishly idealistic.

Qur'an The sacred writings of Islam revealed by Allah to the prophet Muhammad.

Rahil That part of a QASIDAH's (or ode's) structure in Persian poetry—the "disengagement"—that tells of a solitary journey on horseback or camelback, or more metaphorically, of the separation of the poet from the source of his sorrowful memory.

Rasa Indian dramatic theory identifies eight *rasas* (aesthetic emotions) that can focus a drama: the erotic, the heroic, the disquieting, the furious, the comic, the marvelous, the horrible, and the pathetic. Only two are appropriate for the *NATAKA* form, the erotic and the heroic.

Reader-response criticism A critical approach to literature in which the primary focus falls on the reader or the process of reading, not on the author. Reader-response critics believe that a literary work does not possess a fixed idea or meaning; meaning is a function of the perspective of the reader.

Realism Most broadly defined, realism is the attempt to represent the world accurately in literature. As a literary movement, Realism flourished in Russia, France, England, and America in the latter half of the nineteenth century. It emphasized not only accurate representation but the "truth," usually expressed as the consequence of a moral choice. Realist writers deemphasized the shaping power of the imagination and concerned themselves with the experiences of ordinary, middle-class subjects and the dilemmas they faced.

Realpolitik Foreign policy based on practical political expediency rather than moral or ideological considerations.

Recognition Based on the Greek concept of tragedy, recognition, or ANAGNORISIS, is the point in a story when the PROTAGONIST discovers the truth about his or her situation. Usually this results in a drastic change in the course of the plot.

Reformation Also known as the Protestant Reformation, this sixteenth-century challenge to the authority of the Catholic Church caused a permanent rift in the Christian world, with those loyal to the pope remaining Catholic and those rejecting papal authority forming new Protestant faiths such as the Anglican, Lutheran, Calvinist, Anabaptist, and Presbyterian. The Reformation originated—and was most successful—in Northern Europe, especially Germany; its notable leaders include Martin Luther and John Calvin.

Renaissance The revival of art, literature, and learning in Europe in the fourteenth, fifteenth, and sixteenth centuries based on classical Greek and Roman sources. The movement began in Italy, spread throughout Europe, and marked the transition from the medieval to the modern Western world.

Renaissance man A term used to describe someone accomplished in many disciplines, especially in both science and the arts, like Leonardo da Vinci and other figures of the European Renaissance.

Resolution The point in the plot of a narrative work or drama that occurs after the climax and generally establishes a new understanding; also known as *falling action*.

Reversal The point in the plot of a story or drama when the fortunes of the PROTAGONIST change unexpectedly; also known as the *PERIPITEIA*.

Rhyme The repetition of identical or similar-sounding words or syllables, usually accented, in lines of poetry. Rhymes may occur within or at the end of lines.

Rhythm The pattern of stressed and unstressed syllables in prose and especially in poetry that can lend emphasis, reinforce a sound association, or suggest regularity or recurrence. The rhythm of a literary work can affect the emotional response of the reader or listener.

Rishi (Ṛṣi) Sanskrit for sage or holy man.

Romance A medieval tale based on heroic conduct, adventure, or chivalric love, sometimes in a supernatural setting. Medieval romances were composed in France in the twelfth century, spreading to Germany, Spain, England, and other countries in the next several centuries. Later, in the seventeenth century, the romance form was parodied in Miguel de Cervantes' literary masterpiece, *Don Quixote.*

Romantic hero The PROTAGONIST of a romance, novel, or poem who is shaped by experiences that frequently take the form of combat, love, or adventure. The Romantic hero is judged by his actions more than his thoughts, and he is often on a journey that will affect his moral development.

Ruba'i (plural, Ruba'iyat) Equivalent to the quatrain in Western poetry, a *ruba'i* is a very intricate Persian poetic line structure consisting of four lines of equal length, divided into half lines, with the first, second, and fourth lines rhyming.

St. Francis (c. 1181–1226) Founder of the Franciscan religious order, beloved for his gentleness and humility. An account of his life and teachings, *The Little Flowers of Saint Francis,* was published in the century after his death.

Samsara A Hindu term for the cycle of birth, life, death, and rebirth; many Hindu practices are aimed at obtaining release, or *moksha,* from the otherwise endless repetition of life and death.

Samurai Japanese feudal aristocrat and member of the hereditary warrior class. Denied recognition during the Meiji period (1867–1912).

Sangha The Sanskrit word for a fraternity or association often formed out of spiritual or learning communities.

Sanskrit The classical language of ancient India, in which many of the major Hindu religious and literary texts were written.

Satire A literary or dramatic genre whose works, such as Petronius's *Satyricon* and Jonathan Swift's (1667–1745) *Gulliver's Travels,* ridicule human behavior.

Satyr In classical mythology, a minor woodland deity represented as part man and part goat whose chief characteristics are riotous merriment and lasciviousness.

Scansion A system of poetic analysis that involves dividing lines into feet and examining patterns of stressed and unstressed syllables. Scansion is a mechanical way of breaking down verse in order to understand the regularities and irregularities of its METER.

Scene In drama, a subdivision of an ACT.

Scholasticism The dominant philosophical system of the twelfth to fourteenth centuries in Europe, based on the writings of Aristotle and his commentators, including Avicenna (Ibn Sina) and Averroes (Ibn Rushdi). The great Christian Scholastic philosopher, St. Thomas Aquinas, completed his *Summa Theologica* in 1273.

Script The written version or text of a play or movie that is used by the actors.

Sentimentality Extravagant emotion; T. S. Eliot defined this as "emotion in excess of the facts."

Septuagint A Greek version of the Hebrew Scriptures (Old Testament), so called because the ancient tradition was that it was completed in seventy or seventy-two days by seventy-two Palestinian Jews, for Ptolemy II of Egypt.

Sestet A STANZA of six lines; the last stanza of a Petrarchan SONNET is a sestet.

Setting The time, place, and social environment in a narrative or a drama.

Shastra A treatise for authoritative instruction among the Hindu, especially a treatise explaining the VEDAS.

Shi In China, the term used to designate poetry in general.

Shi'ite One of the two great branches of the Muslim faith. Shi'ites insisted on a strict line of family succession from Muhammad and rejected interpretations of Islam construed after the death of Muhammad. They soon were considered heretical by the majority branch, Sunnite (Sunna) Muslims. Present-day Shi'ites primarily occupy Iran and southern Iraq.

Shintoism The indigenous polytheistic religion of Japan, the beliefs of which stress the worship of nature, ancestors, and ancient heroes, and the divinity of the emperor.

Shite The PROTAGONIST or main character in a Japanese *Nō* play.

Shiva (Śiva) The Hindu god of destruction and creation and a member of the supreme Hindu trinity of Shiva, Brahma, and Vishnu.

Shogun A military ruler of feudal Japan between 1192 and 1867. The shogunate was an inherited position in the military that operated under the nominal control of the emperor.

Sikhism The beliefs of those who belong to the Hindu religious sect founded in northern India around 1500 C.E., based on a belief in one God and on a rejection of the caste system and idolatry.

Simile A figure of speech, introduced by *like* or *as*, in which two things are compared as equals.

Smirti (Smṛti) One of the two major classifications of Hindu sacred texts. *Smirti,* which means "memory," comprises Hindu texts other than the VEDAS, which are considered SRUTI, or revealed (heard) texts. *Smirti* may be thought of as a secondary category of sacred literature that includes the Sutras, the Puranas, and the Indian epics the *Ramayana* and the *Mahabharata.*

Sociological criticism School of literary criticism that seeks to place a work of art in its social context and define the relationship between the two. Like Marxist critics, sociological critics are oriented toward social class, political ideology, gender roles, and economic conditions in their analyses.

Soliloquy A dramatic speech in which a character speaks his or her inner thoughts aloud before the audience.

Sonnet A fourteen-line lyric poem. The first basic sonnet form is the Italian or Petrarchan sonnet, which is divided into an eight-line octet and a six-line SESTET (see PETRARCHAN SONNET). The English or Shakespearean sonnet is divided into three four-line QUATRAINS followed by a two-line couplet; the quatrains are rhymed *abab cdcd efef* and the couplet is also end-rhymed, *gg.*

Sophists Literally, "wise men." Greek teachers who provided instruction in logic and rhetoric to pupils who could afford their expensive fees. Rhetoric was a new discipline whose study was observed to provide an advantage in politics and in the courts. *Sophist* came to mean one who used argumentation to undermine traditional beliefs.

Speaker The person or PERSONA who speaks in a poem, often a created identity who cannot be equated with the poet.

Spiritual autobiography An autobiography that gives special importance to self-examination, interpretation of Scripture, and belief in predestination. St. Augustine's *Confessions* (c. 400), detailing a life of sin, conversion, and spiritual rebirth, is generally regarded as the archetypal spiritual autobiography.

Sprezzatura An Italian term that has no equivalent in English, *sprezzatura* suggests a quality of perfect composure and nonchalance, the ability to act with studied artifice while giving the appearance of effortless spontaneity.

Sruti One of the two major classifications of Hindu sacred texts. *Sruti,* which means "hearing," is reserved for the primary sacred texts of Hinduism, the VEDAS, including the Smahtas, the Brahmanas, and the Aranyakas, the most important of which is the UPANISHADS.

Stage directions Written directions explaining how actors are to move onstage. See also SCRIPT.

Stanza A poetic verse of two or more lines, sometimes characterized by a common pattern of RHYME and METER.

Stock responses Predictable responses to language and symbols. See also CLICHÉ.

Stoicism A school of thought founded by the Greek philosopher Zeno c. 308 B.C.E. Stoicism advocated the view that virtue is the ultimate goal of life and that the virtuous seek happiness within by overcoming their passions and emotions while remaining independent of the external natural world, which follows immutable laws.

Stress A syllable receiving emphasis in accordance with a metrical pattern.

Style The distinctive manner in which an author writes and thus makes his or her work unique. A style provides a kind of literary signature for the writer.

Subplot A PLOT subordinate to the main plot of a literary work or drama.

Sufism A devotional movement among certain Muslims emphasizing the union of the devotee with God through ritual and ascetic practices, who hold to a kind of PANTHEISM and practice extreme asceticism in their lives.

Suspense The anxious emotion of an audience or reader anticipating the outcome of a story or drama, typically having to do with the fate of the PROTAGONIST or another character with whom a sympathetic attachment has been formed.

Symbol A representative of something by association. Though a symbol is often confused with a metaphor, a metaphor compares two dissimilar things while a symbol associates two things. For example, the *word* "tree" is a symbol for an *actual* tree. Some symbols have values that are accepted by most people. A flag, for instance, is for many a symbol of national pride, just as a cross is widely seen as a symbol of Christianity. Knowledge of a symbol's cultural context is sometimes necessary to understand its meaning; an apple pie is an American symbol of innocence that a Japanese person, for example, would not necessarily recognize.

Syncretism Combining disparate philosophical or religious beliefs, such as the blending of Christianity or Islam with indigenous religions.

Synoptic Gospels The first three gospels of the New Testament, which give a similar account of the life, death, and Resurrection of Jesus.

Syntax The way parts of speech are arranged in a sentence.

TANAK An acronym used to describe three groupings in Hebrew Scriptures: the Torah (Pentateuch, or first five books), the Nebi'im, (the Prophets), and Ketubim (the Writings); also spelled TENACH.

Tanka A Japanese verse form of thirty-one syllables in five unrhymed lines, the first and third having five syllables each, the second, fourth, and fifth having seven. See also *WAKA*.

Tantrism A minor Hindu tradition written down in scriptures called Tantras. Tantrism holds the supreme deity to be feminine and teaches that spiritual liberation can be won through erotic practices.

Taoism See DAOISM.

Tathagata An epithet for the Buddha that means "thus gone," having attained enlightenment.

Tercets A unit or group of three lines of verse, usually rhymed.

Terza rima A verse form composed of iambic three-line stanzas, with lines of ten or eleven syllables. Terza rima employed most brilliantly in Dante's (1265–1321) *Divine Comedy*.

Tetragrammaton The four consonants of the Hebrew alphabet, YHWH, used to approximate God's secret name; this name and its utterances are believed to contain special powers.

Tezcatlipoca In Aztec mythology, he was the warrior god of the north and the god of sin and misery with an obsidian knife. In Toltec mythology, he was also the brother and/or antithesis of Quetzalcoatl.

Thanatos "Death" in Greek. According to Sigmund Freud, our two primary drives are Eros (love) and Thanatos (death).

Theme A topic of discussion or a point of view embodied in a work of art.

Theocracy Government of the state by God or a god as represented by a person or persons claiming to have divine authority.

Tolkappiyam The formal grammar developed in literary assemblies in and around the Indian city of Madurai between 100 and 250 C.E. created to classify aspects of Tamil poetry.

Tone A manner of expression in writing that indicates a certain attitude toward the subject or the implied audience.

Tour de force A masterly or brilliant creation, production, or performance; the phrase translates literally from the original French as "feat of strength."

Tragedy A dramatic or literary form originating in Greece that deals with serious human actions and issues. The actions are meant to create feelings of fear and compassion in the spectator that are later released (CATHARSIS). Typically, the main character is of a high stature or rank, so his or her fall is substantial. Even though tragedies are sad, they seem both just and believable. The tragedy raises serious moral and philosophical questions about the meaning of life and fate.

Tragicomedy A drama that combines tragedy and comedy and in which moral values are particularly questioned or ridiculed.

Travel narratives Also known as travel literature, a form of narrative that recounts the incidents that occur and the people and things that the narrator meets and sees while visiting a place with which she or he is typically unfamiliar. Prose and poetic accounts about exploration and adventure in unfamiliar lands and places as well as in more or less familiar locations are considered travel narratives. Examples of the genre include the travels of Marco Polo and the travels of Ibn Battuta.

Triplet In poetry, a group of three rhyming lines of verse.

Trobairitz Female troubadours, both members of the nobility and independent artists. See TROUBADOURS.

Troubadours Lyric poets and composers, sometimes of aristocratic rank but more often artists attached to regional courts, who flourished in the south of France in the twelfth and thirteenth centuries. Their compositions in the Provencal language centered on the subject of love. Their work derived in part from Arabic sources in Andalusia, and their influence spread throughout Europe in the thirteenth and fourteenth centuries.

Umrah Known as the "lesser pilgrimage"; in contrast to the *hajj*, which must be performed in the last month of the Islamic calendar year, *umrah* is a pilgrimage to Mecca that can be undertaken at any time.

Understatement A figure of speech that says less than what is intended. In Anglo-Saxon poetry, a special form of understatement known as the litote is an ironic form of address in which the full importance of something is concealed in order to force the listener to discover it by paying close attention.

Upanishads A body of sacred texts dating from the ninth century B.C.E. that provide a mystical development of and commentary on earlier VEDIC texts.

Urdu An Indo-European language closely related to Hindi. Urdu is the official language of Pakistan and is also spoken in India and Bangladesh.

Utopia In literature, a romance or other work describing an ideal place whose inhabitants live under seemingly perfect conditions. Though the term did not exist until coined by Sir Thomas More in 1516, earlier works such as Plato's *Republic* and Bacon's *New Atlantis* can be termed utopias due to the societies they depict.

Vandals Fierce warriors from near the Russian steppes who invaded Roman Gaul (France) in the fifth century C.E. and advanced through Spain to North Africa. They were notorious for their destruction of cities.

Varna Sanskrit word for "color" used in the sense of "class" to indicate the four classes or castes of Hinduism in India.

Vedas The earliest Indian sacred texts, written in Sanskrit, dating from sometime between 1000 and 500 B.C.E.; they contain hymns and ritual lore considered to be revelation, or SRUTI.

Vedic The Old Indic language of the VEDAS, it was an early form of Sanskrit.

Vernacular fiction Fiction that attempts to capture accurately the typical speech, mannerisms, or dialect of a region. The *Satyricon* of the Roman author Petronius is often considered the first work of vernacular fiction.

Waka Traditional Japanese poetry based on Chinese models that rose to prominence in the Heian Period (794–1195). The *waka* is a short five-line lyric consisting of thirty-one syllables with 5-7-5-7-7 syllables to a line. Writing *waka* was an important activity of the Heian aristocracy as well as their court followers. The poetry anthology *Kokinshu* (c. 905) is the most celebrated collection of *waka.* Now generally called *tanka,* these poems are still written today.

Waki Refers to the secondary PROTAGONIST or antagonist in Japanese *Nō* plays; the primary character is known as the shite.

Xiaopin A Chinese form of autobiographical essay that became an important medium in China in the late sixteenth century.

Yahweh A form of the Hebrew name for God in the Hebrew Scriptures.

Yin and yang A pair of opposites derived from a dualistic system of ancient Chinese philosophy; symbolically representing the sun and the moon, *yang* is positive, active, and strong, while *yin* is negative, passive, and weak. All things in the universe are formed from the dynamic interaction of these forces.

Yoni A representation of the vulva, a symbol used in the worship of the goddess Shakti in Hiduism.

Yuefu Chinese folk ballads that, during the Han dynasty, evolved into literary ballads written in quatrains of five-word lines. The ballad typically presented a monologue of dialogue presenting, in dramatic form, some misfortune.

Yugen From the Japanese meaning mystery or profound beauty, *yugen* refers to the aura of spiritual depth and beauty that is the aim of *Nō* drama.

Zajal One of two poetic forms that came to dominate the performance of the GHAZAL, or love poem, which consisted of elaborately rhymed strophes or stanzas in MOZARABIC, without the KHARJA ending.

Zen prominent school of Buddhism that seeks to reveal the essence of the enlightened mind. Zen teaches that everyone has the potential to attain enlightenment but that most are unaware of this potential because they are ignorant. The way to attain enlightenment is through transcending the boundaries of common thought, and the method of study is most frequently the intense, personal instruction of a student by a Zen master.

Zhong Guo The translation of the Chinese characters for "Middle Kingdom," which denotes what today is translated as China.

Ziggurat A temple tower of the ancient Akkadians and Babylonians in the form of a terraced pyramid with each story smaller than the one below it.

Zoroastrianism A dualistic religion founded in ancient Persia by Zoroaster (c. 12th century–7th century B.C.E.). It teaches that two powerful forces—light and darkness, good and evil—are engaged in a struggle that will eventually erupt into a cataclysmic war in which good will prevail, leading to the destruction of the earth.

Zuihitsu Japanese for "following the brush" and translated as "occasional writing" or "essays," *zuihitsu* denotes a genre of Japanese writing mixing poetry and prose that arose primarily among women writers during the Heian Period. Sei Shonagon's *Pillow Book* is an example of *zuihitsu.*

Acknowledgments (continued from p. ii)

Abd al-Qadir Bada'uni, ["Akbar in the Company of Learned Men"] from *Selected Histories (Muntakhab Ut-Tawarikh),* translated by Peter Hardy, revised by Christopher Brunner and David Lelyveld, from *Sources of Indian Tradition,* compiled by William Theodore de Bary et al. Copyright © 1958 by Columbia University Press. Reprinted with the permission of the publisher.

Basavanna, #212 "You Can't Just Do / This Thing Called Bhakti," #251 "Melt My mind, O Lord," #486 "Feet Will Dance," #586 "What of It That You Have Read So Much?," #686 "He'll Grind You into Tiny Shape," and #911 "Mother, / What News Shall I Tell," translated by K. V. Zvelebi from *The Lord of the Meeting Rivers: Devotional Poems of Basavanna,* translated by K. V. Zvelebil. Reprinted with the permission of Motilal Banarsidass Press, Delhi, India.

Vespasiano da Bisticci, "Cosimo de Medici: The Merchant Prince" from *The Vespiano Memoirs: Lives of Illustrious Men of the XVth Century,* translated by William George and Emily Waters. Copyright © 1997. Reprinted with the permission of the Renaissance Society of America.

Campantar, "'Oh God with Matted Hair!' She Cries" (parts 1 through 10) and "Karma Cannot Touch / Those Who Can Cry, 'Lord of the Gods!'" from *The Tevaram,* translated by Indira Viswanathan Peterson, from *Poems to Siva: The Hymns of the Tamil Saints.* Copyright © 1989 by Princeton University Press. Reprinted with the permission of the publishers.

Bartolomé de las Casas, excerpts from *The History of the Indies,* translated by George Sanderlin, from *Bartolomé de las Casas: A Selection of His Writings.* Copyright © 1971 by Alfred A. Knopf, Inc. Reprinted with the permission of Alfred A. Knopf, a division of Random House, Inc.

Baldesar Castiglione, ["The Qualities of the Courtier"] from *The Book of the Courtier,* translated by Charles S. Singleton. Copyright © 1959 by Charles S. Singleton and Edgar de N. Mayhew. Reprinted with the permission of Doubleday, a division of Random House, Inc.

Evliya Çelebi, ["The Court of Abdal Khan, Governor of Bitlis"] from *The Book of Travels,* translated by Robert Dankoff. Reprinted with the permission of E. J. Brill Publishers.

Chandidasa, "How Can I Describe His Relentless Flute," "My Mind Is Not on Housework," "I Brought Honey and Drank It Mixed with Milk," translated by Edward C. Dimock and Denise Levertov from *In Praise of Krishna: Songs from the Bengali.* Copyright © 1967 by The Asia Society, Inc. Reprinted with the permission of Doubleday, a division of Random House, Inc.

Christopher Columbus, excerpt from *The Log of Christopher Columbus* translated by Robert H. Fuson (Blue Ridge Summit, Penn.: International Marine/TAB Books, 1992). Copyright © 1987 by Robert H. Fuson. Reprinted with the permission of the translator.

"The Conquest of Mexico," translated by Angel Maria Garibay K. and Lysander Kemp, from *The Broken Spears* by Miguel Leon-Portilla, translated by Lysander Kemp. Copyright © 1962 by Beacon Press. Reprinted with the permission of Beacon Press, Boston.

Nicolas Copernicus, To His Holiness, Pope Paul III, from *On the Revolutions of Heavenly Bodies,* translated by Edward Rosen. Copyright © 1978. Reprinted with the permission of The Johns Hopkins University Press.

Hernan Cortés, excerpts from "The Second Letter" from *Letters from Mexico,* translated by Anthony Pagden. Copyright © 1986 by Anthony Pagden. Reprinted with the permission of Yale University Press.

Sor Juana Inez de la Cruz, "Love, at First, Is Fashioned of Agitation," translated by S. G. Morley, from *Three Women Poets,* edited by Frank J. Warnke (Lewisburg: Bucknell University Press, 1987). Reprinted with the permission of Associated University Presses. "The Rhetoric of Tears," translated by Frank J. Warnke, from *European Metaphysical Poetry.* Reprinted with the permission of Yale University Press.

Cuntarar, "Life Is an Illusion," from *The Tevaram,* translated by Indira Viswanathan Peterson, from *Poems to Siva: The Hymns of the Tamil Saints.* Copyright © 1989 by Princeton University Press. Reprinted with the permission of the publishers.

Abul Fazl, excerpt from *Institutes of Akbar,* translated by Peter Hardy, from *Sources of Indian Tradition,* compiled by William Theodore de Bary et al. Copyright © 1958 by Columbia University Press. Reprinted with the permission of the publisher.

Galileo Galilei and Johannes Kepler correspondence, translated by Mary Martin McLaughlin, from *The Portable Medieval Reader,* by James Bruce Ross and Mary Martin McLaughlin. Copyright © 1953 by Viking Penguin, Inc., renewed © 1981 by James Bruce Ross and Mary Martin McLaughlin. Reprinted with the permission of Viking Penguin, a division of Penguin Putnam Inc.

Govinda-Dadasa, "When They Had Made Love," "The Marks of Fingernails Are on Your Breast," and "Let the Earth of My Body Be Mixed with the Earth / My Beloved Walks On," translated by Edward C. Dimock and Denise Levertov from *In Praise of Krishna: Songs from the Bengali.* Copyright © 1967 by The Asia Society, Inc. Reprinted with the permission of Doubleday, a division of Random House, Inc.

Hayashi Razan (Doshun), ["On the Mastery of the Arts of Peace and War"], translated by Ryusakku Tsunoda,

William Theodore du Bary, and Donald Keene, from *Sources of Japanese Tradition.* Copyright © 1958 by Columbia University Press. Reprinted with the permission of the publishers.

Jayadeva, excerpts from *Love Song of the Dark Lord: Jayadeva's Gitagovinda,* edited and translated by Barbara Stoller Miller. Copyright © 1977 by Columbia University Press. Reprinted with the permission of the publishers.

David Johnson (trans.), "The Creation of the Earth," "How the Sun and Moon Were Created," "The Creation of Man and Woman," "The Origin of Food," and "The Origin of Ceremony"; "The Myth of Quetzalcoatl"; and "A Defense of Aztec Religion," translated by David Johnson and Armando Jimarez. Reprinted with the permission of the translator.

Kabir, "Go Naked If You Want," and "Pundit, How Can You Be So Dumb?," translated by John Stratton Hawley and Mark Juergensmeyer, from *Songs of the Saints of India.* Copyright © 1988 by Oxford University Press, Inc. Reprinted with the permission of the publishers. "I Don't Know What Sort of a God We Have Been Talking About," and "I Laugh When I Hear That the Fish in the Water Is Thirsty," translated by Robert Bly, from *The Kabir Book* (Boston: Beacon Press, 1977). Copyright © 1971, 1977 by Robert Bly. Reprinted with the permission of the translator.

Ibn Khaldun, excerpt from "Il Muqaddimah," translated by Charles Issawi from *An Arab Philosophy of History: Selections from The Prolegomena of Ibn Khaldun of Tunis 1332–1406.* Copyright © 1981 by Charles Issawi. Reprinted with the permission of The Darwin Press, Inc. ["On dynasties, royal authority, and the caliphate"] from Chapter Three from *The Muqaddimah: An Introduction to History,* translated by Franz Rosenthal, edited by N. J. Dawood. Copyright © 1967 by Princeton University Press. Reprinted with the permission of the publishers.

Louise de Labé, "Kiss Me Again, Again, Kiss Me Again" and "Oh, That I Could Be Crushed to That Dear Breast," translated by Frank J. Warnke from *Three Women Poets* (Lewisburg: Bucknell University Press, 1987). Reprinted with the permission of Associated University Presses.

Miguel Leon-Portilla (trans.), "I, Nezahualcoyotl, Ask This," "Are You Real, Are You Rooted?," "With Flowers You Write," "I Comprehend the Secret, the Hidden," "I Am Intoxicated, I Weep, I Grieve," and "There, Alone, in the Interior of Heaven" from *Native Mesoamerican Spirituality.* Copyright © 1980 by The Missionary Society of St. Paul the Apostle in the State of New York. Reprinted with the permission of Paulist Press. www.paulistpress.com.

Li Zhi, "On the Child Mind," translated by Stephen Owen, from *An Anthology of Chinese Literature.* Copyright © 1996 by Stephen Owen and The Council for Cultural Planning and Development of the Executive Yuan of the Republic of China. Reprinted with the permission of W. W. Norton & Company, Inc.

Martin Luther, ["Here I Stand"] from *Luther's Works: Career of the Reformer, Volume 32,* translated by Roger A. Hornsby. Copyright © 1958 by Fortress Press. Reprinted with the permission of Augsburg Fortress.

Niccolo Machiavelli, "The Prince" from *Machiavelli: The Prince and Other Works,* translated by Allan H. Gilbert (Putney, Vermont: Hendricks House, Inc. Publishers, 1964). Reprinted with the permission of the publisher. ["The Ancient Courts of Ancient Men"] from "Letter to Francesco Vettori," translated by Allan H. Gilbert, from *Machiavelli: The Chief Works and Others* (Durham: Duke University Press, 1965). Copyright © 1965. Reprinted with permission.

Mahadeviyakka, "Like a Silkworm Weaving," "He Bartered My Heart," "Husband Inside / Lover Outside," and "I Love the Handsome One," translated by A. K. Ramanujan, from *Speaking of Siva* (New York: Penguin, 1973). Copyright © 1973 by A. K. Ramanujan. Reprinted with the permission of Molly A. Daniels-Ramanujan.

Nzinga Mbemba, "The Consequences of the Slave Trade" (Originally titled "Affonso of Congo: Evils of the Trade") from Basil Davidson, ed., *The African Past: Chronicles from Antiquity to Modern Times* (Boston: Little, Brown and Company, 1964). Copyright © 1964 by Basil Davidson. Reprinted with the permission of Curtis Brown, Ltd.

Mirabai, "Life without Hari Is No Life, Friend," "Today Your Hari Is Coming," "The Bhil Woman Tasted Them, Plum after Plum," and "I Have Talked to You, Talked, / Dark Lifter of Mountains," translated by John Stratton Hawley and Mark Juergensmeyer from *Songs of the Saints of India.* Copyright © 1988 by Oxford University Press, Inc. Reprinted with the permission of the publishers. #36, 73, 114, 142, 190-191 ["I Donned Anklets and Danced," "Who Can Understand the Grief / of a Woman Parted from Her Beloved?," "Shri Krishna Has Entered My Heart," and "Do Not Mention the Name of Love"], translated by A. J. Alston, from *Devotional Poems of Mirabai.* Reprinted with the permission of Motilal Banarsidass Press, Delhi.

Giovanni Pico della Mirandola, "The Oration on the Dignity of Man," translated by Charles Glenn Wallis (Indianapolis: Bobbs-Merrill / Library of Liberal Arts, 1965). Copyright © 1940 by Charles Glenn Wallis. Reprinted with the permission of Eleanor Van Trump Glenn.

Michel Eyquem de Montaigne, "Of Cannibals" from *The Complete Essays of Montaigne,* translated by Donald

M. Frame. Copyright © 1943 by Donald M. Frame, renewed © 1971. Copyright 1948, © 1957, 1958 by the Board of Trustees of the Leland Stanford Junior University, renewed 1986 by Donald M. Frame. Reprinted with the permission of Stanford University Press.

Nizam Al-Mulk, excerpt from *The Book of Government: Rules for Kings,* translated by Hubert Darke. Copyright © 1960 by Hubert Darke. Reprinted with the permission of Routledge & Kegan Paul/International Thomson Publishing Services.

Nanak, excerpt from *Adi Granth,* translated by Dr. Trilochan Singh, Bhai Jodh Singh, Kapur Singh, Bawa Harkishen Singh, and Khushwant Singh, from *Selections from the Sacred Writings of the Sikhs* (New York: Macmillan and London: George Allen & Unwin, 1960). Reprinted by permission.

Marguerite de Navarre, excerpt from Story 9 ["On the Virtue of Women"], and Story 10 ["Florida and Amadour"] from *The Heptameron,* translated by Paul A. Chilton. Copyright © 1984 by Paul A. Chilton. Reprinted with the permission of Penguin Books, Ltd.

Petrarch, "The Ascent of Mount Ventoux" from *Petrarch: Selections from the Canzoniere and Other Works,* translated by Mark Musa. Copyright © 1985 by Mark Musa. Reprinted with the permission of Oxford University Press. The *canzoniere* are translated by Patricia Clark Smith and are reprinted with the permission of the translator.

Matteo Ricci, ["The Art of Printing and the Making of Fans"], ["Chinese Medicine and Education"], and ["The Literati"] from *The Diary of Matthew Ricci,* translated by Louis J. Gallagher, S.J., from *China in the Sixteenth Century.* Copyright © 1942, 1953 and renewed © 1970 by Louis J. Gallagher, S.J. Reprinted with the permission of Random House, Inc.

Pierre de Ronsard, "To Cassandre," and "To Hélène," translated by David Sanders. Reprinted with the permission of the translator.

Maurice Scève, "The Day We Passed Together for a While," translated by Patricia Clark Smith. Reprinted with the permission of the translator.

William Shakespeare, *The Tempest,* edited by Robert Langbaum. Copyright © 1964, 1987 by Robert Langbaum for Introduction, Annotations and Compilation. Reprinted with the permission of Dutton Signet, a division of Penguin Putnam Inc.

Ibn Sina (Avicenna), ["Mastering the Sciences"] from *Autobiography,* translated by Arthur J. Arberry, from *Avicenna on Theology.* Reprinted with the permission of John Murray (Publishers), Ltd.

Gaspara Stampa, "Love, Having Elevated Her to Him, Inspires Her Verses" and "She Does Not Fear Amorous Pain, But Rather Its End," translated by Frank J. Warnke, from *Three Women Poets* (Lewisburg: Bucknell University Press, 1987). Reprinted with the permission of Associated University Presses.

Bamba Suso, "Sunjata: Gambian Version of the Mande Epic," translated by Gordon Innes with Bakari Sidibe (London: SOAS/University of London, 1974). Reprinted with the permission of the publishers.

Garcilaso de la Vega, "While There Is Still the Color of a Rose," and "Your Face Is Written in My Soul," translated by Edwin Morgan, from Angel Flores, ed., *An Anthology of Spanish Poetry from Garcilaso to Garcia Lorca in English Translation with Spanish Originals.* Reprinted with the permission of the Estate of Angel Flores.

Lope de Vega, "Woman Is of Man the Best," translated by Perry Higman, from *Love Poems from Spain and Spanish America.* Copyright © 1986 by Perry Higman. Reprinted with the permission of City Lights Books. "Stranger to Love, Whoever Loves Not Thee," translated by Iain Fletcher, and "A Sonnet All of a Sudden," translated by Doreen Bell, from Angel Flores, ed., *An Anthology of Spanish Poetry from Garcilaso to Garcia Lorca in English Translation with Spanish Originals.* Reprinted with the permission of the Estate of Angel Flores.

Vidyapati, "There Was a Shudder in Her Whispering Voice," "O Friend, I Cannot Tell You," and "Her Hair, Dishevelled," translated by Deben Bhattacharya, from *Love Songs of Vidyapati.* Copyright © 1963 by Deben Bhattacharya. Reprinted with the permission of HarperCollins Publishers, Ltd.

Wu Ch'eng, excerpts from *Monkey,* translated by Arthur Waley (London: George Allen & Unwin, Ltd., 1942). Reprinted with the permission of the Estate of Arthur Waley.

Zhang Ting-Yu (Chang T'ing-Yü), ["The Voyage of Zheng He"] from *History of the Ming,* translated by Dun J. Li, from *The Civilization of China.* Copyright © 1975. Reprinted with the permission of Pearson Education, Upper Saddle River, NJ.

Zhu Xi (Chu Hsi), "Memorial on the Principles of Study," translated by Clara Yu, from *Chinese Civilization and Society,* edited by Patricia Buckley Ebrey. Copyright © 1981 by The Free Press. Reprinted with the permission of The Free Press, a division of Simon & Schuster Adult Publishing Group.

INDEX